D0989605

FREEDOM

A DOCUMENTARY HISTORY OF EMANCIPATION

1861–1867

SERIES I

VOLUME III

THE WARTIME GENESIS OF FREE LABOR: THE LOWER SOUTH

Planting Sweet Potatoes. Edisto Island, South Carolina.
Photograph by Henry P. Moore; courtesy of The New-York Historical Society, New York City

FREEDOM

A DOCUMENTARY HISTORY OF
EMANCIPATION
1861 – 1867

SELECTED FROM THE HOLDINGS OF THE
NATIONAL ARCHIVES OF THE UNITED STATES

SERIES I
VOLUME III
THE WARTIME GENESIS OF FREE LABOR:
THE LOWER SOUTH

Edited by
IRA BERLIN
THAVOLIA GLYMPH
STEVEN F. MILLER
JOSEPH P. REIDY
LESLIE S. ROWLAND
JULIE SAVILLE

CAMBRIDGE UNIVERSITY PRESS
CAMBRIDGE
NEW YORK PORT CHESTER MELBOURNE SYDNEY

Published by the Press Syndicate of the University of Cambridge
The Pitt Building, Trumpington Street, Cambridge CB2 1RP
40 West 20th Street, New York, NY 10011, USA
10 Stamford Road, Oakleigh, Melbourne 3166, Australia

First published 1990

Printed in the United States of America

Library of Congress Cataloging-in-Publication Data

The Wartime genesis of free labor. The lower South / edited by Ira Berlin . . . [et al.].

p. cm. – (Freedom, a documentary history of emancipation, 1861–1867 ; ser. 1, v. 3)

Includes index.

ISBN 0-521-39493-7 (hard)

1. United States – History – Civil War, 1861–1865 – Afro-Americans – Sources. 2. Freedmen – Southern States – History – Sources. 3. Working class – Southern States – History – 19th century – Sources. 4. Confederate States of America – History – Sources. 5. Slaves – Southern States – Emancipation – Sources. 6. Afro-Americans – Southern States – History – 19th century – Sources. I. Berlin, Ira, 1941– . II. Series.
E185.2.F88 ser. 1, vol. 3
[E540.N3]
973.7 s – dc20 90-2496
[973.7'415] CIP

British Library Cataloguing in Publication Data

Freedom : a documentary history of emancipation, 1861–1867 : selected from the holdings of the National Archives of the United States. Series 1 : Vol. 3 ; The wartime genesis of free labor. The lower South

1. United States. Black slaves. Emancipation, history
I. Berlin, Ira *1941–*
306.3620973

ISBN 0-521-39493-7 hardback

TO

WILLIE LEE ROSE

EXEMPLAR

Other volumes of FREEDOM

THE BLACK MILITARY EXPERIENCE

ed. Ira Berlin, Joseph P. Reidy, and Leslie S. Rowland

THE DESTRUCTION OF SLAVERY

ed. Ira Berlin, Barbara J. Fields, Thavolia Glymph, Joseph P. Reidy, and Leslie S. Rowland

THE WARTIME GENESIS OF FREE LABOR: THE UPPER SOUTH

ed. Ira Berlin, Steven F. Miller, Joseph P. Reidy, and Leslie S. Rowland

Freedmen and Southern Society Project

Ira Berlin, Director

Contents

Acknowledgments

PUBLICATION of *The Wartime Genesis of Free Labor: The Lower South* and *The Wartime Genesis of Free Labor: The Upper South* marks a significant milestone for the Freedmen and Southern Society Project. These volumes bring to a close the first two series of *Freedom*, putting the project roughly at its halfway mark. Having focused on the Civil War years in series 1 and 2, the editors will next turn to the early Reconstruction period.

We could not have come this far without a good deal of help. In *The Black Military Experience* (1982) and *The Destruction of Slavery* (1985), we thanked the men and women who helped found and sustain the Freedmen and Southern Society Project. Our debt to them has not diminished. During the intervening years, many of them have continued in the work, and others have lent a hand. Our gratitude far exceeds this mere mention.

Words, according to Thomas Hobbes, are the money of fools. But, however foolish, we would have no words to trade without the monetary support of both government agencies and private foundations. Our first debt is to the National Historical Publications and Records Commission (NHPRC), particularly to Roger Bruns and Mary Giunta, the successive directors of the Publications Program, and to Richard Jacobs, the commission's executive director. The National Endowment for the Humanities has also been an important and ongoing source of financial assistance. We would like to thank Kathy Fuller, David Nichols, and Margot Backas of the Division of Research Programs for their unobtrusive – yet ever vigilant – oversight of our work. In addition, the project has had a warm friend at the Ford Foundation. Sheila Biddle's understanding and appreciation of *Freedom* goes beyond the call of duty. For this, and for additional material assistance, we are deeply grateful.

Upon completion of our major research at the National Archives, the project moved its headquarters to the University of Maryland. As chairman of the History Department, Richard Price, like his predecessor Emory G. Evans, has been a genial host and valued colleague. In countless ways, he has facilitated our work and advocated our cause in the university's councils. His own pioneering studies of British wageworkers have offered numerous clues to the history of former slaves.

Our next-door neighbor, Louis R. Harlan, offered not only advice and encouragement, but also the temporary use of his office, where proofreading proceeded amid memorabilia of Booker T. Washington and under the watchful gaze of a larger-than-life photograph of Adlai Stevenson.

Indispensable assistance for both volumes of *The Wartime Genesis of Free Labor* came from Leslie Schwalm, who served an apprenticeship as an NHPRC fellow during the 1987–88 academic year, and from Wayne K. Durrill, who joined the project to assist in editing the proceedings of postwar freedmen's conventions. Besides providing a sounding board for many of the ideas in *Wartime Genesis*, both of them shared in the drudgery of proofreading. Wayne Durrill also prepared the indexes, a job requiring intellectual acuity as well as close attention to mind-numbing detail.

Both volumes of *The Wartime Genesis of Free Labor* have benefited enormously from the work of graduate student assistants, who brought to the project an enthusiasm and energy that rejuvenated old hands. We express our gratitude to Mary Beth Corrigan, Margaret Dorrier, Kevin Hardwick, Yong Ook Jo, Cynthia Kennedy-Haflett, Joseph Mannard, Robert Pickstone, Walter Shaefer, Richard Soderlund, Brian Sowers, and Peter Way, each of whom will leave a special mark on the study of the past. Above all, we want to thank Gregory LaMotta, who for eight years has been our eyes and ears at the National Archives. His sharp instincts, intimate knowledge of the labyrinthine stacks, and patient good humor have served us well in tracking down elusive documents and exploring previously untapped records.

Oversight of this sizable force, along with innumerable other duties, fell to the project's administrative assistant and secretary: first Lorraine Lee, then Susan Bailey (returning for a second tour of duty), and now Terrie Hruzd. Each brought her own distinctive skill and style to the task, and each sped and smoothed the work of the editors. Everyone's work was made much easier by Claire Dimsdale, who dispatched a vast array of assignments with an admirable combination of precision and cheerfulness.

As we entered the final stages of work on *The Wartime Genesis of Free Labor: The Lower South*, we called upon several fellow scholars to review parts of the manuscript. Eric Foner read the introductory essay. Lawrence N. Powell and Michael S. Wayne commented on the Mississippi Valley chapter, and Rebecca J. Scott did the same for that on southern Louisiana. Their careful readings saved the editors from a few blunders, raised important questions, and improved the volume in many ways.

After a decade-long association with the people of Cambridge University Press, we remain impressed by their consistently high standards and professional competence. Frank Smith, our editor, has always allowed us to set our own scholarly agenda without forgetting that our object, like that of the press, is to bring volumes before the public. Edith Feinstein and Richard Hollick guided the transformation of a massive and unwieldy manuscript into a book. All authors should be lucky enough to have a copyeditor like Vicky Macintyre. Because she does her job so well, her contributions to *The Wartime Genesis of Free Labor* will be unnoticeable to most readers. We appreciate them very much.

The Freedmen and Southern Society Project could not exist without the magnificent records in the National Archives of the United States and the hundreds of men and women who have built and maintained that institution over the years. We would like to express our appreciation to some of the present generation of archivists who, despite successive reorganizations and budgetary shortfalls, have always found time to answer our queries, point us in the right direction, and sometimes lead us by the hand. To Timothy Connelly, Richard Cox, Robert Gruber, Michael Meier, Michael Musick, William Sherman, Aloha South, and Reginald Washington, our hats are off. Finally, there is Sara Dunlap Jackson, whose knowledge of the records in the National Archives made the project possible and whose deep respect for the people who created those records has established a standard against which every volume of *Freedom* should be measured.

As our dog-eared copy of *Rehearsal for Reconstruction* attests, the work of Willie Lee Rose provided a constant source of information and inspiration as we struggled to understand life and labor within Union lines. In dedicating this volume to Professor Rose, we merely make public our longstanding admiration for her many achievements.

I. B.
T. G.
S. F. M.
J. P. R.
L. S. R.
J. S.

College Park, Maryland
April 1990

Introduction

NO EVENT in American history matches the drama of emancipation. More than a century later, it continues to stir the deepest emotions. And properly so. Emancipation accompanied the military defeat of the world's most powerful slaveholding class and freed a larger number of slaves than lived in all other New World slave societies combined. Clothed in the rhetoric of biblical prophecy and national destiny and born of a bloody civil war, it accomplished a profound social revolution. That revolution destroyed forever a way of life based upon the ownership of human beings, restoring to the former slaves proprietorship of their own persons, liquidating without compensation private property valued at billions of dollars, and forcibly substituting the relations of free labor for those of slavery. In designating the former slaves as citizens, emancipation placed citizenship upon new ground, defined in the federal Constitution and removed beyond the jurisdiction of the states. By obliterating the sovereignty of master over slave, it handed a monopoly of sovereignty to the newly consolidated nation-state. The freeing of the slaves simultaneously overturned the old regime of the South and set the entire nation upon a new course.

The death of slavery led to an intense period of social reconstruction, closely supervised by the victorious North, that lasted over a decade in many places. During this period, former slaves challenged the domination of the old masters, demanding land and the right to control their own labor. Former masters, abetted by a complaisant President, defeated the freedpeople's bid for economic independence and imposed on them new legal and extralegal constraints. But whatever the outcome, the struggle itself confirmed the magnitude of the change. Freedpeople confronted their former masters as free laborers in a system predicated upon contractual equality between employers and employees. They gained, if only temporarily, full citizenship rights, including the right to vote and hold public office.

With emancipation in the South, the United States enacted its part in a world-wide drama. Throughout the western world and beyond, the forces unleashed by the American and French revolutions and by the industrial revolution worked to undermine political regimes based upon hereditary privilege and economic systems based upon bound labor. Slavery had already succumbed in the Northern states and in the French and British Caribbean before the American Civil War, and it would shortly do so in its remaining strongholds in Spanish and Portuguese America. Almost simultaneously with the great struggle in the United States, the vestiges of serfdom in central and eastern Europe yielded to the pressure of the age. Only small pockets in Africa and Asia remained immune, and their immunity was temporary. The fateful lightning announced by the victorious Union army was soon to strike, if it had not already struck, wherever men and women remained in bonds of personal servitude.

For all systems of bondage, emancipation represented the acid test, the moment of truth. The upheaval of conventional expectations stripped away the patina of routine, exposing the cross purposes and warring intentions that had simmered – often unnoticed – beneath the surface of the old order. In throwing off habitual restraints, freedpeople redesigned their lives in ways that spoke eloquently of their hidden life in bondage, revealing clandestine institutions, long-cherished beliefs, and deeply held values. In confronting new restraints, they abandoned their usual caution in favor of direct speech and yet more direct action. Lords and serfs, masters and slaves had to survey the new social boundaries without the old etiquette of dominance and subordination as a guide. Their efforts to do so led to confrontations that could be awkward, painful, and frequently violent. The continued force of these encounters awakened men and women caught up in the drama to the realization that their actions no longer ratified old, established ways, but set radically new precedents for themselves and for future generations.

Moments of revolutionary transformation expose as do few human events the foundation upon which societies rest. Although those who enjoy political power and social authority speak their minds and indulge their inclinations freely and often, their subordinates generally cannot. Only in the upheaval of accustomed routine can the lower orders give voice to the assumptions that guide their world as it is and as they wish it to be. Some of them quickly grasp the essence of the new circumstances. Under the tutelage of unprecedented events, ordinary men and women become extraordinarily perceptive and articulate, seizing the moment to challenge the assumptions of the old regime and proclaim a new social order. Even then, few take the initiative. Some – perhaps most – simply try to maintain their balance, to reconstitute a routine, to maximize gains and minimize losses as events swirl around them. But inevitably they too become swept up in the revolutionary process. Barely conscious acts and unacknowledged motives carried over from the past take on a changed significance. Attempts to stand still or turn back only hasten the process forward. At revolutionary moments all actions – those of the timid and reluctant as much as those of the bold and eager – expose to view the inner workings of society.

Because they thrust common folk into prominence, moments of revolutionary transformation have long occupied historians seeking to solve the mysteries of human society. Knowledge of the subordinate groups who have formed the majority throughout history has proved essential to an understanding of how the world works. Historians have therefore developed special methods for penetrating the often opaque histories of ordinary people, including peasants, slaves, and wage-workers. Some have viewed them over the *longue durée*, translating glacial demographic and economic changes into an understanding of times past. Others have sought such understanding by focusing on particular events, decoding the fury of *carnaval*, the ritual of a bread riot, the terror of the "theater of death," or the tense confrontation of an industrial strike. Almost all have learned from periods of revolutionary transformation. Whatever the historian's approach, direct testimony by the people involved has usually been a luxury. For this reason, the study of emancipation in the United States promises rich rewards not just to those specifically interested in the question, but to all who seek a fuller view of the human past. Encompassing in full measure the revolutionary implications of all transitions from bondage to freedom, emancipation in the American South has left behind an unparalleled wealth of documentation permitting direct access to the thoughts and actions of the freedpeople themselves. Indeed, it provides the richest known record of any subordinate class at its moment of liberation.

THE RECORDS

As the war for union became a war for liberty, the lives of slaves and freedpeople became increasingly intertwined with the activities of both the Union and Confederate governments. Following the war, federal agencies continued to figure prominently in the reconstruction of the South's economy and society. The records created and collected by the agencies of these governments and now housed in the National Archives of the United States provide an unrivaled source for understanding the passage of black people from slavery to freedom. Such governmental units as the Colored Troops Division of the Adjutant General's Office; the American Freedmen's Inquiry Commission; the Union army at every level of command, from the headquarters in Washington to local army posts; army support organizations in Washington, including the Judge Advocate General's Office, the Provost Marshal General's Bureau, and the Quartermaster General's Office, and their subordinates in the field; the Civil War Special Agencies of the Treasury Department; individual regiments of U.S. Colored Troops; various branches of the Confederate government (whose records fell into Union hands at the conclusion of the war); the Southern Claims Commission; the Freedman's Bank; and, most important, the Bureau of Refugees, Freedmen, and Abandoned Lands all played a role in the coming of freedom. (See pp. xxxiii–xxxiv for a list of record groups drawn upon.)

The missions of these agencies placed them in close contact with a wide variety of ordinary people, and their bureaucratic structure provided a mechanism for the preservation of many records of people generally dismissed as historically mute. The Bureau of Refugees, Freedmen, and Abandoned Lands (Freedmen's Bureau) illustrates the point. Although the bureau often lacked the resources to do more than make written note of the abuses of freedpeople brought to its attention, bureau agents scattered across the South conducted censuses, undertook investigations, recorded depositions, filed reports, and accumulated letters authored by ex-slaves and interested whites. Other agencies whose duties focused less directly upon the concerns of former slaves created thousands of similar, though more dispersed, records.

Alongside the official reports in these archival files, hundreds of letters and statements by former slaves give voice to people whose aspirations, beliefs, and behavior have gone largely unrecorded. Not only did extraordinary numbers of ex-slaves, many of them newly literate, put pen to paper in the early years of freedom, but hundreds of others, entirely illiterate, gave depositions to government officials, placed their marks on resolutions passed at mass meetings, testified before courts-martial and Freedmen's Bureau courts, and dictated letters to more literate black people and to white officials and teachers. The written record thus created constitutes an unparalleled outpouring from people caught up in the emancipation process. Predictably, many of these documents requested official action to redress wrongs committed by powerful former slaveholders who only reluctantly recognized ex-slaves as free, rarely as equal. Others, however, originated in relationships entirely outside the purview of either federal officials or former masters and employers. They include, for example, correspondence between black soldiers and their families and between kinfolk who had been separated during slavery. That such letters fell for various reasons into the bureaucratic net of government agencies (and thus were preserved along with official records) should not obscure their deeply personal origins.

Selected out of the mass of purely administrative records, these documents convey, perhaps as no historian can, the experiences of the liberated: the quiet personal satisfaction of meeting an old master on equal terms, as well as the outrage of ejection from a segregated streetcar; the elation of a fugitive enlisting in the Union army, and the humiliation of a laborer cheated out of hard-earned wages; the joy of a family reunion after years of forced separation, and the distress of having a child involuntarily apprenticed to a former owner; the hope that freedom would bring a new world, and the fear that, in so many ways, life would be much as before. Similar records offer insight into the equally diverse reactions of planters, Union officers, and Southern yeomen – men and women who faced emancipation with different interests and expectations. Taken together, these records provide exceptionally full documentation of the destruction of a dependent social relationship, the release of a people from their dependent status, and the simultaneous transformation of an entire society. As far as is known, no comparable record exists for the liberation of any group of serfs or slaves or for the transformation of any people into wage-workers.

However valuable, the archival records also have their problems. They are massive, repetitive, and often blandly bureaucratic. Their size alone makes research by individual scholars inevitably incomplete and often haphazard. The Freedmen's Bureau records, for example, extend to more than 700 cubic feet, and they constitute a relatively small record group. The records of U.S. army continental commands for the period spanning the Civil War era fill more than 10,000 cubic feet. In addition to the daunting volume of the records, their bureaucratic structure creates obstacles for studies that go beyond the institutional history of particular agencies or the documentation of policy formation to examine underlying social processes. Governmental practice provided the mechanism for preserving the records, but it also fragmented them in ways that can hinder historical reconstruction. Assume, for example, that a group of freedmen petitioned the Secretary of the Treasury complaining of a Confederate raid on a plantation supervised by his department. Their petition might be forwarded to the Secretary of War, since the army protected such plantations. He in turn would pass it on to a military field commander, who would send it down the chain of command. If black soldiers provided the plantation guard, the petition might be forwarded to the adjutant general, who directed the Bureau of Colored Troops, who might then send it to the commander of a black regiment. On the other hand, if the Secretary of the Treasury wished to act himself, he could forward it to a treasury agent in the field. Augmented by additional information in the form of reports, depositions, or endorsements on the original complaint, the petition might be passed along to still other federal agencies. In the meantime, the Confederate raiders might have made a report to their commander, perhaps noting the response of the plantation's residents to the foray. Rebel planters, eager to regain their property, might also have a say, addressing the Confederate Secretary of War, his adjutant and inspector general, or a local Confederate commander. At any or all points, additional documents might be added and portions of the original documentation might come to rest. Only a search of the records of all these agencies can make the full story available. In part because of the scope of such an undertaking, individual scholars have been unable to avail themselves of the fullness of the resources of the National Archives. Research has necessarily been piecemeal and limited to one or two record groups or portions of various record groups. Only a large-scale collaborative effort can make these resources available to the public.

THE FREEDMEN AND SOUTHERN SOCIETY PROJECT

In the fall of 1976, with a grant from the National Historical Publications and Records Commission, and under the sponsorship of the University of Maryland, the Freedmen and Southern Society Project launched a systematic search of those records at the National Archives that promised to yield material for a documentary history of emancipation. Over the course of the next three years, the editors selected more than 40,000 items, which represented perhaps 2 percent of the documents they examined. Indexed and cross-referenced topically, chronologically, and geographically, this preliminary selection constitutes the universe from which the documents published as *Freedom: A Documentary History of Emancipation* are selected and annotated, and from which the editors' introductory essays are written.

The editors found it imperative from the outset to be selective. They have focused their attention upon the wartime and postwar experiences of slaves and ex-slaves, but have also sought to illuminate the social, economic, and political setting of the emancipation process. The formation of federal policy, for example, is not central to the project's concerns, except insofar as the preconceptions and actions of policy makers influenced the shape that freedom assumed. Therefore, the volumes published by the Freedmen and Southern Society Project will not undertake a history of the Freedmen's Bureau, the U.S. army, the Bureau of Colored Troops, or any other governmental agency; nonetheless, documents about the operations of these agencies will be prominent when they describe activities of freedpeople and shed light upon the context in which former slaves struggled to construct their own lives. Throughout the selection process, the editors have labored to reconstruct the history of the freedpeople rather than the institutions that surrounded them.

Above all, the editors have sought to delineate the central elements of the process by which men and women moved from the utter dependence slaveholders demanded but never fully received, to the independence freedpeople desired but seldom attained. This process began with the slow breakdown of slavery on the periphery of the South and extended to the establishment of the social, economic, and political institutions black people hoped would secure their independence. The editors have also sought to recognize the diversity of black life and the emancipation process, by selecting documents that illustrate the varied experiences of former slaves in different parts of the South who labored at diverse tasks and who differed from one another in sex, in age, and in social or economic status. Although former slaves, like other men and women caught in the transition from slavery to freedom, wanted to enlarge their liberty and ensure their independence from their former masters, how they desired to do so and what they meant by freedom were tempered by their previous experiences as well as by the circumstances in which they were enmeshed. At the same time, the editors have been alert to the shared ideas and aspirations that American slaves carried into freedom and to those features of emancipation that were common throughout the South – and more generally still, common to all people escaping bondage. These common characteristics and the regularities of the process of emancipation connect the lives of former slaves across time and space and link them to other dependent people struggling for autonomy.

Reflecting editorial interest in a *social* history of emancipation, *Freedom* is organized thematically, following the process of emancipation. At each step the editors have selected documents that illustrate processes they believe are central to the transition from slavery to freedom. The first two series concentrate primarily on the years of the Civil War. Series 1 documents the destruction of slavery, the diverse circumstances under which slaves claimed their freedom, and the wartime labor arrangements that developed as slavery collapsed. Series 2 examines the recruitment of black men into the Union army and the experiences of black soldiers under arms. The remaining series, while drawing in part upon evidence from the war years, explore most fully the earliest years of postwar Reconstruction. They document the struggle for land, the evolution of new labor arrangements, relations with former masters and other white people, law and justice, violence and other extralegal repression, geographical mobility, family relationships, education, religion, the structure and activities of the black community, and black politics in the early years of Reconstruction. The series are organized as follows:

Series 1	The Destruction of Slavery and the Wartime Genesis of Free Labor
Series 2	The Black Military Experience
Series 3	Land, Capital, and Labor
Series 4	Race Relations, Violence, Law, and Justice
Series 5	The Black Community: Family, Church, School, and Society

Each series comprises one or more volumes, and topical arrangement continues within the volumes. Each chapter is introduced by an essay that provides background information, outlines government policy, and elaborates the larger themes. The chapters are further subdivided, when relevant, to reflect distinctive historical, economic, and demographic circumstances.

Also in accordance with the editors' predominant concern with social process, the annotation (both the notes to particular documents and the introductory essays) is designed to provide a context for the documents rather than to identify persons or places. The official character of most of the records means that vast quantities of biographical data are available for many of the army officers, Freedmen's Bureau agents, and others who cross the pages of these volumes. The editors have nonetheless decided against the time-consuming extraction of details about individuals, because to do so would divert energy from research into the larger social themes and reduce the number of documents that could be published, while adding little of substance to the business at hand.

In its aim, approach, and editorial universe, the Freedmen and Southern Society Project therefore differs fundamentally from most historical editing enterprises. Rather than searching out the complete manuscript record of an individual man or woman, the project examines a process of social transformation, and rather than seeking all the documentary evidence relevant to that transformation, it confines itself to the resources of the National Archives. *Freedom* endeavors to combine the strengths of the traditional interpretive monograph with the rich diversity of the documentary edition while addressing in one historical setting a central question of the human experience: how men and women strive to enlarge their freedom and secure their independence from those who would dominate their lives.

SERIES 1

Series 1 of *Freedom* comprises three volumes. Volume 1, *The Destruction of Slavery*, explicates the process by which slavery collapsed under the pressure of federal arms and the slaves' persistence in placing their own liberty on the wartime agenda. In documenting the transformation of the war for union into a war against slavery, it shifts the focus from Washington and Richmond to the plantations, farms, and battlefields of the South, and demonstrates how slaves became the agents of their own emancipation.

Volume 2, *The Wartime Genesis of Free Labor: The Upper South*, and volume 3, *The Wartime Genesis of Free Labor: The Lower South*, concern the evolution of freedom in those areas of the slave states that were held by Union forces for a substantial part of the Civil War (including the border slave states that did not join the Confederacy). Among the subjects they address are the employment of former slaves and free blacks as military laborers; the wartime experiences of former slaves in contraband camps, on government-supervised plantations, and in cities, towns, and military posts; and various kinds of private employment, from evolving labor arrangements with former owners to new forms of independent labor in town and countryside. In so doing, the two volumes also document federal free-labor policies and practices, and the struggle among former slaves, free blacks, Union army officers, Southern planters, Northern teachers and clergymen, Northern businessmen, and federal officials over the meaning of freedom.

In order to give due consideration to the regional differences in society, economy, military occupation, and politics that influenced the evolution of free-labor arrangements, the two volumes of *The Wartime Genesis of Free Labor* are divided geographically. Volume 2 describes developments in Union-occupied parts of the Upper South – tidewater Virginia and North Carolina; the District of Columbia; middle and east Tennessee and northern Alabama; and the border states of Maryland, Missouri, and Kentucky – where small slaveholding units, mixed agriculture, and urban life had characterized the slave regime. Volume 3 documents the evolution of freedom in the plantation regions of the Lower South that were captured and occupied by Union forces – small enclaves in lowcountry South Carolina, Georgia, and Florida, notably the South Carolina Sea Islands; the sugar parishes of southern Louisiana; and the Mississippi Valley from Memphis to just north of Baton Rouge. In order to compare developments in the various regions and to identify common underlying themes, the same interpretive essay introduces each of the two volumes.

Together with *The Black Military Experience*, the single volume that makes up series 2, the three volumes of series 1 document the death of the old order and the birth of a new one in the crucible of civil war.

Editorial Method

THE RENDITION of nineteenth-century manuscripts into print proceeds at best along a tortuous path. Transcribing handwritten documents into a standardized, more accessible form inevitably sacrifices some of their evocative power. The scrawl penciled by a hard-pressed army commander, the letters painstakingly formed by an ex-slave new to the alphabet, and the practiced script of a professional clerk all reduce to the same uncompromising print. At the same time, simply reading, much less transcribing, idiosyncratic handwriting poses enormous difficulties. The records left by barely literate writers offer special problems, although these are often no more serious than the obstacles created by better-educated but careless clerks, slovenly and hurried military officers, or even the ravages of time upon fragile paper.

The editors have approached the question of transcription with the conviction that readability need not require extensive editorial intervention and, indeed, that modernization (beyond that already imposed by conversion into type) can compromise the historical value of a document. The practical dilemmas of setting precise limits to editorial intervention, once initiated, also suggest the wisdom of restraint. In short, the editors believe that even when documents were written by near illiterates, the desiderata of preserving immediacy and conveying the struggle of ordinary men and women to communicate intensely felt emotions outweigh any inconveniences inflicted by allowing the documents to stand as they were written. Fortunately for the modern reader, a mere passing acquaintance with the primer usually led uneducated writers to spell as they spoke; the resulting documents may appear impenetrable to the eye but are perfectly understandable when read phonetically. In fact, reproduced verbatim, such documents offer intriguing evidence about the spoken language. Other writers, presumably better educated, frequently demonstrated such haphazard adherence to rules of grammar, spelling, and punctuation that their productions rival those of the semiliterate. And careless copyists or telegraph operators further garbled many documents. Both equity and convenience demand, nonetheless, that all writings by the schooled – however incoherent – be transcribed according to the same principles as those applied to the documents of the unschooled. Indeed, a verbatim rendition permits interesting observations about American literacy in the mid-nineteenth century, as well as about the talents or personalities of particular individuals.

Therefore, the textual body of each document in this volume is reproduced – to the extent permitted by modern typography – *exactly* as it appears in the original manuscript. (The few exceptions to this general principle will be noted hereafter.) The editorial *sic* is never employed: All peculiarities of syntax, spelling, capitalization, and punctuation appear in the original manuscript. The same is true of paragraph breaks, missing or incomplete words, words run together, quotation marks or parentheses that are not closed, characters raised above the line, contractions, and abbreviations. When the correct reading of a character is ambiguous (as, for example, a letter "C" written halfway between upper- and lower-case, or a nondescript blotch of punctuation that could be either a comma or a period), modern practice is followed. Illegible or obscured words that can be inferred with confidence from textual evidence are printed in ordinary roman type, enclosed in brackets. If the editors' reading is conjectural or doubtful, a question mark is added. When the editors cannot decipher a word by either inference or conjecture, it is represented by a three-dot ellipsis enclosed in brackets. An undecipherable passage of more than one word is represented in the same way, but a footnote reports the extent of the illegible material. (See p. xxxii for a summary of editorial symbols.)

Handwritten letters display many characteristics that cannot be exactly reproduced on the printed page or can be printed only at considerable expense. Some adaptations are, therefore, conventional. Words underlined once in the manuscript appear in italics. Words underlined more than once are printed in small capitals. Internally quoted documents that are set off in the manuscript by such devices as extra space or quotation marks on every line are indented and printed in smaller type. Interlineations are simply incorporated into the text at the point marked by the author, without special notation by the editors unless the interlineation represents a substantial alteration. Finally, the beginning of a new paragraph is indicated by indentation, regardless of how the author set apart paragraphs.

The editors deviate from the standard of faithful reproduction of the textual body of the document in only two significant ways. The many documents entirely bereft of punctuation require some editorial intervention for the sake of readability. However, the editors wish to avoid "silent" addition of any material, and supplying punctuation in brackets would be extremely cumbersome, if not pedantic. Therefore, the editors employ the less intrusive device of adding extra spaces at what they take to be unpunctuated sentence breaks. Although most such judgments are unambiguous, there are instances in which the placement of sentence breaks requires an interpretive decision. To prevent the ambiguity that could result if an unpunctuated or unconventionally punctuated sentence concluded at the end of a line of type, the last word of any such sentence appears at the beginning of the next line.

The second substantial deviation from verbatim reproduction of the text is the occasional publication of excerpted portions of documents. Most documents are printed in their entirety, but excerpts are taken from certain manuscripts, especially long bureaucratic reports, extensive legal proceedings, and other kinds of testimony. Editorial omission of a substantial body of material is indicated by a four-dot ellipsis centered on a separate line. An omission of only one or two sentences is marked by a four-dot ellipsis between the sentences that precede and follow the omission. The endnote identifies each excerpt as such and briefly characterizes the portion of the document not printed. (See the sample document that follows this essay for a guide to the elements of a printed document, including headnote, endnote, and footnote.)

The editors intervene without notation in the text of manuscripts in two minor ways. When the author of a manuscript inadvertently repeated a word, the duplicate is omitted. Similarly, most material canceled by the author is omitted, since it usually represents false starts or ordinary slips of the pen. When, however, the editors judge that the crossed-out material reflects an important alteration of meaning, it is printed as ~~canceled type~~. Apart from these cases, no "silent" additions, corrections, or deletions are made in the textual body of documents. Instead, all editorial insertions are clearly identified by being placed in italics and in brackets. Insertions by the editors may be descriptive interpolations such as [*In the margin*] or [*Endorsement*], the addition of words or letters omitted by the author, or the correction of misspelled words and erroneous dates. Great restraint is exercised, however, in making such additions: The editors intervene only when the document cannot be understood or is seriously misleading as it stands. In particular, no effort is made to correct misspelled personal and place names. When material added by the editors is conjectural, a question mark is placed within the brackets. For printed documents only (of which there are few), "silent" correction is made for jumbled letters, errant punctuation, and transpositions that appear to be typesetting errors.

Although they faithfully reproduce the text of documents with minimal editorial intervention, the editors are less scrupulous with the peripheral parts of manuscripts. To print in full, exactly as in the original document, such elements as the complete return address, the full inside address, and a multiline complimentary closing would drastically reduce the number of documents that could be published. Considerations of space have therefore impelled the editors to adopt the following procedures. The place and date follow original spelling and punctuation, but they are printed on a single line at the beginning of the document regardless of where they appear in the manuscript. The salutation and complimentary closing, although spelled and punctuated as in the manuscript, are run into the text regardless of their positions in the original. Multiple signatures are printed only when there are twelve or fewer names. For documents with more than twelve signatures, including the many petitions bearing dozens or even hundreds of names, the editors indicate only the number of signatures on the signature line, for example, [*86 signatures*], although some information about the signers is always provided in the headnote and sometimes in the endnote as well. The formal legal apparatus accompanying sworn affidavits, including the name and position of the official who administered the oath and the names of witnesses, is omitted; the endnote, however, indicates whether an affidavit was sworn before a military officer, a Freedmen's Bureau agent, or a civil official. Similarly, the names of witnesses are omitted from contracts and other legal documents, but the endnote indicates that the signatures were witnessed.

The inside and return addresses create special complications. The documents in *Freedom* come from bureaucratic, mostly military, records. Therefore both inside and return addresses often include a military rank or other title and a statement of military command and location that may run to three or more lines. Similar details usually accompany the signature as well. Considerations of space alone preclude printing such material verbatim. Furthermore, even if published in full, the addresses would not always provide the reader with enough information to identify fully the sender and recipient. Military etiquette required that a subordinate officer address his superior not directly, but through the latter's adjutant. Thus, a letter destined for a general is ordinarily addressed to a captain or lieutenant, often only by the name of that lesser officer. To bring order out of the chaos that would remain even if all addresses were printed in full, and at the same time to convey all necessary information to the reader, the editors employ a twofold procedure. First, the headnote of each document identifies both sender and recipient – not by name, but by position, command, or other categorical label. For example, a letter from a staff assistant of the Union general in command of the military Department of the Gulf is labeled as originating not from "Lieutenant So-and-So" but from the "Headquarters of the Department of the Gulf." Confederate officials and military units are indicated as such by the addition of the word "Confederate" before their title or command, while those of the Union stand without modification. Most of the time this information for the headnote is apparent in the document itself, but when necessary the editors resort to other documents, published military registers, and service records to supply the proper designations. Second, the citation of each document (in the endnote) reproduces the military rank or other title as well as the name of both sender and recipient exactly as provided in the original document (except that punctuation is added to abbreviations, nonstandard punctuation is modernized, and superscripts are lowered to the line). Thus, the headnote and endnote together communicate the information from the return and inside addresses without printing those addresses in full.

Bureaucratic, and especially military procedures often created document files containing letters with numerous enclosures and endorsements. Although many routine endorsements served merely to transmit letters through proper channels, others reported the results of investigations, stated policy decisions, and issued orders. Indeed, enclosures or endorsements themselves are often valuable documents deserving publication. The editors therefore treat the material accompanying a document in one of three ways. First, some or all of such material may be printed in full along with the cover document. Second, accompanying items not published may be summarized in the endnote. Third, any accompanying material neither published nor summarized is noted in the endnote by the words "endorsements," "enclosures," "other enclosures," or "other endorsements." The editors do not, however, attempt to describe the contents or even note the existence of other documents that appear in the same file with the document being published but are not enclosed in it or attached to it. Clerks sometimes consolidated files of related – or even unrelated – correspondence, and many such files are voluminous. The editors draw upon other documents in the same file when necessary for annotation, just as they do upon documents filed elsewhere, but the endnote is normally a guide only to the material actually enclosed in, attached to, or endorsed upon the published document.

A technical description symbol follows each document at the left, usually on the same line as the signature. The symbol describes the physical form of the manuscript, the handwriting, and the signature. (See p. xxxiii for the symbols employed.)

An endnote for each document or group of related documents begins with a full citation that should allow the reader to locate the original among the holdings of the National Archives.[1] The citation refers solely to the document from which the printed transcription is made; the editors have searched out neither other copies in the National Archives nor any previously published versions. Because all the documents published in *Freedom* come from the National Archives, no repository name is included in the citation. Record groups are cited only by the abbreviation RG and a number. (See pp. xxxiii–xxxiv for a list of record group

[1] Scholars have cited documents from the National Archives in a bewildering variety of forms, many of them entirely inadequate. The editors of *Freedom* have tried to include all the information required to locate a document. They urge similar completeness, if not necessarily their particular form of citation, upon other researchers and publishers.

abbreviations.) For the convenience of researchers, the editors usually provide both series title and series number for each document, but readers should note that series numbers are assigned by the National Archives staff for purposes of control and retrieval, and they are subject to revision. Each citation concludes with the Freedmen and Southern Society Project's own file number for that document, enclosed in brackets. In future the editors plan to microfilm all the documents accumulated during the project's search at the National Archives, along with the various geographical and topical indexes created by the staff. The project's file number for each document will thus serve as a guide both to the microfilm copy of the manuscript document and to other related documents in the project's files.

For ease of reference, the documents published in *Freedom* are numbered in sequence. On occasion, the editors have selected for publication several documents that taken together constitute a single episode. These documentary "clusters" are demarked at their beginning and at their conclusion by the project's logo – a broken shackle. The documents within each cluster bear alphabetical designations next to the number of the cluster.

Because *Freedom* focuses upon a subject or a series of questions, the editors consider the function of annotation different from that required in editing the papers of an individual. The editors seek, in the essays that introduce each section, to provide background information and interpretive context that will assist the reader in understanding the documents that follow, but the documents themselves are selected and arranged to tell their own story with relatively little annotation. When the editors judge annotation to be necessary or helpful, it usually appears in the form of further information about the content of a document or about the historical events under consideration, rather than biographical identification of individuals mentioned in the document. Thus, there are relatively few editorial notes to specific items within a document, but the endnote often describes the outcome of the case or discusses other events related to the episode portrayed in the document. Such annotation, as well as the chapter essays, is based primarily on other documents from the National Archives; those documents are cited in full, and their citations provide a guide to related records that could not be published. Quotations that appear without footnotes in a chapter essay, as well as undocumented descriptions of specific incidents, are taken from the documents published in that chapter. When portions of documents are quoted in endnotes and footnotes, they are transcribed by the same procedures as those employed for documents printed in full, except that terminal sentence punctuation is modernized. Annotation is also drawn from published primary sources, and, with few exceptions, the editors rely upon primary material rather than the secondary literature.

Symbols and Abbreviations

RG 58	Records of the Internal Revenue Service
RG 59	General Records of the Department of State
RG 60	General Records of the Department of Justice
RG 77	Records of the Office of the Chief of Engineers
RG 92	Records of the Office of the Quartermaster General
RG 94	Records of the Adjutant General's Office, 1780s–1917
RG 99	Records of the Office of the Paymaster General
RG 101	Records of the Office of the Comptroller of the Currency
RG 105	Records of the Bureau of Refugees, Freedmen, and Abandoned Lands
RG 107	Records of the Office of the Secretary of War
RG 108	Records of the Headquarters of the Army
RG 109	War Department Collection of Confederate Records
RG 110	Records of the Provost Marshal General's Bureau (Civil War)
RG 153	Records of the Office of the Judge Advocate General (Army)
RG 159	Records of the Office of the Inspector General
RG 217	Records of the United States General Accounting Office
RG 233	Records of the United States House of Representatives
RG 366	Records of Civil War Special Agencies of the Treasury Department
RG 393	Records of United States Army Continental Commands, 1821–1920

Short Titles

Freedom — *Freedom: A Documentary History of Emancipation, 1861–1867.*

Series 1, volume 1, *The Destruction of Slavery*, ed. Ira Berlin, Barbara J. Fields, Thavolia Glymph, Joseph P. Reidy, and Leslie S. Rowland (Cambridge, 1985).

Series 1, volume 2, *The Wartime Genesis of Free Labor: The Upper South*, ed. Ira Berlin, Steven F. Miller, Joseph P. Reidy, and Leslie S. Rowland (Cambridge, forthcoming).

Series 1, volume 3, *The Wartime Genesis of Free Labor: The Lower South*, ed. Ira Berlin, Thavolia Glymph, Steven F. Miller, Joseph P. Reidy, Leslie S. Rowland, and Julie Saville (Cambridge, 1990).

The Elements of a Document

Headnote*

347: Discharged Maryland Black Soldier to a Freedmen's Bureau Claim Agent

Date and place line (reproduced as in manuscript, except printed on a single line at the top of document regardless of location in manuscript)

Salutation (reproduced as in manuscript, except run into text regardless of location in manuscript)

Body of document (reproduced as in manuscript, except extra space added at unpunctuated sentence breaks)

Williamsport Washington Co MD oct the 8 /66

Sir it is With Much Pleser That I seat my self Tu Rit you a few lines Tu Now if you can Git The Bounty That is Cuming Tu us & We hear That The ar Mor for us if The ar Pleas Tu let us Now & if you Can git it With or Discharges if you Can I shod lik for you Tu Du so sum of The Boys ar Giting on Esey A Bout Thear Papars & The Monney Tu The ar so Menney After Them Tu let Them git it for Them & The Tel Them That The Can git it suner Nomor But I still Reman you abdiant survent

Charles. P. Taylor

ALS

Complimentary closing (reproduced as in manuscript, except run into text regardless of location in manuscript)

Signature (reproduced as in manuscript, except titles and identification omitted)

Technical description of the document* (see list of symbols, p. xxxiii)

Charles P. Taylor to Mr. Wm. Fowler, 8 Oct. 1866, Unregistered Letters Received, ser. 1963, MD & DE Asst. Comr., RG 105[a] [A-9641].[b] Endorsement.[c] Taylor identified himself as a former sergeant in the 4th USCI.[d]

Endnote*

a. Full citation of the document: titles and names of sender and recipient exactly as spelled in manuscript; date; and National Archives citation (see list of record group abbreviations, pp. xxxiii–xxxiv)
b. Freedmen and Southern Society Project file number
c. Notation of enclosures and/or endorsements that are neither published with the document nor summarized in the endnote text
d. Text of endnote

Footnotes,* if any, follow the endnote

* Elements marked with an asterisk are supplied by the editors.

Symbols and Abbreviations

EDITORIAL SYMBOLS

[roman] Words or letters in roman type within brackets represent editorial inference or conjecture of parts of manuscripts that are illegible, obscured, or mutilated. A question mark indicates doubt about the conjecture.

[. . .] A three-dot ellipsis within brackets represents illegible or obscured words that the editors cannot decipher. If there is more than one undecipherable word, a footnote reports the extent of the passage.

. . . [5] A three-dot ellipsis and a footnote represent words or passages entirely lost because the manuscript is torn or a portion is missing. The footnote reports the approximate amount of material missing.

~~canceled~~ Canceled type represents material written and then crossed out by the author of a manuscript. This device is used only when the editors judge that the crossed-out material reflects an important alteration of meaning. Ordinarily, canceled words are omitted without notation.

[*italic*] Words or letters in italic type within brackets represent material that has been inserted by the editors and is not part of the original manuscript. A question mark indicates that the insertion is a conjecture.

. . . . A four-dot ellipsis centered on a separate line represents editorial omission of a substantial body of material. A shorter omission, of only one or two sentences, is indicated by a four-dot ellipsis between two sentences.

SYMBOLS USED TO DESCRIBE MANUSCRIPTS

Symbols used to describe the handwriting, form, and signature of each document appear at the end of each document.

The first capital letter describes the handwriting of the document:

A autograph (written in the author's hand)
H handwritten by other than the author (for example, by a clerk)
P printed
T typed

The second capital letter, with lower-case modifier when appropriate, describes the form of the document:

L letter
D document
E endorsement
W wire (telegram)

c copy
p press copy
d draft
f fragment

The third capital letter describes the signature:

S signed by the author
Sr signed with a representation of the author's name
I initialed by the author
no signature or representation

For example, among the more common symbols are: ALS (autograph letter, signed by author), HLS (handwritten letter, signed by author), HLSr (handwritten letter, signed with a representation), HLcSr (handwritten copy of a letter, signed with a representation), HD (handwritten document, no signature).

ABBREVIATIONS FOR RECORD GROUPS IN THE NATIONAL ARCHIVES OF THE UNITED STATES

RG 11 General Records of the United States Government
RG 15 Records of the Veterans Administration
RG 21 Records of District Courts of the United States
RG 45 Naval Records Collection of the Office of Naval Records and Library
RG 46 Records of the United States Senate
RG 56 General Records of the Department of the Treasury

	Series 2, *The Black Military Experience*, ed. Ira Berlin, Joseph P. Reidy, and Leslie S. Rowland (Cambridge, 1982).
Navy Official Records	U.S. Navy Department, *Official Records of the Union and Confederate Navies in the War of the Rebellion*, 30 vols. (Washington, 1894–1922).
Official Records	U.S. War Department, *The War of the Rebellion: A Compilation of the Official Records of the Union and Confederate Armies*, 128 vols. (Washington, 1880–1901).
Statutes at Large	U.S., *Statutes at Large, Treaties, and Proclamations of the United States of America*, 17 vols. (Boston, 1850–1873).

MILITARY AND OTHER ABBREVIATIONS THAT APPEAR FREQUENTLY IN THE DOCUMENTS

A.A.A.G.	Acting Assistant Adjutant General
A.A.G.	Assistant Adjutant General
A.C.	Army Corps
A.C.	Assistant Commissioner (Freedmen's Bureau)
Act., Actg.	Acting
A.D.	African Descent
A.D.C.	Aide-de-Camp
Adjt.	Adjutant
A.G.O.	Adjutant General's Office
Agt.	Agent
A.Q.M.	Assistant Quartermaster
A.S.A.C.	Assistant Subassistant Commissioner (Freedmen's Bureau)
Asst.	Assistant
A.S.W.	Assistant Secretary of War
BBG	Brevet Brigadier General
BG	Brigadier General
BGC	Brigadier General Commanding
BGV	Brigadier General of Volunteers
BMG	Brevet Major General
BRFAL	Bureau of Refugees, Freedmen, and Abandoned Lands
Brig.	Brigadier

Symbols and Abbreviations

Bvt.	Brevet
Capt.	Captain
Cav.	Cavalry
C. d'A.	Corps d'Afrique
C.H.	Court House
Co.	Company
Col.	Colonel
col^{d}, cold., col.	colored
com., comms^{y}	commissary
comdg., cmdg.	commanding
Comdr., Commr.	Commander
Comr.	Commissioner (Freedmen's Bureau)
C.S.	Commissary of Subsistence
C.S.	Commissioned Staff
C.S.	Confederate States
c.s.	current series
C.S.A.	Confederate States of America
Dept.	Department
Dist.	District
D.P.M.	Deputy Provost Marshal
E.C.	Expeditionary Corps
E.M.M.	Enrolled Missouri Militia
f.m.c.	free man of color
Freedmen's Bureau	Bureau of Refugees, Freedmen, and Abandoned Lands
f.w.c.	free woman of color
G.C.M.	General Court-Martial
Gen., Gen'l	General
G.O.	General Order(s)
HQ, Hd. Qrs., Hdqrs.	Headquarters
Inf.	Infantry
Insp.	Inspector
inst.	*instant* (the current month of the year)
J.A.	Judge Advocate
Lt., Lieut.	Lieutenant
Maj.	Major
MG	Major General
MGC	Major General Commanding
MGV	Major General of Volunteers
M.O.	Mustering Officer
M.S.M.	Missouri State Militia
N.C.O.	Noncommissioned Officer(s)
NCS	Noncommissioned Staff
NG	Native Guard
Obt. Servt.	Obedient Servant

P.M.	Provost Marshal
P.M.	Paymaster
P.M.G.	Provost Marshal General
Priv., Pri.	Private
Pro. Mar., Provo. Mar.	Provost Marshal
prox.	*proximo* (the next month of the year)
Q.M., Qr. M.	Quartermaster
Q.M.G.O.	Quartermaster General's Office
Regt.	Regiment, regimental
RG	Record Group
R.Q.M.	Regimental Quartermaster
S.A.C	Subassistant Commissioner (Freedmen's Bureau)
Sec. War	Secretary of War
ser.	series
Sergt., Sgt.	Sergeant
S.O.	Special Order(s)
Subasst. Comr.	Subassistant Commissioner (Freedmen's Bureau)
Supt.	Superintendent
ult., ult^{o}	*ultimo* (the preceding month of the year)
U.S.A.	U.S. Army
USCA Lt	U.S. Colored Artillery (Light)
USCA Hvy	U.S. Colored Artillery (Heavy)
USCC	U.S. Colored Cavalry
USCHA	U.S. Colored Heavy Artillery
USCI	U.S. Colored Infantry
USCLtA	U.S. Colored Light Artillery
USCT	U.S. Colored Troops
U.S.S.	U.S. Ship
U.S.V.	U.S. Volunteers
V., Vols.	Volunteers (usually preceded by a state abbreviation)
V.M.	Volunteer Militia (preceded by a state abbreviation)
V.R.C.	Veteran Reserve Corps

The Wartime Genesis of Free Labor, 1861–1865

AS SLAVERY COLLAPSED during the American Civil War, fundamental questions arose about the social order that would replace the South's "peculiar institution."[1] Amid the tumult and danger of war, former slaves – usually designated "contrabands" or "freedmen" – struggled to secure their liberty, reconstitute their families, and create institutions befitting a free people. But no problem loomed larger than finding a means of support. Having relinquished the guarantee of subsistence that accompanied slavery, freedpeople faced numerous obstacles to gaining a livelihood. Many had fled their homes with little more than the clothes on their backs. Others had been abandoned by their owners. Nearly all began life in freedom without tools or land. How would they feed, clothe, and house themselves? Who would provide for the old, the young, the sick or disabled? For generations the slaves' labor had enriched their owners. Now, in freedom, would they or others benefit from their toil?

Military operations in the slave states compelled Northern officials to confront the same questions. Fugitive slaves poured into federal

[1] This essay is based primarily upon the documents included in this volume, documents published in other volumes of *Freedom*, and unpublished documents in the files of the Freedmen and Southern Society Project. In addition, numerous secondary works have served as guides to the development of wartime labor arrangements: Louis S. Gerteis, *From Contraband to Freedman: Federal Policy toward Southern Blacks, 1861–1865* (Westport, Conn., 1973); W. E. B. Du Bois, *Black Reconstruction in America: An Essay toward a History of the Part Which Black Folk Played in the Attempt to Reconstruct Democracy in America, 1860–1880* (New York, 1935), chaps. 1–5; Eric Foner, *Reconstruction: America's Unfinished Revolution, 1863–1877* (New York, 1988), chaps. 1–3; Leon F. Litwack, *Been in the Storm So Long: The Aftermath of Slavery* (New York, 1979), chaps. 1–4; James M. McPherson, *The Struggle for Equality: Abolitionists and the Negro in the Civil War and Reconstruction* (Princeton, N.J., 1964), chaps. 3–13; Edward Magdol, *A Right to the Land: Essays on the Freedmen's Community* (Westport, Conn., 1977), chap. 4; Benjamin Quarles, *The Negro in the Civil War* (Boston, 1953), especially chap. 13; Lawrence N. Powell, *New Masters: Northern Planters during the Civil War and Reconstruction* (New Haven, Conn., 1980); James L. Roark, *Masters without Slaves: Southern Planters in the Civil War and Reconstruction* (New York, 1977), chaps. 1–3; Armstead L. Robinson, " 'Worser dan Jeff Davis': The Coming of Free Labor during the Civil War, 1861–1865," in *Essays on the Postbellum Southern Economy*, ed. Thavolia Glymph and John J. Kushma (College Station, Tex., 1985), pp. 11–47.

lines, searching for protection and freedom. Other slaves came under Union control as Northern forces occupied parts of the Confederacy. From the first, military considerations encouraged officers in the field and officials in Washington to mobilize former slaves on behalf of the Union war effort. Provision also had to be made for those who could not be usefully employed by the army or navy. Once emancipation became official federal policy, attention turned as well to the task of constructing free labor upon the ruins of slavery. Throughout the Union-occupied South, intertwined questions of labor and welfare forced themselves upon officials concerned chiefly with waging the war.

Federal military authorities were not alone in laying claim to the labor of the former slaves. Antislavery Northerners hoped to demonstrate the superior productivity of free labor, and Yankee entrepreneurs saw profits to be made in the bargain. Slave owners insisted that the former slaves were still theirs by right, and owners-turned-employers argued for preferential access to the labor of people they had lost as property. White Southerners who had never owned slaves saw an opportunity to break the slaveholders' monopoly of black workers. As the confiscation acts, the Emancipation Proclamation, and the success of federal arms extended freedom, the questions of how former slaves would work and for whose benefit assumed ever-greater importance.

In the course of a complex struggle among many contestants, free labor slowly took root throughout the Union-occupied South. Owing more to wartime necessities than to carefully considered plans, the new arrangements were ad hoc responses, not systematic designs for the future. They were restricted, moreover, to the narrow bounds of Union-held territory, themselves subject to the overriding requirements of the war. Provisional by their very nature, wartime labor programs were certain to be revamped or even jettisoned upon the return of peace. Nevertheless, measures adopted as temporary expedients had far-reaching implications. As the victorious North took lessons from wartime developments, precedents solidified that would open certain possibilities and foreclose others. Meanwhile, thousands of former slaves and former slaveholders entered the postwar world already experienced in the ways of free labor. Reconstruction of the defeated South would begin where wartime measures left off.

Four related circumstances influenced the wartime evolution of free labor: the notions of freedom espoused by Northerners, the beliefs and material resources of former slaves and free blacks, the extent and character of federal occupation, and the policies of federal authorities. If no one circumstance operated independently of the others, each was of special significance at particular moments or in particular places.

Free labor emerged in the Union-occupied South as freedom was being redefined in the North. During the first half of the nineteenth century, Northern merchants and manufacturers had reorganized work arrangements and, in the process, gained unprecedented control over production. They thereby elevated themselves to new positions of social and economic preeminence and set in motion changes that ousted artisans from their crafts and farmers from their land. On the eve of the Civil War, most small towns and farming communities had not yet been touched by these revolutionary changes. But in all the major cities of the Northeast and Midwest, as well as many small towns, workshops employing dozens of workers and factories employing hundreds had become common. In these places, wage-workers may have outnumbered landed farmers, propertied artisans, and self-employed shopkeepers.

Changing patterns of ownership and production created overlapping and, often, contradictory conceptions of freedom. From one perspective, freedom derived from a man's ownership of productive property, real and personal, which guaranteed a competency and the ability to establish an independent household. Ownership of productive property ensured respectability within a community and membership in its polity. The ideal citizen was a male proprietor whose control over his own labor and its products underlay both economic and political independence. Since men of independent means could not be bought or bribed, they alone – at least until the 1820s, in most states – could vote, hold office, serve on juries, and enjoy the other manifestations of full citizenship. As heads of households, such men could extend some of the benefits of freedom to others under their jurisdiction – wives, children, servants, apprentices, and journeymen – whom they represented in the polity. Depending on their age, sex, and color, these dependents might travel without restriction, assemble at will, bear arms, testify in court, and enjoy other rights, but they were not and could not be citizens in the fullest sense.

The social and economic changes that eroded property-based independence created a different understanding of freedom. From the new perspective, freedom derived not from the ownership of productive property, but from the unfettered sale of one's labor power – itself a commodity – in a competitive market. "Political freedom rightly defined," proclaimed a Union general, "is liberty to work, and to be protected in the full enjoyment of the fruits of labor."[2] Voluntary rather than obligatory labor, represented by contracts based on mutual consent, became the hallmark of the new order. Ideal citizens thus included not only independent farmers, artisans, and shopkeepers, but also upwardly mobile wage-workers who by dint of ambition, industry, and luck improved themselves. Indeed, to the apostles of the emerging order, the process of self-improvement itself made for better workers,

[2] *Freedom*, ser. 1, vol. 2: doc. 26. The general was Benjamin F. Butler.

better citizens, and better men, thereby affirming the natural – if not providential – origins of the new ideal.

Individual men, able to rise and fall according to their own ability and energy, began breaking away from traditional household structures. By the early nineteenth century, indentured servitude had all but disappeared, apprenticeship was falling into disuse, and the master-journeyman system – increasingly unable to regulate prices, training, or the quality of workmanship – was crumbling. Changes that undermined personal subordination in the workplace also altered domestic relationships. Although fathers retained much of their traditional power and full political rights were not extended to women, the departure of production from the household allowed some women a new authority over domestic life.[3]

As Northerners came to advocate internally generated initiative, rather than personal obligation and external force, as the proper stimulus to industry, they assaulted those social relations that smacked of direct coercion. Southern slaveholders represented everything that advocates of the new freedom despised. By denying the two great incentives to self-improvement – the stick of hunger and the carrot of property accumulation – slaveholders debased both their slaves and themselves

[3] On the transformation of economy and society in the free states, see David Montgomery, *Beyond Equality: Labor and the Radical Republicans, 1862–1872* (New York, 1967), especially chap. 1 and appendix A; Alfred D. Chandler, *The Visible Hand: The Managerial Revolution in American Business* (Cambridge, Mass., 1977), chaps. 1–3; Alan Dawley, *Class and Community: The Industrial Revolution in Lynn* (Cambridge, Mass., 1976); David M. Gordon, Richard Edwards, and Michael Reich, *Segmented Work, Divided Workers: The Historical Transformation of Labor in the United States* (Cambridge, Eng., 1982), chap. 3; Steven Hahn and Jonathan Prude, eds., *The Countryside in the Age of Capitalist Transformation: Essays in the Social History of Rural America* (Chapel Hill, N.C., 1985), chaps. 1–4, 8–11; Peter Dobkin Hall, *The Organization of American Culture, 1700–1900: Private Institutions, Elites, and the Origins of American Nationality* (New York, 1982); Mary P. Ryan, *Cradle of the Middle Class: The Family in Oneida County, New York, 1790–1865* (Cambridge, Eng., 1981); Anthony F. C. Wallace, *Rockdale: The Growth of an American Village in the Early Industrial Revolution* (New York, 1978); Sean Wilentz, *Chants Democratic: New York City and the Rise of the American Working Class, 1788–1850* (New York, 1984). The decline of the master-apprentice system is traced in W. J. Rorabaugh, *The Craft Apprentice: From Franklin to the Machine Age in America* (New York, 1986). For the ideological changes that accompanied and articulated the social transformation, see Eric Foner, *Free Soil, Free Labor, Free Men: The Ideology of the Republican Party before the Civil War* (New York, 1970), chaps. 1–2, and *Politics and Ideology in the Age of the Civil War* (New York, 1980), chaps. 3–4, 6–7; Barbara J. Fields and Leslie S. Rowland, "Free Labor Ideology and Its Exponents in the South during the Civil War and Reconstruction," paper delivered at the annual meeting of the Organization of American Historians, 1984. The changing role of women is analyzed in Nancy F. Cott, *The Bonds of Womanhood: "Woman's Sphere" in New England, 1780–1835* (New Haven, Conn., 1977); Ryan, *Cradle of the Middle Class*; Kathryn Kish Sklar, *Catharine Beecher: A Study in American Domesticity* (New Haven, Conn., 1973); Christine Stansell, *City of Women: Sex and Class in New York, 1789–1860* (New York, 1986).

and created a social order that was tyrannical, exploitative, and corrupt. Only free labor could make for a society of free and independent men.[4]

The new conception of freedom existed side by side with the old, and rather than see them as mutually exclusive, most Northerners embraced elements of both. Indeed, for many of them, the opportunities of the market offered a way to achieve the old ideal of freehold independence. The promise of social mobility bridged the gap between propertyless proletarian and independent proprietor, suggesting that any industrious man could attain independent standing. "There is [no] such thing," declared Abraham Lincoln, "as the free hired laborer being fixed to that condition for life. . . . The prudent, penniless beginner in the world labors for wages awhile, saves a surplus with which to buy tools or land for himself, then labors on his own account another while, and at length hires another new beginner to help him."[5] With similar optimism, Northerners also argued that there was no inherent conflict between the propertied and the propertyless. To the contrary, a "harmony of interests" united capital and labor. Governed by the universal "laws" of political economy, that harmony was embodied in the voluntary contractual relations that joined employer and employee.

A growing number of wage-workers discerned conflict, not harmony, between labor and capital. While struggling to improve themselves, they began to articulate new ideas that denied the preeminence of the market and the right of employers to determine their employees' place in society. Those who subsisted by selling their labor power demanded and received title to privileges previously reserved for property-owning freemen. The suffrage and other political rights became prerogatives of dependent proletarians as well as independent proprietors.[6]

[4] David Brion Davis, *The Problem of Slavery in the Age of Revolution, 1770–1823* (Ithaca, N.Y., 1975), especially chaps. 8–10; Jonathan A. Glickstein, " 'Poverty Is Not Slavery': American Abolitionists and the Competitive Labor Market," in *Antislavery Reconsidered: New Perspectives on the Abolitionists*, ed. Lewis Perry and Michael Fellman (Baton Rouge, La., 1979), pp. 195–218; Foner, *Free Soil, Free Labor, Free Men*; Louis S. Gerteis, *Morality and Utility in American Antislavery Reform* (Chapel Hill, N.C., 1987).

[5] Lincoln's statement appears in his annual message to Congress of December 1861. (Abraham Lincoln, *Collected Works*, ed. Roy P. Basler, Marion D. Pratt, and Lloyd A. Dunlap, 9 vols. [New Brunswick, N.J., 1953–55], vol. 5, pp. 35–53.)

[6] On the development of the American working class during the antebellum years, see Herbert G. Gutman, *Work, Culture, and Society in Industrializing America: Essays in American Working-Class and Social History* (New York, 1976), especially chap. 1; Dawley, *Class and Community*, chaps. 1–3, 5; Gordon et al., *Segmented Work, Divided Workers*, chap. 3; Wallace, *Rockdale*, chap. 4; Wilentz, *Chants Democratic*. Changes in the requirements for suffrage and officeholding are outlined in Richard P. McCormick, *The Second American Party System: Party Formation in the Jacksonian Era* (Chapel Hill, N.C., 1966).

The older ideas about independence corresponded to particular notions of dependence. In a community of independent freeholders, households were responsible for the support of their own dependents, be they children, elderly parents, servants, journeymen, or apprentices. Through networks of family and community, households also succored orphans, the physically and mentally ill, and other unfortunates. When such men, women, and children held no claim upon a particular household, local authorities assigned them to one and provided a subsidy from public funds. Respectable men and women who had fallen on hard times were often supported in their own homes – so-called outdoor relief – both to meet their immediate needs and to maintain the integrity of the community. The care of dependents thus lent support to the social order in communities in which face-to-face relations were the standard. Strangers and those deemed not respectable were either "warned out" of town or given short shrift, no matter how desperate.

The new notions of independence altered ideas about dependence. Relief assumed a new form as mobile, unattached individuals began to outnumber settled householders. In the seaboard metropolises of the Northeast, the arrival of thousands of newcomers from the countryside and from foreign lands transformed neighbors into strangers. In response, associations of benevolent men and women, in alliance with public officials, assumed responsibilities once borne by households. Sponsoring an array of new institutions – schools, poorhouses, penitentiaries, and asylums – these reformers offered a new discipline that would guard against permanent impoverishment in the absence of the traditional rewards and restraints. Reformers wanted to ensure that the freedom of propertyless men and women did not lead to license. They sought to demonstrate that even without a foundation in property ownership, civic responsibility and social discipline could rest upon industry, frugality, and sobriety, the personal virtues taught in common schools and Protestant churches and enforced by the market.[7]

On the eve of the Civil War, the conflicting notions about freedom and independence, work and welfare, were far from reconciled. Fighting a war for national reunification heightened the contradictions. Mobilization under the banner of "Union and Liberty" brought together diverse Northern constituencies with different understandings of both terms: New Englanders and midwesterners, factory workers and

[7] Intertwined ideas of public charity, private philanthropy, reform, and welfare are discussed in Paul Boyer, *Urban Masses and Moral Order in America, 1820–1920* (Cambridge, Mass., 1978), chaps. 1–7; Michael B. Katz, *In the Shadow of the Poorhouse: A Social History of Welfare in America* (New York, 1986), chaps. 1–4; Benjamin Joseph Klebaner, *Public Poor Relief in America, 1790–1860* (New York, 1976); David J. Rothman, *The Discovery of the Asylum: Social Order and Disorder in the New Republic* (Boston, 1971). Robert H. Bremner, *The Public Good: Philanthropy and Welfare in the Civil War Era* (New York, 1980), chaps. 1–5, is especially helpful on the war years.

yeoman farmers, Protestant reformers and Catholic immigrants, antislavery Republicans and proslavery Union Democrats. Contention over the meaning of freedom divided Northerners even as opposition to secession united them.

Southern slaves had their own conceptions of freedom, derived from their experience as slaves within the American republic. Themselves property, they were denied control over their labor and its product. Without independent standing in the eyes of the law, they were subject to the personal will of their owners. Slaves could be sold, disciplined, and moved without recourse, and they had no right to marry, educate their children, or provide for their parents. They could bear arms, assemble, hold property, and travel only with their owners' consent.

Slaves expected the destruction of their owners' sovereignty to open a world of new possibilities. If slavery denied them the right to control their persons and progeny, freedom would confer that right. If slavery required that they suffer arbitrary and often violent treatment, freedom would enable them to protect themselves against such abuse. If slavery allowed their owners to expropriate the fruits of their labor, freedom would at least guarantee compensation if not the entire product of their labor. As free people, former slaves expected to be able to organize their lives in accordance with their own sense of propriety, establish their families as independent units, and control productive property as the foundation of their new status.

But freedom was not merely slavery's negative. Even before the war, slaves established families, created churches, selected community leaders, and carved out a small realm of independent economic activity. An elaborate network of kinship – with its own patterns of courtship, rites of marriage, parental responsibilities, and kin obligations – linked slaves together. Throughout the South, slaves organized churches – formal congregations in cities and on some large plantations, informal gatherings on small farmsteads. Black ministers articulated a different interpretation of Christianity from that heard in the churches of slave owners. In addition to preachers, slaves chose other leaders from their own ranks. Often these were drivers or artisans, but sometimes men and women of no special status in the owners' view.

While subject to their owners' overwhelming power, slaves struggled to increase the possibilities of independent action in all areas of their lives. They pressed for nothing more relentlessly than control over their own labor, denial of which constituted the very essence of chattel slavery. Conceding what they could not alter, slaves worked without direct compensation but claimed the right to a predictable portion of what they produced. They expected their owners to feed, clothe, and house them in accordance with customary usage and irrespective of age, infirmity, or productivity.

Through a continuous process of contest and negotiation with individual owners, many slaves also established a right to some time of their own in which to cultivate gardens, hunt, fish, raise poultry and hogs, make baskets and practice other handicrafts, hire themselves to neighboring farmers and artisans, or receive payment for overwork. Some slaves were permitted to sell the products of such independent activities, often to their own masters and sometimes to others. Although their property had no standing at law, it gained recognition in practice, enabling them to accumulate small and generally perishable resources by which they improved their own lives and gave the next generation "a start." The slaves' self-directed economic activities, like their families and religious congregations, fostered a vision of an independent life and shaped their expectations of the postemancipation world.[8]

While the slaves' ideas about freedom everywhere derived from slavery, slavery was not everywhere the same. Regional and local differences affected the character of emancipation. Many of the four million slaves in the South in 1860 lived and worked alongside their owners, sharing intimately, if never equally, in the daily routine. Others hardly knew their owners, and instead stood at the end of a chain of command that extended from a black driver or foreman through a white overseer before it reached an absentee master. Some slaves had roots in the land they worked that reached back for generations; others were newcomers, recently torn from old homes and transplanted to a strange and distant place. Some slaves spent their entire lives on one great estate, rarely venturing beyond its boundaries. Others lived on small farms or in cities, interacted regularly with nonslaveholding whites and free blacks, traveled widely, and were sometimes rented out by their owners to different hirers. A few privileged slaves hired themselves out, paying their owners a monthly "wage" and retaining for themselves whatever remained.

Slaves also worked in different ways. Most were agricultural workers, chiefly field hands. Although they shared the experience of tilling the soil, the regimen of different crops and particular forms of labor organization fostered divergent patterns of work. Some slave men and women were assigned daily tasks, after the completion of which they could engage in self-directed activities that supplemented their diets and sometimes generated a small surplus. The majority of plantation

[8] The best general studies of Southern slavery in the nineteenth century are Eugene D. Genovese, *Roll, Jordan, Roll: The World the Slaves Made* (New York, 1974), and Kenneth M. Stampp, *The Peculiar Institution: Slavery in the Ante-Bellum South* (New York, 1956). On the family life of slaves, see Herbert G. Gutman, *The Black Family in Slavery and Freedom, 1750–1925* (New York, 1976); on religion, Albert J. Raboteau, *Slave Religion: The "Invisible Institution" in the Antebellum South* (New York, 1978); on the slaves' independent economic activity, Ira Berlin and Philip D. Morgan, eds., *The Slaves' Economy: Independent Production by Slaves in the Americas* (London, in press).

slaves, however, worked from sunup to sundown in closely supervised gangs and had relatively little time to cultivate garden plots or accumulate property of any sort. Still other agricultural slaves, especially those in mixed-farming regions, labored at a variety of seasonally defined tasks that required flexible schedules and considerable freedom of movement. Work outside the field – in artisan shops, in urban warehouses and factories, and in the big house – created other distinctive patterns. The slaves' various work routines influenced both their lives in slavery and their ideas about freedom.[9]

Black people with prior experience in freedom, approximately a quarter-million on the eve of the Civil War, also contributed to the emergence of free-labor relations. Most free blacks resided in the Upper South, where they were so mixed and intermarried with slaves as to have become socially inseparable. Others, particularly those in the port cities of the Lower South, styled themselves "free people of color" and held themselves apart from the mass of rural, black slaves. But no matter how they tried to distinguish themselves, free blacks lived within the close confines of a society that presumed people of African descent to be slaves. Southern lawmakers denied them many liberties enjoyed by white people, forbidding them to travel freely, to testify in court or sit on juries, to bear arms, or (in some states) to hold property in their own names. Yet free blacks were not slaves. They enjoyed the right to marry, establish independent households, control their own labor, and accumulate property. Drawing on their skills and their personal connections with white patrons, a few ambitious free blacks managed to amass considerable wealth and attain a degree of respectability even in the eyes of slaveholders. Their experience engendered a special social outlook and an understanding of freedom that could be as different from that of the liberated as it was from that of the liberators.[10]

No matter what expectations black people brought to freedom, their intentions – like those of everyone else – collided with the realities of war. In some regions of the South, notably the South Carolina Sea Islands and certain areas of the Mississippi Valley, the arrival of federal troops caused slaveholders to abandon both their estates and their slaves. Transformed into de facto freedpeople by their owners' exodus, such former slaves pursued an independent livelihood on their home plantations, surrounded by a familiar landscape, kinfolk, and friends.

[9] The spatial diversity and temporal development of slavery in the United States are captured in Willie Lee Rose, ed., *A Documentary History of Slavery in North America* (New York, 1976), and Ira Berlin, "Time, Space, and the Evolution of Afro-American Society on British Mainland North America," *American Historical Review* 85 (Feb. 1980): 44–78.

[10] Ira Berlin, *Slaves without Masters: The Free Negro in the Antebellum South* (New York, 1974).

In much of the seceded South, however, and in the border states that remained in the Union, slaves gained freedom only by flight, Since solitary fugitives stood a better chance of success – especially early in the war – runaways often had to leave family and friends behind. Many fugitive slaves followed familiar paths to hideaways in forests and swamps; others occupied abandoned farms and plantations. But the vast majority of fugitives sought safety in or near federal encampments, trusting their future to perfect strangers.

Still other slaves secured freedom with their owners in residence. Most notably in southern Louisiana, Tennessee, and the border states, slaves confronted owners who were determined to maintain their old dominance in fact if not at law. Many such slaveholders, professing loyalty to the Union, called upon federal authorities to sustain their claims to black laborers; the officials, hesitant to alienate much-needed allies, frequently complied. Occasionally, even disloyal masters brazenly demanded military backing.[11]

Above all, the march of contending armies determined the possibilities available to former slaves. Where federal lines were secure, freedpeople could sink roots, reconstitute their families, organize churches and schools, and earn a livelihood. Such places were few in number. Enormous though it became, the federal army was never large enough simultaneously to protect the loyal states, defend the occupied regions of the Confederacy, and mount offensives against the rebels. Confederate troops held Union armies at bay during the first two years of the war and enjoyed the ability to counterattack in force well into 1864. Federal lines shifted in the ebb and flow of military campaigns, sometimes incorporating slaves from Confederate territory, sometimes uprooting freedpeople and sending them in search of another safe haven. Certain districts nominally under Union control became the site of guerrilla activity that widened into a war of all against all. If many slaves gained freedom on the run, subsequent events often kept them in motion. Few black men and women passed from slavery to freedom untouched by the uncertainty of military events.[12]

Vagaries of federal policy likewise affected the wartime experience of former slaves. The Union war effort entailed thousands of official decisions, great and small, made by an array of politicians, bureaucrats, and military officers. Although their policies aimed first to secure victory, other considerations also weighed heavily. In the field, soldiers and officers acted to safeguard their lives. In Washington, elected officials and civil servants protected their careers, scrutinizing possible courses of action against their prospects of reelection and advancement. Offi-

[11] The uneven evolution of legal freedom in different parts of the South is described in *Freedom*, ser. 1, vol. 1.

[12] Patterns of federal occupation and their implications for the destruction of slavery are discussed in *Freedom*, ser. 1, vol. 1.

cials, elected and appointed, kept an eye on the interests of their friends, constituents, and political parties. Only incidentally, if at all, did they consider the effect of their decisions upon the freedpeople. Nevertheless, programs implemented to recruit soldiers, to execute a particular military strategy, to bolster the national treasury, or to determine the ownership of captured property had important implications for the lives of former slaves.[13]

Nothing had prepared federal officials for the mobilization that followed the outbreak of war. The army and navy needed tons of food and uniforms, herds of horses and mules, miles of wagons and railroad cars, and thousands of rifles, cannons, and caissons – a veritable mountain of materiel – all of which would have to be purchased by a government that had no national tax save a tariff. It would have been difficult enough to amass and pay for the necessities of war under normal conditions, and these were not normal times. Secession had shaken established patterns of commerce and industry and disrupted financial markets throughout the Union, requiring wholesale reordering of agricultural and industrial production.

The demands of making war exceeded the resources of the peacetime nation and strained the Northern labor force. Whereas the leaders of the Confederacy assumed that slave labor would undergird their war effort,[14] Union officials at first evinced little interest in black laborers, either free or slave. Few in number, generally assumed to be unskilled and untutored, free blacks cut a poor figure in the eyes of most white Northerners, who viewed them as the refuse of slave society. Slave laborers seemed no more desirable or – if desired – attainable. Although slaves constituted a large portion of the laboring population in the loyal border states of Kentucky, Maryland, and Missouri, their services could be secured only with the consent of politically powerful slaveholders. Fearful that such a request might push the border states over the brink of secession, Union officials dared not ask.[15]

Border-state slaves, by contrast, were not deterred by the loyal

[13] Studies of federal policy include Robert P. Sharkey, *Money, Class, and Party: An Economic Study of Civil War and Reconstruction* (Baltimore, 1959); Leonard P. Curry, *Blueprint for Modern America: Nonmilitary Legislation of the First Civil War Congress* (Nashville, 1968); Fred A. Shannon, *The Organization and Administration of the Union Army, 1861–1865*, 2 vols. (Cleveland, 1928).

[14] Confederate mobilization of slave and free-black laborers is discussed in *Freedom*, ser. 1, vol. 1: chap. 9.

[15] On Northern free blacks, see Leon F. Litwack, *North of Slavery: The Negro in the Free States, 1790–1860* (Chicago, 1961). On federal policy regarding slavery in the border slave states, see *Freedom*, ser. 1, vol. 1: chaps. 6–8; *Freedom*, ser. 1, vol. 2: chaps. 4–6; *Freedom*, ser. 2: chap. 4. On early military employment of black laborers in the border states, see *Freedom*, ser. 1, vol. 1: doc. 197; *Freedom*, ser. 1, vol. 2: doc. 131.

standing of their owners. As soon as Union soldiers appeared in the border states, so did runaway slaves. But federal commanders went out of their way to safeguard the property rights of slaveholders. Fugitive slaves who offered their services to the Union army met a stern and sometimes violent rebuke. The heavy work associated with armies on the move therefore fell chiefly upon Northern soldiers themselves, with an occasional assist from private citizens laboring for wages.[16]

The federal government's respect for slavery extended to the seceded states as well. By reiterating a commitment to honor and protect slavery wherever it existed, President Abraham Lincoln and the Republican-controlled Congress hoped to win over not only border-state slaveholders and Northern Democrats but also lukewarm Confederates. Accordingly, when Union armies entered areas in rebellion, commanders disavowed any intention to unsettle relations between master and slave. Judicious policy, a War Department official explained, would "avoid all interference with the Social systems or local institutions" of the seceded states.[17]

While Lincoln and his subordinates courted slaveholders, slaves demonstrated their readiness to risk all for freedom and to do whatever they could to aid their owners' enemy. At every turn, federal soldiers met fugitive slaves bearing information, providing food and drink, and volunteering their labor. Determined to make the most of the presence of the Union army, slaves did whatever they could to ingratiate themselves to the invaders. It did not take long for Northern soldiers to see the wisdom of receiving and protecting them, if only to ease the burdens of military life and prevent the rebels from doing the same. Although officially denied entry to Union army lines, frequently manhandled, and sometimes returned to their owners, slaves continued to offer their services. In time, some found shelter in federal encampments, and many more gained residence in their shadow. Before long, the wisdom of common soldiers began to ascend the chain of command. A glimmer of this dynamic appeared in the border states, where most military operations transpired during 1861 and early 1862; it emerged in full brilliance when Union forces advanced into the seceded South.[18]

Events unleashed by the invasion and occupation of Confederate territory transformed federal policy regarding fugitive slaves and their labor. In May 1861, Union troops reinforced Fortress Monroe, a federal installation in tidewater Virginia. The following November, a joint

16 *Freedom*, ser. 1, vol. 1: pp. 332, 397–99, 495–98, and docs. 127–29, 153–54, 157, 160A–C, 197, 199–201.

17 *Freedom*, ser. 1, vol. 1: doc. 18.

18 See, for example, *Freedom*, ser. 1, vol. 1: docs. 1A, 6, 19, 41, 61, 81, 131A, 160B, 163, 197. The commander of a Union army division in northern Alabama echoed the sentiment of many of his men when he observed that, among local residents, the former slaves "are our only friends." (*Freedom*, ser. 1, vol. 1: doc. 86n.)

army and navy expedition invaded Port Royal Sound, in the South Carolina Sea Islands, to establish a coaling station for the blockading squadron. The presence of federal troops disrupted slavery in both tidewater Virginia and the Sea Islands. At Fortress Monroe, fugitive slaves from the nearby countryside arrived in search of freedom and military protection. At Port Royal, most of the white residents and virtually all the slaveholders fled when Union gunboats drew near, leaving the slaves in possession of the islands' great estates, including their crops of long-staple cotton. In both regions, federal commanders were confronted by large numbers of slaves whose owners were avowed enemies, not wavering friends.[19]

Far from their base of supply, army and navy officers found themselves badly in need of laborers. White Southerners, even those who professed loyalty to the federal government, displayed little inclination to work on its behalf. Northern laborers, whose wages had increased rapidly with the onset of war, proved difficult to lure south. With few alternatives, Union officials followed the traditional army practice of assigning soldiers to various fatigue duties, offering them "extra-duty pay" for work performed on their own time.[20] But the employment of soldiers had its limits, especially with Confederate troops menacing isolated Union outposts.

Military commanders therefore put able-bodied slaves to work. At Fortress Monroe and at Port Royal, runaway slaves soon composed the bulk of the labor force in the army's quartermaster, engineer, and subsistence departments. Navy officers employed fugitive slaves aboard ship and on shore. For those slaves who were able to work, military employment offered food, protection, and freedom in return for their labor. Women, children, and old or disabled people – who, in the eyes of the generals, could contribute nothing substantial to the war effort – posed a problem for Union officers, as no provision had been made for their support. At Fortress Monroe, General Benjamin F. Butler and his successor, General John E. Wool, applied the earnings of contrabands employed as military laborers toward the support of those not so employed. At Port Royal, General Thomas W. Sherman paid military laborers a small wage and issued rations to those unable to work.[21]

Ad hoc employment of fugitive-slave men and meager relief for their

[19] On the Union occupation of tidewater Virginia and the South Carolina Sea Islands, see *Freedom*, ser. 1, vol. 1: chaps. 1–2.

[20] On the military use of Northern laborers in the occupied South, see, for example, *Freedom*, ser. 1, vol. 2: docs. 16, 27; testimony of Gen. Dix before the American Freedmen's Inquiry Commission, 9 May 1863, filed with O-328 1863, Letters Received, ser. 12, RG 94 [K-68]; Capt. R. Saxton to Capt. L. H. Pelouse, 12 Mar. 1862, Letters Received, ser. 2254, SC Expeditionary Corps, RG 393 Pt. 2 No. 130 [C-1642]. On the employment of "extra duty soldiers," see *Freedom*, ser. 1, vol. 2: doc. 6.

[21] *Freedom*, ser. 1, vol. 1: doc. 1A; *Freedom*, ser. 1, vol. 2: doc. 2; see below, docs. 1, 4.

dependents failed to satisfy Northerners who were determined to use any available means to punish treason and reunite the nation. Seeing slavery as the root of the rebellion, practical-minded Republicans had no qualms about accepting fugitive slaves into federal lines, if only to punish the rebels. It was foolhardy not to do so, they argued, for the Confederates had already mobilized slaves in behalf of their own war effort. Abolitionists, black and white, turned that utilitarian argument to their own purposes. Seizing the opportunity to realize the egalitarian promise of the American Revolution, they denounced the narrow ground upon which Lincoln and the Congress were fighting the war. They called for outright abolition of slavery and the employment of former slaves as both soldiers and laborers.

Rather than rely upon the half-hearted efforts of federal commanders, abolitionists mobilized on behalf of the former slaves accumulating within Union lines. During the fall and winter of 1861–1862, antislavery men and women – often in league with other "educated and philanthropic" Northerners – organized contraband relief societies (subsequently known as freedmen's aid societies). These groups gathered clothing, bibles, schoolbooks, and medical supplies for the destitute ex-slaves at Fortress Monroe, Port Royal, and the District of Columbia. Convinced of their ability "to provide for all [the freedpeople's] proper wants," they assured the Lincoln administration that "there is no necessity for any Governmental charity."[22] But the abolitionists and their allies had no intention of confining themselves to rolling bandages and collecting old clothes. They would guide the passage of the former slaves to freedom.

Before long, philanthropic gentlemen and ladies were taking up stations in the Union-occupied South. Most of them were young men and women of high social standing, who had been raised in the abolitionist tradition and saw their service as a culmination of the long struggle against slavery. As teachers, ministers, and physicians, they brought useful skills and a heightened respect for the former slaves' humanity into federal camps. Although these Yankees shared many of the racial preconceptions common among white Northerners, they were sure of both the iniquity of slavery and the superiority of free labor. They assumed that, once freed of the vices of slavery and tutored in the virtues of free labor, evangelical Christianity, and republican citizenship, former slaves would take their place as productive and responsible members of the body politic.[23]

[22] *Freedom*, ser. 1, vol. 2: doc. 4.

[23] On Northern reformers in the wartime South, see Bremner, *The Public Good*, chap. 5; Robert F. Engs, *Freedom's First Generation: Black Hampton, Virginia, 1861–1890* (Philadelphia, 1979), chap. 3; McPherson, *Struggle for Equality*, especially chaps. 7, 11; Frederick Law Olmsted, *The Papers of Frederick Law Olmsted*, ed. Charles Capen McLaughlin and Charles E. Beveridge, 5 vols. to date (Baltimore, 1977–), vol. 4,

Although united in their determination to free the slaves and transform the South, antislavery Northerners did not share a vision of the social order that would replace the slaveholders' regime. They agreed that abolishing property rights in man and substituting the discipline of voluntary contracts for that of the lash were necessary conditions for a free South. But they disagreed about whether those steps were sufficient. A sizable contingent believed that self-ownership without possession of productive property did not constitute true freedom, but thereafter they too divided among themselves. Some of them recommended that freedpeople be required to purchase such property with wages earned after their liberation; the others maintained that years of uncompensated toil entitled the ex-slaves outright to the land they had "watered . . . with their tears and blood." Charles B. Wilder, a Massachusetts abolitionist assigned to Fortress Monroe by the American Missionary Association, regarded wage labor not as an end in itself, but an opportunity for former slaves to "buy a spot of land" where they could "have a little hut to live in with their families like any body else." Mansfield French, a Methodist clergyman sent to the Sea Islands by the same association, urged the government to endow freedpeople with land as indemnification for past injustice. "[T]he negroes had made [the land] what it was and . . . it belonged to them, and them only," he declared.[24]

The freedpeople's Northern friends drew upon their own notions of dependence as well as their ideas of independence. Antislavery men and women were alert to the development of new modes of poor relief. Many of them had ministered to the downtrodden and preached the gospel of industry, frugality, and sobriety in the North's growing cities. To them, destitute former slaves resembled other impoverished people. The imperative to work or starve would bear upon freedpeople no more lightly than it did upon newly arrived foreigners or rural migrants. The need to support themselves and their families and the opportunity to improve themselves and accumulate property would spur former slaves to diligent and faithful labor just as they did other people. "The negro is actuated by the same motives as other men," asserted one opponent of slavery, "& we must appeal to the *human nature* & make it appear for his interest to work & then he *will* work." To be sure, the freedpeople would require temporary assistance. But only temporary. Opponents of

Defending the Union: The Civil War and the U.S. Sanitary Commission, 1861–1863, ed. Jane Turner Censer, pp. 3–4, 20–26, and chap. 4; Joe M. Richardson, *Christian Reconstruction: The American Missionary Association and Southern Blacks, 1861–1890* (Athens, Ga., 1986), chaps. 1–2; Willie Lee Rose, *Rehearsal for Reconstruction: The Port Royal Experiment* (Indianapolis, Ind., 1964), especially chaps. 2–3; Henry L. Swint, *The Northern Teacher in the South, 1862–1870* (Nashville, 1941).

24 *Freedom*, ser. 1, vol. 2: docs. 16, 28, 43; statement of William B. Lucas, 30 Jan. [1864], enclosed in Wm. Henry Brisbane to Hon. Joseph J. Lewis, 15 Feb. 1864, General Correspondence, ser. 99, SC, Records of or Relating to Direct Tax Commissions in the Southern States, RG 58 [Z-3]. See also below, docs. 44–45.

slavery feared replacing one form of dependency with another and believed that charity would create permanent dependency. "Irish souphouses" and other "socialistic institutions" would not make former slaves industrious workers and exemplary citizens.[25]

Agents of Northern aid societies generally received a welcome from federal commanders, who shared many of their ideas about the relationship between private philanthropy and public charity and also saw "the contraband problem" as one of destitution and its relief. This shared perspective propelled some agents of Northern benevolence into positions of authority, with responsibility for distributing government rations and funneling donations from the North to needy freedpeople. At Fortress Monroe, General Wool appointed Wilder to supervise the "Vagrants or Contrabands." In the District of Columbia, where federal officers had initially lodged fugitive slaves in a jail, it seemed fitting to select Danforth B. Nichols, who had once directed a Chicago reformatory, as superintendent of contrabands.[26] Nowhere, however, did Northern reformers play a more prominent role than in the South Carolina Sea Islands.

During the first weeks after the arrival of Union troops, Sea Island slaves supported themselves from the corn and potatoes they had recently harvested and from the larders abandoned by their fugitive owners.[27] But soon, looking to the future, they also began to prepare the fields for a new year's cultivation. Placing their highest premium upon subsistence, they showed no interest in picking the cotton still in the fields or ginning what had already been harvested. Neither had they any intention of planting anew the crop that had "enriched [their] masters but had not fed them."[28]

Although the freedpeople ignored cotton, cotton would not be ignored. War-induced shortage had driven its price to record levels, and the long-staple cotton of the Sea Islands fetched the highest price of all. The partly harvested crop of 1861 immediately drew the notice of Treasury Department agents, who espied a source of revenue for the Union war effort. While the agents urged the freedpeople to gather the cotton still in the fields, offering to pay them for the work, Northern entrepreneurs clamored for an opportunity to operate the plantations the following year.[29]

To abolitionists, far more was at stake than public revenue and

[25] See below, doc. 40; *Freedom*, ser. 1, vol. 2: doc. 4.

[26] *Freedom*, ser. 1, vol. 2: docs. 4n., 60. In coastal North Carolina, Vincent Colyer, who in 1862 had charge of both fugitive slaves and white refugees, was given the title "Superintendent of the Poor." (*Freedom*, ser. 1, vol. 2: doc. 7.)

[27] On the Sea Islands under Union occupation, see Rose, *Rehearsal for Reconstruction*; Julie Saville, "A Measure of Freedom: From Slave to Wage Laborer in South Carolina, 1860–1868" (Ph.D. diss., Yale University, 1986), chap. 2; and below, chap. 1.

[28] See below, docs. 4, 8, 19, 21.

[29] See below, docs. 3, 5–7.

private profit. Inspired by the opportunity to institute free labor on the plantations of some of the South's most notorious rebels, they mobilized under the direction of Edward L. Pierce, a Boston attorney who had briefly supervised former slaves near Fortress Monroe. In February 1862, Secretary of the Treasury Salmon P. Chase – who construed his authority over trade in the occupied South to include operation of the Sea Island estates – appointed Pierce a special agent to oversee cultivation of the 1862 crop and guide the transformation of slaves into free workers. Assisted by freedmen's aid societies in Boston, New York, and Philadelphia, Pierce selected some fifty men to supervise the plantations. A contingent of ministers, teachers, and physicians also joined the enterprise. By March 1862, the flower of Northern abolitionism – young men and women whose mission earned them the sobriquet "Gideonites" – had taken up stations in the Sea Islands.[30]

Prepared to introduce former slaves to the rigors of free labor, the plantation superintendents discovered that their charges had already initiated a new order of their own. To be sure, Sea Island freedpeople generally welcomed the interlopers. They eagerly attended the Gideonites' schools and churches and accepted their gifts of clothing, medicine, and other supplies. But the former slaves contested the newcomers' belief that freedom could be validated only through the cultivation of cotton for wages. Although some plantation superintendents discerned a laudable "republican spirit" in the old slave quarters, they feared that the former slaves would retreat into mere self-sufficiency. Eager to demonstrate the efficiency of free labor in growing cotton and dependent upon revenue from the staple to fund their "experiment," the Northerners insisted that the former slaves take their accustomed place in the cotton fields. When the freedpeople were slow to comply, the superintendents did not hesitate to deny them rations.[31]

The exigencies of war rapidly eroded the sources of subsistence that had enabled the freedpeople to decline work in the cotton fields. Confederate troops raided outlying islands with alarming frequency. Even when they failed to capture and reenslave the inhabitants, the rebels succeeded in ravaging the plantations, burning houses, and carrying off food and livestock. In the wake of such raids, federal commanders relocated former slaves from endangered localities to the more secure islands around Port Royal Sound. There they were forced to rely upon the government for food and shelter. Northern soldiers and sailors also laid claim to the property and people on Sea Island plantations. On

[30] See below, docs. 8, 10, 36; Edward L. Pierce, "Persons recommended by the 'Educational Commission' of Boston . . ." and "Persons approved by the 'National Freedman's Relief Association' of New York . . . ," [Mar. 1862], vol. 19, #80, Port Royal Correspondence, 5th Agency, RG 366 [Q-9]; Rose, *Rehearsal for Reconstruction*, chap. 2.

[31] See below, docs. 10–11, 13, 21.

numerous islands, uniformed Yankees both with and without authorization stripped the estates of useful items. Military employers and Treasury Department cotton agents detailed hands to suit their own needs and convenience, leaving many plantations to be worked largely by women, children, and old people. When fugitive slaves arrived from the mainland, officials quickly siphoned off able-bodied men for military labor and remanded all others to the plantations. The destitute new arrivals added to the burdens of the resident plantation population. Having begun the year with high hopes of subsisting themselves through their own self-directed labor, freedpeople found their goal increasingly difficult to achieve.[32]

Former slaves elsewhere in the South faced many of the same difficulties, and their numbers grew rapidly when the federal army launched its spring campaign. Invasion of coastal North Carolina in March 1862 resulted in the establishment of Union posts at Roanoke Island, New Berne, and other points on the perimeter of Pamlico and Albemarle sounds. By April, army and navy operations had brought additional South Carolina Sea Islands into the Union fold, along with a few Georgia islands and small coastal enclaves at Fernandina and St. Augustine, in northern Florida. Events moved more quickly, and with more momentous implications, in the western theater. By early spring, forces of the Department of the Gulf commanded by General Butler had captured New Orleans and the southern Louisiana parishes between the city and the Gulf of Mexico. At about the same time, federal armies farther north embarked from winter quarters in Kentucky and Missouri for a three-pronged offensive into Arkansas and Tennessee. By midsummer 1862, the Union army had established major posts at Nashville and Memphis, Tennessee; Helena, Arkansas; Huntsville, Alabama; and Corinth, Mississippi; as well as at lesser points along strategic waterways and railroads. These operations in the western theater left Union forces well situated for further strikes into the Confederate interior.

As federal troops advanced, slaves gained their freedom under circumstances as different from each other as they were from those in the Sea Islands. In southern Louisiana, many slaveholders fled their estates, but a substantial proportion remained, proclaiming loyalty to the United States government and demanding that it sustain the slave regime. Eager to reassure slaveholding unionists, General Butler acceded to their entreaties during the first months of occupation. But before long, slaves had successfully challenged their owners and undermined Butler's policy. By the fall of 1862, slave insubordination and flight had disrupted the old order in the sugar parishes and forced Butler to reorganize plantation labor, requiring planters to pay wages and employing federal troops to enforce labor discipline. Taking the

[32] See below, docs. 2, 8, 11–13, 21.

pragmatic stand that such intervention was necessary to save the region's crop, control unruly black workers, and restore peace in the countryside, Butler pushed legal slavery to the edge but stopped short of outright emancipation.[33]

As was true in southern Louisiana, the agricultural year was well under way when federal forces secured footholds in middle and west Tennessee, eastern Arkansas, northern Mississippi, and northern Alabama. Many slaveholders remained in residence, although few possessed the unionist credentials of their counterparts in the sugar parishes. In the vicinity of Union posts, slavery retreated and free labor slowly began to emerge. Federal installations became magnets for fugitive slaves. Most of them were young men who had left their families behind. Although they arrived tired and hungry, they were ready to do whatever was necessary to gain freedom and protection.[34]

Federal commanders had plenty for them to do. With the expansion of Union-held territory during the spring and summer of 1862, the army and navy experienced persistent shortages of laborers. Setting aside reservations about the employment of former slaves, quartermaster, commissary, and engineer officers hired freedmen as artisans, teamsters, and common laborers. Medical officers put freedwomen to work as nurses and laundresses and freedmen as hospital attendants. Individual officers and common soldiers found countless jobs for both men and women, from policing camps to washing clothes and preparing food.

The employment of black laborers received growing support from Washington. As hopes of quick victory and easy reunification dwindled, Lincoln and his advisers became convinced that defeating the rebellion demanded more than the mobilization of Southern white unionists and the conversion of deluded secessionists. It required the destruction of Southern armies, occupation of substantial territory in the Confederate states, and demoralization of those who supported the rebellion. To achieve these goals, the Union needed all the help it could get. "It is a military necessity to have men and money," the President observed in July 1862, "and we can get neither in sufficient numbers or amounts if we keep from or drive from our lines slaves coming to them."[35]

That same month, the Congress and the President ratified the prac-

[33] On Union occupation and the undermining of slavery in southern Louisiana, see *Freedom*, ser. 1, vol. 1: chap. 4. On wartime labor arrangements, see below, chap. 2.

[34] On military developments and the destruction of slavery in the Mississippi Valley (including middle and east Tennessee and northern Alabama), see *Freedom*, ser. 1, vol. 1: chap. 5. Wartime labor arrangements in Union-occupied territory along the Mississippi River are considered below, in chap. 3; those in middle and east Tennessee and northern Alabama are treated separately, in *Freedom*, ser. 1, vol. 2: chap. 3.

[35] *Official Records*, ser. 1, vol. 53, pp. 529–30.

tice of accepting fugitive slaves into Union lines and putting them to work. The Second Confiscation Act and the Militia Act, both enacted on July 17, 1862, declared free the slaves of disloyal owners, authorized the President to mobilize "persons of African descent" against the rebellion, and granted freedom to any slave so employed. Within days, Lincoln ordered his commanders in the seceded states to "employ as laborers" as many black people "as can be advantageously used for military and naval purposes, giving them reasonable wages for their labor."[36] By the fall of 1862, the Union war effort rested in large measure on the labor of former slaves. That dependence enabled federal commanders at last to comprehend abolitionist arithmetic: Every slave employed by the army or navy represented a double gain, one subtracted from the Confederacy and one added to the Union. Some officers learned the lesson too well, adopting dragnet methods of labor recruitment. Slave men who had once begged to enter federal camps found themselves dragooned into service by "*forcible persuasion*."[37]

Most former slaves needed no coaxing. Understanding the connection between Union victory and their own liberty, large numbers volunteered for military labor. Freedpeople in coastal North Carolina, reported one military superintendent, "consider it a duty to work for the U.S. government" and "tabooed" any of their fellows who refused to do so. Accustomed to long workdays under hard taskmasters and eager to secure their freedom, former slaves tolerated conditions that other workers would not. Irish laborers brought to Fortress Monroe, noted Charles Wilder, "are crabbed and will work only so many hours a day." Freedmen, by contrast, "if they are decently paid . . . will work nights or any time and do any thing you want done."[38]

That commitment convinced numerous military employers of the superiority of black workers over Northern and immigrant laborers, and especially over soldiers. Among such employers in the Mississippi Valley, reported a superintendent of contrabands, "the lowest estimate is . . . that one negro is worth three soldiers." Union officers commonly rationalized their preference for black laborers with stereotypes of African docility or the putative ability of black people to withstand the subtropical sun and lowland diseases. While these notions obscured both the commitment of the former slaves to the Union cause and their desperate circumstances, they also reflected the centrality of black workers to the federal war effort.[39]

Military labor assumed different forms, each with its own implica-

[36] *Statutes at Large*, vol. 12, pp. 589–92, 597–600; *Official Records*, ser. 3, vol. 2, p. 397.

[37] On the impressment of black laborers, see, for example, *Freedom*, ser. 1, vol. 2: docs. 19–20, 25.

[38] *Freedom*, ser. 1, vol. 2: docs. 7, 16.

[39] See below, doc. 159; *Freedom*, ser. 1, vol. 2: docs. 27, 62, 206.

tions for the ex-slave employees. Thousands of fugitive slaves found work as personal servants to Union officers or soldiers, or hired on as company cooks or regimental laundresses. So prevalent was the employment of black servants at Helena, Arkansas, in the summer of 1862 that it seemed as if "[e]very other soldier" had one. Living in close quarters and sharing the rigors and camaraderie of camp life, servants often developed strong personal relationships with their employers. Yankee soldiers who hired black men and women simply because "we can get no others" frequently found that they had come to "like them as servants . . . and to feel an interest in their welfare." Such connections offered fugitive slaves a measure of protection from pursuing owners, as well as from hostile Northern soldiers. That same personal dependency also rendered black servants liable to exploitation by their employers, some of whom demanded the performance of degrading duties, refused to pay agreed-upon compensation, or inflicted physical abuse. Women were especially vulnerable to sexual assault. Yet the promise of protection counterbalanced such risks, especially during the first year of the war when the status of fugitive slaves remained largely undefined.[40]

While thousands of former slaves worked as servants, tens of thousands toiled as common laborers. They performed the army's most taxing, tedious, and dangerous tasks: building fortifications, felling trees, constructing roads, laying railroad track, repairing levees, and digging canals. Laborious even under the best of circumstances, such work was often done double-time, in unhealthy surroundings, and under hostile fire. Supervisors drove the workers hard and frequently afforded them insufficient rest and food. Harsh usage took its toll, as debilitated workers fell prey to disease. At one post in southern Louisiana, where federal officers had assumed authority over the maintenance of levees, military laborers toiled for three long months without a single day's rest. Shoeless, clad in rags, living in filthy quarters, and given meager rations of rice and sugar, the laborers endured conditions that moved one Northern officer to declare, "*My cattle at home are better cared for than these unfortunate persons*."[41]

Unlike personal servants, who usually worked for individual employers, laborers stood at the bottom of a vast hierarchy. Most worked in large groups, sometimes encompassing several hundred men (and, occasionally, a smattering of women). In their sheer size, such units exceeded all but the largest field forces in the slave South and rivaled the huge labor gangs on the great antebellum canal and railroad projects. Working under the immediate supervision of white overseers or foremen – usually civilians or junior officers – black gang workers seldom knew the higher-ranking officers who employed them. They were

[40] See below, docs. 150, 157, 160; *Freedom*, ser. 1, vol. 1: docs. 158, 160B; *Freedom*, ser. 1, vol. 2: doc. 119B.

[41] See below, doc. 80; *Freedom*, ser. 1, vol. 2: docs. 4, 52, 90, 102.

subject to an impersonal regimentation and discipline resembling that of unskilled factory operatives. Engineer employees at Fort Clinch, Florida, wore numbers on their hats to facilitate monitoring the work completed by each hand.[42] Such impersonality distanced workers from their bosses. It also encouraged a solidarity with their fellow workers that, among other things, facilitated collective protest against unacceptable conditions.

Many black military workers endured neither the suffocating closeness experienced by personal servants nor the regimentation of gang laborers. Instead, they worked singly or in small groups, driving teams, caring for sick and wounded soldiers, and performing a host of other duties. Like other military laborers, these freedpeople found themselves assigned to tasks shunned by others. Army medical authorities in Washington, for example, put black men to work "cleansing cesspools, scrubbing privies and policing the grounds" – work white civilians spurned and soldiers performed only "under the fear of punishment."[43] The hours were as long as the labor was arduous, especially when "military necessity" demanded prompt completion of a job.

Whether they toiled indoors or out, individually or in gangs, black men and women often found that their work for military employers failed to fulfill the most elemental promise of free labor – compensation. Unlike most Northern wage-labor arrangements, in which workers were responsible for purchasing their own and their families' necessities, military labor was generally accompanied by a guarantee of subsistence in the form of rations and sometimes clothing and shelter. Many military employers made similar provision for the immediate families of their employees, usually deducting the cost from the laborers' wages. Former-slave and free-black military laborers, who had few other resources with which to provide for their families, relied heavily on such allowances. Some federal officers therefore reckoned that the boon of freedom, plus nonmonetary remuneration, was compensation enough. Rejecting the appeal of one group of black military laborers for wages, Quartermaster General Montgomery C. Meigs contended that "[s]ustenance & freedom given at great cost by the United States has fully compensated" the claimants.[44]

For many ex-slaves fresh from bondage, sustenance and freedom were compensation enough, at least at first. But even on Meigs's terms, freedpeople found reason to complain. The quality of rations and clothing issued by military employers often fell below what their owners had

[42] On the scale and organization of military labor gangs, see below, doc. 24; *Freedom*, ser. 1, vol. 2: docs. 52, 90, 102–3.

[43] See below, doc. 20; *Freedom*, ser. 1, vol. 2: docs. 65A–B.

[44] For examples of the monetary and nonmonetary compensation of black military laborers, see below, docs. 8, 15, 24, 64–65, 148, 160; *Freedom*, ser. 1, vol. 2: docs. 2–3, 54–55, 87n.

provided. Even if rations and clothing were furnished to black workers' families, they still required money to meet other expenses, and whenever military laborers had to purchase their families' subsistence, they depended on regular wages.

Few federal officials recognized the depth of this dependence. Confusion within various government bureaus, as well as simple negligence, kept many laborers from receiving compensation. Because of faulty record keeping, hundreds of black men who worked at Fortress Monroe during the first months of the war were still awaiting their wages at war's end. Negligence was compounded by corruption, as the freedpeople's illiteracy and incomplete documentation of their employment made them easy targets for dishonest employers and paymasters. Often, however, the problem stemmed from the enormous wartime strain on the national treasury. At times, the army simply could not meet its payroll.[45]

The complexity of federal policy also contributed to difficulties in paying military laborers. The Militia Act stipulated that black military laborers were entitled to rations and wages of $10 per month (minus $3 for clothing), and Lincoln's executive order called for payment of "reasonable wages." But the law also stipulated that "in proper cases," compensation might be made to loyal slaveholders.[46] Pending official determination of which cases were "proper," many military employers hesitated to pay laborers whose owners might yet enter a claim. In some places, especially in the border states, paymasters issued vouchers or wages to putative owners rather than to the workers themselves. Such procedures made one military employer "ashamed to look a negro in the face." Indefinite and sometimes contradictory instructions from Washington and from field commanders put military employers in an awkward position, because army and navy regulations made them personally liable for improper expenditures. Even officers who wished to pay their workers fully and fairly could not do so without the authorization of superiors and, when proper records were lacking, could not do so at all.[47]

Newly arrived fugitives might endure such shabby treatment for a time, out of gratitude for freedom and the protection of federal arms. But before long, the hard work, the abuse, and the inability to support themselves and their families drove many of them away. Much to the disgust of military employers, black workers "deserted" in large num-

45 See below, docs. 157–58, 160, 226; *Freedom*, ser. 1, vol. 2: docs. 1, 12, 14, 17, 20, 59A, 87.

46 *Statutes at Large*, vol. 12, pp. 597–600; *Official Records*, ser. 3, vol. 2, p. 397; *Freedom*, ser. 2: doc. 64.

47 On complications involving payment of wages to the owners of military laborers who were legally still slaves, see below, doc. 148; *Freedom*, ser. 1, vol. 1: doc. 26B; *Freedom*, ser. 1, vol. 2: docs. 92, 99, 103, 132, 217.

bers to find employers who would treat them decently and pay them regularly.[48]

While affording large numbers of former slaves employment with the Northern army or navy, Union occupation also created opportunities for free labor on different terms. A federal presence over the ridge or around the bend enabled slaves to negotiate new conditions of labor with their masters and mistresses. The slaves pressed for working arrangements that accorded them a measure of self-direction, increased their access to the resources of farms and plantations, or provided compensation. A good many slaveholders met the demands, knowing that if they refused, their slaves would leave them to work for the Yankees. Other farmers and planters, who despaired of making a crop under wartime conditions, abandoned their estates. Often they left their property in the custody of their slaves, who were promised that they could keep a portion – sometimes the entirety – of what they produced. Desperate to salvage some financial return, a few slaveholders renounced slavery altogether and rented land to their former slaves. Other intrepid ex-slaves did not depend upon negotiation to attain independent occupation of land. They simply squatted on abandoned tracts.[49]

Wherever and by whatever means freedpeople secured a chance to farm independently, they demonstrated a preference for food production similar to that exhibited by former slaves in the Sea Islands. They cultivated fields of corn or other grains, planted gardens, raised poultry, and hunted, fished, and foraged in the wild. At times they availed themselves of the smokehouses, corncribs, and poultry yards of the estates, or appropriated hogs ranging in the forests and swamps. As their crops matured, many of them sold or bartered their surplus with Yankee soldiers, neighboring farmers, or the residents of nearby towns. Independent occupation of land could entail a rugged and dangerous existence, especially in disputed territory, but those ex-slaves who managed to gain a foothold clung to their hard-won independence.

In some places, military officials supported the freedpeople's attempts to farm on their own. Charles B. Wilder legitimated the self-organized settlements just inside federal lines in tidewater Virginia, and he permitted other fugitives to "cultivate the Ground and use the property of Rebels in Arms against the Government." At Helena, Arkansas, General Samuel R. Curtis, commander of the Army of the Southwest, went a step further. Deeming the former slaves who had remained on nearby plantations to be the rightful owners of the cotton they had grown as slaves, he and other officers paid them for whatever

48 On turnover among military laborers, see, for example, below, docs. 157, 182; *Freedom*, ser. 1, vol. 2: docs. 3, 16, 56, 92.

49 *Freedom*, ser. 1, vol. 1: doc. 123; *Freedom*, ser. 1, vol. 2: docs. 112–13, 116–17, 127; see below, docs. 104–5, 156.

they brought in. Curtis's policy permitted former slaves to support themselves on the old estates and gave them a small endowment of capital with which to begin their lives in freedom. But Wilder and Curtis had few imitators among federal officials in the occupied South. A military court of inquiry chastised Curtis for his actions.[50]

The war made it difficult and dangerous for freedpeople to farm on their own. Independent black farmers drew the ire of neighboring slaveholders, who attacked them personally or enlisted Confederate raiders to do so. Union troops foraged in the freedpeople's fields, gardens, and stockpens, and sometimes dismantled buildings in which they had taken refuge. Even under agreements with former owners and with guarantees of federal protection, independent black farmers stood on precarious ground, as new terms of employment could revert to the old when lines of military occupation shifted. Nonetheless, a handful of black men and women braved the danger to gain the independence they had long desired. Believing themselves entitled to the land, they sometimes took up arms against those who contested their right to it.[51]

Former slaves in the Union-occupied zones who could not or dared not farm independently sought other ways to earn a living. For all its attendant hardships, the war allowed many freedpeople new latitude to pursue self-directed activities. Army camps and garrisons housed customers aplenty for anyone with cordwood, meat, fish, produce, milk, eggs, or baked goods to sell. Similarly, Union occupation created an unprecedented demand for wood to fuel the engines of steamers and locomotives. Black men and women who as slaves had occasionally sold food or wood now did so routinely, and some managed to support themselves entirely by huckstering or wood chopping. At military posts, where men generally outnumbered women several times over, freedwomen took in laundry or cooked for soldiers; some turned to prostitution to support themselves and their families.[52]

Pursuit of such opportunities often drew former slaves from the countryside. Cities in the Union-occupied South expanded rapidly, particularly those like Washington and Nashville that served as bases for Northern military operations. Their warehouses, arsenals, repair shops, stables, and naval yards employed tens of thousands. Freedpeople in these and other cities and towns also found work catering to enlarged civilian and military populations as barbers, stable keepers, draymen, laundresses, cooks, and domestic servants. The wartime boom allowed some of them to establish businesses of their own. Carpenters became contractors, draymen established their own stables, and cooks opened small restaurants or saloons. Former slaves who lacked marketable skills

[50] On Wilder, see *Freedom*, ser. 1, vol. 2: doc. 5. On Curtis, see below, doc. 151.

[51] See below, docs. 23, 91, 97, 104, 114, 156; *Freedom*, ser. 1, vol. 1: docs. 20, 25A–B; *Freedom*, ser. 1, vol. 2: docs. 12, 112, 116, 127.

[52] See, for example, below, doc. 212; *Freedom*, ser. 1, vol. 2: docs. 7–8, 17, 58.

frequently tried to earn an independent livelihood as peddlers. Some of this entrepreneurship stood outside the law. Cookshops and groceries could serve as fronts for illicit trade, in which contraband or proscribed articles were exchanged for other goods or for cash.[53]

Union-occupied cities and towns emerged as centers of black institutional life. Long-established black churches gained new standing, and Northern missionaries – black and white – founded new congregations. Churches both old and new sponsored schools where former slaves could gain the rudiments of literacy. Mutual-aid societies and other associations took shape to address the particular concerns of members and the general concerns of former slaves at large. In these organized settings, and less formally wherever freedpeople congregated, they discussed old times and new possibilities. By such exchanges, they apprised each other of the going wages, the reputations of various employers, and the opportunities for self-employment.[54]

Yet life in the cities and towns was no easier than in the countryside. Although wages were high, wartime inflation drove prices higher. Even in Washington, where most black military laborers were paid $25 per month, more than twice the rate specified by the Militia Act, former slaves and free blacks had a difficult time making ends meet. Heavy migration swelled urban populations so that the number of workers outpaced expanding employment, creating pitiless competition. Women found their opportunities especially limited and their pay inadequate to support themselves, much less children and other dependents. Former slaves – like other rural migrants – discovered urban housing to be scarce and expensive. The shortage of housing forced black people to reside in alleys, outbuildings, or shanties on the edge of town. Lacking clean water or sanitary facilities, the crowded quarters bred disease, fueling frightful mortality and driving many black city-dwellers back to the countryside.[55]

In city and countryside alike, the changing composition of the fugitive-slave population added to the freedpeople's woes. Beginning in the fall of 1862, the government's guarantee of freedom for all who

[53] On black petty proprietors, see *Freedom*, ser. 1, vol. 2: docs. 10, 20, 97–98, 118. Useful studies of Southern cities under Union occupation include Peter Maslowski, *Treason Must Be Made Odious: Military Occupation and Wartime Reconstruction in Nashville, Tennessee, 1862–65* (Millwood, N.Y., 1978), chap. 6; James T. Currie, *Enclave: Vicksburg and Her Plantations 1863–1870* (Jackson, Miss., 1980), especially chaps. 1–2; Gerald M. Capers, *Occupied City: New Orleans under the Federals, 1862–1865* (Lexington, Ky., 1965), especially chap. 10; Constance McLaughlin Green, *Washington: Village and Capital, 1800–1878* (Princeton, N.J., 1962), chaps. 10–11, and *The Secret City: A History of Race Relations in the Nation's Capital* (Princeton, N.J., 1967), chaps. 4–5.

[54] On urban schools and churches, see *Freedom*, ser. 1, vol. 2: docs. 30–31, 102, 170–72. On benevolent societies, see *Freedom*, ser. 1, vol. 2: docs. 30, 84.

[55] On urban living conditions, see *Freedom*, ser. 1, vol. 1: doc. 107; *Freedom*, ser. 1, vol. 2: docs. 17, 30, 53, 55–57, 59A–B, 64, 66, 76, 179n.

reached Union lines encouraged slaves to flee not individually or in small groups, but en masse. The arrival of families, and sometimes entire plantation units, increased the number of women, children, and old people under federal jurisdiction. The approach of winter added to the rush, as tens of thousands of fugitive slaves made for Union lines in hopes of obtaining food, shelter, and protection during the cold months.[56]

Many Northern officers welcomed the families of black men and women who labored for the government. They offered them shelter and rations not only as a matter of justice, but also because the able-bodied freedpeople made it clear that they would not remain at work if their families were neglected or abused. But other officers saw their employees' dependents as impediments to efficient military operations. Such officials made no provision for their support and did much to discourage them – damning the women as whores and the parents and children as so many "useless mouths."[57] Despite the abuse, the women, children, and old people remained, erecting makeshift villages and scratching out a living as best they could. Their stolid persistence forced federal officials in the field and in Washington to reconsider the "contraband question."

As they had before the war, numerous white Northerners proposed removing former slaves from the United States. From the founding of the Republic, some white Americans had advocated the "repatriation" of black people – particularly free blacks – to Africa or their removal to another nation in the Americas. During the antebellum years, proponents of "colonization" had promoted Liberia as a home for free blacks and manumitted slaves. Despite the vehement opposition of the vast majority of black people, colonizationist sentiment continued to find considerable support among antislavery politicians and their constituents.[58]

Among the proponents of removal was Abraham Lincoln. During the first year of the war, the President entertained various proposals from foreign nations and individual citizens concerning colonization, and in December 1861 he recommended that the government acquire territory outside the United States in which to resettle slaves freed by the First Confiscation Act. Prodded by Lincoln, Congress enacted several measures in support of colonization during the spring and summer of 1862. In April, the law emancipating slaves in the District of

[56] On the changing character of the fugitive-slave population in late 1862, see *Freedom*, ser. 1, vol. 1: pp. 32–34. See also below, docs. 71, 152–54.

[57] *Official Records*, ser. 1, vol. 6, pp. 201–3.

[58] On the colonization movement during the late antebellum and wartime years, see P. J. Staudenraus, *The African Colonization Movement, 1816–1865* (New York, 1961); Floyd J. Miller, *The Search for a Black Nationality: Black Emigration and Colonization, 1787–1863* (Urbana, Ill., 1975); Willis D. Boyd, "Negro Colonization in the National Crisis, 1860–1870" (Ph.D. diss., University of California, Los Angeles, 1953).

Columbia set aside $100,000 to defray the cost of relocating any black people in the District who might "desire to emigrate to the Republics of Hayti or Liberia, or such other country . . . as the President may determine." Subsequent legislation appropriated additional funds for colonization, and the President frequently pledged federal assistance in removing emancipated slaves and free blacks.[59]

Although most black people spurned colonization, a few held so dim a view of their prospects in the United States that it seemed an attractive possibility. During the 1850s, support for emigration had grown among free blacks, who faced harsh discriminatory legislation throughout the nation, mob violence in the North, and threats of deportation and enslavement in the South. While suspicious of the colonizationists' motives, a number of black men and women tried to turn the wartime legislation and the President's proposals to their own purposes. In April 1862, just days after slavery was abolished in the District of Columbia, at least sixty free blacks petitioned Congress to provide a homeland in Central America where they could "secure, by their own industry, that mental and physical development which will allow them an honorable position in the families of God's great world." But the growing Northern commitment to emancipation, embodied in the Second Confiscation Act and in Lincoln's preliminary Emancipation Proclamation, rapidly deflated such sentiment. By the end of 1862, virtually all black Americans had rejected emigration.[60]

While colonization foundered, the transfer of "surplus" contrabands to the North seemed more practical. In the absence of instructions from Washington, some military commanders saw the relocation of former slaves as a convenient way to rid themselves of people who clogged their lines, devoured their supplies, and demoralized their soldiers. Besides, "help" was increasingly hard to find in the free states, as the military enlistment of white men shrank the civilian labor force. Accordingly, in September 1862, General Ulysses S. Grant, commander of the Department of the Tennessee, proposed to transport former slaves from Union encampments in the Mississippi Valley to Cairo, Illinois, where arrangements had been made to hire them to civilian employers. About the same time, General John A. Dix, commander of the Department of Virginia, asked the governors

[59] Jason H. Silverman, " 'In the Isles beyond the Main': Abraham Lincoln's Philosophy on Black Colonization," *Lincoln Herald* 80 (Fall 1978): 115–21; Lincoln, *Collected Works*, vol. 5, pp. 35–53; *Statutes at Large*, vol. 12, pp. 376–78, 422–26, 589–92.

[60] For the petition from free blacks in the District of Columbia, see *Freedom*, ser. 1, vol. 2: doc. 51. On opposition by black people to wartime colonization, see William Seraile, "Afro-American Emigration to Haiti during the American Civil War," *The Americas* 35 (Oct. 1978): 185–200; Ira Berlin, Wayne K. Durrill, Steven F. Miller, Leslie Schwalm, and Leslie S. Rowland, " 'To Canvass the Nation': The War for Union Becomes a War for Freedom," *Prologue* 20 (Winter 1988): 241–42.

of several northeastern states to receive some of the contrabands who had accumulated at Fortress Monroe.[61]

Initially Grant's proposal received approval from the War Department. But the merest whisper that former slaves were to be shipped North evoked impassioned protest in the free states, some of which had erected legal barriers against the immigration of black people. Hostility to such migration crested during the latter half of 1862, as Democrats exploited the "Negro Influx Question" in state and congressional elections. Fearful that federal sponsorship of migration would undermine support for the war, Republican politicians made their objections known to the Lincoln administration. Even abolitionists like John A. Andrew, governor of Massachusetts, opposed the relocation of black people from the slave states. Andrew objected on the grounds that black men should remain in the South and be armed as soldiers, but other Republican leaders cared only that freedpeople stay out of the North.[62]

Determined not to be outflanked by racist Democrats, the Lincoln administration squelched proposals to settle former slaves in the free states. Secretary of War Edwin M. Stanton, who had approved Grant's plan, abruptly reversed himself. After Governor Andrew exposed Dix's scheme to public view, Dix let the matter drop. In his annual report of December 1862, Stanton assured the Northern public that "no colored man will leave his home in the South if protected in that home"; putting freedpeople to work in the South would ensure that they had "neither occasion nor temptation . . . to emigrate to a northern and less congenial climate."[63] By the end of 1862, the Lincoln administration had decided that whatever the fate of the former slaves, it would be in the South.

Unable or unwilling to ship former slaves to Africa, to Central America, or to the North, Union military commanders sought means to support them within the occupied South. From the outset, the war had created unprecedented relief problems, and the number of displaced and destitute people – black and white – increased exponentially as continued fighting suspended agricultural production, disrupted local

[61] *Official Records*, ser. 3, vol. 2, p. 569; see below, doc. 154; *Freedom*, ser. 1, vol. 2: doc. 11; *Freedom*, ser. 2: doc. 41n.

[62] *Freedom*, ser. 1, vol. 2, doc. 13; *Freedom*, ser. 2: doc. 41. On Northern opposition to immigration by former slaves, see V. Jacque Voegeli, *Free But Not Equal: The Midwest and the Negro during the Civil War* (Chicago, 1967), chap. 4; *Freedom*, ser. 2: docs. 30, 194. One Northerner proposed to keep former slaves out of the free states by hiring them to " 'poor white' Southrons," who would be allowed to purchase forty-acre plots from confiscated plantations. Such a solution, he argued, would retain the former slaves' "trained labor on cotton & tobacco." (Robert A. Maxwell, "To Save Fall elections on Negro Influx Question," 25 July 1862, Miscellaneous Letters Received: K Series, ser. 103, RG 56 [X-243].)

[63] *Official Records*, ser. 3, vol. 2, pp. 663, 897–912.

economies, and sent refugees in search of a safe haven. As Union forces occupied Confederate territory, army rations constituted the principal form of aid to impoverished civilians. Whatever the justice of providing relief from federal coffers, other demands upon the treasury encouraged both niggardly assistance and a determination to find alternative sources of support. Northern churches and aid societies assumed part of the burden, but private charity could not begin to meet the need. In some places, Union commanders levied special assessments upon prominent secessionists, on the theory that those who had caused the rebellion should help alleviate the consequent suffering. The assessments, however, were both locally unpopular and difficult to enforce. More important, they, too, were inadequate to the task. With respect to relief for former slaves, federal officials turned increasingly to the idea that able-bodied freedpeople who succeeded in finding employment should be required to support those who remained dependent and unemployed.[64]

Generalizing from longstanding Northern welfare policies, some Union officers insisted first that individual families must care for their own. But in the midst of war, it was difficult for former slaves to fulfill these expectations, however much they struggled to do so. Even when families had fled bondage together or were reunited behind Union lines, they were often separated when military authorities redeployed black laborers or relocated their dependents. In such circumstances, federal officials sought to extend the principle of familial obligation. The idea, in the words of one army chaplain, was to "[keep] families together in responsibility if not in fact."[65]

On the assumption that all Southern black people were members of a single community, federal authorities in some jurisdictions charged relief expenses against the earnings of black military laborers. In September 1862, when a quartermaster in west Tennessee requested instructions regarding provision for black women and children, Quartermaster General Meigs urged that a portion of the wages owed to black military laborers be set aside to assist the needy. "The labor of the men & those women able to work," Meigs reasoned, "should support the whole community of negros at any station." Secretary of War Stanton approved. By the same logic, the War Department authorized a $5 monthly deduction from the wages of black military laborers in the District of Columbia and

64 Bremner, *The Public Good*, pp. 91–92. For examples of assessments upon secessionists, see *Official Records*, ser. 1, vol. 15, pp. 538–39, and ser. 3, vol. 2, pp. 720–25, 731–32; Andrew Johnson, *The Papers of Andrew Johnson*, ed. Leroy P. Graf, Ralph W. Haskins, and Paul H. Bergeron, 8 vols. to date (Knoxville, Tenn., 1967–), vol. 5, pp. 623–25. For an order issued late in the war that proposed to assess "avowed rebel sympathizers" for the care of "sick, helpless, and needy" former slaves, see *Freedom*, ser. 1, vol. 2: doc. 142.

65 See below, doc. 158n.

nearby Alexandria, Virginia. Similar assessments were later made upon black wage-earners in other jurisdictions.[66]

Former slaves expected to support their families and frequently went out of their way to assist the needy, even those to whom they bore no kinship obligations. However, black military laborers objected to taxes that took a large portion of their wages. In the District of Columbia, former free blacks – many of whom had never been slaves – thought it unfair that the federal government tax them for the benefit of destitute ex-slaves, especially since white workers were not similarly assessed. Authorities brushed aside such protests and continued to take deductions for the "contraband fund."[67]

Revenue realized through these levies defrayed some of the expense of supporting former slaves. Even so, it went but a small way toward ameliorating the problems of health, sanitation, and housing created by the presence of large numbers of ex-slaves within federal lines. With winter fast upon them, necessity – as well as humanity – impelled field commanders to establish makeshift bivouacs or "contraband camps" for the reception, relief, and employment of black refugees. In doing so, they placed all freedpeople under direct military oversight and simplified the distribution of rations, clothing, and medical supplies. By the end of 1862, large camps had been established at LaGrange, Bolivar, and Memphis in west Tennessee and at Corinth in northern Mississippi. "Contraband colonies" on the outskirts of New Orleans housed several thousand residents. In the eastern theater, Craney Island, near Norfolk, Virginia, was set aside for unemployed contrabands, as was Camp Barker in the District of Columbia, only blocks from the President's mansion.[68]

As they established separate settlements for former slaves, federal commanders assigned subordinate officers to supervise their labor and welfare. Many of the new superintendents of contrabands came from the ranks of army chaplains, including John Eaton, Jr., and most of his subordinates in the Department of the Tennessee. Some, such as Lieutenant George H. Hanks in the Department of the Gulf, were quartermasters whose duties had involved mobilizing black laborers. Nearly all had connections to Northern aid societies, and a few were themselves agents of those societies. The appointment of the superintendents thus conferred official recognition upon some abolitionists and the organizations they represented. Although their formal incorporation into the Union chain of command gave them new authority, it also signified

66 See below, doc. 153, 166n.; *Freedom*, ser. 1, vol. 2: docs. 54–55.

67 *Freedom*, ser. 1, vol. 2: docs. 56, 66, 69–70, 82.

68 See below, docs. 64–65, 71, 154–55, 160; *Freedom*, ser. 1, vol. 2: docs. 13n., 17–18, 42, 60; Registers of Freedmen at Camp Barker, June 1862–Dec. 1863, ser. 570, Camp Barker DC, RG 105 [A-10092]. See also Cam Walker, "Corinth: The Story of a Contraband Camp," *Civil War History* 20 (Mar. 1974): 5–22.

that private philanthropy would play a subaltern role. The superintendents operated within the framework of military bureaucracy and were subject to the dictates of superior officers.[69]

The new superintendents organized residents of the contraband camps into working parties according to age and physical condition. Healthy men and some women were assigned to the quartermaster, commissary, medical, and engineer departments of the army. The remaining women, children, and old and disabled men did what work they could. Virtually every camp required such freedpeople to police grounds, construct and repair buildings, and generally maintain the premises. Beyond that, the character of their labor depended upon the location of the camp and the timing and circumstances of its establishment. Residents of contraband camps in northern Mississippi and west Tennessee harvested cotton under the direction of government overseers, sometimes from abandoned fields, other times from the fields of resident owners who paid the government for the labor. At Camp Barker, in Washington, the superintendents hired hundreds of former slaves to civilian employers, including slaveholders. Some camps were poorly situated to provide employment. On desolate Craney Island, there was little but make-work; despite the freedpeoples' desire to be "of some account," their superintendent had nothing to offer but unpaid labor refurbishing grain sacks and sewing Union uniforms.[70]

Even in the most favorable circumstances, residents of the contraband camps had to rely upon the government for at least a portion of their livelihood. Not only did the army regularly remove the men and women best able to support themselves and their dependents, but it also made no provision to distribute the earnings of laborers to their relatives and friends. Attempts at self-support were overwhelmed by the continued influx of fugitive slaves. And because most camps were not established until the fall of 1862, their inhabitants could not plant food for immediate consumption. At best, they could forage from nearby woods and abandoned fields.

For all its privations, life in the contraband camps permitted former slaves some latitude in shaping their own lives. Although most residents received only subsistence, some earned modest wages outside the camp, with which they purchased additional food, clothing, and amenities like bibles and schoolbooks or tobacco and liquor. In the camps, many freedpeople reconstituted families separated during slavery or in the travail of war. They eagerly attended schools taught by the agents of Northern aid societies, sympathetic officers and soldiers, or the literate within their own ranks. They organized both informal prayer meetings and formal congregations of the faithful, celebrated wed-

[69] See below, docs. 110, 155, 157n.; *Freedom*, ser. 1, vol. 2: docs. 4n., 22, 64, 72.
[70] See below, doc. 160; *Freedom*, ser. 1, vol. 2: docs. 17–18, 60–61.

dings, and – all too often – mourned the dead. Freedpeople shouldered much of the responsibility for their own medical care – a considerable burden because disease flourished among the crowded, ill-housed, and malnourished inhabitants of the camps. With army physicians and nurses in short supply, black "aunties" and "grannies" ministered to the sick, applying the healing skills they had learned as slaves. Although rude, the contraband camps were the first home in freedom for many former slaves.[71]

The contraband camps and large-scale employment of black military laborers epitomized the transformation of Union policy toward former slaves. By the end of 1862, the necessity of mobilizing former slaves had become apparent to all but the most intransigent federal officials. In defending the Union, declared Quartermaster General Meigs, "it is impossible to cast aside the millions of recruits who will offer themselves for the work, accustomed to the climate, inured to labor, acquainted with the country, and animated by the strong desire not merely for political but for personal liberty." Secretary of War Stanton urged that the Union "turn against the rebels the productive power that upholds the insurrection." "By striking down this system of compulsory labor, which enables the leaders of the rebellion to control the resources of the people," Stanton intoned, "the rebellion would die of itself."[72]

The Emancipation Proclamation, issued by President Lincoln on New Year's Day, 1863, at once ratified developments of the previous year and set new terms for the subsequent evolution of free labor. The proclamation declared free all slaves in the Confederacy, except those in Tennessee and in the Union-occupied parts of southern Louisiana and tidewater Virginia. Congress had already abolished slavery in the District of Columbia and the western territories. The Militia Act had liberated slaves who worked for the Union army or navy. The Second Confiscation Act had extended freedom to those slaves coming under Union control whose owners were disloyal. Now Lincoln's proclamation made emancipation an official aim of the war. Thenceforward, as federal troops advanced into the Confederate heartland, they marched as agents of freedom.[73]

The Emancipation Proclamation closed some doors as it opened others. Whereas the preliminary proclamation of September 1862 had

[71] On everyday life in the contraband camps see, for example, below, docs. 160, 164, 170; *Freedom*, ser. 1, vol. 2: docs. 17–18, 60–61, 72–74.

[72] *Official Records*, ser. 3, vol. 2, pp. 786–809, 897–912.

[73] For the Emancipation Proclamation, see *Statutes at Large*, vol. 12, pp. 1268–69. For the earlier emancipation measures, see *Statutes at Large*, vol. 12, pp. 376–78, 432, 597–600. For an example of federal officers arming former slaves and sending them back to their home plantations as "*missionaries*" of freedom, see *Freedom*, ser. 1, vol. 1: doc. 101.

included the customary pledge to support the removal of freed slaves from the United States, the final edict was silent on the subject. The folly of exiling the very men and women whom Union commanders were trying to mobilize – and who showed no interest in emigrating – seemed increasingly manifest. No less important, the heads of several Central American states had bluntly refused to accept black immigrants. Although Lincoln later gave occasional lip service to colonization, it had become a lost cause. In early 1864 the widely publicized debacle of a government-sanctioned venture in Ile à Vache, Haiti, where unscrupulous Northern promoters abandoned several hundred black emigrants to sicken and die, ended the administration's involvement in such schemes.[74]

While silently rejecting colonization, the Emancipation Proclamation explicitly authorized a larger role for former slaves in the Union war effort. The President enjoined persons freed by the proclamation, "in all cases when allowed, [to] labor faithfully for reasonable wages." More important, he invited black men to support the Union cause as soldiers. Northern free blacks and their abolitionist allies had long viewed military service as a lever for racial equality, as well as a weapon against slavery, and they rushed to accept the President's invitation. In mid-January 1863, Massachusetts Governor Andrew secured permission from Secretary of War Stanton to organize a black regiment, and within weeks volunteers from all over the North were enlisting in the 54th Massachusetts Infantry.[75]

As winter turned to spring, events in the North reemphasized the connection between emancipation and the success of federal arms. In March, Congress authorized the enrollment and conscription of Northern white men. The draft created a firestorm of opposition to the Lincoln administration and to the war itself. In part to shift the burden from Northern whites, the War Department moved quickly to enlist black men, expanding recruitment first to free blacks throughout the North and then to Southern slaves liberated by Lincoln's proclamation and congressional emancipation measures. By the end of April, Secretary of War Stanton had dispatched specially commissioned officers to virtually every part of the Union-occupied Confederacy to organize black regiments. Only the border states and middle Tennessee remained off-limits, and they not for long.[76]

With the nation committed to emancipation and black men marching under the American flag, Northerners contemplated a future in which all black people would be free. To plan for that day, Stanton

74 Boyd, "Negro Colonization in the National Crisis," chaps. 5, 7, 13.

75 *Statutes at Large*, vol. 12, pp. 1268–69. On the recruitment of black soldiers in the North, see *Freedom*, ser. 2: chap. 2.

76 On the expansion of recruitment in the North and its extension to the Union-occupied South, see *Freedom*, ser. 2: chaps. 2–3.

impaneled the American Freedmen's Inquiry Commission in March 1863, instructing its members to recommend "practical measures for placing [the former slaves] in a state of self-support and self-defense, with the least possible disturbance to the great industrial interest of the country," and asking them to suggest how the government might "[render] their services efficient in the present war." In the year that followed, the three commissioners traveled throughout the Union-occupied Confederacy and the border slave states, interviewing military officers, white civilians, free blacks, and former slaves about slavery and freedom, work and property, God and family. In May 1864, the commission submitted its blueprint for reconstructing the South and the nation.[77]

In the meantime, with the beginning of both the spring military campaign and the agricultural season of 1863, the freedpeople's desperate condition required more immediate measures. President Lincoln concluded that it was time for former slaves to start "digging their subsistence out of the ground."[78] His terse formulation struck a sympathetic chord with many Northerners, who agreed that the interests of the Union and of the freedpeople themselves would be best served by putting them to work on land abandoned by their erstwhile owners. In the view of Secretary of War Stanton, the loyalty of former slaves and the treason of their former owners made it both right and necessary to give black people "protection and employment upon the soil which they have thus far cultivated, and the right to which has been vacated by the original proprietors."[79]

Putting the freedpeople to work on abandoned plantations promised to solve many of the problems created by fighting a war for both national unity and universal liberty. By providing former slaves with a way to earn their own food, clothing, and shelter, it would reduce federal expenditures for relief. The resumption of cotton production would stoke the Northern economy and return revenue to the national treasury via wartime taxes on the staple and on commerce in the occupied zones. Furthermore, it would speed the transformation of slaves into free workers. Liberated by the President's proclamation, former slaves would learn to labor for wages in the Union-occupied South.

Its many advantages notwithstanding, the decision to establish freedpeople on abandoned plantations and farms raised numerous practical questions. One of the most important involved ownership of the land. Beyond the customary practices of war, which sanctioned the use

[77] *Official Records*, ser. 3, vol. 3, pp. 73–74. For the commission's preliminary and final reports, dated June 30, 1863, and May 15, 1864, see *Official Records*, ser. 3, vol. 3, pp. 430–54, and ser. 3, vol. 4, pp. 289–382. An excerpt from a supplement to the final report is printed below, as doc. 115.

[78] *Freedom*, ser. 1, vol. 1: doc. 107.

[79] *Official Records*, ser. 3, vol. 2, pp. 897–912.

of captured property for military purposes, Congress had given President Lincoln the legal means to effect lasting changes in Southern landholding. The Second Confiscation Act, which permitted the government to seize real and personal property belonging to disloyal citizens and sell it to loyal ones, provided one tool, but an unwieldy one. Confiscation required formal proceedings in federal courts, which had ceased to function in the seceded states. Moreover, the President had the power to pardon individual rebels, and, at his insistence, Congress had adopted an "explanatory resolution" prohibiting forfeiture of land beyond the life of the offender. Like most Northerners, Lincoln had no taste for wholesale expropriation and, even in wartime, remained wary of any seizure of property by the state.[80]

The Direct Tax Act of June 1862 offered a more straightforward way to transform property holding. In order to collect in the seceded states a federal tax that had been levied upon each state in 1861, the act provided for assessments on individual parcels of land, which would be forfeited to the government if the owner failed to pay. Tax commissioners, appointed by the President for each insurrectionary state, would then assume control, with authority to rent out the property or to subdivide and sell it at auction. In contrast to transactions under the Confiscation Act, the sale of land under the Direct Tax Act would convey fee-simple title, with no restrictions whatsoever. Indeed, as its authors readily admitted, the purpose of the act was less to raise revenue than to "[divest] . . . by law, the titles of rebels to their lands." By the end of 1862, Lincoln had appointed direct-tax commissioners for South Carolina and for Florida, and the South Carolina commission was taking the steps required to put a substantial number of Sea Island plantations on the block. Commissioners were not yet appointed for the other Union-occupied states, however, and the President showed no inclination to speed proceedings.[81]

Only a tiny amount of land within Union-occupied territory had been formally alienated from its owners by the confiscation or direct-tax acts, but the army controlled large tracts by military occupation. Although they lacked authority to determine final disposition of captured or abandoned land, military authorities did not hesitate to use it temporarily for the benefit of the Union war effort, the former slaves under

80 *Statutes at Large*, vol. 12, pp. 589–92. On the framing and enforcement of the act, see James Garfield Randall, *The Confiscation of Property during the Civil War* (Indianapolis, Ind., 1913), chaps. 1–6, and John Syrett, "The Confiscation Acts: Efforts at Reconstruction during the Civil War" (Ph.D. diss., University of Wisconsin, 1971).

81 For the Direct Tax Act, see *Statutes at Large*, vol. 12, pp. 422–26; for a summary of its provisions, see below, doc. 27n. On its authors' intent, see below, doc. 30. On the appointment of direct-tax commissioners, see U.S., Senate, "Letter of the Secretary of the Treasury . . . [on] the collection of direct taxes in insurrectionary districts . . . ," *Senate Executive Documents*, 38th Cong., 1st sess., No. 35.

their jurisdiction, and the nation in general. In doing so, they did not lack for offers of assistance.

Ambitious men with an eye on the soaring price of cotton urged federal authorities to open the South – particularly the rich plantation lands of the Mississippi Valley and the South Carolina Sea Islands – to the invigorating influence of Northern capital. Capitalists, they argued, could transform Southern society more effectively than abolitionist dreamers or government bureaucrats. None was more impatient to bring the plantations "within the reach of private Enterprise" than Edward S. Philbrick, who had spent 1862 as a plantation superintendent in the Sea Islands. Other Northern newcomers to the occupied Confederacy sounded similar themes. For George B. Field, a New York attorney who toured the Mississippi Valley in the early months of 1863 on behalf of Secretary of War Stanton, nothing would ensure public support for emancipation better than a demonstration that "free negro labor under good management can be made a *source* of *profit* to the *employer*." Seeing no contradiction between private gain and public good, would-be planters pledged their lives and their fortunes to recast the plantation South in the image of the North.[82]

Not all Northerners shared this confidence that the interests of private investors would benefit either former slaves or the public at large. From his perspective as superintendent of contrabands in the Department of the Tennessee, Chaplain John Eaton feared the consequences of placing the freedpeople in the hands of speculators. Eaton advocated a system of plantation labor similar to that earlier instituted on the Sea Islands, in which government-appointed superintendents, not private employers, would control agricultural operations and all other aspects of the former slaves' transition to freedom. Meanwhile, on the Sea Islands, the machinations of Philbrick and a "horde" of other Yankees who wished to purchase direct-tax land alarmed the Gideonites, their military allies, and the former slaves. General Rufus Saxton, military governor of the islands, feared that the engrossment of land by private purchasers would put the freedpeople "at the mercy of men devoid of principle," to the detriment of "their future well being." Saxton wanted the national government to "give the negroes a right in that soil to whose wealth they are destined in the future to contribute so largely."[83]

In the end, such misgivings yielded before the promise of Northern entrepreneurs to diminish the government's expenses and increase its revenue. In the South Carolina Sea Islands, the Mississippi Valley, and southern Louisiana, Yankee capitalists gained access to some of the most productive land in the United States. Nowhere, however, did they

[82] See below, docs. 34, 76, 159, 206. On the outlook of Northern planters and would-be planters, see Powell, *New Masters*, especially chaps. 1–2.

[83] See below, docs. 27, 30, 158n.

enjoy as clear a field as they desired. In the Sea Islands, President Lincoln instructed the direct-tax commissioners to reserve a substantial portion of the forfeited land from sale. He also empowered them to bid on behalf of the government for what land was to be offered at auction. In March 1863, when the first direct-tax sales took place, Northern entrepreneurs acquired half the available land. By far the largest purchaser was a syndicate of investors organized by Philbrick.[84]

In southern Louisiana, resident planters obstructed the path of Northern businessmen. Sugar planters claiming loyalty to the federal government retained control over many of the great estates. Heartened by the region's exemption from the Emancipation Proclamation, they pressed General Nathaniel P. Banks, Butler's successor in the Department of the Gulf, to respect their right to manage their plantations and command slave labor. Banks responded by instituting a "voluntary system of labor" that, like Butler's expedient of the previous fall, required small wage payments and promised military enforcement of plantation discipline. Abandoned estates, along with those owned by planters who refused Banks's terms, fell to the department quartermaster, who was authorized to lease them out or operate them under direct government supervision. But because most loyal planters accepted the new regime, however reluctantly, relatively few estates came into government hands. Yankee entrepreneurs leased some of them, but the others were so ravaged by the war or so vulnerable to Confederate attack as to dissuade prospective investors from risking their capital.[85]

Farther north in the Mississippi Valley, Northern planters had a freer hand. In March 1863, Secretary of War Stanton sent Adjutant General Lorenzo Thomas to the valley to inaugurate the recruitment of black soldiers. Traveling in the company of George Field, Thomas soon saw a connection between mobilizing black men, providing for their families, fostering loyalty to the Union, and reestablishing plantation agriculture. Within days of his arrival, he had appointed a commission, headed by Field, to lease plantations to Northerners. Assuming that "the employment and subsistance of negroes [was] a matter to be left to private enterprise," Thomas expected the lessees to hire the families of black soldiers and provide for at least some dependent freedpeople. The leased plantations, protected by newly organized black troops, would unite staple production and many of the relief functions previously borne by the contraband camps.[86]

In most of the Union-occupied Mississippi Valley, however, Thomas's plan could not yet be implemented. At Helena, Arkansas, for

84 See below, docs. 27n., 30, 31.

85 For the orders establishing Banks's system, see below, docs. 81, 84. On the estates leased out or operated by the government, see below, doc. 93.

86 *Official Records*, ser. 3, vol. 3, pp. 100–101; *Freedom*, ser. 2: doc. 194; see below, doc. 162.

instance, where the reach of the small garrison extended barely beyond the town, thousands of former slaves languished in an overcrowded and unhealthy contraband camp for want of securely held plantations. In early 1863, the local commander began transporting them to Cairo, Illinois, and St. Louis, Missouri. Before long, a St. Louis-based network had been established to hire former slaves to midwestern farmers. By the fall of 1863, more than 1,000 had been relocated from Helena to the free states.[87] Midwesterners generally welcomed these migrants. A year earlier, proposals to move black Southerners to the North had sparked Negrophobic hysteria, but circumstances had changed. Even as the conscription of white men created a labor shortage in the North, emancipation and the enlistment of black soldiers engendered a new respect and sympathy for former slaves. Self-interest and sentiment jointly refuted Democratic predictions of race war.

The removal of several hundred former slaves from the Mississippi Valley to the Midwest hardly alleviated the plight of most fugitive slaves or solved the problems of military commanders. Resumption of agricultural production in the South offered the best hope of providing for the increasing number of freedpeople entering Union lines. In 1863, however, secure territory was extremely limited. Adjutant General Thomas found only one promising setting for his plantation-leasing scheme, a small area in northeastern Louisiana that was held by Northern troops operating against Vicksburg. There Thomas's commission rented at least forty plantations to Northern entrepreneurs and a few Southern loyalists. By the fall of 1863, between 3,500 and 5,300 former slaves were living on the leased plantations. Despite the small territory embraced, Thomas believed his plan would eventually "line the [Mississippi] river with a loyal population" of Yankees, emancipated slaves, and native white unionists.[88]

Lured by the prospect of bonanza profits from cotton, Northern lessees bypassed the regions of mixed farming that had also fallen under Union control. No eager capitalists challenged Charles Wilder for land and labor in tidewater Virginia. During the spring of 1863, after receiving Stanton's authorization, Wilder and his fellow superintendent of contrabands, Orlando Brown, settled freedpeople on land abandoned by disloyal owners. Residents of "government farms" literally worked for the government, which supplied rations, livestock, and farm imple-

87 On the relocation, see below, docs. 161, 167; *Freedom*, ser. 1, vol. 2: docs. 162–63, 165, 171.

88 On the extent of territory and number of plantations leased in 1863 under Thomas's system, see below, docs. 180 (which estimates the number of leased plantations at sixty) and 189 (which puts the number at forty). The total number of residents on the leased estates has been estimated by first calculating the average number on twenty-one plantations whose residents were enumerated in October 1863 (see below, doc. 177) and then multiplying that average (eighty-eight per plantation) by each of the two figures for the total number of leased plantations.

ments and, at the end of the year, paid the laborers with a portion of the crop. Some months later Colonel Elias M. Greene, chief quartermaster of the Department of Washington, instituted a similar system on several abandoned estates in northern Virginia, just across the Potomac River from the District of Columbia. However, the number of freedpeople working government-controlled land remained small. As of August 1863, only 1,600 former slaves resided on government farms in tidewater Virginia – about 6 percent of the region's black population. Fewer than 200 worked the abandoned estates near Washington.[89]

While the expansion of Union-held territory made it possible for some former slaves to return to the land, it also changed the character of military labor. The surrender of Vicksburg and Port Hudson in July 1863 gave federal forces control of the Mississippi River and set the stage for offensive operations elsewhere, notably Arkansas and middle and east Tennessee. Union armies on the move had little use for laborers to erect stationary fortifications. Instead, they needed teamsters to drive wagons, hostlers to tend the teams, drovers to herd livestock to the front lines, wood choppers to supply fuel for steamboats and locomotives, and laborers to construct and repair roads, bridges, and railbeds. Naval vessels that patrolled the Mississippi and its tributaries also required a large number of hands. Both the army and the navy needed thousands of workers to operate supply depots and maintain lines of communication. In the most active theaters, Union officers mobilized every black man within their reach. By August, the army was employing 11,000 black laborers in middle Tennessee alone.[90]

During the summer and fall of 1863, black men also enlisted in the federal army in large numbers. The opportunity to don Union blue and strike a blow at slavery drew thousands of ex-slaves and free blacks to recruiting stations in the Union-occupied South. Recruitment officers promptly sent the new volunteers into the field to enlist friends and relatives. Black soldiers also participated in raids and foraging expeditions that brought still more ex-slaves into Union ranks. By war's end, 179,000 black men – the vast majority former slaves – had served in the federal army. More than half of them originated in the Confederate states, from some of which they constituted a substantial proportion of the black men of military age. More than a fifth of such men in

89 On the tidewater farms, see *Freedom*, ser. 1, vol. 2: docs. 16–17, 28; *Freedom*, ser. 1, vol. 1: doc. 13. On those near Washington, see *Freedom*, ser. 1, vol. 2: docs. 63, 77. In the summer of 1864, with farm operations considerably larger than they had been the previous year, only 241 laborers were employed on the northern Virginia farms. (*Freedom*, ser. 1, vol. 2: doc. 77n.)

90 *Freedom*, ser. 1, vol. 2: doc. 95. The 11,000 laborers represented more than one-fifth of the 51,000 black men between the ages of eighteen and forty-five who lived in the entire state of Tennessee in 1860. (*Freedom*, ser. 2: p. 12.)

Arkansas and Mississippi served in the Union army, as did nearly a third of those in Louisiana and almost two-fifths in Tennessee.[91]

Black soldiers often found themselves assigned to menial labor instead of combat duties. Laborers for the quartermaster or other military departments formed the nucleus of several black regiments, which, once mustered into service, continued to work much as before. From the standpoint of their military employers, black soldiers had two advantages over civilians. First, they were subject to army regulations and could not leave their duties at will. Second, in areas where civilian workers commanded high wages, black soldiers performed the same work for lower pay. The combination was too much to resist. Although all Union soldiers performed fatigue duty, black soldiers did more than their share.[92]

Black men struggled to realize their own expectations of martial life. Upon learning that black soldiers earned less than white soldiers, less than white military laborers, and also less than many black military laborers, they often refused to enlist. In Nashville, where black quartermaster employees received $25 per month, more than double the $10 allotted to a black private, "no laborer with his eyes open" would join the army. When they did enlist, even the greenest recruits insisted upon being treated as soldiers rather than uniformed drudges. Before long, some of them had the opportunity to meet their old masters on the field of battle. At Port Hudson, Fort Wagner, Milliken's Bend, and dozens of lesser encounters, black men did a soldier's work.[93]

Large-scale employment of black men as soldiers and military laborers affected plans both to reorganize plantation agriculture on free-labor principles and to provide for destitute former slaves. The mobilization of adult men restricted the pool of laborers available to private planters and government superintendents. Work gangs had to be constructed around able-bodied women, assisted to varying degree by the old and the young of both sexes. Throughout the Union-occupied South, black

[91] On the extension of recruitment to the Union-occupied Confederacy, see *Freedom*, ser. 2: chap. 3. For the number of black soldiers credited to each state, see *Freedom*, ser. 2: p. 12.

[92] *Freedom*, ser. 1, vol. 2: doc. 100; *Freedom*, ser. 2: chap. 10, and docs. 42, 68, 130A, 243, 265. If black soldiers often worked as laborers, black laborers sometimes served as quasi-soldiers. Even before Adjutant General Thomas inaugurated the enlistment of black men in the Mississippi Valley, armed ex-slaves were guarding contraband camps. Black civilians in the valley and elsewhere were often provided with weapons and organized to defend work parties and leased plantations, and black military laborers were liable to duty in local militias. (See, for example, below, docs. 23, 160; *Freedom*, ser. 1, vol. 2: docs. 28, 138; *Official Records*, ser. 3, vol. 4, pp. 874–902.)

[93] *Freedom*, ser. 2: doc. 68. In accordance with the provisions of the Militia Act of July 1862, black soldiers earned $10 per month, $7 in cash and $3 in clothing. On the combat role of black soldiers, see *Freedom*, ser. 2: chap. 11.

women became the backbone of the agricultural labor force.[94] Although the planters would rather have had nothing to do with aged, sick, or disabled freedpeople and preferred not to hire women with numerous small children, they usually had no choice but to accept some of the dependent relatives of their workers. Former slaves spurned employment that entailed separation from their families, and military authorities forbade hiring practices that worsened the government's burden of relief. There remained, however, some dependent freedpeople who had no one to provide for them. To accommodate such unfortunates, federal officials in southern Louisiana and the Mississippi Valley reserved several plantations as "infirm farms," where unemployable former slaves received rations while contributing whatever they could to their own support.[95] The officials also abandoned all illusion that the contraband camps could function merely as receiving depots, from which fugitive-slave men would be inducted into the army and virtually all others hired to plantation owners or lessees.

However genuine their acceptance of the government's responsibility for relief, military officials were overwhelmed by the thousands of slaves liberated by Union victories in 1863. Refugees who sought shelter at contraband camps faced recurrent shortages of food, clothing, housing, and medical supplies. Skyrocketing mortality – the result of wartime privation and of diseases fostered by overcrowding and unsanitary facilities – horrified sympathetic observers. In November 1863, officials of the Western Sanitary Commission ventured the bleak prediction that half the black people in the Mississippi Valley were "doomed to die in the process of freeing the rest." Much to the discomfiture of the Lincoln administration, opponents of emancipation seized upon such reports to support their contention that black people would be worse off in freedom than in slavery. General James S. Wadsworth, who investigated conditions in the Mississippi Valley, deliberately understated the extent of suffering, for fear of putting "ammunition in the hands of the copperheads."[96]

Whereas the contraband camps of the Union-occupied Lower South operated as adjuncts to the plantations, those in the Upper South played a more independent role, chiefly because federal authorities controlled so little abandoned land. In the tiny Union-held enclaves of tidewater North Carolina, where nearly all able-bodied black men had enlisted in the army, contraband camps were established at New Berne

94 On the character of the wartime agricultural labor force, see, for example, below, docs. 36, 163, 165; *Freedom*, ser. 1, vol. 2: docs. 28, 42.

95 See below, doc. 177; Geo. B. Field et al. to the Hon. E. M. Stanton, 16 May 1863, filed with #1315 1886, Letters Received, ser. 12, RG 94 [K-574].

96 See below, doc. 107; James E. Yeatman et al. to His Excellency, A. Lincoln, 6 Nov. 1863, vol. R-S 1863, #342, Miscellaneous Letters Received: K Series, ser. 103, RG 56 [X-12]. See also *Freedom*, ser. 1, vol. 1: doc. 110.

and Roanoke Island to house their families, who had no other means of support. Drawing upon government funds and private donations, Horace James, "superintendent of blacks" in North Carolina, strove to make Roanoke Island a model of life in freedom, with right-angled streets, gardens, and a hospital. Officials in the District of Columbia had similar goals in establishing "Freedman's Village" on the estate of Confederate General Robert E. Lee, across the Potomac River from Washington. Freedman's Village became a showplace to which government officials directed foreign visitors and other dignitaries eager to witness the progress of the former slaves.[97]

In the loyal border states, where slavery remained legal and the recruitment of black soldiers had barely begun, only a few contraband camps came into existence in 1863. Because federal policy in the border states required deference to civil authority and noninterference with slavery, these camps evolved as sanctuaries not for border-state fugitive slaves but for those who had escaped from the Confederacy. Point Lookout, a military installation at the southernmost extension of Maryland's western shore, attracted black refugees from Virginia, among whom mingled a number of Maryland slaves. The post quartermaster employed many of the men and eventually inaugurated an informal contraband camp by issuing rations and tents to the women and children. In Missouri, military authorities established a sizable camp at St. Louis, but not to provide for local fugitive slaves. Instead, it was the arrival of hundreds of freedpeople from Helena, Arkansas, that forced the army to issue rations and set up quarters, first in an abandoned hotel and then at Benton Barracks, on the outskirts of the city. Similarly, the contraband camp at Columbus, on the western border of Kentucky, signaled no offer of protection to slaves from that state. Established in conjunction with the recruitment of black soldiers, the camp, like the new regiments, consisted almost entirely of fugitive slaves from Tennessee. To reduce their unsettling effect upon Kentucky slaves, military officers steadily transferred residents of the camp to nearby Island 10, Tennessee, in the middle of the Mississippi River.[98]

Throughout the Union-occupied South, the desperate poverty of most inhabitants of the contraband camps proclaimed the hollow legacy of chattel bondage. However, not all fugitive slaves traversed the ground between slavery and freedom empty-handed. Quite a few brought personal possessions – clothing, bedding, and cooking utensils – to ease the transit. Some managed to carry away tools and other productive property. A former slave with an axe, a hoe, a wagon, or the implements of a trade stood a better chance of gaining an independent livelihood than one without such tools. Possession of a

[97] *Freedom*, ser. 1, vol. 2: docs. 22, 70–71; Horace James, *Annual Report of the Superintendent of Negro Affairs in North Carolina, 1864* (Boston, 1865), pp. 6–7, 21–26.

[98] *Freedom*, ser. 1, vol. 2: docs. 133, 162–63, 165, 171–72, 205, 209.

horse or mule also improved the possibilities for self-employment. Procured by various means – purchased during slavery, "borrowed" from a former master, picked up as strays, or acquired with the proceeds of wartime labor – draft animals enabled some ex-slaves to set up for themselves. Former slaves with a horse or mule worked as self-employed draymen and wagoners in such cities as Nashville, Memphis, and Washington, whose wartime economies depended heavily upon the transportion of goods. In some rural areas, freedpeople who were similarly endowed bargained with landowners for rental or crop-sharing arrangements. Freedpeople who left slavery in possession of productive property had a wider range of choices than those who owned only their ability to labor.[99]

A few former slaves gained legal control over land in 1863. At the South Carolina direct-tax sales, freedpeople who had pooled their resources purchased as many as eight plantations in competitive bidding. In the Mississippi Valley, about fifteen black men leased land from Thomas's plantation commissioners, and an indeterminable number struck subleasing bargains with Northern planters. Although military authorities in southern Louisiana made no effort to rent land to black lessees, a few elderly and disabled former slaves who had remained on abandoned estates won informal approval to work the land for their own benefit.[100]

If only a minuscule number of former slaves enjoyed either formal or informal possession of land, their control over other productive property was not much more extensive, in part because almost everything fugitive slaves brought into Union lines was subject to expropriation. Military regulations permitted freedpeople to retain their possessions only if they could prove ownership, making it difficult for them to hold any property that was of use to the army. Even when assured that the expropriated livestock, tools, and other goods would be used in the contraband camps or on government-controlled plantations, former slaves could not help but feel a twinge of bitterness as their belongings were pressed into government service. Only rarely did their complaints receive a hearing.[101]

Former slaves were not alone in their protests. Observing that many freedpeople "use their property to make a living," General John Hawkins argued that "[t]he immediate gain to Gov,ment by the seizure is very small compared with the great loss to them." "By letting the property remain in their possission," he asserted, "they will be enabled

[99] For examples of former slaves' ownership and use of productive property, including draft animals, see below, docs. 51, 104, 174–75, 184; *Freedom*, ser. 1, vol. 2: docs. 10, 96–97, 112, 116–17.

[100] See below, docs. 31, 91, 97, 180.

[101] On military policy respecting personal property claimed by former slaves, see below, docs. 35, 160, 175A–B.

next year to cultivate a few acres of ground and the Gov,ment be relieved of their support. By taking it away they or their families are made paupers for perhaps all time to come." But Hawkins's views were rare within Union officialdom, and his superiors rejected his appeal. Draft animals and other items brought into federal lines by former slaves remained subject to confiscation.[102]

Owning little or no productive property, former slaves were perforce dependent upon whatever compensation they could obtain by laboring for an employer. Black military laborers, soldiers, and urban and agricultural workers shared a reliance upon wage work. Accordingly, the amount and kind of compensation and the regularity of payment became important issues, at times critical ones. But in the various settings in which freedpeople became wage laborers, questions of compensation merged with other matters pertaining to control over production, especially the nature and extent of supervision and the length of the workday and workweek. The ex-slaves' experience in bondage had produced sensibilities and expectations opposed to those of former slaveholders and, in many respects, equally foreign to those of Northern planters and military officers. Struggles brought forward from slavery intertwined with those characteristic of free labor. Whereas some matters of contention – including the provision of subsistence, corporal punishment, freedom of movement, and compensation – were common to military laborers, soldiers and sailors, and agricultural and urban workers, others depended upon the particular character of each type of work.

Of all former slaves, black military laborers were perhaps the most fully attuned to the wage relation. Unlike soldiers and plantation laborers, whose work was accompanied by the promise of subsistence for nonworking family members, military laborers usually had to feed and house their dependents from their earnings alone. The amount and frequency of pay therefore weighed heavily in their lives. Although the wages of military employees arrived with greater regularity during 1863, as the federal government's fiscal crisis receded and its bureaucracy gained experience, a substantial number of black laborers found themselves short-changed on account of irregularities or fraud. Nonpayment ranked high among the causes leading black military laborers to "desert," but it was not the only reason. Long hours of work, abusive superintendents, and substandard food, clothing, and shelter all prompted disgruntled workers to search for more attractive employment. To the consternation of military employers, black laborers learned only too well that their new status allowed them to sell their labor power wherever they wished. With the freedom to change employers, however, came the "freedom" to be discharged. Many military laborers experienced periods of unemployment or irregular employ-

[102] See below, docs. 175A–B.

ment, with the accompanying uncertainty of support for themselves and their families.[103]

Black soldiers surrendered the right to change employers, but they gained other rewards, including the respect of their comrades-in-arms and the gratitude of the nation for which they fought. Former slaves expected military service to mean, at the very least, that they would be treated the same as other soldiers, but black soldiers found themselves barred from promotion, assigned to labor gangs instead of combat, issued inferior rations and equipment, and subjected to punishments that, at times, bore uncomfortable resemblance to those meted out by slaveholders. Despite the fact that military discipline rested upon impersonal law rather than personal sovereignty, corporal punishment of any form infuriated men who had known the master's lash.[104]

These burdens aside, black soldiers were guaranteed rations, clothing, and a wage. To be sure, the quantity and quality of rations and clothing frequently fell short of their expectations, and black soldiers complained of the deficiency. But nothing angered them more than the government's failure to pay them at the same rate as their white comrades. Connected as it was with both their ability to support their families and their conviction that equal service merited equal recompense, their demand for equality had special resonance in the wider black community. Their families and friends – along with many Northern abolitionists – joined the soldiers in demanding justice. "We have done a Soldiers Duty," protested a black corporal to Lincoln in June 1863. "Why cant we have a Soldiers pay?"[105]

Farm and plantation workers also wished to enjoy the rights and privileges of free laborers. They especially wanted to erase the hallmarks of personal sovereignty that characterized slavery. At first, some asked little more than the prohibition of corporal punishment and a guarantee of family security. A group of former slaves in southern Louisiana assured an emissary of General Banks that they were "willing to go to work immediately . . . even without remuneration," provided that "they would not be whipped and separated from their families." Objections to the lash extended to the men who had historically wielded it. Steadfastly opposed to working under "Secesh overseers," freedpeople sometimes nominated a replacement of their own, either a fellow freedman or a Northerner who respected their determination not to be commanded by force.[106]

103 See below, docs. 31, 182; *Freedom*, ser. 1, vol. 2: docs. 16–17, 20, 22, 25, 27, 55–56, 60, 62, 70, 82, 92, 99, 102–3; *Freedom*, ser. 2: doc. 45.

104 For the experience of black soldiers, see *Freedom*, ser. 2, especially chaps. 6–11.

105 *Freedom*, ser. 2: doc. 157A. The struggle for equal pay is discussed more fully in *Freedom*, ser. 2: chap. 7.

106 See below, doc. 87. On rejection of overseers, see below, docs. 34, 86, 94, 106C, 116–17, 121; *Freedom*, ser. 1, vol. 2: doc. 43.

With plantation laborers united in opposition, planters courted rebellion if they refused to accede. The consequence of trying to maintain the old order, according to one army provost marshal, was "trouble, immediately – and the negroes band together, and lay down their own rules, as to when, and how long they will work &c &c. and the Overseer loses all control over them." Occasionally, former slaves took matters into their own hands. Armed with sticks, laborers on one plantation drove the overseer away, declaring that "they would make Laws for themselves."[107]

Union military authorities generally sympathized with the freedpeople's efforts to obliterate vestiges of the slave regime. Although they stopped short of removing overseers, army officers prohibited corporal punishment and established procedures for adjudicating disputes between employers and employees. They also required that freed laborers be paid. In their view, prohibiting physical coercion and guaranteeing compensation were fundamental to free labor. To some officers, the principle of compensation mattered far more than its character or amount. "It is free labor if but one cent a year be paid," declared the head of General Banks's "Bureau of Negro Labor," to the ready assent of the general himself.[108]

To the former slaves, Banks's penny represented not the certainty of their liberation but the narrow confines of their freedom. Without exception, military regulations prescribed low wages for plantation hands, substantially lower than the earnings of black soldiers or military laborers. In 1863, monthly wages for the highest-rated field hands ranged from $2 in southern Louisiana to about $6.50 in the Sea Islands and $7 in the Mississippi Valley. The great majority of plantation workers – women, children, and old people, all of whom were rated below first-class hands – earned even less. Like black soldiers and military laborers, plantation laborers received rations in addition to wages but, except in southern Louisiana, had to pay for their own clothing. Unlike black soldiers and most military laborers, plantation laborers also received rations for dependent family members, the value of which, for some large families, may have offset the lower wage rates. Nevertheless, their cash income barely sufficed to purchase blankets, supplemental foodstuffs, medical care, and tobacco. Little or nothing remained to buy items like school books and Sunday clothes, much less to save toward future independence.[109]

Differences in the organization of work and relief gave free labor a somewhat distinctive cast in each region of the Union-occupied South.

107 See below, docs. 90C n., 94.

108 See below, doc. 110.

109 See below, docs. 28, 84, 162. The rate for the Sea Islands, where wages were set by the day rather than the month, is calculated on the basis of twenty-six days of work per month, at $.25 per day.

These differences derived from antebellum practices, particular military circumstances, and the policies of individual commanders. In the Sea Islands, for instance, the antebellum organization of labor by "tasks" left its mark on wartime arrangements. At least initially, military officials and civilian plantation superintendents saw task work as readily adaptable to the requirements of free wage labor, because it assigned responsibility for particular work to particular workers, facilitating both measurement of each individual's labor and payment in proportion to work accomplished. General Saxton issued plantation regulations that organized all steps of cotton production (except harvesting) into daily tasks, each with a precise monetary payment. In effect, federal authorities transmuted antebellum task labor into piecework, expecting that some laborers would redouble their efforts and complete more than one task per day. Piecework also prevailed during harvest, with each worker paid on the basis of the amount of cotton picked. To encourage former slaves to remain at work to the end of the year, wages for planting and cultivation were set at a low level, with picking pegged at higher rates. At the heart of the new regime lay cash payment for work in cotton. With the money they earned, plantation hands were expected to purchase their clothing, whatever food they did not raise, and "luxuries" like tobacco, which in the past had often been provided by the owner. Obligatory labor on provision crops earned no wages at all.[110]

The reorganization of plantation labor was accompanied by new provisions for nonworkers. Except where the estates had been stripped by Union soldiers, Saxton and the plantation superintendents refused to dispense rations, on the grounds that such issues encouraged dependency and resembled the old system of "allowances" from the master. Instead, the laborers on each government plantation collectively produced food for the entire plantation population, workers and dependents alike, on land designated for that purpose. Each family also received a garden plot. Alone among the federally supervised plantation systems, that of the Sea Islands permitted the laborers some voice in decisions about what crops they would cultivate, and in what proportion. The freedpeople clearly preferred food crops. On plantations controlled by private entrepreneurs in 1863, cotton accounted for 40 percent of the cultivated acreage; on those operated under the direction of government superintendents, only 25 percent was in the staple.[111]

In most other respects, however, Saxton's regulations for the government plantations set the standard for those in private hands. In particular, the freedpeople employed by Northern planters expected

[110] For the order establishing the labor system on government plantations in the Sea Islands, see below, doc. 28. For elucidations of its provisions, see below, docs. 31–32, 36.

[111] Calculated from figures in doc. 36, below.

prompt remuneration. One planter complained that he could induce them to cultivate cotton only "by going among them and paying on the spot." Northern entrepreneurs had little choice but to provide garden plots, because the laborers demanded them. To the extent that the planters were therefore able to reduce capital outlays in the form of rations, they found the system acceptable, though they rued the tendency of the laborers to devote their energies to food production instead of additional tasks in the cotton fields. Some laborers failed to complete even a single daily task, leaving the field at midday to work in their gardens.[112]

In another concession to the freedpeople, some Northern planters divided the fields into separate tracts, each worked collectively by the members of one or more households. Edward Philbrick, for one, favored such allocation of land because it gave the laborers "a proprietary interest in the crop." By this arrangement, households or other self-organized work groups in effect supplanted individual task hands. These collective work units allowed the former slaves a greater measure of control over the disposition of their own labor, permitting some family members, for example, to leave the field early to perform domestic tasks, or allowing more experienced workers to assist the weaker and less experienced.[113]

In southern Louisiana and the Mississippi Valley, Union military officials devised a substantially different plan for organizing labor and relief. Both General Banks and Adjutant General Thomas retained certain formal features of the old regime. Plantation laborers continued to be organized into gangs whose composition was determined by the operator of the estate, not the workers. Despite the opposition of the freedpeople, the vast majority of planters – whether former slaveholders or Northern lessees – employed overseers. Hours and conditions of labor were left to the discretion of planters and overseers, subject only to the restraints of custom, the army's ban on corporal punishment, and a vaguely worded insistence that workers receive "proper" and "humane" treatment. The subsistence of plantation residents also remained largely the responsibility of planters, who were required to feed, clothe, and house nonworkers as well as workers. In the view of military authorities, the planters' assumption of that responsibility, together with the risks of planting in a war zone, justified low wages. For their part, former slaves were expected to devote their energy to raising staple crops, not food. Government officials, resident plantation owners, and Northern lessees were of one mind: Cotton and sugar, not corn and potatoes, promised profits for the planters and taxes for the treasury.[114]

112 See below, docs. 32, 34, 40.
113 See below, docs. 31, 34; see also Saville, "A Measure of Freedom," pp. 75–82.
114 For the military regulations governing plantation labor in southern Louisiana and the Mississippi Valley, see below, docs. 81, 84, 162.

Whatever the particular stipulations, military regulation of labor delivered a crippling blow to the master's sovereignty and limited the employer's power. No longer was the planter the court of first and last resort. Freedpeople recognized even the most rudimentary recourse to higher authority as a radical departure from slavery. When an employer trampled on their rights, they protested to the nearest superintendent of contrabands or provost marshal. Throughout the Union-occupied South, employers complained that their laborers appealed even "the least thing," undercutting all discipline. No matter what the decision in any given instance, intervention by federal officials signified the demise of the slaveholder's omnipotence.[115]

Union soldiers, black and white, often interposed their authority on behalf of agricultural laborers. Just as they had disseminated news of freedom, soldiers expounded the rights of free men and women, informing one group of ex-slaves, for example, that "they need never mind a driver any more, that each of them was good as a driver." Some soldiers attempted to redress forcibly the wrongs suffered by plantation workers. From the planters' perspective, black soldiers wielded especially subversive influence. Armed, mobile, and politicized, their very presence demonstrated the freedpeople's new power. Because most black soldiers had themselves toiled in the fields and often had families and friends on the plantations, they identified with those who worked the land and were determined to prevent their abuse.[116]

Plantations that had once been virtual fiefdoms, whose proprietors jealously guarded their boundaries and screened all visitors, became subject to all manner of intrusion. The separation of able-bodied men – most of whom were serving as soldiers or military laborers – from the women, children, and old people who made up the bulk of the plantation work force necessitated frequent visits, because former slaves viewed a secure family life as fundamental to freedom. Planters protested the visits as violations of their private domain, but their complaints availed little. Although military regulations generally forbade plantation laborers to leave an estate without permission, such rules were often honored only in the breach. "[W]e cannot keep our people at home," complained a Sea Island planter, who lamented the effect upon labor discipline.[117] The new permeability of plantation boundaries broke down the isolation of plantation life, permitting rural laborers to gain broader knowledge of the world and to develop solidarity with their counterparts on other estates and with black townspeople.

Within the narrow geographical bounds of Union occupation, the circumstances of plantation life forced all but the most intransigent slaveholders to accommodate the changes wrought by emancipation.

[115] See, for example, below, doc. 32.

[116] See, for example, below, docs. 19, 74, 77, 199; *Freedom*, ser. 2: doc. 55.

[117] See below, docs. 32, 74, 79, 90B; *Freedom*, ser. 1, vol. 2: doc. 21.

Slowly and reluctantly, former masters began to come to terms with the reality of free labor. Few retired the lash voluntarily, and none welcomed the necessity of paying wages, but most planters were compelled to accept at least the rudiments of free labor in order to continue operations. Before long, they even discerned certain advantages in the new order.

Whereas former slaveholders were loath to assume the responsibilities of free labor, they eagerly jettisoned the burdens of mastership. Under the slave regime, they had been obliged to support sick, young, and elderly slaves; under free labor, they derived no benefits from doing so. Employers in the North, they pointedly insisted, bore no such responsibility. Accordingly, many erstwhile slaveholders evicted elderly and unproductive laborers with no consideration for years of service or putative bonds of affection. The wives, parents, and children of black soldiers became special targets of the planters' zeal to "sift out" unproductive former slaves, but anyone unable to contribute labor was liable to be ousted. Masters-turned-employers also refused to provide medical care, declaring that such expenses were no longer their responsibility. "When I owned niggers," announced a Louisiana planter in characteristic fashion, "I used to pay medical bills and take care of them; I do not think I shall trouble myself much now."[118]

The entry of Northerners into the plantation business and the acquiescence of former slaveholders in the requirements of free labor placed relations between planters and laborers on new ground. Even as corporal punishment and the employment of overseers remained live issues, the reorganization of agricultural labor inaugurated new contests over the length of the workday and the workweek. Planters struggled to exact as much labor as possible from freedpeople determined to work less than they had as slaves. In the Mississippi Valley and southern Louisiana, where gang labor predominated, planters tried to hold former slaves to the antebellum standard: dawn to dusk, six days a week, and, during harvest, additional labor at night and on Sunday. Freedpeople resisted such extensive claims on their time, often shortening both the workday and workweek, much to the disgust of former masters, Northern lessees, and federal officials. A government superintendent was chagrined to discover that the hands on one sugar estate "only work five days in the week and then very little." In the Sea Islands, where the task had defined a day's work, the contest centered on Saturday labor, with plantation superintendents and Northern planters insisting that the day belonged to the workweek and freedpeople claiming it as their own.[119]

Like employers elsewhere, planters in the Union-occupied South also

118 See below, docs. 100–101, 106A, 108, 110, 200; *Freedom*, ser. 1, vol. 2: docs. 102, 129.

119 See, for example, below, docs. 19, 21, 100n., 106B.

wanted to pay their workers as little as possible, and at the last possible moment. Federal regulation of wages averted much potential conflict. But even the low rates set by military orders were too high for most planters, who would have preferred to compensate their workers with "a great present" at year's end – maintaining the fiction of their paternal rule and leaving to their own discretion the amount and form of payment. Meanwhile, the former slaves, confined to federally mandated wages, wanted more.

Within the possibilities permitted by military regulations, both planters and workers looked for ways to gain advantage. At times, each found reason to prefer that compensation take the form of a share of the crop rather than cash. Where planters lacked the resources with which to pay cash wages, they gladly acquiesced in laborers' demands for a share. In a good year, a postharvest share wage might return more to the laborers than monthly cash payments, although a short crop would result in smaller compensation. From the standpoint of the planters, share wages offered the important benefit of holding laborers through the entire year, lest they forfeit their portion by leaving before the harvest. Federal officials also encouraged year-long commitments. In southern Louisiana, General Banks offered the option of a postharvest payment instead of monthly cash wages, setting the rate at one-twentieth of the crop, to be divided among the workers. Even when there was no explicit sanction of share wages, freedpeople and planters occasionally negotiated such arrangements on their own.[120]

Gradually former slaveholders and former slaves navigated the terrain of free labor more comfortably. Former slaveholders discovered that wage-earners expected to be paid, and paid promptly. They also came to see advantage in allowing their employees access to the resources of the plantation: the right to cultivate garden plots, to hunt or cut wood in forests and fish in streams, to keep swine and poultry. Such concessions were prized by former slaves, who saw them as a means to labor for their own benefit and to expand control over their own lives. Acceding to their wishes helped employers attract and retain a work force and, at times, permitted reductions in the amount or frequency of monetary compensation.[121] Employers learned not only to cater to the "wants" of the freedpeople, but also to turn them to their own ends. Yankee planters, familiar with the operation of a wage system, pioneered in establishing plantation stores where laborers could purchase items previously beyond their reach. Before long, Southern planters also realized that such stores could help keep their workers on the plantation and provide another source of profit.[122]

120 See below, docs. 84, 86; *Freedom*, ser. 1, vol. 2: doc. 129.

121 See, for example, below, docs. 141, 171.

122 See below, docs. 40, 100, 108; Powell, *New Masters*, pp. 87–93.

While they continued to condemn military regulation as a poor substitute for physical compulsion, planters learned to benefit from the authority of local superintendents or provost marshals. Denouncing anarchy in the quarters and presenting themselves as friends of good order, planters cultivated the goodwill of nearby army officers, who often welcomed the attention and granted them a sympathetic hearing. General James Bowen, provost marshal general of the Department of the Gulf, went so far as to instruct his subordinates that "planters must be regarded as conservators of the peace" on their estates. Planters found the army particularly useful in curbing the former slaves' freedom of movement. Military restrictions against unauthorized travel dovetailed conveniently with the planters' insistence that black workers, once committed to a particular estate, not be allowed to leave except by permission.[123]

Free-labor arrangements, however circumscribed, endangered the old regime, a truth rebel leaders clearly understood. In the summer of 1863, the Confederate high command unleashed a series of raids on the plantations operated by Yankee lessees and reconstructed Southerners. The results were devastating. In the Mississippi Valley, rebel soldiers killed several lessees and hundreds of freedpeople, hundreds more of whom were captured and reenslaved. The attacks thoroughly disrupted the plantation-leasing system, sending panicked laborers and lessees to nearby army posts. Some lessees returned to their homes in the North, and many freedpeople refused to accept work in the countryside. Freedpeople in more secure areas, including the South Carolina Sea Islands and tidewater Virginia, escaped such wholesale terror, but they, too, suffered harassment by Confederate soldiers and guerrilla marauders.[124]

The Confederate raids failed to shake the federal commitment to reconstructing Southern agriculture on the basis of free labor. By the fall of 1863, many erstwhile secessionists were suing for peace. Disloyal planters, reports claimed, were "discouraged and hopeless of the rebellion, and ready to do almost anything that will keep their negroes in the fields." Such accounts were not long in reaching President Lincoln, who liked what he heard. Eager to revive Southern unionism, Lincoln directed his generals, particularly those in the Mississippi Valley, to encourage slaveholders to accept free labor. Adjutant General Thomas endorsed unionist associations in such former hotbeds of secession as Vicksburg and Natchez. Other federal officers courted both long-time loyalists and repentant rebels, promising them protection from Confed-

[123] Bg. Genl. James Bowen to Captain Fitch, 27 Apr. [1863], vol. 296 DG, pp. 594–95, Press Copies of Letters Sent, ser. 1839, Provost Marshal, Dept. of the Gulf, RG 393 Pt. 1 [C-1099]. For examples of military restrictions upon the mobility of rural laborers, see below, docs. 15, 54, 109, 198; *Freedom*, ser. 1, vol. 2: doc. 21.

[124] See below, docs. 96, 168, 177, 196.

erate raiders and assistance in marketing crops and acquiring supplies, if they agreed to compensate their laborers and abjure corporal punishment. Military commanders in Arkansas aided in the formation of a provisional unionist government, while the brightening fortunes of war invigorated antislavery unionists in Louisiana and Tennessee. Sensing the change, Lincoln urged General Banks in southern Louisiana and Military Governor Andrew Johnson in Tennessee to mobilize opponents of slavery in support of loyal state governments.[125]

As the new order spread to areas exempt from the Emancipation Proclamation, federal officials evaluated the success of the labor and welfare arrangements established during 1863. Secretary of War Stanton solicited suggestions from knowledgeable observers, and he dispatched a special emissary, General James S. Wadsworth, to the Mississippi Valley. Equally interested was Secretary of the Treasury Chase, to whose department the President had assigned control over all abandoned and captured "houses, tenements, lands, and plantations" that were not needed for military purposes. Preparing to devise new regulations for leasing plantations and organizing agricultural labor, he, too, sought suggestions from military and civilian authorities. Still other Northerners, stirred by the possibility of remaking the South, needed no invitation to volunteer their views.[126]

Nearly all such commentators agreed that the experience of 1863 had demonstrated the superior productivity of free over slave labor. "Every body admits that the cash System works better than the lash system," declared a treasury agent. Freed black laborers had given the lie to the proslavery dogma "that negroes are very valuable as slaves, but when free, worthless, and unable to take care of themselves." "[I]t is now generally conceded," observed Charles Wilder, "that the labor of one freeman, is worth that of two slaves." From the Sea Islands, General Saxton reported with satisfaction that the 1863 crop had proven beyond doubt "that the cotton fields of South Carolina can be successfully cultivated by free labor, that the negroes will work cheerfully and willingly with a reasonable prospect of reward." Evidence from the Mississippi Valley seemed to bear out Adjutant General Thomas's ear-

[125] *Official Records*, ser. 1, vol. 24, pt. 3, pp. 549–50. On unionist politics in the Mississippi Valley, see below, doc. 182; *Freedom*, ser. 1, vol. 1: doc. 110; *Official Records*, ser. 1, vol. 24, pt. 3, pp. 549–50, 570, 578, 582–88; Lawrence N. Powell and Michael S. Wayne, "Self-Interest and the Decline of Confederate Nationalism," in *The Old South in the Crucible of War*, ed. Harry P. Owens and James J. Cooke (Jackson, Miss., 1983), pp. 29–46. On Louisiana, see LaWanda Cox, *Lincoln and Black Freedom: A Study in Presidential Leadership* (Columbia, S.C., 1981), chaps. 2–4; Peyton McCrary, *Abraham Lincoln and Reconstruction: The Louisiana Experiment* (Princeton, N.J., 1978), chaps. 5–8. On Tennessee, see *Freedom*, ser. 1, vol. 2: doc. 101; *Freedom*, ser. 2: docs. 64–65, 67; John Cimprich, *Slavery's End in Tennessee, 1861–1865* (University, Ala., 1985), chaps. 7–8.

[126] *Official Records*, ser. 3, vol. 3, pp. 872–73; see below, docs. 185–86.

lier prediction "that the freed negro may be profitably employed by enterprising men."[127]

And so it did. Despite unfavorable weather and Confederate raids, lessees in the Mississippi Valley had made money, some of them a good deal of it. Northern planters in the South Carolina Sea Islands had also reaped handsome profits. Even under wartime conditions, the new labor system had fulfilled the prophecy of a New England textile magnate who touted "Cheap Cotton by Free Labor." To judge from the hundreds of Northerners who sought permission to operate plantations in the occupied South for the coming year, the profitability of free labor – at least in cotton-growing regions – had been established beyond cavil. For some Northerners, that was quite enough. In granting the former slaves ownership of their own persons and transforming them into wage-workers, the government had done all it should to secure freedom.[128]

Others disagreed. As long as the war continued, military and political constraints precluded any thoroughgoing overhaul of Southern society, but many Northerners worried that steps taken during the conflict might foreclose options available in peacetime. They therefore viewed wartime labor arrangements with one eye on what was immediately possible and the other on what was ultimately desirable. Because acceptance of the possible did not necessarily imply concurrence on the desirable, observers divided among themselves in complex ways. Their debates focused on four related questions: the condition of black wage-workers in the Union-occupied South as compared with their Northern counterparts; the proper disposition of land controlled by the government; the ultimate political status of the former slaves; and the political status of former Confederates, particularly large property owners.

While acknowledging the productivity of black wage laborers amid the uncertainty of war, many Northerners denounced the limited prospects afforded former slaves under the new regime. Pointing to the meager pay, regimentation of labor, restriction of physical movement, and absence of written contracts and lien laws, they emphasized the extent to which freedpeople were denied rights that Northern wage-earners took for granted. General John Hawkins, whose command included almost all the Mississippi Valley plantations leased out in 1863, attacked the leasing system as a travesty of free labor. Although he expected most former slaves to remain wage laborers, at least for the immediate future, he condemned the terms under which they were

127 Tho. Heaton to Hon. Wm. P. Mellen, 10 May 1864, Letters Received from Assistant Special Agents, Records of the General Agent, RG 366 [Q-169]; *Freedom*, ser. 1, vol. 2: doc. 43; see below, docs. 36, 162, 180.

128 For arguments that cotton and other staples could be produced more profitably with free labor than with slave labor, see below, docs. 7, 36, 70, 93; [Edward Atkinson], *Cheap Cotton by Free Labor: By a Cotton Manufacturer* (Boston, 1861).

working. By renting immense tracts of land to unscrupulous "adventurers" and setting low wages for laborers, the government had ceded control to "a monopoly." Hawkins urged federal authorities to subdivide the great estates into small farms and lease them to Northerners and ex-slaves, multiplying the number of agricultural units and, accordingly, the demand for hired labor. Wage rates, he argued, should be established by the market instead of the government, workers should be permitted to change employers at any time, and employers should have the right to discharge workers for any cause. Only then, Hawkins emphasized, would the labor of the former slaves become "as free as the labor of the northern white man."[129] In two influential reports prepared in late 1863, James E. Yeatman, president of the Western Sanitary Commission, disseminated Hawkins's antimonopoly views to a wider audience, adding his own unflattering judgments about the leasing system and suggestions for its reform. Yeatman thereby established himself as the leading critic of existing policy and gained the attention of Secretary of the Treasury Chase.[130]

Many Northerners concurred with Hawkins and Yeatman in their harsh assessment of free labor in the Union-occupied South. General Wadsworth, Stanton's emissary, was particularly critical of Banks's regulations because they denied what he believed to be the essential right of wage laborers: the freedom to rise to the limits of their own ability. Low wages, inadequate legal protection, and restrictions upon freedom of movement, he feared, would immobilize former slaves at the bottom of the social order, "not as freedmen, but as serfs." James McKaye, a member of the American Freedmen's Inquiry Commission, shared Wadsworth's reservations. "If the only object to be accomplished [were] simply 'to compel the negro to labor' in a condition of perpetual subordination and subjection," he argued, Banks's system would suffice. But it was unacceptable "if the object [were] to make the colored man a self-supporting and self-defending member of [the] community." The freedpeople, maintained McKaye, Wadsworth, and many others, deserved more at the hands of the government.[131]

Among the things they deserved was land to cultivate on their own account. Widespread acquisition by purchase seemed impossible, given the poverty of most former slaves, the insecurity of wartime land tenure, and the absence – except in the Sea Islands – of legal procedures for con-

129 See below, docs. 177, 181.

130 Yeatman, *A Report on the Condition of the Freedmen of the Mississippi, Presented to the Western Sanitary Commission, December 17th, 1863* (St. Louis, 1864), and *Suggestions of a Plan of Organization for Freed Labor, and the Leasing of Plantations along the Mississippi River . . .* (St. Louis, 1864). For a summary of the latter, see below, doc. 189n. For Yeatman's influence on Chase, see below, doc. 186.

131 See below, doc. 107; J. McKaye, "The Emancipated Slave face to face with his old Master: Valley of the Lower Mississippi," [Apr.? 1864], filed with O-328 1863, Letters Received, ser. 12, RG 94 [K-66].

veying forfeited property. But renting was another matter. The government had leased abandoned and confiscated land to poorly capitalized Yankees; surely those ex-slaves who had the experience and resources to work a farm might be similarly favored. The success of the few black farmers who had rented land in 1863 reinforced such reasoning. In the course of debates about the government's leasing policy for the coming year, some Northerners, including James Yeatman, advocated preferential treatment for black lessees. Influenced by their arguments, Secretary of the Treasury Chase directed his subordinates to give special consideration to former slaves who wished to rent land from the government.[132]

A handful of Northerners continued to see the war as an opportunity to endow former slaves with an independent competency. General Saxton maintained that restricting freedpeople to the status of wage laborers would lock them "in the condition of a peasantry only a little higher than chattelism . . . when so many of them had proved their fitness to be owners of the soil." McKaye argued that the interests of both former slaves and the nation would be best served by permitting them to own the land they occupied, for "you can never have in any country a democratic society, or a society substantially, practically free, where the land all belongs to a few people."[133] Asserting the connection between productive property and freedom against those who viewed self-ownership as the ultimate goal, men like Saxton and McKaye revealed the ongoing conflict within Northern society over the sources and meaning of liberty – a conflict that was fast being transferred to the former slave states.

Advocates of redistributing land gained support from the growing number of Northerners who believed that loyal ex-slaves had a better claim to the land than traitorous rebels. The freedpeople's uncompensated labor during slavery and their loyalty during the war, declared one treasury agent, gave them "an equitable lien upon the lands of their masters." Arguing upon similar grounds, General Saxton declared that the freedpeople deserved their former owners' land as a matter of "simple justice." Such Northerners thought it morally wrong as well as politically naive to restore land to former slaveholders while dispossessing former slaves. Fully aware that ultimate settlement of the question would await the end of the war, proponents of a property-based freedom wished to avert wartime policies that might prejudice the outcome. Actions taken during the conflict, they feared, could leave former slaves economically dependent and politically subordinate when peace finally came.[134]

If the constraints of war limited the possibilities for transforming

[132] See below, docs. 107, 186; *Freedom*, ser. 1, vol. 2: doc. 28.
[133] See below, docs. 57, 187.
[134] See below, docs. 47B, 57.

Southern society, those possibilities became narrower still with President Lincoln's Proclamation of Amnesty and Reconstruction, issued in December 1863. The edict offered to pardon most participants in the rebellion (excepting, most notably, high-ranking Confederate military and civil officials), on condition that they forsake the Confederacy, swear allegiance to the United States, and agree to abide by wartime laws and proclamations concerning emancipation. That done, they could again enjoy all rights of property, "except as to slaves." Moreover, the amnesty proclamation proposed a method by which the loyal people of a seceded state could form a government and seek readmission to the Union. The new state governments, Lincoln suggested, might then assume legal control over the former slaves. Although he acknowledged that he lacked constitutional power to dictate terms of reunification, the President hinted that he would welcome state legislation confirming emancipation and providing for the education of former slaves, "which may yet be consistent as a temporary arrangement with their present condition as a laboring, landless, and homeless class." In proposing his own model for reconstructing the South, Lincoln fueled the ongoing debate about the character of the war, the terms of national reunification, and the future of the former slaves.[135]

Widely praised in the North as a magnanimous yet politically shrewd measure, the amnesty proclamation also received high marks from most federal officials in the South. George Field, chief plantation commissioner in the Mississippi Valley, regarded the edict as the foundation for "an enduring and mutually advantageous reconstruction of the Union." Within a month of its issue, two-thirds of the Mississippi Valley plantations leased out during 1863 were restored to their antebellum owners. Field lauded the "amicable connections" that were forming between "*loyal Northern men*" and Southern "*owners* of the soil."[136]

Others took a more skeptical view. Many Northerners feared the consequences of remanding homeless, landless freedpeople to the tender mercies of "loyal" state governments. Under such a reconstruction policy, predicted Wendell Phillips, a noted abolitionist, the restored states would render "the freedom of the negro a sham," leaving the South "with its labor and capital at war." Some Union field commanders, drawing upon firsthand experience with former slaveholders, expressed similar doubts. Disputing the notion that the occupied Confederate states were ripe for readmission, General Napoleon B. Buford, commander of the District of Eastern Arkansas, avowed that he had "not yet seen a man of fortune or standing in the South who was to be relied on as a Union man." Far from accepting the demise of slavery, "every slaveholder sticks to the institution as his only hope for fortune[,]

[135] *Statutes at Large*, vol. 13, pp. 737–39.
[136] See below, doc. 189.

respectability and means of liveing." Northerners in the army and out worried that the Lincoln administration was conceding too much too soon in allowing such "unionists" to reclaim both their political rights and their land.[137]

To the extent that the President's amnesty policy promised to reinstate Southern planters, it also threatened the prospects of former slaves, who expected still more radical changes to follow wartime emancipation. Like Northern critics of federal labor policies, freedpeople objected to the low levels of compensation, restrictions upon freedom of movement, and inadequate protection against fraud or abuse. But their criticism extended beyond the details of wage labor. Freedom from a master, they believed, should mean more than the right to change masters. It implied access to those productive resources, especially land, without which freedom would be compromised.

Not even those Yankees most sympathetic with the aspirations of the former slaves viewed landownership precisely as they did. Land, ex-slaves and Northerners concurred, could provide subsistence and foster independence from former owners. But there agreement usually ended. Former slaves, like many of their contemporaries throughout the world, generally did not view land as property in the abstract or as a commodity whose worth was determined by the market. Instead, they valued it in proportion to labor expended and suffering endured. Given a choice, they preferred to own or occupy not just any plot of ground, but the land where they had been born and reared and in which they and their forebears had invested so much blood and sweat. Land was a link to generations past and future and a foundation for family and community among the living. Nor did former slaves fully subscribe to Northern concepts of absolute property. Instead, rights to particular tracts might bear little resemblance to the specifications of a deed. When left to their own devices, freedpeople often allowed for overlapping rights in any one property; conversely, an individual's use rights might encompass several parcels, not necessarily contiguous. Nonetheless, under the terms of the Yankee occupation, freedpeople desiring to obtain control over land had to comply with the incongruous conventions of the Northerners.[138]

[137] Edward McPherson, *The Political History of the United States of America, during the Great Rebellion* (Washington, 1865), p. 412; Brig. Genl. [Napoleon B. Buford] to Hon. Secy. of War, 11 Dec. 1863, vol. 37 DArk, pp. 240–42, Letters Sent, ser. 4664, Dist. of Eastern AR, RG 393 Pt. 2 No. 299 [C-7539]. See also Berlin et al., " 'To Canvass the Nation,' " pp. 243–44.

[138] See below, docs. 47A, 58; Saville, "A Measure of Freedom," pp. 59–64. See also Ira Berlin, Steven Hahn, Steven F. Miller, Joseph P. Reidy, and Leslie S. Rowland, "The Terrain of Freedom: The Struggle over the Meaning of Free Labor in the U.S. South," *History Workshop* 22 (Autumn 1986): 127–29. On Northern concepts of absolute property, see Morton J. Horwitz, *The Transformation of American Law, 1780–1860* (Cambridge, Mass., 1977).

The most favorable wartime opportunities to acquire land were those afforded freedpeople in the Sea Islands, where absent proprietors had been dispossessed under the Direct Tax Act. Developments in the latter months of 1863 held special promise. Under instructions from President Lincoln, the direct-tax commissioners reserved certain of the forfeited estates for "charitable" purposes, to be sold in twenty-acre tracts exclusively to heads of black households. That policy, which won the favor of two of the three commissioners and several prominent military officials, spared former slaves from having to bid against Northern speculators in order to obtain any land at all. But the freedpeople and many of their advocates – including General Saxton, Mansfield French, and Abram D. Smith, the dissenting tax commissioner – felt that Lincoln's instructions did not go far enough. The total reserved acreage, they pointed out, was far too small to provide a homestead for all black residents of the Sea Islands. They wanted former slaves to enjoy preferred access to any of the forfeited land on the islands, not solely to that on the reserved estates. Hoping to circumvent the instructions, Saxton, French, and Smith encouraged would-be black landowners to settle wherever they wished and lobbied the Lincoln administration to permit the freedpeople to enter preemption claims.[139]

For a time, the strategy worked. On the last day of December, 1863, Lincoln instructed the direct-tax commissioners to permit loyal residents of the Sea Islands to preempt forty-acre tracts on any government-controlled land before it was put up for auction.[140] The news seemed a vindication for the freedpeople of the Sea Islands, many of whom had already staked out a claim "on the old homestead, where they had been born, & had laborered & suffered." Former slaves on some plantations made applications "in mass . . . without the names of the negroes & without designating the particular tracts for each." But preemption evoked strong opposition from Smith's colleagues on the direct-tax commission, whose objections led in February 1864 to a reinstatement of Lincoln's initial instructions. The disappointment of the freedpeople was "almost unbearable." Although a number of them eventually acquired plots on the estates earmarked for "charitable" purposes (110 families by March 1864), the undoing of preemption marked the passing of the former slaves' best wartime hope for landownership.[141]

However disappointing, the opportunities of Sea Island freedpeople to acquire land far exceeded those afforded their counterparts elsewhere in the Union-occupied South. Although the President possessed authority to appoint direct-tax commissioners for every seceded state, by the beginning of 1864 he had done so only for South Carolina, Florida,

[139] See below, docs. 39, 45.

[140] See below, doc. 41.

[141] See below, docs. 39, 42, 45, 49, 62; see also Rose, *Rehearsal for Reconstruction*, chap. 10.

Virginia, and Tennessee.[142] Lincoln's inaction, coupled with the Proclamation of Amnesty and Reconstruction, signaled his intention to use expropriation chiefly to induce Confederates to return to their "proper allegiance," and not as a means to recast Southern society. Although his policy did not foreclose entirely the possibility of providing former slaves with homesteads from the land of disloyal owners, it established a precedent that had momentous consequences in the postwar struggle over land.

The waning possibility of acquiring land was only one source of concern to the freedpeople and their Northern allies in the spring of 1864, as Union armies once more took to the field and the new agricultural season commenced. As earlier, military considerations shaped the evolution of free labor. With the territory under federal control substantially enlarged, especially in the western theater, the army needed every black soldier it could get. Like veterans, the new recruits spent most of their time at noncombat duties, garrisoning towns, guarding railroad bridges, protecting leased plantations and contraband camps, and performing heavy fatigue labor. But increasingly large numbers of black troops traded shovels for rifles. Experienced black soldiers, some of whom had served for over a year, demanded more from military service than did raw recruits, and greater familiarity with official regulations and procedures aided their struggle against the inequities of military service. A handful of black men attained the status of commissioned officers. Of far greater significance for the common soldier, Congress abolished the difference in the pay of black and white soldiers, and Adjutant General Thomas ordered that black regiments perform no more than "their fair share of fatigue duty." Eventually Congress also guaranteed the freedom of all black soldiers' families, whatever the loyalty of their owners and even where slavery remained legal.[143]

The expansion of Union-held territory and the extension of federal supply lines also increased the need for military laborers. In the two major offensives of 1864 – the drive from Chattanooga to Atlanta in the western theater, and the campaign against Richmond and Petersburg in the east – the labor shortage was exacerbated by the scarcity of suitable black men in the contested territory. As a result, laborers and teamsters from previously occupied areas worked endlessly moving supplies and materiel from distribution points in the rear to armies in the

142 U.S., Senate, "Letter of the Secretary of the Treasury . . . [on] the collection of direct taxes in insurrectionary districts . . . ," *Senate Executive Documents*, 38th Cong., 1st sess., No. 35.

143 For the experience of black soldiers, see *Freedom*, ser. 2, especially chap. 6 on black commissioned officers, chap. 7 on the struggle for equal pay, and chap. 10 on disproportionate assignment to fatigue duty (including Adjutant General Thomas's order, doc. 201). The families of black soldiers were freed in March 1865 by joint resolution. (*Statutes at Large*, vol. 13, p. 571.)

field. Black "pioneers," many of them from Tennessee, built miles of corduroy road during the Atlanta campaign. Black men from the contraband camps and towns of tidewater Virginia and North Carolina were dispatched to the James River to dig a canal at Dutch Gap and to construct field works for the troops operating against Richmond.

At times, this heightened demand for military laborers worked to the advantage of black men. Some short-handed quartermasters, commissary officers, and engineers offered premium wages, favorable working conditions, and refuge and support for the families of their laborers. Black women benefited from the construction of general hospitals at Washington, Nashville, Louisville, and St. Louis, which provided employment for hundreds of nurses and laundresses. At the great supply depots, notably Washington and Nashville, black laborers received pay increases along with their white counterparts, and both were paid with greater regularity, as their employers sought to minimize discontent. The War Department eliminated another longstanding grievance when it decided to pay wages directly to black laborers whose loyal owners still claimed them as slaves.[144]

Union military authorities did not always meet their labor needs by increasing the rewards of service. Often they resorted to subterfuge and force, seizing black men without so much as first soliciting volunteers. Sometimes the superintendents of contrabands found themselves forced to do the army's dirty work. Operations against Richmond and Petersburg in mid-1864 led to the impressment of hundreds of men from contraband camps and government farms throughout tidewater Virginia and coastal North Carolina. Elsewhere, too, the opening of a new front or an impending Confederate raid occasioned mass levies that wrenched black men from their homes and sent them to distant places to labor for the army.[145]

The entry of black men into federal service, whether by their own volition or at gunpoint, placed at risk other freedpeople whose livelihood depended upon their labor. To reduce this vulnerability, some military commanders promised to provide "suitable subsistence" to the families of black soldiers. Others, particularly at garrison towns in the

[144] For examples of wage increases for military laborers, see below, doc. 122; *Freedom*, ser. 1, vol. 2: doc. 70; Ass't. Qr. Mtr. General Chs. Thomas to Brig. Gen'l. M. C. Meigs, 22 Jan. 1864, vol. 74, pp. 158–60, Letters Sent, ser. 9, Central Records, RG 92 [Y-681]; unsigned note, [Nov. 1864], enclosed in A.A. Genl. Wm. Fowler to Bvt. Brig. Genl. G. V. Rutherford, 8 Nov. 1866, Letters Received from the Freedmen's Bureau, ser. 34, Central Records, RG 92 [Y-664]. For the policy respecting direct payment of wages to black laborers who, their owners claimed, were legally still slaves, see *Freedom*, ser. 1, vol. 2: doc. 99.

[145] *Freedom*, ser. 1, vol. 2: docs. 36, 40, 47A, 104, 113, 129, 165. In December 1864, an urgent need to repair the levees along the Mississippi River had similar effects; military authorities impressed hundreds of ex-slaves and free blacks. (See below, docs. 131–32.)

Mississippi Valley, tolerated (and sometimes sanctioned) the creation of "regimental villages" near the camps of black troops. In these settlements, the soldiers' kin could share the men's rations and wages and contribute to their own support by cultivating garden patches or working for military or private employers. Such possibilities continued to attract former slaves to federal posts, despite the determined efforts of government officials to assign them to plantation labor. In the Vicksburg area, 3,700 former slaves left contraband camps for leased plantations during a single week in March 1864, yet at week's end the population of the camps had not diminished appreciably.[146]

When the recruitment of black soldiers was extended to the Upper South, contraband camps assumed an importance in both federal policy and the lives of fugitive slaves formerly characteristic only of the Lower South. Given the opportunity to gain freedom through military service, slaves left their owners and enlisted by the tens of thousands. Eventually, 57 percent of Kentucky's black men of military age served in the army, as did 39 percent of those in Missouri and in Tennessee and 28 percent of those in Maryland.[147] Slave men fled to recruiting stations in large numbers, often accompanied by their families. Black women and children also made their way to army posts when their owners, having lost the labor of the men, heaped overwork and abuse upon the remaining slaves or simply refused to support them any longer. The influx of fugitive slaves re-created in Tennessee and the border states the problems of relief that federal officials had earlier confronted in other parts of the Union-occupied Confederacy, but with the added complication that slavery was still legal.[148]

The soldiers' families and other black refugees overwhelmed the resources of established camps such as Freedman's Village and Roanoke Island. Freedman's Village became so crowded that military authorities shunted new arrivals to an employment depot on Mason's Island, in the Potomac River, which itself quickly became overcrowded and disease-ridden.[149] In middle and east Tennessee and northern Alabama, where enlistment of black men did not begin in earnest until late 1863, contraband camps sprang up at major recruiting posts. By June 1864, some 5,500 former slaves were living at seven camps, the largest at Clarksville, Nashville, and Gallatin, in middle Tennessee, and at Decatur and Huntsville, in northern Alabama.[150]

146 See below, docs. 204n., 212; *Freedom*, ser. 1, vol. 2: docs. 26, 33; *Freedom*, ser. 2: docs. 47A–C, 313. On the Vicksburg camps, see below, doc. 200.

147 *Freedom*, ser. 2: p. 12.

148 *Freedom*, ser. 1, vol. 1: docs. 191–92, 237; *Freedom*, ser. 1, vol. 2: docs. 177, 181, 225A–C, 226, 229; *Freedom*, ser. 2: docs. 90B, 91, 106–7, 111, 294, 298, 302.

149 *Freedom*, ser. 1, vol. 2: docs. 47A, 77, 80.

150 On the Tennessee and Alabama camps, see *Freedom*, ser. 1, vol. 2: docs. 108, 110, 114, 123, 129.

In the border states, by contrast, the recruitment of black soldiers crippled slavery without impelling the federal government to sponsor either contraband camps or free labor. Despite the pleas of soldiers' relatives and other runaway and castaway slaves, military authorities refused to provide rations or housing: Since they were legally still slaves, their owners, not the government, were responsible for their care. Orders called upon local commanders to enlist the able-bodied men but turn away all other black refugees.[151]

Border-state black soldiers protested vehemently against such treatment of their families, and they found numerous allies among sympathetic army officers. General William A. Pile, superintendent of black recruitment in Missouri, repeatedly sought permission to transfer fugitive slaves to the contraband camp at Benton Barracks, there to be furnished both protection and rations. Loath to assume responsibility for the fugitives, Pile's superiors instead authorized another officer to remove them to the Kansas border. In central Kentucky, hundreds of black women and children gathered in and near Camp Nelson, which in mid-1864 became the state's largest center of black recruitment. But Union military authorities, from the post commander to Adjutant General Lorenzo Thomas, refused to care for the soldiers' families. Throughout the summer and fall, in a drama that became more somber with each enactment, the women and children were driven from the post, often into the clutches of owners who had received advance notice of the expulsion. A final wholesale eviction, undertaken on a freezing November day, caused such suffering that the ensuing publicity forced military authorities to reverse their policy. At the end of the war, the "Colored Refugee Home" at Camp Nelson sheltered about 1,000 black women and children.[152]

In addition to spawning contraband camps, military enlistment sped the disintegration of slavery, encouraged legal emancipation, and, especially in Tennessee, advanced the development of free labor. Without the direct sanction of military or treasury officials, many slaves negotiated new terms of work, either with their owners or with nonslaveholders who welcomed an opportunity to employ black laborers. Such informal accommodations, usually involving one-to-one bargaining, had appeared with increasing regularity in late 1863 as recruitment diminished the pool of young black men. Private free-labor arrangements proliferated during early 1864, as landowners rushed to secure workers for the coming year. In the Nashville basin and in parts of the border states, farmers and planters made numerous concessions in order to retain "the services of there slaves – or in other words to conciliate &

[151] *Freedom*, ser. 1, vol. 1: doc. 233; *Freedom*, ser. 1, vol. 2: docs. 167, 169, 177, 219; *Freedom*, ser. 2: docs. 93, 102A–C, 105.

[152] *Freedom*, ser. 1, vol. 1: doc. 191; *Freedom*, ser. 1, vol. 2: docs. 176–77, 182, 187, 190, 219, 225A–D, 226–27, 230; *Freedom*, ser. 2: docs. 94, 107, 312A–B.

prevent them from running away." Some promised cash wages; others, to match the terms offered by government employers or to pay "as much as was given to other colored persons"; still others permitted former slaves to cultivate land as renters.[153]

Based on verbal agreement, private free-labor bargains left broad latitude for conflicting interpretation, renegotiation, or abandonment by either party. Employers generally held the balance of power and seldom hesitated to use it. Many of them simply refused to pay what they had promised. Eviction might take place at any moment and for any reason. Families of black soldiers were especially liable to be driven off or denied food and clothing, as was any former slave who showed "a disposition to send his children to school or to favor the *Yankees*." Employers who had lured workers into the field with promises of a postharvest payment often reneged and, instead, drove them away "to save taking care of them during the winter."[154]

The disruptions of war and the continued legality of slavery also hindered the spread of private free-labor agreements – sometimes fatally. In many places, guerrilla bands took direct action against planters and farmers who countenanced any breach of slavery or who introduced black laborers into previously all-white communities. The guerrillas reserved especially deadly venom for the black laborers themselves. Such attacks were widespread in much of Missouri, but by no means confined there. In their struggle to contain free labor, defenders of slavery also deployed the law. Threats of prosecution under statutes that prohibited hiring a slave without the owner's consent deterred many would-be employers from dealing with "slaves" – even when the "slaves" were beyond reclamation by their "owners." Although they eventually capitulated to the new regime, slaveholders and their allies retained many weapons to obstruct its progress. Their bitter resistance prevented free labor from taking root in some areas and stunted its development in others.[155]

Free labor stood on firmer ground in those parts of the Upper South

[153] See below, docs. 231A–B; *Freedom*, ser. 1, vol. 2: docs. 102, 105, 107, 113, 125, 128, 139, 188, 222; *Freedom*, ser. 2: docs. 95–96. In Kentucky, where slavery remained legal until the ratification of the Thirteenth Amendment in December 1865, such informal, unsanctioned, and unstable free-labor arrangements also characterized the summer and fall following the end of the war. (See *Freedom*, ser. 1, vol. 1: docs. 240–41, 245–51, 253–54; *Freedom*, ser. 1, vol. 2: docs. 231–32, 234–36, 238–42.)

[154] *Freedom*, ser. 1, vol. 1: docs. 150A–B, 152, 191–92, 231, 233; *Freedom*, ser. 1, vol. 2: docs. 114, 125, 127, 130, 139, 177n., 181, 193, 222, 226; *Freedom*, ser. 2: doc. 298. On similar developments in the Lower South, see below, docs. 211, 231A–B; *Freedom*, ser. 1, vol. 1: docs. 122–23.

[155] On guerrilla attacks, see *Freedom*, ser. 1, vol. 1: doc. 196; *Freedom*, ser. 1, vol. 2: docs. 141, 178, 186, 193, 195–96, 197n., 199; *Freedom*, ser. 2: doc. 85. On prosecution under antebellum statutes, see *Freedom*, ser. 1, vol. 1: docs. 239, 242, 246, 248–49, 252, 255; *Freedom*, ser. 1, vol. 2: docs. 184, 189, 238–39, 241; *Freedom*, ser. 2: doc. 112.

that were under the jurisdiction of federal superintendents – tidewater Virginia, coastal North Carolina, the District of Columbia, and the immediate vicinity of Union posts in middle and east Tennessee and in northern Alabama. During 1864, only a small proportion of the freedpeople in these areas lived and worked on government-controlled land. A far greater number labored under contracts with local farmers or other private employers. In Union-occupied tidewater Virginia, which had a total black population of approximately 35,000 at the end of 1863, only a few thousand ex-slaves and free blacks cultivated "government farms" as either wage laborers or renters. A similar pattern appeared in middle and east Tennessee and northern Alabama, where probably no more than 1,000 former slaves resided on estates leased out by treasury agents. The impact of federally sponsored labor arrangements extended, however, well beyond their direct participants. Private employers in the vicinity generally had to meet the same standards in order to retain their laborers, and military officials sometimes supervised free-labor contracts between masters-turned-employers and slaves-turned-employees.[156]

Union officers exerted much greater control over labor and relief in the Lower South, where they continued to view the plantations as the proper place to employ and subsist most former slaves. In the cotton-growing regions along the Mississippi River, the government-supervised plantations stretched from Helena, Arkansas, to Natchez, Mississippi, in 1864. They included not only estates leased to Northern entrepreneurs, but also those operated by Southern planters pardoned under Lincoln's amnesty proclamation. In mid-March, an estimated 60,000 freedpeople resided on the leased plantations alone, and the number on owner-operated places probably approached the same dimensions. In southern Louisiana, where the northern boundary of federal occupation reached beyond Baton Rouge, free labor under federal auspices also became more widespread. As of the summer of 1864, 35,000 former slaves were working under formal contracts supervised by the army; about 15,000 more labored under terms similar to those mandated by military regulations, but without written agreements. Meanwhile, in lowcountry South Carolina, Georgia, and Florida, the extent of Union-held territory remained largely unchanged. Approximately 15,000 freedpeople lived within federal lines, most of them on the South Carolina Sea Islands; roughly half were employed on plantations.[157]

In all parts of the Union-occupied South, the struggle between former slaves and former slaveholders involved more people and a broader range of issues than it had during the previous two years. Many of the freedpeople were fresh from bondage, having lately es-

[156] *Freedom*, ser. 1, vol. 2: chap. 3, and docs. 42–43, 105–6C, 109.

[157] See below, docs. 57, 197; Chaplain Thomas W. Conway to Major General N. P. Banks, 9 Sept. 1864, C-228 1864, Letters Received, ser. 1920, Civil Affairs, Dept. of the Gulf, RG 393 Pt. 1 [C-732].

caped to Union lines or fallen under the control of advancing federal armies; others had one or more years' experience in freedom. While recently liberated slaves prepared to fight the old battles, the veterans undertook new ones. More experienced freedpeople not only tutored neophytes in their rights as free men and women, but also led the way. Those who had acquired tools, agricultural implements, and work animals served as exemplars; occasionally, they even employed other ex-slaves.[158]

The interchange between veterans and neophytes proceeded among the employers as well. Planters were an even more diverse lot than plantation laborers, including among their number both newly arrived lessees and old-time proprietors, Northerners conversant with free-labor practices and Southerners entirely unfamiliar with them. Northern entrepreneurs expounded upon the rights of employers and the myriad ways to encourage productivity without resorting to force, while Southern planters shared their technical knowledge of plantation routine and their notions about the peculiar characteristics of black workers. In many instances, exchanges between Northern and Southern planters took place within formal partnerships, in which the latter supplied the land and the former the capital and good offices necessary to resume staple production in a war zone. Like their laborers, planters entered the new crop year with more definite ideas about what they wanted, what they would accept, and what they would not tolerate.[159]

Federal policymakers had also learned from experience, and they, too, acquired new responsibilities. In the Sea Islands, where the government-operated plantations passed into private hands at direct-tax sales in March 1864, General Saxton and his subordinates were reduced to the role of arbiter between private employers and contract laborers. Elsewhere in the Union-occupied Lower South, federal officials continued to supervise plantation labor on both the estates leased out by the government and those operated by antebellum owners. Early in 1864, they revised the regulations governing agricultural labor. Designed chiefly to resolve conflicts that had arisen the previous year, the new guidelines also endeavored to placate Northern critics by requiring terms of agricultural labor more like those in the free states. In the sugar- and cotton-growing regions along the Mississippi River, where labor regulations had been sketchy outlines in 1863, federal officers elaborated more fully the rights and duties of both employers and laborers. The new regulations were particularly specific about the amount and form of compensation, the days and

[158] For examples of freedpeople employing other ex-slaves, see below, docs. 177, 208–9, 216n.; *Freedom*, ser. 1, vol. 2: doc. 58.

[159] On relations between Southern planters and Northern planters, see Powell, *New Masters*, especially chaps. 3–5. See also below, docs. 182, 189, 209.

hours of work, and the use of garden plots and work animals. They addressed, moreover, vexatious questions concerning which plantation residents were obligated to work, whether laborers or employers should pay for food, clothing, and medical care, and who should provide for nonworkers.

Both plantation laborers and planters gained from the new labor codes. For the laborers, improvements were substantial. The regulations increased minimum wages, limited daily hours of labor to ten in summer and nine in winter, and required extra pay for work on Sunday. They gave workers a lien on the crops they produced and codified their right to garden plots. In addition, military authorities urged planters to offer such incentives as compensation for extra work and "appropriation of land for share cultivation." By such means, General Banks believed, former slaves and former slaveholders could prepare themselves "for the time when [the laborer] can render so much labor for so much money, which is the great end to be attained." At the same time, Union officials recognized that wartime conditions prohibited a shift to full monetary compensation. Military orders reinforced the claim of all plantation residents – workers and nonworkers, healthy or sick – to a subsistence, by requiring the plantation owner or lessee to provide food and clothing to all former slaves on the estate.

The new regulations also strengthened the employer's hand. In the interest of maintaining plantation discipline, federal officials barred soldiers from visiting without authorization and prohibited workers from leaving the estates without permission. To secure the fidelity of laborers to year-long contracts, the regulations required monthly payment of only half wages, with the remainder withheld until after the harvest. Once a laborer had "exercised the highest right in the choice and place of employment, he must be held to the fulfillment of his engagements."[160]

Rather than resolving all differences, the new rules became objects of contention, as both planters and laborers tried to turn them to their own advantage. Workers exercised "the power to be idle" until desperate planters were willing to meet their terms. Many former slaves declined to sign contracts until early spring. In February, after Confederate raiders again terrorized leased plantations along the Mississippi River, laborers increased their demands, refusing to return to work without suitable protection and greater pay. The raids were occasional events, but the regular seasonal rhythm of agricultural production also operated both for and against the former slaves. Once workers had "laid by" the crop in the summer, they became expendable until harvest time, when the demand for hands again strengthened their bargaining position. During slack periods, they found themselves liable to dis-

[160] See below, docs. 109, 198.

missal, despite regulations that required planters to support their workers for the duration of the contract.[161]

Sensitive to the dynamics of the new relationship, both plantation hands and planters took care to specify their terms of agreement. Contracting time became an occasion to ventilate grievances from the past and maneuver for future advantage. Laborers took special pains to guarantee their families' subsistence by securing access to gardens, woodlots, and forage, and to insist upon assurances of protection from Confederate raiders. Many workers – a majority in some areas – demanded compensation in a share of the crop instead of a monthly wage. For their part, employers enumerated workers' responsibilities in greater detail, including standards of acceptable deportment. The increased length and specificity of contracts attested to the breadth of the contest.[162]

Both at contracting time and throughout the year, freedpeople sought to allocate the labor of family members at their own and not their employers' discretion. Planters – eager to compensate for the shortage of men by claiming the labor of most women and children – distinguished only between workers and nonworkers, insisting that all of the former should be in the field. The freedpeople, on the other hand, believed that their new status implied greater opportunity for wives and mothers to devote time to child care and to productive labor in house and garden. Moreover, wage scales that accorded female field hands substantially less than their male counterparts offered women scant inducement to labor for the planters. Those whose husbands were at work on the same estate were especially likely to spurn such employment. On one Louisiana plantation the women would work only "on the patches of ground given to their husbands by the overseer"; on another, "[s]ome of the women peremptoraly refuse[d] to work in the field stating that they are ladies and as good as any white trash." The labor of children also became a matter of contest. The planters' insistence upon putting them into field gangs conflicted with the freedpeople's desire that they attend school or perform domestic chores.[163]

161 See below, doc. 130. On the effects of Confederate raids in 1864, see below, docs. 196–97, 209; *Freedom*, ser. 1, vol. 2: doc. 39.

162 For examples of crop-sharing arrangements, see below, docs. 192, 214n. On the prevalence of such arrangements in one Louisiana parish, see below, doc. 129. For examples of nonmonetary compensation for plantation work, see below, docs. 125–26. On plantation laborers' insistence upon physical security, see below, docs. 201, 209.

163 See below, docs. 100n., 116, 199. For examples of former slaves' desire to send their children to school, see below, docs. 21, 110, 217; *Freedom*, ser. 1, vol. 2: doc. 42. On postwar struggles over family labor, which exhibit many of the same themes, see Ira Berlin, Steven F. Miller, and Leslie S. Rowland, "Afro-American Families in the Transition from Slavery to Freedom," *Radical History Review* 42 (Fall 1988): 89–121.

As the range of free-labor relations increased, the struggle between planters and laborers moved beyond matters of production to matters of consumption. During 1864, a growing number of planters established plantation stores that sold a variety of merchandise. The availability of consumer goods, they argued, would "multiply [the workers'] simple wants & stimulate industry." One plantation manager confessed that exhortations about the virtues of honest toil failed to motivate his workers as much as did their desire "to procure a coveted calico dress or straw Hat." For some Northern planters, well-developed purchasing habits and a wide array of merchandise were veritable hallmarks of civilization.[164]

Whatever their boon to civilization, plantation stores also served more immediately useful ends. The ready availability of consumer goods helped keep workers at home, and if their purchases drew them into debt, so much the better. Clever planters learned to manipulate accounts to keep their laborers in arrears. Those who thought they could get away with it set retail prices at levels above the mark-up permitted by government regulations. Some planters-turned-merchant flouted the regulations altogether and required their workers to purchase clothing or rations that were supposed to be furnished free of charge.[165]

Freedpeople appreciated the availability of goods but resented attempts to gouge them. Wherever possible they patronized stores operated by merchants more friendly to their interests. Former slaves in the Vicksburg area took their business to a special "freedmen's store," whose proprietors were prohibited by military order from overcharging. Elsewhere in Union-occupied territory, establishments operated by Northern freedmen's aid societies gave former slaves an alternative to the plantation stores.[166]

Although most former slaves struggled to earn a living wage during 1864, some managed to rise above the status of wage laborer. Several hundred Sea Island freedpeople entered the ranks of small landowners by purchasing plantations cooperatively or by acquiring plots earmarked for "charitable" purposes. In the Mississippi Valley, chiefly around Vicksburg and Helena, a similar number leased land from the government. Possessed of little capital, nearly all the black lessees rented small farms, not large plantations, and they generally worked the land with only the labor of their families, occasionally augmented by hired workers. On a still smaller scale and in more informal fashion, former slaves tended plots on "home farms" administered variously by the Treasury Department, military officials, and representatives of Northern benevolent associations. Such cultivators – whose ranks in-

164 See below, docs. 40, 216. See also Powell, *New Masters*, pp. 87–90.
165 See below, docs. 108, 120A–C, 227. See also Powell, *New Masters*, pp. 90–92.
166 See below, docs. 47A, 225, 227; *Freedom*, ser. 1, vol. 2: doc. 32.

cluded some black soldiers and their families–worked tracts ranging from a few acres to a small homestead.[167]

Some black families in the Upper South also gained access to land through official channels. Superintendents of "Negro Affairs" in tidewater Virginia made about 200 parcels available to black tenants, charging them cash or a share of the crop as rent and otherwise allowing them to control their own farming operations. Similarly, treasury agents in coastal North Carolina leased small farms to former slaves, as well as rights to collect turpentine from the pine forests.[168]

In both Upper and Lower South, black landowners, lessees, and residents of the home farms placed greater emphasis upon subsistence than upon commercial agriculture. Seeking first of all to provide food for their own households, ex-slave farmers generally put most of their land in corn and vegetables. Any surplus could readily be sold to the residents of nearby towns and army posts. When their resources permitted, they added other marketable crops. The chief limit upon such additional production was often the number of workers in the household, a problem that some black farmers solved by hiring additional laborers.[169]

In regions where cotton had been the predominant crop, some black landowners and lessees planted none at all, and those who did generally cultivated modest amounts. Nevertheless, at stratospheric wartime prices, the proceeds of small cotton patches permitted black farmers not only to improve their families' living conditions, but also to purchase livestock, tools, and other productive property. Late in 1864, the superintendent of freedmen at Helena reported that "[a]ll of the colored lessees have made more than a living, and will be ready to begin another year with capital that will enable them to work to better advantage than in the past."[170]

In general, black lessees in tidewater Virginia and North Carolina reaped fewer material rewards than those in the Mississippi Valley. The land they farmed was depleted from years of tillage, and military superintendents lacked both the means and the will to invest in improvements and fertilizer. The only available draft animals were worn-out beasts "condemned" by the quartermaster's department. Many of the leaseholds were too small and unproductive to support the renters and their families. Often the lessees earned a subsistence by working for white farmers in the neighborhood; their share of the crop on their leaseholds thus became "profit for their seasons work." Such arrangements usually involved a division of labor whereby the father hired out for wages while the mother and children worked the rented plot. But,

167 See below, docs. 49, 207–9, 217.
168 *Freedom*, ser. 1, vol. 2: docs. 38, 42–43.
169 See below, docs. 144, 171, 208; *Freedom*, ser. 1, vol. 2: doc. 28.
170 See below, docs. 217, 222A.

depending upon the number of people in the household and their age and sex, the division sometimes differed, reflecting each family's assessment of how best to preserve an independent standing. Although their choices were dictated in part by the local demand for agricultural labor, access to land, however limited, reduced their dependence upon wage employment and often permitted them to engage in such labor for only part of the year.[171]

A large number of freedpeople who had neither the means nor the opportunity to rent land found other ways of earning a living without entering into year-long contracts for agricultural labor. Fishing, oystering, and crabbing provided a means of self-support for former slaves near the water who could afford a modest investment in nets, lines, and perhaps a small boat.[172] Wood yards that supplied fuel for steamers and locomotives offered another alternative, though seldom a means of self-sufficiency. Operated variously by government superintendents, individual landowners, and private contractors, wood yards employed thousands of freedpeople, especially along the Mississippi River and other waterways and in the vicinity of military railroads. Both men and women labored in the wood yards, the men cutting wood and the women cording it. They were paid at piecework rates that probably permitted vigorous workers to surpass the earnings of agricultural laborers. Although taxing, work in the wood yards also allowed considerable control over the hours and pace of work. That measure of self-direction made wood-yard workers reluctant to hire out for agricultural wage labor.[173]

Short-handed planters and farmers complained when former slaves were able to make a living on their own, and they begged military authorities to curtail independent employment. Their appeals met a favorable reception from those officials who viewed year-long contracts for wage labor – not subsistence cultivation or independent jobbing – as the key to social stability. A superintendent of contrabands in the Sea Islands deplored the practice of "getting a precarious livelihood by doing a little at this thing, & a little at that." To encourage "*honest steady* labor" and control "the floating Negro population," military authorities restricted physical movement and confiscated boats. In the Mississippi Valley, superintendents reduced the issue of rations to wood-yard workers as a means of inducing them to hire to planters.[174]

In Union-occupied cities and towns, too, federal regulations often undermined the ability of former slaves to support themselves. Many military officials saw unemployed or irregularly employed black people

171 *Freedom*, ser. 1, vol. 2: docs. 42–43.

172 See below, docs. 53, 55; *Freedom*, ser. 1, vol. 2: doc. 42.

173 See below, docs. 171, 177–79, 193, 200, 210; *Freedom*, ser. 1, vol. 2: docs. 17, 115.

174 See below, docs. 53–55, 210n.

as a threat to good order. Accordingly, they adopted pass systems and vagrancy regulations to "clean out" former slaves who lacked "steady" employment or independent means, thereby treating as criminals those who were self-employed or who earned a living by "chance work." In Natchez, Mississippi, orders ostensibly issued to prevent the spread of "pestilential diseases" virtually forbade any "contraband" to live or work independently of a white employer. The regulations resulted in the expulsion of numerous self-supporting freedpeople, including relatives of soldiers. Their outraged protests were seconded by agents of Northern benevolent societies, provoking a controversy that eventually reached Congress and contributed to the resignation of the general who had approved the "health" orders.[175]

In the border states, the legality of slavery obstructed the development of free labor. Consequently, border-state slaves and former slaves generally had to leave their homes in order to obtain freedom and free-labor employment. The District of Columbia remained an attractive destination for fugitive slaves from Maryland, as did nearby Northern states. Kansas, Illinois, and Iowa received refugees from Missouri, where the continued strength of slavery, guerrilla warfare in the countryside, and the refusal of military authorities to provide contraband camps or free-labor employment made it difficult for fugitive slaves to find work or protection. Meanwhile, Kentucky slaves who could successfully evade civil authorities and military pickets crossed the Ohio River into freedom, especially at Cairo, Illinois; Jeffersonville, Indiana; and Cincinnati, Ohio. Beginning in late 1863, when black recruitment opened in neighboring Tennessee, slave men from southern Kentucky fled to the Tennessee camps, often with their families in tow.[176]

On occasion, federal officials supported the efforts of freedpeople to migrate north; indeed, they attempted to remove freedpeople from "overpopulated" parts of tidewater Virginia, the District of Columbia, and Missouri. Midwestern army chaplains in St. Louis relied on connections in their home states to find employment for hundreds of former slaves. Elsewhere in Missouri, the army sought less to help freedpeople find work than simply to expel them. During the spring and summer of 1864, General Egbert B. Brown ordered the removal of former slaves – chiefly women and children – from military posts in central Missouri to the Kansas border. Although they eschewed the harsh methods of General Brown, officials in tidewater Virginia and Washington also sought to reduce the number of black people under their charge. As new arrivals swelled the ranks of dependent freedpeople, superintendents of "Negro Affairs" in tidewater Virginia worked with Northern

[175] See below, docs. 15, 89, 166, 169, 202A–B, 212.

[176] *Freedom*, ser. 1, vol. 1: docs. 41, 44, 46, 51, 135–37, 144–45A, 190, 194–96, 213A, 219A–B, 224, 227, 228A–B, 232; *Freedom*, ser. 1, vol. 2: docs. 132, 158B, 173, 177, 179n., 194, 224; *Freedom*, ser. 2: docs. 72, 85, 97–98, 303.

benevolent societies and "intelligence offices" (the employment agencies of the day) to transport several hundred black women and children to northeastern cities, where they were hired out as domestic servants. Military officials in Washington used similar tactics to reduce the population of former slaves dependent on the government. Yet, no matter how desperate their condition, most freedpeople refused offers to live and work among strangers in the North. As the end of the war neared, and with it the prospect of freedom on their home ground, they gave even shorter shrift to northward migration.[177]

The deterioration of slavery hastened the progress of legal emancipation. By the end of 1864, unionist governments in Arkansas and Louisiana had ended slavery, as had the new state of West Virginia and the border state of Maryland. During the early months of 1865, Missouri and Tennessee also wrote slavery out of their fundamental law. Meanwhile, congressional passage of a constitutional amendment abolishing slavery and its ratification by a number of Northern states placed further pressure on those Union-held regions of the South in which slavery remained legal. Of the areas exempted from the Emancipation Proclamation, only tidewater Virginia failed to enact emancipation before the end of the war, and citizens in those few Union-controlled counties were scarcely in a position to take such action had they so desired. The loyal slave states of Kentucky and Delaware also refused to act, holding fast to the remnants of chattel bondage until the incorporation of the Thirteenth Amendment into the Constitution. Even in those places, however, slavery's supporters were on the defensive well before the end of the war.[178]

The advent of legal freedom insinuated free labor into the lives of previously unaffected Southerners. The process whereby slaves became employees and slaveholders employers repeated itself on new terrain, with many of the same false starts and dead ends that had characterized such developments earlier in the war. At the same time, increasing numbers of nonslaveholders began bidding for the labor of men and women previously beyond their reach. Eager to hire black workers, they augmented the ranks of Southern supporters of free labor.[179]

177 *Freedom*, ser. 1, vol. 2: docs. 34–35, 41–42, 176–77, 179n., 182, 187, 190, 194; Capt. J. M. Brown to Jos. M. Truman, Jr., 31 Dec. 1864, vol. 60, p. 39, Press Copies of Letters Sent, ser. 527, Asst. Quartermaster & Disbursing Officer, DC Asst. Comr., RG 105 [A-10639].

178 For the legal changes enacting emancipation, see Francis Newton Thorpe, comp., *The Federal and State Constitutions*, 7 vols. (Washington, 1909), vol. 1, pp. 288–306, vol. 3, 1429–48, 1741–79, vol. 4, pp. 2191–2229, vol. 6, p. 3445; Richard O. Curry, *A House Divided: A Study of Statehood Politics and the Copperhead Movement in West Virginia* (Pittsburg, 1964), pp. 100–130; Henry Wilson, *History of the Antislavery Measures of the Thirty-Seventh and Thirty-Eighth United-States Congresses, 1861–64* (Boston, 1864), chap. 13.

179 See, for example, *Freedom*, ser. 1, vol. 2: docs. 154, 159A, 196–97.

Even in the wake of formal emancipation, not everyone accepted the new order. Many erstwhile slaveholders resorted to naked force to sustain their accustomed power over black people. Others, more far-sighted, fashioned new modes of exacting labor. Often they made use of the same state authority that had recently legislated emancipation. In Maryland, former slaveholders drew upon antebellum apprenticeship statutes. Within a month of emancipation, local courts had apprenticed more than 2,500 black children and young adults, generally to their former owners. Reluctant to intervene in the affairs of a loyal state that had voluntarily abolished slavery, federal authorities in Washington overruled orders by the local military commander to "break up the practice now prevalent of apprenticing young negroes without the consent of their parents." Newly freed black people found themselves with little protection.[180]

If some former owners tried to maintain control over their erstwhile slaves, others used emancipation as an excuse to eliminate costly and unwanted responsibilities. Often they simply terminated customary issues of food and clothing. In many places, freedpeople were driven from their homes. In an increasingly familiar scenario, Missouri slaveholders took "unprofitable, and expensive" black women and children "within a convenient distance of some military post, and set them out with orders to never return home – telling them they are free." Freed from the former owner's support as well as his control, such slaves had little choice but to take refuge in cities, contraband camps, or garrison towns. The collapse of the old order heaved up new hardships as well as opportunities.[181]

The steady advance of Union armies accelerated that collapse. Cutting a broad swath of destruction across Georgia, General William T. Sherman and his troops arrived at Savannah in December 1864. Accompanying them were thousands of hungry, footsore slaves who, despite discouragement, had joined their fortunes to those of the Yankee invaders. Their hostile reception by Sherman's army extended in one widely reported instance to removing a pontoon bridge upon which the soldiers had crossed a swift stream; the black refugees who followed were thereby abandoned to the mercy of pursuing Confederates. Many of them drowned when they attempted to swim to safety.[182]

Concerned both about such accounts and about Sherman's longstand-

180 On the forcible maintenance of slavery after emancipation, see, for example, below, docs. 145, 211; *Freedom*, ser. 1, vol. 2: docs. 122, 141, 144–45. On apprenticeship in Maryland immediately following emancipation, see *Freedom*, ser. 1, vol. 1: doc. 151; *Freedom*, ser. 1, vol. 2: docs. 140–43, 146–49, 151–54, 158–60; Richard Paul Fuke, "A Reform Mentality: Federal Policy toward Black Marylanders, 1864–1868," *Civil War History* 22 (Sept. 1976): 222–24.

181 *Freedom*, ser. 1, vol. 1: docs. 152, 196; *Freedom*, ser. 1, vol. 2: docs. 150, 153, 155A, 192–93, 221.

182 Joseph T. Glatthaar, *The March to the Sea and Beyond: Sherman's Troops in the Savannah and Carolinas Campaigns* (New York, 1985), chap. 3.

ing opposition to the enlistment of black soldiers, Secretary of War Stanton journeyed to Savannah in early January. He found Sherman preparing to advance into South Carolina and searching for a way to disencumber his army of its black followers. On January 12, 1865, at Stanton's instance, he and Sherman met with local black religious leaders to ascertain their views about how former slaves could best defend and support themselves. Freedom, declared Garrison Frazier, a spokesman selected by the twenty churchmen, "is taking us from under the yoke of bondage, and placing us where we could reap the fruit of our own labor, take care of ourselves and assist the Government in maintaining our freedom." "The way we can best take care of ourselves," he advised, "is to have land, and turn it and till it by our own labor. . . . until we are able to buy it and make it our own."[183]

Within days, General Sherman responded in a way that addressed both his own pragmatic military problems and the former slaves' fondest hopes. His Special Field Order 15 "set apart" the coastal islands and mainland rice plantations between Charleston and the St. Johns River of Florida "for the settlement of the negroes now made free by the acts of war and the proclamation of the President." The order authorized families of former slaves to occupy as much as forty acres each in the reserved district, for which they would receive "possessory title." Aside from military officials, "no white person whatever" was to reside in the area. "[S]ole and exclusive management of affairs will be left to the freed people themselves, subject only to the United States military authority and the acts of Congress." As the black people who had followed his army through Georgia took up land in the Sherman reserve, thousands of other slaves and ex-slaves set out for the coast, including many lowcountry natives who had been "refugeed" inland by their owners. Their numbers further increased as Sherman's army marched northward through the Carolinas. By the time of the Confederate surrender, about 20,000 former slaves had settled on 100,000 acres in the reserved district. Understanding Sherman's grant as official recognition of their rightful claim to the land, they began to put in crops. Tens of thousands more would join them in the months to come.[184]

As former slaves in lowcountry Georgia and South Carolina took possession of land under Sherman's order, acreage in tidewater Virginia was offered for sale under the Direct Tax Act and the confiscation acts. Hoping to secure "a spot of land" for at least some of the freedpeople under his

[183] Benjamin P. Thomas and Harold M. Hyman, *Stanton: The Life and Times of Lincoln's Secretary of War* (New York, 1962), pp. 343–45. For the meeting with black churchmen, see below, doc. 58.

[184] For Sherman's special field order, see below, doc. 59. On the earliest settlement of freedpeople under its provisions, see Bvt. Maj. Genl. R. Saxton to Maj. Genl. M. C. Meigs, 6 Apr. 1865, "Negroes," Consolidated Correspondence File, ser. 225, Central Records, RG 92 [Y-211].

jurisdiction, Charles Wilder, the local superintendent of "Negro Affairs," joined with representatives of Northern aid societies to buy six estates. He and his partners hoped thereby not only to prevent eviction of the black people occupying the land, but also to subdivide and resell the property to them.[185] The possibility of additional purchases for the same purpose ran aground, however, when the Lincoln administration suspended further sales until deliberations about a bureau of emancipation were concluded. In March 1865, Congress established the Bureau of Refugees, Freedmen, and Abandoned Lands (Freedmen's Bureau), with a mandate to supervise the transition from slavery to freedom in the former slave states, provide for destitute freedpeople and white refugees, and administer the land that had fallen into the hands of the government by confiscation, abandonment, or military occupation.[186]

An expectation that fundamental changes would accompany the return of peace and the organization of the Freedmen's Bureau tempered plans for the new crop year. Unwilling to take steps that might only be undone, federal authorities for the most part continued extant labor arrangements. A proposal to revise labor and welfare policies in southern Louisiana and the Mississippi Valley provoked considerable debate, for it would have sharply increased the wages of plantation workers and made them responsible for their own food and clothing. But, in the end, superiors of the treasury agent who drafted the new rules, including President Lincoln himself, refused to sanction them. Agricultural operations in 1865 therefore commenced under regulations little different from those of the previous year. Throughout the Union-occupied South, nearly everyone – Northerners and Southerners, black people and white – expected the end of the war to bring a full reconsideration of the terms of free labor.[187]

By the spring of 1865, at least 474,000 former slaves and free blacks had taken part in some form of federally sponsored free labor in the Union-occupied South – as soldiers, military laborers, residents of contraband camps, urban workers, or agricultural laborers on government-supervised plantations and farms.[188] In addition, an indeterminable

185 Proceedings of general court-martial in the case of Captain Charles B. Wilder, 1–16 May 1865, MM-2065, Court-Martial Case Files, ser. 15, RG 153 [H-54]; Adjutant General L. Thomas to Hon. Edwin M. Stanton, 5 June 1865, filed as A-1411 1865, Letters Received, ser. 12, RG 94 [K-223].

186 *Statutes at Large*, vol. 13, pp. 507–9.

187 See below, docs. 119, 135, 137, 222A–B. An attempt to revamp the system of relief in the District of Columbia was squelched by Quartermaster General Meigs. (*Freedom*, ser. 1, vol. 2: doc. 77.)

188 The number of black people who experienced some form of federally sponsored free labor can be estimated only roughly. Because many slaves were "refugeed" away from areas that came under Union control and others fled to Union lines from Confederate-held territory, the wartime black population of Union-occupied coun-

number had negotiated private free-labor bargains with their former owners or other employers.[189] Still other former slaves, whose numbers are also impossible to estimate, had left the South to become free workers in the North, some of them under the auspices of official relocation and employment programs, others on their own or with the assistance of individual army officers.

Of the black people who worked under officially sanctioned free-labor arrangements, about 271,000 lived in the plantation regions of the Lower South that came under Union control. Some 125,000 were in the Mississippi Valley.[190] Those in southern Louisiana numbered about 98,000.[191] Another 48,000 experienced wartime free labor in the South Carolina Sea Islands or elsewhere along the south Atlantic coast; two-fifths of these were latecomers who took up land in the Sherman reserve.[192]

ties cannot be derived from the slave and free-black populations of 1860. Official estimates – ranging from systematic censuses to barely educated guesses – exist for some regions. When such figures seem reliable, the editors have used them; when contemporary evidence is lacking or seems unreliable, they have tried to arrive at an estimate by other means.

Louis S. Gerteis has estimated that 237,800 black people were "organized by freedmen superintendents during the war," a category that overlaps, but is not identical to, the one used here. For example, the regional figures that make up his total do not consistently incorporate black soldiers. His geographical focus is also different. While his estimate accounts for most Union-occupied parts of the Confederacy, it does not include such territory in Alabama, Florida, Georgia, and middle and east Tennessee; in addition, it omits the District of Columbia and the border states. (*From Contraband to Freedman*, pp. 193–94.)

189 To the private free-labor arrangements that were individually negotiated throughout the Union-occupied South might be added the more generalized labor systems that began to take shape in Maryland, Missouri, and Tennessee during the final months of the war, following the abolition of slavery by state action.

190 The figure is derived from a report in July 1864 by Colonel John Eaton, which noted that 113,650 former slaves (including soldiers) were engaged in free labor under his jurisdiction. Assuming that new arrivals from Confederate territory increased that number by 10 percent before the end of the war, the total becomes 125,015. (Eaton, *Grant, Lincoln and the Freedmen: Reminiscences of the Civil War* [1907; reprint ed., New York, 1969], pp. 133–34.)

191 According to an official estimate, 80,000 black people (apparently not including soldiers) were living under free-labor arrangements in southern Louisiana in September 1864: 50,000 in the countryside and 30,000 in New Orleans. There is no reason to assume any significant change during the remaining months of the war. Adding to that number the black soldiers recruited in the region (perhaps three-fourths of those credited to Louisiana, or 18,039 men), the total reaches 98,039. (Chaplain Thomas W. Conway to Major General N. P. Banks, 9 Sept. 1864, C-228 1864, Letters Received, ser. 1920, Civil Affairs, Dept. of the Gulf, RG 393 Pt. 1 [C-732]; *Freedom*, ser. 2: p. 12.)

192 Estimates of the number of former slaves who lived and worked under federal supervision in the South Carolina Sea Islands include 16,000 in 1862 (before the opening of black recruitment) and 15,000, exclusive of soldiers, in 1863. The latter number probably did not increase by more than 10 percent (to about 16,500) during 1864; many of the new arrivals were refugees from points in Florida and

In the Upper South, some 203,000 former slaves and free blacks lived and worked under federal auspices. About 74,000 could be found in tidewater North Carolina and Virginia.[193] Perhaps 37,000 were in middle and east Tennessee or northern Alabama.[194] Another 40,000 lived in the District of Columbia, in Alexandria, Virginia, and in the contraband camps on the Virginia side of the Potomac River.[195] In all

Georgia that were held for a time by Northern troops but subsequently abandoned. Perhaps 1,200 additional freedpeople could be found at Fernandina, Florida, and the handful of other coastal outposts that remained continuously in federal hands. Nearly 10,000 black soldiers were credited to South Carolina (5,462), Georgia (3,486), and Florida (1,044); they bring the total to 27,692. Finally, some 20,000 former slaves had been settled in the Sherman reserve by mid-April 1865, making a grand total of 47,692. (See below, docs. 29n., 36; *Official Records*, ser. 3, vol. 4, pp. 118–19; *Freedom*, ser. 2: p. 12; Bvt. Maj. Genl. R. Saxton to Maj. Genl. M. C. Meigs, 6 Apr. 1865, "Negroes," Consolidated Correspondence File, ser. 225, Central Records, RG 92 [Y-211].)

193 The figure for tidewater North Carolina is derived from a census conducted in January 1865, which counted 17,307 black people (evidently excluding soldiers) in the territory under Union control. Adding the 5,035 black soldiers credited to the state brings the total to 22,342. (James, *Annual Report*, p. 4; *Freedom*, ser. 2: p. 12.) The total for tidewater Virginia (52,004) has been reached by adding figures from censuses taken in late 1864, which enumerated 24,850 black people south of the James River (including more than 4,000 soldiers) and 13,305 north of the James (excluding soldiers), plus an estimated 1,000 soldiers in the latter district, plus 12,849 former slaves and free blacks on the eastern shore (the black population of Accomac and Northampton counties in 1860). (*Freedom*, ser. 1, vol. 2: docs. 42–43; U.S., Census Office, 8th Census, *Population of the United States in 1860* [Washington, 1864], pp. 504–13.)

194 Rough estimates can be obtained by beginning with the number of black soldiers recruited in the three regions and assuming a relationship between that figure and the number of other former slaves and free blacks who lived in contraband camps, performed military labor, or worked as agricultural laborers under military supervision. About 18,400 black soldiers enlisted from these areas (assuming that middle and east Tennessee contributed two-thirds of Tennessee's total, and northern Alabama all the soldiers from that state). (*Freedom*, ser. 2: p. 12.) If it is assumed that an equal number of black people participated in other free-labor arrangements, the total becomes 36,800. (The ratio of only one civilian to each soldier is employed because middle and east Tennessee and northern Alabama had relatively few contraband camps—all established late in the war—and very limited government-sponsored agricultural operations; the number of black civilians in federally supervised labor settings was therefore much smaller in proportion to black soldiers than was the case in tidewater Virginia and North Carolina or the occupied regions of the Lower South, where, for every one soldier, between two and nine civilians participated in Union-sponsored free labor.)

195 Estimates for the District of Columbia, Alexandria, and the contraband camps across the Potomac from Washington, D.C., involve consideration of several different sets of figures, as well as an element of conjecture. According to the 1860 census, 3,185 slaves and 11,131 free blacks lived in the District, virtually all of whom presumably had free-labor experience during the war, as did untold thousands of fugitive slaves from Virginia and Maryland. A military census of March 1865, which was almost certainly marred by undercounting, enumerated 16,092 black refugees (excluding quartermaster employees living in government housing, and house servants) in the District, Alexandria, Freedman's Village, and Mason's

the border states combined, probably no more than 52,000 black people took part in Union-sponsored free labor.[196]

Former slaves in the Union-occupied South worked in a wide variety of free-labor settings. Most of the men – about 101,000 in the seceded states and 47,000 in the border states and the District of Columbia – served as soldiers or sailors.[197] Many of them had previously worked as military laborers, along with tens of thousands of men who never entered the armed service. A few thousand women also worked for military employers. Most ex-slave women in Union-held territory, and a sizable proportion of the men, toiled as agricultural laborers on plantations and farms supervised by federal officials. A similar number – mainly women, children, and elderly people – lived in contraband camps, infirm farms, or "regimental villages," where they received rations and occasionally performed remunerative labor. Significant numbers of black men and women found free-labor employment that was not directly sponsored by Union authorities. Most civilian workers in towns and cities did so, and an indeterminable number of rural ex-slaves negotiated new terms of labor on their own. The experiences of soldiers, military laborers, residents of contraband camps, and agricultural and urban workers provided somewhat different perspectives on freedom. These variations were compounded by differences in antebellum status, the character of federal occupation, and the policies of particular Union commanders.

Yet a common thread ran through the diverse experiences. Only a tiny minority of black people in Union-held territory attained the status of independent proprietor or tenant; the overwhelming majority provided for themselves through some form of wage labor. In escaping slavery they had relinquished any claim upon their owners for subsistence, protection, or provision for old age, youth, and illness. Their survival now

Island; other estimates of the number of wartime black migrants to Washington and its vicinity run as high as 40,000. Probably the most useful figures come from a census taken in 1867, which placed the black population of the District alone at 31,937, of whom 22,747 had been resident since at least 1864. Beginning with the latter figure, and then assuming that 17,000 other black people experienced free labor in Alexandria and the northern Virginia camps during the war or else had lived and worked in the District during the war but were gone by 1867, results in a total of 39,747 for the nation's capital and nearby northern Virginia. (*Population of the United States in 1860*, p. 588; *Freedom*, ser. 1, vol. 2: doc. 86; Green, *Secret City*, p. 62; Allan John Johnston, "Surviving Freedom: The Black Community of Washington, D.C., 1860–1880" [Ph.D. diss., Duke University, 1980], pp. 162–66.)

196 Estimates of the extent of federally sponsored free labor in the border states, excepting that for soldiers, are highly conjectural. Although a sizable proportion of border-state black men served in the Union army, few other forms of free-labor employment were available: Military labor was limited in scope, contraband camps few in number, and government-sponsored agricultural operations almost nonexistent. More than 42,000 black soldiers and sailors were credited to the states of Missouri, Kentucky, and Maryland (*Freedom*, ser. 2: pp. 12, 14n.); perhaps an additional 10,000 black people worked in other federally sponsored free-labor settings.

197 *Freedom*, ser. 2: pp. 12 (soldiers), 14n. (sailors).

depended, not upon their place in a system of hierarchical personal relations, but upon the sale of their labor power in an impersonal market. Granted self-ownership but no productive property, former slaves were simultaneously permitted and compelled to work for wages.

Although wartime wage labor did not satisfy the aspirations of former slaves to become freeholders, it broke decisively and irrevocably with slavery. Freedpeople gained proprietorship over their own persons. The new conditions of labor generally prohibited physical punishment, encouraged independent family, religious, and social life, and required compensation. Ex-slave laborers gained rudimentary legal protection, backed by the force of federal arms. They made the most of whatever opportunities the war created. Except for the youngest, oldest, and most infirm, nearly all black people within the Union-occupied Confederacy were self-supporting at the time of Appomattox.[198]

Even in territory still controlled by Confederate forces, particularly those areas adjacent to Union lines, the proximity of free labor and the prospect of universal freedom eroded slave discipline. With freedom within reach, some slaves demanded new terms of labor – an end to corporal punishment, the elimination of overseers, more time to work garden plots, payment in cash or in kind. To slaveholders, such notions smacked of rebellion, to be answered by the lash, sale, or removal to the interior. But as Confederate military hopes dimmed, slaveholders found themselves increasingly unable to wield the old authority. Free labor in the Union-occupied South helped subvert slavery far beyond federal lines.[199]

The advance of free labor within Union-occupied territory and the disintegration of slavery within the Confederacy seemed to vindicate Northerners' faith in the superiority of free over slave labor. Having planted the seeds of free labor in the South, however, federal officials disagreed about how they should be nurtured. Some, like Colonel Samuel Thomas, superintendent of freedmen in the District of Vicksburg, believed the government had done enough. Its job was simply to put the former slave's "labor on an equal footing with white labor . . . [g]uard him against imposition, give him his just dues at the end of each month, . . . and let him work his way up." "Capital does now, and will for some time to come carry on great enterprises," Thomas affirmed, "and a large portion of the human family, both white and black, must labor for this capital at regulated wages, without any direct interest in the result of the enterprise." Arguing that "[o]ur country has enough to bear without undertaking the enormous task of starting out each freedman with a competency," he considered the opportunity for individual self-improvement to be the true boon of freedom.[200]

198 For assessments of the extent of self-support in one region, see *Freedom*, ser. 1, vol. 2: docs. 42–43.

199 *Freedom*, ser. 1, vol. 1: pp. 40–43 and chap. 9, especially docs. 327–31.

200 See below, doc. 209.

Others believed that meddling Northerners had already done too much. Colonel Frank J. White, superintendent of "Negro Affairs" on Virginia's eastern shore, condemned benevolent associations and "enthusiasts" in the army for having made the former slave "dependent upon a bounty that can not last [and] would enevitably render him helpless in the future." White also rejected "communistic" plans to settle freedpeople on abandoned or captured land, on the grounds that they would "[divide], instead of [unite] the interests of the two classes" – former slaves and their former owners – whose futures were necessarily intertwined.[201]

Still others were convinced that not enough had been done to aid the emancipated slaves. Reporting upon conditions in Tennessee shortly after the war, Captain Richard J. Hinton, an officer of a black regiment from Kansas, urged the government to allot land to the freedpeople. "Nothing," he argued, "not even the bestowal of suffrage, will so materially aid [in] destroying the effects of Slavery [as] the creation of a self-reliant independent yeomanry out of the former slaves." Hinton feared that black people would be subject to "the serfdom of capital" if the nation were merely to grant "personal freedom, secure no political or civil rights, and leave the freed class to struggle out of the slough the best way they can with the narrow plank of free labor."[202]

No one knew better than the freedpeople just how deep the slough and narrow the plank. Resolutely determined never again to be slaves, they were nevertheless ambivalent about their wartime encounter with free labor. If the "freedom" of wage work marked their long-awaited liberation from the personal dependency of the past, it also fell far short of the independence to which they aspired. The imminence of Northern victory and the final destruction of slavery therefore encouraged them to become increasingly active in pursuit of their own interests. In so doing, they confounded those federal officials who viewed them as mere objects of policies or a "problem" to be solved. Pointing to their vital contribution to the Union cause, as soldiers and as civilians, former slaves established their claims upon the government that had granted them liberty and in many instances was also their employer. Although frequently couched in the language of supplication, their communications to federal authorities – from local commanders to the President himself – asserted their rights as free citizens and the nation's obligations to them. A group of black men in coastal North Carolina took such ground in a protest against impressment, declaring it inconsistent with "there cause as Freemen and the Rights of their families."[203]

As black people began to assert the prerogatives of citizenship, they

201 *Freedom*, ser. 1, vol. 2: doc. 46.

202 Captain Richard J. Hinton to Captain T. W. Clarke, 31 July 1865, H-47 1865, Registered Letters Received, ser. 3379, TN Asst. Comr., RG 105 [A-6135].

203 *Freedom*, ser. 1, vol. 2: doc. 25.

assumed a more visible place in public affairs. Throughout the Union-occupied South, former slaves and free blacks formed political and quasi-political associations. Such organizations were particularly active in New Orleans, Nashville, and Washington, where federal control dated from early in the war and large antebellum free-black communities were ready to take the lead; but they also appeared elsewhere, especially in localities where black soldiers were stationed. These associations became vehicles by which black people sought to elevate their political status, demanding the right to testify in court, to sit on juries, and to vote. As the movement to reconstruct the South gained momentum, they became an active, though not yet fully sanctioned, force in local politics.[204]

The divisions among federal officials and the burgeoning political presence of black people revealed that if the Civil War had destroyed slavery, the meaning of freedom was no more certain than before the first shots at Fort Sumter. Wartime labor and welfare policies had necessarily rested more upon military exigencies than upon considered decisions about the future of the former slaves. Restricted to the narrow confines of securely held territory and subordinate at all times to the demands of waging war, they bore little resemblance to the requirements of ordinary times. Almost everyone – North and South, black and white – saw peace as an opportunity to begin afresh.

Yet wartime experience did not count for nothing. As the victorious North set about reconstructing Southern society, the labor and relief programs established within Union lines became points of reference for postwar plans. In the course of the debate, both those who equated freedom with independent proprietorship and those who understood it as the unfettered right to sell one's labor power cited wartime developments to bolster their positions. For their part, the former slaves and free blacks who had lived and worked in Union-occupied territory entered the contest with a confidence born of the pivotal role they had played in the Union's triumph and their wartime initiation into the practices of free labor. As freedom burst the bounds of its wartime limitations and advanced into the entire South, more than three and a half million newly liberated slaves joined the half-million who had experienced free labor amid civil war. Their abrupt passage into the American working class as propertyless, unenfranchised free laborers raised fundamental questions about the nation's "new birth of freedom."[205] The answers would affect all Americans.

204 See, for example, below, doc. 139; *Freedom*, ser. 1, vol. 2: docs. 84–85; *Freedom*, ser. 2: doc. 362.

205 The phrase appears in the Gettysburg Address. (Lincoln, *Collected Works*, vol. 7, pp. 22–23.)

CHAPTER 1

Lowcountry South Carolina, Georgia, and Florida

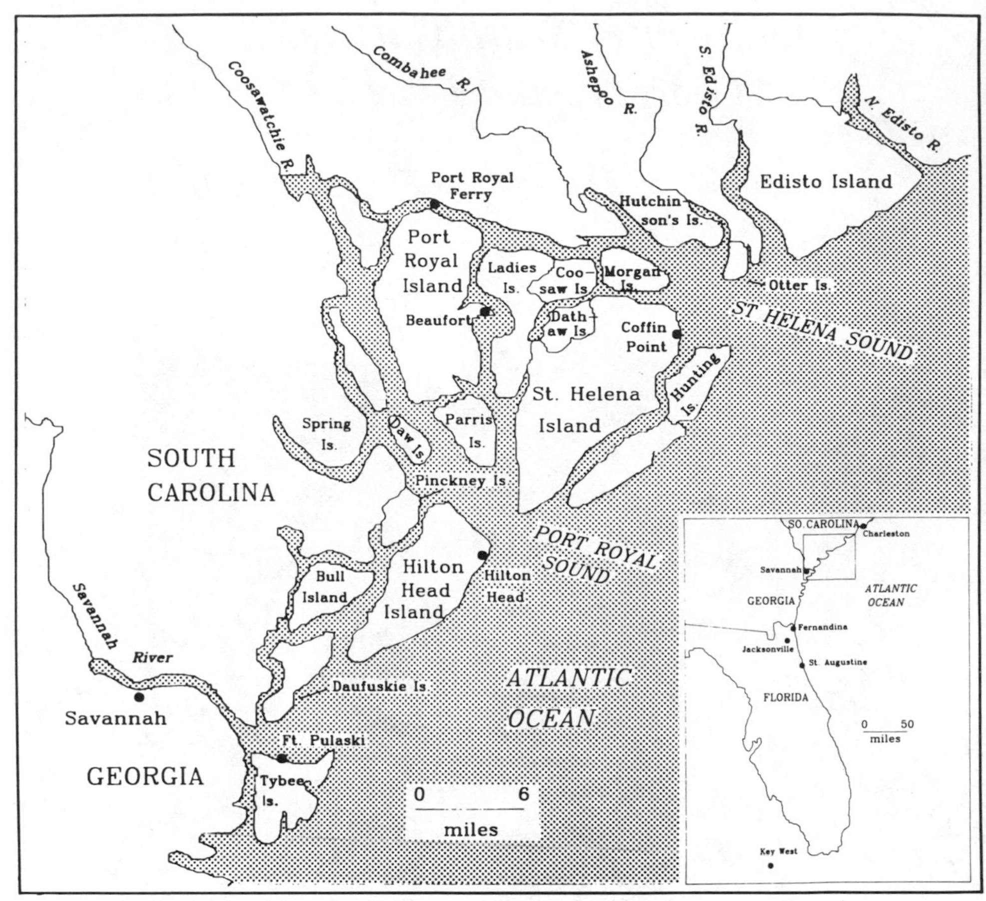

The South Carolina Sea Islands. Inset indicates location on South Atlantic coast.

1

Lowcountry South Carolina, Georgia, and Florida

FROM THE MOMENT the Union flotilla entered Port Royal Sound in early November 1861, fugitive masters and resolute slaves rendered moot the War Department's instructions to "avoid all interference with the Social systems or local institutions."[1] Within days – as the Yankee invaders occupied Port Royal, Hilton Head, St. Helena, Ladies, and nearby smaller islands along the coast of South Carolina – the planter aristocracy vanished. Left behind were great houses filled with fine furniture, fields of long-staple cotton, and thousands of former slaves who had resisted their owners' efforts to remove them to the mainland. Meanwhile, slaves from other islands and from the mainland trickled into Union-occupied territory, avoiding Confederate patrols who worked feverishly to block their paths.

Transformed into de facto freedpeople, ex-slaves seized the moment. Drawing on the special circumstances of antebellum life in the South Carolina Sea Islands – a black majority, large plantations, the slaveholders' seasonal absence, reliance on black drivers, and a task organization of labor – former slaves began to remake their lives on the estates abandoned by their erstwhile owners.[2] Their attempt to establish freedom on their own terms did not go unchallenged. During three and one-half years of Union occupation, army and navy officers, soldiers and sailors, agents of the Treasury Department, and Northern teachers, ministers,

[1] Passages in this essay that lack footnotes should be understood to rest upon the documents included in the chapter. The destruction of slavery in lowcountry South Carolina, Georgia, and Florida is traced in *Freedom*, ser. 1, vol. 1: chap. 2 (see doc. 18 for the War Department's instructions). Secondary accounts of the transition from slavery to freedom in the South Carolina Sea Islands include: Willie Lee Rose, *Rehearsal for Reconstruction: The Port Royal Experiment* (Indianapolis, Ind., 1964); Louis S. Gerteis, *From Contraband to Freedman: Federal Policy toward Southern Blacks, 1861–1865* (Westport, Conn., 1973), chap. 3; Julie Saville, "A Measure of Freedom: From Slave to Wage Laborer in South Carolina, 1860–1868" (Ph.D. diss., Yale University, 1986), chap. 2.

[2] For a discussion of slavery in the Sea Islands, see Rose, *Rehearsal for Reconstruction*, chap. 4. On the task organization of labor, see Philip D. Morgan, "Work and Culture: The Task System and the World of Lowcountry Blacks, 1700–1880," *William and Mary Quarterly* 3d ser., 39 (Oct. 1982): 563–99, and "The Ownership of Property by Slaves in the Mid-Nineteenth Century Lowcountry," *Journal of Southern History* 49 (Aug. 1983): 399–420.

and entrepreneurs offered various and often contradictory blueprints. The former slaves' expectations accorded with those of the newcomers in some respects but conflicted with them in others, and the multisided struggle that ensued attracted national attention. Until the final months of the war, Union-held territory along the south Atlantic coast extended only to a dozen islands in South Carolina and Georgia and a handful of posts in Florida. However, the South Carolina Sea Islands were the first major plantation region of the Confederacy to fall into Union hands and the only one in which wartime reconstruction took place in the entire absence of the antebellum planter class. Consequently, the contest over the meaning of free labor that was waged at Port Royal had ramifications far exceeding the area's narrow geographical bounds.

Former slaves, both natives of the Sea Islands and newcomers from the mainland, viewed the Northern invaders with caution. Mindful of their owners' warning that the Yankees would sell them to Cuba, freedpeople approached federal troops "shyly." But before long, some volunteered to aid the Union cause. Short-handed quartermasters were delighted by the arrival of about 150 fugitive slaves, mostly able-bodied men, during the first two days of occupation. Because of inadequate wharfage, military stores shipped to Port Royal often had to be laboriously landed through the surf. General Thomas W. Sherman, joint commander of the South Carolina Expeditionary Corps, did not hesitate to put the men to work.

Sherman hoped to obtain additional laborers from the "hordes of negroes" remaining on the plantations. Within days of the Yankee invasion, he established temporary bivouacs or "contraband camps" at Beaufort (on Port Royal Island) and at Hilton Head (on Hilton Head Island) to house military laborers and other former slaves. Captain Rufus Saxton, who as chief quartermaster of the expeditionary corps had authority over the military laborers, appointed Barnard K. Lee, Jr., a civilian, to supervise the two camps. Sherman ordered Saxton to organize the laborers into gangs, "keep them comfortably clad," and recommend "what compensation . . . should be allowed them."[3] At first they received only food and clothing, plus rations for their families. By the first of December, wages had been set at $3 to $5 per month for common laborers and $8 for carpenters.

Contrary to Sherman's expectation, former slaves from the Union-occupied islands generally remained on the plantations, while refugees from Confederate territory predominated in the contraband camps. Of the approximately 600 people living in the Hilton Head camp in

[3] Capt. L. H. Pelouze to Capt. R. Saxton, 25 Nov. 1861, vol. 2 DS, p. 103, Letters Sent, ser. 2250, SC Expeditionary Corps, RG 393 Pt. 2 No. 130 [C-1647].

February 1862, 472 had been registered by Lee; nearly three-fifths of them hailed from the mainland or from islands outside Union control. Initially, such refugees welcomed military employment and the rations and shelter that accompanied it. But conditions in the camps were discouraging. Large numbers left after a short stint of military labor, sometimes to live with relatives or friends on nearby plantations. "Many come in and run off," Sherman complained. In January 1862, hoping that higher wages might help stem the exodus, Sherman ordered an increase that accorded common laborers as much as $8 per month and mechanics as much as $12. But because the new terms also required the laborers to purchase their dependents' rations and clothing, the higher pay meant little for men with families to support. In early 1862, an increasing proportion of the camps' inhabitants were women, children, and aged people, rather than men able to work for the army. Sherman disparaged them as "a great many useless mouths." "The negro labor expected to be obtained here," he informed the War Department, "is so far almost a failure."[4]

Meanwhile, on the nearly 200 plantations between St. Helena Sound and Port Royal Sound, some 8,000 former slaves were establishing a new life for themselves. Winter clothing had not yet been distributed when the Yankee gunboats put the masters to flight, but the estates were well-stocked with food and other necessities. Former slaves helped themselves to the pantries and storerooms of the great houses, even as they gathered the sweet potatoes they had planted as slaves. With cold weather fast approaching, much work remained to be done. Animals (some of them belonging to the former slaves) had to be tended, gardens harvested, food stored for the winter, and seed saved for the spring planting. Freedpeople set to work enthusiastically, often under the direction of the same drivers who had supervised their labor during slavery.

The former slaves were not the only people to lay claim to plantation property. Official military foraging parties appropriated food, livestock, and other stores. Soldiers who lacked such authority pillaged on their own, rarely distinguishing between the possessions of planters and those of former slaves. A few days after the occupation of Hilton Head Island, Union soldiers ran riot, "shooting poultry, and plundering the negro Houses of everything of any value." The property slaves had accumulated – often reflecting the efforts of generations – became booty. The soldiers' depredations terrified the freedpeople, who remembered their owners' warnings of Yankee brutality. But they did not undermine the former slaves' determination to support themselves on their home estates.

[4] In addition to the relevant documents in this chapter, see General Orders No. 3, Head Quarters, E.C., 18 Jan. 1862, vol. 60/115 DS, Special Orders, General Orders, & Circulars, ser. 2258, SC Expeditionary Corps, RG 393 Pt. 2 No. 130 [C-1732]; *Official Records*, ser. 1, vol. 6, pp. 201–4.

For all the activity in the fields, the freedpeople displayed little interest in completing the cotton harvest. Although fleeing planters had removed or burned much of the cotton that had been picked and processed, the bulk of the year's bumper crop remained on hand, some of it ginned and bagged, but most of it not yet prepared for market. Union officials resolved not to let such valuable property go to waste. In early December 1861, General Sherman ordered William H. Nobles, formerly an officer in the expeditionary corps, to take custody of the harvested cotton, "employ negroes" to gather what had not been harvested, and pay them with vouchers redeemable for rations and clothing. Meanwhile, higher-ranking authorities in Washington were moving in the same direction. With the cooperation of the War Department, Secretary of the Treasury Salmon P. Chase, who had jurisdiction over captured Confederate property, sent Colonel William H. Reynolds to Port Royal as chief resident cotton agent. A prominent participant in the cotton trade of Rhode Island, Reynolds fully appreciated the value of the Sea Island crop. In late December, General Sherman transferred cotton-collecting operations to him, and Nobles became his subordinate.[5]

Encouraged by a 6 percent commission, the cotton agents swept through the plantations, leaving chaos in their wake. Former slaves complained that the agents expropriated personal possessions in addition to the wagons, carts, mules, and horses needed to transport the cotton crop. Their protests grew louder when they were dragooned to work at picking cotton or loading steamers. Compulsory labor did not suit their expectations of the new order. Often finding it "impossible to hire the negroes by the day," Reynolds instead offered them $1 for every 400 pounds of unginned cotton. Many former slaves accepted these terms, which allowed them more control over when and how they worked. Occasional compliance helped them acquire a bit of change to purchase molasses, salt, and clothing, whose distribution had been suspended by the federal invasion. Freedpeople accommodated the cotton agents to suit their own priorities.

Whereas former slaves on the militarily secure islands enjoyed some possibility of supporting themselves, those on outlying islands faced numerous dangers in trying to do so. Soldiers of the contending armies took turns raiding these islands. Injunctions from federal commanders failed to end the banditry of their subordinates. But if Northern soldiers set peculiar standards of friendship, Confederate raiding parties

[5] In addition to the relevant documents in this chapter, see Wm. Sprague to the Hon. S. P. Chase, 1 Dec. 1861, and Adjutant General L. Thomas to Brig. Genl. T. W. Sherman, 4 Dec. 1861, vol. 19, #10 and #13, Port Royal Correspondence, 5th Agency, RG 366 [Q-310]; General Orders No. 41, Head Quarters E.C., 21 Dec. 1861, and General Orders No. 42, Head Quarters E.C., 24 Dec. 1861, both in vol. 1/3 DS, General Orders, Special Orders, & Circulars, ser. 2256, SC Expeditionary Corps, RG 393 Pt. 2 No. 130 [C-1731].

left no doubt who was the enemy. They not only plundered garden plots and burned cabins, but also attempted to return the freedpeople to slavery and shot those who resisted. Former slaves who remained on the contested islands did so at great risk. Crops betrayed their presence, and the destruction or confiscation of their produce undermined their ability to sustain themselves.[6]

Edisto Island, one of the largest and most populous of the coastal islands, became a battleground between former slaves and fugitive masters. Freedpeople on Edisto resisted repeated attempts by former owners and Confederate troops to remove them to the mainland. In some instances, they took the offensive, attacking rebel pickets and destroying bridges. When these efforts failed to halt the depredations, they reluctantly gathered their belongings and moved en masse from their home plantations to the periphery of the island. There, under the protection of Union gunboats, they built huts and scratched out a livelihood hunting and fishing. By February 1862, when federal forces occupied the island, some 1,200 former slaves had collected at Botany Bay, the largest of the refugee colonies.[7]

The capture of Edisto was only one of several military successes along the south Atlantic coast in early 1862. Northern troops occupied Fernandina and Jacksonville, Florida, in mid-March and Fort Pulaski, Georgia, a month later. When Yankee gunboats moved up the rivers of Florida and Georgia, slaves appeared on the banks in hopes of obtaining protection and freedom. But federal troops could maintain only tenuous control over occupied territory that stretched from Edisto Island, some twenty miles below Charleston, to the Florida Keys. Moreover, military operations often required redeployment of troops and gunboats, rendering once-safe localities vulnerable to Confederate raids. Jacksonville was abandoned by federal troops one month after its occupation, not to be retaken until March 1863. Edisto was given up in July 1862. Proximity to Union arms did not guarantee protection.

In the comparatively secure Port Royal area, former slaves began the 1862 crop season with high hopes. On their own initiative, they expanded their provision fields and garden patches, often into land formerly reserved for cotton. They seemed confident that corn, potatoes, and vegetables, supplemented by the products of their poultry yards and the bounty of the sea and forest, would ensure their independence. But while freedpeople saw the departure of their owners as the dawn of a new agricultural regime, Northerners in the Sea Islands had other ideas.

6 In addition to the relevant documents in this chapter, see Lieut. Danl. Ammen to Flag Officer Saml. F. Du Pont, 29 Dec. 1861, vol. 49, pp. 15–17, South Atlantic Squadron, Letters from Officers Commanding Squadrons, RG 45 [T-612]; *Freedom*, ser. 1, vol. 1: docs. 20–21, 25A–B.

7 In addition to the relevant documents in this chapter, see *Navy Official Records*, ser. 1, vol. 12, pp. 431–32, 516–17, 540.

The abandoned land, abandoned cotton, and abandoned laborers drew the attention of an assortment of Northern civilians who had descended on Port Royal. Admiral Samuel F. Du Pont, commander of the South Atlantic Blockading Squadron, characterized the newcomers as "collectors of cotton, collectors of negro statistics, [and] the people of God." One of the latter, Methodist minister Mansfield French, an emissary of the American Missionary Association, arrived early in the new year. So did a number of abolitionist ministers, teachers, and "philanthropic newspaper correspondents," all eager to prove the wisdom of their antislavery convictions. Northern businessmen were equally determined to demonstrate that Yankee capital and know-how could revitalize the economy of the islands. Free labor, if mobilized by private enterprise and quickened by "New England Skill and Energy," proclaimed one group of would-be investors, would sharply reduce the cost of producing cotton.[8]

While abolitionists and businessmen shared a determination to remake the Sea Islands in accordance with the principles of free labor, they disagreed on the principles themselves. Entrepreneurs eager to gain access to rich cotton lands warned against the dangers of "ill-directed benevolence." They found an ally in William Reynolds, who urged the government to lease plantations to practical men of affairs. "In this way," Reynolds maintained, "another Crop of Cotton might be secured, the negroes properly supported, & profitably employed." But the abolitionists also had their champion: Edward L. Pierce, a young attorney from Boston who had been dispatched to Port Royal by the Secretary of the Treasury to report upon how the former slaves "could best be organized for labor . . . their moral nature addressed and their good will secured." Pierce brought to his assignment solid antislavery credentials and prior experience as superintendent of black military laborers near Fortress Monroe, Virginia. He moved quickly to transform the Sea Islands into a nationally recognized "experiment" in free labor.[9]

Arriving at Port Royal in January 1862, Pierce threw himself into his work. He visited plantations and contraband camps and interviewed federal commanders, treasury agents, and Northern missionaries. In order to discern "their wishes and feelings," he also engaged in "familiar conversations" with former slaves. In February, he submitted an encyclopedic report—at once a census, an inventory, a sociology,

[8] For Du Pont's characterization, see *Navy Official Records*, ser. 1, vol. 12, pp. 540–42.

[9] In addition to the relevant documents in this chapter, see Rose, *Rehearsal for Reconstruction*, chap. 1. For an example of public attention to the Port Royal Experiment, see C. A. Marshall et al. to the Honorable, the Senate and the House of Representatives of the United States in Congress Assembled, [Mar.] 1862, 37A-J7, Petitions & Memorials Tabled, ser. 582, 37th Congress, RG 46 [E-79].

and an anthropology of the Sea Islands. To some extent, Pierce's penchant for detail clouded his view of the former slaves. They appeared to him to resemble a European peasantry, "naturally religious and simple-hearted – attached to the places where they lived . . . and self-interest[ed] in securing the means of subsistence." He was convinced that they yearned for the patronage of powerful white men. "We are yours now, Massa," one freedman obligingly told him. But Pierce was also impressed by their courage in risking all to escape slavery, their self-directed efforts to support themselves on the plantations, and their stubborn determination to have things their own way. His observations created contradictory expectations that became embedded in his own plans for the freedpeople.

Pierce was less ambivalent about the cotton agents and the expectant entrepreneurs allied with them. He denounced Reynolds's scheme to lease plantations to Northern capitalists. Any such system, Pierce argued, would "excite expectations of a speedy fortune, to be derived from the labor of [the former slaves]" and lead inevitably to conflicts between the lessees' "humanity" and their "self interest." He had no doubt which would prevail. Like most Northerners, Pierce felt confident that "voluntary labor with just inspirations" would outperform "compulsory labor, enforced by physical pain." But he questioned the wisdom of trusting the future of the former slaves to private entrepreneurs.

Rather than unleash an orgy of speculation, Pierce proposed to solve the "great social question" by bringing the residents of Port Royal under the supervision of benevolent white Northerners with no pecuniary stake in the outcome of the enterprise. Northern superintendents would live on the plantations, but not as overseers in the antebellum sense. Impressed by the former slaves' familiarity with plantation operations, Pierce believed them capable of handling technical matters. The superintendents' role would be to provide "the moral power of the presence of a white man." Accordingly, they required no practical agricultural experience, only the proper spirit. Under the Northerners' "paternal discipline," former slaves would be protected, educated, assured a secure family life, and paid wages, while they prepared themselves for "the ultimate result" – the privileges of citizenship and landownership. In return for these advantages, "a certain just measure of work, with reference to the ability to perform it" would be expected; "if not willingly rendered, [it was] to be required." The "milder and more effective" compulsions of the new order would include "deprivation of privileges, isolation from family and society, the workhouse or even the prison."

Published in widely circulated Northern newspapers, Pierce's report won the warm approval of Secretary of the Treasury Chase and stirred the abolitionist rank and file. Chase commissioned Pierce a special agent, with authority to implement the free-labor plan outlined in his report. But the federal government allocated no funds for the project except the proceeds of the cotton that had been collected under the auspices of the treasury agents. To provide financial support and personnel for the "Port Royal Experiment," Pierce tapped connections with newly founded freedmen's aid societies in Boston, New York, and Philadelphia.

Abolitionists throughout the Northeast sought admission to the select group who would nurture freedom in the Sea Islands. Pierce set high standards. Seeking tough-minded egalitarians who exhibited both "religious sympathy" and "sound practical sense," he rejected applicants who were "imaginative or fanciful in temperament or conduct," as well as pacifists, who would deprive former slaves of "the little manhood they have left." Considering the tasks at hand to be largely men's work, Pierce accepted only a few women, and they were "ladies of mature years . . . and of *rare* and special fitness." The men and women who passed the test represented the flower of Northern benevolence. Their selection earned them a small salary and a good deal of ridicule. Accorded the derogatory label of "Gideonites" by a generally unsympathetic Northern press, Pierce's chosen few adopted the title as their own, transmuting a name "given in derision" into "a crown of glory."

Landing at Beaufort in early March 1862, the first group of Gideonites were soon dispatched to scattered plantations as superintendents and teachers. When they arrived, the former slaves were preparing garden plots and planting corn. Pierce and his superintendents found them "strongly indisposed" to cultivating cotton. Plantation hands, Pierce learned, "were willing to raise corn because it was necessary for food, but they saw no such necessity for cotton, & distrusted promises of payment for cultivating it. It had enriched the masters, but had not fed them."

The freedpeople's reluctance to plant cotton did not sit well with the Gideonites. While Pierce and the superintendents applauded the former slaves' first steps toward self-sufficiency, they insisted that self-sufficiency not become an end in itself. The viability of free labor, they believed, must be demonstrated through "immediate industrial results" – the cultivation of cotton and the integration of former slaves into the market economy. The "republican spirit" demonstrated by black men and women in reorganizing plantation labor was "not . . . to be encouraged at present." Pierce thought it well to "introduce ideas of independent proprietorship," but all in good time. The day when every former slave could cultivate his own tract of land independently was still in the future.

The plantation superintendents took pains to convince their charges "that labor on cotton was honorable, remunerative and necessary," reminding the former slaves that cash earnings would "enable them to buy clothing and the fitting comforts they desired." Pierce himself insisted "that without the raising of cotton no wages would be paid them – as without it we should have no products of theirs to sell." By applying themselves to the staple crop, he contended, freedpeople would give the lie to their owners' assertion that they would not grow cotton "unless whipped to it." Despite such entreaties, former slaves preferred their patches of corn and vegetables.

Preference aside, necessity soon forced former slaves back into the cotton fields. Although their garden crops might supply much of their subsistence, they needed money to purchase cloth, meat, salt, molasses, sugar, coffee, and tobacco. Army sutlers usually demanded hard cash, not chickens or eggs. Plantation superintendents made access to garden plots contingent upon labor in the cotton fields, as it had been under slavery. The crucial difference was that the prospect of material reward would replace the lash as an incentive to work. From Pierce's perspective, all of this was as it should be. The plantation superintendents were pleased to report at the end of the planting season that about 5,500 acres of cotton had been prepared on the 189 estates under their supervision.

But not everything had gone according to plan. Despite the Gideonites' lectures on the virtues of "compensated labor," plantation hands had received nothing for their spring's work. Many, in fact, had not yet been paid for work performed for the cotton agents, and they expected little better of Pierce's subordinates. Subsequent events bore out their suspicion. The first installment of money for wages, which finally reached Pierce in April 1862, sufficed only to allow each laborer $1 per acre cultivated, and that placed "on account" rather than paid directly. Moreover, freedpeople expected to be provided with food and other necessities as a matter of course. As one superintendent explained, "[t]hey feel entitled already to subsistence from last year's crop of corn because it is the product of their labor under the old state of things." Former slaves particularly resented having to work for the superintendents when they had not received new clothing, rations, or the assorted "extras," such as tobacco, customarily furnished by their former owners. On at least one plantation, they "declared they wouldn't work on cotton without the usual supply of clothes." Nonpayment of wages and scanty provision of needed goods undercut the homilies of free labor that issued from Pierce and the plantation superintendents.

Low wages that arrived late were only one of many problems facing former slaves on the Sea Island plantations. Requisitions by government agents and depredations by individual soldiers – often virtually indistinguishable acts – continued to deprive plantation residents of food, livestock, and tools. Impressment of freedmen by various military employers removed productive workers from the fields. Moreover, the continuing influx of fugitive slaves from outlying islands and the mainland meant that scarce provisions had to feed even more hungry people. By late spring, destitution was widespread on the islands nearest the principal federal posts, especially Hilton Head, Port Royal, and Ladies.

Events on Coffin Point plantation (on St. Helena Island), the largest estate under federal control, illustrate many of the difficulties faced by former slaves and Northern superintendents during 1862. The plantation was under the supervision of Edward S. Philbrick, a young engineer from Boston. Philbrick brought to the Sea Islands a devout faith in wage labor and an unclouded vision of the former slaves' future. He argued forcefully that the freedpeople should be placed "within the reach of private Enterprise in such Employment as they are by nature and experience qualified to compete in with other labor." He had no doubt that growing cotton was "the most Eligible Employment for them."

Philbrick deplored the haphazard operation of the labor system instituted by Pierce. It pained him to see the former slaves "shivering in their cabins & churches for want of sufficient clothing," "crying loudly & with some reason, that we dont treat them so well as their old masters." He squirmed uncomfortably when hungry plantation hands reminded him that the slaveholders had issued beef once a month and provided regular allowances of other goods. He complained of the government's inability to provide basic necessities and, unlike Pierce, stressed the need for superintendents with a knowledge of cotton culture. Philbrick believed that the Sea Island estates could be operated more efficiently by private capitalists than by government agents.

Philbrick's vision of entrepreneurial benevolence also differed from that of William Nobles and the other cotton agents. Philbrick protested that the cotton agents requisitioned laborers, horses, and wagons without his permission. The resulting conflicts, he fretted, diminished his esteem among the freedpeople, especially when the cotton agents demeaned him in their presence. He broadcast his complaints to his superiors in the Sea Islands and to well-connected friends in the North. The cotton agents countered that the plantation superintendents were incompetent. Nobles accused them of hypocrisy: After telling "the poor negroes 'sisters & brothers you are free,' " the Gideonites had proceeded to use them much as they had been used by their "old masters," but with "the additional burden of having first to teach their new masters . . . the most simple rudiments of plantation life & labors." Escalating tension between the cotton agents and the plantation superintendents culminated in Nobles's assaulting Pierce, after which Secretary of the Treasury Chase dismissed Nobles and decided to transfer supervision of the plantations to the War Department once the cotton agents finished their work.

Given such conflicts in plantation administration, military labor looked increasingly attractive to many former slaves. Military laborers had new clothing, tobacco, and ready cash to show for their efforts, not empty promises. The taunts of Northern soldiers and sailors that plantation hands were "great fools" for planting cotton and that "the government would never pay them anything" intensified the frustration. While the Gideonites emphasized that free people everywhere worked for a living, Yankee soldiers assured them that free workers also received regular wages.

For lack of viable alternatives, some plantation laborers left the fields for army depots. Others opted for employment with the dreaded cotton agents. At Coffin Point, able-bodied men joined the agents' picking gangs, while the women and elderly men steadfastly refused to work for "Driver or massa." Instead, they tended their gardens. The "republican spirit" previously noted by the Gideonites had come to represent insubordination of the worst kind.

Federal military operations in coastal Georgia and Florida during the spring of 1862 compounded the unrest among former slaves in the South Carolina Sea Islands. Union authorities needed hundreds of men to maintain fortifications at Key West, reinforce those at Fort Clinch, near Fernandina, and construct new ones on Tybee Island, near Fort Pulaski. With workers available in insufficient numbers at the southerly posts, military employers requisitioned men from Port Royal. But the calls met with resistance. When the War Department ordered General Sherman to send several hundred former slaves to Key West, he found it difficult to amass the requisite number. Worried that such labor would take them far from home and leave their families in uncertain straits, most black men refused altogether or agreed to go only if the government promised to support their families. Perhaps in response to these demands, subsequent requests from the more distant posts specified unmarried men.[10]

General David Hunter, who in late March 1862 assumed command of the newly created Department of the South,[11] envisioned a larger military role for former slaves. Whereas Sherman had confined them to military or agricultural labor and left to his superiors the determination of their legal status, Hunter sought to bring them under arms and establish their legal title to freedom. In early April, he asked the War Department for 50,000 muskets and authorization "to arm such loyal men as I can find in the country." When Washington stalled, Hunter

[10] Colonel Henry Moore to Capt. L. H. Pelouze, 11 Mar. 1862, Letters Received, ser. 2254, SC Expeditionary Corps, RG 393 Pt. 2 No. 130 [C-1642]. General Sherman directed one subordinate to assure the men that "all Contrabands going to Key West will be allowed to leave their families in charge of the Commander of the Post, whose duty it will be to ration and take care of them." (Capt. [Louis H. Pelouze] to Col. Henry Moore, 15 Mar. 1862, vol. 57 DS, p. 78, Letters Sent, ser. 2250, SC Expeditionary Corps, RG 393, Pt. 2 No. 130 [C-1645].)

[11] The Department of the South encompassed all Union-occupied territory in South Carolina, Georgia, and Florida.

acted on his own, ordering the conscription of all black men between the ages of eighteen and forty-five. That was only the beginning. Following the fall of Fort Pulaski in mid-April, Hunter "confiscated" the slaves in its vicinity and declared them free to "receive the fruits of their own labor." A few weeks later, he boldly declared free all the slaves in South Carolina, Georgia, and Florida. President Abraham Lincoln, however, quickly annulled Hunter's emancipation proclamation and rebuked its author.[12]

Returned to their legal limbo between slavery and freedom, black people were of two minds about Hunter. They cheered his grant of freedom, but they were less pleased with his invitation to join the Union army – especially when delivered at gunpoint. To former slaves, impressment was an uncomfortable reminder of the compulsion of the old regime. The conscripts also objected to being removed from those who depended on them for support. At the appearance of press gangs, freedmen took flight; those on one estate suddenly found it "very necessary to go to the woods to split Rails." Employers of plantation hands and military laborers also protested the disruptive effects of Hunter's conscription. Presenting the objections of the plantation superintendents, Pierce complained that the draft threatened the nascent free-labor experiment by removing the most productive workers. Hunter shrugged off all opposition. Although the War Department pointedly ignored his pleas for arms and supplies, he did not disband his black regiment until August.[13]

Meanwhile, the Union troops scattered along the south Atlantic coast remained insufficient to protect more than a few strategic strongholds. In June 1862, the War Department exacerbated the shortage by transferring most of the cavalry serving in the Department of the South to the beleaguered Army of the Potomac. Their departure forced Hunter to evacuate Edisto and several smaller islands. Subsequent reassignments of troops compelled him to uproot a settlement of former slaves that the navy had established on St. Simon's Island, Georgia. Leaving behind the crops they had planted, the residents of these islands became impoverished refugees. By the fall of 1862, some 4,000 displaced former slaves had been transported to Port Royal, too late in the year to cultivate crops of their own.

Responsibility for the care of these new arrivals and all other freedpeople fell to General Rufus Saxton. Formerly quartermaster of the South Carolina Expeditionary Corps, Saxton undertook new duties in June 1862, when Secretary of War Edwin M. Stanton appointed him military governor and chief superintendent of plantations in the Depart-

[12] *Official Records*, ser. 1, vol. 6, pp. 263–64, and ser. 1, vol. 14, p. 333; *Freedom*, ser. 1, vol. 1: pp. 108–9, and doc. 24.

[13] *Freedom*, ser. 2: pp. 38–39, and docs. 1–2; *Official Records*, ser. 3, vol. 2, pp. 50–60.

ment of the South. Adopting the main features of the labor system established by Pierce (who left the Sea Islands to resume his law practice), Saxton put the Port Royal Experiment under military auspices. He appointed four general superintendents of plantations, who supervised some fifty-five local superintendents, teachers, and physicians. Nearly all of them came from the ranks of Pierce's Gideonites, and all subscribed to Saxton's conviction that "negro slavery is a great wrong to humanity." The superintendents oversaw some 16,000 former slaves, both long-time residents and newcomers to Port Royal. Saxton's control over plantation operations reduced the tension between civilian superintendents and military officers that had characterized Pierce's tenure. It also facilitated the payment of wages to plantation laborers, who could now be compensated by army paymasters.

While pressing forward the reorganization of agricultural labor, Saxton and the superintendents struggled to provide for destitute refugees and defend scattered plantations. To help protect the occupied estates, Saxton distributed muskets and ordered the superintendents to form freedmen into militia units. He also sought permission to enroll black laborers whose duties would include safeguarding the plantations. In late August 1862, on the heels of military reverses in Virginia, the War Department approved Saxton's request and also authorized the enlistment of up to 5,000 freedmen as soldiers. Under Saxton, Hunter's dream of a black soldiery was realized. By October, recruitment had begun in earnest. Before long, black troops were conducting forays up the rivers of the mainland, earning the admiration of their fellow freedpeople and the Northern public and escorting thousands of slaves to freedom.[14]

General Ormsby M. Mitchel, who replaced General Hunter in mid-September 1862, shared Saxton's eagerness to recruit black soldiers, but he feared that wholesale enlistment and deployment of the new regiments in operations beyond Port Royal would cripple free-labor agriculture. Removing able-bodied men from the plantation labor force would, he predicted, undermine not only the likelihood of showing a profit, but also the prospect of producing enough food for the local population. Mitchel's own ambitious plan to increase agricultural production by settling up to 200,000 liberated slaves along the south Atlantic coast ran athwart the stern reality that existing Northern forces could barely hold the limited territory already under occupation. He saw additional hindrance in the failure of the federal government either to declare the former slaves free or to establish more definitely the terms of labor. In late October, before he could address these problems, he fell victim to yellow fever. The chief legacy of his brief

[14] In addition to the relevant documents in this chapter, see *Freedom*, ser. 2: pp. 39–40, and docs. 4–5, 207–8; *Freedom*, ser. 1, vol. 1: pp. 110–11, and docs. 31–32.

command was "Mitchelville," a contraband camp on Hilton Head Island that became a self-governing settlement with black officials.[15]

As General Mitchel and others had predicted, the enlistment of black soldiers complicated the lives of former slaves and army commanders alike. Recruitment deprived many plantations of able-bodied men, placing additional burdens on women, children, and the old and disabled. Small garrison towns like Fernandina, Florida, swelled with dependent ex-slaves, chiefly the relatives of newly enlisted soldiers and military laborers. Union officers complained that the soldiers' kinfolk "seem to have no disposition to work . . . but are satisfied to draw their support from the government & live in idleness." They recommended that the soldiers' families be forced to work – if not for the army then at "cleaning streets or such other labor" – or be transferred elsewhere. In fact, the small mainland posts offered scant prospect of either military or civilian employment for anyone other than able-bodied men. Large numbers of unemployed former slaves were simply shipped to Port Royal, shifting to another locality the problem of supporting destitute freedpeople whose fathers, husbands, and sons were serving the Union.[16]

The enlistment of black men also exacerbated the shortage of military laborers. In competition with recruiting officers, military employers found it increasingly difficult to find and retain workers. Assignment of black troops to fatigue duty brought only temporary relief and engendered protests from both the soldiers and their white officers. In March 1863, General Hunter (who in January had returned for another stint as department commander) raised the stakes higher still when he ordered that all "unemployed" men as old as fifty be drafted into the army. Recruiters took a broad view of unemployment, inciting the opposition of military engineers and quartermasters, as well as the conscripted men. Engineers at Fort Clinch, Florida, won exemption for their employees, but elsewhere the competition for able-bodied black men continued to the end of the war.[17]

The growing labor shortage redounded to the advantage of some former slaves. Pilots, blacksmiths, and carpenters earned premium wages. Admiral Du Pont regularly paid skilled black men $12 per

[15] In addition to the relevant documents in this chapter, see O. M. Mitchel to Hon. S. P. Chase, 26 Sept. 1862; O. M. Mitchel to Rev. Dr. Wayland, 13 Oct. 1862, vol. 6*, pp. 38–41, 66–67, Letters Sent by Brig. Gen. O. M. Mitchel, ser. 839, Mobile Units, Dept. & Army of the OH, RG 393 Pt. 2 No. 15 [C-8009]. On Mitchelville, see Edward Magdol, *A Right to the Land: Essays on the Freedmen's Community* (Westport, Conn., 1977), pp. 93, 103. For one of Mitchelville's black officials, see below, doc. 52.

[16] On the scarcity of nonmilitary employment at Fernandina, see *Official Records*, ser. 1, vol. 2, pp. 243–44.

[17] In addition to the relevant documents in this chapter, see *Freedom*, ser. 2: docs. 6A–B, 158A, 198A–C.

month, $2 above the maximum mandated by orders from the Navy Department. Their services, he explained, were "so valuable that I deemed it just to give them advanced pay." Black pilots and engineers made as much as $30 per month. Unskilled laborers also benefited. Noting that "some of my best hands have already left me, because they could obtain higher wages elsewhere," a commissary officer at Hilton Head requested and received authority for an increase from $8 per month to $12. By the fall of 1862, common laborers at the isolated posts of Key West and the Tortugas in southern Florida were earning $2.50 per day.[18]

Whether skilled or unskilled, military labor offered black men a measure of flexibility as well as compensation. Military laborers could visit their families on Sundays or absent themselves for a few days to help with crops. Black soldiers had fewer such opportunities. Their duties often precluded visiting and sometimes took them far from their families. And a soldier's absence from his regiment meant not merely lost wages but arrest and punishment for desertion. If most healthy black men had little choice but to serve the Union army in some capacity, many of them believed that the well-being of their families made military labor preferable to enlistment.

As former slaves struggled to earn a livelihood and meet familial obligations, officials in Washington were taking steps that promised to alter the tenure of the land on which most Sea Island freedpeople made their home and earned their subsistence. In the fall of 1862, the Lincoln administration set machinery in motion to enforce the Direct Tax Act of the previous June. That law, enacted to collect in the insurrectionary states the taxes imposed by a previous revenue measure, established procedures whereby, if property holders failed to pay federal assessments on real estate, title would fall to the government. The land could then be leased out or sold under the supervision of a three-member commission appointed by the President for each state.[19] Fully expecting that secessionists would not rush forward to pay their federal taxes, Congress intended the act to make possible a redistribution of land.

The commissioners for South Carolina arrived in Beaufort in September 1862. Abram D. Smith, a Wisconsin attorney, had helped to draft the Direct Tax Act. William Henry Brisbane, a former Sea Island

[18] In addition to the relevant documents in this chapter, see Flag Officer S. F. Du Pont to Hon. Gideon Welles, 23 June 1862, enclosing a list of black laborers aboard the *Pawnee* and the *Darlington*, [23 June 1862]; and Rear Admiral S. F. Du Pont to Hon. Gideon Welles, 8 Dec. 1862, both in South Atlantic Squadron, Letters from Officers Commanding Squadrons, RG 45 [T-549, T-557]; Capt. Gideon Scull to Captain M. R. Morgan, 25 June 1862, S-124 1862, Letters Received, ser. 4109, Dept. of the South, RG 393 Pt. 1 [C-1308].

[19] *Statutes at Large*, vol. 12, pp. 422–26. For a more detailed summary of the act, see below, doc. 27n.

planter, had left South Carolina for the North after an antebellum conversion to antislavery. With their colleague William E. Wording, they set about surveying and assessing land in St. Helena Parish (which included all the major Union-occupied islands except Hilton Head). Having completed their preliminary duties by December, they scheduled sales for the following February, at which forfeited tracts were to be sold to the highest bidder in lots of up to 320 acres.

The prospect of land sales under the Direct Tax Act delighted Northern entrepreneurs, who saw an opportunity to engross prime plantation land at bargain rates. One-time Gideonite Edward Philbrick organized a consortium of Northern investors to undertake large-scale purchases. Like numerous other businessmen, Philbrick and his associates saw philanthropy and profit as two sides of the same coin. Indeed, he depicted his venture as a continuation of the labor "experiment" initiated by Pierce, but on a sounder basis. After the return of peace, Philbrick conceded, cotton might be grown efficiently "by small proprietors with small capital," including former slaves. But the special circumstances of war and the great goal of transforming slaves into free laborers demanded that private investors with public spirit take the lead.

Former slaves took a different view. Fearful that they might lose the land they had occupied, cultivated, and considered their own, black men and women thronged the tax commissioners' office, seeking information and expressing their desire to obtain legal title. Realizing that they were, in Smith's words, but "tenants at will upon the grace of the Government," they hoped to put their freedom on a more substantial footing. Many of the Northerners in the occupied islands also worried that the auction of tax properties in large tracts would favor speculators. Although they disagreed about how much land was required to undergird the former slaves' freedom – some believing an acre or two sufficient, others insisting on a larger tract – they agreed that open bidding would doom the chances of establishing a class of black landowners.

Some high-ranking military and civil officials shared their reservations. Maintaining that "simple justice" endowed former slaves with "the highest right to a soil they have cultivated so long under the cruelest compulsion," General Saxton feared that their "future well being" would be sacrificed to the interests of "men devoid of principle." Like Saxton, tax commissioner Abram Smith believed that the untrammeled exercise of "private interest" would result in "a change of masters from slaveowners to capitalists." He urged the government to reserve land for sale "in small parcels with the privilege of pre-emption," so that every "freed man may secure himself and family a home at an early day and from his own earnings." Establishing former slaves as landowners would set the Sea Islands on the road to "reformation, advancement in civilization, happiness, wealth, freedom and assured loyalty."

Determined to halt direct-tax sales under the existing provisions, Saxton and Smith lobbied influential friends. Smith journeyed to Washington to confer with Secretary of the Treasury Chase and Republican legislators, while Saxton wrote to Secretary of War Stanton and met with General Hunter. On February 7, 1863, citing the necessity of retaining a portion of the land under governmental control "for the use of the soldiers and the support of the colored population," Hunter postponed the sales. Meanwhile, Smith had persuaded influential members of Congress to amend the Direct Tax Act. By legislation approved on February 6, Congress empowered the President to reserve a portion of the forfeited land for military and other governmental use, placing it off-limits to private investors. To prevent speculators from acquiring valuable land at nominal sums, the amendment also authorized the direct-tax commissioners themselves to bid for any parcel, on behalf of the government, at a rate of two-thirds its assessed value. Soon thereafter, President Lincoln instructed Saxton, Hunter, and the three commissioners to set aside land under the February amendment, and the sales deferred by Hunter's order were rescheduled for early March.

Although the efforts of Saxton, Smith, and their allies did not result in the subdivision of estates and sale to freedpeople on preferred terms, they did keep most of the direct-tax land out of the hands of private purchasers. Prior to the March sales, the commissioners reserved some 40,000 acres in St. Helena Parish. They then bid in another 20,000 at auction, leaving about 20,000 acres (some forty-five plantations) for purchase by private individuals.

Among the purchasers were a handful of freedpeople, who bought as many as eight plantations, totaling about 2,000 acres. To do so, they had formed partnerships, pooling their wages and "funds they had saved from the sale of their pigs, chickens, and eggs." After acquiring title to the land, one such group "divid[ed] off the tract peaceably among themselves."[20] Wealthy Yankees far outstripped such small-scale purchasers. Philbrick snapped up eleven plantations on St. Helena Island, encompassing 8,000 acres, at about $1 per acre, and he leased two other estates. His consortium controlled more than a third of all privately held acreage in St. Helena Parish. Possessed of a vast domain on which more than 900 former slaves would live and work, Philbrick emerged preeminent among the islands' new masters. But the circumstances surrounding his rise embittered his employees. Professing a hope that after the war "the more intelligent and Enterprising of the negroes . . . would become proprietors of the soil," Philbrick promised eventually to relinquish his holdings for just that purpose. Laborers on Philbrick's plantations took his vague promise as a binding commit-

[20] In addition to the relevant documents in this chapter, see Edward L. Pierce, "The Freedmen at Port Royal," *Atlantic Monthly* 12 (Sept. 1863): 310; Magdol, *A Right to the Land*, pp. 175–76.

ment to sell them the land at his cost. His refusal to do so during the war, and his fivefold increase of the asking price when he finally did sell in 1866, kindled bitter dispute.

To the majority of former slaves on the Sea Islands, for whom landownership remained a remote prospect, General Saxton's labor regulations for the 1863 crop season were of more immediate interest than Philbrick's promises. Concerned first about producing enough food, Saxton allotted each adult worker on the government-operated plantations two acres for corn and potatoes, with additional land for each child. Corn was also to be planted to feed the plantation livestock and such supernumeraries as the superintendents of plantations and aged and infirm freedpeople. Plantation hands and the superintendents were to determine jointly how much cotton would be planted, but, in order to increase acreage in the staple, Saxton required that wages be paid only for work on the cotton crop. He also stopped rations except in cases of dire necessity. By these measures, Saxton and the superintendents expected to motivate the freedpeople to perform labor that they were otherwise disinclined to do.

Saxton's labor regulations bore certain formal similarity to antebellum task work. Setting the rate of pay at twenty-five cents per day, Saxton specified how many quarter-acre "tasks" would constitute a "fair day's work" in each agricultural operation except picking, for which he authorized payment of two and one-half cents per pound of cotton. Within these guidelines, plantation hands had some leeway to allocate their labor according to their own inclinations. On most government-operated estates, superintendents assigned tasks to households, rather than to individual workers. "The general way," explained one of Saxton's aides, "is for the head of a family to take so much ground, agreeing to cultivate it in cotton for the government; he then turns his family in and they work it in common." Saxton's regulations also permitted freedpeople to live on the government estates without working the cotton fields, provided they paid rent for their quarters and provision grounds. By exercising such options, ex-slave households gained a measure of control over who worked in what fields, when, and how much.

With their profits dependent upon cotton, not provisions, private planters were even more determined than Saxton's superintendents to overcome the freedpeople's aversion to the staple. Not one of his hands felt "any obligation at all to plant cotton," complained Frederick Eustis, a resident of Massachusetts who had inherited a plantation on Ladies Island. He and other Yankee landowners strove to create that obligation. Certain that former slaves were "actuated by the same motives as other men," Northern planters offered prompt payment of wages. Having seen the detrimental effect of tardy wages in the early days of the Port Royal Experiment, Philbrick made it a point to pay his employees regularly every month. Eustis found it impossible to get workers into the cotton field except by "paying on the spot." Both planters felt themselves vindicated to discover that, when pay was certain, former slaves responded to the stimulus of wages. The new incentives, they believed, even rejuvenated elderly people previously considered too feeble to work. The sight of aged freedpeople diligently at work in the cotton fields seemed to prove the superiority of voluntary, compensated labor. "The great civilizer here," Eustis proclaimed, "is the 'dime.' "

In their struggle with the Northern planters and government superintendents, freedpeople demonstrated their own understanding of the coinage of the new order. They sought as much as possible to feed themselves and earn cash through self-directed pursuits, minimizing the necessity of wage-labor employment. They demanded that private employers, like the government superintendents, allot provision grounds to each family. They sold produce raised on their plots, along with chickens, eggs, fish, and various handicrafts. In these ways, they reduced their dependence on wages.

Plantation hands resisted attempts by the Northern planters to extend their hours of labor or subject them to closer supervision. When Philbrick tried to define the workday in terms of a certain number of hours instead of a fixed amount of work, freedpeople on his estates would have none of it. They engaged in "daily Experiments to test the minimum of labor which would be accepted . . . as a days work." Finding it "nearly impossible to Employ [former slaves] to labor regularly by the day or Month," Philbrick eventually adopted a task-work system similar to that instituted by Saxton on the government plantations. He assigned "temporary allotments" of cotton land to individual families, paying them "by the *piece* or *job*." This system, Philbrick believed, gave each laborer "a proprietary interest in the crop" so that "he feels as if working for himself." Although freedpeople knew full well for whom they were working, they maneuvered for control over their labor and their lives.

Former slaves and their Northern employers also disagreed about the amount of compensation that should be paid for work in the cotton fields. Low wages, the planters believed, forced plantation hands to labor industriously and regularly, inculcating habits that would serve them well in the future. High wages, on the other hand, encouraged them to work only enough to provide for immediate necessities, after which they would turn to other pursuits or indulge in idleness. Viewing the dime literally as the great civilizer, Eustis grumbled that his hands were "spoiled" by receiving a quarter – the daily wage mandated by Saxton, which became standard on private as well as government estates. The freedpeople, on the other hand, based their notions of just remuneration on what their earnings would buy. Those on Philbrick's plantations protested that, in view of inflated prices, money earned by work in cotton was "not enough to sustaine life if wee depended entirely uppon our wages." A good many Northerners agreed with that judgment. Two of Philbrick's own plantation managers acknowledged that wages were "inadequate." A treasury agent who investigated Philbrick's operations concluded that his employees were paid at only half the rate accorded agricultural laborers in the North, although the extraordinary profitability of wartime cotton culture and inflated prices of provisions "would seem to demand that wages should be higher."

To help meet the material needs of their laborers, a number of planters opened stores on their estates. Philbrick boasted five establishments, stocked with "a great variety" of goods, by means of which he hoped "to stimulate labor by multiplying civilized wants." Although he reportedly charged "feerefull prices for every nessary of life," laborers on his plantations purchased "vast quantities of articles which they never had in abundance," including housewares, clothing, and special food items. Such stores served to keep laborers "at home," as well as to return a profit. Schools, the planters found, could also attract and retain workers. By all accounts, the schools on Philbrick's plantations were the most successful part of his enterprise, enrolling over 300 students. Yet not even the combined force of wages, store-bought goods, and Yankee schoolteachers motivated former slaves to the entire satisfaction of the islands' new employers.

For all their disappointments at the hands of the former slaves, Philbrick and the other Northern planters could also count their successes. The private plantations, they boasted, produced more cotton than the government-supervised estates. Only 25 percent of the cultivated land on government plantations was devoted to staple production, compared to more than 40 percent on privately operated estates. While either proportion guaranteed a handsome profit to the employers, former slaves enjoyed their own victories. Even on the private estates a majority of the cultivated land was devoted to corn and potatoes. Although the freedpeople had not dethroned King Cotton, they had reduced his domain. Their resistance to wage work bespoke their desire for independence, preferably undergirded by control over land. "The people here," declared one Sea Island freedman, "would rather have the land than work for wages."

Developments in the closing months of 1863 reopened the land question. In September, President Lincoln instructed the direct-tax commissioners to dispose of the land that had been set aside or bid in for the government in March. Among other things, he directed that fifty-five of the estates reserved for "charitable" purposes be sold in lots of up to twenty acres to "heads of families of the African race," at a price of $1.25 per acre. Lincoln's instructions ensured that former slaves would not have to compete with Northern speculators in open bidding. But they had serious drawbacks in the eyes of the freedpeople and many of their advocates, including General Saxton, Mansfield French, and Abram Smith. The reserved land consisted of about 20,000 acres, an amount insufficient to provide more than tiny plots to most of the Sea Islands' black residents. Moreover, the President's directive effectively denied former slaves ownership of any of the other land that had been forfeited to the government, unless they had the wherewithal to outbid Northern competitors. Few could hope to do so. Consequently, Saxton and others feared, vast tracts were liable to be sold to "persons who had no interests in common with the negro, except the profit to be derived from their labor on the lowest possible terms." The limited extent of the land reserved for "charitable" purposes frustrated the hopes of freedpeople who desired homesteads on the estates where "they had been born, & had laborered & suffered."

Fearing the worst should sales proceed under the September instructions, Saxton, French, and Smith tried to persuade the Lincoln administration to revise its policy yet again. Meanwhile, French and Saxton urged the freedpeople to settle anywhere they pleased on government-controlled land. In early November 1863, Saxton took the process one step further. He issued an order authorizing former slaves who wished to purchase land on unreserved government tracts to enter a description of the desired parcel at his headquarters, along with a cash deposit; a military agent would make bids in their names at the sale slated for February 1864.[21] At the same time, Saxton, French, and Smith hinted that the claimants might eventually be allowed to make purchases through preemption, thereby avoiding competition from speculators. Although such advice had no legal basis at that moment, the advocates of preemption sent French to Washington to lobby Secretary of the Treasury Chase and other leading politicians. Meanwhile, Sea Island freedpeople began staking claims.

French's journey bore fruit. On December 30, 1863, President Lincoln issued new instructions to the direct-tax commissioners, permitting any loyal resident of St. Helena Parish (black or white) to preempt a homestead of twenty or forty acres on government land, at $1.25 an acre, with only two-fifths of the purchase price as a down payment. Plantation laborers welcomed the opportunity to gain independent control over land, even if they did not entirely subscribe to the notions of absolute property embodied in the direct-tax legislation. They "acted promptly and joyfully," Saxton later recalled, "and in an incredibly short time" entered claims "for nearly all the land in the district." Freedpeople on some plantations made applications "in mass . . . with-

[21] Rose, *Rehearsal for Reconstruction*, p. 274.

out the names of the negroes," presumably expecting to divide the land among themselves or to work it collectively. Former slaves separated from their antebellum residences by wartime events journeyed back to Port Royal to claim a portion of "the old homestead."

Smith's fellow direct-tax commissioners reacted with consternation. Objecting to Lincoln's departure from the original notion of "charitable" purposes, Brisbane and Wording raised a host of legal and practical objections to the "squatter sovereignty" of preemption. For one, they argued, former slaves stood in danger of being outmaneuvered by sharp-trading Northerners who were also eligible to preempt. For another, settlement of freedpeople on small plots all over the islands would devalue property and dissuade white purchasers from residing among them "as protectors, teachers and employers." Then too, the government would lose revenue by selling at $1.25 per acre land worth many times that amount. Finally, the two commissioners impugned the motives and character of the advocates of preemption.

While awaiting an official response, Brisbane and Wording simply refused to act on applications to preempt land. General Quincy A. Gillmore, who had replaced Hunter as department commander in June 1863, took their part, and he urged Secretary of the Treasury Chase to reverse the new instructions. In mid-February 1864, to the chagrin of those who supported the preemption policy, Chase suspended it. The sale later that month went forward under Lincoln's September instructions, with freedpeople eligible to apply for the land specifically reserved for them or to bid on other tracts at open auction. Northern entrepreneurs were present in force. Bidding was livelier than the year before and selling prices markedly higher. Few former slaves could compete. Although a significant number of freedpeople eventually acquired plots from the specially reserved land (110 families by March 1864 and about 1,000 by December 1865), their success was scant consolation for those whose claims had been encouraged by the government and then denied in a seemingly capricious reversal.

The disappointment of Sea Island freedpeople was "almost unbearable." Many had selected sites, made down payments, and begun planting crops, only to be dispossessed. They prepared to resist this betrayal. Having no desire to suppress their anger, Mansfield French transformed a funeral service on St. Helena Island into a rally for preemption, urging the freedpeople "to hold on to the land as long and as persistently as [possible]." They hardly needed his encouragement. The residents of one plantation would neither relinquish their claims nor accept refunds of the money they had deposited with General Saxton. Some former slaves resorted to force when new owners attempted to take possession, prompting the purchasers to seek military intervention. On at least one plantation, freedpeople remained in "undisturbed possession" of their preemption claims through the end of 1864, unmolested by military officials. But far more often, claimants were compelled to surrender what they regarded as their inalienable right to the land.[22]

The February 1864 direct-tax sales marked a watershed in the wartime history of the South Carolina Sea Islands. The reversal of preemption closed an opportunity to transform former slaves into freeholders. Although a few "companies" of former slaves leased tracts retained by the tax commissioners for school-revenue purposes, the vast majority of former slaves had to come to terms with the private planters.[23] In the aftermath of the land sales, General Saxton's superintendents also assumed a different role. Once they had directly supervised the operation of numerous estates; now they were confined largely to approving private labor contracts, guarding laborers against fraud, and arbitrating disputes between employers and employees.

The annulment of preemption was not the last of the freedpeople's tribulations. The spring of 1864 brought a new season of military activity, with important effects on the lives of ex-slaves. First, operations against Charleston removed most of the soldiers who had been defending the Union-occupied islands and mainland posts. Then, in July, the War Department demanded several thousand additional soldiers for the Union offensive in eastern Virginia. General John G. Foster, the new commander of the Department of the South, protested that the requisition would reduce his force to dangerously low levels, but he complied. In an attempt to replenish his depleted ranks, Foster ordered his subordinates to "require all the able bodied [black] men to bear arms." He especially targeted laborers on "private (quasi-public) plantations," convinced that women, children, and men exempt from armed service by reason of age or infirmity could keep the estates functioning.[24]

Press gangs of Union soldiers, both black and white, carried out Foster's orders only too well. Among those dragooned into service were boys barely into their teens whose labor was indispensable to the support of their families. The recruiters also hauled in military laborers and arrested "deserters" who, it often turned out, had never enlisted in the first place. Although such tactics filled Union regiments, they alienated the conscripts and jeopardized the welfare of their families. General Saxton, who had repeatedly pledged that no force would be used to fill black regiments, knew that the freedpeople

22 Reuben Tomlinson to Brig. Gen. R. Saxton, 18 Mar. 1864, filed with S-147 1864, Letters Received, ser. 4109, Dept. of the South, RG 393 Pt. 1 [C-1737]; Jno. Hunn to Major General John G. Foster, 8 Dec. 1864, Letters Received, ser. 4109, Dept. of the South RG 393 Pt. 1 [C-1335]. On preemption and its aftermath, see also Rose, *Rehearsal for Reconstruction*, chap. 10; Magdol, *A Right to the Land*, pp. 176–80; Saville, "A Measure of Freedom," pp. 59–65.

23 Most of the so-called school farms were leased to Northerners.

24 See *Official Records*, ser. 1, vol. 35, pt. 2, pp. 142–43, 178, 209, 234–35; *Freedom*, ser. 2: doc. 8.

regarded Foster's impressment as yet another betrayal. Coming hard on the heels of the abrogation of preemption, he reported with sarcasm, it "tended to cool the enthusiastic joy with which the coming of the 'Yankees' was welcomed."[25]

To make matters worse, a failure of provision crops put many black women, children, and old people in desperate straits. Soldiers tried to send home a portion of their wages, but few could spare enough to support their families after providing for their own necessities. Irregular payment of the soldiers' wages exacerbated the problem. Moreover, the rations that General Hunter had promised to furnish their families were dispensed with a miserly hand before being stopped altogether in the summer of 1864. Disheartened soldiers often had little choice but to leave the service. "The black soldiers deserted by the score because their families were starving," explained a brigade commander.[26]

Destitution became distressingly common both on the Union-occupied islands and at the mainland posts. On the islands, the arrival of black refugees from rebel-held areas placed additional pressure on local resources. The increased number of destitute people encouraged some military officials to consider familiar Northern precedents for promoting industry among the poor. At Beaufort, the superintendent of contrabands recommended a poorhouse, believing that forcible segregation would shame the destitute into providing for themselves. If the onus of disgrace failed to motivate impoverished ex-slaves, he suggested that they be compelled to labor in a workhouse or chain gang.

Even in the absence of such Draconian incentives, most freedpeople avoided the dole. They worked hard to piece together a livelihood, generally from the wages of husbands, fathers, and sons in the army and wives, mothers, and children on the plantations. Some demonstrated remarkable ingenuity in making ends meet. A considerable number of former slaves obtained a modest subsistence by hawking goods, taking in laundry, or rehabilitating horses and mules that had been abandoned by the army. Still others turned to the sea to supplement their diet and their income by fishing and oystering. One crippled freedman gathered, washed, and stored two tons of rags before his attempt to sell them initiated a convoluted debate among treasury officials over whether the rags constituted "abandoned property" subject to seizure by the government.

Such efforts at independent employment aroused the suspicion of some military officers, whose determination to keep the freedpeople at "steady labor" on the plantations held fast even as conditions on the plantations worsened. These Northerners looked askance at irregular employment and saw nothing but disorder in working people's "get-

[25] In addition to the relevant documents in this chapter, see *Official Records*, ser. 1, vol. 35, pt. 2, pp. 218–19.

[26] *Official Records*, ser. 3, vol. 4, pp. 226–27.

ting a living by doing a little at this and a little at that." Before long, army provost marshals began tightening restrictions upon the mobility of former slaves. An order by General Foster to confiscate and destroy small boats provoked consternation among the former slaves. As one plantation superintendent aptly observed, seizing their boats would "greatly distress many hundreds of poor men and families, whose dependance for food is chiefly fish, oysters, &c." As he well understood, "great numbers thus live who are unfit for the heavy labor of cultivating the land."

Former slaves in the South Carolina Sea Islands, whose contest over the terms of free labor transpired within a narrow territory decreed by military events and Union strategy, were joined at the end of 1864 by thousands of black people from a wide swath of Georgia. These newly minted freedpeople were ushered into freedom at the hands of General William T. Sherman and his western armies. Cutting free of his lines of supply at Atlanta and living off the land, Sherman's legions moved swiftly toward Savannah, reaching the city just before Christmas. Although Sherman had discouraged any but able-bodied men from following his army, former slaves of all ages and conditions arrived in its train. A rag-tag collection of black people camped in and near Savannah.

As he prepared to swing northward into the Carolinas, Sherman sought first to disencumber himself of the black refugees. Others were equally concerned about the former slaves, though for different reasons. Well-founded reports that Sherman opposed the enlistment of black soldiers and that his men had abused defenseless ex-slaves were provoking public outcry in the North. To investigate such charges and organize relief measures, Secretary of War Stanton traveled to Savannah in early January 1865. There he called a meeting with Sherman and twenty local black ministers and lay leaders.[27]

Garrison Frazier, a former slave who had purchased his freedom before the war, spoke for the assembly. He assured Stanton and Sherman of the loyalty of black people, their commitment to the Union, and their confidence in General Sherman. When asked how former slaves might provide for themselves and assist the government in maintaining their freedom, Frazier declared that "[t]he way we can best take care of ourselves is to have land, and turn it and till it by our own labor." For the time being, the land would be worked "by the labor of the women and children and old men," while the young men served in the army. By obtaining land, he confidently predicted, "we can soon

[27] On the circumstances leading to the meeting with black religious leaders, see Joseph T. Glatthaar, *The March to the Sea and Beyond: Sherman's Troops in the Savannah and Carolinas Campaigns* (New York, 1985), chap. 3; Benjamin P. Thomas and Harold M. Hyman, *Stanton: The Life and Times of Lincoln's Secretary of War* (New York, 1962), pp. 343–45.

maintain ourselves and have something to spare." Questioned about whether his people would rather live "scattered among the whites or in colonies by yourselves," Frazier replied, "by ourselves, for there is a prejudice against us in the South that will take years to get over." Only one of his fellows, a Northern free-black minister, offered a dissenting opinion.

Although Sherman hardly shared all the black leaders' views, he apparently listened closely. Within days of the meeting, he issued Special Field Order 15, which set aside the Sea Islands and mainland rice plantations between Charleston and the St. John's River of Florida, for settlement exclusively by black people. Within the reserved district, the male head of each family could claim as much as forty acres, with soldiers' families entitled to take up claims in the absence of their menfolk. The settlers would receive "possessory title," pending congressional action to resolve the question of ownership. In one fell swoop, it seemed, General Sherman had accomplished what three years of infighting, indecision, and disappointment had not.

Sherman's order opened a new chapter in the wartime reconstruction of the region, even as the war itself was nearing an end. By early April, 1865, General Saxton, whom Sherman appointed "superintendent of settlements and plantations," had located about 20,000 former slaves on 100,000 acres of the reserved district. In the intervening three months, the black population of the Union-occupied coast of South Carolina and Georgia had more than doubled. Meanwhile, Sherman's northward march had liberated tens of thousands more slaves, many of whom made their way to the reserved land. Most of them were utterly impoverished, in part because Sherman's army had stripped the countryside of food. In an ironic turn of events, recently freed slaves from the mainland received possessory title to land on which they had never before dwelled, while lifelong residents of the South Carolina Sea Islands – free in fact since late 1861 and repeatedly frustrated in their efforts to obtain the land they had worked as slaves – remained beholden to Northern entrepreneurs for employment.[28]

Like so much else in the wartime experience of former slaves in the lowcountry, the opening of the Sherman reserve promised more than it ultimately delivered. Possessory titles in hand, black families began establishing subsistence-oriented homesteads. But with ultimate disposition of the land still an open question, it was unclear whether their tenure would be permanent or simply another temporary war measure. That issue, like many others, would not be resolved until well after the

[28] On the earliest settlement of former slaves in the reserved district, see Bvt. Maj. Genl. R. Saxton to Maj. Genl. M. C. Meigs, 6 Apr. 1865, "Negroes," Consolidated Correspondence File, ser. 225, Central Records, RG 92 [Y-211]. On the appropriation of food by Union foraging parties and "bummers," see *Freedom*, ser. 1, vol. 1: docs. 36–38; Glatthaar, *March to the Sea and Beyond*, chap. 7.

military contest had ended. The wartime free-labor "experiment" thus ended much as it had begun: broaching fundamental questions about the meaning of free labor in a way that guaranteed fierce disagreement among former slaves, federal authorities, and Northern entrepreneurs. Before long, former masters would also join the fray.

1: Testimony by the Former Superintendent of Contrabands at Hilton Head, South Carolina, before the American Freedmen's Inquiry Commission

[*Beaufort, S.C. June 1863*]

TESTIMONY OF B. K. LEE, JR.

Mr Lee testified as follows: I have been familiar with the plan pursued here in the treatment of the negroes from the beginning, having come here with the original expedition, and was appointed superintendent of the Contrabands upon the 9th of November, 1861. I commenced with between 60 and 70 at my camp, male and female They were very destitute and were mainly slaves from Hilton Head & St Helena island. They came in rapidly in parties of 10, 20, 50 and 100.

Q What was their condition?

A Very destitute indeed; many had scarcely clothing enough to cover them; their clothing was of coarse material, very dirty. They had no change; in some cases they had taken up their master's old carpets from the floors and were clothed in it, presenting a grotesque appearance. It was necessary to get them into working order at once, and there was little sympathy for the work in the Department. Gen Saxton gave his sympathy; Gen Sherman was very kind when he found them willing to labor. At first he was very strict about passing them to and fro. A man would come in shyly to ascertain if the stories that had been told of us by their masters were true; but when he found that he was treated well, he would be anxious to go home and get his family, and would plead and cry, if opposed After eight or ten weeks Gen Sherman commenced to trust them. As they returned to the Plantations and told their stories they would come in in great numbers. Before we took possession of Beaufort these negroes were employed at Hilton Head in all sorts of occupations. They unloaded vessels in the harbor, and the Harbor master says they were very efficient. We paid them from $3 to $5 per month and rations; we also gave rations to their families, and on the 1st of January their families came in faster than before. I had everything to do with them for eleven months till I was taken sick and went North. I returned again on the 1st of Oct last and commenced my work in Gen Saxton's Department as Paymaster, and have paid all the laborers employed on the Plantations and have visited them, each two or three times.

. . . .

HD

Excerpt from testimony of B. K. Lee, Jr., before the American Freedmen's Inquiry Commission, [June 1863], filed with O-328 1863, Letters Received, ser. 12, RG 94 [K-72]. Two pages of a thirteen-page document. In the omitted passages, Lee described the aspirations of the former slaves for education, their religion, their understanding of marriage and family life, and their desire to acquire land and other property. He also assessed the influence of military service upon black men and made recommendations respecting the settlement of former slaves on land forfeited to the government under the Direct Tax Act of June 1862. Topical labels in the margin are omitted.

2: Aide-de-Camp of the Commander of the 2nd Brigade of the South Carolina Expeditionary Corps to the Commander

Port Royal [*S.C.*] November 11th 1861

Sir In accordance with your instructions I proceeded with a detail of 25 men from the 50th Reg' Penn. on the road towards Braddocks point for about six miles and from thence to Seabrook.

Upon the road I met parties from various Regts with plunder of all descriptions, most of which however consisted of sheep, Pigs and Poultry. Of Co. A. 8" Maine Reg' I herewith transmit names of 8 men viz D. Adams. G. Adams. W. W. Wilkins, N. W. Adams, R. Handly, M. R. Adams, I. R. Adams Serg: E. H. Farnum with one sheep, of 46th N.Y. Reg. under command of 1st Lieut Seldinie Co B. 21 men with a pig and other small articles, also with same party 1st Lt. N. Gangyl of Co. F. with 8 men 8' Maine Co H. H. Rolfe, A. Prescott, Serg: G. Hickerson Corpl E. C. Merriam with a pig. 50th Penn. Co. B. H. Iler, H. Heyneman, G. Egger, I. Heynaman T Taggard, F. B. Fabian, P. H. Herman J. R. Hoffman with one sheep 2d Lieut Patterson 48" N.Y. Co. H. with 3 men with a pig. (I think) New Hampshire 4th Regt. Co I. G. H. Lyman I. Tolman, C. W. Spalding D. J. Wheeler 10 chickens. New York 48th Regt Co G. Private Elmsdorf and two colored Servants 1 pig. At the farm of Squire Wm Pope I found a large number of men from several different regiments shooting poultry, and plundering the negro Houses of everything of any value. I at once gave orders to every man to cease their depredations, and collected them together and placed them under charge of Lieut. M^c^Donald Co. D. 47th Reg^t^ N.Y. with orders to have them report at once to their commanders, and also advised Lt. M^c^D. to place a guard of his own men over a large quantity of corn and cotton which I found upon the place, and to prevent further plundering or Shooting about the farm. He acted upon my advice and is awaiting orders. Lt. M^c^D. reported to me that upon another Farm owned by the same party there was also a large lot of cotton & corn which was under charge of a Capt from same Regiment. I then proceeded to Seabrook and found the Steamer Parkersburg which had loaded all the hard bread and 41 bags Corn which had been taken account of by Capt. Warfield the 10th inst. by the order of Wm Brown Pilot on the Parkersburg. The negroes had been collected near the wharf for the purpose of going on board the St^r^ they had collected as much of their clothing as the time allowed them by W Brown would permit but leaving every thing in confusion. The Lieut in charge of the guard at this place, Hammond had contrary to positive orders given him yesterday when being placed in charge, so soon as the Negroes left their Houses not only allowed his own men to shoot and plunder about the farm but all other Stragglers that came along which I at once protested against and gave orders to himself and men to report to his Commander and placed the guard accompanying myself in charge of the farm and stores. I asked W Brown if he had orders to take the Negroes on board the Steamer and he said he had only verbal orders, and hardly knew who these were from. I advised him to leave them where they were as they had plenty of provisions and plenty of House room. He acted upon my advice and I ordered them back to their Houses and again charged the Lieut in command of the guard to prevent all plundering and to arrest all persons disobeying this order, also to collect any cattle, Horses or Mules he might find at or near the place and put them in proper enclosures. I have no doubt from the appearance of this officer that these orders will be obeyed. I have found all over the Island where I have been, soldiers scattered about, some with arms and others entirely unarmed, all or nearly all, plundering all available property, and shooting ball cartridges to such an extent that it is dangerous to travel about. Balls having repeatedly whizzed over my head to day apparently within a few feet, Although unauthorised to arrest these parties I ordered all to report at once to their Commanders, many of them I am convinced did so; but as I heard shooting in other directions from the course I followed I have no doubt there are now many outside the picket guards. Respectfully Your obed Servant

signed H. S. Tafft.

The Lieut. referred to Hammond belongs to Co. B. Roundhead Reg[t] Penn. Vols.

HLcSr

Lieut. H. S. Tafft to Gen. Isaac I. Stevens, 11 Nov. 1861, enclosed in Brig. Gen. Isaac I. Stevens to Brig. General T. W. Sherman, 11 Nov. 1861, Letters Received, ser. 2254, SC Expeditionary Corps, RG 393 Pt. 2 No. 130 [C-1638]. In the covering letter to General Thomas W. Sherman, commander of the South Carolina Expeditionary Corps, General Isaac I. Stevens, commander of the 2nd brigade, reported that in the two days since Union troops had occupied Hilton Head Island, depredations had "reached an alarming magnitude and threaten the utter demoralization of the troops." The same day, Sherman responded by ordering an end to such "transactions," directing that private property seized by soldiers be turned over to the chief quartermaster of the expeditionary corps, and instructing subordinate officers to "ascertain the names of the perpetrators, that they may be brought to justice." Federal troops, he insisted, must respect "[t]he rights of citizens to be secure in their property." "The first duty of the soldier is the protecton of the citizen. The political character of the citizen is not to be judged and weighed in this manner by the soldier, and there must be by him no molestation of his lawful rights." (*Official Records*, ser. 1, vol. 6, pp. 187–88.)

3: Commander of the South Carolina Expeditionary Corps to a Former Officer in a New York Regiment, and an Order by the Chief Quartermaster of the Expeditionary Corps

Port Royal S.C. Dec[r] 3[d] 1861

– Copy –

Sir, The inhabitants of the deserted Islands having been warned of the destruction of their property by the negroes and invited to return and take charge of their plantations, with a promise of ample protection to all loyal citizens,[1] And such invitation and promise of protection having been set at nought, by their refusal to return, and by several instances of ordering their Cotton to be burned, I deem it proper to take steps for the preservation of as much of this article as practicable, in order that such disposition may be made of it as the Government may direct.

You are therefore appointed an agent of the U.S. Government, to collect, and put into store at the most convenient point occupied by the U.S. Troops such quantities of Cotton as you may find in any part of the State of South Carolina deserted by the inhabitants – A correct and explanatory statement will be made by you weekly to these Head Quarters, Showing, the amount of Cotton stored, its quality, whether baled or unbaled, from whose plantation obtained, and all other information which in your judgment may be necessary to convey a correct idea of its value, and the fixing of its ownership–So that the Government will not be at a loss to dispose of the question of its disposition, or of remuneration to its owners if such questions should arise.

You will employ negroes in picking, Collecting and packing the Cotton, who on your vouchers, properly made out and certified to will be paid by the Quartermaster's Department.

Your services will be Compensated by allowing you 6 per cent on the market value of the Cotton stored as above. Very respectfully &c

HLcSr (Signed) T. W. Sherman

Fort Welles S.C. Dec[r] 6″ 1861

–Copy–

On all the Islands upon which Col Nobles is now collecting Cotton, by authority of the Commanding General, the Cotton, and all the Commissary and Quartermaster's Stores and all other public property captured, must be delivered up to him.

He is directed to take possession of it in the name of the Government, and deliver it to this Department (Signed) By order R. Saxton

HDcSr

Brig'r Genl. T. W. Sherman to W. H. Nobles Esqr., 3 Dec. 1861, and order, Office Chief Quartermaster E.C., 6 Dec. 1861, both enclosed in Brigadier Genl. Isaac I. Stevens to Brigadier General T. W. Sherman, 10 Dec. 1861, Letters Received, ser. 2254, SC Expeditionary Corps, RG 393 Pt. 2 No. 130 [C-1639]. The appointment of William H. Nobles–a civilian–to collect abandoned property raised the ire of General Isaac I. Stevens, commander of the 2nd brigade of the South Carolina Expeditionary Corps, whose headquarters were at Beaufort. On December 10, 1861, when Nobles informed Stevens that, in accordance with General Sherman's and Captain Saxton's orders, he had "taken possession of all the property" on St. Helena, Ladies, and Cat islands, and that his assistant, James A. Suydam, would establish an office at Beaufort, Stevens retorted that he himself would "collect and take charge of" all the "quartermaster and commissary stores" on Ladies Island, although he would not interfere with Nobles's "operations in collecting cotton . . . or the quartermaster or commissary stores you have already collected." Stevens went on to forbid Nobles "to establish an agency at Beaufort, or to interfere in any way with the steps already taken by the commanding general to collect the cotton and the quartermaster and commissary stores on Port Royal Island and its dependencies." (*Official Records*, ser. 1, vol. 6, pp. 200–201.) The same day, Stevens referred to General Sherman copies of his correspondence with Nobles, along with Sherman's letter to Nobles and Saxton's order; his covering letter protested "such orders, as being in derogation of the authority of and the respect due to commanders, as being in opposition to military propriety, and military usage, and as calculated to render the public service inefficient, and to bring it into contempt." Stevens urged Sherman to "admonish [Saxton] to be careful not to give orders, that by inexperienced men in civil life, shall be construed as giving them command and control over General Officers." "I trust," he continued, "that we are not reviving the early experience of the French Revolution, when unscruplous and selfish civillians were given the control of the Armies and Commanders, and when their sirrocco and poisonous breath, blasted the fairest reputations." In an endorsement dated December 11, 1861, on another copy of Saxton's order, Sherman directed Saxton to modify his policy "so as not to prevent Gen[l] Stevens' Qr. Master from collecting means of transportation and subsistence."

1 On November 8, 1861, in a proclamation "To the People of South Carolina," the commander of the South Carolina Expeditionary Corps had stated that the Union army did not wish "to harm your citizens, destroy your property, or interfere with any of your lawful rights or your social and local institutions" (including slavery), but had warned that "rights dependent on the laws of the State must necessarily be subordinate to military exigencies created by insurrection and rebellion." (*Official Records*, ser. 1, vol. 6, pp. 4–5.)

4: Commander of the South Carolina Expeditionary Corps to the Adjutant General of the Army

Port Royal (S.C.) December 15" 1861.

Sir: For the information of the proper authorities, and for fear lest the Government may be disappointed in the amount of labor to be gathered here from the Contrabands I have the honor to report that from the hordes of negroes left on the plantations, but about 320 have thus far come in and offered their services. Of these the Quarter-Master has but about sixty able bodied male hands – the rest being decrepid, and women and children. Several of the 320 have run off. Every inducement has been held out to them to come in and labor for wages, and money distributed among those who have labored. The reasons for this apparent failure thus far appear to be these:

1st They are naturally slothful and indolent, and have always been accustomed to the lash, an aid we do not make use of.

2nd They appear to be so overjoyed with the change of their condition that their minds are unsettled to any plan.

3[d] Their present ease and comfort on the plantations as long as their provisions will last, will induce most of them to remain there untill compelled to seek our lines for subsistence.

Although comparitively few have thus far come in it is therefore probable that in time many will, and if they are to be received and taken care some provision should be made to cover them. They are a prolific race, and it will be found that for every able-bodied male, there will be five to six females, children and decrepid.

It is really a question for the Government to decide what is to be done with the Contrabands. Very Respectfully Your Ob't. Sv't.

T. W. Sherman

P.S. Besides those who have come in there are many still on the plantations employed in gathering cotton. T. W. S

HLS

Brig. Genl. T. W. Sherman to Genl. L. Thomas, 15 Dec. 1861, filed with S-1491 1861, Letters Received, ser. 12, RG 94 [K-126]. Only one day earlier, General Sherman had informed the adjutant general that the "immense" amount of military labor in the Union-occupied Sea Islands was all being "done by volunteer soldiers." "The negro labor expected to be obtained here is so far almost a failure," Sherman had declared. "They are disinclined to labor, and will evidently not work to our satisfaction without those aids to which they have ever been accustomed, viz. the driver and the lash. A sudden change of condition from servitude to apparent freedom is more than their intellects can stand, and this circumstance alone renders it a very serious question what is to be done with the negroes who will hereafter be found on conquered soil." (*Official Records*, ser. 1, vol. 6, pp. 203–4.) No reply to either letter has been found in the volumes of letters sent by the Adjutant General's Office.

5: New Jersey Entrepreneur to the Secretary of the Treasury

"Willards" Hotel [*Washington, D.C.*] Dec. 18. 1861

Sir. I respectfully submit for your consideration, a proposition to open for settlement or colonization, at the earliest practicable period consistent with safety, the country around Port Royal. This region can be profitably occupied in the culture first of the great variety of early fruits vegetables &c: which has been a large business around the cities of Savannah, Charleston and Norfolk, filling the semi-weekly steamers to New York on their return trips during the spring and early summer months. Hundreds of what were known as the "poor whites" in the neighborhood of those places have grown measureably rich thereby. For its influences on the rebels in arms, I suggest this opening, and am satisfied that it is worthy the fostering hand of the Government. Its effect would be to give an opening for this class of men to come out as loyal citizens, either at home or through the lines, for they know that such a settlement would be self sustaining and profitable. The men who would go there would be a hardy industrious race, having no scruples against working with the negroes, whom they would generally employ to assist, and the labor would be of the same character as they had been before employed in. Nor can I but think that its influence would be great on the larger planters, who would look with more dismay on the influx of 500 or a 1000 northern agriculturists and the establishment of a society regularly organized with courts of law &c, than they would on the inroads of an army of a hundred times their number. For the latter could, they know only be maintained there at great cost and their departure would leave the soil to revert, whereas the former is self sustaining, and with a permanency of influence to be by them feared, – at least in their present temper. These men would enter into the cultivation of cotton to a limited extent, and if found profitable for a staple crop, which it would be; they would soon extensively cultivate it. As also any other of the Southern products, which are now cut off from the Northern demand.

The points I suggest will be found as follows. –

1st The establishment of a nucleus for the return of loyal men of the South – if any there are –

2nd The occupation of the Negroes who may come through our lines – in a similar labor to what they have been accustomed to – which I conceive is the great question of the day –

3rd The small risk and expense which the Government would incur in aiding and encouraging it – and for which its beneficial results are fully a recompense –

4th The establishment of a civil government over the negroes by the incomers

4th The great moral influence which would be exerted on the leading men in the rebellion, as inducing them to come to terms, rather than submit to the permanent establishment of such a settlement; on territory claimed by them

In conclusion I remark that this matter is the results of the reflection and consideration of many weeks, and is not a sudden idea, and that if any thing can be done it should be done early before the advent of February. Laws authorizing it would no doubt be requisite, but I do not doubt but that if you should think my suggestions of value, they would be passed at your instance

I have thought the idea of sufficient importance (as have also others) to induce me to come on to Washington to present them, satisfied to so expend my time and money, if I can be of any use to my Country in her emergency

The President to whom I presented these ideas orally expressed himself as desirous that I should have an interview with you and as that was impossible owing to your absence desired me to leave the written communication. I have the honor to be Very respectf[y] your obt serv[t]

ALS Sam[l] H. Terry.

Saml. H. Terry to Hon. S. P. Chase, 18 Dec. 1861, vol. 19, #22, Port Royal Correspondence, 5th Agency, RG 366 [Q-2]. Terry gave his address as "Belleville Essex Co. New Jersey." A penciled notation on the wrapper reads: "file for future reference."

6: Treasury Department Cotton Agent at Port Royal, South Carolina, to the Secretary of the Treasury

FORT WELLES, PORT ROYAL, S.C., Jan 1 1862.

Sir I have just returned from a reconnoissance of St Helena and Ladies Islands, having visited nearly every Plantation on both– I find large quantities of Cotton on these Islands most of which is unginned in the Cribs– I think I shall be able to secure from these two Islands alone more than a million pounds of Cotton after it is Ginned– I find on most of the Plantations corn, and sweet-Potatoes, in sufficient quantities to support the Negroes

I have made arrangements to furnish them with salt molasses & other small stores in moderate quantities deducting the cost of these articles from the amt due them for labor

The plan adopted by Gen[l] Sherman previous to my arrival is, in my opinion the best that can be hit upon for securing *all* the Cotton on the Islands now in our possession, viz the allowing a per centage on the amount collected– In this way we are enabled to secure the services of energetic men, who labor night & day & have thus saved from destruction an immense amount already– *Some* of the military Commandants seem to feel that the saving of Cotton is too small business for them to meddle with, & are very slow to render any assistance or facilities for the carrying out of my instructions– I have reduced the per centage of the collecting agents from six per cent the rate allowed by Genl Sherman to five per cent, which I think is about what it should be– I find it is impossible to hire the negroes by the day, on many of the Plantations, & have authorised my clerks to allow them a dollar for every four hundred pounds of stone cotton[1] which they deliver at the steamboat landing, paying them partly in money & the bal in Clothing & Provisions–

The Negroes seem very well disposed, & quite well pleased with the new order of things here, most of them preferring to remain on the Plantation where they were raised, if they can recieve something for their labor– I would respectfully suggest whether it would not be well to consider the plan of leasing the Plantations in our possession to loyal citazens at a fair rate, under proper restrictions, the Negroes to be paid a fair compensation for their services – In this way another Crop of Cotton might be secured, the negroes properly supported, & profitably employed – The present seems to be a fitting time to try the experiment of producing cotton in one of the oldest slaveholding states with paid labor –

Orders have been issued by Gen[l] Sherman (copies of which I inclose) for the Quartermasters to turn over to me *all* captured property of every description, receipting to me for anything which may be required for the use of the Army As soon as this is done I will forward invoices, & statements of the same – I am very much in need of a Storehouse, & shall be unable to recieve this property, & take proper care of it, until one can be procured

The army have taken among other things many Horses, Mules, Boats; large quantities of Lumber, Corn, Potatoes, &c all of which I will forward statement of as soon as invoices are rec[d] – I found on St Helena Island a German calling himself H. Van Harten who had lived there some eleven years keeping a small store – He said the Planters in his neighborhood owed him about two thousand dollars & he had taken from each Plantation cotton enough to cover the amt due him – I have taken possion of the cotton promising to represent his case to the Department – I think he is a loyal man & his case should be considered, will thank you for instructions in regard to him – I shall ship by the Vanderbilt a quantity of Cotton mostly unginned, will inclose Bills of Lading & invoices before the steamer sails

I hope to hear by the next mail of the appointment of the New York Agent, as I am in want of many things which cannot be furnished here & am consequently compelled to make personal obligations for them I remain very respectfully Your obt Servant

ALS W[m] H Reynolds

Lt. Col. Wm. H. Reynolds to Hon. S. P. Chase, 1 Jan. 1862, vol. 19, #30, Port Royal Correspondence, 5th Agency, RG 366 [Q-3]. On letterhead of the "Head Quarters, U.S. Resident Agent." Reynolds signed as an officer in the 1st Rhode Island Artillery. The orders by General Thomas W. Sherman, commander of the South Carolina Expeditionary Corps, that were said to have been enclosed are not in the volume; for other copies, see General Orders No. 41, Head Quarters E.C., 21 Dec. 1861, and General Orders No. 42, Head Quarters E.C., 24 Dec. 1861, both in vol. 1/3 DS, General Orders, Special Orders, & Circulars, ser. 2256, SC Expeditionary Corps, RG 393 Pt. 2 No. 130 [C-1731].

1 Cotton from which the seed had not yet been removed by ginning.

7: Vermont Investors to the Secretary of the Treasury

Springfield Vt Feb 3d 1862

Sir Yours of the 30 ult was recd at New York. We met Col Reynolds there and had a lengthy conversation with him on the Subject of Employing the persons on the plantations near Port Royal: He fully and emphaticly approved of our Proposition, to Employ them, as he has unduptedly informed you Ere this – according to the promise he made to me at that time, – he did not feel authorised to Execute any perminent arrangement with us in regard to the matter: untill he Should be especialy directed to do so by you: and as he has now Sailed for Port Royal, time will not permit us, to negociate with him further in regard to the matter as it would be to late before an arrangement could be closed With him: for us to plant the crop, – We have our horses plows and supplies to purchase our vessell to charter and the voyage to make before we can begin: all ready time pressess and if we cannot get a decided answer before the 10th inst We shall be compelled, to abandon the Whole project for lack of time and it Will be impossible for any one to Employ them dureing the comeing year after that date: It will be a very disheartning Specticle to the friends of freedom and the union to See Eight thousand persons Entirely under the controll of the government leaft to Starve and Suffer in idleness during the comeing year Simply because the government refused to permitt those abandoned lands to be cultivated – the facts that we Exspect to be able to prove by this Experiment if permitted to go on with the Enterprise, viz, that With New England Skill and Energy to direct, these persons Will grow Cotton 25 per cent cheaper, When Employed as free laborers, at fare Wages than, when compelled to do it as Slaves, – would be worth an untold amount to the cause of Emancipation and human progress – So faforable an opportunety to prove this probably will not occur again for ages, if this one Should be lost. If you do not feel authorised to lease us the lands, we will add the 100,000 dollars that we propose to pay the Govermmment to the Wages of the negroes or hold it Subject to the order of the original Proprietors after this difficulty is Settled, or hold ourselves responsible for what they may be able to recover in an action for trespass after the difficulty is Settled all we ask from the government is thier consent that we may go there and carry on this Enterprise and a promise from them that in case this diffculty is Settled before the crop is picked that they will protect us in our right to gather it. With regard to the Earnestness Skill and Success with which our (Mr Ellis who is the projector and would be the Manger of this Enterprise) has Engaged in the work of furnishing Employment for the destitute poor of New York in past years, the most ample testimony can be obtained from the Rev L. M. Pease. of the Five Points House of Industry N.Y. Geo Kellogg Esq Superintendent of the out door poor of N.Y. and Simeon Draper Esq Presd of the Board of Govoners New York Should you desire it hopeing to receive a decisive answer from you on the Subject by return mail we remain yours Very Respectfully

HLSr Ellis, Britton, & Eaton

Ellis, Britton, & Eaton to Hon. S. P. Chase, 3 Feb. 1862, vol. 19, #46, Port Royal Correspondence, 5th Agency, RG 366 [Q-20]. On January 30, 1862, Secretary of the Treasury Salmon P. Chase had instructed William H. Reynolds, the treasury agent in charge of collecting the 1861 cotton crop at Port Royal, who was then temporarily in New York, to meet with Ellis and report "his views in respect to leasing plantations." (S. P. Chase to Hiram Barney, Esq., 30 Jan. 1862, vol. 1, p. 432, Telegrams Sent: XA Series, ser. 52, RG 56 [X-530].) Reynolds's account of the meeting characterized Ellis's proposal to lease 20,000 acres of Sea Island plantation land as "the most practical, & nearer right than any which have come to my knowledge." "My own opinion," Reynolds continued, "is that the best plan for the Government to adopt at the present time is to lease the lands at a certain sum pr acre, the parties hiring agreeing to employ the Negroes & pay them from ten, to twelve dollars pr month. The Government agent or some officer appointed for the purpose, should represent & decide upon the rights of the Negroes, & protect them from abuses." Noting that the planting season was nearly at hand, Reynolds urged prompt action in selecting an agent to "undertake the management of this business" and placed his own name in nomination. "It is of course very desirable that the Negroes should be properly, & profitbly, employed, & the culture of cotton continued. The only course to be pursued, for securing these objects in my judgement, is, for *some one* to be fully authorised to act on the part of the Government *at once*–" ([William H. Reynolds] to Hon. S. P. Chase, 1 Feb. 1862, vol. 19, #45, Port Royal Correspondence, 5th Agency, RG 366 [Q-5].)

8: Treasury Department Special Agent for the South Carolina Sea Islands to the Secretary of the Treasury

PORT ROYAL [*S.C.*], Feb. 3, 1862.[1]

DEAR SIR: My first communication to you was mailed on the third day after my arrival.[2] The same day, I mailed two letters to benevolent persons in Boston, mentioned in my previous communication to you, asking for contributions of clothing, and for a teacher or missionary to be sent, to be supported by the charity of those interested in the movement, to both of which favorable answers have been received. The same day I commenced a tour of the larger islands, and ever since have been diligently engaged in anxious examinations of the modes of culture – the amount and proportions of the products – the labor required for them – the life and disposition of the laborers upon them – their estimated numbers – the treatment they have received from their former masters, both as to the labor required of them; the provisions and clothing allowed to them, and the discipline imposed – their habits, capacities, and desires with special reference to their being fitted for useful citizenship – and generally whatever concerned the well-being, present and future, of the territory and its people. Visits have also been made to the communities collected at Hilton Head and Beaufort, and conferences held with the authorities both naval and military, and other benevolent persons interested in the welfare of these people, and the wise and speedy reorganization of society here. No one can be impressed more than myself with the uncertainty of conclusions drawn from experiences and reflections gathered in so brief a period, however industriously and wisely occupied. Nevertheless, they may be of some service to those who have not been privileged with an equal opportunity.

Of the plantations visited, full notes have been taken of seventeen, with reference to number of negroes in all; of field hands; amount of cotton and corn raised and how much per acre; time and mode of producing and distributing manure; listing, planting, cultivating, picking and ginning cotton; labor required of each hand; allowance of food and clothing; the capacities of the laborers; their wishes and feelings, both as to themselves and their masters. Many of the above points could be determined by other sources, such as persons at the North familiar with the region, and publications. The inquiries were, however, made with the double purpose of acquiring the information and testing the capacity of the persons inquired of. Some of the leading results of the examination will now be submitted.

An estimate of the number of plantations open to cultivation, and of the persons upon the territory protected by the forces of the United States, if only approximate to the truth, may prove convenient in providing a proper system of administration. The following islands are thus protected, and the estimated number of plantations upon each is given:

Port Royal	65	Morgan	2
Ladies'	30	St. Helena	50
Parry, including Horse	6	Hilton Head	16
Cat	1	Pinckney	5
Cane	1	Bull, including Barratria	2
Dathaw	4	Daufuskie	5
Coosaw	2	Hutchinson and Fenwick	6
			195

Or about two hundred in all.

There are several other islands thus protected without plantations, as Otter, Pritchard, Fripp, Hunting, and Phillips. Lemon and Daw have not been explored by the agents engaged in collecting cotton.

The populous island of North Edisto, lying in the direction of Charleston, and giving the name to the finest cotton, is still visited by the Rebels. A pass near Botany Bay Island is commanded by the guns of one of our war vessels, under which a colony of one thousand negroes sought protection where they have been temporarily subsisted from its stores. The number has within a few days been stated to have increased to 2,300. Among these great destitution is said to prevail. Even to this number, as the negroes acquire confidence in us, large additions are likely every week to be made. The whole island can be safely farmed as soon as troops can be spared for the purpose of occupation. But not counting the plantations of this island, the number on Port Royal, Ladies, St. Helena, Hilton Head, and the smaller islands, may be estimated at 200 plantations.

In visiting the plantations I endeavored to ascertain with substantial accuracy the number of persons upon them, without, however, expecting to determine the precise number. On that of Thomas Aston Coffin, at Coffin Point, St. Helena, there were 260, the largest found on any one visited. There were 130 on that of Dr. J. W. Jenkins, 120 on that of the Eustis estate, and the others range from 80 to 38, making an average of 81 to a plantation. These, however, may be ranked among the best peopled plantations, and forty to each may be considered a fair average. From these estimates a population of 8,000 negroes on the islands, now safely protected by our forces, results.

Of the 600 at the camp at Hilton Head, about one-half should be counted with the aforesaid plantations whence they have come. Of the 600 at Beaufort, one-third should also be reckoned with the plantations. The other fraction in each case should be added to the 8,000 in computing the population now thrown on our protection.

The negroes on Ladies' and St. Helena Islands have quite generally remained on their respective plantations, or if absent, but temporarily, visiting wives or relatives. The dispersion on Port Royal and Hilton Head Islands has been far greater, the people of the former going to Beaufort in considerable numbers, and on the latter to the camp at Hilton Head.

Counting the negroes who have gone to Hilton Head and Beaufort from places now protected by our forces as still attached to the plantations, and to that extent not swelling the 8,000 on plantations, but adding thereto the usual negro population of Beaufort as also the negroes who have fled to both Beaufort and Hilton Head from places not yet occupied by our forces, and adding also the colony at North Edisto, and we must now have thrown upon our hands, for whose present and future we must provide, from 10,000 to 12,000 persons – probably nearer the latter than the former number. This number is rapidly increasing. This week forty-eight escaped from a single plantation near Grahamville, on the main land, held by the Rebels, led by the driver, and after four days of trial and peril, hidden by day and threading the waters with their boats by night, evading the Rebel pickets, joyfully entered our camp at Hilton Head. The accessions at Edisto are in larger number, and according to the most reasonable estimates it would only require small advances by our troops, not involving a general engagement or even loss of life, to double the number which would be brought within our lines.

A fact derived from the Census of 1860 may serve to illustrate the responsibility now devolving on the Government. This County of Beaufort had a population of slaves in proportion of 82 8-10 of the whole, a proportion only exceeded by seven other counties in the United States, viz: one in South Carolina, that of Georgetown; three in Mississippi, those of Bolivar, Washington, and Issequena; and three in Louisiana, those of Madison, Tensas, and Concordia.

An impression prevails that the negroes here have been less cared for than in most other Rebel districts. If this be so, and a beneficent reform shall be achieved here, the experiment may anywhere else be hopefully attempted.

The former white population, so far as can be ascertained, are Rebels, with one or two exceptions. In Jan., 1861, a meeting of the planters on St. Helena Island was held, of which Thomas Aston Coffin was chairman. A vote was passed, stating its exposed condition, and offering their slaves to the Governor of South Carolina, to aid in building earth mounds, and calling on him for guns to place upon them. A copy of the vote, probably in his own handwriting, and signed by Mr. Coffin, was found in his house.

It is worthy of note that the negroes now within our lines are there by the invitation of no one, but they were on the soil when our army began its occupation, and could not have been excluded, except by violent transportation. A small proportion have come in from the main land, evading the pickets of the enemy and our own, something easily done in an extensive country, with whose woods and creeks they are so familiar.

The only exportable crop of this region is the long staple Sea-Island cotton, raised with more difficulty than the coarser kind, and bringing a higher price. The agents of the Treasury Department expect to gather some 2,500,000 pounds of ginned cotton the present year, nearly all of which had been picked and stored before the arrival of our forces. Considerable quantities have not been picked at all, but the crop for this season was unusually good. Potatoes and corn are raised only for consumption on the plantations, the corn being raised at the rate of only twenty five bushels per acre.

Such features in plantation life as will throw light on the social questions now anxiously weighed deserve notice.

In this region the master, if a man of wealth, is more likely to have his main residence at Beaufort, sometimes having none on the plantation, but having one for the driver who is always a negro. He may, however, have one, and an expensive one too, as in the case of Dr. Jenkins, at St. Helena, and yet pass most of his time at Beaufort, or at the North. The plantation in such cases is left almost wholly under the charge of an overseer. In some cases there is not even a house for an overseer, the plantation being superintended by the driver, and being visited by the overseer living on another plantation belonging to the same owner. The houses for overseers are of an undesirable character. Orchards of orange or fig trees usually planted near them.

The field hands are generally quartered at some distance – 80 or 100 rods – from the overseer's or master's house, and are ranged in a row, sometimes in two rows, fronting each other. They are 16 feet by 12, each appropriated to a family, and in some cases divided with a partition. They numbered on the plantations visited from 10 to 20, and on the Coffin plantation they are double, numbering 23 double houses intended for 46 families. The yards seemed to swarm with children, the negroes coupling at an early age.

Except on Sundays, these people do not take their meals at a family table, but each one takes his hominy, bread, or potatoes, sitting on the floor or a bench, and at his own time. They say their masters never allowed them any regular time for meals. Whoever under our new system is charged with their superintendence, should see that they attend more to the cleanliness of their persons and houses, and that, as in families of white people, they take their meals together at a table – habits to which they will be more disposed when they are provided with another change of clothing, and when better food is furnished and a proper hour assigned for meals.

Upon each plantation visited by me, familiar conversations were had with several laborers, more or less, as time permitted – sometimes, inquiries made of them, as they collected in groups, as to what they desired us to do with and for them, with advice as to the course of sobriety and industry which it was for their interest to pursue under the new and strange circumstances in which they were now placed. Inquiries as to plantation economy, the culture of crops, the implements still remaining, the number of persons in all, and of field hands, and the rations issued, were made of the drivers, as they are called, answering as nearly as the two different systems of labor will permit to foremen on farms in the Free States. There is one on each plantation – on the largest one visited, two. They still remained on each visited, and their names were noted. The business of the driver was to superintend the field-hands generally, and see that their tasks were performed fully and properly. He controlled them subject to the master or overseer. He dealt out the rations. Another office belonged to him. He was required by the master or overseer, whenever he saw fit, to inflict corporal punishment upon the laborers, nor was he relieved from this office when the subject of discipline was his wife or children. In the absence of the master and overseer, he succeeded to much of their authority. As indicating his position of consequence, he was privileged with four suits of clothing a year, while only two were allowed to the laborers under him. It is evident, from some of the duties assigned him, that he must have been a person of considerable judgment and knowledge of plantation economy, not differing essentially from that required of the foreman of a farm in the Free States. He may be presumed to have known, in many cases, quite as much about the matters with which he was charged as the owner of the plantation, who often passed but a fractional part of his time upon it.

The driver, notwithstanding the dispersion of other laborers, quite generally remains on the plantation, as already stated. He still holds the keys of the granary, dealing out the rations of food, and with the same sense of responsibility as before. In one case I found him in a controversy with a laborer to whom he was refusing his peck of corn, because of absence with his wife on another plantation when the corn was gathered, it being gathered since the arrival of our army. The laborer protested warmly that he had helped to plant and hoe the corn, and was only absent as charged, because of sickness. The driver appealed to me as the only white man near, and learning from other laborers that the laborer was sick at the time of gathering, I advised the driver to give him his peck of corn, which he did accordingly. The fact is noted as indicating the present relation of the driver to the plantation where he still retains something of his former authority.

This authority, is, however, very essentially diminished. The main reason is, as he will assure you, that he has now no white man to back him. Other reasons may, however, concur. A class of laborers are generally disposed to be jealous of one of their own number promoted to be over them, and accordingly some negroes, evidently moved by this feeling, will tell you that the drivers ought now to work as field hands and some field hands be drivers in their place. The driver has also been required to report delinquencies to the master or overseer, and upon their order to inflict corporal punishment. The laborers will in some cases say that he has been harder than he need to have been, while he will say that he did only what he was forced to do. The complainants who have suffered under the lash may be pardoned for not being sufficiently charitable to him who has unwillingly inflicted it, while on the other hand he has been placed in a dangerous position, where a hard nature, or self-interest, or dislike for the victim, might have tempted him to be more cruel than his position required. The truth, in proportions impossible for us in many cases to fix, may lie with both parties. I am, on the whole, inclined to believe that the past position of the driver and his valuable knowledge, both of the plantations and the laborers, when properly advised and controlled, may be made available in securing the productiveness of the plantations and the good of the laborers. It should be added that in all cases the drivers were found very ready to answer inquiries and communicate all information, and seemed desirous that the work of the season should be commenced.

There are also on the plantations other laborers, more intelligent than the average, such as the carpenter, the plowman, the religious leader, who may be called a preacher, a watchman or a helper, the two latter being recognized officers in the churches of these people, and the helpers being aids to the watchman. These persons, having recognized positions among their fellows, either by virtue of superior knowledge or devotion, when properly approached by us, may be expected to have a beneficial influence on the more ignorant, and help to create that public opinion in favor of good conduct which, among the humblest as among the highest, is most useful. I saw many of very low intellectual development, but hardly any too low to be reached by civilizing influences either coming directly from us or mediately through their brethren. And while I saw some who were sadly degraded, I met also others who were as fine specimens of human nature as one can ever expect to find.

Beside attendance on churches on Sundays, there are evening prayer-meetings on the plantations as often as once or twice a week, occupied with praying, singing, and exhortations. In some cases the leader can read a hymn, having picked up his knowledge clandestinely, either from other negroes or from white children. Of the adults, about one half at least are members of churches, generally the Baptist, although other denominations have communicants among them. In the Baptist Church on St. Helena Island, which I visited on the 22d January, there were a few pews for the proportionally small number of white attendants, and the much larger space devoted to benches for colored people. On one plantation there is a negro chapel, well adapted for the purpose, built by the proprietor, the late Mrs. Eustis, whose memory is cherished by the negroes, and some of whose sons are now loyal citizens of Massachusetts. I have heard among the negroes scarcely any profane swearing – not more than twice – a striking contrast with my experiences among soldiers in the army.

It seemed a part of my duty to attend some of their religious meetings, and learn further about these people what could be derived from such a source. Their exhortations to personal piety were fervent, and, though their language was many times confused, at least to my ear, occasionally an important instruction or a felicitous expression could be recognized. In one case, a preacher of their own, commenting on the text, "Blessed are the meek," exhorted his brethren not to be "stout-minded." On one plantation on Ladies' Island, where some thirty negroes were gathered in the evening, I read passages of Scripture, and pressed on them their practical duties at the present time with reference to the good of themselves, their children, and their people. The passages read were the 1st and 23d Psalms, the 61st chapter of Isaiah, verses 1–4, the Beatitudes in the fifth chapter of Matthew, the fourteenth chapter of John's Gospel, and the fifth chapter of the Epistle of James. In substance I told them that their masters had rebelled against the government, and we had come to put down the Rebellion; that we had now met them, and wanted to do what was best to do for them; that Mr. Lincoln, the President or Great Man at Washington had the whole matter in charge, and was thinking what he could do for them; that the great trouble about doing anything for them was that their masters had always told us, and had made many people believe it, that they were lazy and would not work unless whipped to it; that Mr. Lincoln had sent us down here to see if it was so; that what they did was reported to him or to men who would tell him – that where I came from all were free, both white and black – that we did not sell children or separate man and wife; but all had to work – that if they were to be free, they would have to work and would be shut up or deprived of privileges if they did not – that this was a critical hour with them, and if they did not behave well now and respect our agents and appear willing to work, Mr. Lincoln would give up trying to do anything for them, and they must give up all hope for anything better, and their children and grand children a hundred years hence would be worse off than they had been. I told them they must stick to their plantations and not run about and get scattered, and assured them that what their masters had told them of our intentions to carry them off to Cuba and sell them was a [lie] and their masters knew it to be so, and we wanted them to stay on the plantations and raise cotton, and if they behaved well, they should have wages, small perhaps at first – that they should have better food, and not have their wives and children sold off – that their children should be taught to read and write, for which they might be willing to pay something – that by-and-by they would be as well off as the white people, and we would stand by them against their masters ever coming back to take them. The importance of exerting a good influence on each other, particularly on the younger men, who were rather careless and roving, was urged, as all would suffer in good repute from the bad deeds of a few. At Hilton Head, where I spoke to a meeting of two hundred, and there were facts calling for the counsel, the women were urged to keep away from the bad white men, who would ruin them. Remarks of a like character were made familiarly on the plantations to such groups as gathered about. At the Hilton Head meeting, a good looking man, who had escaped from the southern part of Barnwell District, rose and said, with much feeling, that he and many others should do all they could by good conduct to prove what their masters said against them to be false, and to make Mr. Lincoln think better things of them. After the meeting closed, he desired to know if Mr. Lincoln was coming down here to see them, and he wanted me to give Mr. Lincoln his compliments, with his name, assuring the President that he would do all he could for him. The message was a little amusing, but it testified to the earnestness of the simple-hearted man. He had known Dr. Brisbane, who had been compelled some years since to leave the South because of his sympathy for slaves. The name of Mr. Lincoln was used in addressing them, as more likely to impress them than the abstract idea of Government.

It is important to add that in no case have I attempted to excite them by insurrectionary appeals against their former masters, feeling that such a course might increase the trouble of organizing them into a peaceful and improving system, under a just and healthful temporary discipline; and besides that, it is a dangerous experiment to attempt the improvement of a class of men by appealing to their coarser nature. The better course toward making them our faithful allies, and therefore the constant enemies of the Rebels, seemed to be to place before them the good things to be done for them and their children, and sometimes reading passages of Scripture appropriate to their lot, whithout, however, note or comment, never heard before by them, or heard only when wrested from their just interpretation; such, for instance, as the last chapter of St. James's Epistle, and the Glad Tidings of I[*s*]aiah "I have come to preach deliverance to the captive." Thus treated, and thus educated, they may be hoped to become useful coadjutors and the unconquerable foes of the fugitive Rebels.

There are some vices charged upon these people which deserve examination. Notwithstanding their religious professions, in some cases more emotional than practical, the marriage relation, or what answers for it, is not, in many instances, held very sacred by them. The men, it is said, sometimes leave one wife and take another, something likely to happen in any society where it is permitted or not forbidden by a stern public opinion, and far more likely to happen under laws which do not recognize marriage and dissolve what answers for it by forced separations, dictated by the mere pecuniary interest of others. The women, it is said, are easily persuaded by white men – a facility readily accounted for by the power of the master over them, whose solicitation was equivalent to a command, and against which the husband or father was powerless to protect, and increased also by the degraded condition in which they have been placed where they have been apt to regard what ought to be a disgrace as a compliment when they were approached by a paramour of superior condition and race. Yet often the dishonor is felt, and the woman, on whose several children her master's features are impressed, and through whose veins his blood flows, has sadly confessed it with an instinctive blush. The grounds of this charge, so far as they may exist, will be removed, as much as in communities of our own race, by a system which shall recognize and enforce the marriage relation among them, protect them against the solicitations of white men as much as law can, still more by putting them in relations where they will be inspired with self-respect and a consciousness of their rights, and taught by a pure and plain-spoken Christianity.

In relation to the veracity of these people, so far as my relations with them have extended, they have appeared, as a class, to intend to tell the truth. Their manner, as much as among white men, bore instinctive evidence of this intention. Their answers to inquiries relative to the management of the plantations have a general concurrence. They make no universal charges of cruelty against their masters. They will say in some cases that their own was a very kind one, but another one in the neighborhood was cruel. On St. Helena Island they spoke kindly of "the good William Fripp," as they called him, and of Dr. Clarence Fripp, but they all denounced the cruelty of Alvira Fripp, recounting his inhuman treatment of both men and women. Another concurrence is worthy of note. On the plantations visited, it appeared from the statements of the laborers themselves, that there were on an average about 133 pounds of cotton produced to the acre, and five acres of cotton and corn cultivated to a hand, the culture of potatoes not being noted. An article of *The American Agriculturist*, published in Turner's Cotton Manual, pp. 132, 133, relative to the culture of Sea Island Cotton, on the plantation of John H. Townsend, states that the land is cultivated in the proportion of 7-12ths cotton, 3-12ths corn, and 2-12ths potatoes – in all, less than six acres to a hand – and the average yield of cotton per acre is 135 pounds. I did not take the statistics of the culture of potatoes, but about five acres are planted with them on the smaller plantations, and twenty, or even thirty, on the larger – and the average amount of land to each hand, planted with potatoes, should be added to the five acres of cotton and corn, and thus results not differing substantially are reached in both cases. Thus the standard publications attest the veracity and accuracy of these laborers.

Again, there can be no more delicate and responsible position, involving honesty and skill, than that of pilot. For this purpose these people are every day employed to aid our military and naval operations in navigating these sinuous channels. They were used in the recent reconnoissance in the direction of Savannah, and the success of the affair at Port Royal Ferry depended on the fidelity of a pilot, William, without the aid of whom or one like him, it could not have been undertaken. Further information on this point may be obtained of the proper authorities here.

These services are not, it is true, in all respects, illustrative of the quality of veracity, but they involve kindred virtues not likely to exist without it. It is proper, however, to state that expressions are sometimes heard from persons who have not considered these people thoughtfully, to the effect that their word is not to be trusted, and these persons nevertheless do trust them, and act upon their statements. There may, however, be some color for such expressions. These laborers, like all ignorant people, have an ill-regulated reason, too much under the control of the imagination. Therefore, where they report the numbers of soldiers, or relate facts where there is room for conjecture, they are likely to be extravagant, and you must scrutinize their reports. Still, except among the thoroughly dishonest – no more numerous among them than in other races – there will be found a colorable basis for their statements, enough to show their honest intention to speak truly.

It is true also that you will find them too willing to express feelings which will please you. This is most natural. All races, as well as all animals, have their appropriate means of self-defense, and where the power to use physical force to defend one's self is taken away, the weaker animal, or man, or race, resorts to cunning and duplicity. Whatever habits of this kind may appear in these people are directly traceable to the well-known features of their past condition, without involving any essential proneness to deception in the race, further than may be ascribed to human nature. Upon this point, special inquiries have been made of the Superintendent at Hilton Head, who is brought in direct daily association with them, and whose testimony, truthful as he is, is worth far more than that of those who have had less nice opportunities of observation, and Mr. Lee certifies to the results here presented. Upon the question of the disposition of these people to work, there are different reports, varied somewhat by the impression an idle or an industrious laborer, brought into immediate relation with the witness may have made on the mind. In conversations with them, they have uniformly answered to assurances that if free they must work, "Yes, Massa, we must work to live; that's the law;" and expressing an anxiety that the work of the plantations was not going on. At Hilton Head they are ready to do for Mr. Lee, the judicious superintendent, whatever is desired. Hard words and epithets are, however, of no use in managing them, and other parties for whose service they are specially detailed, who do not understand or treat them properly, find some trouble in making their labor available, as might naturally be expected. In collecting cotton, it is sometimes, as I am told, difficult to get them together, when wanted for work. There may be something in this, particularly among the young men. I have observed them a good deal, and though they often do not work to much advantage, a dozen doing sometimes what one or two stout and well-trained Northern laborers would do, and though less must always be expected of persons native to this soil than of those bred in Northern latitudes and under more bracing air, I have not been at all impressed with their general indolence. As servants, oarsmen, and carpenters, I have seen them working faithfully and with a will. There are some peculiar circumstances in their condition, which no one who assumes to sit in judgment upon them must overlook. They are now for the first time freed from the restraint of a master, and like children whose guardian or teacher is absent for the day, they may quite naturally enjoy an interval of idleness. No system of labor for them, outside the camps, has been begun, and they have had nothing to do except to bale the cotton when bagging was furnished, and we all know that men partially employed are if anything less disposed to do the litte assigned them than they are to perform the full measure which belongs to them in regular life, the virtue in the latter case being supported by habit. At the camps they are away from their accustomed places of labor, and have not been so promptly paid as could be desired, and are exposed to the same circumstances which often dispose soldiers to make as little exertion as possible. In the general chaos which prevails, and before the inspirations of labor have been set before them by proper superintendents and teachers who understand their disposition, and show by their conduct an interest in their welfare, no humane or reasonable man would subject them to austere criticism, or make the race responsible for the delinquencies of an idle person who happened to be brought particularly under his own observation. Not thus would we have ourselves or our own race judged, and the judgment which we would not have meted to us, let us not measure to others.

Upon the best examination of these people, and a comparison of the evidence of trustworthy persons, I believe that when properly organized, and with proper motives set before them, they will as freemen be as industrious as any race of men are likely to be in this climate.

The notions of the sacredness of property as held by these people have sometimes been the subject of discussion here. It is reported they have taken things left in their masters' houses. It was wise to prevent this, and even where it had been done to compel a restoration, at least of expensive articles, lest they should be injured by speedily acquiring without purchase articles above their condition. But a moment's reflection will show that it was the most natural thing for them to do. They had been occupants of the estates; had had these things more or less in charge, and when the former owners had left it was easy for them to regard their title to the abandoned property as better than that of strangers. Still it is not true that they have, except as to very simple articles, as soap or dishes, generally availed themselves of such property. It is also stated that in camps where they have been destitute of clothing, they have stolen from each other, but the Superintendents are of opinion that they would not have done this if already well provided. Besides, those familiar with large bodies collected together, like soldiers in camp life, know how often these charges of mutual pilfering are made among them, often with great injustice. It should be added, to complete the statement, that the agents who have been intrusted with the collection of cotton have reposed confidence in the trustworthiness of the laborers, committing property to their charge – a confidence not found to have been misplaced.

To what extent these laborers desire to be free, and to serve us still further in putting down the rebellion, has been a subject of examination. The desire to be free has been strongly expressed, particularly among the more intelligent and adventurous. Every day almost adds a fresh tale of escapes, both solitary and in numbers, conducted with a courage, a forecast, and a skill, worthy of heroes. But there are other apparent features in their disposition which it would be untruthful to conceal. On the plantations, I often found a disposition to evade the inquiry whether they wished to be free or slave, and though a preference for freedom was expressed, it was rarely in the passionate phrases which would come from an Italian peasant. The secluded and monotonous life of a plantation with strict discipline and ignorance enforced by law and custom, is not favorable to the development of the richer sentiments, though even there they find at least a stunted growth, irrepressible as they are. The inquiry was often answered in this way: "The white man do what he please with us." "We are yours now, Massa" One, if I understood his broken words rightly, said that he did not care about being free if he only had a good master. Others said they would like to be free, but they wanted a white man for a "protector." All of proper age, when inquired of, expressed a desire to have their children taught to read and write, and to learn themselves. On this point they showed more earnestness than on any other. When asked if they were willing to fight in case we needed them to keep their masters from coming back, they would seem to shrink from that, saying that "black men have been kept down so like dogs that they would run before white men." At the close of the first week's observation, I almost concluded that on the plantations there was but little earnest desire for freedom, and scarcely any willingness for its sake to encounter white men. But as showing the importance of not attempting to reach general conclusions too hastily, another class of facts came to my notice the second week. I met then some more intelligent, who spoke with profound earnestness of their desire to be free, and how they had longed to see this day. Other facts connected with the military and naval operations were noted. At the recent reconnoissance toward Pulaski, pilots of this class stood well under the fire, and were not reluctant to the service. When a district of Ladies' Island was left exposed, they voluntarily took such guns as they could procure, and stood sentries. Also at North Edisto, where the colony is collected under the protection of our gunboats, they armed themselves and drove back the Rebel cavalry. An officer here high in command reported to me some of these facts, which had been officially communicated to him. The suggestion may be pertinent that the persons in question are divisible into two classes. Those who, by their occupation, have been accustomed to independent labor, and schooled in some sort of self-reliance, are more developed in this direction; while others, who have been bound to the routine of plantation life, and kept more strictly under surveillance, are but little awakened. But even among these last there has been, under the quickening inspiration of present events, a rapid development, indicating that the same feeling is only latent.

There is another consideration which must not be omitted. Many of these people have still but little confidence in us, anxiously looking to see what is to be our disposition of them. It is a mistake to suppose that, separated from the world, never having read a Northern book or newspaper relative to them, or talked with a

Northern man expressing the sentiments prevalent in his region, they are universally and with entire confidence welcoming us as their deliverers. Here, as everywhere else where our army has met them, they have been assured by their masters that we were going to carry them off to Cuba. There is probably not a Rebel master, from the Potomac to the Gulf, who has not repeatedly made this assurance to his slaves. No matter what his religious vows may have been, no matter what his professed honor as a gentleman, he has not shrunk from the reiteration of this falsehood. Never was there a people, as all who know them will testify, more attached to familiar places than they. Be their home a cabin, and not even that cabin their own, they still cling to it. The reiteration could not fail to have had some effect on a point on which they were so sensitive. Often it must have been met with unbelief or great suspicion of its truth. It was also balanced by the consideration that their masters would remove them into the interior, and perhaps to a remote region, and separate their families, about as bad as being taken to Cuba, and they felt more inclined to remain on the plantations, and take their chances with us. They have told me that they reasoned in this way. But in many cases they fled at the approach of our army. Then one or two bolder returning, the rest were reassured and came back. Recently, the laborers at Parry Island, seeing some schooners approaching suspiciously, commenced gathering their little effects rapidly together, and were about to run, when they were quieted by some of our teachers coming, in whom they had confidence. In some cases their distrust has been increased by the bad conduct of some irresponsible white men, of which, for the honor of human nature, it is not best to speak more particularly. On the whole, their confidence in us has been greatly increased by the treatment they have received, which in spite of many individual cases of injury less likely to occur under the stringent orders recently issued from the naval and military authorities,[3] has been generally kind and humane. But the distrust which to a greater or less extent may have existed on our arrival, renders necessary if we would keep them faithful allies, and not informers to the enemy – the immediate adoption of a system which shall be a pledge of our protection and of our permanent interest in their welfare.

The manner of the laborers toward us has been kind and deferential, doing for us such good offices as were in their power, as guides, pilots, or in more personal service, inviting us on the plantations to lunch of hominy, and milk, or potatoes, touching the hat in courtesy, and answering politely such questions as were addressed to them. If there have been exceptions to this rule, it was in the case of those whose bearing did not entitle them to the civility.

Passing from general phases of character or present disposition, the leading facts in relation to the plantations and the mode of rendering them useful and determining what is best to be done, come next in order.

The laborers on St. Helena and Ladies' Islands very generally remain on their respective plantations. This fact, arising partially from local attachments and partially because they can thus secure their allowance of corn, is important, as it will facilitate their reorganization. Some are absent temporarily visiting a wife, or relative, on another plantation, and returning periodically for their rations. The disposition to roam, so far as it exists, mainly belongs to the younger people. On Port Royal and Hilton Head Islands, there is a much greater dispersion, due in part to their having been the scene of more active military movements, and in part to the taking in greater measure on these islands of the means of subsistence from the planations. When the work recommences, however, there is not likely to be any indisposition to return to them.

The statistics with regard to the number of laborers, field hands, acres planted to cotton and corn, are not presented as accurate statements, but only as reasonable approximations, which may be of service.

The highest number of people on any plantations visited was on Coffin's, where there are 260. Those on the plantation of Dr. Jenkins number 130, on that of the Eustis estate 120, and the others from 80 to 38. The average number on each is 81. The field hands range generally from one-third to one-half of the number, the rest being house servants, old persons, and children. About five acres of cotton and corn are planted to a hand, and of potatoes about five acres in all were devoted on the smaller plantations, and from twenty to thirty on the larger.

The number of pounds in a bale of ginned cotton ranges from 300 to 400 – the average number being not far from 345 pounds per bale. The average yield per acre on fifteen plantations was about 133 pounds.

The material for compost is gathered in the periods of most leisure, often in July and August after the cultivation of the cotton plant is ended, and before the picking has commenced. Various materials are used, but quite generally mud and the coarse marsh grass which abounds on the creeks near the plantations, are employed. The manure is carted upon the land in January and February, and left in heaps, two or three cart-loads on each task, to be spread at the time of listing. The land, by prevailing custom, lies fallow a year. The cotton and corn are planted in elevated rows or beds. The next step is the listing, done with the hoe, and making the bed where the alleys were at at the previous raising of the crop, and the alleys being made where the beds were before. In this process half the old bed is hauled into the alley on the one side and the other half into the alley on the other. This work is done mainly in February, being commenced sometimes the last of January. A "task" is 105 feet square, and contains twenty-one or twenty-two beds or rows. Each laborer is required to list a task and a half, or if the land is moist and heavy, a task and five or seven beds, say one-fourth or three-eighths of an acre.

The planting of cotton commences about the 20th or last of March, and of corn about the same time or earlier. It is continued through April, and by some planters it is not begun till April. The seeds are deposited in the beds, a foot or a foot and a half apart on light land, and two feet apart on heavy land, and five or ten seeds left in a place. After the plant is growing, the stalks are thinned so as to leave together two on high land and one on low or rich land. The hoeing of the early cotton begins about the time that the planting of the late has ended. The plant is cultivated with the hoe and plow during May, June, and July, keeping the weeds down and thinning the stalks. The picking commences the last of August. The cotton being properly dried in the sun, is then stored in houses, ready to be ginned. The ginning, or clearing the fiber from the seed, is done either by gins operated by steam, or by the well-known foot gins, the latter turning out about 30 pounds of ginned cotton per day, and worked by one person, assisted by another, who picks out the specked and yellow cotton. The steam-engine carries one or more gins, each turning out 300 pounds per day, and requiring eight or ten hands to tend the engine and gins, more or less, according to the number of the gins. The foot gins are still more used than the gins operated by steam, the latter being used mainly on the largest plantations, on which both kinds are sometimes employed. I have preserved notes of the kind and number of gins used on the plantations visited, but it is unnecessary to give them here. Both kinds can be run entirely by the laborers, and after this year the ginning should be done entirely here – among other reasons, to avoid transportation of the seed, which makes nearly three-fourths of the weight of the unginned cotton, and to preserve in better condition the seed required for planting.

The allowance of clothing to the field hands in this district has been two suits per year, one for Summer and another for Winter. That of food has been mainly vegetable – a peck of corn a week to each hand, with meat only in June, when the work is hardest, and at Christmas. No meat was allowed in June on some plantations, while on a few, more liberal, it was a dealt out occasionally – as once a fortnight; or once a month. On a few, molesses was given at intervals. Children, varying with their ages, were allowed from two to six quarts of corn per week. The diet is more exclusively vegetable here than almost anywhere in the rebellious regions, and in this respect should be changed. It should be added that there are a large quantity of oysters available for food in proper seasons.

Beside the above rations, the laborers were allowed each to cultivate a small patch of ground, about a quarter of an acre, for themselves, when their work for their master was done. On this corn and potatoes, chiefly the former, were planted. The corn was partly eaten by themselves, thus supplying in part the deficiency in rations; but it was to a great extent fed to a pig, or chickens, each hand being allowed to keep a pig and chickens or ducks, but not geese or turkeys. With the proceeds of the pig and chickens, generally sold to the masters, and at pretty low rates, extra clothing, coffee, sugar, and that necessary of life with these people, as they think, tobacco, were bought.

In the report thus far such facts in the condition of the territory now occupied by the forces of the United States, have been noted as seemed to throw light on what could be done to reorganize the laborers, prepare them to become sober and self-supporting citizens, and secure the successful culture of a cotton-crop, now so necessary to be contributed to the markets of the world. It will appear from them that these people are naturally religious and simple-hearted – attached to the places where they have lived, still adhering to them both from a feeling of local attachment and self-interest in securing the means of subsistence – that they have the knowledge and experience requisite to do all the labor from the preparation of the ground for planting until the cotton is baled, ready to be exported; that they, or the great mass of them are disposed to labor with proper inducements thereto – that they lean upon white men and desire their protection, and could, therefore, under a wise system, be easily brought under subordination – that they are susceptible to the higher considerations, as duty, and the love of offspring, and are not in any way inherently vicious, their defects coming from their peculiar condition in the past or present, and not from constitutional proneness to evil beyond what may be attributed to human nature – that they have among them natural chiefs, either by virtue of religious leadership or superior intelligence, who, being first addressed, may exert a healthful influence on the rest; in a word, that, in spite of their condition, reputed to be worse here than in many other parts of the rebellious region, there are such features in their life and character, that the opportunity is now offered to us to make of them, partially in this generation, and fully in the next, a happy, industrious, law-abiding, free and Christian people, if we have but the courage and patience to accept it. If this be the better view of them and their possibilites, I will say that I have come to it after anxious study of all peculiar circumstances in their lot and character, and after anxious conference with reflecting minds here, who are prosecuting like inquiries, not overlooking what, to a casual spectator, might appear otherwise, and granting what is likely enough, that there are those among them whose characters by reason of bad nature or treatment, are set, and not admitting of much improvement – and I will submit further, that in common fairness and common charity, when by the order of Providence, an individual or a race is committed to our care, the better view is entitled to be first practically applied. If this one shall be accepted and crowned with success, history will have the glad privilege of recording that this wicked and unprovoked rebellion was not without compensations most welcome to our race.

What, then, should be the true system of administration here?

It has been proposed to lease the plantation[s] and the people upon them. To this plan there are two objections – each conclusive. In the first place, the leading object of the parties bidding for leases would be to obtain a large immediate revenue – perhaps make a fortune in a year or two. The solicitations of doubtful men offering the highest price, would impose on the leasing power a stern duty of refusal, to which it ought not unnecessarily to be subjected. Far better a system which shall not invite such men to harass the leasing power or excite expectations of a speedy fortune, to be derived from the labor of this people. Secondly. No man, not even the best of men, charged with the duties which ought to belong to the guardians of these people, should be put in a position where there would be such a conflict between his humanity and his self-interest – his desire, on the one hand, to benefit the laborer, and on the other, the too often stronger desire to reap a large revenue, perhaps to restore broken fortunes in a year or two. Such a system is beset with many of the worst vices of the slave system with one advantage in favor of the latter, that it is for the interest of the planter to look to permanent results. Let the History of British East India, and of all communities where a superior race has attempted to build up speedy fortunes on the labor of an inferior race occupying another region be remembered, and no just man will listen to the proposition of leasing, fraught as it is with such dangerous consequences. Personal confidence forbids me to report the language of intense indignation which has been expressed against it here by some occupying high places of command, as also by others who have come here for the special purpose of promoting the welfare of these laborers. Perhaps it might yield to the Treasury a larger immediate revenue, but it would be sure to spoil the country and its people in the end. The Government should be satisfied if the products of the territory may be made sufficient for a year or two to pay the expenses of administration and superintendence, and the inauguration of a beneficent system which will settle a great social question, insure the sympathies of foreign nations now wielded against us, and advance the civilization of the age.

The better course would be to appoint superintendents for each large plantation, and one for two or three smaller combined, compensated with a good salary, say $1,000 per year, selected with reference to peculiar qualifications, and as carefully as one would chose a guardian for his children, clothed with adequate power to enforce a paternal discipline, to require a proper amount of labor, cleanliness, sobriety, and better habits of life, and generally to promote the moral and intellectual culture of the wards, with such other inducements, if there be any, placed before the superintendent as shall inspire him to constant efforts to prepare them for useful and worthy citizenship. To quicken and ensure the fidelity of the superintendents, there should be a director-general or governor, who shall visit the plantations, and see that they are discharging these duties, and, if necessary, he should be aided by others in the duty of visitation. This officer should be invested with liberal powers over all persons within his jurisdiction, so as to protect the blacks from each other and from white men, being required in most important cases to confer with the military authorities in punishing offenses. His proposed duties indicate that he should be a man of the best ability and character, better if he have already by virtue of public services a hold on the public confidence. Such an arrangement is submitted as preferable for the present to any cumbersome territorial government.

The laborers themselves, no longer slaves of their former masters, or of the Government, but as yet in large numbers unprepared for the full privileges of citizens, are to be treated with sole reference to such preparation. No effort is to be spared to work upon their better nature and the motives which come from it – the love of wages, of offspring, and family, the desire of happiness, and the obligations of religion. And when these fail, and fail they will in some cases, we must not hesitate to resort, not to the lash, for as from the department of war so also from the department of labor, it must be banished,[4] but to the milder and more effective punishments of deprivation of privileges, isolation from family and society, the workhouse or even the prison. The laborers are to be assured at the outset that parental and conjugal relations among them are to be protected and enforced; that children and all others desiring are to be taught; that they will receive wages; and that a certain just measure of work, with reference to the ability to perform it, if not willingly rendered, is to be required of all. The work, so far as the case admits, shall be assigned in proper tasks, the standard being what a healthy person of average capacity can do, for which a definite sum is to be paid. The remark may perhaps be pertinent, that, whatever may have been the case with women or partially disabled persons, my observations not yet sufficient to decide the point, have not impressed me with the conviction that healthy persons if they had been provided with an adequate amount of food, and that animal in due proportion, could be said to have been overworked heretofore on these islands, the main trouble having been that they have not been so provided, and have not had the motives which smooth labor. Notwithstanding the frequent and severe chastisements which have been employed here in exacting labor, they have failed, and naturally enough of their intended effects. Human beings are made up so much more of spirit than of muscle, that compulsory labor, enforced by physical pain, will not exceed or equal in the long run voluntary labor with just inspirations; and the same law in less degree may be seen in the difference between the value of a whipped and jaded beast, and one well disciplined and kindly treated.

What should be the standard of wages where none have heretofore been paid, is less easy to determine. It should be graduated with reference to the wants of the laborer and the ability of the employer or Government; and this ability being determined by the value of the products of the labor, and the most that should be expected being that, for a year or two the system should not be a burden on the Treasury. Taking into consideration the cost of food and clothing, medical attendance and extras, supposing that the laborer would require rations of pork or beef, meal, coffee, sugar, molasses and tobacco, and that he would work 300 days in the year, he should receive about 40 cents a day in order to enable him to lay up $30 a year, and each healthy woman could do about equally well. Three hundred days in a year is, perhaps, too high an estimate of working days, when we consider the chances of sickness and days when by reason of storms and other causes there would be no work. It is assumed that the laborer is not to pay rent for the small house tenanted by him. This sum, when the average number of acres cultivated by a hand, and the average yield per acre are considered with reference to market prices, or when the expense of each laborer to his former master, the interest on his assumed value and on the value of the land worked by him, these being the elements of what it has cost the master before making a profit, are computed, the Government could afford to pay, leaving an ample margin to meet the cost of the necessary implements, as well as of superintendence and administration. The figures on which this estimate is based are at the service of the Department if desired. It must also be borne in mind that the plantations will in the end be carried on more scientifically and cheaply than before, the plow taking very much the place of the hoe, and other implements being introduced to facilitate industry and increase the productive power of the soil.

It being important to preserve all former habits which are not objectionable, the laborer should have his patch of ground on which to raise corn or vegetables for consumption or sale.

As a part of the plan proposed, missionaries will be needed to address the religious element of a race so emotional in their nature, exhorting to all practical virtues, and inspiring the laborers with a religious zeal for faithful labor, the good nurture of their children, and for clean and healthful habits. The benevolence of the Free States, now being directed hither, will gladly provide these. The Government should, however, provide some teachers specially devoted to teaching reading, writing, and arithmetic, say some twenty-five, for the territory now occupied by our forces, and private benevolence might even be relied on for these.

The plan proposed is, of course, not presented as an ultimate result, far from it. It contemplates a paternal discipline for the time being, intended for present use only with the prospect of better things in the future. As fast as the laborers show themselves fitted for all the privileges of citizens, they should be dismissed from the system and allowed to follow any employment they please and where they please. They should have the power to acquire the fee simple of land, either with the proceeds of their labor or as a reward of special merit; and it would be well to quicken their zeal for good behavior by proper recognitions. I shall not follow these suggestions as to the future further, contenting myself with indicating what is best to be done at once with a class of fellow-beings now thrown on our protection, entitled to be recognized as freemen, but for whose new condition the former occupants of the territory have diligently labored to unfit them.

But whatever is thought best to be done, should be done at once. A system ought to have been commenced with the opening of the year. Beside that demoralization increases with delay, the months of January and February are the months for preparing the ground by manuring and listing, and the months of March and April are for planting. Already important time has passed, and in a very few weeks it will be too late to prepare for a crop, and too late to assign useful work to the laborers for a year to come. I implore the immediate intervention of your Department to avert the calamities which must ensue from a further postponement.

There is another precaution most necessary to be taken. As much as possible, persons enlisted in the army and navy should be kept separate from these people. The association produces an unhealthy excitement in the latter, and there are other injurious results to both parties which it is unnecessary to particularize. In relation to this matter, I had an interview with the Flag Officer, Com. Dupont, which resulted in an order that "no boats from any of the ships of the squadron can be permitted to land anywhere but at Bay Point and Hilton Head, without a pass from the Fleet Captain," and requiring the commanding officers of the vessels to give special attention to all intercourse between the men under their command and the various plantations in their vicinity. Whatever can be accomplished to that end by this humane and gallant officer, who superadds to skill and courage in his profession the liberal views of a statesman, will not be left undone. The suggestion should also be made that when employment is given to this people, some means should be taken to enable them to obtain suitable goods at fair rates, and precautions taken to prevent the introduction of ardent spirits among them.

A loyal citizen of Massachusetts, Mr. Frederick A. Eustis has recently arrived here. He is the devisee in a considerable amount under the will of the late Mrs. Eustis, who owned the large estate on Ladies Island, and also another at Pocotaligo, the latter not yet in possession of our forces. The executors are Rebels, and reside at Charleston. Mr. Eustis has as yet received no funds by reason of the devise. There are two other loyal devisees, and some other devisees resident in rebellious districts, and the latter are understood to have received dividends. Mr. Eustis is a gentleman of humane and liberal views, and accepting the present condition of things, desires that the people on these plantations should not be distinguished from their brethren on others, but equally admitted to their better fortunes. The circumstances of this case, though of a personal character, may furnish a useful precedent. With great pleasure and confidence, I recommend that this loyal citizen be placed in charge of the plantation on Ladies' Island, which he is willing to accept – the questions of property and rights under the will being reserved for subsequent determination.

A brief statement in relation to the laborers collected at the camps at Hilton Head and Beaufort, may be desirable. At both places they are under the charge of the Quartermaster's Department. At Hilton Head, Mr. Barnard K. Lee, jr., of Boston, is the Superintendent, assisted by Mr. J. D. McMath of Alleghany

City, Penn., both civilians. The appointment of Mr. Lee is derived from Capt. R. Saxton, Chief Quartermaster of the Expeditionary Corps, a humane officer, who is deeply interested in this matter. The number at this camp are about 600, the registered number under Mr. Lee being 472, of which 137 are on the pay-roll. Of these 472, 279 are fugitives from the main land, or other points, still held by the Rebels; 77 are from Hilton Head Island; 62 from the adjacent island of Pinckney; 38 from St. Helena; 8 from Port Royal; 7 from Spring; and one from Daufuskie. Of the 472, the much larger number, it will be seen, have sought refuge from the places now held by rebels; while the greater proportion of the remainder came in at an early period, before they considered themselves safe elsewhere. Since the above figures were given, forty-eight more, all from one plantation, and under the lead of the driver, came in together from the main land. Mr. Lee was appointed Nov. 10th last, with instructions to assure the laborers that they would be paid a reasonable sum for their services, not yet fixed. They were contented with the assurance, and a quantity of blankets and clothing captured of the rebels was issued to them without charge. About Dec. 1, an order was given that carpenters should be paid $8 per month, and other laborers $5 per month. Women and children were fed without charge, the women obtaining washing and receiving the pay, in some cases in considerable sums, not, however, heretofore, very available, as there was no clothing for women for sale here. It will be seen that, under the order, laborers, particularly those with families, have been paid with sufficient liberality. There were 63 laborers on the pay-roll on Dec. 1, and $101.50 were paid to them for the preceding month. On Jan. 1, there were for the preceding month 127 on the pay roll, entitled to $468.59. On Feb. 1, there were for the preceding month 137 on the pay roll, entitled to something more than for the month of January; making in all due them not far from $1,000. This delay of payment, due, it is stated, to a deficiency of small currency, has made the laborers uneasy, and affected the disposition to work.

On Jan. 18, a formal order was issued by Gen. Sherman, regulating the rate of wages, varying from $12 to $8 per month for mechanics, and from $8 to $4 for other laborers.[5] Under it, each laborer is to have, in addition, a ration of food. But from the monthly pay are to be deducted rations for his family, if here, and clothing both for himself and family. Commodious barracks have been erected for these people, and a guard protects their quarters.

I have been greatly impressed by the kindness and good sense of Mr. Lee and his assistant, in their discipline of these people. The lash, let us give thanks, is banished at last. No coarse words or profanity are used toward them. There has been less than a case of discipline a week, and the delinquent, if a male, is sometimes made to stand on a barrel, or, if a woman, is put in a dark room, and such discipline has proved successful. The only exception, if any, is in the case of one woman, and the difficulty there was conjugal jealousy, she protesting that she was compelled by her master, against her will, to live with the man.

There is scarcely any profanity among them, more than one half of the adults being members of churches. Their meetings are held twice or three times on Sundays, also on the evenings of Tuesday, Thursday, and Friday. They are conducted with fervent devotion by themselves alone or in presence of a white clergyman when the services of one are procurable. They close with what is called "a glory shout," one joining hands with another, together in couples singing a verse and beating time with the foot. A fastidious religionist might object to this exercise, but being in accordance with usage, and innocent enough in itself, it is not open to exception. As an evidence of the effects of the new system in inspiring self-reliance, it should be noted that the other evening they called a meeting on their own accord, and voted, the motion being regularly made and put, that it was now but just that they should provide the candles for their meetings, hitherto provided by the Government. A collection was taken at a subsequent meeting, and $2 48 was the result. The incident may be trivial, but it justifies a pleasing inference. No school, it is to be regretted, has yet been started, except one on Sundays, but the call for reading books is daily made by the laborers. The suggestion of Mr. Lee, in which I most heartily concur, should not be omitted – that with the commencement of the work on the plantations, the laborers should be distributed upon them, having regard to the family relations and the places whence they came.

Of the number and condition of the laborers at Beaufort, less accurate information was attainable, and fewer statistics than could be desired. They have not, till within a few days, had a General Superintendent, but have been under the charge of persons detailed for the purpose from the army. I saw one whose manner and language toward them was, to say the least, not elevating. A new Quartermaster of the post has recently commenced his duties, and a better order of things is expected. He has appointed as Superintendent Mr. William Harding, a citizen of Dawfuskie Island. An enrollment has commenced, but is not yet finished. There are supposed to be about six hundred at Beaufort. The number has been larger, but some have already returned to the plantations in our possession from which they came. At this point the Rev. William Peck of Roxbury, Mass., has done great good in preaching to them and protecting them from the depredations of white men. He has established a school for the children, in which are sixty pupils, ranging in age from six to fifteen years. They are rapidly learning their letters and simple reading. The teachers are of the same race with the taught, of ages respectively of twenty, thirty, and fifty years. The name of one is John Milton. A visit to the school leaves a remarkable impression. One sees there those of pure African blood, and others ranging through the lighter shades, and among them brunettes of the fairest features. I taught several of the children their letters for an hour or two, and during the recess heard the three teachers, at their own request, recite their spelling-lessons of words of one syllable, and read two chapters of Matthew. It seemed to be a morning well spent. Nor have the efforts of Mr. Peck been confined to this point. He has preached at Cat, Cane and Ladies' Islands, anticipating all other white clergymen, and on Sunday, Feb. 2, at the Baptist Church on St. Helena, to a large congregation, where his ministrations have been attended with excellent effects. On my visits to St. Helena I found that no white clergyman had been there since our military occupation began, that the laborers were waiting for one, and there was a demoralization at some points which timely words might arrest. I may be permitted to state that it was at my own suggestion that he made the appointment on this island. I cannot forbear to give a moment's testimony to the nobility of character displayed by this venerable man. Of mild and genial temperament, equally earnest and sensible, enjoying the fruits of culture, and yet not dissuaded by them from the humblest toil, having reached an age when most others would have declined the duty and left it to be discharged by younger men; of narrow means, and yet in the main defraying his own expenses, this man of apostolic faith and life, to whose labors both hemispheres bear witness, left his home to guide and comfort this poor and shepherdless flock; and to him belongs and ever will belong the distinguished honor of being the first minister of Christ to enter the field which our arms had opened.

The Rev. Mansfield French, whose mission was authenticated and approved by the Government, prompted by benevolent purposes of his own, and in conference with others in the City of New-York, has been here two weeks, during which time he has been industriously occupied in examining the state of the islands and their population, in conferring with the authorities, and laying the foundation of beneficent appliances with reference to their moral, educational, and material wants. These having received the sanction of officers in command, he now returns to commend to the public, and the Government will derive important information from his report.[6] Beside other things, he proposes, with the approval of the authorities here, to secure authority to introduce women of suitable experience and purposes, who shall give industrial instruction to those of their own sex among these people, and who, visiting from dwelling to dwelling, shall strive to improve their household life, and give such counsels as women can best communicate to women. All civilizing influences like these should be welcomed here, and it cannot be doubted that many noble hearts among the women of the land will volunteer for the service.

There are some material wants of this territory requiring immediate attention. The means of subsistence have been pretty well preserved on the plantations on St. Helena; so also on that part of Ladies' adjacent to St. Helena. But on Port Royal Island, and that part of Ladies' near to it, destitution has commenced, and will, unless provision is made, become very great. Large amounts of corn for forage, in quantities from fifty to four or five hundred bushels from a plantation, have been taken to Beaufort. On scarcely any within this district is there enough to last beyond April, whereas it is needed till August. On others, it will last only two or three weeks, and on some it is entirely exhausted. It is stated that the forage was taken because no adequate supply was at hand, and requisitions for it were not seasonably answered. The further taking of the corn in this way has now been forbidden, but the Government must be prepared to meet the exigency which it has itself created. It should be remembered that this is not a grain-exporting region, corn being produced in moderate crops only for consumption. Similar destitution will take place on other islands from the same cause unless provision is made.

The horses, mules and oxen in large numbers have been taken to Beaufort and Hilton Head as means of transportation. It is presumed that they, or most of them, are no longer needed for that purpose, and that they will be returned to those who shall have charge of the plantations. Cattle to the number of a hundred, and in some cases less, have been taken from a plantation and slaughtered, to furnish fresh beef for the army. Often cattle have been killed by irresponsible foraging parties, acting without competent authority. There can be no doubt that the army and navy have been in great want of the variation of the rations of salt beef or pork, but it also deserves much consideration if the plantations are to be permanently worked, how much of a draught they can sustain.

The garden seeds have been pretty well used up, and I inclose a desirable list furnished me by a gentlemen whose experience enables him to designate those adapted to the soil, and useful too for army supplies. The general cultivation of the islands also requires the sending of a quantity of plows and hoes.

It did not seem a part of my duty to look specially after matters which had been safely intrusted to others, but it is pleasing from such observation as was casually made to testify that Lieut. Col. Wm. H. Reynolds, who was charged with the preservation of the cotton and other confiscated property, notwithstanding many difficulties in his way, has fulfilled his duties with singular fidelity and success.

Since the writing of this report was commenced, some action has been taken which will largely increase the numbers of persons thrown on the protection of the Government. Today, February 10, the 47th Regiment of New-York Volunteers, has been ordered to take military occupation of North Edisto Island, which is stated to have had formerly a population of 5,000 or 6,000, and a large number of plantations, a movement which involves great additional responsibility. Agents for the collection of cotton are to accompany it.

Herewith is communicated a copy of an order by Gen. Sherman, dated Feb. 6, 1862, relative to the disposition of the plantations and of their occupants.[7] It is an evidence of the deep interest which the commanding General takes in this subject, and of his conviction that the exigency requires prompt and immediate action from the Government.

I leave for Washington, to add any oral explanations which may be desired, expecting to return at once, and, with the permission of the Department, to organize the laborers on some one plantation, and superintend them during the planting season, and upon its close, business engagements require that I should be relieved of this appointment. I am, with great respect, your friend and servant.

PLcSr EDWARD L. PIERCE.

Edward L. Pierce to Hon. Salmon P. Chase, 3 Feb. 1862, vol. 19, #72a, Port Royal Correspondence, 5th Agency, RG 366 [Q-8]. The document is in the form of a clipping from the *New-York Daily Tribune* of February 19, 1862; emendations and corrections in an unidentified handwriting have been incorporated into the text. The documents said to have been enclosed were not printed with Pierce's report. On February 19, 1862, Secretary of the Treasury Salmon P. Chase gave the report his "entire approval." Noting that his department had been authorized to regulate "commercial intercourse with any part of the country declared to be in a state of insurrection," Chase deemed it "in the highest degree essential to commercial intercourse with that portion of the country, that the abandoned estates be cultivated, and the laborers upon them employed." Accordingly, he instructed Pierce to continue as a special agent, charging him with "the general superintendence and direction" of plantation laborers in the vicinity of Port Royal. Observing that "an Association of judicious and humane citizens has been formed in Boston," which, either alone or in conjunction with similar groups in New York and other Northern cities, might sponsor agents, "with the sanction of the Government, to take charge of the abandoned plantations," Chase authorized Pierce to select civilian plantation superintendents, whose salaries would be paid by the private associations and whose food, quarters, and transportation would be furnished by the government. Pierce was also to give "suitable support" to Northern ministers and teachers. (S. P. Chase to Edward L. Pierce, Esq., 19 Feb. 1862, vol. 2, pp. 23–24, Letters Sent Relating to Restricted Commercial Intercourse & Captured & Abandoned Property: BE Series, ser. 14, RG 56 [X-307].)

1 Begun on February 3, 1862, the letter was not completed until February 10.
2 On January 19, 1862, the special agent, Edward L. Pierce, had reported his arrival at Port Royal, to which place he had traveled from his home in Boston. Seeking to clarify his position vis-à-vis William H. Reynolds, the Treasury Department agent in charge of collecting the 1861 cotton crop, Pierce had summarized his own assignment from the secretary: "I was to observe all about the products of the soil – the mode and time of sowing and gathering crops, the capacities and traits of the negroes – how they could best be managed, and kept from being demoralised in this *quasi* interregnum – how for that end they could best be organized for labor and so far as possible their moral nature addressed and their good will secured." (Edward L. Pierce to Hon. Salmon P. Chase, 19 Jan. 1862, vol. 19, #36, Port Royal Correspondence, 5th Agency, RG 366 [Q-4].)
3 On February 1, 1862, Flag Officer Samuel F. Du Pont, commander of the South Atlantic Squadron, had ordered, "No stock or provisions of any kind must be taken without paying a fair price for the same to the negroes." (*Navy Official Records*, ser. 1, vol. 12, pp. 532–33.) The previous November, General Thomas W. Sherman, commander of the South Carolina Expeditionary Corps, had ordered Union soldiers to cease their depredations upon the residents of the islands. (See above, doc. 2n.)
4 In August 1861, Congress had outlawed whipping as a military punishment in the army. (U.S., War Department, *Revised United States Army Regulations* [Washington, 1863], p. 528.)
5 General Order 3, issued by General Thomas W. Sherman, commander of the South Carolina Expeditionary Corps. (General Orders No. 3, Head Quarters E.C., 18 Jan. 1862, vol. 60/115 DS, Special Orders, General Orders, & Circulars, ser. 2258, SC Expeditionary Corps, RG 393 Pt. 2 No. 130 [C-1734].)
6 On February 16, 1862, the Reverend French conveyed to the Secretary of the Treasury some "brief observations" respecting the former slaves on the South Carolina Sea Islands. Some 8,000 to 10,000 were already within Union lines, he reported, "with a prospective increase to twenty or thirty thousand within a few weeks." Those employed by the army (about 1,200) were "comfortably clad & provisioned"; the remainder were "mostly on the plantations, with a very limited supply of provisions; the army having made large drafts for its own use." The latter class, he predicted, would soon suffer for want of food, clothing, and medical care. The former slaves, French asserted, demonstrated "all the evidences of true loyalty, a willingness to support themselves, by their own labor, and are ready, by their prayers & strong arms, to aid our forces, in

their humble way. . . . The strong claims of humanity, as well as the Nation's obligation to God, demand immediate attention to their wants & sufferings." He proposed that Northern ministers, teachers, and doctors, supported largely by private benevolence, but with assistance from the federal government, be sent to the Sea Islands. (M. French to Hon. S. P. Chase, 16 Feb. 1862, vol. 19, #65, Port Royal Correspondence, 5th Agency, RG 366 [Q-7].)
7 The order is printed immediately below, as doc. 9.

9: Order by the Commander of the South Carolina Expeditionary Corps

HILTON HEAD, S.C. *February* 6, 1862,
GENERAL ORDERS, No. 9. THE helpless condition of the Blacks inhabiting the vast area in the occupation of the forces of this command calls for immediate action on the part of a highly favored and philanthropic people.

The occupation of a large portion of this area of country on the 7th of November last, led to an address to the people of South Carolina, briefly setting forth the causes which led to it; its objects and purposes; and inviting all persons to the re-occupation, in a loyal spirit, of their lands and tenements, and to a continuance of their avocations, under the auspices of their legitimate Government, and the protection of the Constitution of the United States.[1]

The conciliatory and beneficent purposes of that proclamation, except in a few instances, have not only been disregarded, but hordes of totally uneducated, ignorant and improvident Blacks have been abandoned by their constitutional guardians, not only to all the future chances of anarchy and of starvation; but in such a state of abject ignorance and mental stolidity as to preclude all possibility of self-government and self-maintenance in their present condition.

Adequate provision for the pressing necessities of this unfortunate and now interesting class of people being therefore imperatively demanded, even by the dictates of humanity alone, an additional duty, next only in importance to that of the preservation of a world revered Constitution and Union, is now forced upon us by an unnatural and wicked rebellion.

To relieve the Government of a burden that may hereafter become insupportable, and to enable the Blacks to support and govern themselves in the absence and abandonment of their disloyal guardians, a suitable system of culture and instruction must be combined with one providing for their physical wants.

Therefore, until proper legislation on the subject, or until orders from higher authority, the country in occupation of the forces of this command will be divided off into districts of convenient size for proper superintendence. For each of these districts a suitable Agent will be appointed to superintend the management of the plantations by the Blacks, to enroll and organize the willing blacks into working parties, to see that they are well fed, clad and paid a proper remuneration for their labor, to take charge of all property on the plantations, whether found there, provided by the Government, or raised from the soil, and to perform all other administrative duties connected with the plantations, that may be required by the Government. A code of regulations on this subject, as well as a proper division of districts will be furnished in due time.

In the meanwhile, and until the Blacks become capable of themselves, of thinking and acting judiciously, the services of competent instructors will be received – one or more for each district – whose duties will consist in teaching them, both young and old, the rudiments of civilization and Christianity – their amenability to the laws of both God and man – their relations to each other as social beings, and all that is necessary to render them competent to sustain themselves in social and business pursuits.

For an efficient and complete organization of this system, there will be appointed two General Agents – one to have a general superintendence over the administrative or agricultural agents, and the other over the educational department.

II. The above system is not intended, in any respect, to interfere with the existing orders respecting the employment of contrabands by the Staff departments of the army, and by the Cotton agents.

III. As the Blacks are now in great need of suitable clothing, if not other necessaries of life, which necessity will probably continue, and even increase until the above system gets into working order, the benevolent and philanthropic of the land are most earnestly appealed to for assistance in relieving their immediate wants. Never was there a nobler or more fitting opportunity for the operation of that considerate and practical benevolence for which the Northern people have ever been distinguished. BY ORDER OF Brig. Genl. T. W. SHERMAN.

PD

General Order No. 9, Head Quarters, E.C., 6 Feb. 1862, vol. 19, #56, Port Royal Correspondence, 5th Agency, RG 366 [Q-6]. Three days later, when he forwarded a copy of the order to Adjutant General Lorenzo Thomas, General Sherman emphasized the "imperative necessity of putting the blacks in the way of avoiding starvation before the planting season expires," and of doing so "without a draw on the commissariat to an extent that would cripple the service." Estimating that at least 9,000 former slaves were already under Union jurisdiction, Sherman asserted that "[t]he present condition of the blacks, daily increasing in numbers and daily diminishing in their resources, must be alleviated both for their own welfare and the great cause itself." (*Official Records*, ser. 1, vol. 6, p. 222.)

1 For the proclamation "To the People of South Carolina," see above, doc. 3n.

10: Treasury Department Special Agent for the South Carolina Sea Islands to the Secretary of the Treasury

New York. March 2d 1862.

Dear Sir

I take this opportunity before leaving for Port Royal to make a more complete report to you of what I have done in fulfilling the purposes of my mission since we parted a fortnight ago.

. . . .

Since we parted I have been laboriously occupied with the business of my commission – as follows: Monday Feby 17", interview at N.Y. with Mr. Barney[1] and Rev. Mr. French;[2] Tuesday Feby 18" to tuesday evening, Feby 25", inclusive, was engaged at Boston, in daily conference with the "Educational Commission", stating the qualifications and number of persons required to aid at Port Royal in organizing and improving the laborers; what aid was to be given by the Government, and for what private contributions must be relied on exclusively; what would be the duties assigned them which they must accept cheerfully and perform with subordination and fidelity. I declined for certain reasons of policy to attend any public meetings, but on evenings met gentlemen and ladies invited for the purpose to private residences, where persons of various professions were present. At Cambridge there were present President Sparks, Professor Parsons & Gray, Judge Washburn, Drs. Wyman & Estes Howe, Rev. Drs. Francis & Peabody, R. H. Dana Jr, & others. Almost the only time given to anything but the business intrusted to me was two half days passed at my mother's.

From Wednesday morning Feby 26" to the present time I have been in New York, occupied constantly with interviews with the "National Freedmen's Relief Assocn", stating the qualifications and other points in the same manner as to the Boston Society – arranging with Mr. Barney and Col. Tompkins[3] about permits – with Capt Eldridge of the Atlantic as to accommodations, – advising with Mr. Suydam and others as to implements and seeds required, – obtaining permits to put a large quantitys of contributed clothing and other articles for the laborers on the Atlantic, and getting the same on board, – asking instructions of Mr. Barney for the Flora, during the first two weeks after her arrival, to aid in transporting persons and implements and rations to the different points, – conferring by letter and telegraph with the persons to come from Boston, and general interviews with those interested in the movement.

To both the Boston and New York Committees, I have said that persons accepted must have in the first place profound humanity – a belief that the negro is a human being and capable of elevation and freedom – every race or individual being entitled to have such a work put in the hands of those who have faith in it; this humanity to be supported by a religious sentiment, church membership not being necessary, but a religious sympathy being required so that it would be a welcome service to attend the meetings of the laborers, read to them the scriptures, and exhort them to practical duties and virtues.

In the second place the person approved must have sound practical sense, not imaginative or fanciful in temperament or conduct, willing to fix himself on a particular plantation or district to which he was assigned and there undertake the regular work of teaching or superintending as the case might be, and feeling that he was best doing his work when he was protecting some 50 or 100 human beings and contributing to their material and moral welfare. These qualities being found, a knowledge of cotton culture was not expected, and a knowledge of farming not required, though the last would be of value; what was most needed being the moral power of the presence of a white man on the plantations to guide and direct, and the laborers themselves understanding their work better than the master or overseer generally did. The applicants might be of different occupations, farmers, mechanics, lawyers, physicians, clergymen, teachers, provided they had the requisite humanity and good sense. Generally they would be required to superintend plantations, adding to this duty, so far as they could, teaching, and a few might be assigned to teaching only.

To the Committees in Boston & New York I have said that being guided by these principles they must select the persons, and, unless some marked unfitness was presented to me, I should approve their nominations without inquiry, leaving to them the honor and responsibility. Except in one case, where I knew a gentleman thoroughly and had already sent for him to aid me, promising compensation from my own funds, I have not suggested any name to either committee, and have only given opinions of applicants when specially desired, always referring applicants to the Committees.

In relation to women to aid in the enterprise I have said that that was particularly within Mr. French's sphere, and I desired that he alone should control as to the approval, but have urged that only ladies of mature years, of established characters, and of *rare* and special fitness should be chosen, and then in a small number – I should prefer only six in all. Both in Boston and here I have named Miss Susan Walker, known in both communities as a person answering my idea of a fit woman to accompany the delegation.

The Boston Committee is composed of George B. Emerson, Dr. Le Baron Russell, Loring Lothrop, Rev. Charles F. Barnard, Mrs. Anna Lowell, & Miss Hannah Stevenson. Mr. Emerson, Mr. Lothrop, & Mrs. Lowell are well known as accomplished teachers; Dr. Russell is a man of excellent sense and practical insight into character; Mr. Barnard has been a City Missionary for some years; Miss Stevenson is known as of the family of Theodore Parker and recently an attendant on Hospitals at Washington. The Committee have done their work diligently and conscientiously, occupying the greater part of their time with it for the last fortnight.

They presented me the names of twenty-nine men and six women, with authority to employ three more, Rev. Mr. Peck, Mr. Rich, & Mr. Boynton, already at Port Royal.

I have to-day upon their arrival here rejected two men and one woman, the latter a wife of one of the men, because they had some scruples about taking an oath of allegiance, fearing it might require them to bear arms. They are non-resistants, as they call themselves. They may be and doubtless are very quiet and well behaved citizens at home, but their peculiar notions imply a want of the best sense, and I did not think, as the enterprise is one which involves cooperation with a Government now putting down rebellion by taking life, that they were the proper persons to participate in it. Besides, although harangues to these laborers about war and bloodshed are to be avoided, it does not seem best to take away the little manhood they have left by inculcating notions of non-resistance. Two of the other five ladies were set aside as being too immature. Twenty-seven men and three ladies are accepted from the Boston Society, with three, and perhaps four, now at Port Royal to be added at my discretion. Of these, three receive only rations from the Government and are not to be paid, having means of their own. One or two more have only their expenses paid, and the rest are paid in sums from $25.00 to $50.00 per month, in no case exceeding the last figure. The Society agrees to pay for only one month, but the persons are employed with the understanding that if desired, and paid the same rates, they are to remain three months.

Of these one has been a successful railroad superintendent, another an engineer, another an auctioneer, others farmers, three or four physicians, and several teachers. One is a son of Dr. R. W. Hooper of Boston, another of Professor Edwards A. Park of Andover, another of Rev. Dr. Gannett of Boston. One is Fred. A. Eustis, the gentleman named in my report.[4] Hereafter I will send more particular descriptions.

Of the ladies, one seems well fitted for the work, and she is accompanied by her daughter, somewhat fitted, but accepted rather as an incident to her mother. The sister of one of the physicians was accepted with him.

Of the list furnished by the New York Society I cannot speak particularly. The Committee only began their work of selection on Thursday last, not having known until my arrival on the previous day what kind of persons was needed and upon what terms they were to be employed. They have handed me a list of twenty-one men and seven women, and I have approved it upon their recommendation and that of Mr. French. I have also approved Miss Susan Walker, Mrs. Walter R. Johnson, and Miss Mary Donaldson, the two latter friends of Miss Walker and coming under your sanction. I will withhold the list until I reach Port Royal, as some may fail to go, and I will give particulars with the list.

At both Boston and New York I have assured all that Government provided transportation and fare for the voyage to Port Royal, and subsistence there, but it did not pay expenses in any general sense, and did not promise compensation, and no one must expect it. For compensation, private benevolence alone must be relied on, and no claim ever made on the Government for expenses or services. I found that a different understanding was prevailing at New York, and a special effort was made to remove it. The suggestion was also made that, except in peculiar cases, where a person having the means desired to connect himself with a worthy movement, and could afford to do so gratuitously, some compensation must be assured, so as to secure fidelity and continuance at their posts during the planting season, or for a reasonable time. I will say that I have spared no effort to remove any fanciful or unfounded impressions as to the character of the services expected, the subordination required, compensation, and otherwise.

The Boston Society has had already some $5000.00 contributed to its funds. It has also forwarded nine large boxes of clothing to Port Royal, and the Atlantic tomorrow will take fifteen more large boxes, all clothing but one, – & one barrel of seeds. These consignments are addressed to me and are at my disposal, except two which are specially reserved for one of the appointees of the "Educational Commission".

I am not advised as to the progress of the New York Society. Their organization was delayed, and on Wednesday last they had less than $1000.00 contributed, but subscriptions when called for will doubtless come in. I am not aware that they have yet forwarded any clothing, but they will doubtless do so soon, as they have a depot for the purpose and some articles contributed.

The "Educational Commission" of Boston desire to remain an independent society and to cooperate with those of New York and other cities. It seems to me clear that it should have this privilege. It was organised first, and has made the earliest and largest contributions. It is well officered, presided over by Gov. Andrew, and is located in a district well calculated to furnish qualified persons for this service. It is however entitled to equality only – not preeminence. Persons to be employed can be furnished by the two societies conferring together, aided by Mr. Barney's intervention.

Many persons already nominated by the New York Society, and a few nominated by the Boston Society, both approved by myself, may fail to go by the Atlantic. They should come by the next steamer. The persons already nominated, and approved by myself, make 48 men and 11 women, besides Miss Walker, Mrs. Johnson, & Miss Donaldson. If more men are needed, as is quite likely, I will inform Mr. Barney from Port Royal.

Under your instructions to Mr. Barney I conferred with him about the purchase of seeds and implements. He had lost the list of seeds which I furnished to him on my way from Washington to Boston. I conferred as to implements and seeds with Mr. James A. Suydam, who is in the confidential employ of Col. Reynolds, and whom you have seen at Washington. I enclose a list of the seeds purchased, making $288.66. It is too small, but I feared to go too high. The Boston Society, as already stated, has contributed a barrel of seeds. I asked a New York gentleman to contribute some, and he has promised to do so. The box obtained from the Patent office has also gone on board the Atlantic. I also enclose a list of all the articles recommended. They will cost about $2600.00 and with the seeds $2800.00. I have not the bills except for the seeds and cannot give exact figures. I enclose Mr. Suydam's minutes of the cost of most of the articles. The implements I am sure are below the requirements, but I remembered your caution of economy.

The blank books are for the superintendents. The sulky harnesses were requested by Mr. Suydam, and I did not feel at liberty to reject them. He needs one himself, the physicans need them, and they should be assigned to those whose duty it will be, in furtherance of the business of the Department, to go much from place to place. The blacksmith works were greatly needed to repair the tools already there & broken. It is unnecessary to explain the need of trace chains, axes, spades, cart hames, yokes, nails, ploughs, hoes, &c –

Let me call your attention to a matter of the greatest possible importance. You remember that I say in my report that the cotton seed is sown about the 20″ of March and through April. The cotton was sent to New York unginned and the seed is here. None of it has been returned to Port Royal, but it should be there by March 10" or 15", so as to give time for distribution on the plantations. I do not know how much or little has been ginned here as yet. I called Col. Reynolds' attention to the matter of cotton seed some time ago at Port Royal, or after his return from Washington. He told me that the seed of each plantation was kept separate, and was to be returned to Port Royal. I now learn that it is not kept separate, but is mixed. I have supposed that the separation and identity of the seed of each plantation was important. The cotton of each plantation has its brand in the European market– Coffin marks his with a *coffin*. Pope's cotton is well known. The Fripp seed is said to be used mainly on Port Royal Island. Now, if we mix the seed, how can we keep up these well known brands, if we desire to do so? But, however this may be, the speedy return of a part of the seed to Port Royal, in sufficient quantities for sowing, is important. Some cotton has been ginned there, and the seed can be used on the plantations from which the cotton itself came.

The suggestion has been made to me that there is a large quantity of condemned army clothing at Washington to be sold, which might be reserved for the purpose of clothing these laborers. I bring the suggestion to your mind, as desired, and leave it.

I note your suggestion that 40 cents per day is too much for the laborers.[5] You understand that they are to pay for everything, except for rent for their small houses, and the corn dealt out will go in part payment of their wages. It took me one half a day in connexion with Mr. [J]. E. Carver to work out the result. I have no pride of opinion on the subject. I hope others will cipher out a more reliable result. But my estimates should not be judged by those who have not devoted an equal amount of care in making theirs. I would give you the data but I have no time.

Mr. Barney, however, has no cotton funds to advance me for the purpose, but hopes for some by March 5". Some money ought to be sent soon to show them that we intend to pay them wages, and to give them confidence in us. Meanwhile we must assure them of a reasonable compensation, charging them for the corn dealt out. I propose that new clothing furnished by the societies should be considered as sold when delivered to laborers set to work by us, and afterwards some arrangement might possibly be made by which the amount could be deducted from the wages and passed over to the societies. If second hand clothing is delivered it should always be considered as a gift. I hope some money, to pay wages, will be sent soon to some authorised agent of the Department.

When I first went to Port Royal I took $100.00 from Mr.

Barney, for expenses. Had I remained there, and my duties not been enlarged, this amount would have nearly sufficed to pay expenses there. My outfit cost $100.00 besides. I have just received from Mr. Barney $100.00, and have made a request for $200.00 more, which, if received, would make $400.00 in all advanced to me for expenses. It may not all be used, and if not will be returned, but the recent enlargement of my duties seemed to justify this requisition. Perhaps this is the proper place to say what I have intended from the first. At our interview at Washington, when the appointment was tendered me, the only subject not considered by us was the rate of compensation. It is still my intention, as it was then, to charge nothing for services, receiving from the Government only remuneration for expenses.

During Thursday, Friday, Saturday, & even to-day, when it was necessary to administer the oaths of allegiance and give passes, on account of the early sailing of the Atlantic tomorrow, Mr. Barney has worked diligently and with a will for this enterprise, giving the better portion of his time to it. The want of attention to it which seemed to exist on Wednesday, when I wrote you, has not existed since, but Mr. Barney has done all he could to further the business. I do think, however, that in this business, particularly in purchases, he needs the aid of some one in whom he has perfect confidence. I should add that the purchases recommended by me were made by Mr. Suydam and Mr. Frederickson, the latter designated here for that purpose by Col. Reynolds.

Since writing the first part of my report I have reconsidered the rejection of one of the ladies from Boston. She was rejected solely because not of sufficient years, being only 21. Her excellent life, devoted to the poor and to missionary labors among the outcast of the city were urged on me, but they did not seem sufficient to justify sending her without some special protector. Finally I referred the case to Miss Susan Walker & Miss Walker advising that she be sent & agreeing to *matronise* her, I reversed my decision, and she has received a permit.

It is time to call your attention to the appointment of my successor whose speciality, I trust, will be the care of plantations and of the laborers on them, leaving to Col. Reynolds the collection of cotton. He should be a man deeply impressed by the great social question, uniting humane sentiments and a well balanced judgment. The sooner he is appointed, the better, – say in a fortnight or three weeks. It will give me great pleasure to introduce him to his sphere of labor, and, with the information and facilities I shall be able to afford him, he will very soon become master of his situation. The suggestion is perhaps worth giving that a store-keeper, who might also be a paymaster may be needed.

I requested Mr. Barney to give the Flora, which left yesterday, instructions to aid me particularly during the first fortnight after her arrival at Hilton Head, in transporting the persons and implements to the plantations. He has given a general instruction, to be made more precise hereafter.

Miss Walker arrived to-day, and I have called on her. She will go on board the Atlantic, which is to leave tomorrow forenoon at 10 o'clock, having orders to that effect from Washington.

You must excuse this hasty report of what has transpired since we parted. It has been the most laborious fortnight I have ever had. I have tried to do everything as if you were looking on, or as you would have done it yourself. I feel conscious of the delicate experiment you have set me to initiate, and I have devoted my whole time and heart to it. I close this at midnight. Yours Respectfully

HLS Edward L Pierce

Excerpts from Edward L. Pierce to Hon. Salmon P. Chase, 2 Mar. 1862, vol. 19, #78, Port Royal Correspondence, 5th Agency, RG 366 [Q-9]. In the omitted passage, Pierce noted his receipt of several orders and correspondence relating to Port Royal. The list ("minutes") of the cost of various articles, prepared by James A. Suydam, is enclosed, as is a list of "articles required for the use of the agency . . . under charge of Edward L. Pierce Special agent." The list of seeds purchased by Pierce is not in the file. On February 24, 1862, the Secretary of the Treasury, Salmon P. Chase, had instructed the collector of customs for the Port of New York, to issue travel permits "to persons going to Port Royal, under the auspices of benevolent Societies formed at New York and Boston," to purchase and forward necessary agricultural implements, and to furnish Pierce "sufficient sums to pay one month's wages to Fifteen hundred laborers, at a rate not exceeding forty cents per day." The same day, Chase had cautioned Pierce that "[t]he most careful economy must be observed, to avoid all grounds of just reproach," reminding him that the only funds with which the Treasury Department could pay plantation laborers were those derived from proceeds of the captured 1861 cotton crop. (S. P. Chase to Hiram Barney, Esq., 24 Feb. 1862, and S. P. Chase to Edward L. Peirce, Esq., 24 Feb. 1862, vol. 2, pp. 28–29, Letters Sent Relating to Restricted Commercial Intercourse & Captured & Abandoned Property: BE Series, ser. 14, RG 56 [X-309, 308].)

1 Hiram L. Barney, U.S. collector of customs for the Port of New York.

2 Mansfield French, a minister and personal friend of Secretary of the Treasury Salmon P. Chase, had been sent to the Sea Islands in January 1862 by the American Missionary Association. There he had consulted with Edward L. Pierce, the Treasury Department special agent, about the government's plans for the former slaves. At the time of his interview with Pierce in New York, he had returned to that city to mobilize the philanthropic community in support of Pierce's plan, which Chase had approved. (See above, doc. 8; Willie Lee

Rose, *Rehearsal for Reconstruction: The Port Royal Experiment* [Indianapolis, Ind., 1964], pp. 26–28.)

3 Daniel D. Tompkins, assistant quartermaster general, whose headquarters were at New York.

4 Frederick A. Eustis was described in the earlier report as "[a] loyal citizen of Massachusetts" and heir to a large plantation on Ladies Island, who "accept[ed] the present condition of things" and wished to see the former slaves on his estate treated no differently than those on plantations owned by disloyal owners. (See above, doc. 8.)

5 On February 27, Secretary of the Treasury Salmon P. Chase had asked the special agent to reconsider his plan to set the wages of plantation laborers at 40¢ per day, since other reports from Port Royal considered that amount too high. "We must not expend more than is absolutely necessary," Chase had warned, "nor give wages, the practical result of which will be to encourage expectations which cannot be gratified in the long run." (S. P. Chase to Edward L. Pierce, Esq., 27 Feb. 1862, vol. 2, pp. 37–38, Letters Sent Relating to Restricted Commercial Intercourse & Captured & Abandoned Property: BE Series, ser. 14, RG 56 [X-311].)

11: Treasury Department Special Agent for the South Carolina Sea Islands to the Secretary of the Treasury

Beaufort S.C. March 14th 1862.

Dear Sir This week has been entirely occupied in selecting locations on Port Royal Island, and forwarding the superintendents to them. I must consult brevity and reserve general matters for a future communication. Let me call your attention to some points requiring immediate action.

1st As to all the points stated in the letter to Mr Barney – a copy of which is enclosed,[1] let me press each and all on you.

2d Cannot something be done to arrest the action of the military authorities in taking cattle whether beef or draught from the plantations? Gen. Stevens[2] told me nearly two months ago that it should not be done, and yet it is done. You have decided to keep up the culture of the plantations. If so – not a horse or mule or cow or pig, should be touched. I grant that there might occur a military necessity, to which everything must yield – but none such has existed. The military authorities allow their horses to run down and when used up, they send off to the Islands and take any that they can get. They have done so in relation to fresh beef – They dont look ahead making a requisition for horses, mules or fresh beef, and dont appear to intend to do so, but look to the plantations now miserably bereft. I mentioned this to you at Washington, and stated the course of things in my published report.[3] Again I call your attention to it.

3ᵈ In my former report I called your attention to the destitution which would soon commence on Port Royal Island and that part of Ladies Island near Port Royal. That destitution *has* now *commenced*. Gen. Stevens said to me a day or two ago, that his orders were, to take what corn could be spared by the negroes, but it had not been complied with and in many cases all or nearly all had been taken. He had given some orders for supplying the negroes from the army stores, – but I find that this work is slowly done. It required no *red tape* to take the corn, but it requires red tape to distribute rations. I told Gen. Stevens this should be done by the army, because it had taken the corn and not we. You remember at Washington I asked you if I should see Mr Stanton on this point, and you said I need not. I presume therefore that you have spoken with him about it. From what Gen. Stevens said to me, I think he means to prevent entire destitution, but it would seem that all doubt as to his power and duty, should be removed by a special order. On this point the following is my record of experiences this week, in my exploration of plantations.

William Elliot no provision or corn, not enough even to plant with

Reynolds – need provisions
R. Oswald – little corn
Ed Rhett – have corn
R. Harrisham – provisions for two weeks
Colin Campbell – nothing to eat.
Tayler Danner – no provisions
Wᵐ Fripp have provision
Wᵐ Barnwell – provision will las until April 1ˢᵗ
Dr Frank Capers – very little provision
Dr Rose have provision.
Mills – no provision
Thos. Stewart just got provision from army.
Mrs. Talbots no provision
Wᵐ Perryclear have provision.
Mrs. Rose nothing to eat for three weeks – go begging.
Mrs Ann Perryclear have provision.
John J Smith have some corn.
John Chaplin no provisions

I should add that where there is this want of provisions there is less work going on.

I take pleasure in saying that Gen. Stevens has cordially aided me, and I think will continue to do so.

He furnished me an army wagon and four horses for transportation of implements and luggage. His cooperation is very essential as I have found this the best centre for operations. I am glad to bear this testimony to Gen. Stevens. Gen. Sherman has issued an order in relation to myself which I enclose, I understand that Col. Reynolds intends to resign his appointment in a few weeks. If so I trust that his successor, will be not only a man of business capacity and fidelity, – but what is of the greatest importance, an entire sympathy with the movement I would press this further but time does not permit. Since I returned I am all the more convinced of the capacity of these people. New facts have come to my knowledge which establish this. On this Island with no master present, they have generally gone to work, and some plantations have been put in excellent order, and notwithstanding the lack of a proper supply of mules. – and all this without a master or overseer. If our army was not here, and white men kept away, a very few superintendents would suffice to put them in complete social order. I never saw before how easy a thing emancipation could be if the slaveholders of their own accord would undertake it. These people are quiet – orderly and industrious, and this, while everything is in chaos and they know not who is to receive the fruits of their labors. Be assured that the success of the experiment here is inevitable. I learn that the negroes on Dr Fullers plantations on Cane and Cat Island are somewhat disorderly. They have been told by other negroes, and white men, that Dr Fuller being a union man, is still to hold them *as slaves*. I am told that Dr F has made a special arrangement with Goverment by which he is to have all his property here, and that he writes to his correspondent here as though he regarded the negroes as still *his property*. This is wrong as I humbly submit. It would be a folly and a crime to put these negroes on a different basis from all their neighbors with whom they are intertwined by kin or friendship. Like the others they are our allies in this war. Treat them otherwise and they will be spies and enemies. Mr Eustis does not do so, but accepts the existing condition of things, – has charge of his mothers plantation, and, is doing all he can to improve the negroes, and make them freemen, and is being a great use to me personally. Besides Dr Fuller, though his civil status may be that of a loyal man, is in entire sympathy with rebellion, and aids it with his influence in Baltimore. Dr Smith, Presbyterian clergyman at Washington assured me the other day that Dr F was a secessionist and Mr Whittridge a leading merchant of that City, certified to the same fact. I do not therefore see why he should be the recipient of special privileges. It would seem to be a good sign that the negroes on his plantation are disturbed. Dr F corresponds with Dr Peck, seems very anxious to get all his cotton, and equally anxious that his connexion with the matter should be kept secret, – probably not desiring to lose caste with the rebels. Dr Peck will discontinue his own agency. I thought it my duty to bring these facts to your attention. Yours truly

ALS Edward L Pierce

Edward L. Pierce to Hon. S. P. Chase, 14 Mar. 1862, vol. 19, #90, Port Royal Correspondence, 5th Agency, RG 366 [Q-11]. The order relating to Pierce, issued by General Thomas W. Sherman, commander of the South Carolina Expeditionary Corps, is not in the file. An appeal by Pierce to General Sherman elicited the latter's pledge, on March 29, "to supply the blacks on the plantations with subsistence wherever it is found that the supplies are exhausted." (Capt. L. H. Pelouze to E. L. Pierce, Esqr., 29 Mar. 1862, vol. 19, #115, Port Royal Correspondence, 5th Agency, RG 366 [Q-13].) Meanwhile, the Secretary of the Treasury applied to Secretary of War Edwin M. Stanton for horses and mules to replace those impressed from the plantations by the army, but Stanton replied on March 25 that he lacked authority to do so. He asked, however, "whether the Treasury Department could not furnish them properly out of the proceeds of the cotton received from Port Royal." (*Official Records*, ser. 1, vol. 6, pp. 249–50.) In April, the Treasury Department forwarded ninety mules from New York to Port Royal, for use on the government-operated plantations. (See below, doc. 21.)

1 A copy of the letter to Hiram L. Barney, collector of customs for the Port of New York, dated March 14, 1862, is in the same file. In it, Edward L. Pierce, the Treasury Department special agent, urged Barney to forward ninety mules, ten horses, and 8,000 to 10,000 bushels of cotton seed for use on the Sea Island plantations, as well as funds with which to pay the laborers, a measure "important so as to ensure confidence and make them trust our promises of payment." Pierce also reported that he would not require as many plantation superintendents as he had originally thought, partly because "on some plantations the negroes are doing very well without any one." He did, however, need three more teachers and two or three mechanics who could teach their trades to the former slaves. Disappointed with some of the men sent from New York, Pierce had applied to "the Boston society" for the additional workers, soliciting men "thoroughly in sympathy with this movement."

2 Isaac I. Stevens, commander of the 2nd brigade of the South Carolina Expeditionary Corps.

3 The report is printed above, as doc. 8.

12: Report by a Plantation Superintendent on St. Helena Island, South Carolina

[*St. Helena Island, S.C. March 18, 1862*]

On Yesterday March 17th I visited Gabriel Capers place, accompanied by Mr Thorpe, to examine as to the particulars of the outrage committed there on the evening of Sat. March 8th. Cuffy the Foreman testified as follows.

On Sat night a party of about 7 seven, apparently sailors, landed in a boat at Scotts and reached Capers at about ten oclock in the evening. They went into the house of Will (the carpenter at Capers) and drank whiskey. They then took Will into the main house to play the fiddle for them, while they danced with the negro girls. Two of them, called by their comrades Mike and Jim, threw the girls down and attempted an outrage.

Will remonstrated and was knocked down. The dance broke up. Mike and Jim were dragged away before any outrage was committed. All the white men went to Cuffys house and sat down, except Mike and Jim. Jim went to the house of one named Plato, but the women ran out, he then went to Cuffys house and attempted an outrage on Cuffys daughter which Cuffy succeeded in preventing. Mike went to the house of one Tim and got into bed with Tim wife. Will the carpenter tussled with Mike and in the affray Will was struck repeatedly and stabbed at. (I saw the cuts in Wills coat) Mike escaped from Will, went into Cuffeys house and saw boy Napoleon standing by the fire. Mike asked what he was doing. He replied "warming himself." Mike stooped picked up a piece of board and struck Napoleon across the face, knocking out one of Napoleons teeth and breaking another (I saw Napoleons mouth, the teeth were mangled as represented.)

All the white men slept in Cuffys house till morning. They then took a horse and buggy and drove to Scotts and thence to Edwin Chaplins, Cuffey following behind. At Edwin Chaplins they shot a cow in the head and the negroes afterwards killed her. Hector (driver at Chaplins) remonstrated. He was struck and knocked down. Cuffey finally got his horse and buggy. Four of them came at night (Sunday night) again to Gabriel Capers in a boat, but Mr Moore (cotton agent), who was at one of the negro houses, quieted them. By this time Mr Salisbury, whom Cuffey had sent for in the morning, arrived and took Mike into custody, taking also the names of his companions. No soldiers or sailors have been to the place since.

The soldiers used to come to the place every Sat. night, but never made serious trouble before.

Will the carpenter – The sailors came and asked him to play on a fiddle for a dance. While playing he was knocked down, the first thing he knew. He rose and scuffled, in the melee he was stabbed at. The sailors then ran to the negro houses after women and Will hid himself. He showed me the cuts in his coat.

Girl Nelly – testified that one (Mike) attempted to violate her in one of the negro houses. She was thrown down but escaped outrage.

Girl Dolly testified an attempt to violate her.

Napoleon said that they knocked his tooth out and showed me his mouth. Napoleon also said that Will, Cuffy and he accompanied Mr Salisbury and Mike to Dr. Jenkins, that then they proceeded in a boat to Hilton Head and laid the matter before Col. Noble. Will confirmed this story. Nobody but Napoleon and Will mentioned it. N. said the name of their ship was John Henry Augustus.

Hector, driver at Edwin Chaplins, said that the sailors came in a buggy and shot a cow, putting two bullets in her head. He was knocked down when he remonstrated. The cow could not walk home and the negroes soon killed her. He showed me the skin of the cow and some bits of the meat. The negroes had eaten most of it.

The accounts of the negroes were extremely contradictory. I think the pith of the matter is, that a party of sailors came to Gabriel Capers and several of them got drunk. They attempted to violate three negro girls, but did not succeed. They struck several negroes, knocked out one mans tooth and stabbed at one, but did not cut him any. They then rode to Edwin Chaplins and as far as I can learn wantonly shot a cow. According to all accounts Mr Salisbury took the matter in charge. Capers place has not been visited since. The transaction took place on the night of Sat March 8th and on the Sunday following.

I think I can find negroes to testify to all the above facts

ADS Wm E. Park.

Report of Wm. E. Park, [18 Mar. 1862], vol. 19, #116, Port Royal Correspondence, 5th Agency, RG 366 [Q-13]. Both Park and David F. Thorpe were plantation superintendents on St. Helena Island, stationed near the Capers plantation. Alfred Salisbury, who assisted in the apprehension of Mike, was an employee of William H. Nobles, a cotton agent.

13: Plantation Superintendent on St. Helena Island, South Carolina, to the Treasury Department Special Agent for the South Carolina Sea Islands

Coffins Point [*St. Helena Island, S.C.*] Mar 26th 1862

Dear Sir I wrote you on the 23d inst. offering some suggestions about providing cloth, thread, soap, salt &c. &c. instead of money for a large portion of the first paymt to be made the negroes. The importance of some such arrangement is becoming more apparent to me every day. The "people" on Fripp's Pine Grove plant^{n} had their patience sorely tried today & broke down under the trial. A Couple of their most active men had just returned from Bay Pt. where they had been cooking for our officers' & earning $10. & $15. a month. Of course they brought decent clothes to wear & tobacco in their mouths & pockets & a little change too. The field hands who have been at work more or less since Dec. packing cotton &c without the first cent for pay Came & asked me if I didnt mean to Do anything for them, holding up their tattered garments 18 months old, & talking about what good times they had when "old massa" was here. They left their tasks half done & some are going to start for Bay Point with the returning cooks. In short their patience is about gone, & I am quite ashamed to go among them with nothing to provide for their wants. They Cant be Expected to work under such treatment & all attempts at Control or organization are *futile*. I might as well have stayed at home as come here and talk smooth but *do* nothing for them. The clothing we have wont give more than one little piece in a whole family. If there are any garments fit for them at Eustis', not already distributed please consider the 400 people here.

I append a list of what the masters used to furnish them, from which you can form an idea of what is needed. for the Coffin & Fripp were liberal men, the present Condition of the negroes demands at least as *much* as they used to get.

Given out in April

For every 200 hands. counting "big & little"

men's blue cotton cloth like our workmen's clothes	550	yds.
men's unbleached cotton shirting, coarse.	600	"
for women's Do. Do. same stuff	600	"
" " frocks, calico, gay colors, Thread &c. to match.	600	"
" " turban, gay hankfs. pieces	100	
for men's heads straw hats "	100	

Coffin gave 12 beeves in summer.
4 Do. at Christmas.
4 bbls. molasses in summer } 250 hands all told.

also from Ap^{l} to June 2 1/2 lbs bacon to every 2 pecks corn.

& 2 hands tobacco per man, every month.

1 qut salt per hand per mo.

4 extra hands tobacco at Christmas.

	Given out in Nov. viz.		
for 200 hands all told	stou't woolen cloth	550	yds
" " "	thinner Do. for women	600	"
" " "	unbleached shirting	1200	"
" " "	turban handkfs pieces	100	
	warm caps.	100.	
	pair shoes	200.	
	Blankets, assorted sizes	67.	

House servants got hose & flannels.

I have written Atkinson at Boston telling him that I had suggested these things to you, & asking him to do whatever he could for you. Of course the thing is on too large a scale for private benevolence, & I merely referred to him as a suitable person to assist in *buying*, provided you dont get Gov[t] clothes ready made. So long as the Gov[t] have been employing these men & owe enough to them for their labor performed to clothe them well, they ought to be made to do it. As an instance of our lack of control: our Driver gave one of the new ploughs to a ploughman today & told him not to use it with oxen but mule. He preferred another plough, an old one, but a hoe-hand took it into his head to try the new plough, yoked the cattle to it & broke the beam in half an hour, & then went home to feed his pig & chickens, leaving his hoe task half done, as about half of them do. Respy yrs &c.

ALS Edw S. Philbrick

Edw. S. Philbrick to Edw. L. Pierce Esq., 26 Mar. 1862, vol. 19, #109, Port Royal Correspondence, 5th Agency, RG 366 [Q-13]. Philbrick's letter of March 23 had reported that the former slaves of St. Helena were "crying loudly & with some reason, that we dont treat them so well as their old masters. They have no *salt* no molasses, sugar or fresh meat. They see the soldiers kill their cattle & sit in idleness (as it seems to them) while their masters gave them a beef once a month & an allowance of the other luxuries. They consider tobacco a necessity, but can't get it at any price." Clothing too was in short supply: "They are all shivering in their cabins & churches for want of sufficient clothing." Accustomed to making their own clothes from cloth issued by their masters, the former slaves "w[d] be glad to Do it now; witness the *Carpet Suits*" they had fashioned out of material scavenged from their owners' houses. "Now can it not be arranged," Philbrick had suggested, "that the first installment of their wages, or such portion as advisable, can be invested in *cloth*, *molasses* salt, *sugar* & a little tobacco, & dealt out to them here at cost prices, to save them from the voracity of the sharks whose teeth are beginning to show at Beaufort?" The former slaves, Philbrick noted, "have shown an alacrity most unexpected to me in preparing the ground to plant, & Call with justice that we shall not cut them short of their accustomed privileges, wh. are by no means extravagant." "[I]f I came here with clothing enough to pay them . . . for their last 2 weeks labor at the hoe," he predicted, "I could get double the amount of work from them during the coming month which I am likely to get." (Edw. S. Philbrick to Edw. L. Pierce Esq., 23 Mar. 1862, vol. 19, #108, Port Royal Correspondence, 5th Agency, RG 366 [Q-13].)

14: Plantation Superintendent on St. Helena Island, South Carolina, to the Treasury Department Special Agent for the South Carolina Sea Islands

Coffin point St. Helena Island. S.C. Mar 27th 1862

Dear Sir I have tried my best since arriving here to keep clear of any collision with the authority assumed and exercised by the agents of Col. Reynolds, and at the same time do what I understood to be my duty towards the interest of the service in which I came here. I have now to say that what little authority I did claim, and which was at first cheerfully recognized by Mr. Salisbury, has since been entirely ignored & set at naught by him, and as his course has been fully sustained by Col Nobles, with whom I had some conversation this morning, I have thought it useless to have any further talk with Mr. Salisbury on the subject, but beg to lay the facts immediately before you.

The morning after I arrived I told Mr. S. that I came here to take charge of the labor of the blacks, & requested him to inform me whenever he needed their services in handling cotton, as I considered it my duty to know where they were all the time. He replied that he had been accustomed to call on the men through their drivers, & should continue to do so. I told him I had no objection to that, but claimed the right to know from him when he wanted them. To this he immediately assented, and we parted with, as I thought, a good understanding on the subject. A day or two after the above conversation I was talking with one of the drivers & in answer to his question as to who was "master" now, I told him I was sent here to take charge of all the labor, but that when Mr. S. wanted him to handle cotton, he was to furnish him with all available facilities, such as laborers teams, &c: that we were employed by the same gov^t & should work for the same ends, and that Mr. S. would control and pay for all labor on cotton of last year's crop & I would control and pay for all labor on this year's crop. Now Mr. Salisbury came to me the same eve'g after the above conversation with the driver, in a considerable flurry, making some incoherent remarks about being "bossed by a nigger" & using very profane language in vague denunciation of something I had done. I coolly asked him what the matter was & learned that the driver had apparently taken occasion to vent some grudge by telling him he had got a new master now & that I was to direct all the work. I told Mr. S. that I supposed our understanding had been sufficiently definite & that I had told the driver nothing more than what was in accordance therewith, & that I hoped he w[d] adhere to it. He then repeated that he would let me know when he wanted the men, & I said that was all I wanted, & told him I would correct any misapprehension on the part of the driver the next time I saw him. Again we parted pleasantly & I have had no unpleasant words with him since. Yesterday morning he told me the Flora was aground near Otter Island & might get here the next tide. I asked him if he was going to haul cotton to the wharf. he said *no*. that it was very uncertain when she would float & that she was in a bad place. I went off to Fripp's plant[n] on foot as usual, & on my way back saw the Flora Coming up to the wharf. Before reaching home I met lots of teams hauling cotton to the wharf, but did not think very strange of it, knowing that I had been away, & that it would be unreasonable to expect them to await my return. I went to Mr. Salisbury at his room in the eve'g, and asked him when the Flora would leave, as I wished to send letters by her. He said she would finish loading "tonight or early in the morning" so as to leave on the morning flood, say 7. o'clock. I accordingly went down to the wharf this A.M. at flood tide & gave my letters to Col. Nobles.

Then for the first time did I learn that several teams from Fripp's, with their men and foremen from both the Fripp plantations were here hauling cotton together with the whole available force of Coffin's. I had expected the latter, but thought it strange that I had not been informed last eve'g about Fripp's foremen and teams being wanted. I was about to ask from Mr. Salisbury an explanation when Col. Nobles, who was close by, accosted me with charges of interference with his business & making a great deal of trouble with the men, & went on with language very disparaging to the Gov[t] & to yourself. I told him if there was any question as to lines of authority between myself & him & his agents, I should not discuss it, and did not consider it my business to talk about it, as I occupied a subordinate position. I merely stated what position I had taken, which had been represented to him as much more authoritative than the reality. He repeatedly said I had no right to any authority whatever among the negroes, that you and all the rest of us were a set of d----d abolitionists come here to supersede Col. Reynolds in the exercise of his duties, & that our only object was to breed discontent among the negroes, using more abusive language about the Gov[t] and yourself. I again checked him by saying any question of his authority or mine must be settled at head quarters & told him I didnt wish to listen to such talk. He told me if I didn't want to hear it, I might go away. He said he told me nothing more than what he had told you, to which I replied that I did not think such language becoming to him, & that he was greatly mistaken if he thought we wished to create any discontent among the negroes, that on the contrary I had done and should continue to do all in my power to make them quiet and industrious. I asked him if he had taken some negroes from here to Beaufort on his last trip, saying that I had heard so, but did not think he would do so. He said he never allowed negroes aboard his boat except he hired them, & that he had hired some here. I asked him if they ran off when reaching Beaufort. "Oh, yes" he could not keep them. I remarked that this seemed very like allowing them to leave the plantation & work their passage off. All this conversation was in the presence of his own agents, some of the negroes, and their drivers, and as he claimed and insisted in their presence that I had no claim to any authority over them except as subservient to their business, which Col. Reynolds & himself did not propose to give into our hands, and as my title to such authority is not of a nature to be understood by the negroes or explained to them by the reading of my papers, I must say that however undignified and ungentlemanly on his part, I consider the occurrence highly detrimental to what authority I had established; for when the blacks consider his language and treatment of me, and have no means of seeing that I am likely to be sustained in the position I took; when they see us walking 10 or 15 miles a day, while every other white man here has all the horses he wants; when they see me living in a room full of *broken* furniture, with no bed to sleep on & with no fresh meat to eat, while other white men have well furnished apartments, kill all the beef they want, & spend their time in riding over the island, the natural inference to men of their calibre is that Mr. Gannet & I are "small fry" & that Col. Nobles & his men are the only ones of much consequence after all. To clinch this comes his orders last night, bringing down the men & teams from Fripp's without saying a word to me, though I gave Mr. Salisbury ample chance to do so; and Col. Nobles accusing me, in the driver's presence, of preventing the proper and orderly management of the work by keeping the men at work in the field when they "should have been here today." (Meaning, I suppose, Fripp's men, most of whom stay at home and dig most industriously and much to their credit, but who, I think, would have been here if they had been so ordered)

Now sir, I have not a bit of personal feeling in this matter, and I told Col. Nobles so, & told him we ought to work in harmony for our Gov^{t} which had sent us both here and which had trouble enough already without our making more, but I must say I am sadly disappointed in finding what little influence I had contrived to establish over the blacks by dint of lectures on the necessity of labor, and a partial organization of their labor with the tone of authority, thus undermined by an unprincipled and disappointed man, who knows well enough what he is about and is avowedly spiteful towards the Administration, yourself, & those under you.

If I had come here from any other motive than a sense of duty and a desire to elevate this degraded race by organizing their labor in a productive form, I should now say I couldn't stop here with any degree of self respect. But it is not a matter of pride or dignity. It is a question of conscience & *duty*. We are here to do what we can with God's help, & must expect to be opposed by the men whose self-interest is in the way. I am for the present nearly powerless. The negroes begin to think I am nobody, and so long as they think so, I cant be of much use. I feel as if my time & their time were being wasted, & precious time it is too for starting the crops. I am confident that if I had been treated as I was promised, things might have gone on smoothly enough, though very disagreeably, for we are surrounded by adverse sympathies, but now that a breach has occurred in the very presence of the negroes, & I am told by the man who brings them their pay in his hand & for whom they have been at work for three months back, and have learned to look to as a man in authority, that I am "encroaching on his authority & interfering with his business, & that I have no right to assume any authority" I must say that the result follows quickly that I *do have none*, till you can build it up.

You may think me sensitive on the subject of horseflesh. I have been accustomed to walking, & regard it no hardship in cool weather, but there is no race in the world with whom a little *state* gives so much power as the African. They have always been accustomed to see men of any power treated as such, and receiving the attention corresponding thereto. They have always seen a white man on a horse, and have got to think it so far a badge of power & caste, that they will hardly lift their hats to a white man on foot. In fact the negroes themselves, while moving about from one plant[n] to another always find some old mule to straddle & look down with contempt upon a "walking nigger". How then must they compare the white man who walks as we do, and he who has plenty of horses as Col Nobles men have?– If you can do anything towards establishing me in the position I took, & proving to these poor fellows that I am of some importance to them, I can be of use & I know how to be.

Perhaps I might have been justified by my papers in assuming the authority which I did not, viz. that I should take care of the labor on cotton as well as in the field, but I refrained from motives of policy, wishing to give Col. Reynolds' men their whole field and reserve my own independently.

I think my ideas about the necessity of authority have your approval. We find the blacks as dependent as children, and as ignorant of social laws as they are of the alphabet. We must stand in the relation of parents to them until such time as they can be taught to stand alone, and as all parental authority should be tempered by benevolence, sound judgement & firmness, backed if necessary by force, so must this undeveloped race be treated if we mean to make men of them, & without such authority judiciously exercised, we shall just as surely fail as does any parent fail in trying to make useful and self-governing men & women of his children without first teaching them to obey. I hope to see you here soon. Till then I trust, indeed I *know*, that everything in your power will be done to advance the object for which we are here.

May God protect these poor people and make men of them. Yrs respectfully

ALS Edw. S. Philbrick

Edw. S. Philbrick to Edw. L. Pierce Esq., 27 Mar. 1862, vol. 19, #106, Port Royal Correspondence, 5th Agency, RG 366 [Q-12]. Two days later Edward L. Pierce, the Treasury Department special agent, informed William H. Reynolds, chief cotton agent for the Treasury Department, that relations between Philbrick and Reynolds's subordinates (William H. Nobles, Alfred W. Salisbury, and Edward Salisbury) had become "intolerable." Nobles, Pierce charged, seemed "determined . . . to thwart the entire movement intrusted to myself and to excite hostility among the negroes against me & the superintendents I have designated." Vowing to "omit no opportunity to free the territory & the negroes of [Nobles's] ruinous influence," Pierce urged Reynolds to "co-operate with me for that purpose" by dismissing him. (Edward L. Pierce to Lieut. Col. Wm. H. Reynolds, 29 Mar. 1862, vol. 19, filed with #114, Port Royal Correspondence, 5th Agency, RG 366 [Q-13].) Instead Reynolds merely referred Pierce's letter to Nobles, who fired off a caustic rejoinder that denounced the charges against him as "untrue in every particular." Ridiculing both the personal pretensions of the plantation superintendents and their ignorance of cotton cultivation, Nobles contrasted the naïveté of Pierce, Philbrick, and their colleagues with his own practical experience in employing 2,000 former slaves to collect the 1861 cotton crop. Unlike the plantation superintendents, he sneered, "I did not . . . represent that it was only necessary . . . to come out here and look profoundly wise to set the negroes to work, and upon the first salutation say to the poor negroes, 'sisters & brothers you are free,' and then use them as they were wont to be used by their old masters in the cotton fields, placing upon them the additional burden of having first to teach their new masters . . . the most simple rudiments of plantation life & labors. Neither did I carry an umbrella under my arm because

I had seen the planters thus represented in the picture books." (Wm. H. Nobles to Edward L. Pierce Esq., 2 Apr. 1862, vol. 19, #119, Port Royal Correspondence, 5th Agency, RG 366 [Q-14].) Meanwhile, on March 30, 1862, Pierce forwarded Philbrick's letter to Salmon P. Chase, Secretary of the Treasury, seconding Philbrick's contention that "Col N– was a most unsuitable man for the place, so far as the welfare of the negroes is concerned," and condemning Alfred Salisbury and Edward Salisbury for exhibiting "the profoundest contempt of the negro." Together, Pierce alleged, the three cotton agents were making "[e]very effort . . . to defeat the movement which has the sanction of the Government and the sympathies of the country." "You must see," he emphasized, "that negroes cannot serve two masters." (Edward L. Pierce to Hon. Salmon P. Chase, 30 Mar. 1862, vol. 19, #105, Port Royal Correspondence, 5th Agency, RG 366 [Q-12].) On the following day, Reynolds forwarded his version of the situation to Chase. Pierce, he complained, had "made himself *personally* obnoxious to me, by assuming authority over those employed by me, & dictating in matters connected with my Department." Conceding the humane motives of Pierce and the plantation superintendents, Reynolds charged "that seven eighths of these Gentlemen are *totally unfit* for the positions which they attempt to occupy." (Wm. H. Reynolds to Hon. S. P. Chase, 1 Apr. 1862, vol. 19, #117, Port Royal Correspondence, 5th Agency, RG 366 [Q-14].) Nobles remained in the Sea Islands for five more weeks, nursing a grudge against Pierce that culminated in a physical attack. As a result of that incident, the military authorities at Port Royal banished Nobles from the islands. (Willie Lee Rose, *Rehearsal for Reconstruction: The Port Royal Experiment* [Indianapolis, Ind., 1964], p. 142.)

15: Headquarters of the 2nd Brigade of the South Carolina Expeditionary Corps to the Superintendent of Contrabands at Beaufort, South Carolina

Beaufort SC. March [28?] 1862

Sir. I enclose to you a series of instructions for the proper regulation of the system of Management of the Department of Contraband negroes resident in this city.

You are instructed to retain within the city such number of contraband Negroes as are requisite for the ordinary labor at the Government works. The remainder you are directed to remove to the plantations for employment in the fields.

In detailing negroes for city duty you will be careful to give the preference to efficient refugees from the main land and the longest dwellers in the city.

Orders permitting negroes to pass from this island to any other shall be issued only from your department on the requisition of the overseer of the plantation on which the applicant may reside, and approved at these Head Quarters, such passes shall be limited to special cases, as illness of a near relative or plantation business. Commanders of posts and Commanders of Cross Roads are empowered upon the written request of the overseer of a plantation to grant a negro a pass to the city of Beaufort, the time allowed being specified thereon, and the negro shall present such pass at the office of the Superintendent of Contrabands in order to obtain a return pass. Dates on passes shall invariably be written in full.

You are instructed to punish at your discretion all negroes absent beyond the time granted by their passes by sending them for penal servitude on public works.

You shall establish a market at Beaufort for the sale of plantation produce, fish &c &c, at stated prices and license resident negroes of good character as retail vendors. The produce shall be conveyed to the city by plantation carts and sold under proper regulations to the retail vendors only by the overseers

The rates of wages of negroes in government employ shall be as follows.

First class mechanics from $9 to $12 per month, with one ration daily

Second class mechanics $5 to per month with one ration daily

Drivers of Gangs from $9 to $12 per month, with one ration daily

First class laborers $6 per month, with one ration daily
Second " " $4 " " "

All persons in this command having negroes employed as servants or otherwise shall be required to report to your dept on the First and Fourteenth of every month, in writing, the names and ages of such servants, their masters names, the rate of pay they each receive, and to what day they were last paid.

The rates of wages of domestic servants shall be as follows
First class servants of either sex $6 per month and board
Second " " " $4 " "
Waiting boys & girls $3 " "
Ostlers coachmen &c $4 " "

The rates of charges for washing by female negroes shall be as follows:
Soldiers under clothing 15¢ per dozen
Finer sorts of " 34¢ "

All servants shall be hired from the Dept of Contrabands under the approval of the Superintendent. The superintendent shall give negroes semi-monthly passes for city use Such passes shall not be transferable, and an abuse of the privilege shall subject the offender to penal servitude on the public works.

You are empowered to furnish for the families of an employee on the government works, at the workmans request hominy, corn, or in lieu thereof hardbread, molasses, coffee, vinegar and salt to an amount not exceeding $3 per month. The amount to be deducted from the mans monthly wages. The supply shall be obtained from the Contraband Commissary Department under your written authority.

You will cause to be arrested negroes found in an intoxicated condition, or creating disturbance or detected in breaking down or carrying away fences, trees and other property: also improper female characters and white men resorting to the negro quarters without permission from the Dept of Contrabands.

Negroes failing to keep their houses and the streets of their locality in a cleanly condition shall be subjected to a penalty or punishment to be approved at these Head Quarters.

Negroes shall not be permitted to pass to or from their work from the Negro quarters except by   street, and only those shall pass who are accompanied by a person detailed from the Dept of Contrabands for that purpose.

You are empowered to provide suitable accommodation with rations for all aged, infirm and destitute negroes and detail an efficient person to carry out this object By order of Brig Gen Stevens

HLcSr (sd). Hasard Stevens

Capt. Hasard Stevens to the Superintendent of the Dept. of Contrabands, [28?] March 1862, vol. 37/89D 9AC, pp. 53–56, Letters Sent, ser. 5075, 2d Brigade, SC Expeditionary Corps, RG 393 Pt. 2 No. 325 [C-1228]. The two blank spaces appear in the manuscript. Two months later, General Isaac I. Stevens (whose brigade had become part of a new district and department structure but whose headquarters remained at Beaufort) issued a circular promulgating new regulations "for the better government of the negro population." They provided that "[a]ll servants of officers and civilians and city negroes shall have their names registered . . . and receive a printed pass monthly," that "[n]o plantation negresses will pass into town, except in cases of sickness of a near relation," that "[n]o plantation negro will stay in town over night," that newly arrived freedpeople must report to the superintendent of contrabands and receive a pass, and that "no Officer or man or citizen will enter the negro quarters after sunset except on actual Governmental service." (Circular, Head Quarters 2d Brigade, North. Dist. Dept. of the South, 24 May 1862, vol. 36/89A 9AC, p. 86, General Orders, Special Orders, Circulars, & Letters Sent, ser. 5077, 2d Brigade, Northern Dist., Dept. of the South, RG 393 Pt. 2 No. 325 [C-1205].)

16: Plantation Superintendent on St. Helena Island, South Carolina, to the Treasury Department Special Agent for the South Carolina Sea Islands

Coffin's Phrogmore Plantation [*St. Helena Island, S.C.*],
March 29th, 1862.

My dear Sir, I present herewith a table of statistics pertaining to the Plantations which you have entrusted to my care, with Mr J. H. Palmer, as teacher and assistant. The table is prepared according to the form proposed by Mr French.

I find most of the colored people well-disposed on all these plantations, and many of the field hands are every day at work in preparing the ground for corn & potatoes; & on some of the estates the planting of potatoes has already commenced. Listing for cotton has also been commenced on two or three of them. But there is a very general complaint among the hands on these estates that they have received no compensation, in any form, from the Government for their labor in getting last year's crop of cotton ready for shipment, as was promised by the cotton-agents, while many of their late associates have been getting $8 per month, besides rations, for their services at Bay Point, Hilton Head & Beaufort. About twenty-five persons who belong on the plantations of which I have charge are now employed at the places named. It is very natural that others should wish to follow their example, and that they should manifest great reluctance to work on the cotton-fields without some substantial evidence that they are to be paid for their labor. I fear that they will lose all confidence in the Government unless something is done immediately to satisfy them that they are to be placed on as favorable a footing as those who have left the estates to find employment at the military posts. My impression is that nothing would tend so much to reassure them & to make them labor efficiently on the plantations as to distribute among them, according to desert, *a certain amount of money in part payment of their wages*. They feel entitled already to subsistence from last year's crop of corn because it is the product of their labor under the old state of things.

I have no doubt that great benefit would result from allowing the negroes a more generous diet than they have heretofore received, if nothing more were added than salt beef, salt pork, and salt fish. The negroes on the sugar estates in Cuba, which I have visited, are very fond of salt fish; and this article constitutes a part of their weekly allowance, the plantain and corn meal being their principal vegetable food.

I have given directions to the drivers to see that the cabins are cleaned as often at least as once a week. They are generally in better condition than I expected. I have also requested the drivers to prepare lime for whitewashing the cabins and other buildings as soon as is practicable.

Mr Palmer is making good progress in the work of instructing both the adults & the children on the plantations under our charge, and all of his pupils manifest great interest in learning to read.

The dwelling-house on the Edgar Fripp Estate is a much more desirable residence than the house which we at present occupy, and we propose to remove thither in the course of a week or two, unless it should be your wish that we should remain longer where we are.

I have nothing further of especial moment to remark upon at present except to say that the two gins now in use on the Phrogmore Estate are somewhat out of repair, and are turning out only about 200 pounds each of cleaned cotton per day instead of 300 pounds, as they might easily do when in good order. New covering for the rollers & new lacing for the driving belts are particularly needed. Very respectfully Your Obedent Servant

ALS Richard Soule Jr.

Richard Soule Jr. to Edward L. Pierce Esq., 29 Mar. 1862, vol. 19, #110, Port Royal Correspondence, 5th Agency, RG 366 [Q-13]. The table said to have been enclosed is not in the volume with Soule's letter.

17: Headquarters of the 2nd Brigade of the Northern District of the Department of the South to the Commander of the Post of Ladies Island, South Carolina

Beaufort S.C. April 7. 1862

Sir The General directs in the execution of orders previously issued that the Military Commandants should sustain the authority of the Agents over the negroes on the plantations, that within the limits of your command you will not hesitate to furnish men to arrest refractory and insubordinate residents and to take measures to keep in confinement negroes who may be guilty of serious offences. M[r] Pierce the Government Agent will confer with you in regard to this matter.

It may be necessary to resort to the ball and chain in extreme cases. If no provision can be made for confinement within the limits of your command, it will then be necessary to send hard cases to Beaufort, with a report. By order of Brig. Gen. Stevens

HLcSr sd. Hasard Stevens

Capt. Hasard Stevens to Capt. Dimmock, 7 Apr. 1862, vol. 37/89D 9AC, pp. 89–90, Letters Sent, ser. 5075, 2d Brigade, Northern Dist., Dept. of the South, RG 393 Pt. 2 No. 325 [C-1231]. General Isaac I. Stevens and his brigade had been involved in enforcing discipline on the plantations even before the arrival of the Northern plantation superintendents recruited by Edward L. Pierce. In mid-February 1862, Stevens had ordered his troops to sustain the authority of treasury agents who were engaged in collecting cotton left behind when plantation owners fled the Sea Islands. At Stevens's suggestion, the cotton agents had "appointed" drivers and "directed them to control and manage the negroes, so they be well ordered, kept on the plantations and be made to get in the remaining crops." "These negroes," Stevens's adjutant had insisted, "must be controled and made to work." (Capt. Hasard Stevens to Capt. Graham, 17 Feb. 1862, vol. 36/89C 9AC, pp. 113–14, Letters Sent, ser. 5075, 2d Brigade, SC Expeditionary Corps, RG 393 Pt. 2 No. 325 [C-1220].)

18: Plantation Superintendent on St. Helena Island, South Carolina, to the Treasury Department Special Agent for the South Carolina Sea Islands

Fuller Plantation [*St. Helena Island, S.C.*] Apr. 11 1862

Dear Sir, It becomes my duty to report some depredations which have been committed on one of the plantations under my charge.

Yesterday a party of soldiers, coming as they said from Otter Island, landed on the estate of Richard Sams on Dathaw Island, caught five sheep and two lambs, tied them, and carried them away in the boat with them.

The Foreman, Hampton, endeavored to persuade the officer commanding not to take them, but he said he did not care a damn about any agent, for he was as much an agent as any one, and he should take just what he wanted – that the agents on the places were keeping them for their own good, and not for the government.

He inquired if they were at work, and who set them to work, and whom they were at work for. They told him they were planting cotton for the government, and were set to work by me. He told them they were great fools, for the government would never pay them anything – if it were going to they ought to have their pay every week – that we were fooling them, and that was all.

About a fortnight ago the lock was broken from the corn-barn by some soldiers from the same place, and Hampton said the officer with them, told the negroes not to say anything about it.

When I visited the plantation today, I found great dissatisfaction, and lack of confidence in my statements, and some disinclination to work, caused by the remarks of these soldiers to them yesterday. And of course my influence over them is much weakened there-by, until I can again gain their confidence which I cannot easily do, if such visits be liable to be made by the soldiers every few days. I am respectfully yours

HLcSr T. Edwin Ruggles

T. Edwin Ruggles to Edward L. Pierce Esqr., 11 Apr. 1862, vol. 19, #128, Port Royal Correspondence, 5th Agency, RG 366 [Q-15]. When Edward L. Pierce, the special agent, instructed Ruggles to undertake a full investigation of the forays onto the Sams plantation, Ruggles conferred first with the Union commander at Otter Island, who replied that none of his soldiers had landed on Dathaw the day the livestock was taken and, moreover, that his troops procured their provisions from other islands. The commander of a navy sloop anchored off Otter Island also denied any knowledge of the incidents described by Ruggles, although he acknowledged that "he furnished himself with fresh provisions from these Islands" and declared "that he should continue to do so until he received further orders." (Edward L. Pierce to Mr. T. Edwin Ruggles, 11 Apr. 1862, and T. Edwin Ruggles to Mr. Edward L. Pierce, Esqr., 15 Apr. 1862, vol. 19, #128–29, Port Royal Correspondence, 5th Agency, RG 366 [Q-15].) Pierce subsequently complained to more senior army and navy commanders about the seizure of property from plantations under his supervision, and, in response, the commanders of the South Atlantic Squadron and of the Northern District of the Department of the South both issued orders forbidding the removal of property from such estates without written authorization. (General Orders, No. 3, Head Quarters: Northern District;–Department of the South, 17 Apr. 1862, Edward L. Pierce to Commodore S. F. Dupont, 21 Apr. 1862, and Edward L. Pierce to Hon. S. P. Chase, 8 May 1862, vol. 19, #125, #127, #151, Port Royal Correspondence, 5th Agency, RG 366 [Q-15].)

19: Plantation Superintendent on St. Helena Island, South Carolina, to a Massachusetts Businessman

Coffins Point St. Helena I. [*S.C.*] April 12th 1862

Copy

Dear Ned I wrote you on the 2d inst, enclosing copy of a communication to Mr Pierce about Col. Nobles &c.[1] After I returned from Hilton Head Mr. P. went down and saw the parties there, but got from Col. N. nothing but abuse and from Col. R.[2] good smooth talk, but nothing satisfactory. Col. R. went off in the Atlantic which sailed on the 4th inst. and doubtless is now at Washington. He told Mr. P. before leaving that he had directed the Salisburys to leave & put the remaining Cotton in his hands, but they are still here at this date. Mr. Pierce's letter to Col. R. complaining of Col. N. & the Salisburys[3] which I delivered in person together with my own communication was given to Col. Nobles & he circulated them among the Salisburys, so they are in a furious state, and are making as much trouble as they well know how to. I did not like to trust Col. R. with these papers for fear he would make such use of them, but Mr. Pierce had more confidence in him, and directed me to do so.

Mr. Pierce's letter to Sec. Chase[4] went in the Atlantic's mail, but as Col. R. is there in person to plead Col. Nobles case, I don't believe Mr. P. will gain his object in getting rid of them, at least not without considerable delay.

I will now give you a sort of diary to show how life is spent here.

Apl. 3^{d} 68 hands in the potato field planting sweet potatoes, swinging their hoes in unison timed by a jolly song, words undistinguishable. They work with a good will, and plant about 13 acres during the day. I walk over to the Fripp's Pine Grove plantation & find the people planting corn, teach school after task is done 3 to 5 P.M. in loft of Cotton House, benches supplied from "Praise house" that is, chapel, and carried back to same after school every day, the chapel being too small for school house. I find an old sulky with shafts and body supplied by a negro carpenter who says the wheels and frame belong to the Gov^{t} but thinks his work in saving the pieces & rebuilding sulky worth $4. I pay the same and take possession of sulky, riding home with an old sore-backed horse and a harness consisting mostly of old hemp.

April 4th Spend most of the forenoon making my sulky harness by sewing together sundry bits of leather picked up at different times, & take out the bits of string with which it was held together. Mr. Gannett gives out a few garments to some worthy women; the other women make a terrible fuss because they don't all get some. Their husbands leave their work and come down on me in a posse & say their wives deserve as much as any (& I dare say they do) All hands agree to wait till we can get clothing or cloth enough to give each family a piece. They dislike this made-up clothing & the first thing they do is to make it over to suit their wants. They have always made all their clothes and their mistress' [&] masters' too except the best suit, so our Northern ladies get no thanks for their sewing.

Sat^{y} Apl. 5. The people on Coffin's hesitate about working Saturdays. I tell them they must work or I shall report them to Massa Lincoln as too lazy to be free. The best part go into the field grumbling about "no clothes, no tobacco, no molasses, no bacon, no salt, no shoes, no medicine &c." which is all very true and unanswerable. I can only say the war has shut up all these things and we can't get them in the North as we used to, but I would do my best to get a little.

I take my sulky and *new* harness and drive off to spend the night with Dr. Wakefield on my way to church to-morrow, stopping at Fripp's as I go along & teaching school.

Sunday April 6th Ride on to the brick church and meet there about 500 negroes from all about the island in their best dresses, of which a good part are very ragged. Meet Mr. Pierce and a lot of our companions. Mr P. says he has no authority to offer any definite pay per acre for cotton planting & I mustn't show favors to my people. I am content with the latter rule, but think it too bad that the people who are so distracted by camp labor at $10. per month, should not have a definite promise for their plantation work. I know if the leasing system had been adopted they would have had this stimulus from the contractors, who know how to use such motives to good advantage. After church I ride on three miles to get some sugar at Mr. Eustis's where our rations have been waiting nearly a week for conveyance. Have a nice dinner and chat with Mr. Eustis & Mr. Hooper & start back about 5 P.M. flies biting like fun; take a bucket of rice & 4 bottles molasses between my feet, and a candle box full of sugar, salt, & bread tied on behind. Twelve miles of fine sandy road give my rations an ample supply of grit especially the bread, & my tired horse can't be induced to go over 2 1/2 miles an hour. For the last three miles I walk by his side with my blanket wrapped about me to keep warm. Splendid moonlight.

April 7th All hands at work in the new Cotton field for the first time this year, working well. Men women and children swinging some 65 heavy hoes, without shoes. The wife of the driver (we have two drivers on this plantation) who left to seek his fortune among the soldiers last week, comes to me & complains that she does not get her allowance of "clabber" (i.e. bonny clapper or milk). I tell her she mustn't expect to get the allowance of a driver's wife now her husband is not here, but must be content with an equal share of milk with all the women. She mutters a good deal but the other women only laugh at her as if to say "that's right."

Steamer Flora comes to our wharf about noon after Cotton. All hands at work loading and hauling to wharf the rest of the day.

Apl. 8 All the men at work loading Cotton. I stroll out through the woods to the cotton field expecting to find the women at work, but find none. On inquiring find Col. Nobles told them to come & get some sugar after the steamer was loaded and they thought best to hang about the steamer till noon. The bbl. sugar is then carried up to house and sold to them for money, each taking what they can pay for. I find Col. N. & both Salisburys in the house removing all the best furniture from the house. I told Col. N.

that Col. Reynolds had promised Mr. Pierce and myself that this furniture should not be removed, that Mr. P. expected to put some more folks on this part of the island and that no other furniture could be found hereabouts fit to use, & I protested against the removal of any of it. Col. N. replied that he knew nothing about any understanding about it and that he had a requisition from Gen. Hunter for some furniture and this was the only place he knew of to get it. He went on abusing me and Mr. Pierce exhausting a choice supply of epithets in presence of his agents and some of the negroes and ended by saying I had told so many lies about him he didn't believe a word I said about the furniture and he should accordingly take it and did so. I go to the Fripp's Point plantation in P.M. Find the people had quit work in middle of forenoon, tasks only half done. Men were all here helping load Cotton & women left to work alone – so (of course) got quarelling, felt discouraged about pay, & declared they wouldn't work on Cotton without the usual supply of clothes. I called them all up and had a grand pow-wow I first heard their complaints, & then told them the usual facts about the difficulty of getting clothing &c. during the war, told how much they had at stake in their own welfare and that of millions of other negroes, and that if they failed to show now that they could work as hard without the whip as they used to work with it, that the Gov^t would be disgusted with them & believe all the stories their masters told us about their laziness &c. &c. hinting that if they didn't raise Cotton enough to pay for all the comforts they wanted the people of the north would say "these islands are not worth keeping, let's take our soldier's away & let the Secesh come back." I told them I had just bought some salt at Beaufort with my own money, meaning to give them a quart all round, but that if they behaved lazy I shouldn't try to do much more for them. They all broke out at this with "Thank you massa" thank you a thousand times! "We *will* work. You shan't call us lazy. We will never work again for old massa & his whip. We only wanted to know if we were sure of our pay, it is so hard living without clothes a whole year, & we get sick putting sea water in our hominy, & haven't had our salt for so many months." A good many promised to make up the unfinished tasks, of the morning, & I called the children together for school, leaving all in good humor. The Driver tells me that Massa Washington Fripp, the brother of his old owner has just been shot near Charleston for refusing to enlist. He was told this by a negro just escaped from the main. He says "our massa didn't like this war: he told other white people it was all wrong & that the Yankees were sure to beat. He would have stayed here with us but didn't dare to, the other white folks would have killed him. He told us before he went off when the Yankees took Hilton Head that we must stay here and work as we used to, & that if we went to the main as the soldiers told us, we should all starve, so we hid in the woods till the soldiers gone, & then came back here and went to work sir, getting ready to plant corn as massa told us, & if you had only come a month earlier sir, we could have planted as much cotton as ever sir, but now it is too late to list much ground, & we can't plant much." I told him to plant all he could & I would do all I could for the comfort of the people. The Flora goes off in P.M. with all the rest of Coffin's Cotton, about 58000 lbs. in all when clean ginned.

Apl. 9th Violent thunder storm in morning, leaving the air clean & cool, about 10 A.M. it clears up & the people go to work. The Flora having unloaded at Beaufort comes back to Fripp's point about 2 P.M. & commences to load their Cotton, calling people away from their work in the field.

Apl. 10th All the men from Coffin's go to Fripp's to help load cotton at daylight; our Driver goes over about 8 A.M. & finds the Cotton all loaded & steamer leaving. Men come back hungry and won't work in field to-day. Women get uneasy without them & quit early. I paddle across to Fripp's Point in a canoe & teach School, paddling back about sunset. The team I had sent to Mr. Eustis's for salt comes back with it & our rations for April, also letters from home up to March 27th Also hear that two boxes clothing have arrived at Eustis's for Mr. Gannett, & I order mule cart sent for them to-morrow Mr. Salisbury informs me he wants a scow crew of 4 good men for several days excursion to the further side of Morgan island to collect cotton. This being an extra piece of civility on his part to *tell me* he wanted the men before taking them I put it down to his credit. I don't like to let the men go, for we are already short by 24 smart young hands of the usual number here, leaving scarce any but women, children and old men to plant; but I have no authority to say no and so assent.

Apl. 11th People all start for the Cotton field in good humor. Driver is called off by Mr. Salisbury to furnish him with the crew: while he is absent from field, the people, mostly women and children, say among themselves "Here are 24 of our husbands and brothers gone to work for their own selves, what's the use of our workg for our Driver or massa. Let's go work for ourselves too and away they scatter, the greater part go to work listing Cotton ground in detached patches, scattered all over 300 acres, in a most republican spirit, but not in a way to be encouraged at present. Some go catching crabs, some go planting corn on their own hook. All leave the field early. I go out and find the Driver utterly discouraged, says it's no use bothering with such people, & he goes to planting in his own patch too. Now this would do well enough in a more advanced state of civilization, but just now it must be treated as chaos & insubordination, for under such a system, the non-workers, old folks, &c. would starve. I walk about among some of them & tell them this day's work will count them nothing on my book, & that if they don't work as the driver tells them, I shall never give them any salt, or clothing or anything else. Visiting Fripp's plantation in P.M. I find all in good order, corn & potatoes all planted & about 15 acres cotton land ready for planting.

April 12. Go out with the people early and see them go to work cheerfully, planting cotton seed. About 20 acres ready on this plantation, which they will plant to-day. I find one man a little saucy to the driver & give him a lecture, sending him about his work. I find my hint about the *salt* has taken effect, & the people appear to work willingly and cheerfully. In fact they are the most docile and easily managed people in the world, & I can only admire the amount of patience exhibited under such untoward circumstances. This plantation shows more demoralization than any other on the island I am told. The reason is plain enough. The 79th N.Y. were quartered here for some time, making a slaughter house of this building where we now live, killing some 80 head of cattle, eating lots of their sweet potatoes & leaving barely enough for seed. The soldiers hired the men for cooks, & told them they were free to do as they pleased now, they need never mind a driver any more, that each of them was good as a driver &c. telling them to go to work each on his own patch, & raise what corn they wanted. Now this may have been meant well enough, but it had a most chaotic effect. Men should be careful how they disorganize labor if they don't substitute a better organization in the place of that they pull down. They ought to have seen that with a rude childlike people like these, any independant individual action was not to be expected to succeed except in isolated cases. They neglected to tell them that they must plant cotton to pay for clothes, & every other comfort which they expected to receive except corn & potatoes. The natural disgust for cotton labor was left to brood till we arrived, & nothing but corn ground was prepared except on Mr. Eustis's who came before. Thanks to the natural good sense of the negroes, they prepared a good deal of land for corn on their own responsibility with no orders from any one but their drivers. I think I may be able to plant 100 acres cotton here and 50 or 60 on each of the Fripp plantations, but can't promise. I hope that the cloth for summer clothes will be forthcoming. I gave a list of the articles furnished by Coffin every 6 mos. to Mr. Pierce a month ago, & Mr. Gannett sent a copy to Mr. Emerson some 2 weeks since. I enclose another copy for you. Mr Pierce thinks northern benevolence will supply it. But I think the Government *ought* to. It is a good large pile when applied to 8000 people.

. . . .

Considering the fact that a limited amt. of clothing has already been supplied both from northern contributions and purchases by negroes with money earned about camps, & by selling eggs chickens &c, the whole of the above amt. would not be required now, but they will doubtless earn enough by the Cotton labor to pay for the whole, & we mean to give out clothing when we get enough to go round, at a low price, charging it to them on account of their Cotton labor as I do the salt, of which I have bought enough to give a quart all round on my 3 plantations once. I suppose Mr. Gannett reports all about the schools, so I say nothing. He teaches 3 daily & I teach one, when not interrupted by other duties. He is working harder than he ought to do when the weather gets hot, but is probably none the worse for it now. I shall endeavor to hold him back bye & bye. We enjoy excellent health. Let us hear from you how matters look at your point of view. Truly yrs,

HLcSr (Signed) E. S. Philbrick

Excerpts from E. S. Philbrick to Ned, 12 Apr. 1862, vol. 19, filed with #154, Port Royal Correspondence, 5th Agency, RG 366 [Q-19]. The addressee was Edward Atkinson, a textile entrepreneur and member of the Educational Commission of Boston, which was sponsoring Philbrick and other plantation superintendents in the Sea Islands. The omitted passage is a list of the clothing and provisions that had customarily been distributed on the Coffin and Fripp plantations; a nearly identical list appears above, in doc. 13.

1 The letter to Edward L. Pierce, a Treasury Department special agent in the South Carolina Sea Islands, had complained about the interference of Treasury Department cotton agents, particularly William H. Nobles, in plantation operations. It is printed above, as doc. 14.

2 William H. Reynolds, chief Treasury Department cotton agent in the Sea Islands.

3 For a summary of the letter, which complained of the conduct of Nobles and his assistants, Alfred W. Salisbury and Edward Salisbury, see above, doc. 14n.

4 Pierce's letter to Secretary of the Treasury Salmon P. Chase, dated March 30, 1862, had urged that Nobles and the Salisburys be dismissed. (See above, doc. 14n.)

20: Commander of the 2nd Brigade of the Northern District of the Department of the South to the Department Commander

Beaufort S.C. May 10, 1862

Sir I have received your letter in regard to raising a regiment of Black troops,[1] What rules shall be observed in this business.

I Nearly all the labor of this command, including carpentering and smiths work is done by negroes. Some two hundred men are thus engaged, shall these be allowed to enlist, thus throwing labor on the white troops. The labor consists in loading and unloading vessels, work on the dock enlarging and repairing the same, work keeping boats and materiel in order, labor with teams and in the bakeries labor cutting wood and timber, labor in cultivating the military farm of this command, labor in policing the town of Beaufort.

2d What rules shall be observed on the plantations, so that the crops no[*w*] put in should be taken care of, and enough be raised for the subsistence of the negroes, Shall the good efficient drivers be allowed to enlist? or shall only a proportion of the able bodied men from each plantation:

3 I estimate there may be 800 able bodied negroes within the limits of my command, between the Ages of 18 & 45 of these 200 are in the quartermasters service at this place. what proportion of the remaining 600 would it be desirable to have enlisted. If one half, they will furnish three companies of one hundred men each

4 Capt Walbridge has reported and is at work to day. Three non-commissioned officers of this command thus far have offered their services. I am Sir very respectfully Your most obt

HLcSr Sg Isaac I Stevens

Brig. Gen. Isaac I. Stevens to Maj. Gen. Hunter, 10 May 1862, vol. 37/89D 9AC, pp. 159–60, Letters Sent, ser. 5075, 2d Brigade, Northern Dist., Dept. of the South, RG 393 Pt. 2 No. 325 [C-1235]. No reply has been found in the records of the Department of the South. Despite his reservations, General Stevens promptly issued the impressment order called for by the department commander, General David Hunter. In enforcing the order, Union soldiers conscripted black men from plantations under the supervision of the Treasury Department, evoking protests from the former slaves, from plantation superintendents, and from the treasury agent in charge of the superintendents. (See *Freedom*, ser. 2: docs. 1–2.)

1 On May 9, 1862, General David Hunter, commander of the Department of the South, had instructed General Henry W. Benham, commander of the

department's Northern District, to have his subordinate officers forward under guard "all able bodied negroes capable of bearing arms." (A.A.A.G. Ed. W. Smith to Brig. Gen. H. W. Benham, 9 May 1862, Letters Received, ser. 2255, Northern Dist., Dept. of the South, RG 393 Pt. 2 No. 130 [C-1633].)

21: Treasury Department Special Agent for the South Carolina Sea Islands to the Secretary of the Treasury

Port Royal [*S.C.*] June 2. 1862.

Sir Upon the transfer of the supervision of affairs at Port Royal from the Treasury to the War Department,[1] a summary of the results of this agency may be expected by you – and therefore this report is transmitted

Your instructions of Feb 19. intrusted to me the general superintendence and direction of all such persons as might be employed upon the abandoned plantations with a view to prevent the deterioration of the estates, to secure their best possible cultivation and the greatest practicable benefit to the laborers upon them.[2] The Department not being provided with proper powers to employ upon salaries superintendents and teachers under the plan submitted in my report of February 3^d [3] enjoined cooperation with associations of judicious and humane citizens in Boston, New York and other cities who proposed to commission and employ persons for the religious instruction ordinary education and general employment of the laboring population. Authority was given to the Special Agent at the same time to select and appoint applicants for such purposes and assign each to his respective duty, such persons when compensated to draw their compensation from private sources, receiving transportation, subsistence and quarters only from the Government. The Educational Commission of Boston had already been organized, and the organization of the National Freedman's Relief Association of New York followed a few days later. Still later the Port Royal Relief Committee of Philadelphia was appointed

On the morning of March 9th forty one men and twelve women accepted for the above purposes and approved by the first two of the above associations, disembarked at Beaufort, having left New York on the third of that month on board the US. Transport, the Steamship Atlantic, accompanied by the Special Agent. The Educational Commission of Boston had commissioned twenty five of the men and four of the women – The National Freedman's Relief Association of New York had commissioned sixteen of the men and five of the women and three women from Washington City had received your own personal commendation. The men were of various occupations, farmers, mechanics, tradesmen, teachers, physicians, clergymen, ranging in age from twenty one to sixty years. Not being provided with full topographical knowledge of the islands, it was necessary for the Special Agent to explore them for locations. At the close of the first fortnight after their arrival, the entire original delegation had been assigned to districts which they had reached. Since then others have arrived viz fourteen on March 23[d], fourteen on April 14th and a few at a later date, making in all seventy four men and nineteen women who having been commissioned by the associations and receiving the permit of the Collector of New York, have arrived here and been assigned to posts. Of the seventy four men, forty six were commissioned and employed by the Boston Society and twenty eight by that of New York. Of the nineteen women, nine were commissioned by the New York Society – six by that of Boston, one by that of Philadelphia and three others not so commissioned, but approved by yourself were accepted. Except in the case of the three women approved by yourself no persons have been received into this service not previously approved by the associations with whom you enjoined cooperation. Of the seventy four men, twenty four were stationed on Port Royal Island, a few of these doing special service at Beaufort, fifteen on St Helena, thirteen on Ladies, nine on Edisto, seven on Hilton Head, three on Pickney, one on Cat and Cane, one on Paris, and one on Daufuskie A few of the above returned north soon after their arrival so that the permanent number here at any one time duly commissioned and in actual service has not exceeded seventy men and sixteen women. The number at present is sixty two men and thirteen women. A larger corps of superintendents and teachers might have been employed to advantage, but as injurious results would attend the overdoing of the work of supervision it was thought best not to receive more until experience had indicated the permanent need.

The following is a list of the islands with the number of plantations and people upon them which have been superintended by the above persons.

	number of Plantations	Population
Port Royal	56	1909
St Helena (including Dathaw & Morgan)	53.	2,721
Ladies (including Wassa, Coosaw – Cat & Cane)	31.	1259
Hilton Head	15	943.
Pinkney	2	423

Daufuskie	3	69.
Paris	5	274.
Edisto	21	1278.
Hutchinson Beef & Ashe	3	174.
	189	9050

The above population is classified as follows – three hundred and nine mechanics and house servants not working in the field, six hundred and ninety three old sickly and unable to work, three thousand six hundred and nineteen children not useful for field labor and four thousand four hundred and twenty nine field hands. The field hands have been classified as under the former system, into full. three quarters, one half and one quarter hands. The term one quarter generally designates boys & girls of about twelve years just sent to the field, the term half applies often to persons somewhat infirm and to women *enceinte*, and the term three quarters applies to those doing less than a full hand and more than a half hand. According to this classification which will aid in arriving at the effective force, the field hands are made up of three thousand two hundred and two full hands, two hundred and ninety five three quarters hands, five hundred and ninety seven half hands, and three hundred and thirty five one quarter hands. Commuting the fractional into full hands according to the custom of the former planter in determining what crop should be required of the laborers, there results the equivalent of three thousand eight hundred and five and a half full field hands. Four thousand and thirty field hands were paid for work on the cotton crop. There is then a difference of three hundred and ninety nine between this number and the entire number of field hands. The number making the difference do not appear to have worked on the cotton. Eighty seven of them are found on Hutchinson Beef & Ashe where they were sent from Otter Island when it was so late as to make it unadvisable to attempt the planting of cotton. The statistics of population and classified laborers were taken some weeks before the payrolls were made and a number of laborers sought employment at the camps in the intervening time. Some of the one quarter hands were not employed on the cotton culture.

The mechanics and houseservants on the plantations have not been profitably employed – the former, because we had not proper stock and tools, and were not authorised to attempt improvements of any permanent or valuable character – the latter, because the superintendents were not accompanied by their families. Both classes were very averse to field labor and occasioned considerable trouble. Some were assigned to the charge of gardens and others went to the camps.

The proportion of old, sickly and disabled is large. The fugitive masters who forced away many of their other slaves, were willing to leave these. The amount of disability among these people is generally quite large, due to moral and physical causes. There appears to be a want of vital energy in them, such as often carries a feeble person safely through great toil and vexation. This may be ascribed partially to their vegetable diet and partially to their former condition which has had nothing in it to give strength to will or purpose. Their bedding and sleeping apartments are unsuitable and at night they sleep on the floor – without a change of clothing. As boatmen they are often exposed and do not properly care for themselves after exposure. During this season small pox has been prevalent and deranged the labor on several plantations. For the purpose of staying it there was a general vaccination and a hospital was established at Port Royal Island and put under the care of a physician employed by one of the benevolent associations. Six physicians have been employed and paid by them. It was an entirely inadequate corps for so extensive a territory particularly as it was impossible to procure for them reasonable means of conveyance.

Since the above statistics were prepared some two hundred fugitives have come to Port Royal and Edisto and have been distributed on the plantations. Besides the table does not include negroes at any of the camps, as Beaufort, Hilton Head, Bay Point and Otter Island who are under the control of the Quartermaster Department these will amount with their families to two thousand persons or more They have not been under the Treasury Department – but they have been instructed by the teachers and attended by the physicians, and they have shared in the distribution of clothing contributed by the associations. The able bodied men have been employed on wages, very much relieving the soldiers of fatigue duty.

Some of the smaller of the above islands have only been visited by the superintendents who are stationed on other islands – the visits being made two or three times a week.

Five of the women have resided at the junction of Ladies and St Helena Islands, The rest have resided on Port Royal, most of those on Port Royal living at Beaufort. Their labors have been directed some to teaching daily schools, and others to the distribution of clothing, to the visitation of the sick among these people and to endeavors for the improvement of their household life. They have been welcomed on plantations where no white women had been seen since our military occupation began. A circle at once formed around them, the colored women usually testifying their gladness by offering presents of two or three eggs. Their genial presence, wherever they have gone, has comforted and encouraged these people, and without the cooperation of refined and Christian women the best part of this work of civilization must ever remain undone.

The superintendents have generally had five or six plantations in charge, sometimes one aided by a teacher having under him three, four and even five hundred persons The duty of each has been to visit all the plantations under him as often as practicable, some of which are one, two, three and even four miles from his quarters, transport to them implements from the store-houses, protect the cattle and public property upon them, converse with the laborers, explaining to them their own new condition, the purposes of the Government towards them, what was expected of them in the way of labor and what remuneration they are likely to receive, procure and distribute among them clothing & food whether issued in army rations or contributed by the benevolent associations, collecting the materials of a census, making reports of the condition and wants of the plantations and any peculiar difficulties to the Special Agent, drawing pay rolls for labor on cotton and paying the amounts, going when convenient to the praise meetings and reading the Scriptures, instructing on Sundays & other days those desirous to learn to read as much as time permitted, attending to cases of disapline, protecting the negroes from injuries and in all possible ways endeavoring to elevate them and prepare them to become worthy and self-supporting citizens. Such were some of the labors cast upon the superintendents, for which as they were without precedent in our history none could have had special experience and for which in many cases of difficulty they were obliged to act without any precise instructions from the Special Agent as he had received none such from the Government. In a very few instances there appeared a want of fitness for the art of governing men under such strange circumstances, but in none a want of just purpose. Many toiled beyond their strength, and nearly all did more than they could persevere in doing. A knowledge of the culture of cotton was found not necessary in a Superintendent, though it would have facilitated his labors. On this point the laborers were often better informed than their former masters. Indeed those persons who might already have possessed this knowledge and applied for the post of superintendent, would have been likely in gaining it to have acquired ideas of the negroes as slaves and of the mode of dealing with them as such prejudicial to their success in this enterprise. The duty to be performed has consisted so much in explaining to the laborers their new condition and their relations to the Government and in applying the best spiritual forces to their minds and hearts that just purposes, and good sense and faith in the work have been of far more consequence than any mere experience in agriculture, and even in the more practical matters those who had the most inspiration for the service were found the most fertile in resources and the most cheerful and patient in encountering vexations and inconveniences. It would not be easy again to combine in a body of men so much worth and capacity and it is but a deserved tribute to say that but for their unusual zeal and devotion under many adverse influences, added to the intrinsic difficulty of the work itself, this enterprise on which Patriotism and Humanity had rested their faith would have failed of the complete success which has hitherto attended it. It is proper to add that an accomplished woman accepted the Superintendence of a single plantation in addition to other duties for which she specially came and carried it [on] successfully.

Upon the arrival of the Superintendents the plantations were generally unsupplied with tools, even hoes, those on hand being the tools used last year and a few found in the shops at Beaufort. Some $3000 worth of ploughs, hoes, other implements and seeds were intended to come with the superintendents The negroes had commenced putting corn and potatoes into their own patches and in some cases had begun to prepare a field of corn for the plantation. No land had been prepared for cotton and the negroes were strongly indisposed to its culture. They were willing to raise corn because it was necessary for food, but they saw no such necessity for cotton, & distrusted promises of payment for cultivating it It had enriched the masters, but had not fed them. Soldiers passing over the plantations had told them in careless speech that they were not to plant cotton. As this was a social experiment in which immediate industrial results were expected, it seemed important that all former modes of culture should be kept up and those products not neglected for which the district is best adapted and which in time of peace should come from it. Besides when a people are passing through the most radical of all changes, prudence requires that all old habits and modes of labor, not inconsistent with the new condition, should be conserved. Particularly did it seem desirable that the enemies of free labor in either hemisphere should not be permitted to say exultingly upon the view of a single season's experiment here that a product so important to trade and human comfort could not be cultivated without the forced, unintelligent and unpaid labor of slaves. Therefore no inconsiderable effort was made to disabuse the laborers of their pretty strong prejudice on this point and to convince them that labor on cotton was honorable, remunerative and necessary to enable them to buy clothing and the fitting comforts they desired. It was not made in vain – and its necessity would in the main have been dispensed with if we had had in the beginning the money to pay for the labor required and the proper clothing and food to meet the just wants and expectations of the laborers. At the same time the importance of raising an adequate supply of provisions was enjoined and with entire success. On this point there was no trouble. The amount of these planted is equal to that of last year in proportion to the people to be supplied and probably exceeds it. The negro patches are far larger than ever before, and as these had been begun before we arrived we were unable to make them equal on the different plantations. They alone in a fair season and if harvested in peace, would probably prevent any famine. On the whole it is quite certain that without the system here put in operation, the mass of the laborers if left to themselves and properly protected from depredations and demoralization by white men, would have raised on these negro patches corn and potatoes sufficient for their food, though without the incentives and moral inspirations thereby applied they would have raised no cotton and had no exportable crop and there might under the uncertainties of the present condition of things have been a failure of a surplus of corn necessary for cattle and contingencies and for the purchase of needed comforts. There is no disposition to claim for the movement here first initiated that it is the only one by which the people of this race can be raised from the old to the new condition provided equal opportunities and an equal period for developement were to be accorded to them as to communities of the white race. But it seems to have been the only one practicable where immediate material and moral results were to be reached and upon a territory under military occupation

The preparation of the ground for planting begins usually about Feb. 1st It was not until March 24th that the superintendence of the plantations under the present system could be said to have been in operation, the first fortnight being occupied by the superintendents upon their stations being assigned in going to them with a moderate supply of implements. The planting, except of the slip potatoes which are planted in July, some cow peas and a small quantity of corn closed on the week ending with May 10th. Each superintendent in response to a call from the Special Agent has furnished a written statement of the acres of cotton, corn potatoes, & vegetables then planted on each plantation in his district, with an estimate of the amount thereafter to be planted, the figures of which have been arranged in a tabular form presenting the amount of each kind on all the plantations on all the islands where agricultural operations are being carried on under the protection of our forces. It is with pleasure that the aggregate result is here submitted. It makes, (adding the negro patches to the corn fields of the plantations) eight thousand three hundred and fifteen 12/100 acres of provisions (corn, potatoes &c) planted, five thousand four hundred and eighty 11/100 acres of cotton planted, in all thirteen thousand seven hundred and ninety five 23/100 acres of provisions and cotton planted. Adding to these the two thousand three hundred and ninety four acres of late corn, to a great extent for fodder, cow peas &c. to be planted, and the crop of this year presents a total of sixteen thousand one hundred and eighty nine 23/100 acres. The crops are growing and are in good condition. They have been cultivated with the plough & hoe and the stalks of cotton have been thinned as is usual at this stage of their growth They are six or eight and in some fields twelve inches high. next month will close the work of cultivation. Notwithstanding the recent withdrawal of six hundred able bodied men from the plantations for military purposes, a very large proportion of the ~~best~~ working force, the spirit of the laborers has so improved that according to present expectations only a small proportion of the above acres already planted will have to be abandoned. The effect of the order will however be to diminish the number of acres to be planted, as the estimate was made just before it was issued

The statistical table presenting the aggregate result is here introduced. The full tabular statement, giving the amount of each crop planted on each of the one hundred and eighty nine plantations also accompanies this report.

	No acres of corn planted	No acres of potatoes (roots) planted	no acres of cotton planted	No of acres of mis cellaneous as vegetables, cow peas rice &c planted	acres of provisions planted by laborers on their own account	Total no of acres planted	No acres of potatoes (slip) cow peas &c to be planted
Port Royal	1646 1/2	176	1257 75/100	81	362 1/2	3523 3/4	540 3/4
Ladies (including Coosaw, Wassa, Cat and Cane)	941	112 3/4	1042 75/100	41	375 1/4	2512 3/4	432 3/4
Hilton Head	381 1/2	49 1/2	659 19/100	13	211	1314 44/100	no return
St Helena (including Da-thaw & Morgan)	1305	238 3/4	1554 57/100	74 5/8	702 3/4	3875 69/100	834 1/2
Paris	164	30 1/4	221	6	157	578 1/4	60
Pinkney & Daufuskie	59	no return	47 60/100	1 1/2	135	243 10/100	no return
Edisto	835 1/4	122	697 25/100	no return	84	1738 1/2	286
Hutchinson Beef & Ashe	00	6	00	2 3/4	00	8 3/4	240
Total	5332 1/4	735 1/4	5480 11/100	219 7/8	2027 1/2	13,795 23/100	2394

Satisfactory as this result is, the crop would have been considerably larger but for several unfavorable circumstances

In the first place the laborers had just passed through four months of idleness and confusion during which the only labor done by the great mass of them was upon the baling and local transportation of the cotton– During this time they had had no assurances as to their future, no regular employment–no care of their moral interests, no enlightenment as to their relations to this war except the careless and conflicting talk of soldiers who happened to visit their plantations and whose conduct towards them did not always prepossess them in favor of the ideas of northern men as to the rights of property or the honor of women. The effects of this injurious season had to be met at the threshold, and as far as could be, removed,

The usual season for preparing for a crop had already advanced six weeks before the superintendence and the distribution of implements commenced. Besides the labor thus lost, there was no time to devise useful plans for abridging it and so conducting it as to be able to ascertain definitely what each had done and to how much each was entitled. The working of all the hands together is not the best mode for this purpose, but we had no time to change the course pursued the year before. In the future it will probably be found that when there is time to arrange accordingly, the best mode will be to assign a piece of land to each laborer and then the amount done and the proportionate compensation due can be more justly fixed. Nothing is found to discourage faithful laborers so much as to see the indolent fare as well as themselves. Even now since the close of planting, some of the superintendents, impressed with this difficulty, have allotted pieces of ground in that way, and they report that this plan works well. It will besides introduce ideas of independent proprietorship on the part of the laborers, not so likely to come from what is called the "gang" system.

The same cause viz the lateness of the season, together with the insufficent means of fencing, required the selection of such fields for cultivation as could be best protected from cattle and not such as could be most easily and productively worked.

There was an inadequate supply of implements when the work commenced. A small quantity, less than that required, was purchased and was to have come with the superintendents, but by some accident the larger part of the hoes and some other articles were left behind and did not come till some weeks later.

The plantations were bereft of mules and horses necessary for ploughing and carting manure. The former owners had taken away the best in many cases and nearly all the workable mules and horses remaining had been seized by our army for Quartermaster and

Commissary service. On a long list of plantations not a mule was left to plough. Others had one only and that one blind or lame, On none was there the former number. The oxen had been to a great extent slaughtered for beef. The laborers had become vexed and dispirited at this stripping of the plantations and they had no heart to attempt the working of them productively. Indeed in some cases it did seem like requiring them to make bricks without straw. At last in answer to a pressing appeal to the Treasury Department by the Special Agent, ninety mules were forwarded from New York, forty arriving at Beaufort on April 18th and fifty on the 21st. Within three days after their arrival they were distributed except some dozen intended for localities not so accessible. This was a most necessary consignment. It made the hand labor available and showed the laborers that the Government was in earnest in carrying on the plantations. The recognition of their complaints at the want of them helped to give confidence. This reinforcement of the implements of labor must have added not far from two thousand acres to the crop of this year and perhaps even more.

Another difficulty was found in the destitution of corn prevalent in many districts as Port Royal, Hilton Head & Paris Islands. In some localities it had been burned by the rebels It had been unwisely taken in large quantities by our army for forage under orders of Gen Sherman, and the result indicated as soon at hand in the report of the Special Agent of Feb 3d [3] had already arrived. The first week after my return here was passed in exploring locations for superintendents on Port Royal. Everywhere I was met with complaints that there was no corn or provisions. A few rations had been doled-out, but only on a few plantations and without system or regularity. It took some two or three weeks there, and longer on other islands to get a system in operation under which the negroes where the corn had been taken or there was destitution, should receive a part of a soldiers ration. From Ladies Island the corn had been taken largely, but it was thought it might be supplied by a possible surplus on St Helena. On these islands there was considerable discontent on account of the exclusive diet of hominy and a great call for meat, molasses and salt. On some of the best conducted plantations these articles had been furnished in small quantities at some seasons. So many cattle had been taken by the army for beef, that following his instructions which required him to prevent the deterioration of the estates, the Special Agent hesitated to continue the slaughter. Salt was twice furnished to these two islands by a special purchase – a quart being given to a family. At length a consignment of two thousand dollars worth of provisions, for which an appeal had been made early in March, consisting of bacon, fish molasses & salt arrived being delayed by many accidents and forwarded by the Port Royal Relief Committee of Philadelphia. Bacon and fish to the amount of three pounds of the former and one pound of the latter to a grown person were distributed May 15th and a distribution of molasses has since been made of one quart to a family– The laborers have been greatly encouraged by this distribution, and if it could have been made earlier or rations could have been issued earlier, the crop would have been increased and we should have been relieved of many grievous complaints the justice of which we were compelled to confess without the power to remove them.

Again, the laborers had but very little confidence in the promises of payment made by us on behalf of the Government. The one per cent a pound which had been promised on the last years crop of cotton, mostly stored when our military occupation began, and for the baling and local transportation of which the laborers had been employed in November and December last had not been paid. This sum, even if paid, was entirely inadequate to supply the needed clothing and other wants, and it would seem that the laborers were fairly entitled upon the taking of the cotton which they had raised, to have been paid for the labor expended by them in raising it or if they were to be paid only for the labor of baling and transporting that they should have been provided with the winter clothing which the masters had not furnished before they left. The destitution of clothing was such as to produce much discontent subsequently relieved to a considerable extent by the benevolent associations. The Special Agent was not provided with funds to pay for labor on this year's crop until April 28th. Then the moderate sum of one dollar per acre was paid for cotton planted by April 23d, being distributed among the laborers according to the amount done by each. This was paid on account, the question of the value of the labor already done being reserved. This payment quickened the laborers very much and the work went rapidly forward until May 10th when the time for closing the regular planting season arrived. Indeed, from the beginning where they could clearly see that they were to receive the rewards of their labor, they worked with commendable diligence. Thus they worked diligently on their negro patches at the time when we had the most difficulty in securing the full amount of proper work on the plantations. Not the least among our troubles was that many able bodied men had gone to the camps at Beaufort, Hilton Head and Bay Point where they were profitably employed on wages, occasionally returning to the plantations where their wives remained to display their earnings and produce discontent among the unpaid laborers on them. No money has been paid for the planting of corn or vegetables, except in the case of a large garden of ten acres it being expected that these products will be consumed on the plantations. A second payment for the cotton planted since April 23d and at the same rate as the first has been made. In all the sum of $5479 65/100 has been paid for 5480 11/100 acres of cotton with ten dollars more for the garden of vegetables. Four thousand and thirty persons received their proportions of this sum. Small as the payment was, the laborers received it with great satisfaction, as if nothing more it was at least a recognition of their title to wages and to treatment as freemen. Accurate pay rolls for each plantation with the name of each laborer and the amount received and certified by the superintendents are preserved.

The order of Maj Gen Hunter[4] forcing the able bodied men to go to Hilton Head on May 12th where a proportion of them still remain against their will, has produced apprehension among these people as to our intentions in relation to them and disturbed the work on the plantations the force of which has been greatly reduced, leaving the women and children over twelve years of age as the main reliance. The Special Agent entered a protest against the order and its harsh execution and the retention of any not disposed to enlist[5] – but the civil being subordinate to military power, no further action could be taken.

The cases of disapline for idleness have been very few and cannot have exceeded if they have equalled forty on the islands. These have been reported to the military authorities and been acted upon by them. The most trouble has been upon plantations lying exposed to the camps and vessels both of the navy and sutlers as on Hilton Head Island and on St Helena near Bay Point where there was considerable discontent and insubordination induced by the visits from the vessels & camps. This trouble, it is hoped, will hereafter be removed by a more effective police system than has yet been applied.

It is not pretended that many of these laborers could not have done more work than they have done or that in persistent application they are the equals of races living in colder and more bracing latitudes. They generally went to their work quite early in the morning say at six oClock and returned at noon often earlier – working however industriously while they were in the field. Late in the afternoon they worked upon their private patches. They protested against working on Saturdays. A contrary rule was however prescribed and enforced, and they did double work on Fridays in order to secure for themselves the day following. As they were making themselves self-supporting by the amount of work which could be obtained from them without disapline it was thought advisable under the present condition of things not to exact more, but to await the full effect of moral and material inspirations which can in time be applied.

What has nevertheless been accomplished with these obstructions, with all the uncertainties incadent to a state of war, and with our own want of personal familiarity at first with the individual laborers themselves, gives the best reason to believe that under the guidance and with the help of the fugitive masters, had they been so disposed, these people might have made their way from bondage and its enforced labor to freedom and its voluntary and compensated labor without any essential diminution of products or any appreciable derangement of social order. In this as in all things the Universe is so ordered that the most beneficent Revolutions, which cost life and treasure, may be accomplished justly and in peace, if men have only the heart to accept them.

The contributions of clothing from the benevolent associations have been liberal, but liberal as they have been, they have failed to meet the distressing want which pervaded the territory. The masters had left the negroes destitute, not having supplied their winter clothing when our forces had arrived so that both the winter and spring clothing had not been furnished. From all accounts it would also seem that since the war began the usual amount of clothing given had been much diminished. That contributed by the associations cannot fall below $10,000. It has produced a most marked change in the general appearance, particularly on Sundays and at the schools and tended to inspire confidence in the superintendents. It would have been almost useless to attempt labors for moral or religious instruction without the supplies thus sent to clothe the naked. A small amount where there was an ability and desire to pay has with the special authority of the societies been sold and the proceeds returned to them to be reinvested for the same purposes. The rest has been delivered without any money being received. In the case of the sick and disabled, it is donated – and in case of those healthy and able to work it has been charged without expectation of money to be paid, that being thought to be the best course to prevent the laborers from regarding themselves as paupers and as a possible aid to the Government in case prompt payments for labor should not be made.

It is most pleasing to state that with the small payments for labor already made, those also for the collection of cotton being nearly completed, with the partial rations on some islands and the supplies from benevolent sources on others, with the assistance which the mules have furnished for the cultivation of the crop – the general kindness and protecting care of the superintendents – the contributions of clothing forwarded by the associations – the schools for the instruction of the children and others desirous to learn – with these and other favorable influences, confidence in the Government has been inspired, the laborers are working cheerfully and they now present to the world the example of a well behaved and self supporting peasantry of which their country has no reason to be ashamed.

The educational labors deserve a special statement. It is to be regretted that more teachers had not been provided. The labor of superintendency at the beginning proved so onerous that several originally intended to be put in charge of schools were necessarily assigned for the other purpose. Some fifteen persons on an average have been specially occupied with teaching and of these four were women. Others having less superintendence to attend to were able to devote considerable time to teaching at regular hours. Nearly all gave some attention to it more or less according to their opportunity and their aptitude for the work.

The educational statistics are incomplete, only a part of the schools having been open for two months and the others having been opened at intervals upon the arrival of persons designated for the purpose. At present according to the reports twenty two hundred persons are being taught on week days, of whom not far from one third are adults taught when their work is done. But this does not complete the number occasionally taught on week days and at the Sunday schools Humane soldiers have also aided in the case of their servants and others. Three thousand persons are in all probability receiving more or less instruction in reading on these islands. With an adequate force of teachers this number might be doubled as it is to be hoped it will be on the coming of autumn. The reports state that very many are now advanced enough so that even if the work should stop here they would still learn to read by themselves. Thus the ability to read the English language ~~and the Scriptures written for the consolation and instruction of all~~ has been already so communicated to these people that no matter what military or social vicissitudes may be in store, this knowledge can never perish from among them.

There have been forwarded to the Special Agent the reports of the teachers and they result in a remarkable concurrence of testimony. All unite to attest the universal eagerness to learn which they have not found equalled in white persons, arising both from the desire for knowledge common to all and the desire to raise their condition now very strong among these people. The reports on this point are cheering, even enthusiastic, and sometimes relate an incadent of aspiration and affection united in beautiful combination. One teacher on his first day's school leaves in the room a large alphabet card and the next day returns to find a mother there teaching her little child of three years to pronounce the first letters of the alphabet she had herself learned the day before. The children learn without urging by their parents and as rapidly as white persons of the same age, often more so, the progress being quickened by the eager desire. One teacher reports that on the first day of her school only three or four knew a part of their letters and none knew all. In one week seven boys and six girls could read readily words of one syllable and the following week there were twenty in the same class. The cases of dulness have not exceeded those among whites. The mulattoes, of whom there are not more than five percent of the entire population on the plantations are no brighter than the children of pure African blood. In the schools which have been opened for some weeks, the pupils who have regularly attended have passed from the alphabet and are reading words of one syllable in large and small letters. The lessons have been confined to reading and spelling except in a few cases where writing has been taught.

There has been great apparent eagerness to learn among the adults and some have progressed well. They will cover their books with care, each one being anxious to be thus provided, carry them to the fields, studying them at intervals of rest and asking explanations of the superintendents who happened to come along. But as the novelty wore away, many of the adults finding perseverance disagreeable have dropped off. Except in rare cases it is doubtful whether adults over thirty years, although appreciating the privilege for their children will persevere in continuous study so as to acquire the knowledge for themselves. Still when books and newspapers are read in negro houses, many inspired by the example of their children, will be likely to undertake the labor again.

It is proper to state that while the memory in colored children is found to be if anything livelier than in the white, it is quite probable that further along when the higher faculties of comparison and combination are more to be relied on, their progress may be less. While their quickness is apparent, one is struck with their want of disapline. The children have been regarded as belonging to the plantation rather than to a family, and the parents who in their condition can never have but a feeble hold on their offspring, have not been instructed to training their children into thoughtful and orderly habits. It has therefore been found not an easy & the to make them quiet and attentive at the schools.

Through the schools habits of neatness have been encouraged. Children with soiled faces or soiled clothing when known to have better have been sent home from the schools and have returned in better condition.

In a few cases the teachers have been assisted by negroes who knew how to read before we came. Of these there are very few. – Perhaps one may be found on an average on one of two or three plantations. These so far as can be ascertained were in most cases taught clandestinely, often by the daughters of their masters who were of about the same age. A colored person among these people who has learned to read does not usually succeed so well as a white teacher. He is [*not*] apt to teach the alphabet in the usual order and needs special training for the purpose.

The Sabbath Schools have assisted in the work of teaching. Some three hundred are present at the Church on St. Helena in the morning to be taught. There are other churches where one or two hundred attend. A part of these, perhaps the larger, attend some of the day schools, but they comprehend others as adults and still others coming from localities where schools have not been opened. one who regards spectacles in the light of their moral aspects can with difficulty find sublimer scenes than those witnessed on Sabbath morning on these islands now ransomed to a nobler civilization.

The educational labors have had incidental results almost as useful as those which have been direct. At a time when the people were chafing the most under deprivations and the assurances made on behalf of the government were most distrusted, it was fortunate that we could point to the teaching of their children as a proof of our interest in their welfare and of the new and better life which we were opening before them.

An effort has been made to promote clean and healthful habits. To that end weekly cleanings of quarters were enjoined. This effort where it could be properly made, met with reasonable success. The negroes finding that we took an interest in their welfare acceded cordially, and in many cases their diligence in this respect was most commendable. As a race it is a mistake to suppose that they are indisposed to cleanliness. They appear to practice it as much as white people under the same circumstances There are difficulties to obstruct improvement in this respect. There has been a scarcity of lime and except at too high prices of soap. Their houses are too small, not affording proper apartments for storing their food. They are unprovided with glass windows. Besides some of them are tenements unfit for beasts, without floors or chimneys. One could not put on a face to ask the occupants to clean such a place. But where the building was decent or reasonably commodious, there has been no difficulty in securing the practice of this virtue. Many of these people are examples of tidiness, & entering their houses one is sometimes witness of rather amusing scenes where a mother is trying the effect of beneficent ablutions on the heads of her children.

The religious welfare of these people has not been neglected. The churches which were closed when this became a seat of the war have been opened. Among the superintendents, there were several persons of clerical education who have led in public ministrations The larger part of them are persons of religious experience and profession who on the Sabbath in weekly praise meetings and at funerals have labored for the consolation of these humble believers.

These people have been assured by the Special Agent that if they proved themselves worthy by their industry, good order and sobriety, they should be protected against their rebel masters. It would be wasted toil to attempt their developement without such assurances. An honorable nature would shrink from this work without the right to make them. Nor is it possible to imagine any rulers now or in the future who will ever turn their backs on the laborers who have been received, as these have been, into the service of the United States.

Special care has been taken to protect the property of the Government on the plantations. The cattle have been taken in such large numbers by the former owners and later by the army, the latter sometimes slaughtering fifty or more head on a plantation that the necessity of a strict rule for the preservation of those remaining was felt. For that purpose the Special Agent procured orders from the military and naval authorities dated respectively April 17 and 26 forbidding the removal of "subsistence, forage, mules, horses, oxen, cows, sheep cattle of any kind, or other property from the plantations without the consent of the special agent of the Treasury Department or orders from the nearest General Commanding" No such consent has been given by the Special Agent except in one case, as an act of mercy to the animal and in another where he ordered a lamb killed on a special occasion and has charged himself for the same in his account with the Department. Your instructions, which expressed your desire to prevent the deterioration of the estates, have in this respect been sedulously attended to. The superintendents have not been permitted to kill cattle even for fresh meat and they have subsisted on their rations and fish and poultry purchased of the negroes.

The success of the movement now upon its third month has exceeded my most sanguine expectations. It has had its peculiar difficulties and some phases at times arising from accidental causes might on a partial view invite doubt banished however at once by a general survey of what had been done. Already the high treason of South Carolina has had a sublime compensation & the end is not yet. The churches, which were closed, have been opened. No master now stands between the people and the words which the Savior spoke for the consolation of all peoples and all generations. The Gospel is preached in fulness and purity as it has never before been preached in this territory even in colonial times. The reading of the English language, with more or less system is being taught to thousands so that whatever military or political calamities may be in store, this precious knowledge can never more be eradicated. Ideas and habits have been planted under the growth of which these people are to be fitted for the responsibilities of citizenship and in equal degree unfitted for any restoration to what they have been. Modes of administration have been commenced, not indeed adapted to an advanced community but just, paternal and developing in its character. Industrial results have been reached which put at rest the often reiterated assumption that this territory and its products can only be cultivated by slaves. A social problem, which has vexed the wisest, approaches a solution. The capacity of a race and the possiblity of lifting it to civilization without danger or disorder even without throwing away the present generation as refuse, is being determined, and thus the way is preparing by which the peace to follow this war shall be made perpetual. Finally it would seem that upon this narrow theatre and in these troublous times God is demonstrating against those who would mystify his plans and thwart his purposes that in the councils of his Infinite Wisdom he has predestined no race, not even the African, to the doom of eternal bondage.

. . . .

ALS Edward L Pierce

Excerpt from Edward L. Pierce to Hon. S. P. Chase, 2 June 1862, vol. 19, #166, Port Royal Correspondence, 5th Agency, RG 366 [Q-22]. Approximately forty-one pages of a forty-three-page report, the remainder of which expressed Pierce's personal gratitude for the assistance rendered him by various individuals and associations, and to the former slaves among whom he had worked. The table showing agricultural operations on each of the 189 plantations, said to have been enclosed, is not in the file.

1 As early as April 1862, the Secretary of the Treasury was planning to transfer to the War Department responsibility for collecting abandoned property and supervising former slaves in the South Carolina Sea Islands. The transfer was effected in mid-June 1862. (See below, doc. 36.)

2 For the instructions of February 19, 1862, see above, doc. 8n.

3 The report is printed above, as doc. 8.

4 On May 9, 1862, General David Hunter, commander of the Department of the South, had ordered subordinate officers in the Sea Islands to forward to his headquarters "all able bodied negroes capable of bearing arms." (See above, doc. 20n.)

5 For the special agent's protest, see *Freedom*, ser. 2: doc. 1.

22: Circular by the Military Governor in the Department of the South

BEAUFORT, S.C., JULY 3d, 1862.

To the Superintendents of Plantations: The season for planting *cow-pease* and gathering *corn-blades* for fodder, being near at hand, you will please give your especial attention to this matter, that the usual quantity for winter's use may be secured. You are authorized to offer the negroes the following prices for work:

For breaking up the ground and planting cow-pease, $1.00 per acre.

For gathering, drying, and storing corn-blades, $1.00 per acre.

For supplying cow-pens with trash, 25 cents per day (requiring as much work per day as the former master did).

For marsh-grass for manure for next year's crop, 30 cents a stack.

This work must not interfere with the careful cultivation of the corn and cotton crops – as from the latter particularly is to be derived the revenue for future operations.

Great care must be exercised in the preparation of full and accurate accounts of the above-mentioned work.

Your attention is also called to the importance of getting in a crop of *turnips* or *ruta bagas*, and of planting a sufficient quantity of *sweet potatoes* for government use, for which you are authorized to pay $1.00 per acre. BY ORDER OF Brig. Gen'l RUFUS SAXTON,

PD

Circular, Head Quarters, Beaufort, S.C., 3 July 1862, enclosed in Brig. Genl. R. Saxton to Hon. Edwin M. Stanton, 10 July 1862, S-1025 1862, Letters Received, ser. 12, RG 94 [K-42].

23: Military Governor in the Department of the South to the Secretary of War

Beaufort South Carolina August 4 1862.

Sir. I have the honor to report that in consequence of the evacuation of Edisto and other islands by our forces some two thousand negroes have been thrown out of employment from the lands they were cultivating, and are now idle, and destitute upon my hands. I am obliged to furnish them with food and clothing at once. I shall be able to provide for a portion of these people on the plantations we still hold, but there will be a large number who cannot be provided for in this way. To keep them from idleness and its attendent evils I am about to introduce an extensive manufacture of rush baskets and expect in this way to make them contribute something towards their own support. There are also on St. Simons island a large number of negroes collected (who have fled from their masters "on the main" land) in the same destitute condition, and at Fernandina I very much regret the necessity which caused the evacuation, or prevents the occupation, of all these islands, by our troops, and I most earnestly, and respectfully call your attention to the importance of a reoccupation as soon as the exigencies of the service will permit. I have distributed from twenty, to thirty muskets to each of the plantations under my charge according to its size. These muskets are placed in an armory under the charge of the superintendent who daily instructs the people in their use. They are held in the different armories always ready for service, in case of an attack. I think in this way a tolerable police force will be organized which will serve as a protection from small guerilla bands and prevent such massacres as that one on Hutchinson Island. I shall take four or five hundred muskets in a day or two to St Simons Island and I hope to obtain enough of this kind of force to hold it without the aid of any other force.

It is my duty to inform you that my authority in this department is not recognized by the military to the extent you intended or my instructions demand,[1] unless something is done for me in this respect I fear that I shall be unable to meet your own expectations or do justice to myself. In a country like this a "Superintendent of Plantations" indifferently supported by the military has no adequate power to meet his great responsibilities. I need it to make my position respected. It shall be my earnest endeavor to do the best I can under the circumstances. I respectfully ask that one regiment may be placed entirely under my own orders as a police force, to give some show of force to my acts, for this purpose I should like to have the 1st Massachusetts Cavalry, I hope that the necessity of this force will be apparent to yourself and that you will give the necessary orders for its assignment to me. I am Sir with Great respect Your obedient Servant

ALS R. Saxton

Brig. Genl. R. Saxton to Hon. E. M. Stanton, 4 Aug. 1862, S-1165 1862, Letters Received, ser. 12, RG 94 [K-42]. Secretary of War Edwin M. Stanton apparently referred Saxton's letter to General-in-Chief Henry W. Halleck, who, by an endorsement of August 12, 1862, in effect denied Saxton's request for control over a regiment. "There cannot be two military commanders in the same Dept acting independent of each other," Halleck ruled. "Either one or the other must have the disposal of all the troops." For accounts of the

Confederate raid on Hutchinson's Island on June 12, 1862, see *Freedom*, ser. 1, vol. 1: docs. 25A–B.

1 The instructions from the Secretary of War, given to General Rufus Saxton on June 16, 1862, upon his appointment as superintendent of plantations and military governor, are quoted below, in doc. 36.

24: Army Engineer at Fort Clinch, Florida, to the Chief of Engineers

Fort Clinch Florida 12th August 1862.

General I have the honor to report, that ever since my return here from Hilton Head S.C. whence I last addressed you I have been engaged in arranging and rearranging the Working parties and preparing the Monthly returns.

There is so much sickness among the men, that I have not refused a discharge to any who ask it since I am able to put the Work in a state of present defence with those remaining, and high priced mechanics are not profitable and will not be until the middle or last of September.

I had thought you might disapprove, my curtailing the length of the working day and therefore determined on my return, to add an hour to it; but I find that two men have been sunstruck and among the soldiers have appeared several similar cases. I have therefore allowed the day-length to remain at eight hours.

I have had but little time as yet to look at the drawings, but shall proceed immediately to their study. I have confined my attention to preparing the Fort so that we may hold it from a land attack.

It has been necessary to reconstruct the labor arrangement.

Under the old system (before the war) Slaves were hired of their masters at a *price per month* Without deduction for loss of time by sickness. Since the war, Slaves have come in on us and have been set to work, not so much because they were desirable men as because they must be supported. As Gen. Hunter and the Quartermasters are able and willing to perform that duty, it seems to me proper, that I should drop the system. Indeed unless especially instructed otherwise, I don't see how I can employ a man unless I need him for the work in hand. For this work, I need the best men – no cripples or laggards.

I have therefore determined not to issue rations to families; – but to employ good men at fair wages and leave the support of families to the proper pillars thereof.

To this end, my payroll is reconstructed and instead of a host of sick–lame and lazy at 15¢, 25¢, 40¢ 30¢ & 50¢ with rations for themselves and families working a day or two and then "loafing" a day or two or pretending sick, I have good laborers at 75¢ a day and one ration. If they are late at roll-call they lose a "quarter." If they are absent a day without good cause or if they are not up to the mark in their work they are discharged. I find the result thus far to be a fewer number of names on the roll, but a larger number of day's work and a better looking body of men about my work.

Every black laborer has a number on his cap; and a time-keeper at every quarter of a day finds out the position of each man on his roll.

In the present condition of things, it becomes necessary to allow the commissary to sell some stores from his goods to the families of our men.

Will you please instruct me as to the manner in which this amount is returned? Is it proper that in my money Statement I should enter such sums as "*money received* during the month"? Accounting for the stores in my subsistence Return?

As to the money deposited with the Agency in N.Y. for this work, Lieut. Dutton was in doubt whether the officer in charge here has anything to do with it in his books. As it is impossible for this officer to be in any manner responsible for its disbursement beyond the judiciousness of his orders, I have supposed, he would limit himself to rendering a proper account of the articles rec'd and ordered.

I shall be glad if you will please instruct me. I have the honor to be sir very Respectfully Yr obt Sevt

ALS Alfred H. Sears.

Capt. Alfred H. Sears to Brig. Gen. Jos. G. Totten, 12 Aug. 1862, S-8823, Letters Received, ser. 18, General Correspondence, Central Office, RG 77 [VV-39]. Sears signed as a captain in the New York Volunteer Engineers. In an endorsement dated September 20, 1862, an aide to the chief of engineers noted that the government customarily provided food to "military employes & their families at cost (including expenses) in cases where it cannot be otherwise procured" and therefore recommended that Sears be authorized to furnish provisions to the workers at Fort Clinch and to their families. The Secretary of War approved the recommendation on the same day.

25: Commander of the Department of the South to a New York Banker

Hilton Head, S.C. Septr 28 1862

My Dear Sir: I have now had time to examine with some care the general outlines of the Department of the South. My general conclusion is, that there are entirely too many troops here, for merely defensive purposes: while the troops will have to be quadrupled for successful operations. You know well my views as to the Government in Washington. If the President and his cabinet would heed at all the opinions of the Commanders of Departments who have been clothed with almost proconsular dignity and power, there would be some chance that in all the Departments some commander might be found who would be able practically to solve the great problem of the war.

I am satisfied that we shall never meet with any success in the prosecution of the war until the north can be firmly united upon some well defined policy. No union can be hoped for upon any platform which does not involve the entire overthrow and destruction of slavery. Many wise judicious and even patriotic men, are even yet undecided in their opinions upon this subject. They are not held back by any sympathy for the South or by any regard for the institution of Slavery. But they dread universal emancipation: first because of the probable injurious influence of a crowd of lazy idle negroes; filling our Camps and demoralizing our Soldiers. Second: they fear that the blacks may be sunk to lower depths of degradation and suffering in consequence of the fact that the government can not care for them while oppressed by the responsibilities of so great a war. Third: they apprehend justly the terrible consequences which would flow from depriving the world for several years of the rich and valuable products of slave labor.

If it were possible then to devise a scheme whereby each of these objections might be fairly met, I have no doubt that the entire North would promptly unite in a demand for universal emancipation. After a close examination of what has been done in this Department, while I believe that there are here furnished the best possible opportunity for the practical application of a wise plan of emancipation. I believe that thus far nothing has been accomplished of any value So far as the working of the plantations on the Island, is concerned it is certainly not a success. I think something better has been done on the neighboring Islands where there are no troops stationed, except a guard. I doubt whether the negros feel that their condition has been at all improved since their escape from the control of their masters Even General Saxton has earnestly appealed to the War Department to be releived from further duty here assigning as a reason that in order to carry out with success, any scheme involving the protection and improvement of the negros he must be clothed also with supreme military command in the Department.[1] I have conversed with a number of persons sent out by the Freedmans Association also with several members of General Saxtons Staff. & I find them all discouraged and not a few ready to Succumb and give up the whole enterprise as utterly impracticable. Nearly all the troops upon the Island and in this Department are from New York, Pennsylvania and the New England States, and I regret to say that while the Western Troops under my Command in Alabama were converted from being protectionists to thorough war abolitionists in this Department not a few Officers and Soldiers who came here abolitionists are now throughly prejudiced against the Negro and are disinclined to show him the slightest favor or countenance.

These facts are certainly not indications of success and I have done what I could to discover the reasons which have produced in this Department results so entirely different from those which were reached in the region of my former command.

The prejudice against the negro has undoubtedly arisen from the fact that many of the officers and Soldiers came to entertain the opinion that the Government through its officials regarded the negros with a special favor and provided for their comfort to the neglect of the Volunteers.

The reasons why so little success have attended the efforts of General Saxton and the benevolent persons who were cooperating with him are to me very obvious: and may be presented briefly as follows First: the negros are not emancipated and made free absolutely by the Government. Second: the remuneration for their labor on the plantations has never yet been definitely fixed. They have thus far received in money three dollars per acre for planting and cultivating the cotton crop and are promised half a cent per pound for picking. Admitting that an industrious hand can cultivate 5 acres of cotton this would [yield?] him $15. and the picking could not give him more than $5 additional. Thus we perceive that no adequate object has yet been presented to induce the negro to labor, and I am certain that the work which has been done, results only from the confidence the black man has in the promise of his white superintendent, that the government will soon make a radical change for the better, in his condition. Third: While these Islands are more secure from attack than the main land yet there never has been any guaranty that the government would continue the military occupation of one of these Islands. Thus Daufuskie has been evacuated, Pinkney Island being given up and even North and South Edisto were abandoned after a most excellent and thrifty crop had been put in the Ground. The black population of these evacuated Islands has been crowded upon the other Islands thus deranging and destroying what little of *System*atic organization had been thus far introduced Under all the discouraging circumstances I am surprised that any valuable results whatever have been reached. I am in no degree affected in my views and opinions as to the successful emancipation of the Slave by what has been done on these Islands. But I greatly fear that a failure here will have a prodigious influence upon the opinions of the north, especially when it is known that the government out of respect to what are called the 'radicals' of the republican party has given General Saxton authority to organize five regiments of blacks and a Corps of fifty-thousand laborers. Such authority in this Department under existing circumstances, can have no other effect than to disappoint and dishearten those who hope that the slave, may rapidly escape from their masters and may soon become auxiliaries to the north in the prosecution of the war. To give a commanding officer such authority at such a time and under existing circumstances is simply absurd – Such is now the deficiency in this Department of a laboring population that day-laborers are receiving at Key West and Tortugas two dollars and fifty cts per diem: while at St Augustine, Fernandina and Fort Pulaski the comd'g officers have made requisitions for negro laborers which cannot be filled.

It is manifest therefore that some great and radical revolution must be effected in the Department before we can hope for any results which will be satisfactory to the North. I have reflected as profoundly as I am able upon this vital subject and in answer to the great question "What shall be done with the negro in case of universal emancipation"? I have reached the following conclusions.

First: Emancipation may be accomplished without the demoralization of the army

Second: Larger and richer crops may be produced from the same soil by the emancipated 'blacks' than by slaves.

Third: The condition of the liberated negros can be greatly improved and under a proper and efficient system, they will become industrious, intelligent, respectable and happy.

I will now give you a brief outline of the scheme which I have ventured to suggest to the War Department, but not of whose execution I am utterly hopeless.

I consider these Islands deserted as they have been by the white population, and readily protected as they are, from destructive raids of the Enemy, as admirably adapted for this first great experiment of liberating and educating the negro. I propose to organize upon each plantation under a competent and honest manager a sort of community to be composed of all the people belonging to that individual plantation. That the culture shall be best possible: the implements the most approved and the seed of the highest quality: that all the hands on the plantation shall be classified: and an exact account be kept of the labor of every hand throughout the year. The crop having been gathered sold and the proceeds realized the entire sum divided by the aggregate Number of days labor by all the hands throughout the year will give the clear value of one days work. This, multiplied by the Number of days work done during the year by each hand will give the amount to be placed to his credit as the result of his years effort.

If to this we add the produce of the gardens and patches what shall be the individual property of the different families on the plantation we shall have the sum total of all the possible earnings and I am satisfied from the investigation I have been able to make that any industrious family will produce $2160. For garden vegatables say $1000.

Cotton	16.700	
Corn	4.500	
Sweet Potatoes	2.760	
Rice	2 160	
Garden Vegatables	1 000	27.120

I do not know the exact number of families: but admitting there are five in each family there will be sixty four on the Island. Dividing the Sum total produced by Sixty-four it will give to each family about $425 To feed and clothe a field hand has generally cost the Master something less than $50 a year Counting the family at three full hands this would require $150 We will add $50 rent to be paid to the Government; and $50 to meet the expenses of better clothing a better mode of living and to pay for schooling and religious instruction. These expenses taken from the gross receipts will leave to each family $175 to be [found] to its credit in the plantation Bank. In five years each family will have accumulated the sum of $875, They will have acquired habits of industry, their children will have been educated and themselves prepared to remove to any field of industry they may elect

I have thus presented to you the details of a single Island merely for the purpose of fixing our ideas. I am confident the measure of success hereby indicated as practicable on this one Island may be extended to all the Islands on this Southern Coast. I am not certain what population can be sustained on these Islands but presume it will not fall below 200.000. It does not at present reach more than 20.000. We have therefore room to accommodate a large population which I trust will soon fall into our hands; by the capture of Charleston and Savannah and the intermediate region on the main land. All the liberated slaves near the coast in the states of South Carolina and Georgia inhabiting a belt say 25 or 30 [meiles] in width may transferred to the Islands. The region thus depopulated of its laboring class will either be deserted by the masters or not. If deserted we will introduce the plantation System. If not the masters will be compelled to hire the negroes who will be sent back from the interior as our army advances.

In case we are successful in the capture of Charleston and Savannah and our army establishes itself firmly on the mainland these Islands with our land forces in front and our Gun Boats in the adjoining waters would require but little military protection and this I propose to obtain from the blacks. To this end I would commence promptly the organization of one or more regiments upon one of the vacant Islands in our possession to be composed of picked men from the entire population. I would thus draw the line broad and deep between our volunteers & regular troops and these experimental negro regiments. After our army shall have advanced to the main land I would turn over the guardianship of the Islands the occupation and holding of the Forts, & Earthworks and military Posts to the black Troops under the command of intelligent white officers Should they prove to be good soldiers and worthy of the trust committed to their charge competent to defend and protect the population whose security has been placed in their keeping then I think we will have reached a satisfactory solution of the Grand Problem of the age.

This same system established briefly above may be readily extended to the Southern part of Florida then to the entire region bordering on the Mississippi river and then successively to the regions in the South which may be overcome and held by the Armies of the United States.

Since the Proclamation of Emancipation has been now issued by the President, the entire subject rises to a dignity grandeur and importance unsurpassed by any that has ever occupied the attention of mankind. Its difficulties have been so great heretofore, so absolutely overwhelming that few have dared even to approach with any hope of a successful solution. But it is useless longer to turn away from it. We are now compelled to face its dread responsibilities & every thinking mind and earnest heart must contribute what it can to aid in the prosecution of the mighty work which now lies before us. Very truly yrs

ALcS O M Mitchel

O. M. Mitchel to Geo. S. Coe, Esqr., 28 Sept. 1862, vol. 6*, pp. 44–50, Letters Sent by Brig. Gen. O. M. Mitchel, ser. 839, 3rd Division, Army of the Ohio, RG 393 Pt. 2 No. 15 [C-8009]. The addressee, George S. Coe, was president of the American Exchange Bank in New York. Between mid-September, when he assumed command of the Department of the South, and late October, when he died of yellow fever, General Mitchel wrote similar letters to President Abraham Lincoln, the Secretary of the Treasury, the Secretary of War, and two leaders of Northern freedmen's aid associations, explaining to each of them his understanding of the war, assessing the situation in the Sea Islands, and outlining his own solution to the "Negro problem." (Maj. Genl. O. M. Mitchel to Hon. the Secretary of War, 26 Sept. 1862; O. M. Mitchel to Hon. S. P. Chase, 26 Sept. 1862; Maj. Gen. O. M. Mitchel to Rev. Dr. Tyng, 30 Sept. 1862; Maj. Genl. O. M. Mitchel to His Excellency Abraham Lincoln, 13 Oct. 1862; and O. M. Mitchel to Rev. Dr. Wayland, 13 Oct. 1862, vol. 6*, pp. 36–44, 61–67, Letters Sent by Brig. Gen. O. M. Mitchel, ser. 839, 3rd Division, Army of the Ohio, RG 393 Pt. 2 No. 15 [C-8009].) On Mitchel's policy and actions respecting fugitive slaves while he was stationed in northern Alabama, see *Freedom*, ser. 1, vol. 1: docs. 85–86, 91A–B.

1 On September 5, 1862, after repeatedly requesting that his authority be enlarged, General Rufus Saxton, military governor in the Department of the South, had asked to be relieved of duty in the department and transferred elsewhere. "[E]ven under the most favourable auspices," he declared, "no one can perform these duties properly unless he has the supreme military control." (Brig. Gen. Rufus Saxton to Hon. Edwin M. Stanton, 5 Sept. 1862, S-2095 1862, Letters Received, ser. 12, RG-94 [K-42].) Saxton was not transferred; he continued as military governor to the end of the war.

26: Superintendent of Contrabands at Hilton Head, South Carolina, to the Commander of the Department of the South, Enclosing a Report on Black Military Laborers and Their Families

Hilton Head, S.C. Sep. 29th 1862

Sir:– I have the honor to submit the within report, agreeably to instructions, exhibiting various statistics relating to contraband laborers employed in Quarter Master's Department. I am very respectfully Your Obedient Servant

ALS

Jas. D. Mc Math

[*Enclosure*] [*Hilton Head, S.C. September 1862*]

No. of Families	Consisting of–	Men	Women	Children
46	man, wife & 1 child each.	46	46	46
64	" " *no children.*	64	64	
27	" " & 2 children each.	27	27	54
19	" " " 3 " "	19	19	57
7	" " " 4 " "	7	7	28
1	" " " 5 " "	1	1	5
1	" " " 6 " "	1	1	6
165		165	165	196

	Widows.			
10	have one child each.		10	10
7	" 2 children each.		7	14
2	" 3 " "		2	6
2	" 4 " "		2	8
	Children having *no parents.*			5
			21	43
	No of Single men.	285		
	" " " women.		50	
	Total No. men, women & children.	450	236	239

Recapitulation.	
Whole No. of Families	165
" " Widows (with children)	21
" " Children having no parents.	5
" " Single women	50
" " " Men	285
" " Married "	165
Whole No. of Men	450
" " " women	236
" " " children	239
Total–	925.

Total No. in Charge of Quar. Mas't Department within the Fortifications		925.
Greatest number of rations drawn to subsist the above	650.	

Compensation for contraband labor varies according to order of Maj. Gen'l Hunter, from *five* to *thirteen* dollars per month, depending on ability; with the exception of foremen in charge of gangs, who receive *twenty* dollars pr. month.

62 contraband laborers, employed in coaling vessels at Seabrook, draw rations for themselves only, their families being supported on the surrounding plantations.

32 contrabands are employed at the two steam-saw mills, drawing rations for themselves only, families being subsisted on the plantations.

Whole no. in charge of Quar. Mast' Dep't, and subsisted by the Government:

Within the Fortifications	925
Outside of " "	94
Total No.	1019

HD

Jas. D. McMath to Major Genl. O. M. Mitchel, 29 Sept. 1862, enclosing untitled report, [Sept. 1862], M-526 1862, Letters Received, ser. 4109, Dept. of the South, RG 393 Pt. 1 [C-1307]. General David Hunter, whose order had set the wage rates, was commander of the Department of the South from April to mid-September, 1862 (and resumed its command the following January).

27: Military Governor in the Department of the South to the Secretary of War

Beaufort, So. Car. December 7th. 1862.

Sir: I have the honor to call your attention to an act of Congress passed during the last session, by which all the lands in this Department which were deserted by their owners, now in rebellion, are confiscated and are to be sold by commissioners appointed for the purpose, to pay the taxes.[1] The said comissioners are now here, busily engaged in assessing the amount of taxes for each estate, and as soon as they have completed this portion of their labor, probably by February 1863, these lands will be advertised and sold at auction to the highest bidder. I regard this law as eminently wise and just, but still it makes no provision for the negoes, who have been for so many years regarded as a portion of the live stock for the plantation, that it is not easy to separate them entirely from its future. The prospect now is, that all the lands on these sea islands will be bought up by speculators, and in that event, these helpless people may be placed more or less at the mercy of men devoid of principle, and their future well being jeopardised, thus defeating in a great measure the benevolent intentions of the government towards them.

To prevent this, and give the negroes a right in that soil to whose wealth they are destined in the future to contribute so largely, to save them from destitution, to enable them to take care of themselves, and prevent them from ever becoming a burden upon the country, I would most respectfully call your attention to the importance of the immediate passage of an act by Congress empowering the President to appoint three commissioners, whose duty it shall be to make allotments of portions of the lands forfeit to the U.S. for nonpayment of taxes, to the emancipated negroes resident thereon, not exceeding three acres to an adult, and one acre to any other person under the age of eighteen, in such proportion of cleared wood land and marsh as said commissioners may deem expedient, on condition of the payment by said person to the U.S. of an annual rent not exceeding one dollar per acre and on such other condition as Congress may see fit to annex. Their attachment to place is a marked trait in the negro character, and in my humble opinion the enforcement of a law of this kind would be the means of establishing them in permanent homes, would insure the careful cultivation of the lands allotted them, and consequently their own independence, and in addition would furnish a large supply of willing laborers who could be hired to cultivate the purchased lands.

Should this plan for a proposed law meet with your approval, and you consider it worthy of consideration by Congress, I think if it were submitted to the Hon: Henry Wilson or Hon: Chas: Sumner they would take measures for its early passage. It appears to me very important that the matter should receive early attention, as in case these lands are all sold I know not what is to become of these poor people. I am, Sir, With great respect, Your ob[t] serv[t]

HLS R. Saxton

Brig. Genl. R. Saxton to Hon. Edwin M. Stanton, 7 Dec. 1862, S-2098 1862, Letters Received, ser. 12, RG 94 [K-52]. No reply has been found in the letters-sent volumes of the Secretary of War or the Adjutant General's Office. Saxton was not alone in his concern about the effects of the direct-tax sales upon the freedpeople. On January 1, 1863, Abram D. Smith, chairman of the South Carolina tax commission, informed Secretary of the Treasury Salmon P. Chase that they were "anxiously inquiring about their destiny, when these lands shall have been sold for taxes." Now mere "tenants at will upon the grace of the Government," they evidenced a "strong desire to obtain permanent and free homes in the region of the country where they were born and reared." But Smith feared that most of the land (which was scheduled for sale on February 11, 1863) would be purchased by capitalists, leaving the former slaves landless. Should that happen, he wondered, "[i]n what manner shall the inhabitants thereon be adequately supported and protected?" Smith doubted "whether the suggestions of private interest, the economical laws of demand & supply, the necessities of labor and the eagerness of capital may be safely left to their ordinary operations and results, without the aid of additional and positive provisions of law." Accordingly, he urged that the government permit the direct-tax commissioners to take "early steps" to have the forfeited estates "subdivided and offered for sale in small parcels with the privilege of preemption." (A. D. Smith to Hon. S. P. Chase, 1 Jan. 1863, General Correspondence, ser. 99, SC, Records of or Relating to Direct Tax Commissions in the Southern States, RG 58 [Z-2].) Smith subsequently visited Washington to discuss the land question with Chase and members of Congress. (See below, doc. 30.) Meanwhile, as Congress considered legislation on the subject, General David Hunter, commander of the Department of the South, took direct action to halt the sale of forfeited land. On February 7, 1863, citing both pending legislation and "military necessities" that "require all the lands . . . for the use of the soldiers and the support of the colored population," he suspended sales "until the pleasure of the Government . . . shall be made known." (*Official Records*, ser. 1, vol. 14, pp. 394–95.) In fact, Congress had already acted. Amendments to the Direct Tax Act, adopted on February 6, 1863, enlarged the power of the tax commissioners to keep forfeited land under the control of the United States and out of the hands of private purchasers. First, the amendments permitted the commissioners, when auctioning off forfeited land, to bid on behalf of the United States for up to two-thirds the assessed value of a parcel; if no other bid exceeded that amount, the land would remain in possession of the government. The amendments also authorized the commissioners, at the President's direction, to bid in for the government such tracts of land as had been selected "under the direction of the President . . . for war, military, naval, revenue, charitable, educational, or police purposes." (*Statutes at Large*, vol. 12, pp. 640–41.) On February 10, President Lincoln issued the instructions called for by the amendments, adding both Saxton and Hunter to the tax commissioners for purposes of selecting the land to be set aside for the government. (Abraham Lincoln, *Collected Works*, ed. Roy P. Basler, Marion D. Pratt, and Lloyd A. Dunlap, 9 vols. [New Brunswick, N.J., 1953–55], vol. 6, pp. 98–99.)

1 The Direct Tax Act of June 1862 had provided for the seizure and sale of land in the seceded states whose owners had not paid their portion of the federal tax levied upon each state in August 1861. The act had authorized the President to appoint three tax commissioners for each state, who were to determine the amount owed for each parcel and give the owners sixty days in which to make good the delinquency. If the tax remained unpaid, title to the land was forfeited to the United States, and the commissioners were empowered to sell it at public auction to the highest bidder, "for a sum not less than the taxes, penalty, and costs." If no private bid equaled or exceeded that sum, title was to remain in the United States, and the commissioners could then either lease the land or subdivide it for sale at public auction "in parcels not to exceed three hundred and twenty acres to any one purchaser." (*Statutes at Large*, vol. 12, pp. 422–26.)

28: Order by the Military Governor in the Department of the South

BEAUFORT, S.C., *December* 20, 1862.

GENERAL ORDERS. No. 12. The following system of labor for the cultivation of the Plantations in this Department, having been proposed by the Superintendents of the Second Division, is adopted for the entire Department, and all the Superintendents are hereby directed to conform strictly to its requirements.

I. The negroes are to be responsible for planting and cultivating sufficient corn and potatoes for their own subsistence. For this purpose, land will be allotted to them as follows:

To each working hand, one acre and two tasks[1] for corn; two tasks for potatoes.

To each child, one task for corn; one-quarter task for potatoes.

The allotments to be made in such field, or fields, as the superintendent may select; but in such manner that when all the tasks in any field or fields are allotted, they shall be contiguous one to another, so as to avoid intermediate spaces of uncultivated land.

The ploughing on these allotted tasks is to be done by the use of the ploughs and oxen, mules, or horses of the plantation, and to be conducted by a ploughman appointed by the superintendent, and acting under his direction exclusively. The distribution of manure, which is to be furnished by the negroes, also to be made by the use of the carts and working animals of the plantation. The ploughman to act as cartman when his services are not needed in ploughing, and to be responsible to the superintendent for the care of the ploughs and working animals, and to be paid for his services at the rate of thirty cents a day.

II. In exchange for the use of the government lands and working animals, and the services of the ploughman, the negroes are to plant and cultivate, in addition to the allotments above stated, as many acres of land as will produce corn enough for the subsistence of the plantation mules and horses, for the use of the superintendent of the district in which the plantation is situated, and also for the subsistence of old or disabled persons for whom no other provision can be made. This additional land is to constitute a part of the negro allotments, or to be annexed *pro rata* to each, and to be at the rate of six acres for every mule or horse belonging to the plantation or used by the superintendent, – one acre for the superintendent himself, one acre and a half for the ploughman, and one acre for every old or disabled person.

When the crop of corn is gathered in, each negro is to contribute, for the purposes mentioned, such a part of the total produce of that negro's allotment as will make the portion contributed bear the same relation to the total produce that the land annexed, as aforesaid, bears to the entire allotment.

III. For the raising of cotton, the negroes are to agree as to the number of tasks or acres they will each plant and cultivate, and these tasks or acres will be allotted in such field or fields as the superintendent may select; but in such manner that, when all the tasks or acres in any field or fields are allotted, they shall be contiguous one to another, so as to avoid intermediate spaces of uncultivated land.

The negroes will be paid for work done on the cotton fields at the rate of twenty-five cents a day; the following standards to be used in determining what shall constitute a fair day's work:

In ploughing, three acres.

In listing, without the use of the plough, in light land, one task and a half; in heavy land, one task.

In listing, after the ground has been broken by a plough, two tasks.

In banking, when no ploughing is done, one task and a half; when a plough is used, two tasks.

In planting, four tasks or one acre.

In the first hoeing, two tasks.

In the first hauling, two tasks.

In the second hoeing, two tasks.

In the second hauling, two tasks.

In the third hauling, when needed as in light land, two tasks.

For picking the cotton, the negroes will be allowed two and one-half cents per pound as picked, or as weighed with the seed; a part of this allowance, say one-half a cent, to be regarded as payment for the labor of picking, and the remaining two cents as additional to the daily wages, and offered to encourage faithful and thorough cultivation.

If any negro fails to do the work required to be done on his task, within a given time specified by the superintendent, he is to call in such other laborers as he may select to do that work, and pay them for it instead of the person to whom the task was allotted.

If any negroes, able to labor in the cotton fields or to perform the general plantation work, should decline doing so, and should at the same time occupy houses or cultivate lands on the plantation, they shall pay a rent, to be determined by the superintendent, but not to exceed two dollars per month for each house, and the land allotted to such negroes, according to the above regulations.

IV. The foreman on the plantation will have the general oversight, under the direction of the superintendent, of all work done in the cotton fields, and will make a true report to the superintendent from day to day of any delinquencies that may fall under his notice. He will also have charge of the plantation buildings and implements, and see that the ploughman takes proper care of the working animals, and that the field-minder attends to his special duties. For this service, when it occupies all his time, he will be paid at a rate not exceeding ten dollars a month, and, when he does not give his whole time to this service, his wages will be reduced at the discretion of the superintendent.

V. Mechanics, field-minders, cattle-minders, cartmen, boatmen, nurses, and others engaged in necessary job-work on the plantation, will be employed and paid as at present. By Order of
R. SAXTON, *Brig. Gen. and Military Governor.*

PD

General Orders No. 12, Headquarters, Beaufort, S.C., 20 Dec. 1862, enclosed in Austin Smith to Hon. S. P. Chase, 15 May 1864, S-97 1864, Letters Received by the Division, ser. 315, Division of Captured Property, Claims, &

Land, RG 56 [X-72]. Labeled on the outside as "Plan for '63." A handwritten marginal notation is omitted. No order regulating the employment and payment of the specialized workers cited in section V has been located among the records of the military governor or in those of the Department of the South and its subordinate commands.

1 When used as a unit of land measurement, a "task" equaled one-quarter acre.

29: Provost Marshal General of the Department of the South to the Commander of the Department

St. Augustine Fla. 2nd May 1863.

General; I have the honor to report as follows respecting the state of affairs relating to my department at the post of Fernandina. Fla.

The general sanitary condition of the post is excellent. I find at this post some 1050 negro women & children who are provided with quarters & rations by the commissary– These people are mostly the wives and children of soldiers in the S.C. Regiment– They have no employment whatever, and seem to have no disposition to work or to endeavor to provide for themselves; but are satisfied to draw their support from the government & live in idleness– It is with difficulty that indifferent house servants can be obtained at $10.– per month The quarters are insufficient and notwithstanding the care & attention of the authorities of the post, I believe that the crowded state of the quarters of these people, without encentives to work & consequently indifferent in all matters of personal cleanliness or other sanitary matters, will breed disease, and I would respectfully recommend that means be taken to remedy this evil before the sickly season arrives.

I would recommend that these families be removed to the neighborhood of the station of the regiment to which their protectors are attached; and that quarters similar to those built at the negro village near Hilton Head, be provided for them– The advantages of this plan, besides uniting and giving each families their own firesides, will be, that they may draw their support from those who are bound to, & by their enlistment are enable to support them; and moreover each one having a portion of ground assigned to them can cultivate it, thereby assisting in their own support & in furnishing fresh vegatables eggs &c &c. to the Soldiers.

I think that the plan of furnishing government rations to these people & thereby offering a premium to idleness, is wrong in principle & pernicious in results Most of them are able bodied people & should be obliged to earn their own living; & had they been required to do so they could at the proper planting season have planted vegatables enough for the entire use of the post, the want of which is now seriously felt – It is my belief where government rations are issued, that there Should be a proper return in labor, and that those so drawing should be required to work in the QM Dept, in cleaning streets or such other labor as they are able to do.

If this or some such system was enforced, I believe that this miserable system of pauperism would soon cease, and that the subjects of it would be greatly benefitted.

A system of apprenticeship for children has been suggested to me, If proper care was taken in placing children & then a general supervision requiring the persons receiving them to educate & learn them some trade or craft by which they can support themselves in the future, I think that it would be a saving to the government, and a benefit to the children. I am General, Very Respectfully Yours.

ALS James F. Hall

Lt. Col. James F. Hall to Maj. Genl. D. Hunter, 2 May 1863, H-243 1863, Letters Received, ser. 4109, Dept. of the South, RG 393 Pt. 1 [C-1316]. Hall signed as lieutenant colonel of volunteer engineers, as well as provost marshal general. A penciled notation suggests that his letter was simply filed at the headquarters of the Department of the South. Three months earlier, the post commander had reported about 1,000 former slaves at Fernandina, of whom only 100 were able-bodied men. Most of the latter were employed by either the engineer at Fort Clinch or the post quartermaster, but a few were working independently – "none are idle that we can find." "We are obliged," he added, "to issue rations to 772 colored persons," all of whom were women, children, or old men. "Some of these people," he observed, "have husbands and sons in the colored Regiment, but as very little, if any, money has come here from the Regiment, we must feed these people or see them starve." (Col. Jos. R. Hawley to Lt. Col. Chas. G. Halpine, 31 Jan. 1863, H-222 1863, Letters Received, ser. 4109, Dept. of the South, RG 393 Pt. 1 [C-1315].)

30: Testimony by a Direct-Tax Commissioner for the State of South Carolina before the American Freedmen's Inquiry Commission

[*Beaufort, S.C. June 1863*]

Testimony of Judge A. D. Smith

Judge A. D. Smith testified: –

I am Chairman of the Board of the United States Direct Tax Commissioners for the State of South Carolina. In the year 1861, at the commencement of the session of Congress in December, M[r]

Senator Doolittle drafted an Act of Congress for the collection of Direct Taxes in Insurrectionary Districts. At the previous special session in July, the United States had levied a direct tax upon all the lands of all the States, but the difficulty was to collect these taxes in insurrectionary districts. The bill of Mr Doolittle provided therefor; but it was not for the mere sake of the taxes that the bill passed. It was for the purpose of giving a title to the lands in these rebellious districts; – divesting, in other words, by law, the titles of rebels to their lands; for Mr Lincoln and a great many others had held, I think erroneously, that the title to real estate could not be confiscated and forfeited in consequence of any acts of rebellion beyond the life of the individual traitor. But the levying of this tax is an undoubtedly constitutional act of Congress; for Congress has the power to levy as well as to declare war. They have levied this tax, therefore; and if I pay my taxes upon my property in Wisconsin it is well; if not, it is sold. If Mr Edmund Rhett owns property in Beaufort, S.C., he is liable; the fact of his being a rebel does not excuse him. We knew beforehand that the rebels would not come up and pay. This bill, therefore, was passed, and I helped Mr Doolittle, being in Washington, at the time, to draw it up; I had then no idea of belonging to this Commission, but after I went home, about the middle of July, I saw the announcement of my appointment in the newspapers, and concluded to accept it.

On coming here I found everything at odds and ends; – no system or policy or anything that looked to a permanent plan. The first necessity was to start a civilization, an education, a domestication of these colored people. They did not want to go away; they were attached to their homes and wanted to stay here provided they could be free and protected. But in order to get that encouragement and hope, they must have the family organized, and a homestead must be given them – they *must have land, land*. A mere military title furnished no security, no permanence; no system could be founded upon it; – it was then necessary to get a permanent title from the Government.

I knew very well, and it has proved so, that these lands being sold for taxes and purchased by private individuals, would require the labor of these people; – for to make these lands valuable, or to preserve value in them, they must be cultivated. Here were the laborers; well, to get their services, they must be paid, and here was your compensated system by a turn of the pencil.

We came here, but we had not a starting point anywhere. All the records, books and maps pertaining to Beaufort had been taken away. Finally, however, we found a corner-stone in the town of Beaufort, and from this we started. We found some old assessment books that had been in the possession of the Collector of Taxes in the town. They were from 1848 to 1859; I think. From these we found out how much real estate each man owned, and knew how many slaves they owned, whether, however, in the City of Beaufort or upon the plantations, we did not know. Then we had a map of the town made, and two of the Commissioners went over all the plantations to find their boundary lines and the number of acres in each.

We knew from the law of the State what their valuation was for the purposes of taxation. I think from the first settlement of the state, but certainly from 1815 to this time, there has been one classification by law of the lands of this State which recognizes their assessed value for the purpose of taxation. I think there are fifteen classes and they range from twenty cents to twenty-five dollars per acre. I cannot find, in looking over the statutes any alteration since 1815. Certain lands of one class, according to their situation, are valued at twenty cents per acre – these are uncultivated or wild lands. These Sea Island lands are generally rated at $4 for the purpose of taxation; so that the assessor or collector came around to Mr Rhett or Mr Hayward and asked him how much land he owned. He answered so many acres at 20 cents and so many at $4, and his word was taken. Well, the act of Congress required the Commissioners to adopt the last assessment prior to the 1st of January, 1861, to settle the valuation of the lands, and having got this description we were about to advertize for sale when some of our friends became frightened lest a horde of speculators might come down here. The law as it first stood required the Commissioners to bid in for the Government all lands, the sale of which would not cover the expense of taxation, assessment and collection, and that would be a very small price to pay for land, because the Commissioners did not feel authorized to bid higher than that amount. General Saxton and Rev. Mr French therefore advised me to go to Washington; that was on the 11th of January. I went and saw Mr Chase, who had just got an order written to suspend these sales, leaving the land in the military possession and subject to all its caprices. The order he had mailed but at my solicitation he sent for it and got it back.

I immediately saw Senator Sumner, who was also frightened and had introduced a bill into the Senate to prevent these lands falling into the hands of speculators. Messrs. Sumner, Collamer, Doolittle, Wilson and a member of Congress from New York who took great interest in the matter but whose name I forget, met with me in consultation upon the subject, and afterwards I drew an amendment to the act to this effect: – that the Government might select such lands and purchase them as Gen. Hunter, Gen. Saxton and the Commissioners might deem a necessity for the military, naval, revenue, charitable, educational and police purposes of the Department, and also giving the land Commissioners power, in their discretion, to bid upon any lands up to two-thirds of their assessed value, so that indeed it might not be a change of masters from slaveowners to capitalists, but that Government might have land enough for them all. I returned here before the passage of the act, but my instructions came here in the same boat, and we went on with the sale of the lands.

[See amendments to the law of June 7, 1862.][1]

Under these amendments the sale came off. Previous to the sale Gen. Saxton assisted the Commissioners to select for purchase by the United States Government, for the purposes already specified, *forty thousand* acres of land in the parish of St. Helena, (Hilton Head having nothing to do with this.) Gen. Hunter was unable to take part in the selection of these lands as he was occupied with his military operations for the attack upon Charleston. At the sale these lands were bid in for the Government, and there were sold to private individuals about twenty thousand acres. Then the Government bid in, over and above the forty-thousand acres, under the two-thirds regulation, some twenty thousand more, making in round numbers a little more than sixty thousand acres; so that in the Parish of St. Helena alone there are reported by the tax list eighty thousand acres. I think this is an under estimate, however, and that there are in reality 100,000 acres, because in almost every instance the lands bid in for the Government overran the quantity stated.

By Col. McKaye– Is there any official map made of these lands?

A. Not of the whole.

Q. Have you any plan for disposing of this property?

A. My idea is that all these lands which have been bought in by the Government should be so disposed of that every man capable of buying a farm should have opportunity to purchase from five to fifteen or five hundred acres. I would not *give* a single cent's worth, because these people must be taught to pay for all that they get. My plan is to sell to these people and to white men also. I want to have the examplar of white enterprise before the colored people. But to put them by themselves, with no Anglo Saxon spirit of intelligence and enterprise to excite their emulation would, I am afraid, result in their deterioration. Therefore I was anxious that there should be men of enterprise and proper moral and social conduct to buy and cultivate some of these plantations.

Col. McKaye– I desire simply to get as briefly as possible your own ideas. Do you think that it would be well for the best interests of the colored people to settle them upon these islands, isolated from white men.

A. No, sir; I do not think that it would.

Q. – Would it do taking these people in their present state of intelligence and civilization to settle them promiscuously – permitting these lands to be disposed of, and the colored people mixing up with such white men as might settle here under a free sale of the land, without any selection – putting these people in relation promiscuously with the selfishness of white men?

A. That depends upon what sort of civil government shall follow in the wake of the army. My plan is this: *First*, if these lands are to be leased there must be rules and regulations governing the hours of labor, and, perhaps, the amount, – at all events the hours – so that provision shall be made against their being overworked – I mean if these lands are leased or sold to white men. If leased, there should be rules and regulations provided for their support; the sum that should be paid them for labor between certain extremes; the hours they should work, and the quantity of land they should have for their own immediate cultivation. And I would make no distinction between white and colored in leasing the plantations or otherwise; there should be no corporal punishment, and I would have a tribunal, if necessary to be appointed under military rule, so organized that the employer and employee could come at once and make their complaints. If the employee on the land worked carelessly or was a mischief-maker, the employer should discharge him, but not whip him – he must be treated like a man and governed by law; and if an employer abuses an employee he can make his complaint and get redress. That they need and for a time must have the guidance of white men is a positive certainty, but the great thing is to inaugurate civil government in some form that shall follow right along in the wake of the army.

Q. Have they any idea of civil government?

A. Some of them, but most of them have not; they depend upon white men.

Q. What is your opinion about removing them as rapidly as possible from military jurisdiction – I mean organizing a distinct authority that shall control and guide the colored men – a government distinct from that of the Commander in Chief?

A. There are a dozen reasons why it should not be mixed up with the military command.

Q. It is your idea that an entirely separate authority should be established?

A. Yes; but the difficulty is in establishing that civil authority without the aid of the military force. I said the same thing last Winter to the President. The great point is to inaugurate some form of civil government that shall begin to teach these people at once, and there is no doubt that the freedman here will be able to support himself.

Q. What is your idea of the propriety of enlisting in the army all the able-bodied men that can be spared from the labor of the plantations?

A. It is the best school in the world. If you could have seen the men who now compose these regiments as they were before, lounging about with a shuffling gait, looking sideways and having a suspicious manner, to contrast their appearance with their present upright and erect carriage, I am sure you would say that it is the very best school. It makes men of them at once – it makes citizens of them, and not only of them but of their wives and children. Their sons and brothers look at them and see how nearly they approach to gentlemen, and want to become so to, and this influence is felt by every member of their families.

Q. Do you think that so far as any military guard is necessary, or wherever military defence is needed, it would be better to be of their own people rather than white men?

A. I think for a time they should be officered by white men, but the body of the force should be black.

Q. What is the effect upon the colored people of contact with the army?

A. It is deleterious.

Q. What plan of Government would you institute for these people?

A. The government of Slavery is essentially barbarous. To change a barbarous to one of civilization and Christianity requires power. Hence a civil government instituted to *reconstruct* society and the South, local and home government, requires a stronger power moving by its own force than to govern a society long accustomed to Freedom. But this governmental power, whatever may be its shape or form, should be so organized as to be educational, in virtue of its own operations; it should be parental though strong, intelligent and kind though firm. Although my whole education and principles of political and social economy have been adverse to sumptuary laws, I firmly believe that something of the kind will be found necessary in the reconstruction of society reorganized by the Freedmen of the South. That this will difficult I do not believe, but that it will be simple, and, to an intelligent mind and good heart, plain and palpable – demonstrating its necessities by its own operations as society shall advance.

Q. Do you think the system under the orders of General Saxton[2] is adequate to the proper control of these people?

A. I think it is the best of which I can conceive under the circumstances in which he has been placed, and that he has done as well as any man could possibly do for the moral and physical elevation of this people.

Q. Do you think that the wages paid them are sufficient–as much as a laboring man should get for his work?

A. Well, some are worth $12 a month and some are not worth $5. I think that the amount they receive is adequate to their support, but in my judgment they are not paid enough.

Q. What do you know of the chastity of the young women among them?

A. I have never seen but one instance of indelicacy.

Q. What is the established general reputation of the colored girls for chastity?

A. I cannot say that it is bad. I have heard loose men say that these women would do anything, but I have no reason to believe it; in two instances young men have come to me and said that white men were trying to seduce their wives.

Q. Have you heard anything leading you to believe that there is a considerable system of paid prostitution?

A. Not until lately, and that was not considerable; there was some I understood at Hilton Head but none at Beaufort. [Judge Smith afterwards stated that he had made inquiry of officers who ought to know and they reported that there was no such practice of paid prostitution.][3]

Q. Do you believe that so far as getting a living is concerned the women are under the necessity of selling themselves for prostitution?

A. No sir; the fact that the demand for labor really exceeds the supply is contradiction sufficient of that. Why, when Gen. Hunter's drafting order was issued there was a universal cry against it because of the scarcity of labor.[4] The women are needed as laundresses and find an abundance of employment.

Q. What is your idea of the best method of taking these people in the army?

A. Well, so far as drafting them is concerned I would conform to the law of Congress, making no distinction between white and colored men.

Q. Have you any suggestions to make respecting these people?

A. Yes, but I do not know that I can say anything until I learn what is the policy of the Government in regard to these lands. I think it is better to initiate measures which will throw these lands promiscuously into the hands of both white and colored men. Here are 63,000 acres, of which probably 10,000 will be wanted for military purposes, but say 20,000, and then 40,000 are left for the use of the Government in taking care of these people. You may calculate that there will be on an average ten to fifteen thousand negroes in the parish of St. Helena, and 40,000 acres will give a little more than five acres to each individual. That is a great deal. Now, I would have the lands offered for sale next January at

$1 or $1.25 per acre and give the right of preëmption to be perfected in October, letting the negro file his right of preemption. As regards their houses I fully approve of the plan of the last houses that Gen. Mitchel constructed at the village of Mitchelville at Hilton Head. In conclusion, I desire to tell you that I was almost overwhelmed with objections against the purchase and occupation of these plantations by white people, because, as it was said, they could not agree with the colored laborers to work upon them for wages. Well, 20,000 acres have been sold and they are all cultivated by the purchasers in their own persons or under their immediate superintendence. The people born and reared upon the plantations thus purchased have all been employed at satisfactory wages, and I have yet heard of but one complaint of abuse or maltreatment. The testimony of all the purchasers is that the negroes have worked well and faithfully, and have told them better than they knew themselves the best method of conducting the cultivation of their lands.

HD

Testimony of Judge A. D. Smith before the American Freedmen's Inquiry Commission, [June 1863], filed with O-328 1863, Letters Received, ser. 12, RG 94 [K-71]. Topical labels in the margin are omitted. Smith's questioner was James M. McKaye, a member of the American Freedmen's Inquiry Commission. On January 1, 1863, Smith had informed Secretary of the Treasury Salmon P. Chase that "[t]he anxiety of [the freedpeople] to obtain a home in their own right, and feel safe in its possession, is intense. Some such measure," he argued, "would seem indispensable to the proper organization of their labor, to the institution of their new form of society, and the establishment of that moral and social police so essential in all societies. . . . the fact that these freed people do manifest such an intense anxiety in regard to their homes, such an ardent desire to remain upon the soil, to own a portion of it, or to cultivate it for reasonable wages, should at least inspire the friends of freedom with a degree of faith in the susceptibilities and vital energy of the people who are to work out the great social and political problems which this rebellion has forced upon the intellect and conscience of the Nation." Smith painted an enthusiastic picture of the rosy future awaiting the Sea Islands if the former slaves were provided with land: "Having the soil, – loyal people skilled in its culture, grateful, docile and hopeful, – rebels absconded or driven out and refusing allegiance, proffered pardon and protection, – their places filled by patriots, their lands yearning for the plow and the spade, – arms and hands eager to leap to their joyful, because voluntary task, – in short, all the elements of reconstruction, reformation, advancement in civilization, happiness, wealth, freedom and assured loyalty, full, devoted and reliable, how can a Government answer to God for its failure to improve opportunities of such a character, means so Providentially furnished, and forego results so humane and magnificent!" (A. D. Smith to the Hon. S. P. Chase, 1 Jan. 1863, General Correspondence, ser. 99, SC, Records of or Relating to Direct Tax Commissions in the Southern States, RG 58 [Z-2].)

1 Brackets in manuscript. The amendments of February 1863 to the Direct Tax Act of June 1862 are summarized above, in doc. 27n.
2 For the principal order by General Rufus Saxton, military governor in the Department of the South, see above, doc. 28.
3 Brackets in manuscript.
4 In May 1862, General David Hunter, commander of the Department of the South, had ordered a draft of "all able bodied negroes capable of bearing arms." (See above, doc. 20n.)

31: Testimony by an Aide to the Military Governor in the Department of the South before the American Freedmen's Inquiry Commission

[*Beaufort, S.C. June 1863*]

Testimony of Captain E. W. Hooper.
Captain E. W. Hooper testified –

Q With whom is the system of authority over the colored people vested – who has control of them?

A General Saxton has control of all persons in the Department of the South not connected with the Military, and of all matters not concerning the Military he has exclusive control.

Q He has in these relations the title and functions of a Military Governor?

A He has the title but the functions are very indefinite. His orders are to take charge of the plantations and all persons in the Department not connected with Military affairs; to make such arrangements for the benefit of the civilians of the Department as may be proper; to make police and sanitary regulations for the well being of society including whites as well as negroes.

Q. General Saxton then has the appointment of all persons connected with the government of the colored people?

A. Yes, sir; entirely except so far as Genl. Hunter and others see fit to encroach on his authority. In relation to the contrabands he reports only to the Department at Washington. He is subordinate to the Commandant of the Department only so far as Military matters are concerned. His jurisdiction as Military Governor is co-extensive with the Department.

Q. He has the appointment of all the persons employed in the care of the laborers on the plantations?

A. Yes, sir.

Q. What are the titles of persons employed in the care of these people?

A. Those having care of the plantations are called Superintendents.

Q. General Saxton has his own Military family, and you are one of his Aids?

A. Yes sir; in addition to being Military Governor, General Saxton is in charge of the post which rather complicates matters; when General Saxton was Military Governor alone he personally attended to the care of the plantations but when he became post Commandant this took up all his time, and I being here at the beginning, he has left me in charge, and does practically little but sign papers.

Q. So far as you have relations with these people you control the whole matter under General Saxton?

A. Yes sir; I have general direction of the business, and under me there are four general superintendents, including Mrs Gage at Paris Island. These four general superintendents have certain islands or territories; their authority is not over the whole, but it is confined to particular localities.

Q. What are the names of these Superintendents?

A. The name of the Superintendent of the 1st division is Henry. G. Judd; he is the Superintendent of Port Royal Island and Barnwell Island; the last being a small island just beyond our picket lines; in his division their are sixty two plantations.

Q How many people has he under him?

A Including Beaufort, he has approximately five thousand.

Q Will you give me the names of the other division superintendents?

A Mr Reuben Tomlinson has St Helena, Ladies and Coosaw Islands; there are about 82 plantations in his division.

Q And how many people?

A He has also about 5000 people. In giving the number of plantations I have stated them as they were previous to the sale,[1] some have since passed into private hands. The next Superintendent is Thos D. Howard; he is general superintendent of Hilton Head Island alone.

Q What number of plantations are upon that Island?

A He has now charge of fifteen plantations. He had twenty including those on Pinckney, and Dawfuskie Islands, but we no longer occupy them.

Q Do you know the population?

A Including those in the Quartermasters Department their are

1,500 or 2,000. The total number of negroes within our lines in South Carolina last spring was 9,050, since which time we have increased 3000, making the aggregate population 12,000. Then we have besides a fourth division of which Mrs Gage is superintendent. This is Paris Island, on which are five plantations and about 500 persons.

Q And how many acres do these plantations include?

A We have no way of ascertaining that, because there is so much land not under cultivation; the Commissioners[2] could not get hold of it [See copy of the Free South containing the best estimate of the number of acres.][3]

Q Several of these plantations have been sold by the tax Commissioners, have they not?

A There have been about 45 plantations sold to private parties, and about 120 are still in the hands of the Government on all the Islands now in the possession of our forces.

Q Are all of these 120 plantations under cultivation for the Government?

A Yes, Sir, more or less every one.

Q Do any of the colored men carry on any portion of the plantations for themselves?

A On all the plantations they have allotted to them so much land for their own subsistance; they plant of it what they please, the only condition being a certain percentage to the government for the fodder of the animals on the place.

Q How much land is allotted for their own use?

A One acre and a half for corn and half an acre for potatoes for each man and woman, and an additional quantity for each child; the government pays for nothing that they cultivate but the Cotton.

Q Have any of the colored men bought plantations?

A Yes, Sir, I bought a plantation for my Servant Henry McMillan who expects to plant enough this season to pay for it and there are 7 or 8 other plantations purchased by negroes singly or in company.

Q On these plantations so purchased does the government have any thing to do with the working?

A No, Sir, except to maintain the Police regulations and to see that the old people in the cabins are taken care of. We do not interfere with their aggricultural arrangements; they plant what they please. We give them all the privileges of passes and so forth that they require. These purchasers hold 45 out of 180 plantations; the people are free and the owners are free, They hire and pay them according to contract; before giving the purchasers possession General Saxton made them sign an agreement not to interfere with the corn lands that were planted before it was known certainly that these lands would be sold.

Q How would it do to have a proper form of contract and make these people enter it?

A I do not believe in government interference; the competition for labor is so great the matter will settle itself.

Q Is the demand for the labor of these people equal to the supply?

A The demand is greater than the supply for able bodied men because the regiments have taken off so many.

Q About how much an acre was paid for these plantations by purchasers?

A About one dollar an acre for the good plantations. I paid three hundred and five dollars for three hundred and thirteen acres, but the title is a little uncertain.

Q What number of acres can a man and his family plant and manage?

A That depends on the size of his family; a man himself can take care of from three to four acres. In the picking season every body turns out to help. Picking is the hardest work and must be done by hand. This necessitates the keeping of a larger number of people on a plantation then are required for the other operations of the crop.

. . . .

Q Who employs the laborers upon the plantations?

A The superintendent is put upon a plantation and told to take care of the people, and do the best he can. He has no distinct instructions save a file of orders giving general directions, excepting in matters concerning rations. His instructions on this point are defined; a very wide discretion is left to the superintendents; when the superintendent comes here he at once reports to me and his name is given to the Quartermaster, Then he is ordered to report to the division superintendent who assigns him a plantation or gets him a boarding house; he goes at his business with the understanding that he is to do the best he can for the people; to settle differences amongst them; to advise them; to teach them, help them in their work; to see that the best crops are put in; to protect them against the soldiers, and to report cases in which the laborers are interfered with; to keep account of the work done on the cotton, &c.,

Q. You pay for the labor of these people in raising cotton?

A. Yes, sir; but only exactly in proportion to the amount planted at first, and as the season advances and it is neglected we cease payment.

Q. What compensation do you give the colored people who work upon the plantations?

A. In brief it is 25 cents a day for field hands' work, but that does not include what they get at the end of the year

Q. How much is estimated at a day's work?

A. Three tasks.[4]

Q. You reserve a portion of the wages of the laborers until the cotton is harvested?

A. Yes, sir; we pay them 25 cents a day for what they do upon the ground; that is before the picking; then for picking we pay them so much per pound, – half a cent per pound for the mere act of picking and then a cent for every pound of seed cotton they bring in to the cotton house, and where the yield exceeds 100 lbs an acre a premium of two cents per pound is given.

Q. Does that constitute the whole compensation given to the laborer?

A. Yes, sir; rations are not issued now except to the destitute; in some instances persons working for the government are destitute, their pay not being sufficient to support them. We principally object to giving them allowances because this matter of allowances was so much like the old system, We have therefore cut them off, and only help them out in this way when the crops have been taken by the soldiers.

Q. Do these people live in their old quarters?

A. Yes, sir, in all cases; but the 3.000 who have come into our lines have been crowded into all sorts of houses wherever they can get them.

Q. On Hilton Head they have built some new houses for themselves; under whose direction where they started?

A. Under General Mitchell's

Q. Where are these persons employed?

A. Mainly in the Quartermaster's Department.

Q. What are the wages paid by the Quartermaster?

A. The Quartermaster pays \$5 a month and soldier's rations which are equivalent to \$8 or \$9 if purchased in the shops; they cost the government about \$7.

Q. What do the Quartermasters pay white men for labor?

A. I believe they cannot get laborers except mechanics; the white men they have here are a grade higher than laborers; a common white laborer could not be procured here for less than \$2 or \$3 a day, consequently none are employed, as negro labor is so much cheaper for the government.

Q. Have you any colored mechanics employed in the Quartermaster's Department?

A. A large number; the ordinary mechanic is paid $10 a month and Soldier's rations by order of the War Department;[5] white mechanics get $3 per day and soldier's rations. If Captn Moore gets hold of an extra fine mechanic he pays him $15 a month and Pilots get as high as $30 a month.

Q. Is a colored man paid as much for the same kind of labor as a white man?

A. I don't think he is; the reason for that is that there was a large supply when we got here seeking work and this pay was very much more than they got before. I advised the Quartermaster not to pay them any more; it did not seem to me desirable under present circumstances.

Q. Have you been in the Quartermaster's Department?

A. No, Sir; but I know a great deal about it.

Q. Can you tell me the comparative amount of labor done by a white and a colored man– suppose you have a man to superintend the labor of a colored man, will he do as much as a white man?

A. I should say a colored mechanic would not do as much as a white; but he will labor with more uniformity, the negroes understand the way to move about in this climate; they move slowly but keep along steadily at it.

Q. Do these people work willingly for wages?

A. I never knew a case where a man had reasonable security of getting wages, even morderate wages, that he was not ready to work.

Q. Are they content with their wages?

A. Yes, as a general thing; except where a person who is doing nothing more than themselves is getting better pay.

Q. Have these people been paid promptly?

A. No, Sir; the chief trouble has been the delay in payment; for instance, all the laborers employed on the plantations and many of those who work for Captain Moore, depending upon the cotton fund for their wages, have not been paid for some time because there was some trouble about the matter of drawing from the fund; the negroes on St Helena received no money for six months.

Q. Is there any clothing furnished to these people?

A. No, sir; except a small amount furnished by charitable persons at the North. When Edisto was evacuated a great many of the people were destitute and General Saxton ordered a certain amount, of the cotton fund, not much, to be expended in the purchase of clothing which was distributed to the needy.

Q. Have the government made any provision for the instruction of these people?

A. No sir; with the exception of a soldier's ration to each teacher, it has never paid for their literary and religious instructions. The teachers in the Schools are paid by benevolent societies in Boston, Philadelphia and New York.

Q. Have the government made any provision for the medical care of these people?

A. Yes, sir; it authorized General Saxton to contract for surgeons; he has about six contract surgeons employed at from $1.000 to $1.200 a year, and they are stationed around at different points. They draw their medical supplies from the Department; their salaries are the same as Assistant Surgeons without the allowances; their business is to attend to the negroes exclusively; in Beaufort there is one Hospital for negroes,

. . . .

Q. In whose hands rest the Police regulations for these people – practically who has the settlement and trial of all cases arising between the colored people themselves?

A. General Saxton has the Police power in these matters concerning the plantations, but he is too much occupied to attend to them personally, and the matter devolved upon me. I found that this was a great burden in addition to my other duties, and we now have a M[r] Dudley of Boston, a member of the Suffolk bar, who is paid the salary of a superintendent. It is his duty to examine into all cases. When a complaint is made to me I refer it to M[r] Dudley and he investigates it informally, between the parties, endeavouring to bring about a settlement.

Q. Then there is no special judicial authority for these people?

A. No, sir; I always make the Superintendent settle any matter of difference if possible, and if the thing is of such a nature that it cannot be settled by him it is refered to the general Superintendent, and if he cannot dispose of it, it is brought to M[r] Dudley; this is all done in an informal way.

Q. Is their any provost-judge in this Department?

A. No, sir; nothing but a Judge Advocate.

Q. Suppose a difficulty arises here between white men upon some question, – a contract for instance, where would it be settled?

A. Wherever such a case has arisen it has been tried before a military commission. In many cases that arise I refer them to M[r] Dudley and advise the parties to agree upon referees and the case is settled in that way; the thing most needed is some regular mode of carrying out the laws – A provost judge would be an excellent thing.

Q. Is there any thing else in relation to the government and management of these people that I have not asked you about?

A. The blacks at Fernandina and S[t] Augustine are respectively under the charge of M[r] Helper and M[r] Brinkerhoff. There are four teachers at Fernandina and two at S[t] Augustine.

Q. Do you think these people understand fully or in part this question of the compensation that they receive for the work they do – do they understand they receive the half cent a pound for picking cotton?

A. Yes, Sir; they understand it as a general thing; many say when you pay them that they want to be made sensible what the money is for; especially is this the case when they are not paid for two or three months. They understand distinctly it is so much a pound for cotton.

Q. How many teachers are there in each large division?

A. In the 1st division there are 29 teachers – six men and 23 women. In the 2nd division there are 23 teachers – 6 men and 17 women. In the 3rd division, Hilton Head, there are 2 teachers, and on Paris Island there is one [Captain Hooper will furnish the number of children in the various schools][6] There is a store kept at Beaufort by a detailed Superintendent, and the goods sold are ordered from New York and paid for out of the cotton fund. They are sold to the negroes at an advance simply, sufficient to pay the cost of transportation; this was done to keep down prices. Then there is a store of the same kind on S[t] Helena Island established by the Philadelphia society – the store is conducted by an old Quaker gentleman, and the society supplies him with goods.

Q. Do any of these people lay up their wages?

A. Yes, sir; many of them; I do not think they are wasteful as a people compared with laborers in the North. They are pretty ready to purchase clothing – somewhat extravagant in that respect.

Q. With whom do they deposit their savings?

A. I think they hoard their money themselves; the paymasters say when they go round that they are always ready to make change for a $5 or $10 bill; sometimes they deposit with private parties; on one occasion a sergeant gave me $22 to keep for his wife.

Q. Has there been anything like an allotment system introduced here?

A. Hardly; Col Higginson's Regiment has been the only one paid off and I went out there at his request and took such moneys from the men as they were willing to deposit with me, I gave each one a receipt, – one of the Superintendents being witness; and from 69 men I received $800; – each of them only keeping back a dollar or two of his pay.

Q. What proportion of their pay went to the families of these soldiers?

A. Well, $700 or $800 went through my hands out of $7.000 or $8.000 paid to the regiment; the wives of these men were constantly visiting them and there must have been a great deal of money handed over to them.

Q. What proportion of the men in that regiment are married?

A. I think a very large proportion.

Q. Would it not be well to introduce among these colored regiments at once a plan for allotting a portion of their wages to their families?

A. Yes, sir; I think some system of this sort might be introduced. At present the wives and families of these men are supplied with rations by the government, if they have no other means of support. My belief is, that with proper management, there would be little difficulty in prevailing on this people to allot a portion of their pay; but they have been so constantly cheated by white men that they do not care to trust strangers; I think that if they were distinctly notified that the rations of their families would be cut off, they would give their money.

Q. Do they know how to count money?

A. They are learning rapidly. There is one great advantage in Greenbacks; they are uniform. They were shamefully treated formerly with old labels from Champagne bottles and similar things.

Q. How do these people compare in intellectual capacity with the humblest white people you have known?

A. They always seem to me, where on first impression I would call them stupid, when I come to watch them, that it is more of the stupidity of the foreigner who does not understand our language when spoken to. I do not think they lack in intellectual capacity.

Q. In relation to their moral condition, what do you think of that?

A. I think the chief trouble of all is the non-obligation of the marriage relation.

Q. Their character for truth and veracity – have they the same consciousness or moral sense about telling the truth as white men?

A. I think they have; because when you hear them say something which you know to be a lie, and tell them of it, they reply "I tell the truth; I would not tell a lie."

Q. I do not mean whether they know the difference between the truth and a lie, but do they understand that in telling a lie they are violating a moral law?

A. Yes, sir; I think they do.

Q. Where these men enter into a contract, have they any sense of the obligation?

A. I think they have; but I do not think that they often understand that they are entering upon a contract when such is the fact. Many complaints are made by Captains of vessels against them for leaving, who fail to specify the time they should stay when they sign the articles; I think it is a misunderstanding.

Q. Where a colored man gives his promise about a particular thing, does he regard his promise?

A. They are of all kinds, and I find the same differences with them in this respect as exist among white people.

Q. Suppose a man gave you a promise that he would do a certain piece of work, would you rely upon it?

A. As a general thing I would depend upon him.

Q. Have these people any sense of what we say of *meum* and teum?

A. They have a sense of *meum* that is certain.

Q. Have they the same sense of the rights of property as white men?

A. Yes; among themselves they are very particular about their rights, – their chickens and pigs; but they would steal from each other as well as from their masters.

. . . .

Q. Are they good at trading?

A. Yes, sir; they are naturally shrewd and sharp, but they do not understand our habits of trading.

Q. Do you think they are frugal?

A. Yes, sir; their pay on the plantations is more than sufficient for their wants, and they save, except in the matter of clothing where they are extravagant.

Q. What pay do the women get on the plantations?

A. They get so much according to the amount of work whether it is done by man, woman or child. The general way is for the head of a family to take so much ground, agreeing to cultivate it in cotton for the government; he then turns his family in and they work in common.

. . . .

HD

Excerpts from testimony of Captain E. W. Hooper before the American Freedmen's Inquiry Commission, [June 1863], filed with O-328 1863, Letters Received, ser. 12, RG 94 [K-82]. Topical labels in the margin are omitted. Approximately twenty-eight pages of a forty-two-page document. In the omitted portions, Captain Hooper provided further details about education and medical care, as well as observations about the social life and customs of freedpeople in coastal South Carolina and Florida, particularly regarding marriage, family relations, sexual behavior, and attitudes toward Union military service and civil government. For testimony by Hooper's former servant, Henry (Harry) McMillan, see below, doc. 33.

1 The direct-tax sale of March 1863.
2 The commissioners appointed by the President to administer the Direct Tax Act in South Carolina.
3 Brackets in manuscript. The copy of the newspaper is not in the file.
4 When used as a unit of land measurement, a "task" equaled one-quarter acre.
5 War Department General Order 91, issued July 29, 1862, promulgated the Militia Act of July 17, which set the wages of black military laborers at $10 per month ($3 of which might be in clothing) and one ration. (*Official Records*, ser. 3, vol. 2, pp. 270–83.)
6 Brackets in manuscript.

32: Testimony by a Plantation Superintendent on Ladies Island, South Carolina, before the American Freedmen's Inquiry Commission

[*Beaufort, S.C. June 1863*]

Testimony of Mr Frederick. A. Eustis.
Mr Eustis testified–
I am a son of General Eustis who owned the plantation on Ladies Island which I now occupy. I came here last year before Mr Pierce was first commissioned and returned North and came back when he came.

Q You are working here under the general system adopted by the authorities?[1]

A Yes, sir.

Q How many slaves were on your plantation before your mother's death?

A I think there were 116 in all, but we had another place near the ferry, besides. At present we have not more than 62,–the young people have all gone away; the draft has taken off a great many. The plantation comprises 607 acres, 200 of which are under cultivation.

Q. Is that about the ordinary proportion of land cultivated?

A. Yes, sir; the practice here is to shift the fences every year, first turning the cattle on one side and then on the other. There is nothing like Northern meadowland here–it is all salt marsh. The marsh grass we use for the cattle; we sometimes feed the mules on moss and they are able to live upon it. When I left here last year there were 400 bushels of corn in my barn but during my absence it was taken away and distributed on other places.

Q. I would like to know what are the principal defects in the present system adopted here in the practical carrying on of work?

A. I think some defects are inevitable owing to the Military status. It is a country we are holding by the bayonet and we cannot keep our people at home. This state of affairs—this instability of the population—demoralizes the negro and unsettles us.

Q. Are the general rules established for the working of the system just in their character?

A I think they are just for the negro and not for the white man, in not giving him authority. It is essential to keep up a mild discipline on the plantations and the negro should have no appeal except in cases of extreme cruelty on the part of the superintendent,— now for the least thing he goes to General Hunter or General Saxton.

Q. You have adopted the general plan of the government in working your plantation?

A. Yes, sir; I took their rules and work upon them.

Q. The whole labor is paid for by the day?

A. Yes, sir; the government limits a day's work by the number of tasks, and a task is a quarter of an acre.

Q. How does this task adopted by the government compare with the task given by negroes during slavery?

A. It is a little easier in light land and rather harder in stiff, clay lands.

Q. Have you any means when entering into a contract with a negro of enforcing that contract?

A. None at all, that is the main difficulty with which I have to contend. The government requires that every negro shall have one and a half acres for corn and half an acre for potatoes for every grown person and so much additional for every child. There is not a negro on my place who feels that he is under any obligation at all to plant cotton. On my plantation there are 150 acres planted in corn and potatoes and about 60 acres in cotton. The only way in which I am able to cultivate the cotton is by going among them and paying on the spot or offering inducements for them to work. The pith of the general order is to have them responsible for planting land for their own subsistence, but for planting cotton they are to agree among themselves. [see general order.][2] I do not feel that I have any hold upon my people if in the middle of July they should say I shall have nothing more to do with the cotton. I think as a general thing they have behaved very well, but when a man has hoed his task I put the money in his hand for his work and that encourages him.

Q. Do they work more willingly, being compensated?

A. I have never seen a people so mercenary in spirit and yet so willing to expend their earnings for provisions.

Q. Do they work more industriously, thoroughly and energetically under the system of compensation than under the old system.

A. Yes, sir; I have no hesitation in saying they do; I think a system of compensated labor might be set on foot which would be very advantageous to the planter. The great civilizer here is the "dime". No man ought to pay a negro more than 10 cents for a day's work. They have been spoiled by the high prices which have been paid them and I think the compensation still too high; for instance, they are paid 50 cents a dozen for eggs. I do not think a negro has any perception of the relative value of money and what it purchases.

Q. I suppose, taking into account the other advantages, he receives, he is paid high wages for his labor?

A. Yes, sir; he gets his homestead for nothing, and 2 acres for provisions and pays no taxes and has no expenses except for clothing and food – his expenses are very light.

Q. Undoubtedly this is an abnormal condition of things; but in making the transition from slavery to free labor will it not be necessary for the government to establish some system of guardianship?

A. Yes, sir; that is my idea. I do not believe in absolute independence; the apprenticeship system is what is needed; they are not prepared for freedom yet; they have just come out of a state of despotism, and when I came here it was a state of absolute licence. There was no law any where; night and day these men were on the backs of mules riding all over the country; but I stopped that by simply issuing two orders, – one was that no negro should leave his plantation until 12 o'clock, and another that he should have no mule or horse; the island was then picketted by the New York Highland Regiment who had orders to challenge every negro and take away his mule. I used to arrest men myself and send them to the pickets and they would give them a farcical examination and dismiss them, which made my authority weaker than it was before.

Q. Are they an orderly set of people?

A. They are the most orderly people I ever saw in my life They are not quarrelsome except with the tongue.

Q. What are their most common vices?

A. Lying is the worst habit they have; they are not so dishonest as they used to be. This fact of their owning personal property has made them all honest. It strikes me in seeing them now and comparing them with what they were, that they have got ahead 50 years. They work in their own corn fields and they work for the government; they are a great deal more industrious than they used to be and are really settling down into a species of order.

Q. What would be the effect of organizing them into Military bodies?

A. I had a theory last year of organizing them into a local militia, giving every man a sort of posse commitatus upon his plantation. I think that the introduction of a Police and Military system among them earlier would have taught them self-reliance. This Military training is teaching them a great deal; they were like a flock of sheep before.

Q What would be the effect upon the secessionists of organizing a large army of colored men?

A. I do not think it would have any other effect than to exasperate them.

Q. Do you not think that teaching them Military tactics and organizing them into large bodies and bringing them into a Military organization would suggest to their masters that they never could be got back into slavery?

A. I do not think they expect to get them back. I find that they have carried them all off to Santee and Columbia. We should have to go along way into the interior to find them now and we do not make much head way in this Department.

Q. Have you any doubt about the fighting qualities of the colored men?

A. I had but I cannot tell what miracle this organization will work; I did not think they would make good soldiers but within a day or two I have read of the splendid fighting at Port Hudson where a whole regiment was destroyed. I am inclined to think that they would make an excellent forlorn hope, but as to the qualities of soldiers I do not think they have them.

Q. What do you think of the feasibility of teaching these people to have regard to the marital relation?

A. Well sir; that would be difficult to manage; it is a matter that troubles me much. I think the people have no moral perception of the crime and no penal statute will touch it; there is a law here about the matter, but you must rely upon their increasing intelligence to bring about a reform.

Q. Do you think that the negroes have a sense of law?

A. He has a profound sense of law—the greatest respect for it—and also a sense of justice. They want few laws and those fully executed, and it must be explained to them that there is no possible escape from the law.

Q. Why will not this feeling make him a good soldier?

A. I think it will in time; but these negroes now have a morbid dread of violence and death. Say to one of them "you do not look well this morning" and he will be lowered 20 degrees in his spirits; but this high sense of feeling a personal interest in their work seems to be changing them in this respect. I never knew during 40 years of plantation life so little sickness. Formerly every man had a fever of some kind and now the veriest old cripple who did nothing under secesh rule will row a boat three nights in succession to Edisto and back again; will pick up the corn about the corn house. There are 20 people whom I know who were considered worn out and too old to work under the slave system who are now working cotton as well as their 2 acres of provisions, and their crops look very well. I have one old woman who has taken six tasks of cotton and last year she would do nothing.

Q. What is the effect with reference to the love and reverence of children for father and mother?

A. I do not think there is much. There is no real domestic life, and that is a thing that troubles me. You cannot get civilization into their houses; they live like pigs, on a fearfully low plane of life; I want to introduce the family table and a meal hour. By making this a law there would be no difficulty. Now every man takes his share of the pot sitting on his haunches before the fire, and I would like authority to furnish every family with table and table cloths, knives and forks and dinner set, and so to establish family relations.

Q. Would it do at all to leave these people perfectly free to do as they liked in free competition with white men – taking white men as they are – without any guardianship adapted to their condition?

A Not at all; white men of very low grade would outstrip them.

Q. Supposing after the war is over these lands are sold promiscuously to white and colored men and they are left here to get on the best way they could – what would happen?

A The extinction of the black race.

Q. Do these people receive proper medical attendance?

A. There are three gentlemen employed to take care of them on Ladies, St Helena and Coosaw Islands. Viz^{d} Dr Lawrence, Dr Wakefield and Dr Bundy; there are about 4000 people; I do not think the compensation enough to induce a good physician to take the place; they are only paid $1000 a year.

Q. How would it do to appoint a Physician with a certain compensation, and leave him to get the remainder of it in the ordinary way?

A. He could not subsist on the living, he would get from the negroes; although I think they should pay now. Otherwise they are on an abnormal footing.

Col McKaye – Attention must be given to this matter. The other day I met an old woman more than 90, and she says since freedom the children are fatter than they used to be. And this is easily explained because the mothers do not have to work in the field up to the time of their accouchement. The good men among the planters always took this into consideration but the bad did not.

Mr Eustis – This year in our Cotton operations we have labored under a great drawback; our seed has been limited to a peck an acre where we should have had a bushel; a bushel an acre is none too much for salt lands. This lack of seed is due to the fact that during the first year of our occupation here the agents appointed by the Treasury Department to collect the cotton carried the seed at one sweep to New York. The cost of cultivation this year, under the government order, including picking, ginning and bagging will be $20 an acre; a bale of cotton contains 300 lbs. I am inclined to think that the introduction of a system of white labor would be a capital idea merely as a matter of instruction to the negro. The maximum product of corn in this region is only 10 bushels to the acre; Irish potatoes, tomatos and water melons grow very well here; grapes do not thrive; yams and the sweet potatoes are produced abundantly; the negroes do not require much meat, but they have an insatiable thirst for molasses. I have used 10 hogsheads.

The first operation of the growing of cotton is "listing" the soil, which costs 25 cents a task or a dollar an acre; then banking and manuring cost 50 cents an acre in addition. This whole system of culture is based upon the old task system and 21 rows, 105 feet in length, make a task. In planting, a day's work is considered one acre at 25 cents per acre. We estimate at the most 3 ploughings to the acre between the rows. The cost of ploughing is 10 cents per acre, so that three ploughings cost 30 cents. Each hoeing costs 50 cents and two tasks constitute a day's work and two hoeings an acre make one dollar. Then come the two "haulings" – the drawing of the dirt up and around the stems. This is done twice at a cost each time of one dollar per acre – making the aggregate cost of cultivation $4.30; this expense however may be increased according to the condition of the land. The picking is agreed upon at 2 1/2 cents a pound and it is estimated that 500 pounds of "stone cotton"[3] are a fair average per acre. The sorting next takes place, when all the yellow pod cotton is thrown out of the stone cotton in order to "bag" nothing but the extra fine pure staple. We make one item only of the "sorting", "ginning", "moting" and "bagging," and that constitutes the whole process, amounting to three cents a pound. If you get then 150 pounds to the acre at a cost of $21.30 for cultivation and sell it for $1,200, you have a pretty large return.

HD

Testimony of Mr. Frederick A. Eustis before the American Freedmen's Inquiry Commission, [June 1863], filed with O-328 1863, Letters Received, ser. 12,

RG 94 [K-80]. Topical labels in the margin are omitted. The "Col McKaye" whose observations interrupted the questioning of Eustis was James M. McKaye, a member of the American Freedmen's Inquiry Commission.

1 The "general system" was embodied in General Order 12, issued by General Rufus Saxton, military governor in the Department of the South, on December 20, 1862. (See above, doc. 28.)
2 Brackets in the manuscript. The order in question was General Order 12, printed above as doc. 28.
3 Cotton from which the seed had not yet been removed by ginning.

33: Testimony by a South Carolina Freedman before the American Freedmen's Inquiry Commission

[*Beaufort, S.C. June 1863*]

Testimony of Harry McMillan. (colored)
Harry McMillan testified—

I am about 40 years of age, and was born in Georgia but came to Beaufort when a small boy. I was owned by General Eustis and lived upon his plantation.

Q. Tell me about the tasks colored men had to do?

A. In old secesh times each man had to do two tasks, which are 42 rows or half an acre, in "breaking" the land, and in "listing" each person had to do a task and a half. In planting every hand had to do an acre a day; in hoeing your first hoeing where you hoe flat was two tasks, and your second hoeing, which is done across the beds, was also two tasks. After going through those two operations you had a third which was two and a half tasks, when you had to go over the cotton to thin out the plants leaving two in each hill.

Q. How many hours a day did you work?

A. Under the old secesh times every morning till night—beginning at daylight and continuing till 5 or 6 at night.

Q. But you stopped for your meals?

A. You had to get your victuals standing at your hoe; you cooked it overnight yourself or else an old woman was assigned to cook for all the hands, and she or your children brought the food to the field.

Q. You never sat down and took your food together as families?

A. No, sir; never had time for it.

Q. The women had the same day's work as the men; but suppose a women was in the family way was her task less?

A. No, sir; most of times she had to do the same work. Sometimes the wife of the planter learned the condition of the woman and said to her husband you must cut down her day's work. Sometimes the women had their children in the field.

Q. Had the women any doctor?

A. No, sir; there is a nurse on the plantation sometimes, – an old midwife who attended them. If a woman was taken in labor in the field some of her sisters would help her home and then come back to the field.

Q. Did they nurse their children?

A. Yes, sir; the best masters gave three months for that purpose.

Q. If a man did not do his task what happened?

A. He was stripped off, tied up and whipped.

Q. What other punishments were used?

A. The punishments were whipping, putting you in the stocks and making you wear irons and a chain at work. Then they had a collar to put round your neck with two horns, like cows' horns, so that you could not lie down on your back or belly. This also kept you from running away for the horns would catch in the bushes. Sometimes they dug a hole like a well with a door on top. This they called a dungeon keeping you in it two or three weeks or a month, and sometimes till you died in there. This hole was just big enough to receive the body; the hands down by the sides. I have seen this thing in Georgia but never here. I know how they whip in the Prisons. They stretch out your arms and legs as far as they can to ring bolts in the floor and lash you till they open the skin and the blood trickles down.

Q What is your idea respecting the treatment of your people by the government – are they not to be taken care of?

A. They are got to be taken care of in this way, – to be protected, because they have not sense enough yet to take care of themselves. I do not want the government to take too much expense on itself for them; I want it to let the colored people feel the weight of supporting themselves.

Q. In speaking of each other do you say "negro"?

A. We call each other colored people, black people, but not negro because we used that word in secesh times.

Q. Do the colored people in their intercourse and dealings with each other tell the truth?

A. It is not always their habit; they learned to talk false to keep the lash off their backs, but now they are getting knowledge and doing better.

Q. If a colored man gives his promise will he keep it?

A. Yes, sir; they know they ought to keep it.

Q. Will they steal from each other?

A. Not so much; they have done it, but they look upon this change as bringing about a different state of things.

Q. What induces a colored man to take a wife?

A. Well; since this affair there are more married than ever I knew before, because they have a little more chance to mind their families and make more money to support their families. In secesh times there was not much marrying for love. A man saw a young woman and if he liked her he would get a pass from his master to go where she was. If his owner did not choose to give him the pass he would pick out another woman and make him live with her, whether he loved her or not.

Q. Colored women have a good deal of sexual passion, have they not – they all go with men?

A. Yes, sir; there is a great deal of that; I do not think you will find five out of a hundred that do not; they begin at 15 and 16.

Q. Do they know any better?

A. They regard it now as a disgrace and the laws of the Church are against it.

Q. They sometimes have children before marriage?

A. Yes, sir; but they are thought less of among their companions, unless they get a husband before the child is born, and if they cannot the shame grows until they do get a husband. Some join a Church when they are 10 years old and some not until they are 30; the girls join mostly before the men, but they are more apt to fall than the men. Whenever a person joins the Church, no matter how low he has been, he is always respected. When the girls join the Church after a while they sometimes become weary and tired and some temptation comes in and they fall. Sometimes the masters, where the mistress was a pious woman, punished the girls for having children before they were married. As a general thing the masters did not care, they liked the colored women to have children.

Q. Suppose a son of the master wanted to have intercourse with the colored women was he at liberty?

A. No, not at liberty; because it was considered a stain on the family, but the young men did it; there was a good deal of it. They often kept one girl steady and sometimes two on different places; men who had wives did it too sometimes; if they could get it on their own place it was easier but they would go wherever they could get it.

Q. Do the colored people like to go to Church?

A. Yes, sir; they are fond of that; they sing psalms, put up prayers, and sing their religious songs.

Q. Did your masters ever see you learning to read?

A. No, sir; you could not let your masters see you read; but now the colored people are fond of sending their children to school.

Q. What is the reason of that?

A. Because the children in after years will be able to tell us ignorant ones how to do for ourselves.

Q. How many children have you known one woman to have?

A. I know one woman who had 20 children. I know too a woman named Jenny, the wife of Dagos, a slave of John Pope, who has had 23 children. In general the women have a great many children – they often have a child once a year.

Q. Are the children usually obedient?

A. There are some good and some bad, but in general the children love their parents and are obedient. They like their parents most, but they stand up for all their relations.

Q. Suppose a boy is struck by another boy what does he do?

A. If he is injured bad the relations come in and give the boy who injured him the same hurt. I would tell my boy to strike back and defend himself.

Q. How about bearing pain – do you teach your children to bear pain?

A. Yes, sir.

Q. When a colored man was whipped did he cry out?

A. He would halloa out and beg, but not cry for pain, but for vexation.

Q. Did they try to conceal their whippings and think it a disgrace?

A. Yes, sir; they tried to conceal it; a great many are marked all over and have not a piece of skin they were born with.

Q. Have they any idea of the government of the United States?

A. Yes, sir; they know if the government was not kind to them they could not keep their liberty. When the war began a great many of us believed that the government could not conquer our masters because our masters fooled us. They told us we must fight the Yankees who intended to catch us and sell us to Cuba to pay the expenses of the war. I did not believe it, but a great many did.

Q. What would the colored people like the government to do for them here?

A. They would like to have land – 4 or 5 acres to a family.

Q. How many here could manage and take care of land?

A. A good many. I could take care of 15 acres and would not ask them to do any more for me.

Q. Suppose the government were to give you land, how long would you take to pay for it – five years?

A. I would not take five years; in two years I would pay every cent. The people here would rather have the land than work for wages. I think it would be better to sort out the men and give land to those who have the faculty of supporting their families. Every able bodied man can take care of himself if he has a mind to, but their are bad men who have not the heart or will to do it.

Q. Do you think the colored people would like better to have this land divided among themselves and live here alone, or must they have white people to govern them?

A. They are obliged to have white people to administer the law; the black people have a good deal of sense but they do not know the law. If the government keep the masters away altogether it would not do to leave the colored men here alone; some white men must be here not as masters, but we must take the law by their word and if we do not we must be punished. If you take all the white men away we are nothing. Probably with the children that are coming up no white men will not be needed. They are learning to read and write – some are learning lawyer, some are learning doctor, and some learn minister; and reading books and newspapers they can understand the law; but the old generation cannot understand it. It makes no difference how sensible they are, they are blind and it wants white men for the present to direct them. After five years they will take care of themselves; this generation cannot do it.

Q. Do you think the colored men are willing to fight for their liberty?

A. Yes, sir; if the government will protect them and give them a chance; but they must have white officers.

Q. Suppose the government protect the colored men against their masters and sell the land, half to the colored, and half to the white, what would be the effect – would not the colored man sell his land to the white man.

A. I think he might; some of them are lazy and they do not understand how to take care of themselves against the white man; it is necessary to have some one here to do justice to both parties.

Q. Would the colored men like to go back to Africa?

A. No, sir; there is no disposition to go back, they would rather stay where they are.

Q. Are there physicians enough here to take care of the sick?

A. I do not think there are doctors enough; the islands are very large. If you send for the doctor, he will come; probably if you send for him one day you will see him a day or two afterwards. They do not get out of bed to go when called.

HD

Testimony of Harry McMillan before the American Freedmen's Inquiry Commission, [June 1863], filed with O-328 1863, Letters Received, ser. 12, RG 94 [K-78]. Topical labels in the margin are omitted, as is a penciled interlineation that was evidently added at a later date.

34: Northern Planter to the American Freedmen's Inquiry Commission

13 India St Boston August 17th 1863

Gentlemen In reply to your circular letter soliciting information respecting the Freedmen that have come under my notice & the resulths of such thoughts as I have bestowed upon the subject of their treatment. I beg to present the following hasty sketch of the conclusions I have arrived at with allusions to the experience from which such conclusion are drawn.

In order to "place the Colored people of the United States in a condition of self support & self Defence" I suppose it will be generally admitted that the first & best means to be taken is to bring them within the reach of private Enterprise in such Employment as they are by nature and experience qualified to compete in with other labor.

Of course agriculture in their native states & localities is by far the most Eligible Employment for them. There right Could be secured from the imposition of grasping Employers by regulations, similar to those Existing in other places where a healthy competition of Employers exists. So long as the tenure of the soil and chattel property are rendered insecure by Military Events, but little private enterprise can be enlisted in the work, but the isolated position of the island at Port-Royal seems to render them more favorable to an Experiment of this kind than any other point at present.

With a view to try such an experiment on a large scale and with a more liberal supply of Capital then any one, man could feel like risking during the present unsettled state of the country I entered into an association with several other Gentlemen of this City in March last for the purchase of land at the tax sale at Port Royal and for the Employment upon it of such labor as could be had in the cultivation of the well known staple of the Sea Islands while such a combination is perhaps the best way of meeting the uncertain condition of things.

It cannot be regarded as best for the permanent success of a Community; for under the ordinary condition of peace there is no reason why Cotton should not be successfully raised by free labor by small proprietors with small capital Cotton culture is unlike that of sugar in as much as it is not mixed with manufacture and does not require the machinery of a mill and outlay of a considerable fixed capital to prepare the crop for market. So that it seems that no state of things could be so advantageous for the success of the community as the division of the land into a number of small freeholds.

The competition of these small proprietors, with the minute

attention and supervision of labor secured by their self interest, is the surest guarantee for the success of agriculture by free labor. It is to be hoped that with the return of peace there would be a large Emigration from the north, and a large number of discharged soldiers from our army, as well as of the more intelligent and Enterprising of the negroes who would become proprietors of the soil.

The apparent success of the present crop at Port Royal, not only on the Estates which I bid in, but upon all of those which fell into private hands if followed by success in harvesting and marketing the crop, as there is every reasonable probability of doing at present, would Encourage similar undertakings in future.

It seems to me to be very important, not only to the welfare of the laborers immediately concerned, but as test of the practicability of their being usefully Employed upon the soil upon as large a scale as possible that the remainder of the lands on the Port Royal Island now in the possession of our force, should be brought within the reach of private Enterprise at the earliest moment after the harvesting of the present crop which will be done before Christmas. Possession could then be given in time for the preperation of the ground for a new crop, which ought to begin as soon as June [*January?*] 1st.

At the sale of March last, there were only about fifty Estates sold to private hands. There were about one hundred and twenty Estates bid in by the commissioners on behalf of the U.S. Government although in many cases there were bona-fide bidders present, who wished to become settlers.

Now as I under stand the act of June 1862 under the provision of which these Estates were sold and offerd for sale, those which were bid in for the U.S. can be sold or leased to private parties by the tax commissioner, as directed by the Prest.[1] In case any more land should be offerd for sale, I should be ready to extend my present arrangement where I should not come in competition with actual settlers, who may wish to buy land.

In case any such should present themselves, it would be manifestly for the advantage of the community that the land should be sold to them rather then to any combination of men.

As it may be of interest to you to hear of the attempts already made in detail towards the re-organization of labor which have come under my notice I will attempt a short history of our expenses [*experiences*] in that work.

Having to deal with large numbers of laborers and large areas of land, where the old organization had melted away, from the sudden removal of its only stamina [*stimulus*] the, lash. we found the people timid Even to suspicion, & little inclined to believe what we had to say to them by way of advice. The white race had they far been known to them as a sort of natural Enemy, against which it behoved Every man to be on his guard, and it was only after a *personal acquaintance with* the character of their *individual Employers* that they could be induced to believe Enough of our promises to feel any confidence in our disposition to *pay* for their labor. In this state it was nearly impossible to Employ them to labor regularly by the day or Month with any satisfactory result Their previous life had been such as to Educate them most thoroughly in the art of shirking & had faild to give the labor that pride in the faithful performance, which can arise only from self respect and requited labor When at work by the day. some few of the older and more faithful hands began by doing a fair days work as re[quired] of all The young and careless ones. found of play, and less serious in their intentions invariably began by shirking, and continued by a serious of daily Experiments to test the minimum of labor which would be accepted by their Employers as a days work.

The faithful ones soon followed their Example, not wishing to furnish more labor for their money than did the lazy ones.

The result was soon found to be the Entire failure to accomplish anything regular or definite. An attempt was then made to fix a standard for a days work, and to record Every day, by means of the reports of the black foreman; the Exact amount of work done by Each hand.

Here a new trouble arose in the lack of organization and the difficulty of creating any.

All systems of day wages presuppose an independent, unprejudiced foreman who Enjoys the confidence of the laborers and who controls the time and manner doing the work; he must also keep a record of the amount of work done by Each laborer and be responsible to his Employer for the correct preformance of the work.

The black drivers appointed by the former masters. had always been in the habit of doing this duty, reporting to the overseer Every night all cases of dilinquency, which were duly punished by the lash.

But the position of this driver was purely artificial.

Selected from among the crowed from whom he was distinguished only by a slightly superior animal Energy and mental Endowment, but not by any peculiar Education he was sustained in his authority merely the power of the owner represented by the lash.

Now that this power had vanished. the driver had lost his prestige and in place of it was the object of hatred and jealousy among the crowed, almost every one of whom had old scores to settle with him. His authority was a cypher, and he could not be relied upon to render an account of the work done daily by the several hands simply because Each hand had been at work when & how it pleased him, or her to go. In the absence of any men, who Enjoyed the confidence of those people to a degree to enable any authority to be used, after trying a change of foremen with little success, we cast about us for some means by which the result of each mans labor could be made to show for itself in the crop to be judge of at the amount produced. The Eagerness with which this proposal was sezed by the negroes themselves was an Earnest of its success.

The planting had already been done by working in the old fashioned "gang" but the field was readily divided in such lots or patches as could be managed by single families, and a share of the field assigned to Each for the season in such proportions as they desired. The responsibility of the crop was thus thrown upon Each family separately, to the Extent of its patch in the field and a price per lb was offerd for the cotton.

But the daily wants of the people could not wait for the harvest of the crop, without some help. Some partial payments must be made which the crop was growing in order to keep up the interest in the work inspired confidence in their current wants. It was Evident that all payments of this sort must be made with great caution in order that they might be proportioned, as nearly as possible to the amount of labor actually performed To secure this end, the field were mapped so that riding over them I could always tell on whose patch, I happened to stand at any moment.

Occasional Examinations were made of the state of the crop & the thoroughness of the cultivation For every hoeing 50 cents per acre was paid, the payment being made monthly as nearly as possible.

The success of this system has Exceeded our hopes The division of the land into these temporary allotment gives the laborers a proprietary interest in the crop & he feels as if working for himself. The more Efficnt and endustrious soon showed the Effects of their industry by the superior condition of their crops.

Their care and attention soon gave evidence, that they understood the details of cultivation and needed no help on that subject which we could afford.

They took an evident pride in the condition of their crops. The more industrious soon ridiculed the lazier, for the neglected appearance of their fields and view [*vied*] with each other in the excellence of the cultivation.

The above experience relates to those cases, where large numbers of laborers fell under the management of a limited number of employers. In cases where small proprietors begin by working in the field themselves, with a few negroes, or by spending the greater part of the time in the immediate supervision of the labor. I have no doubt that the negroes could be advantageously hired by the day or month.

Such a course, by keeping the control of the work, in the hands of white men, who have a larger share of forethought and energy than the negroes, besides acquired knowledge would conduce to the misprovement of their methods of culture; the introduction of new manners, implements &c. Still the system which our circumstances forced us to adopt, i.e. the tempory allotments of land to separate families, certainly tends to the advancement of the laborer, by developing in him a degree of self-reliance forethought and industry and may in the end be attained, with many of the good results which would be gained, by a more intelligent supervision, and control.

As the welfare of the negroes and the value of their services may be greatly enhanced, by such rudiments of education, as can readily be given them, any system of government, which looks to the permanent good of the community, will provide for this. The children learn, and a small number of the adults with great eagerness. There are now five teachers at work, upon the estates which I bought, their salary, being charged to the [general?] expenses of the work. At some future time the people will perhaps provide for the education at their own expense, but during the present state of society, some provision should be made for furnishing such privileges, either at the expense of the Govt or the proprietors of the soil. Very respectfully Your obedient Servant

HLcSr Edw. S. Philbrick.

Edw. S. Philbrick to Robert Dale Owen et al., 17 Aug. 1863, filed with O-328 1863, Letters Received, ser. 12, RG 94 [K-83]. Topical labels in the margin are omitted.

1 For the provisions of the Direct Tax Act of June 1862, see above, doc. 27n.

35: Commander of the U.S.S. *Midnight* to the Commander of the U.S.S. *Vermont*

Sapelo Sound Ga September 10th 1863

Sir In one of the buildings on the Plantation on the South end of St Catharines Island thare is some eight hundred to one thousand lbs of ungined cotton which has laid thare for over two years.

The Negroes on the Island tell me they gathered it in and housed it after the whites all left the Island and some thirty bales was left to rot in the field.

They hav asked me to let them sell it to any Sutler that might chance to touch here for Small Stores. They supoart themselves hav never asked for any rations from the ship besides suplying us with many things. would I be doing right to let it be sold it will soon all be Spoiled as it lays Verry Respectfully Your Obedient Servant

ALS Nicholas Kirby

Acting Master Nicholas Kirby to Commander Wm. Reynolds, 10 Sept. 1863, Area 8, Area File, RG 45 [T-14]. In an undated endorsement, William Reynolds, commander of the *Vermont*, referred Kirby's letter to the commander of the South Atlantic Blockading Squadron, who directed: "If the property comes within the law – it should be taken for the US – which can alone dispose of it." On October 5, 1863, Reynolds transmitted that ruling to Kirby, with the following elaboration: "If it can be shown to your satisfaction that this cotton was raised by the negroes themselves, after the whites left the place, it might *probably* be disposed of for their benefit; if on the contrary, it is a portion of the property left by the rebels on their abandonment of the island, it must be taken on account of the United States." ([William Reynolds] to Act'g. Master Kirby, 3 Oct. [1863], vol. 2, p. 63, Letters Sent by Comdr. William Reynolds, Letterbooks of Officers of the U.S. Navy at Sea, RG 45 [T-680].)

36: Military Governor in the Department of the South to the Quartermaster General

Beaufort – So: Car: October 2" – 1863.

Sir, In reply to your communication of August 27", I have the honor to report that I have had no direct duties connected with the Quartermaster's Department, except as the Commander of U.S. forces on Port Royal Island. Capts. James P. Low & John H. Moore, Assistant Quartermasters, have been directed to make reports on this head.

Under your instructions to make a report of the operations under my charge during the year ending June 30" 1863, I have the honor to make the following report.

The charge of the conquered territory, estates, and inhabitants within the limits of the Department of the South, having been transferred from the Treasury Department to the War Department, I received; on the 16" of June, 1862, the following order from the Secretary of War:

War Department
Washington City– D.C.
June 16″– 1862.

Brigadier General R. Saxton

You are assigned to duty in the Department of the South, to act under the orders of the Secretary of War. You are directed to take possession of all the plantations heretofore occupied by rebels, and take charge of the inhabitants remaining thereon within the Department, or which the fortunes of the war may hereafter bring into it, with authority to take such measures, make such rules and regulations for the cultivation of the land, and for the protection, employment, and government of the inhabitants, as circumstances may seem to require.

You are authorised to exercise all sanitary and police powers that may be necessary for the health and security of the persons under your charge, and may imprison or exclude all disorderly, disobedient, or dangerous persons from the limits of your operations.

The Major General Commanding the Department of the South will be instructed to give you all the military aid and protection necessary to enable you to carry out the views of the Government.

You will have power to act upon the decision of Courts Martial which are called for the trial of persons not in the military service, to the same extent that the Commander of a Department has over Courts Martial called for the trial of soldiers in his Department: and so far as the persons above described are concerned you will also have a general control over the action of the Provost Marshals.

It is expressly understood that, so far as the persons and purposes herein specified are concerned, your action will be independent of that of the other Military Authorities of the Department, and in all other cases subordinate only to the Major General Commanding.

In cases of need or destitution of the inhabitants, you are directed to issue such portions of the army ration, and such articles of clothing, as may be suitable to the habits and wants of the persons supplied, which articles will be furnished by the Quartermaster and Commissary of the Department of the South, upon requisitions approved by yourself. It is expected that by encouraging industry, skill in the cultivation of the necessaries of life, and general self-improvement, you will, as far as possible promote the real well-being of all people under your supervision.

Medical and Ordnance supplies will be furnished by the proper officers, which you will distribute and use according to your instructions.

You will account regularly with the proper Bureaus of this Department, and report frequently–once a week at least.

Yours truly
(Signed) Edwin M. Stanton–
Secretary of War.

My operations under this order commenced on the 28″ of June, 1862, and extended over the Islands of Port Royal, Barnwell, Paris, Ladies, Coosaw, Wassa, Cat, Cane, St. Helena, Morgan, Hilton Head, Pinkney, Edisto, St. Simons, and smaller adjacent islands, and the settlements of Fernandina, Key West, and St. Augustine in Florida.

The system which with some modifications has been pursued in the management of the various interests of this novel department had already been inaugurated by the Hon. Secretary of the Treasury, by sending Mr. Edward L. Pierce, as a special agent of the Treasury Department, to organize the labor of the freedmen. His able report is already before the country.[1]

The freedmen were found to be in a destitute condition, bewildered and astonished at the strange events transpiring around them. My first duties were to provide for their immediate necessities, organize their labor, and fit them to become self-sustaining, establish schools for the education of all who had a desire to learn – in fact, to demonstrate to the world that which has been denied and disbelieved by the friends of African Slavery, – the fact that the cotton and rice fields of the South can be cultivated by the labor of freedmen. I shall endeavor to show how well this great principle has been established in South Carolina.

The Hon. Secretary of the Treasury, with a wisdom and sense of justice which will ever redound to his honor, decided that the cotton which was raised by the negroes, and in their possession in a crude state when our forces took possession of these Islands, belonged to them and should be expended for their benefit. In this view the Hon. Secretary of War heartily coincided. The cotton was accordingly collected, and after the expenses of its collection and preparation for market were paid, a fund remained with which to carry on the work. And it is from this fund that all the direct expenses of my operations have been paid.

At first my operations extended over one hundred and eighty-seven plantations, besides the towns of Beaufort, Fernandina, St. Augustine, and Key West, and the Island of St. Simons. To carry on my work about fifty-five Superintendents were appointed at a Salary of fifty dollars per month, each having several plantations under his charge, and whose duty it was to organize the labor of the people, attend to the proper preparation of the lands for the crops, to keep an account of the work performed by each laborer – in short, to come in immediate contact with the people. In addition, General Superintendents, with a Salary of $1000 – per annum, were appointed, each to take charge of several Islands and exercise a general control over the Special Superintendents and Teachers. The Superintendents so appointed had most of them been on the ground for several months, under the Special Agent of the Treasury Department, and were men well qualified for their positions. On July 18," 1862, I issued the following order:

Headquarters –
Beaufort – S.C.
July 18" – 1862 –

General Orders – }
N° 2 }

I. The following are announced as General Superintendents of the Divisions to which they are respectively assigned.

Mr. H. G. Judd, of the 1" Division, (Embracing Port Royal, Paris, Barnwell, Cat and Cane Islands.)

Mr. Richard Soule Jr., of the 2" Division (comprising St. Helena, Ladies, Wassa, Coosaw, Dathaw, and Morgan Islands)

Rev. Thomas D. Howard, of the 3" Division, (consisting of Hilton Head and Pinckney Islands.)

II. Superintendents of Districts will in all cases of minor importance apply for information and instructions to the Division Superintendents, who will forward the communications received by them to these Headquarters only when expressly so requested by their writers, or when the importance of the Subject seems to them to require it.

III. The District Superintendents will send in their Reports on the 1" and 15" of every month to the General Superintendent of their Division; whose duty it shall be to furnish consolidated semi-monthly Reports to these Headquarters, and to receive thence and promulgate such orders as may from time to time be issued by the General Commanding.

IV. The Reports will be upon printed forms to be supplied by Capt – George Merrill A.A.G., to whom these and all other official communications from the General Superintendents will be addressed.

By order of
Brig^{r} Genl R. Saxton
Commanding – "

All Superintendents were required to subscribe to the following Oath;

"I, believing that negro slavery is a great wrong to humanity, do solemnly swear that I will faithfully perform, to the best of my ability, my duty as Superintendent of Plantations in this Department, and, as such, will use all the means in my power so to educate and elevate the people under my control as to fit them to enjoy the blessings of freedom. That, to the best of my knowledge, I will deal fairly and honestly with them, and respect, their rights. That I will not engage in trade with them for my own profit, or appropriate any of the proceeds of their labor to my own personal advantage, – So help me God."

As this was a new work, entirely experimental at the outset, and with no precedent to guide the way, its perfect organization was of course only to be a process of time, gaining a little light each day as the work went on. For the crop already growing when I took charge, I decided to pay the negroes fair wages for their work, and that the Government should have the proceeds of the crop. Nothing, however, was paid for labor on the crop of corn and sweet potatoes raised by the laborers for their own support. The orders appended will show the rates of wages paid under this plan. Some 5480 acres of cotton, 5332 acres of corn, & 735 acres of sweet potatoes were growing at the time I took charge. Some 16,000 people were under my charge, the majority of them being old men, women, and children, as most of the able-bodied men had been taken away by their masters in their exodus.

Unfortunately, after all the expenses of cultivating the fertile Islands of Edisto and Pinckney, and when the crops were nearly ready to harvest, Major General Hunter, Commanding the Department, deemed it necessary to evacuate them. About 2000 acres of the most promising portion of the crop were thus lost, and 2000 people thrown upon my hands entirely destitute. This was a serious blow, interfering much with my operations generally, even upon the Islands not evacuated, because these 2000 bewildered, and in a measure discouraged, people had to be crowded on to plantations where there was no suitable shelter for them, and but little chance to work or earn money until the next season. Subsequently, the evacuation of the Island of St. Simons, on the coast of Georgia, and of the settlement at Georgetown, S.C. threw upon my hands about 1000 people in a destitute condition. And in the endeavor to provide for the pressing wants of so many unfortunate persons my other operations have been necessarily in great measure interfered with.

The next serious drawback to the visible success of my operations was the appearance of the "cotton worm", a well known enemy to the crops of the Sea Islands, and the destruction by it of the greater portion of the crop which had before promised a very fair result. After the cotton crop had been gradually reduced by the above misfortunes, and others incident to operations in a military department, the portion which remained uninjured was collected and ginned here, and subsequently sold by the Collector at New York for about fifty thousand dollars. And this, considering all the unfavorable circumstances before mentioned may be reckoned a success.

Sufficient corn, potatoes, &c were produced to support the entire resident population. Rations have been issued to this class of persons only in return for what was taken from them for forage by the Army, and what was destroyed, in the neighborhood of camps and picket Stations, by the depredations of soldiers. Of course a simple ration had to be issued to refugees who had come within our lines too late to plant crops. But many of these persons did not long remain dependent on the government, for they soon found friends or work.

On January 30″, 1863, I issued the following order;

Headquarters,
Beaufort – S.C.
January 30″ – 1863 –

This circular is issued for the guidance of Division and Plantation Superintendents in this Department.

As a General Rule, the people on the Plantations are to draw no rations whatever from the Commissariat; for the presumption is, that the laborers on each plantation have corn enough, raised last year, to support themselves and their families until the next harvest.

Where they are destitute of corn, they must be destitute either by their own fault, by their own misfortune, by the act of the Government, or by some combination of these causes.

Where they are destitute of corn by the act of the Government, they ought, as a matter of Justice, to be furnished with a simple ration from the Commissariat, equivalent to the ordinary allowance of corn to which they have been accustomed.

Where they are destitute of corn by their own misfortune, they ought, as a matter of charity, to be furnished with a simple ration, provided they have themselves no other means of support.

Where they are destitute by their own fault, they are to draw nothing; except in cases where, in the sound judgment of the Superintendent, the giving a ration will produce a better effect for the future than the discipline of want.

In no case is a ration to be given to any person who refuses to do what he can to earn a living.

Rations are not to be issued, as a matter of course, to *all* the people on any plantation, but there must be some special reason in each case why the person drawing a ration from the Commissariat should be made an exception to the general rule.

It is very desirable both for the good of the Government and of the people under your charge, that the latter should not be dependent on the Commissariat any more, or any longer, than is absolutely necessary.

The Division Superintendents and Plantation Superintendents are expected to use good sense in applying the above general principles, and to apply them to all cases with strict impartiality –

By order of R. Saxton
E. W. Hooper, Brig[r] Gen[l] & Mil: Gov:
Capt. & A.D.C.

In justice to the colored people I must mention that they have suffered most grievous wrongs, both in persons and property, from bad men among the soldiers. In many cases their little patches upon which they relied for their own sustenance were invaded, and the products stolen, or destroyed in mere wantoness. There have been outrages committed which disgraced civilization. I am happy to say, however, that the perpetrators were not countenanced or upheld by the majority of the army here. Those brave officers and men who came to do battle for their country and the Right, have ever been willing to regard the rights of the freedmen. It is also encouraging that as the work progresses these outrages become less and less frequent, and the rights of these people are now almost universally recognized by the officers and men in our army. But these depredations have tended greatly to discourage industry the past year, as is shown conclusively by comparing the results of my operations on plantations near camps and distant from them.

Profiting by the experiences of the last season, and for the purpose of avoiding late planting &c, the programme contained in General Orders N° 12, (appended and marked "A"), issued on December 20" 1862, was adopted for the coming Season.[2] This system has been found to work admirably.

General Orders N° 1, issued February 5" 1863, (appended and marked "B") will explain the system by which the laborers have been paid.

The drafting into military service of every able-bodied man capable of bearing arms, proved another serious drawback to the agricultural operations, coming as it did at the critical season of plowing and planting, and leaving all the work on the plantations to be performed by old men, women, and children. And hundreds of these, finding plenty of work and ready pay with the Army preferred following it to working on the plantations.

Another interruption occurred from the sale of the lands for unpaid taxes.[3] This sale took place at an unfortunate time, throwing the laborers into confusion at a time when they should have been occupied only with their work. By this sale also large tracts, including most of the plantations which were profitable last season, passed into the hands of private persons, who could afford to carry on their plantations on a more liberal scale than I felt authorised to do, and who may therefore fairly expect a more profitable result than the Government. As an evidence of the usefulness of the negroes, and as an indication of the great demand that there must be in the future for their free labor to cultivate the vast fields of the South, it is proper to state that the purchasers of these plantations offer the negroes every inducement to remain upon them and work for fair wages.

Notwithstanding discouragements, the work has still progressed until now we have, on the lands retained by the Government, 2701 acres of cotton, 5499 acres of corn, and 1809 acres of sweet potatoes, rice, ground-nuts &c, &c. And on the private lands there are now 1732 acres of cotton, 2004 acres of corn, and 540 acres of sweet potatoes &c, &c. This makes a total of 14,285 acres of crops, as the industrial result upon the plantations this year, or on an average 3 1/5 acres to each "working hand" upon the plantations: And it must be remembered that all these working hands are women, children, and disabled men.

Enough has been done to demonstrate that the cotton fields of South Carolina can be successfully cultivated by free labor, that the negroes will work cheerfully and willingly with a reasonable prospect of reward, and that as a race they are eminently fitted to provide for themselves. Their wants are few and simple, they are exceedingly anxious to acquire property, are fond of the soil, and the idea that they may become owners of it fills them with delight.

There being no means in my hands to provide for the education of the freed children it was agreed between charitable associations in Boston, New York, and Philadelphia and myself, that they should send as many teachers as could be successfully employed. By their liberality and humanity schools have been established throughout the Department, and old and young of both sexes are being taught to read and write. Experienced teachers, who have taught in public schools at the North, and are now teaching in our schools here, report that the progress of the scholars here does not compare unfavorably with that of white children at the North. They all manifest an intense desire to learn to read, and seem to have an intuition that it is by the means of education they are to rise in the scale of being. Their freedom was of course a gift without price to them, and next to that the labors of these devoted teachers will prove of far greater benefit to them than anything else that has been done for them.

When these brave and self-sacrificing men and women, who seek to lift up the ignorant and down trodden, are rewarded, the name of "Gideonite" which was given in derision will become a crown of glory.

Some 1941 children attend school regularly within this Department, and during the planting and harvest seasons it is a common sight to see troops of children going to school after having completed their tasks in the cotton field.

In carrying out this great work of Education, too much cannot be said in praise of the good work done by the "Educational Commission" of Boston, Gov. Andrew, Pres^{t}, Dr. Le Baron Russell, Chairman of the Committee on teachers; the "National Freedman's

Relief Association" of New York (Dr Stephen H. Tyng) & Francis George Shaw Esq. Pres[t]; and the "Port Royal Relief Committee" of Philadelphia, Stephen Colwell, Esq, chairman. Without their aid the work of Education could not have been carried on. They have sent down to us large numbers of experienced teachers, thousands of school books, and many thousand dollars worth of clothing for the destitute, and their noble charities have been of the greatest benefit to the naked and hungry. These societies have expended for the benefit of the freedmen here, during the past year, not less than sixty or seventy thousand dollars, and they are still continuing to furnish us with an abundance of excellent teachers at a great expense to themselves. Besides this, the Societies in New York and Philadelphia are doing a great service for the freedmen and for the Government by carrying on at their own risk upon these Islands, stores for the sale, at the lowest possible price which will make the stores self-supporting, of such articles as the freedmen must have. These stores have been established at my urgent request. Before their establishment, I found it absolutely necessary, in order to prevent the gratuitous issue of large quantities of rations and clothing, to open stores on account of the Government, for the sale to these destitute persons of the common necessaries of life, at prices just sufficient to cover the cost and selling expenses. These stores tend very greatly to encourage the idea of self-dependence, and are a great stimulus to the people to work diligently and earn money, for the value of money in their eyes is, naturally, affected by the ease or difficulty of exchanging it for the necessaries and comforts of life.

While I have endeavored by every means in my power to make the people under my charge understand that they must not become paupers on the bounty of others, and have striven – with a very satisfactory result – to inculcate the principle of self-dependency there are yet to some extent cases of such utter destitution, especially among recent refugees, that it is absolutely necessary to give to them.

It is principally by Education that this race is to be raised from the mental and moral degradation which this accursed system has entailed. It has blunted their intellects, darkened their moral natures, and crushed out their manhood more completely on these Islands than in any other portion of the Country, for the reflected light of the free institutions of the Northern States could not be shut out from the cities or from the main-land of the South so completely as it has been from these isolated plantations. The Superior intelligence evinced by some of the older slaves, and especially those who were themselves imported from Africa, shows that this race has been sinking, under the influence of Slavery, lower and lower into the depths of barbarism and ignorance.

On the 28" of August, 1862, I received the following order from the War Department:

"War Department
Washington City – D.C.
August 25" – 1862.

General,

Your dispatch of the 16" has this moment been received.[4] It is considered by the Department that the instructions given at the time of your appointment were sufficient to enable you to do what you have now requested authority for doing. But in order to place your authority beyond all doubt, you are hereby authorised and instructed.

1" – To enrol and organize in any convenient organization, by Squads, Companies, Battalions, Regiments and Brigades, or otherwise, colored persons of African descent for volunteer laborers to a number not exceeding fifty thousand, and muster them into the service of the United States, for the term of the war, at a rate of compensation not exceeding five dollars per month for common laborers, and eight dollars per month for mechanical or skilled laborers, and assign them to the Quarter Master's Department, to do and perform such laborer's duty as may be required in the Military Service of the United States, and wherever the same may be required during the present war, and to be subject to the rules and articles of war.

2" – The laboring forces herein authorised shall, under the order of the General-in-Chief, or of this Department, be detailed by the Quarter Master General for laboring Service with the armies of the United States; and they shall be clothed, and subsisted after enrolment, in the same manner as other persons in the Quartermaster's service.

3" – In view of the Small force under your command, and the inability of the Government at the present time to increase it, in order to guard the plantations and settlements occupied by the United States from invasion, and protect the inhabitants thereof from captivity and murder by the enemy, you are also authorised to arm, uniform, equip, and receive into the service of the United States such number of volunteers of African descent as you may deem expedient, not exceeding five thousand, and may detail officers to instruct them in military drill, discipline, and duty, and to command them. The persons so received into service, and their officers, to be entitled to, and receive the same pay and rations as are allowed by law to volunteers in the service.

4" You will reoccupy, if possible, all the Islands and Plantations heretofore occupied by the Government, and secure and harvest the crops, and cultivate and improve the Plantations.

5" – The population of African descent that cultivate the lands, and perform the labor of the Rebels, constitute a large share of their military strength, and enable the white masters to fill the Rebel Armies, and wage a cruel and murderous war against the people of the Northern States. By reducing the laboring strength of the Rebels, their military power will be reduced. You are therefore authorised by every means in your power to withdraw from the enemy their laboring force and population, and to spare no effort consistent with civilized warfare, to weaken, harass, and annoy them, and to establish the authority of the Government of the United States, within your Department.

6" – You may turn over to the Navy any number of colored volunteers that may be required for the naval service.

7" By recent act of Congress,[5] all men and boys received into the service of the United States, who may have been the Slaves of Rebel Masters, are, with their wives, mothers, and children declared to be forever free. You, and all in your command, will so treat and regard them.

Yours truly
(Signed) Edwin M. Stanton –
Secretary of War –

Brigadier General Saxton –

In pursuance of this order, I at once proceeded to organize colored soldiers. All the able bodied men in the Department were enrolled. The command of the 1" So: Car: Reg[t] was given to Col – T. W. Higginson, and it enjoys the honor of being the first regiment of freedmen volunteers ever mustered into the United States Service. It is thoroughly drilled and instructed, and is as efficient for service as any regiment in this Department. It has already in several actions vindicated its efficiency, courage, and claim to respect. No body of men can show a fairer record than the 1" South Carolina Volunteers.

The Command of the 2" Reg[t] So: Car: Vols – was given by the War Department to Col. James Montgomery. I assisted to the extent of my power in raising, arming, and equipping it. As it has passed out of my control, I leave its appropriate Commander to speak of its merits.

The 3" So: Car: Reg[t] is commanded by Col. Bennett – As it is composed principally of Quartermaster's employees, it has had no opportunity for military distinction. It has, however, performed a vast amount of labor at Department Head Quarters, as useful as any service it could have rendered in the field.

The 4" So: Car: Reg[t] is to be commanded by Col. Littlefield, commissioned by the War Department, and is now in the process of organization. It cannot be filled until our successes have extended our lines, as all the able-bodied men are now in the Military Service.

One great difficulty I have had to contend with is the want of shelter for the refugees who are constantly coming into our lines. The houses on the Islands being completely filled, and tents proving very expensive as well as unserviceable dwellings, I built temporary shelters of logs; but now having a good saw-mill in full operation, I am enabled to build small cottages, at very trifling expense. These are located in advantageous positions, on government lands, so that each house will be surrounded by about ten acres of land, which is considered sufficient for a moderate sized family. The negroes perform the labor on the houses after the location is fixed, and finish them off to suit their own convenience. It is proposed by the Tax Commissioners to sell these lands to the negroes at a moderate price, with easy terms of payment. They will gladly purchase them, and undoubtedly bring them to a high degree of cultivation. The theory of selection and reservation was to alternate the plantations sold to private individuals with those reserved by Government for the negroes; thus by a judicious location of houses a supply of labor will always be at hand which can be hired at reasonable wages to cultivate the land. It is my belief that if this system is properly carried out, the amount of cotton produced will be far greater than that yielded under the slave labor system. With the limited means at my disposal these building operations will go on slowly, but the cottages being of the slightest construction I expect to have, before the winter season, comfortable shelter for a large number of houseless, homeless ones. With the exception of rations to my employees and to the destitute, and the services of five surgeons furnished by the Medical Department, all my expenses have been defrayed from the proceeds of the cotton raised by the negroes. The total proceeds of cotton sent from here and sold by the Collector at New York, for the benefit of those who raised it, were more than seven hundred thousand dollars; and after deducting the cost of collecting &c, and the expense of operations here under Edwd L. Pierce, Special Agent of the Treasury Department, and the expense of my own operations up to this time, a very large balance still remains in the hands of the Hon. Hiram Barney Collector at New York.

The prospect for this year's crop of cotton is very good, and I doubt not it will pay this year's expenses. The crop of corn, sweet potatoes, &c is amply sufficient to support the resident population, as also many of the refugees, until another harvest.

When the vast amount of labor at a cheap rate that the negroes in this Department have performed for the Army, and the supplies of various kinds that they have produced, are considered, it is my belief that the Government will not be found the creditor of the negroes.

It has been my endeavor to introduce the most rigid system of economy into all the details of these operations. My duties have been difficult and arduous. I have been slandered and maligned, and have met steady and persistent opposition. All this however has not changed my purpose to carry out faithfully the instructions given me from the Department when I took charge of this novel work. The Members of my Staff, and the devoted men and women who have aided me in my work deserve well of the country. Many of them have fallen victims to the climate and have gone to their reward. They can have the assurance that they have helped to settle one of the greatest questions of the age, in demonstrating that it is possible to elevate the freedmen, that they are fit for the blessings of Liberty, and that the cotton and rice fields of the South can be cultivated by free labor.

Untutored and degraded as these people are, they contemplate being free with intense delight, and the first of January, 1863, was a day which will ever be remembered in this Department. I issued the following order which was responded to by thousands of freedmen throughout the Department, with such manifestations of joy and satisfaction as evinced that the President's glorious Proclamation of Emancipation was understood and appreciated;

> "A happy New Year's Greeting to the colored people in the Department of the South—
>
> In accordance, as I believe, with the will of our Heavenly Father, and by direction of your great and good friend, whose name you are all familiar with, Abraham Lincoln, President of the United States, and Commander in Chief of the Army and Navy, on the 1st day of January, 1863, you will be declared "forever free".
>
> When in the course of human events there comes a day which is destined to be an everlasting beacon-light, marking a joyful era in the progress of a nation and the hopes of a people; it seems to be fitting the occasion that it should not pass unnoticed by those whose hopes it comes to brighten and to bless. Such a day to you is January 1st, 1863. I therefore call upon all the colored people in this Department to assemble on that day at the Headquarters of the 1st Regt of South Carolina Volunteers, there to hear the President's Proclamation read, and to indulge in such other manifestations of joy as may be called forth by the occasion. It is your duty to carry this good news to your brethren who are still in Slavery. Let all your voices, like merry bells, join loud and clear in the grand chorus of liberty—"We are free," "We are free"—until listening, you shall hear its echoes coming back from every cabin in the land,—"We are free," "We are free."
>
> (Signed) R. Saxton
> Brig Genl & Mil: Gov:

In addition to these duties as Military Governor, I have had the command of the U.S. forces on Port Royal Island.

In making this Report of my operations, some of the better traits of the negro character have been noticed. It is due to Truth that their vices should not be concealed. They are very human. Many of them are immoral, untruthful, and ungrateful. This poor reward for the exertions and labors of those who have charge of them might discourage a superficial observer, but not one who looks deeper—at the cause. The cases of ingratitude should be excused, because in many cases they do not understand or appreciate our efforts in their behalf. And in their immorality it is evident we see but the legitimate fruits of a system which has never held up to them any high standard of morality, has blunted their sensibilities, disregarded their rights, and as a consequence made them regardless of the rights of others. But delivered from the influences which have so long crushed them, with the same laws and institutions to govern and protect them in their rights as white men, and with the teachers remaining in their noble work, the negroes will soon make rapid strides towards improvement. The elevation of the race is sure, and the Country need feel no apprehension regarding the future of the freedmen— I am very respectfully Your obt: Servant

HDS R Saxton

Capt. R. Saxton to Brigadier General M. C. Meigs, 2 Oct. 1863, Annual, Personal, & Special Reports of Quartermaster Officers, ser. 1105, Personnel, RG 92 [Y-501]. Saxton signed as an assistant quartermaster, as a brigadier general of volunteers, and as military governor. The blank space in the oath appears in the manuscript. The orders said to have been appended are not in the file. In February 1864, Saxton reported "the final result" of agricultural operations in 1863. The freedpeople on the Sea Island plantations retained by the government had produced "sufficient food for their own subsistence," as well as 470,000 pounds of unginned cotton, the proceeds of which would "pay all contingent expenses." In addition, he estimated, freedpeople on the plantations that had been sold to private individuals had produced "fully as much more" in the way of cotton. Even after taking into account the government's assistance to refugees who were unable to work or had arrived late in the agricultural year, Saxton concluded that "when the final balance is struck between all the freedmen have received from the Government and all it has paid out for them in this department the balance will be against the Government and in favor of the freedmen." (*Official Records*, ser. 3, vol. 4, pp. 118–19.)

1 Pierce's report is printed above, as doc. 8.
2 The order is printed above, as doc. 28.
3 The sales, which took place in March 1863, auctioned off land that had been forfeited to the government under the Direct Tax Act.
4 In his dispatch of August 16, 1862, General Rufus Saxton, the military governor, had requested authority "to enroll as laborers in the employ of the Quartermaster's Department a force not exceeding 5,000 able-bodied men

from among the contrabands in this department," the enrolled men to receive wages of $8 per month for common laborers and $10 per month for mechanics and "to be uniformed, armed, and officered by men detailed from the Army." Among other duties, they would guard the former slaves who were working on plantations within Union lines. (*Official Records*, ser. 1, vol. 14, pp. 374–76.)
5 The Militia Act, adopted on July 17, 1862. (*Statutes at Large*, vol. 12, pp. 597–600.)

37: Commander of a South Carolina Black Regiment to the Headquarters of the Department of the South

Camp Bennett Hilton Head SC November 30" 1863.

Captain I have the honor most Respectfully to request that the families of men of 3[d] S.C. Infty be furnished with rations until such time as their pay will be raised and enable them to furnish means for their support. In making this request I would respectfully call the attention of the General Comdg[s] to the following facts.

On the Organization of this regiment the families of the men, received rations by Gen[l] D. Hunter's orders,[1] those rations have from time to time been curtailed, and now they are entirely taken away, some of the men have large families unable to procure sufficient food and are in a deplorable condition. – The pay of the men being only seven dollars ($7) per month, and being obliged to remain in Camp to attend to their military duty they are unable to render the least assistance towards the support of those who are depended upon them; while Colored men employed in the *Quartermaster's* Department receive from 10 to 25 dollars per month, with ample opportunity for the cultivation of the soil, do receive full rations for their families thereby causing great dissatisfaction among the men of this Command Hoping that the above will meet with the approval of the General Comdg. I am Cap[t] Very Respectfully Your most Ob[t] Ser[t]

HLS Aug's. G. Bennett

Lieut. Col. Aug's. G. Bennett to Captain Wm. L. M. Burger, 30 Nov. 1863, enclosed in Col. Wm. B. Barton to Brig. Genl. R. Saxton, 5 Dec. 1863, Letters Received, 21st USCI, Regimental Books & Papers USCT, RG 94 [G-302]. In an endorsement dated December 2, General Quincy A. Gillmore, who had succeeded Hunter as commander of the Department of the South, directed that "application for subsistence stores should be made to Brig. Gen'l Rufus Saxton," military governor in the department. Three days later, the commander of U.S. forces at Hilton Head, South Carolina, forwarded Bennett's letter to Saxton, affirming in a covering letter that the families of soldiers in the regiment were indeed "in a suffering condition" and urging that "measures should be taken for their immediate & permanent relief." On December 11, in an endorsement on the covering letter, Saxton's adjutant conveyed the general's "opinion that a habit of dependence upon the government for food and clothing ought to be discouraged among the freedmen, even at the risk of some suffering." Accordingly, rations would be issued "only to those in extreme destitution, unable to help themselves, and having no relatives who can support them." General Saxton, the adjutant concluded, "would be very glad to see the colored soldiers in this Department paid fully and fairly, as other soldiers are, but he does not think it best to regard as 'destitute' persons the families of men who are receiving seven dollars a month, beside rations and clothing for themselves."

1 General Order 17, issued on March 6, 1863, by General David Hunter, then commander of the Department of the South, had called for a draft of all able-bodied black men between the ages of eighteen and fifty. A portion of the order had stated that "[u]ntil other arrangements can be made, the families of all negroes thus drafted will be provided for by orders which General Saxton has authority to issue." Hunter had added, however, the following qualification: "[I]t is hoped and confidently believed that, in the present scarcity of labor . . . few such families will be thrown upon the Government for support." (*Official Records*, ser. 1, vol 14, pp. 1020–21.)

38: Commander of the U.S.S. *Vermont* to the Commander of the South Atlantic Squadron

[*Port Royal Harbor, S.C.*] Dec. 9 [*1863*]

Sir: I have rec'd your letter in repect to distributing the contrabands on board this ship, if they can be used more advantageously elsewhere, and beg leave to say that without these Contrabands, the work which devolves on this ship cannot be carried on.

When I took command of the Vermont a year ago, there were then One Hundred and Eighty Contrabands on board besides her crew and have not seen the day since, when they could be spared.

This ship has to wait upon every vessel that comes here, more or less, with boats & working parties, besides attending to her own economy, discharging vessels, &c. &c. and I shall be at a loss to get along if her complement should be weakened. In fact I cannot get time to attend properly to the requirements of the Ship herself, as I have to meet so many demands for labor outside of her.

HLc [*William Reynolds*]

[William Reynolds] to Admiral, 9 Dec. [1863], vol. 3, p. 32, Letters Sent by Comdr. William Reynolds, Letterbooks of Officers of the U.S. Navy at Sea, RG 45 [T-692].

39: Direct-Tax Commissioner for the State of South Carolina to the Commissioner of Internal Revenue

Beaufort So Ca. Decr 12th 1863

Dear Sir, The impression is upon my mind that the notice of the sales of lands in St Helena Parish on the 18th of February next, forwarded to you by the mail of last week, was not first handed to me for my signature. If my name is not thereto I authorize you to add it, so that the names of the three commissioners may appear to the advertisement.

I was surprised to see in the Free South the Instructions of the President to this Commission.[1] Who furnished the copy I am not informed. It was not ordered or sanctioned by our Board. Judge Wording says he knew nothing about it. I am thus particular in naming this matter lest you may consider it an indecorum to have it thus published without the approval of the Department first obtained.

I see that a writer in the New-York Herald has been making a furious attack upon our Commission. I presume it is Lieu^t Co^l Halpine, who was chief of Gen. Hunter's Staff. The statements are utterly false.

I think it proper to inform you that I have heard from different persons who have been present that speeches have been made to the negroes at their gatherings on the Sabbath, urging them to adopt the squatter sovereignty plan and prevent white men if possible bidding against them at the public sales. Mr French, Chaplain on General Saxton's staff advocates this plan; and to me he tried to underrate the President's Instructions. Judge Smith goes out with Mr French on these appointments. I was told by the best authority that they got the negroes on St Helena Island, at their church, to adopt some very violent resolutions. The negroes consequently in some instances have been placing stakes for themselves on lands not selected for them, and I fear, instructed as they are, they will be either greatly disappointed or may give us some trouble. The true friend of the negro, it seems to me, ought to encourage white men to purchase plantations among them as protectors, teachers and employers; and their own homesteads, so generously allowed them by the Government, will thereby be greatly increased in value intrinsically.

You have doubtless observed that some of our documents are signed by only two of the Commissioners, or simply by myself as Chairman. Judge Smith has refused to put his signature to papers where my name appears as Chairman. I have, therefore, to secure his signature to important papers, as land sale advertisements, waived my position as chairman and allowed his name to come first. I see that the Free South of this day's issue recognizes him as Chairman. That paper does all it can to depreciate Judge Wording and myself and to exalt Judge Smith, whose squatter sovereignty and such like ideas suit the proprietors better, than our rigid adherence to the Law and to the interests of the Government. I hope, however, through it all to secure your and the Secretary's approbation, and finally to see my work with the blessing of God crowned with success.

We have received the Forms and the Books, except the Book entitled "Certificate Book C", being for "Heads of Families of the African Race". The loose sheets have come but not the Book. I am, Dear Sir, with the greatest respect Yours Truly

Wm Henry Brisbane

You might read this letter to the Secretary of the Treasury.

ALS

Wm. Henry Brisbane to Hon. Joseph J. Lewis, 12 Dec. 1863, General Correspondence, ser. 99, SC, Records of or Relating to Direct Tax Commissions in the Southern States, RG 58 [Z-2]. Brisbane's fellow commissioners were Abram D. Smith and William E. Wording. No reply has been found in the records of the direct-tax commission or of the commissioner of internal revenue.

1 President Abraham Lincoln's instructions, issued on September 16, 1863, pertained to land in St. Helena Parish that had been forfeited under the Direct Tax Act and then bid in for the federal government during the tax sale of March 1863 (and thus remained in the hands of the commissioners). Lincoln directed the commissioners to sell much of that land at public auction, in tracts no larger than 320 acres to any one purchaser. He also instructed them to exempt numerous named plantations from auction, including twenty "reserved for the use of the United States, for war, military, naval, revenue and police purposes"; portions of about thirty-five, designated "for school purposes," which were to be leased out by the commissioners and the proceeds applied to the education of black and poor white youths; and about fifty-five that were to be divided into parcels of up to 20 acres and sold to "heads of families of the African race," one parcel per family, at not less than $1.25 per acre, "for the charitable purpose of providing homes . . . so as to give them an interest in the soil." (Abraham Lincoln, *Collected Works*, ed. Roy P. Basler,

Marion D. Pratt, and Lloyd A. Dunlap, 9 vols. [New Brunswick, N.J., 1953–55], vol. 6, pp. 453–59.)

40: Northern Planter to a Direct-Tax Commissioner for the State of South Carolina

Beaufort S.C. Jany 14th 1864

Dear Sir In reply to your request to give you a statement of the result of my Enterprise in Employing negro labor upon the plantations purchased by me in this department in March last, I would state, that although the books are not yet written up, to show the Exact cost of the year's work, I can in general terms, give some information which, as far as it goes, may be taken as perfectly reliable, & may be of some use, considering the great social & political question at issue.

I purchased at the sales in March 1863, Eleven plantations, and hired of another purchaser two more, including a little over seven thousand acres in all. being mostly upon St. Helena Island. Although two months later than the usual period for beginning to work on land for a cotton crop, I succeeded in organizing the negro population residing on these lands, to a limited Extent, and planted the following amt. of crops, offering the same rates of pay that had been Established by Genl Saxton on the Govt plantations.[1]

Cotton crop	13 plantations	814 acres
Corn "	" "	700 "
Sweet potatoes	" "	150 "

The population resident on these lands consisted of about 950, including all the infirm & children. If I had been able to Employ the able bodied men, I should have had about 500 working hands, but as this portion of the labor was drafted by Genl Hunter for the Military service, I had to do what was done with the help of women, Children & old men, about 400 in all. making an area planted of over 4 acres to the hand. The provision crops were assigned to the separate families for culture and for their exclusive benefit, except a tax of 2 bushels of corn per acre, to feed the mules. Each family took the responsibility of feeding itself from the land so assigned, & took the crop to their own houses, when harvested. The cotton crop was also assigned in definite portions to each family as they chose & all labor paid for by the *piece* or *job*. Each family having a separate portion of the field to cultivate, the hoeing was paid for per acre and any neglect of culture was followed by a withholding of the pay. In order to inspire confidence & encourage industry payments were made promptly at the End of Every month, taking great care to assign the money Exactly in proportion to the amt. of work actually done upon the crop. The picking of cotton was paid for by the pound. The payments for cultivation were less than the labor was worth, but the final payment for picking was double what the labor for picking was worth, so that it might be regarded as a premium on successful culture, stimulating the laborer to a feeling of proprietary interest in the crop, & throwing the whole responsibility of the crop upon him. Of course a great variety of individual character was thus developed. The result has been to cultivate self reliance & stimulate ambition & intelligence to a degree highly satisfactory. The entire crop will be about 73,000 lbs of ginned cotton, or about 90 lbs. per acre. The crop under the slave system averaged about 135 lbs. per acre for Sea Island cotton. It must be remembered that we worked with little or no manure, & began the work on the crop at least two months later than the usual period with scarce any live stock. Under these circumstances I am fully satisifed with the result. It has exceeded my anticipations. We have been at work throughout under grave disadvantages, sufficient to discourage many men from such an undertaking. We have been surrounded by camps, with their manifold temptations. We were deprived of the usual lines of intercourse with the rest of the world, & could obtain our supplies with great difficulty. Moreover we had to contend with the ingrained prejudice on the part of the negro to work on cotton, believing it as he has been taught to, to be for the white man's benefit & not for his own. This feeling is fast wearing away however, & will soon disappear.

Under all these drawbacks, the cost of the crop I have raised here this year will not far Exceed if it does at all, the cost per lb. of producing the same staple under the old system. This is said by writers in DeBow's review to have been 30 to 40 cts per lb.

As to the quality of the staple we have grown, I will say, that I have sent average samples of it to Liverpool where it has been valued, Nov. 20th '63 at 50^{d} sterling per lb.

Our expenses have been chiefly in labor, the rates of which are based upon the enormous prices paid now for the necessaries of life by the negroes, viz. coarse cotton cloths & shoes, *rice*, *sugar*, *tobacco*, bacon, &c. with all of which articles they provide themselves by purchase.

The greatest difficulty to be encountered in Employing negro labor lies in their ignorance & lack of confidence in our promises, a difficulty which has been in no way removed by their intercourse with our soldiers, who are too apt to take advantage of their helplessness. Next to this is the disposition to lie idle after earning money enough to supply their simple wants. But I have found both of these rapidly disappearing. The negro is actuated by the same motives as other men, & we must appeal to the *human nature* & make it appear for his interest to work & then he *will* work. With a view to multiply their simple wants & stimulate industry, I have placed within their reach by purchase a great variety of new food, articles of useful domestic ware, clothing adapted to their wants & tastes &c. &c. They purchase readily vast quantities of articles which they never had in abundance before, such as soap, candles, pots, ovens, knives & forks, pails, brooms, spoons, tin ware, sieves, fine shoes, hose, flannels, underclothing, hats. also, flour, rice, sugar, molasses, coffee, herring, mackerel, bacon, beef &c &c.

I have spent in wages & shall spend in the course of this month, which will prepare my crop for market, the sum of $20,000– and I find that the sales of articles like the above already reach $15,000– during the same period. My course has been to offer these articles at cost, with a view to keep my laborers at home, away from the sutlers, and to stimulate labor by multiplying civilized wants. My last cargo of supplies was taxed one thousand dollars by the Special agt. of the Trs. Deptmt, & these laborers have to pay rather higher prices now than before this tax was levied. The sutlers & merchants at Hilton Head being exempt from the tax, are beginning to attract some of my customers, who are not long in finding out where to buy cheapest.

One great source of influence with these simple people has been my school system. Believing that under private Enterprise the schools ought no longer to be dependent upon charity, I have supported five of them on my lands at the cost of the proprietors, charging it to the crop, which, at present prices has an ample margin of profit for such a trifling burden. The whole cost of these schools will be about $3,000 per an. & they accommodate some 300 pupils, nearly all of whom have already learned to read.

I have thus produced an amt. of cotton equal to two thirds the old average crop per acre, on 814 acres, and at a cost of about 30 cents per lb. here. while, under the old system, enjoying all the advantages of a thorough organization, open commerce, & long experience the slave holders failed to produce the same staple at a lower price, as their advocates have already shown, in their peculiar organ, De Bow's review. I feel very sure, that after the present difficulties shall have passed away, which are inseparable from the military occupation of the district, & when we shall have an unrestrained intercourse with the North, when the competition of the camps for labor shall have ceased, & laborers shall have a free &

open market for their services, & have the choice of Employers, that any just and equitable man can raise cotton or any other product here at far less cost than under any system of compulsory labor. Moreover the more open the labor-market is, the more can be accomplished. I am satisfied that no restrictions can be placed upon their labor to advantage. It must be *entirely voluntary*. Any half way system of pupilage or apprenticeship will fail, as compared with a perfectly free intercourse between Employer & Employed. Very respectfully yrs &c,

ALS Edw[d] S. Philbrick

Edwd. S. Philbrick to Hon. W. E. Wording, 14 Jan. 1864, General Correspondence, ser. 99, SC, Records of or Relating to Direct Tax Commissions in the Southern States, RG 58 [Z-1].

1 The wage rates, established in December 1862 by General Rufus Saxton, military governor in the Department of the South, are printed above, in doc. 28.

41: Circular by the Military Governor in the Department of the South

Beaufort, South Carolina, January 16, 1864.

Copy.

Circular.

The following instructions, which have been received by the U.S. Direct Tax Commissioners, are announced for the information and benefit of all concerned:

Treasury Department, Dec. 30, 1863.

Gentlemen: – By direction of the President I transmit the following instructions, which you will observe in disposing of lands struck off to the United States. You will consider them as applying to all lands in your district which are now, or may be hereafter owned by the United States, except such as are or may be set apart for military, naval, school or revenue purposes, and the plantations on St. Helena Island known as "Land's End" and the "Ben Chaplin Place," and the City of Beaufort on Port Royal Island.

All previous instructions or parts thereof which conflict with those now given, are hereby rescinded.

Yours Respectfully,
(signed) S. P. Chase.

To U.S. Direct Tax Commissioners.

Additional Instructions To The Direct Tax Commissioners For The District Of South Carolina, In Relation To The Disposition Of Lands.

1. You will allow any loyal person of twenty-one years of age or upwards, who has at any time since the occupation by the national forces, resided for six months or now resides upon, or is engaged in cultivating any lands in your district owned by the United States, to enter the same for pre-emption to the extent of one, or, at the option of the pre-emptor, two tracts of twenty acres each, paying therefor One dollar and twenty-five cents per acre. You will give preference in all cases to heads of families and to married women whose husbands are engaged in the service of the United States, or are necessarily absent.

2. You will permit each soldier, sailor or marine actually engaged in the service of the United States, or any who may have been, or hereafter shall be honorably discharged, to pre-empt and purchase in person or by authorized agent at the rate of One dollar and twenty five cents per acre, one tract of twenty acres of land if single, and if married, two tracts of twenty acres each, in addition to the amount a head of family, or married woman in the absence of her husband, is allowed to pre-empt and purchase under the general privilege to loyal persons.

3. Each pre-emptor, on filing his claim and receiving his certificate of pre-emption, must pay in United States notes two fifths of the price and the residue on receiving a deed for the parcels of land pre-empted, and a failure to make complete payment on receipt of the deed will forfeit all rights under the pre-emption, as well as all partial payments for the land.

4. When persons authorized to purchase by pre-emption desire to enter upon and cultivate lands not yet surveyed, they may do so; but they will be required to conform in their selections as nearly as possible to the probable lines of the surveys, and to take and occupy them subject to correction of title and occupation by actual surveys when made.

5. In making surveys, such reservation for paths and roadways will be made as will allow easy and convenient access to the several subdivisions entered for sale and occupancy by pre-emption or otherwise.

Approved Dec. 31, 1863 (signed) A. Lincoln.

These instructions it will be seen apply to all, soldiers as well as citizens. The Superintendents and Teachers in this Department are hereby directed to give their entire attention to the carrying out of these instructions, and to assist the people to the extent of their power in locating, staking out their claims, and securing their title deeds under this order of the President, which, in its beneficient results is to be second only to the Proclamation of Emancipation. I also recommend the people to lose no time in pre-empting their claims and in preparing their grounds for the coming harvest. The foundation of all national wealth and prosperity is in the soil. No people can be truly prosperous who neglect its cultivation.

Freedmen, you should plow deep, plant carefully and in season, cultivate diligently, and you will reap abundant harvests. First provide for an ample supply of corn and vegetables, then remember that cotton is the great staple here. I advise you to plant all you can of it. So profitable was its culture in the old days of slavery that your former masters said "Cotton is King." It is expected that you will show in a Free South that cotton is more of a king than ever. R. Saxton, Brig. Gen. and Military Gover[nor]

HDc

Circular, Headquarters U.S. Forces, Beaufort, South Carolina, 16 Jan. 1864, enclosed in Brig. Genl. Ed. R. S. Canby to the Secretary of the Treasury, 18 Feb. 1864, vol. 3, pp. 115–16, Letters Received from Executive Officers: AB Series, ser. 82, RG 56 [X-125].

42: Direct-Tax Commissioner for the State of South Carolina to the Commissioner of Internal Revenue

Beaufort So Ca. January 16th /64

Sir, I have the honor of acknowledging the receipt of yours of the 6th Instant received an hour ago.

You therein say "I notice in your advertisement of lands offered for sale on the 18th Feby next that you have included therein several plantations that were sold to individuals at your previous sale, say" "Rice Park" "Woodland"– "Campbell Pine Land" on Port Royal Island, why has this been done?"

I do not know from what source you received your information; but our books accord with the fact that these places were bid off to the United States at the Tax sale in Feby last.

As yet we have nothing but incomplete or rough plats of what has been surveyed. As soon as we have any thing completed & fully established a copy thereof shall be forwarded to you.

Your construction of the 11th Section[1] is precisely that which is given unanimously by our Board. I refer to the clause relating to credit to soldeirs, sailors or marines.

I perceive that your letter was written apparently without having in mind the effect of the new instructions of the President and Secretary of the Treasury, forwarded to us through Mr French, and bearing date Decr 30th 1863,[2] upon the land sales advertised for the 18th of February. And this confirms me in the idea I had previously expressed that they could not have passed under *your* eye. I am sorry to inform you that they will, unless *speedily* rescinded, have a very disastrous effect not only upon the public sale but upon the entire interests of the trusts committed to us. This scheme was carefully kept from Judge Wording and myself; nor was the document placed in our hands until the Arago having departed with the mail it was too late for us to write you. How Mr French could have succeeded in getting Mr Sumner & Mr Chase to give us such instructions so plainly at variance with the 11th section of the law will be as difficult of solution as his success in getting a press established here under the name of the Secretary & by leaving Mr Barney to foot the bill. If the Government will investigate the doings of Mr French I am satisfied that the confidence of Mr Chase & Mr Sumner in him will not be such as to be very much influenced by his communications. I am sure those gentlemen must have trusted greatly to him for the data upon which those instructions were issued. They are crowded with business & must necessarily depend more or less upon those in whom they have confidence in making up their minds what to do. In this case there is a mischief accomplished which ought not to be overlooked.

Mr French arrived here with those instructions last Monday or Tuesday. Instead of bringing them to our office immediately, they were kept out of our hands & from our knowledge until yesterday (Friday). He was with Judge Smith soon after his arrival, & *may* have told him of them, but neither he nor Judge Smith allowed us to see them until the mail had departed & General Saxton had prepared his orders for publication based upon those instructions.[3] As soon as Judge Wording & myself had read & studied these Instructions I immediately went to General Saxton & entreated him to delay the publication of them & to suspend action upon them until we could communicate with the authorities in Washington. He refused to do so. I then entreated him to wait one week for consideration. This he also declined. I then entreated him to wait 24 hours to give us an opportunity to reflect upon the matter and to allow us to present the objections we had to them fully & fairly. This he agreed to do, & immediately came over to see Judge Wording with me & to hear what we had to offer. But he was so entirely unfitted at the time for the consideration of the subject that it was utterly impossible to get him to listen to a connected argument, or to give the slightest indication of a disposition to grant the request for delay until we could confer with the Department. He has issued his orders to his Agents to go immediately forward & divide up the lands. As Judge Wording & myself anticipated would be the case, the orders had scarcely issued from the printing office before applications were presented by gentlemen occupying the premises for preemption of two of the very best improved lots on St Helena Island, one of 20 & the other of 40 acres with a fine mansion house on each, which, under the instructions, they will get (if we grant the applications) for fifty dollars. Another has filed his application for eighty acres of some of the best wood land adjoining the new habitations which General Saxton has had built for the refugees, & which had been selected by me under your approval & that of the Secretary & President for the benefit of the colored people. Already too are wholesale applications made by General Saxton's brother & others for the freedmen in mass on certain plantations without the names of the negroes & without designating the particular tracts for each. In our meeting this afternoon Judge Smith presented a series of resolutions for us to adopt that we lay aside all other business (although the sales of this Town are to commence on Monday) until we carry out this pre-emption plan. He was then himself really unfit to attend to such important business. It was entirely new to us & we wished for time to deliberate, & therefore for the present laid his resolutions on the table.

Lands upon which we have been expecting to realize at the sales from five to ten dollars an acre will under these new instructions bring only one dollar & a quarter; & probably most of them will be taken by those who have no intention of settling them, but who are keen enough to be first in securing them for speculation. The negroes instead of being all supplied with homesteads will not have land enough for one fourth of them. They have already been greatly distracted by the course taken by General Saxton independently of our required duties under the law, & the Instructions of Sep 16 1863,[4] & now they will be out of all heart at their prospects. Mr French has already appointed to attend the meeting for religious worship to morrow at the Baptist Church on St Helena, & convert it into a meeting for himself & General Saxton & others to lay their plans about the land before the negroes & superintendents. The negroes will be confused beyond measure, and while they will be wondering what it all means keen sighted white men will be traveling over the Islands to see where to locate their pre-emptions.

But if all this be *law*, I as a Commissioner and my truly honest & upright colleague Judge Wording will carry it out in its letter & spirit so long as we remain in Office. But to our view to make these new instructions law, will require an Act of Congress. Certain lands were selected agreeably to the law as a charity to the negroes that they might have small homesteads.[5] These lands are taken by the new Instructions out of that charitable selection and opened to any white man who is loyal however well off he may be. Thus being taken from under the head of a charity where is the law by which this land can be sold (and remember it is improved land) except at public auction to the highest bidder?

Under the law there is no authority whatsoever for the pre-emption of improved lands.

Again the law requires that the soldier, sailor or marine shall have the right to purchase the land at public sale, & pay down only one fourth of the purchase money, & the balance in three years. The new Instructions require him to pay two fifths of the money at once.

As the Instructions therefore are inconsistent with the law how can we give a valid title under them?

General Saxton tells us that the responsibility is upon the President & not upon us if we carry out the instructions. But we do not so view it. The Secretary & the President have no time to examine these details. They have placed us here to carry out the provisions of the law, and they have a right to expect of us that they be informed correctly and truly in all matters for which they are to be held responsible by their sanction.

Can we look on and see these lands disposed of upon the *paltriest* scale or any other scale of speculation, and satisfy our conscience with the plea that it is the President's responsibility? He ought to turn us out of office forthwith, if he had an idea that we could be guilty of such dereliction of duty. Can we under the shelter of the President's responsibility violate the law that we are sworn to carry out, and expect that he himself whose name has been the synonym of honesty would justify us in using *his* name for such a purpose?

I have much personal regard for Gen. Saxton on account of his large heartedness & kindly disposition to a long oppressed race, and for his readiness to afford me every facility to carry on my work for the benefit of that people; but I have deeply lamented from the first that I saw he had some in his confidence and his counsels who have talent enough to insinuate themselves into his favor & *carry their* points by *seeming* to *follow* him. As Judge Wording and myself were not willing to bend ourselves to the rule that the end sanctifies the means, and we would not counsel with men who acted upon such a rule, care has been taken that we should not know what was going on in their deliberations; & that General Saxton himself might not consult with us means have been adopted to impress him with the idea that we were negligent of the interests of the colored people, whilst to him must the negroes look to save them from the grasping power of heartless speculators. Thus have M[r] French & his co-adjutors brought these poor ignorant people into a state of bewilderment that gives the best opportunity for speculators to take the advantage of them.

Judge Wording & myself have earnestly desired to give every advantage that could honestly be given to the negroes and the soldiers to get the good of these lands. And my life has shown that the negroes could have no truer friend than myself. But I am not writing this to speak of myself, and I thus write only to make out completely the logical point of this communication. The same spirit which made me twenty six years ago sacrifice home property & friendships the Secretary knows me well enough to believe will develope itself through life. Yet I do not claim to be more a friend to the negro than to the soldier who stands by his country & faces the cannon's mouth in her holy cause. But I cannot look on and see what I am now seeing here and not feel that both soldier & negro are to be sacrificed to a "zeal without knowledge" on the part of some, cupidity on the part of others, and though last not least to a meddlesome spirit which has from first to last been a hindrance to the successful operations of this Commission.

Pardon me, Sir, for this long letter and accept the renewed assurances of my highest esteem. I have the honor to subscribe myself Your Obedient Servant

ALS Wm Henry Brisbane

Wm. Henry Brisbane to Hon. Joseph J. Lewis, 16 Jan. 1864, General Correspondence, ser. 99, SC, Records of or Relating to Direct Tax Commissions in the Southern States, RG 58 [Z-2]. In the margin, William E. Wording, Brisbane's fellow commissioner, noted, "I fully concur in the above statements and propositions." The letter of January 6, 1864, to which the commissioners were responding, has not been located in the records of the direct-tax commission or in those of the commissioner of internal revenue. The preemption policy that so discomfited Brisbane and Wording delighted General Rufus Saxton, military governor in the Department of the South, who urged the freedpeople to avail themselves of its provisions and directed plantation superintendents and teachers to assist them in doing so. (See doc. 41, immediately above.) When, by early February 1864, Brisbane and Wording had "refused to carry out" the preemption instructions, "on the ground, as they assert, of their illegality," Saxton protested to the Secretary of War, pointing out that the third commissioner, Abram D. Smith, "the only lawyer on the Board, pronounces them legal and just, and has done everything in his power to have them carried out." (*Official Records*, ser. 3, vol. 4, pp. 118–19.) But other military officials in the Department of the South disagreed with Saxton about the merits of preemption. On January 31, 1864, General Quincy A. Gillmore, the department commander, warned Secretary of the Treasury Salmon P. Chase that if the new instructions were carried out, "the colored man will be the sufferer . . . by being thrown into competition with white men and speculators," whereas under the earlier policy – setting aside for "charitable" purposes land that would subsequently be sold exclusively to former slaves – the freedman "was protected by a carefully prepared law and the liberal and humane instructions issued under it." Gillmore recommended "that the new instructions be revoked entirely and the old order of things restored." (Maj. Gen.

[Quincy A. Gillmore] to Hon. S. P. Chase, 31 Jan. 1864, Letters Sent, pp. 148–49, Q. A. Gillmore Papers, Generals' Papers & Books, ser. 159, RG 94 [V-121].) In the end, critics of preemption carried the day. On February 11, 1864, Chase directed Brisbane to "regard the recent instructions touching preemption as suspended until otherwise ordered" and to proceed under previous instructions. "It is greatly regretted," Chase wrote, "that differences of opinion exist in the Board of Commissioners as to the most certain and efficient mode of protecting the interests and promoting the welfare of the laborers on the plantations, but so long as such differences exist in fact, the judgment of the majority must govern unless for good cause the President shall see fit otherwise to direct." (S. P. Chase to Dr. W. H. Brisbane, 11 Feb. 1864, vol. 1, p. 91, Letters Sent to Collectors & Assessors of Internal Revenue, State Officers, Banks, Corporations, Etc.: GS series, ser. 26, RG 56 [X-124].)

1 Section 11 of the Direct Tax Act of June 1862 authorized the tax commissioners, under the direction of the President, to sell at public auction land that had been bid in for the United States at direct tax sales, in parcels no larger than 320 acres to any one purchaser. Men who had served in the U.S. military service for at least three months could acquire such land by paying one-fourth of the purchase price at the time of sale, with the balance due within three years. Any nonlandowning head of family residing in the district in which the lands were situated might, under rules established by the commissioners, "have the right to enter upon and acquire the rights of preëmption in such lands as may be unimproved and vested in the United States." (*Statutes at Large*, vol. 12, p. 425.)
2 The new instructions are quoted in doc. 41, immediately above. Mansfield French, who transmitted the instructions to the direct-tax commissioners, was a Northern minister working among the freedpeople in the Sea Islands, and a personal friend of Secretary of the Treasury Salmon P. Chase.
3 Saxton's order is printed immediately above, as doc. 41.
4 For the President's instructions of September 1863 to the direct-tax commissioners, see above, doc. 39n.
5 Amendments to the Direct Tax Act, adopted in February 1863, had provided that when land forfeited under the act was to be sold at public action, tracts selected under direction of the President "for war, military, naval, revenue, charitable, educational, or police purposes" could be retained in possession of the government; a few days later, the President had ordered the direct-tax commissioners and two army officers to make such selections. (See above, doc. 27n.) Subsequently, by instructions of September 1863, the President had ordered that the land earlier reserved for "charitable" purposes be divided into twenty-acre plots and sold to black heads of family for not less than $1.25 per acre. (See above, doc. 39n.)

43: Diagram of Plots Selected for Preemption by Freedpeople on Port Royal Island, South Carolina

[*Port Royal Island, S.C. January 25, 1864*]

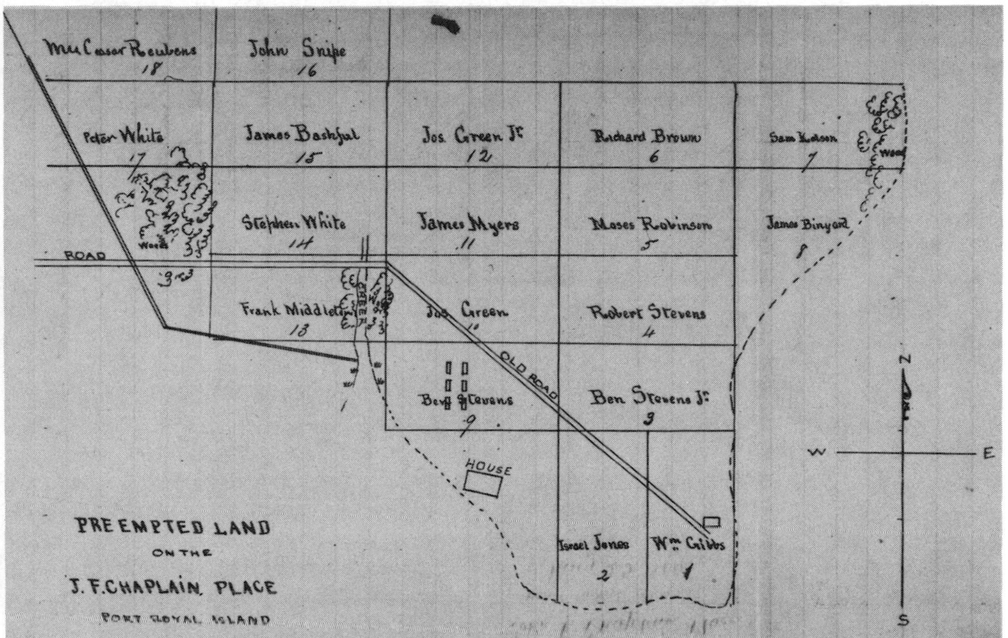

"Preempted Land on the J. F. Chaplain Place," [25 Jan. 1864], enclosed in Wm. G. S. Keene to the honorable the direct tax commissioners for the district of South Carolina, 25 Jan. 1864, Preemption Papers, ser. 113, SC, Records of or Relating to Direct Tax Commissions in the Southern States, RG 58 [Z-33]. The covering letter reported that the eighteen freedpeople (seventeen men and one woman) wished "to purchase by pre-emption 360 acres of land on the 'John F. Chaplain place,' being twenty acres to each . . ., according to the plot herewith submitted."

44: Former Plantation Superintendent on St. Helena Island, South Carolina, to a Direct-Tax Commissioner for the State of South Carolina

St. Helena Island S.C. Feb 15" 1864

Dear Sir, In accordance with your request I will state as nearly as I can from memory, what transpired at our church yesterday.

The pastor of the church, Rev. Mr. Phillips, died two days ago, and the funeral Services were held in the church yesterday. The Rev. Dr. Peck preached the Sermon. Rev. M. French was present and, after Dr. Peck's Sermon, spoke at length, addressing the widow and the bereaved church and then to close up dragged in the land question. He said he had come over partly to attend the funeral and partly to sympathize with and comfort them in view of the "cloud of sadness" which was passing over them in consequence of the action of the Gov^t^ at Washington in suspending the late "Instructions" to the Direct Tax Commissioners authorizing preemption of land.[1] He showed the people how happy they were a few weeks since when he and others were there to tell them of their right to preempt; and also showed them how sad they were then (at the funeral) on account of the suspension of those "Instructions" He tried hard to comfort them! and exhorted them still to believe the Government friendly to them.

He gave it as his own opinion, that they (the negroes) would be sustained in all they had done in preempting and working the land; but, if they should *not* be sustained, (I do not pretend to give his precise words but give the substance of his advice to the people,) he exhorted them still to hold on to the land as long and as persistently as possibly, and to give the Authorities or Gov[t] as much trouble as possible in dispossessing them of it.

The taste he displayed in introducing such a subject at a funeral Service, and that the funeral service of the pastor of the church which he was addressing, and in the presence of the widow of the deceased, is submitted to your judgment, but the loyalty to our Gov[t] of such advice as he gave to the negroes is not a matter of *taste*.

The negroes are becoming disgusted with such proceedings.

Many of them said to me yesterday, we don't want to hear any more about land on Sundays; we've heard enough, we want to hear the Gospel.

If such meddlers as Mr. French were out of the Department the negroes would be better off. With much respect I am very truly Your Ob[t] Serv[t]

ALS J. M. Fairfield

J. M. Fairfield to Dr. Wm. H. Brisbane, 15 Feb. 1864, enclosed in Wm. Henry Brisbane to Hon. Joseph J. Lewis, 15 Feb. 1864, General Correspondence, ser. 99, SC, Records of or Relating to Direct Tax Commissions in the Southern States, RG 58 [Z-3]. The direct-tax commissioner, William H. Brisbane, forwarded Fairfield's letter to Joseph J. Lewis, commissioner of internal revenue, characterizing its author as "a highly respectable gentleman who resides on St. Helena Island." Brisbane urged that Mansfield French, who had been sent to the Sea Islands by the American Missionary Association, "be removed from the Department" for inciting "a spirit of resistance" to the government's reversal of the preemption policy. Under the same covering letter, Brisbane forwarded a letter from Solomon Peck, who had officiated at the funeral. Peck confirmed that French had urged the freedpeople "to hold fast at *any & every hazard* the lands which they had staked out," assuring them that the government would eventually accede to their wishes. According to Peck, French had further proclaimed that if the government did not grant the right of preemption, he hoped the freedpeople "would give them all the trouble they could." (Solomon Peck to Rev. Wm. H. Brisbane, 15 Feb. 1864.)

1 On February 11, 1864, the Secretary of the Treasury had suspended instructions to the South Carolina direct-tax commissioners that would have permitted preemption claims upon land scheduled to be sold later the same month. (See above, doc. 42n.) The suspended instructions are quoted above, in doc. 41.

45: Northern Minister to the Commissioner of Internal Revenue

Beaufort. S.C. Feb 23 '64

Dear Sir. I promised to advise you from time to time about affairs in this Department. I regret not having done so, especially, as matters have gone so badly. We seem to be retrograding rapidly. The sale of public lands, which, under the late instructions, were all to be preempted, has wrought immense mischief.[1] The surveys have been now turned, mostly, to the account of speculators. and the public lands (or those designated for auction sales) are going off rapidly & at too high prices for the freedmen, while, as yet, very few lots have been sold to the freedmen, from even the lands specially set apart for them. On the reception of the late instructions, only 19 deeds had been given, & up to this date. only 43 deeds are given, and those for tracts of ten, & five acres. More land was sold yesterday to speculators, than all that has been deeded to the freedmen. Supposing the late instructions would remain in full force, the people scattered all over the islands laid their claims, commenced listing & preparing the lands for planting. Some had commenced building, many had moved several miles to get a good home, & on the old homestead, where they had been born, & had laborered & suffered. Now *all* such, as were so unfortunate as to locate on lands originally selected for sale, are being sold out. The disappointment to them is almost unbearable. They see neither justice nor wisdom in such treatment. The white man loves power & money, and is sharp enough to grasp both, when he can. I fear for the freedpeople & our country. I could hardly express my surprise, when I was told by Dr.

Brisbane,[2] that you urged the sale of the lands. I was sure you must labor under a mistake, that you certainly did not want to deprive these unfortunate creatures of homes. The Dr. Said the lands, set apart originally, were enough for them.[3] I replied, so they are if no man is to be allowed over five or ten acres, and you intend to keep them dependent, & discourage them from enlisting as soldiers, & if you too, wish to crowd them together & form an exclusive negro settlement, a measure perfectly abhorrent to their feelings, as well as ruinous to their future elevation. The school farms,[4] so far as leased, are all let to white men, & that which originated in a benevolent intent, is working, in my humble opinion, only evil. The lessee tries to appropriate the laborers to his own interest, & scarcely any residents of plantations out of which school farms are taken, have preempted. They are at the mercy of the lessee. Mr Chase never did himself more honor, or a greater good to this people & through them to the country, than when he adopted the late policy of preemption. Disabled white soldiers, & colored soldiers, poor civilians here from the North seized the opportunity of securing homes. This plan, if left undisturbed, would have put S. Carolina, where she would be compelled, in all future time, to behave herself. None but speculators objected, Yes, there is another class who did, I mean anti-slavery and anti-negro men. Now speculators are buying the lands. One man fraudently in the name of office[*r*]s, bought 330 acres, was arrested, confessed his guilt & is now a maniac. My heart has never, for the last two years, been so sad, nor have the people during that time seen so dark an hour– Our Berachah is turned into a Bochim.[5] Why Providence has permitted this calamity I know not. Mr. Chase would never, never have done as he has, had he *fully known* the facts.[6] Thousands are fervently praying that God would yet, by some means, turn back this wave of trouble and protect the people. By what means, we cannot tell. We are now all adrift.

I know your heart is fully with us, & that you would be glad to do all in your power for the cause. I know of no way to undo the harm, but to *confirm all properly made claims* of the *people to their twenty acres*. The promulgation of the instructions was like the bursting of noon-day after a night of darkness of a century. I regret the sudden departure of the Str. & I must here close. Yours most sincerely

ALS M. French.

M. French to Hon. Mr. Lewis, 23 Feb. 1864, General Correspondence, ser. 99, SC, Records of or Relating to Direct Tax Commissions in the Southern States, RG 58 [Z-4].

1 The sale had commenced on February 18, 1864. The "late instructions" to the South Carolina direct-tax commissioners, which had included provisions for preemption of small acreages, are quoted above, in doc. 41.
2 William H. Brisbane, one of three direct-tax commissioners for the state of South Carolina.
3 In February 1863, in accordance with amendments to the Direct Tax Act, the President had instructed the South Carolina direct-tax commissioners to set aside for "charitable" purposes a portion of the land forfeited for nonpayment of taxes. (See above, doc. 27n.) The following September he had directed that the properties so reserved be divided into 20-acre plots and sold to black heads of families, but he had also ordered that most of the other land under the commissioners' control be sold at public auction in units of up to 320 acres. (See above, doc. 39n.) By contrast, new instructions of December 1863 (later suspended) had made all land under the commissioners' control subject to preemption in 20- or 40-acre tracts (excepting only certain properties reserved for "military, naval, school or revenue purposes") by "any loyal person" who was then residing or had resided since the federal occupation on any of the land forfeited to the government. (Quoted above, in doc. 41.)
4 Forfeited estates that had been reserved by the government "for school purposes"; they were leased out by the direct-tax commissioners and the proceeds used to support the education of black and poor white children. (See above, doc. 39n.)
5 Berachah ("blessing") and Bochim ("weeping") allude to episodes in Old Testament chronicles. After divine intervention saved Judah from invasion by vastly superior forces, King Jehoshaphat and his subjects "assembled themselves in the Valley of Berachah; for there they blessed the Lord." (2 Chron. 20:1–26.) At Bochim, an angel appeared before the Israelites to convey God's displeasure with them for merely occupying Canaan and placing its inhabitants under tribute, rather than obeying His instructions to expel them. As punishment, God decreed that the Canaanites "shall be *as thorns* in your sides, and their gods . . . a snare unto you." (Judg. 1:1–2:5.)
6 On February 11, 1864, Secretary of the Treasury Salmon P. Chase had suspended the instructions that permitted preemption, directing the direct-tax commissioners to proceed instead under the President's instructions of September 1863. (See above, doc. 42n.)

46: Headquarters of the Department of the South to the Direct-Tax Commissioners for the State of South Carolina, and a Reply by One of the Commissioners

HILTON HEAD, S.C. Feby 25th 1864.

"Copy"

Gentlemen, The Major General Commanding having been informed that persons desiring to bid at the land sales[1] have been deterred therefrom by threats that violence would be used by parties claiming preemption rights, to prevent them from entering into or retaining possession of the premises. I am instructed by him to inform you that bids may be made at these sales freely under his assurance, hereby given, that the purchasers will be protected in all their rights as such, if necessary by armed force.

You are at liberty to publish this letter for the information of all concerned, and you are requested to report promptly to these Headquarters the names of any officers or soldiers who by threats or otherwise are exciting apprehensions of the nature referred to I have the honor to be Very respectfully Your obt. servt.

HLcSr (Signed) Ed. W. Smith

[*Beaufort, S.C. late February 1864*]

. . . .[2]

as the sales are to be kept open sixty days we hope that we shall have all ready before the time expires. *In the mean time we shall allow the laborers or freed people to go on preparing the soil for the crop of the season, with the guarantee that purchasers shall not deprive them of the fruits of their toil.*" Such was the guaranty given to the government and by the commissioners to the people. Is it possible that the commanding General could have been advised of this when he dictated the note just recieved, volunteering "armed force" to summarily dispossess the people, drive them from the grounds they have planted or prepared to plant, without hearing, without trial, but by "armed "force" alone; in behalf of the large purchasers, yielding to the clamor of greedy avarice, and scouting the appeal of the poor and the oppressed? There must have been some strange misconception taking hold of the mind of the commanding General for the moment, which his better judgment cannot fail to correct when properly informed. Indeed I cannot but believe that he is groping in the dark, both as to the law, and the policy of the system which the government desires to inaugurate here.

I am not aware that the bidders, or would-be bidders have been intimidated by the threats of which you speak. The prices for which the lands sold, and again resold by speculative purchasers, would seem to invalidate the correctness of the commanding General's information in that behalf. Should any such frightful threats become so serious as to defy the authority of the Military Governor, he will doubtless apply to the commanding General for all necessary aid.

But, I desire to ask, if the commanding General assumes the authority to eject the preemptioners, in favor of speculators by "armed force," from their homes, from the grounds which they have planted with the assurance that they should "not be deprived of the fruits of their toil" – this assurance made to the government by the commissioners; – and this too with out any process of law; with out giving them any opportunity to settle judicially the rights in dispute between them and the (so called) speculators? Does he intend to issue execution first, then try, hear and determine afterwards. In other words will he execute the alleged culprit, and try him afterwards.

The turning out tenants by military force without hearing, (even tenants by sufferance) is such a monstrosity of administration as would shock the conscience of christendom –

The military Governor is vested with ample authority to administer justice between all conflicting claimants here. The commissioners need no menaces of "armed force" to be placed at their disposal. The assumption that such a necessity exists, is alike derogatory to the fidelity of the commission and to the delicacy of the commanding General. Some strange misapprehensions must have siezed upon his mind, or some foolish reports must have been made to him, to induce him to interfere in a matter which is foreign to his functions, and especially in a manner which would seem to overleap the line of demarkation between civil and military or even *quasi* civil & *quasi* military administration.

There has not been, to my knowledge any action of this Board requesting the interference of the commanding General. His premature assumption of judicial functions, to determine private rights by the bayonet, to eliminate and define estates, not by due course of law, but by the tramp of soldiers and beat of drum is, at least novel in the history of modern war; superceding titles and muniments of title, uprooting tenancies without inquiry, and desolating homes of loyal citizens without the poor privilege of being heard, or their titles or claims of title adjudicated.

Does the commanding General desire to be understood as assuming the functions of the United States courts, anticipating their judgment, and executing their presumed decree upon, and in respect of such rights of pre-emption and possession as may have been required while the instructions of the 31st Dec. 1863 were in full force and effect?[3] Does the Commanding General understand that the instructions of Dec. 31. 1863 are merely suspended, not revoked or abrogated? Can he be pre-advised of the judgments of the courts in the premises? and is he willing to become the voluntary ally of the one party or the other? and especially of the strong against the weak? to give to the strong, by "armed force" the "nine points" in the law viz: possession, driving out the weak claimants, to submit or starve? If such is the purport of his order I desire to be fully advised in the premises in order that the Government may be also advised of the exact position taken by him in the premises. If, while the preemption instructions were in force certain persons acquired possessory rights, and became so to speak "terre tenanants" does he assume to dissolve such rights by "armed force"? In short what means this new order of ejectment? this writ of lead and steel instead of ink and parchment?

I will assure the commanding General that in October 1862 when I came down here in charge of this commission I brought with me orders from the Secretary of War to the military commanders to afford me all necessary protection and facilities for the transaction of our business. The Board have applied from time to time to the Military Governor for such helps as we needed, and it gives me great pleasure to say, never in vain. There has been no event brought to the knowledge of the Board requiring such a promulgation as is contained in your note. The Board has never asked for such, nor has any necessity for such been intimated at any meeting of the Board.

Whenever the ordinary course of administration of our functions become impeded by interventions which we cannot over come, we shall certainly apply for a sufficient *posse commitatus* to carry out the law as its behests shall have been deliberately declared.

As all the lands prepared for sale are sold, I have not caused your note to be published, but if it is the desire of the commanding General I will cause the same to be published in the Free South Very respectfully Your Obt. Servt

ALfS A. D. Smith

Lt. Col. Ed. W. Smith to Messrs. Brisbane, Wording & Smith, 25 Feb. 1864, filed with S-147 1864, Letters Received, ser. 4109, Dept. of the South, RG 393 Pt. 1 [C-1737]; A. D. Smith to [Edward W. Smith], [late Feb. 1864], Q. A. Gillmore Papers, Generals' Papers & Books, ser. 159, RG 94 [V-322]. The military governor in the Department of the South was General Rufus Saxton.

1 Sales of land forfeited to the government under the Direct Tax Act, which had begun on February 18, 1864.
2 The first page of the letter is missing.
3 The instructions, issued by the President to the direct-tax commissioners for South Carolina, had authorized the preemption of small tracts of land. Owing to objections raised by two of the three commissioners, as well as by the department commander, the instructions were suspended on February 11, 1864. (See above, docs. 41 and 42n.)

47A: South Carolina Freedmen to the President

St Helena Island S.C. Mar 1st 1864

Sir Wee the undersigned. beleaveing wee are unfarely delt with, Are led to lay before you, these, our greaveiences first; then our petetion. And wee here beeg, though it may be long, You will beare kindly with; Reade & answere uss, And as now so, henceforth, our prayrs shall asscende to the Throan of God, for your future success on Earth. & Tryumph in Heaven.

For what wee have receaved from God, through you, wee will attempt to thank you, wee can only bow our selves, and with silent lips feel our utter inability to say one word, the semblence of thanks. Trusting this our Petetion in the hands of Allmighty God, and your kindness, wee now say, Let there be what success may in stor for you and your Armies, Wither our freedom is for ever or a day, wither as Slaves or Freemen, wee shall ever, carry you & your kindness to us in our hearts, may Heaven bless. you.

Our greaveincess

Mr Edward Philbrick. (A Northern Man) has bought up All our former Masters Lands under falls pretences;

To wit

He promis'd to buey in, at public sale, with our consent all the Lands on the following Plantations,

Mr Coffin's Place, Mr. Coffin's Cherrie Hill, Maulbuery Hill place. Big House place. Corner place. Dr Fuller's place, Pollawanney place, Mary Jinkins'es place. Hamelton Frip place, Morgan Island, & John Johntson's place, of Ladies Island.

Before bueying he promised to sell to us again any ammount of the Land at $1.00 one Dollar pr Acre wee wish'd to purchas, Said sail was to be made when ever the Government sold the balance of its Land to the People resideing thereon,

On the 18th day of last month sailes of Publick Lands began in Beaufort, & what doo wee see to day, on all the Plantations our Breathern are bucying thr Land. getting redy to plant ther cropps and build ther Houses, which they will owne for ever

Wee hav gon to Mr Philbrick & Ask'd him to sell us our Land, and get for an answere he will not sell us one foot, & if he does sell to any one he will charge $10.00 Ten Dollars pr Acre. Wee have work'd for Mr Philbrick the whole year faithfully, and hav received nothing comparatively, not enough to sustaine life if wee depended entirely uppon our wages, he has Stors here chargeing feerefull prices for every nessary of life, and at last the People have become discouraged, all most heart broken.

He will not sell us our Land neither pay us to work for him; And if wee wish to work for others where wee might make something, he turns us out of our Houses, he says wee shall not live-on his plantation unless wee work for him, If wee go to Gen[l] Saxton he tells us if Mr Phlbrick sees fit he will sell us the Land according to agreement If not then wee must go on Government Land where wee can buey as much as wee please, But, the Tax Commissioners say they cannot sell to us unless wee are living on the Plantations now selling, Wee go to the Sup[t] Gen[l] of the Island; Mr Tomlinson, he says work For Mr Phibrick for what ever wages he sees fit to pay if wee do not Mr Philbrick may drive us off the Land and wee shall not taks our Houes with us, He says, 'Mr Philbrick bought everything Houses Lands & all.

Why did Goverment sell all our Masters Land's to Mr Philbrick for so trifling a sume; we are all redy & willing of truth anxious to buey all our Masters Land, & every thing upon them; and pay far more than he did for them

Wee will not attempt to lay all our greaveinces before you as t'will take much to long we will only mention one cas which exceedes anything done in our Masters time Charl's Ware an agent of Mr Philbrick's turn'd the cloths of a Colard Girl over her head turned her over a Barrel, & whipd her with a Leathern Strap She had been confined but two days before & allthough the case was reported to Mr Tomlinson Sup[t]. Gen[l] the Agent still retains his place, Thiss is shamefull, wee blush [*to*] write or send it you but the truth must be told, But you may ask what wee would have done,

If possible wee Pray for either one of theese two things.

Petetion

1st Either let Mr Philbrick be compeeld to live up to his promises with us, and sell us as much Land as wee want for our owne Homes at a reasonabele price, giving us cleare deeds for the same.

2nd Otherwise wee pray Goverment to repurchas the Land of Mr Philbrick and then let us farm it giveing one half of all that is rais'd to the Goverment wee would much rather this and will furnish everything ourselves and will warrent there will be but few feet of Ground Idle. As Mr Philbrick has broken his part of the contract is Government bound to keep thers?

And wee will her mention, that many of us told Mr Philbrick not to buey the Land as wee wanted it our selves.

3rd And wee furthermore beeg that an Agent may be sent us, who will see not wrong; but right done us one who will deal justly by us, Wee doo not want a Master or owner Neither a driver with his Whip wee want a Friend

Trusting this may be lookd upon kindly beeging a immediate answer that wee may know what to doo Wee are with very great respect your most Humble & Obdt Srvt's

HLSr [*19 signatures*]

[*Endorsement*] Please answer to ~~care~~ of John S Smallwood Beaufort SC

The writer of this would meerley say in conclusion, that were the Grounds Farmed by the Cold people Government would make more in one Year than would pay for two plantations at $1.25 pr Acre. It does not require then an agent on every Plantation one man could attende at leas six or eight Very Respec[t] Submitted by

John S. Smallwood

John H. Major et al. to his Exelency Abraham Lincoln, 1 Mar. 1864, General Correspondence, ser. 99, SC, Records of or Relating to Direct Tax Commissions in the Southern States, RG 58 [Z-5]. The petitioners were all men, and all of them signed with an "X." Their names and the body of the petition are in the same handwriting, apparently that of Smallwood (not himself one of the petitioners). The names appear in a column headed "The Petetioners," and the marks in a column headed "There Marks." The Secretary of the Treasury instructed Austin Smith, a special agent who was on his way to the Sea Islands, to investigate the freedmen's complaints; for Smith's report, see doc. 47B, immediately below.

47B: Treasury Department Special Agent to the Secretary of the Treasury, Enclosing Statements by the Agent of a Northern Planter and by a Northern Plantation Manager

Beaufort [*S.C.*] May 15th 1864

Dear Sir, Just before leaving Washington, there was placed in my hands a copy of a Petition to the President of the United States signed by John H. Major & 18 others, Colored Freedmen, residents of St. Helena's Island S.C. complaining of abuses, with a request that I would examine into the matter.

For particulars of the charges, see petition on file in the Department.

I went to Coffin's Point plantation on St. Helena's Island on the 21st of April, that being the residence of Mr Soule the chief superintendant upon the plantations bought by Mr. Philbrick, to examine into the matter.

I took the statements in writing of Mr. Soule & Mr Gannet two of the superintendents, which, with certain exhibits, I herewith send to you. I also examined the books of the Tax Commissioners in regard to the sales of the lands, and took their verbal statements, and those of others in regard to the representations made by Mr. Philbrick at the time of the sale of the lands. I did not reduce to writing these statements, but from all the testimony & statements and exhibits, I deduce the following facts.

In March 1863, Mr. E. S. Philbrick, for himself & 13 others (whose names & residence are stated in the testimony) purchased 11 of the best plantations on St. Helena's Island, at a cost of a trifle over 97 cts an acre. The plantations containing 6030 acres, cost, 5860 dollars.

Mr. Philbrick had been here about a year before the tax sales took place, in the character of Superintendent, and as agent of some Boston society. He was sent out as the friend of the negro, an Abolitionist, & Philanthropist. In that character he had an opportunity to visit all the plantations, & was well prepared to make good selections.

Before & at the time of the sales he represented that he was buying for the benefit of the Freedmen.

This was fully believed by the Commissioners as well as by Gen. Saxton, Mr. French & others, warm & earnest friends of the negroes. Whether these representations actually prevented others from bidding it would be impossible to determine, but they were of a character to produce that effect. Under these representations he bid off 11 plantations, comprising some of the best lands, & most desirable locations on St. Helena's Island.

The Coffin Point & Cherry Hill plantations (the former the most beautiful I have seen on the Island) had been bid in by the Commissioners for the government on the 9th day of March 1863. Mr. P. neglected to bid on them for the reason that he understood that there would be some obstacle to getting possession, but afterwards, finding his information had been incorrect, he made an application to the Commissioners in writing, requesting them to open the bids on those plantations, & offer them for sale again. Genl Saxton, having entire confidence in Mr. Philbrick's professions & believing that his bids would inure to the benefit of the Colored freedmen, endorsed & approved his application, and the next day, a majority of the Commissioners (Dr. Brisbane dissenting as I understand) decided to waive their bids, in behalf of the United States and put them up for sale again, and they were bid off by Mr. Philbrick (who raised upon the bid of the Commissioners) & were struck off to him. The Coffin Point place of 1438 acres for

	#1150.00
& the Cherry Hill place of 300 acres for	380.00
making 1738 acres for	#1530.00

In his written request to the Commissioners, after stating the preliminaries, Mr. P. used this Language,

> "I do hereby respectfully request, *on behalf of the interests of the U.S. Government, of the laboring population now resident upon said estates, and my own wishes*, that the lands above mentioned be again offered at public sale at the earliest opportunity."

This letter is now in possession of the Commissioners.

The above are facts about which there is no dispute.

I saw the Gen[l] Superintendant Mr. Soule & two plantation Superintendants, Mr. Ware & Mr. Gannet, who all admit, that Mr. Philbrick promised to let the negroes have lands for homes, *when the war should close*, They think he is acting in good faith, and intends to fulfil his promises, Though they admit that the wages he pays are inadequate, And Mr. Soule promised to write to Mr. Philbrick (who is in Boston) & advise him to raise their wages. Their wages are not equal to the wages paid to white people at the North for the same character and amount of labor, while the groceries, and other necessaries furnished them, are much higher here than at the North, though they are furnished to them at fair prices, considerably less than the prices of the same articles at Beaufort.

By reference to the last exhibit it will appear, that the average wages paid to said Major & one of the other Complainants last year, was #0.474 per day (and this is a full average of the wages paid them generally) and there was more than 4 months during the year, that they were not employed, and received no pay. The wages offered this year are a little better, by the task, but Mr. P. has not as yet decided to give them the bacon & molasses which he gave last year. Yet, the wages offered this year are admitted to be less than the wages paid to white laborers at the North for the same amount & kind of labor, Whereas, the profitableness of the cotton crop, the hardships & exposure in raising it, & the high price of all necessary articles of food & clothing here, would seem to demand that wages should be higher than at the North. And the wages of white laborers is nearly double.

The use of a little land is furnished to each family, on which 10 bushels of corn per acre and other things in proportion can be raised. Mr. P. reserved to himself 2 1/2 bushels of corn to the acre, (although he did not take last year but 1 1/2) and the blade of the corn, which is used for wintering the stock, is also reserved. But the crop of corn & potatoes do very little more than pay for raising,

& they receive no other Compensation for the time employed in raising those crops. They also have some priveliges of raising fowles & eggs, and pigs, for their own use & for sale. How much these privileges are worth I am unable to state; with their cheap mode of living & dressing, they manage to support themselves and lay by a little something every year, but if they lived & dressed as Northern laborers do, their wages would not support & clothe them.

It is proper to state, to show the profitableness of the cotton crop here, that after deducting the costs & expenses of carrying on the 11 plantations & cultivating the same, including the expenses of schools &c. from the proceeds of the last years crop, there remained a net profit of about #70,000.

Schools are kept on the premises of Mr. Filbrick, for the Education of the colored children. Whether they are paid for by himself or by benevolent associations North, I do not know. I supposed, at the time of the examination that they were paid for by him & his associates.

There are about 900 blacks residing on these 11 plantations, of which 371 are adult working hands. There were raised of cotton (for Philbrick) 814 acres, of potatoes (belonging wholly to Negroes) 122 acres, of Corn (chiefly for Negroes) 763 acres.

2[d] As to the charge of cruel whipping,

Mr. Ware did whip a very immoral & bad girl in the manner charged, but not under the circumstances, nor with the severity stated. It was *3 or 4 weeks* after her confinement, instead of 2 days. It was contrary to Mr. P.s instructions, And in fact, corporeal punishment is not allowed. It is the only case of corporeal punishment which has occurred. It was very much regretted by the person who inflicted it, & I am satisfied it will not occur again.

I went to Coffin Point in company with Mr. Cooly, one of the Tax Commissioners, & Mr. Graves of Chicago, who kindly assisted me in making my investigations.

In the evening, at the request of Mr. Soule, & the plantation superintendents, also of Mr. Tomlinson, general superintendent of Schools, Major & his associates (the Complainants) came to see me, & we had a long conversation with 3 of them.

They understood Mr. P. to promise to let them have homesteads at $1. an acre, *when the Commissioners should sell the lands,* which were bid in by them for the government. Those lands were sold on St. Helena's Island last March, & as Mr. P. has refused to sell them lands unless they will pay him $10. an acre, they think he does not mean to fulfil his promise.

They say he tells them the lands are worth $10. an acre, and that he means to sell to the man that will pay the most. They say they cannot understand why the government should sell their houses to Mr. Philbrick. That the houses were always Called theirs by their masters, and that if Mr. Philbrick owns their houses, they must work for him for whatever wages he may see fit to pay, or he can turn them out of their houses, and they have no where else to go. They think the wages he offers are too small, and although they were to work for him upon the plantation, they had, up to the time I had the conversation with them, refused to receive any wages, because they would not, by receiving wages, place themselves in a condition to be Considered as having assented to the Contract. (I am not certain that this applies to the whole 19, but it applies to some of them.) I have understood since that they have consented to receive their wages.

I cannot but think that Mr. Philbrick & the eminent philanthropists whom he represents, mean to do right in the end, That they think they are paying fair wages, & mean, when the war is over, to furnish the negroes (who were raised upon these plantations, were left in possession when their masters fled, & continued in possession to the time of the sale) with homesteads at the price of $1.00 an acre. Yet I think it would be better if their hopes were no longer deferred.

In view of the large profits realized upon the investment, these gentlemen can well afford to grant homesteads to these people at a nominal price. Justice & equity demand that the freedmen should be provided with homes. They are all loyal citizens. We found them in possession of the lands & houses. They had made all the improvements, built all the houses, were the loyal portion of their masters families, had never received any pay, and should be deemed as having an equitable lien upon the lands of their masters for compensation for what they had done. If the law does not hold these men to the fulfilment of their promises, public opinion will.

If they should decline to do so, I hope the government will inquire into the validity of their titles, at least to the plantations known as Coffins Point, & Cherry Hill.

It is at least a matter of question, whether Filbricks title to those plantations is not defective. Having been bid off by the commissioners for the U.S. Government, did they not become "*functus officio?*" Was not the title then in the United States? And could the Tax commissioners waive or relinquish that title? Could they divest the United States of that title without readvertizing & selling in the manner required by the 11th Section of the Act?[1]

But I trust that the fulfilment of Mr. Filbricks promises will render all action in the premises, on the part of the Government, unnecessary. I am, most respectully Your Obt. Servant

HDS Austin Smith

[*Enclosure*] [*St. Helena Island, S.C.*] 21st day of April 1864
The Philbrick Case.

Richard Soule Jr.

Is the Gen[1] Agent of Mr. Philbrick. Mr. P. is in Brookline Mass.

Mr. P. bot. 11 Plantations on St. Helena Island. The slaves were residing on the plantations. There were 933 of them, but that includes 2 plantations that he hired last year making 13. There are probably about 900 on the plantations that he bought.

I was in Beaufort when the plantations were sold, and when he bought most of them, was there when the sale commenced, I am not aware that he made any representations at the time of the sale. The people were none of them present. I heard no conversations between him & the people before or at the time of the sale– After the sale I heard conversations between him and several persons that belonged to the plantations. The purport of what he said was that he would be willing to sell them land when the war was over, but did not think it best for them to have the land now. I never heard him state any price. He employed these people to work for him last summer, on the terms prescribed by Genl Saxton in Genl. Orders No. 12, for the Govt. Plantations[2] which is hereto annexed marked Exhibit A–, and in addition to that he allowed them bacon & Mellasses, viz. 2 lbs. of bacon & 2 qts of Molasses per month, for each acre cultivated by them, for 4 months, fr. May to August inclusive. Also he supported 5 schools, on the places that he bought.

The annexed statement, marked Exhibit B, shows, the amt. pd for labor, in the several districts, also the cost [here] of the Bacon & Molasses, distributed, in addition to the wages, And the amt. paid for supporting the schools last year, & the salaries of the teachers this year, which he is to pay–

Acres of cotton raised	814.
" " potatoes belonging wholly to Negroes–	122.
" " corn, belonging chiefly to Negroes–	763.

There were 371 adult working hands.

Mr. Philbrick only retained 1 1/2 bushels of corn to the acre. (The government would have been entitled to 4 bu. pr acre, but did not take but about 2 1/2)

The average crop of corn was about 10 bu. to the acre–

The hands employed by Mr. Filbrick never complained that they had not enough to eat, and in my opinion they had enough to eat, and laid up mo[ne]y besides.

They raised enough on the lands furnish[ed] them to support them much more comfortably than they were supported by their former masters. The Amt. allowed by their former masters was 8 bu. of corn pr head & 11 bu of potatoes, per annum.

There can be no doubt that they had enough to eat. Out of their wages they laid up a good deal of mo[ne]y, and have this spring bought 2 mules on the plantation that Major lives on – one at #231 and one at #196, Also a pair of oxen at #99, These were bought by 3 several families,

They had an opportunity to make a good deal also on Eggs & oysters, and pigs and fowls, so that in fact they actually purchased & paid for merchandise to the amount of #28,000, which is more than the whole amt. of their wages, and besides they had mo[ne]y to spare, to buy stock and land, They made a good deal of mo[ne]y on the sale of vegetables,

They worked by the task, and did much or little, as they pleased, They earned and were paid for the time actually worked, on an average 55 cents a day, and a portion of that time each day was generally employed on their own patches.

As I do not know who made the compl[t] to the President I cannot state any thing about them particularly. The family of Major lived upon a plantation of which William C. Gannett is the superintendent. These hands appear to be contented & satisfied to work for Mr. Philbrick & are to work for him this year, at much higher rates – Where we gave 25 cts last year, we give 40 cents this year. And in about the same proportion for all the work, but it is not settled yet whether he will give them the pork & molasses this year.

Mr. Philbrick represents a company of men composed of the following persons,

Edward S. Philbrick –	Brookline	Mass.
Ja[s] M. Barnard		"
Geo. B. Blake	Brookline	"
W[m] Endicott –		"
R C. Greenlief		"
Tho[s] Ho[w]e –	Brookline	"
W[m] D. Philbrick	"	"
Geo. M. Soule	"	"
J. H. Stephenson		"
Cha[s] A. Wh[ting]		"
Edward Whitney		"
Alfred Winson	Brookline	Mass
Henry Winson	Philadelphia	Pen
J. M. Forbes –	Milton	Mass –

The object of these men in making these purchases was to try the experiment of employing negroes at wages, to see if they would work as well as under their masters, and also to show which was the most economical, which would produce the greatest profit to the landowner – & the result has proved very satisfactory. I think it has proved that paid labor is more profitable to the Landowner than slave labor–

Mr. P. has promised to sell the negroes land when the war is over, and I believe it is his intention to furnish [homes] [then] to all who are worthy.

In regard to the prices charged to the laborers for goods, we commenced by charging 10 percent above the first cost & transportation, &c. we found that did not cover the expense, & then we added ten percent more, After that the government taxed us 5 percent upon the goods brought here, and we then added 5 percent more, making 25 percent above first cost. At the close of the year we found we had made a little less than 10 pr. c. on the amt. of goods sold, and have about #10,000 worth of goods on hand.

This enables us to sell flour now at #9. a barrel, while in Beaufort it is sold from 10 1/2 to 12 dollars a barrel. We sell them sugar at 18 cts a pound, while a similar quality of sugar is (I think) 25 cts in Beaufort, some sugar we sell as low as 16 cts.

We sell them other things in about the same proportion, compared with ordinary Beaufort prices.

Richard Soule Jr,

W[m] C. Gannett, says,

I have charge of 2 plantations belonging to Mr Filbrick on St. Helena, to wit, the 2 plantations that belonged to William Fripp, & I suppose the plantations on which the petitioners reside from the fact that Mr. Major lives there, & I had Charge of them last year. They worked at the same wages and fared the same as the hands on the other plantations. In regard to the fare, and wages, and general prosperity of those hands, I Can say the same that Mr. Soule has said above in regard to the hands generally. John H. Major did no work himself for Mr. Philbrick. His Children worked, as well as the average. Major's wife was sick & did not work.

They did not suffer for want of food. John H. Major worked at Hilton Head, as I understand for 20 or 25 dollars a month. He has bought a horse (since January I think) for which he paid 105 dollars, I understand has one or two watches, and he appears to have plenty of mo[ne]y–

No corporal punishment is allowed on any of the plantations, and none has ever occurred but in a single instance which was not authorized, That punishment was inflicted on a very bad and immoral girl, was much less severe than represented in the petition, and has never been, and will never be allowed to be repeated.

HDS W. C. Gannett

Austin Smith to Hon. S. P. Chase, 15 May 1864, enclosing statements of Richard Soule, Jr., and of W. C. Gannett, 21 Apr. 1864, S-97 1864, Letters Received by the Division, ser. 315, Division of Captured Property, Claims, & Land, RG 56 [X-72]. The "exhibits" cited by Smith and Soule are all in the file, as is a list of the names, acreage, and selling prices of the plantations purchased by Philbrick. In endorsements dated May 18, 1864, Dennis N. Cooley, who had been appointed to the South Carolina direct-tax commission in March, approved the findings and recommendations of Smith's report, as did General Rufus Saxton, military governor in the Department of the South. Cooley concurred "*especially*, in the recommendation that the Government inquire into the validity of Mr Philbrick's title." Not until January 1866 did Philbrick sell any of the estates he had purchased, and then only the two Fripp plantations were offered to the former slaves, evidently at $5 per acre. (Elizabeth Ware Pearson, ed., *Letters from Port Royal, 1862–1868* [1906; reprint ed., New York, 1969], pp. 315, 324–26.)

1 Section 11 of the Direct Tax Act of June 1862 provided, among other things, that the tax commissioners give sixty days' public notice before selling land that had been bid in for the United States. (*Statutes at Large*, vol. 12, p. 425.)

2 General Order No. 12, issued on December 20, 1862, by General Rufus Saxton, military governor in the Department of the South. It is printed above, as doc. 28.

48: Northern Businessman to a Massachusetts Congressman

Beaufort S.C. March 2[d] 1864

Dear Sir Having made arrangements to go into business here I desire my son to come out to assist me. Will you use your influence to procure a Pass for him and much oblige Yours truly

E. P. Hutchinson

My son's name is Ezra A. Hutchinson

P.S. owing to the conflicting instructions which have been issued to the Tax Commissioners, the negroes have been much confused and exceedingly dissatissatisfied and in some instances refuse to work and in one instance I heard of today they threatened to shoot the purchase[r] which so alarmed him tha[t] he dared not venture among them and was enquiring of the commissiones what his remedy might They thought a Military force would be detailed to secure justice to him if found unavoidable E. P. H.

ALS

E. P. Hutchinson to Hon. J. B. Alley, 2 Mar. 1864, General Correspondence, ser. 99, SC, Records of or Relating to Direct Tax Commissions in the Southern States, RG 58 [Z-22]. Endorsements.

49: Direct-Tax Commissioner for the State of South Carolina to the Secretary of the Treasury

Beaufort S.C. March 21, 1864.

Sir: The Rev. J. W. Parker, D.D. of Cambridge Mass., who is now here as an agent of the Baptist Home Mission Society of the United States, looking after the church property of that denomination in this District, informs me, that a gentleman named Williams, an Englishman by birth, and a former correspondent of the "*Liberator*" and who has hitherto been employed as a superintendent on the plantations on St Helena Island, has submitted a statistical document in relation to the disposition of the lands in this parish, within a few weeks, to a society in Boston, called the "Educational Commission," of which Dr. Parker is a member, and in whose hearing, the document was read. Mr. Williams further stated, that he had been favored with an audience by you, and had strong hopes, that "something would be done for the colored people." I once saw that statement above referred to, in the "Free South," but cannot now find it. It is not however based upon the records in our Office, as Mr. Williams has not examined them to my knowledge or to the knowledge of our clerk, and from my recollection of the statement, it is quite incorrect in facts, and his conclusions thereon, are of course, quite erroneous. The following are the statistics as taken by me from our records today:

Lands upon which taxes have been paid in the Parish of St. Helena S.C., and redeemed from tax sale	2469	Acres.
Lands reserved for Town,	599	"
" reserved for military or naval purposes*	13368	"
Educational Lands[1]	5090	"
Lands reserved for charitable purposes[2]	20430	"
" sold at tax sale in March, 1863.†	21342	"
" bid in to us and sold under the 11th section of Act approved June 7th 1862.[3]	18689	"

*These embrace principally the small islands washed by the ocean, have never been cultivated, and are valuable only for the timber which is needed by the Government.

†1900 acres are included in this, which constitute an island on the ocean which has never been cultivated and has but little

timber. The sands composing this island are continually changing and shifting under the influence of the tides, and the island was purchased by the only man living on it, a non-slaveholder who had taken the oath of allegiance and was the equitable owner of a portion of it. –

The assertion, that the best of the lands were, sold, and are to be sold at public auction, cannot be proved, because it is not so. Mr. Philbrick being an old superintendent and well acquainted with the lands, bought several good plantations, it is true, and Dr. Lawrence bought one that had very fine improvements upon it, but generally the lands selected for educational and charitable purposes, are the best, in quality and position, of the parish. As to the lands sold at auction this spring, they have been sold in parcels of 40, 80 or 160 acres, some of 200 acres, and but one parcel of 320 acres, and several colored soldiers have purchased at the auction sales.

I have noticed also in the "*Free South*" the following objections of Mr. French to our instructions of Sept. 16th 1863:[4]

> *Objections to the instructions of the President for the disposition and the sale of lands in South Carolina.*
>
> I. *Compelling* on the part of the freedmen a choice of location which will require nearly all of them to leave their former homes and settle among comparative strangers, a measure no less repugnant than injurious to them in the infancy of their freedom.
>
> II. *A moral discrimination* as to the parties purchasing is required, which it is believed will make the commissioners obnoxious to the people, and foster jealousies, and persecution against the preferred parties.
>
> III. The settlement of the freedmen *so exclusively by themselves*, as the instructions require, is not agreeable to them, nor do their friends believe it to be favorable to their elevation.
>
> IV. The instructions seem to provide that the persons employed in the army, navy, or marine corps must buy lands, if at all, for their families at the public sales, upon which they cannot attend, and if they could, they could not compete with other sagacious parties, whose means far exceed the ability of these poor, but well-deserving classes of men.

The *first* objection is not true in point of fact. Instead of "nearly all" only one half in any event, would vacate the old plantations on which they have resided, and quite a number of these have purchased at the auction sales of the lands. Of course those sold by the Government last spring, are now beyond its control, and not to be taken into account. Besides, the removal is in practice, but two or three miles and is a physical and moral as well as an intellectual benefit to the people. It secures a greater acquaintance with the world about them, and has a tendency to prevent inter-marraige among relatives.

As to the *second* objection it amounts to nothing in the way of producing the results spoken of. As to the phrase "preferring such as by their good conduct meritorious services or exemplary character, will be examples of moral propriety and industry to those of the same race," it was only designed to prevent notoriously bad men from settling among an industrious and well behaved community.

The *third* objection is not true in fact. All the plantations have been selected *alternately*, except five on Paris Island and two on Coosa Island, among which there are still three school farms, and the five on Paris Island were selected on account of their freedom from the danger of rebel raids.

As to the *fourth* objection: It would require a *much longer time* for persons employed in the Army Navy or Marine Corps, to select the lands which they desire to preempt, and establish their claim among conflicting claims, before the Commissioners, and the sutlers, traders, superintendents and others would be quite as sagacious (having superior knowledge of localities) in preëmpting as in purchasing at auction sales, and the three years time without interest under the 11th section of the act of Congress, gives the soldier a decided advantage over the civilian.[5]

In the moral constitution of Mr. French, there is an obliquity or an inaccurateness, (to say the least), which entirely unfits him for business. In saying this, I but reiterate the sentiments of nearly all the friends of freedom in this Department.

A great deal, I have reason to believe, has been said, about the danger of the population who cannot purchase lands for themselves, being thrown on the Government for support. There is no foundation for this fear. Labor is scarce and nearly twice as much is being paid to laborers for most kinds of labor, as was formerly paid by the Government.

There is here as well as elsewhere in all free communities, a mutual dependence of capital upon labor and labor upon capital. Horses, mules and farming implements from the North, are constantly arriving on private account, and are being put to proper use, to the mutual benefit of all concerned.

The amount of the proceeds of the sales of plantations thus far, since Feby 18th, 1864, is $73794 of which $62101 has been paid or secured to be paid by soldiers and sailors, white and black, claiming privilege under the 11th section of the act. About 110 families of freedmen have purchased homesteads on the selected lands at $1 25/100 an acre.[6] All the lands for sale at auction on Ladies and St Helena Islands, are sold, and we have under the 9th and 10th sections of the act of Congress,[7] leased those plantations on Port

Royal Island not sold, for the current year, subject to the sale, to responsible persons, some to freedmen and some to white men, as we could find opportunity, and have made rules and regulations in respect to the employment of the persons residing thereon, which we will soon submit to your approval. We propose that the residents be allowed to plant what they please in corn and potatoes, and that the lessees furnish seed, mules, hoes, ploughs, and other implements and personal care, attention and protection, and share equally the cotton crop with the laborers. With this the people are well satisfied, as with the animals and ploughs of which there was till lately a great scarcity, they can accomplish much more than with the hoe alone. All able-bodied black men are drafted into the army, or are in the Quartermaster's Department, and the laborers are women, old men and small boys.

This letter is of course unofficial, but under the existing state of facts, and knowing the deep interest you feel in the welfare of the freedmen, and how desirous you are of knowing the truth in respect to them, I deemed it proper, though not requested, to write you this private letter. Very truly, Your friend.

HLS W. E. Wording

W. E. Wording to Hon. S. P. Chase, 21 Mar. 1864, Miscellaneous Letters Received: K Series, ser. 103, RG 56 [X-252]. The objections by the Reverend Mansfield French are in the form of a newspaper clipping (in the same file) that was originally attached to the handwritten letter. Passages in the clipping that precede and follow French's statement are omitted.

1 Land forfeited to the government that had been reserved "for school purposes"; it was to be leased out and the proceeds applied to the education of black and poor white children. (See above, doc. 39n.)

2 Land forfeited to the government that had been reserved for "charitable" purposes and was subsequently to be subdivided into twenty-acre plots and sold to black heads of families. (See above, doc. 39n.)

3 Section 11 of the Direct Tax Act authorized the direct-tax commissioners, at the direction of the President, to sell at public auction land that had been forfeited to the government, in plots not to exceed 320 acres to any single purchaser. (For a summary of the act, see above, doc. 27n.)

4 The instructions are summarized above, in doc. 39n.

5 Section 11 of the Direct Tax Act allowed Union soldiers and sailors to buy land at auction by paying one-quarter of the purchase price at the time of sale and the balance within three years; other purchasers were to pay the full amount at the time of sale. President Lincoln's instructions of September 16, 1863, simply reiterated those provisions. (*Statutes at Large*, vol. 12, p. 425; Abraham Lincoln, *Collected Works*, ed. Roy P. Basler, Marion D. Pratt, and Lloyd A. Dunlap, 9 vols. [New Brunswick, N.J., 1953–55], vol. 6, pp. 454–55.)

6 The "selected lands" were those that had been reserved for "charitable" purposes.
7 Sections 9 and 10 of the Direct Tax Act authorized the direct-tax commissioners to lease to loyal persons land forfeited to the government that had not been sold at auction. (*Statutes at Large*, vol. 12, pp. 424–25.)

50: Army Surgeon to a Treasury Department Special Agent at Beaufort, South Carolina

Beaufort S.C. April 28th 1864

Dear Sir Charles Gelston a poor old lame colored man: in the course of the last four or five months; has collected some three or four thousand pounds of rags.

A fortnight or three weeks ago I think, he requested me to help him to make sale of them urging that he was in great want of means: and that if I would only be so kind as to help him to sell them, he would be at once relieved of his embarrassment. I accordingly, in the early part of April sold his rags to Mr. Newbould as Charles' Agent in the transaction. But in a few days afterward; I met Mr. Brown, the Treasury Agent, who said to me, "Did you sell those rags to Mr. Newbould? yes sir I did as Charles' agent" He then added "Dont you know that you did very wrong Sir, that you had no right to have anything to do with the rags, that they are Government property?" I answered, I did not sir. He said, well sir, "I could have you at once dismissed from the service sir; and Mr. Newbould sent out of the Department." I explained to Mr. Brown, that Charles had gathered these rags from the streets, and garbage hauled out and thrown away in the woods by the scavengers; where the Regiments or individual soldiers had thrown away their old clothes: and that in one instance he had supplied fifty old sacks at 15 cts each in which to pack the rags. And that I had seen Charles bring in his little lots of dirty rags from the streets and from the woods; and wash, and dry, and pack away perhaps 50 lbs. per day. But Mr. Brown says "no difference, he cant have them. I can only allow him 25/c [25 *percent*] for picking the rags"

Now Charles has to pay rent for barn and house in which to keep his rags; and 25/c will not pay his rent he says if Mr. Brown dont soon come to his help.

Mr. Augustus White a very respectable young man here, tells me that he heard one of Mr. Brown's clerks tell Charles when he was commencing to pick rags, that he might have all the rags he could gather, and dispose of them as his own, or words to that effect.

I submit the above for your consideration in the hope that

justice will be done to the poor laborer, as well as to the Government Very respectfully Your obdt. Servt

ALS W. J. Randolph

A.A. Surgeon W. J. Randolph to Hon. Austin Smith, 28 Apr. 1864, enclosed in Austin Smith to Hon. S. P. Chase, 14 May 1864, S-98 1864, Letters Received by the Division, ser. 315, Division of Captured Property, Claims, & Land, RG 56 [X-71]. In his covering letter, the special agent, Austin Smith, reported that Albert G. Browne, supervising agent of the Treasury Department's 4th Special Agency, had seized the rags from Newbould and was holding them as abandoned property. Smith put to Secretary of the Treasury Salmon P. Chase the following question: "are rags, gathered up from the ditches & hedges, where they have been thrown away as useless & valueless, to be deemed 'Abandoned Property'?" Smith ventured his own opinion that they were not, that the rags "only became *property*, when they acquired a *value* by being gathered & washed, & prepared for market." "This is a small matter," Smith admitted, "but it is one which may be distorted. . . . I should be sorry to have the government represented as competing with the negroes in the rag picking business." In a draft reply dated June 13 (in the same file), Chase ruled that "[o]ld rags scattered about, or thrown away, are not abandoned property," and, accordingly, "this Department has no jurisdiction in this matter." However, Chase's letter was apparently never sent, and he resigned his office in late June, leaving his subordinates uninformed of any decision. Four months later, when the question came to the attention of Chase's successor, William P. Fessenden, he directed Browne to turn the rags over to either Gelston or Newbould, "according to evidence of ownership." (W. P. Fessenden to Albert G. Browne, Esq., 19 Oct. 1864, vol. 8, pp. 40–41, Letters Sent Relating to Restricted Commercial Intercourse & Captured & Abandoned Property: BE Series, ser. 14, RG 56 [X-71].)

51: Affidavit of a South Carolina Freedman

State of South Carolina District of Beaufort Parish of St. Helena
28th day of May A. D. 1864

William Mitchell being duly sworn doth depose and say, that he was a slave belonging to the estate of Mrs Eustiss called "Motley" on the main land & was raised there– That after the war broke out, and in the month of May 1862 he came to Beaufort and after staying there about two weeks, Genl. Stevens took him for a guide on an expedition to Pocotaligo– That he went with Genl. Stevens on said expedition, and that Genl. Stevens told him he should get a mule, and that whatever he got should be his deponent's property. He got a mule on the "main" and brought it over, from the estate of Daniel Hayward a rebel. With the mule and a wagon he made up with the help of others he brought over his mother and another slave, belonging to the Eustiss estate. That he had the mule on the Eustiss Estate on Ladies Island till last of July 1862 when Capt Hooper brought him over here in Beaufort to work in the Quarter Masters Department, and he left the mule on the Eustiss plantation – Genl. Stevens always called the mule the property of this deponent, and it was generally understood & known to be such. That the said mule as he believes ought not to be considered as captured or abandoned property, as Genl. Stevens expressly awarded the same to him as a reward for his services. – that said mule is now in possession Harry McMillan, and he claim said mule by virtue of some sale. But deponent insists that the said mule is the fruit of his own toil and services, and that he ought to have the free and full possession, control and ownership of him

his
HDSr William X Mitchell
mark

Affidavit of William Mitchell, 28 May 1864, Correspondence Received by Supervising Special Agent Browne, 5th Agency, RG 366 [Q-185]. Sworn before a justice of the peace.

52: South Carolina Black Minister to the Commander of the Department of the South

Mitchelville S.C. August 12 1864

Dear Sir a bought (8) this evening I was Call a pon by a Man Who Stated that thair was three men in his house trubling his wife on the Pretence of hunting Recrutes which he Ses that he have paper indors by You on my a Rival at the house i Saw the 3 men who had commited to Rape on the Person of his wife there are as i Suppose to be officers of the 25 Ohio Reg & was under the influent of Licor thay also took thair Sholder Straps of there Coat & Pin it on the inside i have 4 or five witness if Requierd: We have been trubled very often by these officers & Sailers & i think a stop aught to Put to it Gen I Have the Honer to Remain your obediant Servant

Revd Abram Mercherson

ferther thay Say that thay are Recruteing colored men for Solders & thay had with them 3 Bottle of Licor of Sum Kind & thay gave Adam Bowin & Several others Sum of it i genl Several of the 2nd US Batery men col here & thay Stand Redy to assist me in Keeping

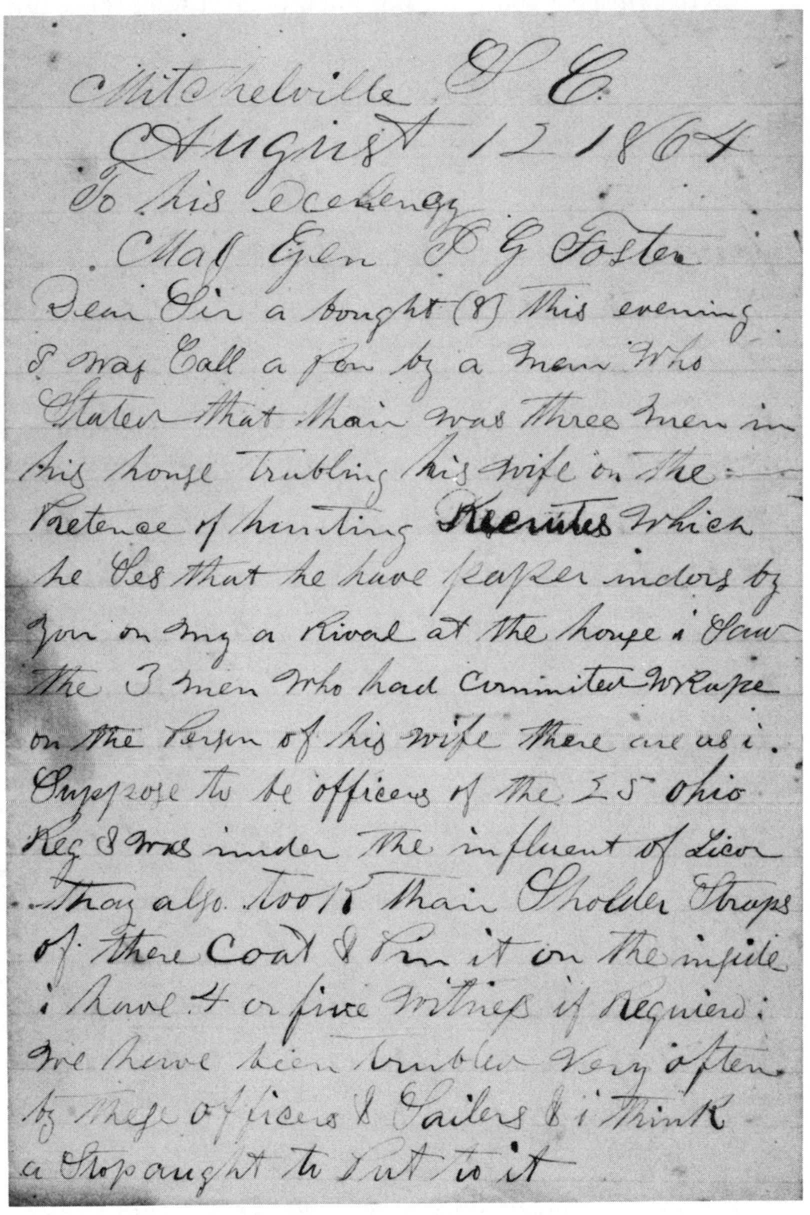

Mitchelville S C
August 12 1864
To his Excelency
Maj Gen J G Foster
Dear Sir a bought (8) this evening
I was Call a Pon by a Man Who
Stated that thair was three men in
his house trubling his wife on the
Pretence of hunting Recruites Which
he Ses that he have paper indors by
you on my a Rival at the house i Saw
the 3 men Who had Committed Wrape
on the Person of his wife there are as i
Suppose to be officers of the 25 ohio
Reg & was under the influent of Licor
thay also took thair Sholder Straps
of there Coat & Pin it on the inside
i have 4 or five Witness if Requierd:
we have been trubled very often
by these officers & Sailers & i think
a Stop aught to Put to it

Document 52

order in the Village if you will grant Promission i Dont think that eny officers or Saler aught to have these Night Pass to come over to the Villag for thay will not Behave them Selves as men these col Soildier over here gen are faithfull in the Discharge of there Duty Sum of them i have none ever Since i arive on the island Your obd. Servent Rev[d] A Mercherson

ALS

Revd. Abram Mercherson to his exelency Maj. Gen. J. G. Foster, 12 Aug. 1864, M-268 1864, Letters Received, ser. 4109, Dept. of the South, RG 393 Pt. 1 [C-1327]. By an endorsement of the same date, the department commander referred Mercherson's letter to the provost marshal general of the department: "The rule is for no men to be allowed to visit Mitchelville at night. Why is not this carried out? and who gives passes for this purpose." No response has been found in the records of the Department of the South. The authority of Abram Mercherson over the freedpeople in Mitchelville may have been officially sanctioned. By October 1864, if not earlier, he was a magistrate; on the fourth of that month, the department's provost marshal general ordered that the guard of black soldiers stationed at Mitchelville be directed "to arrest persons whom *Father Murchison* (Magistrate) may designate for any riotous or disorderly conduct." (Lt. Col. James F. Hall to Col. M. S. Littlefield, 4 Oct. 1864, vol. 209/475 DS, p. 62, Letters Sent by the Provost Marshal General, ser. 4270, Dept. of the South, RG 393 Pt. 1 [C-1327].)

53: Acting General Superintendent of Contrabands in the South Carolina Sea Islands to the Provost Marshal General of the Department of the South

Contraband Office Beaufort S.C. August 25 '64

Colonel: In accordance with a request made by you at this office some days since concerning measures to be instituted to lessen the number of idle & dissolute persons hanging about the central Posts of the Department & traveling to & from between them, desiring my opinion thoughtfully made up as to what measures would be best, I write this note, at a somewhat late day on account of sickness. I write with some delicacy withal inasmuch as it would seem to come from an office which would give the weight of an extended experience touching the matter, whereas the person who has acquired the experience & has manifested a well-tried ability withal is absent on furlough home. However, having had considerable experience in dealing with the people & having thought much of what their best interests demand I will write what I think.

Had I the control of the negroes the first thing I would endeavor to do, & the thing I think of most importance to be done, is to Keep all the people possible on the farms or plantations at *honest steady* labor. As one great means to this end, I would make it as difficult as possible for them to get to the centres of population. – Young women particularly flock back & forth by scores to Hilton Head, to Beaufort, to the country simply to while away their time, or constantly to seek some new excitement, or what is worse to live by lasciviousness. This class of persons is as great a curse to the soldier as to themselves. All persons in town or at posts should be peremptorily sent to the country if they have not *steady* employment. There are numbers who would wash or hire themselves out just enough to answer the order, but that should not suffice. This getting a precarious livelihood by doing a little at this thing, & a little at that is the very curse of the people. So far as possible they should be compelled to *steady labor*. Hence I would allow no peddling around camps whatsoever. Fishing I would discourage as much as possible unless a man made a livelihood of it. All rationing I would stop utterly, & introduce the poor house system, feeding none on any pretense who would not go to the place provided for all paupers to live. This wo'd cut off rations by 3/4 their present amount. Then to be fed by the public would soon come to be a disgrace as it should be. All persons out of the poor house & running from place to place to beg a living I would treat as vagabonds, & also all persons, whether in town or on plantations, white or black, who lived without occupation should either go to the poor house or be put in a place where they *must work* – a work house or chain gang, & if women where they could wash iron & scrub for the benefit of the public. Under a military order those at present charged with the care of negroes would cheerfully labor to carry out such suggestions, and after the system was well instituted their labors would be made less by it – Some one must take care of the poor but the diminution in expense of rations would well nigh pay for it & I doubt if a new officer would be needed. At any rate there is not the least doubt in my mind that a military order should be made *stringent* to take care of the floating Negro population, nor that it sho'd be made very much more difficult to get into centers of population by greatl restricting passes. Very Respectfully

ALS A. S. Hitchcock

[*Endorsement*] [*Hilton Head, S.C. August 29, 1864*] Respectfully forwarded

This is certainly a well considered and sensible document –

As regards the use of boats, I think the recommendation of Mr. Hitchcock is evidence that no injury or injustice will be done to the

Negroes, by taking them away, and in a military point of view, I think by them having them, it gives opportunity for desertion and communication with the enemy, and I recommend that no private boats be allowed in the Department except on Special permits from Dept Head Quarters. Genl orders N° 122[1] if faithfully carried out will meet the other suggestions of Mr Hitchcock James F. Hall Lt Col & PMG

[*Endorsement*] [*Hilton Head, S.C.*] The within is approved– A circu= letter or an order should be drawn up to promulgate the requisite rules. J. G. Foster MGC Aug 30. 64

A. S. Hitchcock to Col. Hall, 25 Aug. 1864, H-371 1864, Letters Received, ser. 4109, Dept. of the South, RG 393 Pt. 1 [C-1325]. On September 6, General Foster issued an order incorporating many of the recommendations of Hitchcock and Hall; it is printed immediately below, as doc. 54.

1 In General Order 122, issued on August 22, 1864, General John G. Foster, commander of the Department of the South, had complained that "[t]he number of idle persons, of both sexes, found loitering around the Camps and Posts of the Districts of Beaufort and Hilton Head is subversive of good order and military discipline, and is a fruitful source of vice and disease." Accordingly, he had ordered district provost marshals to "arrest all such persons, either white or black" and put them to work at such labor as district commanders might direct. Black people arrested under the order were to be reported to the superintendent of contrabands in the department and held "subject to his order." (General Orders No. 122, Head Quarters, Department of the South, 22 Aug. 1864, vol. 31 DS, p. 151, General Orders, ser. 4124, Dept. of the South, RG 393 Pt. 1 [C-1325].)

54: Order by the Commander of the Department of the South

Hilton Head, S.C., Sept. 6, 1864

PRINTED

GENERAL ORDERS NO 130. It having been reported to these Headquarters, that quite a number of small boats and dug-outs, are now in the hands of, and used by, both white persons and negroes in this Department; therefore, in order to carry out more fully the provisions of General Orders 122 current series from these Headquarters,[1] and to prevent the possibility of said boats and dug-outs from being used, for the purpose of carrying deserters or smuggling goods to the enemy, it is hereby ordered:

I. That all small boats, of whatever description, now in the hands of any person in this Department, not used for military purposes by the Provost Marshal of any Post or District, shall be immediately taken charge of and guarded in a secure place by the Provost Marshal of the District or Post in which the boats are found.

II. All sailing boats, such as are now used between Hilton Head or Beaufort, shall be registered at the office of the Provost Marshal of each District, or Post where said sail boats ply. These boats must also have the regular permit to trade between these points; said permit must contain the names of the crew, and the purpose for which such boat is used. All boats of this description that have not been properly registered according to the provisions of this section of the order, within ten days after the date of the same, shall be immediately seized and confiscated to the US. Government.

III. The practice of allowing negro women to wander about from one plantation to another, and from one Post or District to another, on Government transports, for no other purpose than to while away their time, or visit their husbands serving in the ranks of the Army, is not only objectionable in every point of view, both to the soldiers and to themselves, but is generally subversive of moral restraint, and must be discontinued at once. All negro women, in future found wandering in this manner, will be immediately arrested, and compelled to work at some steady employment on the Plantations. By Command of Major-General. J. G. Foster.

HD

General Orders No. 130, Head Quarters, Department of the South, 6 Sept. 1864, vol. 31 DS, pp. 164–65, General Orders, ser. 4124, Dept. of the South, RG 393 Pt. 1 [C-1334].

1 For a summary of General Order 122, see above, doc. 53n.

55: Plantation Superintendent on St. Helena Island, South Carolina, to the Military Governor in the Department of the South

St Helena Island S.C. September 12th 1864

Sir, Agreeably to your request I have to inform you that the work of seizing and destroying the boats belonging to owners of plantations, & people on these Islands, was commenced this morning, and is rapidly progressing

An order from Maj. Gen Foster requires "that all boats" be

immediately taken charge of, and guarded in a secure place," but Mr. Holden, who is in charge of Mr Well's plantations near Eddings Point, on St. Helena, says the men sent to execute this order, carry away some, and destroy more, and others say the same course is taken on other places

If the object is to detain, temporarily, the boats, and then allow their return, the loss and damage might probably be borne, but their destruction or removal will greatly distress many hundreds of poor men and families, whose dependance for food is chiefly fish, oysters, &c, and great numbers thus live who are unfit for the heavy labor of cultivating the land

The extensive failure of the provision crops this season will make boats more necessary than they would otherways be, and their destruction will make it necessary to ration many hundreds & perhaps thousands of people, or they will have to suffer

The larger boats should be regarded as a military necessity as they are the principal means of carrying the quanities of produce, vegtables &c, required by the Army, Navy and people living at Hilton Head, Beaufort, &c, as well as carrying supplies to the plantations, many of which are accessible only by water, and many of the boats thus used are worth considerable sums of money, and if destroyed cannot be replaced, as neither materials nor labor can be obtained.

At the present time most of the boats on plantations are used for cu[tt]ing marsh grass for animals, and for manure for cotton for the coming year.

I enclose herewith a copy of the order as published in the Palmetto Herald, and beg most earnestly to protest against the destruction of boats under cover of it, and hope no effort will be spared to secure its revocation, or at least to have all boats preserved, and speedily returned to their owners I am, sir, most respectfully Your most obedient servant

(signed) Theodore Holt,

P.S. Since the above was written I learn that a more recent order allows some boats to be registered, but the small boats of the poor people should be carefully preserved and returned as soon as possible, if any necessity exists for there seizure. I am Respectfully &c, &c, &c, (signed) T. Holt,

HLcSr

Theodore Holt to Brig. Gen'l. R. Saxton, 12 Sept. 1864, Letters Received, ser. 4109, Dept. of the South, RG 393 Pt. 1 [C-1334]. The newspaper copy of the order referred to by Holt – General Order 130, issued by General John G. Foster, commander of the Department of the South – is not in the file;

another copy is printed immediately above, as doc. 54. Contrary to the impression conveyed by Holt, General Order 130 itself, and not a subsequent directive, permitted the owners of some boats to retain them by registering them with a provost marshal. General Rufus Saxton, the military governor, forwarded Holt's letter to General Foster, noting in an endorsement that "thousands of these poor people live by fishing, and taking away their boats, takes away their living." Declaring himself "fully satisfied that no possible harm can result from allowing the negroes to keep their boats," Saxton charged that "some person whose officiousness is only equalled by his want of knowledge of the facts has greatly exaggerated and missrepresented . . . the danger of allowing the negroes to retain their boats." Saxton urged Foster to "modofy his [order] so as not to deprive the S.C. people of their Chief means of support." In an endorsement dated September 20, 1864, Foster reiterated his determination to establish "order and system" in the "retention of boats by the blacks." "If the Sup^{ts} [of plantations] will certify that the boats are necessary," Foster suggested, "they can have them by simply registering them." But some superintendents themselves reported "that the wholesale use of the boats by the negroes is an incenitive to idleness, and tends to a precarious living rather than those habits of steady industry which I would like to see established. Moreover," Foster concluded, "I have evidence that these boats in the hands of free blacks employed by rascally whites at Beaufort, have been engaged in smuggling."

56: Permit from the Provost Marshal of Hilton Head District

Hilton Head S.C. Oct 11th 186[4]

This is to certify that *Commodore Perry*, *Mark Hagany* and March *Hayne* (colored men) having at their own expense constructed a foot bridge from Mitchelville to Hilton Head are allowed to collect fare from all persons crossing the same except Soldiers on duty at the following rates until further orders.

Three tickets five cents– Ten tickets fifteen cents Twenty tickets Twenty five cents. Each ticket good for one crossing. Any person refusing to pay toll at the above rates will be liable to arrest.

HDcS Joseph T Pratt

Permit from Capt. Joseph T. Pratt, 11 Oct. 1864, vol. 209/475 1/2 DS, p. 1, Letters Sent by the Provost Marshal, ser. 1398, Dist. of Hilton Head, Provost Marshal Field Organizations, RG 393 Pt. 4 [C-1636]. The same day, Captain Pratt authorized Abram Murchison, a black justice of the peace at Mitchelville, "to open a Subscription Book for the purpose of raising money to defray the expenses of constructing the foot bridge." Murchison was to "take note of all money subscribed and present the same at [Pratt's] Office twice each week." Once $420 was raised, "the bridge will be paid for in presence of

G. Pillsbury Supt of Contrabands and the travel on said bridge shall then be free to the Public without cost." (Permit from Capt. Joseph T. Pratt, 11 Oct. 1864, vol. 209/475 1/2 DS, p. 2, Letters Sent by the Provost Marshal, ser. 1398, Dist. of Hilton Head, Provost Marshal Field Organizations, RG 393 Pt. 4 [C-1636].)

57: Military Governor in the Department of the South to the Secretary of War

Beaufort South Carolina December 30th 1864

Sir: I have the honor to report my doings for the current year, under the special instructions of June 16th 1862. from the War Department.[1]

The lands in the possession of our forces having been sold by auction under the direction of the Direct Tax Commissioners, have passed into the hands of private persons, or are under the control of the United States Direct Tax Commissioners. My jurisdiction and responsibility concerning them having ceased, I have no agricultural operations to report.

My official action under those instructions has been limited to the establishment and enforcement, as far as it was in my power, of regulations for the sanitary condition and police of the Department, and for the protection of the freedmen in their industry and its products. I have also established civil courts of justice, boards of referees, and Military Commissions, for the settlement of all matters at issue between residents of this Department not in the military service. Many of the freedmen had by industry and thrift acquired considerable property. To provide for the contingency of their dying without providing for its disposition, I appointed a Board of Trustees in each General Superintendency, to take charge of such property, and administer it for the benefit of the legal heirs. The details of their organization are stated in Circular N° 3 herewith appended.

In order to protect the freedmen against oppression or fraudulent treatment by employers who might be disposed to take advantage of their ignorance of affairs and comparative helplessness, as well as for a general measure of security and just dealing between employers and employed, I directed that all persons employing the freedmen in agriculture should make written contracts with them, signed by both parties and witnessed by the Superintendents, stating clearly and precisely the terms and conditions. The contracts were subject to my approval. These regulations were published February 10th 1864. in Circular N° 3 hereunto appended.

To protect the Freedmen from being defrauded by sharpers, ever ready to prey upon their simplicity, and chiefly to induce in them habits of carefulness and prudence, I established August 27th 1864, the "South Carolina Savings Bank," at Beaufort. All sums deposited in this Bank are to be invested in interest bearing bonds of the United States. There have been deposited in this Bank since its establishment sums amounting in the agregate to about $65.000 by depositors. The establishment of the Bank was announced in Circular N° 5, appended herewith.

In consequence of authentic reports that speculators were buying cotton of the negroes in advance of the harvest, at prices much below the probable value of the crop, I issued August 30th 1864. Circular N° 6, declaring such contracts as not binding upon the people, and giving them a lien upon the crops upon which they had labored. It was ordered that no cotton should be shipped from the Department until satisfactory evidence had been given that all just claims for labor had been settled, and a permit thereupon issued from these Headquarters. Purchasers of cotton from the negroes were required to obtain a certificate from the Superintendent that the sale was fairly made, and with a due regard to the probable market value of the cotton. Violations of these regulations subjected the offenders to the penalties prescribed in Circular N° 6, appended.

It is my wish in this report to call your attention to the economical results of the year in connexion with a general resumê of the operations of the Department, and to a brief review of my administration. –

. . . .

The number of negroes under my superintendence [*in 1863*] was about 15,000. Of these 9,000 were engaged in productive or compensated labor as soldiers, agricultural laborers, mechanics, employees in the Quartermaster's Department, house and officer's servants; and others engaged in various handicrafts. Those who required support from the Government were lately arrived refugees and persons who by reason of age or bodily infirmity were unable to earn their subsistence, and had no relatives or friends present to depend upon.

The increasing industry and thrift of the Freedmen is illustrated by the decreasing amount of Government expenditure for their support. The whole expense on that account for 1863. was $41,544. But while the monthly average was $3,462. the expenditure in December was less than $1,000.

The operations conducted under my supervision, and those carried on by white purchasers of lands, have proved only the availability of the negroes as an agricultural peasantry, that the rich staple of the

Sea Islands can be successfully cultivated by free labor moderately compensated. They have also proved that the lash is a gratuitous abomination. But the prudence, forethought, industry, and ability to calculate results necessary for an independent owner and cultivator has so far been proved, that those qualities may be safely assumed as elements in all reasoning upon the problem, *What to do with the negro?*

As an illustration of the general capacity of the Freedmen, a few plantations were purchased by the negroes, and a few leased by them of the Government by companies, usually the late slaves on the plantations hired. They all managed their respective lands on their own account, and have all shown an industry, sagacity and prudence, that will not compare unfavorably in its results with white men in similar circumstances.

I was early convinced from general considerations, and by personal experience and observation in the Department, that to lay a sure basis for the substantial freedom and permanent improvement of the negroes, that they should be owners of the land they cultivate. In view of their past wrongs, present condition, and the circumstances in which they came under the special guardianship of the Government, it seemed to be the dictate of simple justice that they have the highest right to a soil they have cultivated so long under the cruelest compulsion, robbed of every personal right, and without any domestic or social relations which they could protect. As a mere question of wages withheld and accumulated for generations, they would seem to have paid for it many times over, to have established a claim to it that must be held valid under any code of natural or civil law, for when our forces came, we found them in possession. With these convictions I had the honor to suggest to you in communications of December 27th 1862. and January 6th 1863. the justice and importance of putting them in possession of a suitable portion of the confiscated lands in the Department.[2] In September. 1863. the President issued instructions to the Tax Commissioners, pursuant to an Act of Congress, to sell by auction to the highest bidder all the unreserved lands, in lots not exceeding 320 acres, reserving a limited quantity to be offered at private sale for $1.25 per acre, to negro families according to the number of persons in the family, but no family to have more than 20 acres. I issued a Circular inviting the Freedmen to, and suggesting a method by which they might avail themselves of the opportunity to purchase. This Circular marked "A" is herewith appended.

It was soon evident that by this plan less than one-half of the negroes could receive allotments of two acres each, while the great bulk of the lands would come into the hands of speculators, persons who had no interests in common with the negro, except the profit to be derived from their labor on the lowest possible terms. To put the lands at auction in large lots, was virtually to place them beyond the reach of the Freedmen. In a free competition of their weakness, poverty, and ignorance of affairs, with the practiced shrewdness and ample means of persons eager to grasp the prizes offered here to speculation, their chances could be stated only by very small fractions or minus quantities.

The provisions of the Act of Congress are supposed to have been suggested by the Chairman of the Tax Commissioners. In my judgement he has made a great mistake. The result of his plan must be to fix the people for a long time in the condition of a peasantry only a little higher than chattelism, and that too when so many of them had proved their fitness to be owners of the soil, and some their competence to manage large estates. These considerations were presented to the Treasury Department, and on December 30. 1863. new instructions were issued to the Tax Commissioners by the President,[3] giving limited pre-emption rights, at the rate of $1.25 per acre, to all loyal persons of twenty-one years of age, then residing upon, or who at any time since the occupation by the United States forces, had for six months resided upon, or been engaged in cultivating any lands in the district. Additional rights of pre-emption were given to soldiers, sailors or marines, in the service of the United States. These instructions seemed to me eminently wise and just, and their universal application to the whole of the southern country would have solved the whole problem of its future, and inaugrated such a measure of prosperity as the world has never seen.

I communicated these instructions to the people in a Circular of January 10th 1864. marked "B," and herewith appended, urging them to select their lots and file their claims with the Tax Commissioners, without delay.[4] They acted promptly and joyfully, in accordance with my suggestions, and in an incredibly short time claims of pre-emption for nearly all the lands in the district were presented to the Tax Commissioners, and the payment required tendered.

The majority of the Commissioners, Hon A. D. Smith dissenting, refused to allow the claims or accept the money tendered, or in any way to recognize the instructions. On the contrary, they immediately forwarded such representations to Washington that soon after, the last instructions were suspended by the Secretary of the Treasury. I am not aware that they have ever been revoked. The land sales proceeded according to the original instructions, and the homes of these people were sold over their heads, at prices beyond their limited means.

The Commissioners refused to notify the intended purchasers of the conflicting claims which might arise, from the pre-emptions made in good faith. While the instructions were in force, many of the Freedmen had not only staked out their lots and filed their claims, but had begun their preparations for putting in crops. The action of the Commissioners proved a sad blow to their hopes, and the disappointment and grief of all were in proportion to their previous exultation in the certain hope of soon becoming independent proprietors, free men upon their own free soil; for their attachment and love of the soil is one of the marked traits in the negro character. No violence however was committed, nor to be reasonably apprehended, although the Commissioners thought it necessary to call upon the Major General Commanding for military protection.[5] An appeal to force to settle conflicting claims between themselves and the purchasers need not have been feared.

Besides the confusion of conflicting titles occasioned by these sales, not the least noticeable result is the uncertainty in the minds of the Freedmen, induced by previous occurrences and increased by these proceedings, as to our ultimate purposes toward them. In connexion with this subject may I be permitted to refer to the proceedings of the "United States Commission for the Relief of the National Freedman." This is an organization constituted by delegates from the various Freedmen's Relief Associations of the North, whose main object is to "secure such legislation by Congress, and such co-operation on the part of the Government, as will give the greatest efficiency to the efforts made for the relief and elevation of the Freedmen." The first meeting of the Commission was held in Washington in February last. It was then resolved to address the President "on the expression of their earnest desire that means be adopted to give to the slaves made free by the power of the Government, a legal and just possession of adequate land for their residence and support, as rapidly and as early as the responsibilities of the Government shall render possible." These land holders may be needed in the future to defend the soil they own as well as tax-payers and producers.

. . . .

The whole number of colored troops recruited in the Department, both by myself and others, falls much short of the number contemplated in your instructions.[6] This failure is owing to several causes. When first invited to enlist, the negroes had hardly learned to realize the promised change in their condition, to comprehend as a possibility that they had been so suddenly lifted out of the utter degradation of chattelism, to the dignity of the right of bearing arms. They were far from being sure of their freedom. Several occurrences had led them to doubt our good faith, who professed to come as their deliverers. They were fully aware of the contempt, oftentimes amounting to hatred, of their ostensible liberators. They felt the bitter derision, even from officers of high rank with which the idea of their being transformed into available soldiers was met, and they saw it was extended to those who were laboring for their benefit. When their own good conduct had won them a portion of respect, there still remained wide-spread distrust of the ultimate intention of the Government. A large number was required as laborers in the various Departments of Government service. But one of the chief causes of failure is the fact that comparatively few of the negroes are physically fit for soldiers. Many suffer under some visible or concealed infirmity produced by the rigor, cruelty, and barbarity of their treatment, and the evidences of the most unsanitary conditions of life on the plantation. In these circumstances, the recruiting went on slowly: when the Major General Commanding (General Foster) ordered an indiscriminate conscription of every able bodied colored man in the Department. As the special representative of the Government in its relation to them, I had given them earnest and repeated assurances that no force would be used in recruiting the black regiments. I say nothing of this order in referrence to my special duties and jurisdiction, and the authority of the Major General Commanding to issue it. But as an apparent violation of faith, pledged to the Freedmen, it could not but shake their confidence in our just intentions, and make them the more unwilling to serve the Gov[t]

The order spread universal confusion and terror. The negroes fled to the woods and swamps, visiting their cabins only by stealth and in darkness. They were hunted to their hiding places by armed parties of their own people, and if found, compelled to enlist. This conscription order is still in force. Men have been seized and forced to enlist who had large families of young children dependent upon them for support, and fine crops of cotton and corn nearly ready for harvest, without an opportunity of making provision for the one, or securing the other. Three boys, one only fourteen years of age, were seized in a field where they were at work, and sent to a regiment serving in a distant part of the Department, without the knowledge or consent of their parents. A man on his way to enlist as a volunteer was stopped by a recruiting party. He told them where he was going, and was passing on, when he was again ordered to halt. He did not stop, and was shot dead and left where he fell. It is supposed the soldiers desired to bring him in and get the bounty offered for bringing in recruits.

Another man who had a wife and family was shot as he was entering a boat to fish, on the pretence that he was a deserter. He fell in the water and was left. His wound though very severe was not mortal. An employee in the Quartermaster's Department was taken, and without being allowed to communicate with the Quartermaster, or settle his accounts, or provide for his family, was taken to Hilton Head and enrolled, although he had a certificate of exemption from the military service, from a medical officer. I protested against the order of the Major General Commanding, (General Foster) and sent him reports of these proceedings, but had no power to prevent them. The order has never to my knowledge been revoked. It was generally beleived that the commission with which I was entrusted was given with a view to a critical test experiment of the capabilities of the negro for freedom and self support, and self-improvement; to determine whether he is specifically distinct from, and inferior to the white race, and normally a slave and dependent; or only inferior by accidents of position and circumstances, still a man, and entitled to all the rights which our organic law has declared belong to all men by the endowments of the Creator. I believed myself charged with a mission of justice and atonement for wrongs and oppressions the race had suffered under the sanction of the national law. I found the prejudice of color and race here in full force, and the general feeling of the army of occupation was unfriendly to the blacks. It was manifested in various forms of personal insult and abuse, in depredations on their plantations, stealing and destroying their crops and domestic animals, and robbing them of their money. The women were held as the legitimate prey of lust, and as they had been taught it was a crime to resist a white man, they had not learned to dare to defend their chastity. Licentiousness was wide-spread. The morals of the old plantation life seemed revived in the army of occupation. Among our officers and soldiers there were many honorable exceptions to this; but the influence of too many was demoralizing to the negro, and have greatly hindered the efforts for their improvement and elevation.

There was a general disposition among the soldiers and civilian speculators here to defraud the negroes in their private traffic, to take the commodities which they offered for sale by force, or to pay for them in worthless money. At one time these practices were so frequent and notorious that the negroes would not bring their produce to market for fear of being plundered. Other occurrences have tended to cool the enthusiastic joy with which the coming of the "Yankees" was welcomed.

Their disappointment at not getting the lands they had selected at the invitation and under the supposed guarantee of the Government, I have referred to. They had been promised land on conditions they were ready and offered to fulfill. The land was denied to them. They could not understand the reasons of law and expediency why the promise was broken to the hope.

When they were invited to enlist as soldiers, they were promised the same pay as other soldiers. They did receive it for a time; but at length it was reduced, and they received but little more than one-half what was promised.[7] The questions of the meaning and conflicts of statutes which justified this reduction, could not be made intelligable to them. To them it was simply a breach of faith. It is first of all essential to the success of the efforts of the Government in their behalf, that the negroes shall have entire confidence in its justice and good faith. These things fill them with doubt and apprehension. They know as yet very little of political mechanisms, or gradation of authority; and hence every white man is in their eyes the Government.

Their conceptions are too confused to enable them to distinguish clearly between official acts and the wanton outrages of individuals. I had no independent power to prevent or punish these violences and wrongs. The aid and protection in my operations, which the Commander of the Department was instructed to afford, were not always promptly or efficiently rendered.

. . . .

The experiment with the Freedmen in this Department is a success. The only use I wish to make of this catalogue of difficulties is, as an illustration of the fact, which forms the summary and substance of this and all other true reports of the Freedmen in their new conditions, amid all their obstructions, and in spite of all, they have made constant progress and proved their right to be received into the full communion of Freemen. They have shown that they can appreciate freedom as the highest boon; that they will be industrious and provident, with the same incitements which stimulate the industry of other men in free societies; that they understand the value of property and are eager for its acquisition, especially of land; that they can conduct their private affairs with sagacity, prudence and success; that under freedom's banner these sea islands are not destined to become a howling wilderness, but will flourish more than ever, when cultivated by freemen; that they are not ignorant from natural incapacity, but from the brutishness of their former condition; that they are intelligent, eager, and apt to acquire knowledge of letters, docile and receptive pupils; that they aspire to, and adopt, as fast as means and opportunity admit, the social forms and habits of civilization; that they quickly get rid of, in freedom, the faults and vices generated by slavery, and in truthfulness and fidelity and honesty, may be compared favorably with men of an other color, in conditions as unfavorable for the development of those qualities; that they are remarkably susceptible of religious emotions, and the inspirations of music; that in short, they are endowed with all the instincts passions, affections, sensibilities, powers, aspirations and possibilities, which are the common attributes of human nature. They have given the highest proof of manhood by their bravery and discipline on many a battle-field, where defeat, they well knew, had for them no mercy. They have conquered a recognition of their manhood and right to be free, and vindicated the wisdom and justice of your first order, to place arms in their hands, (which I had the honor of receiving and executing.) The senseless prejudices and bitter contempt against their race is disappearing before their peaceful and orderly conduct under their trials and provocations, their patient hope and heroism in war. Events for four years have been disciplining the mind of the nation to prepare it to give them full recognition and ample justice.

In this view, it may be that the obstacles which beset their earlier path towards freedom were blessings, normal elements for the solution of the great problem of their manhood and their rights, as the attrocities and diabolisms, the murders and martyrdoms, the countless sacrifice of noblest lives in this war, may have been necessary to convince the American people of the utter and irredeemable barbarism of slavery, and to inspire them with a determined purpose to build themselves up into a new nation and a new union, upon the enduring foundation of Justice, Freedom, and equal rights of all men.

It has been my earnest endeavor to carry out to the extent of my ability your views and purposes with regard to the people committed to my charge and to inaugrate in this Department the wise and humane policy contemplated in your instructions to me.

In the hope that I have been in some degree successful, I am Sir With great respect Your Obedient Servant

HLS R. Saxton

Excerpts from Brig. Genl R. Saxton to Hon. Edwin M. Stanton, 30 Dec. 1864, S-2775 1864, Letters Received, ser. 12, RG 94 [K-236]. Twenty-six pages of a thirty-seven-page report. In the omitted passages, Saxton noted his appointment as military governor and superintendent of plantations, and summarized events of 1862 and 1863 that he had described more fully in an earlier report (printed above as doc. 36). He also reported upon the enlistment and military performance of black soldiers and the education of former slaves, and elaborated upon the complaint that his authority had been repeatedly overridden or ignored by the department commander and his subordinates. None of the circulars said to have been appended are in the file, and none have been found in the files maintained by Saxton as military governor, the records of the

Department of the South, or the records of the War Department. One has been located elsewhere; it is printed above, as doc. 41.

1 The instructions are quoted above, in doc. 36.
2 No letter dated December 27, 1862, has been found; however, in a letter of December 7, 1862, General Rufus Saxton, the military governor, had argued that land forfeited to the government should be made available in small parcels to former slaves. (See above, doc. 27.) In the letter of January 6, 1863, Saxton had warned that the sale to "[s]peculators" of land controlled by the government under the Direct Tax Act would render 18,000 freedpeople homeless. Furthermore, "[t]he prospect of the sale of the lands has so alarmed the negroes, that I fear it will interfere with the proper planting of the fields." There was, he had argued, "but one solution of the question. It is for Congress to pass a law for the bidding in of the lands by the Government for the purpose of securing the title, and afterwards allotting portions of them among the emancipated negroes." (Brig. Genl. R. Saxton to Hon. Edwin M. Stanton, 6 Jan. 1863, S-1570 1863, Letters Received, ser. 12, RG 94 [K-52].)
3 The instructions are quoted above, in doc. 41.
4 The circular (which was issued on January 16, not January 10) is printed above, as doc. 41.
5 On February 25, 1864, General Quincy A. Gillmore, commander of the Department of the South, had offered to use "armed force," if necessary, to enforce the claims of purchasers of direct-tax land. Although the other direct-tax commissioners presumably requested Gillmore's intervention, they did so without the knowledge of Abram D. Smith, the third commissioner. (See above, doc. 46.)
6 The instructions, dated August 25, 1862, are quoted above, in doc. 36. They authorized Saxton to enlist as many as 5,000 black soldiers.
7 On the pay accorded black soldiers and the protests arising therefrom, see *Freedom*, ser. 2: chap. 7, especially docs. 158A–F.

58: Account of a Meeting of Black Religious Leaders in Savannah, Georgia, with the Secretary of War and the Commander of the Military Division of the Mississippi

[*New York, February 13, 1865*]

THE FREEDMEN IN GEORGIA.

Report of the Conference between Secretary Stanton, Gen. Sherman and the Colored People of Savannah.

In the course of a very interesting and eloquent sermon, by Mr. Beecher, at Plymouth Church, last evening, in support of the rights of the black man to universal suffrage, in common with all men, Mr. Beecher read the following report of a meeting recently held at Savannah between the Hon. Edwin M. Stanton, Secretary of War, and Major-Gen. Sherman, on the one part, and a number of colored cl[ass le]aders, deacons and divines, on the other. The [report] was placed in Mr. Beecher's hands by the Secre[tary of] War himself, who, during his recent visit to Gen. Sherman at Savannah, held, in conjunction with the General, the conference with these representatives of the colored population, in order to learn their views as to what they desired should be done in their behalf by the Government. Mr. Beecher stated that the document was a verbatim phonographic report of the questions that were put and the answers elicited. It is a most remarkable paper:

MINUTES OF AN INTERVIEW BETWEEN THE COLORED MINISTERS AND CHURCH OFFICERS AT SAVANNAH WITH THE SECRETARY OF WAR AND MAJOR-GEN. SHERMAN.

HEADQUARTERS OF MAJ.-GEN. SHERMAN,
CITY OF SAVANNAH, GA., Jan., 12, 1865–8 P.M.

On the evening of Thursday, the 12th day of January, 1865, the following persons of African descent met by appointment to hold an interview with Edwin M. Stanton, Secretary of War, and Major-Gen. Sherman, to have a conference upon matters relating to the freedmen of the State of Georgia, to-wit:

One: William J. Campbell, aged 51 years, born in Savannah, slave until 1849, and then liberated by will of his mistress, Mrs. May Maxwell. For ten years pastor of the 1st Baptist Church of Savannah, numbering about 1,800 members. Average congregation, 1,900. The church property belonging to the congregation. Trustees white. Worth $18,000.

Two: John Cox, aged fifty-eight years, born in Savannah; slave until 1849, when he bought his freedom for $1,100. Pastor of the 2d African Baptist Church. In the ministry fifteen years. Congregation 1,222 persons. Church property worth $10,000, belonging to the congregation.

Three: Ulysses L. Houston, aged forty-one years, born in Grahamsville, S.C.; slave until the Union army entered Savannah. Owned by Moses Henderson, Savannah, and pastor of Third African Baptist Church. Congregation numbering 400. Church property worth $5,000; belongs to congregation. In the ministry about eight years.

Four: William Bentley, aged 72 years, born in Savannah, slave until 25 years of age, when his master, John Waters, emancipated him by will. Pastor of Andrew's Chapel, Methodist Episcopal Church–only one of that denomination in Savannah; congregation numbering 360 members; church property worth about $20,000, and is owned by the congregation; been in the ministry about twenty years; a member of Georgia Conference.

Five: Charles Bradwell, aged 40 years, born in Liberty County, Ga.; slave until 1851; emancipated by will of his master, J. L.

Bradwell. Local preacher in charge of the Methodist Episcopal congregation (Andrew's Chapel) in the absence of the minister; in the ministry 10 years.

Six: William Gaines, aged 41 years; born in Wills Co., Ga. Slave until the Union forces freed me. Owned by Robert Toombs, formerly United States Senator, and his brother, Gabriel Toombs, local preacher of the M.E. Church (Andrew's Chapel.) In the ministry 16 years.

Seven: James Hill, aged 52 years; born in Bryan Co., Ga. Slave up to the time the Union army came in. Owned by H. F. Willings, of Savannah. In the ministry 16 years.

Eight: Glasgon Taylor, aged 72 years, born in Wilkes County, Ga. Slave until the Union army came; owned by A. P. Wetter. Is a local preacher of the M.E. Church (Andrew's Chapel.) In the ministry 35 years.

Nine: Garrison Frazier, aged 67 years, born in Granville County, N.C. Slave until eight years ago, when he bought himself and wife, paying $1,000 in gold and silver. Is an ordained minister in the Baptist Church, but, his health failing, has now charge of no congregation. Has been in the ministry 35 years.

Ten: James Mills, aged 56 years, born in Savannah; free-born, and is a licensed preacher of the first Baptist Church. Has been eight years in the ministry.

Eleven: Abraham Burke, aged 48 years, born in Bryan County, Ga. Slave until 20 years ago, when he bought himself for $800. Has been in the ministry about 10 years.

Twelve: Arthur Wardell, aged 44 years, born in Liberty County, Ga. Slave until freed by the Union army. Owned by A. A Solomons, Savannah, and is a licensed minister in the Baptist Church. Has been in the ministry 6 years.

Thirteen: Alexander Harris, aged 47 years, born in Savannah; free born. Licensed minister of Third African Baptist Church. Licensed about one month ago.

Fourteen: Andrew Neal, aged 61 years, born in Savannah, slave until the Union army liberated him. Owned by Mr. Wm. Gibbons, and has been deacon in the Third Baptist Church for 10 years.

Fifteen: Jas. Porter, aged 39 years, born in Charleston, South Carolina; free-born, his mother having purchased her freedom. Is lay-reader and president of the board of wardens and vestry of St. Stephen's Protestant Episcopal Colored Church in Savannah. Has been in communion 9 years. The congregation numbers about 200 persons. The church property is worth about $10,000, and is owned by the congregation.

Sixteen: Adolphus Delmotte, aged 28 years, born in Savannah; free born. Is a licensed minister of the Missionary Baptist Church of Milledgeville. Congregation numbering about 300 or 400 persons. Has been in the ministry about two years.

Seventeen: Jacob Godfrey, aged 57 years, born in Marion,

S.C. Slave until the Union army freed me; owned by James E. Godfrey – Methodist preacher now in the Rebel army. Is a class-leader and steward of Andrew's Chapel since 1836.

Eighteen: John Johnson, aged 51 years, born in Bryan County, Georgia. Slave up to the time the Union army came here; owned by W. W. Lincoln of Savannah. Is class-leader and treasurer of Andrew's Chapel for sixteen years.

Nineteen: Robt. N. Taylor, aged 51 years, born in Wilkes Co., Ga. Slave to the time the Union army came. Was owned by Augustus P. Welter, Savannah, and is class-leader in Andrew's Chapel for nine years.

Twenty: Jas. Lynch, aged 26 years, born in Baltimore, Md.; free-born. Is presiding elder of the M.E. Church and missionary to the department of the South. Has been seven years in the ministry and two years in the South.

Garrison Frazier being chosen by the persons present to express their common sentiments upon the matters of inquiry, makes answers to inquiries as follows:

First: State what your understanding is in regard to the acts of Congress and President Lincoln's proclamation, touching the condition of the colored people in the Rebel States.

Answer – So far as I understand President Lincoln's proclamation to the Rebellious States, it is, that if they would lay down their arms and submit to the laws of the United States before the first of January, 1863, all should be well; but if they did not, then all the slaves in the Rebel States should be free henceforth and forever. That is what I understood.

Second – State what you understand by Slavery and the freedom that was to be given by the President's proclamation.

Answer – Slavery is, receiving by *irresistible power* the work of another man, and not by his *consent*. The freedom, as I understand it, promised by the proclamation, is taking us from under the yoke of bondage, and placing us where we could reap the fruit of our own labor, take care of ourselves and assist the Government in maintaining our freedom.

Third: State in what manner you think you can take care of yourselves, and how can you best assist the Government in maintaining your freedom.

Answer: The way we can best take care of ourselves is to have land, and turn it and till it by our own labor – that is, by the labor of the women and children and old men; and we can soon maintain ourselves and have something to spare. And to assist the Government, the young men should enlist in the service of the Government, and serve in such manner as they may be wanted. (The Rebels told us that they piled them up and made batteries of them, and sold them to Cuba; but we don't believe that.) We want to be placed on land until we are able to buy it and make it our own.

Fourth: State in what manner you would rather live – whether scattered among the whites or in colonies by yourselves.

Answer: I would prefer to live by ourselves, for there is a prejudice against us in the South that will take years to get over; but I do not know that I can answer for my brethren. [Mr. Lynch says he thinks they should not be separated, but live together. All the other persons present, being questioned one by one, answer that they agree with Brother Frazier.][1]

Fifth: Do you think that there is intelligence enough among the slaves of the South to maintain themselves under the Government of the United States and the equal protection of its laws, and maintain good and peaceable relations among yourselves and with your neighbors?

Answer—I think there is sufficient intelligence among us to do so.

Sixth—State what is the feeling of the black population of the South toward the Government of the United States; what is the understanding in respect to the present war—its causes and object, and their disposition to aid either side. State fully your views.

Answer—I think you will find there are thousands that are willing to make any sacrifice to assist the Government of the United States, while there are also many that are not willing to take up arms. I do not suppose there are a dozen men that are opposed to the Government. I understand, as to the war, that the South is the aggressor. President Lincoln was elected President by a majority of the United States, which guaranteed him the right of holding the office and exercising that right over the whole United States. The South, without knowing what he would do, rebelled. The war was commenced by the Rebels before he came into office. The object of the war was not at first to give the slaves their freedom, but the sole object of the war was at first to bring the rebellious States back into the Union and their loyalty to the laws of the United States. Afterward, knowing the value set on the slaves by the Rebels, the President thought that his proclamation would stimulate them to lay down their arms, reduce them to obedience, and help to bring back the Rebel States; and their not doing so has now made the freedom of the slaves a part of the war. It is my opinion that there is not a man in this city that could be started to help the Rebels one inch, for that would be suicide. There were two black men left with the Rebels because they had taken an active part for the Rebels, and thought something might befall them if they stayed behind; but there is not another man. If the prayers that have gone up for the Union army could be read out, you would not get through them these two weeks.

Seventh: State whether the sentiments you now express are those only of the colored people in the city; or do they extend to the colored population through the country? and what are your means of knowing the sentiments of those living in the country?

Answer: I think the sentiments are the same among the colored people of the State. My opinion is formed by personal communication in the course of my ministry, and also from the thousands that followed the Union army, leaving their homes and undergoing suffering. I did not think there would be so many; the number surpassed my expectation.

Eighth: If the Rebel leaders were to arm the slaves, what would be its effect?

Answer: I think they would fight as long as they were before the bayonet, and just as soon as soon as they could get away, they would desert, in my opinion.

Ninth: What, in your opinion, is the feeling of the colored people about enlisting and serving as soldiers of the United States? and what kind of military service do they prefer?

Answer: A large number have gone as soldiers to Port Royal to be drilled and put in the service; and I think there are thousands of the young men that would enlist. There is something about them that perhaps is wrong. They have suffered so long from the Rebels that they want to shoulder the musket. Others want to go into the Quartermaster's or Commissary's service.

Tenth: Do you understand the mode of enlistments of colored persons in the Rebel States by State agents under the Act of Congress?[2] If yea, state what your understanding is.

Answer: My understanding is, that colored persons enlisted by State agents are enlisted as substitutes, and give credit to the States, and do not swell the army, because every black man enlisted by a State agent leaves a white man at home; and, also, that larger bounties are given or promised by State agents than are given by the States. The great object should be to push through this Rebellion the shortest way, and there seems to be something wanting in the enlistment by State agents, for it don't strengthen the army, but takes one away for every colored man enlisted.

Eleventh: State what, in your opinion, is the best way to enlist colored men for soldiers.

Answer: I think, sir, that all compulsory operations should be put a stop to. The ministers would talk to them, and the young men would enlist. It is my opinion that it would be far better for the State agents to stay at home, and the enlistments to be made for the United States under the direction of Gen. Sherman.

In the absence of Gen. Sherman, the following question was asked:

Twelfth: State what is the feeling of the colored people in regard to Gen. Sherman; and how far do they regard his sentiments and actions as friendly to their rights and interests, or otherwise?

Answer: We looked upon Gen. Sherman prior to his arrival as a man in the Providence of God specially set apart to accomplish this work, and we unanimously feel inexpressible gratitude to him, looking upon him as a man that should be honored for the faithful performance of his duty. Some of us called upon him immediately upon his arrival, and it is probable he would not meet the Secretary with more courtesy than he met us. His conduct and deportment toward us characterized him as a friend and a gentleman. We have confidence in Gen. Sherman, and think that what concerns us could not be under better hands. This is our opinion now from the short acquaintance and interest we have had. (Mr. Lynch states that with his limited acquaintance with Gen. Sherman, he is unwilling to express an opinion. All others present declare their agreement with Mr. Frazier about Gen. Sherman.)

Some conversation upon general subjects relating to Gen. Sherman's march then ensued, of which no note was taken.

WAR DEPT. ADJT. GEN.'S OFFICE
WASHINGTON, Feb. 1, 1865.

I do hereby certify that the foregoing is a true and faithful report of the questions and answers made by the colored ministers and church members of Savannah in my presence and hearing, at the chambers of Major-Gen. Sherman, on the evening of Thursday, Jan. 12, 1865. The questions of Gen. Sherman and the Secretary of War were reduced to writing and read to the persons present. The answers were made by the Rev. Garrison Frazier, who was selected by the other ministers and church members to answer for them. The answers were written down in his exact words, and read over to the others, who one by one expressed his concurrence or dissent as above set forth.

E. D. TOWNSEND, Asst.-Adjt.-Gen.

Mr. Beecher said that Secretary Stanton had remarked that it was the first time in the history of this nation when the representatives of this government had gone to these poor, debased people to ask them what they wanted for themselves. "What do you want for your own people?" was the question which had been put to them; and the speaker concluded that it was upon the basis of this conference that Gen. Sherman had formed his recent order, in relation to the freedmen of his department,[3] which has been so severely criticized at the North, but for which, now that the facts are known, he should be still further honored and admired.

Mr. Beecher concluded by stating that Gen. Grant had been heard, in the presence of several distinguished officers, to give the opinion that, for picket and guard duty, the negroes made the best soldiers in the world. He had not tested them in the matter of endurance, the quality displayed by our troops in the terrible succession of battles, called the Battle of the Wilderness, but could otherwise answer for their military capabilities, and, on the whole he considered them equal to any soldiers in the world.

PD

Clipping from *New-York Daily Tribune*, [13 Feb. 1865], "Negroes of Savannah," Consolidated Correspondence File, ser. 225, Central Records, RG 92 [Y-199]. A small hole in the clipping accounts for the bracketed letters in the first paragraph.

1 Brackets in the original.
2 The act, adopted on July 4, 1864, permitted agents from Northern states to recruit soldiers among black men in the Confederate states, crediting them against the draft quotas of the Northern states. (*Statutes at Large*, vol. 13, pp. 379–81.)
3 Special Field Order 15, issued on January 16, 1865; it is printed immediately below, as doc. 59.

59: Order by the Commander of the Military Division of the Mississippi

IN THE FIELD, SAVANNAH, GA., January 16th, 1865.

SPECIAL FIELD ORDERS,
No. 15.

I. The islands from Charleston, south, the abandoned rice fields along the rivers for thirty miles back from the sea, and the country bordering the St. Johns river, Florida, are reserved and set apart for the settlement of the negroes now made free by the acts of war and the proclamation of the President of the United States.

II. At Beaufort, Hilton Head, Savannah, Fernandina, St. Augustine and Jacksonville, the blacks may remain in their chosen or accustomed vocations – but on the islands, and in the settlements hereafter to be established, no white person whatever, unless military officers and soldiers detailed for duty, will be permitted to reside; and the sole and exclusive management of affairs will be left to the freed people themselves, subject only to the United States military authority and the acts of Congress. By the laws of war, and orders of the President of the United States, the negro is free and must be dealt with as such. He cannot be subjected to conscription or forced military service, save by the written orders of the highest military authority of the Department, under such regulations as the President or Congress may prescribe. Domestic servants, blacksmiths, carpenters and other mechanics, will be free to select their own work and residence, but the young and able-bodied negroes must be encouraged to enlist as soldiers in the service of the United States, to contribute their share towards maintaining their own freedom, and securing their rights as citizens of the United States.

Negroes so enlisted will be organized into companies, battalions and regiments, under the orders of the United States military authorities, and will be paid, fed and clothed according to law. The bounties paid on enlistment may, with the consent of the recruit, go to assist his family and settlement in procuring agricultural implements, seed, tools, boots, clothing, and other articles necessary for their livelihood.

III. Whenever three respectable negroes, heads of families, shall desire to settle on land, and shall have selected for that purpose an island or a locality clearly defined, within the limits above designated, the Inspector of Settlements and Plantations will himself, or by such subordinate officer as he may appoint, give them a license to settle such island or district, and afford them such assistance as he can to enable them to establish a peaceable agricultural settlement. The three parties named will subdivide the land, under the supervision of the Inspector, among themselves and such others as may choose to settle near them, so that each family shall have a plot of not more than (40) forty acres of tillable ground, and when it borders on some water channel, with not more than 800 feet water front, in the possession of which land the military authorities will afford them protection, until such time as they can protect themselves, or until Congress shall regulate their title. The Quartermaster may, on the requisition of the Inspector of Settlements and Plantations, place at the disposal of the Inspector, one or more of the captured steamers, to ply between the settlements and one or more of the commercial points heretofore named in orders, to afford the settlers the opportunity to supply their necessary wants, and to sell the products of their land and labor.

IV. Whenever a negro has enlisted in the military service of the United States, he may locate his family in any one of the settlements at pleasure, and acquire a homestead, and all other rights and privileges of a settler, as though present in person. In like manner, negroes may settle their families and engage on board the gunboats, or in fishing, or in the navigation of the inland waters, without losing any claim to land or other advantages derived from this system. But no one, unless an actual settler as above defined, or unless absent on Government service, will be entitled to claim any right to land or property in any settlement by virtue of these orders.

V. In order to carry out this system of settlement, a general officer will be detailed as Inspector of Settlements and Plantations, whose duty it shall be to visit the settlements, to regulate their police and general management, and who will furnish personally to each head of a family, subject to the approval of the President of the United States, a possessory title in writing, giving as near as possible the description of boundaries; and who shall adjust all claims or conflicts that may arise under the same, subject to the like approval, treating such titles altogether as possessory. The same general officer will also be charged with the enlistment and organization of the negro recruits, and protecting their interests while absent from their settlements; and will be governed by the rules and regulations prescribed by the War Department for such purposes.

VI. Brigadier General R. SAXTON is hereby appointed Inspector of Settlements and Plantations, and will at once enter on the performance of his duties. No change is intended or desired in the settlement now on Beaufort [*Port Royal*] Island, nor will any rights to property heretofore acquired be affected thereby.

BY ORDER OF MAJOR GENERAL W. T. SHERMAN:

PD

Special Field Orders, No. 15, Headquarters Military Division of the Mississippi, 16 Jan. 1865, Orders & Circulars, ser. 44, RG 94 [DD-38].

60: Two Contracts between Northern Planters and South Carolina Freedpeople

[*Beaufort?, S.C. February? 1865*]

Statement of Agreement between James Millett and laborers on the

Lonesome Hill
Paul Chaplin } Pln't
Parsonage

Spreading manure pr. task[1]	.20
Listing ground " "	.60
Banking " " "	.30
Planting " " "	.15
Hoeing " " " ea. time.	.30
Thinning " " " " "	.10
Hauling " " " " "	30
Ploughing " " acre	.25
Picking & Sorting pr. lb.	.03
Blades pr. 100 lbs.	50
Cutting marsh pr. cord	60

Each hand that plants cotton shall have 6 tasks for corn & potatoes with one task to each child

Every full hand must plant 2 1/2 acres cotton.

From each acre of corn on Lonesome Hill & Parsonage two bush. shelled corn will be taken

HDSr [*32 signatures*]

[*Endorsement*] The within agreement is accepted by the laborers as binding, except that on the Lonesome Hill Pln'. the laborers refuse to give the proprietor any corn, unless he shall cause their corn land to be ploughed free of expense to them. C. F. Williams Gen'l. Sup't.

[*Dathaw Island, S.C. February 27, 1865*]

Article of agreement made & entered in to between W. T. Calkins and H P Kellam of Dathaw Island South Carolina party of the first part, and

Bess Perry, Grace Perry,[2] Will Mack,[2] Rose Mack,[2] Ellen Mack,[2] Juno Mack,[2] Isaac Jenkins, Hanah Jenkins,[2] Lucynda Jenkins,[2] Thomas Jenkins,[2] Lydia Upright,[2] Phebe Washington,[2] Tamer Chism,[2] Mol Chism[2] William Roach[2] Mariah Roach[2] Mary A Polite,[2] Brutus Bronson and Dorcas Bronson Inhabitants of Inlet Plantation Dathaw Island South Carolina party of the Second part

witnesseth that each and every one of the Said party of the second agrees to Cultivate the land plant and attend properly three acres of Cotton and Pick Sort Gin mote and Sack the Same all the above work to be done in the proper time and in good order They farther agree to pland one task of Corn each attend the same & gather the Corn & blades to feed the Horses & mules to be used in the Cultivation of the above mention Cotton & Corn

The Said party of the first part agrees to furnish to the party of the Second part the use of Horses or Mules Harnes & Ploughs Sufficient to do the team work in the Cultivation of the above mentioned Cotton & Corn

The Said party of the Second part are to have one fourth part of all the Cotton they rase and the use of one & a half acres of land to plant with Corn Potatoes & other vegitables for their own benefit

This contract is to remain in force until the first day of January 1866

Given under our hands this 27" day of February 1865

W. T. Calkins
HDS H. P. Kellam

[*Endorsement*] The within contracts have been read and explained to the laborers whose [*names*] are endorsed upon them, and they have signified their intention to work for the season of 1865 on the terms proposed, C. F. Williams Gen'l. Sup't.

Contract between J. A. Millett and Peter Middleton et al., [Feb? 1865], and contract between W. T. Calkins and H. P. Kellam and Bess Perry et al., 27 Feb. 1865, Labor Contracts for the Beaufort District, ser. 3106, Beaufort SC Subasst. Comr., RG 105 [A-7365].

1 When used as a unit of land measurement, a "task" equaled one-quarter acre.
2 The notation "yes" has been added next to the name.

61: Commander of the U.S.S. *New Hampshire* to the Commander of the South Atlantic Squadron

Port Royal Harbor. S.C. May 15th 1865.

Copy.

Sir: – Contrabands whose families are in distress, are continually applying to me to be discharged, and allowed to join their families.

Some of these men escaped to the squadron, without being able to bring off their families, and Shipped as the only resource left to them.

Land is now being apportioned out to these people to Settle upon, and as the Squadron can Spare a certain proportion of the Contrabands, who belong to it, I respectfully request that I may be authorized to discharge such men whose cases merit it. – Very Respectfully Your Obedt. Servt.

HLcSr (Signed) Wm Reynolds

Commander Wm. Reynolds to Rear Admiral John A. Dahlgren, 15 May 1865, enclosed in Rear Admiral J. A. Dahlgren to Honorable Gideon Welles, 16 May 1865, South Atlantic Squadron, Letters from Officers Commanding Squadrons, RG 45 [T-583]. In his covering letter to the Secretary of the Navy, the squadron commander reported that he had "directed the Commander of the Naval Depôt. – at Port Royal to discharge all contrabands . . . who shipped on that Station; – upon application being made by them to return to their families; – where their services can be spared."

62: Direct-Tax Commissioners for the State of South Carolina to the Secretary of the Treasury

Charleston So. Ca. Dec 11th 1865

Sir We have the honor of requesting your attention to a few lines on the subject of the sales by the U.S. Direct Tax Commissioners to "Heads of Families of the African race". Under President Lincoln's instructions of September 16th 1863[1] a number of plantations which had been bought in by the United States for the purpose, at the sales for delinquent taxes, amounting to over twenty thousand acres in the Parish of St Helena, already have been in great part divided up by careful survey into small tracts of ten acres each and sold for sums of from twelve and a half to fifteen dollars per tract to the heads of colored families, as fast as the survey has advanced. Thus not far from a thousand families in the Parish actually paid for their homesteads, and many more are occupying small patches under the pledge that when surveyed so that they could be properly described they may pay for them and get a certificate of sale on each of such parcels. On all of these plantations under the system of survey adopted there has been opportunity for Some sales to be made, so that nearly every plantation has been partially disposed of and so cut into as to entirely unfit it for such cultivation as could be made profitable to the former proprietors, it not being anticipated that the Government could ever be disposed, after the solemn pledge given to the colored people, to withdraw from sale to them the lands thus selected for their homesteads. The people are profoundly distressed on account of your order to stop the sales[2] and even those who already have paid for their lands, and obtained their certificates of sale are having their faith shaken in their titles to them. Upon some of these lots not yet paid for they have erected their habitations and have their families dwelling in them and cultivating the surrounding acres having had full confidence in the instructions given by President Lincoln to the Commissioners.

It has cost the government a considerable amount to divide these lands into small parcels and the divisions being now nearly completed it would seem to be throwing away that much money if it is not to be returned by the contemplated sales to the Negroes.

The Commissioners do not know whether you had it in mind that these selected lands were included when you worded your order to Suspend *all* sales and we hope to hear from you that such was not your intention.

We most respectfully submit to your consideration the importance of carrying out in letter and spirit the instructions of Sept 16th 1863. We verily believe that if these selected lands be now otherwise appropriated than to those who have been cultivating them in anticipation of purchasing there may arise serious legal difficulties in dispossessing them, notwithstanding the usual forbearance and patince which these people generally exhibit.

The Plantations on Hilton Head. Pinckney and several other Islands in St Lukes Parish bought in by the United States for Similar purpose as the above named lands in St Helena Parish, although not yet actually surveyed into small lots are also in numerous instances occupied by persons who have built on them in expectation of purchasing: and these include the town of Mitchelville containing not less than two thousand inhabitants. If now these occupants do not have the opportunity to purchase they will feel that they have been deceived by the Government in defence of which many of them have bravely fought while others have lost their husbands, sons and fathers. It would be an exhibition of extraordinary meekness if under such circumstances none of them should feel bitterly towards those who may come in with authority from the United States to divest them of what was sacredly set apart for their homesteads. We would not have it understood that we do not feel for those who by the issues of war have lost this property, nor that we are unwilling the Government should take measures to mitigate the severity of their losses; but we cannot but think that some other method of alleviation would be better for them, for the negroes and for the country than the violation of the pledged faith of the Government.

We cannot but be profoundly interested in this not only for the sake of the good name of the Government but because we have ourselves been personally the medium through whom the pledge has been made, and you will therefore be disposed to hear with the more patience our earnest entreaty that you will permit us to proceed with this Class of sales We have the honor to subscribe ourselves Your obed^{t} humble Servants

Wm Henry Brisbane
W. E. Wording
Willis Drummond

HLS

Wm. Henry Brisbane et al. to Hon. Hugh McCulloch, 11 Dec. 1865, Letters Received Relating to the Direct Tax, ser. 180, RG 56 [X-2]. Each commissioner signed his own name; the body of the letter is in yet another handwriting. On December 26, 1865, an assistant secretary of the treasury replied that the commissioners' letter would "be considered at the earliest practicable moment," but no later response has been found among the records of the Treasury Department. (J. F. Hartley to William Henry Brisbane et al., 26 Dec. 1865, vol. 2, p. 300, Letters Sent to Collectors & Assessors of Internal Revenue, State Officers, Banks, Corporations, Etc.: GS Series, ser. 26, RG 56 [X-2].)

1 For a summary of the instructions of September 1863, see above, doc. 39n.

2 On May 17, 1865, in conformity with a directive from Secretary of the Treasury Hugh McCulloch, the commissioner of internal revenue had suspended land sales under the Direct Tax Act. In early December 1865, McCulloch recommended that the suspension be continued until the former Confederate states "shall have an opportunity of assuming (as was done by the loyal States) the payment of the tax assessed upon them." (U.S., House of Representatives, "Report of the Secretary of the Treasury on the State of the Finances for the Year 1865," *House Executive Documents*, 39th Cong., 1st sess., No. 3, pp. 29–30, 91–92.)

CHAPTER 2
Southern Louisiana

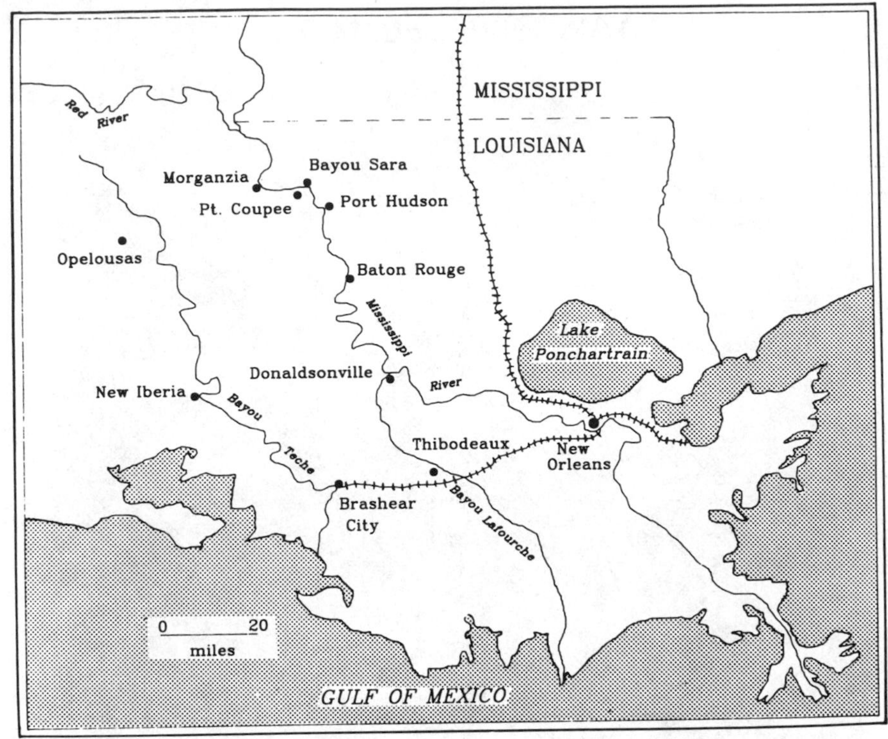

Southern Louisiana

2

Southern Louisiana

UNION OCCUPATION of southern Louisiana set in motion both the collapse of slavery and the development of free labor.[1] Although slavery would remain legal until September 1864, when it was abolished by a new state constitution, military and political circumstances led federal commanders to institute wage labor as early as the fall of 1862. The legality of slavery and the continued residence of a large segment of the antebellum planter class – many of whom professed loyalty to the national government and expected it to sustain their mastery – complicated but could not arrest the process. Implementation of even the most rudimentary wage relations corroded slavery without fully satisfying the demands of slaves, ex-slaves, or other opponents of slavery, including urban free people of color, native white unionists, and assorted Northerners, both military and civilian. At the same time, efforts by the Lincoln administration to engineer Louisiana's return to the Union focused national attention on the occupied parishes. Local contests over federally sponsored labor arrangements became part of a broader debate about the war aims of the North, the meaning of free labor, and the terms of national reconciliation.

[1] This chapter focuses on the wartime evolution of free labor in the sixteen sugar-growing parishes that came under federal control during 1862 and were subsequently administered by the Union army as the Department of the Gulf. A few documents pertain to the cotton-growing parishes between Baton Rouge and the Red River, on the northern fringe of territory added to the department in 1863. (Developments in northeastern Louisiana are considered below, in chapter 3.) Passages in this essay that lack footnotes should be understood to rest upon the documents included in the chapter. Secondary works concerning wartime labor arrangements in southern Louisiana include Louis S. Gerteis, *From Contraband to Freedman: Federal Policy toward Southern Blacks, 1861–1865* (Westport, Conn., 1973), chaps. 4–6; Peyton McCrary, *Abraham Lincoln and Reconstruction: The Louisiana Experiment* (Princeton, N.J., 1978), especially chap. 3; William F. Messner, *Freedmen and the Ideology of Free Labor: Louisiana, 1862–1865* (Lafayette, La., 1978); C. Peter Ripley, *Slaves and Freedmen in Civil War Louisiana* (Baton Rouge, La., 1976); Armstead L. Robinson, " 'Worser dan Jeff Davis': The Coming of Free Labor during the Civil War, 1861–1865," in *Essays on the Postbellum Southern Economy*, ed. Thavolia Glymph and John J. Kushma (College Station, Tex., 1985), pp. 11–47; Charles P. Roland, *Louisiana Sugar Plantations during the American Civil War* (Leiden, Netherlands, 1957); J. Carlyle Sitterson, *Sugar Country: The Cane Sugar Industry in the South, 1753–1950* (Lexington, Ky., 1953), chap. 10.

Soon after capturing New Orleans in April 1862, Northern troops under General Benjamin F. Butler, commander of the Department of the Gulf, gained control over the banks of the Mississippi River (the "coast," in local parlance) from the Gulf of Mexico to Baton Rouge. Later that year, military operations west of New Orleans brought the area between the Mississippi and Bayou Lafourche into federal lines. Union-occupied territory in southern Louisiana thus embraced both the largest city in the South and a substantial rural hinterland. The swampy countryside was home to nearly nine-tenths of the region's 117,000 slaves, a majority of whom lived on large sugar estates along the Mississippi River and various bayous, outnumbering free inhabitants many times over. With slave populations commonly exceeding one hundred, the sugar plantations of southern Louisiana were among the South's largest slaveholding units, rivaled only by the rice estates of lowcountry South Carolina and Georgia.

New Orleans, by contrast, was populated largely by free people. Roughly two-thirds of the 216,000 white people in southern Louisiana resided in Orleans Parish, as did about four-fifths of the region's 14,000 free blacks. The city's white residents, most of them nonslaveholders, included large numbers of immigrant and Northern-born artisans and laborers. Its free people of color, many of them light-skinned, French-speaking, and formally educated, were well represented in the ranks of shopkeepers, professionals, and self-employed artisans. Enjoying a degree of wealth and respectability unique among Southern free-black communities, the free people of color prided themselves on their achievements and generally distanced themselves from the mass of darker-skinned, illiterate slaves.[2]

In both countryside and city, Union occupation marked the beginning of the end of slavery. Many slaveholders retreated to the Confederate interior, forcing their most valuable slaves – chiefly young men – to

[2] For a list of the Union-occupied parishes and an accounting of their population, see *Freedom*, ser. 1, vol. 1: p. 188n. On slavery and the plantation economy, see Sitterson, *Sugar Country*, chaps. 2–9; Joe Gray Taylor, *Negro Slavery in Louisiana* (Baton Rouge, La., 1963); Roderick McDonald, "Goods and Chattels: The Economy of Slaves on Sugar Plantations in Jamaica and Louisiana" (Ph.D. diss., University of Kansas, 1980). On New Orleans, see Roger W. Shugg, *The Origins of Class Struggle in Louisiana: A Social History of White Farmers and Laborers during Slavery and After, 1840–1875* (Baton Rouge, 1939), especially chaps. 4, 6; John W. Blassingame, *Black New Orleans 1860–1880* (Chicago, 1973), especially chap. 1. On the free people of color, see Laura Foner, "The Free People of Color in Louisiana and St. Domingue: A Comparative Portrait of Two Three-Caste Slave Societies," *Journal of Social History* 3 (Summer 1970): 406–30; David C. Rankin, "The Impact of the Civil War on the Free Colored Community of New Orleans," *Perspectives in American History* 11 (1977–78): 379–416, and "The Origins of Negro Leadership in New Orleans during Reconstruction," in *Southern Black Leaders of the Reconstruction Era*, ed. Howard N. Rabinowitz (Urbana, Ill., 1982), pp. 155–89; Herbert E. Sterkx, *The Free Negro in Ante-Bellum Louisiana* (Rutherford, N.J., 1972).

accompany them. Their remaining slaves tried to scratch out a living on the abandoned estates, but necessity eventually drove many of them to the camps of federal troops. Meanwhile, emboldened by the presence of the Yankees, slaves whose owners had stayed at home increasingly resisted the accustomed routine. When their owners or overseers attempted to compel obedience, they too sought asylum at Union posts.[3]

In the face of deteriorating slave discipline, resident slaveholders sought guarantees of their mastership. At first, Butler lent a receptive ear. Like his superiors in Washington, he hoped that the federal presence would encourage both unionists and disaffected rebels to declare fealty to the Union. Taking for granted the loyalty of nonslaveholders and urban workingmen, Butler wooed the local gentry by offering to protect the property of those who disavowed the Confederacy. In June 1862, he reported to Secretary of War Edwin M. Stanton that "[t]he planters and men of property are now tired of the war, well-disposed toward the Union, only fearing lest their negroes shall not be left alone." Eager to promote any sign of loyalty, especially among wealthy and prominent planters, President Abraham Lincoln approved Butler's course.[4]

Solicitude for unionist slaveholders dictated Butler's policy regarding fugitive slaves. Although he considered slavery "a curse to the nation," he accepted "the fact of its present existence." Accordingly, he instructed subordinate officers to accept only those fugitive slaves whose labor was needed for military purposes. Butler refused to sanction wholesale "confiscation" of human property when loyal people were among its owners. Moreover, he hesitated to assume the burden of feeding and sheltering runaways. Given the number of destitute white people already receiving military relief, it was "*a physical impossibility*" to accommodate fugitive slaves.[5]

The determination of the slaves soon rendered Butler's position untenable. Runaways of all ages and physical conditions presented themselves at Union camps, defying attempts to categorize them according to their military usefulness. They found allies among some of Butler's subordinates. At Camp Parapet, a few miles upriver from New Orleans, General John W. Phelps welcomed all fugitives, gave short shrift to pursuing owners, and authorized slave-liberating raids upon nearby plantations. His forthright policy enraged slaveholders and angered General Butler, with whom he dueled verbally throughout the summer of 1862.[6]

3 On Union occupation and the collapse of slavery in southern Louisiana, see *Freedom*, ser. 1, vol. 1: chap. 4.

4 *Official Records*, ser. 1, vol. 15, pp. 422–24, 465–67, 483–84, 502–4; ser. 3, vol. 2, p. 141.

5 *Freedom*, ser. 1, vol. 1: doc. 61.

6 *Freedom*, ser. 1, vol. 1: docs. 58–63; *Freedom*, ser. 2: docs. 9–10, and pp. 41–44.

In August, after a heated exchange about Phelps's unauthorized recruitment of black soldiers, Butler finally prevailed and Phelps resigned.[7] But by that time, Butler had adopted much of his adversary's position. The dictates of his superiors, including President Lincoln, facilitated the reversal. "[C]ommon humanity," the President advised, demanded that escaped slaves "must not be permitted to suffer for want of food, shelter, or other necessaries of life." Acting upon authority recently granted by the Second Confiscation Act and the Militia Act, he directed Butler to accept all fugitives, putting the able-bodied to work for "reasonable wages."[8]

In view of changing military circumstances, Butler found the new policy increasingly congenial. Already his short-handed army had come to depend upon black laborers, both among the regiments in the field and in the quartermaster, engineer, subsistence, and medical departments. A Confederate offensive in August 1862 necessitated an even greater reliance on black men – free as well as former slave, and not only as laborers. Fearing an assault on New Orleans, Butler bolstered his fighting force by incorporating free-black Native Guard regiments into his command.[9]

The army's eagerness to employ ex-slave military laborers and free-black soldiers did not necessarily guarantee a warm welcome for the black women, children, and old people who also escaped from their owners. They took refuge in New Orleans and in makeshift settlements on the outskirts of the city. At Camp Parapet and nearby Carrollton, several thousand former slaves crowded into "contraband colonies," some of which had originated during Phelps's command. There they lived a hand-to-mouth existence, sleeping in cast-off army tents and subsisting on rations doled out by military officials or supplied by kinsmen who were working for the army. Many died of disease and exposure.

The growing population of the contraband colonies and the corresponding disruption of agricultural production worsened an already serious problem of relief. The flight of slaves left many plantations virtually deserted, their valuable sugar cane "standing to waste." In September 1862, Butler warned General-in-Chief Henry W. Halleck that many people in southern Louisiana – white and black – were living on the verge of starvation. In response, Halleck remanded "[t]he matter of feeding the negroes" to Butler's discretion, specifying only that he "economize the expenses as much as possible." To do so, Halleck suggested that he adopt "measures . . . to make them earn their own living."[10]

[7] *Freedom*, ser. 2: docs. 9–10.
[8] *Official Records*, ser. 3, vol. 2, p. 200. For the Second Confiscation Act and the Militia Act, see *Statutes at Large*, vol. 12, pp. 597–600.
[9] *Freedom*, ser. 2: docs. 11, 127.
[10] *Official Records*, ser. 1, vol. 15, pp. 558, 572.

Officers in charge of the contraband colonies were already requiring labor in return for subsistence. At Camp Parapet, Lieutenant George H. Hanks, a quartermaster from Connecticut, organized former slaves into squads of several families, each supervised by a Northern soldier. The men were assigned to military labor, and some of the women cooked for them. Those who demonstrated "a disposition to work regularly" received rations and clothing for themselves and their families; the "idle and worthless" went hungry. General Thomas W. Sherman, a division commander with headquarters at Carrollton, insisted that those ex-slaves employed in his camps as servants, cooks, and military laborers be duly registered; all others were consigned to the contraband colonies, from which they were forbidden to "stroll away." Sherman also ordered deductions from the earnings of black military laborers to cover the cost of their own clothing and the rations and clothing issued to their families.

While thousands of rural slaves fled to New Orleans or to the contraband colonies, their counterparts who remained at home struggled with would-be owners and overseers to redefine the terms under which they would labor. Some slaves refused to work altogether; others called for dismissal of overseers; still others demanded wages. In Plaquemines Parish, the slaves on one estate drove off the overseer, swore they would "not allow any white man to put his foot on [the place]," and appropriated plantation property "for their own benefit."[11] Unable either to prevent their slaves from running away or to control those who stayed at home, some planters hired white laborers from New Orleans to harvest their crops.[12] Others asked Union commanders to provide laborers from among the fugitive slaves who had accumulated in their camps. Amenable to such requests, General Sherman directed Lieutenant Hanks to accommodate the planters "if the negroes [were] willing to go."

Few were willing, especially when the would-be employer was their former owner. One woman informed Hanks that she would "go anywhere else to work, but you may shoot me before I will return to the old plantation." Hanks appreciated the former slaves' reluctance in such instances, but he had no sympathy for objections to plantation labor in general. Determined to get freedpeople out of the contraband colonies, he forced them to accept offers of wage employment. During the har-

[11] *Freedom*, ser. 1, vol. 1: doc. 66B.

[12] In late October 1862, the colonel of a Union regiment recruiting white men in New Orleans noted that enlistments had come to a standstill because "so many of the unemployed laborers are now being engaged by the planters to work on their plantations in the place of negroes who have run away." (Act. Col. Chs. J. Paine to Major George C. Strong, 22 Oct. 1862, enclosed in Major General Benj. F. Butler to Hon. Edwin M. Stanton, 22 Oct. 1862, G-825 1862 Letters Received, ser. 12, RG 94 [K-29].)

vest season of 1862, the population of the colonies declined from 3,000 to 600.

General Butler himself soon took a direct hand in the evolving labor arrangements. In October 1862, he placed Charles A. Weed, a Northern civilian, in charge of harvesting sugar on the abandoned estates south of New Orleans "for the benefit of the United States." Weed was authorized to requisition black laborers from the contraband colonies, to hire white laborers if necessary, and to draw rations and supplies from the quartermaster and subsistence departments. He appointed Northern civilians to manage some of the government-controlled plantations. In addition, Weed reportedly furnished black laborers to individual Northerners (including General Butler's brother) who had entered into private contracts with resident planters.[13]

Later that same month, Butler concluded an agreement with planters in Plaquemines and St. Bernard parishes that pledged military enforcement of labor on the estates of unionist slaveholders who agreed to pay wages to their slaves. The federal government would require "all the persons heretofore held to labor" to work "as they have heretofore been employed" under the supervision of "Loyal Planters and overseers." In return, Butler banned corporal punishment and required wages of $10 per month for able-bodied men, smaller amounts for women and children. Loyal planters who agreed to Butler's terms could call upon Northern soldiers "to preserve order and prevent crime." Planters who were disloyal or who refused the bargain received no military assistance, and their slaves could hire themselves to any cooperating employer.

Union military successes soon opened a larger territory to Butler's labor system. In November 1862, during the peak of the sugar-grinding season, federal troops invaded the Lafourche district, west of New Orleans. Butler directed their commander to put fugitive slaves to work saving the crop "for the owners that are loyal, and for the United States where the owners are disloyal."[14] He also appointed a three-member Sequestration Commission to seize the property of secessionists, protect that of unionists, arrange to harvest the crop on abandoned estates, and regulate labor according to the terms previously instituted in Plaquemines and St. Bernard. Within weeks the commissioners had assigned about a dozen abandoned plantations to Northern managers who were to supervise operations, keep accounts, and pay the workers from government funds.

Although federal policy increasingly focused on plantation agriculture, not all fugitive slaves in the Union-occupied parishes worked in the fields. In late 1862 and early 1863, military authorities detailed

[13] In addition to the relevant documents in this chapter, see *Official Records*, ser. 2, vol. 5, pp. 792–94; Messner, *Freedmen and the Ideology of Free Labor*, pp. 36–41.
[14] *Freedom*, ser. 1, vol. 1: doc. 69.

hundreds of men and women from the contraband colonies to repair levees along the Mississippi River. At first, they toiled alongside white workers paid by the government. Soon, however, unpaid black workers constituted the entire force.[15] They labored long hours with insufficient food and rest. At Kenner, Louisiana, the former slaves assigned to the levees "worked from sunrise till dark, Sundays included," for three months. Most were barefoot and clad in rags. Their living quarters consisted of an old barn, tattered tents, and shanties fashioned of dismantled fences. "*My cattle at home are better cared for than these unfortunate persons*," protested the commander of a nearby brigade.

Behind reinforced levees, the sugar harvest proceeded to Butler's satisfaction. His makeshift wage-labor scheme had achieved the immediate goals of saving the crop and keeping the slaves and former slaves at work, while also helping to mollify unionist slaveholders and punish disloyal ones. A successful harvest with wage-workers, Butler believed, would convert planters to the cause of emancipation. Slavery was "doomed" in the Union-occupied parishes, he assured President Lincoln, presenting him with a barrel of sugar produced by free labor.

Such optimism was only partly warranted. Butler's labor program had indeed crippled slavery, but it neither settled the status of "persons held to labor" by loyal owners nor convinced slaveholders – unionist or otherwise – of the superiority of free labor. While professing a willingness to accept the federal regulations, some planters and overseers insisted that all of their own former slaves be hired to them. A few likened the new arrangements to antebellum slave hiring and claimed the wages their former slaves earned by working for other planters. A good many defiantly refused to surrender "the right to use the whip." Sooner their fields lie idle than be worked by free laborers.

Former slaves also found much to dislike in the new arrangements. Military regulations forbade whipping, but planters continued to rely upon overseers accustomed to driving slaves, not supervising free workers. Moreover, a great many plantation operators, both Southern planters and Northern managers, failed to pay their harvest hands. Many – probably most – of the laborers dispatched from the contraband camps to the plantations were dismissed with no compensation.[16]

The free-black soldiers of the Native Guard regiments reinforced the former slaves' objections. They listened to their grievances, encouraged them to confront or quit abusive employers and sometimes advised them "not to work[,] as they were free." On occasion they avenged ill-

[15] Capt. Edward Page Jr. to Lieut. Col. Rich. B. Irwin, 19 Dec. 1862, P-24 1862, Letters Received, ser. 1956, Field Records – Banks' Expedition, Dept. of the Gulf, RG 393 Pt. 1 [C-826].

[16] In addition to the relevant documents in this chapter, see B. Genl. W. H. Emory to Capt. Hoffman, 27 Jan. 1863; E-31 1863, Letters Received, ser. 1756, Dept. of the Gulf, RG 393 Pt. 1 [C-532].

treatment. Soldiers in the 2nd Louisiana Native Guard arrested a Northern plantation manager for his abuse of women workers, threatened his life, and, he charged, fired shots at him. The effect, he complained, "was to show the hands that they the Soldiers was masters and, that obediance was due them, and not me." Armed, mobile, and cloaked with the authority of the federal government, black soldiers by their very presence emboldened former slaves to press for more favorable terms of labor.[17]

With one eye on developments in the countryside, General Butler kept the other on local political events. Elections for the U.S. House of Representatives were scheduled to take place in the Union-occupied parishes in December 1862, and, as the day drew near, Butler struggled to mediate factional quarrels among white unionists – particularly proslavery planters, on the one hand, and emancipationist smallholders, shopkeepers, and urban workingmen, on the other. When the polls closed, unionist voters had elected two representatives, thereby earning the exemption of thirteen Louisiana parishes from the Emancipation Proclamation.[18] Although their power had been severely compromised by the federal labor policy of late 1862, planters took heart from the continued legality of slavery and prepared to resist further inroads.

General Nathaniel P. Banks, a former governor of Massachusetts who assumed command in southern Louisiana just after the elections, was even more respectful of unionist slaveholders than Butler had been. Shortly after his arrival in New Orleans, Banks took pains to correct their widespread "misapprehension and misrepresentation" regarding the intentions of the federal government. If Louisiana returned promptly to the Union, he suggested, slavery might be preserved. He pointedly directed slaves to remain on the plantations and took steps to calm the planters' fear of servile insurrection during the Christmas holidays.[19]

Pleased by his conciliatory gestures, some slaveholders thought Banks might restore their accustomed supremacy. In January 1863, a delegation of sugar barons from Terrebonne Parish took their troubles to the new commander. Military occupation, they reported on behalf of nearly 200 fellow planters, had destroyed the old modes of exacting labor while failing to institute new ones. The slaves had repudiated their authority. "[N]egroes led astray by designing persons" fancied

[17] In addition to the relevant documents in this chapter, see *Freedom*, ser. 1, vol. 1: doc. 72.

[18] The exempted parishes are listed below, in doc. 81n. The preliminary Emancipation Proclamation of September 1862 had provided that any seceded state or portion of a state that signified its loyalty to the United States by electing congressional representatives would, "in the absence of strong countervailing testimony," be considered no longer in rebellion and therefore exempt from the final decree. (*Statutes at Large*, vol. 12, pp. 1267–68.)

[19] *Freedom*, ser. 1, vol. 1: doc. 74. On apprehensions of a Christmas insurrection, see *Freedom*, ser. 1, vol. 1: docs. 70–72.

that "the plantations & everything on them belong to them." On some estates, they "refused to work on any terms." Field hands were destroying fences, slaughtering livestock, riding draft animals, and traveling where and when they pleased. To end this "State of anarchy," the planters requested "such power & authority as will enable us to preserve order & compell the negroes to work so as to make the crops necessary for the support of our families & of the negroes themselves."

Although he acknowledged the continued legality of slavery, Banks was convinced that "the laws and the spirit of the age" demanded freedom. In a carefully worded order, issued in late January, he charted his course. Duly noting the exemption of southern Louisiana from the Emancipation Proclamation, he nevertheless prohibited the recapture of fugitive slaves, because it created a "disturbance of the public peace." Furthermore, he insisted, "labor is entitled to some equitable proportion of the crops it produces." "To secure the objects both of capital and labor," the Sequestration Commission would "establish a yearly system of negro labor, which shall provide . . . food, clothing, proper treatment and just compensation for the negroes." Promising to enforce labor discipline on behalf of planters who acceded to his terms, he forbade slaves and former slaves to "wander . . . without employment"; those who disobeyed would be compelled to perform unpaid labor on public works. He also directed his quartermaster to put unemployed black people to work on abandoned estates, which were to be operated by government agents or "suitable" private planters.

Early the following month, the Sequestration Commission issued its regulations for plantation labor, in the form of a contract between the U.S. government and individual planters. Its provisions applied not only to privately controlled estates – where the majority of slaves and former slaves lived – but also to plantations leased out or operated by the government. The contract provided that army provost marshals would "induce the Slaves to return to the Plantations where they belong" and require them "to work diligently and faithfully . . . for one year." For their part, the planters had to eschew corporal punishment and compensate their "slaves" with food, clothing, and either a small cash wage to each worker (from $1 to $3 per month, according to sex and occupation) or one-twentieth of the crop to the workers collectively. As the commissioners assured the planters, the contract did not involve "the surrender of any right of property in the slave." Nor, Banks emphasized, did it constitute an agreement between employer and employee. Only the Sequestration Commission and the planters were parties to the contract; the former slaves' presence on an estate constituted "proof of their assent." Hailing the commission's regulations as the most practicable solution to the labor question, Banks reported that "Representative Planters" had pronounced them "acceptable," as they "ought to be to all those who seek the welfare of the Negroes."

In practice, however, the new policy satisfied no one. Planters condemned the "voluntary" labor system as a violation of slavery's fundamental tenet: the sovereign power of the master, backed by the authority of the state. To slaveholders in St. James Parish, the regulations represented "an attempt to reconcile things which, in their nature, are utterly incompatible." "The master who pays wages to his slave," they reasoned, "either hires his own property to himself or is divested of it," and a slave who could legally "leave the service of his master when he pleases, and . . . sell his services to another person" was virtually free. In their view, Banks's system amounted "to an actual and immediate emancipation" in parishes explicitly exempted from the Emancipation Proclamation. Planters in Terrebonne Parish pronounced themselves willing to pay wages but skeptical of "[d]eriving any benefit from the arrangement." Monetary incentives, they insisted, would not motivate black people to work; "some *coercion* is absolutely necessary." Aware that federal troops were forbidden to serve as a slave patrol, they suggested that Banks permit civilians to do so. If they could not piece together the remnants of slavery, planters wanted to fashion free labor according to their own design.

Whereas slaveholders would accept nothing less than military sanction of their sovereignty, slaves would accept nothing less than unconditional freedom. In their view, federal occupation meant the end of slavery, notwithstanding the contrary provisions of the Emancipation Proclamation. In practice, most black people in the sugar parishes could no longer be claimed as slaves, but they wanted explicit confirmation of both their liberty and their rights as free workers. The federal labor program fell far short. Vowing that they would "rather die" than work under Banks's terms, the laborers on one estate threw down their tools and "left in a body."[20]

Ex-slave laborers especially contested official limitations upon their physical movement. Banks's strictures against vagrancy, which in effect bound them to a given plantation for an entire year, violated their conviction that freedom conferred the right to come and go as they pleased. The restrictions hampered efforts to visit or reunite with kinfolk on other estates, to leave abusive employers, or to market produce and livestock within the local provision economy. Regarding unimpeded mobility as essential to their new standing, former slaves defiantly moved when it suited them. Union officers charged with keeping laborers on the estates found the task formidable, especially since force was forbidden. "To prevent in ordinary times negroes from running away was difficult," reported one provost marshal, "now, tis simply impossible."

Even when the laborers remained on the plantations, they refused to

[20] Gerteis, *From Contraband to Freedman*, p. 90.

work as before. On the many estates that continued to be populated by their antebellum residents, the former slaves' shared experience and knowledge of their former owners fostered collective action to redress common grievances and pursue common objectives. As one army officer observed, they exhibited "a spirit of independance – a feeling that they are no longer slaves, but hired laborers; and demand to be treated as such." When planters and overseers insisted on treating them otherwise, the result was "trouble, immediately – and the negroes band together, and lay down their own rules, as to when, and how long they will work &c &c. and the Overseer loses all control over them." Workers sometimes drove off "Secesh" overseers and insisted on selecting their replacements. In a few instances, they refused to be "overlooked" by anyone.[21]

Former slaves also had their own notions of what constituted proper remuneration. Wages of $2 and $3 per month for able-bodied men struck them as less than "reasonable," especially when black military laborers and soldiers were earning $10. Although plantation hands, unlike employees of the army, also received food and clothing for family members too old or young to work, the compensation still seemed paltry. Dissatisfaction with their wages, together with a conviction that their years of unrequited toil warranted indemnification, underlay the former slaves' belief that they were entitled to property on the plantations. They seized crops, tools, and livestock, smashed fences for firewood, and dismantled sugar-milling machinery to sell as scrap. According to one provost marshal, they had "their heads so full of freedom" that they refused to wait until the end of the year to collect their pay.

To meet the demands of the former slaves, a few planters offered shorter workdays, payment for overwork, or plots of land for independent cultivation. Some of the inducements derived from antebellum practices that allowed slaves gardens for their own use, time in which to tend them, and the right to market the produce, as well as to hunt, fish, forage, gather moss, and cut wood. Former slaves sought to expand such independent activities. Planters who came to terms, reported a provost marshal in mid-1863, "have had less negroes leave them, and have much better crops than the average." Those who refused did so at the peril of losing their laborers.

Struggles over the terms of agricultural labor also raged on the abandoned plantations supervised by Captain Samuel W. Cozzens, an aide to Banks's quartermaster. Of the fifty-seven plantations under his jurisdiction in May 1863, fourteen were leased to private individuals (many of them Northerners) and another fourteen were operated by overseers employed by the government. Nearly all the remainder –

[21] In addition to the relevant documents in this chapter, see Wm. F. Gourand to B. F. Flanders, 26 Dec. 1863, Incoming Correspondence of the Supervising Special Agent (Group C), 3rd Agency, RG 366 [Q-84].

those plantations most devastated by the war and most vulnerable to Confederate raids – fell to Lieutenant (later Colonel) George Hanks, who in February 1863 became superintendent of a new agency, the Bureau of Negro Labor. Most of the estates under his control served as receiving depots for fugitives from Confederate-held territory. As rapidly as possible, he hired the new arrivals to private planters and lessees or government overseers.

Cozzens strove to demonstrate that free labor was not only "more beneficial to the negro," but also "more economical to the planter." But his overseers, no less than those on private plantations, found it impossible to exact "perfect obedience." The former slaves, he reported, were "indisposed to work" until they were provided with food and clothing, "discontented and unhappy" unless supplied with tobacco. Their demands extended, moreover, beyond subsistence and the retention of customary privileges; they objected to gang labor under overseers and to military restrictions upon freedom of movement. Despite their best efforts, Cozzens's agents could not prevent laborers "from leaving, the plantations at will, and Stealing or Committing depredations upon neighboring places." Some "obstinate" former slaves "refused to work themselves or to allow others around them to do so." But Cozzens would brook no insubordination. He subjected uncooperative workers to the stocks, a punishment which, in his view, exerted "a most salutary influence not only upon the offenders but upon the others around them." Ultimately, however, such measures failed of their object, becoming yet another bone of contention.

Different conditions prevailed on a handful of estates that had been abandoned by their owners but not yet assigned to Cozzens. The former slaves on these places struggled to support themselves amid the devastation of war. On one, whose owner had removed his able-bodied slaves to Texas, a small group of aged men and women remained in residence. With old tools and debilitated work stock, they cultivated corn and vegetables and harvested cane for their own use. Their hard-won independence impressed a Northern observer, who praised the "*joint Stock Company*" for having "succeeded beyond rebel Expectations in living without the assistance of white men." "No White men in Louisiana," he concluded, "could have done more or better than these Negroes."

But former slaves who attempted to work independently faced numerous difficulties. On the Potts plantation in Terrebonne Parish, about sixty freedpeople grappled with the disruptions of war and the strictures of federal policy. Early in 1863, having received permission from the parish provost marshal to "do something for ourselves, until the Government could do something for us," they began to plant some sixty acres of land. Their tenure did not, however, remain uncontested; near the end of the planting season, a prospective lessee claimed authority over the estate. The freedpeople were outraged. "We have had a hard struggle to get along," they asserted, "and we feel it hard now that we have succeeded in making ourselves in a measure independent, to have to [turn] it all over to someone else." They defended their right "to work the land already broken up and planted on equal shares with the Government." With the assistance of a sympathetic Union army officer and the consent of the plantation's absentee owner (a Northerner), the former slaves retained control to the end of the year, raising substantial crops of corn and cane. According to an agent of the Treasury Department, they realized "larger returns" than any of the plantations "managed by inexperienced Govm't agents or soldiers." Yet independent control over this or any other abandoned plantation remained precarious. The claim of black squatters might be abruptly superseded by a decision to operate the estate under government auspices, forcing them to work for wages on land they regarded as theirs by right.

Whether they labored independently or for wages, former slaves in the sugar parishes sooner or later encountered the provost marshals who administered General Banks's labor policy. These officers of junior rank were expected simultaneously to uphold the government's end of the contract between the planters and the Sequestration Commission and to referee conflicts that arose between employers and employees. Their dual role – at once agent and arbiter – further complicated the task of reconciling the irreconcilable interests of planters and laborers.

In carrying out their duties, the provost marshals relied upon orders from superior officers and upon their own notions about the proper role of military authority in enforcing "voluntary labor." General James Bowen, provost marshal general of the Department of the Gulf, generally saw the planters as natural allies in the work of maintaining order. "In the present condition of affairs," he declared, "planters must be regarded as conservators of the peace on their respective plantations." Accordingly, he instructed his subordinates to permit plantation owners, managers, and overseers to administer "such corrections . . . as may by law be permitted to masters over their apprentices" or to army officers over enlisted men. Although Bowen directed the provost marshals to fine or jail anyone who exceeded the limits or otherwise violated Banks's orders, they felt considerable pressure to favor the employers. Inducements from the gentry, ranging from sumptuous dinners to outright bribes, reinforced the tendency.[22]

Despite such temptations, some provost marshals displayed greater sympathy for lowly former slaves than for haughty planters. Black workers hastened to submit their grievances to such officers, much to the annoyance of plantation owners and overseers, Northern lessees, and managers of government plantations. "[I]f you find it necessary to

[22] In addition to the relevant documents in this chapter, see Bg. Genl. James Bowen to Captain Fitch, 27 Apr. [1863], vol. 296 DG, pp. 594–95, Press Copies of Letters Sent, ser. 1839, Provost Marshal, Dept. of the Gulf, RG 393 Pt. 1 [C-1099].

punish a Negro," complained a government agent, "one of the others run off to Thibodeaux to the Provost Marshall and report, you will be ordered to appear then to answer the charge, and while you are gone the others rest." Whatever the outcome of a complaint, freedpeople recognized the significance of their new right to appeal to higher authority.

When a provost marshal shared the planters' contempt for their workers, however, the right could prove a mockery. Captain Silas W. Sawyer, for example, served as virtual overseer for the planters of St. Bernard Parish. Determined to prevent former slaves from leaving the plantations, he assaulted one man for attempting to enlist in the Union army. On another occasion, he flouted a direct order from Colonel Hanks to permit a black soldier to reclaim his wife and children; instead, Sawyer arrested the soldier and complained that such directives "disorganize [plantation laborers] and make them uneasy." There would be no "uneasy" black people under Sawyer's rule.

For former slaves seeking an alternative to wage labor on the plantations, New Orleans offered the attractions of occupational diversity, unrestricted mobility, and greater freedom from oversight. As increasing numbers of black people – both longtime residents and newly arrived fugitives – claimed their liberty in the city, slaveholders mounted a desperate attempt to reverse the tide. Former slaves and free blacks lived in constant fear of being kidnapped and forced to work on the plantations. Masters and mistresses who had permitted their slaves to live on their own or to hire their own time abruptly revoked the privilege. To forestall flight, scores of urban slaveholders jailed their slaves. The municipal police not only arrested fugitive slaves at the instance of their owners, but also locked up "vagrants," a category that at times embraced virtually any black person found on the streets.[23] Northern military officials sometimes collaborated in the arrest of unoffending former slaves and free blacks. In March 1863, General Bowen ordered the provost guard in New Orleans to detain all black people who lacked "regular habitation or Employment" and convey them to Colonel Hanks, who would assign them to military or plantation labor. In the resulting sweep of the city, the guard arrested numerous self-supporting men and women.

Military events in the spring and summer of 1863 had important implications for black people in both city and countryside. Operations between Bayou Lafourche and Bayou Teche liberated thousands of slaves, many of whom took refuge in New Orleans when the Union army subsequently evacuated the region. An ensuing campaign against Port Hudson extended federal control into the cotton-growing parishes immediately north of Baton Rouge. With the fall of Port Hudson in

[23] On the jailing of slaves and free blacks in New Orleans to prevent their running away or to punish the families of men who enlisted in the Union army, see also *Freedom*, ser. 1, vol. 1: docs. 75–76, 78; *Freedom*, ser. 2: docs. 10, 295.

early July, hard on the heels of the rebel surrender at Vicksburg, Northern forces held sway over the entire Mississippi River.

The campaigns enlarged the territory under federal occupation and increased the number of former slaves subject to free-labor employment. They also prompted a more extensive mobilization of black people for military purposes, disrupting established labor arrangements. The army required laborers in great numbers: teamsters and dock hands to transport supplies, common laborers to fell trees and construct earthworks, cooks and servants to assist soldiers in the field, nurses and laundresses to care for the sick and wounded. Many black workers preferred such employment to agricultural labor under the regulations of the Sequestration Commission. "While camp lines are open and easy work found therein," complained one provost marshal, "negroes will not work upon plantations."

When General Daniel Ullmann arrived in southern Louisiana in April to recruit a brigade of black troops, enlistment in the Union army offered yet another alternative. Whereas the Native Guard regiments had consisted largely of urban free blacks, rural freedmen predominated in the new units. Large-scale recruitment generated a three-sided competition in which army recruiters, military employers, and planters all bid for the services of black men. Planters who came out last made their objections known. Prominent unionists, including members of the state's newly elected congressional delegation, pressed Banks to ban recruiting on the estates. In May, he obligingly declared a moratorium, which he ordered Ullmann to observe "scrupulously."[24] Grudgingly withdrawing his recruitment officers, Ullmann condemned Banks's labor system as "a virtual rendition of the negro to slavery" and an obstacle to enlistment. But removal of the recruiters did not halt enlistment. Many freedmen gladly forsook ill-paid field labor to fight for freedom at higher wages, and some were surreptitiously pressed into the service. Whether voluntary or involuntary, enlistment depleted the supply of black men available to the planters.[25]

The recruitment of black soldiers undermined plantation discipline by dramatizing the limits of the planters' power. In St. Bernard Parish, according to the local provost marshal, a group of "Recruiting negroes" seized carts and mules and assembled seventy-five black men and women who "went singing, shouting & marauding through the Parish." The recruiting party promised free passage to New Orleans for "all the negroes who desire it," provoking "great insubordination and confu-

[24] M.G.C. N. P. Banks to Brig. General Ullman, 5 May 1863, and M.G.C. N. P. Banks to Brig. Genl. D. Ullman, 8 May 1863, vol. 5 DG, pp. 132–34, 149, Letters Sent, ser. 1738, Dept. of the Gulf, RG 393 Pt. 1 [C-617].

[25] In addition to the relevant documents in this chapter, see *Freedom*, ser. 2: doc. 51. On black enlistment in southern Louisiana more generally, see *Freedom*, ser. 2: chap. 3.

sion." Elsewhere, a planter lamented the "change [that had] come over" his laborers when they became aware of "a chance of avoiding Labor by enlisting in the Service." Planters protested, but to little avail.[26]

Unable to prevent plantation laborers from running away to enlist, Banks attempted a more systematic regulation of recruitment. In late August 1863, he appointed a "commission of enrollment" to supervise the enlistment, employment, and education of "persons of color." One month later, he ordered the commission to begin conscripting able-bodied black men between the ages of twenty and thirty. The draft threatened to remove hundreds of men during the harvest and grinding season, when their labor was essential to the operation of the sugar mills. A pledge to exempt irreplaceable workers "in cases of necessity" and to furlough recruits to work the harvest failed to appease the planters. They appealed to Adjutant General Lorenzo Thomas, who, in mid-November, suspended recruitment. Although Thomas's reprieve addressed the planters' immediate needs, it also underscored the extent to which their authority had become subordinate to that of the army.[27]

If the Union army compromised Banks's labor system, the Confederate army attempted to eradicate it. In June 1863, during the siege of Post Hudson, rebel troops mounted a counteroffensive in the Lafourche region, briefly threatening New Orleans. They operated under the command of General Richard Taylor, himself the owner of a plantation in St. Charles Parish that had been seized by federal authorities. The attack neither returned New Orleans to Confederate hands nor dislodged the federal chokehold on Port Hudson. But it wreaked havoc on the government-supervised plantations. Confederate soldiers recaptured several thousand former slaves and forced thousands more into the swamps and canebrakes.[28] Of thirty-three plantations controlled by Lieutenant Hanks, to which more than 12,000 black refugees had been assigned, only one escaped devastation. Months later, many of them remained unoccupied, and those that had resumed operations suffered shortages of supplies and draft animals.

Meanwhile, responsibility for the "government plantations" had been placed in different hands. In mid-July 1863, General Banks's quartermaster transferred the abandoned estates to Benjamin F. Flanders, supervising agent of the Treasury Department's 5th Special

[26] In addition to the relevant documents in this chapter, see *Freedom*, ser. 2: doc. 55; Andrew Robinson to Major General N. P. Banks, 23 Mar. 1863, R-43 1863, Letters Received, ser. 1920, Civil Affairs, Dept. of the Gulf, RG 393 Pt. 1 [C-719].

[27] *Official Records*, ser. 1, vol. 26, pt. 1, pp. 704, 740–41, 803.

[28] On the Confederate attack and its effects, see, in addition to the relevant documents in this chapter, *Official Records*, ser. 1, vol. 26, pt. 1, pp. 210–14, 217–20, 223–24.

Agency.[29] Viewing them chiefly as sources of revenue, Flanders concentrated his attention on the plantations already leased out and on any others that seemed likely to generate a profit. He appointed Captain Cozzens – who as military superintendent had demonstrated similar concern for profitability – to head operations. He also appointed civilian "inspectors of plantations" to monitor conditions on the government-supervised estates, adjudicate labor disputes, and supervise payment of the laborers.[30] Taking their cue from Flanders, the inspectors showed little interest in unproductive or war-ravaged places, particularly those on the fringes of Union-held territory. Nor did they assume responsibility for the support of former slaves whose age or physical condition disqualified them for field work. Colonel Hanks's Bureau of Negro Labor remained in charge of such people. Their numbers increased markedly as plantation owners and lessees continued to "sift out" unproductive workers. Evicted freedpeople joined newly arrived fugitive slaves at army camps scattered throughout the Union-occupied parishes and at the contraband "depots" in and near New Orleans.

The swollen ranks of the poor and dependent – white as well as black – faced a bleak winter. Since the Treasury Department, not the army, now received all funds generated by the government-supervised plantations, General Banks urged General-in-Chief Halleck to exact from treasury officials a commitment to support aged and infirm freedpeople. In October, Halleck instead advised Banks to prohibit the planters from evicting such people and to take control of any property needed to provide for the destitute. Banks promptly did so, and Flanders and his subordinates thereafter played a subaltern role with respect to both the disposition of abandoned property and the supervision of former slaves.[31]

President Lincoln, too, encouraged Banks to exert greater influence in civilian affairs. In the closing weeks of 1863, he directed him to help organize a state government that would abolish slavery and apply for readmission to the Union. Although far from assured of success, Lincoln's goal seemed attainable, for the political balance in southern Louisiana had shifted considerably since the beginning of the year. Federal sponsorship of free labor had strengthened indigenous oppo-

[29] Benj. F. Flanders to Hon. S. P. Chase, 17 Sept. [186]3, vol. 119, pp. 169–71, Letters Sent by the Supervising Special Agent, 3rd Agency, RG 366 [Q-87]. Not until October 1863 did the War Department order Union military commanders elsewhere in the Union-occupied South to turn over such property to treasury agents. (*Official Records*, ser. 3, vol. 3, p. 872.)

[30] In addition to the relevant documents in this chapter, see Benj. F. Flanders to Sir, [June 1864], F-53 1864, Letters Received by the Division, ser. 315, Division of Captured Property, Claims, & Land, RG 56 [X-75].

[31] In addition to the relevant documents in this chapter, see *Official Records*, ser. 1, vol. 26, pt. 1, pp. 735–36; ser. 3, vol. 3, pp. 925–26.

nents of slavery and convinced numerous others that reunion could proceed only on the basis of universal freedom.[32]

Former slaves and most free people of color had held that position from the first. "[F]reedom and liberty is the word with the Collered people," declared a New Orleans "colored man," probably a soldier. "[L]iberty is what we want and nothing Shorter." He spoke for thousands of his fellows when he urged the federal government to "[d]eclare freedom at onc and give us Somting to fight for." But black people in southern Louisiana could not vote, and it was by no means certain that the antislavery wing of the unionist movement, itself beset by internal divisions, could carry the day against a powerful conservative faction determined to block emancipation.[33]

The further Banks ventured into the political fray, the more his labor policies came under public scrutiny. As efforts to readmit Louisiana gathered momentum, assessments of plantation labor in the Department of the Gulf assumed national importance and Banks's measures received increasingly harsh criticism. Some of the negative judgments came from emissaries of the Lincoln administration. General James S. Wadsworth, dispatched by the War Department to investigate conditions along the Mississippi River, worried that former slaves might emerge from the war "not as freedmen, but as serfs." Granted legal protection against their former owners and access to the courts, they would become self-supporting laborers and "peasant cultivators"; without such safeguards, the former slaveholders would so limit their freedom as to make it a mockery. Military restriction of mobility and regulation of wages, Wadsworth charged, furthered the designs of the former owners by denying former slaves the freedom to find the best market for their labor. A restored state government could cite the army's "system of management" as a precedent for measures circumscribing the ex-slaves' liberty. To prevent such an outcome, he recommended that political reconstruction be suspended until the war was over, emancipation was secure at law, and the former slaves had "got the idea of freedom into their heads so that they cannot be reenslaved."

Like Wadsworth, James M. McKaye of the American Freedmen's Inquiry Commission feared that the "temporary arrangement" instituted by Banks established a dangerous precedent. Instead of allowing

[32] Abraham Lincoln, *Collected Works*, ed. Roy P. Basler, Marion D. Pratt, and Lloyd A. Dunlap, 9 vols. (New Brunswick, N.J., 1953–55), vol. 7, pp. 1–2; McCrary, *Abraham Lincoln and Reconstruction*, chaps. 5–7.

[33] For the New Orleans "colored man," see *Freedom*, ser. 2: doc. 54D. For the political activities of the free people of color, see Donald E. Everett, "Demands of the New Orleans Free Colored Population for Political Equality, 1862–1865," *Louisiana Historical Quarterly* 38 (Apr. 1955): 43–64; Rankin, "Impact of the Civil War on the Free Colored Community" and "Origins of Negro Leadership"; Ted Tunnell, *Crucible of Reconstruction: War, Radicalism, and Race in Louisiana, 1862–1877* (Baton Rouge, La., 1984), chap. 4.

wages and the provision of food and clothing to be negotiated in accordance with "the capacities or wishes of the employed or the competition of the labor-market," Banks had set rates of pay by decree and made the workers' living conditions entirely dependent upon "the employer's sense of what is needful." His regulations failed to "recognize the Freedman's right to intervene in his own affairs" and gave insufficient attention to "the great end of educating him to self-control, self-reliance and . . . the exercise of the rights and . . . duties of civilized life." On the whole, McKaye averred, Banks conceded too much to the former slaveholders at a moment when national unification demanded their destruction as a political force. To punish the slaveholders, ensure the welfare of the former slaves, and preserve republican institutions, McKaye recommended a national policy of legal protection for the liberty and property of the freedpeople, including full civil and political rights, and "the ultimate division of the great plantations into moderate sized farms" owned and operated by former slaves and white yeomen.[34]

Sensitive to criticism from such well-placed sources, Banks took the offensive. The former slaves, he maintained, "readily accept the necessity of continuous and faithful labor at just rates of compensation, which they seem willing to leave to the Government." Taking issue with those who condemned military regulation of labor relations, he insisted that government supervision was necessary for the protection of both employers and employees "until the new order of things shall be better understood" by all parties. His plan bore "no color of serfdom," Banks proclaimed; it was "a transition from absolute slavery to absolute freedom."[35]

In January 1864, he took steps to speed the transition. Provisions of the state's constitution and laws that pertained to slavery, he announced, were "inconsistent with the present condition of public affairs, and plainly inapplicable to any class of persons." He therefore declared them "inoperative and void" and forbade their enforcement by any official chosen in the forthcoming state elections. Banks's proclamation – virtually a declaration of emancipation – dashed the hopes of those Louisiana unionists who had expected a reconstituted state government to sustain slavery.[36]

Having dispatched the old labor system, Banks proceeded to revise

[34] James McKaye, "The Emancipated Slave face to face with his old Master: Valley of the Lower Mississippi," [Apr. 1864], filed with O-328 1863, Letters Received, ser. 12, RG 94 [K-66].

[35] M.G.C. N. P. Banks to Hon. J. M. McKaye, 28 Mar. 1864, filed with O-328 1863, Letters Received, ser. 12, RG 94 [K-66]; [Nathaniel P. Banks], *Emancipated Labor in Louisiana* (New York? 1864), p. 19.

[36] Proclamation, Headquarters, Department of the Gulf, 11 Jan. 1864, General Orders (Printed), ser. 1763, Dept. of the Gulf, RG 393 Pt. 1 [C-1074].

the new one. Although represented as a continuation of the previous year's guidelines, General Order 23, issued in early February 1864, in fact embodied substantial changes. References to black workers as "slaves" and "fugitives from service or labor" disappeared. Compensation increased. "[R]espectful, honest, faithful labor" now merited between $8 per month for a "first class hand" and $3 for a "fourth class hand," but at least half of each month's pay was to be withheld until the end of the year. Alternatively, the laborers on an estate might collectively receive one-fourteenth of the net proceeds of the crop. The new regulations required employers to provide medical care to both workers and their dependents, in addition to rations, clothing, and housing. They limited the workday to ten hours and gave laborers a lien upon the crop as security for wages. Moreover, they ordered planters to furnish garden plots and encouraged them to offer "perquisites for extra labor" and "land for share cultivation." Such incentives, Banks suggested, would prepare the former slaves and former slaveholders "for the time when [the laborer] can render so much labor for so much money, which is the great end to be attained."

Declaring work "a public duty, and idleness and vagrancy a crime," Banks was determined to enforce the "universal law of labor." Eventually, he proposed, employers might allow "faithful hands" to rent "extensive tracts," but for the time being former slaves would have to work for hire. In choosing an employer, they "exercised the highest right" and must thereafter abide by a year-long contract. To maintain plantation discipline, Banks extended the prohibition against military recruitment and preserved existing restrictions upon mobility.

For the plantations leased out or directly operated by the government, Samuel Cozzens, the Treasury Department's superintendent of plantations in southern Louisiana, espoused an even more restrictive version of free labor. His plantation regulations, designed to supplement Banks's order, gave employers wide-ranging power "to govern hands," including the right to levy sizable fines for breaches of discipline. In a direct blow at the freedpeople's participation in the local provision economy, Cozzens forbade them to raise pigs, cattle, or draft animals and required the immediate sale of all such livestock in their possession. He also prohibited the cultivation of cotton or sugar cane in their garden plots.

Commencement of the planting season saw federal officers redouble their efforts to return to the countryside the thousands of black refugees who had collected in New Orleans. Colonel Hanks's Bureau of Negro Labor had authority over such people, some of whom received rations and shelter at an abandoned cotton press that served as "rendezvous" and employment office. Hanks's agents hired them out as fast as employers requested them. But many former slaves managed to elude the bureau by "slip[ping] off during the night" or finding "friends here in town who are willing to harbor them." New Orleans continued to shelter disaffected plantation laborers, as well as newly arrived refugees from the Confederacy.

Freedpeople who were unfit for the rigors of plantation employment posed problems for a system premised upon "the universal law of labor." To the fullest extent possible, General Banks expected young, aged, disabled, or sick freedpeople to reside with relatives who were at work on the plantations. In order to obtain the labor of the able-bodied, planters would have to feed and clothe their dependents. Those former slaves who were unable to support themselves and had no relatives upon whom to rely were assigned to "infirm farms" near Donaldsonville and Baton Rouge. There they drew government rations, and those who could do so tended crops of cotton, corn, and vegetables. In the summer of 1864, the two places provided for a total of 800 people, but military officials had no intention of permitting them to become havens for any but the most desperate former slaves. Fewer than 20 of the 300 freedpeople at the Donaldsonville farm were fit for labor, Colonel Hanks believed, "and those are needed to take care of the old."[37]

When black men and women accepted employment on plantations, they demanded not only wages but also control over the pace of work, access to land and other resources for independent production, and recognition of their right to keep poultry and hogs. Their resistance to the constraints of government regulations pitted them by turns against their employers, military provost marshals, and treasury officials. In April 1864, a plantation inspector in Terrebonne Parish found the freedpeople "impressed with the idea that they were under no kind of obligation to work for their employers on Saturday" and convinced that "their contracts did not require them to remain at any one place longer than they were pleased." He was able to correct these "erroneous ideas" by reading Banks's order to them, but other officials met stiffer opposition. When the laborers on another Terrebonne estate refused to work, the local provost marshal forced them back into the fields under an armed guard. Soon, however, they disarmed and beat the sentry, and "it was only after considerable effort that a showing of submission to orders was obtained."[38]

Of all the controversies between planters and laborers, perhaps the most far-reaching involved overseers. To the freedpeople, the overseer was both a detested remnant of slavery and a constant reminder of the regimentation of wartime free labor. Former slaves found it especially

[37] Col. Geo H. Hanks to Maj. George B. Drake, 26 July 1864, filed with C-92 1864, and Col. Geo. H. Hanks to Maj. Geo. B. Drake, 6 Aug. 1864, H-114 1864, Letters Received, ser. 1920, Civil Affairs, Dept. of the Gulf, RG 393 Pt. 1 [C-729].

[38] T. J. Henderson to Capt. S. W. Cozzens, 30 Apr. 1864, vol. 72, pp. 61–73, Reports of Inspectors of Plantations, 3rd Agency, RG 366 [Q-115].

galling to work under men whose habits had been shaped by the old regime, but they also came to resent Northern "managers." Ultimately, the overseer's provenance and title mattered far less than his position in the plantation hierarchy. At times, smoldering resentment flared into fiery confrontation. When a new overseer attempted to establish himself on one estate, the laborers rebelled. "[E]very man, woman and child on the plantation" blocked his passage, and one former slave proclaimed that "the quarter belonged to them and no d----- white man should live there." If he tried to "set foot" in the former overseer's house, "they would burn powder and lead round it all night." Wisely, he chose not to try.

Wartime developments, especially the enlistment of black men into the Union army, guaranteed that many conflicts would focus upon the labor of freedwomen, who constituted an increasingly large majority of the plantation work force. Planters and overseers – whether Southern or Northern – expected all able-bodied hands to labor in the fields; former slaves insisted upon their own right to determine who would work where. In their scheme of things, caring for children, cultivating garden plots, and tending livestock and poultry took precedence over raising staple crops. Women whose households included wage-earning men or older children were especially likely to spurn labor in the field gangs. Freedwomen on one estate refused to cultivate any crops except those in their gardens. Rejecting instructions to join other workers in the fields, women on another plantation served notice that they were "ladies and as good as any white trash."

A contest over gardens emerged in tandem with the struggle over field labor. Freedpeople asserted their right to grow what they pleased and dispose of it as they wished. Although most of them raised vegetables for their own tables or for local markets, a few also grew cotton. Planters objected that allotting land to the laborers for their own use encouraged them to neglect the plantation fields and tempted them to augment their independent harvests through pilferage. Cozzens's regulations sustained the planters. On the Potts estate, where the former slaves who had supported themselves in 1863 had to work for a lessee in 1864, conflict surfaced early in the season. Smarting from their reduction to the status of wage-workers, the freedpeople defiantly claimed "the right to plant cotton or anything else they pleased" in their gardens. But a treasury agent ruled against them. Independent economic activity by former slaves, such officials assumed, should not extend to the cultivation of staple crops.

Planters parried their laborers' every demand and endeavored to turn free labor to their own advantage. Despite military orders to the contrary, they scuttled responsibilities characteristic of the old order, including the support of nonworking plantation residents. Attempting to shift the burden of subsistence, some of them restricted rations, forcing the freedpeople to purchase food at the plantation store or to sustain themselves from the products of their gardens and hen houses. A good many planters refused to pay their laborers' medical expenses. Under slavery, a master's interest encouraged provision of medical care; under free labor, an employer's interest called for discharging sick workers or at least charging lost time and doctors' bills against their wages.

Planter-employers also became adept at manipulating relations of credit to increase their laborers' dependence. Northern lessees pioneered in this area, but former slaveholders learned quickly. As early as January 1864, a Union army physician reported that planters were reducing their employees to debt by charging them not only for "luxuries" like tobacco and coffee, but also for house rent, shoes, and clothing, all of which they were contractually bound to furnish without charge. One provost marshal likened such practices to "the Peonage System which prevails in Mexico." By August 1864, so many employers had reneged on their obligations that Banks sternly reminded them of their responsibilities and directed the provost marshals to enforce compliance.

As Northern lessees and native planters came to adopt similar tactics, former slaves discovered that Yankees long accustomed to free labor were little more likely than former slaveholders to permit them the independence they prized. Determined to extract the maximum profit during their short tenure, lessees pressed their laborers hard. "[M]any of these new men," complained an army officer, "are imprincipled & came down here with a little money, not intending to settle in the country, but merely to enhance their fortunes by a year's operation & to do so regardless of the laborers."

Wartime events frequently upset the best-laid plans of both lessees and resident planters. In the summer of 1864, wholesale recruitment of black soldiers once again intensified the competition for agricultural laborers. Amid fears that a Confederate offensive would jeopardize plantation agriculture and political reconstruction, General Banks rescinded the ban on recruitment and ordered a new draft.[39] A contingent of planters eager to retain their laborers urged Banks to conscript black men working outside the official labor system rather than plantation hands. They targeted city-dwellers who "work just enough to exist" and "vagrants" who had "escaped from Plantation labor" to live in the swamps, where they "cut wood on public and private property for a few days and then idle the balance of the time." When impressment officers attempted to act upon the planters' proposal, they obtained only a handful of conscripts, including some well-to-do free people of color.[40] Having failed to hold the recruiters at bay, the planters begged Banks at least to leave them enough men to harvest the sugar crop. In re-

[39] *Official Records*, ser. 1, vol. 41, pt. 2, pp. 350–51.
[40] *Freedom*, ser. 2: docs. 58A–C.

sponse, he allowed each planter to retain one-fifth of the hands on his estate who were liable to conscription – an exemption large enough to include all coopers, sugar makers, and other skilled laborers. As he had done the previous summer, Banks also agreed to furlough new recruits for the harvest if military circumstances permitted. But these concessions failed to silence the complaints of planters and their advocates, including many treasury officials.[41]

Recruitment was only one component of the crisis besetting southern Louisiana's plantation economy during the summer of 1864. Natural calamity exacerbated the disruptive effects of military occupation and emancipation. Sugar production had declined precipitously since the beginning of the war. During the grinding seasons of 1862 and 1863, planters who doubted the efficacy of free labor had processed their entire cane crop, including that portion normally reserved for seed. They had also failed to repair or replace damaged sugar-mill machinery. By 1864, many of them had shifted to cotton, which required a smaller capital investment and fewer skilled laborers. The change proved disastrous. The cotton crop enjoyed an auspicious beginning, but by late summer it had been decimated by the army worm. Both native planters and Northern lessees took steps to cut their losses. They scrimped on rations and clothing and drove off now-unneeded workers. A few – chiefly lessees – abandoned their plantations altogether, leaving their employees without wages or food.

The short crop and resulting evictions increased the number of freedpeople dependent on the government. They came under the supervision of Thomas W. Conway, a former army chaplain who became head of the Bureau of Negro Labor in August 1864. His predecessor, Colonel Hanks, had departed in disgrace when a military commission uncovered rampant corruption. Himself a silent partner in a leased plantation, Hanks had accepted "bonus" payments from planters for supplying them with laborers, and so had his subordinates. "[T]here is hardly a man in the Office with clean hands," the commission concluded.[42]

Conway struggled to reorganize the bureau, which he pointedly renamed "Bureau of Free Labor," and to redress the wrongs perpetrated upon plantation workers. To prevent planters from dismissing their employees without pay, he forbade them to sell their crops without first satisfying the laborers' lien. When a planter was unable or unwilling to pay, Conway seized the crops. He also collected wages owed to black soldiers who had been conscripted from the plantations before the harvest.[43]

[41] *Official Records*, ser. 1, vol. 41, pt. 2, pp. 429, 518–19; *Freedom*, ser. 2: doc. 60.

[42] Col. Harai Robinson et al. to Major George B. Drake, 20 Aug. 1864, filed as H-42 1864 (supplemental), Letters Received, ser. 1756, Dept. of the Gulf, RG 393 Pt. 1 [C-549].

[43] Thomas W. Conway to Major General S. A. Hurlbut, 1 Feb. 1865, Letters Received, ser. 1920, Civil Affairs, Dept. of the Gulf, RG 393 Pt. 1 [C-746].

In addition to its oversight of plantation laborers, the Bureau of Free Labor remained in charge of dependent freedpeople and refugees from the Confederacy. It operated an orphan asylum in New Orleans for some sixty children, an employment depot in Algiers (across the river from New Orleans), the infirm farm near Baton Rouge, and two "home farms," one in Iberville Parish and the other in St. Charles Parish. Freedpeople who refused offers of employment from "suitable" employers were sent to the home farms to labor without pay under military superintendents. But it seldom came to that. Despite the various disruptions of the summer of 1864, Conway reported, some 50,000 freedpeople in southern Louisiana were working on the plantations for wages: 35,000 under written contracts governed by General Banks's regulations, and an estimated 15,000 without formal contracts but under essentially similar arrangements. At any given moment, only 1,000 or so were supported by the government.[44]

Conway had scarcely assumed his new office when the army's jurisdiction over plantation labor once more came into question. In early July, Congress had granted the Treasury Department broad authority over abandoned land – including that previously worked under military auspices – and charged treasury agents with responsibility for "the employment and general welfare" of those former slaves not employed as soldiers or military laborers.[45] The measure could scarcely have been more ill-timed. By authorizing a change of administrative responsibility in the middle of a crop, Congress inadvertently opened new possibilities for conflict and confusion.

Few of them went untested. In late July, William P. Mellen, general agent of the Treasury Department's special agencies, propounded regulations (issued in the name of the Secretary of the Treasury) to govern plantation labor throughout the Mississippi Valley, including the Department of the Gulf. Mellen's plan differed markedly from that of Banks. It proposed a considerably higher scale of wages: $15 to $25 per month for men and $10 to $18 for women, half of which would be reserved until the end of the year. From these higher wages, however, laborers would have to purchase their own food and clothing. Mellen also proposed to replace military control over plantation labor with a system administered by civilian appointees of the Treasury Department.

Mellen's regulations met immediate resistance from military offi-

[44] Another 30,000 black people, Conway noted, were living and working in New Orleans. In addition to the relevant documents in this chapter, see Thomas W. Conway to Major General N. P. Banks, 9 Sept. 1864, C-228 1864, and Thomas W. Conway to Major General S. A. Hurlbut, 1 Feb. 1865, both in Letters Received, ser. 1920, Civil Affairs, Dept. of the Gulf, RG 393 Pt. 1 [C-732, C-746]; Thomas W. Conway to Major General E. R. S. Canby, 1 July 1865, filed as L-51 1865, Letters Received, ser. 15, Washington Hdqrs., RG 105 [A-8745].

[45] *Statutes at Large*, vol. 13, pp. 375–78.

cials, especially Colonel John Eaton, Jr., general superintendent of freedmen in the Department of Mississippi and the state of Arkansas. Eaton objected both to changing the terms of plantation labor in midyear and to substituting civilian for military authority. He urged treasury officials to suspend the regulations. Hoping to avoid conflict with the War Department and awaiting congressional action regarding a federal bureau of emancipation, William P. Fessenden, the newly appointed Secretary of the Treasury, agreed in August to postpone implementation of the new policy until the following February.[46]

But Fessenden's decision was slow to reach officials in southern Louisiana. Not until December did Benjamin Flanders, the chief treasury agent in the region, learn that Mellen's regulations had long since been suspended. Meanwhile, Flanders and local military authorities were busy making plans for 1865, ignorant of Fessenden's directive. General Stephen A. Hurlbut, who succeeded Banks as commander of the Department of the Gulf in September 1864, and his superior, General Edward R. S. Canby, commander of the Military Division of West Mississippi, both wanted to relieve the army of the "embarrassment" of providing for freedpeople other than soldiers and military laborers.[47] Accordingly, in late October, Hurlbut instructed Flanders to assume jurisdiction over such former slaves and over the plantation labor system. While Secretary of the Treasury Fessenden believed that the military authorities remained in charge, military commanders in southern Louisiana were directing his subordinates to take control.

The change of administration intensified the debate over free labor, as warring constituencies sought to influence policy. In devising a plan for 1865, Flanders solicited suggestions from planters, who did not have to be asked twice. Individually and collectively, they lambasted Banks's system and proposed alternatives. They urged strict enforcement of restrictions on mobility and of the prohibition against laborers' raising livestock. Some planters called for reinstatement of corporal punishment, the only means of exacting "obedience, honesty and faithful labor" from "a people entirely oblivious of moral obligations resulting from their contract."

Flanders received their suggestions with respect. Conway denounced them. Rejecting the assumption that "*Capital* shall control *labor*," Conway countered that "[l]abor is as important as capital, if not more so." The planters, he argued, were the rump of a landed aristocracy, which, though crippled by the war and emancipation, still required close scrutiny by federal authorities. He proposed that Flanders call a public meeting to "take the voice of the colored people themselves into account."

Flanders did not see fit to summon such a gathering, but black

[46] See below, docs. 222A–B.

[47] *Official Records*, ser. 1, vol. 48, pt. 1, pp. 492–93.

people, free and freed, were already making their views known. Much of what they had to say concerned Louisiana's new constitution, ratified by white unionists in September 1864. Although it abolished slavery and gave black people access to the state courts, it denied them the suffrage. This political settlement especially disappointed the free people of color who, though disfranchised, had been active in the unionist movement. They saw in the shift from military to treasury jurisdiction an opportunity to press their claims for equal citizenship. Both publicly and privately, they urged Flanders – himself a leader of the unionist faction that favored universal manhood suffrage – to overhaul the plantation labor system and appoint black men to some of its administrative positions.[48]

Even as the free people of color maneuvered, the special social niche long accorded them was shrinking. Federal officials increasingly ignored their claim to a status distinct from that of former slaves. In April 1864, for example, a plantation inspector ruled that "a free born negro was as much bound by his contract and by the terms of General orders No 23 as any contraband" and therefore required a free-black man who had changed employers to return to the one with whom he had initially contracted.[49] Similarly, in December 1864, when orders went out to impress all the able-bodied black men in Baton Rouge for labor on the levee, free men of color were caught in the dragnet along with former slaves. Objecting to being thus "placed on an equality with contrabands," they protested that their more privileged status had been "well ascertained, and defined long before . . . the present rebellion" and demanded to be "treated as freemen." But military exigencies, like the new civil law, recognized no distinctions between free and freed.

Although the differences between the free people of color and newly liberated freedpeople would continue to engender different outlooks, wartime developments brought their worlds closer together. In January 1865, at a "convention of colored men" dominated by urban free men of color, a large majority of the delegates refused to recognize either the new state constitution or the government elected under it. One faction, associated with the New Orleans *Tribune*, went a giant step further, opposing military regulation of labor and advocating the right of all workers – whatever their color or antebellum status – to seek the best market for their labor. They formed a "bureau of industry" to monitor conditions on the plantations, advise the freedpeople of their rights, and facilitate their "coming and going freely and at will." As the interests of the free people of color increasingly converged with those of

[48] On the politics of the "free state" constitution, see McCrary, *Abraham Lincoln and Reconstruction*, chaps. 5–8; LaWanda Cox, *Lincoln and Black Freedom: A Study in Presidential Leadership* (Columbia, S.C., 1981), chaps. 2–4; Tunnell, *Crucible of Reconstruction*, chaps. 2–4.

[49] T. J. Henderson to Capt. S. W. Cozzens, 30 Apr. 1864, vol. 72, pp. 61–73, Reports of Inspectors of Plantations, 3rd Agency, RG 366 [Q-115].

the former slaves, the freemen sought less to distinguish themselves from the freedmen than to establish themselves as their leaders.[50]

The free people of color, like the military authorities and other interested parties, assumed that administration of plantation labor would be transferred to treasury officials in February 1865, when Banks's General Order 23 expired. Early that month, Mellen reissued his regulations of the previous July. In the intervening months, however, they had come under attack from all sides. Criticism focused on the requirement that laborers purchase food and clothing for themselves and their families out of the half of their wages received each month. Even men earning the highest rates would have difficulty supporting a family on half-pay; lower-paid women and elderly and infirm men could not hope to do so. General Hurlbut feared that the new policy, intended to foster independence by throwing the freedpeople upon their own resources, might instead trap them in debt and reduce them to "a state of peonage."[51] Even Mellen's own subordinates disapproved of his regulations. Without supporters, they became a dead letter. Within two weeks of their reissue, President Lincoln had nullified them, directing military officials to retain control.[52]

The following month, General Hurlbut issued plantation regulations that continued the essentials of Banks's policy, including mandatory year-long contracts and restrictions upon freedom of movement. They required planters to supply their laborers' food, clothing, and medical care, and established minimum wages of $6 to $10 per month for men and $5 to $8 for women, one-half paid quarterly, the balance at the end of the year. Addressing subjects disputed during the previous season, Hurlbut permitted plantation laborers to grow whatever they wished in their garden plots, but forbade them to raise any animals except poultry. While authorizing planters to reduce the wages of workers who lost time on account of illness, he yielded to the laborers' demand for more time of their own by ending the official workweek at noon on Saturday. To provide for dependent freedpeople, he levied an annual tax of $3 per black laborer, $1 to be paid by the laborer and $2 by the employer.

[50] "State Convention of the Colored People of Louisiana," in *Proceedings of the Black State Conventions, 1840–1865*, ed. Philip S. Foner and George E. Walker, 2 vols. (Philadelphia, 1979–80), vol. 2, pp. 243–53. See also Ripley, *Slaves and Freedmen*, pp. 74–75; Messner, *Freedmen and the Ideology of Free Labor*, pp. 109–11; Rankin, "Impact of the Civil War on the Free Colored Community."

[51] M.G. S. A. Hurlbut to Lt. Col. C. T. Christensen, 1 Mar. 1865, vol. 9 DG, pp. 248–49, Letters Sent, ser. 1738, Dept. of the Gulf, RG 393 Pt. 1 [C-762].

[52] See below, doc. 222B. See also Lt. Col. C. T. Christensen to Major General S. A. Hurlbut, 2 Mar. 1865, C-132 1865, Letters Received, ser. 1920, Civil Affairs, Dept. of the Gulf, RG 393 Pt. 1 [C-742]; W. P. Fessenden to Hon. Z. Chandler, 30 Jan. 1865, vol. 8, pp. 476–82, Letters Sent Relating to Restricted Commercial Intercourse: BE Series, ser. 14, RG 56 [X-385].

Hurlbut's plan drew sharp criticism, especially from the New Orleans free people of color. At a public meeting in mid-March, they adopted resolutions demanding absolute freedom of contract, an end to restrictions on mobility, and abrogation of taxes "imposed on account of color." They also called for the establishment of a "tribunal of Arbitrators composed partly of Freedmen," to which the decisions of local provost marshals could be appealed. Declaring military regulation of labor "inconsistent with freedom," they urged that the Bureau of Free Labor be abolished and Conway removed.

Hurlbut defended his course and lashed out at his critics. Citing a "bitterness of feeling" between antebellum free blacks – some of whom had owned slaves – and former slaves, he denied that the freemen could speak for the freed. The former were "striving for social equality," he insisted, the latter "for personal freedom." Military oversight of plantation labor was necessary for the protection of the former slaves, who in fact welcomed it. Conway likewise denounced the free people of color for inducing "ignorant Freedmen" to believe "that they are oppressed and wronged by the Gov^{t}." Hurlbut stood by both his labor regulations and Conway's bureau.[53]

In 1865, as before, federally supervised wage labor on the plantations was the lot of most black men and women in southern Louisiana. But, drawing on their increasing familiarity with the ways of free labor, many freedpeople struck better bargains than the terms prescribed by Hurlbut's order. Increasingly common were share-wage contracts, under which the laborers received part of the proceeds of the crop – sometimes as much as one-third. On a few estates, chiefly in Lafourche and Terrebonne parishes, freedpeople received permission from the Treasury Department to rent government-controlled estates, thereby avoiding wage labor. The black lessees were soon working crops of corn, vegetables, cotton, and, occasionally, sugar cane. In some instances, the rented land was apparently subdivided into plots worked by separate families; in others, the fields were worked collectively by the members of a "company."[54] Such self-directed cultivation attested to the freedpeople's desire for independence and suggested how they themselves might have reorganized plantation labor if given the opportunity.

In southern Louisiana, however, the character of Union occupation and the policies of the federal government prevented the extension of such independent work arrangements to more than a few hundred former slaves. Most proprietors of plantations had either remained at

53 In addition to the relevant documents in this chapter, see Thomas W. Conway to Lt. Col. George B. Drake, 29 May 1865, C-142 1865, Letters Received, ser. 1920, Civil Affairs, Dept. of the Gulf, RG 393 Pt. 1 [C-747].

54 In addition to the relevant documents in this chapter, see C. L. Dunbar to Capt. H. Stiles, 26, 27 Apr. and 6, 25 May 1865, vol. 72, pp. 235–37, 254–57, Reports of Inspectors of Plantations, 3rd Agency, RG 366 [Q-126].

home throughout the occupation, or, by 1865, had returned under the terms of President Lincoln's Proclamation of Amnesty and Reconstruction. As a result, the federal government controlled relatively little abandoned or confiscated land. Moreover, treasury officials were reluctant to subdivide estates, so that still less was offered for rent in small tracts. Equally important, only a handful of former slaves had the capital or the access to credit that were necessary to operate even a modest farm.

In the early months of 1865, as the Lincoln administration's effort to readmit Louisiana generated national debate, both federal authorities and private citizens evaluated the state's wartime experience and considered its implications for the future. Prominent among the commentators were General William F. Smith and James T. Brady, who were commissioned by the Secretary of War to investigate official corruption in the lower Mississippi Valley. When they arrived in southern Louisiana, they turned their attention to the labor system administered by the army, taking testimony from military authorities, treasury agents, and planters.

Asked by the commissioners for a description of conditions on his plantations, William J. Minor, one of the antebellum South's largest slaveholders, painted a bleak picture of uncontrollable laborers and diminished production. "The only certain remedy," he candidly proposed, was "to take us back under the [U.S.] Constitution & establish things as they were, but perhaps under some other name [than slavery]." Minor repudiated the state government elected in 1864 and anticipated the day when the "old citizens" could legislate a system of compulsory labor as thoroughgoing as bondage itself. By allowing white Southerners to "manage their affairs in their own way," agreed another sugar baron, federal authorities could effect a lasting restoration of the Union. Anything else "would be mere hollow truce."

Determined as these former slaveholders were to turn back the clock, their testimony also revealed just how much had changed. Unable to command labor by force, they now relied on military officials to maintain plantation discipline. Not only could they no longer buy and sell slaves, but they were forbidden to contract with their laborers for longer than a year at a time. Their interest in schemes to import workers from tropical countries attested to their realization that the old order was beyond resuscitation. Former slaves, mobilized to protect their freedom and possessed of "a physical ability to resist," would not permit encroachments on their newly won rights.

Freedpeople shared their former owners' apprehension about the future, but for different reasons. The federal government had aided their fight against slavery, initiated their transformation into wage laborers, and eventually confirmed their status as free people. But it had neither placed them in a position to earn an independent livelihood, guaranteed them all the rights of free laborers, nor endowed them with full citizenship. Although the wartime introduction of free labor had resolved certain momentous issues, it left a great many others unsettled and some barely addressed. When the struggle on the battlefields came to an end, the contest over the meaning of free labor had just begun.

63: Surgeon at a New Orleans Military Hospital to the Medical Director of the Department of the Gulf

US. General Marine Hosp– [*New Orleans, La.*] Aug 15th 1862

Doct We need 30 colored women for washi[ng] and cleang, and 50 colored men. If these are now to be had at the Custom House send them up at once. I am informed that there is a large number of them to be had at Camp Parapet. The need is of the most pressing character. Yours Very Truly

ALS Rufus King Brown

[*Endorsement*] We have great need of much help at this Hospital & I therefore recommend these persons may be sent there Charles McCormick Med Director Dept Gulf New Orleans La *Augt 15 1862*

Brig. Surg. Rufus King Brown to Doct., 15 Aug. 1862, #423 1862, Letters Received, ser. 1756, Dept. of the Gulf, RG 393 Pt. 1 [C-506]. The same day, General Benjamin F. Butler, commander of the Department of the Gulf, ordered General John W. Phelps, the commander at Camp Parapet, to "forward to the General (Marine) Hospital 50 colored men and 30 colored women, as their labor is absolutely necessary for the proper care of the sick." (Order, Headquarters Department of the Gulf, 15 Aug. 1862, vol. 2 DG, p. 269, Letters Sent, ser. 1738, Dept. of the Gulf, RG 393 Pt. 1 [C-506].)

64: Order by the Commander of a Brigade in the Left Wing, Department of the Gulf; and an Order by the Brigade Quartermaster

Camp Parapet [*La.*] Sept [*1862*]

After this date all the male negroes, within and about the Camps, will be organized into squads of Fifty or less in number with the woman and children belonging to each squad, under the charge of a private Soldier, who will be furnished with a Roll Book, in which he will enter the names of his squad, designating the married and single and the number of children.

Rations will be drawn for those of the squads that show a disposition to work regularly and for their wives and children and for the sick and disabled. The idle and worthless will not be fed

A. Commissioned Officer will be detailed to superintend (under the direction of the Qr. Master) all the negroes; He will see that the men in charge of squads, report with them every morning at 7 oclock for work. They will labor at such works as may be assigned them untill 12 Oclock when they will be dismissed for dinner untill 2 oclock P.M. at which hour they will resume labor, untill 6 oclock P.M.

Rations will be drawn for these squads, every third day; this to enable the chiefs of squads to designate the Idle and worthless men for whom if they miss Two days labor out of three no rations will be drawn.

The chiefs will designate those present and absent as is done by the Orderly Sergeants of Companies The superintending Officer will have a careful supervision of these matters, as it is the only means in our power by which we can control the labor, and make the presence of these people useful. They will be mustered for Inspection every sunday morning.

It is expected that it will require Twenty men to take charge of these people as chiefs of squads, and these should be sober, Careful & reliable men, who will conscientiously discharge their duties.

The superintending Officer will see that each squad, are at their alloted work regularly at the working hour. The women attached to each squad, will Cook for all the men of the squads, so that no ablebodied men will be left in their quarters under any pretence to Cook.

The Commandants of Regts ands Corps will hand into the Quarter Masters Office Twenty four hours if possible in advance a statement of what work they may need to have done in or about their respective Camps for Cleanliness and Sanitary purposes The Commanders of Regiments are requested to send in the names of Privates as chiefs of squads of the qualifications mentioned above for this duty.

It is intended that hereafter no soldier shall be set at any labor, not strictly military, that can be performed by negroes except as a punishment for offences. For that purpose they will take their places in the working gangs with the negroes so that a soldier who misbehaves may understand what his position will be and govern himself accordingly.

The Chiefs of squads will present their ration returns to the superintending Officer, this return will include those only who have made Two days work out of three, and the really sick. This Officer will consolidate the returns, and draw from the Commissary the full amount needed

Quarter Master Hanks will call upon the Commandants of the Respective Regiments for Two Non Commissioned Officers from Each Reg[t] to assist him in the duties above indicated

HDS Tho[s] W Cahill

[*Camp Parapet, La. September? 1862*]

Instructions for the Non-Commissioned Officers in command of Contraband Colonies at Camp Parapet.

1st

No transfers from one Colony to another will under any circumstances be allowed.

2[d]

The Officer in command of the Colony will assign new arrivals to squads as his judgment may dictate.

3[d]

A perfect system of registration will be complied with. The *name*, *age*, *residence*, *masters name*, *date of arrival*, whether *married or single*, *sex*, N° of *Children*, *age of Children*, their *sex* and "*remarks*" will be writen under their respective heads.

Under the head of "*remarks*" the cause of absence whether by death, desertion or transfer, and all else necessary to account fully for every member of the Colony will be carefully stated opposite their respective names

4th

Roll calls will be at the same hours, as those of the Brigade, immediately after retreat each day the commandants of Colonies will hand to the Supervising Officer a report of their commands showing fully their numerical and Sanitary condition.

5th

The chiefs of squads will daily note upon their roll book the delinquents from duty and report the same to the chief of the Colony who will inquire into the cause of the delinquency, and unless a good and sufficient cause therefor is apparent, he will withold from said delinquent his rations for the next three days.

6th

The Chiefs of squads will report promptly to the Quarter Master with their men for duty every morning (Sundays excepted) at 8 o:clock, and every afternoon at 2 o:clock.

HDS Geo H Hanks

Order by Col. Thos. W. Cahill, Head Quarters Left Wing, Sept. [1862], filed with Lt. Geo. H. Hanks, Instructions for the Non-Commissioned Officers in command of Contraband Colonies at Camp Parapet, [Sept.? 1862], both filed as Sept. 1863, Letters Received, ser. 1860, Defences of New Orleans, RG 393 Pt. 2 No. 95 [C-1005]. The final paragraph of Cahill's order is in his own handwriting. A notation on the wrapper erroneously dates the two orders as September 1863.

65: Order by the Commander of the 1st Division of the Department of the Gulf

Carrollton, La., October 17, 1862.

GENERAL ORDERS No. 14. After a careful examination into the condition of the contrabands who have found their way into the limits of this command, and who, under existing laws and the unfortunate condition of affairs, are forced upon the guardianship and control of the military authorities of the United States, it is found that the camps are infested with large numbers of them, under the pretence of services as cooks, waiters, policemen, etc., but who, in fact, in their present situation, are not only of little practical advantage to the service, but are rapidly demoralizing this command, and destroying the usefulness of the soldiery. It is found too, that recent attempts to render the contrabands useful to the Government as well as of service to themselves, have been foiled, to a great extent, through a licentious and destructive course pursued towards them by many of this command.

For the welfare of the contrabands, and to save them from idle and vicious habits, it is necessary that they should work; and as they are yet too ignorant, thoughtless and improvident to think and act judiciously for themselves, they must be subjected to wholesome rules and restraints. The police of the parish too, demands this: theft, robbery and vagrancy must cease.

It is therefore ORDERED—

I. Hereafter, no contrabands other than the recognized servants of officers, those hereinafter allowed as assistants in company kitchens, and those on duty in the Staff Departments, after being regularly received into service and enrolled for that purpose, will be permitted at any time within the camps, and the commanding officers of camps will be held responsible that this order is faithfully carried out.

Commanding officers of camps, guards and provost guards, etc., will cause their vicinities to be habitually patrolled, day and night, and all contrabands, not on duty, found outside of their colonies without a written pass signed by their superintendents, will be taken up and confined, or sent back to their colonies.

The Provost Guard in Carrollton will be responsible that no contrabands but those on duty there remain in the place.

II. The superintendents of contrabands will keep all the contrabands they may have enrolled, or may hereafter enrol, in their colonies or places of residence, when off duty, so that all able-bodied men and women be at all times in readiness for any service required of them. No contraband will be allowed to stroll away from his colony without a written pass from the superintendent.

III. The contrabands will be disposed of as follows:

1st. The officers of the Staff Departments will receive into the service of their Departments all able-bodied contrabands the service may require, and on the last day of every month render a monthly report of the contrabands hired, agreeably to Form 2, Quartermaster's Department, Army Regulations, to the Chiefs of their Departments.

The pay of the contrabands will be rated according to the value of their labor, but not to exceed $10 per month in any case. Each person thus employed will receive one ration daily in kind.

Clothing will be furnished by the Government to the contrabands thus employed, but not to exceed the value of $3 per month for each person, and the money value of the clothing issued will be deducted from their pay established as above.

2d. Officers may supply themselves with the number of servants they are entitled to by law from the contrabands, at a fair compensation agreed upon between themselves, when they are not required for the public service.

3d. When not required for the public service, two contrabands per company may be employed as *assistants* in the company kitchens, but only with their own consent, and on condition that they shall be compensated by the company.

4th. It is believed that the above dispositions will absorb every able-bodied contraband; those which remain, viz: the decrepid and sick, will receive all proper attention from the superintendents of contrabands and the officers of the Medical Department.

IV. No contraband will receive rations from the Government unless enrolled for service in the Staff Departments as above, or unless sick or decrepid, and unable to work; except that, the wives and children of contraband employees may receive rations as follows: to each person over 14 years of age, one ration; to each person upwards of 2 and under 14 years of age, half a ration. The money value of the rations, thus furnished at cost price, will be deducted from the pay of the employees.

When found absolutely necessary to issue clothing to the families of employees, its money value at cost price will be deducted from his or her wages. By order of BRIG. GEN. SHERMAN.

PD

General Orders No. 14, Headquarters 1st Div., Dep't of the Gulf, 17 Oct. 1862, filed with Lt. Geo. H. Hanks to Capt. R. O. Ives, 17 Jan. 1863, H-184 1863, Letters Received, ser. 1756, Dept. of the Gulf, RG 393 Pt. 1 [C-537]. On January 19, 1863, in response to an inquiry about the adequacy of the rations allotted to black military laborers, General Thomas W. Sherman forwarded this printed copy of his general order, with an endorsement explaining its rationale. The contrabands' "peculiar state of transition," Sherman declared, "has produced among them, ignorant and unreflecting as they are, such strange ideas of liberty that it has been found difficult to keep them at work." Previously, slaves who came under federal control "had been indulged in idleness to such an extent as to render labor almost forgotten by them." Since the enforcement of his order, however, "a gradual improvement [had] taken place. But still many of them are so irregular at work that it has been found impracticable to enrol them for pay *by the month*."

66: Order by the Commander of the Department of the Gulf

New Orleans, November 1, 1862.

GENERAL ORDERS No. 88.

I. No person will be arrested as a slave, by any Policeman or other person, and put in confinement for safe keeping, unless the person arresting knows that such person is owned by a loyal citizen of the United States.

II. The Inspector and Superintendent of Prisons is authorized to discharge from confinement all slaves not known to be the slaves of loyal owners. By command of MAJOR-GENERAL BUTLER.

PD

General Orders No. 88, Headquarters Department of the Gulf, 1 Nov. 1862, General Orders (Printed), ser. 1763, Dept. of the Gulf, RG 393 Pt. 1 [C-1086]. Later that same month, General Butler ordered that all slaves confined in the New Orleans police jail be discharged after ten days unless their "reputed owners" paid all outstanding jail fees, and that no slave should thereafter be incarcerated unless the fees were paid in advance, "the slave to be released when the money is exhausted." "This is the course taken in all countries with debtors confined by creditors," Butler reasoned, "and slaves have not such commercial value in New-Orleans, as to justify their being held and fed by the City, relying upon any supposed lien upon the slave." Butler also appointed a commission to determine the amount of jail fees owed by the U.S. government on account of black people who had already been released from jail and set to work at military labor. (General Orders No. 99, Headquarters Department of the Gulf, 21 Nov. 1862, General Orders [Printed], ser. 1763, Dept. of the Gulf, RG 393 Pt. 1 [C-1086].)

67: Commander of the Department of the Gulf to the Secretary of War; Enclosing, First, a Memorandum of a Contract between the United States and Planters in Two Louisiana Parishes and, Second, an Order by the Department Commander

New-Orleans, November 14th *1862.*

Sir; I have addressed you directly in this despatch because the subject relates to other matters than the movements of troops in the field.

As you may have learned from the despatches to General Halleck, I have moved Brig Genl Weitzel into the La Fourche country, and have taken possession of the richest portion of Louisiana. Thousands of hogsheads of sugar of the value of at least a Million of Dollars ought at once to pass into the hands of the United States, together with much other property. I have therefore organized a Commission to take charge of the whole business so as if possible to save this property to the United States. and have put the ablest and most honest men I have at the head of it.

I annex the copy of the Order No 91, and of the Memorandum of Contract which will explain themselves.

The experiment of free labor which I am trying, is succeeding admirably and I hope large results, not so much in profit to the United States as in example.

Will you allow me to avail myself of this note to ask of you reinforcements. I have had none save my free native guards (colored), and while they are doing good service, still I find trouble because they are not formally recognized by the Department. I have the honor to be Very Respectfully Your Ob'dt Servant

HLS Benj F Butler

[*Enclosure*] [*New Orleans, La. late October?, 1862*]

Memorandum

of an arrangement entered into between the Planters, loyal citizens of the United States, in the Parishes of St. Bernard and Plaquemines, in the State of Louisiana, and the Civil and Military authorities of the United States in said State.

Whereas many of the persons held to service and labor have left their masters and claimants and have come to the city of New Orleans and to the Camps of the army of the Gulf, and are claiming to be emancipated and free, And whereas these men and women are in a destitute condition, And whereas it is clearly the duty, by Law, as well as in humanity of the United States to provide them with food and clothing, and to employ them in some useful occupation,

And whereas it is necessary that the crop of cane and cereals, now growing and approaching maturity in said Parishes shall be preserved and the Levees repaired and strengthened against floods;

And whereas the Planters claim that these persons are still held to service and labor, and of right ought to labor for their masters, and the ruin of their crops and plantations will happen if deprived of such services,

And whereas these conflicting rights and claims cannot immediately be determined by any tribunals now existing in the State of Louisiana;

In order therefore to preserve the rights of all parties, as well those of the Planters as of the persons, claimed as held to service and labor and claiming their freedom, and those of the United States, and to preserve the crops and property of loyal citizens of the United States and to provide profitable employment at the rate of compensation fixed by act of Congress for those persons who have come within the lines of the army of the United States,[1]

It is agreed and determined that the United States will employ all the persons heretofore held to labor on the several plantations in the Parishes of St. Bernard and Plaquemines belonging to loyal citizens as they have heretofore been employed and as nearly as may be under the charge of the Loyal Planters and overseers of said Parishes and other necessary directions.

The United States will authorize or provide suitable guards and patrols to preserve order and prevent crime in the said Parishes.

The Planters shall pay for the services of each able-bodied male persons Ten (10) Dollars per month, three (3) of which may be expended for necessary clothing, and for each woman   dollars, and for each child above the age of ten (10) years and under the age of sixteen (16) years the sum of   dollars, all the persons above the age of sixteen years being considered as men and women for the purpose of labor.

Planters shall furnish suitable and proper food for each of these laborers and take care of them and furnish proper medicines in case of sickness,

The Planters shall also suitably provide for all the persons incapacitated by sickness or age, for labor bearing the relation of Parent child or wife of the laborer so laboring for him.

Ten hours each day shall be a day's labor, and any extra hours during which the laborer may be called by the necessities of the occasion to work shall be reckoned as so much towards another days labor, Twenty six days of ten hours each shall be deemed a month's labor except in the month of December, when twenty shall make a month's labor, It shall be the duty of the overseer to keep a true and exact account of the time of labor of each person and any wrong or inaccuracy therein shall forfeit a months pay to the person so wronged.

No cruel or corporal punishment shall be inflicted by any one upon the persons so laboring or upon his or her relatives, but any insubordination or refusal to perform suitable labor or other crime or offence shall be at once reported to the Provost Marshal, for the district and punishment suitable for the offence shall be inflicted under his orders preferably imprisonment in darkness on bread and water.

This arrangement to continue at the pleasure of the United States.

If any Planter of the Parishes of St. Bernard or Plaquemines refuse to enter into this arrangement or remains a disloyal citizen, the persons claimed & to be held to service, by him may hire themselves to any loyal Planter or the United States may elect to carry on his plantations by their own agents and other persons than those thus claimed may be hired by any planter at his election. It is expressly understood and agreed that this arrangement shall not be held to effect, after its termination, the legal rights of either master or slave; but that the question of freedom or slavery are to be determined by considerations wholly outside of the provisions of this contract, provided always that the abuse of any master or overseer of any person laboring under the provisions of this contract shall after trial and adjudication by the military or other courts emancipate the person so abused.

HD

[*Enclosure*] *New Orleans, November* 9, 1862.

GENERAL ORDERS No. 91. The Commanding General being informed, and believing, that the District west of the Mississippi River, lately taken possession of by the United States troops, is most largely occupied by persons disloyal to the United States, and whose property has become liable to confiscation under the Acts of Congress and the [P]roclamation of the President,[2] and that sales and transfers of said property are being made for the purpose of depriving the Government of the same, has determined, in order to secure the rights of all persons as well as those of the Government, and for the purpose of enabling the crops now growing to be taken care of and secured, and the unemployed laborers to be set at work, and provision made for payment of their labor–

To order, as follows:

I. That all the property within the District to be known as the "District of Lafourche," be and hereby is sequestered, and all sales or transfers thereof are forbidden, and will be held invalid.

II. The District of Lafourche will comprise all the territory in the State of Louisiana lying west of the Mississippi river, except the Parishes of Plaquemine and Jefferson.

III. That

Major Joseph M. Bell, Provost Judge, President,

Lieut. Col. J. B. Kinsman, A.D.C.

Capt. Fuller (75th N.Y. Vols.), Provost Marshal of the District, be a Commission to take possession of the property in said District, to make an accurate inventory of the same, and gather up and collect all such personal property, and turn over to the proper officers, upon their receipts, such of said property as may be required for the use of the United States Army; to collect together all the other personal property, and bring the same to New Orleans, and cause it to be sold at public auction to the highest bidders, and after deducting the necessary expenses of care, collection and transportation, to hold the proceeds thereof subject to the just claims of loyal citizens and those neutral foreigners who in good faith shall appear to be the owners of the same.

IV. Every loyal citizen or neutral foreigner who shall be found in actual possession and ownership of any property in said District, not having acquired the same by any title since the 18th day of September last, may have his property returned or delivered to him without sale, upon establishing his condition to the judgment of the Commission.

V. All sales made by any person not a loyal citizen or foreign neutral since the 18th day of September, shall be held void, and all sales whatever, made with the intent to deprive the Government of its rights of confiscation, will be held void, at what time soever made.

VI. The Commission is authorized to employ in working the plantation of any person who has remained quietly at his home, whether he be loyal or disloyal, the negroes who may be found in said District, or who have, or may hereafter, claim the protection of the United States, upon the terms set forth in a memorandum of a contract heretofore offered to the planters of the Parishes of Plaquemine and St. Bernard, or white labor may be employed at the election of the Commission.

VII. The Commissioners will cause to be purchased such supplies as may be necessary, and convey them to such convenient depots as to supply the planters [in] the making of the crop; which supplies will be charged against the crop manufactured and shall constitute a lien thereon.

VIII. The Commissioners are authorized to work for the account of the United States such plantations as are deserted by their owners, or are held by disloyal owners, as may seem to them expedient, for the purpose of saving the crops.

IX. Any persons who have not been actually in arms against the United States since the occupation of New Orleans by its forces, and who shall remain peaceably upon their plantations, affording no aid or comfort to the enemies of the United States, and who shall return to their allegiance, and who shall, by all reasonable methods, aid the United States when called upon, may be empowered by the Commission to work their own plantations, to make their own crop, and to retain possession of their own property, except such as is necessary for the military uses of the United States. And to all such persons the Commission are authorized to furnish means of transportation for their crops and supplies, at just and equitable prices.

X. The Commissioners are empowered and authorized to hear, determine, and definitely report upon all questions of the loyalty, disloyalty or neutrality of the various claimants of property within said District; and further, to report such persons as in their judgment ought to be recommended by the Commanding General to the President for amnesty and pardon, so that they may have their property returned; to the end that all persons that are loyal, may suffer as little injury as possible, and that all persons who have been heretofore disloyal, may have opportunity now to prove their loyalty and to return to their allegiance, and save their property from confiscation, if such shall be the determination of the Government of the United States. By command of MAJOR-GENERAL BUTLER.

PD

Maj. Genl. Benj. F. Butler to Hon. Edwin M. Stanton, 14 Nov. 1862, enclosing agreement between the planters of St. Bernard and Plaquemines parishes and the United States, [late Oct.? 1862], and General Orders No. 91, Headquarters Department of the Gulf, 9 Nov. 1862, filed as G-838 1862, Letters Received, ser. 12, RG 94 [K-30]. The blank spaces left for the wages to be paid to women and to children appear in the manuscript memorandum.

1 Section 15 of the Militia Act, approved on July 17, 1862, set the wages of black military laborers employed under its provisions at $10 per month ($3 of which was deducted for clothing). (*Statutes at Large*, vol. 12, pp. 597–600.)
2 The First Confiscation Act of August 1861 authorized the seizure of property

used on behalf of the Confederacy; the Second Confiscation Act of July 1862 provided for the seizure and sale of property owned by persons disloyal to the Union; President Lincoln's proclamation of July 25, 1862, warned persons in rebellion "to return to their proper allegiance to the United States" or face forfeiture of their property under the July 1862 act. (*Statutes at Large*, vol. 12, pp. 319, 589–92, 1266.)

68: Member of the Sequestration Commission to the Commander of the Department of the Gulf

Thibodaux [*La.*] Nov– 19– *1862*–

General: Gen. Weitzel referred to me an Order for 150 negroes– brought by Mr Weed–

Allow me to state the facts– Probably from 1500 to 2000 negroes have been enlisted & run off to New Orleans– Very many have returned to the Plantations they left and are now at work– The Quartermasters & Commissaries have many in their employ, & claim their services as a military necessity– I have a train of 80 to 100 carts sparsely manned with drivers & a few men to load & unload the carts–

Gen. Weitzel has 150 men from the Com. at work on a military road– Thus are the negroes at the disposal of the Commission employed.

I could not fill Mr Weed's Order without stopping my train and giving him nothing but teamsters whom it is difficult to replace–

As the Order was not to me, I refused to stop the train & reported to Gen. Weitzel– He approved my decision & thus the matter rests–

Furthermore Mr Weed positively refused to take the women & children of the train; and I doubted very much whether the Major General commanding would stop the hauling of 250 to 300 Hds of sugar by the Com. to work plantations below the city.

I think a little effort around Algiers & a few miles above it, might pick up plenty of hands that have left this vicinity–

I await Orders however, while I beg leave to remain, General, very respectfully Your obedient servant

ALS T. K. Fuller

Capt. T. K. Fuller to Maj. Gen. Butler, 19 Nov. 1862, #814 1862, Letters Received, ser. 1756, Dept. of the Gulf, RG 393 Pt. 1 [C-511]. Captain Fuller was also provost marshal of the District of Lafourche, which was commanded by General Godfrey Weitzel. A search of the records of the Department of the

Gulf revealed neither a reply to Fuller's letter nor any order issued in response to it. Charles A. Weed, a Northern civilian, had, on October 13, 1862, been appointed by General Benjamin F. Butler, the department commander, to "take charge" of sugar plantations between New Orleans and Fort Jackson, Louisiana, that had been abandoned by their owners, and to harvest growing crops "for the benefit of the United States." Butler had directed officials in charge of contraband camps to accommodate Weed's requests for laborers, empowered Weed "in scarcity of Contrabands" to "employ white laborers at $1.00 per day," and ordered the quartermaster and commissary departments to furnish Weed with provisions and supplies. (Special Orders No. 441, Head Qts. Dept. of the Gulf, 13 Oct. 1862, vol. 27 DG, p. 171, Special Orders, ser. 1767, Dept. of the Gulf, RG 393 Pt. 1 [C-965].)

69: Testimony in the Trial of Four Louisiana Slaves before a Military Commission

New Orleans Nov. 21′ 1862.

United States v George Windberry & als	Upon being arraigned the Prisoners pleaded severally that they were *not guilty*, when the following witnesses being duly sworn testified –

. . . .

Henry Clement Millandon.

Know the Prisoners – they belong to my father Laurent Millandon. they have been living on the Estrella Plantation in the Parish of Jefferson – Knew Mr McKay in his lifetime – early in the year 1862 he went to take charge of the Estrella Plantation as overseer – and was overseer of the Plantation Estrella Oct 9th last – He was alone there without any other white persons – the Plantation was four miles from the front or River Plantation. & about 10 miles from the city –

On the morning of the 9th I rode down to the Plantation found McKay who complained of the conduct of the boys particularly George. I summoned before me George. I said to him McKay complained of his impudence. & that he must not behave in that manner, he answered me roughly saying it was a lie, I also told him Mr McKay believed it was him who attempted to enter his house one night after he was abed. Geo denied it in a very rough manner. I told him I did not pretend to keep any body on the Plantation by force – and that any [one] who was not satisfied might leave – but as for him or any of them to undertake to rule the

Plantation I would not allow it – I was talking to him politely – & if he did not cease his rough manner I would slap him – He said I dare not do it – I then struck with my whip on the head – I don't remember precisely what took place next – only that we fell down together, we were next up, I with my pistol in my hand. which I kept before him until he retreated a few steps when he turned and ran. I fired sideways to scare him. My desire was to tie him and take him to the pickets – two minutes afterwards I saw him coming towards me with an axe in his hand – when about 40 yards distance from me he was stopped by one of the boys. I think Ceasar – they had a scuffle and after a while George disappeared – the deceased was a spectator of this scene but took no part in it – I then gave orders to the boys I met among whom were Ceasar, and Sam'l Hall another boy, to have the boy George secured & carried to the front plantation and delivered to Capt Lyons comdg. pickets at the Canal, to whom I was going to report. a few moments after my Cousin & myself after talking with M^c^Kay went off to the front plantation leaving M^c^Kay there. it was then 7 1/2 or 8 o'clock a.m.

When I had got about half way between the two Plantations, I overtook the boy George going in the same direction – as I passed – he halloed don't shoot me and jumped into the cane. I said, "Geo I don't want to shoot you – you can go wherever you please" – He replied, "I want you though, me," I turned my horse towards him and said, "well come on then if you want me" – He did not come – I then turned & rode towards the pickets he following running & shouting – when I reached the picket (there were two sentinels together) I pointed to the boy coming and told them to stop him and detain him until I could go to cap't Lyons and report him. I went to cap't Lyons & reported. I then went towards my house – while on the way & near my house I met, the boy, Sam'l Hall – who told me what was going on, on the back plantation the "Estrella" – in consequence of what he told me I again went immediately to Cap't Lyons – Soon after Cap't L. & about 10 or 12 men, soldiers came, and we proceeded towards the Estrella Plantation When we arrived at the first-named picket I did not see the boy George – When we had got about 30 or 40 Acrés from the River we met the boy George – [mounted] on the overseer's horse, with one of his pistols on his person – Cap't L. arrested him & ord[d] him to report himself to the picket & took away the pistol – some ten acres farther, we met a cart, Freeman (boy) was in it. the boys James Wilcox. Sam Picker, Hanson. & I think W[m] Picker was driving – all slaves, belonging to the plantation – In the cart we found the body of M[c]Kay, the deceased, dead – Cap't L. stopped the cart and asked if the man was dead. one of the boys answered he is dead now– Cap't L. asked who Killed him– the boy Freeman, replied very quietly, "I Killed him sir–" Cap't L. then asked him for the gun which he held in his hand–& asked whose gun it was & how long he had it–? He replied the gun was his own & he had it a long time– it was a single-barrel musket of large calibre–for ball– Cap't L. also took away from the boys in the cart several balls, some shot, powder, and caps a double-barrelled shot gun & a pistol belonging to the overseer– he then arrested the boys–and marched them forward to the front Plantation– when we got to the pickets we found the boy George waiting– He joined us & we went on to the front Plantation, where they were left with the guard– The body of deceased was left at the hospital at my house–on the front plantation– the boy, Sam Picker, was wounded on the lip– that evening I saw the boy, Ceasar, at the Hospital, he was wounded in the left shoulder I think by a pistol bullet–

The employment of Freeman & George, was that of chopping wood, of Sam Picker of cutting hay, & of Ceasar that of his trade a cooper on that morning– Ceasar & George were the only two of the Prisoners I observed at the quarters that morning–

Deceased was about 47 yrs old–was of Kind disposition–rather ascetic–unmarried–lacked force of character–had not much agricultural skill and on the whole was unfitted for the place– there were 175 negroes all told on the place–& about 16 or 18 missing. Deceased had a gun (double barrel shot) & a pair of Pistols in his house.

Deceased always told me that Ceasar, was the only boy that he could trust or was not afraid of on the Plantation–

I never had any complaint of George before–

. . . .

New Orleans, November 24th 1862.

The whole Court met this morning according to adjournment, After the transaction of other business. the farther examination of this case was resumed–

James Wilcox– }

Am slave of Millandon on Estrella Plantation, Know deceased since last spring. Know the Prisoners– On that day, I was in the woods. & heard of the difficulty with George– I picked up my tools, saw. 2 axes, & measuring pole–& came home– after I got to my quarters, I heard a report of a gun, Soon after I saw Ceasar, coming holding one of his arms with the other–& some of the boys met him & helped him to his house– I asked what was the matter my wife said Mr Mackey shot your brother– I looked &

saw my brother – Sam Picker coming with his jaw tied up – I asked Sam what M[c]Kay shot him with he said he shot him with a gun, but didn't Know whether it was with shot or a ball – I then asked what he was doing there – he said he was not there but had been working with the hoeing gang, and as he came along home by the house of M[c]Kay he shot. By that time I heard another report of a gun or pistol – from overseers house & saw Freeman dodge at the report – Freeman then said, that M[c]Kay's ball had just missed his face – but he would try not to miss him – M[c]Kay then passed through the opening between the door and stancil to see the effect of his shot – as he did so, Freeman fired at him – and shot him through the arm and in the right side – "here's a man gentleman that has caused me to shoot him, he shot at me first and now I have shot him and I never had a [wry] word with him in my life," this was said as M[c]Kay was coming out of his house – there were there beside Freeman & myself, Sam Picker, Hanson & the folks were standing off at a distance – Freeman was not in the yard of the overseer at the time – I didn't see any of the boys in the yard – M[c]Kay ran out flourishing his pistol – and ran towards the driver's house – just as he got to the driver's house he fell We then went to him and picked him up – I heard but one shot fired at him – we laid him over the gutter hitched up a cart, laid him in the Cart, put in his pistols gun powder &c, in the Cart with him, & then started to the pickets with him – while on the way to the pickets he died – as he fell he struck his forehead upon the edge of a tub or foot-bucket that stood at the door of the driver's house – I think that was the way in which he was wounded in the forehead – no lick was struck him he was shot – after we put him in the Cart Hanson and I went into his house to get his gun &c. I then saw several shot in the door at the place where he stood when Freeman fired – it was the door farthest from the quarters and next to the Kitchen – He lived about half an hour after he was shot – didn't speak to any of us – I said to him when we went to take him up "Well Mr M[c]Kay your pistol has brought you to your ruin." he raised his hand up with his pistol still in it – when we ran away from him. just as Mr M[c]Kay was shot George came up as though he was coming from the front Plantation – Geo' asked how we shot him – Freeman said he shot him – Geo said he came to get his things and he wasn't going to stay another moment on the place. he helped to put him in the cart – Geo said to us after we put M[c]Kay in the cart – "well boys I suppose this affray come about me – if young master hadn't come down and shot and missed the first time I suppose this affray wouldn't have been. I'll go along to the pickets with you – ". Freeman said, "yes, you'd better go along, I have done something I never had to do in my life before–" never Knew of any previous difficulty– between Freeman & M^c^Kay– When I first saw Freeman he was standing between his quarters and the overseer's house, nearer to his quarters, had his gun in his hand, that's the time he was shot at– nobody was nearer to the overseer's house at that time than Freeman–

. . . .

Freeman – Pris examined –

I had this gun, a musket, about 2 yrs bo't it of an Indian– I only used it for hunting. I had been over in the swamps next the sugar-house to my traps– I heard racket at the overseer's house. then I heard a report of a gun. then M^c^Kay shot at me. I saw Ceasar & asked him if he thought M^c^Kay shot at me– He said yes, he says he had orders to shoot & would shoot. I went to my house, got my gun, and said to myself–if he shoots at me again I will shoot him. My gun was loaded– I said nothing more to Ceasar, I next saw Ceasar–he was shot– M^c^Kay then saw me and shot at me, I then shot him– Wilcox was standing at the Driver house– it was loaded with buck-shot & some small shot with it– I was not present in the morning when Master was there– I was in the woods– Didn't see Geo' that morning–had nothing to say to him– I didn't speak with any of the boys except Ceasar– I can't blame any of the boys but myself– I wouldn't have shot him if he hadn't shot at me– When M^c^Kay ran out with his pistol. I ran away–

No one of the boys advised me to shoot Mr M^c^Kay– When M^c^Kay shot at me I made up my mind that if he shot again, I would shoot him– I was cross– M^r^ MaKey would be alive today if Millanden had not given him orders to shoot– Here the evidence closed–

. . . .

HD

Excerpts from proceedings of a military commission in the case of George Windberry et al., 21 & 24 Nov. 1862, MM-499, Court-Martial Case Files, ser. 15, RG 153 [H-5]. The four defendants–Freeman Washington, George Windberry, Sam Picker, and Ceasar McQueen–were charged with murdering their overseer, William P. D. McKay. Windberry, Picker, and McQueen were acquitted; Washington was found guilty and sentenced "to be hung by the neck until he be dead."

70: Commander of the Department of the Gulf to the President

New-Orleans, November 28th *1862.*

Dear Sir; I am exceedingly obliged for your kind note enquiring for the success of our experiment in attempting the cultivation of sugar by free labor, and am happy to report it is succeeding admirably. I am informed by the Government agent who has charge that upon one of the plantations where sugar is being made by the negros who had escaped therefrom into our lines and have been sent back under wages that with the same negros and the same machinery by *free labor* a hogshead and a half more of sugar has been made in a day than was ever before made in the same time on the plantation under slave labor.

Your friend Col Shaffer has had put up to be forwarded to you a barrel of the first sugar ever made by *free black labor* in Louisiana and the fact that it will have no flavor of the degrading whip will not I know render it less sweet to your taste.

The planters seem to have been struck with a sort of Judicial blindness and some of them so deluded have abandoned their crops rather than work them with free labor.

I offered them as a basis a contract the copy of which is enclosed for your information.

It was rejected by many of them because they would not relinquish the right to use the whip, although I had provided a punishment for the refractory by means of the Provost Marshal as you will see "preferably imprisonment in darkness on bread and water." I did not feel that I had a right by the Military power of the United States to send back to be scourged at the will of their former, and in some cases infuriated masters those black men who had fled to me for protection, while I had no doubt of my right to employ them under the charge of whomsoever I might choose to work for the benefit of themselves and the Government. I have therefore caused the negros to be informed that they should have the same rights as to freedom if so the law was on the plantation as if they were in camp, and they have in a great majority of instances gone back willingly to work and work with a will. They were at first a little adverse to going back lest they should lose some rights which would come to them in camp, but upon our assurances are entirely content.

I think this scheme can be carried out without loss to the Government, and I hope with profit enough to enable us to support for six months longer the starving whites and blacks here. A somewhat Herculean task!

We are feeding now daily in the City of New Orleans more than

32.000 whites, 17.000 of which are British born subjects and mostly claiming British protection, and only about 2.000 of whom are American citizens – the rest being of the several Nationalities who are represented here from all parts of the globe.

Beside this we have some ten thousand negros to feed besides those at work on the plantations, principally women and children.

All this has thus far been done without any draft upon the Treasury, although how much longer we can go on is a problem of which I am most anxiously seeking a solution.

I take the liberty to enclose to you a Synopsis of our report of the Relief Commission published weekly, which may be interesting upon this topic. (The Synopsis only shows the free-colored before the war.)

Of course our operations are mostly yet unorganized and without that completeness necessary to insure success, but I hope to get them in such form that they will work. The operations of General Weitzel in the Lafourche country, the richest sugar planting part of Louisiana, have opened to us a very large number of slaves, all of whom under the Act are free,[1] and large crops of sugar as well those already made as those in process of being made.

I do myself the honor to enclose to you the order that I have made to meet this state of things (Order No 91) to protect the rights of the United States and of all concerned from the rapacity of swindlers and speculators – and the effects of disloyalty. All the inhabitant of this portion of the country are rapidly returning to their allegiance and the Elections are being organized for Wednesday next, and I doubt not a large vote will be thrown.

I found Dr Cotman to be one of the candidates in the field, but, as he had voluntarily signed the Ordinance of Secession as one of the convention which passed it, and had sat for his portrait in the cartoon which was intended to render those signers immortal – which was painted and exhibited here in the shop-windows in imitation of the picture of our signers of the Declaration of Independence, and as the Doctor had never by any public act testified his abnegation of that act of signing – I thought it would be best that the Government should not be put to the scandal of having a person so situated elected, although the Doctor may be a good Union man now. So I very strongly advised him against the Candidature. It looked too much like Aaron Burr's attempt to run for a seat in Parliament after he went to England to avoid his complications in his Mexican affairs and his combat with Hamilton. It is but fair to say that Dr Cotman, after some urging, concluded to withdraw his name from the Canvas.

Two good *unconditional* Union men will be elected. I fear however we shall lose Mr Bouligny. He was imprudent enough to run for the office of Justice of the peace under the secessionists, and although I believe him always to have been a good Union man and to have sought that office for personal reasons only, yet this fact tells against him. However Mr Flanders will be elected in his district and a more reliable or better Union man cannot be found.

But to return to our Negros. I find this difficulty in prospect. Many of the planters here while professing loyalty and I doubt not feeling it, if the "institution" can be spared to them, have agreed together not to make any provision this Autumn for another crop of sugar next season. Hoping thereby to throw upon us an immense number of Blacks without employment and without any means of support for the future. The planters themselves living upon what they may make from this crop. Thus no provision being made for the crop either of corn, potatoes or cane, the Government will be obliged to come to their terms for the future employment of the negros or to be at enormous expense to support them.

We shall have to meet this as best we may. Of course we are not responsible for what may be done outside of our lines, but here I shall make what provision I can for the future as well the cereal and root crop as the cane. We shall endeavor to get a stock of cane laid down on all the plantations worked by Government and to preserve seed corn and potatoes to meet this contingency.

I shall send out my third Regiment of Native Guards (colored) and set them to work preserving the cane and roots for a crop next year.

It cannot be supposed that this great change in a social and political system can be made without shock and I am only surprised that the possibility opens up to me that it can be made at all. Certain it is I speak the almost universal sentiment and opinion of my officers that Slavery is doomed. I have no doubt of it, and with every prejudice and early teaching against the result to which my mind has been irresistibly brought by my experience here I am now convinced:

1st That labor can be done in this State by whites more economically than by blacks as slaves.

2nd That Black labor can be as well governed, used, and made as profitable in a state of freedom as in slavery.

3rd That while it would have been better could this emancipation of the slave have been gradual, yet it is quite feasible, even under this great change, as a Governmental proposition, to organize, control and work the negro with profit and safety to the white, but that this can be best done under military supervision. Of which, allow me to say, I do not desire the charge.

I must close by apologizing for this very long and discursive letter, but I am consoled by the thought that it is entirely at your option to read as much of it as it pleases you to do. I am very truly Your friend & servant

HLS Benj. F Butler

Maj. Genl. Benj. F. Butler to The President, 28 Nov. 1862, G-839 1862, Letters Received, ser. 12, RG 94 [K-31]. Of the documents said to have been enclosed, only a copy of the "contract" – a memorandum of agreement between General Butler and planters of Plaquemines and St. Bernard – is in the file. Both the memorandum and Butler's General Order 91 are printed above as doc. 67. Butler wrote to the President in response to a letter of November 6 from Lincoln, who had pronounced himself "much interested" to learn that some planters in southern Louisiana "were making arrangements with their negroes to pay them wages" and asked "to what extent . . . this is being done." Lincoln had also inquired about the efforts of John E. Bouligny and other Louisiana unionists to organize an election for representatives to the U.S. Congress. (Benjamin F. Butler, *Private and Official Correspondence of Gen. Benjamin F. Butler during the Period of the Civil War*, 5 vols. [Norwood, Mass., 1917], vol. 2, p. 447.)

1 Presumably the Second Confiscation Act, adopted on July 17, 1862, which declared free the slaves of disloyal owners and, by forbidding federal soldiers to return any slave to any claimant, in effect freed any slave who came within the lines of the Union army. (*Statutes at Large*, vol. 12, pp. 589–92.)

71: Superintendent of Contrabands in the 1st Division of the Department of the Gulf to the Commander of the Division

[*Camp Parapet?, La.*] Dec. 1st 1862

Sir Herewith I have the honor to enclose statement showing the condition of the Contraband department at present date.

The report shows that less than 33 per cent of the entire number are available as laborers upon the public works, a large proportion being women, children, and infirm persons, whom the government has yet as far as I have been able to ascertain no means of making either useful or self supporting, and I beg leave to offer a suggestion which to my mind appears feasible. Viz. that the confiscated and unoccupied plantations within the military lines be taken, these people colonized upon them under the supervision of a faithful officer or agent of the government, thus by causing them to be producers of the staple products of this climate they will become not only self supporting but an element of strength to the government as they have formerly been to its enemies. their present condition is wretched in the extreme poorly sheltered in comfortless huts, and scantily-clothed, the mortality among them the past month has been fearfully excessive, as to my certain knowledge more than 250 have been buried from among those under my charge, and I fear that unless something is done to make them more comfortable the mortuary report for the next three months will be proportionately greater as the cold and rainy season advances.

In concluding this lengthy communication I beg leave to call your attention to the existence of a number of vacant buildings in the vicinity of the brick yards, near the river, below Carrollton which in my opinion might be made available for sheltering a large number of those who are now needing such comforts. I have the honor to be, Sir, Very respectfully Your ob't Serv't

HLS Geo. H. Hanks

Lieut. Geo. H. Hanks to Brigr. Gen'l T. W. Sherman, 1 Dec. 1862, Letters Received, ser. 1860, 1st Division, Dept. of the Gulf, RG 393 Pt. 2 No. 95 [C-1001]. The statement said to have been enclosed is not in the file.

72: Louisiana Planter to the Provost Marshal General of the Department of the Gulf

[*Plaquemines Parish, La. late December 1862*]

Dear Sir Allow me to call your attention to certain plantations of my neigborhood which are being worked (as it is said for the benefit of the United States), by certain parties under the management of M[r] Weed –[1] It might be well to see that the United States have received full credit for what has been derived from them as I have no doubt full charges will be made on the other side –

They are now entirely out of fuel and the works are stopped and it therefore is necessary to save the crops to take active measures either to roll off the crop or to dispose of the Cane to the best advantage so as to realise all possible for the government – They have also promised to pay the negroes that are working on those places by the month as yet they as far as I can learn, have not received their wages – I think this subject is worthy of enquiry by the proper department – If the same manager is to be retained it might be well to examine into all past transactions –

I would also beg leave to call the attention of the proper authorities to the fact that a band of speculators of whom M[r] A. J. Butler is the principal has now posession of many estates and are de[riv]ing one half of the sugar crops of such estates and the facts can be proven that said parties were the only ones who seemingly had the power by Miltary force of the United States to restore negroes to the places which had been abandoned by the working force and that only could be done after Contracts of ruinous compensation by the innocent owners was made –

I Contend that the power which was given to Contractors especially the military power was an abuse, and was used to the prejudice of the innocent parties who had a right to rely on the protection of the government and that the government had no right by its officials to produce such a Condition on the plantations as would drive the owners to such villanous contracts in the hope of saving what they Could from what seemed to them a settled purpose to ruin them –

I enclose for your perusal one of these Contracts by which a poor widow with six children was Compelled to make such a Contract in the hope of being able to preserve something –

If A J Butler & M[r] Weed had not themselves the power to restore the negroes they derived it from some higher power as it can be proven that the working force was returned under the bayonets of the United States and we have a right to presume that the negroes were induced to leave the plantations in order to drive the proprietors to these Contracts by which they were to surrender one half their property to save the balance – Your earnest attention is asked to these matters as the widow and the orphan may yet be saved as no portion of her sugar crop has yet been disposed of –

Please excuse the liberty I take in bringing this matter before you but knowing as I do the earnest desire of the Commanding General and his officers to do justice to our people I do not hesitate to address you in the hope that at all events it may lead to a full enquiry if nothing more into these abuses I have the honor to remain Your ob s[t] & friend

ALS Bradish Johnson

Bradish Johnson to Col. Clarke, [late Dec. 1862], J-5 1862, Letters Received by the Provost Marshal General, ser. 1390, State of LA, Provost Marshal Field Organizations, RG 393 Pt. 4 [C-965]. The contract said to have been enclosed is not in the file. Andrew J. Butler, a Massachusetts entrepreneur, had taken part in numerous speculative business ventures in and about New Orleans in 1862, while his brother, General Benjamin F. Butler, was commander of the Department of the Gulf. In one such undertaking, he had purchased the growing crop of a large sugar estate for $25,000, and hired black laborers "at a fair rate per day" to harvest and mill it. George S. Denison, a federal internal revenue agent who visited the plantation in November, had declared the operation a triumph for free labor: "I . . . never saw negroes work with more energy and industry. This single experiment refutes theories which Southern leaders have labored, for years, to establish." Denison also noted that, following Andrew Butler's example, other Northern entrepreneurs were working plantations near New Orleans on similar terms and "with the same success." (Benjamin F. Butler, *Private and Official Correspondence of Gen. Benjamin F. Butler during the Period of the Civil War*, 5 vols. [Norwood, Mass., 1917], vol. 2, pp. 426–28.)

1 Charles A. Weed, who in October 1862 had been appointed by General Benjamin F. Butler, commander of the Department of the Gulf, to supervise the harvest on abandoned sugar plantations below New Orleans. (See above, doc. 68n.)

73: Commander of U.S. Forces at Baton Rouge, Louisiana, to the Headquarters of the Department of the Gulf

Baton Rouge [*La.*] Dec 29th 1862

Sir. There are in this vicinity a large number of Union citizens, many of whom are planters and have taken the oath of allegiance since our occupation of this post. I have been informed though I have not seen the order that by the provisions of one of Genl. Butlers orders where the negroes left the plantations of Union citizens, – negro labor would be furnished to put in crops &c.[1] I have been asked if it be the intention of the Maj Genl comdg – the Dept. to carry out this policy or any similar to it – I do not believe that however desirable it may be that Union citizens should be protected in their labor in making their crops that it is practicable at this time and place to give such protection owing to the numbers that would be required. The contraband question atogether appears to me to be an expensive and growing inconvenience I have now upwards of six hundred and the number increases, daily – I have one hundred at work on the intrenchments one hundred on the dyke, and what of the remainder are fit for duty – with the Qr. M and Com. Dept. The gang on the dyke will be increased tomorrow and daily hereafter as they can be spared from other work.

I have received information from several sources that the enemy are establishing a camp or post at Clinton. have also been informed that two Regiments were ordered from Port Hudson on to that point.

I have the honor to enclose a report of a skirmish which took place on the morning of the 29th inst between a scouting party lead by Capt Godfrey 1st La Cavalry and the enemys advance guard near Eli Browns plantation on the Clinton road – Our cavalry behaved very gallantly and was well and successfully handled under the circumstances.

I think it quite important at this time that some action be taken defining the extent to which protection shall be given to Planters who have taken the oath of allegiance. My understanding of the wishes of the Maj. Gen. Comdg. the Dept. is that such Planters be allowed as far as practicable to continue their planting and their usual trade in the products of their plantations through the U.S. authorities at New Orleans. The practical working of the present state of affairs is this. All or nearly all of the plantation hands come within our lines and planters in consequence are unable to use their plantations. If some means could be found to remedy this I think it would result in public good. – I am Sir Very Respectfully Your Obedient Servant

HLcSr (Signed) C. Grover

Brig. Gen. C. Grover to The Asst. Adjt. Genl., 29 Dec. 1862, vol. 128/233 DG, pp. 65–67, Letters Sent, ser. 2134, U.S. Forces Baton Rouge & Grover's Division, RG 393 Pt. 2 No. 120 [C-925]. In a reply dated January 1, 1863, the adjutant of General Nathaniel P. Banks, commander of the Department of the Gulf, informed General Grover that Banks "expects to be able to make such arrangements as will place it in our power to furnish the loyal planters upon equitable terms with the labor necessary to secure their crops." He added that Union officers could "require the negroes who come within our lines, to labor either on the public works or on plantations," but were forbidden to "restore the negroes to servitude, or place them at work under their former masters." (Lieut. Col. A.A. General to Brig. Genl. C. Grover, 1 Jan. 1863, vol. 4 DG, pp. 115–16, Letters Sent, ser. 1738, Dept. of the Gulf, RG 393 Pt. 1 [C-616].)

1 General Order 91, issued on November 9, 1862, by General Benjamin F. Butler, then commander of the Department of the Gulf, had established the Sequestration Commission, with authority to furnish planters with laborers from among the fugitive slaves in Union lines, provided that the planters paid wages, refrained from corporal punishment, and abided by other regulations. (See above, doc. 67.)

74: Louisiana Slaveholder to the Commander of the Department of the Gulf

Parish of Jefferson [*La.*] January 2[d] 1863

General I have the honor of addressing to you the present letter in order to bring to your knowledge certain facts the most aggravating and important nature of which has a claim to your benevolence and to the protection of your authority.

I am a planter in this Parish, and my property consists of a small plantation on the right bank of the Mississippi opposite the Canal of the Barataria Company.

Close to my place there is a picket of the Native Guards colored men under command of an officer by the name of Villevert and a colored man equally. Out of 20 slaves twelve have left me, I have as yet delayed any application to you, knowing the many calls that are daily pressing on your time: but the men composing the said picket have taken the liberty to carry away from my place about 50 cords of wood, and my industry being in vegetables they have entirely destroyed and picked up my garden, and taken also my horses, mules, carts with all harness and saddlery articles; they have moved away the hay from out my store or ware-house, and they are constantly destroying my fences to make fire with, and not long ago one of my mules was crippled by them. Finally, they have seized the person of my driver, tied him and flogged him, and he was obliged to fly away; he took refuge in my family in this city and has been threatened of death by them, and he dares not turn back on the place.

I can well account for the many painful necessities impending on a state of war, but that a loyal citizen the father of Ten children, possessing no other livelihood than his industry for himself and family, and if it should add any little title to the protection of the United States authorities a veteran of 1814 & 15, should be thus dealt with, without any mention of multiplied vexations and personal insults, I can little conceive, and it is to the power and discretion vested into your hands, General, that I resort to put a stop to a state of things and deeds which must call the shame and blush of the very first soldier of the white race having any sense of military pride and who cannot but know that the peaceful and loyal citizen should not be molested.

In the name of my nearly ruined family, I sollicit your kind and benevolent protection I am Sir, very respectfully Yours

F Fazende

[*In another handwriting*] Frances Fazande, 145 Main Street

HLS

F. Fazende to Major General P. N. Banks, 2 Jan. 1863, F-52 1863, Letters Received, ser. 1756, Dept. of the Gulf, RG 393 Pt. 1 [C-534]. No reply has been found in the letters-sent records of the Department of the Gulf. About the same time, a planter in St. James Parish complained that black soldiers had repeatedly "visited" his plantation in November and December 1862, "influencing all my negroes to leave me," and taking mules, farm implements, and other property. "At a heavy expense I sent up white labor [from New Orleans] to take off the crop, but am unable to do so for want of mules, Carts and harnesses–" (J. Burnside to United States Sequestration Commission, 14 Jan. 1863, Records of the Sequestration Commission, ser. 1947, Dept. of the Gulf, RG 393 Pt. 1 [C-1058].)

75: Attorneys for a Louisiana Planter to the Commander of the Department of the Gulf

New Orleans, January 3. *1863.*

General, Mr. D. C. Osborne, is an old client of ours, and a very respectable sugar planter in the adjoining parish of Jefferson. He is infirm and almost blind. His plantation became disorganised from the desertion of fifty negroes out of his total force of sixty, and he made a contract with Dr. B. F. Smith to take off his crop, the Dr. agreeing to supply the laborers and Osborne to pay them. A portion, about eight, of the negroes put upon Osbornes place by Smith, were slaves of Mr. Riviere Gardere, who has notified Mr Osborne not to pay the said eight slaves for their labor but to pay him, Gardere. Hereupon, a negro Ben Howard, one of the eight procured and brought to Mr Osborne, the letter which we enclose herewith, dated "Contraband office Janry 2, 1863 and signed G. H. Hanks Lieut. and supt. of Contrabands". On consulting us yesterday we advised Mr. Osborne to seek an interview with Lieut. Col. R. B. Irwin, A.A.G. and if told by him that all was right, to pay the negroes accordingly; but Mr. Osborne informs us that Lt. Col. Irwin told him that he did not know Lieut. Hanks or the office from which the letter purported to emanate. Under these circumstances we beg leave respectfully to invite your attention to the matter; it is one of moment, and will be the precendent of a large class of cases. Must Mr. Osborne pay the negroes, or must he pay the master; he is ready and willing to pay either, but of course wishes to be protected by an adequate order against any after demand when payment shall once have been made. We remain, Very respectfully Your obdt. servts

HLSr Durant & Hornor

Durant & Hornor to Major General N. P. Banks, 3 Jan. 1863, D-24 1863, Letters Received, ser. 1920, Civil Affairs, Dept. of the Gulf, RG 393 Pt. 1 [C-691]. The letterhead provides the full names of the two attorneys: Thomas J. Durant and Charles W. Hornor. The next day, Colonel Richard B. Irwin, the department commander's adjutant, informed them that their letter had been received, but that the letter from Lieutenant George H. Hanks had not accompanied it. (Hanks had been appointed superintendent of contrabands in the 1st Division of the Department of the Gulf during the tenure of General Benjamin F. Butler, the previous department commander.) (Lieut. Col. [Richard B. Irwin] to Mess. Durant & Hornor, 4 Jan. 1863, vol. 4 DG, p. 126, Letters Sent, ser. 1738, Dept. of the Gulf, RG 393 Pt. 1 [C-691].) Neither Hanks's letter nor any further correspondence from Durant and Hornor pertaining to D. C. Osborn has been found in the letters-received files of the Department of the Gulf. The previous September, Osborn and several relatives had appealed to General Butler for protection from four former slaves who had recently returned to their estate with "an *Order* to the other Negroes, to rise and murder the whole family–and plunder and burn the Plantation." (*Freedom*, ser. 1, vol. 1: doc. 68.) Planters were not the only ones in doubt about the status of fugitive slaves who had been hired during the 1862 sugar harvest. In late January 1863, a Union officer at Gretna, Louisiana, reported that every day he was called upon by "[s]everal Contraband" who had been dismissed by their employers after completing the harvest. In order to obtain new employment, he believed, they would need "[p]asses or *some Paper* from an Officer that will protect the *employer* in [hiring them], and the contraband from arrest." Indeed, many of the former slaves had already "been arrested and made to pay a snug little sum" before being released. (Capt. John S. Clark to Col. Richard B. Irwin, 30 Jan. 1863, C-119 1863, Letters Received, ser. 1756, Dept. of the Gulf, RG 393 Pt. 1 [C-526].)

76: Northern Plantation Lessee to the Commander of the Department of the Gulf

New Orleans Jan[y] 3 /63

General I have in my employ more than Four hundred negroes engaged in taking crops from plantations on the upper coast right bank

I have finished on two of them and within a fortnight shall have closed work on the remaining one

Most of these negroes are the slaves of disloyal men and under any construction of existing laws and executive proclamations will not be again under the control of their former masters. The same is the case in regard to a large number of plantations on this coast now worked by hired runaway slaves

These negroes must have immediate employment to prevent their necessities from forcing them into acts of robbery and violence; and if any crop is to be made on these plantations another year prompt measures must be taken to remove the standing cane which has soured, and to prepare the ground for the purpose of Cropping

I desire to lease from the Government and work with hired negro labor under such regulations as may be hereafter established the following named abandoned plantations belonging to persons now in the Confederate service viz

Capt Ranson	Parish S[t] Charles	right bank
Col R Taylor	" do	do
Capt[n] M Becnel	" S[t] John Baptiste	do

I propose to pay for the lease of each of these plantations a sum to be computed at the rate of Ten dollars for each Hogshead of Sugar produced

I believe each plantation will yield about Five Hundred Hogsheads

I would respectfully beg as early a reply to this proposition as may be practicable as the negroes are becoming demoralized by idleness and until a decision is made as to their future disposition I am at the cost of their subsistence without any equivalent in labor It would be prejudicial to every interest to turn them loose upon the coast Very Resp[y] Yr ob[t] serv[t]

ALS Geo M. Chapman

Geo. M. Chapman to Major Gen. N. P. Banks, 3 Jan. 1863, Records of the Sequestration Commission, ser. 1947, Dept. of the Gulf, RG 393 Pt. 1 [C-951]. Endorsement. Chapman wrote a similar letter to the provost marshal general of the state of Louisiana, in which he argued that only by "[e]ngaging at once in preparing the plantations & putting in a crop for the ensuing year" could fugitive slaves be "used so as to provide themselves & families with sustenance and at the same time be of advantage to the Government and to the property lying along the River." Private businessmen, Chapman asserted, could conduct such agricultural enterprises more effectively than the government, because "[g]overnment operations of this character have never been found to be managed with the same energy & economy that mark those managed by individuals and have seldom returned any profit to the Treasury." "Individual energy," he predicted, "will succeed in procuring the plant cane and starting the work before government can possibly organize a system & procure the necessary agents and assistants to carry it into effect." Accordingly, he urged that abandoned plantations be placed under the control of "individuals who will work them with the labor that will otherwise have no recourse but thievery for its support." ([George M. Chapman] to Colonel, [Dec.? 1862], filed as A-12, Letters Received by the Provost Marshal General, ser. 1390, State of LA, Provost Marshal Field Organizations, RG 393 Pt. 4 [C-951].)

77: Northern Plantation Manager to the Commander of the Department of the Gulf

Raceland Plantation [*Lafourche Parish, La.*] Jan. 5 1863

Sir– As manager of this Plantation I desire to mak complaint against Capt. Carter, Lieut. Watson, & Trask, of Co. C. 2nd Reg. La. N.G. for interfering with work on this place

Having come to this Country as guid to Gen Weitzels Brigade and then by the Generals advice and concent I have undertaken to save if possible a part of the Sugar crop that was spoiling in the field. After making satisfactory arangements with the owners of the place I employed hands at $15 per month for good men and others in proportion to what they could do On the 10th of last Nov. I commenced with every prospect of success all the hands working well and seemed Satisfied and contented Capt Carter was Camped on the Rail Road near my place his men was allowed to go upon the place as they pleased some eight or ten Hhds of Sugar was taken from the place Theas Soldiers was so much with my hands that very little work could be done I asked the Officers repeatedly to keep their men away that the work might go on they promised to do so but have since acknowledged themselves unable to controul their men I was arrested taken to the Camp where they threatened to shoot me and then let me go wieth no punishment nor did they charge me with any crime; and I do not know what the arrest was made for. I suppose it was to show the hands that they the Soldiers was masters and, that obediance was due them, and not me. They tell my hands that there is no necesity of their doing any work that the Government will feed and care for them whether they work or not; and language to this effect is repeated to them every day They try every means to excite the hands to insubordination by telling them that I am a Rebel and calling me other names to profane or obscean to be repeated here, Thay have threatened my life four or five times cocking and caping their muskets pointing them at my head and declairing with an oath that thay would blow out my brains, and when I go to the Camp to complain to the Officer the threats are repeated Many shoots have been fired at me in the night I saw the flash of their guns and heared the balls whisel theas Soldiers were about here with their muskets a short time befoe the fireing and I suppose it was them that did it

I believe thay intend to take my life when thay can do it and eccape punishment Many of my hands (the wimen) spend most of the day time in the Camps and return with a gang of Soldiers at evening to carous the night away. Thay have so demorlized the hands that I was obliged to stop the Mill at a lose of not less than two thousund Dollars in spoiled Cane and Lost fuel. I have now been under arrest for two days by orders of Lieut. Watson for Assault & Battery I have asked for a tryal but have not had it nor do I expect it soon as Lieut Watson has gon to New Orleans I have not been informend where or when the aleged crime was commited. I do not know that I have given them cause for offence unless my desire to be let alone is one and they have never asked a favor of me that I have not granted if it was in my power to do so I cannot go ahead with the work on this place unless I can controul the labor I pay for

Sir As a Loyal Citizen of the State of Illinois I respectfully clame that protection due the Subjects of the United States Respectfully yours Truly

J. A. Pickens

P.S. Gen. Butler, Gen. Weitzel, Col. Thomas of the 8th Vt. Reg. Lieut. Col. Kinsman of Gen, Butlers Staff know me to be a Loyal man J A Pickens

ALS

J. A. Pickens to Major General Banks, 5 Jan. 1863, inexplicably filed in Letters Received, 6th USCI, Regimental Books & Papers USCT, RG 94 [G-285]. Endorsement. All three officers cited by Pickens – Captain Hannibal Carter, Lieutentant Frank L. Trask, and Lieutenant George F. Watson – were free men of color who held commissions in the 2nd Louisiana Native Guard. (*Freedom*, ser. 2: p. 310n.) Captain Carter, to whom Pickens's letter was referred, gave a very different account of events on Raceland Plantation. Before Pickens even arrived on the scene, Carter had himself induced "a number" of slaves to remain at work, had placed a guard on the plantation at the owner's request (after an overseer had been "threatened by some of the hands"), and had ordered the slaves to return sugar and household furniture that they had appropriated for their own use. Captain Carter acknowledged that soldiers of his company had made unauthorized visits to the plantation, but insisted that the offenders had been punished, as had the soldiers who threatened Pickens. Carter denied having advised plantation hands not to work; to the contrary, he and his fellow officers had "endeavored to impress upon their minds the neccessity of labor." He also disputed Pickens's charge that the black soldiers had caused the "demoralization" of the work force. The sugar mill had indeed been shut down, but the cause was "lack of hands": "numbers [had] left on account of cruel treatment," and "sickness [had] so thinned [Pickens's] forces that it was not possible to continue." The cause of Pickens's arrest, Carter explained, was his abuse of women workers on the plantation; among other misdeeds, he had evicted "a woman with her suckling babe only because she was a soldiers wife." (Capt. Hannibal Carter to Col. N. W. Daniels, 8 Feb. 1863, inexplicably filed in Letters Received, 6th USCI, Regimental Books & Papers USCT, RG 94 [G-285].)

78: Louisiana Black Sailor to the Provost Marshal General of the State of Louisiana

New Orleanes January the 7 1863

Dear Genarl Franch Genarl Butler Promest Me if i Went in the Sivest that My Fambely Should be taken Car of by the Govenment but i dou not think that it is so For My Sister has been in Jail now very nere a Month Suffern and i Would Wish to Gite her out if there is any Possibely Chance of douingin so i think that it is hard that she has been Keep in there so For nothingin For as hard as tames is at the Prasent no one Could Pay Wages house Rent For it is as Mouch as pepel Can dou to Gite somthingin to Eate less payingin Rent. Wages her Master put her in there on that Corse this Case Cane be prove by White. Black so i Will ask of you intesede of Giten her out if you so pleas For i think that she has been in there Most Longe or nouff Suffern She has not Got very Good health For hes has not been Longe Sence been out of her Child bad [. . .] taken and put in Jail and i see that Som of tha Wemen that Was in there For the Sam Caste so i think that My sister oughter to Com out to Rose Rossan 585 Gratman St Wachman that taken her is 371 her Brother George W. F. Johnson borde of the U.S Ship Pampero Gulf Squrd off Pilot town also you Will Pleas to answer this Letter and if i Can Gite her out you Will beso Kinde as Give Me a permitt to Go in and See her For i Lern that the ponish them slily in Jail and i Woulden For to be ille treted What Sowever because She has Misscarried a Childe

AL [*George W. F. Johnson*]

[George W. F. Johnson] to Genarl Franch, 7 Jan. 1863, Miscellaneous Records, ser. 1796, Dept. of the Gulf, RG 393 Pt. 1 [C-1062]. It is unlikely that Johnson received a reply to his letter (which was evidently intended for Colonel Jonas H. French, provost marshal general of the state of Louisiana) or that his request was acted upon; file notations on the wrapper identify the sender as "No Name" and give no indication of further action. For another complaint regarding the jailing of slave women in New Orleans – particularly the relatives of black soldiers – for arrears of rent, see *Freedom*, ser. 2: doc. 295.

79: Louisiana Planters to the Commander of the Department of the Gulf

[*Terrebonne Parish, La.*] Jany 14th 1862 [*1863*] –

General, The undersigned, comtee, appointed by the citizens of the Parish of Terre Bonne – La – to lay before you the deplorable condition of their once florishing & happy Parish –

Respectfully reprisent – that – nine tenths of all the horses, saddles & bridles & at least two thirds of all the mules, carts, wagons & harness necessary to carry on the plantations have been seized by the U.S. (to say nothing of cattle, hogs, sheep poultry & other things necessary to support our families & negroes) consequently many planters are not able to haul necessary supplies from the depots nor will they be able to dilever at depots & landings the Sugar & molasses now in their Sugar-Houses – neither will they be able to cultivate their crops this year – Large quantities of corn *necessary* for the use of the planters their negroes & teams remain in the fields, & without carts teams & harness must so remain & be entirely lost – That – many of the negroes led astray by designing persons, believe that the plantations & everything on them belong to them, the negroes – They quit work, go & come when they see fit – Ride off at night the mules that have been at work all day – Fences are pulled down gates & bars are left open – Cattle, & sheep hogs & poultry are killed or carried off & sold – Negroes in numbers from one plantation to an other at all hours night & day – They travel on the rail road – They congregate in large numbers on deserted plantations – All these things are done against the will & in defiance of the orders of their masters. – In Some instances negro Soldiers partially armed have been allowed to visit the plantations from which they inlisted – In a word we are in a State of anarchy. – The time has come when preperations for planting & cultivating the crops of 1863 should be made. – But without teams, & the ability to command the labour of our negroes, nothing can be done. – Unless a full crop of corn can be grown this year Starvation Stares us in the face – In the rear of famine march insurrection & pestilence –

General – We ask relief from our present evils & security for the future. – To obtain these ends, we respectfully suggest – That – To each planter be restored not less than half of all the team, carts, wagons & harness, that he has heretofore used in the cultivation of his plantation, & that they be secured to him to be used in the cultivation of his plantation or plantations if he has more than one – That no person be allowed to hire or employ in any way a negro or colored person without the written permission of his or her owner or the known agent of the owner – Which written permission the party employing or hiring a negro or colored person must be able to produce when called on in justification of himself – Some plan should be adopted to compell negroes hired to remain & complete their contracts – This object would be furthered by arresting & returning to their owners or employers all negroes absenting themselves without leave of their owners or employers. –

Negroes should not be allowed to enter the lines of encampment without passes from their owner or employer – Those who do so should be promptly expelled – otherwise the foregoing suggestions will be fruitless. – Furnishing negroes or colored persons in any way with any kind of intoxicating liquor or drink should be strictly prohibited – On some places the negroes have refused to work on any terms – We ask such power & authority as will enable us to preserve order & compell the negroes to work so as to make the crops necessary for the support of our families & of the negroes themselves. –

To make a crop of 1.000 – Hoags of Sugar & 2000 – barrels of Molasses requires the labour of 150 – hands & an outlay of some $25.000 – in money – Too large a sum to risk on an uncertainty – Hence it is all important that we should have undoubted security for the future use of the labour of our negroes, our teams, carts, etc – Without this security for at least twelve months, we fear not attempt will be made this year (1863) to grow either corn or cane in the Parish of Terre Bonne. – Without bread the negroes must Starve, revolt & become a heavy charge on the Govt. of the U.S., while disease will decimate their ranks. – But by a prompt & decided course, requiring obediance & work from our Slaves the Govt. may save the country & especially the poor negroes from Such dire calamities. –

W. J. Minor Andrew McCollam
HLS Frs E Robertson T. Gibson

W. J. Minor et al. to Major Genl. Banks, 14 Jan. 1862 [1863], M-108 1863, Letters Received, ser. 1920, Civil Affairs, Dept. of the Gulf, RG 393 Pt. 1 [C-710]. Each signature is in a different handwriting; the petition is in that of Minor. Appended are three virtually identical documents, each dated January 8, 1863, and signed by various "Citizens" of Terrebonne Parish (about 170 in all), delegating Minor, Robertson, McCollam, Gibson, and one John M. Pelton to represent "the condition of things in this Parish & indeavour to obtain some amelioration of our grievances so as to justify us in attempting to grow our usual crops, which it would be unwise in us to attempt to do, under, existing circumstances."

80: Commander of the Guard at Kenner, Louisiana, to the Headquarters of the 3rd Brigade of the 2nd Division, Department of the Gulf; and the Brigade Commander to the Headquarters of the Defenses of New Orleans

Kenners [*La.*]. Jan'y 27. 1863

Lieut J H Metcalf AAAG. The order of Col Nickerson, directing me to report the state of the Hospital and Quarters of the Contrabands at this place, was received this PM.

I had intended either to have made a written or verbal report this week.

Last Monday (the 19th) I took Doct Sangar through the Hospital and Quarters to show him the condition I had found them.

He stated he should make a report of affairs to Gen Sherman

When I took charge here I found a lot of clothing on hand. Lieut Hopkins, whom I relieved, stated he had delivered but few articles. And advised me there was no necessity for my doing so.

The following day I visited the Quarters &c which I found in a very bad state. There were about 12 or 15 sick in Hospital.

They had a few old blankets and a little hay for bedding – some had nothing but the bare boards. The building is an old house formerly used as one of the negro Quarters on the plantation. It has a chimney, with a fire place on each side of it, in the center, but in the top there was a large hole, and the sides have cracks between the boards, consequently the rain and wind have free access.

Doct Norcom of this place is the surgeon. He visits them every second day and oftener if called upon. He informs me that he has urged upon those in command the necessity of procuring suitable clothing and blankets, especially for the sick, but without success. He says he has been able to aid the sick but little, although he has sufficient medicine at his command, owing to the want of a suitable building and clothing for them. The chimney was in one corner at first, and of but little use towards warming the room untill he had negros detailed to make one in the center. It was a month before it was completed owing to the overseers taking the men off to work on the levees.

The sick are in charge of a mulatto man who understands administering medicine. As rations they have one lb rice and 1/4 do of sugar each per day.

The Quarters are an old barn – three building made by the negros out of fence materials, and some dozen old tents.

Excepting the first named none have any windows, or chimneys. The only way for the smoke to escape is by the door, or through the cracks between the boards. But few have fireplaces, the only method of heating being by fires built on the ground. Bunks of rough boards are built around the sides. The only bedding consists of a few quilts and blankets with a little hay.

The reason the negros gave for their filthy condition was that they had no time to clean up in. On inquiry I found they have worked from sunrise till dark, Sundays included, since last Sept. Many have worked three months without losing a single day. I directed some of the old men to clean the Quarters which in a degree has been done. Capt Page[1] gave me permission to allow them Sundays which I did last Sunday for the first time, and also gave a liberal ration of soap which they all very much needed.

The men were in a shocking condition in regards clothing Many were entirely barefooted, and others nearly so – Others with no shirts, and a majority without pants excepting in the most ragged state. In this condition they worked daily on the Levees.

Hardly an article of clothing had been issued, excepting about 75 pairs of shoes, and not a single blanket.

I immediately issued all the clothing on hand consisting of about 120 jackets, shirts, hats and pants There were no shoes on hand To make them in any way comfortable there is wanted about 150 suits of clothing – 150 prs of shoes and 150 blankets. Capt Page informed me a week since that he had drawn on QM Crowel for them. I have not seen or heard since from him

The rations are given out every day. Either Sergeant Hagerthy or myself have attending to issuing them in order to be sure that the proper persons receive them.

Many of the women are in even a worse condition than the men as regards clothing. From 5 to 16 work daily on the levee, more would if they had shoes Their rations we issue once a week. They receive 2 qts of meal and 2 lbs pork for a week.

Yesterday we issued to 248 men – 19 sick and 74 women, Total 341 The total number of deaths has been 78. None have died since I have been here

I will in a few days make another report. Yours Respectfully

Charles L Stevens

Capt Page has a patrol of *citizens, armed,* between Fellsons and Judge Rost's to prevent negro's from coming down by there without a pass. I have been informed several have been stopped.

ALS

Bonnet Carre [*La.*] Jan 28th 1863.

Captain. I send report upon condition of Negroes at Kenner. They are in no better condition here. But I can do nothing. By order I have turned them all over to Capt. Page. He has not been here for a week, and appears to know or care but little about them. The work ordered on levee is all done here. Much more is to be done above, but no one here is authorized to do it. As Capt. Page is absent all work must be suspended. "Some peculiar attraction" has ruined the efficiency of the Captain. The Negroes here are without proper clothing or shelter. *My cattle at home are better cared for than these unfortunate persons*, who seem just now to be the subject of words.

Mr. Hollingsworth's plantation is entirely deserted of Negroes. He has a plenty of untenanted huts, which if we could have orders might be occupied by the Negroes now at this place.

There is not the least difficulty in putting this whole matter in shape. Every person should be enrolled as he comes into camp. – where from – to whom he belonged &c – and a weekly or daily report forwarded to Provost Marshal General, or Chief of Contrabands which shall clearly account for condition and whereabouts of every man. As it is, I doubt if those who have come in here can be properly accounted for. A frequent inspection would keep those whose duties it may be to look after them, informed. The manner in which the business is conducted here, I find on inquiry to be very loose. There are about two hundred and ten (210) here under charge of a Sergeant, a very faithful and intelligent man. He informs me that his instruction in the matter does not reach the point suggested. If the General will give me the authority, though I do not desire the job, I will show you an organization, such as will not only enable you to know the exact condition of all Negroes here, whenever you desire to look, but put them in condition to be serviceable for any work, now or in future, which Gov'mt may require. Their rations should only be drawn on actual returns; births – deaths – absences &c – should be noted and reported – Sunday morning inspections should be enforced, and such rules and regulations as seem needful and proper should be provided. This *may* all have been provided for and more. I only make the suggestion, and hope soon to see the improvement in their condition here, which is so much needed. Genl. Sherman's order relating to contrabands has not been complied with I think.[2] I should like to see it carried out more fully Respectfully Your Obdt Sv't

HLS F. S. Nickerson

Lieut. Charles L. Stevens to Lieut. J. H. Metcalf, 27 Jan. 1863, enclosed in Col. F. S. Nickerson to Capt. A. Badeau, 28 Jan. 1863, Miscellaneous Records, ser. 1796, Dept. of the Gulf, RG 393 Pt. 1 [C-1063]. In an undated endorsement on Lieutenant Stevens's report, Colonel Nickerson pointed out that the rations issued to the black levee workers fell short of the amount he had mandated. On January 29, Nickerson reported that the fugitive slaves in his camp now numbered nearly 300, and that, in the absence of Captain Page, he had himself ordered them to work on the levee, deeming it "a '*military necessity*' " to do so. Two days later, General Thomas W. Sherman, commander of the defenses of New Orleans, sanctioned Nickerson's actions and directed him to send "[a]ll able-bodied contrabands not required up there" to Camp Parapet "for work on fortifications." (Col. F. S. Nickerson to Capt. W. Hoffman, 29 Jan. 1863, and endorsement of Bg. Gen. T. W. Sherman, 31 Jan. 1863, vol. 102 DG, Letters Received, ser. 1859, Defences of New Orleans, RG 393 Pt. 2 No. 95 [C-1063].)

1 Captain Edward Page, Jr., provost marshal for the parishes of St. Charles, St. John the Baptist, and St. James.
2 For the order, issued by General Thomas W. Sherman on October 17, 1862, see above, doc. 65.

81: Order by the Commander of the Department of the Gulf

New Orleans, January 29, 1863.

GENERAL ORDERS No. 12 The Proclamation of the President of the United States, dated January 1st, 1863, is published in General Orders for the information and government of the officers and soldiers of this command, and all persons acting under their authority. It designates portions of the State of Louisiana, which are not to be affected by its provisions. The laws of the United States, however, forbid officers of the army and navy to return slaves to their owners, or to decide upon the claims of any person to the service or labor of another; and the inevitable conditions of a state of war unavoidably deprive all classes of citizens of much of that absolute freedom of action and control of property which local law and the continued peace of the country guaranteed and secured to them. The forcible seizure of fugitives from service or labor by their owners is inconsistent with these laws and conditions, inasmuch as it leads to personal violence, and the disturbance of the public peace, and it cannot be permitted. Officers and soldiers will not encourage or assist slaves to leave their employers, but they cannot compel or authorize their return by force.

The public interest peremptorily demands that all persons without other means of support be required to maintain themselves by labor. Negroes are not exempt from this law. Those who leave their employers will be compelled to support themselves and families by labor upon the public works. Under no circumstances whatever can they be maintained in idleness, or allowed to wander through the parishes and cities of the State without employment. Vagrancy and crime will be suppressed by an enforced and constant occupation and employment.

Upon every consideration, labor is entitled to some equitable proportion of the crops it produces. To secure the objects both of capital and labor, the Sequestration Commission is hereby authorized and directed, upon conference with planters and other parties, to propose and establish a yearly system of negro labor, which shall provide for the food, clothing, proper treatment and just compensation for the negroes, at fixed rates, or an equitable proportion of the yearly crop, as may be deemed advisable. It should be just, but not exorbitant or onerous. When accepted by the planter or other parties, all the conditions of continuous and faithful service, respectful deportment, correct discipline and perfect subordination, shall be enforced on the part of the negroes by the officers of the Government. To secure their payment, the wages of labor will constitute a lien upon its products.

This may not be the best, but it is now the only practicable system. Wise men will do what they can, when they cannot do what they would. It is the law of success! In three years from the restoration of peace, under this voluntary system of labor the State of Louisiana will produce threefold the product of its most prosperous year in the past.

The Quartermaster's Department is charged with the duty of harvesting corn on deserted fields, and cultivating abandoned estates. Unemployed negroes will be engaged in this service under the control of suitable agents or planters, with a just compensation in food, clothing and money, consistent with the terms agreed upon by the Commission, and under such regulations as will tend to keep families together, to impart self-supporting habits to the negroes, and protect the best interest of the people and the Government. BY COMMAND OF MAJOR GENERAL BANKS:

. . . .

PD

Excerpt from General Orders No. 12, Headquarters, Department of the Gulf, 29 Jan. 1863, Orders & Circulars, ser. 44, RG 94 [DD-10]. The omitted portion reprinted the Emancipation Proclamation, which exempted the following Louisiana parishes from its provisions: St. Bernard, Plaquemines, Jefferson, St. John the Baptist, St. Charles, St. James, Ascension, Assumption, Terrebonne, Lafourche, St. Mary's, St. Martin's, and Orleans (which included the city of New Orleans).

82: Quartermaster in Charge of the New-Orleans, Opelousas, and Great Western Railroad to the Commander of the Department of the Gulf

Algiers, [*La.*] January 30th *1863.*

Sir. An employee of this road, a contraband named Adam Mobley, reported at the Office yesterday noon that his wife and daughter had been seized by two City Policemen, at Gretna, and forcibly carried to their former mistress in New Orleans. I immediately placed an order for the arrest of the kidnappers, and return of the negroes, in the hands of Capt OBrien, commanding the Provost Guard in this place. An arresting party, commanded by a Lieut, proceeded to New Orleans, made the arrest, and were returning with the whole party. They were met by Mayor Denning who ordered their release on the ground, that the seizure of the negroes was by civil authority and denying my right to arrest. I soon after met the Lieut and again ordered him, to rescue, if need be, by force, the two negroes. This he informs me he was enabled to do by your decision in the case.

Another negro. Dan Claiborne an employee, and bearing a Workman's Ticket, was arrested early in the week by two policemen under the direction of the former owner and lodged in jail at New Orleans, He was released this morning and immediately reported here.

Other and similar cases have been reported. Policemen make these arrests to obtain the reward offered by owners, who lodge their negroes in jail for punishment. It interferes materially with the operation of the Road.

This statement is made in accordance with your request and I most respectfully ask what course I am to pursue in the protection of employed contrabands and their families, as I am liable to come in conflict with the civil Authority. Very respectfully Your Obedient Servant.

HLS L Colburn

Lt. Col. L. Colburn to Major Gen. N. P. Banks, 30 Jan. 1863, C-129 1863, Letters Received, ser. 1756, Dept. of the Gulf, RG 393 Pt. 1 [C-527]. On letterhead of the railroad. A notation on the wrapper reads merely "File," and no reply has been found in the letters-sent volumes of the Department of the Gulf.

83: Chaplain of a Connecticut Regiment to the Sequestration Commission

New Orleans La Feb 3rd 1863

Having, in accordance with instructions recieved from you, examined most of the plantations therein designated I beg leave to submit the following report.

Plantation	Manager	Sugar Made	Sugar Shipped	Molasses Made	Molasses Shipped
Mad Lanaux	Tripler	none		none	
A Lanfear 1	"	95 Hds			
" " 2	"	120 "	95 Hds.		100 Bbls
P. Suave		24 "		{ 67 Bbls. 55 Tierce }	
Mad Meyrone	Woodard	84 "	40 "	200 Bbls	100 "
Payne	"	144 "	60 "	165 "	100 "
L Ransan	Chapman	Cane cut but no Sugar made			
John Williams	Bennie	{ 36 Hds 16 Crush[d]	33 Hds. 8 Crush[d] }	138 Bbls	132 "
Raceland		128 Hds–	128 Hds–	300 "	300 "
Gaillard		106 "		60	
Brashear	Breed	128 "	92 "	200 "	74 "
Waf[or]d	E. W. Smith	102 "		not measured	
Taylor	Chapman	36 "			

On most of these plantations the negroes have been brought to work from other places and have been promised $10 per month (on the Raceland $15. per month) the clothing furnished them to be charged On the Williams and Brashear places only, have the hands been fully paid. Mr. Woodard was to pay off the hands on the Payne place as soon as they finished work. In several instances no money has been furnished by the Commission for payment. The accounts of the Raceland place were to be forwarded immediately to the Commission for approval and settlements.

The three Cage plantations viz. Woodlawn, Ashland, & Ranch were 25 miles from Tibodeaux. It was impossible to visit them. Capt. Goodrich Provost Marshall. of La Fourche had just visited them and informed me that the hands of the woodlawn and Ranch plantations were making sugar on woodlawn. Mr. Tu[re]gon overseer. How much had been made he did not know. One Fox was reported to have sold 70 Hds. of old sugar and removed it. The matter was being investigated.

The Taylor place was left without any guard, and cane from it has been ground on the LaBranch Plan. Adjoining. Fences are down, and the valuable copper work of the sugar works was reported stolen, cost about $20,000.

It was reported also that 350 barrels had been shipped to Ransan's place for what is termed "cistern bottoms." and were being filled.

On plantations managed by energetic men who desired free labor to succeed, the negroes worked well, especially where a soldier or two had been stationed to preserve order. Woodard, Bennie and others found no trouble. but where the former overseers had been retained who desired "all *their* slaves to be sent back" the Negroes were represented as unwilling to work well –

From my observation I have no doubt but Planters and others who desire to manage plantations can well afford to pay the hands $10 per month. if means are used to secure their faithful labor. It is essential that work be commenced immediately as the old crop and rubbish must be removed, and I would suggest that either the Provost Marshalls of the districts [or] an agent appointed for the purpose by the Commission be empowered to arrange terms immedeately with agents on unocupied places so that negroes may be employed who are now living on deserted places, and also a crop may be raised for their food & support the coming year.

I find also that the presence of undiciplined soldiers who are allowed to wander at will over these plantations has been most pernicious, especially the colored soldiers, who incited those at work faithfuly to spend their time in idleness telling them not to work as they were free. Many of the colored hands would gladly enlist and would be no injury, if decently disiplined to guard any rail road or property.

Applicants for the managing of places the coming season are waiting impatiently for arrangements to be made with the Commission so they can enter upon their duties. On the Potts plantation a man named Culwell is reboiling old molasses has put up 100. Bbls Augustin Babin for four years overseer there desires to work the place. I beg the Commission to consider the neccessity of immediate action in the work of arranging these plantations for a new crop. Most respectfully submitted Your Obt. Servt.

ALS Ja[s] H. Bradford

Jas. H. Bradford to U.S. Sequestration Commission, 3 Feb. 1863, Records of the Sequestration Commission, ser. 1947, Dept. of the Gulf, RG 393 Pt. 1 [C-820]. Bradford was chaplain of the 12th Connecticut Infantry.

84: Circular by the Sequestration Commission, Enclosing a Contract Form

[*New Orleans, La.*] *February*, 6, 1863

CIRCULAR.][1]

In accordance with the agreement between the Military authorities and the Planters, based upon General Orders No. 12, January 29, 1863,[2] the Provost Marshal of each parish is authorized to receive the signatures of Planters to said agreement, (a printed copy of which is herewith inclosed,) and is ordered to carry out in good faith the provisions of the agreement on the part of the authorities.

He will, in good faith, offer all fair and legal inducements to the negroes within his district, in whatever condition or service they may be found, to return to their families and the plantations where they belong.

When any negro has acquiesced in the terms proposed, the Provost Marshal will see that he fulfils his engagements for one year, in good faith. He shall be required to remain upon the plantation to which he is bound, to work faithfully and industriously, and maintain a respectful and subordinate deportment toward his employer.

The Provost Marshals are ordered to prohibit the harboring and employment of negroes laboring upon plantations under this agreement, by other parties, either civil or military.

All negroes not acquiescing in the proposed agreement, not otherwise employed, shall immediately be put to labor upon the public works, and all negroes found in the country, cities, villages, or about the military stations, without visible occupation or means of subsistence, shall be arrested as vagrants, and put to labor upon the public works or the Quartermaster's plantations.

The Provost Marshals will also see that the agreement entered into by the Planters in regard to the negroes is faithfully and fairly carried out.

It is not expected that an individual contract is to be made with the negroes who return to their plantations or remain upon them. Such arrangement would be impracticable. The fact that they return or remain is to be taken as proof of their assent. The officers of the Government who advise and assist their return will feel that they are responsible that the advantages promised shall be secured to them.

BY ORDER OF THE U.S. SEQUESTRATION COMMISSION. Approved:
N. P. BANKS

PD

[*Enclosure*]

DEPARTMENT OF THE GULF,

Headquarters, U. S. Sequestration Commission,

New-Orleans, February 5, 1863.

The officers of the Government will induce the Slaves to return to the Plantations where they belong, with their families, and when returned will require them, and those remaining upon the Plantations to work diligently and faithfully on the Plantations for one year, to maintain respectful deportment to their employers, and perfect subordination to their duties, upon condition that the Planters or other employers will feed, clothe, and treat them properly, and give to them at the end of the year one twentieth ($\frac{1}{20}$) part of the year's crop, or a fixed monthly compensation, in cases where it may be more convenient, as follows:

Mechanics, Sugar Makers, Drivers, &c., - - - - -	Three Dollars Each.
Able-bodied Field Men, - - - - - - -	Two " "
Able-bodied Field Women, House Servants, Nurses, &c., - -	One " "

The proportion reserved for the slaves, shall be divided into shares, and distributed according to the value of their labor, as follows:

Mechanics, Sugar Makers, Drivers, &c., - - - -	Three Shares Each.
Able-bodied Field Men, - - - - - - - - -	Two " "
Able-bodied Field Women, House Servants, Nurses, &c., - -	One " "

All negroes not otherwise employed will be required to labor upon the public works, and no person capable of labor will be supported at the public expense in idleness.

(Signed) E. G. BECKWITH,

Colonel, President Sequestration Commission.

The undersigned hereby accept the arrangement above proposed, and agree to carry it out, on their part, for one year from the date thereof, it being distinctly understood that the crop referred to means the commercial crop, and the acceptance of this contract does not imply the surrender of any right of property in the slave or other right of the owner.

Circular, Headquarters, Department of the Gulf, Office of the Sequestration Commission, 6 Feb. 1863, enclosing contract, Department of the Gulf, Headquarters, U.S. Sequestration Commission, 5 Feb. 1863, Letters Received, ser. 1860, Defences of New Orleans, RG 393 Pt. 2 No. 95 [C-1003]. On February 7, General Banks distributed copies of the contract and the circular to all commanders, provost marshals, and provost judges in the Department of the Gulf, characterizing the proposed labor arrangement as "an effort . . . to provide work for the Negroes, and to maintain the cultivation of Plantations upon a system compatible with the laws and the spirit of the age." "It is acceptable to a large number of Representative Planters," Banks declared, "and I am sure it ought to be to all those who seek the welfare of the Negroes." Accordingly, he asked his subordinates to assist in informing all interested parties about the system and, especially, "in explaining to the negroes the advantages of the plan to their race, to the planters and to the Government."

Banks concluded by inviting correspondence from "any one interested in the subject, if improvement upon the plan can be suggested." (Major General N. P. Banks to all Commanding Officers, Provost Marshals, Judges, etc., etc., 7 Feb. 1863, Letters Received by the Provost Marshal, ser. 1516, St. James & St. John Baptiste Parishes LA, Provost Marshal Field Organizations, RG 393 Pt. 4 [C-765].)

1 Bracket in the original.
2 See above, doc. 81.

85: Louisiana Planters to the Commander of the Department of the Gulf

[*St. James Parish, La., February? 1863*]

The undersigned, loyal citizens and planters of the Parish of St James, having been informed by Peter. M. Lapice Esq. Deputy Provost Marshall of said Parish, that their views and opinion on the practical results of General Orders N° 12 issued under date of the 29th January 1863,[1] would be taken into consideration by Gen. Banks, beg leave respectfully to represent,

That the object of said order being to promulgate the proclamation of the President of the United States, dated January 1st 1863, which is published with it, for the information and government of the officers and soldiers of the Department of the Gulf the undersigned have nothing to say in regard to said order so far as it applies to those parts of the Department where slavery is abolished by the President's proclamation.

But the undersigned find in the proclamation of the President that the Parishes composing the First and Second Congressional Districts of Louisiana are exempted from this general rule. Slavery is not abolished in those Parishes, but on the contrary it is expressly maintained as if the proclamation had not been issued, because they have recognized the authority of the Federal Government, by electing Representatives to the Congress of the United States.

"Slavery is the obligation to labor for the benefit of the master, without the contract or consent of the servant." Slaves have no freedom of action, because they are wholly under the control of another. The President, in his last annual message, has besides emphatically declared that slaves are property, and that emancipation is the destruction of property.[2] The voluntary system of labor mentioned in General orders N° 12 may be the best for those portions of Louisiana where slavery is no longer permitted under the President's proclamation. Men must do what they can, when they cannot do what they would. But in the opinion of the undersigned, the enforcement of this voluntary system of labor in the two Congressional Districts of the State where slavery is maintained, would be an attempt to reconcile things which, in their nature, are utterly incompatible. The master who pays wages to his slave, either hires his own property to himself or is divested of it. If the slave is free to leave the service of his master when he pleases, and to hire himself or sell his services to another person, he thereby obtains freedom of action and becomes a free man. The undersigned are thus led to the conclusion that the enforcement of the provisions of the General Orders N° 12 relative to a voluntary system of labor, over the whole Department of the Gulf, without excepting the two Congressional Districts of the State expressly excepted by the President's proclamation, is equivalent to an actual and immediate emancipation of all the slaves of the State of Louisiana.

The inevitable conditions of a state of war cannot be said to demand such a sacrifice, since the President's proclamation of the 1st of January is predicated upon that same military necessity and yet maintains Slavery in those two Congressional Districts.

An institution like that of Slavery, when it has stood for centuries, cannot be suddenly overthrown, without producing disasters in the country where it exists, which it takes many long years to repair.

The undersigned are firmly convinced that should Gen. Banks concur with them in opinion, that voluntary or free labor cannot be governed by the same rules as forced or slave labor, without changing entirely the status of the slaves, he might easily find the means of enforcing in the First and Second Congressional Districts of the State a system of regulations which would effectually prevent the loss of crops, the danger of overflows, and other calamities with which the planters are now threatened.

The undersigned are aware that the laws of Congress forbid officers of the Army and Navy to return slaves to their owners, but they beleive that the interdiction is not extended to the civil authorities. Should the constitutional right of bearing arms be restored to loyal citizens in these two Congressional Districts and the Sheriffs be authorized to organize police guards or patrols in conformity with the ordinances of the Police juries, the Slaves could, in the opinion of the undersigned, be made to return to and labor steadily on the plantations of their owners, without leading to personal violence or disturbances of the public peace, the more especially if the wise and salutary provisions against negro vagrancy contained in General Orders N° 12 are carried strictly into execution, and if the prohibition to officers and soldiers to encourage or assist slaves to leave their masters is rigidly enforced.

The undersigned having thus expressed with candor their opinion on the practical results of the system of voluntary labor, mentioned in General Orders N° 12, hope that upon reflection, Gen. Banks will adopt such measures as may relieve them from the apprehensions which they now feel in reference to the execution of said orders. The whole is very respectfully submitted

HLS [*13 signatures*]

D. Tureaud et al. to Major General N. P. Banks, [Feb.? 1863], filed as P-96 1863, Letters Received, ser. 1920, Civil Affairs, Dept. of the Gulf, RG 393 Pt. 1 [C-715]. Each of the signatures appears to be in a different handwriting. No reply has been found in the letters-sent volumes of the Department of the Gulf. In nearby Terrebonne Parish, the spokesman for another group of slaveholders offered similar advice regarding the enforcement of labor discipline under General Banks's order. He characterized the planters as "perfectly willing" to pay their laborers a portion of the crop but skeptical about "[d]eriving any benefit from the arrangement." Contending that "no *inducement* can ever be sufficient" to return black laborers to their accustomed tasks, he insisted that "some *coercion* is absolutely necessary," lest they "continue to roam about becoming more demoralised and irreclaimable than they now are." Like the planters of St. James, he proposed that the civil police be allowed to wield "the authority formerly held under the laws of the state to Arrest and imprison" fugitive slaves. If such a course were followed, he suggested, "a great portion of these troubles would cease"; otherwise, "unless something is [done] quickly both Planters and slaves will sink in Irretrievable ruin." (A. Robinson to Major Gen. Banks, [Feb. 1863], Letters Received, ser. 1845, Provost Marshal, Dept. of the Gulf, RG 393 Pt. 1 [C-715].)

1 See above, doc. 81.
2 In support of his proposal to compensate slaveholders who agreed to gradual emancipation, President Lincoln had argued, in his message to Congress of December 1, 1862, that "the liberation of slaves is the destruction of property – property acquired by descent, or by purchase, the same as any other property." (Abraham Lincoln, *Collected Works*, ed. Roy P. Basler, Marion D. Pratt, and Lloyd A. Dunlap, 9 vols. [New Brunswick, N.J., 1953–55], vol. 5, pp. 518–37.)

86: Provost Marshal of Three Louisiana Parishes to the Provost Marshal General of the Department of the Gulf

Camp Weitzel, La. Febry. 16th *1863*

General, I beg to reply to a communication received by me this day over the signature of Maj. Genl Banks comd'g. this Dept.[1]

I have been upon the coast and brought in close connection with the negroes for the past nine mos. and can truly appreciate any effort which will releive this dept. and its subordinate officers from the anxiety felt on their behalf.

Agreeable to your late orders I have communicated with the planters on the subject of employing the negroes and, at the end of the season giving them a share of the crop; I have read and explained to the negroes the communication from the Sequestration Commission[2] and advised them to work faithfully upon their plantations that the result might be favorable to their own interests.

In the two cases I have tried the result has not been favorable– On the Rost plantation where they have a very kind and good overseer the entire negro force refused to work and claimed the right to go to the camp: I have therefore sent them all down to Lieut Hanks Supt. of Contrabands at Carrollton as they could not be supported in idleness and had already began to steal the plantation cattle and kill them for their own use or to sell. In the other case the planter entered into the arrangement and called his negroes up before me when I explained the order and told them that their master had entered into this agreement for the next year; That they should be well clothed & fed and that, at the end of the year they should receive one twentieth (1/20) of the year's crop for their own use; I told them that I stood as representative of the Govt. and would see that their master carried out faithfully his part of the contract. This was yesterday, and last night eight of his hands run away; He now calls upon me to fulfil my part and see that his negroes are returned to him; this I cannot do; as an officer of the U.S. army I cannot and will not assist in any way in returning slaves to their masters, and here General comes the great difficulty in carrying out the late orders.

Let me if you please review the last circular from the commission.

By Art. 1st I am ordered to carry out in good faith the provisions of the agreement on the part of the authorities. This cannot be done unless a large force can always be at the command of the Provost Marshal, for no one man either civil, or military can control the negro force upon one plantation and when you remember that in my district I have nearly thirty plantations which will require a force of at least four thousand negroes, how is it possible for me to keep them in control or to require them to remain faithfully upon their plantations. 2nd I have offered upon two plantations all fair and legal inducements for the negroes to remain and they refuse so to do, in what manner can I carry out the wishes of the Comd'g. General? 3rd Negroes have on one plantation acquiesced in the terms proposed and the same night run into camp limits; as I am required by art. 3rd "to see that the negro fulfils his engagements for one year in good faith" what shall I do when he leaves and violates that engagement? Art. 3rd says "he shall be required to remain upon the plantation to which he is bound for one year" and I would most respectfully ask what means are to be furnished me to fulfil that requirement? 4th I have already entered into an agreement with a planter that, so long as he fulfils his part of the contract, I will answer on the part of the Govt. that the other part shall be carried out in good faith: He now calls upon me to maintain that position; his negroes who are bound to him by the Govt. refuse to work and a portion have already run away, how can those be returned and the ballance made to work?

The planters are perfectly well satisfied with the circular and are willing to enter into all of its requirements but they will insist that I, as representative of that Govt. carry out in every particular my share of the contract.

How is this to be done? What we have seen upon two plantations, will I am sure be the case upon many others; to prevent in ordinary times negroes from running away was difficult, now, tis simply impossible. Already agreeable to Art. 5th I have sent to Carrollton abt. 300 negroes and must in a few days send as many more—six hundred in six days, but I have no use for them here as they will not work.

This trouble will increase, negroes have their heads so full of freedom or of living in camp without work that they are not willing to wait one year for their pay, and planters cannot afford to pay for their crops until after the rolling season and they know their profits. I shall gladly carry out your views on the subject Genl and will do every thing in my power for the welfare of the negroes as well as for the interests of all loyal planters, but pardon me if I say other orders are needed. On this question we must commence back and prevent negroes entering camps to remain: The number of negroes now within camp lines must be nearly if not quite six thousand; this number will increase, and, while camp lines are open and easy work found therein negroes will not work upon plantations; To carry out the view of this circular & your order, orders should be issued prohibiting negroes coming into the lines; those now in should if possible be handed over to the civil authorities who should be made responsible for them to the Govt. and by them let out to planters. I would suggest that a weekly report be sent in from all Provost Marshals, Supt. of works & Supt. of Contrabands of the number of negroes under their charge both working and sick and if the lists are correct you will be surprised at the number Govt. are feeding without any remuneration— most respectfully asking your advice on this subject I beg to remain, General, your ob't. sv't

HLS Edward Page Jr.

Capt. Edward Page, Jr., to Brig. Genl. James Bowen, 16 Feb. 1863, Letters Received, ser. 1845, Provost Marshal, Dept. of the Gulf, RG 393 Pt. 1 [C-787]. Page was provost marshal for the parishes of St. Charles, St. John the Baptist, and St. James. No reply has been found in the records of the provost marshal general of the Department of the Gulf.

1 Probably the circular letter from General Nathaniel P. Banks, commander of the Department of the Gulf, dated February 7, 1863, which solicited the aid of local provost marshals in explaining to planters and laborers the plantation labor system established by the Sequestration Commission and invited suggestions for its improvement. (See above, doc. 84n.)
2 Presumably the contract form (February 5, 1863) and accompanying circular (February 6, 1863) that set forth the commission's plantation labor regulations and described the duties of local provost marshals in enforcing them. Both are printed above, as doc. 84.

87: Louisiana Free Man of Color to the Commander of the Department of the Gulf

New Orleans, February 22[d], 1863.

General: As I have already stated to you, as soon as I reached Donaldsonville, I travelled about and tried to get all the informations I could; and after a very short while, I found out easily that but very few persons had any knowledge of your last orders.[1] There is two ways to account for such a state of things in that section of the country: *First*, there is no mail going to Donaldsonville, and consequently but few papers reach that place; *Second*, there is still in Donaldsonville and vicinity some persons sympathizing with the Rebels; these persons are continually on the alert; they are generally the first ones to get the news; they always catch the newspapers before any body else; if the news are favorable to their cause, they spread them around rapidly; if it happens that the news are contrary to their wishes, then the papers disappear before any one can get a glance at them, with the exception of a few devoted brother Rebels.

In the four days that I passed in Donaldsonville and vicinity, I managed to get in contact with as many different persons as I could, and belonging almost to all classes of Society.

The rich planters, as far as I could see, are those who seem to me to be the most strongly opposed to any proposition which would purport to take away from them even a particle of their former savage authority. But I do earnestly believe that by catechizing them constantly and actively, it would be easy work, after a short period, to bring them to understand that, not only God and humanity, but their interest commands them to follow the dictates of the progresses of ages. This class of planters argues constantly, and often times on the most trifling points; but by conceding momentarily to them some little ground to stand upon in the discussion, it is easy to turn them, and then to fight and defeat them, and drive them from their positions.

But this class of planters, though the wealthiest, is not the one, in my candid opinion, which ought to attract the most the attention of your administrative powers.

The farmers or planters who possess but a few negroes, are those, I earnestly believe, in whom may be placed some confidence, and whom will more faithfully abide to the orders of the Government and return more promptly to their former allegiance to the United States. I conversed and discussed with them as much as with the others, and I found the great majority of them willing to admit readily that they had been odiously deceived when they were induced to vote for secession; and, furthermore, many of them assured me that it was only the fear of the return and momentary Sojourn of the Rebels among them, that prevented them to renew immediately their oath of allegiance to the Government of the United States. Their present deportment makes me believe that they spoke to me with all sincerity.

As to your last orders concerning negro labor, this class of planters made but few objections. On the contrary, many of them acknowledged that they thought it was the only course to pursue for the present.

I do not think necessary to speak to you of the adopted citizens, of the foreigners not naturalized and of the population not owning any slaves. Their sympathy for the Government of the United States is too well known: I did not come in contact with any one of them opposed to your vews on the matter which makes the object of this report. I am very much inclined to assure you, on the contrary, that you will find, in that class of people, a great number of the most devoted supporters of your measures.

I will now speak of the last and the most interesting class of the population of that section of the country, – the negroes, the slaves.

I explained to them what were your wishes, – that they had to work for their living, – that *liberty* did not signify *idleness*, – that the presumption was that those who would not willingly go to work to support themselves, intended undoubtedly to steal their brothers' earnings, – that it was only by constant labor and good conduct that they would succeed in winning the sympathy of the white population, and obtain that great blessing for which this beautiful country is now almost all over in a blaze, liberty! – &c., &c. – They listened to me with great attention and devotion, and assured me that they were, all of them, willing to go to work immediately on the plantations or for the government, even without remuneration, if I would only promise to them that they would not be whipped and separated from their families, – in fact, requesting only to be treated with humanity. Some of them begged of me, with tears in their eyes, to inform you of their willingness to humbly submit to your orders, and tell you to put them to work at once, and that you would soon have the satisfaction to hear that you could trust their word. The fact is that many of them are now working at the Fort, merely for their daily food, – and many more could be had at the same rates, if their services were needed. And do not think that it is because they are starving, as it has been reported, – no, I have seen many with some money, – but simply to show that they are aware that they have to labor for their daily bread. I remain, General, Your most devoted servant,

ALS Frank F. Barclay

Frank F. Barclay to Major General Nathaniel P. Banks, 22 Feb. 1863, B-152 1863, Letters Received, ser. 1920, Civil Affairs, Dept. of the Gulf, RG 393 Pt. 1 [C-686]. Barclay, formerly the editor of *L'Union*, a New Orleans newspaper with a large readership among the city's French-speaking free people of color, may have been one of the prominent free blacks sent by General Nathaniel P. Banks, commander of the Department of the Gulf, to investigate the response of rural ex-slaves to his plantation labor policy. ([Nathaniel P. Banks], *Emancipated Labor in Louisiana* [New York? 1864], p. 7.) In early March 1863, after a second trip to Donaldsonville (a post on the fringe of federally controlled territory northwest of New Orleans), Barclay informed Banks that at least 800 freedpeople were living there, "the most of them idle and entirely destitute of the necessaries of life." Some 120 were employed at the fort, but "more by humanity than by necessity, half that number being amply sufficient for the amount of work they have to do." All the unemployed, but able-bodied, men and women were, he assured Banks, "very willing to go to work on the plantations sequestered by the Government and for the remuneration proposed by you, because they know well that you will not allow whipping and separation of families." They did not, however, "care to return to their former owners . . . because they have been too unmercifully used and abused by the overseer, and are constantly threatened with the return of the Rebels, who will, they are told, hang them or whip them to death." Above all, they desired "to be under the protection of the paternal Government of the United States." (Frank F. Barclay to Major General Nathaniel P. Banks, 5 Mar. 1863, B-153 1863, Letters Received, ser. 1920, Civil Affairs, Dept. of the Gulf, RG 393 Pt. 1 [C-686].) Barclay was not alone in discerning differences in the reactions of great planters and smallholders to Banks's labor system. In June 1863, the provost marshal of Plaquemines Parish described "*fifty* or *sixty* small farms where the labor is conducted on a small scale in the cultivation of Rice,

Corn, &c," and whose proprietors voiced "little complaint . . . inasmuch as their ambition and desires are satisfied with a mode of living that is the same from year to year." The large planters, by contrast, "have an idea that, unless they can go on as in former years, with the unlimited control of their slaves, free to punish them as they please, they will certainly be '*ruined*' – and Louisiana become a *wilderness*." The planters, the provost marshal suggested, would continue to "complain just as long as the Federal Army holds the least restraint over them in regard to servile labor" and, in particular, as long as they were "not . . . allowed to inflict corporal punishment, and, as they say, make the slave *fear* them." (Lieut. Enoch Foster, Jr., to Capt. Henry L. Pierson, 8 June 1863, Miscellaneous Records, ser. 1896, Provost Marshal, Dept. of the Gulf, RG 393 Pt. 1 [C-813].)

1 Presumably General Order 12, issued January 29, 1863. (See above, doc. 81.)

88: Louisiana Slave to the Commander of the Department of the Gulf

New Orleans March 4 [*1863*]

To Your Honour Major General Banks I earnestly request of your honour to grant a hearing in behalf of myself an^{d} husban^{d}, My mistress has hired me out at the rate of ten dollars a month an^{d} times are so dull that I proposed giving my ma^{d}ame eight dollars a month she would not accept of it an^{d} said I should come home an^{d} she would find a place for me in the work house or in the parish prison where she has my husband Charley Jones for five months I have a son who is home with my ma^{d}ame an^{d} I dont want to go home but I am willing to pay a liberal price until so times get better So I entreat of your honour to look an^{d} examine my case for I shall do whatever you a^{d}vised me to do anything that is just an^{d} right I earnestly request of you to ansure this an^{d} lete me [*know*] what I should do for to releive my mind for I am afraid she may come an^{d} deman^{d} me an^{d} take me to prison any moment when I am willing to give my ma^{d}am a liberal amount for my time Receive this an^{d} tele me what I shal do I remain your Obeden^{t} Servant

ALS Edith Jones

Edith Jones to Your Honour Major General Banks, 4 Mar. [1863], J-21 1863, Letters Received, ser. 1920, Civil Affairs, Dept. of the Gulf, RG 393 Pt. 1 [C-705]. No reply has been found in the letters-sent volumes of the Department of the Gulf.

New Orleans March 4

To Your Honour

Major General Banks

I earnestly request
of your honour to grant a hearing in
behalf of myself an husband. My mistress
has hired me out at the rate of ten
dollars a month an times are so dull that
I purpose giving my madame eight dollars
a month she would not accept of it
an said I should come home an she
would find a place for me in the work
house or in the parish prison where she
has my husband Charly Jones for
five months I have a son who is here
with my madame an I dont want to
go home but I am willing to pay a
liberal price until so times get better
So I entreat of your honour to look
and examine my case for I shall do
whatever you desire me to do anything
that is just an right I earnestly
request of you to answer this an tell

Document 88

89: Five Letters from the Provost Marshal General of the Department of the Gulf to the Provost Marshal of Orleans Parish, Louisiana

New Orleans, 5th March *1863.*

Captn C. W. Killborn P.M. You will cause all vagrant negroes having no regular habitation or Employment to be arrested by the Provost Guard as vagrants and sent to Lieut Hanks, Supt of Negro Labor, Corner of Orange & New Levee Streets in order that they may be placed at work upon plantations or upon Government works

ALS James Bowen

New Orleans, 5 March *1863.*

Captain Kilburn Provost Marshal You will cause all negroes now confined in the prisons of this city not charged with crime or misdemeanors but confined merely on the charge of vagrancy to be released and sent to Lieutenant Hanks, Superintendant of Negro Labor, at his recieving depot, Cotton Press Corner of Orange & New Levee Streets

ALS James Bowen

New Orleans, 14 March *1863.*

Captain Kilburn P.M. The order in respect to the arrest of idle negroes [was?] made to the end that the streets of the City might be freed from vagrants. Where there is evidence in the appearance of persons stopped by the guard or if they shall have passes from their employers approved by competent authority the guard will permit them to pass

ALS James Bowen

New Orleans, 18 March *1863*

Captain Kelburn P.M. I apprehend that the order for the arrest of vagrants is made an instrument of oppression rather than for the correction of an evil

The purpose of the order is simply to prevent vagrancy and in cases of negroes being well or comfortably dressed or following any lawful vocation they are not to be molested or in case of being stopped by the guards they give satisfactory statements of themselves they will be permitted to go free from arrest

ALS James Bowen

New Orleans, 18 March *1863.*
Captain Killborn P.M. There is reason to believe that many persons have been improperly arrested and are now detained by the police authorities in the City prisons as vagrants among whom are it is stated the wives and mothers of soldiers of the U.S.

Be pleased to take such measures as will discharge all persons arrested by the Provost Guard from custody as vagrants either by freeing them from arrest or turning them over to L[t] Hanks, Sup[t] of negro labor –

ALS James Bowen

Brig. Genl. James Bowen to Captn. C. W. Killborn, 5 Mar. 1863, Brig. Genl. James Bowen to Captain Kilburn, 5 Mar. 1863, Brig. Genl. James Bowen to Captain Kilburn, 14 Mar. 1863, Br. Genl. James Bowen to Captain Kelburn, 18 Mar. 1863, and Bg. Genl. James Bowen to Captain Killborn, 18 Mar. 1863, Letters Received by the Provost Marshal, ser. 1497, Orleans Parish LA, Provost Marshal Field Organizations, RG 393 Pt. 4 [C-968].

90A: Anonymous Louisiana Unionist to the Commander of the Department of the Gulf

New Orleans, April 3[d] 1863.
Dear Gen[l], the writer of this beg leave to State the following facts. which can be proved. by overwhelming testimony.

George Johnson. alias Merritt. is a regularly enlisted man, in Company B. Captain. W[m] B. Barrett. 2[d] Regiment Native Guards. La Vols. and has a family consisting of wife and three children.

Recently four whitemen, pretending to be acting under authority of Capt Sawyer. Provost Marshall of St Bernard. came to the residence of the wife of George Johnson. N[o] 90 Circus St. and kidnapped her. carried her down to the plantation of Dr T. B. Merritt. Eleven miles down the Mexican Gulf Rail Road. and there subjected her to the most cruel and unmerciful treatment. the Overseer of the plantation. whose name is Stamply. beat her unmercifully with a Stick. he afterward turned her clothes over her head, and Struck fifty two lashes. at the time he was thus punishing her. the Driver. remarked. M[r] Stamply. if you dont be careful. you will Kill that woman. thereupon, Stamply drew his Revolver. and pointing it at the Driver; Said, God damn you, if you Say another word. I'll blow your brains out. the Yankee's have turned all you Niggers fools. and I intend to Kill all the niggers I can. and it will not be long. before all the Yankee's in Louisiana were killed off. and those who were not Killed. would have to run off.

On last Sunday. March 29th 1863. Dr's Merritt. and Knapp. and Maj. Walker. met at a Station on the Mex. Gulf. R.R. and had with them the woman before mentioned. who had been previously brought there in the cars. they proceeded down the road to the plantation of one Ducrow. they then and there whipped her unmercifully and cruelly, for the purpose of making her tell where the other negroes were. and to give up her Ration certificate, which they called. 'Damned Yankee Documents' as to the documents, she could not give them up, as they were in this city. as to the negroes. she Knew nothing of their whereabouts. her name is Arana Johnson, This woman is the property of a man named Patton. a Rebel. now at Vicksburg, he was one of those who fired into the fleet. as it came up the River. last April, Patton is also married to a Daughter of Dr Merritt,

There is concealed. Somewhere in the vicinity of the plantations of these gentlemen, a large quantity of Medicine, which they intend to Smuggler to the Rebels. the woman Knows where it is concealed. and will show the proper authorities the Spot. She is now at Dr Merritt. Plantation. they having found out. that further concealment would not do.

General, if you will investigate this matter, it will be of no use to apply to Capt Sawyer the Provost Marshall. down there. as he is in league with the planters. and, tell them to treat the negroes as they please that he will take good care to see that nothing Shall be known at headquarters, and especially of this case. of pesecuting the wife of a United States Soldier.

Capt. Sawyer is Selling Soldier rations to the planters down there.

It is but recently that an old man was starved to death. by being confined in the Stocks. and allowed nothing to eat. from which he died.

There are a great many union persons down there. who all say that it is a Shame that this woman Should thus be persecuted. and that if it were known at head quarters. it would not be allowed to exist.

I am heart. head. and hand for the union. and hope to see it shortly put down this Rebellion and with it the vile and wicked institution of Slavery. Knowing the facts here in Stated, my own feeling will not Suffer me to remain Silent. that the proper remedy. may be applied. feeling that if Known at head quarters the parties offending may brought to

HLSr *Justice*

Justice to Major Genl. N. P. Banks, 3 Apr. 1863, filed as A-38 1863, Letters Received, ser. 1756, Dept. of the Gulf, RG 393 Pt. 1 [C-522]. Presumably in response to this complaint, the department commander directed Lieutenant George H. Hanks, superintendent of Negro labor, to investigate conditions on the Knapp and Merritt plantations. Hanks's report is printed immediately below as doc. 90B. Meanwhile, Colonel Charles W. Drew, commander of another Louisiana black regiment (the 4th Native Guard), reported to the provost marshal general of the department that the relatives of several of his men had also been abused by planters in St. Bernard Parish. One woman's owner had sent her from New Orleans to a plantation in that parish, where she was whipped "very badly." The daughter of another soldier "was kept in the stocks a long time and then given one hundred & fifty lashes." "Nearly every day," Drew charged, "the wife of some Soldier is spirited away . . . to that Parish." According to Drew, Dr. F. A. Knapp, a dentist in New Orleans who owned a plantation in St. Bernard, "is the instrument used to accomplish their object, That of making those who enlist all the trouble they can." (Col. Chas. W. Drew to Brig. General Bowen, 7 Apr. 1863, Letters Received, ser. 1845, Provost Marshal, Dept. of the Gulf, RG 393 Pt. 1 [C-522].) The provost marshal general forwarded a copy of Drew's report to Captain Silas W. Sawyer, the provost marshal of St. Bernard Parish, with instructions to "cause the persons charged to be arrested and if guilty to be severely punished" and to return the abducted woman to her home in New Orleans. (Brig. Genl. James Bowen to Captain Sawyer, 7 Apr. 1863, vol. 296 DG, p. 485, Press Copies of Letters Sent, ser. 1839, Provost Marshal, Dept. of the Gulf, RG 393 Pt. 1 [C-522].)

90B: Superintendent of Negro Labor in the Department of the Gulf to the Commander of the Department

New Orleans April 8th 1863.

Sir. I have the honor to report that I have just returned from the parish of St Bernard where I visited the plantation of Drs Merritt and Knapp. when within about two miles of Dr Merritts plantation I met a Negro whom I had yesterday sent with a polite note to Dr M– requesting him to allow the wife and two children of the Negro to accompany him to their own homes. he reported that the overseer of the place caused him to be imprisoned over night and told him that Hanks was a d----d scoundrel. and in the morning chased him away towords the City for over 1/2 mile giving him no opportunity to see his wife and Children or to procure a particle of food. I immediately went to the plantation. called for the Proprietor, was informed that he was absent. I then called for the manager, he had gone to the Provost Marshall's Office. I found the Negro'es at dinner called them out into line and proceeded to take the names of those who did not belong to Dr M. while doing this the Manager rode up, I informed him who I was, and that I had come there to attend to a little business which had been intrusted to me.

Having finished interrogating the Negro'es, I told them that they should not be allowed to leave the place, that they must work as faithfully as in former years and try and make a good crop, that their share would be larger than If they made only a small one, the result of my inventory of names, was, that about Twenty adults and a number of Children had been brought there under Coercive Circumstances; a large proportion of them were the property of a man in the Rebel army whose estate is Confiscated.

I called the manager aside so as not to intefere with his discipline, and asked him why he retained those people? who all assured me that they desired to return to their own plantation to work. He replied that he had the permission of the *owner's agent* to keep and work them, (bear in mind that the owner is a rebel)

I then questioned him in regard to his conduct in imprisoning and maltreating the messenger whom I had sent with the letter to Dr Merritt? He replied that "he "would'nt allow no strange niggers to come on to his plantation." I quietly told him that if he persisted in disregarding the Millitary authorities, he would be likely to get into trouble, I also informed him that It had been frequently reported that several of the planters of that parish were in the habit of whipping their Slaves cruelly, and that there were others method of punishment quite as salutary and less obnoxious. he said that he would whip his Niggers if they were saucy or disobedient. I told him that it would not be permitted he still persisted; saying that if he was managing a plantation for me, he would do it as I directed, but that as he was managing for Dr M. he would do it to suit *him*. I replied that furthur argument was unneccessary. I then requested him to release the wife and Children of the Negro whom I had sent the day before, he refused to do it. I replied that I would do it for him. he said he should object. I told him he was at liberty to do so, but that his objections would not prevent the execution of the order. he said he would go and state the case to the Gen. I replied that I would save him the trouble as I should report upon it, Having delivered the woman and Children to the husband, I proceeded to visit the plantation of Dr Knapp. Here I was received with civility, the proprietor accompanying me over his broad acres, which were in a fine state of Cultivation, and exhibited every indication of thrift, enterprise and discipline. I visited each laborer without disturbing or embarrassing the labor, took the names of those who were not owned by Dr Knapp numbering about twenty adults. most of them were sent there by their owners, or their Agents, if the owners were absent. I interrogated them. they said they were well fed and that there had been no Corporal punishment upon the place recently. I think that the many complaints against several planters of this Parish is occasioned by the injudicious manner in which they have procured their laborers viz. accepting all fugitives who could be arrested by, or at the instance of their reputed owners. the coercion neccessary to arrest and convey them thither causing much excitement among the blacks and their sympathizers both Civil and Millitary.

It is also my opinion from what I learned in conversation that certain members of the police of this Parish have unauthorizedly arrested Negro'es, and having subjected them to the lash, have thus coerced them into submitting to be hired out to the planters. I found a policeman overseeing a large gang upon a new Levee which is being built upon Dr Knapps plantation but which is apparently a superfluous piece of work, as the Levee in front of it is in a good state of repair. I questioned these Negro'es and found that none of them belonged in the Parish, nearly every one was arrested and brought there, and all but one disired to return home, some of them are nearly naked and all are locked up in a brick building every night without blankets and only boards to lie upon. Dr Knapp informed me that he had nothing to do with them, that the work was under the direction of the Provost Marshall.

Having finished my investigation, I accepted the proffered hospitality of the proprietor by partaking of a bountiful dinner. returning I called at the plantation of Maj Walker, found 70 Laborers at work, he informed me that they were working more cheerfully and better than formerly. the fact that none of his Negro'es have ever left him is I think conclusive evidence that he is kind and humane to his laborers. I have been thus explicit and minute in my report knowing that the parties visited will probably make their statement of the case. Knowing the extreme sensitiveness of the planters upon the subject I endeavored to perform my unpleasant duty with extreme courtesy and hope my visit may prove salutary in preventing further atrocities or inhumanity. I have the honor to be Sir Very Respectfully Your Ob[t] Serv[t]

HLS Geo. H. Hanks

Lieut. Geo. H. Hanks to Maj. Gen. N. P. Banks, 8 Apr. 1863, H-84 1863, Letters Received, ser. 1920, Civil Affairs, Dept. of the Gulf, RG 393 Pt. 1 [C-701].

90C: Provost Marshal of St. Bernard Parish, Louisiana, to the Provost Marshal General of the Department of the Gulf, Enclosing an Order by the Superintendent of Negro Labor in the Department

Pa St Bernard [*La.*] 17th May 1863

Genl Enclosed please find order of Liut Hanks to Dr Merritt to deliver to George Johnson (Colored) his wife and Three Children. I would respectfully ask if Such Orders are to be complied with I think they Should come from you. I have arrested the Overseer Stamply and Sent him out of the Parish Dr Merritt is very sick and there is no white man on the place the Negroes were getting along very well and well contented but Such orders disorganize and make them uneasy, and I think if Liut Hanks had wished the woman and children it would have, been much better to have Sent a white Soldier or officer not a Former Slave of the Plantation.

yesterday, whilst I was at the Lake with those Registered Enemys, A man by the name of Furniss claiming to be a Special Policeman came into the Parish and Visited the difernt Plantations telling the Negroes if they did not wish to work they could leave he went to one house where the owners were all away opened the house went to the Desk, &c when the Owner returned he found him in Possession of his place Such things tend to make the Negroes unhappy and if they are continued in the Planters will neve be able to make there Crops. they were getting along very well and were contented if let alone

I would therefore ask for instructions in the matter, if they are to Visit all Plantations or only when they hear of Cruel Treatment Said Furniss had a negro Soldier with a Pass to go to Dr Knapps which Expired on the 15th he was arrested by my Picket Some ten miles below Knapp. I Send him and the man Johnson, up under Guard, and await your Orders in the case of his wife and children Respect your obt Servt

ALS S W Sawyer

[*Enclosure*] New Orleans May 16th 1863

Dr Merritt Parish St Bernard Deliver to Geo Johnson U.S. Soldier his wife Arian Johnson and her three children

ADS Geo. H. Hanks

S. W. Sawyer to Brig. Genl. James Bowen, 17 May 1863, enclosing Lt. Geo. H. Hanks to Dr. Merritt, 16 May 1863, Letters Received, ser. 1845, Provost

Marshal, Dept. of the Gulf, RG 393 Pt. 1 [C-779]. Two days later, in a letter to the commander of the defenses of New Orleans, Sawyer inveighed against "Officers, or men representing themselves as Officers of Genl Banks Staff visiting the different Plantations and telling the Negro's if they did not wish to work, they could leave the Place, that no one had a right to Keep them." As evidence of the disruptive effects of such interference from headquarters, Sawyer maintained that Hanks should have sent white soldiers to undertake the release of George Johnson's family, rather than put such an order into the hands of the black soldier himself. Sawyer also described, with indignation, the visit by Furniss to several plantations on May 16. The police officer, Sawyer charged, had "asked the Negroes if they were satisfied, telling them if they were not, that he would take them away (or words to that effect) and as the height of a Negros ambition is to have nothing to do and plenty to eat," Furniss's advice had "as a matter of Course" made the laborers "uneasy." On another plantation in the parish, the workers had "Armed themselves, with sticks, with Lead on the end . . . driving the overseer into his house saying they would make Laws for themselves." Significantly, Sawyer noted, the rebellious laborers had named their "Officers" after Union army commanders, "[c]alling one Col. Thomas, one Col. Stafford, &c." (Capt. Silas W. Sawyer to Brig. Genl. T. W. Sherman, 19 May 1863, Letters Received, ser. 1845, Provost Marshal, Dept. of the Gulf, RG 393 Pt. 1 [C-779].)

91: Louisiana Freedmen to the Provost Marshal General of the Department of the Gulf; and Statement of the Commander of Camp Hoyt, Louisiana

Camp Hoyt Terre Bonne [*La.*] April 5th /63.

Sir We the undersigned Negroes residing on Major Potts Plantation Parish Terre Bonne La. respectfully submit to you the following statement;

Captain Goodrich Provost Marshal at Thibodeaux told us to go on and cultivate the land on the Plantation, and do something for ourselves, until the Government could do something for us and gave orders for all the Stray Mules belonging to the plantation to be brought in, so that we could work the land, and we understood that we were to be protected in our labor– We have about 60 Arpents of land broken up a large portion of which is already planted, and the balance ready for planting. Now a Mr Wright comes on the plantation with Authority from the Government to work it and claims the result of our labor– We have had a hard struggle to get along and we feel it hard now that we have succeeded in making ourselves in a measure independent, to have to [*turn*] it all over to someone else.

We have at present on the place about 14 men, 23 women 10 of whom are old and with Children, 24 Small Children & Babies. Under the circumstances we think it but just that we should be allowed to work the land already broken up and planted on equal shares with the Government.

We therefore ask your aid and assistance in having secured to us what was promised us by Provost Marshal Cap't Goodrich – and the posession of the property we [*have?*] and land acquired by our labor.

Henry Norvall	Littleton Saunders,
Claiborn Thomas,	Thos Essex,
Thornton Boller,	Phil Sergeant,
Thos Mathews,	Parker Williams,
Jefferson Rounds,	Nelson McClenny,

HLSr

Terre Bonne Louisiana April 5 1863,

At the request of some of the contrabands on the plantation of Major Potts I have visited the plantation & certify to the following facts.

1. They appear to be of unusual respectability & bear a good character, giving all the evidences of neat, thrifty & industrious laborers,

2. They have broken up & partially planted with corn as nearly as I can compute about sixty arpents of land and have acquired some corn & cotton seed sufficient I should judge for planting this ground.

3 From what I can learn they have thus far received no aid from the government but have supported themselves creditably by their own exertions & labor – although a very large proportion are aged men, women & young children.

ADS *Charles C Nott.*

Henry Norvall et al. to Brig. Gen'l Bowen, 5 Apr. 1863, enclosed in statement of Col. Charles C. Nott, 5 Apr. 1863, N-13 1863, Letters Received, ser. 1920, Civil Affairs, Dept. of the Gulf, RG 393 Pt. 1 [C-712]. Endorsement. The body of the freedmen's petition and all the signatures are in the same handwriting. Nott signed as a colonel in the 17th New York Infantry. A search of the letters-sent volumes of the Department of the Gulf revealed no evidence of a reply, but the freedpeople evidently remained in control of the plantation during 1863. In August of that year, an agent of the Treasury Department reported that the Potts estate "has been Cultivated by the negroes without the assistance of any white man; they have made sufficient Corn for their own use and some to sell; Cane sufficient for Forty or Fifty Hhds may be ground and there is sufficient wood at the sugar House for one hundred Hhds." "The Negroes," he continued, "are contented and happy and larger returns will be found from the management of this place than any one I have seen managed by inexperienced Govm't agents or Soldiers; no supplies are furnished them and they are better clothed than any I have seen on other plantations." "Their confidence in the Government is very limited," the agent noted, "and they are in constant fear of the rebels." He concluded with a categorization of the sixty residents of the estate: nineteen men (sixteen ranked "No. 1," one "No 2," and two nonworkers); twenty-six women (nineteen "No 1," four "No 2," three nonworkers); and fifteen children. (H. Stiles, "Report 'Potts Plantation,' " 18 Aug. 1863, vol. 71, pp. 54–55, Reports of Inspectors of Plantations, 3rd Agency, RG 366 [Q-110].) For the fate of the freedpeople on the Potts plantation in 1864, see below, doc. 114.

92: Testimony by the Former Commander of the Department of the Gulf before the American Freedmen's Inquiry Commission

[*Boston, Mass. May 1, 1863*]

Testimony of Major-General B. F. Butler.

At the request of the Commission, General Butler appeared before them, in Boston, May 1st, and after some informal conversation, in the course of which the General referred to his Order in reference to the employment of the freedmen of Louisiana on the plantations,[1] and to the objection made by the planters to his restriction in the matter of punishment, (the Order vesting all correctional power in the Provost Marshal,) the General said–

I feel inclined to call your attention to this matter, because I believe that, if you look at it with minds sharpened to see how the negroes can be freed, instead of being edged the other way, you can find reasons for believing that eight out of every ten of the negroes of Louisiana are free. The masters claim them now, I know; and they used to claim them of me; but those claims did not amount to a great deal. I see by the paper that the negroes are required, by Gen. Banks, to work on the fortifications for nothing, or for their masters, at two or three dollars a month – three dollars for skilled labor, two dollars for ordinary field hands. The Act of Congress gave them ten.[2]

Question [by Mr. OWEN][3] – Have you any doubt of the general disposition of the negroes to work, if they are employed at fair rates of wages, and paid regularly?

Answer, No more than I have of any other class of laborers. Take Mr. Zunt's plantation. That plantation was sold for $25.000, and the man who bought it (Mr. Weare) came and asked me if the negroes might go back. I said, "Yes; only you must pay them ten dollars a month, and make ten hours a day's work. In the grinding season, when you have to work them nearly all night, you must pay them for two day's work, if they work twenty hours instead of ten, and let them understand it and go to work." He said he would; and afterwards I went down to the plantation, with the French Admiral, and the man who had charge of the negroes told me he had no trouble with them. There was only one ugly fellow, he said, who insisted that he must be supplied with tobacco extra. "I get more labor out of them," said he, "than was ever got out of the negroes on this plantation before. I can make a hogshead & a half more sugar a day, with the same help, than I could with slave labor." I had some of the first crop of sugar made there by free black labor barrelled up, and sent it to President Lincoln, and wrote him a letter,[4] which he answered. I do not know as there will be any harm in my sending copies of those letters to you. Wherever the planters employed the negroes, they were made to employ them upon those terms.

Q. What is your opinion of their capacity as soldiers?

A. They are good soldiers, precisely in propor[*tion*] to their intelligence, like anybody else. If I was getting up a company of soldiers, I would like in the first place, the Senior Class of Harvard University; next, intelligent Yankee farmers and mechanics; next, intelligent Irishmen; next, intelligent Germans; and the negroes, in the scale of their intelligence. There is this advantage in favor of the negroes as soldiers – they are all disciplined. I do not mean that they are drilled in the Manual, but I mean, they have learned a thing we never can learn – at least, not until after three or four years, and then very imperfectly – and that is, to do as they are told. If they are told to shoulder a musket in a given way, they have no lingering idea that there may be a better way than that. If a Yankee is told to shoulder a musket in a particular manner, he immediately sets himself thinking if that is the best way. It is habit of mind; it is discipline, in other words; it is what we get into our soldiers only after long drill.

Q. Don't you find them earnest in their desire to learn?

A. Oh, very earnest. No trouble about that. Another thing about them is, that they are gregarious in fright, and in that particular the exact opposite of the Yankee. If a crowd of Yankees gets frightened, it is "Every one for himself, & God for us all," They scatter – every one seeking safety alone. Now, the negroes have been accustomed to stand in a body against master and overseer; they segregate – they run to each other.

Q. The negroes you enlisted were enlisted as volunteers?

A Entirely; and without bounty; and, at the time I left them, without pay.

Q Do you think it wise to draft them?

A No; there is no occasion to draft them. Give them fair play.

Q Equal rights and equal protection, whether as prisoners or in the ranks?

A Give them *fair play*; and "fair play" means what the words express. If a man is fit to be a soldier and fight for the country, if he is intelligent enough, he is fit to be an officer; and a great wrong has been committed, if the newspaper reports are true, in the Department of the Gulf, in making all the colored officers resign.

. . . .

Q Then you don't think there is any risk of servile insurrections?

A Not if you will arm the negroes, and give them officers of their own color. Do you suppose if the French General at St. Domingo had given Toussaint a captaincy, there would have been any trouble? I have always thought not. I can hardly conceive of a greater injustice than has been done in compelling the resignation of these colored officers.

Q And not only great injustice, but an injustice which is pregnant with dangerous consequences?

A The consequence is, that Gen. Banks has been ever since filling up one regiment. They don't understand it, & won't enlist. There is another thing in which colored soldiers excel our troops, and that is, in the art of taking care of themselves. Our soldiers have depended more on their mothers, wives and daughters. None of our soldiers know how to cook. The blacks have always been accustomed to cook for themselves. The able-bodied woman was reckoned a field hand as well as the man, and it was about an even chance whether a healthy woman or a not over-healthy man did the cooking. In New Orleans, it was especially so, because there the cooks were generally men, and they lived well, I assure you– They will cook & wash & take care of their clothes better than white soldiers.

Q Do you think they are more punctilious as guards or sentinels?

A They are more exact, inasmuch as they are more obedient. They only do exactly what they are told to do. It is simply–"You can't come here." They have never been allowed to take any responsibility; they have never been allowed to do any thing except what they were told to do. They are more punctilious, because better disciplined.

Q [by Dr. HOWE].[5] I should like to know whether, in your opinion, there is any call for a supervision of these men, to prevent vagrancy and idleness, and make them support themselves, any more than for poor whites?

A No, Sir; there is the same call as there would be if they were poor whites. Suppose you should put here four millions of unemployed white laborers at once, without a dollar of their own, and with a disorganized state of society, there would be cause for supervision here, wouldn't there? You are doing precisely that there. They are vagrants—"with no visible means of support." They come within our statute definition.

Q [by Mr. OWEN][5]– To what extent do you believe the guardianship of the Government over these men is necessary or expedient?

A My belief is, that both over the whites and blacks at the South, there has got to be, for a series of years, a military supervision; that we have got to go back to the original idea of Territorial government, which was that of military supervision. We must remember that it is only a few years since all the Territories were governed through the War Office, and the Governor of a Territory was a military officer.

Q [by Dr. HOWE].[5] In that case, would you leave negro labor to regulate itself, the same as white labor?

A Precisely,—under the same laws. I don't make any distinction between poor negro labor and from white labor. I don't see any occasion to make any distinction. I should make the distinction in intelligence, rather than in color, if I was going to make any.

I found a very queer set of people down in Louisiana, who would interest you very much. In La Fourche Parish, through which the bayou La Fourche runs, (for "bayou" does not mean, as I had always supposed, an area of the sea, or lagoon, but a canal,) there are a lot of small holdings, differing from the great estates, with small houses and little narrow plats of ground, on each side of the bayou, running down to what used to be the swamps, but which are now large plantations; holdings of perhaps fifty or sixty acres apiece, inhabited by a very simple people, of French extraction, & speaking that language largely. A quiet, agricultural people, who sustain themselves by raising a few bales of cotton annually and shooting game for the market, and rejoice in the name of "Cajans." I was curious to know how they came by that name, and at last I found out that they were our old friends the Acadians, who had moved down there. It was the whole story of "Evangeline." Then I found another set of men, with a name that has a very curious derivation. There are a lot of Greeks, Sicilians, Maltese & Corsicans in New Orleans—in fact, all the Meditteranean islands are represented there. The whole fruit & fish trade is in their hands. These men from the Meditteranean isles are all known by the general name of "Dagos." It is the commonest phrase in the world. It bothered me to trace that out, and I could not find anybody who could give me any aid; but when I went back to the old Spanish name, "Hidalgo," I had the clue, and I find that

"Hidalgo" had been corrupted into "Dago," and now all who go there from the shores of the Meditteranean are called "Dagos."

Q Did you find any disposition in the colored people to come North?

A Yes, Sir, I found that dispositon, and I took away three. They desired to get North, for they were in continual fear that New Orleans would be retaken, as the secesh people all told them it would. There are only 24000 colored people in New Orleans, out of a population of 170,000. The hardest labor done in the city is done by white men. They pave the streets, work on the levee, dig the canals. But when you get out into the parishes, you will find a different state of facts. Here is a matter to which your attention might be well turned – the proportion of the property of Louisiana that is invested in slaves. I learned from the State Auditor's Report, that in 1860, the entire taxable property of Louisiana amounted to $316,000,000, of which $153,000,000 was slaves, and $163,000,000 all other property. I was surprised to find whole parishes in this condition (& they do not tax slaves under ten years of age) – with three millions of taxable property, two millions of it in slaves, and only one million in all other kinds of property; and there would not be more than $32,000 of money at interest out of the three millions. All the other personal property would be a mere bagatelle.

Q [by Dr. Howe].[5] That has been the favorite investment for the last thirty years in the South.

Gen. Butler. Well it might be. A negro that would bring $1500 could be let for $30 a month; sometimes they bring as much as $40 or $50 a month; I give rather an average. One of the men who came on with me was a barber, who brought $50 a month.

As I was saying just now, the difficulty is that a good many of the negroes there want to get North, because they are not quite sure things are to remain at the South as they are. I would come North if I were they. If I could go the plantation negroes and say to them – "Go back to work on the plantations, and you shall have all the rights coming to you that you would have if you came into my camp," they would all go there and stay; but if they thought they would have a little better protection and additional rights, if they came to my camp, they would come there, instead of living in their comfortable cabins on the plantations.

Q [by Dr. Howe][5] Suppose there were entire emancipation throughout the South, would the movement of the negroes, in your opinion, be northward or southward?

A It would be southward.

Q [by Mr Owen][5] Did you find much difficulty in getting white soldiers to treat the negroes properly?

A No, not the least. The only trouble was, that the negroes made gentlemen of all my soldiers. They were so willing to aid the soldiers, that they would carry their knapsacks & muskets for them, and if you went out with them on a march, you would see the negroes relieving the soldiers in that way – one negro carrying a man's gun, and another his knapsack. I had no difficulty with the men; but I did have some with the women, and was obliged to make some stringent regulations in regard to them, because the women are all brought up to think that no honor can come to them equal to that of connection with a white man; and I am sorry to say, that white men are not all above taking advantage of this feeling. I found some difficulty in that respect, but there were no quarrels between the negroes and the soldiers; and I assure you that quarrels between white and black soldiers were unknown and unheard of while I was there. But you will get your eyes open in regard to the terms "black" and "white," before you get back, as I did

Q [by Dr. HOWE][5] If there should be an entire emancipation of the slaves throughout the South, do you not think it would have an effect upon the emigration of free labor from the North?

A Oh, yes, a very great effect. It would have precisely this tendency. I suppose, (to illustrate what I mean,) that Irishmen coming over here to dig our railroads & canals, and do our work as the laboring population, has had a tendency to make our sons railroad engineers, conductors, locktenders, &c. – the next grade above. Now, I suppose that there would be such an opening, with all this labor being broken up into small numbers, as would carry our soldiers there, with the expectation of hiring it.

Q Then it would open a new and rich field for Northern enterprise and emigration?

A Oh, certainly. I think we had better confiscate the land, but whether we do or not, they will go down there & get it; they *will* have it. The Yankee isn't going to work forever where he has to turn out big rocks every Spring, when he can go where, to use the language of an astounded Vermonter, "there isnt a stun to throw at a dog."

Q [by Mr OWEN][5] Do you think we have to anticipate, in the future of the war, any secret insurrections by the negroes?

A I hope so.

Q But do you think it likely they will occur?

A As soon as they find out that they can help themselves, they will do it; but they would a great deal rather have our assistance.

Q [by Dr. HOWE][5] Have you any knowledge of the views of the Northern soldiers generally with regard to staying at the South?

A I think a large portion of the soldiers in Louisiana will go back there. Those who have not very strong ties here I think would remain, almost universally; and, indeed, I have known many discharged soldiers to stay.

Q Would not that have the effect to carry Northern ideas and institutions there?

A Yes, if you got rid of slavery; but if you do not get rid of slavery, you carry Southern ideas into Northern hearts; for the worst secessionists, the most accursed of all the accursed rebels, are Masstts men who have gone there and got thoroughly imbued with Southern ideas.

Slave property, as a marketable commodity, had gone out entirely in Louisiana, before I left. I could buy the best negroes in Louisiana for $250. I think that, take them all through, you might safely put it down that the remuneration to the masters should be $100 apiece, with gradual emancipation;– it should be only gradual emancipation.

Q In what way?

A Take it that all born after a certain time should be born free– about as in Western Virginia.[6] I think any change should be gradual. All natural changes are gradual. It was a gradual change in this State, a gradual change in New Hampshire, and a gradual change every where. Only make it just, that is all, and then you need not trouble yourselves about its certainty. This thing, once started, will not go backward.

. . . .

HD

Excerpts from testimony of Major-General B. F. Butler before the American Freedmen's Inquiry Commission, [1 May 1863], filed with O-328 1863, Letters Received, ser. 12, RG 94 [K-86]. About sixteen pages of a twenty-three-page document. Topical labels in the margin are omitted. The first omitted portion, which concerned black officers in the Department of the Gulf, is printed in *Freedom*, ser. 2: doc. 127. Butler's questioners were Robert Dale Owen and Samuel Gridley Howe.

1 General Order 91, issued by General Butler on November 9, 1862, while he was commander of the Department of the Gulf. (See above, doc. 67.)

2 In early February, 1863, General Nathaniel P. Banks, Butler's successor as commander of the Department of the Gulf, had approved a contract offered by the Sequestration Commission to Louisiana planters, under which black laborers were to receive from $1 to $3 per month (although not necessarily in the employ of their former masters); if they refused plantation employment, they were to labor on the public works without pay. (See above, doc. 84.) The act of Congress in question was the Militia Act of July 1862, which set the pay for black military laborers at $10 per month (minus $3 for clothing). (*Statutes at Large*, vol. 12, pp. 597–600.)

3 Brackets in manuscript.
4 See above, doc. 70.
5 Brackets in manuscript.
6 The constitution of the state of West Virginia, ratified in March 1863, provided that, as of July 4, 1863, all slaves under the age of ten would become free on their twenty-first birthday, all slaves between the ages of ten and twenty-one would become free on their twenty-fifth birthday, and all children of slaves would be born free. (Francis Newton Thorpe, comp., *The Federal and State Constitutions, Colonial Charters, and Other Organic Laws of the States, Territories, and Colonies*, 7 vols. [Washington, 1909], vol. 7, pp. 4013–33.)

93: Aide-de-Camp of the Chief Quartermaster of the Department of the Gulf to the Chief Quartermaster

New Orleans May 15" 1863

Colonel In obedience to your order of 12th Febr'y last, I proceeded to take charge of such abandoned Plantations as were placed in possession of the Chief Quarter Master by the Major General, Commanding the Department of the Gulf, and which were turned over to you by the U.S. Sequestration Commission. Viz:

The "Point Celeste" Plantation in Parish of Plaquemine formerly belonging to McManus & Griffin and worked the last season by C. A Weed on account of U.S. Government. I found the plantation in very bad order, it having been stripped of everything available. I appointed Mr Geo. R. Ward, overseer at a salary of One Thousand ($1.000⁰⁰) Doll's per annum.

I have on this place 227 Acres of Cane and 145 Acres of cotton in good condition with a fair promise of a fine crop. There is also 332 Acres of Corn, a portion of which is in bad condition owing to the large quantity of wet land that we have been unable to properly drain with the small draining machine on the place. There is upon this Plantation a total of 117 hands, of which 29 are invalids and children. The monthly consumption of provisions here is 13 Barrels Pork and 60 Bushels of Corn for the hands. With a fair season I have no doubt but this place will pay a handsome profit to the Government

The "Sarah" Plantation in the same Parish formerly owned by W. F. Smith (also abandoned) like the "Point Celeste" was stripped of nearly everything valuable when I took possession of it. I employed as overseer Mr Jas. M. Silvant at a salary of Eight hundred ($800⁰⁰) Dollars per annum. Upon this place I have 300 Acres of

Cane and 60 acres of corn planted, all looking well and with a prospect of a good crop. Here I am working 29 hands in addittion to which there are 12 Women & children unable to labor. The Monthly Consumption of provisions is 4 Brls Pork and 50 Bushels Corn, in addittion to which I have been obliged to feed the Mules with oats as they were in such bad Condition I could not otherwise properly work them.

The "Oakland" Plantation formerly belonging to Jas. N. Brown and the "Star" Plantation formerly belonging to Dr P. A. Borland in the same Parish I have rented. the former for one half the Nett profits of the Crop, the other for the Sum of One thousand ($1.000^oo^) Dollars – for after a careful inspection of the place and its Condition, I was fully satisfied that it could only be worked at an expense instead of a profit to the Government, the soil being naturally very hard and unproductive, and the place destitute of very many of the most necessary articles for properly Cultivating it. In addition to which I found the Sugar Mill and its Machinery in such bad Condition that a Crop Could only be taken off after spending at least Five thousand ($5.000^oo^) Dollars in necessary repairs.

In the Parish of Terrebonne I have Ten abandoned Plantations of which I am working only the "Hopkins" Plantation on Bayou Black, for the U.S. Government. Upon this place I have installed Mr Horace Bell as overseer at a salary of One thousand ($1.000^oo^) Dollars per Annum. I have upon this plantation 240 acres in Cane, about 75 acres in Corn and some 10 acres in Potatoes. There are 43 working hands and 29 Children unable to labor –

The Monthly Consumption of provisions upon this place is 6 Barrels Pork and about 100 Bushels Corn. The Crop looks well, although it has suffered greatly for want of rain. The promise is good for a fair Crop.

The several Plantations formerly owned by Messrs J. H. Quitman J. R. Robinson A. G. & D. S. Cage, J. R & W. A. Bisland, J. Bronson Jr and J. C. Potts, have all been rented for one half the Nett, profits of the Crop, and a good and Sufficient bond taken for the proper Cultivation of the places as is invariably done in all Cases where I have rented Plantations.

From all that I can learn I do not think the Bisland places have been properly managed, or that it was any part of the rentors desire to raise Crops upon these places, but rather to keep the negroes together until such time as the owners might return to claim their abandoned homes. I have therefore cancelled the orders heretofore made relative to these places and have placed them in Charge of Mr Wm Fielder to work for the benefit of the Government. I have found a disposition on the part of the Provost Marshalls in some of the Parishes to unwarrantably intefere with the management of the places – This only breeds discontent among the hands and engenders in them a refractory Spirit, which it was becoming exceedingly difficult to Control while at the same time it rendred the Lessees of the different plantations careless and extremely negligent in obeying orders emanating from this office. This renders the task of properly managing the different places, very much more laborious than would otherwise be necessary. I am happy however to be able to state that upon properly representing the Case to Brig. Gen. James Bowen Provost Marshall General of the Department of the Gulf, he at once gave me Such orders as will I am quite confident prevent any Conflict hereafter between the Provost Marshalls and my overseers.

The "Ellis" Place belonging to the heirs of T & T. Ellis is in possession of two minor heirs who are working it for themselves reserving the share due to U.S. Government.

In the Parish of St. Charles there are seven abandoned plantations and one belonging to Madame Davis Lanaux & Son which was seized because the negroes refused to work for the owners, and it thus became a resort for runaway negroes which rendered anything like discipline on the other plantations entirely futile. In addition to these reasons both the proprietors are noted Rebels who have thrown every obstacle in the way of properly Cultivating the plantations for the Government, and have labored long and faithfully to make a Crevasse upon their place, which was only prevented by great expense and diligence. This plantation with those formerly belonging to Ezra Davis, Geo. E. Payne & Geo. E. Wailes have been placed at the disposal of 1st Lieut. Geo. H. Hanks who is working them as Supt of negro labor, for the U.S. Government.

The Plantations formerly belonging to Judge P. A. Rost, and J. W. & S. McCutcheon on the left Bank of the Mississippi have been rented upon the usual terms. In this Parish I am working the Plantations formerly belonging to Mayronne Bros and Gen. R. Taylor. Upon the Mayronne place, I have 1073 in Cultivation, Viz: 555 acres of Cane – 308 acres of Corn and 210 acres of Cotton and am working 240 hands in addition to which there are 67 women and children unable to labor. The monthly Consumption of provisions on this place is 25 Barrels Pork and 300 Barrells Corn. The prospect of a Crop upon this place is very good

Upon the Taylors place I have a total of 1323 acres in Cultivation of which 911 acres are in cane and 412 acres in Corn. The prospect for a fine Crop of Sugar on this place is better than upon any other place under my charge. There are upon the place, 351 hands of which 71 are women and children unable to labor. The monthly consumption of provisions is 30 Barrels Pork and 350 Bushels Corn. These two places are under the charge of Mr Jno. L. Murphy an old and successful overseer who is employed at a salary of Twenty five hundred (\$2500^{00}) Dollars per annum, he employing an under overseer at a Salary of \$1.000^{00}. Upon the Taylor place is a good saw mill (situated in a fine Cypress Brake) and Capable of cutting 5.000 Feet of lumber pr day. This mill I have nearly completed the repairs upon and will soon have the same in running order. The Sugar Mill upon the plantation is much out of repair and will require a large expenditure before it can be used for grinding the crop. Upon both these places I have felt greatly the want of a sufficient number of mules to properly Cultivate the Crops – So many have been reclaimed by parties Claiming to be loyal owners, and the difficulty of procuring enough to supply the deficiency has been great, that up to this time I have been utterly unable to overcome it

In the Parish of Ascension, I have thirteen abandoned places of which seven have been placed in charge of Lieut. Hanks to work on account of the Government. Viz: The Mt. Houmas plant^{n} owned by Heirs of Henry Doyal Dec^{d}, the Linwood place formerly owned by J. M. Brown the Jas. Martin. the Trasimond Landry (Lower place) the Tournillion place, the James Hewitt place and the Miles Taylor's place – One, the "Home" place of Trasimond Landry has been rented upon the usual terms. In this Parish I am working on Government account Five Plantations all of which are under the immediate charge of Mr G. W. Graves who was employed by you at such a salary as he formerly received

Upon the "Ashland" Place formerly belonging to Duncan F. Kenner, I have 850 acres in Cultivation of which 450 acres are in Cane, 250 of which is very fine, also 400 acres in Corn which promises well. I have upon this place 295 hands of which 35 are quite old and 80 are children all unfit for labor. The monthly consumption of provisions amount to 16 Barrels Pork or 3.200 pounds Bacon and about 300 Bushels Corn.

Upon the "Bowden" Place owned by the same party, I have 850 Acres in Cultivation of which 570 Acres are in Cane in very fine Condition and 280 Acres in Corn which promises very well. Upon this place I have 196 hands of which 57 are infirm and children and unable to labor. The Monthly consumption of provisions amounts to 12 Barrels Pork or 2400 lbs Bacon – For this place I have an overseer employed at a salary of One thousand (\$1.000^{00}) Dollars.

Upon the "LeBlanc" plantation formerly owned by Trasimond Landry I have 700 Acres in Cultivation of which 475 acres are in Cane which promises a fair Crop and 225 acres in Corn not first rate. On this place I have 73 hands of which 13 are old and children, unable to labor. The monthly Consumption of provisions is 6 Barrels Pork or 1200 Pounds Bacon. Upon this place I have an overseer employed at a salary of Twelve hundred ($1200^{oo}) Dollars pr year

On the "Hermitage" Plantation formerly owned by L. A. Bringier, I have 348 acres of Cane in Cultivation, but have only been able thus far to properly work 178 Acres as I have not the requisite number of hands to labor, and have not yet been able to procure them. In addition to this I have planted 160 acres of corn which looks fair. Upon this place I have 72 hands of which 22 are unable to labor. The monthly Consumption of provisions amounts to 5 Brls Pork or 1.000 pounds Bacon. The above four places, more especially the "LeBlanc" and "Hermitage" Plantations suffered severely from a large and very formidable crevasse which occurred upon the LeBlanc place in April last. In addition to the fact that I was obliged to take the entire force from all of the above places for nearly three weeks in order to repair the levee, at a season when every hour of time was very valuable, the water Covered a large portion of the Crops to their great damage. They have however nearly recovered from the effects of this misfortune and give a good prospect for a Crop.

Upon the "Point Houmas" Plantation formerly belonging to Ex. Gov. J. L. Manning of South Carolina. I have 950 Acres of land in cultivation of which 500 Acres are in Cane and 450 acres in Corn all of which is very fine. There are upon this place 195 hands of which 79 are unable to labor. The monthly Consumptions of provisions is 12 Barrels Pork or 2400 pounds Bacon. Upon this place I have an overseer employed at a Salary of One thousand ($1.000^{oo}) Dollars pr annum.

In the Parish of Lafourche I have thirteen abandoned Plantations, one of which belonging to the minor heirs of J. W. Tucker Dec^{d} has been placed in charge of the "Dative Tutor" appointed by the Court for the benefit of the heirs. The plantations belonging formerly to Jno. Williams & C. M. Gillis & Gary, have been rented upon the usual terms. Those places formerly belonging to Geo. Tucker, R & J. H. Tucker, C. L. Matthews, Gen. Braxton Bragg, L. L. Johnson, Col. Vick and R. Pugh have been placed in possession of Lieut. Hanks to work for the Government.

In the Parish of St. Mary there are Eight abandoned places, three of which have for sometime been occupied by U.S. Troops. The "Vincent" Plantation I am working for the Government, more for the purpose of Keeping the negroes employed than from any profit which I expect to realize from its cultivation.

I am unable to make a report upon the plantations in this Parish as they have all been so much disturbed by United States troops that nearly if not quite all the expenditures have been made useless by Military necessity.

The Monthly Consumption of provisions upon the places worked in this Parish is 5 Barrels Pork or 1,000 Pounds Bacon.

– RECAPITULATION –

Total	Number	of Plantations	Rented	14
"	"	"	Worked	14
"	"	"	Returned to heirs	2
"	"	"	Turned over to Lieut. Hanks	23
"	"	"	Idle or occupied by troops	4
Total	"	Abandoned Plantations in my charge		57

" *in course of Cultivation*

Cane	4.576 Acres
Corn	2.712 "
Cotton	355 "
TOTAL	7.643 ACRES

Total Number of *Hands* 1.719
" *quantity of Meat used per Month*
134 Barrels Pork or *26.800* Pounds Bacon

The usual Meat rations is 5 Pounds pr week for each working hand and half rations for old people and children unable to labor

Upon all the places under my charge I found the negroes suffering for want of proper and suitable clothing, and indisposed to work until such was furnished them – this I have been obliged to do. I also found that the negroes upon all the places were in the habit of receiving a Certain amount of tobacco per week, and that unless they were supplied with the usual rations, they were discontented and unhappy – I have therefore been obliged to furnish tobacco for all the working hands at the rate of about 3/4 of a pound per week.

I have also given such of the Negroes (Heads of families) as performed their task better than the majority, weekly rations of Coffee at the rate of One pound per Month, not to exceed ten rations per week.

Corporeal punishment has been entirely abolished upon all of the places under my charge.

In conclusion I would most respectfully beg leave to state that thus far, the wisdom of the plan matured and put into Successful operation by Major General Banks, for working these plantations has been most happily demonstrated.

I have found with but very few exceptions that the negroes when properly clothed and fed are willing, nay anxious to work under their agreement; and upon most of the plantations under my charge the overseers have assured me, that the negroes labor better and more faithfully under the present, than under the old regime.

In a few instances when negroes were obstinate and refused to work themselves or to allow others around them to do so, I have been obliged to resort to the Stocks and have [. . .] such into Confinement until the time that the Consented to return to labor. In every instance I have found this punishment to exert a most salutary influence not only upon the offenders but upon the others around them.

Taking into Consideration the many, very many disadvantages under which we have been obliged to labor in properly organizing and perfecting the different gangs of laborers – many of them coming from different parts of the Country, entire strangers to the overseers as well as to each other, together with the fact that many of the places were almost entirely Stripped of the necessary implements and animals for properly Cultivating them I have no hesitation in giving it as my opinion that under the present system of labor, as large if not larger Crops can be raised at a much less expense to the planter than heretofore. The only obstacle which has thus far presented itself, is the difficulty which has been experienced upon some plantations, by my overseers in properly restraining the negroes from leaving, the plantations at will, and Stealing or Committing depredations upon neighboring places.

This cannot be entirely remedied while the "army" is Stationed in the Country, and Soldiers are allowed to rove unmolested over the different plantations interfering at will with the overseers management and rules. No plantation can be successfully worked unless the overseer has full control of the laborers, and most perfect obedience must be exacted from them or all attempts at Cultivation will prove a failure.

But of one thing I am Convinced beyond the peradventure of a doubt, and the facts will Show the assertion to be true, that the system devised and put into successful practice by Major Gen. Banks will effectually settle the long mooted and much vexed question, "Can the Cotton and Sugar plantations of the South be *successfully* Cultivated by free labor" and will most positively demonstrate that not only is free labor more beneficial to the Negro, but that is more economical to the planter. I have the honor Colonel to be most respectfully Your Obd't Serv't

HLS Sam[l] W. Cozzens

Cap't Saml W. Cozzens to Col. S. B. Holabird, 15 May 1863, C-77 1863, Letters Received, ser. 1920, Civil Affairs, Dept. of the Gulf, RG 393 Pt. 1 [C-665].

94: Provost Marshal of Jefferson Parish, Louisiana, to the Provost Marshal General of the Department of the Gulf

Carrollton [*La.*], June 11th *1863.*

Gen'l In reply to the questions proposed in circular of May 22nd,[1] I have the honor to report, that I immediately called a meeting of the planters, and those working plantations in this Parish, and obtained from them, and from all other available Sources what information I could, which is as follows, Viz

1st As to the number of negroes unemployed in the Parish–

It is impossible to give a correct estimate, except of those in the Contraband Colonies, under the charge of Capt B. M. Pratt Supt of Contrabands of this district Viz

Women unemployed	237
Children do	188
Sick & Infirm – women & men	160
Total	585

He keeps all of his able bodied *men* employed. There is a number of negro men, women & children, in the Parish, outside of the Contraband Colonies, and plantations the most of whom, claim to be at work for, and supporting themselves, which number it is, impossible for me to estimate.

2nd As to the number unemployed on the 1st day of Febuary last, I am also unable to state correctly! as both Capt Pratt, and myself were appointed since that time; but according to the best information I could obtain, there were in the colonies (then under the charge of Lieut Hanks), unemployed, about Thirteen Hundred (1300).

The number of those outside of the colonies, and Plantations, must have been much larger *then*, than now, as I have, since I have been here, sent a considerable number of vagrant and idle negroes from all parts of the Parish, to work on Govt works; and am now almost daily sending them to the nearest military officer in charge of negroes, requesting that they be employed.

3rd As to the condition of the Crops, There is, on an average, not much, if any more than one half as much Land planted, as in previous years; and the crop will probably, not much exceed one Quarter, of that of previous years. (This is the estimate of the Planters)

4th As to whether there is sufficient labor employed, to cultivate, and gather the crop.

There are, generally, sufficiently numbers of negroes on the plantations, to cultivate and gather the crop now planted, if *they would* all *work well.*

5th As to the general sense of the planters in regard to the present system of negro labor–

They say that the system is well enough, if properly carried out–that is, if the negroes were *forcibly* "required to work diligently & faithfully"–but they (the planters) complain, that they have no control over the negroes–that they only work when they choose, and the planter has no power to compel them to work, and that the consequence is, that a large proportion of them, either do nothing, or but little! which is the cause of the present condition of the crop.

The Provost Marshal tells the negroes what they must do, (either to work faithfully, under the Contract, *for wages*, or for Gov't *without wages*). He sees that they remain on the plantations, as far as he is able, and instructs all guards, to see that the contract is carried out–and when notified that any negroes, can not be made to work, takes them away, and sends them, to be employed on Gov't Works.

But the Planters say that this does not, in many cases, prove effectual– They want a military guard, of one or two men stationed on every plantation, or, a sufficient guard in each neighborhood, who shall be instructed to *compel* the negroes to work–or they want, in some manner, to be authorized, and sustained in using force themselves.

6th As to whether the negroes are contented, and well treated–

They are as well contented as could be expected, under the present state of things, and my observations is, that they are, generally, well treated–for although I tell all whom I send to work under this Contract, to notify me immediately if they are not treated well and I will attend to it, and I have visited many of the plantations, a number of times, I have had but very few complaints of that nature.

Although this report is probably already too long, you will pardon me if I make a single suggestion in regard to this system of negro labor, as the result of my observations in this particular.

I think that much of the trouble in many of the cases referred to, is caused in this way. The planters and overseers do not sufficiently appreciate, or regard, the change that has taken place, especially in respect to this institution of slavery– The negroes come back on to the plantation, with altogether different feelings, from those of former times– They have obtained in the camps, and whereever they have been, and they exhibit, a spirit of independance–a feeling, that they are no longer slaves, but hired laborers; and demand to be treated as such. They will not endure the same treatment, the same customs, and rules–the same language–that they have heretofore quietly submitted to,

This feeling is in many cases, either entirely ignored, or not sufficiently respected, by those who have charge of them on the plantations, and the consequence is, trouble, immediately–and the negroes band together, and lay down their own rules, as to when, and how long they will work &c &c. and the Overseer loses all control over them, I am led to believe that this fault exists in many of these cases, because I have talked with planters who seem to have recognized this feeling, and who have caused it to be respected–at least, in a measure– They have also given them Land to plant, and a portion of the time each week to work on it– They have given them reasonable tasks, and an opportunity to work, and get extra pay, after their tasks were finished &c &c. and I have noticed that these planters have had less negroes leave them, and have much better crops than the average– All of which is respectfully submitted,

HLS John W. Ela

Capt. John W. Ela to Brig. Genl. James Bowen, 11 June 1863, Letters Received, ser. 1845, Provost Marshal, Dept. of the Gulf, RG 393 Pt. 1 [C-778]. The same series contains the responses of numerous other local provost marshals to the provost marshal general's questions.

1 The circular, issued on May 22, 1863, by order of the provost marshal general of the Department of the Gulf, directed each local provost marshal to answer the following questions: "How many negroes are unemployed in your Parish? How many were unemployed on 1st Feby? What is the condition of the crops in your Parish? Is there sufficient labor employed to cultivate and gather the crops? What is the general sense of the planters in regard to the present condition of negro labor? Are the negroes contented and are they well treated?" (Captain Henry L. Pierson Jr. to Provost Marshal, 22 May 1863, vol. 430/1004 DG, Letters & Orders Received, ser. 1560, Brashear City LA, Provost Marshal Field Organizations, RG 393 Pt. 4 [C-778].)

95: Special Inspector to the Provost Marshal General of the Department of the Gulf

New Orleans, July 8th *1863.*

General In accordance with orders recieved from Lieut Col Hopkins Chief of Police I proceeded to the Parish of St Bernard and arrived there July 7th 10 Oclock A.M. I then went to Merrits plantation and saw a negro who told me he had been arrested by a Policeman in New Orleans on or about last May, from there he was sent by Rail Road to Mr Merrits plantation Parish of St Bernard, and since detained and held a prisoner against his will. At no time has he been the property of said Merrit.

I next saw a negro named "Gabel" who can read & write, and is working on Canfields plantation, he stated that about three weeks ago he had told Capt Sawyer (then Provost Marshal) that he wished to go to New Orleans for the purpose of enlisting in the army of the United States. Capt Sawyer told him to go back, at the same time striking and kicking him. The negro fearing to return to his master hid himself in the woods for the period of 8 or 9 days, in attempting to reach New Orleans he was captured by our Pickets who took him to the office of Capt Sawyer about 9 miles distant. Capt Sawyer there knocked him down, kicked and beat him in the most brutal manner – and while bleeding profusely from a wound in the head inflicted by said "Sawyer" he was returned to his master under a guard, when the following punishments were inflicted "Viz'

1st 18 hours in Stocks.

2nd 6 hours with his hands tied together in front and elbows confined below his knees by means of a stick, his shirt being pulled up over his shoulders so that the mosquitoes might bite him

3d Six hours in Stocks and twenty five lashes on the bare back, then made to beg the pardon of his master

I next visited Bassets plantation, I there saw a negro named "Daniel" who stated that Sometime during the month of May he was in company with three other negroes in Algeirs where they were arrested by two soldiers, taken to the City of New Orleans, and from thence to Capt Sawyer the Provost Marshal of Parish of St Bernard. They were there kept for a number of days doing work according to Captain Sawyers orders and finally sent by him to Mr Bassetts plantation, where they now remain, I afterwards called on Mr Bassett pretending to be in search of a negro who had stolen goods from me, during said conversation with him he remarked that all negroes procured from the Provost Marshal were paid by him, the said Basset, two dollars per month, besides clothes and victuals in compensation for their the said negroes services.

I then returned to the Headquarters of the Provost Marshal and seeing a number of Soldiers around the place I entered into conversation with them, again pretending that I was in search of a "Negro Thief" who had been stripped and tied to a tree by order of Captain Sawyer and then left for the mosquitoes to bite him,

Two or three of the soldiers spoke very eagerly and said "that Negro you will find nine miles from the Headquarters cutting wood"

I then asked them to be certain about it, when a negro man named "George Russel" who was present, replied "I know he is up there"

I afterwards saw the same negro (George Russel) privately who made the following statement

The negro in question was first stripped of all his clothing except his shirt, his hands were lashed together then elevated above his head and tied to a tree. This was all done by soldiers of the United States Army Captain Sawyer walked past the negro and laughed at him while he the said negro was tied in the said manner.

All this was done between the hours of seven & nine P.M. when the mosquitoes are most plentiful. I then saw the negro who had been so treated, and he confirmed all that had been said as regards his ill treatment I remain General most respectfully your Obedient Servant.

HLS Ephraim Q Patterson

Special Officer Ephraim Q. Patterson to Brig. Genl. James Bowen, 8 July 1863, Letters Received, ser. 1845, Provost Marshal, Dept. of the Gulf, RG 393 Pt. 1 [C-780]. On letterhead of the provost marshal general. For earlier accounts of abuse of black laborers by planters in St. Bernard, and allegations regarding the complicity of Captain Silas W. Sawyer, see above, docs. 90A–C.

96: Superintendent of Negro Labor in the Department of the Gulf to the Commander of the Department

New Orleans July 12th 1863.

General, It is my duty to report to you the condition of the Department placed under my charge.

Previous to the 16th June I was occupying with my laborers, thirty-three plantations upon which were sheltered and subsisted, twelve thousand, one hundred and eighty nine negroes. The laborers were working cheerfully, the crops were looking finely and the sanitary condition of the negroes who had suffered much from exposure during their migration was improving.

The labor department had become systematized and all visible indications were in favor of ultimate success. Upon the day referred to the enemy suddenly appeared in force at Plaquemine and commenced depredating upon, and devastating all plantations cultivated under the direction of any government agent. While they would leave unmolested those occupied by their owners, their special efforts at destruction were directed to the government plantations They drove away the animals and the young able-bodied Negroes, abused and maltreated the old and defenceless, and when possible captured the managers and treated them with severity. Some of their proceedings were too atrocious to be believed.

An Officer of the Gun-boat New London reports that at a place near Donaldsonville they massed the wretched, defenceless Negroes immediately in range of the shells of the Vessel thus causing the destruction of many lives. I made every exertion to get to their assistance and with partial success, bringing away several thousand and saving considerable property.

I think that out of the thirty three plantations occupied under my direction, only one remained unmolested. I am now engaged in caring for the Negroes as best I can, until such time as they will be able to reoccupy the plantations.

I herewith enclose copy of a report made July 1st to the Quartermaster's Department – marked A. and copy of Telegram dated June 30th marked B. which until recently I supposed was forwarded to you, but was not, in consequence of the destruction of the line.

Sincerely regretting that circumstances over which I had no control, have temporarily blasted my prospects of success yet trusting that the recent achievements of the noble Heroes of the 19th Army Corps, will speedily cause the enemy to evacuate the territory recently occupied by my laborers, I have the honor to be Sir, Most Respectfully Your Ob'dt Servt.

HLS Geo. H. Hanks

1st Lieut. Geo. H. Hanks to Maj. Genl. N. P. Banks, 12 July 1863, H-86 1863, Letters Received, ser. 1920, Civil Affairs, Dept. of the Gulf, RG 393 Pt. 1 [C-702]. In his report of July 1 to the quartermaster's department, Hanks enumerated thirty-three plantations in the parishes of St. Charles, Ascension, St. John the Baptist, Iberville, and East Baton Rouge, all of which had been under his control prior to the Confederate attack described in his letter, and most of which had been abandoned as a result of the raid. In the second enclosure (the telegram of June 30), Hanks praised the performance of some thirty "plantation negroes" who had "fought bravely and sustained their share of the casualties" in fending off a Confederate assault on Donaldsonville. Several months later, Hanks recounted the history of the freedpeople living on the estates that were raided by rebel troops in June 1863. Most of them were "Sable refugees" who had come into the lines of the Union army during its spring campaign in southwestern Louisiana. By June 1, 1863, 12,000 such people had come under Hanks's care, many of them sick as a result of "the privations experienced during their migration." "[O]n one day," he noted, "6000 came in via Brashear City and for several days I had from 15 to 30 carloads sent me daily." Overwhelmed by the number of refugees, Hanks had housed more than 5,000 in cotton presses in New Orleans, and had run "a line of flat boats towed by mules up Bayou Lafourche for the purpose of distributing them wherever shelter could be obtained" on abandoned plantations. (Col. Geo. H. Hanks to Hon. B. F. Flanders, 12 Sept. 1863, vol. 71, pp. 14–16, Reports of Inspectors of Plantations, 3rd Agency, RG 366 [Q-108].)

97: Report by an Inspector of Plantations in the Treasury Department 5th Special Agency

New Orleans August 18″ 1863

On the 14th of August, I visited the plantation Evacuated by the rebel, Dick Robinson; Some of the hovels are occupied by five or six negroes in a destitute condition – The dwelling house is abandoned and stripped of the little furniture it contained, one fine Piano is in the possession of Mrs Baker in the town of Houmas – The old negroes appear to share the old house of their Master, it is open to the weather and is in a very filthy condition; the miserable hovels occupied by the Negroes are fast going to decay; the Sugarhouse also is in a very miserable Condition

The Negroes remaining on the plantation have cultivated Small parcels of ground, and made Sufficient Corn and vegetables to Supply them; they have Some Cane, I have given them written permission to grind it for their own use – These Negroes have succeeded beyond rebel Expectations in living without the assistance of white men –

Robinson took all his good or able Negroes to Texas, and left these old and crippled ones to starve – No White men in Louisiana could have done more or better than these Negroes & they well deserve the reward of their labor (the Crop) and the Encouragement of the Government – One old waggon, two Condemned Mules – two old ploughs and Six old hoes Comprise the inventory of this *joint Stock Company* – The condition of the Negro Cabins, no floors, no chimneys, built of pickets without regard to Comfort or Convenience, and their venerable appearance Confirms the Stories of cruelty related by the old Negroes of Dick Robinson the planter who made annualy 600 Hhds Sugar –

This plantation is situated 82 miles above this City on the Grand Cailloux, Parish Terrebonne, I could not obtain any Correct information of the size of the plantation

HDcSr H. Styles

H. Styles, "Report Dick Robinsons Plantation," 18 Aug. 1863, vol. 71, p. 49, Reports of Inspectors of Plantations, 3rd Agency, RG 366 [Q-109].

98: Memorandum of a Visit by Army Recruiters to Plantations in St. Bernard Parish, Louisiana

[*New Orleans, La.*] Sept. 3[d] [*1863*]–

Monday 31st Aug– Capt Lyon Lt Reynold. [. . .] visited Maj Walker's place. took wood book givn him by overseer on demand, & sent to woods & collected the hands cutting wood– Stripped & examined all the negroes Selected 71. & took them off– Maj Walker absent at the time–

The negroes say that these officers told them–that now was the time for them to decide about being free or being slaves for life– That they could take their families to N.O. & they would be supported at Govt Expense–

Then called up the women &c and made them a speech– Telling them that they were as free as he himself although their skin was a little darker than his– That they might work as much or as little as they pleased–&c &c–

When Maj Walker arrived they had left– He went to meet Maj Yarrington– Finding him, he asked for his authority, & he exhibited a letter from Major Plumley directing him to proceed to the Parish of St Bernard & recruit 100 volunteers–directing him specially to go to plantation of D[r] Knapp, & get the 100 there, as he understood D[r] K. had more negroes than he needed– Maj Walker states that there were 11 taken from his place 29 from D[r] Knapp's. 12 from D[r] Merritt & 5 from Ducros. 2 from Widow Ducros–

To D[r] Merritt Capt Lyon said "let us once get them enrolled, and then even Gen[l] Banks could not get them away"–

D[r] Merritt states that colored soldiers were sent among his hands to induce them to enlist, and they sent word back that they had better enlist voluntarily, or otherwise they would be forced in–

HD

"Abstract of visit of Major Yarrington to plantations of Dr. Knapp, Ducross et. al.," 3 Sept. [1863], filed as Y-14 1863, Letters Received, ser. 1756, Dept. of the Gulf, RG 393 Pt. 1 [C-547].

99: Provost Marshal of St. John the Baptist Parish, Louisiana, to the Provost Marshal General of the Department of the Gulf

Bonnet Carre, La., September 23[d] *1863*

Col I am obliged to feed about 200 negro men, women & children, issue 150 Rations about 50 are working as woodchoppers,

Waggoners Hostlers & carpenters &c– The remainder are old, sick, disabled or children, with a few women, whose husbands are in the army and have so many children or are in such condition, that they cannot support themselves Many of the old and decipped are from the Parish of St James, and *say* they have been driven away by their owners, or forced to leave on account of cruel treatment, and not being furnished with food to eat–

These people have spent their best days in the service of their masters, now their masters should be made to support them in their old age and disabled condition–

Previous to my taking charge of these contrabands, Capt King was issuing about 400. Rations to them. Have reduced the number to 150– have sifted them all I can unless you will authorize me to send back these old and disabled people to the plantations where they belong, and let their masters support them– Can send away some of the woodchoppers have 23 such as they are, have wood enough cut for this Post for the winter– Can keep them cutting and get the wood out for Government Boats. found only two chopping wood when I came here–

Will you please give me instructions in relation to the whole matter I am Sir Very Respectfully Your Obt Ser[vt]

ALS Winslow Roberts

Capt. Winslow Roberts to Col. E. G. Beckwith, 23 Sept. 1863, Letters Received, ser. 1845, Provost Marshal, Dept. of the Gulf, RG 393 Pt. 1 [C-785]. In an undated endorsement, the provost marshal general referred Captain Roberts's letter to the headquarters of the Department of the Gulf, asking, "Should not Col. Hanks [the military superintendent of Negro labor] take charge of these people & the Quarter Master at Bonnet Carré employ all that are able to get wood for gov't use?" General Nathaniel P. Banks, the department commander, was himself uncertain about the proper disposition of dependent freedpeople who had been driven off plantations. On October 16, 1863, he informed General-in-Chief Henry W. Halleck that plantation lessees in southern Louisiana, who preferred to employ only able-bodied black men and women, were removing the "disabled and infirm" to uncultivated plantations and expected the military authorities to support them. For Banks's letter and the War Department's instructions respecting dependent ex-slaves, see below, doc. 101. On November 6, 1863, Colonel John S. Clark, General Banks's aide-de-camp and a member of the department's "commission of enrollment," penned an endorsement returning Roberts's letter to the provost marshal general with Banks's instruction regarding responsibility for dependent freedpeople. The local provost marshals, Clark acknowledged, were responsible for "caring for the negroes temporarily," but those "*Plantations* from which have been driven the families and wives of soldiers in the United States Army must support them either by being quartered upon them or by levying a contribution. . . . The land and property of the country must support the people." Turning to Captain Roberts's original question, Clark indicated that the enrollment commission "fully endorsed" the view that aged and infirm former slaves, "[having] spent their best days in the service of their masters," were "in return . . . entitled to a support." He therefore instructed Roberts "to send back the old and disabled people to the plantations where they belong and *compel* their masters to support them or use the Plantations for their support."

100: Treasury Department Inspector of Plantations to the Superintendent of Plantations in the Treasury Department 5th Special Agency

Donaldsonville [*La.*] Sept 27th 1863–

Sir– I have the honor to submit to you the following report, in relation to the condition of the Plantations, heretofore visited by me, and those now visited since my last report, as also to the course pursued in regard to Police regulations by me established, and which I trust will meet your approbation–

I will first state, that on leaving the City of New Orleans, I received a communication from Col Hanks, authorizing me to pass over to Mr. Harry McCall–100 Negroes, to be taken from the "Old Hickory," "Belle Grove" (Andrews plantation), "White Castle", "Magnolia," and Richland."

On my arrival, I proceed with Mr. John A. Brett, who was sent to aid me, together with Mr. Hansom, the Overseer of McCall to carry out the instructions. I have delivered over to him up to date 85–the Balance, as soon as I can– Accompanying this, you will find a list of the names, and also that of the Plantation, from whence taken–

I regret to state, that I cannot give a more favorable account, in regard to the "Old Hickory" plantation

Since my last report, 9 others have died among them, the woman that was insane, and the one that had puerperial fever– There are now 54 sick, many in such a state that recovery is impossible; the Doctor has not been there. I have this day seen him, and he complains the medicines that were ordered to be sent up by the Special Agent, Hon B. F. Flanders, have not arrived; the poor creatures, are in a truly destitute condition–no one to care for them– the Agent has been gone over a month, having been ordered to join his regiment. I succeeded in obtaining 2 oz of Dover's powder, which I have given out in 15 gr doses to those suffering with dysentery– I solemnly declare that I have never in the course of my life, witnessed so much misery, as I have at this place– there are living skeletons– Women, nude, lying in their filth on the bare ground, their clothes rotten from the filth–

On entering the Hospital, the moans, and cries came, –"Master, for Gods' sake, give us a little water, give us something, to ease our pain." One poor girl, suffering from "*Brusa*"– Mr. Hanson declared to me, that he never beheld such a sight, and would not believed it, had it been told. It is unnecessary for me to dwell upon the subject, I only ask, that I be permitted to place someone in charge of them, until removed, or something done for them.

The Andrews plantation– At this place I found things there as usual, with the exception, that of an increase of sickness; there being 15 Sick in Hospital–

The Agent here, doing nothing, or causing any work to be done– I found the negroes, devoid of discipline, doing just as they pleased, riding from place to place, stealing every-thing they can lay their hands on, from the Planters around; this I found to be the Case on every plantation on which the Government has placed Negroes in charge of detached soldiers, who knew nothing of Negro management. I took from them the Horses, and directed the Agents, that under no circumstance whatever, to let them have them, and not to permit the Negroes to leave the premises– I also caused them to be called together, and told them, that they would be punished, if they disobeyed–

At "White Castle," I stopped for the night– I found there, a number of planters, who had come to see me, as they heard I was on my way up, and wished to represent their grievances– I informed them, I had no power, but would report their Condition, and in the meantime, I would do all I could do, to put a stop to the negroes running about– I also told them of the instructions I had given, and would give to the Agents in Charge–

On Friday night, 9 Negroes from the Adams Plantation, went to Mrs Stone's, armed; they drove off the Overseer, and proceeded to shoot the Hogs, they carried off three– On Saturday morning (yesterday), I proceeded to the Adams place, and arrested 7, out of the 9. Two escaped to the Cane–

Among the Number arrested, was the negro Charles, who had murdered another, five weeks ago– I took them all to the White Castle, after giving them a lecture, and requiring them to give security, they promising to behave, and Mr. Wade Gilbirt, becoming security, I discharged them– The Boy Charles, I had cuffed, and put in the stocks, and left him in charge of Mr Brett, and I proceeded to this place, with Mr. Post, the Agent–he for his Rations, and I to report to the Provost Marshal here–

I sent word for him to be brought down; to be turned over to the Prov. Marshal; Mr. Brett was also to assist Mr. Hanson in bringing down the Negroes– It appears from the statement of Brett, that he permitted the Boy, to be taken out of the stocks last evening, and kept out all night, that this morning he left without ordering him to be put in again, the Boy escaped, handcuffs and all–

I am at a loss to account for such an act– I shall proceed immediately to secure him– I took from this Boy, an Enfield Rifle, which he said the "Yankees gave him; the Boy Milton escaped with a Revolver– Crawford had stolen the shot gun, he had from Mr. Read, the Agent, who has a permit from Genl Weitzel to keep the same; they all had Horses, which of course they had stolen, but which they also declared the Yankees gave them– Some of the Negroes, I arrested on the Road without passes, and with Horses in their possession, told me that Capt Miller, the Commissary of Negro Subsistence here, gave them– I took them from them, and left them at Plantations, to be held subject to your order–

The Richland, and Magnolia places are a nuiscance, as well as the others; Mr. Ricour, the Agent has caused some weeds to be cut down at the "Magnolia," since my last visit– I must here call your attention to a subject of a serious nature. On visiting the places, and asking how many there are on the place, the Agents have many of them, given me a much greater number that I found, on mustering them. On the "Andrew's place" for instance, according to my former report, there were in all 202. Now the Agent tells me there are 221, an increase, you will perceive– On mustering, I found but 194. Now at the Adam's plantation where I arrested the negroes, I found a number secreted there, unknown to the Agent Mr. Read, or to the Overseer; they had been there for weeks–The Agent in the meantime, drawing rations in full, for all.

Again, at the Richland Plantation, I found two Agents, one Mr. Hubbard, a paroled prisoner, the other, Mr. Edmond D. Holdridge a detached soldier, both placed there by Lieut, now Col Hanks, each at a salary, as they say of $\$50^{00}$ pr month– What their duties are, I cannot conceive, unless to superintend, a luxuriant growth of Weeds. Hubbard was absent, but returned the evening I was there. I found the same system pursued– I was told there were 318, on examination, I found 279– Hubbard, had on his own responsibility, hired out [10?] Hands to Mr. Thompson, 10 to Capt Rauteford, and so on; the same state of things at the "Magnolia", a larger number, given, than were actually there; in fact every place, except the White Castle.

I found at L. Marreneaux, F. Marreneaux, and Schlaters' places, that the Govt hands placed there by Col Hanks, had been removed by his order, and the places restored; they as well as Mrs. Shiff, and Mrs. Sigur, having taken the Oath, soon after the issuing of the order of Major Genl Butler–[1]

The two ladies named, are now suffering deeply from the Conduct of the negroes, on their respective places.

I know not what remedy to suggest, in regard to the Condition of things. I would however state, that at the meeting of the Loyal Planters referred to, a number stated, that they desired to secure the services of hands to work their places – In view of relieving the Government as much as possible, and also of placing the negroes at work, so as to keep them out of mischief – I gave those desirous of taking them, orders on the Agents on the White Castle, Richland, Magnolia, and Andrews plantations, to let them have the hands they required, not to separate families however, and to take a receipt, mentioning names &c – The terms agreed upon were as follows including the McCall. They to give them their rations, to take care of them if sick, to pay them in Cash $7.50/100, that is Five Dollars, pr mo out of the Rolling season, and $2^{50} pr month more during the Grinding Season, for watching during the night. I trust these arrangements, will meet your approbation; by it the Government gains, and the Negro is kept out of mischief – I also made it a distinct understanding, that the Government shall have the privelege of sending their Agent, to visit the Plantations and to ascertain how they are treated &c –

The Planters refused to give them clothes – it is necessary that they be furnished as soon as possible, as many have no shoes, and what clothes they have, are worn out, and in rags; the women need clothes very much.

I learned from the Planters, that there are several distilleries above the Town of Plaquemine, managed, and carried on by negroes, who have stolen all the Copper pipes &c from Plantations, and that the liquors made, are of a villainous character.

Shall I break them up, and ship the Copper to you? Since my arrival here, Major Grover Provost Marshal, informs me, that he is daily called on by Planters, from this Parish and Assumption, complaining of the Depredations of the Negroes from the Govt places, particularly the Hewett place, and this Town, and the Miles Taylor plantation; he says he is at a loss what to do. I told him, I could do nothing; he begged of me to report to you the state of things – I therefore propose, if you will carry out in writing, what you stated to me – viz – placing me in Charge of the right Bank of the La Fourche, this town – 5 miles on the left side, and 5 miles down the River, I will put a stop to the Negroes running about, and robbing – on this you may rely on my doing – As regards the Agent on the Hewett place, name Fitzlaw, from what I can learn, he is not of any use, only to ride up and down, from that place to this, as regards the representations made as to crops on that place, I am of the opinion, that the Government will not realize as much as they anticipate; not having any control, it is out of character, to say any-thing further – they need wood &c –

May I ask the favor of your transmitting to me at as early a moment, your instructions, as the situation of affairs, require immediate action – This place is filled up with Contrabands, whom the Military complain of; they should be set to work as soon as possible – You mentioned also, that I should take charge of the Commissary Dept, here – Capt Miller, who had charge, has not been here for a month, and things are badly managed, no system about it – I learn further, that it is a Sale store, and that the Government Coffee, has been sold at the rate of $8 pr 100lbs, and other articles –

I consider it a useless tax on the Government to have the Negroes scattered as they are, on so many places. I mean by that the unemployed; I would therefore recommend, as I presume the Richland, Magnolia, Old Hickory, and Andrews plantations will be given up, that arrangements be made to place them all on the Miles Taylor place, as it is near Donaldsonville, where Medical Attention can be obtained, and let the negroes be placed there, as a convalescent Camp, until they are able to go to work. Something must be done, as I remarked with the Negroes, here, I will proceed to set those to work, who are able, the same as the others, and on the same terms, if you so order.

I have this moment been waited on by Mr. Profit, the Overseer on the Chas Kock place; Major Grover, Prov. Mar, sent him to me; he says that Mr. Kock hired 36 Government hands, and that they refuse to work, he wishes to return them; I have no authority to receive them, or make them work. Please send instructions.

I cannot close this report, without calling your attention to a course of Conduct, disreputable in character, as being pursued by some Agents – For instance, at the Andrews place, the Agent there has in his quarters, a negro girl, with whom, he cohabits, and places at the same table with himself –

At the White Castle, the Agent there, has a Colored prostitute, taken from Donaldsonville; he places her at his table, has a saddle and horse for her to ride about the plantation, and a boy to ride behind her when she goes out – At the Richland, the two Agents, have each a negro girl, who sit at the Table with them. To say the least, such things should be put a stop to, as the example set to the Negroes, causes them to be insolent and overbearing – Besides which, there are ladies living on two of these places, who are forced to see this Conduct. Trusting that my course as pursued, will meet your favor, and waiting your immediate answer, and asking that Mr. Brett be allowed to return to me at the earliest moment, as I shall wait your further order, before going up the River, and hope to be directed to take from those, who have no right to hold, the Horses, Buggies &c that should be on your hands. I have the honor to remain Your obdt Serv't–

W. H. Wilder–

Note– I have this moment learned that the Agent on the Hewett plantation (Fitzing) has hired to Mr. James Cranford a number of negroes, from that place.

Is it by your order? Every hand is needed there to secure the crop– The accompanying note speaks for itself; as I said, this Agent is a nuisance– Mr. Brett informs me that the Agent at the Andrews plantation has in his possession, a sack of Coffee, which he, the Agent, said had been sent from the Commissary Dept as over rations, to be sold to buy luxuries, for themselves.

That they were out of Coffee now at the Commissary Dept, and had sent to him, to return the sack of coffee, by a negro Boy, but he would not do so, as he wanted to sell the same, as he had instructions from Lieut Hanks to sell the Rations– I ordered the Agent to ration the negroes, that were being removed to McCalls place for 3 days; this I told him to do, because I was not certain, of their being able to leave under that time; they were however, removed, and he did not even give them one ration– This Agent drew rations, for all on the plantation, two days ago– I look upon this Agent, as a dishonest man, moreover he says that the Shiff place, shall not be given up, and that Hanks will see that it is not done.

This fellow had the impudence, to take the Negro girl Victoria, in a Buggy, up, and down the Coast– I saw him on my way up, with Mr. Brett, with her in a Buggy– For the sake of the Department over which you preside, and as my instructions are, to report the condition of things, I recommend the immediate disposal of this man, as he is a disgrace to the Government, and you will please send me an order to that effect– W. H. Wilder–

HLcSr

W. H. Wilder to S. W. Cozzens, Esq., 27 Sept. 1863, Miscellaneous Letters Received: K Series, ser. 103, RG 56 [X-241]. None of the documents referred to as enclosed are in the file. About the same time, another inspector of plantations described as "entirely disarranged" the "labor system" on the government plantations in Lafourche Parish. The laborers, who had been receiving government rations since May 1863 (but, according to their own complaint, neither wages nor clothing), believed, he reported, "that they are free and the U.S. Government will support and take care of them." They generally avoided work in the cane fields of the government plantations, while, at the same time, a number of able-bodied men had hired to private planters for the grinding season, at premium wages of $8 to $10 per month. On one government estate, the inspector complained, the laborers "only work five days in the week and then very little." Many fell short of even that standard. "Some of the women peremptoraly refuse to work in the field stating that they are ladies and as good as any white trash." On all of the government plantations, however, black workers had cultivated and harvested crops of corn, which they claimed as their own and "stored . . . in Ware Houses attached to their cabins." "The fact is sir," the inspector asserted, "the negroes do as they please and what work they please." In order to make the government estates self-supporting, he advised, their managers should be given "power to punish insubordinate negroes according to military law." Under the existing arrangements, "if you find it necessary to punish a Negro, one of the others run off to Thibodeaux to the Provost Marshall and report, you will be ordered to appear there to answer the charge, and while you are gone the others rest, during grinding." (Jno. C. M. Conner to S. W. Cozzens, 29 Sept. 1863, vol. 71, pp. 81–83, Reports of Inspectors of Plantations, 3rd Agency, RG 366 [Q-111].)

1 Presumably General Order 91, issued on November 9, 1862, by General Benjamin F. Butler, then commander of the Department of the Gulf. The order's ninth section had provided that hitherto disloyal persons who had remained at home and not aided the Confederacy could, after "return[ing] to their allegiance," be permitted "to work their own plantations, to make their own crop, and to retain possession of their own property." (See above, doc. 67.)

101: Commander of the Department of the Gulf to the General-in-Chief

New Orleans, 16 October, *1863.*

General.

I. – Thus far in my admistration I have not troubled the Goverment *about negroes.* When I arrived at new orleans, I found many thousand in idleness. I set them all to work for wages, *wherever they pleased to go.* What with the system of compensated labor – by the goverment and by individuals universally adopted – and their enlistment as soldiers, they were all employed and all supported by their labor. – With the exception of the brief period when the enemy occupied a portion of country west of the missippi, there has not been a day when I would not gladly accepted ten twenty, fifty thousand negroes, in addition to those I found here from any part of the country – We had estimated their labor, on goverment plantations at near a quarter million dollars for the year. The condition is now changed. – I have in obedience to orders from the Goverment turned over to agents of the Treasury Department all plantations and plantation property[1] The disposition of this property that is made is a matter of public interest – Those who have leased them, prefer in working them, the able bodied men and women to the disabled and infirm – They are daily sifting them out placing the helpless, on plantations, as I am informed, that are and have been uncultivated – I am officially notified of the fact that they are there. It is expected the military authorties are to support them.

To day I receive information that large numbers of negroes are coming into Brashear from the Teche Country. They are of course nearly all incapable of providing for themselves. The Rebels have run into Texas, and upper Louisiana all that are valuable. The govermnt finds itself in this position – The lessors of Goverment plantations, and the enemy turn over to us, all their helpless men women children we turn over, very gladly, all plantation property to the Treasury Department – Does the support of the infirm and poor negroes, go with the property to which they naturally belong, or is it a charge upon the army as military expenses, and fastened upon the war Department and paid out of the war estimates and appropriations? If the latter, I desire an order to that effect and means provided for defraying the cost. It is a pressing and important subject here, increasing in magnitude daily, and I beg instruction as to my course. The process pursued will bring us tens of thousands before winter is over.

II – When I assumed command of this department, I found *eleven thousand families* supported at the public expense. By exposing frauds, cutting off the contributions to families of Soldiers in the Rebel army who do not seem entitled to support at our hands, and requiring our Soldiers *where they are regularly paid* to support their families, I have reduced the number of families receiving rations to *Five* thousand Five hundred instead of *Eleven* thousand and the number of rations from 143,000 to 72,250 – The coming winter will I fear be one of terrible suffering here. The People are becoming poorer every hour, and some supplies, as of coal and wood, are insufficent for the wants of the Goverment to say nothing of the people. Hitherto these expenses, have been paid out of rents, contributions levied upon Rebel property etc etc – This property is now turned over to the Teasury officers. I do not complain of this. The admistration of these charities and providing for the negroes, has been a labor of far greater intensity and suffering than the creation of an army and the conduct of campaigns – My inquiry is: ought not these charities to go with the only property out of which they can be properly paid? ought the expense of supporting from *six* to *ten* thousand families, as will be this winter, to be considered as a part of my *military expenses* and charged to war appropriations? If it be so, I request that orders may be given without delay to that effect, and means, provided therefor –, The calls upon us are very urgent, increasing in number, and come from families hitherto beyond want. I have the honor to be with great respect Yours: etc etc:

N. P. Banks

[*In the margin*] a part of the anticipated increase in the number of families, arises from the number that are evicted in the process of reducing the tenements to the possession of the Goverment.

ALS

M.G.C. N. P. Banks to Major General W. H. Halleck, 16 Oct. 1863, B-392 1863, Letters Received Relating to Military Discipline & Control, ser. 22, RG 108 [S-10]. Henry W. Halleck, the general-in-chief, submitted General Banks's inquiries to the Secretary of War and then, in a reply dated October 26, 1863, transmitted the secretary's instructions that Banks issue "such orders and regulations" as might be necessary to provide for dependent freedpeople, and to appropriate "such plantations, houses, funds, and sources of revenue as you may deem most suitable" for the support of "suffering families." Halleck reminded Banks that the Department of the Gulf was "a theater of actual war," in which "all civil authorities . . . must act in subordination to the general commanding," and he directed Banks to "enforce the laws of war against all classes of persons and all kinds of property within your command." (*Official Records*, ser. 1, vol. 26, pt. 1, pp. 775–76.) Banks subsequently followed the principle, as expressed by his aide-de-camp, that "[t]he land and property of the country must support the people," and he took steps to prevent the "sifting out" of dependent freedpeople onto government charity. (See, for example, above, doc. 99n.)

1 War Department General Order 331, issued on October 9, 1863, had directed Union army officers to turn over to the supervising agents of the Treasury Department's special agencies all captured and abandoned "houses, tenements, lands, and plantations," except those required for military purposes. (*Official Records*, ser. 3, vol. 3, p. 872.) For all practical purposes, however, abandoned plantations in the Department of the Gulf were already under the control of the Treasury Department's 5th Special Agency, and had been since July. (Benj. F. Flanders to Hon. S. P. Chase, 17 Sept. [186]3, vol. 119, pp. 169–71, Letters Sent by the Supervising Special Agent, 3rd Agency, RG 366 [Q-87].)

102: Collector of U.S. Internal Revenue in the District of Louisiana to the Secretary of the Treasury

New Orleans, October 23, *1863.*

Unofficial (Plantations)

Dear Sir, I have spent four days this week on a tour of inspection upon government plantations on the river above the city, together with Gov. Shepley and Capt. Cozzens, the superintendent of plantations. I think best to give you the result of my observations, at the risk of repeating what, perhaps, has been already said by others. To the successful management of these plantations during the present year, there have been four great obstacles.

First; the negroes employed upon these plantations were generally cheated out of their pay last year, and it is hard to inspire in them a confidence that they will be properly paid this year.

Second; you are aware, perhaps, that every autumn cane is picked out and preserved for planting next year. The first year's crop is called "plant-cane." The cane is planted once in four years. After the first year's growth, it is called "rattoon-cane." Plant cane yields nearly twice as much per acre as rattoon. No one went to the trouble of putting in plant cane last year, and on the gov^{t} plantations this year the growth is wholly rattoon, and the yield is correspondingly low.

Third; the care of the plantations was undertaken too late in the season, as the military authorities did not organize the labor until February. The plantations were turned over to the Treasury Department only some three months ago.

Fourth; the manufacture of sugar is very laborious, and requires uninterupted and skilled labor. Just at the beginning of the grinding Gen. Banks put in force his "negro conscription" system, taking off from the plantations, in direct violation of his agreement with the planters, and from gov^{t} plantations, all the hands between the ages of 20 and 30. The loss of this class of laborers, severe as it has proved, has not been as damaging as the manner in which the orders to conscript were enforced. The cane fields have been driven through and trampled by the horses of the recruiting parties, labor wholly suspended, all the hands, at least as many as could escape, breaking for the swamp and brakes The effect of this has been very disastrous to the crops, not only of the planters generally, but on the gov^{t} plantations, occurring as it has at the most critical moment in the year. So far as the gov^{t} plantations are concerned, this has now been stopped.

On the plantations worked by the government we expected a clear profit of nearly ($500.000.) five hundred thousand dollars.

I found the negroes well fed, clothed, satisfied and industrious on all the gov^{t} plantations.

These plantations on the river are not favorable for cotton, but considerable cotton is being raised. It is sugar land, and the cane this year looks well. For "rattoon cane" it is a very good crop.

It is of the utmost consequence that all these plantations should remain in the possession of the Treasury Department during the next year. We pledge ourselves, in that case, to make a large profit to the gov[t], and illustrate successfully on a grand scale free negro labor.

On every plantation a large amount of cane has been "matted," which will become "plant-cane" next year, and while this has diminished this year's crop, it will largely increase that of next year. Machinery and buildings have all been repaired, and carts, mules, &c., replenished – which had been seized by military authority or stolen or destroyed by rebels.

None of the obstacles in our way this year will exist the following year. Everything is provided for success. So far as I have any direction of the matter, I shall endeavor to have religious privileges provided for the negroes, and a system of primary instruction for each plantation. In this case the gov[t] cannot neglect the moral and educational interest of its *protegés*.

These plantations must not be put into court for confiscation at present. They would sell for a trifling part of their value, and in most cases, private liens upon them would consume the entire proceeds. The negroes without protecting care would be ruined, and the odium of the suffering caused them would fall upon the government. It would be proper for the District Attorney here, Mr. Waples, to be instructed by the Atty. General, not to take legal proceedings against the abandoned plantations during the next year at least.

I have appointed a young man, Capt. Davis, whose term of service in the army has lately expired, to be inspector of plantations, acting under the direction of Capt. Cozzens, the superintendent. By my direction he went today to the Teche and Opelousas, to examine, inventory, and report upon all the abandoned plantations within our lines in that country, with a view to working them next year, so far as practicable.

I think we shall make this year eight or ten thousand hogsheads of sugar, four or five hundred bales of cotton, and a large quantity of sirop and molasses. The unusual expenses of repairing machinery, &c., will, however, much diminish the profits. Very Respectfully, Your obed. servt.

HLS George S. Denison

George S. Denison to Hon. S. P. Chase, 23 Oct. 1863, Miscellaneous Letters Received: K series, ser. 103, RG 56 [X-222].

103: Affidavits of Two Louisiana Freedmen

[*Terrebonne Parish, La.*] 21st day of November 1863

Ruben Win colored sworn according to law deposes and says, that he lives on the Quitman plantation on grand Caillou parish of Terrebonne that on Thursday last the overseer of said plantation Mr Bauvais reproved his wife Marcelline who is far avanced in the family way, about her work, and when she said that it was not her who cut the stubble to high, said Bauvais got down from his horse and struck her with a cane some ten times, and that afterwards he struck her with the handle of a cane knife over the head some five or six times, that his wife went off [. . .][1] to him said deponant, who was about fifty yards from her, that said Bauvais, who had got on his horse, rode over her, making her fall down, that deponant went to Mr Pelton, who is agent of the plantation. to complain to him about the bad treatment of his wife – that Mr Pelton said that it was not right for the overseer to illtreat his wife. that when deponant came back the same evening to the plantation, and had told the overseer that he had complained to Mr Pelton, said Bauvais first struck him in the [face] with his fist, and then struck him with his gun violently on the stomach twice, said Bauvais then had his gun cocked, he had also a pistol with him

his
Ruben X Win
mark

Henry White colored sworn says that he is the father of the negro woman Marcelline, that on the evening when Mr Beauvais had been beating Marcelline he spoke to her, examined her wrist, which was swollen. and told her to go to her cabin. that he would see next day if Mr Bauvais had the right to beat the people on the place. that then Mr Bauvais struck him with his fist on the stomach and knocked him down

his
Henry X White
mark

HDSr

Affidavits of Ruben Win and Henry White, 21 Nov. 1863, Miscellaneous Records, ser. 1896, Provost Marshal, Dept. of the Gulf, RG 393 Pt. 1 [C-816]. Sworn before a provost court clerk. On November 24, the overseer, Pierre E. Beauvais – against whom Win had lodged a complaint of assault and battery – levied a countercharge of disorderly conduct. "The negro man Ruben does not belong on said plantation," Beauvais stated, but "came there some time last spring and agreed to work faithfully, which he has not done." Moreover, Win had "threatened the lives of some the negroes on the plantation," including the driver, had "tried to persuade the people on the plantation to quit working at several times," and had "quit the work deponant had put him to and interfered with deponant's authority as overseer." Presumably as a result of Beauvais's complaint, Win was "confined in jail to be put on the levee until his trial." (Affidavit of P. E. Beauvais, 24 Nov. 1863, Miscellaneous Records, ser. 1896, Provost Marshal, Dept. of the Gulf, RG 393 Pt. 1 [C-816]; entry of 24 Nov. 1863, vol. 389 DG, p. 52, Miscellaneous Records of District & Parish Provost Marshals, ser. 1758, Subordinate Provost Marshals in the Dept. of the Gulf, Provost Marshal Field Organizations, RG 393 Pt. 4 [C-816].) No further information about the outcome of either complaint has been found in the surviving records of the provost marshal general of the Department of the Gulf or in those of the provost marshal of Terrebonne Parish.

1 Two illegible words.

104: Testimony by a Louisiana Freedman before the Southern Claims Commission

[*New Texas Landing, La. November 16, 1871*]

Deposition of John King (col.) claimant in answer to Interrogatories, Set N° I, relative to his loyalty to the Government of the United States during the rebellion.

The said claimant, John King, (col.) residing on Blue Bayou, a mile and a quarter from New Texas Landing, in the parish of Pointe Coupée and State of Louisiana, aged fifty nine years, being first duly sworn to tell the truth, the whole truth and nothing but the truth relative to the above named claim testified as follows:

Answer to First Interrogatory –

I lived with a man by the name of Dix on Racoursi cut-off, about four miles from New Texas Landing in the parish of Pointe Coupée, and State of Louisiana. I was a slave owned by William Dix and was on his plantation in person during the said six months [*July–December, 1863*]. My business was that of a laborer, making cotton and corn.

Answer to Second Interrogatory –

I lived on the same place as above stated from the 1st of April 1861 to the first of June 1865. I was there in person during this period. I was a laborer on Mr. Dix's plantation. I did not change my residence during the whole rebellion.

Answer to Third Interrogatory –

I lived within what during the first part of the war would have been the rebel lines, but after the formation of the camp at Morganza my residence might be considered within the Federal lines, and the Federals frequently visited the section in which I lived, but never remained there. The Yankees were there ten times where the Confederates were once.

. . . .

Answer to Seventeenth Interrogatory–

I was never arrested by the officers of either the Confederate or Federal Government, but the Yankee officers would frequently take me to assist in carrying things to and from the Gunboats, for which I never received any pay, and then they would send me home afoot. I never took any oath to support the Union government, but they frequently questioned me about our harboring confederate soldiers or whether any were hidden about to bushwhack them, etc. . . .

Answer to Nineteenth Interrogatory–

I was threatened by John Prior because I acted as guide to the Yankees. . . .

Answer to Twenty-first Interrogatory–

No, But [*Union*] soldiers frequently came to my house and Kitchen, and took what they wanted.

Answer to Twenty-second Interrogatory–

I was always willing to help them in any way in my power. When they made raids into my section, they took me as a guide, and I was very willing to go, and do the best service I could.

Answer to Twenty-third Interrogatory–

Yes, I had a son in the Union army. I have never heard of him since he went into the service. I don't Know what company or regiment he joined, as he went down the river from here in a skiff and joined the army at Port Hudson. I have never seen him since, and do not Know, whether he is alive or dead. I had no relatives in the confederate service. I gave my son a suit of clothes which cost me twenty dollars, that he might be able to go.

. . . .

Answers of claimant to Interrogatories, Set N° II, relative to the property taken from him by the Federal forces.

Answer to First Interrogatory–

Yes, I was present.

Answer to Second Interrogatory–

Yes, I saw taken by Federal soldiers one horse, one mule, one cow, one heifer and one yearling, six head of hogs fattening, one thousand pounds of bacon, ten dozen chickens, thirty barrels of sweet potatoes, one barrel of sugar weighing two hundred and fourteen pounds, one half barrel of syrup containing twenty two gallons.

Answer to Third Interrogatory–

I saw no others taken.

Answer to Fourth Interrogatory –

The mule was taken in July, 1863, by the Illinois cavalry from William Dix's plantation on Raccourci Island where I was living. The horse was taken about the 1st of November in the same year from the same place by the cavalry stationed at Morganza. All the other articles specified in my answer to the second Interrogatory were taken from my residence, as above stated, on the last day of December, 1863, by Col. Dickey who came to my residence on board of a transport and landed near my cribs.

Answer to Fifth Interrogatory –

Nearly all the colored people on the Dix plantation were present, but I will mention, as present, the names of Gabriel Carter, Maria Carter, Franks, Warren Johnson, Eliza Harris, and Lucinda Headon.

Answer to Sixth Interrogatory –

When the mule was taken, I Know that an officer was present who commanded the regiment who said his home was in Illinois, but I do not Know his name. A soldier in the presence of this officer took hold of the mule in the lot, and I told him that it was my mule, he replied that he was going to take him and that he had orders to do so. When the horse was taken, there was an officer, commanding the force, present, but I do not Know his name, nor his command except that it was cavalry stationed at Morganza. He took me with him as a guide through Raccourci Island to show him the way and where the Confederates had hidden things. I rode my own horse, and, when he got to the river, he told that I had been faithful, but that he must have my horse for service for a few days, and that then he would send him back. But he never returned the horse to me. When the other articles of property specified above, as taken on the last day of Christmas, 1863, Col. Dickey was present, and saw the things taken, and he made the special order in my presence to take the bacon to the transport because it was so fine. I begged him not to take the things, and he told me he was going to leave me some and promised to pay me for what he took, but he never paid me anything, and he left me only a half a shoulder.

Answer to Seventh Interrogatory –

The mule was ridden away; the horse I surrendered to the officer in command, and the other articles were taken by the soldiers, and carried aboard the transport at the landing. Nothing more which I recollect, was said on the several occasions of taking my property, than I have stated in my answer to the last interrogatory.

Answer to Eighth Interrogatory –

The mule was ridden away and I loaned the horse. The cattle were taken on board the transport, some slaughtered and some alive by the soldiers. The hogs were killed and carried aboard, and the other articles were either carried by the soldiers or hauled in carts.

Answer to Ninth Interrogatory –

I do not Know farther than I have above stated to what place it was removed. I do not Know where the transport went to, but I heard it went to Port Hudson.

Answer to Tenth Interrogatory –

I am well satisfied that it was taken for the use of the soldiers of the various commands that took the property. Col. Dickey said he must have the bacon for that purpose, and I saw the hogs and part of the cattle Killed and dressed for their use.

Answer to Eleventh Interrogatory –

I made complaint personally to the officers commanding the forces which took my property, and begged them not to take it, but they said they were obliged to do it to conquer the country; that if they did not do it, the rebs would, and that would enable them to fight against the Yankees; and that by taking such things they would be starved out and be obliged to surrender.

Answer to Twelfth Interrogatory –

I did not ask for a receipt or voucher, because I would have been afraid to Keep it about me, and the officers never offered me any, but they told me by word of mouth, that they would pay for the property which they had taken.

. . . .

Answer to Fifteenth Interrogatory –

The mule was of good size and in excellent flesh, considered number one, between six and seven years old, and he would not have brought less than a hundred and fifty dollars on the block. The horse was good size and in fair working order and a very good work and saddle horse. The cavalry Kept him for cavalry services. When he was taken, he could have been bought for one hundred dollars, and I Know he was fully worth that sum. The cow, the three year old heifer forward with calf, and the yearling were fat and good beef. The cow was seven or eight years old, and she was then worth forty dollars. The heifer could not have been bought much cheaper, and the yearling was worth ten dollars. The hogs were fattening and none of them would weigh less than one hundred and fifty pounds and some would weigh over two hundred. The six hogs together were well worth fifty dollars. The chickens were worth from three to three and a half dollars a dozen. The sweet potatoes at that season were worth three dollars a barrel. The sugar (214 pounds) was worth seven cents, what I had just paid for it per pound, and the syrup was worth about twenty five cents a gallon.

Answer to Sixteenth Interrogatory –

I had just bought the sugar and had never opened the barrel. The syrup was in a whole barrel and measured at the bung it was half full. A whole barrel full would hold forty four gallons. I Know the weight of the bacon from the number and weight of the hogs. There were seven hogs weighing two hundred and fifty pounds each dressed, and the whole meat had been made into bacon. I had never used any of it, as it was then hanging up in the smoke house and being smoked about two weeks. I Know the number of chickens because I was in the habit of counting them every after they went to roost by candle light. I did this so as to Know when any were missing. The other people did the same thing with their chickens and we each had a different mark so as to tell when they got mixed, and I measured my sweet potatoes when I banked them nearly two months before and I had never used any out of the bank which the soldiers took from me.

. . . .

Interrogatory propounded by the Special Commissioner –

How did it happen that, being a Slave at the commencement and during the continuance of, the war, and as such not being allowed to acquire and hold property by the State law, you still managed to accumulate and hold in your own right the several Kinds and amounts of property which you swear the Federal forces took from you, for which you bring this claim against the Government of the United States?

Answer: My old master was William Dix who himself lived at Natchez, Miss – and left his colored people upon his plantation on which I resided, to cultivate it. He Kept a wood yard on the Mississippi river for the purpose of selling wood to Steamers, which usually sold for from two and a half to three and a half dollars per cord. He required of each of his best choppers of whom I was one, to cut him twelve cords a week, and gave each of us choppers all the wood which we could cut over twelve cords, and gave us his teams without charge to haul it to the river. I have several times had as many as fifty cords of my own wood on the bank at once. Besides this we were allowed to cut down timber nights and Sundays and on any day of the week after we had each cut our twelve cords, and at odd times did the hauling with his teams. With the proceeds of the sale of the wood thus earned we bought and held by the permission and Kindness of our master the property herein described and claimed as our own. I was always through my task by Thursday at dinner and had the rest of the week to cut for myself. Two crops before the close of the war my master, wishing to Keep his hands at home on the plantation, told us all that if we would stay there and cultivate and take care of the place, we might have all we could make from cultivating it for division among ourselves. We accepted the offer, and made a great deal of money by this means, which no person could by law take from us when we had our master's permission, and the close of the war found us with plenty of greenbacks.

his
HDSr John X King
mark

Excerpts from testimony of John King, 16 Nov. 1871, claim of John King, Pointe Coupée Parish LA case files, Approved Claims, ser. 732, Southern Claims Commission, 3rd Auditor, RG 217 [I-86]. Sworn before a special commissioner of the Southern Claims Commission. The questions that correspond to the enumerated responses are not in the file. According to other documents in the same file, King had submitted a claim for $550.48 as compensation for the following property: one horse, one mule, three cattle, six hogs, ten dozen chickens, and assorted provisions. He was awarded $271. Also in the file is testimony by Frank Banks, a former slave who had lived on the same plantation as King before and during the war; he recalled that King had purchased the horse and mule from his owner when the latter was preparing to leave the plantation for Natchez. King had "got them very cheap beeing the bosses head man and having managed well the boss wished to encourage him." The sugar and syrup claimed by King had been purchased locally. As those items were not furnished to the slaves on the plantation, Banks explained, "we would go to some sugar house and buy them from the colored people." (Testimony of Frank Banks, 16 Nov. 1871.)

105: Freedmen's Bureau Agent at Bayou Sara, Louisiana, to the Executors of a Louisiana Planter's Estate

[*Bayou Sara, La.*] Feby 12 [*1866*]

Messrs Jed Smith & Edward Converse. Executors Carmena Estate.

Complaint has been entered at this office by Luke Carney John Johnson and nine (9) other freedmen representing the Laborers on the plantation during the Year 1864 That during the winter of 1863–4 all the white population having deserted said plantation.

Jed Smith one of the parties addressed called upon said freedmen and urged them not desert to the plantation and go over to the Yankees. but to remain and take care of it and that all they could raise in the way of crops &c should belong to them and be their compensation for so remaining and Keeping up the place.

That under these promises and with full faith in the same. they did remain. take care of the plantation and raised a crop of corn and Cotton. That the Corn was donated. sold to. by you. or taken by. the rebel army. and that sometime last summer You came upon the plantation had the Cotton some nine (9) bales taken away and sold and that You have never accounted to them for the same or Compensated them in any way for their labor.

You either one or both will please furnish this office with information as to the Circumstances under which You took and disposed of this Cotton – to whom it was disposed of. for what Consideration

Why. you have failed to account for it – to said freedmen and owners with such other information in regard to the transaction as will lead to an early adjustment of the Claim

This paper will please be returned accompanied by the desired information

HLc [*A. H. Nickerson*]

[Captain A. H. Nickerson] to Messrs. Jed Smith & Edward Converse, 12 Feb. [1866], vol. 227, pp. 13–14, Letters Sent, ser. 1512, Bayou Sara LA Agt., RG 105 [A-8667]. Jed Smith, one of the executors, responded that the claims of the freedpeople were "without any foundation either in fact or reason." The executors, he claimed, had made no contract or agreement with the laborers, nor had they sold the corn and cotton raised on the plantation in 1864; the crops had been taken "by force, alternately, by both of the contending armies" without their consent. Moreover, according to Smith, Captain Nickerson's predecessor as Freedmen's Bureau agent had already dismissed the freedpeople's claim. When Nickerson nevertheless reiterated his request for information regarding the disposition of the crop and hinted broadly that the executors could expect still further investigation and prosecution, Smith admitted that he and his coexecutor had sold the cotton and used the proceeds to pay creditors of the estate. "We as Executors were powerless to make any other disposition . . . and emphatically deny that the . . . freedmen upon said estate ever had any just equitable or legal interest, ownership or property in the cotton in question or the proceeds of the Same." (Jed D. Smith to Capt. A. H. Nickerson, 13 Feb. 1866, and Jed D. Smith to Capt. A. H. Nickerson, 27 Feb. 1866, Unregistered Letters Received, ser. 1516, Bayou Sara LA Agt., RG 105 [A-8667]; [Captain A. H. Nickerson] to Smith & Converse, Executors, 14 Feb. [1866], vol. 227, p. 16, Letters Sent, ser. 1512, Bayou Sara LA Agt., RG 105 [A-8667].) The surviving Freedmen's Bureau records for Bayou Sara reveal nothing further about the case.

106A: Statement of Two Louisiana Freedmen, and an Order by the Superintendent of Plantations in the Treasury Department 5th Special Agency

New Orleans Dec 19th 1863 –

Harry Locket, and Henry Jones (colored men) of the W. A. Bisland Plantn, Parish Terrebonne, state –

That the working hands on the aforesaid Plant'n have made upward of 100 Hhds Sugar; that they have worked the Plantation, and found their own provisions durg Eight months of the year –

That about the 1st of Oct, a Mr. Pierce came on the Plantation, and stated to the People that he had rented the place from the Govt –

That Mr. Pierce has only clothed, and fed the working hands on the place, leaving the Old Men and Women, and the young children (about 100 in number) to find them-selves –

That Mr. Pierce says he is only going to pay the Hands, 1/20 of the Crop –

We respectfully ask for the People on the W. A. Bisland Plantn, that we be paid more than 1/20 of the Crop, as it has been by our own exertions, that any crop at all has been made – Very Respectfully

his
Herry Locket. X
mark

HDSr Henry. Jones

New Orleans Dec. 19th [*1863*]

Mr. S. E. Pierce, Lessee of the Wm and John Bisland Plant'ns, will be required before any portion of the Crop, now upon said Plantations can be shipped to this City by him, to pay each male field hand on the Places, ten dollars ($10.00) pr month; each female field hand Eight Dollars, ($8.00) pr month, and each of the old persons and those too young to labor, two dollars and fifty cents ($2.50) pr month, in lieu of proper clothing which should have been furnished them – The time to be computed from Feb 1st 1863 to Jan 1st in each instance

The above amounts to be paid in the presence of, and certified to, by an Officer from this Office, and to be deducted from the gross proceeds of the Crop

HDS S. W. Cozzens

Statement of Herry Locket and Henry Jones, 19 Dec. 1863, enclosed in W. H. Wilder to S. W. Cozzens, Esqr., 1 Jan. 1864, #15575, Case Files of Claims for Cotton & Captured & Abandoned Property, ser. 370, Miscellaneous Division, RG 56 [X-516]; order by S. W. Cozzens, 19 Dec. 1863, vol. 123, p. 53, Outgoing Correspondence of the Plantation Bureau, 3rd Agency, RG 366 [Q-113]. The statement of Locket and Jones was witnessed by an official of the Treasury Department's 3rd Special Agency; the signatures are in a different handwriting, apparently that of Jones.

106B: Treasury Department Inspector of Plantations to the Superintendent of Plantations in the Treasury Department 5th Special Agency

New Orleans Jany 1st 1864

Sir I[*n*] pursuance to verbal instructions from you received directing that I proceed to the Two Plantations known as the Bislands' in the Parish of [*Terrebonne*] and which are under Lease to Mr [*S. E.*] Pearce. That I make investigation as to the Follow

First – The manner in which the Negroes have been treated
Secondly The Number of Rations received by each
Thirdly The Amount of Clothing by each received
Fourthly The Number of hands on each place
Fifthly The Amount of Crop made and
Sixthly What arrangements was made or what promises held out by the Lessee to the Negroes as to the Amount to be paid each person

I now beg leave to submit the following report together with the Accompanying Documents

On my arrival at the William Bisland or Upper Plantation I deemed it proper before examining the Overseer Mr Jas C Davis to take the statements of some few of the hands after doing so to examine him & then to visit each cabin and learn from the Negroes themselves what complaints if any they had to make. The first Person called was.

Abner Fleming The Driver on the Plantation

I[*n*] reply to the questions propounded by me He says

"I have been well treated by Mr Pierce since he took charge. I have had enough to eat except for two weeks after we started Rolling then we had no meat Mr Pierce was not there and had been absent sometime Mr Davis the overseer bought Four Hogs, and One Beef and gave us, he then went to New Orleans and got Pork since then we have had meat I have received clothing viz

One Shirt – One Jacket One Pair Pantalons One pair shoes I received meal and 10 lbs Pork for myself and wife Mr Pierce also gave me a Barrel of Flour and to pay me extra besides the amount I was to be paid out of the Crop which as I understood was to be 1/20. – I know Harry Lucket he belongs on this place. Do not know Henry Jones no such person on this or the other Plantation I never heard of him as being here or there.

Henry Lucket – I belong to this (Wm Bisland) Plantation I cannot exactly recollect when Mr Pierce took possession it was in the fall. I believe last September – Mr Van Bergen was the gentleman before him he came, as it were one day went away and Mr Pierce came. the time was short Mr Van Bergen however sent 30 Barrells of Pork I stated when in New Orleans it was only 20 Barrells I since recollected that it was 30 Barrells, Mr. Van Bergen came and wanted us to work in the same manner as we had been doing in rebel times by this I mean to work as we used to do under our Master. we told him we would not do any such thing. he then went away he left no Agent. we used up the Pork he brought and after it gave out we provided the best we could for nearly Six Months. Mr Pierce then came and made proposals that if we would go to work He would act fair He would give us Three Hogsheads He take three and give the Government (ie give them 1/3) Mr Pierce being present at this mans examination asks will you swear that I told you so – He replies – I wont swear to it but I so understood you and so did the rest of us. all on this place.

I have not been treated well by Mr Pierce I do not mean by that, that he has abused or punished me or the rest. I mean to say he has not given me and the rest enough to eat since he came here he did not for Three weeks give us any meat during that time I had to look out for my self and family the best I could. I did get during that time and only once fresh Pork. I wont say now as it was during the three weeks it was about One month ago since that time had enough meat.

I have received from Mr Pierce One Jacket One Pair Pantaloons, 1 Pair shoes. no shirt – since he came here. we used to get from Master Two suits a year one suit in April and the other in September or October – I have a wife and One child Ten years old – My wife has worked about One month my child has not worked – I have worked every day except when sick – I have lost Twenty seven days in all. none of us work on Sunday – we have not been asked to. I got 3 Pounds of meat before Rolling since Rolling commenced I get 4 pounds my wife got none until she worked she gets 3 Pounds – child none I get in all Seven Pounds a week. besides meal no coffee. got little whiskey since Rolling.

I Know Henry Jones the person who signed the statement I did in New Orleans (see statement annexed)[1] he does not live on this or the other Plantation I believe he lives on the Bayou Black– I met him in the Cars when on my way to New Orleans– I told him what I was going to New Orleans to tell the Government at the Custom House how bad we folks had been treated and as we had been cheated by Mr Fox and Mr Caldwell out of our labour we expected Mr Pierce would as they had.– Mr Fox and Cadwell were the people that had the charge of the place He did not know anything about the Plantation only what I told him. and he signed the paper for me, I was chosen by Abner Fleming the Driver and all the other people on the place.

Milly Anderson– I have not had enough to eat since Mr Pierce came here not as much as when master was here. I have had no clothes since mistress left except one piece Mr Caldwell gave and another Mr Pierce gave me that is all I have received I have Three Pounds of Meat a week I have no family–

Edmond Reeve– I have a wife and three children one Sarah aged 12. Adeline 8 & Monroe 6– since Mr Pierce came we have not been well treated I got but 3 pounds of meat a week before Rolling Now I get 4 Pounds My wife and children get no Rations they have not received any clothes– I have received only one shirt and one pair shoes. Mr Pierce agreed to give 1/3 the Crop

Lydia Reeve wife of above corroborates his statement and further says she is not able to work nor is her oldest child able to tend the carrier– she further says that her husband has to purchase provisions for their support. they were to get 1/3 the Crop.

Alick Butler–states I work and so does my wife I have Five children none work they are too young the eldest is 12 years. We have not been treated well by Mr Pearce. we do not get enough to eat before Rolling commenced my wife & self got together 6 pounds a meat a week. My children get no Rations I get meal also– I have received the following clothing one shirt– one Pair Pantaloons, one coat, one pair shoes My wife and children received None.

Jane Butler corroborates the above statement of her husband–

. . . .

I deem it unnecessary to add the names of others I found on a thorough examination of the Negroes on this Plantation that they all agreed to the same statement as to not having had enough to eat– I found however a disparagement as to the amount of Crop that they were to receive some stating 1/3 others 1/20 it is true that the majority state 1/3 as the portion to be allotted them yet many state this on hearsay. as for instance Henry Lucket told them that Capt Pierce said so.

I now add the statement of Mr James C Davis the Overseer as follows

Mr Pierce came here in Sept last about the 12th I believe– I entered on my duties as overseer on this place on the 20th of that month– I then received instructions from Mr Pierce to feed all the hands that worked & no others– I accordingly gave them Four pounds of Meat until the Rolling commenced when he ordered me to increase the same One half Pound more which I have done– I was overseer on the John Bisland or lower plantation during the time it was in his Bislands possession– The Negroes received during the same time as at the present One & a half Barrells a Pork per week They now receive of Mr Pierce 1/2 Barrell more making Two Barrells per week at this Plantation they also received during Mr Bislands time One & a half Barrells they now get from Mr Pierce Two Barrells of the best quality Pork.– The negroes have also had as extra Rations 4 1/2 Barrells of Beef–2 Barrells of Mackerel. they have had also 17 Barrells of Wheat flour, Tobacco has also been given out as rations also since the Rollig commenced 4 Barrells of Whiskey has been got & they receive a dram. regularly–

I made out a list of all the names as I thought of those on the Plantation & gave it to Mr Pierce so that he could obtain shoes & clothing for those that did work– I however forgot some names & when the clothing came there was not enough– it fell short as I found out on distributing– The clothes came in a Bale I also found that even enough had not been sent according to the list I handed him & called Mr Pierces attention to the fact– He said he could not see how that was. we found however that the Bale had been cut open on its way no doubt from New Orleans to this place and some taken out as there were more Jackets than Pantaloons–

There lacks now but 5 or 6 suits of clothes to complete the number for those that worked– as to shoes all have had shoes at this plantation at the lower plantation some were too large some 21. pairs & Mr Pierce took them back to Exchange for smaller & I expected them here daily. & then all would have. been furnished who are to receive–

As to the treatment of the Negroes they have not been worked hard– previous to the Rolling they did not work on Saturdays, since then they do. they do not work on Sundays nor have they been asked to. do so– they have not worked in rainy weather– they have at all times received full rations– I have never given those that did not work Rations– The Negroes have been very kindly treated by Mr Pearce so much so that I remonstrated with him as to his giving them Wheat flour unless it was his intention to keep it up. this was when he got the 17 Barrells. I told him he would have to get at least 100 Barrells

I have had to go to the quarters to start the Negroes out to work at one time they refused to turn out. I threatened to go to New Orleans & report them and I did start they sent a messenger to me to say they would work to come back they did go to work

I was present when Mr Pierce bargained with the Negroes. – he told them he would give them what the Government allowed them & that was 1/20 of the Crop I told them so myself they agreed to it –

Mr Van Berger came to the Plantation he saw some of the Negroes he then came to me and asked me how much seed cane there was – In reply I asked him – if he was going to have the places. for another year – He replied I shall see about it – he took dinner with me after dinner he ask me to allow him to take Isaac M^c^Murry the Driver to New Orleans with him that he would see that he came back – I consented & he M^c^Murry did return. a difficulty then took place since that time

I would also state that we got short of Meat for about 2 weeks after Rolling commenced there was Meat sent to the Depot at Algiers to be forwarded here but the Government was using the Rail Road and it could not be forwarded until after they got through transporting Troops & Baggage &c. which was for two weeks –

The Number of Deaths on this Plantation have been Three since Mr Pierce came is Three Two Children and old Man.

. . . .

Mr Pierce on conversing with him informed me as also did Mr Davis who neglected to state the same in his examination That the Negroes had in there possession some 50 mules & Horses which they claimed as their own besides Hogs which the Negroes that owned them fed from the Corn Cribs on the Plantations. – That he Tasked the woodcutters 1 1/2 Cords. per day and for every cord over he paid them 50 cents – That he paid the Coopers One Dollar for every Three Barrells and One Dollar for evey 4 Hogsheads

That he has promised to pay the Drivers – Sugar Makers – and Engineers $50 each after the Crop is over – I found on examination of the persons that such was the agreement.

. . . .

I Now proceed to lay before you the statements of the hands on the John Bisland Plantation, remarking that I found a less number of complainants at this than the other – To save uncessary time & labour in the perusal of this my Report I would Respectfully say that I examined some 28 of the most intelligent of the hands they stated that they had had enough & not enough to eat of the No 28 some 15 had not had enough and claimed that they were to receive 1/3 of the crop I append the statement of Solomon Moses. – who says I am treated well I have enough to eat – I have worked every day – I have Meat enough – I get Tobacco and Whiskey – all have been treated well, I am a field hand and I take care of the Horses. & see about things around the house Mr Pierce agreed to give us 1/20 of the crop

Martha Lawson, house servant – My husband was hung by the Rebels so I heard Mr Pierce told me in consideration of the loss of my husband he would give me a share in the crop the same as the others which was to be 1/20 since Mr Pierce came I have had plenty to eat & he has given me clothes as also my Three children I am not able to work now as I expect to be confined every day –

Martha Boland I have been treated well get enough to eat. have clothes given me so has my husband I work about the house understood we were to get 1/20 of the crop.

Victor Varries f.m.c. says I am the overseer on this Plantation (John Bisland) The hands are well treated some complain some dont. about not getting enough to eat – I think they get enough. the complaints are about 1/2 I understood that the hands. were to get 1/20 of the Crop. and no more – they have all had clothes except a few – they have had shoes except a few. the shoes came but were too big & Mr Pierce took them back to New Orleas to change. for small – I dont feed those that dont work

I now close the examination without making any comments thereon as I would consider it out of place and. a presumption on my part and submit the same to your better judgment

In. conclusion I would now state that the Number of Hogsheads of Sugar made on the William Bisland or upper Plantation is 112
On the John Bisland or Lower 60
Total 172

I learn that no more can be made & that the cane yet to be ground will make nothing but Molasses. There will be made at the upper Plantation as the overseer informed me say 500 Barrells.
The lower Plantation about 200 "
Total 700

I was unable to get. a statement as to the Number of Barrells of Corn raised

Three of the hands have raised some cotton which they have disposed of. at the rate of Eight cents per pound All of which is respectfully submitted

ALS W H Wilder

Excerpts from W. H. Wilder to S. W. Cozzins, Esqr., 1 Jan. 1864, #15575, Case Files of Claims for Cotton & Captured & Abandoned Property, ser. 370, Miscellaneous Division, RG 56 [X-516]. The omitted portions include additional testimony by freedpeople on the William Bisland plantation and an accounting of rations, clothing, and other items issued to the laborers. Accompanying Wilder's report are lists of the freedpeople on each of the two Bisland plantations. On the William Bisland estate were a total of 163: 92 adults (44 men, of whom 24 were aged forty or older; 48 women, of whom 21 were forty or older) and 71 children. Those on the John Bisland plantation totaled 127: 57 adults (27 men, of whom 16 were forty or older; 30 women, of whom 14 were forty or older) and 70 children. John P. Van Bergen, a native of New York, had leased the William Bisland plantation for a brief period in the spring of 1863. He may also have been an agent of the owners; by mid-May, his lease had been canceled by Union military officials, who were then in charge of leasing plantations, on the grounds that his principal purpose was not to cultivate the plantation "but rather to keep the negroes together until such time as the owners might return to claim their abandoned homes." At the end of the year, charging that his lease had been wrongfully nullified, Van Bergen laid claim to one-half of the profits, in accordance with the lease. (See above, doc. 93; John P. Van Bergen to the Honl. Benj. F. Flanders, 23 Dec. 1863, filed with #13844, Case Files of Claims for Cotton & Captured & Abandoned Property, ser. 370, Miscellaneous Division, RG 56 [X-528].) Meanwhile, members of the Bisland family were maneuvering to regain control of the estates. By late December, Fannie A. Bisland had arranged to lease the plantation of her husband, John Bisland; and Joshua Baker, that of William Bisland, who was Baker's son-in-law. (Case of Joshua Baker, 23 Dec. 1863, and case of Mrs. Fanny A. Bisland, 28 Dec. 1863, vol. 17, pp. 73–76, Claim Records, 3rd Agency, RG 366 [Q-92].) Pierce did not take kindly to his loss of control over the two estates. According to an affidavit by Wilder, dated January 12, 1864, and filed with his report of January 1, he had himself overheard Pierce instruct two freedmen not to permit Van Bergen or Fannie Bisland to enter the John Bisland plantation, but to "drive them off"; and if they attempted to enter the locked house, "to knock them down." To this one of the men replied that "he could do no such thing that he could not forget his old Mistress – & would receive her if she came." Surviving loyalty to Mrs. Bisland quickly evaporated, however, when she attempted to send a new overseer onto the plantation to assume control; for his reception, see document 106C, immediately below.

1 Printed immediately above, as doc. 106A.

106C: Louisiana Former Slaveholder to Her Mother

Terre Bonne [*La.*] Jan. 12th [*1864*]

My dearest Ma Mrs. Winder is here and intends to leave this morning for home, she advises me to write to you and let her send the letter to the city, about trying to get some servants for me there. There is no disposition among my house servants to return, they have taken a house near Houma and of course so long as they can live in that way they are not going to return to me. None of the people in the quarter are willing to work for me either, indeed, before this reaches you, you will probably hear of the *rebellion* on the place about Mr. Grey's (the overseer) coming there. On Sunday he sent his baggage down ahead of him and towards evening came himself in the buggy. He stopped here for a few moments and I told him I thought he would have a good deal of trouble before he could bring them straight, but never dreaming of the trouble he did have. He says, when he came in sight of the plantation, the bell commenced ringing furiously, and by the time he crossed the bridge every man, woman and child on the plantation had collected around the overseer's house. Before he quite reached the house, one of the men seized the bridle and told him he should not set foot in that house, that the quarter belonged to them and no d----- white man should live there. He tried to speak to them but they shut him up immediately and told him they did not want to hear a word from him. That he should not come on the place unless he could show a written order from Gen. Banks and if Gen. Banks himself said that he was to come there, he should not live down there but must live at the house with *Mrs. Bisland*. Mrs. Bisland had no right to come there and give orders. &c &c. They said too much for me to begin to tell you what they did'nt say. He says every man woman and child were talking at the same time, one man told him if he went to live in that house they would burn powder and lead round it all night. When he started off, he told them his baggage would have to stay there all night as the mules would not pull it any further, they at first refused to let it stay there but at last consented to let it remain there till morning, under the cane shed. Mr. May (the guard) was here when Mr Grey came up and told his story, he was very much excited and started off to Thibodiaux to get a squad of soldiers to come down and arrest some of the ring-leaders. He has not yet returned but we look for him to day, if a severe example is set in this instance; something may be done, if not all the white people will have to leave and give the parish up to the negroes. Mr. May seemed to be very much impressed with the necessity of doing something with them. Tell Uncle, I think he ought to come *here* from the city and stay until things get quiet. I forgot to mention that as soon as Mr. Grey left Aragon to return, that two negroes rode past him on their way to Hope Farm, and just before he reached there, the bell commenced ringing there and such shouting and rejoicing that we could hear it, way up here. This shows a concerted movement between the two places. – I wish you would get me a washerwoman and cook, if you can. I am more determined than ever to take charge down there since this affair, and if the government will support me in it I will do so, Mr. Grey says he is going there if they kill him in the attempt. The whole parish is interested in putting this down. I have five rooms cleaned and ready to go into and the house looks very well, so that if I could get some one to cook and wash for me I think I could move very soon. You might try and get a good old negro woman for cook, but I should prefer a white woman for a washerwoman. However you can exercise your own judgment about it. Try to get them as reasonably as you can. I dont like to incur this expense but dont know how I can avoid it, and after all I dont know but what it will be almost as cheap, as I wont have to clothe them. I think Uncle had better report this case to the authorities in the city, for they have made similar threats on several places; that no overseer or white man shall come on the places. I would write more but Mrs. Winder is waiting. All well but the weather is still as bad as can be. Do bring me a letter from John when you return. Yours as ever.

ALS Fannie

Fannie to My dearest Ma, 12 Jan. [1864], Incoming Correspondence of the Supervising Special Agent (Group C), 3rd Agency, RG 366 [Q-92]. The writer, Fannie A. Bisland, had leased Aragon plantation, which was owned by her husband, John R. Bisland, for the 1864 crop year. Her letter eventually reached officials of the Treasury Department's 5th Special Agency, who were already attempting to settle difficulties on Aragon and on Hope Farm plantation (owned by William A. Bisland) that stemmed from a dispute between black laborers and S. E. Pierce, who had leased both estates in 1863. (See docs. 106A–B, immediately above.) On January 15, 1864, the superintendent of plantations in the 5th Special Agency directed that further investigation be made into Pierce's conduct, as well as "into the difficulty existing between Mrs. Bisland, and the negroes on the Plantations." (Order by S. W. Cozzens, 15 Jan. 1864, vol. 123, p. 88, Outgoing Correspondence of the Plantation Bureau, 3rd Agency, RG 366 [Q-113].) By April 1864, perhaps as a result of her own overseer's inability to exercise authority over the laborers on Aragon, Mrs. Bisland had turned over its management to Joshua Baker, a kinsman who had leased Hope Farm. (T. J. Henderson to Capt. S. W. Cozzens, 30 Apr. 1864, vol. 72, pp. 61–73, Reports of Inspectors of Plantations, 3rd Agency, RG 366 [Q-115].)

107: Testimony of a War Department Special Inspector before the American Freedmen's Inquiry Commission

[*New York? January? 1864*]

Testimony of Gen. Wadsworth.

Q General, I would like to ask you, in a general way, whether you were encouraged or discouraged by what you saw at the South?[1]

A Highly encouraged. At the beginning of the war, I was hardly a Republican. I thought slavery should be restricted to the ground where it stood, but was opposed to interfering with it there. I dreaded insurrections, massacres, and violence; and when we sent that expedition to South Carolina, although I wished it to go, I looked upon it with dread. I believed there would be massacres there. I believed sudden emancipation impossible, except at an enormous sacrifice of life. I have changed my mind about that. I believe now that sudden emancipation is the only way to free the slaves. The first moment you begin to talk to the slave of freedom, and tell him that in so many years he is to be free, or that his children are to be free, you spoil him for a slave. You see the effects of such a course in the two Districts which the President most unfortunately excepted in Louisiana, although it does not seem to have much effect, because the planters cannot sustain slavery, and have to pay their slaves wages to keep them on the plantations They are "demoralized," as the whites call it, & are not getting on half so well as they are in the other Districts, where they get wages, and are acknowledged as free. The docility of these people! I had never any doubt that the blacks would work for wages, because that had been settled here by many years of experience. We have 80,000 blacks in this State, and no portion of the population keeps so clear of the poor house & the jail as the blacks. The statistics of the city of Washington alone, where they have always had a large free colored population, would settle the whole question of slavery, and those statistics ought to be got at. There is no one point where the whole thing could be so well brought to a nut-shell as at Washington.

Q How is it about the lease system on the Mississippi?

A My report is in fact apologetic on that matter, though not avowedly so.[2] That system was imperfectly commenced, in the midst of fighting and war. I think that is the only way to dispose of the lands, because to put a Gov't agent on them is folly. The Gov't, under that system, retains control of the matter, for all practical purposes, just as much as if there were a Gov't agent there. I found that the lessees had generally tried to do their duty; the difficulty had been the want of means. A class of men with very small capital were the only ones who embarked in it at first. Clerks in the Quartermaster's Department went into it, with only a few hundred dollars. They got credit for food, but they could not get credit for clothes, and for months they could get nothing down the Mississippi. They strove under immense disadvantages. The negroes came to them from the depots, diseased with measles, small-pox, whooping-cough, and all those diseases which people take when they are brought together suddenly in masses, and to which, when living on isolated plantations, they had not been exposed. They were taken out of the depots, and carried all those diseases with them to the plantations; and sometimes they would be four or five days in the depots without food. I am afraid there will be a great deal of suffering there from this terrible cold weather, if it has extended to that region. When I left there, there were 12000 in those depots. In Banks's Department, so much of the country had been freed from guerillas, that every man had been taken from the depots. The applications exceed the number coming in. Three hundred came in from the Teche country while I was there, and they were all turned off in three days.

Q I observe that by the Articles of Agreement which were drawn up by the Commissioners, the amount of wages to be paid the men is mentioned as $7.00 per month.[3] I do not understand whether or not that was compulsory or not on the negro. Is it left for the negro to make his own bargain with the employers, and does the Gov't say the rate of wages shall not be under $7.00 a month, or is that the fixed price?

A The tendency has been to make these people accept the $7.00. From the docility of these people, the tendency has been to leave the Gov't to make the bargain for them. Notwithstanding all that, you must look at the other side. Up to this time, the Gov't has not been able to get lessees who would take them for any thing, though they have held out great inducements to lessees to take them. I went round to several young men I knew, and men with a little capital, and asked them, "Why don't you take hold of this thing?" and pointed out the advantages. Well, they said they hadn't heard of it. I thought that was one point in which the Commissioners had been a little lax: they had not advertised the thing. Seeing, when I was there, that there was no hope for these people in the depots, that was the great evil pressing upon us for a remedy. I said to them, "Why don't you take hold of this thing?" and I got two or three to take hold of it, who took out two or three hundred from the depot at Natchez. I did not protest against the low rate of wages, because that was not the point of danger and suffering at that moment. The difficulty was not that these people were getting too little, but that you could not get them on to the plantations from the depots; and I thought that, for the first year, it was very well that the lessees should make great profits, and that it did not make much difference whether the freedman got seven or ten dollars a month the first year, if he could only get his living; the principal point was, to save his life. When I was there, the rate of mortality was at the rate of 25 per cent. per annum, at the depots; and yet the men in charge said it was all over. At President's Island, just below Memphis, where there were 1600 of these people, I got hold of this thing, and made a very searching examination. Capt. Cole was the Superintendent, and there were twenty-six white men, detailed soldiers, on the island. I called the white men all up, and told them, "Here are 1600 negroes, and you have not done as much work as twenty-six white men ought to have done." I went over how much wood they had cut, and how much crop they had got in, and I said, "Here is no such amount of work as you white men alone ought to have shown, if you had been employed by the month. You are very comfortable; but here are these people in a terrible condition." And I referred to the place where we had found a dead child that morning – just four stakes stuck up, and blankets thrown over them. I was very severe with them, and they were constrained to admit the truth of what I said. Then they talked about the mortality, and I made the calculation, & found it amounted to 25 per cent. per annum. And yet the doctor said the worst was over! I would not like to have this statement made public, for it would only be to put ammunition in the hands of the copperheads.

Q When was that?

A That was about the 15th of November.

Q Without referring to the past – for I entirely agree with you, that it would not be fair that it should be brought up against the Gov't, for the emergency & the practical difficulties were so great that it was impossible to hit upon the right system at once – don't you think we ought to express our opinion very strongly, that there ought to be no interference fixing the rate of wages for the negro?

A Oh, certainly. I was going to say, that I saw, particularly in Gen. Banks's Department – not so much in Gen. Thomas's, for he is perfectly right on this question; I don't know whether Gen. Banks is or not; he is so conservative, so non-committal, and so afraid of committing himself, that I don't know what he thinks – a strong tendency, to make the negroes stay on the plantations. If a negro is found off the plantation, the Provost Marshal takes him up, and asks him where he belongs. He says he belongs on a certain plantation, but had some difficulty with the overseer, & came away. "Then" says the Provost Marshal, "you must go to work on the levee, without wages." That is the police system of the country. I protested against that. I said, "You are going to hand over these people to your successors – who will be but half-converted, at the best – not as freedmen, but as serfs." I did not have an opportunity to see Gen. Banks about it, but I talked with Gen. Bowen, the Provost Marshal, and I called the attention of the Allotment Commissioners [*commissioners of enrollment*] to that great evil, and I got Gen. Thomas to issue an order that the men at work on the levee should be paid.

When these people first come in to the depots, you must take them, like children, get them on the plantations, and make the first bargain for them, no matter whether it be for seven or ten dollars a month; but just as soon as possible you must say to them, "Now, you must make your own bargains." I think the tendency to establish a system of serfdom there is the great danger to be guarded against. Well, this regulation of the wages is one point. If the Gov't regulates the wages, the Gov't makes them serfs, not freemen. The tendency of the police arrangements in Louisiana is to make them serfs, and to hand them over as serfs to the local authorities, when the State is reconstructed, who will quote this system of management in support of the system which they will undoubtedly try there, to make them serfs, and eventually hand them over to slavery. I will tell you why I thought it best to put the best face upon this matter in my Report. I saw the evil effects here at the North of the statements that have been made of the sufferings of these people in the depots. The Northern people did not reflect that this was an unavoidable incident of the war; that it only related to one-twentieth or one fiftieth part of the slave population – to that portion only that came into the depots; that it was temporary, and that the white soldiers have suffered in the same way. But the opponents of the system held it up as the natural fruits of emancipation. They held it up as the inevitable consequence, and they said – "Look at your system! See that terrible mortality! Do you want to take the lives of one quarter of these people to carry out your system?" You see what effect it could have upon those who did not reflect upon it.

Q What do you suppose to be the total number of negroes enlisted throughout the United States?

A I only know as to that district, that the number given in my Report – 27000 – is substantially correct. Very little has been done in that direction in Grant's army. I made the estimate in talking with Mr Stanton about it, and we concluded there must be 45,000.

Q General, I want to ask you one thing. I have been to Washington recently; and my principal object in going there was to see Mr. Eliot, who is the Chairman of the Committee on Emancipation. That Committee had prepared and introduced a bill, which would not have amounted to much, I think; but they had been consulting before I got there, and they had agreed to various modifications. I had three interviews with Mr. Eliot, and some members of the Committee, and finally they agreed upon a bill which is virtually the same as that we recommended. Now, what I want to ask you is this – whether you think, from your experience, it would do to let the "Assistant" Superintendents have charge of the land & the leasing of it?

A It does not matter who has charge of it, if he is properly appointed. There was a collission when I left there as to the authority for leasing these lands, and a very bad state of things. Gen. Thomas had been going on with these three Commissioners – Mr. Field, Mr. Dent, and Mr. Montague – whom he had appointed very hastily, and having a very narrow field of choice. Two of them were men who ought not to have been appointed, because they were themselves large lessees – Mr. Dent & Mr. Montague; and when I got there, I found that he had recommended their removal, and the appointment of others. The other gentleman, Mr. Field, I think a very good man, and was very much impressed by him. But when I was there, the order came to transfer all these abandoned plantations to the Agents of the Treasury;[4] and Gen. Thomas said, "What are we to do? This interrupts our leasing." I said, "No; you go right on leasing the plantations, and get these people out of the depots; your plan is a good one, substantially; it requires some modification as it is developed, but go on, and I will satisfy Mr. Chase that you are right; and if the agents of the Treasury Dep't take the plantations, they will adopt your system." Gen. Thomas & Mr. Field agreed to go on and give leases, and when I got to Washington, I gave Secretary Chase my Report, and a private letter, saying that Mr. Dent and Mr. Montague were not fit men; and Mr. Chase sent Mr. Mellen (the Agent of the Treasury at Vicksburg) my Report and letter, as his instructions, and told him to go right on with the system of leasing; so that the transfer of the business from the War Depa't to the Treasury would cause no delay in getting the plantations occupied and in getting the negroes out of the depots.[5] Now, whether the agents are appointed by the Secretary of War, or of the Treasury, or by the Commissioners of Emancipation, is not material; only the Commissioners must be men of character and earnest in the work, who will select good agents. One man, perhaps, is as good as three men. I know if I were going to lease plantations on the Mississippi, I would just as lief do it myself, as to divide the responsibility between two Commissioners, and be obliged to have a meeting whenever anything was to be done.

Q The question is this: whether, in order to settle the question of the disposition of the colored people in the valley of the

Mississippi, it is not necessary that the authority for the care and disposition of the colored people should be identical with the authority for disposing of the plantations?

A Undoubtedly. That is what I called their attention to in Washington. I said, "The War Department is now taking charge of these contrabands, and supporting them in the depots, and the Treasury Dep't takes the plantations; and nothing but great good nature and good sense have prevented collisions already." There were the elements of collission every day.

Q You are aware, General, that the instructions of the Secretary of War to this Commission were to examine into the condition of the fugitive freedmen, and to report what was necessary for their protection and improvement, and in what way they can be made most instrumental in suppressing the rebellion. Now, I would like to ask you your views in regard to the amount of guardianship or protection that is really necessary for these people, & in regard to its duration?

A The duration must depend entirely upon the animus of the masters. Take the State of Mississippi, for example. If the people of the State of Mississippi, when it is reorganized, adopt in good faith the emancipation of the negroes as a fixed fact, then the Gov't can very soon withdraw all its agents; but if there continues to be there, as there is in Louisiana, a disposition to restore slavery, under another name – as one man very frankly said – "We are ready to give up the name of "slavery", we care nothing about the name; but we must have a certain control over these men" – the Gov't must continue to exercise a certain sort of protection over these people.

Q How far do you think this protection ought to go?

A That depends upon the efforts that are made to restore them to slavery. It is to be a sort of war between freedom and slavery; and sufficient protection should be afforded to prevent the return of these people to slavery. But as soon as you have taken them out of the depots, and got them at work on the plantations for a year, you have disposed of them; they will take care of themselves. You have then got to settle who owns the plantations – whether the lessees or the old masters. There will be a thousand troublesome questions arising, but, whoever takes these people, you may dismiss them from your care.

Q You don't think, then, that it will be necessary to continue the system of guardianship, except to see that they have fair play for one year?

A No, I don't say that; but I should say, a few years; not more than five years; perhaps not more than three. And, to prevent any alarm in the public mind that this was to be a permanent system, I should say, that it should not extend beyond five years. In fact, I don't think it need continue a great deal over a year. These people will take care of themselves. The relations between the negro and the master are very well established. After the next year, I think we can say to the negroes, "You must make your own bargains."

Q But there is one thing that must be taken into consideration in all this matter, and that is this, (as you have yourself intimated,) that there will exist a very strong disposition among the masters to control these people, and keep them as a subordinate and subjected class.

A Undoubtedly, they intend to do that.

Q It seems to me, that the great thing is, to establish by law, so that it shall be universally considered fixed, the position which these people are to occupy.

A Yes. I will tell you what you want. You want a general Act of Emancipation, and to make it so broad as to cover every form of serfdom and peonage; and you, want that made constitutional, and recognized by the Supreme Court, so that these people can go into court, and get their rights.

Q There is one other question I want to ask you. This, of course, is a mere matter of opinion, but as you have seen so much of these people, and been all through this country, your opinion would be of value to us. Have you any doubt that, in the end, these two races can live amicably together?

A I can have no doubt of it, when I know they *have* lived amicably together over a hundred years.

Q I mean, both free?

A Both free. I have not the slightest doubt of it. I think there will be developed, in time, a tendency to segregation, from the antagonism of the whites to the blacks, and that the blacks will gradually work off towards the malarious regions, and become peasant cultivators, and that the whites will occupy the regions free from malaria. But, in the mean time, the blacks & the whites will live together, and the blacks will continue. I think there is in the black race an incompetency for the acquisition of property to a large amount. The acquisitiveness of the blacks does not carry him much beyond independence; and therefore I think the whites will gradually crowd them out of the healthy regions. In the mean time, it would be destructive to us to move them from these regions. Take that cotton belt: if we were to drive them off and export them, we should inflict the most terrible blow upon ourselves possible. Therefore they will remain there, generally, not exclusively, as laborers; there will be some black planters, and some peasant cultivators, the holders of small masses of property; but they will go on amicably with the whites. They are only too docile. That is the difficulty we have to contend with – their excessive docility. It is because of that docility, that we must exercise a certain guardianship over them, and suspend reconstruction until we have thoroughly emancipated them, and got the idea of freedom into their heads so that they cannot be reenslaved, and, if possible, got it into the Supreme Court. If we can only get the Supreme Court so that they will recognize the rights of the blacks, then the question is settled. Congress can at once pass a law declaring that in the United States Courts, the testimony of blacks shall be received.

. . . .

Q In making arrangements for the care of the families of our colored soldiers and laborers, what would you think of such an arrangement as this? Where there are only small numbers of them, I suppose they can get places; but suppose there are three or four hundred families, what should you say to taking an abandoned plantation, building for each family a cabin, giving them a couple of acres, fenced round each cabin, and then work those among them fit to work, – say those from thirteen to eighteen, and those above 45, – for four or five hours a day on the plantation, giving them the rest of the time to work on their two acres; and then following the soldier or the laborer with the system of allotment, so as to get back from his wages a fair amount to support this establishment?

A I am afraid it would be too complicated to be carried out by Gov't instrumentality. You must not undertake to do too much. The moment you undertake to do too much by Gov't instrumentality, you break down. And there is really no trouble on that score. If I were free to go on to a plantation, and had the wish to do it, I could go on to one tomorrow, and agree not to take a single laborer to it but the wives and children of soldiers, to take good care of them & support them handsomely, and make money raising cotton at 25 cts. a pound. At this moment, in Banks's Department, the wives and children of the soldiers are all sought after. There is no trouble there. That is on the sugar plantations, too, where women and children are not so valuable as in the cotton region. I wouldn't want a better future for myself, if I were a young man, than to take one of those cotton plantations, and agree to employ nobody on it but the wives and children of colored soldiers.

Q This, then, is your idea – that the first thing to be done is to endeavor to get suitable persons to lease this property, and to let the women and children go on to it; and not to resort to the other plan, except in cases where you could not get them taken?

A Yes; but there would not be any such cases. I can assure you of that fact. You will have no trouble upon that point. I will tell you where I am very anxious. My efforts were addressed first to relieving a pressing evil, which was this evil in the depots. My next idea was to try to establish a system of peasant cultivation. I talked a great deal about that. I did not say much about it in my Report; but if the Gov't will make Mr. Field the Commissioner, he is fully up to that idea, and will carry it, out. There are now half a dozen plantations that have been leased to blacks, and they have done wonderfully well. Take some plantation that will be sure to be confiscated, like Davis's or Perkins's, and establish a system of peasant cultivation.

Q Where are those plantations?

A Davis's is some ten or fifteen miles from Vicksburg. Perkins's is some thirty or fifty miles below that place. He had some 16,000 acres, and burned what cotton he had, and his houses. I wanted to try that system at Goodrich's Landing. I said "Here is a fine place to try the experiment of peasant cultivation;" but it seemed that Mr. Dent, one of the Commissioners, had applied for the plantation, and although I requested him to give it up, he was not willing to do so. There were five thousand soldiers there. The gin house had been burned, and nothing had been grown upon the plantation.

Q What is your idea in regard to what ought to be the Gov't policy touching the permanent disposition of the confiscated lands?

A My idea is, that very little land will be ultimately confiscated. When the Southern people come back and say – "We have done with this thing; it is all up and we are now going to support the Union," the military commandants will put them back on their estates; particularly if they acknowledge the Proclamation,[6] and say, "We consider slavery done with." The military commanders are doing that now; and the tendency will be in that direction. These people will recover their lands; but I will tell you where there is going to be a great change. A great many of these people are dead; the lands of others are heavily mortgaged; and then there are tax titles coming in; and in one or the other of these ways, the ownership of this property is going to change, and change very rapidly. But that there will be a general confiscation and a dispersion of the men, I do not believe. I can hardly say that I think it is the policy of the Gov't to do it, unless it becomes necessary to do it to carry out the policy of emancipation.

Q That is the question that concerns us, in any policy we may recommend. Now, can you have a body of peasant cultivators in the South, and any thing like a Democratic society in the South, or even a loyal society, unless you do dispose of the lands? Is it possible?

A Yes, I think it is possible. I think that natural causes will bring it about. If you put these lands into the market, they will be bought by Northern men, and they will carry out the same system that Southern men are now carrying out, under our system; that is, they will employ these people. I want to see that change go so far as to make sure of that result; but I don't think that, practically, it will go further than that. I don't think there will be a general dispersion of the people of the South. I think, however, that some estates will be confiscated; others will be lost to their owners by tax sales; others by the foreclosure of mortgages; and others will be sold, in consequence of the death of the head of the family; and I shall be willing to have them sold. I saw at Natchez a lady – a sister of the wife of Senator Gwinn, whose husband had died from disease contracted while in the rebel service. She had three little children. She came in at Natchez, & went up on the boat with us, and I got acquainted with her. She was a sensible woman, and very humble. Two of her children were at school, but her plantation had been abandoned, & she had no means to keep them there. She came in and said she was willing to take the oath. I said to her: One of two things is open to you. Before the question of confiscation is raised, go and sell your estate. There were difficulties about that, because her children were minors, and there were no courts to authorize the sale. She saw that, and mentioned it, and I saw it. Then I said, "The next best thing is to find some Northern man who will lease your estate, and take a lease from the Gov't too, which will protect him"; and she said she would try to do that. I should not myself care to confiscate that plantation. I should be perfectly willing that that woman should hold the plantation in that way, or sell it, and have the proceeds for her children. Now, that is an illustration of numerous cases that will occur.

Q You say – and I entirely agree with you – that it is very desirable there should be peasant cultivators. Now, what do you think ought to be done in regard to helping these people to land? – for the Gov't will undoubtedly have to confiscate a large amount, such as that which belongs to those who are excluded from the Proclamation.[7]

A If the Gov't was competent to manage business as you or I could manage it, if it were our private business, it would be very simple. I would take one of those great estates, lay out a road through it, and divide it into ten, twenty, or fifty lots, and go on the plantations adjoining, or wherever there was a whole family at home – husband, wife and children, (because you could not put a woman on a lot; she must go to work on the plantation for wages,) and I would say to the man – "Here are ten acres; you may have these ten acres for $10 an acre, payable in ten years." He would be able to pay for it very easily – perhaps out of the proceeds of his first crop. He could raise two or three bales of cotton, and sell it in the pod. That is a very natural division of labor; just as in our neighborhood, one man owns a threshing machine, and goes round among the farmers, and threshes their grain. This peasant wants a yoke of oxen, or a pair of mules, and a cow. How is he to get them? All that is very easy for you or I to settle, but it would require very complicated machinery for the Gov't to manage it; and therefore I do not believe that the Gov't can do a great deal in that direction. I think it will grow up itself.

Q Can it not do one thing?– Can it not adopt the plan of selling out this confiscated property to a considerable extent in small holdings?

A Oh, yes; that it ought to do. But that must not be done too soon; because, if it is, there won't be a single negro found, within a radius of ten miles from any plantation, who will be able to come in and buy. You must wait until the negro has had a little time to fit himself for the change. Wherever I went, I would inaugurate a system of peasant cultivation; and I know that I could inaugurate such a system to a very considerable extent, if I were to go there. It will be very troublesome. You have got to take an ignorant negro, and explain to him how he is to hire a man to plough his land, and how much he ought to give of the crop for that service; how he is to get his cabin put up, and where he is to get the stuff to finish it. There is a vast deal of labor about it, and you have got to let it grow up gradually; although, as I have said in my Report, if the Commissioners favor it, it will naturally grow up.

Q Cannot the Commissioners lease these great plantations in small holdings?

A To a certain extent, they can.

Q And give to the actual occupant a right of preemption?

A Yes. But I tell you, it is pretty difficult to do it. There is a vast deal of difficulty about it. You must find a man who is fit for such a position. Some are too idle, or too ignorant, or too drunken for it. You have got to build him a house, and find a team for him. There is a vast deal of labor, which would discourage any man but one who is determined to carry it out, and a man of character and energy. But the system will grow up, if it is inaugurated in a few instances; for the moment one peasant cultivator is found to be doing well,–having his little homestead, his mules, and his pig and his poultry,–the other men will want the same things; because with all their ignorance, they have all the instincts, propensities and asperations, that the most cultivated man has, but in a fainter degree, and without the intellect to acquire the objects they desire. They have the same love of home, and the same desire to own the soil they live on, that we have.

Q Don't you think it would be well to throw the leasing of the lands into the hands of the Bureau of Emancipation, which Congress proposes now to establish?

A I believe the chances would be better if the whole thing were under one system of management, than to have it beating about, as it is to-day, between the Treasury and the War Departments. It is a most absurd state of things. The only way to settle it, is to put it all in the hands of the War Department, or in the hands of the Treasury Department, or else have an independent system; and the thing is so important, that I think it would be best to have a Bureau for it. The disposition of the land & the slaves must go together.

Q There is a large amount of abandoned property which the Secretary of the Treasury has so far taken charge of; and he has several hundred agents to take & secure abandoned property at the present time. That would have to be separated from the other, would it not?

A No; the abandoned property on the plantations should go with the plantations. It was only by the aid of the abandoned property that we started this leasing system at all – the mules, ploughs, hoes, and other implements that were left on the plantations.

Q How would it do to put all the abandoned property under the control of the Emancipation Bureau?

A So far as it is plantation property, that ought to be done, undoubtedly. You might possibly draw a distinction between abandoned property on the plantations, and that in cities and towns. To-day, the great stumbling-block in the way of leasing plantations is the want of the necessary material to carry them on. There is not a plough or a mule on some of the finest plantations. If there were any left, the neighbors have carried them all off. A man must have from two to fifteen thousand dollars capital to carry on a plantation, as I said in my communication to the *Post*. I would want no better business than to go back to Livingston Co. [*N.Y.*], and select twenty young men of character and industry, and go back to Natchez, and put those men on abandoned plantations, and say to them – "I will furnish you with capital, and you must give me one-half the net profits. I will have a bookeeper, to see that the accounts are all right, and the cotton must be sent me to sell."

Q What do you think – because that question has been put to me very strongly, growing out of some suggestions of Maj. Stearns[8] – of the organization, at the North, of a company to furnish capital to young men who will go there and do just what you propose?

A I think it would be rather hazardous business for a company; because you then have, in addition to the risks of the system – and there is some risk in it, from guerrillas, dishonest lessees, and the failure of the crop – all the risks that attend the management of any corporation.

Q Suppose you find twenty men, who will furnish $5000 apiece, or an aggregate capital of $100.000?

A That would be a very good enterprise. I think the capital is going there now, and the men are going there. I think there is no necessity of doing it as a measure of philanthropy. Gen. Thomas thought that in sixty days from the time I left, he would be able to lease plantations enough to take all the people out of the depots. I don't think he will be able to do it in that time, however.

Q Where is Gen. Thomas now?

A The last I knew of him, he was up at St. Louis. He had been very sick, but was getting better, and was going back.

Q What part of the territory is the most advantageous for this enterprise?

A I should go, by all means, to the cotton region. That begins at the mouth of Red River, coinciding with the northern line of Eastern Louisiana, and extends up to the Kentucky line; that is 500 miles in a straight line. The centre of that is about Vicksburg. Cotton can be raised as far down as Baton Rouge, and even lower, and they are going into it there; but it is not a good cotton country. West Tennessee is a great cotton country. The cotton line does not extend to the tropics, by any means, although they raise cotton at the tropics, as they raise horses there.

Q Do you consider Tennessee a good cotton country?

A Southern Tennessee is the best cotton country. Its value gradually diminishes as you go North or South. I should say, there is not a great deal of difference until you get 200 miles below. When you get South of Baton Rouge, it falls off pretty rapidly, and there is a falling off when you get to Memphis. Half a dozen men have already gone from Livingston Co. to raise cotton in this region, and they have done well. Take the case of those lessees who took plantations last Spring. They took them in the midst of all the devastation of war. They were Northern men, who knew nothing about raising cotton, and made very bad management in many respects; and in July, the rebels came in and dispersed the negroes, and burned the gins. They had not the industry to mow down the cotton, and when the lessees went back, they found it standing. They collected the negroes, and harvested the crop; and with all these drawbacks, there is scarcely one who has not made money, and some have made $20.000. There was one negro, named Sancho, (or some such name,) who came in about the first of April, with sixty or eighty negroes from his plantation. He had been the driver, and was undoubtedly a good man, for these negroes all depended upon him; whatever Sancho said, they believed. They brought in several cows, and four or five mules. Mr. Field put them on a plantation which a white man had leased, but who evidently was not going to get more than a third of it into cotton. Sancho built his houses some time in April, put in a crop of cotton, was driven off by guerrillas, – making a very good fight himself, with four or five of his men, and being wounded – came in again and harvested his cotton; and to-day, Sancho has $16,000 in his pocket.

Q Has Davis's plantation been leased?

A No, Sir. It is so situated that it cannot be protected from guerrillas. I got Gen. Thomas to issue an order which I think will be of great importance in the future. There were a lot of abandoned muskets at his disposal – they were good arms, however, that had been abandoned by our soldiers, or taken from the enemy – and I got him to put on these plantations as many muskets as there were men to use them. At Goodrich's Landing, Sancho and some men went out and drove off a party of guerrillas; there was not a white man among them. You cannot make Sancho a slave again; he has fought, and has been wounded. The quickest way to elevate the race is to put arms in their hands. I got Gen. Thomas to send arms to Island No. 10, where there were two white companies. There were some 800 people on the Island, but not three men, I think, fit for military service. I called up the men – about 100 – and said to them, "Here you are upon an island; don't you think you could hold the island, if you had a hundred muskets, & had a little time to practice with them? Couldn't you prevent a boat landing here?" "Oh, yes," they said; "give us muskets, and we can take care of this island." I got Gen. Thomas to take away the two companies of white soldiers, give these people arms, and let them defend themselves. The moment you put in the hands of one of these poor, humble, depressed men, a musket, and tell him to defend himself, the element of manhood is developed at once, and then they should have every facility to learn to read, so that they can operate together. One great difficulty I had was in getting information to them. They had all to be called up, perhaps 200, and the necessary information given to them in that way. You have got to educate these people, give them new ideas, & tell them what will be their share of the work. All that you could easily do, if they could read, by circulating tracts; and something can be done in that way even now, because some of the negroes can read, and they will gather the others around them. That is one difficulty in the way of carrying out the system of peasant cultivation. You have got to explain to each individual man what you want, and make each one understand the whole system.

Q Suppose we were to get into this bill of Mr. Eliot a clause, that these Assistant Commissioners of Emancipation should have charge of the abandoned property properly belonging to plantations, and have charge of the leasing of the property; and suppose that then you instruct them, when it is necessary, to lease these plantations to persons having capital, Northern men or others; and where they find among the negroes that have been entrusted to their charge, any one to whom they can lease lands, in holdings of ten, twenty, thirty or forty acres, to let them have such holdings – would not the whole thing then go on?

A Exactly; that is what I urged upon the Commissioners. Mr. Field was fully impressed with its importance, and did not need any urging; and he promised, if he stayed there, to carry it out wherever he could. He promised to take the plantation at Goodrich's Landing, and divide that up for one; and that he would inaugurate the peasant system of cultivation wherever he could. You will find a great many difficulties about it; more, perhaps, than you imagine. I would have a Gov't agent or inspector to go over and inspect these plantations once every two or three months, because the Gov't is really responsible for the management of these plantations while they lease them; and under this inspector, you could inaugurate the system of peasant cultivation; but I don't think we can force it along very rapidly. I never went on a plantation, that I did not find some trouble existing on it. But the first thing we have to do, for the next two or three years, is to save these people from perishing. You have got to inaugurate a system that will keep them alive for two years; and if you do that, you may be very well satisfied with your two year's work. And while you are doing that, have the other thing in your mind. Now, to prevent their perishing, what must you do? You must have these plantations worked. You cannot subdivide them to any great extent. You have got to get lessees upon the system of making the old owner acknowledge the finality of the Proclamation, & make him go on and give wages to his negroes. Our great effort must be to prevent any terrible mortality. Take the State of Georgia, which is crowded with negroes. You suddenly break up that system, and let these negroes fail to raise a crop of corn, and you will have a mortality that will sweep off 100,000 of these people. I do not really dare to estimate how many people have died on the Mississippi River. We have done all we could, and if they have died, they have died as our soldiers have died, unavoidably.

Q At present, then, the whole leasing system is in the hands of the Treasury Dep't?

A To-day, I suppose it is.

Q And you suppose that Mr. Field has been appointed as Commissioner?

A I suppose he is, if he will consent to remain. But Gen. Thomas consented to go back, and go on with the leasing, because he felt the importance of it.

Q Where are these people?

A The largest depot is at Presidents Island, below Vicksburg [*Memphis*], a couple of miles. There are 1600 there. Then on the main land, on the east side of the river, there are 800. Just above there, three or four hundred have been sent out to cut wood. There is a great deal of suffering among them, from the neglect of the men who employ them to provide adequate shelter; and if they have this extreme cold out there, there will be great mortality among them— many will actually perish. Then at Island No. 10 there are 800; at Goodrich's Landing, 1000; and at Helena, 500. I summed them all up, and made the number about 12000; but my impression was that there were considerably more than that. Really, I have no doubt that there are 25000 of these people who ought to be got on the plantations; and Gen. Thomas promised to go back and go on leasing the plantations, as if no order had been issued transferring them to the Treasury Dep't, and to continue the system until somebody appeared to take his place. Well, Secretary Chase has ordered his agents to go on with the system, and act in harmony with Gen. Thomas.

Q How many agents has the Treasury Dep't who have authority to lease plantations?

A Not one, that I know of. Mr. Mellen, at Vicksburg, is the man who really has the whole thing in his hands. He is in the Dep't of Mississippi; when you get to Louisiana, then the special agent of the Treasury at New Orleans, Mr. Flanders has it in charge; and there, the Treasury has managed this matter for six or eight months. The Treasury took the business to this extent: where they found a plantation that it would pay them to take, they took it, and they took just as many negroes as they wanted. The Commissioner of Allotment [*Enrollment*] have the negroes in charge; and they have given them out under contracts, which are very naked, meagre things. I took them, and made emendations, which they promised to adopt.

Q Who are these Commissioners of Allotment?

A Col. Clark is one of them; Maj. Plumly another, and I forget the name of the third. But Maj. Clark did all the work.

Q He is at New Orleans?

A He is at New Orleans. These Commissioners hire the negroes to the planters. Many of them, who are proslavery men, come to the Commissioners to get laborers. An old acquaintance of mine, from Philadelphia, Harry McCall, came in one day, when I was there, and began to talk with me. I met him very cordially, for I did not know what his views were; but I soon found he was exceedingly pro-slavery. He said, "I don't agree to this thing, but I must secure my crop." Then I took up the question of the treatment of the negroes, & the medical attendance that was furnished them; and he said, "I don't take such care of the negroes as I would if they were my slaves, of course; it isn't for my interest to do so." I turned to the Commissioner and said, "I wouldn't let that man have a single negro. I wouldn't let any man go to a planter the owner of which expresses the ideas that he does. He don't adopt our ideas, and he ought not to have these people." I said to Mr. McCall, "I would not let you have a man, unless you promised to provide proper medical attendance." There was nothing in the contract requiring the lessees to furnish medical attendance, and of course these poor people, their wages not being paid regularly, had no means to send for a physician. I laid down the law to Mr. McCall pretty strongly; much to his amazement, and to the amazement of the Commissioner, who had not been accustomed to talking in that style to gentlemen down there. Well, Mr. McCall gave in, and said, "What do you want me to do?" I showed him my emendations in regard to medical attendance, and told him he must sign them; and I said, "Next year, you must sign a contract to furnish these people with a school. You have got a plantation with two hundred people, and you must support a school, and provide reading matter for them." Well, he gave in, came to the terms, and got some negroes.

You see, the result of the system in Louisiana to-day is (we must not disguise the fact from ourselves) practically to make these people *adscripti glebæ.*[9] My great fear is, that some of our own friends, some foolish fellows, will hurry on reconstruction, and the new State authorities will come in and say, "You are Emancipationists, you are Abolitionists; and you leave these people *adscripti glebæ;* and we will just go on with your system." That is the great source of danger there now. I talked with Gen. Bowen a great deal about that, and I asked him what his regulations were. He said, "If they won't stay on the plantations, we put them on the levee, without wages." That is not making them freemen. I got Gen. Thomas, as I have said, to issue an order, that these men at work on the levee should be paid. I saw it was no use to contend with these men in detail – A, B and C. You have got to get the law on your side, and the Administration on your side. I talked to a pro-slavery and secession planter, who lives in the La Fourche District, near

Tibodouville, who had eight sons, of whom four were in the rebel army, and who scarcely professed to be a Union man, only he said he was not in favor of secession. He avowed his hope and expectation that slavery would be restored there in some form. I said, "Do you suppose you could return these people to slavery, if we went away and left them now?" He laughed to scorn the idea that they could not. "Can you take these men who have had arms in their hands, and make slaves of them?" I asked. "Yes," he replied; "we should have no trouble about that. We should take the arms away from them, of course." And he went on with the general argument in favor of slavery – that the whites would have to leave the country if the blacks were freed, &c. He said the negroes had been greatly demoralized by what had taken place, and it would take a great while to restore the excellent discipline that existed before the war; but still, they could be returned to slavery. And I think he was right. I know that any energetic man could go on to a plantation, crack his whip, tell these people that all this talk about freedom was bosh and they must go to work, and make them obey him. Some of those who have been in the army would go North, others would go to the swamps, and the whites would have a great deal of trouble; but they would hunt the fugitives up, and capture or kill them, and in ten years they would have a system of slavery even more severe than before, because they would have to exercise greater severity in order to maintain their authority. That was the purpose of all these people; and there is our great source of danger. I advocated the leasing system in preference to the system of Treasury agents, because those agents are not laying the foundations of freedom, in any respect. They have, in almost every case, taken an old French overseer, and put him on the plantations. Now, if the fifty plantations which they are carrying on by these old French overseers had each a northern man upon it, imbued with our ideas, and with no sort of an idea of restoring slavery, there would be fifty intelligent, influential men on our side. As it is we have not got a man on our side. These old overseers would be very glad to see the old system reestablished – it would be much easier for them.

Q Do you think the Secretary of the Treasury would object to this whole matter being placed under the control of a Bureau of Emancipation?

A I don't think he would; although when I talked with him about this collision of authorities, and the obvious impropriety of giving the land to one Dep't & the negroes to another – (I was rather in favor of recalling the order which transferred the lands to the Treasury, and leaving them in the hands of Gen. Thomas, who, although not a working man, is very thorough and honest in his

purpose) – I thought the Secretary did not seem to see it in that light; he did not quite like to give up the great power and patronage it placed in his hands.
HD

Excerpts from testimony of Gen. [James S.] Wadsworth before the American Freedmen's Inquiry Commission, [Jan.? 1864], filed with O-328 1863, Letters Received, ser. 12, RG 94 [K-87]. About thirty-nine pages of a forty-three-page document. The omitted portion included sundry observations about slavery. Topical labels in the margin are omitted.

1 On October 9, 1863, General James S. Wadsworth, a native of upstate New York who had served as military governor of Washington, D.C., had been ordered by the War Department to inspect black troops and examine the condition of black civilians in Union-occupied areas along the Mississippi River. Beginning his tour in late October at Cairo, Illinois, he traveled down the river to New Orleans, west by land to Brashear City, Louisiana, thence back to New Orleans and farther downriver some seventy miles before returning to Washington in December 1863. (*Official Records*, ser. 3, vol. 3, pp. 872–73; see also below, doc. 185.)
2 In a report to the War Department dated December 16, 1863, Wadsworth had given a largely favorable assessment of the plantation-leasing system established by Adjutant General Lorenzo Thomas in the Mississippi Valley. It is printed below as doc. 185.
3 The terms proffered by the commissioners of plantations in the Department of the Tennessee governed leased plantations on the west bank of the Mississippi River, virtually all of which lay in the Louisiana parishes across from Vicksburg, Mississippi. (See below, doc. 162.)
4 War Department General Order 331, issued October 9, 1863, directed Union army officers to turn over to the supervising agents of the Treasury Department's special agencies all captured and abandoned "houses, tenements, lands, and plantations," except those required for military purposes. (*Official Records*, ser. 3, vol. 3, p. 872.)
5 For Wadsworth's report and Chase's letter, see below, doc. 185.
6 The Emancipation Proclamation of January 1, 1863.
7 A reference to President Lincoln's Proclamation of Amnesty and Reconstruction, issued December 8, 1863, which offered "full pardon" – including restoration of all property rights, "except as to slaves, and in property cases where rights of third parties shall have intervened" – to former rebels who took a prescribed oath of allegiance. Certain categories of people were, however, ineligible to apply; they included: civil or diplomatic officers of the Confederate government, high-ranking Confederate army and navy officials, persons who had left the U.S. Congress or resigned a commission in the U.S. army or navy to support the Confederacy, and persons who had failed to treat captured black Union soldiers, seamen, or military laborers lawfully as prisoners of war. (*Statutes at Large*, vol. 13, pp. 737–39.)

8 Major George L. Stearns, commissioner for the organization of black troops in middle and east Tennessee.
9 Slaves who served the owner of the soil and were legally transferred with the land when it was conveyed.

108: Surgeon of Government Plantations in Ascension and Assumption Parishes, Louisiana, to the Supervising Agent of the Treasury Department 5th Special Agency

Donaldsonville – La – January 9, 1864

Honb[le] Sir, Having heard from D[r] W. H. Hire of your liberal politics towards the col[d] people and as you are the highest Government Officer over the Treasury Department, I take the liberty of writing to you in the hope of obtaining your influence in promoting a measure for the medical relief of the destitute col[d] population in these two Parishes (Ascension and Assumption) – You, of course, may be aware that I was placed here to afford medical aid to the col[d] people on the Government Plantations in the Parishes of Ascension & Assumption – but lately the Planters have commenced to discharge the col[d] laborers, in many cases bringing the unfortunate creatures into their debt – thus – the Planters hire the col[d] laborer – for 3 1/2 lb salt Pork – per week and #7. per month – Now out of this #7. they deduct rent for the cabin – tobacco – coffee – shoes – clothing – so that at the end of the month – there is nothing *absolutely* due to the col[d] man – but often is in debt to the Planter – If the col[d] man become sick, he is left to Nature to live or die as he receives no medical aid whatever and if he ask for any, the Planter Sends for a rebel physician who attends the Planter's family and who always feels largely for the Planter, but for the negro, contempt and disdain expressed by such language – as that used by D[r] [Mey] "Oh! God damn the nigger – God damn their soul, – I wish they were all dead – they are only fit to lie and steal" – I have heard him say so – in public – Every physician up here wishes for the rich respectable practise of the Planters family – and invariably he sides with the Planter always against the col[d] man – Now the laborer knows this very well and they look to the Government for protection against oppression – It is not agreable to speak of myself but I must do it in this connexion – I am willing from my heart to attend to every sick col[d] man who sends for me in both of those parishes – viz – Assumption and Ascension – simply and solely for the ordinary pay I now receive from the medical Director for attendance on the Gov[mt]

Plantations– I ask no more– as for medicine, the Provost Marshalls of both Parishes aught to pay for it out of the Parish funds– This is the system of gratuitous relief to the destitute–but the Government should exact a small *trifling* tax from each Planter which would be so small that really it would be like taking a drop out of the ocean– they would not even miss it– If you use your influence to have such a system of dispensaries for affording medical relief to the destitute col[d] poor, you would evidently do for them a most benevolent act– besides the Government would be at no loss for the trifling "little"–collected by the Provost Marshalls of each parish from the Planters would *more* than pay every expense–

The Small Pox–the *worst* variety–is now raging among the poor col[d] people in this neighborhood– they are applying to me in town for vaccination for the children– I have written to Major Plumley for vaccine matter for them but as yet have received no answer– doubtless he will send it as it will be given to him gratuitously at the Hospital– Trusting that you will act as senator and Father not only for the white rich people but also for the poor despised colored man–I remain most respectfully Your Sincere well wisher and of every supporter of the holy Republican party

John. E. Tallon M.D.

P.S. It is proper to tell you that the Planters obtain no physician whatever for the sick col[d] laborer– he may discharge him and get a healthy laborer in his place I have made careful inquiry into the matter they *used* to have the family physician–a rebel of course– now no physician whatever is ever sent to the sick col[d] man

ALS

A.A. Surgeon John E. Tallon M.D. to Honble. B. Flanders, 9 Jan. 1864, Incoming Correspondence of the Supervising Special Agent (Group C), 3rd Agency, RG 366 [Q-90]. Tallon signed as "Government Physician for sick 'Contrabands' at Donaldsonville &[c]."

109: Order by the Commander of the Department of the Gulf

New Orleans, February 3, 1864.

GENERAL ORDERS No. 23. The following general regulations are published for the information and government of all interested in the subject of compensated plantation labor, public or private, during the present year, and in continuation of the system established January 30, 1863:[1]

I. The enlistment of soldiers from plantations under cultivation in this Department, having been suspended by order of the Government, will not be resumed except upon direction of the same high authority.

II. The Provost Marshal General is instructed to provide for the division of Parishes into police and school districts, and to organize from invalid soldiers, a competent police for the preservation of order.

III. Provision will be made for the establishment of a sufficient number of schools, one at least for each of the police and school districts, for the instruction of colored children under twelve years of age, which, when established, will be placed under the direction of the Superintendent of Public Education.

IV. Soldiers will not be allowed to visit plantations without the written consent of the Commanding Officer of the Regiment or Post to which they are attached, and never with arms, except when on duty, accompanied by an officer.

V. Plantation hands will not be allowed to pass from one place to another except under such regulations as may be established by the Provost Marshal of the Parish.

VI. Flogging and other cruel or unusual punishments are interdicted.

VII. Planters will be required, as early as practicable after the publication of these Regulations, to make a Roll of persons employed upon their estates, and to transmit the same to the Provost Marshal of the Parish. In the employment of hands, the unity of families will be secured as far as possible.

VIII. All questions between the employer and the employed, until other tribunals are established, will be decided by the Provost Marshal of the Parish.

IX. Sick and disabled persons will be provided for upon the plantations to which they belong, except such as may be received in establishments provided for them by the Government, of which one will be established at Algiers, and one at Baton Rouge.

X. The unauthorized purchase of clothing, or other property, from laborers, will be punished by fine and imprisonment. The sale of whisky, or other intoxicating drinks, to them, or to other persons, except under regulations established by the Provost Marshal General, will be followed by the severest punishment.

XI. The possession of arms, or concealed or dangerous weapons, without authority, will be punished by fine and imprisonment.

XII. Laborers shall render to their employer, between daylight and dark, *ten* hours in summer, and *nine* hours in winter, of respectful, honest, faithful labor, and receive therefor, in addition to just treatment, healthy rations, comfortable clothing, quarters, fuel, medical attendance, and instruction for children, wages per month as follows, payment of one half of which, at least, shall be reserved until the end of the year:

For first class hands	$8 00	per month.
For second class hands	6 00	do.
For third class hands	5 00	do.
For fourth class hands	3 00	do.

Engineers and foremen, when faithful in the discharge of their duties, will be paid $2 per month extra. This schedule of wages may be commuted, by consent of both parties, at the rate of one fourteenth part of the net proceeds of the crop, to be determined and paid at the end of the year. Wages will be deducted in case of sickness, and rations, also, when sickness is feigned. Indolence, insolence, disobedience of orders, and crime, will be suppressed by forfeiture of pay, and such punishments as are provided for similar offences by Army Regulations. Sunday work will be avoided when practicable, but when necessary, will be considered as extra labor, and paid at the rates specified herein.

XIII. Laborers will be permitted to choose their employers, but when the agreement is made, they will be held to their engagement for the year, under the protection of the Government. In cases of attempted imposition, by feigning sickness, or stubborn refusal of duty, they will be turned over to the Provost Marshal of the Parish, for labor upon the public works, without pay.

XIV. Laborers will be permitted to cultivate land on private account, as herein specified, as follows:

1st and 2d class hands, with families	*one* acre each;
1st and 2d class hands, without families	*one half* acre each;
2d and 3d class hands, with families	*one half* acre each;
2d and 3d class hands, without families	*one quarter* acre each;

To be increased for good conduct at the discretion of the employer. The encouragement of independent industry will strengthen all the advantages which capital derives from labor, and enable the laborer to take care of himself and prepare for the time when he can render so much labor for so much money, which is the great end to be attained. No exemption will be made in this apportionment, except upon imperative reasons, and it is desirable that for good conduct the quantity be increased until faithful hands can be allowed to cultivate extensive tracts, returning to the owner an equivalent of product for rent of soil.

XV. To protect the laborer from possible imposition, no commutation of his supplies will be allowed, except in clothing, which may be commuted at the rate of $3 00 per month for first class hands, and in similar proportion for other classes. The crops will stand pledged, wherever found, for the wages of labor.

XVI. It is advised as far as practicable, that employers provide for the current wants of their hands, by perquisites for extra labor, or by appropriation of land for share cultivation; to discourage monthly payments so far as it can be done without discontent, and to reserve till the full harvest the yearly wages.

XVII. A Free Labor Bank will be established for the safe deposit of all accumulations of wages and other savings; and in order to avoid a possible wrong to depositors, by official defalcation, authority will be asked to connect the Bank with the Treasury of the United States in this Department.

XVIII. The transportation of negro families to other countries will not be approved. All propositions for this privilege have been declined, and application has been made to other Departments for surplus negro families for service in this Department.

XIX. The last year's experience shows that the Planter and the Negro comprehend the Revolution. The overseer, having little interest in capital, and less sympathy with labor, dislikes the trouble of thinking, and discredits the notion that anything new has occurred. He is a relic of the past, and adheres to its customs. His stubborn refusal to comprehend the condition of things, occasioned most of the embarrassments of the past year. Where such incomprehension is chronic, reduced wages, diminished rations, and the mild punishments imposed by the Army and Navy, will do good.

XX. These Regulations are based upon the assumption that labor is a public duty, and idleness and vagrancy a crime. No civil or military officer of the Government is exempt from the operation of this universal rule. Every enlightened community has enforced it upon all classes of people by the severest penalties. It is especially necessary in agricultural pursuits. That portion of the people identified with the cultivation of the soil, however changed in condition, by the revolution through which we are passing, is not relieved from the necessity of toil, which is the condition of existence with all the children of God. The revolution has altered its tenure, but not its law. This universal law of labor will be enforced upon just terms, by the Government, under whose protection the laborers rests secure in his rights. Indolence, disorder and crime, will be suppressed. Having exercised the highest right in the choice and place of employment, he must be held to the fulfilment of his engagements, until released therefrom by the Government. The several Provost Marshals are hereby invested with plenary powers upon all matters connected with labor, subject to the approval of the Provost Marshal General, and the Commanding Officer of the Department. The most faithful and discreet officers will be selected for this duty, and the largest force consistent with the public service detailed for their assistance.

XXI. Employers, and especially overseers, are notified, that undue influence used to move the Marshal from his just balance between the parties representing labor and capital, will result in immediate change of officers, and thus defeat that regular and stable system upon which the interests of all parties depend.

XXII. Successful industry is especially necessary at the present time, when large public debts and onerous taxes are imposed to maintain and protect the liberties of the people and the integrity of the Union. All officers, civil or military, and all classes of citizens who assist in extending the profits of labor, and increasing the product of the soil, upon which, in the end, all national prosperity and power depends, will render to the Government a service as great as that derived from the terrible sacrifices of battle. It is upon such consideration only that the Planter is entitled to favor. The Government has accorded to him, in a period of anarchy, a release from the disorders resulting mainly from insensate and mad resistance to sensible reforms, which can never be rejected without revolution, and the criminal surrender of his interests and power to crazy politicans, who thought by metaphysical abstractions to circumvent the laws of God. It has restored to him in improved, rather than impaired condition, his due privileges, at a moment when, by his own acts, the very soil was washed from beneath his feet.

XXIII. A more majestic and wise clemency human history does not exhibit. The liberal and just conditions that attend it, cannot be disregarded. It protects labor by enforcing the performance of its duty, and it will assist capital by compelling just contributions to the demands of the Government. Those who profess allegiance to other Governments, will be required, as the condition of residence in this State, to acquiesce, without reservation, in the demands presented by Government as a basis of permanent peace. The noncultivation of the soil without just reason, will be followed by temporary forfeiture to those who will secure its improvement. Those who have exercised, or are entitled to the rights of citizens of the United States, will be required to participate in the measures necessary for the re-establishment of civil government. War can never cease except as civil governments crush out contest, and secure the supremacy of moral over physical power. The yellow harvest must wave over the crimson field of blood, and the representatives of the people displace the agents of purely military power.

XXIV. It is therefore a solemn duty resting upon all persons, to assist in the earliest possible restoration of civil government. Let them participate in the measures suggested for this purpose. Opinion is free and candidates are numerous. Open hostility cannot be permitted. Indifference will be treated as crime, and faction as treason. Men who refuse to defend their country with the ballot box or cartridge box, have no just claim to the benefits of liberty regulated by law. All people not exempt by the law of nations, who seek the protection of the Government, are called upon to take the oath of allegiance in such form as may be prescribed, sacrificing to the public good, and the restoration of public peace, whatever scruples may be suggested by incidental considerations. The oath of allegiance, administered and received in good faith, is the test of unconditional fealty to the Government and all its measures, and cannot be materially strengthened or impaired by the language in which it is clothed.

XXV. The amnesty offered for the past, is conditioned upon an unreserved loyalty for the future, and this condition will be enforced with an iron hand. Whoever is indifferent or hostile, must choose between the liberty which foreign lands afford, the poverty of the rebel States, and the innumerable and inappreciable blessings which our Government confers upon its people.

May God preserve the Union of the States!

By command of Major General Banks:

PD

General Orders No. 23, Headquarters, Department of the Gulf, 3 Feb. 1864, General Orders (Printed), ser. 1763, RG 393 Pt. 1 [C-1078]. Banks's order for the Department of the Gulf, with minor modifications, later formed the basis of an order, issued by Adjutant General Lorenzo Thomas in March 1864, that governed plantation labor in the Military Division of the Mississippi. See below, doc. 198.

1 The order establishing the labor system for 1863 was published under the date of January 29 (not 30) of that year. See above, doc. 81.

110: Testimony of the Superintendent of Negro Labor in the Department of the Gulf before the American Freedmen's Inquiry Commission

[*New Orleans, La.*] Feb 6th 1864

Deposition of Col. Geo. H. Hanks, of the 15th Regiment Corps d'Afrique, a member of the Commission of Enrollment.

I came here in May, 1862, as a lieutenant in the 12th Connecticut; General Butler was then in command; I am now Superintendent of Negro Labor for the Department of the

Gulf; about 2,500 negroes came under my control in August, 1862; in February, 1863, I was appointed Superintendent of Contrabands under Brig. Gen. T. W. Sherman; the negroes came in scarred, wounded, and some with iron collars round their necks; I at once placed them on abandoned plantations; I also set them at work on the levee and fortifications; at one time 1,500 were at work; their families remained with them; I do not know the extent of the colored population of the Department; but steps have been taken to ascertain it, and I will inform the Commission when the result is known; we paid the negroes wages but once; rations and clothing were given them; we had not the slightest difficulty with them; they are more willing to work and more patient than any set of human beings I ever saw.

In October, 1862, previous to the arrival of Gen. Banks, there was a great demand for laborers to take off crops; applications would be made to Gen. Sherman for laborers from the contraband camps; he would endorse the requests: "no objection if the negroes are willing to go;" I forced them to labor for wages; there had been much sickness and mortality among the negroes; A "family" of 205 persons came 30 miles to our camp; they came from the plantation of V. B. Marmillon, who had 1,450 acres of cane in cultivation; among these people could be found nearly every species of mechanic and artisan; I called them up and informed them that the Government had taken possession of old master's crop, and that they were needed to take it off, and would be paid for their labor; all assented; when the time came for their departure, however, none would go; I afterward ascertained that the master, whom they termed "Old Cottonbeard," had boasted, in the presence of two colored girls, how he would serve them when they returned; these girls walked at night a great distance to my camp and informed the negroes; one of them said to me: "Master, I will go anywhere else to work, but you may shoot me before I will return to the old plantation;" the planters make great endeavors to recover their own negroes; they have even hired men to steal them from my camp; I gave orders to shoot any one caught at this business; one planter offered me #5,000 to return his negroes; it is very rarely that one will return home; they are very reluctant to do so; there is a general dislike to return to old masters; this year the dislike has very much lessened, in consequence of their appreciation of freedom, and they do not now hesitate to return for wages; those who have remained at home are suspicious of foul play, and feel it necessary to run away to receive their freedom, to illustrate: two weeks ago five colored men came from Bayou Black with passes to see me on business; said they came for advice; master had taken oath and returned home; they had not been paid for several months' labor; I had them paid; in case of neglect or refusal to pay laborers I seize the crops; I told these men they were free; said they were told they were *not* free; told them if they were willing to work for their master he would pay them; the negroes now begin to comprehend the fact of their freedom, and that they have a right to demand the protection of the Government; a negro soldier *demanded* his children at my hands; I endeavored to test his affection for them, when he said: "Lieut., I want to send them to school; my wife is not allowed to see them;" I said they had a good home; said he: "I am in your service; I wear military clothes; I have been in three battles; I was in the assault at Port Hudson; *I want those children*; they are my flesh and blood;" I sent a soldier for the children, when the mistress refused to deliver them; she came with them to the office and acknowledged the facts; she affirmed her devotion to them, and denied that the mother cared for them; I told her even an alligatress would protect and nurse her young; she had bribed them to lie about their parents, but I delivered them up to the father; I knew a family of five who were freed by the voluntary enlistment of one of the boys; he entered the ranks for the avowed purpose of freeing the entire family; his name was Moore, and he was owned by the Messrs. Leeds, iron founders; he was the first man to fall at Pascagoula; he said, upon starting: "I know I shall fall, but you will be free."

I soon reduced the number of contrabands in my camp from 3,000 to 600; and relieved Government of the expense of maintaining them; after the crops were taken off they began to return, until I again had 3,000; Gen. Banks arrived on December 14, 1862; on February 24 he issued General Order No. 12–his first important order relative to the negroes; on January 29, 1863, I was ordered to report at headquarters;[1] I told him I was ready to assist in the execution of the order, providing it was not to be tortured or construed into returning slaves to their owners; he replied: "No." Said I: "It is free labor if but one cent a year be paid the negroes; he replied that he was glad I comprehended his meaning and purposes; I received an order appointing me Superintendent of Negro Labor for the Department; he left everything in my hands; I addressed the negroes in their camps; told them there must be no idleness; gave them permission to elect whether they would return home (under protection) or go elsewhere; 1,500 to 2,000 consented to return home rather than accept a new place; in each case I sent a printed circular to the master, stating that while Government guaranteed a faithful performance of duty on the part of the negroes, it would also see that they received proper treatment; I put them on plantations, under wages, under Government protection; this is now the plan of treatment adopted in the Department.

A guardianship is necessary for the negroes; owners and speculators will make capital of them; they are defenseless unless protected by the authorities; Government must establish a protectorate; it will be absolutely necessary for the Government – for some years to come – to establish a guardianship to protect the negro against the cupidity and superior intelligence of the white race; the present generation of negroes would scarcely be able to maintain their status and enter into competition with the present white population of the Department; the next generation will be educated into the general ideas and conditions of freedom; they have very indefinite ideas of our system of government; they have been educated to a government of force; they are tractable, patient, and easily governed; if civil government be established here, and military rule withdrawn, there is the greatest danger that the negro would become subject to some form of serfdom; they had much better be slaves; with the present feeling of the Southern whites against them, to be left without national guarantees for the maintenance of their civil rights as freemen would be worse than Slavery; a property interest would at least dictate some care for their physical well-being; the planters see that Slavery is dead but the spirit yet lives; they are even more rampant to enslave the negroes than ever before; among slaveholders, loyalty is exceedingly rare; the non-slaveholders are much more loyal; without guarantees for the negro he would have no safety save in a protectorate; the disposition of the planters toward their own hired slaves is by no means friendly; they submit to the terms dictated by Government because obliged so to do; said a planter to me: "When I owned niggers I used to pay medical bills and take care of them; I do not think I shall trouble myself much now;" Mr. Marmillon refused to work his plantation because, after taking the oath of allegiance, he could not obtain his own negroes; the planters accept the idea of freedom under compulsion; a change for the better, however, is taking place in some parishes; the letting of plantations to Northern men has a powerful effect; I told a planter that it was the express order of Gen. Banks that the negroes must be educated, and he said he would have no one teach his negroes; I told him he then could not plant; the negroes willingly accept the condition of labor for their own maintenance, and the musket for their freedom; they are rapidly acquiring a sense of their position in this struggle; they are a very devotional people, and through that channel can be easily taught; I have had frequent exhibitions of their trust in God relative to freedom; I have known them to pray to God to "bless the d----d Yankees;" I cannot speak highly of the integrity of plantation negroes; they have little moral sense, and will lie and steal; the negroes were formerly whipped for stealing from their own masters, but not punished for robbing a neighboring planter; they have no ideas relative to chastity; I think, in general, negro women willingly allow white men to copulate; girls at thirteen are fully experienced; family relations have not generally been maintained among the negroes; colored schools were established here on September 1, 1863; we have now about thirteen hundred pupils; outside the city there are no colored schools under our organization; the colored people manifest the greatest anxiety to educate their children; they thoroughly appreciate the benefits of education; I have known them to go with two meals per day in order to save fifty cents per week to give some indifferent teacher; the negro children learn more rapidly than whites, because creatures of imitation; it is absolutely necessary that the disposition of the lands and the management of the colored people should be placed in the same hands.

HD

Testimony of Col. Geo. H. Hanks before the American Freedmen's Inquiry Commission, 6 Feb. 1864, filed with O-328 1863, Letters Received, ser. 12, RG 94 [K-220]. Revisions and marginal notations in another handwriting, evidently made by the commission at a later date, are omitted.

1 The dates of General Order 12 and of the order for Hanks to report at headquarters are confused. General Order 12 was issued on January 29, 1863, and Hanks received his appointment to head the Bureau of Negro Labor on February 27, 1863. (See above, doc. 81, and Special Orders No. 58, Headquarters Department of the Gulf, 27 Feb. 1863, vol. 28 DG, pp. 172–76, Special Orders, ser. 1767, Dept. of the Gulf, RG 393 Pt. 1 [C-1097].)

111: Testimony of a New Orleans Free Man of Color before the American Freedmen's Inquiry Commission

New Orleans Feb 9th 1864

Deposition of J. B. Roudanez, a Creole mulatto, of New Orleans.

For many years I was employed as a mechanic on plantations; I am thoroughly acquainted with slave life on the plantations; in general, the slaves have one given name, to which they affix that of their master; the colored families are not always kept together; some have their families with them, but the family relation is not well maintained; the slaves are not permitted to eat at a family table; under the old French rule, rations were served out to persons; as a general custom, of late years, the cooking was done for the entire force by regular details; the negroes came with their buckets, got their share, and ate it by themselves; they were lodged in cabins built for them; they fixed beds for themselves, and made their own furniture; there were generally two or four rooms to cabins; one room would be given to a family; the young people were lodged separately, but married couples lodged by themselves; families had usually a room twelve feet square; in relation to child-bearing, the feeling of planters was divergent; some planters desired the negro women to have children, and some did not; some planters worked the women as hard as the men; in some instances they were obliged to labor in every stage of conception; these statements relate exclusively to the sugar plantations; the planters were indifferent in regard to the chastity of their negresses; there were many illicit children; generally speaking, the young masters were criminally intimate with the negro girls; it was their custom; the girls copulate at fourteen years, and under; have known girls to be mothers at that age; some of the French planters had children by slave women; the planters' sons preferred these half-sisters for concubines; the practice of copulation was so frequent among negro girls that a chaste one at seventeen years was almost unknown; some were kept at work while with child, and others sent to labor one week after confinement; sometimes they were compelled to labor up to the moment of conception; they usually performed men's labor; to this there were some exceptions; ordinarily, they were given one month to recover; mothers were permitted to nurse children one half hour three times a day; have heard, but do not know, of women being taken with labor pains in the field; slavery on the plantations had no regard for family relations.

As to punishments and discipline: Some planters were very severe; in these matters there was a great difference; whipping was the common mode; some were confined at night in the stocks for days or weeks; they were whipped with a paddle usually; a paddle is a piece of wood about sixteen inches in length, covered with sole leather nailed over it to the width of a hand; this was used when it was not wished to mark the slave; when the paddle was used the negro was stripped naked and held by others; both sexes were subject to this species of punishment; the number of blows was prescribed in advance, and were inflicted on the posterior; 16 to 30 was the usual number; sometimes a whip was used; this is made of cowhide; is seven feet long, and has a hempen cord with knots for a lash; the cord is about 1/8 of an inch in thickness; the lash was a foot in length; when whipped, they were stripped from the middle of the back downward; still another mode of punishment was to put round the neck an iron collar with branches one foot in length; heavy iron rings were also put round the legs, with a chain tied up to the knee; these were common methods of punishment; I have heard of negroes having been bound to stakes and given two or three hundred lashes; have heard of instances of great cruelty to negroes; sometimes women with child were forced to lie down and receive the lash – a hole being dug underneath them large enough to admit the pregnant stomach; negroes were sometimes branded with the owner's mark; on some plantations this was done with a red hot iron; ears were sometimes clipped to show ownership; between the wife and favorite women of the planter there was often the greatest jealousy; the planters were generally in the habit of cohabiting with their slave women; in consequence wives often made false statements against these favorites and had them whipped; for fear they would not be punished, wives often had them whipped in their presence; the slave relation was often the source of great domestic difficulty; the fact of cohabitation was well known to both parents and children; there was no provision for the instruction of the negroes; none was permitted; the planter did not desire to have their negroes become religious; many secret religious meetings were held; they were dispersed when the facts were ascertained; they would frequently repair to the woods to pray; as a general rule, they are very religious; their general character for truth is good; they are not in the habit of lying; they sometimes had not enough to eat or to wear, and in consequence would take what was needed; in general they were not thieves; one-fourth to one-tenth of the negroes are colored; I know some plantations where one-half or three-fourths are colored; many colored children were the offspring of planters; these were generally made house servants; I think the pure negro lives the longest; I have known both negro and colored women to have fifteen children each; slave women prefer to cohabit with white men rather than black; mixed children are considered more creditable; the negroes are much more virtuous since the Proclamation of Freedom; the females are more chaste, because an honest livelihood is open to them; cohabitation was prompted by the wants of the colored women; such as dress, clothing, etc.; their religious instruction is much better than formerly; they are fond of religious meetings, and generally attend them; there are very few freemen who have not joined themselves to some religious society; they are mostly Methodists and Baptists; among those born in the State Catholicism universally prevails; an idea obtained from the old Spanish settlers yet retains its hold: horse-shoes are nailed upon the door-steps to insure good luck.

The hours of labor on sugar plantations are from fifteen to eighteen hours per day for the year; at certain seasons they are obliged to labor a great part of the night; they are usually called at 3 or 4 A.M.; overseers have power over all field hands; those inside the house yard are house servants; the overseer is usually expected to produce a certain crop with a fixed number of hands; all are obliged to obey him in preference to the master; he is generally much more cruel than the master; kind-hearted planters sometimes select cruel overseers; sometimes a field hand is called away by the master, when he is whipped by the overseer for obeying the planter; should he refuse his master, *he* would whip him; as a general rule, overseers have intercourse with the slave women; if one resists, some occasion is found for her punishment; bloodhounds are in ordinary use for catching runaway slaves; *some whites make this a profession.*

As to the present management and conduct of the officers having the freemen in charge here and on the plantations – more especially Provost Marshals, – I am free to declare that they have not done justice to the slaves; they do not see that Gen. Banks's orders are carried out; on many places whipping is still permitted; in October last a slave was beaten by his master with a stick; he complained to Capt. O'Brien, Provost Marshal of the parish of St. James, who took him home and helped his master to wash his head; he then told the negro to stay there and the master would not again whip him; many employers last year cheated the negroes out of their wages; I think it best for the negro that his remuneration be left open to competition; also better for the employer. In some instances last year the planters paid their negroes more than was prescribed; both parties were perfectly satisfied; the order requiring the laborers to remain for one year upon the plantations where they engage is, in my opinion, right.

Generally speaking, the condition of the colored people has greatly improved since their freedom was acknowledged; they endeavor to find employment; they appreciate their newly-discovered rights very highly; I think if left free in a community by themselves they would be capable of self-government; they will endeavor to their utmost ability to discharge satisfactorily their civil duties; they have no idea of government; often they discuss political questions; in Louisiana they have had a certain kind of political education; they often discuss the question of the fitness of their respective masters to hold political power; there are one or more on each plantation who have secretly learned to read; they secretly read newspapers; the day following that on which the news of the execution of John Brown reached New Orleans I sat out for a plantation 75 miles distant; a slave gave me the details of the execution; a negro in the sugar-house asked the master for a paper to clean some machinery, and he retained and read it; he secretly read it to the entire force; whenever a slave was known to be able to read and write he was punished severely.

HD

Testimony of J. B. Roudanez before the American Freedmen's Inquiry Commission, 9 Feb. 1864, filed with O-328 1863, Letters Received, ser. 12, RG 94 [K-221]. Revisions and marginal notations in another handwriting, evidently made by the commission at a later date, are omitted.

112: Acting Superintendent of Negro Labor in the Department of the Gulf to the Headquarters of the Department, Enclosing a Letter from the Supervisor of a Contraband Depot to the Superintendent of Negro Labor

New-Orleans, February 15th *1864*

Sir I have the honor to respectfully enclose the report of Mr Willey in charge of the Picayune [*cotton*] Press, the rendezvous for the colored Refugees under my supervision, and to request that a company of soldiers be stationed at that place to preserve order and decorum. I have the honor to be Very Respectfully Your obt. Sert

HLS Geo. R. Bell

[*Enclosure*] Office of the Picayune Press
[*New Orleans*] Feb. 5th 1864.

Dear Sir. I respectfully suggest to you the propriety of obtaining, if possible, a guard for the purpose of protecting the property and enforcing proper regulation of affairs at this Press,

To my certain knowledge, there are many able bodied persons here, who are in the habit of getting their rations and staying here at night, and wandering about the city during the day, either as vagrants or obtaining jobs of work about the levees. Such persons it is almost impossible to hire out for we can never find them when they are wanted.

I have very good reasons for believing that many idle and vagrant negroes in the city are in the habit of secretly obtaining rations from the contrabands in the press, and when there is a large number of people here, it is impossible to distinguish those who actually belong to the Press, and who are entitled to draw rations from those who are not.

Soldiers and others are in the habit of visiting the Press, and creating disturbances among the people.

If any of the colored people here are dissatisfied, they easily find friends here in town who are willing to harbor them; and this is very often the case, when it is attempted to make up a gang to go on to a plantation – they slip off during the night and it is impossible to find them when they are wanted.

I think that one company of well disciplined colored troops, with their officers, would be sufficient for all the wants of the Press.

I am very anxious to have better regulations and discipline here among the colored people, but it is impossible as matters now are; often I find some refractory or discontented man who refuses to leave and go to work when he is needed, to the great disappointment of the planters as well as ourselves, and we believe that the presence of a military force would ensure obedience.

In case we have several hundred people here, some efficient means of keeping them in their place will be absolutely necessary.

Hoping that these suggestions will meet your approval; – I remain, – very respectfully your obedient servant

ALS N Willey –

Capt. Geo. R. Bell to Brig. Genl. C. P. Stone, 15 Feb. 1864, enclosing N. Willey to Col. Geo. H. Hanks, 5 Feb. 1864, Letters Received, 4th USCC, Regimental Books & Papers USCT, RG 94 [G-73]. Bell signed as a captain in the 37th Illinois Infantry. In an endorsement dated February 15, the headquarters of the Department of the Gulf directed the commander of the defenses of New Orleans to detail a black cavalry company to serve as a guard at the Picayune cotton press.

113: Regulations by the Superintendent of Plantations in the Treasury Department 5th Special Agency

[*New Orleans February? 1864*]

REGULATIONS!

1st. The Inspector of Plantations will be present at each pay day, keep a correct account of the amount of money paid each hand, together with a full and complete record of every transaction in his office.

2d. Settle all difficulties between employer and employee, arising under lease.

3d. See that proper quality and quantity of Rations are issued, and proper amount and quality of clothing is issued to employees.

4th. Inspect the plantation and report if it is cultivated according to lease.

5th. Report all derilictions of duty on part of employer or employee, promptly to this office.

TO GOVERN HANDS.

1st. All hands to be in the field within one half hour after bell rings.

2d. Each hand two hours late in the field, without proper excuse, shall be docked one half day's labor for each two hours so absent.

3d. No hand shall be allowed to leave a plantation without a pass from the manager, and no hand allowed to leave the parish without a pass from Inspector of Plantations, endorsed by Provost Marshal. Every hand found off the plantation, without a proper pass, will be docked one day's work for each offence.

4th. Half hour shall be allowed for breakfast each day, and two hours each day for dinner.

5th. No hand shall be allowed to roam at will over plantations in the night, and any hand found out of his or her quarters after 9 o'clock, each night, without proper excuse, shall be fined one half day's work.

6th. No hand shall be allowed to ride on horses or mules belonging to the plantation without proper permission from lessee or overseer, and each and every person guilty of such offence shall forfeit the amount of two days' work.

7th. No hand shall be allowed to keep any horse, mule, hog, pigs, or cattle on any plantation on which he may labor, the value of those now owned by any negro or negroes, on any leased plantation, shall be assessed by the parish Inspector of Plantations, and either purchased by the lessee, or permitted to be sold by owner.

In case of questions materially affecting the interests of either party to a lease, the Inspector of Plantations shall forward a certified statement of the case to the Superintendent of Plantations for his decision. Any party deeming himself aggrieved by any decision of the Inspector of Plantations of the parish, may appeal the same to the Superintendent of Plantations, or to the Provost Marshal of the Parish, as he may deem proper, whose decision in the case shall be final, he first notifying the Superintendent of such appeal.

8th. No hand cultivating any part or parcel of ground under the permission of the Major General Commanding, shall be allowed to plant any Cotton or Sugar Cane upon the land so cultivated by him upon his own account, but shall devote his time and land to the raising of corn or vegetables.

No hand shall be hired on any of the leased or private plantations without a written permission from last employer, or from the Inspector of Plantations of the Parish.

9th. Hands leaving Plantations without proper authority, wherever found shall be forced to return, and employers of said hands fined according to the offence ~~for~~ each hand so employed by the Provost Marshal of the Parish.

BY ORDER OF

S. W. COZZENS,

Superintendent of Plantations.

Regulations by S. W. Cozzens, [Feb.? 1864], filed between P-76 and P-77 1864, Letters Received, ser. 1920, Civil Affairs, Dept. of the Gulf, RG 393 Pt. 1 [C-736]. Although this printed copy bears no evidence as to its date of issue, Cozzens's regulations probably date from about February 15, 1864, when he transmitted a slightly different handwritten version to a subordinate "inspector of plantations." (S. W. Cozzens to Mr. Charles L. Dunbar, 15 Feb. 1864, vol. 123, pp. 119–21, Outgoing Correspondence of the Plantation Bureau, 3rd Agency, RG 366 [Q-307].)

114: Provost Marshal of Terrebonne Parish, Louisiana, to the Superintendent of Plantations in the Treasury Department 5th Special Agency

TERREBONNE PARISH, La., *Houma,* March 2nd *1864.*

Sir If any thing can be done by way of cultivating the Plantation of Major Potts in this Parish Please do it under the superintendance of some white Man– The place is a pest and nusience to this parish if not done I shall be compelled to turn out these hands altogather

Let this man have it and relieve me if you can Respectfully Your Obt Svt

ALS John. W. Lee

[*Endorsement*] Respt. Referred to Brig Gen Bowen Provost Marshall Genl. This place was not rented last year because Capt. Nott of Your office interceeded in behalf of Bishop Potts of Pennsylvinia who is the real owner of the place, and who requested that the old slaves who were on the place might be allowed to cultivate as much of it as they could for their own benefit, without paying rent, hoping that they might by industry acquire a little competence–

These wishes have been regarded this year as well as last and I have refused to rent the place

I have always heard that these parties now on the place were quite industrious & worthy S. W. Cozzens Supt Plantatns

Capt. John W. Lee to Capt. Couzins, 2 Mar. 1864, Incoming Correspondence of the Plantation Bureau, 3rd Agency, RG 366 [Q-98]. For Captain Charles C. Nott's role in securing the Potts plantation for the independent occupation of former slaves during 1863, as well as a petition by several of the freedmen, see above, doc. 91. Despite Cozzens's intervention on the ex-slaves' behalf with respect to the 1864 season, the Potts plantation was turned over to a lessee only a few weeks later. Having previously operated the place as independent producers, the freedpeople did not take kindly to being reduced to wage laborers and subjected to army and treasury regulations. In late April 1864, a plantation inspector reported that they had "recently set up a claim to the right to plant cotton or anything else they pleased in their respective patches," contrary to regulations that forbade the cultivation of staples on garden plots. The plantation inspector had "decided adversely" to the laborers' claim and, he reported, "[t]hey are quiet about it now." (T. J. Henderson to Capt. S. W. Cozzens, 30 Apr. 1864, vol. 72, pp. 61–73, Reports of Inspectors of Plantations, 3rd Agency, RG 366 [Q-115].)

115: Report by a Commissioner of the American Freedmen's Inquiry Commission

[*New York? April? 1864*]

The Emancipated Slave face to face with
his old Master.
[Valley of the Lower Mississippi.][1]

Of all portions of the slave region to which the Commission have had access, the valley of the Lower Mississippi affords the most interesting field for the observation and study of the slave system, as well as of the great changes which, at the present moment, slave society is everywhere undergoing. Unlike most other sections visited by the Commission, here are found all the elements of that society still in existence, but in a state of revolution and transformation. Here, facing the broad river on either side, still stands the great, white mansion of the planter; by its side, just without its shadow, the long rows of cabins, called the negro quarters, and a little in the rear, the great quadrangular structure, usually of brick, with its tall chimney, known as the sugar-house. In many instances the old master still occupies the mansion and the negroes their old quarters, but under circumstances and in relations quite new, strange and full of anxiety to both.

During a recent personal visit to many of these mansions and negro quarters many important facts came to light and important suggestions occurred not elsewhere presented.

In most other sections visited by the Commission, slave society had been observed in a state of total disruption. Either the master or the slave on both had become fugitives. In South Carolina the masters had absconded, leaving their habitations and their slaves. In Virginia and North Carolina, as well as in many localities in the SouthWest held by our armies the emancipated could only be seen as fugitives, and the old masters not at all. On the contrary, in such portions of the valley of the Lower Mississippi as are within our military lines and especially in the river region of Louisiana, many of them still stand face to face in the presence of the great revolution and of the trials to which it summons both.

. . . .

If in the preceding cursory survey of the present state of things in the valley of the Mississippi I have succeeded in presenting the two constituent elements of the old slave society in their true light, it cannot fail to suggest the intrinsic nature of the antagonisms that stand in the way of the successful introduction of the free-labor system there, and of the political re-construction based upon it. Every analysis of slave society, everywhere, brings us to a like conclusion. The difficulty is not with the emancipated slave, but with the old master still enthralled by his old infatuation.

. . . .

Every diagnosis of the malady under which the body politic is writhing and staggering in the present hour, discloses its nucleus in the old mastership. That in this mastership is the seat of the disease, containing the pestiferous virus by which the whole nation has been infected. That this seed of national dishonor, dissolution and death was brought from Africa and landed upon the banks of James River, Virginia, in the Autumn of that same year, 1620, in which the Pilgrims with the germs of our national life, civilization and glory landed upon Plymouth Rock. That this fatal virus has spread and increased in virulence, for more than two hundred years, until the glow of the fever had come to be mistaken for the bloom of health; until the summits of the mountainous social carbuncle generated by it had come to be regarded as the heighths of national culture, wealth and glory. Let us thank God, that it has burst at last and opened up to the eyes of all men its loathsome depths, so that the merest tyro in the science of social and political health and statesmanship need no longer be mistaken as to its nature or as to the treatment proper for its cure.

In all manner of official proclamations and manifestoes it has been repeatedly declared, that the war on our part was waged alone for the preservation of the Constitution and the re-establishment of the Union. But what would be the value of the letter of the Constitution unless quickened by the spirit of the "self-evident truths" of the great Declaration–"that all men are created equal, endowed by their Creator with the inalienable rights of life, liberty and the pursuit of happiness?" And what would the Union be without the inherent principle of cohesion, the living unity, founded in these truths?

Reunion then and the preservation of the essential life of the Constitution demand, not alone the release of the slave population from their bonds and the degradation thereby imposed upon them, but the deliverance of the master-population also, wholly and forever, from their mastership and from the fatal delusions and depravations that are inherent in it. This is the primary necessity of any rational attempt to establish free-labor and a better social order in the Slave States, the very first step towards any wise or well-founded re-construction. In no other way can the rebel States ever be rehabilitated with a truly loyal, democratic, concurrent citizenship.

And this brings me to speak of the means, which in the judgment of the Commission are deemed necessary to give practical effect to the acts of Congress and the President's Proclamation of January, 1863, "to the end that the colored population thereby emancipated may defend and support themselves."

Their recommendations embrace three principal measures, which, with more or less completeness, have been, heretofore, in their several preliminary Reports, and are herewith, in their final Report, submitted to the War Department.

The object of the first of these measures is to secure, beyond any possible peradventure or doubt, the civil right of the colored man to personal freedom, by placing that right in the new order of things, on the same broad basis as that of the white man.

This is to be effected most surely by an amendment of the Constitution of the United States. That measure is already before Congress and although not exactly in the form recommended by the Commission, yet it is believed sufficient, especially if accompanied with other legislation in the same spirit and with a like intent, to accomplish the great object proposed; and every true lover of his country's permanent peace, prosperity and honor cannot but await with the greatest anxiety its final consummation.

The second is a measure of scarcely less importance, and considering the exigencies of the approaching crisis and the present temper and disposition of the master class, even more immediately urgent than the first.

Whenever civil authority shall be re-established in the rebel States and they shall be re-admitted to the Federal Union, the greater portion of the civil and political rights of their inhabitants necessarily fall under the jurisdiction and control of State authority. In all these States the colored people, even such of them as have been always free, have been uniformly debarred the enjoyment of all political and many civil rights. Unless therefore the emancipated population have secured to them their civil and political rights by national authority antecedent to such re-admission, they will stand in imminent danger of being defrauded of any practical freedom, notwithstanding "the acts of Congress and the President's Proclamation."

In the language of a witness whose intimate acquaintance with the spirit of the master class gives great weight to his words: "they had much better be slaves, with the present feelings of the Southern whites against them, than to be left without national guarantees for the maintenance of their rights as freemen."[2]

It is the producing class – that class whose whole life is devoted to toil – that under every form of civil government is most in danger of being made the victims of the leisure, capital and opportunities of the non-producing class. Under the most favorable circumstances therefore, it is this class who most need to be fenced about with civil and political guarantees. But the circumstances and position of the emancipated population are most unfavorable and critical. Without their own volition, without previous preparation and as a measure of national self-preservation, they have been suddenly precipitated into new and wholly untried relations with an antagonistic, far more able and adroit class. To leave them in this position defenceless and at the mercy of their old masters would, in its cruellest meaning be, to keep with them "the word of promise to the ear and break it to the hope."

Nay, not only the national honor but future national peace and well-being demand that the national Government should secure to these people now, while they are still under the sole jurisdiction and control of that Government, the permanent possession of such civil and political rights, as will enable them "to defend and support themselves" against the machinations and schemes of any class or power to subject them again to any form of slavery or serfdom.

To this end I cannot too earnestly urge that Congress be invoked to fix and establish by law, antecedent to and as a condition precedent to re-construction, the civil rights of the emancipated population; and at the same time to provide for the future enjoyment by all free persons of color of the fundamental right of citizenship in a free government, the right to the elective franchise, based upon the acquisition, on their part, of such qualifications only as are deemed essential in their white fellow-citizens.

Another matter intimately connected with the foregoing, and as I believe profoundly involving the existence and future prosperity of free society in the Southern States, is the disposition to be made of the confiscated estates and other lands in these States. No such thing as free democratic society can exist in any country where all the lands are owned by one class of men and are cultivated by another. Such ownership of the lands of a country constitutes the basis of the most permanent and oppressive aristocracies. Upon this foundation stood for a thousand years the feudal aristocracy of France. And to-day the aristocracy of England maintain their supremacy upon the basis of the partition and tenure of the soil of England, robbed by William the Conqueror from the original owners, the people of England, and granted in large estates to his captains. So incompatible has that tenure become with modern civilization and the well-being of society in that country, that the wisest statesmen there are beginning to apprehend the most fearful consequences from its continued existence.

In the sugar and cotton producing portions of the South, almost all the cultivated soil has been hitherto held in large tracts by the master class. I need not stop to argue the utter incompatibility of such a state of things with the existence of a free, independent, democratic yeomanry, or with the development of free democratic institutions. The poor whites of the South are a sufficient illustration of its pernicious influence and effect upon a whole community of the same race with the land-holders.

If not for the sake of the emancipated colored people, then for the sake of these poor whites, these most pitiable men of our own race, this whole scheme and tenure of the mastership should be overthrown. The great necessity, as I have before intimated, from another point of view, which at the present hour lies upon the People and Government of the United States is not so much a political as a social reconstruction of the Southern States. Any well founded plan for the former, to be effectual and permanent must include the latter. And for the latter the initiation of a policy on the part of the National Government which shall have for its aim the ultimate division of the great plantations into moderate sized farms, to be held and cultivated by the labor of their owners is of the utmost importance.

I am aware that an opinion has been hitherto generally entertained that sugar and cotton cultivation could only be profitably carried on upon large estates and by the employment of large gangs of laborers; principally because a large capital is necessary to the erection of the sugar-mills, cotton-gins and other machinery connected with the production of these commodities. All the investigations of the Commission go to show that this opinion is but a part of the system of slavery and has no foundation in the necessities of the case. There is, in reality, no more reason why the sugar cane should be raised and converted into sugar by the planter alone than there is that wheat should be converted into flour only by the farmer who raises it. And so with the raising, ginning and baling of cotton. On the contrary, a proper division of labor in the raising and manufacture of sugar and cotton would almost inevitably lead to a great developement in their production, while at the same time it would tend not only to mitigate the labor but to secure the industrial prosperity and independence of all those employed in that production; and thus constitute an entirely different order of social relation and condition in these States. I consider this a matter next in importance to the permanent security of the civil and political rights of the emancipated population, and beg leave to recommend it to the earnest attention of the National Authorities.

And finally permit me once more to call the attention of Government to the third of the measures proposed by the Commission. The establishment of some uniform system of supervision and guardianship for the emancipated population, in the interim of their transition from Slavery to freedom. No one acquainted with the facts could hesitate a moment as to the necessity and propriety of such a system; not only for the sake of the emancipated but for the general interest of the Government and country.

. . . .

HDS J. M[c]Kaye

Excerpts from J. McKaye, "The Emancipated Slave face to face with his old Master: Valley of the Lower Mississippi," [Apr.? 1864], filed with O-328 1863, Letters Received, ser. 12, RG 94 [K-66]. About 20 pages of a 104-page essay, itself a supplement to the final report of the American Freedmen's Inquiry Commission. The omitted portions included: a survey of slavery, emancipation, and wartime labor arrangements in the lower Mississippi Valley, drawn largely from testimony taken by the commission; passages from a letter by General Nathaniel P. Banks, commander of the Department of the Gulf, that argued for the necessity of government supervision over all labor, not only that of former slaves; and a broadly drawn comparison of Southern slaveholders with the French nobility during the *ancien régime*. Denouncing any sort of aristocracy as antithetical to republican principles and democratic institutions, McKaye noted that in France "[i]t took the reign of terror and the guillotine to cure that ancient noblesse of their delusions." Seeing the American Civil War as "[t]he culmination of the masters' infatuation," he suggested that their conduct might warrant "a somewhat similar kind of providential surgery for them."

1 Brackets in manuscript.
2 A marginal notation, marked with an asterisk, refers to the testimony of Colonel George H. Hanks, for which see above, doc. 110.

116: Provost Marshal of Plaquemines Parish, Louisiana, to the Provost Marshal General of the Department of the Gulf

Parish of Plaquemines, La. May 3d *1864*.

General I have the honor to submit for your consideration the following report

Complaint was made to me Friday April 29– 64, that several colored laborers on the Oakland plantation had refused to work, I immediately sent P. Holton, a Police Officer of this Parish to investigate and ascertain their reasons for so doing– They could or would not give him any reason–and some of them were very insulting to him– He then attempted to arrest one of the ring leaders when he was beset upon by at least twenty with hoes, Shovels & hatchets– not having any assistants he was obliged to leave the plantation without accomplishing anything, On his reporting the facts to me I proceeded to the said Oakland plantation and found them in a riotous & insubordonete state–None of them at work– I called them all before me and asked, them separately if they had any complaint to make, Their answer was that they had none, except that they did not want to work on the plantation, with Mr Desbin as Overseer, they did not charge him with being dishonorable in any respect but simply said that in their Judgement a change of Overseer wold be benneficial, Their complint appearing to me to be trifling, I then read to them General Orders No 23 issued from Head quarters Department of the Gulf February 3d 1864,[1] After explaining the same to them I assured them that the said General Orders would be strictly enforced both one the employer and employees, and told them that a repetetion of their present conduct would be followed by a punishment such as [. . .] provide in such cases, and at the same time told them if they had any complaints to make that they were at liberty to make them to me at any time, they then informed me that they were satisfied and would go to work on the following day which they did and are now in a peacable and quiet state, on enquiry I find that Mr Desbins character was very exemplary and that he treats those in his employ with the utmost respect, Very Respectfull Your Obedient Servant

ALS E. R Clark

Capt. E. R. Clark to General, 3 May 1864, Letters Received, ser. 1845, Provost Marshal, Dept. of the Gulf, RG 393 Pt. 1 [C-796]. Captain Clark's quelling of the unrest on Oakland plantation was undoubtedly made easier by the involvement of George T. Converse, a Treasury Department inspector of plantations. After learning that the laborers would not work and had driven the parish policeman from the estate, Converse discharged three "ring-leaders" (who were confined in the parish jail in irons) and "made them forfeit all back pay due them." (George T. Converse to S. W. Cozzens, 1 May 1864, vol. 72, p. 77, Reports of Inspectors of Plantations, 3rd Agency, RG 366 [Q-114].) It was not the first time that Converse had punished insubordinate laborers on the plantation. Only three weeks earlier, he had interceded after thirteen women refused to work "except on the patches of ground given to their husbands by the overseer." Acting upon the principle that all able-bodied freedpeople "*should work* for the benefit of the plantation . . . or in some way pay rent for the quarters they occupy," Converse directed that one-half of the pay owed to the offenders' husbands be withheld "until such a time as the women shall see fit to work for the Plantation." (George T. Converse to Capt. S. W. Cozzens, 6 Apr. 1864, vol. 72, pp. 54–55, Reports of Inspectors of Plantation, 3rd Agency, RG 366 [Q-114].)

1 See above, doc. 109.

117: Treasury Department Inspector of Plantations to the Superintendent of Plantations in the Treasury Department 5th Special Agency

Parish La Fourche [*La.*] Johnson Plantation. June 16th 1864

Sir. On several of the government plantations in this Parish, little or no discipline exists, without which it will be impossible to make a crop— The hands on all these places can be made to work and I propose to do it. I may require the assistance of the military in so doing but as I have asked their aid several times and received no satisfaction, I shall not ask again. It is on this account I make this special report.

Can not an order be had from General Bowen to the Provost Marshal of this Parish to furnish me with a guard when I need it or at any rate not to interfere with me in the discharge of my duties.

While on this subject, I may as well report the following.

One day in last week, a negro sergeant of the 4th Cold Cavalry came to the Bragg Plantation (with proper passes &c) to visit his wife. meeting the overseer in the road he drew his sword on him and compelled him to make room for him (Sergt) Of course the overseer was considerably provoked at this—but did nothing— Later in the day when I visited the plantation the overseer informed me of the fact, and requested me to see the negro— I asked the negro for his pass, and while getting it, he commenced to use the worst possible language towards the overseer, and myself. Upon this, (as his pass was out) I ordered him from the place. He went to the Provost Marshal who gave him a pass to return—enclosed and marked A. When he returned he talked with great impudence to me swearing and cursing all the time, threatening to "Knock Hell" out of any one that troubled him &c I then went to the Provost Marshal myself and asked him to have the sergeant taken away from the plantation – He gave me an order to that effect – subsequently however he gave the sergeant an order to go on the place and stay there as long as he pleased; and informed the overseer if he (Prov) ever heard of a *U.S. Officer* being insulted, or molested, he would "smoke the person high"

Of course every hand on the plantation knew what had happened, and they acted the next day pretty much as they pleased.

There is no use trying to do anything if this is all the satisfaction that can be had from the military.

Please let me know what can be done in reference to the enquiry made in the first part of this report. Respectfully.

HLcSr (Signed) George T. Converse

George T. Converse to Capt. S. W. Cozzens, 16 June 1864, vol. 72, pp. 95–96, Reports of Inspectors of Plantations, 3rd Agency, RG 366 [Q-119]. The pass referred to as enclosed was not copied along with the letter. General James Bowen, who Converse wished would take steps to provide him with military assistance, was provost marshal general of the Department of the Gulf. Within a month, Converse had evidently received such assistance and had instituted stern disciplinary measures against unruly laborers on several government plantations. Aided by a detail of soldiers, he discharged eighteen "of the most refractory" hands from one estate and twelve from another; on a third plantation, punishment took the form of "forfeiture of pay, extra work, &c." "The remainder of the hands," he noted with satisfaction, "probaly taking the hint, have gone to work with much more energy than has been seen before," and the workers on two neighboring government plantations, "knowing what had befallen their comrades, have conducted themselves in a decent manner since." Converse thanked the local army commander and provost marshal for furnishing soldiers "to assist me in cleaning out these places." (George T. Converse to Capt. S. W. Cozzens, 16 July 1864, vol. 72, pp. 106–8, Reports of Inspectors of Plantations, 3rd Agency, RG 366 [Q-119].)

118: Superintendent of Negro Labor in the Department of the Gulf to the Provost Marshal General of the Department

New-Orleans, July 29" *1864.*

Sir. Complaint is made at this office by two colored men named Sanford Thomas and Charles A. Butler, both residing on Dick Taylor (Government) Plantation, that Major Bradley Provost Marshal of St. Charles Parish has issued an order prohibiting the raising of cotton by the negroes on their own patches, and compelling them to sell all their hogs. to two certain men whom he shall designate.

I would therefore respectfully request. that an investigation of this matter be ordered, and the laborers be protected in their rights. Very Respectfully Your Ob'd't Serv[t]

HLS Geo. H. Hanks

[*Endorsement*] Provost Marshals office. Parish of St. Charles [*La.*]. August 2nd 1864. Respectfully returned to the A. Pro Marshl. Genl. with the following report. Their are no negroes in the parish cultivating cotton, owing to the regulations published by Capt Cozzens Sup[t] of Govm[t] Plan[tns] some months ago.[1] I came here on the 10th of May and the first order I issued was that negroes should be allowed to raise cotton and I have always enforced that order. although no cotton was cultivated. yet it will have the desired effect next year. As to the Hogs, many planters complain of negroes stealing their corn & feeding the Hogs. On one plantation alone (La Branche) 100 barrels were stolen. I consulted with Co[l] Hanks, regarding the matter & proposed that the hogs should be sold & a satisfactory price paid to the negroes where it was known the negroes had no means of feeding their Hogs.

Where I know they have corn & can support their hogs without stealing I have allowed them to retain them Others I have ordered to be sold according to the enclosed copy of regulations which I think prevents fraud or imposition on either negroe or planter. As I can account for *every single* hog owners name, weight of hog & price paid. I am particular that the negroe shall receive a proper price for his hog – Very respectfully. J. H Bradley Maj & Pro Marshl

Col. Geo H. Hanks to Col. Chickering, 29 July 1864, Letters Received, ser. 1845, Provost Marshal, Dept. of the Gulf, RG 393 Pt. 1 [C-800]. Other endorsements. In the same file is a copy of the "regulations" forwarded by Major Bradley, as they appeared in a letter of July 25, 1864, authorizing one "T. S. Johnson Esqr" of St. Charles Parish "to purchase all the Hogs in the fourth fifth and Sixth patrol districts," subject to the following conditions: a deputy provost marshal was to witness each sale; the price paid had to be satisfactory to the owner of each hog; a tax of ten cents per hog was to be collected and "appropriated to the building of a church for the colored people"; no plantation owner, lessee, manager, or any other person could purchase hogs without Bradley's permission; and Johnson was to furnish Bradley with a list of "all Hogs bought. From whom bought. and the prices paid for them, & the weight." (Major J. H. Bradly to T. S. Johnson, Esqr.) Also in the same file are affidavits (sworn before Bradley on August 2, 1864) by Sandford Thomas and Charles A. Butler, the freedmen who had reportedly gone to New Orleans and complained to Colonel Hanks. Thomas confirmed that he had asked Hanks "if we be permitted to raise one hog apiece on the Taylor plantation. And told him that the order was issued from the Court House that we were to part from all Hogs." He further stated that he had indeed told Hanks that two men had been appointed to buy hogs from the freedpeople, but had not claimed that the freedpeople were compelled to sell. Thomas also confirmed that the policy prohibiting plantation laborers from raising cotton and cane on their garden plots had been established before Bradley became provost marshal, "[n]or has Major Bradly ever prevented or interferred with us in the raiseing of our crops." Butler swore that he had not been in New Orleans with Thomas when the complaint was entered. According to subsequent endorsements, the documents were all forwarded to the headquarters of the Department of the Gulf, and, on August 9, General Nathaniel P. Banks sternly disapproved Bradley's "order of sale." "No such proceedings can be justified," he declared. "They are open to great abuses."

1 The regulations, probably issued in mid-February 1864, had prohibited the cultivation of cotton or sugar cane on garden plots, which were to be devoted "to the raising of corn or vegetables." (See above, doc. 113.)

119: Plantation Regulations by the Secretary of the Treasury

[*Washington, D.C. July 29, 1864*]

FREEDMEN.

REGULATIONS OF THE SECRETARY OF THE TREASURY,

SERIES JULY 29, 1864.

Providing for the employment and general welfare of all persons within the lines of National Military Occupation within Insurrectionary States, formerly held as Slaves, who are or shall become free.

Agents to carry out these Regulations.

I. The Regulations relative to the employment and general welfare of freedmen will be carried into effect by the same Agents, and under the same supervision as are provided under the Regulations concerning commercial intercourse.

Freedmen's Home Colonies.

II. There shall be established in each Special Agency one or more places to be known as "Freedmen's Home Colonies," where all freed persons within the Agency may be received and provided for in pursuance of these Regulations.

Superintendent of Freedmen – His Duties.

III. A Superintendent of Freedmen will be appointed for each one of these Colonies, under the general direction of the proper Supervising Special Agent. Superintendents will make such arrangements as shall be necessary at each Colony to provide temporary shelter and care for persons received there, and also such buildings as are proper for the permanent use of those retained there; and will obtain such working animals and other agricultural implements of labor and other supplies as may be necessary and proper for the economical conduct of these establishments. They will also keep books of record in which shall be entered the name, age, condition, former owner, residence, and occupation of each person received in these Colonies; also, the marriages, births, and deaths occurring therein; also, all departures, and by whom those departing are employed, for what purpose, at what place, and on what terms.

Classification of Freedmen and their Wages.

IV. All persons of proper age and condition to labor, when received shall be classified by the Superintendent as follows: Sound persons, over 18 and under 40 years of age, shall be classed as No. 1 hands; over 14 and under 18, and over 40 and under 55, No. 2; over 12 and under 14, and over 55, No. 3. Persons suffering from any physical defect or infirmity, but able to work, shall be classed as he considers proper. The minimum rate of wages of No. 1 males shall be $25 per month; No. 2, $20; No. 3, $15. Nos. 1, 2 and 3, females, $18, $14, $10. These rates shall not restrict mechanics and others from contracting for higher wages if they can do so.

Employment to be Provided for Freedmen of Proper Age.

V. Superintendents will see that all persons so received, registered, and classified, who are able to labor, are promptly provided with employment by lessees or others desiring their labor, upon the terms specified, and they will permit none over the age of twelve, capable of labor, to remain in idleness; and they will, as far as possible, obtain from planters and others the names and other particulars above specified, of all freed persons in their employ or within their knowledge in the district within which these Colonies are located, a record of which shall be kept by them as above provided, and they will do what they consistently can to see that all such persons are provided with employment at rates equal to those above specified, and that the helpless among them are properly cared for.

Applications for Laborers to be Received and Recorded.

VI. Superintendents will receive and record all applications for the labor of freedmen, that those received may be promptly furnished with employment. Planters and others employing parents will be required to take their children with them, unless the parent prefers to have them remain, in which case Superintendents will see that provision is made to apply sufficient of the wages of the parent to support the children at the Colony.

Written Agreements to be made between Employers and Employes, and Conditions.

VII. Superintendents shall see that written agreements are made between the employer and the employé, by which, in addition to the wages above fixed, the employer shall agree to furnish, without charge, sufficient quarters for the laborers, a separate tenement for each family, with proper regard for sanitary condition, one acre of ground for garden purposes to each family, fuel, medical attendance, and schools for children; also, that laborers shall be paid for full time, unless they are sick or voluntarily neglect to work; that one-half their monthly wages shall be paid to the laborer during each month, and the other half at the end of the term of employment; that, in case the laborer violates his contract by voluntary absence or continued neglect to work, the half wages due to him shall be forfeited, one half to the employer, and one half to the Government to aid in supporting the helpless; that any wages due to the laborers, under the agreement, shall be a first lien upon all crops produced, and that no shipment of products, shall be made until the Superintendent shall certify that all dues to laborers are paid or satisfactorily arranged; that no labor in excess of ten hours per day shall be required, but if more shall be performed at the request of the employer, extra payment shall be made therefor; that the employers shall keep on hand and sell to their employés at actual cost on the plantation, a sufficient supply of wholesome food and proper clothing for themselves and their families.

Interest in Profits of Labor may be given instead of Wages.

VIII. In case any person employing Freedmen to labor on plantations shall wish to give an interest in the profits of their labor instead of the wages above fixed, and the laborers desire to accept the same, an agreement in writing may be made accordingly, subject to the approval of the proper Superintendent.

Where civil courts are established within reach of parties complaining under these agreements, they may seek redress there; but if no such courts are within reach, then the complaining party may state his case to a Superintendent, who, after hearing both parties, shall decide between them. Either party may appeal to the proper Supervising Special Agent, whose decision shall be final.

Care of Aged and Infirm Freedmen.

IX. Aged or infirm Freed persons, and orphan children under twelve years of age, and others unfit for regular labor who cannot be otherwise provided for, will be retained and provided for by Superintendents, and each Superintendent will see that all such persons under his care perform all such labor as is proper, considering their condition; and he will employ as many hands, at regular rates as may be requisite for producing on the plantation all things that can be raised, necessary to the support of the establishment, and no more; and he will require all freed persons temporarily there to labor without wages, until they can be employed elsewhere. He will provide such medical attendance and schools as are necessary and proper.

Home Colonies may be Assigned to Associations upon certain Conditions.

X. Any Association or combination of Associations desiring to improve the condition of Freedmen, will have assigned to their care and general charge such Freedmen's Home Colonies as they may desire, and as they can give satisfactory assurance of their ability to provide for. Superintendents for any such Colonies will be appointed upon the nomination and in pursuance of the wishes of such Associations, and every proper facility for the execution of their purposes will be given by the Supervising and Assistant Special Agents. Associations, desiring to operate under this clause, are notified that the Secretary reserves the right to revoke or modify this regulation whenever, in his judgment, the public interests will be promoted by such action.

Reservations of Land for Freedmen's Labor Colonies.

XI. For the purpose of promoting habits of industry and self-reliance among Freedmen, and to encourage them to locate in Colonies, and to enable them to work advantageously, there will be reserved in the respective Special Agencies such contiguous, abandoned, and confiscable lands and plantations as may be proper for that purpose, for the exclusive use and cultivation of Freedmen, which reservations will be called Freedmen's Labor Colonies. Over each of these Colonies there will be appointed a Superintendent for leasing small tracts therein to such Freedmen as are able to work them; and such lessees shall be subject to the same conditions and entitled to the same rights and privileges as other lessees.

Labor Colonies may be assigned to Associations on certain Conditions.

XII. Any Association, or combination of Associations, desiring to aid lessees in such Colonies who have not sufficient means to cultivate without aid, will have set apart to their beneficiaries such part or the whole of any one of these Colonies as they shall give satisfactory assurance of their ability to provide for; and in case they agree to provide the necessary working animals, agricultural implements, seeds, and other aid which may be necessary for the cultivation of the whole of any such Colony, such Superintendent will be appointed as may be desired by the Association. Associations desiring to operate under this clause are notified, that the Secretary reserves the right to revoke or modify this Regulation whenever, in his judgment, the public interests will be promoted by such action.

Schools will be Established.

XIII. Schools will be established within these Home and Labor Colonies sufficient for the education of all children there under the age of twelve years, teachers for which will be provided by the Superintendent or by the Association, as the case may be.

Penalties for Ill Usage of Freedmen.

XIV. Ill usage of Freedmen by lessees or others employed by them, will be regarded as sufficient ground for the forfeiture of the contract between lessee and laborer, or, if the case be an aggravated one, of the lease of a plantation. Superintendents will promptly and fully investigate complaints of this character, and if they prove to be well-founded, they will annul the contract for labor as above.

If, in their opinion, this action is inadequate, they will report the case to the proper Supervising Special Agent, who may, if he thinks proper, cancel the lease, subject to appeal to the General Agent.

Expenses to be approved by Secretary – Copies of all Papers to be Transmitted.

XV. All expenses must be authorized and approved by the Secretary of the Treasury. Each Superintendent, on the first of every month, will furnish the Secretary of the Treasury and the proper Supervising Special Agent with copies of all records, agreements, and other papers under his charge, and also a monthly statement of accounts, of all receipts and expenditures, with vouchers for all money paid out. Supervising Special Agents will render a monthly account current of all receipts and expenditures within their respective Agencies under these Regulations, accompanied with vouchers for all money paid by them.

PD

Regulations of the Secretary of the Treasury, 29 July 1864, enclosed in Wm. P. Mellen to Hon. Wm. P. Fessenden, 6 Feb. 1865, M-760 1865, Letters Received by the Division, ser. 315, Division of Captured Property, Claims, & Land, RG 56 [X-109]. Part of a printed compilation of Treasury Department regulations and military orders concerning the leasing of plantations, the shipment of plantation supplies and plantation products, and the employment of freedpeople. Although issued in the name of the Secretary of the Treasury, the regulations were drafted by William P. Mellen, general agent of the Treasury Department's special agencies, in accordance with an act of Congress of July 2, 1864, which transferred from military to treasury authorities the supervision over "the employment and general welfare" of ex-slaves in the Union-occupied South. (*Statutes at Large*, vol. 13, pp. 375–78.) Shortly after the regulations were issued, military officials objected to a transfer of authority in the middle of the crop year, and also to particular provisions of the treasury plan; in response, the Secretary of the Treasury suspended the regulations until after the harvest. (See below, doc. 222B.)

120A: Company Commander in a Louisiana Black Regiment to the Provost Marshal of St. Mary's Parish, Louisiana

Berwick City La Aug 24" [22"] 1864

Sir Numerous complaints having been made to me by men of my Co in regard to the treatment their wives and children were receiving on a goverment plantation worked by Mr Smith not far from Brashear City caused me to pay some attention and partially investigat the case; it appears that the wife (Katrina) of Jesse Segvola of my co. having fallen sick he refuse to furnish either rations or medicines the woman has been for weeks subsisting upon what she could beg from others; I have been creditably informed that he has curtailed the allowance of those who are able to work and not allowing any thing for children compelling Laborers to buy provision from him at exorbitant prices so much so that the majority of laborers on his plantation are indebted to him more than their wages or share of the products of the plantation will amount to.

Hoping you will as a friend of humanity and an officer of U.S. will see Justice done. I have the honor to be Very Respectfully Your Obedient servant

ALS Jas M White

Capt. Jas. M. White to Capt. Stearns, 24 [22] Aug. 1864, Letters Received & Sent, ser. 1519, St. Mary's Parish LA, Provost Marshal Field Organizations, RG 393 Pt. 4 [C-1017]. Captain White commanded Company "C" of the 93rd USCI. Endorsements indicate that the provost marshal instructed a deputy to investigate conditions on the Wofford plantation; for the deputy provost marshal's report, see doc. 120B, immediately below.

120B: Deputy Provost Marshal of St. Mary's Parish, Louisiana, to the Provost Marshal of the Parish

Brashear City, La., Aug. 23" *1864.*

Sir I submit to you the following report in Case of the treatment of the wives & Children of soldiers on the Wofford Plantation by Capt. E. N. Smith:

1st in case of Katrine Segola it appear by the overseers Statement & his books that she has in the last 3 month worked 11 1/2 days & has had rations issued up to the 7th of this month. & the reason that she did not get them the last time was because she did not come after them untill it was dark & then she was told to come in the morning & she failed to come. her statement is, that she is & has been sick the most of the time & that Capt. Smith would not issue to her the last two weeks. it appears by others statements that she is not able to work in the field as a field hand. & I would say the same Judging by her looks.

2nd In reference to short rations of other hands. by the overseers own statement he issues 5 lbs of Pork and one Peck of corn meal pr. week, & salt. his statemet is corroberated by the most of the hands,

3d In reference to exhorbitant prices I examined the books & find that the following is a list of prices,

Rice.	.20 cts per lb.	Demins.	.60 cts. pr. yd. (for Dresses)
Butter	.65 " " "	Check	.35 " " " "
Coffee	.70 " " "	Campachy hats	.60 cts a piece
Tobacco	$1.25 " " "	Fur hats	$2.00 & $3.00" "
Corn Meal.	.50 " " peck	Mollasses	.25 cts. pr. quart
Pork	.25 " " lbs	Soap	.35 " " *Bar*
Candles	.40 " " "		
Shoes (Russett)	$2.75 pr pair		
" (black).	2.50 " "		

The hands on the place agrees as to the correctness of the abov list of prices of clothing & provisions that they buy of capt Smith.

3dly In reference to rations to Children, the overseers statement is that they have never issued to the children at all but in lieu. have given them ground to work for their own use, on which they raise such things as they desire.

4th In reference to the Majority of hands being in dept to Capt. Smith I examined his books & find that on the Wafford place he has 48 working hands & that 22 of them are somewhat in dept to Capt. Smith. some to a considerable an extent but the majority but a verry small amount. I will also state that out of some 12 diffrt articles mentioned in "Gen. Orders 92"[1] that he (Capt smith) only issues 3 of them viz. Meat, Meal, & salt but claims that allowing them to have small pieces of ground to cultivate that they can raise such articles as will be of as much benefit to them as the articles not issued. & that he does not give them Medicine, but Charges them for what they get, such as so much a dose or so many pills for so much; as I noticed on some of the hands books that he would charg .15 cts for a dose & 10 cts for 4 pills, &C. Yous verry respectifully

ALS W. W. Mason

Lt. W. W. Mason to Capt. Albert Stearns, 23 Aug. 1864, filed with Capt. Jas. M. White to Capt. Stearns, 24 [22] Aug. 1864, Letters Received & Sent, ser. 1519, St. Mary's Parish LA, Provost Marshal Field Organizations, RG

393 Pt. 4 [C-1017]. On August 25, the provost marshal of St. Mary's Parish forwarded to Captain James M. White of the 93rd USCI the portion of Lieutenant Mason's report that referred to the wife of "Jesse Segoola," a soldier in White's company. While suggesting that in this instance "the fault was *partly* her own," the provost marshal disclosed that "the result of the investigation has decided me to put in force a plan which I had contemplated for some time past," and he forwarded a circular letter that he had drafted. (Capt. Albert Stearns to Capt. Jas. M. White, 25 Aug. 1864, in the same file.) The circular is printed immediately below, as doc. 120C.

1 General Order 92, issued by the commander of the Department of the Gulf on July 9, 1864, is printed below, in doc. 120C.

120C: Circular Letter by the Provost Marshal of St. Mary's Parish, Louisiana, and an Order by the Commander of the Department of the Gulf

Brashear City, La. 1864.

Sir. I enclose to you a Copy of General Order No. 92. which provides what shall constitute a ration "for each Laborer on the plantations." This order will be rigidly enforced.

I have heard rumors that on some of the plantations in this Parish, the laborers are charged for their rations and medicines during the time they may happen to be sick, also that some are charged for their rations during stormy weather, when they are unable to work upon the crops, this is clearly in violation of Sec. 12. of Gen. Order No. 23.[1] and must cease. The planter and not the laborer must take the risk of the weather, and he can deduct wages only, for sickness, unless it is clearly "feigned sickness" of which the Provost Marshal must be the judge, see Sec. 13. Gen. Order No. 23.

The practice appears to prevail upon most plantations to give no rations to Children under 12 years of age, the enclosed Order provides that they shall each have one half a ration.

I also learn that laborers have been discharged from plantations without previous notice being given at this Office, Sec. 13 of Gen. Order No. 23 provides that they "will be held to their engagement for the year," if there is any just cause why they should be discharged, it must be decided upon by the Provost Marshal, in accordance with Sec. 7. of the same Order.

It is reported that many planters are charging exhorbitant prices for articles sold to their laborers, Sec. 3 of the enclosed Order regulates the profit upon "articles of Merchandize" so sold, and must be adhered to. An Officer will soon be detailed to inspect your accounts of such sales.

It is with pain that I learn that many laborers are kept constantly in debt to their employers, this is as bad as the Peonage System which prevails in Mexico, and in direct violation of Sec. 12 of Gen. Order No. 23.

The Negro has been down-troden and oppressed long enough, and it is time that he should receive some just reward for his labor, and I trust that you will aid me in accomplishing this just result. I remain very respectfully your Obedient Servant.

PD [*Albert Stearns*]

New Orleans, July 9, 1864.

GENERAL ORDERS No. 92. In accordance with orders from the War Department, establishing the rations of certain persons, it is hereby ordered, in pursuance thereof:

1. That the weekly ration of each laborer on the plantations shall consist of not less than the following amount and variety, viz:

5 Five pounds pork or bacon or
8 Eight pounds beef.
5 Five pounds fresh ground cornmeal.
2 Two pounds flour or soft bread.
1 One pound beans or peas.
9 Nine ounces sugar.
1 One gill vinegar.
1 One gill molasses.
1/2 One half ounce adamantine or star candles.
4 Four ounces soap.
3 Three ounces fine salt.
3 Three pounds of potatoes or other suitable vegetables.

Children under (12) twelve years of age will receive half rations, for which no charge will be made, and the sick shall be furnished with coffee, tea, rice, or other suitable farinaceous diet.

2. Laborers must be invariably paid in United States currency, and the money counted out to the laborer in the presence of an officer, duly authorized by the Provost Marshal of parish in which the parties reside.

3. Employers who sell articles of merchandize to their employees, will not be permitted to charge them more than 10 ten per cent advance on the nett cost of the articles.

4. Any violation of these regulations will be considered a fraud upon the laborer and punished accordingly.

The Parish Provost Marshals are entrusted with the enforcement of this order, and their attention is particularly directed to paragraph

IX General Orders No. 23, [current series][2] in regard to sick and disabled persons, also to paragraph XII of same order, with reference to medical attendance. BY COMMAND OF MAJOR GENERAL BANKS:
PD

Capt. [Albert Stearns] to Sir, [Aug.] 1864, and General Orders No. 92, Headquarters, Department of the Gulf, 9 July 1864, both enclosed in Capt. Jas. M. White to Capt. Stearns, 24 [22] Aug. 1864, Letters Received & Sent, ser. 1519, St. Mary's Parish LA, Provost Marshal Field Organizations, RG 393 Pt. 4 [C-1017]. The blank space in the dateline of the circular appears in the original. The circular was probably printed between August 23 and 25, although portions may have been drafted earlier.

1 For General Order 23, issued by the commander of the Department of the Gulf on February 3, 1864, see above, doc. 109.
2 Brackets in the original; the order is printed above, as doc. 109.

121: Statement of a Louisiana Overseer

[Johnston] & Grisott Plantation
[*Jefferson Parish, La.*] Augt. 30th 1864

This is to certify that on the 9th of Augt. /64 I found Thom Peterson on the above named– Plantation without a pass I therefore arrested him and ordered him to my house where the following named Negros– followed me to my House and demanded the release of Petterson or I should be put to Death Some of them wish to hang me others wished to Cut me to Pieces– Petterson wished to be allow to Preach [when] he advised them to arrest [. . .] and myself and deliver us to Col– Hanks or to the Negro Soldiers at Fort Banks also to Search the House for all the armes the could find which was done Six or Eight that followed Thom Petterson were arrested and Sent to Prison and the [case] reported to Col Brown the Provost Marshal but nothing was ever done.

On the Evening of the 25th Inst 5 of them returned and demanded there discharge I replyed that I had discharged them Some time ago and offered them Papers to that Effect that it was now late, but come in the Morning and the Should have them But as the were not working on this Place I wished to know if the had a Pass to come heare the replyed the had not I then Stated to them that the Should leave this Place within one Houre or I would arrest them in about one Houre I took Mr [. . .] Gun and went Down through the quarters to See if the had left when I reached the Gate I heard tow men talking I Hailed them no answer a Second time and no answer I then Caled to them if the did not answer I would Shoot I then Haled a third time and no answer and then discovered the were Making there Escape I then– raised my Gun to fire but the Gun [. . .] the Second Barrel went of by axcident I then returned to the House loaded the one Baril returned through the quarters to the Sugar Mill where I heard Some Persons talking I hailed them but got no answer I waited a little to See who would come out but no one coming and the Steam Boat coming to the landing I went to the Boat and on my return from the Boat I was fired upon from a corn field not Seeing any one I turned round and fired where I Saw the Corn Shake I returned to the House and while Sitting on the fronet Gallery a Pistol was fired at me the Ball Striking the dore about one foot above my Head and [. . .][1] a number of Shot was fired at me on my left the also Stricking the fronet of the House

HDS James Aiken

Statement of James Aiken, 30 Aug. 1864, Letters Received, ser. 1482, Jefferson Parish LA, Provost Marshal Field Organizations, RG 393 Pt. 4 [C-1022]. The outside wrapper notes only that the statement concerned "negro Preacher Tom Peterson," and no evidence of any action taken in response to Aiken's complaint has been found among the surviving records of the provost marshal of Jefferson Parish.

1 Two illegible words.

122: Order by the Commander of the Department of the Gulf

New Orleans, September 7, 1864.

GENERAL ORDERS NO. 122. The recent strike among Boiler Makers and Machinists, the wages demanded by Mechanics and Laborers being exorbitant and greatly beyond the regulated prices for such labor, and some action being imperatively required in order that public interests may be protected and public work properly prosecuted; it is hereby ordered that, the required number of Mechanics of the various classes be detailed from the enlisted men of this Command for duty in the Quartermaster's Department to be furloughed for the time being, and that the colored persons conscripted under General Orders, No. 106 from these

Headquarters,[1] that are rejected by the examining surgeon as not meeting the standard for recruits for military service, shall be delivered to the Quartermaster's Department as laborers.

Extra pay will be allowed all such, as a matter of public expediency and necessity as follows: – White Mechanics, $30.00 per month; Colored Mechanics of the 2nd and 3rd class of skilled labor $15.00 per month. Colored laborers taken under the order above cited, $20.00 per month with rations and clothing not to exceed $2.50 per month.

In order to carry out the foregoing provisions, Commanding Officers of Regiments in this Department will, immediately upon receipt of this order transmit to the Chief Quartermaster a list of all Mechanics in their respective commands, such list to include Boiler Makers, Carpenters, Bricklayers, Blacksmiths, and all other Miscellaneous Mechanics. Upon receipt of such lists the Chief Quartermaster will make requisition for such men reported on his list as he may need, upon receipt of which immediate orders will be given for their detail and furlough, provided such requisition does not exceed 100 white and 400 colored mechanics.

The Superintendant of recruiting service for colored troops will report daily to the Chief Quartermaster the colored laborers, heretofore referred to, taken from plantations and rejected by the Examining Surgeons. BY COMMAND OF MAJOR GENERAL BANKS

PD

General Orders No. 122, Headquarters, Department of the Gulf, 7 Sept. 1864, General Orders (Printed), ser. 1763, Dept. of the Gulf, RG 393 Pt. 1 [C-1083]. For those black men who were employed as military laborers after being judged physically unfit for service as soldiers, the wages of $20 per month prescribed by General Banks's order compared favorably with those they would have received as plantation laborers ($8 per month for "1st class" hands) or as soldiers ($10 per month). (For the wages of laborers and soldiers, see above, doc. 109, and *Official Records*, ser. 3, vol. 3, pp. 250–52.)

1 General Order 106, issued by General Nathaniel P. Banks, commander of the Department of the Gulf, on August 2, 1864, provided for the conscription of all able-bodied black men between the ages of eighteen and forty. Local provost marshals, furnished with "lists of the employers and the number of men to be taken from each," were to gather the eligible men and forward them to recruiting stations. To enable planters to retain "indispensable" skilled workers, the order permitted them, subject to the "discretion" of the local provost marshal, to exempt one-fifth of their adult male employees from conscription. It also specified that conscripted men who were rejected by the army surgeons as physically unfit for military service would be returned to their employers and that, military circumstances permitting, soldiers re-

cruited from plantations would be temporarily furloughed to assist in the harvest. (*Official Records*, ser. 1, vol. 41, pt. 2, pp. 518–19.) For an example of a conscription order issued in accordance with General Order 106, see *Freedom*, ser. 2: doc. 59.

123: Louisiana Planters to the Union Commander at Baton Rouge, Louisiana

Baton Rouge [*La.*], September 13th, 1864.

Sir, We, the undersigned Planters in the immediate vicinity of Baton Rouge, hereby respectfully petition you to issue an order similar in character to the following, namely, to prohibit ALL persons within the lines *purchasing* or *selling* cotton in smaller quantities than ONE BALE *or its equivalent in Bags*, without a special permit, and if a negro, the additional permit of the planter by whom he is employed. Our object is to prevent as far as possible, irresponsible and dishonest parties from plundering our fields, gin houses, etc.

HLS [*15 signatures*]

John M. Nelson & Co. et al. to the Military Commander of Baton Rouge, 13 Sept. 1864, N-4 1864, Letters Received, ser. 760, Dist. of Baton Rouge & Port Hudson, RG 393 Pt. 2 No. 13 [C-850]. On September 22, General Francis J. Herron, commander of the District of Baton Rouge and Port Hudson, issued an order along the lines suggested by the planters, forbidding "the transfer or sale of cotton in less quantities than a bale or the equivalent in bags" without the permission of the district provost marshal. Herron's order required that persons desiring to make such sales provide "satisfactory evidence of title and reliability," but did not stipulate that black people had to receive the permission of their employers. (General Orders, No. 12, Headquarters Dist. of Baton Rouge and Port Hudson, 22 Sept. 1864, vol. 144/253 DG, p. 38, Orders, ser. 761, Dist. of Baton Rouge & Port Hudson, RG 393 Pt. 2 No. 13 [C-850].)

124: Treasury Department Inspector of Plantations to the Supervising Agent of the Treasury Department 3rd Special Agency

New Orleans, Sept. 22 /64

I desire to call your attention to the Necessity of leasing the Government plantations in this Department, for the Comeing Year, at the earliest moment possible.

The failure of the Present Cotton Crop and the Necessity of

Providing for the future, is more obvious than at any other time, Some of the Lessees intend abandoning the plantations, and others are Sure to do likewise, unless some proceedings are taken to arrest the Calamity, the employees left to their own resources, and the Property exposed to Serious depredation,

I shall immediately, instruct the deputy Inspector, to notify all Lessees, who intend to abandon the estates that No Such proceedings will be permitted, There are many of the Lessees who will be heavy loosers the present year, and are anxious to invest in Sugar, the Comeing year, To enable them to do so. it is Necessary to insure to them the privilege of occupying the plantations the Comeing year, by So doing they will be induced to plant all their present Crop of Cane. Otherwise their interest will Compel them to grind or make sugar of all the Seed Cane, thereby rendering the plantations destitute of Cane Seed, and worthless to future Lessees, except for the uncertain Culture of Corn or Cotton, the loss of which has So far discouraged planters as to cause them to abandon its production, and should the Seed Cane be ground, there will be no possible chance of leasing the plantations the comeing year

I respectfully request therefore that instructions be issued to this department authorising the immediate leasing of all Government plantations on the same terms as of last year, which Considering the high price of plantation Supplies, and ordinary risks to Lessees if the existing rate of wages of Genl Banks order N° 23[1] is to be continued.

The recent Military order Conscripting the able bodied Male laborers[2] has been enforced to the letter on the Government plantations, depriving Lessees of all the valuable laborers, and Creating great distress among the employers, Many Complaints have been made by Lesees of the partiality of the Conscripting officers in the discharge of their duties, whilst nearly all the able men have been taken from their plantations Many private plantations have hardly, been visited,

The plantation of H M Coll, who employs over 100 working hands has lost only 4 hands by Conscription, Some of these planters have letters of Protection from Genl Banks, and Seem to be exempt from the execution of all Military orders, Many hands lately Conscripted as Soldiers have been rejected by the Army Surgeons, and Sent to work on the Government Fortifications, thereby depriving Lessees of all the effective laborers on the plantation, Many of the exempt planters are Known to be rebel sympathizers, and two, Doct Stone, & Mr Randolph, only returned from "Dixie" in May last, Should this State of affairs Continue to exist, there is No prospect of leasing Government Property the Comeing year. and some other plan will be necessary for the Security of the Property. and the maintenence of the Women and children dependent on their management.

I would respectfully request, that their Statements and Complaints be referred to the proper authorities, that some action may be taken, Many acts of injustice without warrant or Necessity have been Committed by the Military, and complaints have been made to officers of the Command or to the Provost Marshals of the respective districts, Satisfaction is Seldom or Never obtained, and the Special protection of Genl Banks appears to be Necessary for our interests

By your instructions, an order was issued by Capt Cozzens[3] on the 31st May, to the Department Inspectors, requesting an estimate of all old Iron, Copper and Brass on plantations, Returns have been made showing about (60) Sixty tons Most of which has been Collected and Can be shipped or Sold, there have been proposals within the past few days for the purchase of the Same, I think it Can be sold on the plantations for Nearly the Same price as in this city, I require a Special order to close the sale.

I will shortly submit my views for your consideration, on the Management and disipline Necessary on Plantations, I regret to Say, I have found a disposition among planters and Lessees generally, to impress the Negro with a Sense of dependence, and to make him More degraded and miserable, if possible, than under the old System of labor

I find Some plantations where they Say they were better off with their old Masters and would be glad of his return, this feeling among them is the result of bad Management and indiscretion on part of Lessees, or the intention of the enemies of Freedom,

I have found in my experience that the Negro is Susceptible of flattery and Kind influence and requires some encouragement and instruction in the principles, of independence, a branch of education rendered more necessary under the present State of affairs than formerly.

I desire to discourage idleness, and induce Lessees to Sacrifice one immortal dollar, for the grand experiment of Free Labor.

I desire to impress you with the Necessity, of immediate Action on the points of this Report, and request your instructions or orders. Respectfully Submitted

ALS H. Stiles

H. Stiles to B. F. Flanders, 22 Sept. 1864, Incoming Correspondence of the Supervising Special Agent (Group C), 3rd Agency, RG 366 [Q-89]. The problems reported by Stiles were addressed on the same day by General Stephen A. Hurlbut, commander of the Department of the Gulf. Hurlbut ordered all sugar plantation owners, lessees, and managers to reserve one-fourth of the cane harvest for seed, reminded planters that all plantation products were subject to a laborer's lien for wages, and forbade the sale of such products until "the just claims of laborers for wages" were met. (*Official Records*, ser. 1, vol. 41, pt. 3, pp. 297–98.)

1 See above, doc. 109.
2 General Order 106, issued by General Nathaniel P. Banks, commander of the Department of the Gulf, on August 2, 1864, which provided for the conscription of all able-bodied black men between the ages of eighteen and forty. (For a summary, see above, doc. 122n.) Although General Order 106 had provided that men who were rejected by the army surgeons as physically unfit for military service would be returned to their employers, Banks's General Order 122 of September 7, 1864, revised that policy, providing instead that such men were to be turned over to the quartermaster's department and put to work as military laborers. (See above, doc. 122.)
3 Captain Samuel W. Cozzens, the Treasury Department's superintendent of plantations in southern Louisiana.

125: Louisiana Planter to the Supervising Agent of the Treasury Department 3rd Special Agency

Bayou Black [*La.*], Nov. 15th 1864.

Dear Sir, Having learned with pleasure that the whole subject of negro labor for this District, has been handed over to you, to reorganise and if possible to reduce to a practical system,[1] I, as an interested party, take the liberty of submitting for your consideration a few suggestions.

As much emphasis has been laid upon the great favors received, and the small compensation returned, by the planter, I propose to show that the negro receives more compensation, than any other class of laborers of like capacity in the country.

First	House rent per year ———————————	$60.
2d	Fuel, ten cords of wood, (I am rather under than over)	30.
3d	Clothing, two suits a year ———————————	30.
4th	Pork, per year ———————————	65.
5th	Meal and other articles of food ———————————	60.
6th	Medical attendance ———————————	10.
7th	1 1/2 acres of land at the expense of the planter which if properly cultivated, will produce 40 Bbls. Corn, worth at present prices	100.
8th	Wages, say $10. per month, for not one in ten will exceed, or even come up to ten months work in a year.	100.
		$455.

Thus, the handsome sum of $455. is paid annually to the negro. In addition to the above, every negro is allowed to keep a poultry yard, and feed invariably from the planter's crib, which, they do, be it said to their everlasting credit, with no stinted hand. Some of my hands have told me that they realize $40. a year from the sale of eggs and poultry.

Now Sir, all of this is given for the lowest order of labor. Search the world for a like compensation for even a higher order of labor, such as mechanics can render, and you will search in vain. To all of this, the planter would willingly submit, if he could receive for his heavy outlay, respectful, obedient and faithful labor.

I think I have said enough to convince you, that increased wages will be a great hardship upon the planter. I am in favor of making it optional with the planter to give a portion of the crop, or wages.

I would suggest that you divide the hands into five classes, beginning at $2. per month and increasing at the rate of $2. per month for each class. Should you think proper to give $12. per month to some hands, then have six classes.

An equitable division of wages cannot be made, with a less number of classes, and the planter is the only one that can correctly classify his hands.

I think well of your own suggestion, that no negro will be permitted to leave his home unless the planter refuses to comply with the rules and regulations fixed upon by yourself.

If increased pay would produce obedience, honesty and faithful labor, I for one would willingly submit to it, but twenty year's experience convinces me that the negro has little, or no ambition to provide for the future. Hence corporal punishment is the only means that will effect it. Two thousand years experience, I may say has devised no other means. Witholding rations, is only an incentive to theft, which the planter has little or no means to guard against. Hence this will, I fear, be ineffectual. The question here may be asked, what is to be done? and if you find it difficult to solve satisfactorily a question that has cost the lives of a million American citizens (to say nothing of foreigners and negros) in the last four years, no one will be very much astonished. Your task is a difficult one, and much is expected from you, hence, if you *partially succeed*, you will be entitled to the lasting gratitude of the planters, now borne do[wn] and struggling with difficulties that require the greatest fortitude to resist. I regret to be obliged in candor to say that, the government of the Provost Marshals has not been satisfactory.

And in place of the Provost government, I would suggest, that a permanent Police, holding their office and receiving their instructions from you, be appointed for each Parish, having their

Head Quarters in the central part of the Parish, and whose duty it shall be to visit the plantations from time to time, for the investigation of all complaints – inflicting such punishments as you may authorize for neglect of duty. And in all extreme cases, reporting to you. They should in order to give weight to their action, be authorized to call on the nearest military power, or the citizens to assist in enforcing their authority. In visiting the plantations, they should go armed, and be authorized to prevent strolling soldiers from going on plantations to interfere, either with the negros or the proprietors.

Much trouble has resulted from negroes being allowed to keep horses and hogs. It is true, that the Regulations of 1864. *prohibits* negroes from keeping either horses or hogs,[2] but unfortunately the Regulations have not been enforced. You justly remarked in our last conversation that the *certainty* of *mild* punishment, would be more *effectual*, than *severity* if uncertain. The difficulty and interruption to the business of the place, attendant upon taking a delinquent before the Provost Marshal, is so great, that the negroes soon learn that the planter prefers to suffer wrong, than to attempt to get redress.

But if it was known that your Police would appear at short intervals to investigate all complain[ts] it appears to me, that the effect would be salutary.

The amount of wages, and the time and manner of paying, have given far less trouble, than the inability to enforce the contracts with a people entirely oblivious of moral obligations resulting from their contract.

If you succeed in enforcing the contracts, the planters will owe you much. Your most obedient servant,

ALS A. M^c^Collam.

A. McCollam to B. F. Flanders, 15 Nov. 1864, Incoming Correspondence of the Supervising Special Agent (Group C), 3rd Agency, RG 366 [Q-77]. No reply has been found in the letters-sent records of the supervising agent.

1 Benjamin F. Flanders, supervising agent of the Treasury Department's 3rd Special Agency, had assumed "the charge and control of freedmen" in the Department of the Gulf on November 1, 1864. In his order transferring control to Flanders, General Stephen A. Hurlbut, the department commander, provided that all military orders respecting the ex-slaves were to remain in effect until modified or revoked by Flanders. (*Official Records*, ser. 1, vol. 41, pt. 4, pp. 293–94.)

2 Regulations issued in February 1864 by the superintendent of plantations in the Treasury Department's 5th Special Agency (which, in late July 1864, became the 3rd Special Agency) forbade laborers on plantations leased out or operated by the U.S. government "to keep any horse, mule, hog, pigs, or

cattle." (See above, doc. 113.) The regulations did not apply to plantations operated by their owners.

126: Treasury Department Inspector of Plantations to the Supervising Agent of the Treasury Department 3rd Special Agency

New Orleans La Nov[r] 16, 1864.

Sir:– As a sample of the way in which rations have been issued by the Commissary at Thibodaux to freedmen, I copy as follows from my memoranda made at the Joseph W. Tucker Place, Hubert Murray, manager.

"The families drawing rations from Govt."

Sarah Williams has two children, husband in the army. fed by Mr Murray, draws rations also from Government. Owns 3 Hogs– 20 Bbls Corn. 80 lbs Cotton in seed, and a dozen chickens.

Lydia & Tamar, draw two rations, gone to Thibodaux with a load of hay on their own account.

Priscilla has three children and draws rations from Govt. for them. Didn't note her circumstances.

Eliza Ann and one child, draws for both. Didn't note her circumstances.

Little Susan and two children. draws for the three. Has hogs, chickens and 80 Bbls Corn.

Lair & Davy, draw for both.

Big Susan and six children, needy, draws for the seven.

Rachel, Nancy and one child needy.

Dinah and two children, has 60 Bbls Corn, 100 lbs cotton in the seed and pigs.

Mary OHanda and two children.

Allen, three children, has 30 Bbls Corn, 3 large hogs– 7 pigs– 150 lbs cotton in the seed, 17 hens.

Huldah.

Elizabeth & three Children, Husband in Govt Employment at Thibodaux.

In explanation of the foregoing it is proper to state that Mr Murray's hands worked for a portion of the crop instead of wages, and this was commuted by allowing them one day in a week, (Saturday). This time they employed in working land for themselves. This accounts for their comparatively large crops of Cotton and Corn.

Mr Murray informed me that he advanced rations and clothing, provided mules for ploughing their land, and allows them to cut hay on their own account and mules & wagons to market it with. Four loads of hay went to Thibodaux in this way last Saturday. Very Respectfully,

ALS Jotham W Horton.

Jotham W. Horton to Hon. B. F. Flanders, 16 Nov. 1864, Incoming Correspondence of the Supervising Special Agent (Group C), 3rd Agency, RG 366 [Q-76]. The same day, in another letter to the supervising agent, Horton reported that rations had been issued from the military commissary at Thibodaux to 241 freedpeople during November: 15 men, 121 women, and 105 children, most of whom resided on "a few plantations within a few miles of Thibodaux." Such rations were to be discontinued, he noted, until he and military authorities completed an investigation of the number and circumstances of the freedpeople who were receiving them. (Jotham W. Horton to Hon. B. F. Flanders, 16 Nov. 1864, Incoming Correspondence of the Supervising Special Agent (Group C), 3rd Agency, RG 366 [Q-76].) No reply to either of Horton's letters has been found among the letters-sent volumes of the 3rd Special Agency.

127: Northern Black Physician to the Supervising Agent of the Treasury Department 3rd Special Agency

New orleans Nov 17 /64

Dear Sir– As I have been over the River and examined the Condition of the Freedmen at the Foundry at Algiers[1] and Returned to report to you on the same day, I failed to see you and as I have called 4 times to see you and can not get to make the Report verbaly I do it by letter– I found the People doing as well as could be expected situated as they are. the most complaint I heard was of not getting Meals regular they tell me that they do not get but two a day Breckfast at 11. A.M. dinner at 6 or 7. P.M. that is too long for Children to wate or old Persons *either* the Cooking is done in the lower Room on the dirt Flower in Pots & Skillits of which they say they have not enough to cook for all & have it redy in due season– the Room will be cold and uncumfortable for winter– I found 2 sick that should be in the Hospittal which the man in charge said he would have done– The above is a correct Report of the Freedmen in Algiers at the Foundry They all seem to want one of our own Collor to have the charge of them and I think so to– I should like to have an Agncy under you a mong my People in the Department of the Gulf– I am confident that a good Collared (man) can do more good a mong my People than any White Man *can*, my People want a *Black man* a mong *them* a *man* who has the good of his *Race* at heart – one that will instruct them a*right* and incourarge them when they do good – a *Man* of *Ideas*, *will*, and *courage* – I think that collored men are the most suitable for taking charge of Government Plantations cultivated by Freedmen Hospitals for Freedmen *&c.* now Sir with thise facts set forth if you think you have any employment for me at a Salery that would justify a man to take hold of the great task you can let me know through the Postoffice – the place and time to have an interview – You will find me or my Wife at 164 Girod St who will tell you where I may be or address me through the Postoffice – Yours Respectfuly

ALS Dr R. I. Cromwell

R. I. Cromwell to Mr. B. F. Flanders, 17 Nov. [18]64, Incoming Correspondence of the Supervising Special Agent (Group C), 3rd Agency, RG 366 [Q-81]. Cromwell, a native of Wisconsin, had come to New Orleans in 1864. During the fall of 1864, after Benjamin F. Flanders, supervising agent of the 3rd Special Agency, assumed control over the employment and general welfare of former slaves in the Department of the Gulf, free blacks in New Orleans sought to participate in the formulation and administration of Treasury Department policies. Shortly after Cromwell wrote to Flanders, James H. Ingraham, a free man of color who was president of the Progressive Union Association, inquired "on behalf of numerous '*Colored Citizens*' " whether Flanders intended "to give employment to *Competent Colored men* In the practical working of The Bureau of Free Labor." (James H. Ingraham to Hon. B. F. Flanders, 30 Nov. 1864, Incoming Correspondence of the Supervising Special Agent [Group C], 3rd Agency, RG 366 [Q-85].) No reply to either Cromwell or Ingraham has been found in the records of the 3rd Special Agency.

1 The Belleville Iron Foundry in Algiers (directly across the Mississippi River from New Orleans) was being used by Union military officials as a refuge for freedpeople who were unable to work.

128: Superintendent of the Bureau of Free Labor, Department of the Gulf, to the Supervising Agent of the Treasury Department 3rd Special Agency

New Orleans, Nov. 22nd *1864.*

Dear Sir: Last nights meeting demonstrates how intensely the Planters of this country hold the notion that *Capital* shall control *labor*. We saw clearly enough that they ignore the fact that labor has claims as weighty as are those of capital, and if we lose sight of this fact especially at this time, when the great future is being moulded, we will commit an error which will be hard to rectify.

The capitalist, who employs labor should understand that there are considerations of justice which are as applicable to the laborer as to him. Labor is as important as capital, if not more so. The fundamental laws of Political Economy establish clearly enough that to ignore the right of the laborer to demand as much for his work as he can possibly receive, would be an injury and an injustice of which no Government should be guilty. I agree with you fully that this subject is so momentous that we must deal with it cautiously. Most of the Planters have a disposition to *grind* the negroes. They want to have "all to say" in the premises; and they want things in the way that suits *them*.

I propose, in justice to the negroes, that you hear the other side of the question – and in a public way, No man knows better than yourself that among the negro population can be found intelligent men who appreciate the claims of the poor laborers. From the statements of some of these men of color, and from others who study the welfare of the negro, I am inclined to think that a meeting of this character should be called. Otherwise we will be accused of being *one sided*.

Your "hits" were good, and well aimed; but let us do the colored man the justice of giving him a voice in a matter about which he has an unquestionable right to speak. Not only are we to take the voice of the colored people themselves into account, but we must bear in mind that the moral sense of the loyal people of this Country will demand at our hands the absolute right of the Freedmen to just as much protection as it is possible for us to give them, not only in regard to their general welfare, but especially in regard to their right to have their *work*, their services, their toil, placed upon the scale of absolute justice, there to be regarded as the equal in every respect, of the capital which now seeks a sweeping and dangerous preeminence.

These hints were in my mind and I throw them out as "a drop in the bucket". I have the honor to be Very Respectfully Your Obdt. Servt.

HLS Thomas W Conway

Thomas W. Conway to Hon. B. F. Flanders, 22 Nov. 1864, Incoming Correspondence of the Supervising Special Agent (Group C), 3rd Agency, RG 366 [Q-71]. The planters' meeting of the previous evening, held in the New Orleans Chamber of Commerce, had appointed a committee "to draw up rules and regulations for the better administration of the plantations of Louisiana, and the management, payment and feeding of the freed laborers," and to propose such changes in the Treasury Department's plantation regulations "as they deemed of vital importance to the agriculture of the State." The committee's report, presented on November 22, asserted that "[t]he whole study, aim and object of the negro laborer now is, how to avoid work, and yet have a claim for wages, rations, clothes, etc." The committee therefore recommended that employers be permitted to punish "insolence, disobedience, improper behavior, or contempt of superiors . . . 'as formerly' "; that workers be compelled to perform "ten hours faithful work" per day, by corporal punishment "in obstinate cases"; and that they be forbidden to keep livestock, or to "*leave the plantation for the purpose of visiting or trading*," without the employer's permission. These proposals, Conway later maintained, "*if approved and enforced . . . would have brought the freedmen again into bondage, in fact, if not in name*," bringing "anarchy to the country, and utter prostration to the planting interests themselves." The planters, Conway believed, had "lost sight of the fact, that though the freedmen are, as a general thing, not learned, they possess sufficient intelligence and good sense, to resolve never again to be reduced to slavery." (Thomas W. Conway, *The Freedmen of Louisiana: Final Report of the Bureau of Free Labor, Department of the Gulf, to Major General E. R. S. Canby, Commanding* [New Orleans, 1865], pp. 7–9.) Benjamin F. Flanders, the supervising agent of the Treasury Department's 3rd Special Agency, did not incorporate the planters' recommendations into his own proposals for revising the treasury regulations; nor is there any evidence that he pursued Conway's suggestion about a meeting at which black people could air their views about plantation labor policy. For Flanders's proposals, see below, doc. 130.

129: Provost Marshal of St. John the Baptist Parish and St. James Parish, Louisiana, to the Provost Marshal General of the Department of the Gulf

Deslondes [*La.*], Dec. 4th 1864.

Col, In reply to the enclosed order requesting information concerning the assessment made by me towards defraying the expenses of the new Levee now in course of construction in this Parish, I would respectfully submit the following. As Gen. Order No –, dated at Head-Quarters, Dept of Gulf, Sept 30th 1864, Office Pro. Marshal Gen'l, did not designate any particular mode of assessment, I assessed a tax, of one half of one per. cent, upon the real estate owners in this Parish (Right Bank) as per. communication dated Nov. 26th 1864, for the following reasons.

1st. Real estate being the basis of all taxation, and all would suffer alike in case of overflow.

2d Any other mode of taxing would be unequal as most of the residents of this Parish, on the Right bank are men of small fortunes who work their estates themselves with the assistance of free negroes, consequently could not furnish laborers or mules but whose real estate is equally benefitted with those in better circumstances.

Another weighty reason is, that the owners of several of the large plantations on the Right Bank, would not, through prejudice to hiring *Contraband Labor*, as they call it, cultivate, but let their Plantations to poor whites. This is the case with Mr. V. B. Marmillion, who I understand is the Author of a petition, to the Maj. Gen. Com'd'g, praying that the assessment of said tax may be suspended for the present.

He had no laborers that I could obtain, and I am credibly informed when I ordered mules and dump carts to be seized in order to facilitate the work, he divided his mules among the poor whites and I could only obtain three after a peremptory order. His real estate is equally benefitted with others, and his conduct patterned after by those less opulent, he being at present the largest land owner within the Parish on the Right Bank.

Another reason, why I assessed a tax on the real estate, is that the laborers with few exceptions have been working for one-fourteenth (1/14) of the crop, which having proved a failure, are left with nothing to obtain the many little comforts sought after by them, and have gladly accepted this work with the prospect of a little ready money which I have promised them. Without this tax they would have been compelled to remain on their employers hands earning nothing until Dec. 31st 1864.

The owners of real estate in the rear of this Levee are poor, and the value of their real estate unimproved as per. assessment of 1861. is $7.900, which if sold would not bring sufficient to pay for the Levee if made by contract.

The amount of taxable real estate on the Right Bank of this Parish is $854,960. a tax of one half of one per. cent would give $4274.80 from which must be deducted the tax on the Whitehead Estate held by Gov^{t} which is $450. also a tax on the Estates of Dr. A. G. Wiendahl and M. B. Hydel, who are with Gov^{t} assistance building large Levees on their estates, which in the aggregate amounts to $825 leaving the sum of $3449.80 from which must be deducted certainly the odd hundreds, as amounts of unpaid taxes from various causes which will leave $3000, which will not be sufficient to pay laborers, Engineers, teams and many other incidental expenses. A very significant fact is observable that the poorest class upon whom the burden of taxation falls with equal severity have come forward and in several instances paid their assessment, with expressions of gratitude that the Government have taken upon itself to construct a New Levee at this, the most difficult and dangerous point on the river in this State (owing to the swampy character of the soil) and are constructing a substantial levee for their protection

Trusting that the above will meet your approval, and that the order suspending the collection of the assessment will be immediately removed that the many obligations for which I am responsible may be cancelled I am Col with much respect Your Ob[t] Serv[t]

ALS Geo J. Darling,

Capt. Geo. J. Darling to Col. Harai Robinson, 4 Dec. 1864, Papers Relating to Levees, ser. 1882, Provost Marshal, Dept. of the Gulf, RG 393 Pt. 1 [C-1071]. The order said to have been enclosed is not in the file, and neither it nor any of the other issuances from the provost marshal general referred to by Captain Darling has been found among the surviving records of that office. The provost marshal general had been in charge of "[t]he repair, extension and preservation of the Levees" in the Department of the Gulf since at least January 1864, with authority to make assessments on estates adjoining the levees and to require proprietors to furnish "such labor as may be equitable and practicable" for making repairs. The unnumbered "general order" of September 30, 1864, was probably a circular of that date by the provost marshal general, Colonel Harai Robinson, which, according to his own summary, empowered local provost marshals to supervise levee repairs in their respective jurisdictions. (General Orders, No. 7, Headquarters, Department of the Gulf, 21 Jan. 1864, General Orders [Printed], ser. 1763, Dept. of the Gulf, RG 393 Pt. 1 [C-1075]; Col. [Harai Robinson] to Major General S. A. Hurlbut, 1 Jan. 1865, Papers Relating to Levees, ser. 1882, Provost Marshal, Dept. of the Gulf, RG 393 Pt. 1 [C-1069].) The day following Darling's letter, Thomas P. May, a Louisiana unionist who held an appointment with the Treasury Department, wrote Robinson in support of Darling, warning that unless the assessments for St. John the Baptist Parish were collected, "the work will stop & that whole region [be] inundated." Like Darling, May accused V. B. Marmillion of having "gotten up" the petition that led to suspension of assessments, adding that the planter was "an infernal rebel & would like very much to see things go to the d---l." (T. P. May to Col., 5 Dec. 1864, Papers Relating to Levees, ser. 1882, Provost Marshal, Dept. of the Gulf, RG 393 Pt. 1 [C-1071].) The petition purportedly originated by Marmillion has not been found among the letters received by the headquarters of the Department of the Gulf or by the provost marshal general.

130: Supervising Agent of the Treasury Department 3rd Special Agency to the Secretary of the Treasury

New Orleans, December 8th 1864

Sir, Since the charge of the Freedmen within the limits of this Agency devolved upon me, I have devoted to the subject of their proper management, the most serious attention and careful study, and have come to the conclusion that the Regulations of July 29th,

1864, respecting Freedmen,[1] are inadequate for the purpose for which they were designed; and that other provisions are necessary, both to the welfare of the Freedmen, and to secure the co-operation of the Planters in the employment of the Freedmen.

Cotton has always been considered a very unsafe crop in lower Louisiana which is the only portion of the State within the lines of Union military occupation; But stimulated by the high price of Cotton, and by the large profits obtained by the few who tried it successfully in 1863, our Planters were induced to embark the past year in its culture with free labor as regulated by the orders of General Banks,[2] of which they had greater distrust even, then of the crop. The crop turned out a disasterous failure, and, *in the opinion of the Planters* the labor regulations of General Banks have proved equally so.

Through neglect for two years past, the Sugar Cane has to a great extent, run out; and it would require at least two years of effort, under the most favorable circumstances, to bring the Sugar culture up to its former remunerative standard.

While the planters have attained to the conviction that the abolition of slavery is an accomplished fact; not one of them is converted to the belief that free labor, can adequately replace the old System.

Therefore it is to be feared that the planters will discontinue the cultivation of their Estates, & that the entire management and support of the Freedmen in this Department, (about Eighty thousand in number) will consequently be thrown upon the Government, This will be the result if the wages of the freedmen are fixed too high, or the regulations or measures adopted for the supervision of the laborers are insufficient to meet the views of the planters. – On the other hand, if the wages are fixed so low that the freedman can only pay for his food and clothing such as he has been accustomed to; and if the restrictions placed upon him, leave him no more liberty or privileges than he had under a master, he will be apt to avail himself of the only advantage which he knows that emancipation has given him – the power to be idle.

The case therefore requires the most delicate and judicious handling.

That the matter may be placed before you in the clearest lights in every particular, I have induced Mr S. M. Swenson and Hon Thos. H. Duval, gentlemen of high character, great intelligence and experience, and liberal views, and who have assisted me in devising plans and rules for the Government of the freedmen, to proceed to Washington to explain the subject minutely; and I sincerely hope that the views entertained by me, may be so elucidated as to meet with your approval.

The plan upon which it is proposed to conduct the labor system, and the care of the indigent freedmen, is as follows.
1st To establish a Bureau of freedmen in the city of New Orleans, with a general superintendent thereof, with the necessary clerks for the proper accountability, and the general transaction of all its branches. With this office will be also connected a Depot in or near this city, to take immediate charge of refugees and transient persons, to aid them in obtaining employment &c &c.
2nd – To appoint assistant Superintendents for each Parish, or such District as can be properly attended to, – these assistants to be bonded and sworn officers,: and their duties will be to guard the freedmen from all impositions and frauds that might be practised on them by their employers; to aid the freedmen in obtaining employment under voluntary agreements; to supervise the entering into such agreements, and explain their terms and binding effects, which will stipulate the term of service (not to exceed one year,). the wages agreed upon, (including rations); the time of labor each day, and other duties,: they are also to be charged with the supervision and assistance in making Indentures of apprenticeship; To visit each plantation as often as once a month; and to inspect the Quarters, Hospitals, Schools, Rations &c, and to hear complaints and settle disputes; to impose fines, and distribute rewards, to act as ~~magistrate~~ arbitrators between the employer and employees, under a set of rules which has been elaborated for the government. of freedmen, and their employers, and to which I invite your attention. They shall also be required to take a census immediately of all the freedmen within their respective districts, showing the name, age, sex, birthplace, color, status of Parents, health, occupation, mental and moral character, religion, marital condition and education; the number attending day and Sunday Schools; births, deaths and marriages, and the productions within their district. This census will afford the means of determining hereafter the physical, mental and moral progress of the freedmen. The assistants will also be enjoined to aid the freedmen in all matters in which they are incompetent to act for themselves; to encourage industry, sobriety, economy & morality; and to hold them to a strict observance of their duties under the agreement and rules referred to.

The general plan was submitted to the Planters of Louisiana, at a meeting in this city, and they unanimously agreed that the system would be satisfactory, and that they believed it would redound to the benifit of all interested in the agricultural prosperity in this State. At this meeting I also suggested, that in order to relieve the Government of the expense of Superintendents, a contribution of one dollar a year should be assessed upon each employer for each laborer employed by them under agreement, and also upon each laborer. To this proposal they also readily agreed, as they anticipated much benifit from the aid in the governance of the freedmen, who unfortunately do not generally, understand, that all classes, whatever their condition, are subject to law and good order. But with the aid of the Superintendents, who are especially charged with the guardianship of their rights and privileges, as well as their duties, it is hoped that they will be more readily governed, and thus promote mutual satisfaction and Kindly feelings between the employer and the laborers.

3[d] – To establish Home Colonies in accordance with Section II and IX of the Regulations; for these Colonies, I propose to reserve several abandoned estates, and to assign to each a Superintendent, who shall also report to the general Superintendent, and receive instructions through him, – for this purpose a plan has been elaborated in all its details (a copy of which is herewith enclosed) for your perusal and approval.

I propose also to establish a System of premiums and rewards, for good conduct and efficiency among the freedmen, to be bestowed upon the most deserving, both on the Colonies and in the Parishes, and to assign colored men on the Colonies to the management of the Farm, Garden and Workhouse, whenever such can be found properly qualified, or can be made such by experience.

In respect to the labor Colonies contemplated in Reg Sec XI, I deem it premature to establish them at present, as the tenure by which the abandoned Estates are now held by the Government is incomplete, and almost all these abandoned Estates are encumbered with mortgages; to satisfy which may involve the sale of the Estates under foreclosure.

I have thus briefly stated the outline of the plan I proposed for inauguration here: for the particulars thereof, as well as the departures from the Regulations of the Treasury Department deemed necessary, I beg to refer you to the bearers of this whom I recommend as worthy of your confidence and kind consideration. I have the honor to be Very Respectfully Your obt Servt

ALS Benj. F. Flanders

Benj. F. Flanders to Hon. Wm. Pitt Fessenden, 8 Dec. 1864, F-134 1865, Letters Received by the Division, ser. 315, Division of Captured Property, Claims, & Land, RG 56 [X-104]. The plan for establishing "Home Colonies," said to have been enclosed, is not in the file. On the meeting between Flanders and Louisiana planters, held on November 21, 1864, see above, doc. 128. Unaware of decisions taken by his superiors in the Treasury Department, Flanders was operating under the erroneous belief that he, as supervising agent of the department's 3rd Special Agency (roughly coterminous with the military Department of the Gulf), had charge of freedpeople within the agency. Congress had indeed adopted legislation that charged the Treasury Department with responsibility for the welfare of former slaves within Union lines, and William P. Fessenden, Secretary of the Treasury, had, on July 29, 1864, issued regulations pertaining to freedpeople and plantation labor. (See above, doc. 119.) Soon thereafter, however, Fessenden had been persuaded not to supersede existing military arrangements until the end of the 1864 crop year, and he had therefore suspended the regulations. (See below, doc. 222B.) Unaware that Fessenden had postponed the department's assumption of control, Flanders assumed that the regulations were in force. Consequently, he had requested and, on October 28, 1864, received an order from the commander of the Department of Gulf (who shared his misconceptions regarding the treasury regulations) transferring control over the former slaves from the military authorities to Flanders. (*Official Records*, ser. 1, vol. 41, pt. 4, pp. 293–94.) Finally, on November 26, 1864, in response to a letter from Flanders questioning certain provisions of the regulations, the Treasury Department enlightened the misinformed supervising agent, explaining that the department was not in charge. Flanders had not yet received that letter when he devised his "plans and rules for the Government of the freedmen," submitted them to the planters' meeting, outlined them in his letter of December 8 to Fessenden, and forwarded them to Washington at the hands of Swenson and Duval. When at last he learned the true state of affairs, Flanders "confess[ed] that in the matter of the Freedmen, I have been under wrong impressions, and have acted somewhat too hastily." Fortunately, he assured Fessenden, he had as yet made no changes in the preexisting military arrangements, and he therefore expected "[n]o difficulty or embarrassment . . . in the Continuance of Military Control in the matter." (Benj. F. Flanders to Hon. W. P. Fessenden, 12 Dec. 1864, F 135 1865, Letters Received by the Division, ser. 315, Division of Captured Property, Claims, & Land, RG 56 [X-105].)

1 The regulations, which concerned the leasing of abandoned plantations and employment of freedpeople, had been drafted by William P. Mellen, general agent of the Treasury Department's special agencies, and issued in the name of the Secretary of the Treasury. (See above, doc. 119.)
2 General Order 23, issued by General Nathaniel P. Banks, commander of the Department of the Gulf, on February 3, 1864. (See above, doc. 109.)

131: Provost Marshal at Morganzia, Louisiana, to the Commander of U.S. Forces at Morganzia

Morganza La Dec 9th /64

General I have the honor to most respectfully call your attention to the following facts

The Steamer Starlight arrived here this morning at 1.30. bringing under charge of Lt W. B. Stickney A.A.Q.M Bureau Free

Labor–Sixty one (61) Males and five (5) females all colored. to commence a work requiring some 500 Strong Men

They were collected by him under Special order No 133 H[d] Qrs Dp't Gulf Prov Marshal Generals Office to take from the various depots for "Freedmen" all able bodied Laborers to be employed on the Levee at Morganza.

The parties brought range in age from Fourteen to Seventy two years & of the entire party not Ten can be classed as able bodied Laborers, nor are there over Twenty who are in any way fit to do any work.

Some of them state that they were taken from their sick beds and one is helpless from a shot wound received a short time since. In fact the entire party are worthless for the use for which *they* were collected.

and it is an outrage upon humanity and Confidence of these people to retain them at this place, where so little can be done for their Comfort.

Requesting information in regard to the disposition I shall make of them I am Sir Very Respectfully Your Obedent Servant

HLS Alex D Bailie

[*Endorsement*] Head Quarters, Dept. of the Gulf New Orleans Dec 12" 1864 Respectfully referred to Rev. T. W. Conway, Sup't. of the Bureau of Free Labor for report By command of Major Gen'l Hurlbut: C. S Sargent. 1 Lieut 2 La Vols & A.A.A.G.

[*Endorsement*] [*New Orleans, December 12 or 13, 1864*] Respectfully returned to Dept. H[d] Qrs. On the 4th inst I was ordered to report to the Provost Marshal Gen[l] Dept. of the Gulf, the number of Freedmen in my charge who were able to work. I reported from my Returns, 363 persons, 108 men and 255 women. This number I was ordered to hold subject to the order of the Provost Marshal Gen[l] On the 5th inst I reported 132 wood choppers employed near Baton Rouge by the Quarter Masters Dept and had permission to have them taken instead of the women, excepting a few who could be taken as cooks. Lt. W. B. Stickney. A.A.Q.M. was ordered on the 6th inst. to proceed and take "all able bodied laborers from the various Depots for Freedmen to be employed on the *Levee* at *Morganza*" The officers in charge of these persons were ordered beforehand to have them in readiness. On the arrival of the Steamer to convey them, but few could be found, and such as were taken, were to be taken good care of, as was promised by the Provost Marshal, Gen[ls] Dept. Lt. Stickney reports that instead of having made any preparation for the comfort of the number ordered (363) who, it was expected were to be employed two months on the Levee, it was found that nothing had been done no tents or cabins, or any other means of shelter were in readiness excepting an old Flat Boat in the river. It is further reported by Lt. Stickney that the Pro. Marshal wanted him to remain with the boat till he built a cabin for them. It could hardly be expected that so peremptory a demand for these people, coupled with an expressed necessity for immediate supply of such laborers as could be had including even women – could be carried out without finding some too old or infirm for the service required, *but, if the Provost Marshal had made appropriate preparations there need have been no suffering and those unfit for the service could have been returned.* Thomas. W. Conway Supt. Bureau of Free Labor Dept Gulf.

Capt. Alex D. Bailie to Genl. D. Ullman, 9 Dec. 1864, B-1594 1864, Letters Received, ser. 1756, Dept. of the Gulf, RG 393 Pt. 1 {C-559}. An earlier endorsement by General Daniel Ullmann, military commander at Morganzia, had referred Captain Bailie's letter to the headquarters of the Department of the Gulf, and a final endorsement forwarded it to Colonel Harai Robinson, provost marshal general of the department, who, in a penciled notation, directed a subordinate to have Bailie "send those [freedpeople] unfit to work to Mr Conway." Bailie and other military officials had been attempting for weeks to muster a force of black laborers to repair the levees in Pointe Coupée Parish, especially the Grand Levee near Morganzia. On November 5, 1864, General Hurlbut had ordered that every planter in the parish whose plantation fronted the Mississippi River "shall at once report to the Provost Marshal at Morganzia, all able bodied hands on his place, to work on the levees." (Special Orders, No. 300, Head Quarters Department of the Gulf, 5 Nov. 1864, vol. 31 DG, pp. 39–46, Special Orders, ser. 1767, Dept. of the Gulf, RG 393 Pt. 1 {C-559}.) That order having failed to raise the necessary force, Union officers turned to other measures. On December 11 and 12, upon the order of Colonel Robinson, military officials undertook a massive impressment of ex-slave and free-black men in Baton Rouge to work on the levee at Morganzia. (See doc. 132, immediately below.) But as of January 1, 1865, the number of laborers was still inadequate to the task. The superintendent of levees at Morganzia reported that only 240 were regularly at work; another 36 were "on the sick list," 16 had "gone astray," and still others were "without shoes and not fit to work." The women among them, he complained, were "good for nothing . . . too lazy to cook or do anything." Colonel Robinson agreed that it had been "almost impossible to procure laborers"; moreover, little progress was being made by those who were at work. Black laborers, Robinson opined, "cannot make more than one or two cubic yards per day, while an Irish navvy will make from eight to ten." Arguing that failure to repair the Grand Levee would have grave consequences, he urged that if it were deemed "a military necessity to have these repairs made . . . a sweeping conscription of some 3000 negroes must be adopted at once"; alternatively, "let the work be done by contract, and by white labor." By mid-January Captain Bailie's force had dwindled still further, to 215: "171 Working men and boys, 15 Women cooks. 29 Sick." Several of the workers had "eluded the Guard and gone astray," a dozen had died, and "about twenty [had] become worthless" and were "sent back to the post from which they were taken." (F. T. Rotthaas to J. W. R. Bayley, 1 Jan. 1865, Papers Relating to Levees, ser. 1882, Provost Marshal, Dept. of the Gulf, RG 393 Pt. 1 [C-1068]; Col. [Harai Robinson] to Major General S. A. Hurlbut, 1 Jan. 1865, Papers Relating to Levees, ser. 1882, Provost Marshal, Dept. of the Gulf, RG 393 Pt. 1 [C-1069]; Capt. Alex D. Bailie to Colonel H. Robinson, 16 Jan. 1865, vol. 391/959 DG, p. 20, Letters Sent by the Provost Marshal, ser. 1408, Morganzia LA, Provost Marshal Field Organizations, RG 393 Pt. 4 [C-944].)

132: Louisiana Free Men of Color to the Commander of the Department of the Gulf; and Provost Marshal of Baton Rouge, Louisiana, to the Headquarters of the District of Baton Rouge

[*Baton Rouge, La. December 1864*]

The undersigned free colored citizens of Baton Rouge, whose status has been well ascertained, and defined long before the breaking out of the present rebellion, beg leave to call your attention to the grievances to which we have been lately subjected, and ask for relief in the premises– We would premise by saying that we are loyal to the Government of the United States, and that many of us are property holders and tax-payers, who have been liberally educated, & that our position in the social scale has always been respected– Such being the case we respectfully claim not to be placed on an equality with contrabands– But from the scenes lately enacted in this place, we have been treated as if we belonged to the lowest and most degraded class– Our places of business, & our private residences have been forcibly entered, and many of us, as well as those in our employment have been forcibly dragged from home & business, & incarcerated in the old ruin of the Penetentiary at this place, herded up with a set of contrabands from all parts of the country, exposed to disease & the inclemency of the weather, our business neglected & our families suffering during our forced absence– We beg leave respectfully to say that this is not in accordance with the benign intentions of the Government towards the colored population, which were intended to ameliorate, instead of degrading that class– We are aware that we owe fealty to the Government that protects us, and that fealty we are ever ready & willing to render to that Government. But at the same time we claim to be treated as freemen, and contend that we should be exempt from the rule which tends to place us on a level with contrabands, or those who have heretofore been slaves. We trust therefore, that for the future where orders are issued for the impressment of laborers on public works, that a distinction will be made between persons of our status & the class above alluded to; at least that we shall be treated as freeman. We claim it as an act of justice, and pledge ourselves as freemen that whenever stands in need of our services to defend the cause of the Union & Liberty, they will ever find us ready to respond to the call Resptly submitted

HDS [*51 signatures*]

Baton Rouge, La., Jany 2nd *1865*

Major In obedience to the order of the General Comdg Dis'ct of Baton Rouge of this date endorsed on the petition of certain free colored citizens of Baton Rouge La., I have the honor to submit this report.

On the 10th day of Dec 1864 I received a telegram from Colonel Harai Robinson, Pro Marshal General Dept of the Gulf, a copy of which is enclosed marked ("A".

I considered the order urgent and imperative & immediately sent orders to the commanding Officers of the several Patrol Districts of the City, of which a copy is submitted marked "B."

The work of impressment was begun simultaneously in all parts of the City on the morning of Dec 11th 1864.

The Negroes as fast as they were taken up were placed in a vacant wing of the Penitentiary: this place was selected as it combined security and comfort.

An Officer was detailed to take charge of them, – rations were drawn &c &c.

This officer was instructed to receive all Negroes brought by the Guards until he had at least one hundred and twenty five (125.) He was then to consider exemptions and reduce the number to (100) one hundred as called for by the order of the Pro. Mar. General.

By the 12" Dec. 1864, the work was completed and the negroes ready for shipment – they were not ordered away for several days. I suppose nearly or quite (200) Two hundred passed through the hands of the Officer in charge before they were finally sent away.

The question of physical disability was the main point considered in making exemptions. The Negroes were sent to Morganzia & I am informed are now at work there on the Levees.

I do not consider any one responsible for the manner in which this order of impressment was executed but myself. It was carried out with as great a regard for humanity as was consistent with what was supposed to be imperative necessity. I am at a loss to know how the signers of the petition could have been greatly injured by the execution of the order and still be in Baton Rouge with the power of petition. The question of loyalty was not considered in determining who should perform a duty imposed upon all who live upon the banks of the lower Mississippi – white and black – bond and free – Neither is it evident that those who have always been free, own property &c. are necessarily more loyal than those who have once been slaves. This petition is the first indication that I have seen that there exists in this community a class of persons who claim exemption not only from the duties imposed upon them by just laws and Military Authority, but from those made imperative by the physical conformation of the country and the providence of God. I am with great respect Your Obedient Servant

ALS Geo E Smith

S. W. Ringgold et al. to the Generals Commanding the District and Department of the Gulf, [Dec. 1864], and Capt. Geo. E. Smith to Major Geo. W. Durgin, Jr., 2 Jan. 1865, both filed as S-1 1865, Letters Received, ser. 760, Dist. of Baton Rouge & Port Hudson, RG 393 Pt. 2 No. 13 [C-852]. Endorsements. The signers of the petition appear all to have been men, each of whom signed his own name. The date of the first endorsement on the undated petition indicates that the protest was drawn up before December 26, 1864. Both enclosures cited by Captain Smith are in the same file: Enclosure "A," the telegram of December 10 from Colonel Harai Robinson, ordered Smith immediately to impress 100 "able-bodied Negroes . . . and hold them in readiness so they can be sent to Morganzia at a moments notice" to repair the levee. Enclosure "B," Smith's Order 25 (also dated December 10), directed his subordinate officers "to impress all able-bodied male Negroes within their respective districts" (excepting officers' servants and employees of the quartermaster's department) and convey them under guard to the penitentiary. Many of the signers of the petition had joined in an earlier protest against the forcible induction of free-black men into Union military service in the same manner as former slaves. "The evil we complain of," they had written (in November 1863), "is, that we are hunted up in the streets, in the market house, and other places whilst engaged in our daily avocations, and marched off to the Penetentiary, where we are placed with contrabands, and forced into the service." Insisting that "we were born free, have lived free, and wish to be treated as freemen," they had asked to be subject to the procedures for registration and draft that applied to loyal white men. (*Freedom*, ser. 2: doc. 57.)

133: Louisiana Freedmen to the Superintendent of Plantations in the Treasury Department 3rd Special Agency

Terrebonne [*Parish, La.*], January 8th 1865.

Honorable Sir, We the undersigned Colored People residing on Wood lawn Plantation ask your honorable attention to our humble appeal that you will please give us the opportunity of working the Place among ourselves and you confer a great blessing and favor upon us. We are willing to make any arrangements for the interest of ourselves and the Government. Yours most respectfully

HLcSr ("S'gned") [*28 signatures*]

Charles Harris et al. to Honorable Captain Stiles, 8 Jan. 1865, vol. 72, p. 244, Reports of Inspectors of Plantations, 3rd Agency, RG 366 [Q-126]. The twenty-eight names listed on this copy of the petition are all those of men; beneath them appears the phrase, "and many others." The petition evidently received a favorable hearing; in April 1865, a Treasury Department inspector of plantations reported that twelve "companies" of freedpeople were at work on Woodlawn plantation, "eight of which are doing very well, as far as work is concerned but are suffering for want of supplies." At the beginning of 1865, similar "companies" of former slaves were permitted independent occupation of other plantations in Terrebonne and the adjoining parish of Lafourche. Another treasury inspector reported in January that freedpeople on several Lafourche plantations, having worked for white lessees in 1864, now evinced "a great desire to cultivate the land on their own account, and without exception they promise diligence, good order, obedience to regulations, and the faithful care and return of the property entrusted to them." Accordingly, he granted "permits for the occupation & cultivation of the land" to freedpeople on three estates, though he acknowledged that "want of Stock, and the limited means of the laborers for purchasing the same, will doubtless prove a serious obstacle to their success." By late April, an inspector who had visited all the plantations in the two parishes that were being worked independently by former slaves, was able to "certify, that taking into consideration their limited means in stock and supplies . . . they are well advanced with their work." He recommended, however, that a "Freedmen Aid Association" assist particular "companies" by providing cotton seed and draft animals. (G. P. Davis to Capt. H. Stiles, 21 Jan. 1865, and C. L. Dunbar to Capt. H. Stiles, 26 Apr. 1865, vol. 72, pp. 217–24, 235, Reports of Inspectors of Plantations, 3rd Agency, RG 366 [Q-126].) For a still later report on the plantations occupied by freedpeople in Lafourche and Terrebonne, see below, doc. 144.

134: Permit from the Superintendent of Plantations and the Supervising Agent of the Treasury Department 3rd Special Agency to a Louisiana Free Man of Color

[*New Orleans, La.*] January 13th [*186*]5

Jack Jerinan. F.M.C. ex-manager of the Robert Tucker Plantation, in the Parish of Lafourche, is hereby authorized to take charge of the Robert Tucker Plantation, in the Parish of Lafourche for one year, from the 13th day of January 1865 to the 1st day of January

1866. The said Jack Jerino shall take proper care of all property entrusted to his care, and of the fences and buildings thereon. In Consideration of which, he shall have the use of one hundred acres of land for Cultivation, he shall receipt to the agent of this Dept for all impliments or tools rec^d from government Agent, an order for which, is issued with this permit, he shall Comply with all orders, & regulations regarding labour, that may be issued from this Office. The following named persons constitute a portion of the employees, together with such others as he will deem necessary.

Robert Tucker
Allec Scip
Sipio Singellary
Mon Singellary
Morgan Fuller
Ben Jackson.
Israel [. . .]
Martin Benedict
Robert Singellary
Marc Frasor
Jacob Young
Levy Anderson.
Jerry Redd
John Webb.
David Buttler
Dotson Robertson
Wm Decato
David Ross
Petter Field
Allison
Robert Allen
Richard Tollerable
Erren Hunt.

H. Stiles
HDpS — Benj. F Flanders

Permit by H. Stiles and Benj. F. Flanders, 13 Jan. [186]5, vol. 123, pp. 303–5, Outgoing Correspondence of the Plantation Bureau, 3rd Agency, RG 366 [Q-100]. On May 25, 1865, a Treasury Department inspector of plantations found only twenty laborers at work on the "Bob Tucker" plantation under the direction of "Jacques Jeriman." They were cultivating a total of 110 acres: 70 in corn ("good" condition) and 40 in cotton ("all but 5 acres poor and in need of Cultivation.") (See below, doc. 144.)

135: Testimony by the Superintendent of the Bureau of Free Labor, Department of the Gulf, before the Smith-Brady Commission

New Orleans, January 28" *1865.*

Thomas W. Conway, being duly sworn, testified as follows:

"I have no rank military, – have been in the service as chaplain & came to this Dept. in that capacity. I was first assigned to duty in connection with the freedmen, by Order dated 11"th of Feb. 1864, & entered upon my duty as soon as I could reach this place. When I first reported, I was ordered to report to the Supt.; my Order did not state that I was Asst. Supt. although I assisted the Supt. & registered the names of freedmen in the Dept. & was assigned to that special duty. I was appointed Supt. on the 15th of August 1864. I have nothing to do with the leasing of plantations.

My duties are the observance & carrying out the labor regulations established by the Dept. Comndrs for the freedmen; – to see that the benefits prescribed to freedmen by these Orders, are secured to them, – that they are not abused or defrauded out of their wages, or denied the benefits to which they are entitled under that & other Orders;[1] also, to receive all contrabands coming into the city from any points of our military lines & to provide for them; also, to receive any vagrants who may be picked up here or in any town or city within our lines & to provide for them, – giving them proper care while they are in my hands & securing for them employment & wages. I have only met a few who are not willing or cannot hire out, who are generally old persons & whom I send to one of our home colonies, somewhat in the nature of a penal colony, where they are kept & obliged to do what they can. I also attend to the matter of passes given to freedmen from the city to points out of it, – to any point within our lines, – under certain restrictions prescribed by the military authorities.

I have hardly known for three months, whether I am under Treasury or Military Regulations, for the reason that the special agent of the Treasury stated, in answer to an inquiry from Gen. Hurlburt, that he was ready to take charge of the freedmen, which charge was transferred to him, excepting certain duties belonging to the present year as established by the military authorities, which were to be performed by me under those authorities.[2] The extent to which these duties were to go, was not specified, but the military retain control of winding up the affairs of the year, – such as securing the payt. of wages on the plantations. It was the intention to only conclude these obligations, but practically it has been found that Gen. Hurlburt intended the Treasury to take charge of those who are unemployed, – which has been partly done.

My system in reference to finding employment for negroes who have come in from beyond the lines to my office, or who have been brought in by military guard, has been to send them to the employment depot at Algiers. When applications were made by planters or Qr. Mstrs., I first ascertained whether they were worthy of taking charge of these persons. If I considered them so, I gave an Order to the Supt. of the depot to have laborers hired out to them, if the terms were suitable, – the parties making a selection in the depot. A man cannot however be separated from his family & the party hiring must take family & all, – a practice which has been always observed. The prices were fixed by the military authorities & also have been fixed by the Treasury Dept., – but are not the same. The prices that I have been claiming, are, – to a first class laborer, eight dollars a month, everything found, – the rations being specified. The classification of laborers has been generally determined between the Prov. Mrshls. & the planters, – the gage having been, – the ability of a man. That classification is not made until they get to the plantations, although it could be before, if the employer saw fit. There might have been some collusion between these parties & the system of classification is open to that objection as it might lead to that; still I think it is very improbable that such collusion did occur. There are four classes of laborers, who receive three, four, six & eight dolls. per month, respectively. I say that I consider any collusion improbable, – for the reason that the classification is one of those things which appears unimportant as compared with other matters wherein collusion would be more probable, – such as in relation to the final & monthly statement. It has been the custom to let a man know his classification grade & men hired were not, to my knowledge, compelled to go with any person, as I directed the consultation of a laborer & the decision to be made by *him* as to whether or no he would go with a particular individual, but if any appeared to wish to remain idle upon our hands I compelled them to work for wages, with parties whom I knew to be suitable or to go upon our home farm & there work without wages. In such a case as the latter, the whole family were sent & were there taken care of: if they were helpless, they were taken care of, but if able to work, those who could so were permitted to go & work for wages, while the vagrant, – the head of the family, – would be taken alone to the farm. There are very few, if any instances of that kind. As a class, I find them ready to work, but not ready to be hired out. They object to being hired out to the old slave holders, – very generally. The majority of the plantations are worked by the old owners, but the abandoned plantations are generally worked by new men. There *was* not formerly any objection among the negroes to being hired out to this last class, although there is *now*, – arising from the fact that the freedmen are treated worse by them, if anything, than by their old employers, – for the reason that many of these new men are imprincipled & came down here with a little money, not intending to settle in the country, but merely to enhance their fortunes by a year's operation & to do so regardless of the laborers, their own dignity & behavior.

The Prov. Mrshls. have jurisdiction over their own parishes & I know that they are in the habit of visiting all the plantations & making inquiries into the treatment of the laborers & the general behavior of the employers. When they find anything done not in accordance with the contract, they sometimes report the evils & have, by Order issued, the power to correct them. It would seem that they should, in order to make my bureau complete, report those inspections to me & allow me to judge in regard to correction, – which has not been done, as a general rule. I have frequent communications with the Provost Marshals, – & receive reports of abuses &c from them through the P.M.G., though my bureau is not under him, but under the direct Orders of the Comndg Gen.

The giving of bonds by planters has not been practiced in order to secure faithful performance of their obligations, although the Treasury agent required, – in the lease of an abonded plantations, – a bond covering the payt. of the laborers & the rent of the plantation. If a man is owner of a plantation which has not been abandoned, no bonds are required. We establish a lien however upon the produce, which works better than the giving of bonds would. That is done under the provisions of the military labor Order issued in last February – Gen. Order No. 23, – under Gen. Banks. There was also a supplementary Order issued by Gen. Hurlburt, the intentions of which was to enlarge the provisions established by his predecessor & to suit existing circumstances; – the failure of the crop.[3] On account of this failure, there was so little produce out of which to realize anything that there was danger that the laborers would not be paid for their work, & hence increased restrictions were rendered necessary, that their pay should come out of what was derived from their services. I have only known one case where neither the crop or the lessee could be held for payt., – that is where the crops amounted to nothing & the lessee had no means belonging to him, which we could command. That is the only instance which I know of, where laborers have been obliged to go without their pay.

Planters living on their own plantations are not allowed to make their own bargains with their own negroes, independent of our military regulations. I control all laborers on plantations within the

Dept. of the Gulf, – or rather I control their treatment. Planters have to enter into some contract to pay their negroes. I require returns of the ages & wages of every laborer, by which means I know the exact condition of each one as far as wages are concerned, – which does not include house servants who, – both here & elsewhere, – have never been considered as coming under the regulations. None of them ever come under my care, – nothing but refugees from outside the lines & the broken down remnants of the old slave system upon the plantations. We do not interfere with planters who have hired servants who formerly belonged to them or worked upon an adjoining plantation, but simply require a record of the fact from the employer. If the wages given on such occasions do not come up to the requirements of the Dept. Order, I direct an alteration, – through the Prov. Mrshll, – which I have done to quite an extent.

Where a man is selected from an employment depot, who has a family, I require that the family be taken also. We require that these families have quarters suitable to them, – though not always a house; – still we do not allow two families to be put in one room, – nor would that be tolerated by themselves. Employers are obliged to furnish rations to the children of such a family without charge, while all members of the family are supposed to work, – all over eleven years of age, – & are classified under the same heads as the remainder of the freedmen. The employer enters into an agreement to care of them, in addition to the amount he pays to the head of the family & is allowed to get what work from them that he can, – but not without charge.

I have received the pay due to those freedmen who have been conscripted, – an order having been issued that all pay due them up to the time of conscription, be collected if not paid to them at the time. I circulated blanks, through the P.M's., to these planters, requiring the name of the conscript & the time of commencing work, the months of work, & the wages per month, the date of conscription & the amount due him at the time of conscription.[4] I have about ten thousand dollars of that money on my hands. Gen. Hurlburt issued an Order to the Comndr's of colored troops in whose regts. these conscripts were serving, to return the names of them to me, so that I could forward this money to them. I have also been compelled to enforce this lien, in some cases, upon produce in order to secure means to pay the laborers, – which I have done by stating the case to the Comndg. Gen, who issues an Order directing the seizure of the produce, or the party receiving it, to pay into my hands enough to pay the laborers. Some negroes on the plantations have been deserted by people leasing them, – with their pay in arrears. – That was generally done after the sale of the products & sometimes at the time of the sale. I have only had one case where I was too late to get hold of these products, though I am satisfied that the parties intended to avoid their obligations, in many cases.

Our home plantation is worked directly by govt. So far as raising of crops is concerned, we should have raised one very good crop upon it, – had it not been destroyed by the worms, – which would nearly have reimbursed the govt. for all its expenses. We had one other place for a home depot which we kept as a sort of poor house.

As to the cost of this system to the govt., Gen. Hurlburt's Order required me to give such returns as would ascertain this fact, but as the office had not been organized at the beginning of the year & expenses were incurred without keeping a proper record, until I took charge, it is not possible to say exactly.

In regard to distributing this money which I have received for conscripts, I find two columns in the returns of Regtl. Comdrs; – one of which contains the old names of the freedmen & the other, those by which they enlisted. By Ascertaining from what plantations they are, – I am able, in nearly every case, to determine the individual, – as I also find the plantion, employer & parish from which he comes. It has lately become a practice among the freedmen to assume two names & probably two thirds of them are enrolled in my office, in that manner. Under the old system they have but one, – the majority of them. When enlisted or conscripted, they are always put down with two names & any one who has not had two names before, generally takes one then or is given one by the enlisting officer, – generally taken that of his father, if he had two names or that of his mother if she had. Sometimes they take the name of their employer or where they don't like that, assume a new one.

In regard to the term of the negroes service, there has been some conflict of powers. The leases made by the govt. agents here, extended from the first of January to the first of Jan., while Gen. Banks order issued in February, established the labor year as extending from the first of Feb. to the first of Feb. We have so far remedied this as to enable the next year to commence on the first of Feb. We have made no agreements for the coming year. In cases where the lease of a plantation only extends to the first of Jan., Gen. Hurlburt instructed me to allow the labor obligation to expire providing the laborers would remain until the first of Feb. & would not be driven off until that time, when new arrangements could be made for the year, under new leases from the Treasury Dept. In case of a planter whose lease expired on the first of Jan. & who didn't wish to re-lease his plantation, he could not be held for the support of the negroes until the first of Feb., We simply insist that the negroes shall, in such a case, remain on the place. Where a person has re-leased his plantation, we hold him up to his obligation, until the first of February. I am informed that almost all of the plantations have been leased for the present year, though some have not. The new contracts have never been given us. We allow matters to go on under the old contract, until a new one can be procured by the party, if he chooses to employ the negroes & they, in turn, choose to stay.

The classification & rates of labor have never been changed, though the last Treasury Regltns, require a change.[5] I do not think that the allowing a negro a certain pay & his supporting himself, – I don't believe it is going to work. Under the regulations, a third class female laborer receives but ten dollars a month & is compelled to support herself & her children also: half of her wages are to be reserved, – thus compelling her to pay current expenses out of five dollars a month which she cannot do & must resort to stealing in order to live.

The monthly ration prescribed to the negro amounts to about seven dollars a month, – not more than that.

Considering these people as absolutely requiring a certain amount of guardianship, I consider the Treasury Regltns. open to objection. Considering the improvident character of the race, provisions should only be issued them for a short time, – not longer than for a week's supply. I have never been consulted as to my general views upon these subjects or upon the particular one of which I have just spoken, but have only had short discussions relative to particular points.

As to sources from which I have derived funds to carry on my operations, – we had the Corp D'Afrique fund, realized, I think, by the sale of certain cotton captured from the enemy & retained here for the purpose of managing the freedmen & paying the expenses of their treatment, which was the original object of the fund. Since that fund was exhausted, the proceeds realized from the product of the home farm, have been turned over to a special agent who has used that partly (& it amounted in the whole to some ten thousand dollars) in pay[t] of expenses. Another source of revenue, is from the P.M.G's. office. I make no disbursements myself, though I sometimes draw money from the planters, for incidental expenses & furnish vouchers. There are daily expenses on account of the home plantation & the employment depot, the wants of both of which are presented to me; I fill the list of purchases to be made & take bills to Mr. Flanders who draws his check & pays them, on vouchers I take to him. I don't become responsible for any money. The negroes at the home farm have usually ben fed by the Commissary out of govt. supplies. I know of but instance in which Mr. Flanders has paid for rations. Although the freedmen are under the control of regulations of the Treasury Dept., they are still fed by the Military Dept. & regulated by the latter. The military Regltns. have never been suspended & are now the only ones in force here. I do not think that the Treasury Dept. has sought to take the control of the freedmen, out of the hands of the military. Mr. Flanders has never appeared to exhibit the amount of interest & energy in the cause that it requires, & although I have written him very often in regard to the details & necessities of the freedmen, I cannot say that, I have ever had one single answer to my letters. I have frequently seen my letters upon his desk & the inattention given to the matter has been a great source of embarassment, although there is no greater necessity existing in the country than the adoption of measures for the support of these people & the furnishing them with employment. I have received no aid whatever from Mr. Flanders or from any agent of the Treasury under his Orders, in the efforts which I have made in the cause of the freedmen, but my aid has been received principally from Gen. Hurlburt who has met all the necessities of the case, in a very active way. I should recommend the continued superintendence of the military over this cause, for the coming year, for the reason that their machinery is in full operation & can, with proper diligence, be made much more effective than it has been during the past year; any change must embarass us to such a degree as to throw the country into chaos. I would therefore say, – let the old system continue, – at least the main features of it, – & attempt no radical change at this particular time. It is essential both to the interest of the planter & the negro, that contracts should be made as soon as possible & the old one can be renewed much more easily than to attempt to carry into force, new Regulations.

. . . .

HD

Excerpts from testimony of Thomas W. Conway, 28 Jan. 1865, Testimony Received by the Commission, ser. 736, Smith-Brady Commission, RG 94 [AA-1]. In the remainder of his testimony, Conway described the charges made against his predecessor, Colonel George H. Hanks, chiefly that of accepting bribes from planters in return for furnishing them with laborers. He also suggested that the Smith-Brady Commission (which was investigating corrupt practices in Union-occupied parts of the lower Mississippi Valley) look into allegations that both Benjamin F. Flanders, supervising agent of the Treasury Department's 3rd Special Agency, and Hilas Stiles, superintendent of plantations in the special agency, were themselves involved in operating plantations. For Stiles's testimony before the commission, see doc. 136, immediately below.

1 The principal military order governing plantation labor in the Department of the Gulf during 1864 was General Order 23, issued by General Nathaniel P. Banks on February 3, 1864. (See above, doc. 109.)
2 See above, doc. 130n., for a description of the circumstances that, between late October 1864 and mid-January 1865, created confusion about whether military orders or treasury regulations were in force. For the order by General Stephen A. Hurlbut, commander of the Department of the Gulf, that transferred control over freedpeople to Benjamin F. Flanders, the supervising agent of the Treasury Department's 3rd Special Agency, on November 1, 1864, see above, doc. 125n. In fact, however, the Treasury Department had not intended that Flanders assume control, and the military system remained in operation until February 1, 1865.
3 General Order 138, issued by General Stephen A. Hurlbut on September 22, 1864, announced that all plantation products were subject to a laborer's lien for wages, and it forbade the sale of such products until "the just claims of laborers for wages" were met. (*Official Records*, ser. 1, vol. 41, pt. 3, pp. 297–98.)
4 The procedures for collecting wages owed to black men who had been conscripted from plantations were set forth in a circular dated August 16, 1864, issued by Conway with the approval of General Nathaniel P. Banks, then commander of the Department of the Gulf. (Chaplain Thomas W. Conway to Sir, 16 Aug. 1864, Letters Received, ser. 1845, Provost Marshal, Dept. of the Gulf, RG 393 Pt. 1 [C-731].)
5 Plantation regulations issued by the Treasury Department on July 29, 1864 (but suspended almost immediately thereafter), set the wages of laborers according to age and sex, in contrast to General Banks's order, which based them upon a laborer's ability to work, apparently without regard to sex. The treasury rules provided for higher monthly wages than did the military orders, but required that one-half be withheld until the end of the year and that laborers purchase their food and clothing out of the portion received monthly. (See above, doc. 119.)

136: Testimony by the Superintendent of Plantations in the Treasury Department 3rd Special Agency before the Smith-Brady Commission

New Orleans, February 3" *1865.*

H. Styles, being duly sworn, testified as follows:

I am Superintendent of Plantations & received that appointment from Mr. Flanders. I believe that appointment to be within his control as Special Agent of the Treasury Dept. I think my commission dates from the 1st of November 1864. I have been a permanent resident of New Orleans since about 1839 or /40. I am not a planter but have resided in the country, – put up machinery, sugar mills &c for the planters. I was interested in a plantation, –

last year, – for the first time. I have an interest in it now: it is Dr. Wardhal's plantation, who resides on it, & I lease it from him. It is not in the possession of the govt. in any way, – it is thirty five or six miles up the river.

My duties, as Superintendent, are, – to have general supervision of the department, employ the subordinate officers who belonged to it & to lease out the plantations. Fifty one or two are already leased. Part of these plantations have been seized as abandoned & part have been turned over by the military authorities.

. . . .

The new regulations with reference to freedmen, are not yet published but soon will be.[1] It will only require a short time to put them into operation. They propose to made a change in regard to wages of the negroes, – giving twenty five dollars a month to the first class, – twenty to the second & eighteen to the third class, – the women being classified lower. Rations are not furnished them but are charged to them & the planter is obliged to see that they have rations, – to furnish supplies & sell them to the negroes at cost. Speaking from my knowledge of the negro & planting, I think the proper mode would be to give them a share of the crop. I think that the plan of selling them their provisions, – if done equitably & honestly, – is advantageous to both parties, for the reason that under the regulations of last year they were fed on many plantations, whether they worked or not, – even if they lost through indolence, two or three days out of the week, but where they have to purchase provisions & only get their half wages every month, they must labor in order to live. I do not favor this plan of payment of half wages as I do not consider it sufficiently provides for the case of a man who has a family to support, & Mr. Flanders is of the same opinion, but Mr. Mellen says that if they don't get enough wages they must get enough in some other way. The planter has redress in case a negro is indolent, as he may pay him off & discharge them, – bringing the case before the Superintendent of Plantations under Mr. Conway. He [a planter][2] cannot discharge a man without the permission of some government officer & must have some proof of charges against the party. It rests with some government officer to say that a man shall or shall not be discharged & although injustice is no doubt done on both sides, I think that the planter is sufficiently protected

I could not tell what was the gross amount of my receipts from the rents of plantations, last year, without reference: the income was quite small, – ten or twelve thousand dollars.

. . . .

I can make no estimate as to what may be received from the rent of plantations this year. I can estimate pretty closely on sugar, but cotton is very uncertain, – as uncertain in LaFourche district as here. The cotton crops are more certain above Baton Rouge, – which is true of both sides of the river.

The negro is not necessitated to buy all his rations as each one is entitled to an acre of ground. I think that their rations will amount to about two dollars a week or nine dollars a month. He has twelve dollars & a half paid him monthly, – thus leaving him three dollars a month over & above the cost of rations, out of which he must clothe himself, buy his tobacco & support his family. Mr. Mellen provides for the support of the helpless children & sick, by requiring the planter to support them, – for doing which he is paid by government: that is, I suppose the expense is to be deducted when he comes to settle for his rent. On account of this provision, the negro may live on his wages, – for if he has more of a family than he can support, he may say that they are helpless, in which case they must be supported.

. . . .

I think that the regulations of Mr. Mellen, so far as labor is concerned, will apply as well & as much to plantations hired from private parties as to those leased by me. I think it is a little "heavy" to saddle the government with those children who may be declared helpless & do not think that the negro is entitled to more consideration in the way of wages than a white laborer whose children are not taken care of. I cannot see the wisdom of legislating on this question of labor, though I think that in the present condition of affairs, some legislation is necessary for the negro. I think that the negro is capable of taking care of himself to the extent of making his own purchases. If there was any Court of Justice in which he could apply a law by which he could recover, I believe he could follow up an employer who didn't pay. I also think that the negroes are capable of conducting plantations. I do not think that negroes would decline to work at important seasons or would leave one plantation, – at such times, – to hire out on another. It is the general impression of the men of most experience, – whom I know throughout the State – that if the labor system was set aside & legislation on that subject prevented so as to let every negro hire himself at the best wages he could procure, all would go on & be attended with a great deal better success than we are achieving under this system of coercion. The United States has been at great expense in providing for the support of these negroes. On year before last, I think that two hundred thousand dollars ($200,000) were received for rents, from confiscated & seized property & it has not taken a good portion of that to keep up the offices necessary to get it. The rents for plantations amounted, – in

1863, – amounted to ten or twelve thousand dollars, but in 1864 they amounted to nearly two hundred thousand dollars. In regard to the system I would devise to regulate labor in this State & to regulate the relations between the planter & the negro, – I would first establish a regular time for labor, – say ten hours a day, – as making a day's work, which would prevent the coercion of the laborers. Then I would let each one look out for himself, – first establishing courts in every parish as near as might be necessary, – either a Justice of the Peace or Provost Marshal's Court to which complaints might be referred. I would permit the men to hire themselves for the month or year & then if a planter became dissatisfied because labor was not performed, – give him the power of discharging such workman, – upon proper proof. I would have the planter comply with his obligations in regard to payment for labor & in short place the negro upon a level with a white men. The courts would of course be necessarily such as did not involve much expense. You have no idea of the disposition which the negroes manifest to be located. It is almost impossible to drive them from their homes. If a negro can be free he prefers to remain where he was born & has lived & with reference to the contrabands, it is only a question between their love of liberty & love of locality. Some law should of course be made to prevent vagabondism, but as a general thing our laboring class is as much, if not more, disposed to labor than the same class at the North. In this State there is field enough for labor if all who wished could become owners of land, but the great misfortune is that there is no way of dividing up the large estates, – to run which requires a great deal of capital. If we had plantations of two hundred & fifty or three hundred acres, there would be plenty who would pitch in & create a call for labor. The most intelligent man of whom I know, – Judge Baker, – says that we don't want any legislation on the subject of labor.

HD

Testimony of H. Styles [Stiles] before the Smith-Brady Commission, 3 Feb. 1865, Testimony Received by the Commission, ser. 736, Smith-Brady Commission, RG 94 [AA-2]. In the omitted portions, the superintendent of plantations, Hilas Stiles, further discussed his official duties, the procedures for leasing plantations, and his own involvement, with Benjamin F. Flanders, supervising agent of the Treasury Department's 3rd Special Agency, in operating a leased plantation.

1 The "new regulations" were those of the Treasury Department, drafted by William P. Mellen, general agent of the department's special agencies, and originally issued in July 1864, only to be suspended until February 1865,

when an amended version was issued. (See above, doc. 119, and below, doc. 137.)
2 Brackets in manuscript.

137: General Agent of the Treasury Department Special Agencies to the Secretary of the Treasury, Enclosing an Order by the Commander of the Military Division of West Mississippi

New Orleans, February 6th *1865*

Sir: I arrived here on the 20th ult, and since then have been diligently engaged with Maj. Gen. Canby in preparing such a system for the employment and welfare of freedmen in his Military Division as would, so far as possible make them self-supporting, and tend to their general improvement, and also facilitate and encourage planting. Supervising Special Agents Orme and Flanders, have co-operated with me. Admiral Lee happened here opportunely, and has cordially joined in our consultations.

We have conferred as fully as possible with the especial friends of Freedmen here, also with as many of those proposing to lease abandoned and confiscable plantations, and resident owners proposing to work their own plantations as could be seen from Memphis to this place.

Enclosed herewith please find the local rules and military and naval orders, which have been made, so as to harmonize as far as possible the various opinions and interests. The local rules I submit for your approval.

The success of the system will depend very much upon the good judgment, fidelity and practical business capacity of Agents and Superintendents, the just and considerate conduct of planters towards those employed by them, but even more upon the proper co-operation of Military Commanders. Lacking this, no system can be made successful in the present condition of the Country.

Gen. Canby has conferred with me in a spirit of frank sincerity, and has discussed the whole subject fully and fairly. His personal convictions are against all planting and trading at the present time. But these he yields to the desire of the Government, and promises his best efforts to carry out its policy in such manner as in his judgment will best insure success.

You will see that the system contemplates the employment of freedmen by their former owners whose plantations are in such interior localities as may be within the range of Military or Naval supervision and control" provided that such owners come in and register their plantations agreeing to pay their hands, and perform all the requirements of the regulations[1] &c.

I was very desirous that Genl. Canby should himself designate the lines of occupation, along and near the Mississippi and other Rivers as embracing all plantations of persons who should register and cultivate them under the regulations so long as they should observe all Military orders, maintain peace and good order in their neighborhoods, and observe good faith towards the Government. This he was unwilling to do, preferring to leave that subject, and also the extent of military protection to local commanders. I regret his decision in these particulars, as it leaves what I regard as the important points in the system, to the discretion of officers entertaining different views and subject to changes and uncertainty prejudicial the interests involved. Still I shall go on and do the best I can with department and District Commanders.

You will observe that the order of Gen Canby turns the Freedmen over to your care. I have declined to assume any control over them, or to have any liability incurred on their account by the Supervising Special Agents until you direct it to be done after full report as to their condition and the prospect of employment without danger of having your arrangements frustrated by Military orders. I have consented however that the superintendent heretofore acting under military orders may adopt the regulations and local rules as the bases of his action, and continue to perform his duties, under military orders, but in pursuance of those regulations. By so doing the contracts with them, the leases and registrations for the current year will all be made in compliance with the regulations, so that when you assume charge of them, you have only to put in your own machinery to work out the system so begun.

I hope to get the order of Genl. Hurlbut, commanding this Department, tomorrow. If so I shall start up the river at once. I am very Respectfully Your Obt Servt

HLS — Wm P. Mellen

[*Enclosure*] *New Orleans, La., February 1st*, 1865.

GENERAL ORDERS, No. 13.

The foregoing regulations of the Treasury Department, in relation to leased and registered plantations and the care and support of freedmen in the valley of the Mississippi, are published for general information,[2] and the following rules will be observed in carrying out the policy of the Government in relation to these interests:

1. The plantations to be leased, or registered under Articles 1 and

3, of these regulations,[3] will be limited to the banks of the Mississippi River, such of its tributaries and other communications as are under our control, and to such interior localities as may be within the range of military or naval supervision and control.

2. The limits of military occupation, under the orders of Department Commanders, will be so far extended as to include any colonies, plantations, farms or other industrial occupations that may be established, leased, registered, or otherwise authorized in accordance with the provisions of Articles 1 and 3 of the aforesaid regulations.

3. In the establishment of colonies or in leasing plantations, upon which freedmen are or may be employed, care will be taken that they are not so distant from the military posts that are or may hereafter be established as to expose the freedmen, so employed, to the danger of being carried off, and again reduced to a state of slavery.

4. The troops to be employed, in the protection of plantations, will be posted in strong positions for the protection of districts and not of isolated plantations or individual interests. The points, so occupied, will be selected by Department or District Commanders, and will be so fortified and armed as to be able to resist an assault and hold out until relieved.

5. Such protection will be given to these interests as may be consistently with the general prosecution of military action, but it will at all times be held subordinate to the necessity of employing troops for offensive military operations, and the troops, so employed, with the exception of such as may have been raised for this special service, will be regarded as in the field and held in the state of preparation directed by existing orders. Whenever it may become necessary to withdraw any of the troops so employed, care will be taken to bring the negroes to a place of security within the new lines, and to give to the lessees such protection, in removing their property, as may be necessary and practicable.

6. Owners or lessees of plantations or the parties engaged in other pursuits, under the authority of the aforesaid regulations, will be required to construct stockades or such other temporary defences as may be necessary to secure their laborers, stock and other property from the danger of being carried off or destroyed by small raiding parties of the enemy.

7. The hospital, post, and other taxes, heretofore levied by military authority upon the products of leased or registered plantations, cultivated in accordance with the provisions of Articles 1 and 3, of the aforesaid regulations, are abolished, it being understood that a moiety of the sums realized from the products

delivered, under the provisions of Article 5,[4] are to be turned over to the military authorities of the District, in which the plantations are located, in lieu of the said taxes.

8. Freedmen, employed on leased plantations or other industrial pursuits, duly authorized under the foregoing regulations, will not be taken from their employment except by voluntary enlistment or by draft, ordered by the Commander of the Division or the Commander of a Department, nor will they be impressed for labor without the authority of a Department Commander except under some immediate and pressing necessity.

9. The horses, mules and other stock, and the provisions and other supplies, intended and necessary for the cultivation of leased plantations, home colonies or other duly authorized pursuits, will not be subject to seizure or impressment except in case of immediate necessity and under such rules as may be established by Department Commanders.

10. Commanders of Districts will act in concert with the Treasury Agents in regulating the quantity and character of supplies to be allowed, and will determine the manner and route by which they are to be sent in, and products brought out. Supplies and products so "permitted" will not be subject to seizure or detention except for manifest fraud in character, quantity or destination.

11. As the care and support of freedmen is devolved upon the Treasury Department, by the law of July 2d, 1864,[5] all persons of that class, now under the control of the army except such as are in the military service by enlistment, contract or hire, and all unemployed freedmen, who may hereafter be found, at or in the vicinity of any military posts within the insurrectionary districts, will be turned over to the proper Agent of the Treasury Department. Commanders of Departments will give the necessary orders for these transfers but will previously arrange with the Supervising Special Agents the term of transfer so as to avoid any embarrassment to either branch of the service. Proper directions will also be given for the disposition of any public funds or property connected with these establishments and for the fulfilment of any contract or obligations that have been entered into under military authority. Officers or Agents of the Army, now on duty in connection with establishments of freedmen, will be relieved and returned to their proper duties as soon as they can be replaced by the Agents appointed by the Treasury Department.

Department and District Commanders will establish such supplementary regulations as may be necessary to carry out fully, the objects and intentions of the aforesaid regulations of the Treasury Department and of this order, and will give to the Officers and

Agents of that Department, any facilities and assistance that may be needed in the performance of their duties.

BY ORDER OF MAJOR GENERAL E. R. S. CANBY:

PD

Wm. P. Mellen to Hon. Wm. P. Fessenden, 6 Feb. 1865, enclosing General Orders, No. 13, Headquarters, Military Division of West Mississippi, 1 Feb. 1865, M-760 1865, Letters Received by the Division, ser. 315, Division of Captured Property, Claims, & Land, RG 56 [X-109]. Other enclosures, including copies of the July 1864 treasury regulations (see above, doc. 119) and Mellen's "Local Rules." Besides specifying new terms for leasing and registering plantations (described below, in notes 3 and 4), the "Local Rules" provided that a portion of the crop share paid to the government might be used to compensate a lessee or owner for losses caused by Confederate raids or for the expense of supporting "helpless freed persons" on his plantation. Lessees and owners were warned that permits to purchase and transport supplies were subject to suspension if Confederate forces threatened. The "Local Rules" also revised the plantation labor system outlined in the July regulations. Whereas those regulations had required laborers to purchase their own food, the new rules allowed lessees or owners, at the request of their employees, to "furnish them with board at an agreed monthly price." Other revisions clarified contractual obligations and established procedures for their enforcement. The new rules also required plantation lessees to "work the land awarded to them under their own supervision, or that of substitutes" approved by the local treasury agent, and they ordered employers to keep an itemized account with each laborer, open to examination by treasury officials.

1 The regulations, written by the supervising agent, William P. Mellen, had been issued in the name of the Secretary of the Treasury on July 29, 1864, but, in response to protest from military authorities, had shortly thereafter been suspended until the conclusion of the 1864 crop year. (See above, doc. 119, and below, doc. 222B.)

2 Part of a printed compilation, this copy of General Order 13 is preceded by the Treasury Department regulations of July 29, 1864, which were being reissued in the department's 1st, 2nd, and 3rd special agencies (roughly coterminous with Union-occupied portions of Arkansas, Mississippi, Louisiana, Tennessee, and northern Alabama), and by William P. Mellen's "Local Rules . . . Concerning the Employment of Freedmen, Etc.," issued February 1, 1865, which amended the earlier regulations.

3 Article 1 of the "Local Rules" provided that "[a]bandoned and confiscable plantations, within the lines of national military occupation . . . may be leased to loyal persons by the proper Agents of the Treasury Department"; article 3 provided that "well disposed persons" who were living on plantations that were not abandoned or confiscable, and who agreed to abide by treasury regulations for employing freedpeople, could register their estates with treasury officials.

4 Article 5 of the "Local Rules" required that, in consideration of "the protection and privileges conferred by the Government," plantation lessees turn over to the Treasury Department not less than one-eighth of the crops produced, and plantation owners not less than one-tenth – except for those lessees and owners engaged in sugar planting, who were to pay a share of "not less than one-thirtieth . . . in addition to the cane left for seed."

5 The law charged officials of the Treasury Department's special agencies with providing for "the employment and general welfare" of ex-slaves in the Union-occupied South. (*Statutes at Large*, vol. 13, pp. 375–78.)

138: Order by the Commander of the Department of the Gulf

New Orleans, March 11th, 1865

GENERAL ORDERS No. 23.

The Regulations heretofore published by Mr. W. P. MELLEN, General Agent, Treasury Department, in relation to Freedmen and labor, not having been recognized by the Secretary of the Treasury,[1] the following orders are prescribed for the hiring and government of laborers within the State of Louisiana.

HOME COLONIES.

1. The Home Colonies, already established by Orders from these Headquarters, are hereby continued under said Orders.

SUPERINTENDENCY.

2. Mr. THOMAS W. CONWAY, as Superintendent, with such Assistants as he may designate, will be obeyed and respected by all persons in the discharge of their respective duties.

REGISTRY OF PLANTATIONS.

3. The system of Registry of Plantations, as prescribed in Mr. Mellen's Regulations and the Military Orders in relation thereto,[2] will continue and be in force as therein required.

HIRE AND COMPENSATION OF LABORERS.

4. Voluntary contracts heretofore made between Planters and Laborers, or which hereafter may be made, will be submitted to the Superintendent of Freedmen, and if found by him to be fair and honest to the laborers, will be by him confirmed and approved, and stand as the contract of the parties thereto for the present year. But all such contracts must secure support, maintenance, clothing and medical attendance to the laborer.

5. The following schedule will be observed in all other cases, as the Rule required by the Government.

In addition to just treatment, wholesome rations, comfortable clothing, quarters, fuel, and medical attendance, and the opportunity for instruction of children, the Planter shall pay to the Laborer as follows:

Male Hands – First Class, $10 per month.
Second Class, $8 per month.
Third Class, $6 per month.
Female hands – First Class, $8 per month.
Second Class, $6 per month.
Third Class, $5 per month.
Boys under 14, $3 per month.
Girls under 14, $2 per month.

These classes will be determined by merit and on agreement between the Planter and the Laborers.

6. Engineers, Foremen and Mechanics will be allowed to make their own contracts, but will always receive not less than $5 per month additional to first-class rates.

7. One half of the money wages due will be paid quarterly as follows: On the 1st days of May, August and November, and final payment of the entire amount then due on or before the 31st day of January.

PENALTIES.

8. Wages for the time lost will be deducted in case of sickness; and both wages and rations where the sickness is feigned for purposes of idleness; and in cases of feigned sickness, or refusal to work according to contract, when able so to do, such offender will be reported by the Provost Marshal to the Superintendent, and put upon forced labor on public works, without pay.

The Laborers must understand that it is their own interest to do their work faithfully, and that the Government, while it will protect and sustain them against ill treatment, cannot support those who are capable of earning an honest living by industry.

9. Laborers will be allowed and encouraged to choose their own employers, but when they have once selected, they must fulfil their contract for the year, and will not be permitted to leave their place of employment (except in cases where they are permitted so to do for just reasons, by the authority of the Superintendent), and if they do so leave without cause and permission, they will forfeit all wages earned to the time of abandonment and be otherwise punished as the nature of the case may require.

10. Planters and their agents will be held to rigid accountability for their conduct toward the Laborers, and any cruelty, inhumanity or neglect of duty, will be summarily punished.

TIME OF LABOR AND PERQUISITES OF LABORERS.

11. The time of labor shall be ten hours, between daylight and dark in Summer, and nine hours in Winter, of each day, except Saturday and Sunday.

The afternoon of Saturday and the whole of Sunday shall be at the disposal of the Laborer.

On Sugar Estates, at the proper season, the hands will take their regular watches, the night work of which and the Saturday afternoons and Sundays, if positively necessary, shall be paid for as extra work.

Laborers will be allowed land for private cultivation at the following rates:

1st and 2d Class hands, with families, one acre each.
1st and 2d Class hands, without families, one-half acre each.
2d and 3d Class hands, with families, one half acre each.
2d and 3d Class hands, without families, one-quarter acre each.

On these allotments they will be allowed to raise such crops as they may choose for their own use and benefit, but will not be permitted to raise or keep animals except domestic poultry.

POLL TAX.

12. For the purpose of reimbursing to the United States, some portion of the expenses of this system, and of supporting the aged, infirm and helpless, the following tax will be collected in lieu of all other claim under these Regulations:

From each Planter, for every hand employed by him between the ages of 18 and 50, Two Dollars per annum.

From each hand between the same ages, One Dollar per annum.

This sum will be payable and be collected on the 1st day of June next, and will be paid over to the Superintendent of Freedmen, for disbursement.

Measures will be taken to collect the same Poll Tax from all colored persons not on plantations, so that the active labor of this race may contribute to the support of their own helpless and disabled.

GENERAL DUTIES.

13. Provost Marshals in the several Parishes, are charged with the general supervision and welfare of the laborers, reporting on these subjects frequently to Mr. T. W. Conway, Superintendent, and will use all possible exertion by themselves and their deputies, to see that industry and good order are promoted, and that the contracts under these orders are faithfully performed by both parties. Orders heretofore issued and published so far as they are not changed or modified by this order, will remain in force.

14. This order shall be deemed and taken to have effect from the 1st day of February last, and all contracts entered into in relation to the labors of the present year will be held to be controlled amended and governed by the terms and conditions of this order.

LIEN AND SECURITY FOR LABOR.

15. All crops and property on any plantation where laborers are employed will be held to be covered by a lien against all other creditors to the extent of the wages due employees, and such lien

will follow such crops or property in any and all hands until such labor is fully paid and satisfied. BY COMMAND OF MAJOR GENERAL HURLBUT:
PD

General Orders No. 23, Headquarters Department of the Gulf, 11 Mar. 1865, Orders & Circulars, ser. 44, RG 94 [DD-51]. General Hurlbut's order also formed the basis for an order, issued on March 23, 1865, by the commander of the Department of the Mississippi, that governed plantation labor in that jurisdiction (the Mississippi counties and Louisiana parishes in the cotton-growing region north of the Red River). (See below, doc. 222Bn.)

1 For the Treasury Department regulations, originally issued in July 1864 but shortly thereafter suspended until February 1865, when they were reissued in amended form, see above, docs. 119 and 137. On the refusal of the Secretary of the Treasury to recognize the regulations, see below, doc. 222B.
2 For the army and treasury policies respecting registration of plantations, see above, doc. 137.

139: New Orleans Free People of Color to the Commander of the Department of the Gulf, and the Latter's Reply

New Orleans March 21st 1865

General At a mass meeting of the colored Citizens of New-Orleans, held at the Economy Hall on Friday March 17th 1865. The following resolutions, were passed unanimously. And the undersigned were appointed to forward a copy of the resolutions to you, for your consideration.

Resolutions

Whereas: The labor system established by Maj. General Banks – which does not pratically differ from slavery, except by the interdiction from selling and whipping to death, the laborers. were only intended by its promoter to be a temporary one.

Whereas: Some enlargement of the liberties of the laborers was contemplated to gradually take place, and were really to be introduced unless Emancipation be a by-word. and the boon of freedom a falsehood intended to deceive the world. and.

Whereas: An abridgment of the liberties of the black, will have for effect, the strengthening of the hands, of the enemies of our beloved country, who have been asserting for several years, that the emancipation movement at the North, was a shame, that the United States government was not in earnest, on the abolition question, and did not intend to treat the negro better than the southern slaveocrats do. thereby damaging before the world, the honor and the social cause of the American Union, and

Whereas: There is no pratical liberty for the laborers, without the right of contracting freely, and voluntarily, on the terms of labor and

Whereas: The right of traveling is guaranteed by the National Constitution, to all Citizens, and any particular restriction put upon any particular class of Americans, on account of color, is unconstitutional. and

Whereas: Equal taxation, and reciprocal obligations between all classes of citizens, are the natural consequences of equality before the law. and have become the recognized principles of all liberal governments: and

Whereas: Congress has discountenanced the growing interference, with the rights and privileges of the Freedmen, by refusing during two successive sessions, the proposed organization of a Freedmen's Central Bureau and

Whereas: A liberal policy can only be conceived and carried out by men of liberal spirit and progressive tendencies. Be it therefore

Resolved: That the right of the employee to freely agree and contract, according to his best judgment, with his employer, for the term of labor, is the unquestionable attribute of every freeman.

Resolved: That as freinds of freedom, equal rights, and liberty, we enter our protest against every restriction put on the traveling facilities on account of color.

Resolved: That we denounce, to the world, the attempts, and wishes of the former slaveowners to transform, the boon of Liberty, solemnly offered to the American Slaves into a disguised bondage.

Resolved: That while we are prepared for any sacrifice dictated by philanthropy and patriotism, we earnestly protest, against any tax imposed on account of color.

Resolved: That it is highly important to institute, in this city a tribunal of Arbitrators composed partly of Freedmen, to decide in the simplest, but in the most equitable way the cases of appeal, from the decisions rendered, on matter of labor, by the Provost-Marshals – of the parishes.

Resolved: That we consider the existence of a Bureau of Free-labor as inconsistent with freedom, and we pledge ourselves, to use our most active efforts, to have it abolished by the proper authorities, in order to make room for complete freedom.

Resolved: That new ideas want new men, that the past has shown, that we cannot expect any decided progress, in the conduct of labor, so long as superintendant Thomas W. Conway remains at the head of the Bureau of free Labor of Louisiana.

Resolved: That it is shall be the duty, of the Officers, of this meeting to respectfully transmit the above preambles and resolutions, to the Commanding General of the Department of the Gulf, and to have published in the New-Orleans Tribune in French and English, and in the liberal press throughout the North.

General

You will please give an answer to this communication at your earliest convenience.

The undersigned can be addressed at N° 82 Baronne street. We are General Respectfully Your Obedient Servants

James H. Ingraham.
Dr A. W. Lewis } Committee

HLS

New Orleans March 23" 1865.

Gentlemen, Your Communication of 21" March has been considered by me.

It consists of Preambles that do not state facts and resolutions that are based upon false views. I hope you have been led into these mis-statements by error rather than wilfully, although I can scarcely believe you could have been so singularly misinformed.

If instead of assembling in Mass meetings and wasting your time in high sounding Resolutions you would devote Yourselves to assisting in the physical and moral improvement of the Freedmen you would do some practical good. As it is you do not in any respect represent the "Emancipated Freedmen of Louisiana," nor are you doing their cause any good. The Mass Meeting which you claim to represent was not composed of "Freedmen" but of the Free Colored People of New Orleans, free by the Old Laws of the State, and some at least of them in the old system themselves slave holders.

Between them and the "slaves" there was always and is now bitterness of feeling. You are striving for social equality, they for personal freedom. The first is not a thing that can be reached by laws and orders but can only come from the social tastes prejudices or inclinations of the people where you live; the Second is the Creature of Law and can be secured by the sanctions of Law.

Your Statement that the condition of the Freedmen is but little better than slavery is notoriously untrue, and I believe you know it.

I believe that you have wilfully inserted in your resolutions for publication statements that you must know to be baseless.

The Freedmen is paid for his labor, The slave is not.

The Freedman's wife and family are his – The Slave's are not.

Free Education is given to the Freedman and his children. To the slave it is forbidden.

The Freedman can bring suits and be a witness – The slave cannot.

These things you know to be true and yet your falsify and deny these great facts.

You know further perfectly well that without some supervision on the part of the United States these Freedmen would be cheated of their labor, induced into contracts that would ruin them and even if fair contracts were made would be uncertain as to their fulfilment. You know this because you have seen it, because you have reported it, because you have ask for the assistance of Military officers to remedy it.

You also know that as a Rule these payments have been Enforced by the military authorities rigorously and that many a hard working man now has his money that otherwise would have been robbed of his dues.

These results can only be obtained by control and supervision of the contracts by the Government officers. There must be some tribunal to ascertain and secure these rights. Freedmen may make contracts as they please, but the contract must be approved and registered and will be so done unless manifestly unfair to the Laborer.

This is provided for in General Orders N° 23[1] If they do not make such contract they can adopt that made by the terms of the order.

They cannot be allowed to lie around doing nothing, because then they become paupers and thieves and fall upon the Government for support.

The Freedmen and the Planters are charged a Capitation Tax, Two Dollars to the Planter, one to the hand to aid in supporting the disabled and helpless.

I have never heard of an undustrious working man who objected to it.

Are you willing with your knowledge of Society here to have the military officers withdraw all control and leave these questions of Labor of Freedom and of rights to such Civil authority as exists in this State.

You well know that you are not? for I receive constant complaints from you in relation to invasion and neglect of your rights.

Your cannot do away with the effects of two centuries of wrong upon White and Black in a day or a year, you must take time and slow processes of Education to root out such prejudices and habits of thought.

It is more than probable that an entire generation must grow up under new auspices before all this ill effect can be done away.

You must wait and work. Not call meetings and pass resolutions but work faithfully and slowly to educate the public mind both of whites and blacks, for the future.

It is true that this system prescribed in order of General Banks, and continued by me is temporary to be succeeded in its turn by other step of progress.

Whenever the time comes in which the Freedman can safely appeal to society and the Civil Courts for his rights when invaded, this military supervision will cease. I do not believe that this time has yet come.

No one will rejoice more than I when it shall come.

Until then under some form or other their paramount rights of living and of Education will be secured to them under the best plan that experience shall devise. and under such control as to officers as the United States may determine.

I differ Entirely from you as to Mr Conway and consider his services valuable and therefore retain him.

I consider your proposal of a mixed Tribunal of arbitration impracticable and decline to establish it.

I shall however forward your Communication and this reply to the Secretary at War to be laid before proper authorities.

Of course I shall be glad to have your assistance as far as it may go in advancing the condition of the Laborers, but in as much as you are not responsible for your acts and I am for mine, I shall not change a system adopted without facts and reasons satisfactory to my mind. Very Respectfully

HLcS S A Hurlbut

James H. Ingraham and Dr. A. W. Lewis to Major General S. A. Hurlburt, 21 Mar. 1865, I-5 1865, Letters Received, ser. 1920, Civil Affairs, Dept. of the Gulf, RG 393 Pt. 1 [C-750]; M. G. Comd'g S. A. Hurlbut to James H. Ingraham and Dr. A. W. Lewis, 23 Mar. 1865, vol. 9 DG, pp. 327–30, Letters Sent, ser. 1738, Dept. of the Gulf, RG 393 Pt. 1 [C-750]. Hurlbut did in fact forward to the War Department copies of the committee's letter and his own reply, apparently without comment. Received on April 8 by the Adjutant General's Office, they were submitted to the Secretary of War on the same day. File notations reveal nothing further, aside from an indication that, on June 2, 1865, the copies were received at the headquarters of the Freedmen's Bureau, among whose records they are filed. (G-2 1865, Registered Letters Received, ser. 15, Washington Hdqrs., RG 105 [A-8749].)

1 Issued by the commander of the Department of the Gulf on March 11, 1865. (See above, doc. 138.)

140: Testimony by a Louisiana Planter before the Smith-Brady Commission

New Orleans, April 25th *1865.*

Wm. J. Minor having been duly sworn testified as follows.

Q What is your age?

A Fifty-seven.

Q Where do you reside?

A I am residing, at present, in the Parsh. of Terrebonne, La, but my native residence is Adams Cty. Miss. – I have been residing here pretty nearly ever since the war began, – on my estates.

Q What do your estates consist of?

A I have three sugar estates.

Q The extent of them?

A About four thousand acres in Terrebonne.

Q You are what we call a sugar planter?

A Yes Sir.

Q Have been for how many years?

A Since 1829.

Q Giving your personal & practical attention to that pursuit?

A Yes Sir.

Q Please to state, in your own way, the difference between your present and former condition of your estates and sugar planting generally, – so far as it is within your knowledge with reference to the periods, of just before the war and during the war & now?

A On my own particular estates the sugar interests are almost entirely broken up. Previous to the war, I made on these three estates some fifteen hundred hhds of sugar. The year previous I made that on all three, I mean,. Last year I made only eight hhds. on the three estates, but that was in part owing to the season. Year before last was a very good season, I made only three hundred & sixty hhds. & that was owing in a great measure to the inability to control labor. The negroes were just emancipated & you could not make them work & they would not work. They were working for a portion of the crop, but I am satisfied that I left one hundred & fifty hhds on the field.

Q What do you mean by working for a portion of the crop?

A They were to have a portion of proceeds of the crop, one twentith of the crop I think it was, under Gen. Banks first order,[1] – & though I went into the field & cut twenty sticks & told them that "for each you leave in the field you lose one," – they said they "didnt care," – they "could afford to lose it." There was no means to make them cut a cane & you could not get the binders to bind all the cane or the cartmen to put it in the cart & therefore I am satisfied that I left that amount in the field & not withstanding my practicle instruction they didn't care; so my estates have been reduced since the war, – although I have done better than nine-tenths of my neighbors, – have been reduced all of three fourths, but my loss last year can not be attributed to the system of labor.

Q What is the prospect of a crop for the present season?

A As bad as it was last year, – if we have as bad a season. If the season is a good one, I may make about a tenth of a crop; – that is, if I save seed to plant next year.

Q What is the remedy that your reflections have suggested for this state of affairs?

A That is very difficult to tell. The negroes are working much better this year than last, – working on the same plan then as now. Last year, when I told them that if they didn't work, it would be deducted & that "for those days you lose you will not be paid," – the answer was, "we can afford to lose'

Q To what do you attribute the improvement?

A From increased experience. The found that this running about & going as they were disposed to do caused them a great deal of suffering in mind & body & they are becoming more desireous to return to their masters & working more under the old system than they did. They feel satisfied, – a good many do at least, – that they can rely upon their old owners to be paid, though a good deal of pains have been taken to deceive them by telling them that their old owners would have less feeling for them than new masters. Many were told that & thought so probably, – on account of Gen. Banks order that one half of the wages should be retained until the end of the year, to be paid,[2] – because there was designing people who told them that this retention was designed to cheat them out of it & that they would never get it. But a great many of them, I suppose nine out of ten, – were paid up, & they have more confidence in getting their back wages, – for they are retained the same way this year.

Q Can you state what proportion of Sugar plantations, which before the war were worked are now entirely disused?

A I don't know exactly, but I suppose that not more than one in ten is worked as a Sugar plantation.

Q Have the proprietors left for the Confederacy?

A No Sir, – not to that extent.

Q What is the reason?

A The difficulty has been to control the labor, Sugar planting is an artificial culture, as you may say, in this state & we are obliged to do certain things at certain times; for instance the cane crop must be saved between the 1st Oct. & 1st Jan. & all out after that may be considered a total loss. The inability has been to get labour to take off the crop – that is to make the sugar within the time prescribed, in the lease for labour. We have generally a frost by the 15th Nov.

that kills the cane & all standing will sour within ten days, though that is obviated to some extent by [windrow]ing, – that is, putting the stalks of one row over those of the other after it has been cut down. The cane put up in that way & good sugar made out of them in six weeks after this is done, but cane left standing will sour in four or five days, – sometimes in two or three & sometimes in five or six. Last year, & for two years, these negroes have taken it upon themselves to decide whether we should winrow the crop or not, – though working for a-twentieth. I told them if they didn't come to terms, I would send for Provt. Mshl. & have them put off the plantation and that was the only way I could get them to work & then they didn't cut as much in three days as they used to in one day & not as well. With this uncertainty the planters have abandoned the sugar interest almost entirely. Then there is another thing, – a man does not realize the full benefit of his planting unless he can insure his crop for three years. At the first year we grind the planting cane & the next year it comes up from the stubble, – the roots left in the ground, – & in good land there comes up the crop of rattoon which make as much as the cane almost, – & sometimes in very fresh land we make another crop & that year, we use that as seed, – & unless a man can do this, he cannot reap the full benefit of his planting for three years. One acre of good planting cane will plant three acres & if very superior five acres. An acre of can that will plant five acres will make two hhds. sugar which would be worth, at twenty cts per pound, four hundred dollars & thus every acre of cane we keep of that description is worth four hundred dollars of sugar. Planting seed is a very expensive article therefore, and has sold for four or five hundred dollars an acre. When this trouble came on & the people found they could not control the labour, they only saved a little seed & preferred to grind up the cane for which they could realize money on the sugar, – instead of, to keep the cane as seed & run the risk of lacking the labour, to derive full benifit from planting it. That is the trouble in La., for this is a very poor cotton Country & unless this matter is so arranged that we can grow sugar, it will be almost lost. We have rains & a wet season here which lasts from four to seven weeks, which comes just in the time when the cotton ought to be fully opened & in the best condition to pick. If this county don't grow sugar, it won't grow any thing of much account for it can't compete with the lands above Morganzia in regard to growing cotton.

Q What effect has this new system or policy upon the negroes, generally?

A The negroes, generally, are becoming rapidly demoralized. On all well regulated plantations, previous to this matter, excessive drinking was prohibited, also gambling, beating of wives, excessive punishment of children – & the running about at nigh was stopped. But now they are now beating their wives to excess; they are rapidly learning to gamble to excess & as they can get whiskey almost every where they please, they are drinking to excess & consequently are quarrelling & fighting. I have had three or four instances of wife-beating on my own plantation in the last two or three months, where men have tied their wives up to the house & whipped them, One man, an elder of a church, tied up his wife & beat her with an ox whip.

Q What was done in that case?

A Nothing, – she would not complain. One great trouble is the religous fanaticism they are acquiring; this man who beat his wife so severely was an elder of the Church, but she suspected him of being too intimate with another man's wife & complained of him to the governing committee of the Church, & he was dismissed, whereupon he trumped up some excuse & gave her a sever beating. In former times they were not allowed to beat their wives & were admonished that they should not break up their marriage relations for trifling causes. We compelled them to remain together & would not allow them to be divorced until they had tried each other some time longer. The marriage relation has been encouraged & sustained, – ever since I can recollect, – among the negroes & though not married by any ceremony of the church or a licensed parson, they were married by their own preachers & considerd themselves as much married as now, when they are married by a white one, licensed.

Q They were married by their own ministers?

A By their own ministers & frequently the whiteman of the family read the service, – the masters or the young masters or overseers or somebody, – at any rate there was always a marraige ceremony, though the african hadn't much of a marriage ceremony. Now they ar fast becoming demoralized in this respect. There are designing preachers among them who hold long meeting from eight or nine oclock until morning, in the course of which the wemon become hysterical & the men pick them up & hold them & all that sort of stuff. This occurs on my plantation twice a week & then they have a meeting on Sunday. The negroes get a sort of enthusiastic feeling & then get tired & back slide & become worse than ever. Something should be done to regulate this. On my plantation, before the war, they were allowed to have preaching on Sunday & prayer meeting during the week, but not to keep them up beyond ten oclock & they promised to do the same now but they now sit up all night & are not qualified to work the next day. At these meeting they collect from all parts of the country & negroes will come & preach sermons who have been dead for twenty years & for three, four, five & six years is a very common thing. They preach very bad doctrine too;— one feller preached that he was the servant of Christ &, as such, was not required to work except for him & that the same doctrine applied to them that joined his Church,—that the Lord put them in possession of my houses & none but the Lord could put them out. I informed him that the Lord would appear to him in the shape of Capt Benjamin & a squad of cavalry, if they didnt quit within a certain day, when they sent down a delegation to find out if the Govt. would put them out for me. & having ascertained it was so, this elder than ran off with another man's wife. Another feller preached up the doctrine,—not in the pulpit but in private—that there is no immorality for those to live together who are clean sheep which he considers himself & all the sisters of his church. In ordinary times I should have dethroned such a man from the ministry myself, but now the Govt. Committee do that & then after a while will reinstate such characters.

Q So far as you know does this extend to other plantations?

A Yes Sir.

Q What is the opinion entertained among gentlemen of the South who are in favor of the reconstruction of the Union, as to the mode of remedying these difficulties which you have described & restoring plantations to their value?

A The only certain remedy that we know of is, to take us back under the Constitution & establish things as they were, but perhaps under some other name.

Q Retaining the institution of slavery?

A Yes Sir, I think this state & all the states would come back under the Constitution Sir. I am the more inclined to think so because I was one of those who were altogether opposed to going out in the beginning. I have been anxious for a restoration under the Constitution from the first day of secession up to the present day.

Q Suppose that the administration should carry out the policy of treating the states as never having gone out of the Union, for the reason that they could not leave it, but regard slavery as abolished,— what would be the practical effect of that?

A I think that there would be an immense reduction of products & that this from being a very large market would dwindle down one-fifth & perhaps, for a few years, one-tenth. My own opinion is that if slavery is completely abolished this county will have ceased to have been a sugar growing country.

Q What will be substituted for it?

A Nothing except a little rice which cannot be grown in competition with those countries where they have irragation, though we have that here now in seasons like the present, but at the last season it could not be done & there are only patches, where the spring rains irragate, that rice in grown in this country.

Q To what extent do you think that white labour could be employed?

A I don't think that white labour could ever make sugar or Cotton in this state because the white man can not bear the climate or sun & he can get as much as we can afford to give, elsewhere. I am supposing that after Peace these articles will come in from other Countries, when the price must necessarily come down, & then we wont be able to control white labour at all. A man won't come here from a healthy, high state, like Ohio, when we can't afford to give them any more to make our crops here than they can get to make corn in the west. If those men can live there they won't come down here to live among mosquitos & mud, – for it rains here almost every day in some seasons – . When they can get their usual wages in a more pleasant climate than this, where they are free from the mosquitos & the fevers of this Country, they won't come down here & work for the same wages & therefore I don't think that we can ever control white labour here, to any extent. When emancipation is perfected, we will have to get "Cooly labour" or some other, – labourers that can stand this Climate.

Q How would it do with regard to European emigrants?

A They would not do at all, for they die like sheep & our own american people can stand the climate better than Europeans. When we bring negroes from Kentucky or Northern Va. here, they are only required to do half labor the first year until they are acclimated with a great deal of care. Negroes are much better adapted to bear the heat, can live almost where alligators can, don't care for mosquitos & sleep in mid-summer with their heads rolled up in a blanket.

Q How does the civil administration make itself felt in this Dept. under the new system?

A We have had but little of it until lately, when it attempted to levy three or four years taxes at once upon us. In my parish we have been saddled with a most terrific set of officials, – police jurors sheriffs &c, & a great many men never heard of before the war. I knew but one single man in the police jury & he couldnt read or write, nor can a member of his family, though living with a free school within five miles of him, where he could send his children for three or four dollars a year, – where I paid three hundred dollars myself for school tax. He is a white man & has worked for me many years. We had free schools here under the old system.

Q How long ago were they first established?

A Fifteen or twenty years.

Q What does the police jury do?

A It regulates the Internal affairs of the parish.

Q Of what number does it consist?

A Thirteen, – one for each ward. It levies taxes, builds public buildings, – like school houses &c – & looks after public roads &c.

Q What is the judicial system?

A We have a State Circut judge I belive, who holds Courts twice a year.

Q And under the new system?

A It is the same.

Q With civil & criminal jurisdiction?

A Yes Sir. We have had one or two courts held there, I think, since the reorginization of the civil govt.

Q What has been the extent of white imigration to your section of the Country since the war broke out?

A It has been very small. There have been a few men who have opened trade stores & a few who have leased plantations. I don't think that one hundred & fifty men have gone into the parish since the war.

Q How many have leased plantations?

A I don't know, but not over fifty I suppose, – perhaps twenty-five or thirty. The great immegration has been, of men opening trade stores.

. . . .

Q Did the people of the state of La., as far as you know, take any part, as a general thing, in this election for Gov. under the new system?

A No Sir, I don't think they did as a general thing, because the people considered it a fore gone conclusion that certain men were to be elected, & as they were opposed to those men, they didn't consider it of any use to take any part.

Q If the legal voters of the State, voted at an election for Gov; – would not they have the majority?

A I think they would, – without the Army vote.

Q But the Army vote would give a majority against the old residents?

A Yes Sir.

Q Are there not a great many men qualified to vote who are absent from their homes in this State in the Confederate Army?

A Yes Sir.

Q Could you form any idea how many?

A No Sir, – not the slightest.

Q Suppose it was inevitable that slavery should be teated by the

General Govt as abolished, & the state, under its constitution, should be controled by resident of La. having views similar to yours, legislating over labou generally. with a view to prevent idleness, drunkedness & the other evils which you have particularized, – how much then would remain, if the laws were vigorously executed, of these difficulties among the colored men?

A In case the state should come into the Union & the old citizens recovered the control of the state Govt. – then the laws that they would pass, – if not interfered with by the General Govt. & fully executed, – would, in a great measure, remedy these evils of which we complain, but this is based upon the assumption that the old citizens get possession of the Govt., for otherwise we could not rely upon it at all; & I dont think that the laws passed by people who have jost come here, would remedy the evils of which we complain. I dont doubt that the state can be carried back by force, but I should depreciate very much the necessity of forcing the South back in the Union. I am an American, body & soul, & as such, I speak. If the South is forced back into the Union, I don't think that we shall have peace, but that in case of a foreign war we should have secession again immediately.

Q What do you mean exactly "by the South's being forced back"?

A Suppose you subjagate this country & hold it for a while, & then give it back to the citizen & withdraw the force; it will be merely a temporary peace & the moment this country gets into a foreign war with a power of any strength, – there are many in the South who will contrive to get us in a foreign war, if we don't get into it, – & the moment that begins & a force is thrown into the Southern States there are many men in the South to join it & then, with a foreign Navy against us, we will have another [desolating?] war, – in my judgement. I was opposed to Secession, because I didn't perceive the right or necessity for it, but I think the "personal liberty bill" was the beginning of this war. I think that we must have a reconstruction under the Constitution, that we may send our represenativ & establish things as they were befor the war. I have lost more negroes by death on my plantation since the war commenced than in the ten years previous, – from their refusal to go to the hospital, which we have on our plantations, provided with a hospital nurse & a regular physician & visited by the planters once a day, usually. Another cause, is the introduction of these epidemics produced by their running about here & there. A year & a half ago a positive Order was issued by Gen. Banks, – which was enforced however only a very little while, – prohibiting them from going about –[3]

HD

Excerpts from testimony of Wm. J. Minor, 25 Apr. 1865, Testimony Received by the Commission, ser. 736, Smith-Brady Commission, RG 94 [AA-3]. The omitted portion concerned an annual compilation of statistics of sugar production published by P. A. Champonier before the war.

1 The "order" – actually a contract offered to planters in February 1863 by the Sequestration Commission (with the approval of General Nathaniel P. Banks, commander of the Department of the Gulf) – had provided that plantation laborers might receive compensation of one-twentieth of the crop (to be divided among them) instead of wages in cash. (See above, doc. 84.)
2 Banks's General Order 23 of February 3, 1864, which had governed plantation labor during the 1864 crop season, provided that, when laborers were working for cash wages, "at least" one-half of the amount due them "shall be reserved until the end of the year." (See above, doc. 109.)
3 On January 19, 1864, Banks had cited "[c]onsiderations of public health" in prohibiting "all unnecessary communication or travel by plantation laborers between the different parishes of the State, or between plantations of the same parish," except under regulations established by local provost marshals. (*Official Records*, ser. 1, vol. 34, pt. 2, p. 111.)

141: Testimony by a Louisiana Planter before the Smith-Brady Commission

New Orleans, April 25th, *1865.*

Tobias Gibson, having been duly sworn, testified as follows.

Q. Please state your age and place of birth

A. I am sixty four years of age and was born in Adams County, Mississippi.

Q. What has been your occupation?

A. I have been a planter, – a cotton and sugar planter, – for about forty years.

Q. Where have your plantations been?

A. First in Miss, and then in the Parish of Terrebone La,

Q. How long in Louisiana?

A. Thirty six years,

Q. You have principaly devoted yourself during this time to the sugar interest?

A. Yes Sir, but raised cotton here for several years however.

Q. You have heard the statement of Mr. Minor, just completed?

A. Yes Sir.

Q. Do you agree with him in his experience and opinions, and if not, state in what particulars your views are different, – and add such new suggestions as you may think proper.

A. I do agree with him fully, – in the main,

Q. You experience has been the same in regard to the effects produced upon labor, and the plantations and your pecuniary interests during the war,?

A. Yes Sir, I subscribe to every thing he has said.

Q. And have you observed among the negroes the same tendency to demoralization, under the new system, that he has?

A. Precisely.

Q. And in the same forms?

A. Precisely, and think it is getting worse. I think they are laboring better than they did, but ascribe that to a different cause from what Mr. Minor did. I think in the first place, that the class of persons not disposed to work are in the army and the mass of the population left are compelled to work because of large families and inability to leave home. I don't think it arises from any disposition to work, but that it is the necessity which forces them to. Formerly the army favored them and gave them rations, but now there is no army and they therefore stay at home and work better than they did. Those who are subject to the draft dread it as they do a pestilence, having seen the consequences to those who have gone into the army, and will do any thing I tell them to do if I will only keep them out of the army. – and have now a great apprehension for working for the "Yankees" as they call them, who don't pay them or treat them as their old masters did and they realize that they are better off with their "old masters" than with their new. They have their homes and have been addressed by their present employers in language which they comprehend, because they see the truth of it. They have their houses, gardens and pigs and make a good deal of money by working half Saturdays, which they have, as formerly, – and they make a great deal of money so; they have a thousand comforts at home and realize a real profit by staying there, rather than going on to abandoned plantationes which strangers have, who only care for money; – hence it is, I think, that it not from any motive or disposition to labor that they do better and I don't think they do it any better now than before, but they realize the change and are compelled to labor. We have now only inferior laborers who are retained on plantations by their families.

Q. Be good enough to state, as the result of your knowledge of public sentiment in this state and your own reflection and experience, what, – in the state of things, – if the state of Louisiana should be left as a state of the Union with what sovereign power the United States secures and slavery treated as abolished – would be the effect of regulating this matter of labor by civil enactments by old residents?

A I think there would be an amelioration, – both in regard to labor and its character, as it would be regulated by persons accustomed to the management of negroes and it would be legislative instead of arbitrary, but there would be insuperable difficulties, in my mind, to that, – for if the negroes are free at the end of the year to go and choose their masters, it breaks up the sugar interests, because we have to have a series of years provided for in respect to labor, in order to reap any benefit from it, Sugar is the only article we can produce here by any labor, but as soon as negroes get any money they will not do anything at all, but are a perfect nuisance, – and unless we have some organization and can have for some years, we can not make any sugar. You must, before October, put up your seed for the ensueing year and you must do that before any frost, – and then you have a guarentee of seed, but not of labor, and it subtracts very largely to put up this seed; so that without an absolute certainty, – without any contingency whatever, – that you will have labor for the ensueing year, no prudent man can work at the business at all. There must be some method moreover of making a party to whom a negro applies for work certain in regard to that negroe's status as it relates to his former master. In order to make this labor valuable, you must make labor press upon capital and import labor – but I hardly know what that is. History proves that the labor of free negroes can not be made profitable. The negro population is so large in comparison with the white, and the territory so great, that I don't see how it is possible that the parties can exist free together. The negro now feels himself as good as a white man and will only work when it is necessary for him to do so. He will become proprietor, in a small way, which breaks up plantations, for it requires large estates and improvments to carry on sugar plantations and none of less than five hundrend acres can be carried on, – though in regard to cotton it is different, because the improvement is comparitively cheap; but in sugar a very large measure of the capital is in improvements which are constantly deteriorating and hence the Northern idea that large estates may be distributed into small ones, is erroneous and impractacable. The idea that a large proportion of the population is opposed to slavery, is not the case, but they are as much in favor of it as I am, – and I was a tolerably large slave owner, – knowing as they do that the value of their property depends upon that same thing.

Q. How many slaves have you lost?

A. I suppose not more than about a third.

Q. Was that owing to the army or their running away?

A. The most of it is in consequence of the negroes leaving the plantation and going into the camps with the army, when the women and children died off; a good many went first voluntarily into the army; a good many have been drafted and put into the army and on account of the lack of care among them and in consequence of demoralization, they have died. We have also a pestilence among them and I have lost a large number from smallpox and the mumps are now universal on my plantation.

Q Was this new at that time?

A. Yes Sir, – never had an epidemic on the plantation before. We never had the yellow fever or cholera on our plantations, because our police regulations were such that fewer negroes died than white men. My negroes are prohibited only from going [in] to the army, but can go any where else. They have big meetings at "Minor's," but nobody asks them for a pass, because they have no right to do it, – and if I meet my own negro and he tells me he is going to "Miner's," to meeting, I have no power to arrest him. He takes the mules out at night and goes where he pleases, though I have the stables locked – It is only where the military are that these orders can be carried out and many of the military wink at it and give them very bad advice

Q. What is the age at which a negro begins to labor in the field, usually?

A. We have negroes put to work at twelve years of age as water carriers, – for each gang has to have pure rain water, – and negro boys from twelve to fifteen act as water carriers. I don't think they can be considered as laborers in the field with the plow or hoe, until about fifteen.

Q. What is the average of life?

A. I think that the number of deaths in proportion to the population, is quite as small as with the whites If you mean that as regards the present, I have already stated.

Q. When your plantation was under good working order., under the old system, – before the rebellion, how many men would be at work a day, – on an average?

A. Do you mean in proportion to the whole number?

Q. Actually at work?

A Of the force?

Q. Yes.

A Of the men?

Q. Yes.

A. You consider the mechanics as working in field or all at labor?

Q. Say all that labor.

A. Of the men capable of laboring, – there are a large number superanuated, – not at work, but whom we support, – but of those at an age to labor, there are at least ninteen twentieths that are at work. There is not more than one out of twenty, sick, and that is the only exception, – except that we have a large number that have passed from fifty five to sixty years of age whom we don't require to work regularly as field hands, – about fifty five is about the average according to my views.

Q. What would be the average age of those in the field, – literally speaking – ?

A. I should say about thirty three,

Q. What is your opinion of the practacability of introducing the apprenticeship system under a state law, – by which a negro could bind himself until his majority, in the same manner that apprentices bind themselves to mechanical pursuits at the North, where the master stands legally in the same relation as parent to the child, with power of restraint, imprisonment or punishment.

A. I would be a poor judge, as I can't look upon them as only slaves or free. The difficulty would arise from this, – that at the North your apprentices are taken from home and are appenticed to some art. Here every man wishes to keep his negroes at home and then you incorporate on the same estate those in a quasi state of slavery – and you have their parents and the whole of the rest of the plantation to interfere with you exercise of authority over them, which you have not over the latter; – and therefore you create as sort of antagonism. If I went to correct these apprentices, under a law, they say "I am not going to see my son or daughter punished and I will fight for it first," and nine out of ten are against you, with a physical ability to resist you and they wont allow you to punish them. If you threaten to send to the Provost Marshal or to send them off the place, – or have reason to complain of one very decidedly, they are all against you at once, If the people are obliged, – if terms are made with the people of the Southern states so that they can return under the Constitution to manage their affairs in their own way, subject only to the Constitution of the United States, my impression is that the people will return voluntarily to the Union, but that any thing but that would be mere hollow truce.

HD

Testimony of Tobias Gibson, 25 Apr. 1865, Testimony Received by the Commission, ser. 736, Smith-Brady Commission, RG 94 [ΛA-4].

142: Testimony of Two Louisiana Planters before the Smith-Brady Commission

New Orleans, May 2nd *1865.*

Henry E. Laurence, being duly sworn, testified as follows;

Q. Where do you reside?

A. My home is on Berwick's Bay, Parish of St. Mary, on the

Opelousas R.R; – commenced to reside in that Parish in /49, as a planter of both cotton & sugar, – have a cotton plantation about eighty miles North.

Q. What is its present condition?

A. The houses & everything have been destroyed. I ceased working this plantation in /62 when the Federal forces took possession of Berwick's Bay. I was obliged to move all my negroes to a small plantation this side of the Bay where they all are, except those who have been conscripted. I have been with my brother on the Magnolia plantation & my negroes are all working well, I give them a fourth of the profits of the cotton this year, because I cannot be there to attend to it myself, – am raising no sugar this year. I furnish everything but have no overseer except one whom they elected among themselves, – an old servant in whom I have confidence.

Q. Have you observed any demorilization among those negroes since the rebellion broke out?

A. No Sir, – can't perceive a bit of change in them, – they are as respectful, confiding & dependent as ever. My brother has the Magnolia plantation, forty five miles below the City & the other, fifteen miles, on the same side, – about two hundred & thirty negroes on the first & a hundred & ten on the last. He has lost seven or eight since I have been there. The negroes have so improved in all respects that they are now in a position equal to that which they held before the war. They have confidence in the course which the Govt. is pursuing & that their employers will pay them

Q. Some gentlemen who reside in La. & other districts have given as their opinion that there is no system can possibly be adopted by which sugar plantations can be made profitably worked if the negroes are not kept in slavery as before, – your opinion?

A. I don't & never did think so, but know to the contrary, – if a negro is to have a status & be made responsible for his contracts, – that is the only thing I conceive to be necessary to enable us to work our lands, – for they will be vagrants if they chose & are permitted to be. Assuming La. to be a State with authority to regulate its own concerns without any interference from the Gen. Govt., I think that free negro labor can be made successful. I have kept my own statistics & am fully satisfied not only that slave labor was most terribly costly but that the whole cotton country of the U.S. can & will be as successfully worked, – if not more so, – with free labor, white or black, & that before ten years the product would be larger than ever, – if perfect peace & confidence is restored. With the exception of the over-flowed delta of the Mississsippi, the health of the healthy Northern man, – or the same of any other nation, – will

be as good in this country as in any other part of the U.S. Sugar is not as successful & sure as cotton, but cotton is a perfect success.
HD

New Orleans, May 2nd *1865.*

E. Laurence, having been duly sworn, testified as follows;

Q. Please give your views on the testimony of your brother.

A. I agree with him & wish to say a few words for myself. My brother's statement & my own will probably give you a better idea of affairs than you would get from most people as my negroes are old family servants who have been well cared for in every respect. When the war came, I persuaded them to remain with me & they have been very happy & contented. Last year I raised about four hundred & fifty hogshead of sugar, but we have had two very bad years, – but the present season bids fair to be a good one. We generally plant from November to April. It is NOT necessary to cut the cane before the first frost, – as has been suggested to the contrary, – but we cut & winrow it after it has been killed by the frost. I think that sugar & cotton plantations through the South, – from my former knowledge & experience, – can be carried on successfully with free negro labor & proper state laws regulating labor, – & have always said so.

Q. Don't you believe that there is a certain set of gentlemen engaged in planting who feel disposed, because they take offence at the Act of Congress,[1] not to make any exertion in regard to that matter?

A. Yes Sir, – there is no question about it & I know one case personally where a most intelligent planter, a foreign subject, who has had all his negroes at home, has lost a hundred thousand dollars in crops by not meeting things as they were & are.
HD

Testimony of Henry E. Laurence, 2 May 1865, and testimony of E. Laurence, 2 May 1865, Testimony Received by the Commission, ser. 736, Smith-Brady Commission, RG 94 [AA-7]. A notation at the end of each document indicates that the Laurence brothers were examined together.

1 Presumably the law, adopted on March 3, 1865, that created the Bureau of Refugees, Freedmen, and Abandoned Lands (within the War Department), to oversee the transition from slavery to free labor, much to the chagrin of those Louisiana planters who had hoped that the restoration of civil authority in their state would permit them to make labor arrangements without federal interference. (*Statutes at Large*, vol. 13, pp. 507–9.)

143: Statement of a Louisiana Freedman

New Orleans December 21′ 1865

Statement of VIRGIL LOYD

Virgil Loyd, states and declares that he and Ten others Freedmen residing in the Parish of St John Babtist in January 1865 – entered into a written contract with D Z Leve also residing in St John Baptist by the stipulations whereof. said Freedmen were to work on the Plantation of said *Levee* known as the Donnoi Plantation in the Parish of S[t] John [th] Baptist and receive from said Levee also Four Dollars each in advance. which was paid – and 4 lb[s] meat & one peck meal weekly as rations only – if anything more was received it was to be paid for – On the 17th day of Febuary 1865 – the Freedmen all went to work under that contract – which was to have been signed having been agreed to by Capt Darling then Pro Vost Marshall for that Parish but before that was done. Capt Darling was Captured by the *Confederates*. This contract contained this other material stipulation, that Virgil Loyd Leader and the Ten other[s] his associates were to have in compensation for their labour on said Plantation in working and producing the crop one *entire* FIFTH of every THING raised and produced on the Plantation, the said Leve. furnishing the draft animals seed and necessary implements to be employed in the working said Plantation raising the crop In the month of May 1865 – Leut Rich succeeded Capt Darling as Pro vost Marshal, of the Parish of St John the Baptist, at which time said Loyd and his associates made him acquainted with the contract and its stipulations under which they had been all the year – (including January 1865 – and which was solemnly confirmed on the 17″ day of February 1865 –) been at work. performing strictly and fully all its stipulations. on their part; and they continued to so to work and comply with all its Stipulations. on their part – and had made and laid by the crop and were employed in hauling and cording wood for Sale on the Banks of the Mississippi River for the said Levee near the end of July 1865 When the Said Leut Rich, without the consent and in gross violation of the rights of said Freedmen instigated thereto by the said *Levee*, broke and Changed the Contract to the predjudice of the said Freedmen, by threats and artifices employed upon the other Freedmen in the absence of their leader and head contractor, by which he undertook to Substitute a new contract requiring and compelling the Freedmen parties to this contract to accept from Mr *Levee* Eight Dollars per month for the benifit of Mr Levee – and compelled and frightened them into signing this Substituted Contract. by the others *which Virgil Loyd refused to agree to or, to sign,* and which was *extorted* from the others – a peice of and act of injustice, appealing strongly for investigation and relief and *redress*, The original contract required the Freedmen to work and labour on the Plantation until the crop was made and laid by which they on their part honestly and faithfully performed. and as herein stated on the part of Mr Levee the other contracting party were these the Freedmen rights violated, and they robed of their labor. and up to this time they are without relief– The facts herein stated can be substantiated – by the production of the written contract which went into the possession of Mr *Levee*, by Captain Darling – by the overseeer – *Mr Vicknell*, by Capt Morse – late of the Freedmen *Beaureau*. In confirmation of this recital of the facts by the Freedmen and although this statement refers to the Conduct of Leut. Rich, unfavorably and as the Freedmen understand it – they believe he could not fail to corroborate and confirm it – The cotton raised on the Plantation is now in the hands of Mr [Brown?] N° 45 New Levee St office up stairs, out of the proceeds whereof the Freedmen[s] claim [herein?] can be enforced as he is in possession thereof as Factor or Agent of Mr *Levee*, and there remains cane and Corn and potatoes on the Plantation – The Freedmen to this contract have been before Capt Morse and have caused Mr L*evee* to be there also and Mr Levee, then and there acknowledged he had wronged these Freedmen in attempting to have this contract violated and changed and promised on Thanksgiving day the 7th of December to pay them the one Fifth of the entire Crop produced on the Plantation. But this agreement & promise to them has not been complied with and fullfiled. because Mr Levee has been pemitted to go back to the Plantation to bring here *the contract* more than two weeks *since*. but in the Same spirit, of Fraud and injustice which he had as hereinbefore stated, made without the Knowledge or consent of the Freedmen he Mr Levee, has again instigated and employed Leut Rich, who has consented to perform in this respect that part, to make substitute and antedate a Contract for the benifit of Mr Levee, to derive and rob these Freedmen of their rights under said contract – And that too after Capt Morse – *had* – investigated this subsituted and fraudulent contract and decided against its validity and appeal to Captain Morse for confirmation of this statement

ADS Virgil Loyd

Statement of Virgil Loyd, 21 Dec. 1865, L-324 1865, Letters Received, ser. 1303, LA Asst. Comr., RG 105 [A-8580]. The statement is headed "For. Maj Genl Baird Assist Com[r] for L[a]" and was evidently submitted at the headquarters of General Absalom Baird, the Freedmen's Bureau assistant commissioner for Louisiana. From Baird's office it was eventually referred to Lieutenant J. D. Rich, Freedmen's Bureau agent at Bonnet Carré. Rich's reply (in the same file) made little effort to disguise his annoyance with Virgil Loyd. Dismissing the freedman's statement as "perfectly groundless and *entirely false*," Rich recounted events as he saw them – making no mention of the verbal agreement made by the freedpeople and D. Z. Levet in January 1865. Instead, he began his account in April 1865, when he had drawn up a "regular Gov't contract" between Levet and his employees, in accordance with General Order 23 (issued by the commander of the Department of the Gulf the previous month). Rich had visited the Levet plantation, "explained [the contract] to them all," and warned them "to make no outside verbal contract." Failing – or refusing – to understand that Loyd's complaint stemmed from this military abrogation of the private agreement made in January, Rich asserted that Loyd's description of a change in the contract was "as false and ungrounded as anything can be." "If he was a white man," the lieutenant fumed, "I should certainly complain of him and have him brought before the Courts of justice." But instead, Rich "earnestly recommend[ed] that [Loyd] have his pay turned over to the Bureau of Free Labor as a lesson to him which may be of benefit to him in after years." (2″ Lieut. J. D. Rich to Brevet Colonel M. A. Reno, 29 Dec. 1865; for General Order 23, see above, doc. 138.) Lieutenant Rich's exasperation antedated Loyd's complaint to the assistant commissioner. In November 1865, Levet's employees had stopped work and complained to Rich "that they [had] made a Verbal contract with Mr Levet which he [would] not fulfill." After Rich's visit to the plantation in April, they reported, Levet had told them that the new military contract "did not amount to anything and that he [Levet] wished them to work well and he would give them one fifth of the next proceeds of Crop." Rich's response to the freedpeople's complaint had shown no awareness that Levet's promise to pay them a share of the crop had constituted, not a new verbal contract, but a restatement of the agreement made in January. On that occasion, too, Rich had suggested a stiff punishment for deviating from the military contract – this time for the employer: "I would resply ask permission to fine Mr Levet . . . One Hundred Dollars for tampering with his men and trying to evade Orders & Contract. I think it would be a good lesson for him, as he well knew that he had no right to do so just to get more Labor." (2″ Lieut. J. D. Rich to Lieut. D. G. Fenno, 22 Nov. 1865, R-195 1865, Letters Received, ser. 1303, LA Asst. Comr., RG 105 [A-8580].)

144: Tabular Report by a Treasury Department Inspector of Plantations

[New Orleans?, La. mid-June? 1865]

Report of Inspection of Gov[t]. Plantations being worked in the Parishes of "Terrebonne and Lafourche, for the year 1865. (by Freedmen.)

Date of Inspection	Name of Company	Name of Plantation	No of Laborers	No. acres of Corn	No. ac. of Cotton	No. ac. stubbles Cane	No. ac. Plant Cane	No ac[rs] Cultivated	Remarks.
May 11	G. Hunter	Woodland	52	165	35			200	Divided and worked by 12 Companies, seven of which have very good crops of cotton & corn
23	Madison Rose	Johnson	15	150	15		2	167	Very good Cotton and Corn crops Cane middling, land well cultivated.
"	Palin Alexander	"	8	42	10			52	Cotton and Corn middling good.
"	Kenny Morrison	"	8	30	20			50	About 8 acres good cotton, ballance poor, Corn good.
"	Lige Sears	"	18	75	21			96	Corn 30 " good balance not up Cotton 10 acres good ballance poor.
"	Henry Jordan	"	8	25	17			42	[*Corn*] 10 [*acres*] poor [*balance*] middling Cotton 10 [*acres good ballance poor*]
24		Vicks.	28	75	50	5	8	138	[*Corn*] middling Cotton 18 acres, very good cane, 3 acres good, ballance neglected and suffering for want of cultivation.
25	Peter Matthews	Geo. Tucker	17	90	38	25	3	156	60 acres good corn ballance poor, Cotton very good, Cane about 15 acres good ballance thin, lined with corn.
"	Joe King	" "	15	60	22 1/2			82	Joe King's Co. 25 acres Corn good. ballance poor. Cotton 4 acres middling, ballance poor.
"	Jacques Jeriman	Bob Tucker	20	70	40			110	Corn good, Cotton all but 5 acres poor and in need of Cultivation
June 13	J. Adams, & A. Lewis	D. A. Landry	8	45	50			95	15 acres Cotton very good. Balance doing well. Corn good, place well worked.
14	Nelson Hill	H. Doyal	147	250	110		9	369	35 acres Cotton good 75 acres Cotton poor 50 " " " 200 " Corn middling

HD

("signed") C. L. Dunbar

C. L. Dunbar, "Report of Inspection of Govt. Plantations being worked in the Parishes of 'Terrebone and Lafourche, for the year 1865 (by Freedmen)," [mid-June? 1865], vol. 72, pp. 256–57, Reports of Inspectors of Plantations, 3rd Agency, RG 366 [Q-126]. Limitations of space make it impossible to align the "Remarks" column exactly as in the manuscript; therefore, for reasons of clarity, bracketed words replace some of the ditto marks that appear in the original.

145: Headquarters of U.S. Forces at Port Hudson, Louisiana, to a Louisiana Former Slaveholder

Port Hudson La. June 23[d] 1865.

Mrs. Adams The General Comdg directs that I call your attention to the case of a colored man. Louis Jones. formerly your slave. He reports that you demand half of his wages. from this date as *your right* and that you have taken all the money earned by him during the past three years. He also states that you claim this money on the ground. that he is *not free*. In order that you may not longer entertain such erroneous *ideas*. or again attempt to take or claim the wages of a man over whom you have no control. you are hereby informed that by the Proclamation of the President of the United States. the late *Abram Lincoln*. all the colored men. women and children in this part of Louisiana were declared *Free* from the 1st day of January 1863. This with the advice and consent of the Senate & House of Congress. By the recent amendment of the Constitution. Congress. abolished all slavery.[1] and your pretended rights over the said Louis Jones ceased on the 1st day of January 1863. In regard to the money you have already taken from him. no action will be taken at present. But you will please to understand that you have no right to his services or any other person without you pay them an equivalent for their labor. I am Madam Very Respectfully Your ob't. servant.

HLcS E. G. Manning

1st Lt. E. G. Manning to Mrs. Adams, 23 June 1865, vol. 173 DG, pp. 259–60, Letters Sent, ser. 2100, U.S. Forces Port Hudson LA, RG 393 Pt. 2 No. 118 [C-912].

1 The Thirteenth Amendment had been adopted by Congress in January 1865 and submitted to the states, but it was not ratified until the following December.

CHAPTER 3
The Mississippi Valley

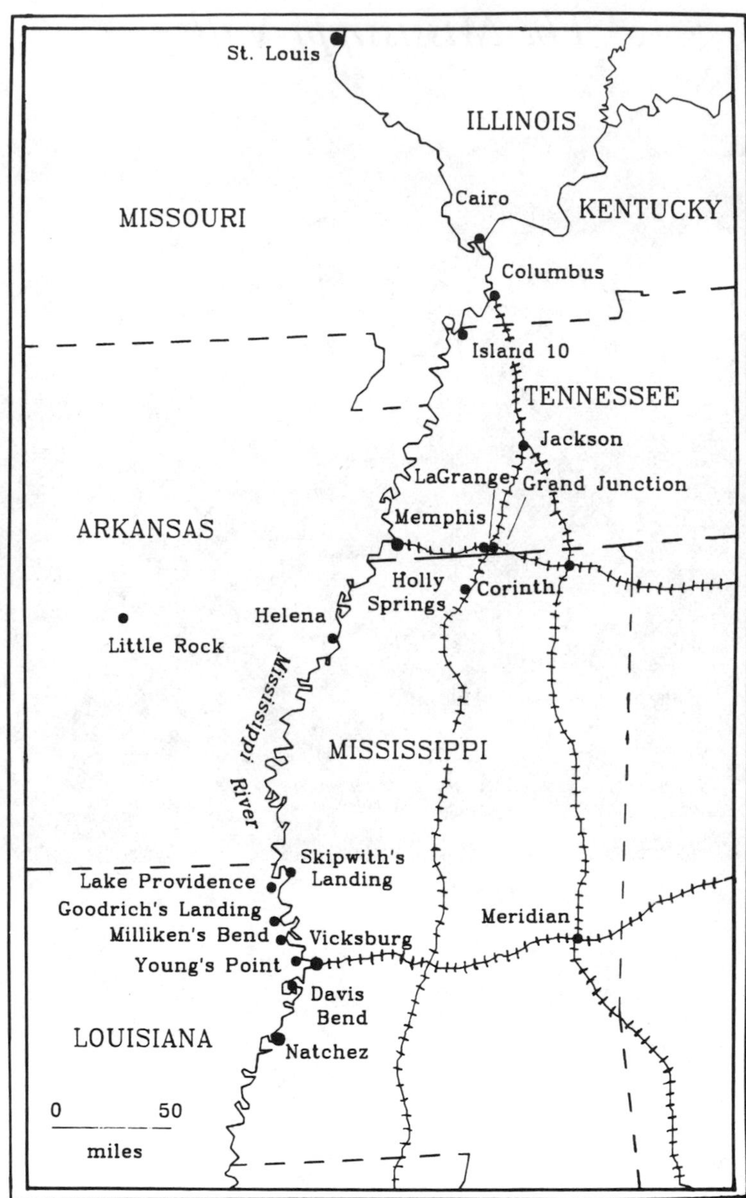

The Mississippi Valley

3

The Mississippi Valley

UNION MILITARY OCCUPATION transformed the Mississippi Valley from the heartland of slavery to a testing ground for free labor.[1] The first Northern invaders marched under orders forbidding any interference with slavery, but the flight of slaves to Union lines and the army's need for laborers soon gave rise to ad hoc measures for their employment and welfare. After emancipation became a stated aim of the war rather than an unintended result, federal authorities considered questions of labor and relief in conjunction with the larger task of constructing a new social order. The stakes were high. The Mississippi Valley contained the nation's major inland waterway, rich cotton plantations, and a large population of former slaves who could be either a resource or a liability to the Union. Establishing a viable free-labor regime along the Mississippi River promised to restore cotton production, generate revenue for the national treasury, weaken the Confederacy, and help the freedpeople support themselves.

Beginning in the spring of 1863, federal authorities in the Mississippi Valley reorganized plantation labor on the basis of compensation instead of servile obligation. Former slaves became wage-workers. Among their employers were Northern entrepreneurs drawn south by the lure of quick profits, who received privileged access to land and laborers. Other Northerners – army and navy officers, military superintendents of contrabands, and treasury agents – also made claims upon the labor of the freedpeople. Meanwhile, in hopes of benefiting from changes they could not prevent, a growing number of native planters renounced the Confederacy and hired former slaves to work their es-

[1] This chapter concerns the wartime evolution of free labor in west Tennessee, eastern Arkansas, western Mississippi, and northeastern Louisiana. Developments in southern Louisiana are considered above, in chapter 2; middle and east Tennessee and northern Alabama are considered in *Freedom*, ser. 1, vol. 2: chap. 3. Passages in the present essay that lack footnotes should be understood to rest upon the documents included in the chapter. Secondary accounts of the wartime development of free labor in the Mississippi Valley include James T. Currie, *Enclave: Vicksburg and Her Plantations, 1863–1870* (Jackson, Miss., 1980), chaps. 1–4; Louis S. Gerteis, *From Contraband to Freedman: Federal Policy toward Southern Blacks, 1861–1865* (Westport, Conn., 1973), chaps. 7–10; Lawrence N. Powell, *New Masters: Northern Planters during the Civil War and Reconstruction* (New Haven, Conn., 1980).

tates. Mindful of what was at stake, Confederate regulars and guerrillas tried to disrupt, if not eradicate, the federally supervised labor arrangements. To a degree unmatched in other Union-occupied parts of the South, ongoing warfare affected the character of the new order, repeatedly upsetting the plans and reshaping the expectations of all participants. Wartime obstacles notwithstanding, by the end of the conflict more former slaves had experienced free labor in the Mississippi Valley than in any other region.

By mid-1862, the Union army had established strategic strongholds in west Tennessee, northern Mississippi, and eastern Arkansas, subverting slavery in the vicinity of federal posts. The Army of the Tennessee, commanded by General Ulysses S. Grant, controlled Memphis and the railroad line east to Corinth, Mississippi. West of the Mississippi River, General Samuel R. Curtis's Army of the Southwest held Helena, Arkansas. Union gunboats plied the river from Cairo, Illinois, headquarters of the western navy, to Helena and beyond. With federal forces already in possession of New Orleans, the strategies of both belligerents increasingly focused upon the territory between Helena and the mouth of the Red River, above Baton Rouge, Louisiana. The contested area boasted some of the largest and most productive cotton-growing estates in the South, and slaves constituted a sizable majority of the population. Plantations with 100 or more slaves, relatively rare in west Tennessee, northern Mississippi, and eastern Arkansas, were common in the alluvial district south of Helena.

As Union troops positioned themselves to move farther south, thousands of slaves near Memphis, Corinth, Helena, and other posts fled their owners. At first most of them were young men who left family and friends behind. Some of the fugitives made straight for federal camps. Others, eager to escape bondage but suspicious of the Yankees' intentions, headed for the woods. Slaveholders, too, took flight – but away from, not toward, the invaders. They carried with them what property they could, including their most able and valuable slaves. Forsaking their other worldly goods, they instructed the slaves left behind to fend for themselves.[2]

Both enabled and obliged to support themselves, abandoned slaves appropriated as their own the fields they worked, the livestock they tended, and the houses they inhabited. Sometimes joined by fugitive slaves from the surrounding countryside, they eked out a livelihood cultivating corn and vegetables, hunting and gathering, and raiding the fields, stockpens, and smokehouses of nearby plantations. But sustaining an independent existence in a war zone tested the fortitude of

[2] On the collapse of slavery in the Union-occupied Mississippi Valley, see *Freedom*, ser. 1, vol. 1: chap. 5.

even the hardiest. Those freedpeople who inhabited the no man's land between hostile armies braved reprisals by vindictive slaveholders, assaults by rebel guerrillas, and depredations by straggling soldiers. Foraging parties from both armies seized food and draft animals at will, often depriving the squatters of their means of subsistence. A few intrepid ex-slaves remained on the abandoned estates despite the risks. But most could not maintain themselves in such catch-as-catch-can fashion. Fearing for their safety, they joined the exodus to Union lines.

Many slaves near federal posts neither fled to the Yankees nor squatted on abandoned land, but exploited their owners' apprehension that they might do so. Wary slaveholders tightened discipline, subjecting their slaves to closer surveillance and harsher punishment. But such measures failed as often as they succeeded, and some owners found themselves forced to negotiate if they wished to keep their slaves at work. They promised relief from onerous tasks, exemption from corporal punishment, and expansion of customary rights to garden plots. A few offered payments in cash or a share of the crop to "faithful" laborers. One west Tennessee farmer, convinced by the summer of 1862 that "all slaves would be free at the end of the war," told his slaves "that they were free to go or stay, as they might choose," but that those who stayed would receive half the cotton they produced. Some of them declined the offer and departed, but others remained for the duration of the war. A slaveholder near Helena left his slaves under the jurisdiction of an overseer, instructing them to "do the best they could." They continued at their work, but with an understanding that they would receive a share of the cotton crop in addition to standard issues of food and clothing. Slaves near the zone of federal occupation often chose to remain at home under such quasi-free labor arrangements rather than hazard the uncertainties of life with the Yankees.[3]

Not least of the uncertainties was how to support themselves and their families once within Union lines. Only healthy men willing and able to work for the army could count on protection and rations, much less wages. Throughout the first half of 1862, official policy barred most fugitive slaves from federal camps, even as the demands of waging war encouraged local commanders and ordinary soldiers to accept and employ them. Attempting to subdue a vast territory from a handful of scattered positions, the Union army required legions of laborers, teamsters, cooks, personal servants, laundresses, and hospital attendants; the navy called for hundreds more, both ashore at Cairo and aboard ship. By July 1862, when Congress and the President directed that all fugitive slaves be received and those fit for military labor be so employed, thousands of black men and a few hundred black women were

[3] In addition to the relevant documents in this chapter, see *Freedom*, ser. 1, vol. 1: doc. 123; affidavit of Geo. D. Martin, 15 Nov. 1864, filed with lease of George D. Martin, 14 Nov. 1864, Leases of Plantations, Helena Dist., 2d Agency, RG 366 [Q-34].

already at work for the Union. In some jurisdictions, their employment was the rule. "Every other soldier in the Army of the South West has a negro servant," observed the post commander at Helena. The ex-slaves' readiness to work increasingly generated a reciprocal readiness to employ, feed, and shelter them.[4]

Whereas able-bodied black men were greeted with open arms, black women, children, and old people often got the cold shoulder. But rather than return to their old homes, most took up residence within or just outside army lines, forcing local commanders to address their needs. With few explicit instructions from Washington, officers responded according to their own understanding of legal obligation and military exigency. Some refused to extend government support to any former slave not employed by the army. At Memphis, General William T. Sherman, commander of a division of the Army of the Tennessee, furnished food, clothing, and tobacco to black men engaged in military labor, but nothing to their families. Nor did the laborers receive wages with which to provide for the women, children, and old people. Uncertain whether ex-slave laborers or their owners were entitled to compensation, Sherman ordered that payment be withheld, pending "a fair and equitable settlement" after the war. The laborers' families had to shift for themselves.[5]

General Curtis took a more expansive view of the army's role in providing for former slaves. Of the fugitives who received "free papers" upon reaching his army, Curtis employed hundreds of men to construct fortifications at Helena, promising them $10 per month and feeding and sheltering their families. He also encouraged slaves who had remained on abandoned estates to sell cotton and other property to government agents (himself included) and thereby gain "the necessary means of sustenance." Furthermore, he transported to Cairo at their own request several hundred former slaves "not . . . needed in the Public Service."[6]

[4] On the transformation of federal policy respecting fugitive slaves in the Mississippi Valley, see *Freedom*, ser. 1, vol. 1: chap. 5. On the employment of ex-slaves as military laborers early in the war, see, in addition to the relevant documents in this chapter, *Freedom*, ser. 1, vol. 1: docs. 82–83, 90, 93–94; clipping from *New-York Daily Tribune*, 27 Jan. 1863, "Negroes," Consolidated Correspondence File, ser. 225, Central Records, RG 92 [Y-25]; Ulysses S. Grant, *The Papers of Ulysses S. Grant*, ed. John Y. Simon, David L. Wilson, John M. Hoffman, Roger D. Bridges, and Thomas Alexander, 16 vols. to date (Carbondale, Ill., 1967–), vol. 5, pp. 199, 272–73.

[5] In addition to the relevant documents in this chapter, see *Freedom*, ser. 1, vol. 1: docs. 92, 94; *Official Records*, ser. 1, vol. 17, pt. 2, pp. 169–71; *Navy Official Records*, ser. 1, vol. 23, pp. 472–73, 475.

[6] In addition to the relevant documents in this chapter, see Earl J. Hess, "Confiscation and the Northern War Effort: The Army of the Southwest at Helena," *Arkansas Historical Quarterly* 44 (Spring 1985): 56–75. On the "free papers" issued by Curtis, see *Freedom*, ser. 1, vol. 1: p. 259 and doc. 95.

Whatever their status with local military authorities, fugitive slaves within Union lines lived in difficult circumstances. Most had arrived with only the personal belongings they could carry. Many were ill or exhausted by their trek. Some, however, had been able to plot their escape with more care, raiding the plantation storehouse or appropriating a mule before striking out. A few had spent months "laying up their money . . . preparing to leave their masters." But risks remained even for those who had planned carefully and reached Union lines unscathed. With shelter scarce, the "contrabands" dwelled in condemned army tents and shanties constructed of any available material. Often they fell victim to diseases that spread rapidly in such crowded and unsanitary surroundings. Their few possessions were regularly confiscated by army quartermasters under orders to seize what was militarily useful or by individual soldiers under no orders at all. Most able-bodied ex-slave men found military employment, as did some women, but their earnings were often insufficient to feed and clothe dependents. Many women, children, and old people foraged for food or planted gardens; others performed odd jobs in army camps. But their poverty and their uncertain standing with military authorities left them vulnerable.

The plight of the former slaves attracted the attention of sympathetic Northerners in and out of army ranks. In some places, federal soldiers – most often chaplains – worked to alleviate destitution and disease. But the task was daunting, and they appealed for assistance. In letters to home-state newspapers and benevolent societies and in petitions to their superiors, they described the privations of the freedpeople, praised the services of black military laborers, and called for a national commitment to aid former slaves who, having escaped bondage, now suffered in freedom.

Partly in response to such appeals, the War Department began to affirm the necessity of providing for all fugitive slaves who reached Union lines. Secretary of War Edwin M. Stanton sanctioned the course of a local commander at Helena who had housed and fed black women and children over the objections of General Frederick Steele, Curtis's successor. Quartermaster General Montgomery C. Meigs instructed a subordinate at Jackson, Tennessee, to provide for all the fugitive slaves in his jurisdiction. Meigs also suggested that a portion of the wages owed to black military laborers be withheld and the resulting fund used for the welfare of the unemployed. "The labor of the men & those women able to work should support the whole community of negroes at any station," Meigs declared. Although the War Department continued to give local commanders broad latitude in dealing with former slaves, a proliferation of inquiries from the field forced officials to begin formulating general guidelines.

The growing number of black refugees tested the policies improvised by field commanders. With winter approaching, many of the former slaves who had been abandoned by their owners drifted toward federal lines rather than endure hunger and rebel depredations. News of President Lincoln's impending Emancipation Proclamation emboldened other slaves to flee to the Yankees. Although the destitute new arrivals required immediate relief, military employers had use for only a fraction of them. In mid-September 1862, General Grant settled the families of black military laborers in a "Contraband Retreat" near Corinth, under the supervision of an army chaplain.[7] A few weeks later, he ordered more than 600 freedpeople transported from there to Columbus, Kentucky, and Cairo, Illinois. The commander at Cairo offered to arrange their hire to civilian employers, and Secretary of War Stanton approved. But as news of the intended transfer spread, white midwesterners, inflamed by race-baiting Democrats, protested any movement of former slaves into the free states. When Republican politicians warned of an electoral backlash, Stanton abruptly annulled the plan.[8]

Worried that the black refugees would encumber his army, but forbidden to relocate them to the North, Grant sought advice from his superiors. Former slaves, he informed General-in-Chief Henry W. Halleck, were entering his lines "by wagon loads." In response, Halleck directed him to employ at military labor those who were physically qualified and to put the others to work picking cotton in abandoned fields.[9] Meanwhile, Grant placed John Eaton, Jr., an army chaplain from Ohio, in charge of fugitive slaves near LaGrange, Tennessee, and authorized him to establish a contraband camp at the nearby railroad town of Grand Junction. In December, he designated Eaton general superintendent of contrabands in the Department of the Tennessee. Eaton, in turn, appointed subordinate superintendents, mostly fellow chaplains, to assist in supervising the former slaves at other posts.[10]

New arrivals swelled the population of the first contraband camps, while the advance of Grant's army toward Vicksburg necessitated new ones. By early 1863, according to Eaton's estimate, more than 22,000 former slaves had come under the purview of his superintendents: nearly 3,700 at Corinth; 1,700 at Grand Junction; some 1,400 in camps near Memphis and another 2,500 "living about town"; 5,000 at

7 *Papers of Ulysses S. Grant*, vol. 6, pp. 54–55; Special Orders No. 195, Headquarters, District of West Tennessee, 15 Sept. 1862, vol. G4 DT, pp. 336–37, Special Orders Issued, ser. 2734, Dist. of West TN, RG 393 Pt. 2 No. 171 [C-2239].

8 *Official Records*, ser. 3, vol. 2, pp. 569, 663. On Northern opposition to immigration by Southern ex-slaves, see V. Jacque Voegeli, *Free but Not Equal: The Midwest and the Negro during the Civil War* (Chicago, 1967), chap. 4.

9 *Papers of Ulysses S. Grant*, vol. 6, pp. 315–17.

10 In addition to the relevant documents in this chapter, see John Eaton, *Grant, Lincoln and the Freedmen: Reminiscences of the Civil War* (1907; reprint ed., New York, 1969), chaps. 1–3; Ulysses S. Grant, *Personal Memoirs of Ulysses S. Grant*, 2 vols. (New York, 1885), vol. 1, pp. 424–26.

Cairo; a total of 2,500 at Columbus, Kentucky, and Jackson and LaGrange, Tennessee; nearly 2,400 at Lake Providence, Louisiana; and roughly 3,000 at unspecified other points.

The contraband camps served as receiving depots, hiring centers, and temporary settlements. Union soldiers forwarded incoming fugitives to the nearest camp, whose superintendent assigned them to labor according to their sex, age, and physical condition. Most of the able-bodied men joined military labor gangs, which were detailed wherever necessity dictated. Some women and a few children also found employment with the army, but most women and children either worked around the contraband camps or were hired to civilian employers, chiefly as domestic servants. Residents of several camps harvested cotton and corn from abandoned fields or labored for landowners who employed them through the superintendents.

Eaton and his subordinates assumed responsibility for the welfare as well as the work of the freedpeople. Army surgeons ministered to the sick, quartermasters distributed blankets, and commissaries of subsistence issued rations. The superintendents of contrabands also tapped the resources of midwestern churches and freedmen's aid societies. Donations of clothing, medical supplies, garden seed, and tools, although never quite adequate to the task, alleviated much misery.

The superintendents of the contraband camps sought not only to sustain but also to remake the lives of their charges, transforming dependent former slaves into self-sufficient citizens. In Eaton's view, years of bondage had destroyed the freedpeople's ability to "follow their own undirected, unaided, fortunes" and distorted their understanding of the "relation between their industry and their comfort." Nor had they developed "the innate love of possession, on which is based the acquisition of wealth, and all the relations of property." By inculcating such values, Eaton hoped in time to make the former slaves independent. But at the outset, he believed, most of them required "a guardian." "Strict Supervision . . . down to the minutest details" thus became a virtue, not simply a wartime necessity. Generally sharing Eaton's vision, the superintendents organized schools as systematically as they dispensed rations and scrutinized the freedpeople's domestic life as closely as they monitored their work routine. A handful of teachers and ministers sponsored by Northern aid societies also took part, equally intent upon remaking the former slaves in their own image.[11]

The residents of the contraband camps took aid where they could

[11] In addition to the relevant documents in this chapter, see Chaplain John Eaton, Jr., to Lt. Col. Jno. A. Rawlins, 29 Apr. 1863, filed with O-328 1863, Letters Received, ser. 12, RG 94 [K-89]; [John Eaton, Jr.,] to Hon. Henry Wilson, [Feb.?] 1863, and [John Eaton, Jr.,] to Robert W. Carroll, 9 Feb. 1863, vol. 74, pp. 13–23, Letters Sent by John Eaton, ser. 2027, General Supt. of Freedmen, MS Asst. Comr. Pre-Bureau Records, RG 105 [A-4000, A-4002].

find it, but they also pursued their own objectives. They welcomed the chance to "make their own money and protect their families." Some of them set out from the camps to their old homes in hopes of "recruiting" kin and friends.[12] Seizing the opportunity to give their unions legal standing, husbands and wives sought out army chaplains and civilian ministers to conduct marriage ceremonies. The inhabitants of the camps also attended schools and organized religious congregations, often presided over by leaders from their own ranks.

For all its privations, life in the contraband camps afforded former slaves some latitude within which to assert their independence. The freedpeople at Corinth, supervised by Chaplain James M. Alexander, transformed the makeshift "Contraband Retreat" into a thriving community. By the end of 1862, they had constructed sturdy log cabins, as well as a church, a hospital, and a commissary. They policed the streets and acted as their own guards. They worked for the army when called upon and harvested crops from abandoned fields. Come spring, they tended gardens. Far from being an expense to the government, the freedpeople at Corinth supported themselves and, by Alexander's reckoning, returned a surplus of more than $3,000 per month to the U.S. Treasury.[13]

But at Corinth, as elsewhere, the fate of former slaves depended upon the fortunes of the Union army. The widely dispersed locations of federal posts exposed the contraband camps to rebel raids, and redeployment of federal troops put once-secure areas at risk. Military developments thus jeopardized the efforts of former slaves to support themselves and reconstitute their families – and sometimes even to maintain their freedom. Beginning in late December 1862, after Confederate forces overran the supply depot at Holly Springs, Mississippi, Union officers moved most of the fugitive slaves in west Tennessee to the relative safety of Memphis. But many were left behind in the confusion, some to be captured and reenslaved.[14]

Former slaves within Union lines owed much of the insecurity in their lives to rebel raiders, but they had federal authorities to blame for erratic payment of their wages. Nonpayment stemmed from numerous causes. Although the Militia Act of July 1862 provided that black military laborers be paid $10 per month, some Union officers continued to question the legality of payments to former slaves who might yet be claimed by loyal owners. At Helena, General Steele reneged on Curtis's pledge to pay the laborers who worked on the fortifications,

[12] For an account of armed contrabands from Corinth "recruiting" slaves behind Confederate lines, see *Freedom*, ser. 1, vol. 1: doc. 101.

[13] In addition to the relevant documents in this chapter, see Cam Walker, "Corinth: The Story of a Contraband Camp," *Civil War History* 20 (Mar. 1974): 5–22.

[14] On the evacuation of Holly Springs and its aftermath, see Eaton, *Grant, Lincoln and the Freedmen*, pp. 25–28, 30–32.

insisting that wages be withheld until it was determined whether the workers or their putative owners should collect. By the end of 1862, black military laborers at the post were owed as much as $50,000. But even when commanders were willing to compensate ex-slaves, any number of circumstances might intervene to delay or prevent payment. Negligence or outright fraud by subordinate officers frequently made it impossible for black workers to document their employment and hence to collect their wages. Bureaucratic entanglements and budgetary shortfalls delayed the disbursement of funds. For whatever reasons, former slaves all too often received nothing more than subsistence during their first experience with free labor. "The services of a large number have been stolen outright," affirmed one superintendent.[15]

Former slaves had reservations about a system of wage labor in which the laborers received no wages. Residents of the contraband camp at Grand Junction, observed its superintendent, exhibited a "considerable disposition to escape labor, having had no sufficient motives to work." Other superintendents concurred. Eaton himself recognized the difficulty of teaching former slaves the duties and benefits of freedom "without a proper use of the motives inspired by reward for labor." He recommended (without success) that the money owed to former slaves be invested in U.S. securities, believing it unwise to pay cash to the workers "until they are prepared for its proper use." He also approved the plan, adopted at Corinth, of crediting part of the wages owed black laborers to a fund for the benefit of dependent former slaves.[16]

Nonpayment of wages forced military laborers to seek alternative means of support. Some hired themselves to private employers who offered better wages and delivered on their promises. Large numbers of freedmen performed intermittent stints of military labor between periods of private employment, independent production, and leisure. Turnover among military laborers ran especially high at Fort Pickering in Memphis, where fewer than 400 of the 2,000 freedmen on the labor rolls appeared for work on any given day.[17] The coming and going of black military laborers often left the army short-handed. When newly arrived fugitive slaves or workers detailed from other posts failed to fill the vacancies, military officials resorted to force. The necessity of impressment revealed both how indispensable black workers had become to the Union war effort and how difficult it was to retain them without compensation.

[15] In addition to the relevant documents in this chapter, see clipping from *New-York Daily Tribune*, 27 Jan. 1863, "Negroes," Consolidated Correspondence File, ser. 225, Central Records, RG 92 [Y-25].

[16] In addition to the relevant documents in this chapter, see Chaplain John Eaton, Jr., to Lt. Col. Jno. A. Rawlins, 29 Apr. 1863, filed with O-328 1863, Letters Received, ser. 12, RG 94 [K-89].

[17] Chaplain John Eaton, Jr., to Lt. Col. Jno. A. Rawlins, 29 Apr. 1863, filed with O-328 1863, Letters Received, ser. 12, RG 94 [K-89].

Events in the early months of 1863 radically altered the circumstances in which former slaves in the Mississippi Valley lived and worked. The Emancipation Proclamation, issued on the first day of the new year, declared free all slaves in the seceded states of the valley, with the notable exception of Tennessee. It also announced the government's intention to enlist black men as soldiers, and encouraged the freedpeople to "labor faithfully for reasonable wages."[18] In the ensuing months, military operations against Vicksburg freed thousands of slaves and forced rebel masters to abandon some of the largest and most productive cotton plantations in the South. While increasing the number of freedpeople dependent on the government, the campaign also gave Union authorities control over land on which the refugees could support themselves and, more than likely, produce a substantial surplus. The former slaves, Lincoln and members of his administration concluded, "had better be set to digging their subsistence out of the ground."[19]

A broad array of Northerners shared that conviction, but they differed among themselves over how best to achieve the goal. Some, including Chaplain Eaton, proposed that Union-occupied plantations be operated under direct government supervision. In early 1863, Eaton made plans to cultivate fields near several existing contraband camps and to relocate freedpeople from Cairo and Columbus to Island 10, near the border between Kentucky and Tennessee, where abandoned land was available for cultivation. Those former slaves not suited for labor with the army would work crops "planted & gathered in common," under the close direction of the superintendents of contrabands.

With cotton prices at an all-time high, other observers hoped that returning former slaves to the fields would promote private gain as well as the public good. George B. Field, a New York attorney with ties to Secretary of War Stanton, recommended that abandoned plantations on the west bank of the Mississippi below Memphis be leased to Northern investors, who would hire black workers at wages regulated by the government. Such arrangements, Field emphasized, would at once enable the freedpeople to support themselves and demonstrate that cotton production with free labor "can be made a *source* of *profit* to the *employer*."

Field's suggestion struck a responsive chord in the Lincoln administration. In late March 1863, shortly after meeting with Field, Secretary of War Stanton dispatched Adjutant General Lorenzo Thomas to the Mississippi Valley. Thomas, a career army officer whose antebellum service had included a stint in Mississippi, was charged chiefly with recruiting black soldiers, but he quickly grasped the connection between that mission and the reorganization of agricultural production.

[18] *Statutes at Large*, vol. 12, pp. 68–69. For an official explication of changes in federal policy signaled by the proclamation, see *Freedom*, ser. 2: doc. 50.

[19] *Freedom*, ser. 1, vol. 1: doc. 107.

Sharing Field's faith in private investment, he proposed to lease abandoned estates to Northerners and Southern unionists, who would employ those freedpeople not suited for service as military laborers or soldiers. Newly recruited black soldiers, meanwhile, would garrison federal posts along the Mississippi River, protect the contraband camps and leased plantations, and safeguard "commercial intercourse on this great 'inland sea.' " This course, Thomas hoped, would "[line] the river with a loyal population" of liberated slaves and white unionists.[20]

In many Union-occupied parts of the Mississippi Valley, however, military and political circumstances worked against Thomas's strategy. West Tennessee was particularly ill-suited. Because Tennessee was exempt from the Emancipation Proclamation, slavery remained legal. Yet there was no legitimate civil authority to enforce bondage, and Union military officials, "both from choice and under orders," disregarded the master-slave relationship. In and around Memphis, slaves comported themselves as though they were free. Moreover, months of intermittent warfare, extensive foraging by both armies, and the movement of slaves to the city had desolated much of the countryside. In addition to military laborers, some 5,000 former slaves relied upon the federal government for support. Condemning the contraband camps as a "tremendous failure and a mere excuse for misplaced charity," General Stephen A. Hurlbut, commander of the 16th Army Corps, sought Lincoln's permission to hire former slaves to private employers. But few black people were willing to leave Memphis to toil as agricultural laborers in unsafe rural areas. Hurlbut himself realized that the legality of slavery and the menace of rebel guerrillas threatened the freedom and security of former slaves employed in the countryside.[21] Nevertheless, he and his subordinates expelled a great many freedpeople from Memphis, only to find them "constantly returning." Eventually he established a new contraband camp on President's Island, just below the city, to which he relocated residents of other camps as well as black "vagrants."[22]

A few hundred miles downriver, in northeastern Louisiana, condi-

20 For Stanton's order dispatching Thomas to the Mississippi Valley, see *Official Records*, ser. 3, vol. 3, pp. 100–101. On Thomas's recruitment and plantation policies, see, in addition to the relevant documents in this chapter, *Freedom*, ser. 2: pp. 116–19, 484–85, and docs. 194–95.

21 In addition to the relevant documents in this chapter, see *Freedom*, ser. 1, vol. 1: doc. 107; Maj. Genl. S. A. Hurlbut to Lt. Col. Jno. A. Rawlins, 26 Mar. 1863, vol. 1/18 16AC, p. 83, Letters & Telegrams Sent, ser. 385, 16th Army Corps, RG 393 Pt. 2 No. 7 [C-8600].

22 John Eaton, Jr., to Col. Smith, 22 May 1863, vol. 74, p. 54, Letters Sent by John Eaton, ser. 2027, General Superintendent of Freedmen, MS Asst. Comr. Pre-Bureau Records, RG 105 [A-4001]. On the wartime history of President's Island, see Capt. T. A. Walker to Brig. Gen'l. Davis Tillson, 8 July 1865, enclosed in Capt. T. A. Walker to Brig. Genl. Davis Tillson, 8 July 1865, Unregistered Letters Received, ser. 3522, Memphis TN Subasst. Comr., RG 105 [A-6512].

tions better suited Thomas's plans. The advance against Vicksburg had placed in federal hands a number of cotton plantations owned by disloyal proprietors, and in early April 1863 Thomas appointed three "commissioners of plantations," headed by Field, to institute a system of rental to private investors.[23] With only limited territory safely under Union control, they began by leasing out about forty estates along a seventy-five-mile stretch of the river. Eager to implement the new system speedily, they offered the land in large tracts to Northerners already on the scene, including cotton speculators and civilian employees of the army.

Thomas declared the leased plantations off-limits to Union foraging parties and ordered local commanders to protect them from Confederate raids. He also directed military authorities, upon the request of the plantation commissioners, to supply each lessee with "as many negroes . . . as he may desire" – thereby denying the freedpeople any choice of employer. The laborers were to remain on the plantation until the following February. Thomas's labor regulations forbade corporal punishment and set wages at $7 per month for men and $5 for women. Children between the ages of twelve and fifteen were to receive half the wages of adults; those under twelve were exempt from field labor. The regulations required lessees to bear the expense of feeding and housing the laborers and their families, but the cost of clothing would be deducted from the laborers' wages. The new terms, announced the commissioners, were "based upon the presentation of *motives* to the African in contrast with the *lash*."[24]

The primary motive was the expectation of a wage, not the stimulus of independent enterprise. Although the commissioners later permitted some fifteen former slaves to rent small farms from estates whose lessees failed to fulfill their agreements, the vast majority of black workers on the government-sponsored plantations were wage hands, not independent farmers. Their employers chose the crops to be planted and organized labor as they saw fit, subject only to Thomas's stipulations. The commissioners encouraged the Yankees' propensity to raise cotton

[23] The other commissioners were Chaplain Lark S. Livermore, superintendent of contrabands at Lake Providence, Louisiana, and Captain Abraham E. Strickle, an officer in the subsistence department. Only Field served to the end of the year. Strickle died soon after his appointment, and Livermore resumed his duties as a chaplain. (Gerteis, *From Contraband to Freedman*, p. 126.) Thomas replaced them with two civilian appointees: Lewis Dent, a Northern lessee (and General Grant's brother-in-law), and Robert V. Montague, a Louisiana planter. Shortly after appointing the original commissioners, Thomas authorized two chaplains, Jacob G. Forman and Samuel Sawyer, to supervise the leasing of plantations in Union-occupied Arkansas. (Special Orders No. 12, 18 Apr. 1863, L. Thomas Letters & Orders, Generals' Papers & Books, ser. 159, RG 94 [V-321].)

[24] For the commissioners' characterization, see Geo. B. Field et al. to Hon. E. M. Stanton, 16 May 1863, filed with #1315 1886, Letters Received, ser. 12, RG 94 [K-574].

rather than food and forage crops, which meant that all plantation residents were dependent upon rations provided by the lessees. Neither the commissioners nor Thomas objected when most lessees worked their employees in gangs or hired "managers" who had served as overseers under the old regime. "The cultivation of cotton under slave labor," Thomas later wrote, "is the result of experience. Now, under compensated labor, the nearer it can approach this, the better, and the further we depart from it, the worse."[25] Before long, some "experienced" native planters in the vicinity of the leased plantations also accepted Thomas's terms. Unable to enforce slave labor and therefore compelled to make the best of a bad bargain, they acquiesced to emancipation and hired ex-slave laborers – sometimes including their own former slaves – through the commissioners.

Federal military operations made it difficult for freedpeople to support themselves outside the contraband camps or the government-supervised plantations. In the Vicksburg area, Grant's army displaced numerous independent settlements of former slaves, impressing the men as laborers or soldiers and seizing food and livestock. The relatives of such men, noted one Union officer, complained "that they (the old, with numerous old women and children) had enough to support them until the soldiers . . . carried off their chickens, or killed their pigs or their milk cows."[26] No longer able to feed themselves, they had little choice but to seek refuge at the nearest contraband camp. Once there, they came under the jurisdiction of the plantation commissioners.

Military seizure of "contraband" goods also undercut the efforts of former slaves to work on their own account. Freedpeople who exited slavery in possession of livestock, wagons, farm implements, and other productive property often had it confiscated by federal quartermasters, irrespective of its provenance or military value. Adding insult to injury, the quartermasters supplied some of the draft animals and other confiscated goods to the plantation lessees. Such forcible redistribution of resources outraged General John P. Hawkins, whose District of Northeastern Louisiana encompassed most of the plantations leased in 1863. Because the Emancipation Proclamation entitled them to freedom, Hawkins contended, it was "no crime" for slaves to appropriate their owners' possessions to escape bondage. By allowing them to retain such property, the federal government would enable the freedpeople "to cultivate a few acres of ground" without outside assistance; "[b]y taking it away they or their families are made paupers for perhaps all time to come." But Hawkins's argument failed to persuade his superiors. Gen-

[25] Adjutant General L. Thomas to Mr. William P. Mellen, 22 Feb. 1865, General Letters Received, Records of the General Agent, RG 366 [Q-162].

[26] In addition to the relevant documents in this chapter, see Col. Richd. Owen to Col. Scates, 9 May 1863, vol. 3 13AC, pp. 162–65, Letters Received, ser. 5536, 13th Army Corps, RG 393 Pt. 2 No. 352 [C-7624].

eral Sherman held that a former slave had "no right to the property of his former owner, unless by special gift." Considering their own claim nothing more than common justice, freedpeople took little comfort from Sherman's codicil that the army might temporarily permit them to use the seized property.

In the absence of ready alternatives, several thousand freedpeople in the Vicksburg area accepted employment on the leased plantations. As much as they disliked the prospect of working in gangs under the supervision of overseers, they generally preferred such employment to remaining in crowded and unhealthy "depots." Those who were reluctant to work for the lessees found themselves forcibly escorted to the plantations, where they again had to acclimate themselves to new surroundings among strangers. Owing to patterns of flight from bondage and the widespread employment of healthy young men by the Union army, the labor forces of the leased estates seldom included large numbers of people who had lived and worked together as slaves; instead they were assembled from the fragments of numerous antebellum plantation communities. Women and children made up an increasingly large proportion of the whole. The lessees' preference for able-bodied workers caused further fragmentation, as elderly, sick, and disabled people were left behind at the contraband camps. To provide for the former slaves who were unwanted by either lessees or military employers, the plantation commissioners reserved several estates as "infirm farms."[27]

While the Yankees struggled to reorganize plantation agriculture on the basis of wage labor, the rebels set out to destroy it. In a series of attacks on the "government plantations" in June 1863, Confederate soldiers torched buildings, commandeered tools and livestock, killed dozens of former slaves, and kidnapped hundreds more – 1,200 by one estimate.[28] Thousands of panicked plantation laborers retreated to the safety of the contraband camps and Union army posts. Many of them vowed never to return to the estates. Those who later went back to reclaim possessions or tend growing crops found the plantations devastated.

The lessees, too, were shaken by the raids. Fearing for their lives, a large number abandoned the enterprise altogether. Others returned to the plantations to recoup their losses – often at their laborers' expense. An inspector commissioned by General Hawkins reported in October that not a single lessee had fully complied with the terms of his contract

[27] On the establishment of the infirm farms, see Geo. B. Field et al. to Hon. E. M. Stanton, 16 May 1863, filed with #1315 1886, Letters Received, ser. 12, RG 94 [K-574].

[28] In addition to the relevant documents in this chapter, see *Official Records*, ser. 1, vol. 22, pt. 2, pp. 578–79, 856–57; ser. 1, vol. 24, pt. 2, pp. 457–61, 466; ser. 1, vol. 24, pt. 3, p. 1049.

and many had shown "utter disregard of even the commonest principles of humanity . . . in their treatment of the contrabands." To turn a profit, the lessees overcharged for goods, stinted rations, and failed to pay wages. Even when plantation hands were duly credited for their work, deductions for lost time and for clothing and other supplies reduced their meager earnings. "[A]t the end of the year," Hawkins acidly observed, "the Negro has less money than was usual with him when a slave," along with "the consolation of knowing he has been worse fed and worse treated." Hawkins castigated the lessees as "adventurers[,] hangers-on of the Army and the like[,] men who cared nothing how much flesh they worked off of the negro provided it was converted into good cotton at Seventy five cents per pound." "Cotton closes their eyes to justice," he concluded, "just as it did in the case of the former slave master."

While the plantation-leasing system floundered, recruitment of black soldiers flourished. Thousands of black men joined the Union army during the spring and summer of 1863. Recruiting parties routinely visited the plantations and inducted black men into the service – sometimes by force. Those who were impressed resented having to leave their families, abandon growing crops, and forfeit wages. Whether the new soldiers went willingly or not, planters had reason to complain, because recruitment removed their most valuable field workers. The protests of former slaves might easily be ignored; not so those of the proprietors and lessees. By June, they had raised such an uproar that General Thomas banned recruiting on the government-supervised plantations. But Thomas's directive scarcely slowed enlistment. The capture of Vicksburg in early July, Natchez a few weeks later, and Little Rock in September brought thousands of former slaves under federal jurisdiction. Army recruiters had a field day. By the end of the year most Union authorities had concluded that since newly arrived fugitive slaves volunteered in such numbers, it did more harm than good to impress black men who were already at work for planters or military employers.[29]

Northern occupation and the enlistment of black men altered the balance of power in the newly conquered territory. Former slaves increasingly demanded and won concessions from their former owners. Some erstwhile slaveholders offered wage arrangements similar to those on

[29] On recruitment in the Mississippi Valley, see, in addition to the relevant documents in this chapter, *Freedom*, ser. 2: chap. 3; Brig. Genl. Jas. S. Wadsworth to the Adjutant General U.S. Army, 16 Dec. 1863, enclosed in S. P. Chase to Wm. P. Mellen, Esquire, 17 Dec. 1863, Letters Received from the Secretary of the Treasury, Records of the General Agent, RG 366 [Q-142]. In November 1864, Adjutant General Thomas himself noted that many more black regiments could have been raised in the Mississippi Valley but for the army's need for black men as military laborers. (*Freedom*, ser. 2: doc. 62.)

the leased plantations, and a few held out more attractive terms. Shortly after federal troops reached Natchez, one freedman later recalled, his mistress announced "that she did not want us to leave" and offered to "rent us land or pay us wages and protect us." Expediency, if not conviction, forced many resident planters to accept the rudiments of free labor.[30]

Federal authorities in the Mississippi Valley, hoping to cultivate unionist sentiment among the local gentry, encouraged such conversions. Once former slaveholders acquiesced to free labor, military officers exempted their field hands from conscription, forbade seizure of their livestock and tools, and helped them obtain supplies. By denying such benefits to disloyal proprietors, the army led many to reconsider their allegiance. General Sherman outlined the minimal conditions to planters near Vicksburg: "You must do as we do, hire your Servants and pay them. If they don't earn their hire, discharge them and employ others." Few planters adopted the new ground rules enthusiastically, and some secretly supported the rebellion while giving lip service to the Union. But for most, self-interest overrode Confederate patriotism.[31] Taking advantage of their former owners' readiness to negotiate, many freedpeople remained on their home plantations on new terms.

For former slaves who were unwilling or unable to stay on the old estates, Union army installations offered the best hope of finding freedom, protection, food, and work. The newly occupied cities of Vicksburg and Natchez attracted thousands of black refugees. Their arrival delighted army recruiters but taxed relief facilities. When hastily organized contraband camps filled to overflowing, former slaves crowded into abandoned dwellings and built shanties near regiments of black troops. Residents of these makeshift quarters struggled to piece together a livelihood, taking odd jobs, tilling gardens, and sharing the pay and rations of black soldiers, who defended the "contraband family camps" and "regimental villages" against the objections of local planters and some Northern officers.

Even when the will was present, the Union army often lacked the means to provide for newly arrived refugees. Officials in the Vicksburg area put as many as possible to work on leased plantations, but military conditions elsewhere precluded that solution. At Helena, where Union control extended barely beyond the picket lines, Adjutant General

[30] In addition to the relevant documents in this chapter, see testimony of Wallace Turner, 5 July 1873, claim of Thomas Turner, Adams Co. MS case files, Approved Claims, ser. 732, Southern Claims Commission, 3rd Auditor, RG 217 [I-193]; *Freedom*, ser. 2: doc. 52.

[31] On the military policy of "calculated magnanimity" and its sanction by the Lincoln administration, see Lawrence N. Powell and Michael S. Wayne, "Self-Interest and the Decline of Confederate Nationalism," in *The Old South in the Crucible of War*, ed. Harry P. Owens and James J. Cooke [Jackson, Miss., 1983], pp. 29–46.

Thomas's commissioners succeeded in leasing out only two estates, which provided for a few hundred former slaves at most. Many times that number lived in a contraband camp just outside the town, dependent upon the uncertain largess of the government and vulnerable to Confederate raids – one of which, in July 1863, destroyed the camp and scattered its residents.[32]

Unable to protect and provide for the growing number of fugitive slaves, federal officials at Helena resorted to shipping them north. Beginning in early 1863, successive commanders of the District of Eastern Arkansas sent "boatloads" of freedpeople to St. Louis. There, Chaplain Samuel Sawyer, a superintendent of contrabands, hired them to local unionists and to applicants from midwestern states. But the northward relocation came to an abrupt end in October, when General Hurlbut ruled that thereafter the former slaves "must be employed & fed where they are." In response, General Napoleon B. Buford, the commander at Helena, moved hundreds of freedpeople to Islands 63 and 66, in the Mississippi River, where the men cut wood and the women and children corded it. Such wood yards – some of them supervised by private contractors, others by government superintendents – became the largest employers of former slaves in the Helena area. But the islands could not support all the new arrivals from the interior, thousands of whom gathered in a reconstructed contraband camp.

Throughout the Union-occupied Mississippi Valley, the government's inability to accommodate the ex-slave refugees forced them to be self-reliant. Drawing upon skills learned in bondage, they worked to alleviate suffering and improve themselves. With disease rampant and physicians in short supply, black "grannies" ministered to the sick. Even when army hospitals were available, freedpeople generally preferred to provide their own medical care through established ties of family and community. In similar fashion, former slaves who had learned to read and write joined teachers sponsored by Northern aid societies in tutoring the unlettered, and "old patriarchs" conducted religious ceremonies and burial services as they had before the war.

Blind to evidence of self-organization among the former slaves, Adjutant General Thomas saw only their destitution. Touring the Mississippi Valley in August 1863, he was alarmed to find tens of thousands of freedpeople living near Union army posts without visible means of support. To reduce the government's relief expenditures, he ordered ex-slave women, children, and old men to remain on their home estates; those who had left were "encouraged" to return, provided

[32] In addition to the relevant documents in this chapter, see Major W. G. Sargent to Col. John Eaton, Jr., 1 Mar. 1864, enclosed in Major W. G. Sargent to A.A. General C. H. Dyer, 17 May 1864, Miscellaneous Letters & Reports Sent & Received, ser. 272, Dist. of Little Rock, RG 393 Pt. 3 [C-254].

their former owners treated them as free and paid them wages.[33] To better protect the contraband camps and government-supervised plantations, he authorized the enlistment of black men unfit for regular military duty into "invalid" regiments. John Eaton, the general superintendent of freedmen, was promoted to colonel of one of the regiments. By the fall, companies from the new units were scattered along the Mississippi River as guards for the camps and plantations.[34]

Having revised the army's policy respecting former slaves, Adjutant General Thomas drafted a rose-colored report of the leasing system in the Mississippi Valley. Despite the unavoidably late planting season and the disruptions of rebel raids, he boasted, his scheme had demonstrated the viability of free labor. "[N]ot one of the lessees will loose money," he predicted, "but all derive a profit." The former slaves, he averred, were well treated and "perfectly contented." Tossing aside contradictory evidence – much of it furnished by Union officers in the field – Thomas pronounced his system "a complete success."

The adjutant general touted his plan as a basis for reconstructing the entire South. Many planters, he believed, had come to regard slavery and the Confederacy as lost causes. Eager to save their property from confiscation and recoup their fortunes, they seemed "perfectly willing to hire the negroes and adopt any policy the Government may dictate." Thomas himself favored a program of conciliation that would encourage erstwhile secessionists to join Southern unionists and Yankee lessees in rebuilding plantation agriculture. In late October 1863, he authorized planters "of undoubted loyalty" to occupy and manage their own property, whether their unionism was longstanding or of recent vintage. Even proprietors of dubious loyalty might be permitted to operate their estates, provided they joined in partnership with "a loyal citizen."[35] President Lincoln soon proffered a similar invitation. His Proclamation of Amnesty and Reconstruction, issued in early December, allowed most repentant rebels to reclaim their property, aside from their slaves, upon taking an oath signifying allegiance to the Union and acceptance of emancipation.[36]

Many planters in the Mississippi Valley assented to Lincoln's terms. Forming alliances of convenience with Northern investors, army officers, and simon-pure unionists, they resumed control over their estates. In 1864, the number of federally supervised plantations operated by

[33] In addition to the relevant documents in this chapter, see *Freedom*, ser. 1, vol. 1: doc. 110; *Official Records*, ser. 3, vol. 3, p. 1044.

[34] On the invalid regiments recruited in the Mississippi Valley (which became the 63rd and 64th USCI), see Eaton, *Grant, Lincoln and the Freedmen*, pp. 107–12.

[35] In addition to the relevant documents in this chapter, see *Freedom*, ser. 1, vol. 1: doc. 110; Circular, 27 Oct. 1863, enclosed in L. Thomas to Col. E. D. Townsend, 19 Apr. 1864, filed as A-1370 1864, Letters Received, ser. 12, RG 94 [K-578].

[36] *Statutes at Large*, vol. 13, pp. 737–39.

antebellum owners (alone or in partnership) exceeded the number operated by Northern lessees. George Field welcomed such "amicable connections" between "*loyal Northern men*" and "the *owners* of the soil." In his view, this "union of interests" portended "an enduring and mutually advantageous reconstruction of the Union."

Ex-slave laborers took a dimmer view of developments on the plantations. Whether they had worked for Northerners or Southerners, most of them ended the 1863 season with little or nothing to show for their work. By supplementing their meager wages with earnings from independent labor, a few families managed to acquire draft animals, tools, or a bit of cash with which to better their prospects. But the mass of black agricultural laborers could barely support themselves from their wages. Dissatisfied with the result of their first year as free workers, large numbers left the plantations in what one Northern observer characterized as "a general stampede."[37]

With the harvest season at an end and lessees and landowners busily making arrangements for the new year, numerous Northerners in the Mississippi Valley voiced misgivings about the Union-sponsored free-labor system. The program adopted by Adjutant General Thomas, critics charged, offered too much to Yankee speculators and former secessionists and too little to former slaves. At the very least, argued General Hawkins, freed laborers in the South were entitled to the prerogatives of free workers in the North, including wages commensurate with the value of their labor, the right to select their own employers and negotiate for better terms, and legal recourse against delinquent employers. Many Northerners, both military and civilian, shared Hawkins's conviction that the wages established for plantation labor were shamefully low, especially in light of the soaring price of cotton. Moreover, the employers bore few contractual obligations to either the government that permitted them to operate the plantations or the workers whose toil made the estates productive. General James S. Wadsworth, an emissary of the War Department who inspected the contraband camps and leased plantations in late 1863, argued that plantation lessees and owners who benefited from the freedpeople's labor should be required to sustain schools and churches and to help support the unemployed and dependent. If private enterprise was to take the lead in establishing free labor, Wadsworth and others insisted, it must be held accountable.[38]

For some Northerners, the failure of individual employers to advance the welfare of the freedpeople called into question the presumption of congruence between private profit and public good. Colonel Eaton

[37] In addition to the relevant documents in this chapter, see William Burnet to W. P. Mellen, Esq., [early Jan.? 1864], B-68 1864, Letters Received by the Division, ser. 315, Division of Captured Property, Claims, & Land, RG 56 [X-22].

[38] In addition to the relevant documents in this chapter, see above, doc. 107.

worried that "[s]chemes of money-making" had won out over the "loyal and benevolent . . . impulse of the country." He invited Northern freedmen's aid societies to sponsor plantations on which former slaves would work not as wage-workers but as independent cultivators of small plots "under the kindly but faithful care of some worthy friend of [their] race." Prominent philanthropists, notably James E. Yeatman of the Western Sanitary Commission, advocated a similar role for private benevolence as a counterweight to private cupidity.[39]

Some critics of Union-sponsored free labor in the Mississippi Valley cited the government's reluctance to subdivide plantations as an obstacle to truly free labor. By failing to break up large estates, General Hawkins argued, the government was squandering a golden opportunity to restructure Southern society. Complaining that the plantation commissioners simply replaced "one negro-landed Aristocracy" with another when they leased government-controlled plantations in "immense tracts," he proposed dividing the estates into small farms for settlement by former slaves and Yankee farmers. Land monopoly, in Hawkins's view, was incompatible with free labor. General Wadsworth agreed. Convinced that market forces would transform the great plantations into yeoman farmsteads after the return of peace, Wadsworth envisioned a future in which many former slaves would become "Peasant Cultivators" possessed of small tracts of land. The government, he believed, could speed that process by offering abandoned and confiscated land for rent or purchase in small parcels.[40]

In two widely publicized reports written in late 1863, James Yeatman drew together the disparate threads of criticism and offered detailed suggestions for reforming the plantation-leasing system. To discourage absentee speculators and encourage leasing by freedpeople and Northern yeomen, Yeatman urged that each lessee be allowed only one estate, preferably no larger than 200 acres. To promote industrious habits among plantation workers, he called for written contracts, with compensation ranging from $15 to $25 per month for men and $12 to

[39] Col. John Eaton, Jr., to Levi Coffin, 10 Nov. 1863, vol. 74, pp. 89–91, Letters Sent by John Eaton, ser. 2027, General Supt. of Freedmen, MS Asst. Comr. Pre-Bureau Records, RG 105 [A-4006]; James E. Yeatman, *A Report on the Condition of the Freedmen of the Mississippi, Presented to the Western Sanitary Commission, December 17th, 1863* (St. Louis, 1864), and *Suggestions of a Plan of Organization for Freed Labor, and the Leasing of Plantations along the Mississippi River . . .* (St. Louis, 1864). See also Friends' Association of Philadelphia, *Statistics of the Operations of the Executive Board of Friends' Association of Philadelphia . . . for the Relief of Colored Freedmen . . .* (Philadelphia, 1864), pp. 9–26. On the activities of Yeatman and the Western Sanitary Commission in the Mississippi Valley during 1863, see James E. Yeatman et al. to His Excellency A. Lincoln, 6 Nov. 1863, Miscellaneous Letters Received: K Series, ser. 103, RG 56 [X-12].

[40] In addition to the relevant documents in this chapter, see above, doc. 107.

$20 for women. The laborers would buy their own food, clothing, and other necessities from those earnings. Government-sponsored "Infirmary Farms" would provide relief and employment of last resort, while vagrancy laws would "govern and regulate those who are unwilling to perform labor." Convinced that the government's responsibility to the former slaves extended beyond organizing their labor, Yeatman also advocated that freedpeople be required to legalize their marriages and that lessees be required to provide schools. Such policies, he argued, would enable the government to "exercise a wholesome guardianship over these new-born children of freedom" while making them "realize that they are freemen."[41]

Yeatman's suggestions came just as the Treasury Department was preparing to assume control over confiscated and abandoned land in Union-occupied territory.[42] Upon consultation with Yeatman, Secretary of the Treasury Salmon P. Chase decided to revamp the leasing system established by Adjutant General Thomas. He instructed William P. Mellen, supervising agent of the Treasury Department's 1st Special Agency,[43] to draft regulations for the Mississippi Valley that would both encourage the leasing of land to former slaves and require higher wages and stronger legal protection for plantation laborers.

The regulations issued by Mellen in January 1864 bore the stamp of Thomas's critics. They forbade any lessee to rent more than one plantation, but placed no limit placed upon its acreage. Minimum monthly wages ranged from $15 to $25 for men and $10 to $18 for women (classified according to age), with each household allotted one acre of ground for its own use. Instead of cash wages, laborers could negotiate with employers to work for "an interest in the profits." Unlike Thomas, Mellen made the laborers responsible for supplying their own food and clothing, hoping thereby to abandon the "old system of support under slavery" for "that usual in the employment of free labor."[44] "Home farms" supervised by civilian treasury agents would serve as labor-contracting centers and as places of refuge for sick and aged people. The

41 Yeatman, *Report on the Condition of the Freedmen*, p. 16, and *Suggestions of a Plan of Organization for Freed Labor*.

42 The change of administration was prompted by an executive order of October 1863. (*Official Records*, ser. 3, vol. 3, p. 872.)

43 Treasury Department regulations of September 1863 established five "special agencies" to administer federal trade policy in the Union-occupied South. The 1st Special Agency embraced those parts of Alabama, Mississippi, Arkansas, and Louisiana that were "occupied by national forces operating from the north." (U.S., House of Representatives, "Report of the Secretary of the Treasury, on the State of the Finances, for the Year Ending June 30, 1863," *House Executive Documents*, 38th Cong., 1st sess., No. 3, pp. 410–22.)

44 Wm. P. Mellen to Hon. S. P. Chase, 11 Feb. 1864, Letters Sent, Records of the General Agent, RG 366 [Q-138].

agents were also to oversee contracting, ensure payment of wages, and protect laborers from fraud and abuse. A tax on plantation products would defray the expense of supporting unemployed freedpeople. Mellen's regulations also required that husbands and wives solemnize their marriages and that children attend school. Thus did Mellen overturn the existing system, which in his view considered "the profit of the planter exclusively, without . . . tending to the improvement of the freedmen in his new relation."[45]

Virtually as one, planters condemned the treasury regulations. Protesting that the government had shown bad faith, lessees who had already contracted with the plantation commissioners complained that the new tax and higher wages would drive them to bankruptcy. Adjutant General Thomas and former commissioner Field (now himself a plantation lessee), amplified the planters' grievances. They also warned that Mellen's system would undermine enlistment by offering black agricultural laborers as much as $25 per month while black soldiers received only $10. Dismissing Yeatman as a misguided visionary, Thomas condemned the treasury plan as "beautiful in theory, but utterly impracticable."[46]

As Mellen's subordinates in the Mississippi Valley assumed their new duties, jurisdictional disputes and substantive disagreement widened the breach between army and treasury officials. Colonel Eaton protested the transfer of authority from military superintendents to civilians who in reality were powerless unless backed by military force. Treasury agents routinely came into conflict with Eaton's subordinates, whose responsibilities overlapped with those of the newcomers. Confusion and mutual recrimination were the inevitable result.

Dissatisfaction with the treasury regulations did not long deter Northern lessees, whose optimism about large profits overrode their misgivings about higher wages. Most were willing to accept the new dispensation if they could be assured of military protection. Defying rebel attack, they applied to lease plantations on the fringes of Union-held territory. In their pursuit of revenue, the treasury agents gladly complied, assuming that federal troops would do their part.

Events proved them wrong. In February 1864, General Sherman withdrew forces from the Mississippi River to strike at the interior railroad depot of Meridian, Mississippi. Confederate guerrillas seized the opportunity to raid exposed plantations, destroying quarters and cotton gins, appropriating livestock and supplies, and kidnapping or murdering laborers and lessees. Fearing for their lives, thousands of plantation workers fled to the nearest Union post. Near Helena, guerrillas brazenly threatened to "annihilate the race" should any freed-

[45] [William P. Mellen] to Wm. Burnet Esq., 10 Mar. 1864, Letters Received by Assistant Special Agents, Natchez Dist., 2nd Agency, RG 366 [Q-49].

[46] *Official Records*, ser. 3, vol. 4, pp. 235–36.

people go to work on government-sponsored plantations.[47] Lessees demanded protection, and treasury officials appealed to the army and navy. But neither local commanders nor military authorities in Washington held the security of the plantations foremost among their priorities.

In the aftermath of the raids, Adjutant General Thomas blasted the Treasury Department's administration of plantation labor, arguing that "military authorities must have command of the negroes." The argument swayed his superiors. In late February – with Mellen's regulations only six weeks old – President Lincoln instructed Thomas to "take hold of and be master of the contraband and leasing business." However "well intended" the treasury plan, Lincoln feared, it might "fall dead within its own entangled details."[48]

Thomas quickly exercised mastery. His Order 9, issued in early March, largely reproduced the labor policies adopted by General Nathaniel P. Banks in southern Louisiana.[49] It left Mellen's leases in force and retained many of the treasury regulations, but revised the provisions respecting compensation of laborers and administration of the system. Thomas's order cut wages to their 1863 levels, while again obliging employers to furnish food and clothing. It placed matters of law enforcement under the control of military provost marshals rather than civilian superintendents, prohibited Union soldiers from visiting the government-supervised estates without special authorization, and forbade laborers to leave the plantation on which they were working without their employer's permission. Although not entirely supplanted, treasury agents were thereafter confined to arranging leases, collecting revenues, and regulating commerce. Military authorities and agents of Northern aid societies assumed supervision over the home farms. With only minor revision, the system established by Thomas's order governed federally supervised agricultural labor in the Mississippi Valley for the rest of the war.

Lessees welcomed the adjutant general's coup, but plantation laborers protested the arbitrary reduction of their wages and the imposition of new restrictions. In some cases, they flatly rejected the new terms. Former slaves on one estate near Helena noted with scorn, "We used to work so in Secesh times." Their Northern employer agreed that Thomas's regulations "would do to govern slaves" but were "not prctical among free people." Many laborers opposed the employers' resumption of responsibility for their subsistence. They "will not consent to a change,"

[47] In addition to the relevant documents in this chapter, see E. L. Floyd et al. to the Supervising Special Agent Treasury Department, 1 Feb. 1864, General Letters Received, Records of the General Agent, RG 366 [Q-30].

[48] In addition to the relevant documents in this chapter, see *Official Records*, ser. 3, vol. 4, pp. 124, 138.

[49] For Banks's system, see above, doc. 109.

reported a treasury agent at Vicksburg; "they are so much better satisfied to do for themselves, 'like *white folks*.' "[50]

However much laborers and employers disagreed about Thomas's labor policy, they unanimously censured the government's feeble efforts to protect the plantations. Only those estates near garrison towns or army camps were safe; elsewhere within Union lines, Confederate raiders and local guerrillas generally operated with impunity. On many plantations – a majority, according to some observers – raiders prevented cotton planting on any but the smallest scale. One by one, Northerners abandoned the leasing business in disgust. Their laborers, who had seen family and friends murdered or carried off by rebel marauders, stood in constant dread of reenslavement.

Among its other effects, the warfare in the countryside complicated the efforts of planters to procure and retain workers. Would-be employers had to recruit laborers from among the freedpeople at contraband camps, home farms, and military posts. Prospective employees often turned down offers that involved removal to dangerous locations, and Colonel Eaton's superintendents generally respected their decision. Some former slaves found reasons not to work on any plantation, wherever situated. Wives of black soldiers, complained one treasury agent, "openly refused to work, on the ground that the Recruiting Officer promised them the government would take care of them." Frustrated Northern planters complained of having been "deceived by the [government's] promise of an abundant supply of labor."

In the rush to obtain hands during the early months of 1864, former slaves acquired new bargaining power. Many of them demanded and received wages well above those stipulated in Thomas's order. As a result of large-scale enlistment in the Union army, able-bodied men were in especially short supply; near Vicksburg, some declined offers of $50 per month. Planters found themselves bidding for the services of able-bodied women and older children, who increasingly formed the bulk of their labor forces. Such competition, noted Colonel Samuel Thomas, Eaton's chief assistant, "actually settle[d] the troublesome question of what wages shall be paid. A planter must pay well and punctually, or he will not get laborers to do his work." A sizable number of freedpeople exacted attractive crop-sharing arrangements in lieu of cash wages; some received as much as one-half the crop, plus rations. Besides better compensation, former slaves also pressed for greater access to the productive resources of the plantations. Many concluded agreements that provided substantial plots of land for independent cultivation or permitted them to cut and sell cordwood from plantation woodlots.

[50] In addition to the relevant documents in this chapter, see C. A. Montross to W. P. Mellen, Esq., 17 May 1864, #941, Case Files of Claims for Cotton & Captured & Abandoned Property, ser. 370, Miscellaneous Division, RG 56 [X-515].

The tug of war over the terms and conditions of labor continued even after freedpeople accepted employment on the estates. Employers – whether Northerners or Southerners – sought to mold them into a tractable, dependent work force; former slaves resisted all efforts to dominate them. The struggle embraced virtually every aspect of plantation life. Some contests turned upon such hallmarks of slavery as the use of force. Former slaveholders showed particular affinity for corporal punishment, but many Northern planters resorted to it as well. "[M]oral suasion" by Yankee employers, one superintendent of freedmen caustically observed, "often consists of the use of a club." Former slaves abhorred these vestiges of bondage and fled or refused to work when confronted with them.[51]

Freedpeople also rebuffed attempts by their employers to control the pace of work and the length of the workday. Guided by their own sense of the proper balance between labor and leisure as well as the seasonal demands of various crops, plantation hands refused to perform "steady labor" over the ten-hour workday mandated by Thomas's regulations. They arrived in the fields late, left them early, and took midday dinner breaks that exceeded specifications. They attended to domestic duties and their garden plots when they should have been hoeing cotton. Planters countered with measures ranging from "exhorting & precept" to monetary incentives and penalties. When these failed, they summoned the local provost marshal. Nevertheless, as one officer admitted, "[t]he Freedmen regulated the matter to suit themselves, and quit work when they thought they had done as much as they ought."[52] One Northern plantation manager estimated that the former slaves worked one-third less under free labor than they had under slavery.

By the fall of 1864, struggles between planters and laborers were proceeding in circumstances greatly changed since the spring. Because of short cotton crops – the result of unfavorable weather and damage by the so-called army worm – the demand for hands shrank, and with it much of the workers' leverage. "Superfluous" laborers represented costly liabilities to employers with heavy debts and little cotton to pick. Endeavoring to shift their losses to their employees, many planters and lessees discontinued rations, refused to pay wages, and drove off unwanted hands. Former slaves working for a share of the crop fared little, if any, better, as a small crop meant correspondingly small compensation.

The uncertain rewards of wage labor only reinforced the freedpeople's determination to live and work independently. In 1864, several hundred black families, chiefly in the vicinities of Vicksburg, Lake

[51] In addition to the relevant documents in this chapter, see John Eaton, *Report of the General Superintendent of Freedmen, Department of the Tennessee and State of Arkansas for 1864* (Memphis, 1865), p. 30.

[52] Eaton, *Report of the General Superintendent of Freedmen*, p. 59.

Providence, and Helena, did so by leasing land from the Treasury Department. Most of them farmed small tracts, but a few cultivated 150 acres or more, either with hired labor or cooperatively with other black lessees. Near Vicksburg, some 180 black lessees tilled roughly 6,000 acres, employed about 380 laborers other than family members, and supported themselves and nearly 1,300 other people. Near Helena, about 30 former slaves leased tracts on the plantation of Confederate General Gideon J. Pillow. Numerous other former slaves struck private rental agreements with individual landowners or sublet land from Northern lessees.

Black renters generally resisted the cotton mania that had brought Northern planters to the Mississippi Valley. They sought to ensure their subsistence before devoting land to commercial crops, and they also understood that large cotton fields invited rebel raids. Accordingly, many black farmers contented themselves to grow corn and vegetables and raise pigs and barnyard fowl. When nearby towns or army camps provided a market, they sold surplus produce, poultry, meat, and eggs. Most of those who raised cotton did so on a small scale. Yet with high wartime prices, a two-acre patch could yield enough to pay expenses and allow a cash surplus. A few black lessees who put large amounts of land in cotton realized profits of thousands of dollars.

Only the most fortunate former slaves possessed sufficient capital to rent land, but a good many men and women of lesser means managed to support themselves without resort to wage labor. Some simply took up residence on abandoned estates that had escaped the attention of federal authorities, planted gardens, and subsisted by hunting and foraging until their crops matured. The squatters lived a precarious life, but for many the rewards outweighed the dangers. Government-supervised home farms offered a safer setting in which former slaves, depending on their means and the number of laborers in their households, tended plots that ranged from small gardens to farms of ten acres or more. At home farms established on the Pillow plantation, near Helena, on the Birney plantation, across the Mississippi River from Vicksburg, and at Davis Bend, Mississippi, downriver from Vicksburg, former slaves produced corn and vegetables for domestic consumption and for sale. Those on the Pillow estate also grew considerable amounts of cotton. Shortages of draft animals, tools, and seed limited agricultural operations on the home farms, but as long as the freedpeople could wrest an independent living from the soil, they abjured wage labor.

The success of those former slaves who cultivated land on their own during 1864 led many Northerners to advocate allowing more of them to do so the following year. The black lessees in the Helena area, reported Chaplain James I. Herrick, had all "made more than a living, and will be ready to begin another year with capital that will enable them to work to better advantage." By contrast, the wage laborers on nearby plantations had been able to save little or nothing of their earnings. Herrick urged that in the future the abandoned plantations be leased exclusively to former slaves, who would thereby become "a self supporting and self directing people, a comfort to themselves, and strength to the nation." His proposal won the enthusiastic support of General Buford, the commander at Helena.

Surveying the entire Mississippi Valley, Colonel Eaton was equally impressed with the former slaves' ability to support themselves – even to prosper – in difficult circumstances. As of July 1864, he estimated, nearly 114,000 freedpeople were under his jurisdiction. Of that number, more than 41,000 were employed by the Union army as soldiers or laborers; the remaining 72,500 lived and worked on plantations, at wood yards, in cities, or in "freedmen's villages." The ex-slaves associated with the army earned monthly wages, and the vast majority of the others were "entirely self-supporting, – the same as any industrial class anywhere." Only 10,000 were being fed by the government, and one-third of these were black lessees and their families, the cost of whose rations would be repaid from their crops.[53] By the end of the year, the black lessees had produced larger crops per acre than had wage laborers; moreover, Eaton reported, they had "saved sums varying from one hundred dollars to ten thousand," whereas the wage hands had "rarely laid up any[thing]." The evidence was conclusive: "The Freedmen do best for themselves & the Gov't as independent cultivators of small farms."

Events at Davis Bend – where Confederate President Jefferson Davis, his brother Joseph Davis, and other prominent rebels owned large plantations – dramatized both the opportunities and the constraints facing freedpeople within Union lines.[54] The flight of the owners during the first year of the war left the area in the hands of former slaves, to whom federal gunboats provided protection and occasional employment. After the surrender of Vicksburg in July 1863, Davis Bend became part of the larger network of contraband camps and leased plantations. Colonel Samuel Thomas, superintendent of freedmen for the District of Vicksburg, used the site as a hiring depot and a refuge for former slaves incapable of military service or plantation labor. What had been a self-sustaining independent settlement quickly became one of the largest contraband camps in the Mississippi Valley.

Although the freedpeople at Davis Bend shared Colonel Thomas's determination that they support themselves without expense to the government, they faced a spate of setbacks in attempting to do so. In

[53] Eaton, *Grant, Lincoln and the Freedmen*, pp. 133–34.

[54] On Davis Bend, see, in addition to the relevant documents in this chapter, Currie, *Enclave*, chap. 4; Janet Sharp Hermann, *The Pursuit of a Dream* (New York, 1981), chaps. 2–3; Steven J. Ross, "Freed Soil, Freed Labor, Freed Men: John Eaton and the Davis Bend Experiment," *Journal of Southern History* 44 (May 1978): 213–32.

February 1864, Thomas settled at the bend several thousand former slaves liberated by General Sherman's expedition to Meridian. The refugees were crowded into livestock pens and jerry-built hovels. Colonel Thomas hired hundreds of them to planters and lessees from all over the Mississippi Valley, but the continued arrival of newcomers from the interior thwarted efforts to reduce overcrowding. Moreover, the amount of land available for the former slaves shrank when treasury agents leased part of Joseph Davis's plantation to Northern investors and restored other land to professedly loyal claimants. In late March, however, Adjutant General Thomas reserved the remainder of Davis Bend exclusively for the former slaves. Colonel Thomas subsequently organized a 500-acre home farm on Jefferson Davis's estate and rented 2,000 additional acres to seventy black farmers, who worked plots ranging from 10 to over 150 acres each.

Protected by several companies of black soldiers, the independent farmers at Davis Bend fared well, raising abundant crops of corn and vegetables. In addition, some cleared modest profits from cotton, despite the ravages of the army worm. Residents of the home farm also produced more than enough to feed themselves. With Eaton's approval, Colonel Thomas expanded the leasing program in 1865. The local superintendent of freedmen organized nearly 200 "companies," each numbering between three and twenty-five freedpeople "wishing to work lands upon their own account." By the end of the war, the residents of Davis Bend had demonstrated that, when given access to land and protection from rebel raids, former slaves could support themselves.

For thousands of former slaves, the cities of Memphis, Helena, Vicksburg, and Natchez offered still other ways to make a living. Because of the presence of federal troops – largely black soldiers – urban freedpeople enjoyed security from Confederate attack. The cities also provided an alternative to the isolation and monotony of plantation life. Thriving local economies, the result of war-related commerce and greatly enlarged urban populations, created new employment possibilities. Black artisans could earn a livelihood at their trades, and freedmen who had acquired draft animals and wagons could work as draymen. Laundresses were in great demand, and black women could often avoid live-in domestic service by taking in washing. Families of black soldiers could live near their loved ones and supplement the soldiers' wages with earnings from "chance work." The cities also offered a rich organizational life, including benevolent societies, churches, and schools, some of them established by Northern aid societies and others by black people themselves. After tasting life in the city, many freedpeople considered the plantations unpalatable. Despite crowded and unhealthy living conditions, high rents and food prices, and the risk of unemployment, the river cities continued to attract ex-slave immigrants from the hinterland.

Short-handed planters and harried federal officials attempted to reverse this migration. To rid the towns of unemployed or irregularly employed black people, they instituted systems of passes or compulsory registration. Freedpeople who lacked proper documentation might be expelled from town, exiled to a nearby contraband camp, or hired to planters. Various motives were at work. Colonel Eaton's subordinates often denied passes to former slaves who wished to work in urban trades, lest new entrants jeopardize the livelihood of established practitioners. Other efforts to remove freedpeople from cities, however, uprooted black residents who were earning a living on their own. In an episode early in 1864 that became a cause célèbre, a military officer at Natchez singled out "*idle* negroes" as sources of "*loathsome* and *malignant diseases*." He therefore ordered the expulsion of every former slave who was "not employed by some *responsible white person* in some legitimate business" and did "not reside at the domicil of his or her employer." The mass evictions that ensued swept up self-supporting freedpeople as well as the sick and unemployed. Black town folk and sympathetic Northerners mounted an indignant protest that eventually reached the halls of Congress and led to the resignation of the general who had sanctioned the offending order. But a determination to relocate ex-slaves from city to countryside – or at least reduce the influx of new migrants – remained characteristic of federal policy in the Mississippi Valley.

During the winter of 1864–1865, the architects of that policy redoubled their efforts to expand the scope of plantation agriculture under free labor. But with Union victory imminent and a growing number of erstwhile Confederates reclaiming their estates under Lincoln's amnesty proclamation, circumstances were changing rapidly. Yankee capitalists increasingly formed partnerships with native proprietors instead of leasing plantations in their own right.[55] The transfer of estates from federal control to that of amnestied owners also diminished the amount of land available for lease to black people. Most former slaves who had hoped to rent a small tract from the government found their ambitions thwarted, while some who had previously held leases could not renew them and instead had to seek wage work.

Anticipating that the labor and welfare measures instituted as wartime expedients would be neither necessary nor desirable after the return of peace, federal officials quietly began to reduce the army's involvement in the day-to-day management of free labor. Colonel Samuel Thomas believed that the government ought thenceforth do no more than place the former slaves' labor "on an equal footing with white labor." The legitimate sphere of state power did not include "the

[55] In March 1865, the Treasury Department's assistant special agent for the Vicksburg district noted that "[r]egistering of places by owners is far in the advance of leasing." (C. A. Montross to Hon. Wm. P. Mellen, 3 Mar. 1865, Letters Received from Assistant Special Agents, Records of the General Agent, RG 366 [Q-178].)

enormous task of starting out each freedman with a competency." "Capital does now, and will for some time to come carry on great enterprises," he asserted, "and a large portion of the human family, both white and black, must labor for this capital at regulated wages, without any direct interest in the result of the enterprise." In accordance with this view, Thomas and other federal authorities increasingly assumed the role of mediator between the interests of capital and labor, with a tacit acceptance of capital's preeminence.

Former slaves in the Union-occupied Mississippi Valley ended the war in a variety of different circumstances. Nearly all had gained useful experience as free laborers: bargaining with employers, demanding more favorable working arrangements, collecting wages, spending and, in some cases, saving the fruits of their toil. A few had parlayed their earnings into a modest competency, undergirded by control over land or ownership of livestock and tools. But for every ex-slave so situated, many more entered the postwar world empty-handed. Large numbers were still trying to collect wages owed them for military labor or to settle disputes with civilian employers.[56] Their wartime experience as propertyless free laborers, no less than their years of toil in bondage, shaped their understanding of what freedom should mean and braced them for the struggle ahead.

[56] On the continuation of wartime labor disputes into the postwar period, see, in addition to the relevant documents in this chapter, *Freedom*, ser. 1, vol. 1: docs. 122–23.

146: Testimony by a Tennessee Freedwoman and by a Tennessee Freedman before the Southern Claims Commission

Memphis, Shelby Co. Tennessee 23[d] day of November 1871

The said Witness, Leah Black, who resides in Memphis, Tennessee aged 49 years, being first duly sworn to tell the truth, the whole truth, and nothing but the truth, relative to the above named claim, testified as follows:

(Examined at her own instance by the Commissioner)

I am the Claimant in this case, I resided in April 1862 about 2 miles from Somerville, Fayette Co. Tenn. together with my husband and 4 Children, all boys. My husband had bought himself free and cultivated about 80 acres of land on lease.

At that time we owned 2 horses, 7 Cows, about 63 hogs, about 200 chickens, 23 geese; that was all of Stock, – further about 250 Bushels Corn as near as I can guess, 4 Stacks of fodder. The month of April was nearly out when there came a party of Union Soldiers, numbering from 20 to 30 or more, I could not tell how many, they were scattered over all the yard, They took our 2 horses. This was in the afternoon, just after dinner. I saw them take Corn, fodder, chickens, geese, our 2 horses, and some Cows; they also killed some hogs.

. . . .

My husband James Black was absent at the time. He came home soon after and tried to follow the soldiers. He did not go far & came soon back.

They told him to go Wednesday to Bolivar to get his horses.

After he got home Guerillas or Confederate Soldier came there and got into a quarrel with my husband about some fodder and killed him.

About an hour or 10 in the night, while my husband laid there dead, another party of Soldiers came to our place; I don't know whether they were the same as in day time. There was a heap of them, but I don't know how many, say about 40, I could not see them all, and they then took all the balance of our stock, all the chickens but a few, all of the geese, all but a little Corn, and all the fodder except a little that was in the Stable loft.

I saw them take all there was left, I was then right at home. It was a dark night, I just could see them moving about; I stood just under my door.

I heard a Command given to take all the things, but I don't know whether it was given by an Officer; it was obeyed though, for all our stock was taken.

. . . .

We cultivated 80 acres of ground. All of it was in Cultivation and we held a three years lease from M[r] Claspers, which had just expired when the soldiers took our things. We could have stayed another year on the place and would have stayed if our things had not been taken away.

My husband had bought his freedom about 5 or 6 year before the above mentioned event, and I had been married to him about 5 years before he bought himself free. He was formerly the Slave of Pinkney Reed at Somerville, while my master was James Martin, near Somerville. I was not a free woman when we married, but belonged to James Martin.

We had 4 Children during our Marriage, all boys, of which two only are alive. I and my children became free only after the Proclamation of the President.

My two living boys are about 19 and 17 years of age. One died 5 years & the other with 1 years age

After my husbands death I went with my 4 children to Bolivar. There was no Administrator appointed that I know of. We did not own any ground and I packed up the things that were left, household goods, and went away under federal protection.

. . . .

her
HDSr Leah X Black
mark

Memphis Shelby Co Tennessee, 23[d] day of November 1871

The said Witness, Leah Black, who resides in Memphis, Tenn. aged 49 years, being first duly sworn to tell the truth, the whole truth, and nothing but the truth, relative to the above named claim, testified as follows:

. . . .

Interrogatory 2. Where did you reside from the 1st of April, 1861, to the 1st of June, 1865? Where were you *personally* during that period? What was your business or occupation during that time? Did you change your residence during that time? If so, when, and where was your new residence?

Answer: About May 1862 I went to Bolivar, where I staid 2 or 3 weeks; from there I went to La Grange, where I staid until 3 days before Vicksburg was taken; then I came to Memphis & to Presidents Island, where I staid about 6 mths & then came to Memphis & lived there all the while. I washed & ironed for a living.

. . . .

Interrogatory 22. Did you ever *do* anything for the United States Government or its army, or for the Union cause during the war? If so, state fully what you did.

Answer: I worked on a Government farm at La Grange for pay

. . . .

her
HDSr Leah X Black
mark

Memphis Shelby Co Tenn. 27th day of November 1871

The said Witness, Fountain Day, who resides about 5 miles S.E. from Memphis Tenn. aged about 27 years, being first duly sworn to tell the truth, the whole truth, and nothing but the truth, relative to the above named claim, testified as follows:

Interrogatory 1. When did your acquaintance with Ja[s] Black dec'd & Leah Black the said claimant, begin? Where did you then reside; and what was your occupation?

Answer: I first knew them when I was about 9 years old, in Fayette Co Tenn. – I was a boy, belonging to Mr. Wiley Day, &

they lived about a mile from me, on Mr. Glaspar's place– They rented a piece of ground there–

Interrogatory 2. Was your acquaintance with said claimant intimate throughout the war, or any portion of it and if so, to what extent?

Answer: I knew them very well, & before the war I visited them every Sunday–& did afterwards often up to the time James Black was killed–

Interrogatory 3. How far from said claimant's residence did you reside during the war, and how often did you see him and under what circumstances?

Answer: I lived about 1/2 a mile from them up to the time I went into the service– I went into the 59th Col'd Inf. in the U.S. volunteer army–

Interrogatory 4. Did you converse often, and if so, how often, with the claimant, about the war, its causes and progress?

Answer: I did very often with her–about twenty times–

Interrogatory 5. Were you an adherent of the Union cause, and how did the claimant regard you as to your adhesion and sympathies?

Answer: I was–and she knew it– I saw her often inside the Federal lines– she was in Camp "Shiloh" of the colored people, & also on President's Island, while I was in the service–

Interrogatory 6. What did claimaint say to you at any time during the war, concerning the war, its causes, or the Union cause; and what did he say at any time during the war, concerning his sympathy with and adherence to the cause and government of the United States? State the occasion and circumstances of any such conversations and who were present.

Answer: She told me once that if she hadn't left home when she did, the rebels would have killed her as they did her husband– She also said she wished her sons could grow up and go into the service as I had– She told me these things in the colored people's camp in Memphis–

Interrogatory 7. Did you know, during the war, what were the sympathies and opinions of the claimant, and if so, how did you know them?

Answer: I couldn't tell– she told me she was satisfied about her property as she knew the Union soldiers got it–

. . . .

Interrogatory 10. Do you know how the said claimant was regarded during the war by his loyal neighbors? If yea, state the same fully.

Answer: I heard the colored soldiers speak well of her– They visited her often–

Interrogatory 11. Did the said claimant ever contribute any money or property to aid the Union cause, or the Union army, or did he ever give information to the officers or soldiers of the Union army, in aid of their movements and cause? If yea, state the same fully.

Answer: She frequently brought victuals to camp for the colored soldiers – myself among them – and told us she had worked and earned money to buy them with – This was when she was living in the government camp –

Interrogatory 12. Was the said claimant ever molested or threatened with injury to himself, his family or his property, on account of his Union sentiments? If yea, state the same fully.

Answer: I heard that her husband was killed on that account, and I helped to bring him home after he was killed. I found his body about 300 yards from his house in a path in a field, about a mile from the main road – He was dead – It was about dusk – It was in the first or second year of the war – He had been shot in his right side with a shot-gun –

. . . .

Int. 14 – What did James Black ever say to you about the war –

Answer – He said once that he would be glad if the Yankees would whip them – This was about two weeks before he was killed – It was 2 years after that when I enlisted –

The witness further states as follows in regard to the taking of property –

Once during the war when I was 12 or 13 years old a Yankee force came to the place where I was living – Mr. Wiley Day's place – They came from Bolivar & I think they were making on to Memphis. It was the first time I had seen any Federal soldiers. It was a whole army corps – Genl. Hurlbut's – Five or six cavalry men, with a Captain, made me go with them to find some horses – I told them I could find some, and I showed them to Jim Black's – He was not at home – claimant was there – The soldiers got two horses, one from the stable & one from the lot, and led one off & rode off the other – and went to their camps, on the Brownsville road, about a mile away – They had just come there that day and remained camped there a week or 10 days – I don't remember what I heard said when the horses were taken – I heard the Captain say something about orders but I don't remember what – I don't know his name – This party took nothing else –

These were sportly looking horses – I don't know their age – Black had had one of them about 2 years & had lately bought the other – I didn't know what horses were worth then – I saw Black buy the last horse & pay for it & he said he paid \$150.⁰⁰ – He paid Greenbacks – I never saw the horses afterwards –

I was there once afterwards when 5 or 6 cavalry soldiers came there, early in the morning, and saw them lock up the corn crib – and then went away – There was an officer with them – He talked to Leah Black but I don't know what he said – The crib was in the lot near the house – I didn't look into the crib – I heard them say a year before that, that they had put 200 bushels of corn in the crib and hadn't used any out –

I wasn't there when the soldiers came and took the corn – nor did I see them take any other property – I know that Jas Black had 200 chickens & 27 geese & 4 stacks fodder – I counted them all often – He had 70 acres of ground, rented – I don't know how many acres of corn he raised – He had 2 wagons – & 7 head of cattle & 63 hogs – I counted them – And further this deponent says not & hereto subscribes his name –

HDS Fountain day

Excerpts from testimony of Leah Black, 23 Nov. 1871 (twice), and excerpts from testimony of Fountain day, 27 Nov. 1871, Claim of Leah Black, Shelby Co. TN case files, Approved Claims, ser. 732, Southern Claims Commission, 3rd Auditor, RG 366 [I-252]. All sworn before a special commissioner of the Southern Claims Commission. On printed forms with spaces for the answers, which are handwritten. According to other documents in the same file, Leah Black had submitted a claim for $1,434.50 as compensation for the following property taken by Union soldiers: 2 horses, 7 cows, 63 hogs, 23 geese, about 200 chickens, 250 bushels corn, 4 stacks of fodder, and 2 wagons. She was allowed only $350, the commissioners having disallowed her claim for the hogs, poultry, fodder, and wagons, on the grounds that she had not proven they were taken for the use of the army.

147: Commander of the U.S.S. *John P. Jackson* to the Commander of the Mortar Flotilla

Off Vicksburg [*Miss.*] July 1st 1862

Sir: It becomes my duty, to report to you, that in carrying out my instructions, in compliance with the act of Congress,[1] and instructions from the Navy Department, in relation to Contrabands,[2] I was compelled to receive, all those seeking refuge, on board the U.S. Steamer "Jackson," my vessel being stationed at the head of the line of the Fleet, and first meeting those coming down the river.

Up to the morning of the 24th of June, I had enlisted, and given shelter to forty seven persons, including men, women, and children who had sought protection of my vessel, under a flag of truce.

The enclosed list, includes only those taken from the Island, and from intelligence I received from those already in my custody, and from efforts made by some I had permitted to return; that accessions would soon be made, to the number of two thousand; for the purpose of constructing the "cut off," I deemed it expedient to establish a camp on an Island in the River, near the anchorage of the squadron.

Twenty of the men on the Island, were regularly enlisted from time to time, under the law governing such cases, and were employed as Coal [passers?], and other various duties on board, and to whom clothing, and rations had been regularly issued. They were at this time engaged on the Island, cutting wood for this vessel, the "Jackson" at the time being without coal, and no supply vessel in the squadron.

An Officer came on board my vessel, and informed me, that he came by order of Comm[dr?] Craven of the "Brooklyn", to demand all contrabands in my custody, and all others that may be found on board of any vessel, belonging to the "Mortar Flotilla."

I informed him, that I had a large number of "contrabands" in my custody, consisting of men, women, and children; but not having accomodations on board the Steamer, I had placed them in camp, on the Island, where my men were employed, cutting wood for the "Jackson", by your order.

I directed the Officer to return to Commander Craven, and inform him, that I would immediately confer with Commander Porter in person and ordered him not to remove or molest any person on the Island, until I received Comm[dr?] Porters instructions what to do. I assured the Officer, that the contrabands would be safe in my charge, until Commander Porter could communicate with Commander Craven.

I also directed the Officer, to inform Commd[r?] Craven that Twenty of the men, were regularly enlisted on board my vessel, and to whom issues of clothing and rations had been made, and that I would require written order for thier transfer, and receipts for thier accounts.

I proceeded immediately to inform you of the demand of Commander Craven, and while on board the "Octoraro," the Officer or Officers sent by Commander Craven, removed from the Island, all the "contrabands" I had placed there On returning to my vessel; I learned that the Island containing much public property, was left without protection.

The forty "Contrabands" taken from the Island, belonged to, or were claimed by persons residing on plantations, for three hundred miles distant; the whole were taken as alledged, to be returned to thier owner, a women, residing opposite Vicksburg, who had been on board the "Iroquois" and "Brooklyn", and represented herself as a loyal subject to the union, but I have reasons to know, from reports from her own negroes, and from information obtained by my Officers; that she is the wife of a notorious Rebel, both husband and wife have ever, and continue to afford, aid and comfort to the enemy, and since the return of her negroes, has had concealed in her house, a Rebel spy for several days, who would have been captured by a party from my ship, but for the assistance of the woman, who aided his escape.

The barbarous and inhuman treatment received by these unoffending slaves at the hands, and under the direction of this woman, since thier restoration, can only be understood by seeing them since thier scourging.

I am pained to think, that I should have been the innocent cause of this brutal chastisement, that took place almost within sight and sound of our Squadron, when I had promised them immunity from punishment, as I believed I had authority to do, under the instructions contained in the circular of the Secretary of the Navy, concerning "Contrabands."[2] Many of those who were returned to thier owners by Commander Craven, assured me they were induced to leave thier masters, by reports amongst them, that they would never again be returned, after once reaching the Ægis of our Flag and guns.

Under the peculiar circumstances that I am situated, having no Paymaster on board and being held responsible pecuniarily, for issues of public property under my charge I have to request that, I may be instructed how to proceed, in order to protect myself from the responsibility I have assumed under your verbal orders, and at the same time, to be governed in future, to prevent a recurrance, of the very humilitory position I have been placed in, by this unwarranted and unofficial act, of Commander Craven I have the honor to be, very respectfully, your obedient servant,

ALS Selim E. Woodworth

Acting Lieut. Commander Selim E. Woodworth to Commander D. D. Porter, 1 July 1862, enclosed in [David D. Porter] to Gideon Welles, 4 July 1862, Mortar Flotilla, Letters from Officers Commanding Squadrons, RG 45 [T-701]. Enclosed is a list of forty contrabands: twenty men, whom Woodworth had enlisted "under instructions from Navy Department, for general Service in the 'Mortar Flotilla,' " and supplied with clothing, tobacco, and rations; nine women, to whom he had issued rations; and eleven children. Under the same covering letter to Secretary of the Navy Gideon Welles, David D. Porter, commander of the Mortar Flotilla, also forwarded copies of three letters he had himself written to Captain Thomas T. Craven, commander of the Sloop of War *Brooklyn*, on June 24, 1862, regarding Craven's instructions to hand over slaves who had taken refuge aboard the U.S.S. *Octorara* and other vessels in the flotilla, presumably so that Craven could return them to their owners. Welles immediately referred all the documents to Craven, who confirmed that he had permitted claimants to search for runaway slaves and had requested that "officers who had them in charge . . . deliver them up to their lawful owner's." That admission prompted Welles to condemn Craven's actions as "not warranted by instruction, by usage or by law [and] in derogation of each." (Gideon Welles to Capt. T. T. Craven, 16 July 1862, and Gideon Welles to Captain T. T. Craven, 26 July 1862, vol. 67, pp. 326, 390, Letters to Officers, RG 45 [T-701].)

1 The additional article of war adopted by Congress on March 13, 1862, which prohibited the employment of Union troops – army or navy – in returning fugitive slaves to their owners. (*Statutes at Large*, vol. 12, p. 354.)
2 On April 30, 1862, the Secretary of the Navy had announced that "[t]he large number of persons known as 'contrabands' flocking to the protection of the United States flag affords an opportunity to provide . . . acclimated labor" for ships' crews; accordingly, he "required" all flag officers "to obtain the services of these persons for the country by enlisting them freely in the Navy, with their consent, rating them as boys at $8, $9, or $10 per month and one ration." (*Navy Official Records*, ser. 1, vol. 23, pp. 80–81.)

148: Order by the Commander of the 5th Division of the Army of the Tennessee

Memphis [*Tenn.*] July 22d 1862.

General Orders, No. 60. Whilst negroes are employed on public works, fortifications, driving teams and such public works, they will be subsisted by the Officer in charge, by a Provision Return, specifying number and how employed, which Return must be approved at Head Quarters.

As the negro receives no specific wages, the Commy may issue to the negroes at the rate of one pound of chewing tobacco per month, the bills of purchase for which are to be sent to the Chief Engineer of the District for payment.

The Engineer in charge of the Fort will purchase necessary clothing, such as shoes and pants for the negroes and issue to them keeping an accurate account of the issues that the value of the clothing be charged to the proper party on the final settlement of accounts.

The Bills of purchase will be sent to the Chief Engineer of the District for payment.

A Register and Time Table of the negroes employed on the Fort will be kept by the Engineer in charge, or by some one under his orders, giving the name and description of the Negro, whether a slave or refugee, and the name of Master, that a fair and equitable settlement may be made at the "end of the war." By order of Major Gen[l] W. T. Sherman

HDc

General Orders, No. 60, Head Quarters, 5' Division, 22 July 1862, Orders, W. T. Sherman Papers, Generals' Papers & Books, ser. 159, RG 94 [V-313]. General Sherman's conditional acceptance of fugitive slaves as military laborers stood in contrast to the course he had adopted only one month earlier at LaGrange, Tennessee, when he declared that "[t]he well settled policy of the whole army is now to have nothing to do with the negro" and ordered the ejection of all fugitive slaves from the camps of his division. (*Freedom*, ser. 1, vol. 1: doc. 88.) In early August, after learning of the provisions of the Second Confiscation Act and the Militia Act, Sherman further modified his policy to conform with his understanding of the laws. (See *Freedom*, ser. 1, vol. 1: doc. 94.)

149: Quartermaster at Helena, Arkansas, to the Chief Quartermaster of the Army of the Southwest

Helena Ark 24th July 1862

Capt There is a perfect "Cloud" of negroes being thrown upon me for Sustenance & Support. Out of some 50 for whom I drew rations this morning but twelve were working Stock all the rest being women & children

What am I to do with them If this taking them in & feeding them is to be the order of the day would it not be well to have some competent man employed to look after them & Keep their time, draw their Rations & look after their Sanitary Condition &c &c As it is, although it is hard to beleve that such things can be, Soldiers & teamsters (white) are according to Common report indulging in intimacy with them which can only be accounted for by the doctrine of total depravity. This question of what shall be done with these people has troubled me not a little & I have commenced my enquiry in this maner hoping that the matter may be systematized Respectflly Your ob[t] St

ALS B O Carr

A.A.Q.M. B. O. Carr to Capt. F. S. Winslow, 24 July 1862, #2360 1862, Letters Received, ser. 4676, Army of the Southwest, RG 393 Pt. 2 No. 299

[C-245]. In an endorsement dated July 25, the chief quartermaster referred Carr's letter to the headquarters of the Army of the Southwest, with a recommendation that "some competent commissioned officer . . . be detailed as General Superintendent of Colored free men." Notations on the wrapper suggest that the letter and endorsement were filed without further action, and apparently no such officer was appointed at Helena until January 1863. (See below, doc. 157.)

150: Commander of the Post of Helena, Arkansas, to the Commander of the Army of the Southwest

Helena [*Ark.*] Aug 22. 1862

General Every other soldier in the Army of the South West has a negro servant. While this Continues, it will be impossible to get laborers for the Fort. Unless there is a stringent order made at once by you, I cannot see how we are to get on with the work. Truly Yrs

ALS C. C. Washburn

C. C. Washburn to Maj. Gen. Curtis, 22 Aug. 1862, Unentered Letters Received, ser. 2594, Dept. of the MS, RG 393 Pt. 1 [C-112]. A notation on the wrapper reads simply, "File," and no reply has been found in the letters-sent volumes of the Army of the Southwest.

151: Testimony by the Former Commander of the Army of the Southwest before a Military Court of Inquiry, and Testimony by Two Former Arkansas Slaves before the Court

[*St. Louis, Mo. March 20, 1863*]

Major General *S. R. Curtis* continued his testimoney as follows:

. . . .

Ques. by Court Are Negroes at the South understood to be owners of Cotten. If so was the Cotten bought from them [*at Helena, Arkansas, during the summer of 1862*], that which was their own Crop, or did it include that abandoned by their masters?

Ans. The [*Confederate*] Cotten burners were always in front of our lines burning all the cotten they could find. The masters induced the negroes to hide away as much as they could in their quarters and in the Cane brake. In that way almost every negro had a bale, or two, of Cotten which I allowed them to sell

Ques. by Court. Would not this cotton you have described as

having been secreted by the Negroes at the instigation of their Masters be included in that species of property which you have designated as the Spoils of War? being that belonging to Rebels– If so, was it necessary to give all the proceeds to the Negroes to induce them to bring it forth?

Ans. It might possibly be considered Spoils of War. But the Negroes ran into my lines by thousands and had to be provided for. by selling this Cotten he got the necessary means of sustenance, this was particularly the case with the Negroes of the estate of Pillow. The Plantations were stripped by our Soldiers and the Negroes must have perished, If I had not [*resorted*] to some such means to save them from starvation. By disposing of this Cotten which they raised and concealed about 400, of the Pillow Negroes got away North in rather comfortable circumstances So with the Negroes of many other plantations about there. The Negroes were left free to make their own bargains, but vast numbers of them took counsel and advice from officers, where controversies arose in the Negroe Gangs as to the sale and disbursement, the matter was referred to myself and other officers and proper directions given to prevent injustice among themselves.

. . . .

[*St. Louis, Mo. June 27, 1863*]

David Haywood (Colered), Private, Company "A" 1st Regiment Mo. Infantry (Colored) being first duly sworn, testified as follows.

Question by the Court State to whom you belonged in the first part of the year 1862, where you resided and how if at all you became free?

Ans. I belonged to General Gidion J. Pillow of Tennessee, I lived on one of his farms in Arkansas, 8 Miles from Helena. I was set free by Major General Curtis. (A Copy of Special Orders No 445 of July 25th 1862 emancipating this Negro is hereto attached Marked "A")[1]

Q. by. Ct. What work did you do on the plantation?

Ans. For three months in the year, I was fore ploughman, ploughing myself, and seeing that all the rest ploughed, during the rest of the year I was wagoner, hauling Cotton to Helena, there were between 40 and 50 working hands on the place, this place was called the field cane place.

Q by Ct. About how many bales of Cotton, did you raise last year?

Ans. About 275.

Q by Ct. How much of this was burned?

Ans All but about 30 bales.

Q. by Ct What was done with the cotton, that was saved from the burners?

Ans. The boys sold it. General Curtis bought it. He paid me at the rate of $50 00/100 per bale. Between 200, and 300 for 5 Bales It was paid in Greenbacks, and Gold, The first payment was made in gold by Dr. Guthrie to me, and three others. He paid us $50 00/100 a piece in gold, the balance was paid by General Curtis himself in Greenbacks, I made the bargain for myself with General Curtis, me and the three others sold 20 bales to General Curtis, He told me to turn it over to the Quarter Master–

Q. by Ct. How were you employed after the money [*army*] came to Helena?

Ans. I was Steward for General Curtis

Q. by Ct. What if anything do you know of any other cotton being sold by the Negroes from the Pillow Plantations?

Ans I don't know of any other being sold from the Field cane Plantation, I saw General Curtis pay Negroes from the Jerome Pillow Plantation $500 at one Payment, He would call me in as a witness as to whether these Negroes belonged to Jerome Pillow, I don't know at what rate a bale or pound he paid them, He made some other Payments to them afterwards,

Question by the Court. How many of the canefield Plantation Negroes received money from General Curtis for the cotton you sold him, and how much did each one receive?

Ans. About 15 or 20 of them got paid, General Curtis paid me, and the three who first went with me $50 00/100 a piece He afterwards paid those three $50 00/100 or $60 00/100 a piece, He paid me altogether about $250 or $300, at different times whenever I asked him for money, but whether it was all for cotton, or not, I cannot say, I was with General Curtis as Steward for about 6 Months, and this sum includes all the Money paid me by him. I know the General to have paid others of the boys from $15 to $30 dollars–

Q by Ct. When, and where were these Payments made?

Ans He made the first Payment two or three weeks after he got to Helena, at his Head Quarters. He never made any Payments in St Louis, If any of the Negroes belonging to the Pillow Plantation would go to him, he would call on me to know if they belonged to the Pillow Families. If I said they did he would always give them Money from 10 to 20 dollars, He did that at Helena, and here too, I can't say whether this was for cotton or not.

Q. by Ct Did General Curtis buy cotton from all the Plantations, and how much?

Ans. I don't know except what the negroes told me.

Q. by Ct. Was much cotton taken from the Plantation of Jerome Pillow?

Ans. Jerome Pillow claimed to be Loyal, and his place was not much touched, the Negroes did not sell much cotton from this place, so they all told me.

Q. by Ct What became of the Negroes of the Pillow Plantations?

Ans Nearly all of Gideon Pillow's Negroes went upon a SteamBoat to Cairo, sent by General Curtis, Paid nothing for their Passage, this was very soon after the Army came.

Q by. Ct Did these people all have Money?

Ans Most all

Q by Ct. How did they get it?

Ans. Every way, selling cotton, selling Mules. and horse.

Sam Washington (Colored) being first duly sworn testified as follows:

Q by Ct. Where did you live in 1862?

Ans. Middle Farm, Philips County, Arkansas belonging to General Pillow

Q by Ct. Were you set free, By whom?

Ans I was set free by General Curtis, Have got my papers but not here.

Q by Ct. How much cotton was on the Middle Farm when the Soldiers came to Helena?

Ans As near as I can come at it, there was 80 bales, there was about 550 bales before they came in, and burned it, they burned it all but these 80 Bales which were hid.

Q by Ct. What was done with these 80 Bales?

Ans. There were 20 Bales raised by the colored folks on their own Ground that year and the year before, General Curtis had them sold, and divided among fifty farm working hands who were on the place, I got for me, and my boy $53 00/100. The cotton was sold in the lump, and the money divided equally among us fifty four, The balance General Curtis hauled up to Helena, and I don't know what became of it, Mr Hansom bought the 20 bales from us on the Plantation, and paid us for it there, we hauled it up on the bank of the river at Helena, for Mr. Hansom, Mr Hansom was an army Docter, in uniform, The boys on the middle farm got one of them to go up, and see General Curtis, and he said General Curtis sent Dr Hansom to sell it for us, and paid us the money. I don't know who bought the cotton. The stock, and cattle on the farm had been taken before, we were never paid any thing for that.

Q. by Ct. When, and how did you come north?

Ans. Nearly five hundred of us came North. the last of August, to Cairo, on steam Boat. Captain Smith had charge of us, We did not pay anything for the trip, The most of us stopped at Cairo, A good many of them came to St. Louis.

Q. by Ct. How did you live after the troops came in?

Ans. When the soldiers came there they divided the meat on the Plantation with us. and General Curtis sent us out some flour.

HD

Excerpt from testimony of Major General S. R. Curtis, 20 Mar. 1863, and testimony of David Haywood and of Sam Washington, 27 June 1863, vol. 1, pp. 16, 21–22, and vol. 2, pp. 558–62, Proceedings & Report of Court of Inquiry on Sale of Cotton & Produce at St. Louis Missouri, ser. 27, RG 159 [J-1]. According to other documents in the same volumes, the military court of inquiry had been established in February 1863, by order of General-in-Chief Henry W. Halleck. The three-member body, headed by General Irvin McDowell, was instructed to investigate whether Union officers "have been engaged, or directly or indirectly participated in traffic in Cotton or other produce on the Mississippi River or its tributaries, . . . have granted licenses or permits for trade, . . . [or] have used or permitted the use of Government transportation, or other public property for private purposes." (Special Orders No. 88, Head Quarters of the Army, 23 Feb. 1863, vol. 1, pp. 1–2.) Much of the investigation concerned cotton trading in the vicinity of Helena, Arkansas, during the summer of 1862, when General Samuel R. Curtis was in command of the Army of the Southwest. (He became commander of the St. Louis-based Department of the Missouri in September 1862.) In the report of its investigation, dated July 2, 1863, the court found that Curtis had acted improperly in paying slaves from the Pillow plantations for cotton they brought into Union lines. While acknowledging that the slaves might have had a legitimate claim to any cotton raised on their own, the court concluded that most of the cotton on the estates was the property of their rebel owners and therefore "should have been turned over to some officer of one of the administrative branches of the Staff and regularly accounted for." Instead of permitting the destitute fugitive slaves to support themselves from money they received for the cotton, Curtis should have provided for them "in a regular systematic manner by the proper staff Officers On proper returns made by some officer having knowledge of the number, and condition of these negroes." (Vol. 2, pp. 575–84.) For a secondhand account by Confederate General Gideon J. Pillow of events on his Arkansas plantations during Curtis's command at Helena, see *Freedom*, ser. 1, vol. 1: doc. 92.

1 The order, issued in the name of General Samuel R. Curtis, commander of the Army of the Southwest, declared "Haywood Pillow & Wife" to be "confiscated as being contraband of War," pronounced them "forever emancipated," and permitted them to pass northward from the lines of the army. General Curtis issued virtually identical freedom papers – some of them on printed forms – to hundreds of other Arkansas slaves. (See, for example, *Freedom*, ser. 1, vol. 1: doc. 95.)

152: Commander of the Post of Helena, Arkansas, to the Secretary of War

HELENA, ARKANSAS. Septembr 6th 1862.

Sir There are now at this Post about 400 negroes who are employed on the Fortifications. I have had them collected together onto one camp and they are in charge of a commissioned officer, who has drawn for their rations and clothing & promised them wages. There are also here otherwise unprovided for, 500 women & children who are refugees from their masters. They were in a most deplorable condition suffering for both food & covering. Gen. Curtis instructed me to take care of them which I have been doing as well as I could. I have them in a camp by themselves and have provided them with tents & food, drawing for them about half rations. I am advised by Genl Steel now in command here that this feeding of women and children is wholly unauthorised and that I am personly involving myself by continuing it. Many of these women & Children came into the Army from a long distance. They could not get back to their masters if they desired it, and to turn them out to starve is an act of cruelty which I wish to avoid. Many, if not most of these people have free papers given them by Genl. Curtis.[1] Shall I continue to feed them? I have the honor to be Your Obdt Svt

HLS C. C. Washburn

Brig. Genl. C. C. Washburn to Hon. E. M. Stanton, 6 Sept. 1862, W-1251 1862, Letters Received, RG 107 [L-18]. Endorsement. In the same file is a copy of a reply from the War Department sanctioning General Washburn's actions to date, and instructing him to continue to provide food and clothing to needy contrabands and to "give employment to such of them as are able to work." (P. H. Watson to Brig. Genl. C. C. Washburn, 30 Sept. 1862.) On September 28, John S. Phelps, military governor of Arkansas, complained from his headquarters at Helena that the town was "filled with contrabands, who have been forcibly in many instances brought from their plantations," and among whom "[m]uch sickness and mortality prevails." Phelps charged that General Samuel R. Curtis (who had only recently left Arkansas to become commander of the Department of the Missouri) had issued free papers to fugitive slaves upon no further evidence of their claim to freedom than "the statement of the negroes themselves," and he suggested that Curtis had ordered the construction of fortifications chiefly "to give employment to the slaves." Phelps also noted that some of the freedpeople at Helena had "gone up the river" to the North. (*Official Records*, ser. 1, vol. 13, pp. 683–85.)

1 For an example of the "free papers" given to former slaves by General Samuel R. Curtis, commander of the Army of the Southwest, see *Freedom*, ser. 1, vol. 1: doc. 95.

153: Assistant Quartermaster of the District of Jackson, Tennessee, to the Quartermaster General

Jackson, Tenn 9th Sept *1862*

General: Quite a large number of fugitive slaves have come into camp, and been turned over to me by the District Provost Marshal for employment. As the number will probably continue to increase I write for instructions as to what provision should be made for them. So far, the Negro men under my control have been profitably employed, and an additional number probably can be, but there are women and children among them, and I am at a loss to know how they can be made serviceable to the Gov't, and if they cannot be; I am without knowledge of any law or regulation of the Deptm't which would authorize me to provide for even their most pressing wants. They come penniless – and without food – necessary clothing or camp equippage – relying wholly upon the bounty of the Gov't. Shall that bounty be extended to them, and if so, in what manner, and to what extent I doubt not this question has met with a solution by you, and I respectfully request such instructions as you may deem proper to give me. Very Respectfully

HLS G L Fort

[*Endorsement*] [*Washington, D.C. September? 1862*] Respectfully referred to the Secretary of War for his instructions in the case –

I think that a temporary measure would be to credit the men able to labor with the proceeds of their labor paying them only a portion & applying a sufficient sum to the feeding & clothing & shelter of the women & children. The labor of the men & those women able to work should support the whole community of negros at any station. Respectfully M C Meigs QMG

[*Endorsement*] War Departmt Oct. 4th 1862 Approved and the Quarter Master General directed to issue the necessary instructions for carrying into effect his recommendation By order of the Secretary of War P. H. Watson Asst Secy War

Capt. G. L. Fort to Brigr. Genl. M. C. Meigs, 9 Sept. 1862, "Slaves, Fugitive," Consolidated Correspondence File, ser. 225, Central Records, RG 92 [Y-44]. A penciled notation, presumably by an official of the Quartermaster General's Office, reads: "What Genl Instructions shall be given? Shall a circular be issued." But neither a reply to Captain Fort, nor any circular setting forth the policy outlined in Meigs's endorsement, has been found in the records of the quartermaster general. Although Fort doubted that fugitive-slave women could be of service to the Union, a few black women had earlier found military employment at Jackson. In mid-August 1862, an army surgeon had requested that the employment of five such women, who were working as hospital attendants, "be authorized by a regular detail." "[T]heir services are absolutely necessary," he urged, "and could scarcely be dispensed with at the present time." However, the surgeon's superior officers not only denied his request, but also allowed a provost marshal to return the women to their owners, in violation of the March 1862 article of war. (Brig. Surg. J. D. Strawbridge to Sir, 15 Aug. 1862, enclosed in Brig. Surg. Jas. D. Strawbridge to Brig. Surg. Holston, 11 Sept. 1862, Registered & Unregistered Letters & Reports Received, ser. 2732, Dist. of West TN, RG 393 Pt. 2 No. 171 [C-8000].)

154: Chaplain of a Wisconsin Regiment to the Secretary of War; Enclosing a Letter from Three Northern Chaplains, a Colonel in an Ohio Regiment, and an Iowa State Agent to the Secretary of War

Corrinth [*Miss.*] Sept. 19th 1862

Dear Sir. Having been assigned by Gen. Grant to superintend the contrabands of this part of the army, & having learned something of their condition & circumstances, & also the expressed wishes of many Officers & soldiers of the Army with respect to this unfortunate class of persons, I thoght proper to write you & ascertain if some arrangement cannot be adopted by which we can place them in positions of safety & comparative comfort. I have under my charge at present about two thousand. I have sent six hundred of this class to Columbus by order of Gen. Grant, & my fear is that having no one whose special business it is to take charge of them that they may be left to suffer duing the approaching winter –

Therefore I would suggest that you appoint if it be consistent to do so some reliable person who shall have them wholly in charge – Many Officers of all grades have conferred with me to whom I have submitted this plan – & without an exception they generally approve of it – The work while I can conceive much labour & responsibility connected with it, might be an interesting work one which would furnish a reward to the one who performs it –

Many at the North would employ these contrabands, & are now in great numbers applying to me for them, but having no orders to do so I cannot comply –

To day a Lady from Ill. called on me & pledged one thousand dollars as a donation to begin the work, another stands ready to make a similar pledge –

I would therefore suggest that a suitable person be at once

appointed with proper authority to execute these plans, & that he have the right at least for the time being if not permantly to employ one or two more Agents as his assistants – I think it might be an easy matter to clothe the persons in question with a slight expense to the Gov[t] from the contributions of friends North – Since writing this the memorial accompanying it has been handed me which I now send you – I should be happy to serve as my Brethren recommend should I be appointed to the responsible position – Yours truly

ALS J. B. Rogers

[*Enclosure*] Corinth Miss. Sept. 18, 1862.

Sir; In view of the fact that the unavoidable issues of the present war, have throwen upon our hands, thousands of controbands, who must be provided for in Some manner or other, many of whom cannot be made useful in the army, being women, children and aged men, coming to us as many of them do in the most destitute circumstances, *it becomes a matter of no minor importance,* as to how these persons Shall be provided for, until Such time as the Government, Shall be able to decide upon the proper disposition of them. Futhermore, in-as-much as Genl. Grant, has detailed Chaplain Rogers of the 14 Wis. Vols. to receive and provide for temporally, all contrabands coming into our lines, which work he has been doing for the last five or Six days, and the fact that we this day have had an interview with Genl. Grant, who tells us that he has no power to act in this matter beyond what he has done, but refers us to you, telling us also that he has Already received orders from you, to remove at the earliest day all this class of persons to Cairo Ill. which places them beyond his jurisdiction. Being Some what familiar, by force of circumstances, with the difficulties of the Subject in question, we are led to beleive that a Statement of Some of the facts concerning this class of persons and some Suggestions in refference to thier future, would be acceptable to you and the President.

1. We already have upon the books of this division of the army Some 2000, besides hundreds Still in the Regiments not yet accounted for, and yet they have just commenced to come within our lines. The men and many of the women are employed in the Army, while the Sick and greater number of women and children are Still in the hands of Chaplain Rogers. Families are being broken up, husbands Seperated from their wives, and children from their parents. Many of them are destitute of clothing, most of them are incapable of providing for themselves. The turning them lose promiscuously and unrestricted into the free States would be alike injurious to the peace of the country and the good of the colored

race. yet if some efficient measures are not adopted by the Gov. and that very Soon, thousands of them must Suffer if not perish during the coming winter from cold and disease.

2. We would Suggest in accordance with what we Suppose to be a part of your plan: That all the controbands who cannot be usefully employed in the Army, as fast as they enter our lines, be Sent to Some Safe and Suitable place and if need be places, where they can be Suitably provided for and instructed, that they may not be wholy disqualified for whatever position Government may think best for them to occupy when this war is ended.

3. (a) If any persons in the free States are desirerous of employing either male or female controbands, that they be permitted to do So, provided Such persons can give evidence of responsibility and will in writing become responsible for the return and Stipulated wages of Such persons So employed, or a Satisfactory account of the Same, when ever the Government may demand it; provided Such employers be permitted to make Such return to the Agents of the government at any time previous to the final Setlement above named.

(b) That all employers, – government included, – be required to pay one fourth of the Stipulated price for the labor of all controbands so employed, into the hands of a Suitable person appointed by the Sec. of war, as a fund for the benefit of the whole class and to be so employed by those in charge, under the direction of the Sec. of war or his agent.

4. We reccommend Chaplain Rogers, as a Suitable person to be placed in charge of the whole department of controbands of the South West, and that he have two other efficient and Suitable persons associated with him, who Shall Superintend the departments of instruction, employment, food and clothing. That these persons for the present, that no additional expence be laid upon the Government, be detailed from the Army And that these Superintendants be permitted, through the proper chanels, to detail as many clerks and employees as may be necessary to properly arrange and conduct this work

5. That the Government, So far as it can and So long as needed, Supply food and clothing through the Superintendants of these Several departments.

6. That the officer in charge of the department be granted all necessary transportation for himself, assestants and goods. With much Respect we are, your Obet. Servants,

James M. Alexander
Joel Grant
Joseph Warren
R. N. Adams
Ira M. Gifford

HLS

Chaplain J. B. Rogers to E. L. Stanton, 19 Sept. 1862, enclosing James M. Alexander et al. to E. M. Stanton, 18 Sept. 1862, H-1523 1862, Letters Received, RG 107 [L-20]. The body of the enclosure is in Alexander's handwriting; each of the signatories wrote his own name. Rogers, Alexander, Grant, and Warren were chaplains of, respectively, the 14th Wisconsin, 14th Missouri, 12th Illinois, and 26th Missouri infantry regiments; Adams was lieutenant colonel of the 81st Ohio Infantry, and Gifford identified himself as "aid to Gov: of Iowa & State agent." No reply has been found in the records of the Secretary of War. On September 3, 1862, Rogers had been ordered by the commander of the Post of Corinth to assume supervision over "all the contrabands, Women and children," who were not employed as hospital attendants, cooks, or laundresses, and to establish a camp for them. (Special Orders No. 37, Head Quarters Corinth Miss., 3 Sept. 1862, Letters Received, ser. 6103, 4th Division, Dist. of Memphis, Army & Dist. of West TN, RG 393 Pt. 2 No. 403 [C-8926].) General Ulysses S. Grant, commander of the District of West Tennessee and the Army of the Tennessee, subsequently recognized Rogers's authority over the Corinth "Contraband Retreat." (Special Orders No. 195, Headquarters, District of West Tennessee, 15 Sept. 1862, vol. G4 DT, pp. 336–37, Special Orders Issued, ser. 2734, Dist. of West TN, RG 393 Pt. 2 No. 171 [C-2239].) But no orders extending Rogers's authority beyond Corinth or directing him to send fugitive slaves to Columbus, Kentucky, have been found in the records of Grant's command. Apparently, Grant did not officially designate a superintendent of contrabands until November 1862. (See doc. 155, immediately below.)

155: Order by the Commander of the Department of the Tennessee and 13th Army Corps

LaGrange, Tenn, Nov 14" 1862.

Special Field Orders No 4 Chaplain J Eaton Jr, of the 27th Regt Ohio Infantry Vols., is hereby appointed to take charge of all fugitive Slaves that are now or may from time to time come within the military lines of the advancing army in this vicinity, not employed and registered in accordance with General Orders, No 72, from Headquarters District of West Tennessee,[1] and will open a camp for them at Grand Junction, Tenn, where they will be suitably cared for and organized into companies and set to work picking, ginning and baling all cotton now out standing in the Fields.

Commanding officers of troops will send all fugitives that come within the lines, together with such teams, cooking utensils and other baggage as they may bring with them to Chaplain Eaton Jr at Grand Junction, Tenn.

One Regiment of Infantry from Brig. General McArthur's Division will be temporarily detailed as Guard in charge of such contrabands, and the Surgeons of said Regiment will be charged with the care of the sick.

Commissaries of Subsistence will issue on the requisitions of Chaplain J Eaton Jr, omitting the coffee rations and substituteing Rye. By order of Maj. Genl. U S Grant.

HDc

Special Field Orders No. 4, Headquarters, 13th Army Corps, Dept. of the Tennessee, 14 Nov. 1862, Orders & Circulars, ser. 44, RG 94 [DD-41]. On December 17, Grant issued a general order (No. 13, Headquarters 13th Army Corps, Department of the Tennessee) that significantly expanded both Eaton's jurisdiction and his authority. Appointing Eaton general superintendent of contrabands in the department, it directed him to organize fugitive slaves "into working parties in saving cotton, as pioneers on railroads and steamboats, and in any way where their service can be made available," and also authorized him to hire them to "private individuals." "In no case," Grant insisted, "will negroes be forced into the service of the Government, or be enticed away from their homes except when it becomes a military necessity." The order also stipulated that the contrabands "be clothed, and in every way provided for, out of their earnings so far as practicable," and instructed Eaton to oversee the distribution of clothing and other goods donated by charitable organizations "for the benefit of negroes." (John Eaton, *Grant, Lincoln and the Freedmen: Reminiscences of the Civil War* [1907; reprint ed., New York, 1969], pp. 26–27.)

1 Issued by General Ulysses S. Grant on August 11, 1862, the order authorized the employment of fugitive slaves as military laborers and officers' servants, and required the registration of those so employed; at the same time, it mandated the exclusion of unregistered fugitives from Union lines and prohibited Union soldiers from "enticing Slaves to leave their Masters." (General Orders No. 72, Head Quarters, District of West Tennessee, 11 Aug. 1862, vol. G3/4 DT, p. 90, General Orders & Circulars Issued, ser. 2733, Army & Dist. of West TN, RG 393 Pt. 2 No. 171 [C-391].)

156: Affidavit of a Mississippi Former Slaveholder, and Affidavits of Two of His Former Slaves

[*LaGrange, Tenn.*] 6" day of June 1866.

Personally appeared before me Geo. Gorman of Marshall Co. Miss and testified as follows.

In the year 1862, beleiving that all slaves would be free at the end of the war. I called my slaves to me and informed them that they were free to go or stay, as they might choose, but that those who staid at home might have all the cotton they made. The corn was to be cribbed for the use of the place Either in the latter part of 1862 or the fore part of 1863, I contracted with my negroes to work for half of the cotton, and the corn still to be raised for the use of the place; none to be sold by me or themselves, or removed by them. This contract was to last during the continuance of the war and was binding on the negroes during the war provided they remained at home. A portion of them remained and fulfilled the contract during the years 1862, 3 and 4.

At the end of the year 1865 they concluded to leave the place, and then they claimed a portion of the corn. I denied the justice of their claim and refused to deliver the corn to them. They then appealed to S. H. Melcher. Supt Bureau RF and AL at La Grange Fayette Co Tenn. Supt Melcher appointed a day to hear the case. I was sick and could not attend and wrote to him to that effect and stated in my letter that I could prove to him the contract if that would satisfy him. He may have summoned me more than once but I have no recollection of it.

Supt Melcher finaly gave an "exparte" hearing in the case and sent me an order directing me to give the negroes what they claimed and at the same time ordered me to pay $50 as a fine or costs in the case, the receipt for which I have in my posession. The said Supt Melcher said if I refused to obey the order that a regiment would be sent to enforce the order at my expense, that is the expenses of their transportation. The first lot of corn taken by the order of Supt Melcher was in January of this year. The last lot was seven and a half barrels and taken during the Month of May. Mr Baum of La Grange came in person and took the last lot. I being sick in bed at the time was unable to do anything

HDS *Ge^o Gorman*

[*LaGrange, Tenn.*] 6th day of June 1866.

Personally appeared before me Harry Gorman. (Col) and testified as follows

My name is Harry Gorman, I formaly was a slave belonging to Mr Geo Gorman of Marshall Co Miss. Was present in the year 1862 when Mr Gorman told us we were free to go or stay, as we choose. If we remained at home we were to have half the cotton we raised: the corn raised was to be cribbed and kept for the use of the place. If we left we were to leave all things as they were turned over to us. The corn was not to be sold by Mr Gorman or ourselves nor to be removed by either party. I considered this contract binding

his
HDSr Harry X Gorman
mark

[*LaGrange, Tenn.*] 7" day of June 1866.

Personally appeared before me Jessie Gorman. (Col) and testified as follows

My name is Jessie Gorman I reside in Fayette Co Tenn and am in the employ of Mr John Baum. I formaly was a slave belonging to Mr Geo Gorman of Marshall Co Miss. I left Mr Gorman in the Spring of 1863 and returned to him in March 1864. On my return to Mr Gorman he told me as I had begun late to work for him and had a bad start he would give me all I could make on the farm that year. At the end of the year in dividing the crop he did not by me as he agreed but gave equally to all. We filled his corn cribs as they were turned over to us and the balance of the corn we divided amongst ourselves. Nothing was said about the corn until August 1865. when we were about gathering it. he then insisted that all the corn raised was to be left on the place. We divided the corn after it was gathered he Mr Gorman consenting to the division and told us to take care of our corn for we would need it.

his
Jessie X Gorman
Mark

HDSr

Affidavit of Geo. Gorman, 6 June 1866, affidavit of Harry Gorman, 6 June 1866, and affidavit of Jessie Gorman, 7 June 1866, all enclosed in Capt. F. M. H. Kendrick to Capt. Mch. Walsh, 11 June 1866, Unregistered Letters Received, ser. 3522, Memphis TN Subasst. Comr., RG 105 [A-6531]. All sworn before a Freedmen's Bureau inspector. According to other documents in the same file, several freedmen who worked on George Gorman's farm in 1865 had brought suit against him in January 1866 for corn that they claimed was theirs. In testimony before Samuel H. Melcher, the Freedmen's Bureau superintendent at LaGrange, Tennessee (there being no bureau official in their home county in Mississippi), they had disputed Gorman's account of the terms of their employment, contending that he had promised them half the cotton they produced and all the corn in excess of "six loads." However, testified one of the freedmen, "when we talked of working somewhere else, Maj. Gorman said we should not have an ear of corn and refused to allow it moved." Melcher had decided in favor of the freedmen, permitting them to remove their corn from Gorman's farm and ordering Gorman to pay court costs of $50. (S. H. Melcher to Bt. Brig. Genl. B. P. Runkle, 6 June 1866, enclosing testimony of Ben, Henry, and Ernst, 8 Jan. 1866, and testimony of Harry, 12 Jan. 1866.) A search of the records of the Freedmen's Bureau subassistant commissioner at Memphis and of the Tennessee Freedmen's Bureau assistant commissioner revealed nothing further about the case.

157: Superintendent of Contrabands in the District of Eastern Arkansas to the Commander of the Department of the Missouri, Enclosing a Letter from a Committee of Chaplains and Surgeons to the Commander of the Department

Helena– Ark. Jany 26th 1863–

General, I herewith send a paper unanimously adopted by the Chaplains Association of the Army of the Eastern District of Arkansas.

Since its adoption, a number of the Chaplains accompanied the expedition of Gen. Gorman up White river, & several circumstances have delayed the transmission of a copy to your Head Quarters–

Before leaving, Gen. Gorman, (to whom I forwarded a copy as Secretary of the Association at the suggestion of a personal friend of the General,) made some radical changes with reference to the contrabands– The Hospital Steward & the contract Surgeon were discharged from the negro hospital, & Capt. Richmond relieved of his command, I was ordered to report to Gen. Gorman, & placed in charge of this office, & of the Hospital & instructed to take charge of this post of duty as Superintendent of Contrabands– By order of Col. Bussy Rev. J G. Forman Post Chaplain, was joined with me as Associate Supt– The Hospital had been under the charge of Dr Jacks Editor of Helena Shield–who authorized two negro nurses to whip the patients with leather straps–at their discretion– A radical change of course was demanded– I have had Dr. Cravens Assistant Surgeon of 1st Ind. Cavalry detailed as "Contraband" Surgeon–& he has entered upon his work with diligence & promptness– Miss Mann a niece of Horace Mann, representing the Sanitary Commission, has volunteered her services in behalf of the invalid contrabands & her help will be very valuable–

I have received a call from Col. Shaw, who comes by your orders to form a regiment of contrabands for U.S. service– Believing that such an organization is eminently desirable for many & obvious reasons, I hoped that he would be aided by those in command. The present system is disheartening to both races– The laborers do not receive that protection & care they should have– Few of them have comfortable shoes or boots, & yet they are expected to wade through the deepest mud along the river bank in loading & unloading government stores– They are suffering for want of clothing– Most of them have received no money as yet for their services & there is no sutler arrangement for them to procure tobacco or other real or imagined necessities– The soldiers here & there plunder them– When Gen. Gorman's expedition returned over fifty contraband families were turned out of their cabins into the wet

& mud, to make room for the soldiers, & upon a requisition being made for tents to supply them, none could be had – Such things constantly occurring embarass the operations of this office & constantly also weaken its effective force – The hands seek for passes through the lines & hundreds of them return to their old homes – Two days since a number, by some process, were passed into Mississippi, & their labor is lost to the Government – If Col. Shaw should succeed in organizing the contrabands as contemplated by the President's Proclamation[1] many of these matters might be remedied – & the Government much more effectively served – Very respectfully –

Samuel Sawyer

Gen. Gorman has suggested that the women & children be sent up the river as soon as practicable – A boat load is ready to go – S. S.

ALS

[*Enclosure*] Helena Arkansas Dec 29th 1862

General The undersigned Chaplains and Surgeons of the army of the Eastern Destrict of Arkansas would respectfully call your attention to the Statements & Suggestions following

The Contrabands within our lines are experiencing hardships oppression & neglect the removal of which calls loudly for the intervention of authority. We daily see & deplore the evil and leave it to your wisdom to devise a remedy. In a great degree the contrabands are left entirely to the mercy and rapacity of the unprincipled part of our army (excepting only the limited jurisdiction of capt Richmond) with no person clothed with Specific authority to look after & protect them. Among their list of grievances we mention these:

Some who have been paid by individuals for cotton or for labor have been waylaid by soldiers, robbed, and in several instances fired upon, as well as robbed, and in no case that we can now recal have the plunderers been brought to justice –

The wives of some have been molested by soldiers to gratify thier licentious lust, and thier husbands murdered in endeavering to defend them, and yet the guilty parties, though known, were not arrested. Some who have wives and families are required to work on the Fortifications, or to unload Government Stores, and receive only their meals at the Public table, while their families, whatever provision is intended for them, are, as a matter of fact, left in a helpless & starving condition

Many of the contrabands have been employed, & received in numerous instances, from officers & privates, only counterfeit money or nothing at all for their services. One man was employed as a teamster by the Government & he died in the service (the government indebted to him nearly fifty dollars) leaving an orphan child eight years old, & there is no apparent provision made to draw the money, or to care for the orphan child. The negro hospital here has become notorious for filth, neglect, mortality & brutal whipping, so that the contrabands have lost all hope of kind treatment there, & would almost as soon go to their graves as to their hospital. These grievances reported to us by persons in whom we have confidence, & some of which we know to be true, are but a few of the many wrongs of which they complain– For the sake of humanity, for the sake of christianity, for the good name of our army, for the honor of our country, cannot something be done to prevent this oppression & to stop its demoralizing influences upon the Soldiers themselves? Some have suggested that the matter be laid befor the Department at Washington, in the hope that they will clothe an agent with authority, to register all the names of the contrabands, who will have a benevolent regard for their welfare, though whom all details of fatigue & working parties shall be made though whom rations may be drawn & money paid, & who shall be empowered to organize schools, & to make all needfull Regulations for the comfort & improvement of the condition of the contrabands; whose accounts shall be open at all times for inspection, and who shall make stated reports to the Department– All which is respectfully submitted

committee { Samuel Sawyer
Pearl P Ingall
J. G. Forman

HLSr

Chaplain Samuel Sawyer to Major Gen. Curtis, 26 Jan. 1863, enclosing Samuel Sawyer et al. to Maj. Gen. Curtis, 29 Dec. 1862, #135 1863, Letters Received Relating to Military Discipline & Control, ser. 22, RG 108 [S-3]. Sawyer's letter of January 26 is headed "Head Quarters of Public Works." In the enclosure, the text and all three signatures are in the same handwriting. Endorsements referred both letters to the headquarters of the army, where they were filed without reply. Sawyer, who was chaplain of the 47th Indiana Infantry, had been detailed as superintendent of contrabands at Helena by General Willis A. Gorman, commander of the District of Eastern Arkansas, on January 8, 1863. Captain George N. Richmond had apparently been in charge of black military laborers at the same post. (Special Order No. 356, Head Quarters Dist. of Eastern Ark., 22 Nov. 1862, and Special Order No. 7, Head Quarters District Eastern Arkansas, 8 Jan. 1863, vol. 42/108 DArk, pp. 161–62, 202–3, Special Orders, ser. 4686, Dist. of Eastern AR, RG 393 Pt. 2 No. 299 [C-7544].)

1 The Emancipation Proclamation, issued January 1, 1863, which, after proclaiming the freedom of all slaves in those states still in rebellion, announced

that the federal government would receive former slaves "of suitable condition . . . into the armed service of the United States to garrison forts, positions, stations, and other places, and to man vessels of all sorts." (*Statutes at Large*, vol. 12, pp. 1268–69.)

158: General Superintendent of Contrabands in the Department of the Tennessee to the Headquarters of the Department

Steamboat Magnolia Mississippi River Expedition Feb. 14th 1863
Colonel: The ocurrence of questions which I have not the power to answer compels me to submit them for the consideration of the General Commanding, & his instructions–

I Pay of contrabands

1st In hospitals

(a) Men & women render service & receive vouchers signed by Surgeon in charge & by Genl commanding Post: but Paymasters do not pay; and I am informed the pay department consider the exigency as yet unprovided for.

(b) Often are given no vouchers, by reason of the officer's doubting, what is legal & proper, & these persons labor on month after month with only rations, shelter, & donations of clothing from the benevolent for compensation.

(c) Colored women employed as cooks, laundresses &c– Some see no legal provision for their pay; others put them on the same footing with colored men; others still would give them vouchers at the rate of six dollars, others at the rate of eight, and others still at the rate of twelve dollars per month.

(d) Shall men & women be compensated the same for service in hispitals for colored persons as in hospitals for soldiers?

2nd Generally– (a) Shall all officers employing contrabands as cooks, teamsters &c. for Government, be held to give them the proper vouchers, if not the money? and shall these vouchers be as good in colored hands as in white?

(b) It happens that fifty women, work two days cleaning buildings for hospitals; or that one hundred men work one day loading or unloading Government stores:– ought not the proper vouchers to be given for the work, & the money collected by the local supt. & credited to the individuals performing the labor?

Thousands of days of such labor pass unpaid. Paid, the amount may be put over against the support of these individuals & the balance paid those who earn it.

II Funds found on deceased colored persons; and moneys due for services: if heirs are known & within our lines, I have ordered them paid over to them; if no heirs, in some cases, they have been used as hospital funds: as the amount is likely to increase, ought there not to be some proper provision, for investing it in United States securities as a fund to be expended for the benefit of orphaned contrabands?

III In clothing these persons we have been greatly aided by donotions from loyal persons in the North. These donations in a number of instances have been charged freight as private goods. Can not some general provision be made, so that all such donations properly certified can come forward at Government expense?

IV Shall soldiers detailed in this service be allowed extra pay? It would seem to be just that those should, who act as clerks, commissaries, foreman, &c, who do proper extra duty; & that those who act as guards should, not.

V The camp at Cairo is obnoxious to the people of Illinois. They need laborers but are prejudiced against blacks.

Various difficulties have been reported to me in connection with that camp.

So far the influx at other points has prevented my giving it any personal attention; in going there as I hope to, shortly, shall I examine into the feasibility of its removal?

VI Shall any attempt be made at agriculture on islands in the River? or on its banks where the laborers can be safe?

The soil so productive, is deserted; cotton, one its leading products, for the culture of which these ignorant persons are prepared – men, women & children – without any additional skill, must for a time bear a high price; the organisation is provided in Gen[l] order No. 13:[1] soon the present nakedness of these persons will be covered by the donations of benevolent persons & by issues of the Government; this support goes on; besides they will ere long need another supply, & multitudes more are pressing in equally destitute; ought either government or charity to be taxed to meet the demand, – when the [season] is here with these facilities for their doing it by their own labor, with additional advantages to their health & their moral & social condition?

Imperfect provisions, just now, may turn thousands back to continue enriching their disloyal masters, & supporting the rebellion by their otherwise loyal labor, notwithstanding the President has announced the policy of withdrawing them.

Although I am perplexed with these and other facts & inquiries in my endeavors to carry out Order No. 13,[1] I am more & more assured of the correctness of the principles it indicates for my guidance.

Hoping soon to be able to submit a full report – the blanks for which have already gone to the different posts – of all matters under my supervision[2] I remain Your Obd't Serv't

ALS John Eaton Jr.

[*Endorsement*] Head Quarters, Dept. of the Tn. Before Vicksburg, Feby 16th /63, Respectfully refered to H^{d} Qrs. of the Army with the request that instructions be sent covering such of these inquiries as are not already provided for by law or Gen. orders.

If it is the design of the Government to cultivate Southern fields with the numerous Contrabands coming into the Federal lines I would suggest Lake Providence as a most suitable place for a colony. The plantations are in a high state of cultivation, well improved as to quarters, and the place easily protected, U. S. Grant Maj. Gen.

Chaplain John Eaton Jr. to Colonel, 14 Feb. 1863, #150 1863, Letters Received Relating to Military Discipline & Control, ser. 22, RG 108 [S-4]. Another endorsement. Eaton signed as chaplain of the 27th Ohio Infantry. No reply has been found in the records of the Headquarters of the Army or the Department of the Tennessee, and more than two months later, Chaplain Eaton complained that the "[d]ifficulties" regarding the pay of black laborers remained unresolved. "Can we expect to elevate this people," he asked rhetorically, "without a proper use of the motives inspired by reward for labor?" (Chaplain John Eaton, Jr., to Lt. Col. Jno. A. Rawlins, 29 Apr. 1863, filed with O-328 1863, Letters Received, ser. 12, RG 94 [K-89].) In the meantime, Eaton made preparations to employ freedpeople in growing crops on abandoned land near contraband camps. From the Cincinnati Contraband Relief Commission he solicited seed and farm implements for agricultural operations at Corinth, Mississippi, where a camp was already established, and at Island 10 (in the Mississippi River near Tiptonville, Tennessee), where he hoped to relocate former slaves from Cairo, Illinois, and Columbus, Kentucky. (J. E., Jr. to Robt. W. Carrol, [Feb.? 1863], vol. 74, pp. 23–26, Letters Sent by John Eaton, ser. 2027, General Supt. of Freedmen, MS Asst. Comr. Pre-Bureau Records, RG 105 [A-4003].) Eaton also communicated his views respecting the former slaves to the chairman of the Senate Committee on Military Affairs. He recommended that the able-bodied men be organized as soldiers or military laborers, and that all others remain under federal supervision in contraband camps. The camps, Eaton urged, should be "regulated by a method of business which keeps families together in responsibility if not in fact [with] the husband and father made responsible for the Support of his family." He also advocated federal supervision of abandoned plantations on which crops would be "planted & gathered in common" by black laborers, who would also be permitted to cultivate (in their spare time) "[s]eparate plots peculiarly their own in manner of management and results." Suitable locations for such labor "[might] be found on Islands or banks of the [Mississippi] river possibly protected by an armed organisation of blacks." This plan, Eaton concluded, would at once secure the Union's hold over the river, effect "the Speediest restoration of Government authority & unity and the reduction of its expenses," and ensure "the fit and certain elevation of the coloured race." ([Chaplain John Eaton, Jr.] to Hon. Henry Wilson, [Feb.? 1863], vol. 74, pp. 16–23, Letters Sent by John Eaton, ser. 2027, General Supt. of Freedmen, MS Asst. Comr. Pre-Bureau Records, RG 105 [A-4000].)

1 See above, doc. 155n.
2 For a compilation of replies to Eaton's questions regarding the condition of contrabands at various federal posts, and a summary of his report, see below, doc. 160.

159: Superintendent of Contrabands at Lake Providence, Louisiana, to a Northern Attorney; and the Attorney to the Secretary of War

Providence, La Feb. 19" 1863

Dr Sir: – Your note of this morning is at hand & I cheerfully answer your interogations.

1st We have 1250 [*freedpeople*] in aggregate that have come in within the last twelve days, & I think of this number 700, are able bodied men & all in travling distance wo'd crowd to the river Bank.

2 From my observation & conference with them, the efficient men wo'd gladly take arms & often *beg* the privilege. I have often tried to intimdate them with Davis threat, if found in arms,[1] but the right men *have* NO *fear of it*.

I see no reason why they wo'd not become the best of soldiers for these times, & this region –

3d There is a superabundance of everything in this region for black & white only use the negro to secure it, for he knows its whereabouts.

4 Their condition beggars description, for want of clothing many of them at least, & of their disposition to labor, the lowest estimate is by those overseeing them, that one negro is worth three soldiers others say four.

5" I have known but one negro in arms here, & he went out with an old gun (as I understand it) on his own hook as the saying goes, & got into a skermish, he killed one man dead – *took two prisoners*, (& has now one of the double barreled shot guns) making one of them wade a bayou up to his neck to get it & when with my clerk he saw a rebel, & made for him under cover of a fence, till he halted & shot at him, & the reb, cry out "O Lord," but did not get him.

I gave him a note to Gen. M^c^Arthur & Col. Ditzler comd^g^ post, gives him a mule & I hear he is like a pointer dog ahead looking up the game.

The information they give of property &c Gen M^c^Arthur has sent but one boat, & then he found all reliable & truthful that the negro said.

I have much information by them of treasures of all kinds, & almost in all places that sho'd we remain here, I think the Gen. will look after, especially secreted forage & cotton. They bring inteligence of telegraphs, bateries, & operators, & seem well posted (the inteligent portion especially) in passing events.

My own conviction is, if they were brigaded along the banks of the river on each side, those from 18 to 45 years of age, we have crippled successfully for the future the [*Confederate*] war power in these states. I have the honor to be respectfully Your ob^t^ servant

ALS L. S. Livermore

Washington March 20th 1863

Hon E M Stanton Secy of War At the Suggestion of a number of officers of the Army of the Mississippi, whose views regarding the employment of Negroes as Soldiers, are believed to be in harmony with the present policy of the administration and who are Sincerely desirous of Seeing them armed and brought to bear against the enemy in that part of Louisania and Arkansas lying between Vicksburgh & Napoleon at the Mouth of the Arkansas River, I have appeared here to represent their wishes and also to state Some facts regarding the present condition of that particular Section derived from personal observation during the last Six weeks. These facts bear mainly upon the present number of whites and blacks, their Sentiments, condition as to food & clothing willingness to bear arms &c, The region refered to embraces the Parishes of Madison and Carroll in Louisania & the counties of Chicot and Desha in Arkansas. Stretching over two hundred miles on the West side of the Mississippi River. I have been in three of these Parishes and counties on Scouting and foraging expeditions, And have conversed with intelligent and I believe loyal gentleman in them all. from their statements I believe the following estimate will be found very nearly correct.

	Madison.	Carroll,	Chicot,	Desha,	total
White population	700,	2500,	1200,	1600.	6000.
Black D^o^	12.000	13.000,	9000,	3500.	37,500

Thus you will observe that taking the whole population the proportion of colored to white is over Six to one. The white population is composed almost entirely of old men, women & Children, who with very few exceptions are bitterly hostile to our government. Men capable of bearing arms are scarcely any where found except as spies or guerrillas, these number about one thousand,

Negroes every where are anxious to come within the lines and but for the close vigilance of Masters and overseers, would do so in very large numbers. As it is their arrivals at Lake Providence average about one hundred per day

And this notwithstanding *they are generally discouraged* by our *officers* from coming with in the lines– on this point I speak from positive knowledge. Were systematic efforts made by the Military authorities. There can be very little doubt that a force of Eight or ten thousand able bodied men could be mustered into service within the next forty days which would afford ample protection for the region referred to, while the numerous Abandoned and forfeited Plantations lying on the River would afford comfortable places of refuge for the families of those thus organized for Military purposes.

These noncombatants, under proper management can be profitably employed in cultivating the soil at once. thereby rendering themselves self sustaining–instead of becoming a burthen to the goverment. The able bodied men formed into regiments, and posted in the rear of the Settlements, would afford ample protection to the cultivators of the soil, bsides rendering the navigation of the Missippi perfectly safe from guerrilla attacts which are now so annoying to our Transports, There is found in all that region west of the Mississippi & below Napoleon an abundance of corn, Sweet potatoes, cattle sheep, swine. & mules to answer the demand of those who might flock there for protection during this season, In clothing and shoes the whole population white & black are extremely destitute– Particular pains have be taken to ascertain the disposition of the Negoes of that district to bear arms–and no doubt is entertained by those conversant with the subject of their entire willingness and in many cases eagerness to enlist as soldiers, So little doubt have the gentlemen I represent of their ability to raise immediately a large and efficient force that they ask Nothing in the way of outfit, except arms, ammunition, and clothing. They ask no food. No horses or mules, no waggons, No tents (except for officers) the country will afford all these, without cost. They firmly believe the negro can fight and are willing to organize and direct his energies against the rebellion and that with them they can conquer. defend & cultivate that region thus demonstrating the question, whether the Negro can battle successfully for his freedom & country & maintain himself when free, With reference to the present support of the large negro population which would come in, It is suggested that of the one hundred & fifty Plantations lying on & Near the west bank of the Mississippi between Vicksburgh & Napoleon, Not over ten of them but what are subject to confiscation and nearly all have been abandoned. Not one Single Plantation between Vicksburgh & Napoleon present any signs of a design to Cultivate, the present season, Wood it not therefore be good policy to treat that description of property As is done in Memphis where several hundred Abandoned buildings are said to be rented for the benefit of goverment,

The abandoned plantations could easily be rented to enterprising at a certain rate per acre for the present season, with the agreement on the part of the Lessee to employ as laborers none but negroes & to pay them such wages as is usual for that description of labor, The rate to be fixed by goverment,

If this can be done the present season (& I believe it can) It would be of great importance as establishing the fact that in *Agriculture* free negro labor under good management can be made a *source* of *profit* to the *employer*. This point once established on the scale proposed, would divest the whole question of emancipation and the production of cotton with free negro labor of most of the difficulties which at present surround it. Should the plan proposed prove successful in the district alluded to. It may be easily extended so as to embrace the whole region between Memphis & New Orleans, thereby furnishing complete protection to the commerce of the Mississippi Valley, besides furnishing the black population, Now idle, with immediate employment that shall render them self sustaining. In my interview with you on Monday next I will furnish you with the names of those officers at present in the army of the Mississippi who are willing to undertake the organization. Very Respectfully &c

ALS Geo B Field

L. S. Livermore to Geo. B. Fields, Esqr., 19 Feb. 1863, and Geo. B. Field to Hon. E. M. Stanton, 20 Mar. 1863, both filed as L-89 1863, Letters Received, ser. 360, Colored Troops Division, RG 94 [B-600]. The military commander at Lake Providence endorsed Livermore's letter, describing him as "a truthful and reliable gentleman." The "interogations" to which Livermore responded have not been located. Although no report of Field's meeting with Secretary of War Edwin M. Stanton, slated for March 23, 1863, has been found in the records of the War Department, the views expressed in Field's and Livermore's letters evidently accorded with those of the secretary: On March

25, Stanton dispatched Adjutant General Lorenzo Thomas to the Mississippi Valley under orders to "observe particularly the condition of that class of population known as contrabands," to organize the men fit for service as soldiers and military laborers, and to provide for the employment and support of the women, children, and aged or disabled men. (*Official Records*, ser. 3, vol. 3, pp. 100–101.) Field accompanied Thomas to the valley, and two weeks later, Thomas appointed both Field and Livermore commissioners for leasing abandoned plantations. (See below, doc. 162.)

1 On December 23, 1862, Confederate President Jefferson Davis had ordered "[t]hat all negro slaves captured in arms be at once delivered over to the executive authorities of the respective States . . . to be dealt with according to the laws of said States." (*Official Records*, ser. 2, vol. 5, pp. 795–97.) Black Union soldiers captured by the Confederates thus would be treated not as prisoners of war, but as runaway slaves (to be returned to their owners) or as insurrectionary slaves (to be punished by whipping or execution).

160: General Superintendent of Contrabands in the Department of the Tennessee to the Headquarters of the Department

April 29, 1863. Memphis [*Tenn.*].
[Copy.][1]

Sir– Ordered by the Gen'l. Comdg. to assume general supervision of the Freedmen in this Department, Dec. 7, A.D. 1862,[2] I have the honor to present the following summary statement.

Undertaking duties so new, so perplexing, involving such hostilities, so minute in their details, so sweeping in their consequences, & so vital to the issue of those most dear to the heart of every citizen loyal to Union and Liberty, & among persons so violently condemned as worthless, I was fortified against my misgivings by the orders & instructions of the General, & his considerate attention, always given to the questions on my hands, however unusual or unique for the consideration of a Commander in the field. The necessary incompleteness and unsatisfactoriness of all undertaken for these persons, and of this report, are understood by one so familiar as he is with the chaos of uncertainties, necessities & changes, in the midst of which all this labor is performed. Negroes, in accordance with the Acts of Congress, free in coming within our lines, circulated much like water;– the task was, to care for & render useful. They rolled like eddies around military posts; many of the men employed in accordance with Order No. 72, District

West Tennessee;[3] women and children largely doing nothing but eating and idling, the dupes of vice and crime, the unsuspecting sources of disease. Already the numbers were large; a camp had been gathered and was progressing finely at Corinth under Chaplain Alexander – their the women & children had picked to their own advantage all cotton accessible; at Bolivar, large amounts – to whose advantage I am unable to say; at Grand Junction, in accordance with Order No. 4,[4] with advantage to themselves and profit to the Government; and at Cairo, a camp for their reception and care.

Struggling after an increased settlement of first principles, by which to direct the efforts committed to my discretion, the necessity of accurate, extended, minute observation was apparent. Fine-spun speculations parted like gossamer before the [events?] in the affairs of these people. All theories available interlocked with the main facts. Endeavoring to gather what had been observed, and converge their light upon the path before us, tabular forms and a series of questions were sent to each Superintendent. I present the substance of their reports.

Tabulated Items.

		Total	Field Hands	House Servants	African	Mixed	Carpenters.	Blacksmiths	Teamsters	cooks	Laundresses.	Seamstresses	Read	Write	Have children	Deaths	Births	Cases of sickness	Married
J. M. Alexander	Men	658			219	438	48	36	180	200			120	30		80		300	438
Post Superintend'nt.	Women	1440			360	1080				600	150	80	40	10	1260	65		400	1080
Corinth, Miss.	Children	1559														44	45	200	
Chaplain 66th Ill.	Total	3637 [3657]			579	1518	48	36	180	800	150	80	160	40	1260	189	45	900	1518
Chaplain J. Grant	Men	353	307		303	50	6	10	23	4			3		157	35		205	177
Post Superintend't	Women	464	367	19	387	77				28	30	20	5		260	32		234	207
Gnd Junction, Tenn	Children	891			772	119										52	75	262	
	Total	1708	674	19	1462	246	6	10	23	35 [32]	30	20	8		417	119	75	701	384
A. S. Fisk, Chaplain	Men	361	317	8	165	152	10	7	11	8		8	18		140	43		53	
Post Superind't	Women	320	218	12	126	92				42	21		7		136	60	21	47	
Memphis, Tenn.	Children	701	701		440	261												84	
	Total	1382	1236	20	731	505	10	7	11	50	21	8	25		276	103	21	184	
Total of above three		6747	1910	39	2772	2269	64	53	214	885 [882]	201	108	193	40	1953	411	141	1785	1902

Memphis, Tenn	2500	– living about town – not fed by, nor yet under care of Supt.
La Grange	750	Chaplain A. B. Morrison, Supt. No statistics given.
Providence, La.	2380	L. S. Livermore " " " "
Cairo, Ill	5000	J. B. Rogers " chiefly gone North
Jackson, Tenn.	800	No Supt. chiefly in Government employ.
Columbus, Ky.	1000	Reported by Rev. Mr. Wright. See Appendix A.
Estimated	3000	at points & in Regiments not included in above.
Sum Total	22177	Those gathered at Helena, Arkansas, not included.

Some of these, in various ways, have gone back to slavery – others found Northern homes.

Answers to Interrogatories.

Interrogatory 1st What of their clothing, when they entered and since?

Answers.

Corinth Very poor, with exceptions. Some came dressed in suits borrowed from those over them. Now, good by their own earnings, & by donations.

Cairo Was very poor, many of them having hardly enough to cover their nakedness. A few well dressed, & clothes for future use.

Grand Junction# Of those coming earliest, much worn; of those later, most needy– since supplied by Government, & donations from loyal States.

[*Footnote*:] #After being at Grand Junction a month, taken away by General Order, I left Lt. McClarren in charge, who in turn was succeeded by Chaplain Grant. The answers for Grand Junction were furnished by Assistants David L. Jones and W. G. Sargent, continuously there; from all other points by Superintendents, as per table.

Holly Springs and Memphis Very poor– supplied since by Govermnt and donations.

Memphis Included in the above Chaplain J. R. Locke first in charge at Memphis.

Bolivar Very indifferent

La Grange In nearly every instance, very destitute.

Providence Many, not enough to cover their nakedness;– few, to make themselves comfortable;– clothing arriving from the North.

Interrogatory 2d Have they been sheltered by tents, houses, or cabins?

Answers.

Corinth First tents; finally, chiefly by cabins, built by themselves.

Cairo. Old barracks.

Grand Junction. Houses, and old tents.

Holly Springs & Memphis. " " " " & in some cases no shelter.

Memphis. Tents. Building log cabins.

Bolivar. Board cabins.

La Grange Old houses, then tents.

Lake Providence. Deserted houses.

Interrogatory 3d When did you commence issuing the contraband ration?[5]

Answers.

Corinth. Last of November, 1862.

Cairo. Issued soldiers' rations, on assuming control of camp.
Grand Junction As soon as the ration was determined.
Holly Springs & Memphis On the 27th December, 1862.
Memphis From the first.
Bolivar. January 1st. 1863.
La Grange From the first.
Providence. " " "

Interrogatory 4th Have you varied from it since? If so, how & why?

Answers.

Corinth. Flour, when corn-meal could not be had; never have had hominy. The soap is insufficient.

Cairo. Varied from soldiers' rations somewhat, substituting rye for coffee. I have drawn the same in kind & quantity as is furnished to soldiers, excepting to children, as follows: Children from 2 to 5 years old 1/4; from 5 to 15, 1/2

Grand Junction. Never, except when could not obtain full rations.

Holly Springs & Memphis. Part of the time, 1/2 and 1/4 rations.

Memphis. No variation.

Bolivar. Never, except when on 1/2 rations.

La Grange Never; do well on it.

Providence Never.

Interrogatory 5th What of the property brought in by them, its amount and disposition?

Answers.

Corinth. Horses, mules, wagons, cotton, oxen, &c., estimated at $3000 – all turned over to Quartermaster.

Cairo. None whatever.

Grand Junction Oxen, yokes, chains, wagons, mules, horses; – generally, in poor condition; used for employing and caring for contrabands, as per order. Much taken from them by officers and soldiers.

Holly Springs & Memphis. 15 horses and mules – 15 pairs oxen. 12 pairs turned over to U.S. Quartermaster. Otherwise used for benefit of freedmen.

Memphis. Included in the above, and brought by Chaplain Locke on removal of freedmen from Holly Springs.

Bolivar. Teams; large number turned over to Quartermaster. Value not known – part used in camp.

La Grange Two ox-teams. They were allowed to sell them.

Providence. Turned over to Quartermaster.

Interrogatory 6th What of hospitals in connection with your camp; their management, & character of diseases treated?

ANSWERS.

Corinth. Surgeon Humphrey treated diseases in hospital Surgeon McCord in camp. Those in hospitals visited twice a day; those in camp, once a day. In camp, we have a bathing trough to wash all the dirty & filthy, when necessary. Surgeons, both kind & faithful. Health of camp improving. *Diseases* – Pneumonia, rapid in its progress, sometimes terminating fatally in twelve hours after the attack; typhoid and congestive fevers, of a low grade; measles, sometimes terminating in gangrene of the feet, requiring amputation.

Cairo. Three hospitals – male, female, and pest house. Measles, pneumonia, small pox. Two surgeons.

Grand Junction. About 50 sick in hospital – balance treated in quarters. Diseases as above.

Holly Springs & Memphis. *Diseases* – Diarrhoea & pneumonia.

Memphis. Hopital not under charge of Superintendent. Its condition wretched in the extreme. Lack of medicines, of utensils, of vaccine matter. No report of admissions, of diseases, of deaths, or discharges. No attention to sick in camp by surgeon. Sent assistants out of my own office, having some Knowledge of medicine, but surgeon refused vaccine matter & medicines. Improvement at date. *Diseases* – Pnuemonia, fevers, small pox. See appendix B

Bolivar. One hospital. Not more than 10 or 12 inmates at a time. *Diseases* – Pnuemonia & measles.

La Grange. Hospital under Dr. Welsh – common diseases; mostly pneamonia. Pest Hospital well managed by Dr. Wilson.

Providence. Difficulty in obtaining surgeons & medicines. One surgeon.

Interrogatory 7th The situation of your camps with respect to town and troops – how guarded and regulated?

Answers.

Corinth. Location good – half mile from any troops – wood plenty – abundant water from deep well dug in camp, costing $50 – paid from their own earnings. Cabins, nearly 100, from [*form*] three sides of a square. Church & Commissary buildings occupy the fourth Grounds ditched & regularly policed. Until about Feb'y 1st, was guarded by a company of white soldiers; since by blacks, organized under authority of Gen. Dodge, drilled & managed by two soldiers. Black guards have lea[r]ned readily, & discharged their duty with the highest degree of satisfaction to camp and garrison commanders.

Cairo. Location of camp grounds, low, wet & unpleasant. Only guards, freedmen – have rendered efficient service

Grand Junction. Two camps near troops – no guards since first patrol was removed, until lately. As a consequence, the freedmen suffered robbery and all manner of violence dictated by the passions of the abandoned among the soldiery.

Holly Springs and Memphis. As far as possible, separate from troops. Freedmen arranged in families; to some extent, their own guards.

Memphis. Camp two miles from town – on high bluff, easily drained; water from river; in the midst of wood. No soldiers near, except guard of eight from convalescent camp. One man regulates camp – another directs the working men, who are divided into squads of eleven; – the most intelligent selected as leader. Each three or four of squads are under a white foreman, who directs and credits their work, notes and supplies their necessities.

Bolivar. One & half miles from town – guarded in part by soldiers, and part by colored police.

La Grange Near depot – troops all around.

Providence. In the midst of town and troops – great evils resulting.

INTERROGATORY 8TH What coöperation or opposition from the army?

ANSWERS.

Corinth. Now, no opposition from the army or any of its members, but their highest approbation.

Cairo. No coöperation – little opposition.

Grand Junction. No coöperation – any amount of opposition; – in some cases, unable to procure suitable rations, quarters or guards.

Holly Springs and Memphis. No opposition; always coöperation from Gen Grant & Commanders at Holly Springs & Memphis.

Memphis. From the commander of the Post, every reasonable facility. Sometimes embarrassment in obtaining Quartermaster supplies. Many soldiers and some officers manifest only bitterness and contempt, resulting, among the abandoned, in the violence and abuse of these helpless people, in addition to the injuries heaped upon them by the vicious & disloyal in the community.

Bolivar. None of either worthy of note.

La Grange. All favors possible, especially from Col. Loomis, Commander of Post:

Providence. Little coöperation – considerable interference.

INTERROGATORY 9TH What of the work done for individuals or Government, by men, by women?

ANSWERS

Corinth. All men, except the infirm, & few for camp, employed. All women, save those having large families or small children;– generally reported industrious & faithful, when half treated. Many have worked from 2 to 12 months, and never received a cent or rag yet as reward–alike as private servants & Government employees.

Cairo. Many in Quartermaster's Department and Post Hospitals. Cannot give definite numbers.

Grand Junction. All men, but the feeble, employed by Government, or individuals, or in camp; have cut wood & lumber, handled goods, erected defences. 160 went to Vicksburg.– many in Quartermaster & Commissary Departments. Women & children pick cotton for Government and private individuals.

H. Springs & Memphis. Large amount for each.

Memphis. Average able-bodied men for the month 85. Erecting cabins,–preparing camp,– many have been turned over to different Departments, sometimes most grossly abused–as, for instance, worked all day in water, drenched, nearly frozen, and then driven to tents for shelter, to sheds for sleep, without covering, and almost without fire and food, they have come back to die by scores. Wages seldom paid–none in hospitals. The services of a large number have been stolen outright.

Bolivar. None for individuals– large amount for Government–building fortifications, cutting wood, rolling logs, running sawmills, and in Quartermaster's Department and Hospitals. No general system of pay.

Providence. Digging canal– picking cotton.

INTERROGATORY 10 How many assistants?

ANSWERS.

Corinth. Ten–all unfitted for regular service.

Cairo. Sept., none; October and November one;– during winter, three, detailed soldiers.

Grand Junction For Nov. and Dec., four; afterwards, five & six.

Holly Springs & Memphis Six.

Memphis Nine.

Bolivar Three.

Providence No report.

INTERROGATORY 11 What, if any, means of instruction?

ANSWERS.

Corinth. No school. About 100 books, from which they are

taught incidentally, besides Sabbath services, & talks by the Superintendent.

Cairo. School taught eleven weeks gratuitously by Job Hadley, wife & niece.

Grand Junction. None, save incidentally.

Holly Springs & Memphis. Very little religious instruction.

Memphis. School taught two months before the designation of any Superintendent here. gratuitously, by Miss L. Humphrey, of Chicago, See Report. School-house soon to be built.

Bolivar. Many taught to read by Mr. Richards, carpenter.

La Grange. None but incidental and occasional divine service

Providence " " " " " " "

INTERROGATORY 12. What of the motives which induced those under your care to change their relations to their masters?

ANSWERS.

Corinth. Can't answer short of 100 pages. Bad treatment – hard times – lack of the comforts of life – prospect of being driven South; the more intelligent, because they wished to be free. Generally speak kindly of their masters; none wish to return; many would die first. All delighted with the prospect of freedom, yet all have been kept constantly at some kind of work.

Cairo. All have a repulsive idea of going back into slavery, but would prefer going back to their old places, if they could be free there.

Grand Junction Cruel treatment, or being pressed into the rebel service, or driven South, or because they were bewildered by the presence of our army.

Holly Springs & Memphis. Universal desire to obtain their freedom.

Memphis. Destitution at their old homes, or the running away of their masters, or the fear of being driven South, or simply because others came away. Many chose to be free, and so abandoned their masters.

Bolivar. Fear of going South, or severe treatment, or desire for liberty

La Grange. Most have a tolerably well developed idea of freedom, and long to enjoy it.

Providence. As above – very many abandoned by their masters.

INTERROGATORY 13 What of their intelligence?

Corinth. Far more intelligent than I supposed. Some are men of fine intelligence and correct views.

Cairo. Their common intelligence is good – much better than we had supposed.

Grand Junction. Exhibit intelligence greater than has been attributed to their race; very shrewd in escaping from their masters and in shirking work, if so disposed.

Holly Springs & Memphis. House servants much more intelligent than field hands. All learn rapidly – are intuitive, not reflective – need line upon line

Memphis. Higher than I had expected – keen & bright when they wish to understand; – stupid and idiotic when they do not.

Bolivar. Better than many suppose; good as any could expect under the circumstances.

La Grange. As good as that of men, women & children anywhere, of any color, who cannot read.

INTERROGATORY 14 What of their notions of liberty?

ANSWERS.

Corinth. Many, if not most, have correct notions – believe they must work – anxious for pay – put no value upon money in spending it.

Cairo. Indefinite; anticipate having it as the result of the war.

Grand Junction Ideas of liberty are freedom from restraint and labor – need instruction.

Holly Springs and Memphis. Generally correct. They say they have no rights, nor own anything except as their master permits; but being freed, can make their own money and protect their families.

Memphis. A slander to say their notion of liberty is idleness – that is their laziness. Their notions of liberty have no more to do with their love of ease in the black than in the white race.

Bolivar. Varies. Don't seem to realize that labor is attendant on liberty.

La Grange No answer.

Providence No answer.

INTERROGATORY 15 What of their notions of property?

ANSWERS.

Corinth. Beyond the possession of a little kitchen plunder, they seem generally to have but little idea. Many are dishonest – the result of a system which compels them to steal from their masters. Have met many who have a high sense of honor, and are strictly honest.

Cairo. Wholly childlike. Having had nothing to provide for, they have no ripeness of judgment in regard to accumulating.

Grand Junction Entirely undeveloped

Holly Springs and Memphis. Generally strong desire to make money or get property; – when theirs, they use it much as whites do. Many have been laying up their money for months, preparing to leave their masters.

La Grange. Good enough.

INTERROGATORY 16. What of their notions of honesty?

ANSWERS.

CORINTH. Included in answer to Inter. 15.

Cairo. Have little idea of honesty.

Grand Junction. Large proportion act upon the principle of getting what they can by any means, while others are perfectly honest.

Holly Springs and Memphis. They do not consider it dishonest to take from their masters. I making them feel that I have placed confidence in them, I have seldom been disappointed.

Memphis. I verily believe that their habits in this particular have not been so thoroughly prostituted by the influence of all the centuries of their degradation in slavery as have those of our patriot soldiery, in two years of war.

Bolivar Most seem to be honest; many prove to be otherwise.

La Grange Equal to soldiers.

INTERROGATORY 17. What of their disposition to labor?

ANSWERS.

Corinth. So far as I have tested it, better than I anticipated. Willing to work for money, except in waiting on the sick. One hundred and fifty hands gathered 500 acres of cotton in less than three weeks – much of which time was bad weather. The owner admitted it was done quicker than it could have been done with slaves. When detailed for service, they generally remained till honorably discharged, even when badly treated. I am well satisfied, from careful calculations, that the freedmen of this Camp and District have netted the Government, over and above all their expenses, including rations, tents, &c., at least $3000 per month, independent of what the women do, & all the property brought through our lines from the rebels.

Cairo. Willing to labor, when they can have proper motives.

Grand Junction. Have manifested considerable disposition to escape labor, having had no sufficient motives to work.

Holly Springs and Memphis. With few exceptions, generally willing, even without pay. Paid regularly, they are much more prompt.

Memphis. Among men, better than among women. Hold out to them the inducements, – benefit to themselves and friends, – essential to the industry of any race, and they would at once be diligent and industrious.

Bolivar. Generally good – would be improved by the idea of pay.

La Grange. No report.

Providence. " "

INTERROGATORY 18 What of their religious notions and practices?

ANSWERS.

Corinth. Very religious – always orthodox – mostly Methodists, Baptists & Presbyterians. Notwithstanding their peculiar notions, when any one dies, they often pray & sing all night.

Cairo Naturally religiously inclined. During my six months' connection with them, I have not heard over ten colored men swear. Their religious meetings are both solemn and interesting.

Grand Junction. During the cold months, no house for church. Their religious notions & practices have failed of any marked manifestation. Show a strong religious inclination.

Holly Springs and Memphis. Great majority religious – Baptists or Methodists. Their notions of the leading doctrines of the Bible are remarkably correct. Justification, repentance, faith, holiness, heaven, hell; are not troubled, like educated white men, with unbelief.

Memphis. Notions of doctrine better than to be expected. Practices not always in accordance with their notions, as is also true of other colors. Have been taught to make their religion one of feeling, not necessarily affecting their living. If one finds himself susceptible to religious excitement or sentiment, he is a religious man, though at the same time, he may lie, steal, drink, and commit adultery.

Bolivar. Exceeding those of the whites in the army.

La Grange. Good, but full of superstition.

Providence. Not answered.

INTERROGATORY 19 What of their marital notions & practices.

ANSWERS.

Corinth. All wrong. All entering our camps who have been living or desire to live together as husband and wife are required to be married in the proper manner, and a certificate of the same is given. This regulation has done much to promote the good order of the camp.

Cairo. Their idea of the marriage relations and obligations is very low.

Grand Junction Most of them have no idea of the sacredness of the marriage tie, declaring that marriage, as it exists among the whites, has been impossible for them. In other cases, the marriage relation exists in all its sacredness without legal sanction.

Holly Springs and Memphis. The greater number have lived together as husband and wife, by mutual consent. In many cases, strongly attached and faithful, though having no legal marriage.

Memphis. They know what marriage is among the whites, but have yielded to the sad necessity of their case. Generally, I believe the men to be faithful to the women with whom they live, and the women to reward their faith with like truth. Free and married, they will maintain the marital relations as sacredly as any other race.

Bolivar. Have had no opportunity for correct notions and practices.

La Grange. Loose & by example.

Providence. No answer.

INTERROGATORY 20 What is your opinion of the possibility of arming the negro?

ANSWERS.

Corinth. I can see but one answer. That the negro is better than the white man, I do not see; nor do I, why we should fight for our country and exempt him. I do not doubt he will make a good soldier, especially for Southern climates. Blacks have made better guards for our camps than whites. Most of the officers & men in this Division are in favor of arming the negro at once, believing it will be the best means of ending the war.

Cairo. Should be at once armed. Many of them are bold – willing to fight, and are capable of rendering good service as soldiers.

Grand Junction. Have had no experience in this matter, but find they will unhesitatingly follow into any danger, so long as their leader exhibits no sign of fear. I am confident, that with competent and brave white officers, they will make the best of soldiers.

Holly Springs and Memphis. I believe in giving them their freedom by their swords. Policy and humanity say, Arm the negro. History affords all the necessary precedents for liberating slaves and arming them as soldiers, to fight in defence of their country. Blacks fought in the Revolutionary struggle, and in the war of 1812. Let them fight in the war for their own liberty.

Memphis. Yes, arm him! It will do him worlds of good. He will know then he has rights, and dare maintain them – a grand step towards manhood. Arm him! For our country needs soldiers. These men will make good soldiers. Arm him! – for the rebels need enemies, & heaven knows the blacks have reason to be that. Once armed and drilled, the black man will be an enemy the rebels will neither love nor despise. Arm him, & let the world see the black man on a vast scale returning good for evil, helping with blood and life the cause of the race which hated, oppressed & scorned him.

Bolivar. When the pickets at this place were attacked of a night, their coolness and readiness for the fight convinced me of their fitness for soldiers.

La Grange. Arm them at once. We can hurt the rebels more by the use of the negro than by any other means in our power. Arm him – use him; do it speedily. Why leave him to labor for our enemy, & thus keep up the strife? Arm him – he is a man – he will fight – he can save the Union. I pledge you & the world they will make good soldiers.

The above figures & extracts are from competent witnesses of widely different opinions, having under their observation all the diversities of the black race, in great numbers, from all the possible conditions of slavery.

Testimony seldom appears in a form more worthy of belief or more fitly the source of information, and the basis of opinions. These facts give very clearly the results of the abuses heaped upon American slaves, their present social, intellectual and moral condition, their skill at labor, their aptitudes, and suggest inferencies of the utmost consequence, in reference to their

Management.

. . . .

HLcSr (Signed) John Eaton, Jr.

Excerpt from Chaplain John Eaton, Jr., to Lt. Col. Jno. A. Rawlins, 29 Apr. 1863, filed with O-328 1863, Letters Received, ser. 12, RG 94 [K-89]. Interrogatory numbers and italicized place names appearing in the margin of the manuscript have been inserted into the body of the text. Topical labels in the margin are omitted, as are three numbers that were interlined into the table and whose meaning is not evident. In this copy, filed among the records of the American Freedmen's Inquiry Commission and probably furnished to the commissioners in late 1863, Eaton signed as chaplain of the 27th Ohio Infantry and general superintendent of freedmen; his title when the report was written was general superintendent of contrabands. The appendices referred to in the report are not in the file. The questionnaire to which Eaton's subordinate superintendents responded had been circulated in February 1863. (See above, doc. 158.) In the remaining twenty-six pages of the fifty-seven-page report, Eaton surveyed the condition of freedpeople in the Department of the Tennessee and offered suggestions for their management. He lauded the contributions of black military laborers, presenting calculations to show that the amount the government saved by using black workers instead of white ones exceeded the amount expended for the support of all the ex-slaves in his jurisdiction by more than $42,000 per month. Eaton urged the enlistment of black men as soldiers and outlined a system for the employment and support of black women, children, and those men who could not serve as soldiers or military laborers. Noting that nothing in the freedpeople's experience had taught them "the force or inviolability or sacredness of contracts," he also emphasized that even within Union lines "their labor has been without compensation" and hence they had not "had the best illustration of the nature of agreements." Close supervision would be required to teach them "[c]orrect notions of liberty." Eaton advocated that superintendents of freedmen oversee the employment of former slaves, hiring as many as possible to private employers, and directing the labor of the unemployed and dependent on abandoned plantations. He also called for a stringent system of registration to prevent freedpeople from relocating, changing employers, or revising the terms of their employment without the permission of the local superintendent. Such a scheme, Eaton suggested, would routinize the employment of black laborers and curb vagrancy – particularly in cities. The superintendents should also "lay at once the foundations of society" by establishing "schools supported by tax upon property or income from labor," "enforcing the laws of marriage," affording opportunities for religious instruction, and regulating trade. Military supervision, in short, should meet "every exigency arising in the affairs of these freed people, whether physical, social or educational, so far as is possible and is accordant with the genius of our free institutions, and the spirit of american christian civilisation."

1 Brackets in manuscript.
2 General Order 13, 13th Army Corps, Department of the Tennessee, issued by General Ulysses S. Grant on December 17 (not 7), 1862, designated Chaplain John Eaton, Jr., general superintendent of contrabands in the department and outlined a system for the reception, relief, and employment of fugitive slaves. (See above, doc. 155n.)
3 Issued by General Ulysses S. Grant on August 11, 1862. For a summary, see above, doc. 155n.
4 Special Field Order 4, issued by General Ulysses S. Grant, commander of the Department of the Tennessee, on November 14, 1862. (See above, doc 155.)
5 Although not standardized by the War Department until January 1864, the ration issued to contrabands was usually a modified soldier's ration, with smaller quantities and less variety. A soldier's daily ration consisted of 12 ounces pork or bacon, or 1 1/4 pounds beef; 1 3/8 pounds soft bread or flour, 1 pound hard bread, or 1 1/4 pounds corn meal; plus comparatively small amounts of the following, issued for every one hundred rations: peas or beans, rice or hominy, coffee or tea, sugar, vinegar, candles, soap, salt, pepper, potatoes, and molasses. (U.S., War Department, *Revised United States Army Regulations* [Washington, 1863], p. 244.) On November 17, 1862, the commander of the Department of the Tennessee ordered that the contraband ration was to include cornmeal instead of flour; hominy instead of peas, beans, and rice; parched and ground rye instead of coffee; smaller amounts of sugar and soap than the soldier's ration; and no candles. Tea and sugar were to be issued weekly rather than daily. (General Orders, No. 7, Headquarters, 13th Army Corps Department of the Tennessee, 17 Nov. 1862, vol. 13/21 DT, pp. 14–15, General Orders, ser. 4792, Dept. of the TN, RG 393 Pt. 1 [C-2240].)

161: Commander of the District of Eastern Arkansas to the Commander at Cairo, Illinois

Helena Ark. March 11th 1863

Sir I found on assuming command at this point that there was a very large number of contrabands within the lines – more than could be used to any advantage in the government Service, and that they were a very greate burden upon the government and were quite devoid of any facilities for getting a livelihood or taking care of themselves I have for these reasons been shipping some of them to the North. I send you to day 100. of them They will be less of a burden to the government and can be made more useful, and more cheapely fed there than here. I am Sir Very Truly Your Obdt Servant

HLcS B M Prentiss

Brig. Genl. B. M. Prentiss to Commanding Office Cairo Ills., 11 Mar. 1863, vol. 37 DArk, p. 50, Letters Sent, ser. 4664, Dist. of Eastern AR, RG 393 Pt. 2 No. 299 [C-7529]. In attempting to alleviate the problem of relief at Helena by transporting former slaves to Cairo, General Prentiss was following a precedent established by General Samuel R. Curtis, who, in the summer of 1862, as commander of the Army of the Southwest, had authorized several such shipments. (See above, docs. 151 and 152n.) At the same time, however, Prentiss expanded the scope of northward removals from Helena, adding a new destination – St. Louis – and increasing the numbers transported. On March 3, 1863, for example, he had ordered that 450 blacks, accompanied by Chaplain Samuel Sawyer (superintendent of contrabands at Helena), be shipped to St. Louis, headquarters of the Department of the Missouri – which had been commanded by General Curtis since the previous September. (*Freedom*, ser. 1, vol. 2: doc. 162.)

162: Adjutant General of the Army to the Secretary of War, Enclosing a Plan for the Leasing of Plantations

Millikens Bend Louisiana April 12. 1863.

Sir I have the Honor to enclose a plan which after mature deliberation has been adopted for the occupation and Cultivation of plantations on the West side of the Mississippi. This plan has been submitted to General Grant & other practical men who are unanimous in their Approval several gentlemen of Capital have already applied for lands to cultivate and but for the lateness of the season (It should have been adopted four weeks ago) I would have no doubt of its success. – As it is by energy on the part of the

Appointed Agents it is hoped to accomplish much in demonstrating that the freed Negro may be profitably employed by enterprising men– As we are sure of the possession of persons and property on the West side of the river we shall endeavour to draw our supply of Contrabands, stock, grain, &c. from the East side of the Mississippi thereby weakening the enemy to that extent.– I shall give immediate publicity through the plan in the hope of inducing persons of enterprize & capital to come here and engage in the matter. I have the Honor to be sir your Very Obedient Servant

HLS L. Thomas

[*Enclosure*] [*Milliken's Bend, La. April 10, 1863*]

I. The Government of the United States, in order to secure the safety of commerce and navigation on the Mississippi river, have determined to locate on and near its bank a loyal population, who will protect (–instead of destroying, as is now done–) the freedom of commercial intercourse on this great "inland sea." That this policy may the more speedily receive its initiation, George B. Field, Capt. A. E. Strickle and Rev. L. S. Livermore are hereby appointed Commissioners, whose duty it shall be to superintend the letting of Plantations to persons of proper character and qualifications, and to see that the mutual obligations between the negroes and their employers, or superintendents, shall be faithfully performed; to attend in some measure to their moral and intellectual wants; and generally to carry out the policy of the Government regarding the negroes that are to be put to agricultural pursuits.

II. It being deemed the best policy, as far as possible to make the employment and subsistance of negroes a matter to be left to private enterprise, plantations will be placed in possession of such persons as the Commissioners shall deem of good character and pecuniary responsibility; and, in lieu of rent, a tax will be collected upon the product of the land, payable to such agents as the Treasury Department shall designate–care being taken to secure, as far as possible the just rights of employer and employed. In all cases the negroes will be furnished with enough clothing for comfort, in advance of their earnings, in consequence of their present extreme destitution; and in no case will negroes be subjected to corporeal punishment by the lash, or other cruel and unusual modes.

III. Upon entering into the occupancy of plantations, Inspectors will visit each plantation, and take an inventory of all property upon the estate. Crops yet ungathered will be turned over to be gathered by the Lesee, upon such terms as shall secure to the Government its fair share; while all moveable property, stock, grain &c, will be taken possession of by the Government, or sold to the Lessee, if he so desires, at their appraised value, payable out of the proceeds of the plantation in the Fall: the appraisers to be appointed by the Commissioners, unless otherwise designated by the Government.

IV. After the Lessee shall have taken possession of the plantation, as many negroes, of average quality, as he may desire, shall be turned over to him, upon the order of the Commissioners; the Lesees entering into bonds to employ them until the first of February, 1864, and to feed, clothe and treat humanely all the negroes thus turned over (– the clothing to be deducted from their wages, and to be furnished at cost.)

V. If it shall be found impracticable (in consequence of the lateness of the season) to find persons of sufficient character and responsibility to give employment to all the negroes coming within the lines of the Army, the Commissioners may appoint superintendents, under whose supervision the soil may be cultivated for the exclusive benefit of the Government; or may have the plantations worked upon such terms as, in their judgment, shall be best adapted to the welfare of the negroes, taking care that, in all plans adopted, the negroes shall be self-sustaining, and not become a charge upon the Government.

VI. The wages to be paid for labor shall be as follows: For able-bodied men, over fifteen years of age, seven (7) dollars per month; for able-bodied women, over fifteen years of age, five (5) dollars per month; for children between the ages of twelve and fifteen, half-price; children under twelve years of age shall not be used as field-hands: and familes must be kept together, when they so desire. The tax on the product of the plantations, in lieu of rent, shall be at the rate of two (2) dollars per bale of four hundred (400) pounds of cotton, and five (5) cents per bushel of corn and potatoes.

VII. Whilst military protection will not be guaranteed for the safety of persons engaged in cultivating the soil, yet all troops will be required to give protection, when it can be done without injury to the service; and it is confidently believed that the military organization of the negroes will afford all the protection necessary.

VIII. Commanders of the Army will render the Commissioners such military assistance as may be necessary – without injury to the service – for the execution of their duties. The Commissioners will report their proceedings to the Secretary of War every two weeks. Given under my hand, at Milliken's Bend, La., April 10, 1863, by authority of instructions from the Secretary of War.

HDS L. Thomas

Adjt. Genl. L. Thomas to Hon. Edwin M. Stanton, 12 Apr. 1863, enclosing a plan for the leasing of plantations, 10 Apr. 1863, filed as A-808 1863, Letters

Received, ser. 12, RG 94 [K-62]. On April 1, shortly after beginning his investigation of the condition of former slaves at federal posts in the Mississippi Valley, Adjutant General Thomas had offered his first suggestions for organizing ex-slaves "for their own good and for the benefit of the government which has declared them free." Thomas deemed it unwise "to collect them in large bodies," employing "only what our armies require for laborers and teamsters" and leaving the remainder to survive on government charity. He rejected as impolitic the shipment of large numbers of freed blacks to the free states against "the prejudices of the people," or to the border slave states, where they "might again, to some extent, be reduced to slavery, or kidnapped and carried as slaves far beyond our lines." Assuming, therefore, that most former slaves would remain in the South, Thomas proposed that they be kept within Union lines and "put in positions to make their own living," the able-bodied men as soldiers and military laborers, and the women, children, and disabled men "placed on the abandoned plantations to till the ground." Regiments of black troops could "give protection to these plantations," operate against guerrillas, and perform garrison duty. (*Freedom*, ser. 2: doc. 194.)

163: Louisiana Plantation Lessee to the Commander of a Black Brigade

Millikens Bend La. May 17– 1863

Col. Shepard Comdg. Brigade of African decent. The undersigned begs leave to call your attention to the conduct of Recruiting officers now engaged in Recruiting for the Brigade you now comand.

On thursday or friday last one Mr. Griffith came to the Dr. Harding plantation (now leased to me by the commissionors) and forced eight (8) men against their will to join his regiment and also warned them in case they resisted he would bring an armed force and would compel them to go regardless of their reluctance.

The colered people now living on the plantation leased by me earnestly insist that I appeal in their behalf to the Millitary authorities for the purpose of having some regulations made to protect them while laboring peacebly in the field and at the same time not allow Recruiting officers to force them into the ranks as soldiers unless there is some law authorizing them to do so. I will also say that it not only retards my Business but makes great confusion among families when men are forced into the ranks against their will Very Respectfully Your obedient servant

ALS J. E. Walker

J. E. Walker to Col. Shepard, 17 May 1863, filed as 17 Apr. 1863, Letters & Orders Received by Forces under the Department of the Gulf, ser. 1753,

Dept. of the Gulf, RG 393 Pt. 1 [C-605]. On May 24, Colonel Isaac F. Shepard, the brigade commander, forwarded a copy of Walker's letter to Adjutant General Lorenzo Thomas, noting in a covering letter that he could "hardly doubt" the allegation against Griffith, since he had himself spoken to black men who claimed that Griffith "threatened to shoot them" if they did not enlist. Shepard also enclosed a circular he had issued on May 19 to correct the "misunderstanding of the mutual rights and duties" of plantation lessees and recruiting officers. Both plantation laborers and black recruits, the circular insisted, were entitled to "*the rights of personal liberty*" and to "*kindness and protection* in the lawful discharge of chosen duties." While Shepard's policy was intended to allow black men the "*privilege*" of voluntary enlistment, it did not authorize recruiting officers "to enter at will upon the plantations" and force unwilling men into the service. The circular therefore directed that plantation laborers who had been impressed "be allowed to return to the Lessees at once," and it forbade recruiters "to tamper with the hands" on a leased plantation without the lessee's permission. (Isaac F. Shepard to General, 24 May 1863, enclosing J. E. Walke to Col. Shepard, 17 May 1863, and Circular, Headquarters African Brigade, 19 May 1863, S-13 1863, Letters Received, ser. 360, Colored Troops Division, RG 94 [B-499].) Adjutant General Thomas sustained Shepard's policy. On June 13, he ordered recruiters not to "interfere with the blacks on the leased plantations, such blacks being under contract with their employe[r]s." (Special Orders No. 35, 13 June 1863, L. Thomas Letters & Orders, Generals' Papers & Books, ser. 159, RG 94 [V-19].)

164: General Superintendent of Contrabands in the Department of the Tennessee to the Corresponding Secretary of the American Missionary Association

Memphis [*Tenn.*] May 18th 1863

Dr Sir your letter to Mr Wright or myself was received Some days Since and its contents carefully noted,

M Carrathers, Mrs Olds, & Miss Warren have Since arrived,

The condition of affairs near Vicksburg is Such as to render it undesirable it seems to me to put laborers into the field then where– there are So many now repening for the harvest this side, that will Soon open,

If you or Mr Whipple could visit here you would understand many things to your advantage in locating your missionaries.– Say come down the river visit the different points & then on your return See friends of the cause in the West at St Louis, at Chicago, & Cincinati and I am confident your personal views of these great interests would not only be benefitted but great good arise from the increased unity of effort,

There are many things to be Seen & heared but I have advised M Carrothers to locate for the present at Helena. Where there is quite a camp as yet but partially organized greatly needing laborers, He appeared to think Miss Warren had better go with him but as I understood matters I felt unwilling to take the responsibility of advising that, I suggested that he go and try matters and if he could on personal knowledge either immediately or weeks hence advise her going there She could go down any time meanwhile her hands could immediately be put at Work now waiting to be done at Corinth, La-Grange, & Memphis, Twenty five more teachers could be well employed at these three places, each of these camps as well as Island 10 is getting in condition to render teaching most available I Shall advise Miss Warren to remain at Corinth for the present the three teachers there have now about 500 different pupils & I fear very much the effect of these labors upon their health, Mr Carrouthers will accompany the ladies there examine matters of fitting himself for his labors and then return I have been furnished by Genl Webster (by the way a bro of the Rev Webster of Hopkinstown Mass) Supt of M,R,R, transportation for all in all Such cases Genl Thomas reached here from below last Tuesday night by his invitation I went with him to Corinth Thursday He Spoke at five different points, all the troops turning out to hear him Many citizens were present He announced every where with great distinctness the policy of the Government & its determination that these people Should be every where received & well treated by the Army, and that the men Should be armed and every officer and man not carrying out its commands punished, The enthusiastic approbation & Men was especially Surprising to those of us who know how Strong were their prejudices how bitter their opposition a few months ago This is the work of the Lord, At Corinth there was an immense gathering of the troops in the morning to hear the General who was followed by Genl Oglesby, Dodge & Sweeny & others the enthusiasm was unbounded. There followed an imposing review of all the various arms of the Service unwearied in his efforts the General accompanied with other Generals & their various Staff officers in the afternoon visited the camp of the Colored people So long under Charge of Chaplain Alexander its Sterling Superintendent, They rode through the various Streets all as they ever are nicely policed, looked into the cabins examined the drill of the colerd Soldiers the General putting Some of them through the manuel of arms to the great amusement of all present, he commended their execution as excellent then followed the culminating Scene the School children with banners flying with their teachers, the women, the men, the Soldiers each in their places as nearly as possible as Chaplain Alexander has them assembled twice a day for roll call to the number of 2400 forming three Sides of a Square and the cavalcade of Officers the fourth The children Sang very finely under charge of M[r] Pierce Several of the songs they have learned the general – addressed them briefly & pertinently telling them he lived where their great friend President Lincolm lived and Saw him daily, that the President had Sent him out here So far to tell them they were free & to tell all the Soldiers they must receive them, treat them kindly, provide work for them and pay them, feed them if hungry, clothe them if naked and to make Soldiers of the Strong & healthy men So that they might fight for the liberty of their wives & children and against the rebellion, which has raised great armies to overthrow our great and good Government upon them as Slaves the President had made them free to overthrow that rebellion by taking away the laborers which furnished it food & clothing & now he was going to use them further for the overthrow of the rebellion by putting arms in their hands to fight against it, Will you fight Soldiers? yes I know you will, I have Seen many black Soldiers, Half the guns at the late great battle of Grand Gulf were manned by blacks I have ten thousand black Soldiers down the river, I want two Regiments or more here I have just Seen how well you can drill, I tell you these things not only because I am commanded to do So by the President but because I feel them, I was raised by Slaves I once owned Slaves, I know what all the prejudices are upon this Subject but I have over come them, I expect the whole Army as good Soldiers & Officers to over come them, We give you the opportunity & you must improve it, All these people, these teachers are to help you, This is the great opportunity afforded your race, Will you improve it & make men & women, christian citizens

I know you can, I am a Soldier & have been most of my life in the Army, but for more than twenty years I have been Superintendent of the Sab School connected with my church we have had our colerd classes & my observation of your people through all the South assures me too that you can learn readily that you can be christian men & women as well as Soldiers,

I Shall tell the President of what I have Seen here to day and he will be very glad to know that you are doing So well," Vociferous cheers rolled up from the depths of their hearts for the President for the good news, for the General cheer following cheer, their echoes flying along the defences erected by Beauregard & over the field red with the blood of friends & foes of liberty & union, The company then rode through the acres upon acres of garden So free from weeds, So full of finely growing vegitables & took a look at the hundreds of acres of cotton cultivated by their free hands, then at the hospitals in excellent condition, then at the School house & the cotton field planted & to be cultivated by School children for the benefit of the School, Chaplain Alexander was deeply moved by this authoritative recognition of the Success of his efforts to prove this people capable of improving their freedom and as he parted with the General turned to me and Said now I am prepared to die, No one can know how much he has endured to attain this Success, As I returned to the camp at night I found one portion celebrating the day of *jubilo* with a dance and another class with prayer meeting in which neither the General nor those laboring for their good were forgotten One Speaker Said most significantly I am a Soldier I am Soldiers to of the Cross, The Lord Jesus– christ is the captain of our Salvation He is never conquered He can bring us forth, He conquers the Sea & brought his people through on dry land He conquered the wild beasts & delivered Daniel from the lions jaw, He conquered the fire around worthies, I will trust in the Lord the captain of my Salvation, The General Spoke at Six different places as we returned Saturday, Sincerely yours &c

John Eaton Jr

P,S, Among the many calls given I have been running this off Rev M Connor has come in from Wheeling V[a] his wife & two other teachers are with him all reported by Presbytery. he says on the Same boat is a young man from the Commission (Cincinati) and man & wife from where he dont know, on their own responsibility expecting to be Supported by tuition

I hope Schools can after a while be Self Sustaining, but I fear the moment has not arrived Still there are those now in this town who could Support a School if the authorities would protect it, yours &c J E Jr

HLcSr

John Eaton Jr. to Revd. S. S. Jocelyn, 18 May 1863, vol. 74, pp. 48–52, Letters Sent by John Eaton, ser. 2027, General Supt. of Freedmen, MS Asst. Comr. Pre-Bureau Records, RG 105 [A-4005]. Five days later, in a letter to the president of the Cleveland Contraband Relief Commission, Eaton expounded on the significance of the adjutant general's personal statement of government policy. Until Thomas arrived in the Mississippi Valley, Eaton's work had proceeded "without any formal authority from Washington," but Thomas had "Set the broad responsible Seal of the Government upon it by authority of the President." Eaton also noted that Chaplain James M. Alexander, the superintendent of contrabands at Corinth, Mississippi, had already organized nearly a full regiment of black troops. (Chaplain John Eaton Jr. to H. B. Spelman Esqr., 23 May 1863, vol. 74, pp. 55–58, Letters Sent by John Eaton, ser. 2027, General Supt. of Freedmen, MS Asst. Comr. Pre-Bureau Records, RG 105 [A-4005].)

165: Absentee Mississippi and Louisiana Planter to the Secretary of War

Staten Island [*N.Y.*]. – May 30th. – "63.

My Dear Sir. Owing to the violation of "protection papers" given us (as well known & acknowledged Unionists) by Genls Grant & McPherson, – & Admiral Porter – I am necessitated to thus apply to Headquarters for papers which WILL REALLY "protect" us in our rights as thoroughly loyal citizens. for while one party appropriated books, curtains, &c; &c; in the name of the "Treasury Dep'mt" – other individuals (as officials under the recent "*impressment*" permits) came to our various estates, & (despite the *imperative* & written orders of above Commanders) removed – by *main force* – all our male negroes (saving some few who managed to escape by flight or concealment) from the different plantations. Now – as these blacks had been FREED & HIRED, – & were perfectly willing to remain on home ground – it seems rather hard that they should have been seized & carried off – to serve as soldiers – or – (as is most generally the case) *field laborers* – for enterprising speculators *hiring* lands from Genl Thomas. – & while Genl Thomas can impress *all* able bodied negroes – & the Treasury Dep'mt take all the cotton – "protection papers" from Genls Halleck & Grant – & the Admiral – are of no avail or benefit. for as "*protected*" Unionists – WE have (on *nine* plantations) been robbed, plundered, & outraged without even a *show* of decency or justice. (& this, too, under the strongest papers from the Chiefs of Army & Navy!) – The perfect mania for cotton speculation & planting on the Mississippi river is certainly a great incentive to fraud & injustice. & having recently made a brief visit to that region I have seen FOR MYSELF that Unionist & rebel both fare alike. for cotton & negro labor *must* be had. & the political views of the lawful owners are unheeded – where plunder is to be obtained. – This is a *plain statement* of a *plain case.* & I have but given bare facts – & stated my own experience. Gen' Grant & the Admiral *desire* to protect & shield us. (for they know & recognize our rights as long suffering – devoted Unionists.) but – what protection *can* they give – when there is "higher law" & conflicting authority to veto & annul their commands? We have a *right* to demand justice & protection from our rulers. & therefore – My Dear Sir, – do I appeal to you in this *grave* case of wrong & violence. trusting that you will correct the *outrageous* abuses which are of daily occurrence on the Miss. river. abuses too – committed on Unionists – under cover of the flag, & in the sacred name of the Union & Law! It may be (most probably *will* be) that Gen' Thomas will say that *he* "gave no *especial* orders for impressment on *our* places, – & knows nothing of the case." nevertheless – his *officials* acted under his authority. & as we have lost our laborers, – & redress is unobtainable – all I ask is – *authentic* papers from *you* – in order that we may not *again* be invaded – & again robbed & insulted. for – if we are *worthy protection* – can we not have it? There is now little left to take – as our property is *wellnigh ruined*. & nothing remains save to apply the torch. – but – as we have been notified that the blacks taken from our places – will be allowed (as *armed soldiers*) to return to the estates to visit their families there – it will probably not be long (unless you kindly interfere) before *fire* completes the wanton destruction of a once noble property. No loyal citizen can obtain permission to purchase needful supplies of food or clothing – for the starving half-naked blacks (women & children) that remain on the plantations. while every greedy speculator is able to furnish himself with all requisites for feeding & clothing *his impressed* laborers. – I am merely stating *facts* – which cannot be denied or disputed. & have myself *witnessed. shameful* thefts on that river – which are doubtless kept concealed from Washington authorities. – As a Northern & Union woman I implore your interference. – & you can readily understand that Gen[l] Thomas will hardly be informed of deeds (by his officials) which common honesty would force him to punish. If the impressment of *free* & *hired* negroes (from Unionists) is approved of by the War Dep'mt – we must – of course – bow to our hard fate as law-abiding citizens; but – if "protection papers" have ANY meaning or power – may I beg *your endorsement* to them. For further information respecting our loyalty (& that of D[r] Duncan's family) I refer you to Mr Seward, – Gen' Halleck, – Mr Alexander Hamilton, D[r] George Schuyler, – Mr Thurlow Weed, – Gen' Crawford, – Gen[l] Scott, – & can – if desired – send you any number of letters from the most influential men in the country. – With many apologies for this long letter – & with assurances of high respect – I remain, My Dear Sir – yours very truly

Mary Duncan.

[*In the margin*] My address is care of "Duncan & Sherman. Bankers. New York."

ALS

Mary Duncan to Honble. Edwin Stanton, 30 May 1863, D-24 1863, Letters Received Irregular, RG 107 [L-98]. A penciled endorsement on the wrapper instructed a War Department clerk: "Answer That the Secretary of War regrets that the disturbed state of that section of that Country renders it impossible to prevent or remedy the evils complained of at present," but that her letter would be forwarded to General Ulysses S. Grant, commander of the Department of the Tennessee, "for such action as he may find just and practicable." On July 11, 1863, Grant instructed a subordinate officer to investigate the Duncans' complaint regarding military impressment of their laborers. "If their negroes have been carried off, find out where they are and who carried them off. . . . Arrest the parties engaged in this transaction, and all officers among them send to me under guard." Grant noted that he had "received instructions from Washington to protect all loyal persons found in the South," which "mention[ed] the Duncans, in particular, as being entitled to protection. They have gone so far as to acknowledge the freedom of their slaves, and made . . . regular contracts with them to pay wages, and employ them just as negroes are employed on leased plantations." (*Official Records*, ser. 1, vol. 24, pt. 3, pp. 500–501.) However, recruitment officers denied the truth of Mary Duncan's allegations. They had "never even used *harsh words*" to enlist the Duncans' laborers, avowed one recruiter; "we told them as we did all others that they would be most likely kept along the river to guard the plantations where their families would be at work, as that was the understanding we had of the policy layed down by *Gen Thomas*." Another officer recalled that in several recruiting visits to the Duncan plantations, he had "noticed a great dissatisfaction among the Colored people," who "complained that they were poorly cared for, over worked and had but little to eat." Convinced "that their condition could not be made worse than it was at that time," the men had been "willing and even anxious" to enlist. (*Freedom*, ser. 2: doc. 53.)

166: Superintendent of Contrabands at Memphis, Tennessee, to the Commander of the 16th Army Corps

Memphis Tenn June 11th 1863

Sir You instructed me the other day. to consider the matter of organizing and making useful the Blacks in this Town. Allow me to outline a plan, which appears to me feasible.

No voluntary system will answer as private parties will pay higher than Goverment wages besides the disorganized condition of society affordes opportunity for a life of theft and crime more attractive to many Blacks as well as Whites than Military service or any form of Labor

The essential things in any other than a voluntary plan *are to find know and locate all*,

Your own order concerning the registrations of citizens suggest's the efficient plan here

On penalty of ejection from their quarters or even of expulsion from our lines, let all Black be ordered for registration at the Contraband Office, such as were made free by their masters, or free born, will have papers to show it, let them prove some lawful means of livelihood and be registered accordingly.

Let all the Contrabands free by Military authority be examined and the able bodied be allowed to seclect between Military service. and such other forms of labor as Military authority shall direct.

Let no colored person be suffered to find employment except in the Engineer. Quartermaster Commissary. Ordinance, Military Rail

Road, and Hospital Departments or by special contract made through the Superintendent of Contrabands

Let all others. employing Black, not now slaves be required to report them to the Supt of Contrabands, and submit their engagements to him no engagement to be valid without his approval

Let all wages except those paid by the above Departments, be paid through the Supt

Let a tax of ten (10) per cent be levied upon all wages received above six (6) Dollars per Month to constitute a fund for the sustenance of the sick and infirm. for the procurement of such articles as the Gov[t] does not supply, and such implements and facilities for the conduct of contrabands affairs as may be required

Let all colored families be quartered as the Supt may direct in town or Camp, premits

The permit stating date of registration, and form of service to be kept always at the quarters, any person not having it to be ejected

Every registered person except such as enter the Military service should be furnished a written statement of the working company to which he is assigned.

Any person without such statement properly signed to be arrested, and brought to the Office for registration

Such a plan as this I think can be enforced and by it the services of a large number of Blacks be made available to the government Very Respectfully Your Obdient servant

HLS A Severance Fiske

A. Severance Fiske to Major General S. A. Hurlbut, 11 June 1863, #6026 1863, Letters Received, ser. 391, 16th Army Corps, RG 393 Pt. 2 No. 7 [C-8616]. General Stephen A. Hurlbut, the corps commander, referred Fiske's proposal to Chaplain John Eaton, Jr., general superintendent of contrabands in the Department of the Tennessee, who approved it and suggested that its implementation would curb idleness and crime, improve "the sanitary condition of the city," and help fill black regiments. Anticipating objections by "philanthrophists" to the proposed tax on the wages of black laborers, Eaton argued that such a levy would "contribute to meet the expenses of Govt" and ensure that a portion of the pay of "the husband and father" would go to "support his wife and children," as well as to aid "entirely dependent" freedpeople. "This slight tax," he insisted, would mark "a step in the education of the black man by introducing him to some knowledge of his relations to the expense of the family & the state." (Chaplain John Eaton Jr. to Lt. Col. H. Binmore, 23 June 1863, vol. 74, pp. 47, 59–60, Letters Sent by John Eaton, ser. 2027, General Supt. of Freedmen, MS Asst. Comr. Pre-Bureau Records, RG 105 [A-4004].) Within weeks, the commander of the District of Memphis had established a registration system similar in some respects to that proposed by Fiske, but without the tax on wages. (See below, doc. 169.) Apparently, no such tax was imposed anywhere in the Mississippi Valley until September 1863, when Adjutant General Lorenzo Thomas (presumably after consultation with Eaton) ordered that 10 percent be deducted from the wages of black people who earned $6 or more per month at either military or private employment, the fund thus created to be administered by the superintendents of freedmen for the relief of "the sick and otherwise dependent." (Special Orders No. 63, 29 Sept. 1863, L. Thomas Letters & Orders, Generals' Papers & Books, ser. 159, RG 94 [V-28]; see also John Eaton, *Grant, Lincoln and the Freedmen: Reminiscences of the Civil War* [1907; reprint ed., New York, 1969], pp. 127–29.)

167: Commander of the District of Eastern Arkansas to the Commander of the Department of the Missouri

Helena Ark. June 16. 1863.

General– I have under my charge in this District several hundred contrabands, disabled men, women and children–such as cannot be made in any way available in carrying on the war, yet who deserve care and kind treatment at our hands, and who are thus a burden and an encumbrance to the army and the cause. No employment offers itself for them here–sickness rages fearfully among them in this unhealthy location–and they are a great source of embarrassment– To better their condition and save their lives I send a boat load of them north, with instructions to report to you– They can there find employment among loyal people,–as many others have heretofore done when sent from here–but if turned adrift here, they can be useful to no one but the enemies of the Government–

I am working to advantage all of this class of people who can possibly be used, in any manner, in carrying on the war– It is that portion of them who can only sicken and die here, but who may be made useful, or at least can be easily taken care of, that I am sending north–

I am aware that many complaints may be made concerning this action–but I assume all the blame that may properly attach to it–believing it to be my duty to do what may tend to relieve these loyal people.

I trust, General, that facilities may be rendered these people to obtain employment and to receive care–thus making them a means of usefulness instead of a mere source of encumbrance– I remain, General, Your most obdt. servant

ALS B M Prentiss

Major General B. M. Prentiss to Major General J. M. Schofield, 16 June 1863, filed as E-116 1863, Letters Received, ser. 2593, Dept. of the MO, RG

393 Pt. 1 [C-123]. General Prentiss had been transporting freedpeople from Helena to St. Louis since March, with the cooperation of General Samuel R. Curtis, the previous commander of the Department of the Missouri. (*Freedom*, ser. 1, vol. 2: docs. 162–63, 165.) General John M. Schofield, who had succeeded Curtis in late May, evidently permitted the practice to continue: A notation on Prentiss's letter reads merely "file," and several hundred freedpeople were shipped from Helena to St. Louis that summer. (*Freedom*, ser. 1, vol. 2: doc. 171; Special Orders No. 128, Head Quarters, Dist. of East. Ark., 12 July 1863, Special Orders No. 136, Head Quarters D.E.A., 21 July 1863, and Special Orders No. 145, Head Quarters Dist. East. Arkansas, 31 July 1863, vol. 42/109 DArk, pp. 327–28, 335–36, 346, Special Orders, ser. 4686, Dist. of Eastern AR, RG 393 Pt. 2 No. 299 [C-7547].)

168: Commander of the Mississippi Squadron to the Secretary of the Navy

Flag Ship Black Hawk [*Mississippi River*] July 2, 1863

Sir On the 29th of June I received a communication from General Dennis, commanding the Post at Young's Point, informing me that our black troops at Goodrich's Landing had been attacked and the Rebels were getting the upper hand of them.

I had already dispatched a gunboat to that point, but sent off another without delay. I also directed General Ellet to proceed with the Marine Brigade to the scene of action and remain there until every thing was quiet.

The headmost vessel of the Brigade ("John Raines") arrived there as the Rebels were setting fire to the socalled Government Plantations and supposing her to be an ordinary transport they opened fire on her with field pieces, but were much surprised to have the fire returned with Shrapnel which fell in among them killing and wounding a number. The result was a retreat on the part of the Rebels, and the escape of a number of negroes whom they had imprisoned.

The Gunboat "Romeo" also came from up the River about this time, and hearing the firing hurried to the scene of action; the Commander soon discovered the Rebels setting fire to the plantations, and commenced shelling them. This he kept up for a distance of 15 miles chasing them along the river bank, the Rebels setting fire to every thing as they went along.

The result was an almost total destruction of houses and property along the River front in that vicinity.

The Rebels carried off about 1200 negroes who were employed working on the so called Government Plantations.

I am much surprised that this has never been attempted before, for the temptation to plunder is very great and there is nothing but the black Regiments to protect the coast. I have no great confidence in their ability to do so unless protected by white Soldiers and gunboats.

If it is intended to have the Navigation of the Mississippi free and unobstructed I would recommend that this leasing of property on the River be stopped. It leads to a great deal of injustice in the first place, offers strong temptations to the Rebels to infest the river, and is a great expense to the Government for which it will get no return.

If this plantation system continues this River will never be safe for transports without double the number of gunboats we now have, and it will require a large army to protect the negroes.

General Ellet landed his forces, and in company with a black brigade proceeded to chase the Rebels who were making a hasty retreat when they found there was a force after them. It was no part of their system to fight, they only came to plunder and carry off the negroes. General Ellet found the road strewn with broken carts and furniture, which the Rebels left in their haste to get away from our forces.

He pursued them as far as Tensas River where they had crossed, burnt the bridges and entrenched themselves for a battle. This was soon offered them and our artillery opened on them and soon put them to flight, notwithstanding it was reported that they had twenty field pieces.

General Ellet not knowing the country very well and having only a small force with him deemed it proper not to pursue the Rebels much further; he sent two hundred infantry across the Bayou and found that the Rebels were retreating to Delhi leaving all their plunder, splendid furniture, pianos, pictures &c strewn along the road.

The unexpected re-inforcement of the Brigade and the gun boats saved the whole of the black troops. It is only a temporary peace though, for as long as the blacks remain in such small numbers, so long will they be an object of attack. The party who made this attack on the so called Government Plantations are the same that attacked Milliken's Bend some short time since; they are a half starved half naked set, and are in hopes of capturing some of the transports with clothing and provisions. They have not done so as yet, and I think the precautions I have taken will prevent their doing so at any time.

. . . .

David D Porter

HLS

Excerpt from Acting Rear Admiral David D. Porter to Hon. Gideon Welles, 2 July 1863, Mississippi Squadron, Letters from Officers Commanding Squadrons, RG 45 [T-515]. The remainder of the letter discussed increasing the size of the Marine Brigade. According to notations on the wrapper and in the margins, the Navy Department made a copy of the letter for the Secretary of War, but omitted Admiral Porter's criticism of the plantation-leasing system. General Ulysses S. Grant, commander of the Department of the Tennessee, shared Porter's doubts about the practicality of providing military protection for the leased plantations opposite Vicksburg. Two days before the Confederate attack at Goodrich's Landing, he had cautioned the general-in-chief that he would probably have to remove the troops that had been guarding the plantations, leaving the estates unprotected. "The location of these leased plantations," he had pointedly noted, "was most unfortunate, and against my judgement." (*Official Records*, ser. 1, vol. 24, pt. 1, pp. 43–44.) In his report of the Confederate raid, General Alfred W. Ellet, commander of the Marine Brigade, expressed shock at "the sight of the charred remains of human beings who had been burned in the general conflagration," presumably those of "sick negroes whom the unscrupulous enemy were too indifferent to remove." (*Navy Official Records*, ser. 1, vol. 25, pp. 215–16.) A Union cavalry commander, passing through the site several days later, confirmed that "[i]n some instances the negroes were shut up in their quarters, and literally roasted alive," and also reported that he had found "[y]oung children, only five or six years of age . . . skulking in the canebreak pierced with wounds" and women "shot down in the most inhuman manner." (*Official Records*, ser. 1, vol. 24, pt. 2, p. 516–18.)

169: Order by the Commander of the District of Memphis

Memphis Tenn 17" July 1863.

General Orders N° 75 –

I. All Idlers, Vagrants, and persons without lawful occupation, or means of support, found within the District of Memphis after ten days from this date will be arrested and confined at hard labor in Fort Pickering –

II. All owners of Slaves within the District of Memphis must within twenty days report to the District Provost Marshal the name age and description of such slave –

III. Every free Negro or mullatto and every contraband within the District must within twenty days enter into the employment of some responsible white person who will be required to report name age and description of such free negro or contraband and nature of contract to the Provost Marshal of the District

IV – All Negroes and Mulattoes failing to find service or employment with some responsible white person will immediately remove to the Contraband Camps under charge of Captain Fiske

Superintendent of Contrabands By order of Brig Genl James C Veatch
HD

General Orders No. 75, Head Quarters Dist. of Memphis, 17 July 1863, vol. 20 DWT, p. 78, General Orders Issued, ser. 2843, Dist. of Memphis, RG 393 Pt. 2 No. 181 [C-8508]. General Veatch's order purporting to check "vagrancy" virtually prohibited black people in Memphis from working for black employers or undertaking any form of self-employment – even when they had long labored as independent artisans or petty proprietors. It proved, however, nearly impossible to enforce. In October 1863, Captain Charles H. Cole, superintendent of contrabands in the District of Memphis, complained: "I labor under a great inconvenience in consequence of the manner in which the negro is '*stood for*' by citizens – who get the Provost Marshal passes by the Dozen and give them to the negroes – to evade conscription. and Keep them from being employed by Government. and the result is that after a few days work. they get out of employ and go to stealing gambling &c for subsistence." Despite his best efforts, Cole lamented, "Memphis is full of lazy – indigent negroes who live in holes and corners." (Capt. Charles H. Cole to Brig. Gen'l. L. Thomas, 20 Oct. 1863, filed with C-26 1863, Letters Received, ser. 360, Colored Troops Division, RG 94 [B-487].)

170: Army Surgeon to the Secretary of War

Vicksburg [*Miss.*] July 27th 1863

Sir: Learning that you take great interest in the organization and general condition of the negro regiments now organizing in this and other Departments, and having been appointed to inspect these regiments from Lake Providence to Sherman's Landing, I take the liberty of sending you a copy of my report of the above inspection.

In the same district I found about ten thousand women and children, who, having left their plantations, were roving about without adequate support or protection. My report on the condition of these contrabands, forms the conclusion of this report. Respectfully Your Obedient Servant

James Bryan

Report.

The ground indicated is about eighty miles in extent, on the right bank of the Mississippi, stretching up the river from Vicksburg. Like the banks of this stream generally, the ground is flat, and in some places wet, the overflow of the river being guarded by a single or double levee. The exact points occupied by the negro regiments, counting from above, are Goodrich's Landing, about ten miles below Lake Providence, and Milliken's Bend, ten miles above Young's Point. Outside of these encampments, however, are numerous contraband family camps, which extend along the shore down to Sherman's Landing. It does not come within the province of the letter of the order, to report upon the contrabands, but I have understood that the Medical Director is desirous that the inspection should extend also to them.

. . . .

Contrabands.

I shall speak of the contrabands, as distinct from the soldiers, in the following particulars.

First. They are the families of soldiers and others, and consist of women, children, and worn out old men. The women and children are profitable to the slave dealer. It is said, for instance, that some of the quasi agents of the government, have an understanding with the guerillas to supply them with negroes at the following rates. A male $300, a female $200, a likely child $100. Some of those agents, it is said, in times of raids, are found leading the rebels to their spoils.

The greater number of contrabands, however, are necessarily children, who suffer very much from exposure and want of proper protection.

Second. Many of the children are capable of moderate employment, which would support them well. The mothers also, and other young and middle aged women, are most of them vigorous and able, if properly employed, to support themselves confortably with their young children. The aged blacks, broken down by years and toil, are still able, during the short period of their existence, to do light work of some kind. I am informed that the most successful and wealthy planters, allow no old persons to be entirely idle, but keep them occupied at such light work as may be suitable to their years or strength. Occasionally I found one of these who knew how to read, whose talents might be well employed in teaching the younger children the elements of an education. Their burials and other religious services, conducted chiefly by these old patriarchs, are very impressive and calculated to sustain the religious tone of the race. The diseases found amongst the children, are very much the same as those seen among the children of the poor in the large cities of the North. Their mortality in this wandering life, appears to be very great, and the affectionate mother weeps over the dying babe with the sad reflection that a few simple medicines, with the comforts of life, would have been sufficient to prolong its existence. They are more independent in their habits than many suppose. Their own "grannies", who are generally youngish or middle aged mulatto women, are well skilled in most of the simple and many of the scientific medical agents of our art. These "grannies" are an institution fostered by the economical planter. He selects an intelligent young woman, places her under the special guidance and instruction of the plantation Doctor, who carefully teaches her the effects and doses of medicines, which she administers to the sick during his absence. These "grannies" are found among the contrabands not unfrequently, and if well supplied by the government with medicines, would do great good with them. The great number of children and old persons in these camps, give them much the character of a hospital, and I would suggest that the government, in addition to securing the services of these grannies, appoint medical men, in the ratio of one to three thousand, to distribute medicine and prescribe for the sick. The Surgeon might also draw rations in the absence of other officers, and see that his patients are properly fed. There is not, in my opinion, any necessity for the establishment of a hospital for this class of people; they are bound together by family ties and will not willingly be separated. These attachments are not easily broken. In times of sickness and distress, they prefer assisting their relatives, to neighbors or strangers.

Finally. As the arrangements for the contrabands in their present unsettled condition, must necessarily be temporary, I have only the two suggestions above named to make. The final distribution of these laborers, and their employment in different avocations of life as free men and free women, must be left to the wisdom and power of that great Government, which, now, with outstretched arms, breaks the shackles of their long enduring slavery, and bids a nation of four millions of people, be forever free.

One suggestion, however, I would add; it is that the children be immediately instructed in the elements of an English education. Large numbers of elementary books, primers, spelling books &c, should be distributed among them, and good white teachers be employed by government to instruct all the black children within the Federal lines. All of which is respectfully submitted.

ALcS

Excerpts from Surgeon James Bryan to Hon. E. M. Stanton, 27 July 1863, B-108 1863, Letters Received, ser. 360, Colored Troops Division, RG 94 [B-612]. The omitted portion discussed the health of, and hospital facilities for, black troops. Bryan had conducted the inspection under an order from the medical director of the Department of the Tennessee, issued on June 24, 1863, that instructed him to "report on the condition of the Hospitals of the Negro

Regiments from Lake Providence to Shermans Landing." (In James Bryan file, Personal Papers of Medical Officers & Physicians, ser. 561, Medical Records, Record & Pension Office, RG 94 [KK-6].) Bryan was not alone in recognizing the medical skills of black women, or in proposing that the government facilitate their work by providing them with medicines. In February 1863, Chaplain John Eaton, Jr., general superintendent of contrabands in the Department of the Tennessee, had suggested that the Cincinnati Contraband Relief Commission include "common medicinal herbs" among its charitable donations. "[T]he colored people," he explained, "have been accustomed to manage the use of these and some of the 'Aunties' do this with Skill and success." ([Chaplain John Eaton, Jr.] to Robert W. Carroll, 9 Feb. 1863, vol. 74, pp. 13–15, Letters Sent by John Eaton, ser. 2027, General Supt. of Freedmen, MS Asst. Comr. Pre-Bureau Records, RG 105 [A-4002].)

171: Assistant Inspector General of the Department of the Tennessee to the Chief Commissary Officer of the Department

Vicksburg [*Miss.*], Aug 12th 1863

Colonel, I have the honor to communicate for your information the following, from the report of Captain A. C. Mathews, Act. Asst. Inspr. Genl, sent under special instructions to Lake Providence and Goodrich's Landing.

At Lake Providence "I noticed three fields of Cotton 'tended by Contrabands– One was the Plantation of the rebel General Sparrow and another that of A M Black–the other unknown. *On these plantations there is a great deal of fruit. The negroes raise Corn, beans, peas, potatoes, melons*, &c, *much of which I notice them selling*,"

On Island 82 a man named Smith, employing Contrabands to labor in cutting Cord Wood, paying them ($1.80) One Dollar and Eighty Cents pr week–sells government rations to these Contrabands at exorbitant rates#. "pork at 18 Cents pr pound and other articles at the same ratio."

It may not be improper to state that this report is based upon the evidence of Contrabands.

The General desires that you take such steps as you may think proper to prevent fraud on the Government, in these & similar Cases: Very Respectfully Your Obdt Servt

HLcSr (Signed) J. H. Wilson

Lt. Col. J. H. Wilson to Lt. Col. Robert Macfeely, 12 Aug. 1863, vol. 21/40 DT, pp. 41–42, Letters Sent, ser. 4757, Inspector, Dept. of the TN, RG 393 Pt. 1 [C-2033]. Freedpeople who had access to garden plots frequently sold surplus produce at nearby army camps and towns. During the summer of

1863, such trade became especially lively in the Vicksburg area, where it was regulated by military orders that established regular market hours and promised vendors security from "imposition or violence." (G. Orders No. 7, Head Quarters. 13th Army Corps, 27 June 1863, vol. 12/31 13AC, pp. 5–6, General Orders Issued, ser. 5541, 13th Army Corps, RG 393 Pt. 2 No. 352 [C-8792].) But the promise was often honored only in the breach. In August 1863, for example, a Union officer complained that pickets on the outskirts of the city were "making a regular practice of robbing and abusing persons bringing in fruit and vegetables." Indeed, such incidents occurred so frequently that some federal troops were "cut off . . . from fruit & vegetables almost entirely." (Endorsement of Capt. J. B. Gorsuch, 8 Aug. 1863, on Lt. Col. S. Kent to Captain Gorsuch, 8 Aug. 1863, and J. B. Gorsuch to Colonel, 8 Aug. 1863, both filed as K-140 1863, Letters Received, ser. 4720, Dept. of the TN, RG 393 Pt. 1 [C-2006].)

172: Order by the Adjutant General of the Army

Vicksburg, Miss, August 18. 1863.

Special Orders N° 45.

Under instructions from the Secretary of War, the undersigned hereby announces his return to this region of the Country for the purpose of continuing the organization into the military service of the United States of all able bodied male persons of African Descent who may come within our lines, or who may be brought in by our troops, or who may already have placed themselves under the protection of the Federal Government, also to take such measures as may prove most beneficial for the welfare of all women, children, aged and infirm persons of African Descent who have sought refuge within our lines, or may hereafter do so.

In future all able bodied male negroes of the above class, will at once be organized, by such officers as may be detailed for that duty, into the Military service of the United States, when they will be assigned to Regiments composed of persons of African Descent, now in process of formation, or to be formed hereafter.

It has become apparent that the system of receiving all negroes who may have sought the protection of our Government, and allowing them to remain in many instances in a state of almost inactivity, has become, at times, not only injurious to the interests of the service, but to the welfare of the negroes themselves, resulting in habits of idleness, sickness and disease.

It is further considered expedient that all children and females of negro descent, who may hereafter be desirous of seeking refuge within the lines of the United States troops, be advised to remain on the plantations, or elsewhere where they have been heretofore in a state of servitude, provided such place be under the control of the Federal troops. All such negroes will receive the protection of this government while they remain in the locations that may be designated; and all such persons as may be authorized to occupy plantations or other places, will be permitted to employ those females and children in any capacity most suited to their ability.

All male negroes who are incapacitated by old age, ill-health, or in any other respect, from serving in Regiments of African Descent, will be duly cared for and assigned, as heretofore, to the nearest camp for such persons. By order of the Secretary of War:

HDcS L. Thomas

Special Orders No. 45, 18 Aug. 1863, L. Thomas Letters & Orders, Generals' Papers & Books, ser. 159, RG 94 [V-17]. As Adjutant General Thomas explained it to the Secretary of War a few days later, the crowding, disease, and mortality among former slaves who had gathered at Union camps along the Mississippi River, and whose numbers were "daily increasing," had prompted his decision "that the old men, women and children be advised to remain on the plantations" and that ex-slaves in the contraband camps who wished "to return to their old homes" be "encouraged to do so, in cases where we are satisfied their former masters will not run them off or sell them." Thomas's new policy also reflected his conviction that many planters in the valley "now see it is vain to resist our arms, and only see utter ruin to themselves as the war goes on." According to Thomas, such planters realized that slavery "cannot again exist in regions passed over by our armies," seemed "perfectly willing to hire the negroes and adopt any policy the Government may dictate," and desired "that their States should resume their position in the Union with laws providing for the emancipation of slaves in a limited number of years." (*Freedom*, ser. 1, vol. 1: doc. 110.)

173: Commander of the 15th Army Corps to the Commander of the 17th Army Corps

Camp on Big Black [*Miss.*], Septbr. 1" 1863

Dear General– Yours of Aug. 31" is received. I will strengthen my Picket (now 2 Regts.) at Oak Ridge by two more Regts. and a Battery to morrow and will order a picket of four Comps. to be sent to the valley road east of Haines Bluff. Our Telegraph at this moment is interrupted, and as soon as it operates, I will despatch to you the same assurance. –

The Negros at Blakes plantation have been for some time a nuisance. I think it would be advisable for you to send up and bring them *all* into Vicksburg – the available men to work on the

Forts and the woman & children to be sent to Island 10. – It is represented to me, that there is an Officer there who does not attempt to control or restrain them; – for they wander all about the country, doing no good but infinite mischief. – The negroes naturally cluster about the old Negro inmates of abandoned plantations, and put on the Majestic air of Soldiers. – I have had occasion to punish some of these already. –

I have read with pain the narrative of James Pearce, Thos H. Hill and others of Deer Creek. – When Citizens represent to you, that Genl Sherman sends Negroes out, to kill and plunder, you may safely assure them, that it is not only false, but the very reverse of my practise On the contrary, I have done more than most persons to restrain the violence and passion of the Negro. – But I do say, and have said to these very planters, both before they *would have* War and since, that by breaking up the only earthly power, that could restrain the negroes, by openly rebelling against the Government of the United States they prepared the way for those very acts, against which they now appeal to us to shield them. – I know the parties named and have been on their plantations, and with the exception of Mr. Fore, who is simply one, who acts neither way, the others were esteemed Secessionists, – Rebels. – The Hill's were notoriously so. We cannot undertake to guard them in their isolated swamps, and all we are bound to do in the name and cause of humanity is to invite them into our Lines for personal Safety and to leave their property to revert to a state of nature for the use of alligators and negros. This is not our Act, but the natural, immediate and necessary result of their own conduct. –

It is in this very Deer Creek country that are nursed and harbored the Banditti who fire on our Boats at Greenville Point and of all the poeple of this Region, they least of all are entitled to the generous protection of any Government. Because they profess not to have done this with their own hands, they claim to be Non combatants, but I was there on Hills and Fore's plantations, last winter – and know they were not our friends. They fled from us, gave us no information, but on the contrary, aided Ferguson in his efforts to entrap the Gunboats.

I deplore the calamity, that has now overtaken them, but repeat it is the natural fruit of their own conduct With great Respect

HLcSr signed W. T. Sherman

Maj. Genl. W. T. Sherman to Maj. Genl. J. B. McPherson, 1 Sept. 1863, Letters Sent, pp. 107–8, W. T. Sherman Papers, Generals' Papers & Books, ser. 159, RG 94 [V-314]. The "narrative" of the residents of Deer Creek (in Warren County, Mississippi) has not been found, but it presumably described the events of August 25, 1863, when, according to the report of one "citizen," twenty-three armed black men had killed eleven white civilians. (Lieut. Col. S. Kent to Lieut. Col. Jno. A. Rawlins, 29 Aug. 1863, vol. 20/36A MDM, pp. 97–98, Letters Sent & Orders Issued, ser. 4769, Provost Marshal, Dept. of the TN, RG 393 Pt. 1 [C-2031].) On September 7, General Sherman informed H. W. Hill, chairman of a "Meeting of Citizens of Warren County," that the Union army bore no obligation to protect disloyal whites from "[t]he Negroes . . . that now fill the Country"; in supporting the rebellion, they had forfeited the right to such protection. "In due season," Sherman promised, "the Negroes at Roache's and Blake's will be hired, employed by the Government or removed to Camps where they can be conveniently fed, but in the mean time no one must molest them or interfere with the agents of the U.S. entrusted with this difficult and delicate task." If the former slaves were armed, Sherman continued, "it is for self defence, and if they mistake their just relation to the Government, or the poeple, we will soon impress on them the Truth." The Union army, he advised, could neither "hire Servants for the poeple, who have lost their Slaves" nor "detail negros for such purposes. You must do as we do, – hire your Servants and pay them. – If they don't earn their hire, discharge them and employ others. – Many have already done this and are satisfied with the results. –" (Maj. Genl. W. T. Sherman to H. W. Hill, Esqr., 7 Sept. 1863, Letters Sent, pp. 122–24, W. T. Sherman Papers, Generals' Papers & Books, ser. 159, RG 94 [V-316].)

174: Testimony by a Mississippi Freedman before the Southern Claims Commission

Natchez Miss August 17, 1873

Littleton Barber being duly sworn doth depose & say my name is Littleton Barber I am 59 years of age reside about three miles from Natchez and am by occupation a farmer

Int 2 During the war I resided in this County upon the Waller Irwin place was a slave. when the Union troops Came to Natchez in July 1863, I came away from my masters place and got into the Union lines where I resided during the remainder of the War, When I left my masters place I rode my own mule that I purchased from a Texas Drover two or three years before for $\$65^{00}$ I had been in Natchez but a short time, when I traded the mule with Thomas Johnson I gave him $\$35^{00}$ to boot and got a fine black horse, that Johnson had,. Johnson owned the horse and had worked him in a dray for over two years, When I got the horse I hired him out at $\$1^{00}$ per day draying, and I went to work on the Steam Ferry between this place & Vidilaia, I had more than $\$100^{00}$ of my own money that I made by overwork upon the plantation, I worked on the Steam Ferry "till the close of the War, I was never outside of

Adams County during the War except when I went across to Vidalia on the Ferry boat I was kept close at work on the farm untill the union soldiers came I always determined to get away the first chance that I got and I done so, My master is yet living in this county on the old place his name is Waller Irwin. I am not indebed to him, do not work on his land, and am not connected with him in any way, I never took an oath to the Confederate States – I never had anything to do with them in any way was never employed in a military or a naval capacity or as a laborer in any way – I just made corn & cotton from the time that the war Commenced "till the union Soldiers got here, when I came into the lines, and worked on the Steam Ferry and for the quartermaster there till the war ended – I was never arrested by any government – never had any property but the mule, never was injured on account of my Union Sentiments, took good care that no white persons heard me say anything, Col Farrar hung too many men who just said that they were for the Union. I used to talk to a few of my own color about our chances for freedom and always told them that the only thing that we could do would be to watch & pray – I always was for the Union and would have done anything that I could to have helped it along. When I got to the Union troops I tried to enlist, but they would not have me. Said I was too weakly – I would have been willing to have joined & served for nothing –

In regard to the property, Claimant Says,

I did not see the property taken, the first notification I had that it was seized – was when Capt Organ of the Colored Heavy Artillery Regiment with his Company went across on the Ferry Boat to Vidalia – this was some time in September 1863 – I saw my horse with the soldiers. I asked What they were doing with my horse they said that they wanted him and that they seized him on the streets,

. . . .

His
Littleton X Barber
mark

HDSr

Excerpt from testimony of Littleton Barber, 17 Aug. 1873, claim of Littleton Barber, Adams Co. MS case files, Approved Claims, ser. 732, Southern Claims Commission, 3rd Auditor, RG 217 [I-183]. Sworn before a special commissioner of the Southern Claims Commission. The questions that correspond to the enumerated responses are not in the file. According to other documents in the same file, Barber had submitted a claim for $135 as compensation for the horse taken by Union soldiers. He was awarded the full amount.

175A: Affidavit of a Louisiana Black Soldier

Goodrichs Landing La Sept 21, 1863

Private Joseph Rogers Co. (C) 10th La. Vols AD Deposes and says That sometime in the month of Feby last he came within our lines at Lake Providence bringing with him a sorrel mare given to him by his Master "L. E. Strouse", That soon after his arrival Chaplain Livermore borrowed the mare for his own use and promised to return or pay for her, That said Chaplain Livermore still retains the mare and refuses to give her up or pay for her

his
Joseph X Rogers
mark

HDSr

Affidavit of Joseph Rogers, 21 Sept. 1863, filed with Adjt. Gen'l L. Thomas to Brig. Gen'l J. P. Hawkins, 11 Oct. 1863, Letters Received, ser. 2016A, Dist. of Northeastern LA, RG 393 Pt. 2 No. 109 [C-899]. Sworn before an army officer. On the same day, an endorsement by General John P. Hawkins, commander of the District of Northeastern Louisiana, referred the affidavit to Chaplain Lark S. Livermore, who had been superintendent of contrabands at Lake Providence, Louisiana, when Rogers reached federal lines. In the same file is Livermore's reply, also dated September 21, which claimed that the mare had belonged to the overseer on the plantation where Rogers was a slave and that Rogers had simply absconded with it when he fled. Livermore acknowledged that he had seized the mare and several mules brought in by Rogers and other fugitive slaves from the same plantation, but claimed that he had turned them over to the post quartermaster, as required by standing orders regarding "contraband property," and that the quartermaster had subsequently authorized him to use the mare. Not persuaded by Livermore's explanation, General Hawkins immediately ordered him to return the mare to Rogers. Matters did not rest there, however. On October 11, 1863, according to other documents in the same file, Adjutant General Lorenzo Thomas (who had apparently acquired from Livermore the papers about Rogers's claim), called the attention of General Ulysses S. Grant, commander of the Department of the Tennessee, to "the subject of the right of negroes to Mules and other property claimed by them as given to them by their former masters, or brought with them when they left their former homes, captured &c." Later that day, Thomas informed Hawkins of Grant's opinion: "The General denies the right of the negroes to such property, and regards it as the property of the United States to be turned over to the Quartermasters Department." At the same time, Thomas returned to Hawkins the papers about Rogers's claim, with an endorsement noting that Grant's decision "covers this case." (L. S. Livermore to Gen. J. P. Hawkins, 21 Sept. 1863, with endorsements by Brig. Genl. John P. Hawkins, 21 Sept. 1863, and by Adjt. Genl. L. Thomas, 11 Oct. 1863; Adjt. Gen'l L. Thomas to Brig. Gen'l J. P. Hawkins, 11 Oct. 1863.) In the meantime, General

Hawkins had himself written to Grant's headquarters respecting the right of ex-slaves to property they brought with them into Union lines. (See doc. 175B, immediately below.)

175B: Commander of the District of Northeastern Louisiana to the Headquarters of the Department of the Tennessee

Goodrichs Landing [*La.*] Oct. 9. 1863.

General, A nice and peculiar question has come up in this District as to the rights of a negro, coming into our lines from the country occupied by the enemy, to the property he may bring with him such as mules oxen or wagons, When the case has been brought up before me I have decided the right of property in favor of the negro. President Lincolns Proclamation gives legal freedom to the slaves, The masters in the lines of the enemy deprive them. of this right and attempt to hold them contrary to law, I hold it no crime that the slave should attempt to escape this wrong and in so doing has a right to make use of the facilities that might assist him in his escape by taking horse, mule or any thing else of his masters that might help him to get away, We have a distinguished precedent for this when the children of Israel went out fugitive slaves from the Egyptians, Again, I think the negro should hold the property as his own which he has secured by his energy and effort, and that it is a very small thing on the part of a Government that should be magnanimous towards such persons to take it away from him, By letting the property remain in their possission, they will be enabled next year to cultivate a few acres of ground and the Gov,ment be relieved of their support, By taking it away they or their families are made paupers for perhaps all time to come, The immediate gain to Gov,ment by the seizure is very small compared with the great loss to them, As the wealth of a Gov,ment consists in the prosperity of its Citizens, and as these people have been declared Citizens of the United States nothing is gained to Gov,ment by interfering with the individual prosperity of any one of them, Many of them now use their property to make a living, when planting season comes they will be able to do a great deal better if they have half a chance, I am willing to run this District without instructions, without troubling the Department Commander on delicate questions that may arise, and would not write now only that General Thomas intends to refer the matter to Dept. H[d] Qrs. for decision and I wished to present my views of the question. I am Genl, Very Respectfully Your Obdt, Servt,

ALS John P. Hawkins

[*Endorsement*] Hd. Qrs. Dept. & Army of the Tenn. Bridgeport Ala. Decbr. 23. 1863. Respectfully returned. The negro on his becoming free, has no right to the property of his former owner, unless by special gift. All property belonging to their former Masters brought within our lines by negroes should be taken charge of at once by the Government, through its proper agent, the Qr. Mr. Department Should the good of the Service and the future prosperity of the country demand it, the negro can be allowed the use of such property after it has been taken in charge by the Government By order of Maj. Genl. W. T. Sherman R. M. Sawyer Asst. Adjt. General.

Brig. Genl. John P. Hawkins to Brig. Genl. J. A. Rawlins, 9 Oct. 1863, Letters Received, ser. 2016A, Dist. of Northeastern LA, RG 393 Pt. 2 No. 109 [C-899]. By the time Hawkins's letter reached General Ulysses S. Grant, to whose headquarters it was addressed, Grant had been promoted to the command of the Military Division of the Mississippi; consequently, he referred it (without comment) to General William T. Sherman, his successor as commander of the Department of the Tennessee. Meanwhile, however, Grant's own opinion regarding property brought into Union lines by fugitive slaves had already been conveyed to General Hawkins. (See doc. 175A n., immediately above.)

176: Louisiana Planter to the President

No 111 Broadway New York Sept 1863

To His Excellency Abram Lincoln President of the United States Permit me to request your special attention to the following statement

I am a citizen of Louisiana, I remained on and in the occupation of my Estate until last April, When I rented two of my home places to Judge Dent, and subsequently requested the commissioners appointed by Gen[l] Thomas to appoint Agents to manage the other three home places until the first of Febuary 1864 – and on the 15″ day of April last (1863) I left my home under a permit of Gen[l] Grant for the purpose of bringing my family and the minor heirs of the Estates of Oliver I Morgan and Alexander C Keene of which Estates I am Agent north to a place of safety

The object of this statement is to request an official Government Order requiring the Government Agents or others in occupancy of said Estates and places to deliver possession of each and every of them to me as the owner Guardian or Agent on the first day of Febuary 1864

My home Estates Carrol Parish L[a] Embraces			8000 Acres
of which there was in cultivation			4000 "
Viz – Planted in cotton	3000	Acres	
" " " corn	1000	"	

On the above Estates I had 423 Negroes Viz from

1 to	5	years old	63
5 "	10	" "	50
10 "	15	" "	40
15 "	45	" "	196
Above	45	" "	74
			423

Average half males & half females

The above labor produced in 1860 –	3119	bales pressed cotton
1861 –	1890	" " "
1862 –	2760	" " "
	7769	Average 2589 bales per annum

[*To the right of the brace*] Having in 1861 refused to loan my cotton to the Confedrate Government they burned it And in 1862 having refused to sell my cotton to the Confedrate Government they burnt all except 142 bales making 4508 bales burned by the Confedrate Government

This year (1863) owing to the deranged state of the district and late planting, the Estates will not produce over 500 bales of cotton

I have had twenty years experience in New England in the employment of a large number of men (free laborers) in manufacturing, and I have had five years experience in Louisiana in the employment of a large number of negroes (Slave laborers) in raising cotton, and a comparison of the workings, and practical results of the two systems – or paid labor and slave labor, has satisfied me that the free or paid labor system – is the true, practical and most profitabl system or plan, for adoption by the planting interest of the south

I shall on receiving the solicited government authority for my reinstatement and occupancy of the aforesaid Estates, at once proceed to my home in Carrol Parish L[a] and make arrangements for cultivating the Estates upon the Government system, or plan of paid free labor. and upon a scale of cultivation equal to that of any former years, and will assume the responsibility of being one to prove to the Nation, that the Government policy of paid free Colored labor, is the true economical policy or System, for cultivating the lands of the Southern States

Conscientously entertaining these sentiments and views on the question of colored labor, I shall devote my best efforts and influence in my neighborhood and in the state to induce men of position and influence to adopt my views practically and join with me in perfecting the organization of local and state political associations to bring the state back into the Union, with an ordiance for immidiate or gradual Emancipation I am with due respect Your obedient Servant

HLcSr Horace. B. Tebbetts

Horace. B. Tebbetts to His Excellency Abram Lincoln, Sept. 1863, #746, Case Files of Claims for Cotton & Captured & Abandoned Property, ser. 370, Miscellaneous Division, RG 56 [X-502]. Endorsement. Tebbetts, through his attorney, also sought an interview with the Secretary of the Treasury to discuss making his plantations "the nucleus for a great practical introduction of free labor into Louisiana." "The largest capitalists in N York," the attorney wrote, "stand ready to supply all the Capital, needed, to purchase or lease as much Cottonland as possible and to carry the enterprise to success." By December, the "Louisiana Company" had been incorporated under the laws of New York State. According to a promotional circular, the company's "motive and mainspring" was the restoration of "Order out of confusion in the Southern States . . . [through] the employment of free in the place of compulsory labor" in cotton production. The company's introduction of "healthful industry" would "lead others to unite in similar efforts" and thus bring the South "in to the great brotherhood formed and held together by the bond of intelligent labor." The circular promised capitalists both unsurpassed returns on their investment and an opportunity to demonstrate "the feasibility of the successful employment of free colored labor, by affording practical examples, on a large scale, by which the plans of the Government will be more speedily carried out, and the new order of industry sooner established." (Henri Lovie to Hon. Salmon P. Chase, 7 Sept. 1863, and "CIRCULAR OF THE LOUISIANA COMPANY," [Dec.? 1863], enclosed in T. D. Lincoln to Hon. S. P. Chase, 23 Dec. 1863, all in Miscellaneous Letters Received: K Series, ser. 103, RG 56 [X-233].)

177: Inspecting Officer in the District of Northeastern Louisiana to the Headquarters of the District

Goodrich's Landing Dist. N.E. La. October 10th 1863.

Captain: I have the honor to make the following report of my tour of duty up to the present time, as Inspecting Officer to enquire into the condition of the Contrabands in this District, as required by S.O. No. 14 from District Head Quarters.[1]

In my report I have divided the contrabands into three classes. 1st, those on plantations controlled by Government Lessees: 2nd: those on what are called Infirmary Farms, and in camps controlled by Government Agents, and 3rd: the floating population, including those in the temporary employ of Government Contractors for wood, etc,

The estimates I have made of the numbers of Contrabands on plantations & in camps the number of deaths, and the amount of crops and stock on the places may not be perfectly correct, as I had in most cases to depend on the statements of negroes and interested parties, modified by my own Judgement. I regret to state that in no case have I found a strict compliance with the terms of their contracts on the part of Lessees of plantations, and in too many an utter disregard of even the commonest principles of humanity and the rights of individuals, in their treatment of the contrabands. Generally the negro has been treated by those employing him, as a mere brute, from whom the greatest amount of labor should be gained at the least possible expense: and not as a free citizen with personal rights and immunities. No schools have been established, with one or two exceptions, and those have been taught by intelligent negroes who were on the plantations and who were unfit for other labor. Almost nothing has been done to raise the negro to a higher level, or to convince him that our Government is in earnest in its declarations that he is a free man with all a freeman's rights and privileges. In this District during the past summer he has been in a far more servile and pitiable condition than when a slave under his master.

Some it is true have a false idea of their freedom and its responsibilities, thinking that it releases them from all restraint, and are consequently roving the country stealing and committing depredations on property: but it has been demonstrated that the majority, if stimulated by the right kind of treatment, proper wages, and a prospect of bettering their condition, would labor faithfully and steadily: while some show a capacity for management an energy and executive ability that would do credit, to men of better education and a whiter skin. The contrabands in the District are generally much in want of clothing, and unless it is furnished before winter they will suffer much from its want. Many who had a supply in the spring have been robbed of it or had it burned in their quarters. I have in my report given the condition of the contrabands on each plantation & camp.

Contrabands on "Infirmary Farms"

These are plantations on which were placed by the Government Commissioners, aged and infirm contrabands and their families, who could not be disposed of on the leased plantations. Two of these known as the Savage and Front Raliegh plantations are situated on the river a mile & a mile and a half respectively below Goodrich's

Landing: the others known as the Richardson Blackman, Stone, Hardison and Carry plantations, are situated west of the "telegraph road" leading from Goodrich Landing to Millikens Bend. The majority of these contrabands depend on Government for subsistence, which they draw weekly from the Commissary for Contrabands" at Goodrich Landing.

The ration issued, consists of bacon, flour, salt and rye coffee, and occasionally rice, beans and sugar. Some of these contrabands have planted cotton, corn, potatoes and other vegitables, which have generally yeilded fine crops: but no system seems to have been adopted to compel them to support themselves, and therefore many well able to work are idle. What crops there are, on these places, are due solely to the exertions of a few individuals. In some cases Government has furnished mules. The remainder of the stock on these places has been collected from the abandoned plantations in the vicinity. A portion of the negroes are earning a good living by the sale of vegitables, by day's work, and by cutting wood.

The health on these places is generally good at present: but there has been a great deal of sickness and mortality amongst them during the past summer. The supply of medicines has been very limited. On the "Savage" farm, a hospital is established for Contrabands, and also a pest house for small pox cases. The Surgeon in charge Dr H. H. Littlefield has been there but a short time: but his hospital shows evidence of great improvement in cleanliness and system. Medical supplies and hospital stores are greatly needed.

On one farm, the "Savage," there is a school of about twenty children taught by a lame negro, which is the only instance of any effort being made for the mental improvment of the children on these farms.

Only an approximate estimate can be made of the numbers on the farms, the number of deaths, or the amount of the crops.

Below is given the estimate which I have made of the persons and crops on these farms.

Total number of Contrabands:	1057
" " of Field hands	304
" " " Sick	95
" " Deaths	300
No of acres of Cotton	189
" " " Corn	245
" " " Potatoes and Other Vegitables	52
No. of Mules	26
" " Cattle	42
" " Hogs	15.

Contrabands on Leased Plantations.

The "Bell Plantation" leased by Cha's Hays and Co. is situated about three miles below Goodrich Landing on the river. The Lessees have been absent from the plantation for nearly three months. Since July 1st but little has been furnished for the comfort of the contrabands employed. Rations have been limited, and recently the negro in charge, has purchased rations from his own means to supply the hands. But few medicines were on the place, and the contrabands had applied to and recieved medical assistance from the army surgeons at Goodrich's Landing. No clothing has been furnished, although the blacks are much in need of it and no school established. The sickness of the Lessee Mr Hayes may be a partial excuse for the neglect of the colored people on the place. The total number of contrabands, is ninety (90). No. of field hands, sixty (60). No. of deaths during the season, twenty three (23). No. of acres of cotton four hundred (400). No. of mules sixty (60): of cattle thirty (30). of hogs thirteen (13).

Since my first visit to this place the Lessees have returned, and the negroes are better provided for than before.

The plantation leased by Mr Newman, the owner, is the next below on the river. The care of the contrabands is quite good although the full ration required has not been issued, although perhaps that lack may have been compensated for by the issue of vegetables etc, which have been furnished them. No school has been organized for the children. The number of contrabands on the place is one hundred & thirteen (113). No. of field hands forty four (44). No of sick five (5): No. of death during the season, eleven (11). No of acres of cotton one hundred & seventy (170): of corn fifty (50). No. of mules thirty five (35), of cattle twelve (12). The Lessee complains of the want of power to make the negroes work.

The plantation known as the (Back) Raliegh place is situated one and a half miles below Goodrich's Landing and the same distance back from the river. The contrabands here are in good condition in regard to health. The ration furnished is meal, salt and fresh meat. A little rice, flour, sugar and coffee has been kept for issue and sale. There is no school. A small quantity of clothing has been furnished, and a few have recieved wages. Medicines have been furnished in good quantities. The number of persons on the place is about one hundred and fifty (150) Number of field hands seventy two (72). No of deaths during the past season fifteen (15). No. of acres of cotton four hundred (400). of corn thirty (30). No of mules forty (40) of cattle ten (10). The crop of cotton is being gathered in by the field hands. Since the first visit to the place, I find that *no rations* are issued to persons unfit for work. The Henderson place, situated about half way between Goodrich Landing and Milliken's Bend, on the river, and leased by J. Williams & Co. shows the evidence of good management, and of consideration for the wants of those employed.

Rations of meal, flour, meat, molasses, grits and beans are issued: and coffee, sugar etc are kept on hand for sale at reasonable prices to the contrabands. Money has been paid when called for in sums of from two to twenty dollars. The Lessees intend the purchase of at Memphis or St Louis as soon as the cotton crop can be forwarded. The number of persons on the place is two hundred and twenty (220). No. of field hands one hundred and eighty eight (188). No. of acres of cotton six hundred (600) No. of bales. three hundred (300) No. of mules thirty two (32).

The Harris' places leased by John Dunham, adjoins the Henderson place below. The contrabands on this place I found badly cared for and discontented. Meal and a little salt pork is issued to them and they are allowed the privilege of killing cattle and hogs on the plantations and in the woods. There are on the places two hundred, and eleven persons unfit for work, old, infirm, or maimed or children, who have to be supported, and only seventy (70) field hands, The number of deaths has been, during the past season, sixty three (63), No. of acres of cotton four hundred (400). No of bales of cotton three hundred (300). There is no school on the place, & the place has evidently been badly managed, The negroes are allowed to prowl around nights and steal mules, hogs and cattle, from the neighboring plantations.

The Harding place, three miles back from Millikens Bend has been abandoned since this Lessee Mr Walker was taken prisoner by the rebels in June last. A few contrabands, about thirty in number, have returned there and have commenced picking the cotton, of which it is estimated there will be two hundred bales. No attention has been paid to these negroes by any one. They have been living on fresh meat killed in the woods, and on the corn obtained on the place– It is reported that the cotton crop is claimed by Mr Dunham Lessee of the Harris places.

The "Compromise" and "Parham" places leased by Farmer and Dunlap: the "Orkney & Buckner places leased by J. W. Green lying back from Millikens Bend have been neglected by the Lessees during the summer: but they have returned within a few days to secure what crops there are on the places. I could not learn that any rations had been issued to the negroes since the fore part of summer. The negroes have subsisted mainly on the corn and meat obtained from the country around.

The "Outpost" plantation a part of which is leased by Duke & Hotchkiss is situated two miles back from Goodrich Landing. The treatment of the negro in the main seems to be good. The ration issued is mainly salt meat, meal & molasses, Sugar, flour and Tobacco are kept for sale to the hands at reasonable prices, though at an advance on first cost. The crops are small. The cotton may average one half bale per acre –

The portion of the place leased by Sancho, Humphrey, and Jackson, seems to be quite well managed. About sixty (60) persons are in thier employ, thirty (30) of whom are field hands They are well fed, and most of them have a supply of vegitables raised on the place. No wages have been paid by either of the lessees, on this plantation. The negroes have depended for medical attendance, on the army surgeons A school has been established, taught by a black man, in which the children seem to make good progress in reading. The number of deaths on the whole place during the season has been about forty (40). The colored Lessees will make about two hundred bales of cotton, and have eighty (80) acres of corn.

The plantations leased in the name of R. V. Montague, & Montague and Clary, known as the Wilton, Buckner, Albion, Steam boat, Mound and Keene Richards places, I found, with the exception of the two latter in an entirely neglected condition. The Lessees had paid but little attention to them since the raid made by the rebels on the 28th day of June last. At that time all the quarters and gins on the places were burned with the exception of those on the Wilton place, and the negroes captured or driven from the plantations and scattered. Many of them came to Goodrich Landing and were there furnished with rations from the Government. At the time of visiting the plantations I found on the Wilton place about one hundred contrabands who had returned, and on the Buckner Albion and Steam boat places fifty more, all in a most neglected condition. The quarters were very filthy and there was much consequent sickness. The exposure of these people after being driven from their quarters, caused a great deal of sickness and death. But five barrels of meat had been furnished since last June, no other rations. No wages have been paid and no clothing furnished. Nothing even has been paid for the labor done in gathering in the old crop of cotton which was picked last spring.

The contrabands have evidently been totally neglected, and the terms of the contract disregarded by the Lessees. About four thousand acres of cotton were planted on these places, which will yield probably from three to five hundred bales. Two places originally leased by R. V. Montague and Clary, the Mound & Keene Richards places, have been subleased by a Mr Campbell, who now has charge of them. The contrabands on these places seem much better cared for than on the others, are all at work and quite well supplied with rations. The number of contrabands on these places is one hundred and seventeen (117) of field hands ninety seven (97). No school is established, and no medicines furnished. About three hundred and fifty acres of cotton are being gathered. The number of mules on the place is twenty (20): of cattle twenty (20). The plantations leased by H. B. Tibbetts & L. Dent, Lewis Dent, and Ledbetter and Dent, known as the "Benjamin," "Concord" "Bodine," and "Benton" places, situated near and above Transylvania Landing, suffered much by the raids made upon them last summer by the rebels: but I found that many of the negroes who then left had returned, and were living in temporary quarters, prepared for them; the quarters on most of the places having been burnt down. The hands are kept employed, were paid one months wages in the spring, and are now paid one dollar per hundred pounds for picking cotton. Shoes and a few other articles of clothing have been furnished them during the season. A good supply of rations is furnished and the negroes seem contented, and are humanely treated. There are nearly four hundred (400) persons on these places: one hundred and sixty (160) of whom are field hands. Quite a number are sick from exposure and diseases contracted during the summer while they were driven from their quarters. Between three and four hundred bales of cotton will be made on these places, this season. The corn crop will be very light.

The plantations leased by [Deweese?], Alexander & Smith known as the "Noland" Bledsoe, Nutt & Neely places are situated near the Omega Landing above Milliken's Bend. On these places are about one hundred and eighty contrabands. The ration issued to them is mainly meal and salt meat: occasionally molasses is issued. The rice, beans and hominy required by contract is but rarely furnished. No food of a better kind for the use of the sick is issued or even kept for sale: and but little medicine is furnished. A little clothing has been furnshed them at exorbitant prices. From eight hundred to one thousand bales of cotton will be made on these places, an amount which would fully justify the Lesses in a liberal and humane treatment of those employed. The contrabands are much in need of clothing & unless it is furnished soon, they will suffer for the want of it.

Some other plantations, the "Dr Noland–" & "Holly Grove" places, have been entirely abandoned, and have no crops worth gathering.

ALS Julian E. Bryant

[*Endorsement*] H[d] Qrs Dist. N.E. La Goodrichs Landing Oct. 14, 1863 Respectfully forwarded to Dept H[d] Qrs with the recommendation that the report be forwarded to Washington for the information of the Secy of War. The report does not half show the hardships and ill treatment the free negroes are subjected to and if better policy for them cannot be introduced, and humanity, is a matter of consideration we had better call back their former masters and let them take charge of them. If a proper policy is adopted they will become good industrious Citizens, but the present treatment will make vagabonds of them and is doing it just the same as it would make of white people. If the vacant lands here can be divided into farms of from 80 to 200 acres and the farmers of the north invited down to farm for one year every farmer would make a moderate fortune the first season and the labor of the negro be in the market and in demand for what it is worth and the competition would insure his proper treatment. As it is now and will be under the system of large leases a monopoly controls the labor and treatment, any one who has seen the emigration to California to dig for gold can know how the people of the west would flock here to cultivate for one year, the banks of the Miss. River would be thickly populated in three months with a loyal people and the profits to them would be greater than ever realized from the California or Pikes Peak gold mines John P. Hawkins Brig. Genl. Comdg.

Major Julian E. Bryant to Captain, 10 Oct. 1863, filed as T-9 1863, Letters Received by Adjutant General L. Thomas, ser. 363, Colored Troops Division, RG 94 [V-69]. Other endorsements.

1 The order, issued on September 16, 1863, by General John P. Hawkins, commander of the District of Northeastern Louisiana, had designated Major Julian E. Bryant, 1st Mississippi Infantry A.D., a temporary "Inspecting Officer" and directed him "to inquire into the Condition of the Contrabands in this Dist. including those under the care of Government Agents. the floating population & those in the employment of Government Lessees." (Special Orders No. 14, Hd. Qrs. Dist. N.E. Louisiana, 16 Sept. 1863, vol. 208/432 DG, p. 21, Special Orders, ser. 2019, Dist. of Northeastern LA, RG 393 Pt. 2 No. 109 [C-2167].)

178: Commander of the District of Eastern Arkansas to the Headquarters of the 16th Army Corps, and a Reply by the Corps Commander

Helena, Ark., Oct[r] 10th, *1863.*

Sir The helpless condition of women and children in the contraband camp at this Post, is such, that I request permission of

Gen[l] Hurlbut to send them in installments of 100 at a time to the Free States where they will be received. I find Chaplain Jonathan Thomas of the 56" Ohio here, who is a suitable man to take charge of them. I suggest that I be allowed to order Transportation for them by Steamers to places in Iowa, Indiana and Ohio. that he be furnished five dollars for each person out of the Provost Marshal's fund at this place to pay necessary expenses above transportation and rations

It is estimated that there are nearly 4000 negroes in this vicinity,

The healthy men can all get employment as Wood Choppers or servants (they can support themselves and families). The Camp contains about 700 persons, who draw rations. and there are not men enough in it, to cut and draw the fuel necessary for this season of the year. I only propose to send off the women and children, who could earn a support if distributed with farmers families Your Obd[t] Serv[t]

HLS N. B. Buford

[*Memphis, Tenn.*] Octr 14, 1863

General Your favour of the 10th is received. It is impossible to send the contrabands at and near Helena North – They must be employed & fed where they are.

Had any thing like ordinary care & foresight been exercised by the Chaplains who have pretended to look after them they would have been comfortably prepared for winter out of their own labour.

But this whole business has been thrown into the hands of men utterly incompetent by education & position to control these people – and who in many instances have neglected their trust.

Orders now require that these Camps be in the hands of Military officers who must reduce this black chaos into order and the Chaplains be confined to their legitimate duties

More time & money has been squandered than can ever be repaid or accounted for.

Industry must be enforced for a time upon this people, until it becomes a habit.

You will cause a Return to be made of all contrabands of both sexes within your command not actually taken up on Military Rolls, and report the same with the names of the Military officers in charge as soon as practicable

Let the ages be set forth also, and the physical ability Your obt Servt

ALS S A Hurlbut

Brig. Genl. N. B. Buford to Lt. Col. H. Binmore, 10 Oct. 1863, #11572 1863, Letters Received, ser. 391, 16th Army Corps, RG 393 Pt. 2 No. 7 [C-8628], and Maj. Gen. S. A. Hurlbut to Brig. Genl. N. B. Buford, 14 Oct. 1863, General & Special Orders Received & Other Records, ser. 4687, Dist. of Eastern AR, RG 393 Pt. 2 No. 299 [C-7565]. Forbidden to transport freedpeople from Helena to the North, General Buford placed large numbers of them in camps on Islands 63 and 66 in the Mississippi River, where the men cut wood for Union steamers. But new accessions of black refugees thwarted his efforts to reduce the population of the camp at Helena, which had grown to at least 1,400 by the following December. (Brig. Genl. [Napoleon B. Buford] to Capt. T. H. Harris, 19 Nov. 1863, Brig. Genl. [Napoleon B. Buford] to Capt. Kincaid, 25 Nov. 1863, Brig. Genl. [Napoleon B. Buford] to Major Genl. Steele, 14 Dec. 1863, and Brig. Genl. [Napoleon B. Buford] to Captain G. F. Work, 30 Dec. 1863, vol. 37 DArk, pp. 222, 226–27, 243–44, 252–53, Letters Sent, ser. 4664, Dist. of Eastern AR, RG 393 Pt. 2 No. 299 [C-7537, C-7538, C-7540, C-7542].) In early 1864, however, the expansion of plantation leasing in the Helena area created a great demand for laborers, and most of the freedpeople at the Helena camp were hired out to plantation lessees. By the beginning of March, the superintendent of freedmen in the state of Arkansas was reporting, "we can now hire out . . . many more freedmen than we have now in our midst." (Major W. G. Sargent to Col. John Eaton Jr., 1 Mar. 1864, enclosed in Major W. G. Sargent to A.A. General C. H. Dyer, 17 May 1864, Miscellaneous Letters & Reports Sent & Received, ser. 272, Dist. of Little Rock, RG 393 Pt. 3 [C-254].)

179: Testimony of an Arkansas Freedman before the Southern Claims Commission

[*Helena, Ark.*] 6– day of June 1873

Robert Houston (colored) claimants evidence continued

I was borne a Slave in Buckinham Co– Va.– I was brought to Memphis Tenn. at the beginning of the war by a negro trader named A M Boyd with 40 or 50 other slaves– From here Mr Boyd sent me with the others to Chico Co– Ark– to work on his Plantation– This was in the winter of 1861–before the fireing on Fort Sumpter.– Then I was put to work on Mr Boyds Plantation with the others makeing corn.– After a time the Yankees took Memphis and the Gun & other Boats were passing up & down the river.– the Confederate Authorities made a requizition on Boyd my Master for a large number of Slaves to work in breast works.– Boyds Father in Law–in charge would send only one– then went to Lake Village and made a Speech against the order saying it was death to put the negroes to work in the swamps

The requisition was repeated and demand for all his slaves when

Mr Hedspeth – in charge told all of us Slaves to put out to the woods and he would send us provissions till we could get to the Yankees – and he had to leave the country – We stayed in the woods about three weeks then made our way to the Miss – river and got taken on Marine Fleet and hired to work at $60. per Month. – for two Months. A few days before the two months were up I was taken with the small Pox – when I was put off on Island 76 – There were a good many here cutting wood. When I got able to work I was seperated from the others – and told by one seeming to have control to go by myself on the other side of a Slew and I might have all the wood I could cut & sell. I then built me a Shanty on that ground & went on cutting as I was able. – I remained here for a long time or till I cut & hawled out – to the river 150 cords – intending when I made enough to go to farming. When this much cut and put up then came the Federal Steam Boat South Western and took all of us men and wood here to Helena and swore us into the Army service – This steamer took this lot of wood at different times as she was forageing up & down the river. – When called upon I went into the Union Service very willingly, having by this time learnt something of the principles & object of the war. From my first information of the war my actions feelings and Sympathies have all the time been for the Success and maintainance of the Union Cause & all the time willing and desireous to fight or do any thing else in my power, in that behalf – I never done any thing to my knowledge to aid, assist or countenence the rebellion and could never be induced to go in that direction.

The way I got at the quantity of wood taken was this – When cut I ranked it all up and measured with a four foot stick except 25 cords or about that laying as it was cut which I do not charge for – There was 125 cords so put up and this steamer South Western got all of it also sent teams in the woods & took the 25 cords Scattered. – At this time Steam Boats were paying for this kind of wood $\$3^{50}$ per cord for wood: – & I consider this worth that much I asked the officer for pay when they commenced takeing it – It was Lieut – Hadlock – He consulted with other officers – then come back and said part would be paid when we get to Helena. and asked how much I expected for it I told him $\$3^{50}$ the same as others got. – then he gave me a receipt for it, At Helena he said I must wait for the Pay Master to come – Then when I enlisted, he was not permitted to pay – must wait till mustered out & take it with Bounty money – After I was mustered out I made unsuccessful attempts for pay till finally the receipt was worne out and lost

HD

Testimony of Robert Houston, 6 June 1873, claim of Robert Houston, Phillips Co. AR case files, Approved Claims, ser. 732, Southern Claims Commission, 3rd Auditor, RG 217 [I-132]. Sworn before a special commissioner of the Southern Claims Commission. According to other documents in the same file, Houston had worked as a woodcutter for at least three months before the seizure of his wood in late December 1863 or early January 1864. He submitted a claim for $562.50, the value of 125 cords of wood, but the commissioners rejected as "improbable" his assertion that he had been entitled "to have & own all the wood he could cut," maintaining that he had "[d]oubtless" been a wage laborer who "was to have pay for his work." They estimated Houston's "interest" in the property to be "about $1.00 per cord" and awarded him $125. (Testimony of Mingo Scott, 6 June 1873; summary report, [Dec.? 1875].)

180: Adjutant General of the Army to the Secretary of War

Natchez Mississipi October 15th 1863

Sir I recently passed a few days at Goodrich's Landing, La, fifty miles Above Vicksburg, one of my purposes being to ascertain the condition of the leased plantations, to what extent the cultivation of cotton had been carried, and especially to know, whether the cultivation of plantations could not be carried on as well by hired freedmen as by slaves.

The gathering of cotton is now in full operation, and it may be too soon to report fully the result; but the facts in my possession are sufficient for a judgement on the experiment.

As previously reported, the season had advanced fully two months from the time cotton should have been planted; which was unavoidable, though the system was put into operation as soon after my coming to this country as was possible. The lessees therefore labored under great disadvantages in this respect, for most of them had just to run the furrow to plant the seed, then plant their corn; relying on subsequent time to break up the ground between the furrows of cotton and exterminate the weeds. The necessity of withdrawing the troops from Louisiana to augment the forces operating against Vicksburg, left the line of plantations, some sixty in all, without adequate protection when the Rebels made the attack on Milliken's Bend (where they were signally defeated) and made raids on the plantations; scattering and driving off the Negroes and stock. This occured at the time when it was important to cultivate the crops. Some time elapsed before the hands could be collected and they induced to recommence work. The consequence was, fully one half of the crops were not worked at all, and in other cases where some work was done, the weeds and plants had to grow up together, the ill weeds overtopping the cotton plant. The Army worm attacked all the late cotton destroying from one fourth to a third of the crop– Still under all these disadvantages, not one of the lessees will loose money, but all derive a profit. I know that they are satisifed with the experiment; all desire to release for another year. The negro lessees, of whom there are some fifteen will make from four and five bales, up to, in one case one hundred and fifty, and it is a fact, that the cotton they have raised for themselves, owing to better cultivation, is of a higher grade than that of the white lessees. Some of the negroes have cultivated by themselves and families, whilst others have employed their fellow freedmen.

The freedmen have all worked for wages, according to a scale fixed upon by the Board of Commissioners and at a higher rate, I understand, than was adopted in the Department of the Gulf.[1] They have been well and more abundantly fed, than they were when held in slavery. Schools have been established upon the plantations and the lessees have felt it a duty, by every proper means, to elevate this unfortunate race. As a general rule they greatly prefer working with nothern men, whom they regard as their friends, to working with Southerners, even their former owners, and I hazard nothing in saying that the net proceeds on a crop by a Northener, who has paid his hands wages, will exceed that of a Southerner, who has cultivated by slaves, the number of acres being the same in both cases. Those employed have thus been of no expense to the Government, but have supported themselves and families. They are perfectly contented and look forward with hope to a future elevation of character. The experiment adopted, hastily and from necessity, with many misgivings, I now regard as a complete success.

The number of bales of cotton raised on these plantations, will not much, if any, fall short of eight thousand bales, giving to the Government some one hundred and fifty thousand (150.000) dollars of revenue. The lessees will also pay to the Quartermaster's Department for mules, utensils &c furnished or found on the places, some one hundred thousand (100.000) dollars. The charge in lieu of rent is two dollars a bale, making sixteen thousand (16.000) dollars The Government share on some few plantations, abandoned by the lessees, may sell for one hundred and fifty thousand (150.000) dollars. I desire this money, or as much as may be necessary, set aside as a fund, necessary to pay the expenses of this year and of the year commencing January 1st 1864

I purpose to continue the same system for the next year, but of necessity on a much more enlarged scale, as our forces now cover and protect a much larger extent of country on the Mississipi

River. The parish of Concordia, La, alone will throw on our hands a large number of plantations on which the crops for the present year will have to be gathered, and then planted for the next year. Northern Union men will be invited to come here and engage in the work, until we make if possible the whole negro population self supporting.

The present Commissioners will continue to act until December 31st and lease the plantations for the next year, when they desire to withdraw to attend to their private business. For the next year the work will be very laborious and I desire three persons to take their places and I would suggest at salaries sufficiently large to secure active, upright business men. I would fix the salaries at five thousand (5.000) dollars per annum. A Secretary and Treasurer will also be necessary, who should give bonds for the faithful disbursment of the funds to be placed in his hands. His salary might be three thousand (3.000) dollars. I know of no persons for these positions, and, if you approve, I request that you appoint the new Commissioners and Treasurer. I can not too urgently press upon your attention the necessity of employing the very best men that can be found.

It is a significant fact that while Army posts on the river have been frequently fired into by the Rebels, not a single shot has been fired from that line of the river covered by leased plantations, extending for seventy five (75) miles above Vicksburg, which shows the importance to commerce of lining the river with a loyal population I have, Sir, the honor to be Very Respectfully Your Obedient Servant

HLS L. Thomas

Adjutant General L. Thomas to Honble. Edwin M. Stanton, 15 Oct. 1863, filed as A-615 1863, Letters Received, ser. 12, RG 94 [K-60]. On November 4, 1863, upon receiving the adjutant general's report, Secretary of War Edwin M. Stanton suggested to Thomas that involvement with the plantation-leasing system was distracting him from "the paramount object," the recruitment of black soldiers in the Mississippi Valley; and the following day, the War Department forwarded a copy of its General Order 331, issued October 9, which prepared the way for transferring the leasing system from military control to the Treasury Department by ordering that most abandoned plantations be placed under the supervision of treasury agents. (Asst. Adjt. Genl. E. D. Townsend to Brig. Genl. L. Thomas [two letters], 4 Nov. & 5 Nov. 1863, vol. 36, pp. 42–43, Letters Sent, ser. 1, RG 94 [K-60]; *Official Records*, ser. 3, vol. 3, p. 872.)

1 Plantation regulations in the Department of the Gulf, issued in February 1863, set minimum cash wages at $3 per month for artisans and drivers, $2

for male field hands, and $1 for female field hands, the employer to furnish clothing free of charge; alternatively, laborers might (with the consent of their employer) collectively receive one-twentieth of the proceeds of the crop, to be divided among them, in lieu of monthly wages. (See above, doc. 84.) Minimum wages for laborers on leased plantations in the Department of the Tennessee were $7 per month for men and $5 for women, minus the cost of clothing supplied by the employer. (See above, doc. 162.)

181: Commander of the District of Northeastern Louisiana to a New York Abolitionist

Goodrichs Landing [*La.*] Oct. 21, 1863.

Sir, Allow me to introduce myself. I graduated at West Point in 1852 and since that time have been an officer in the U.S, Army. Last April I was appointed Brig. Genl of Vols and assigned to duty in command of a Brigade of Colored troops, I went into the business of organizing them looking on the negro as so much bone and muscle out of which to make a soldier, in my intercourse with him I find he has a great deal of human nature in him, pretty much as is found in a white man, whether good or bad his virtues or vices affect him pretty much as they do the white man, He is now uneducated and degraded, or rather depressed, something should be done to give him a chance and elevate him, Mr Lincoln's Proclamation makes him free in name, his surroundings should be such as to make him so in reality, For years I have heard of you as an Abolitionist, read some of your speeches made at Abolition Meetings As far as speeches go every thing has been accomplished in that direction that they can influence, Negro freedom has been declared and those who once spoke for him should now work for him otherwise their labor will all have been in vain. The success and progress of our Army has released the negro from his master and in the majority of cases driven away the owners of Plantations, the Negroes and plantations remained, the question was what to do with both, In the latter part of last March the matter was taken hold of by the War Dept. and through the Agency of Agt. Genl. Thomas the lands (some of them) were leased to Northern men for one years cultivation the Negroes were placed on the plantations and hired at the rate of Seven dollars per month for men and five dollars for women, The time is counted, twenty six working days to the month and every day deducted that the negro does not work either on account of sickness or weather So that instead of working by the month he is working by the day for the merest pittance, All the bargain is on the side of the white man and at the end of the year the Negro has less money than was usual with him when a slave, and has the consolation of knowing he has been worse fed and worse treated, the only difference perhaps in his favor being that he has not been flogged, though killing may be resorted to as usual The other day a Negro being killed (shot) by the Overseer on a plantation near here, The man is now being tried by a Military Commission by my order; I want to see how many good people there are who are willing to *do* something for the negro, I believe you are reputed rich and I have seen statements of your generosity for humane purposes, I do not want one cent from you in this way, You might give all you are worth and the result in the amelioration of the negro not be noticeable. This would be only tampering with the evil not eradicating it, all evils have a root the only cure is to extirpate it, The evil here is this, Last Spring Genl Thomas appointed three Commissioners to lease the abandoned plantations, The season was far advanced and every thing had to be done in a hurry, Several large plantations were in many cases leased to one man the lessees generally were adventurers hangers-on of the Army and the like men who cared nothing how much flesh they worked off of the negro provided it was converted into good cotton at Seventy five cents per pound, The negro was hired to him and the contract mentioned some unimportant matters that were very seldom lived up to, about quantity of food and supply of medicines in case of sickness, Something was also talked of as to schools for the children, but cotton has been the main thing, the Negro is only a nigger, In the programme last spring it would have been difficult to arrange matters well, but in the coming season there is time to think and consider the *best* policy to pursue, There are now three Commissioners, Mr Dent, Mr Montague and Mr Field, the two former are lessees of several large plantations, the latter has relatives who are lessees and next year he intends going into it largely himself, The Adventurer, the Gambler and the Projector have control over the interests of thousands of helpless human beings and every one of them interested in making rules and decisions against their interests, Cotton closes their eyes to justice just as it did in the case of the former slave masters, I want men in authority here who care at least as much for the negro as for cotton, To get justice done the negro we must have a large white population here or lease to him the lands, genrally he has not the capital for farming, to get the large population the lands should be divided into small tracts say from eighty to two hundred acres and the farmers of the north be invited to come down here and cultivate them, Eighty and two hundred acres represent eighty and two hundred bales of cotton, worth *at least* Sixteen and forty thousand dollars The northern farmer by coming down here and cultivating only for one season could return home with more money than he ever dreamed of possessing, the title to the land need not be a consideration with him, no more than was that of the gold mines of California to the miner who worked them – when he dug his gold he could leave, I lived at Fort Kearney N[*evada*]. T[*erritory*]. during the California and Pikes Peak emigration and saw the great number of our Western men who went to those countries, encountering great dangers and hardships, and with less favorable chances of success than is in coming here, If a proper plan could be adopted – the same class of people would leave their farms and flock here by the thousands There is a greater gold mine here than was ever known in California or Pikes Peak and accessible by stamboat and rail road from all parts of the Northern States, The lands to be occupied are all along the Miss. River from Memphis to New Orleans, up the White and Arkansas Rivers and probably Red River, All these small tracts can be settled and the population would be great enough to form a militia sufficient for their own protection, they would at least do a great deal towards it, Gov,ment would furnish what else was needed, The ownership of the soil here will change during and after the war, Slavery will be done away with, and the labor education of the slave holder will prove of no use to him, free labor will be an annoyance to him and if he can sell his lands and get rid of the trouble he will do it, If these lands can now be divided those who cultivate them next year will in the majority of cases be the purchasers, Which is best for our country, that the lands shall be held in small farms or in immense tracts by leasing in small tracts we render probable the former, by leasing in large tracts we insure the latter, We have just subverted one negro-landed Aristocracy, if we can avoid it let us not establish another in its place, The people have fought this war and should derive whatever benefits may accrue from it, not the Speculators and contractors and hangers on of the Army and those in league with them, Next Feby the leases expire, new leases will then be made, the Commissioners in fact are making them now. the other day a man passed up the river having just procured a lease of 3200 acres enough for thirty men of reasonable ambition, to-day I hear of a Qr masters Clerk, a person of no capital, leasing four or five large plantations, I cite these as showing the style in which the business is being done, a few more leases will probably be given out and then perhaps the three Commissioners will vote to each other a division of the remainder as the three Roman Triumvirs divided the Roman Territory among them, A few land holders will constitute a monopoly that will control negro labor, and treat it as they please, as they now do, I want a large population so that labor will be respected, will be in the market and be paid according to the demand for it, There must be no rule contracting the labor of the negro for one year or one month, it is strength contracting with weakness and results in oppression the labor of the negro must be as free as the labor of the northern white man, There must be freedom for the employer to discharge at any time and freedom for the negro to leave at any time– this relation between them will make each respect the rights of the other– In fact I want no laws for the negro as if he were a child and had to be taught every thing for under this guise of protection we rob him of every right, I never saw people more willing to work and do what is right, and like a white man they know when they are justly or unjustly treated, they are generally in low spirits as to their future and something should be done for them soon, give them enough employers or send for their former masters and tell each one to claim his slaves, his treatment of them was parental compared to what we now permit, I will except those who are soldiers, those are cheerful and sprightly because their Officers bound by regulations and law, treat them well and as men all the rest have a vagabondish look because treated as niggers, The gist of my letter is, Abolish the Commissioners, annul their acts, get a large loyal population south and make the labor of the negro so much in demand that he will be treated as a human being Respectfully

John P. Hawkins

[*In the margin*] I wish no publication of this neither as a whole nor extracts

[*In the margin*] For knowledge of myself I refer you to Genl. Canby. Comdg New York Surgn Chas M^c^Dougall Broome St N,Y, Dr Godfrey Aigner no 96 Franklin St NY or City Dispensary

[*In the margin*] I would like Robert Dale Owen & Mr How Commissioners to investigate the condition of freedmen to see this letter, they are in New York Schools to educate them are also wanted, they are anxious to be taught a small tax on lessees would support them,

ALS

Brig. Genl. John P. Hawkins to Hon. Gerritt Smith, 21 Oct. 1863, filed with O-328 1863, Letters Received, ser. 12, RG 94 [K-88]. Gerrit Smith, to whom the letter was addressed, evidently honored General Hawkins's request that it be shown to Robert Dale Owen and Samuel Gridley Howe, members of the American Freedmen's Inquiry Commission; it is filed among the Mississippi Valley records of the commission. Topical labels in the margin are omitted.

182: Commander of the Mississippi Squadron to the Adjutant General of the Army, Enclosing a Letter from a Mississippi Freedman to His Son

Flg Ship "Black Hawk" Cairo [*Ill.*]– Octo. 21st 1863

Dear General I have just received your communication respecting freed Negroes, and their capabilities for maintaining themselves. I have scarcely ever yet met with a Negro who has not been able to support himself, they are naturally astute at making money, and when they are not it is an exception to the rule. The character of the Negroe depends very much on the Plantation from which he had been taken, On some Plantations it has seemed to be the policy of the owners to keep the Negroes in ignorance, and to treat them like brutes, while in the majority of cases, they seem to have been well taken care of, and have had some degree of education, – Many of them have been allowed to trade and resere their profits to themselves, and they all have money, more or less, when they come to us. Quite a number of them have good trades, and we have now in the fleet Contrabands who are considered our best mechanics. (All our fireman and coal heaver's are Negroes – they soon learn the business, and are rated and receive pay accordingly. We have now about 814 contrabands performing the duty of coal heavers and fireman, and we have altogether (counting officer's servants, cooks &c.) 1049).

The Servants are all inteligent, and could make more money out of the service than in it. It must be reccollected however that we generally select the best men for the Navy, and regect those who are physically unable to perform duty. The latter are however properly provided for. There is a great demand somewhere for Negro labor, for we find them constantly deserting, notwithstanding the good pay they receive, and the good treatment, so different to what they have been accustomed to. I think the natural disposition of the Negro is to run away, and be idle; they have been dreaming of freedom all their lives, and their idea of freedom is to have nothing to do. They are the most docile race I ever saw, and with fewer vices considering the training they have had. When they have been partially, or well educated, they seem to be perfectly correct, and ambitious to do something for themselves. The Plantations of Joseph, and Jefferson Davis, at Palmyra, offer a strong contrast to many on the River. The Negroes seem more inteligent than those I have seen elsewhere, and many of them are very well educated I found some with quite a mechanial genius. The people on those two plantations are now maintaining themselves, under the charge of a Gunboat. After our army got to the rear of Vicksburg the Negroes belonging to Joseph and Jefferson Davis escaped from the place where they had been located back of Vicksburg, and succeeded in getting back to the old place where they claimed our protection.

Many of them enlisted in the Gunboat service but the majority concluded it was best to stay on the Plantation, and go to work for themselves The officer in command of the Gunboats drew up rules and regulations for them, and gave an old Patriarch Negro charge of the party. There has been no trouble amongst them whatever, and they have all been set to cutting wood for the use of the Steamers on the River, and the Gunboat people see that they are not defrauded. We have driven a lot of cattle out of the Plantation, which the Negroes guard, and we allow them a fair proportion for themselves. Thus they maintain themselves, for I forbade the commander giving them any food, while there was any to be obtained elsewhere. In the Spring they will all go to work planting cotton on their own account, and you will find that they will raise more than they ever did before. I have talked to a great many Planters about allowing their Negroes a certain per centage on all they raised instead of paying them regular wages, and I am sure that they would under that system, realize more than they ever did before.

The System of leasing out Plantations is a bad one. No one can tell except those who have seen it, what evils it has led to. It has benefitted no one, and has been the means of having many of the Plantations destroyed. The people who enter into the business are greedy adventurers, who have no interest beyond getting one crop, which if a large one enriches them. They treat the Negroes brutally, and chastise them worse than their former masters did. They enter into an agreement with the former owner to go shares, and work the property togeather, the intruder agreeing to give the owner the Government protection. In a short time the former takes chief control and elbows the owner out, who generally join a Guerrilla band, come back and burn the Plantation kill half the Negroes and carries of the rest in irons to Texas. This is a fair history of more than half of these transactions. The banks of the Mississippi have been made scenes of ruin and desolation owing to the Plantation system. The worst of it is they are known as Government Plantations, when the Government in fact have nothing to do with them, and derive not the least benefit from them. The Rebels will continue to drive off the Negroes whenever they can, and no Plantation will ever be worked successfully except by the former Master, who should be encouraged to stay on his farm

There is no doubt in my mind but that nine out of ten are Rebels in their hearts, but still interest is stronger with them than patriotism. They have tried their remedy out of the Union, and they would be too happy to get back again on any terms. Let them have the old men, women and children, who will make more money for them at a proper rate of compensation than all their laborers ever made before. Then take the able bodied Negro and make him guard the Forts. I think I could take a regiment of them and make them stand up against any Rebel Regiment in the South, flattering myself that they would go through a better system of drill and discipline than I have yet seen adopted amongst them. My opinion, however, is not asked in this matter, and I am wandering from the subject

Besides the 1000 men we now have employed many have deserted and are getting employment elsewhere.

I have sent up River about five hundred women and children, and I believe they are all employed and maintaining themselves. The women all sew and wash well, and in a short time after getting to Cairo set up on their own account. I know that of all those who have been brought up by us, and allowed to go on shore, none ever come back for assistance. They get a piece of land, and go to work building houses. The plan of putting the Negroes together in large crowded camps is a bad one, it engenders disease. vice and profligacy of all kinds, and demoralizes the white Soldier who guards them and he sinks to their level in a very short time. The Negroes had better be allowed to go back to their Plantations if they wish it, and seek a maintainance there; many of them go back when they can do so.

I enclose a letter written by one of my "Protege's", he was a man belonging to Joseph Davis and is as well educated as most white people and as sensible a man as I ever met with. He is also an ingenious mechanic – his family are all well educated, they are now in Cincinnati and doing well. I think they were attached to M[r] Davis, who was a kind master, and there slavery, was only nominal Still they prefer freedom, and I dont see how so inteligent a man could have consented to remain so long a Slave. I have already extended this letter beyond reasonable bounds, and could have given the statistices you asked for on one page – Still I never like to do anything by halves. I could write a large book on what I have seen of the Negro. With my best respects, I remain, General Yours Very Truly & Respy,

David D Porter

I omitted to mention that the pay of the negroes in this Squadron, ranges from ten to twenty five dollars per month.

HLS

[*Enclosure*] Cincinnati [*Ohio*] Oct 14th 1863

My Dear son: Your letter of 9th inst came to hand yesterday I am sorry to hear of your indisposition your mother with myself feel much concern about your health and as you have had such frequent attacks hope you may get leave to visit us if only until you recover your health, I think you would be benefited by coming to see us. Should you be able to come you will on arriving call at Mrs Capt Richardson's N° 284 and Sis will accompany you to where we live. My respects to the Admiral.

I suppose you are pretty fully posted in the news of the day which is quite favorable politically.

Write as soon as you can that we may know how you are.

Your mother & Beck join in love to you. Your father

Ben Montgomery

Direct 915 Central Avenue as before

ALS

Rear Ad. David D. Porter to General Lorenzo Thomas, 21 Oct. 1863, enclosing Ben Montgomery to My Dear son, 14 Oct. 1863, P-17 1863, Letters Received by Adjutant General L. Thomas, ser. 363, Colored Troops Division, RG 94 [V-67]. On October 8, Adjutant General Lorenzo Thomas, who was at Goodrich's Landing, Louisiana, "collecting statistics respecting the freed negroes for the purpose of making a report to the Secretary of War," had asked Admiral Porter for information regarding former slaves employed by the Mississippi Squadron. (Adjt. Genl. L. Thomas to Admiral D. D. Porter, 8 Oct. 1863, Mississippi Squadron, Letters from Officers Commanding Squadrons, RG 45 [T-827].)

183: Testimony by a Former Resident of Mississippi before the American Freedmen's Inquiry Commission

Louisville, Ky., Nov. 19, 1863

Testimony of Sam'l B. Smith, Esq.

I lived two years on a large cotton plantation near Natchez, Miss., and have had a good opportinity to see slavery in all its phases My interests were all there; the friends of my early manhood were there, and I could have succeeded better in my profession there than anywhere else; but I saw enough of niggerdom when I was down there to satisfy me.

Q. Have you seen any thing in the habits of the slaves to prepare them to take care of themselves; to look after their property, &c.?

A. Yes, Sir. The negroes there are a better class than those in other parts of the South. On the plantation where I was, there were 400 negroes. The plough gang, as we called them, consisted of about seventy-five, and I think I can say without hesitancy, that there was not a man among them who was not perfectly capable of taking care of himself. They were thrifty, intelligent men. There are two classes of remuneration allowed the slaves of the South, according to the peculiar views of the planter. On the large number of lesser plantations, the privilege of the negro is to have his corn patch, or his cotton patch, or his tobacco patch, independent of the master, and he raises his crop at night, after he has done his day's work, or on Sundays. That is the usual way, on the small plantations of giving something to the negro. On the smaller plantations, the negro always owns something. On the larger plantations, it is not so. On the plantation where I was, the negro had a task to perform, and after that, he received so much pay, either for overwork in picking cotton, or ploughing. That was his property. He used it in any way he pleased. He sent commissions to buy goods at Nashville, or bought of the traders, or of the other negroes. I never saw a plantation where this was not permitted to a certain extent. The negroes living on the river had better opportunities to trade, and were better able to take care of themselves, than those in the interior, because they had had more experience in trading.

Q. Do you look upon that experience as of any value in fitting them to become self-supporting

A. I think so. They all knew the value of money. They knew very well what things were worth, and could calculate. There were scarcely any of them that could not. They could cipher, and Keep complicated accounts. For instance, they would keep in their heads the amount to which they were entitled for their labor, so that they would know, at the end of the week, whether they received enough. The cotton is weighed out each day, and they have to remember, at the end of each day, what they have done over, so as to know, at the end of the week, what they are to receive.

Q. Are there any habits which would lead them to be forecasting – to provide for the next season or the next year?

A. Not to any extent.

Q. How is it with regard to their houses? Are they responsible for keeping them in order?

A On the smaller plantations, they are; on the larger, they are under the penitentiary system, or rather, the barrack system. On the large plantations, the negro quarters are in a square, surrounded by a high fence, with the houses, without any windows, opening on the outside, and then a picket fence between the houses, and four gates. I was there ten or eleven years ago, and since that time, slavery has become a great deal more violent, so to speak. A great many more privileges were allowed to the negroes than are now allowed them. The tendency even then was to use them with more violence.

Q Was that in consequence of the growth of great plantations?

A Decidedly. The man I lived with – to show you who he was and what he was – was the candidate on the Coöperation ticket in Adams Co., Miss., and was elected by an overwhelming majority, and was the only member of the Convention that refused to sign the Ordinance of Secession. The supporters of the Cooperation ticket at the South were those who advocated having the whole South go out together. It was a conservative movement to prevent going out at all My friend was a good Union man, a good Clay Whig, and an Emancipationist. I saw the operation of tightening the reins while I was out there, and we had very frequent conversations about it. His idea was, that it was a necessary consequence of the institution. For instance, although he was as kind a man as ever lived in the world, he kept his bloodhounds, as a matter of humanity. Of course, the slaves are kept there by force, exactly as you would keep a conquered country by military force, and it is better for them to keep down insurrections. So the slaveholders keep these dogs to prevent their slaves from running away, and so prevent suffering. The more facilities they had for overtaking them, the less danger there was of their running away.

The whole tendency at the South for years has been to increase the larger plantations. The man of immense wealth was buying up the little plantations and concentrating the negroes. The tendency was, as I told you, to take away the capacity of the negroes to take care of themselves.

Q. On these smaller plantations, where they lived in separate houses, did the care & management of the houses devolve upon the negroes?

A. Entirely; and so it was on the larger ones, but it was under the supervision of the overseer. He always used to visit the houses, and often at night, and was obliged to do it, in order to keep any degree of virtue. There being no relation of husband and wife, in order to prevent universal concubinage, they had to visit those families that were kept in houses.

Q Why did they want to prevent it?

A The reason was, that if they did not prevent it, the slave women would have no children. To show you the difference, the plantation I was on was changed from a small to a large one, by the purchase of a large number of negroes by my friend, who was obliged to buy them in order to secure a debt. Among those negroes, the average births had been a very small per cent., because the owner had permitted a universal concubinage; but this young man, knowing how the thing worked, and being compelled to make some new regulations, put them into families; and I think the increase was more than 150 per cent. more than it had been for four or five years previous. Among well-organized plantations, the family relationship is kept up with great care, both as a matter of prudence for the master and of kindly feeling to the slaves. A large family has a house to itself.

Q Now, on the small plantations, where the negro had his house by himself, was it his lookout, for instance, to see that the house was made tight for the next winter?

A Oh, yes, it was his business, but it was mighty little taken care of. On the larger plantations, that was a part of the regular business of the master or the overseer, and those houses were much better kept. The tendency was to adopt the barrack system where I was. But that is not at all true with regard to the plantations on the upper Mississippi. There, very few introduced the barrack system. It was introduced on the lower Mississippi from Louisiana, and was brought there from Cuba. Dr Duncan, who was a true-hearted Union man, and one of the wealthiest men in Natchez, never adopted it. I should say his negroes were abundantly able to take care of themselves. He had six plantations, side by side, the houses in a row instead of in a square, and he was very careful in keeping up the family intercourse. I have understood that both Dr. Duncan and Dr. Mercer (who is also one of the richest men in the South) are now hiring their negroes.

Q Should you have any apprehension in throwing these people upon their own resources, simply giving them protection?

A Not the slightest. I think if the planter can be induced to stay at home and hire his own negroes, that they can be organized at once, under their lead, to the profit of both the negro and the master.

Q That is, without any Government interference?

A Not at all. All they want is the protection of the Government, to prevent their being run off. That is the great danger. When the planter is satisfied it is for his interest to hire his laborers, then of course they will not be run off, because the thing is settled. But you know the great difficulty at the South has been, that the use of free labor would not be tolerated for a moment. That prejudice has got to be taken away altogether Now, one of the most successful men we have here – Mr. W. P. Hahn – who is in Government employ, building the hospitals at Baton Rouge and New Orleans, was giving his experience in the use of labor, (and he is one of the most practical men I have ever seen, & the most sensible,) and he said that cotton at the South could be raised with the largest amount of profit by free labor; that he was satisfied of that when he was at the South, and made preparations to hire several plantations, for the purpose of trying the experiment of free labor; but the moment it was noised about among the planters, he was called upon and told that that wouldn't do; that free labor or hired labor should never be used, and he had to give it up. That they considered necessary for the security of their institutions. He says, if he was a few years younger, he would go down there now, and get the Gov't to grant him land, and he wouldn't thank any man to give him a million of dollars for his profits in ten years.

I have always taken very great interest in the black men, and my intercourse with them on the plantation was very free. I knew them intimately, and talked with them freely. The gentleman I lived with was a very sensible man, and we never hesitated to talk with perfect freedom. He was in favor of emancipation and said, "I would give up my negroes [and his property was worth a million of dollars][1] if I could find some way of getting rid of them." Mr Hahn believes that white labor is just as practicable as black, and says that an Irish laborer could carry his hod to the top of a four story building in the middle of August just as well as a black man, and could withstand the miasma there, too. In fact, on the New Orleans and Lake Ponchetrain Railroad, which runs through a swamp, where they were obliged to drive piles 15 or 16 feet, in order to get a foundation, they gave up their slave labor, after spending hundreds of thousands of dollars, and employed white men, selling their slaves, whose constitutions had been broken down, at a great sacrifice.

Q What is your opinion of the comparative virility of the blacks and mulattoes?

A. I think the blacks are much superior. The mulattoes cease almost altogether to produce in the third generation. I think the cross between a yellow woman and a white man is better than the cross with a black man. It is very difficult to form an opinion, because it is very seldom they go back. You scarcely ever see a cross between a full-blooded negro and a yellow woman; it is more uncommon than the cross between a white woman and a black man – because that is not uncommon. I knew well a ferryman on the Wachita river, whose mother was a white woman and his father a black man. He was a free voter, but it was notorious in the neighborhood that he was a half-blooded negro. I knew a gentleman who was very respectable, and who was admitted into society, whose half sisters – half a dozen of them – were negroes. I knew a number of cases in the vicinity of Natchez where that intercourse was kept up; and if it was so there, what must it have been in the country? I believe the instances at the South where a yellow woman breeds with a full-blooded black man are fewer than where a black man has breeded on a white woman. It is true that owners and overseers cohabit with the negroes, but they always regret it. I never knew one who had done so who did not say that it was the misfortune of his life, especially in any civilized region; The negroes are blacker at the South & Southwest than here. The mulattoes are more intelligent, but less docile, and more apt to be ferocious than the blacks.

HD

Testimony of Sam'l B. Smith, Esq., before the American Freedmen's Inquiry Commission, 19 Nov. 1863, filed with O-328 1863, Letters Received, ser. 12, RG 94 [K-90]. Topical labels in the margin are omitted.

1 Brackets in manuscript.

184: Testimony by a Mississippi Freedman before the Southern Claims Commission

[*Adams County, Miss.*] 23[d] day of February 1878

Claim 19.537
William Hardin
vs.
The United States

Personally appeared before me Edward J Castello Special Commissioner William Hardin the claimant in the above claim who being duly Sworn by me deposes and answers as follows

Question What is your name, your age, your residence and how long has it been Such and your occupation

Answr My name is William Harden I am about forty years of age I live in Adams Conty State of Mississippi I have been living here about Sixteen years. I keep a wood yard in the neighbourhood of Natchez

Q Are you the claimant in the above claim

A I am nobody has any interest in the claim but myself

Q Were you a Slave or a Freeman during the war

A I was a Slave

Q To whom did you belong

A I belonged to Edward Hicks of Jefferson County in this State

Q When did you become free

A I left home before 1863 but returned to my master in 1863 I remained at home about two months then I came to Natchez I had been in the Pioneer Corps at Vicksburg for over two months left there and came to Natchez and enlisted in the 6th US

Heavy Artillery Company C and Served with the regiment until I was discharged in May 1866

Q Did you own this property you claim to have been taken from you before or after you became free

A I owned part of it before I actually became free

Q What portion did you own before you became free

A One Cow and Calf One yearlin calf

Q How did you keep the Stock you claim to have had before you were free

A It ran around on the place under the Care of my father

Q When did you come possessed of the other Stock you claim as having been taken from you

A My father had money of mine that I had Saved up while I was a Slave and after I came to Natchez and while I was a Soldier my father came to me and told me he could by a nice mare If I would agree to it I told him to by the mare and Send her to me by my brother which he did at the Same time my father and brother brought in The Horse, mare, mule, Cow Calf, an and yearling Calf all of which my father had bought with my money I had the Stock brought in to Natchez to keep it from falling into the hands of the Rebels My brother remaned in Natchez to take care of the Stock under my care

Q What became of the Stock after you brought it to Natchez

A I had the Stock taken to whare my wife lived opposite the Carrell in the City of Natchez and the Stock remained there from October 1863 until December of the Same year when it was taken by the Yankeys

Q What was taken and by whome was the property taken

A one Horse, one Chestnut mare, one Bay Mule, one Cow and Calf, one young heiffer, they were taken by the Yankey Soldiers and all the Stock was taken at the Same time and in daylight My brother was taking them to the river to watter them

Q Did you See the Stock you mention taken or were you present when it was taken

A I was not present I was on duty at the time they were taken

Q What became of the Stock after it was taken

A The Stock was taken to Headquarter Correll in the City of Natchez. I Saw the Horse, Mare and the Mule after they had been taken by the Yankeys I never Saw the Cow Calf or heiffer I Saw my Mule in the Post team often, The mare I saw in the possession of a Yankey officer he was riding her I dont know his name nor his rank The Horse I Saw often he was used in Company A the Company was mntd Infantry

Q How did you or whare did you get the means to pay for this property you claim to have been taken from you by the Yankeys

A My Master allowed me to work a Small piece of ground and I raised corn, vegeta[bl] Turkeys chickens and Geese and I brought all I raised to market and Sold it and the money was by me placed in the hands of my father for Safe keeping Some times my master would buy from me and pay for what he bought that was the way I made the money and my father bought the Stock with my money and with my consent

Q Is your master Still living

A I am almost posetive he is

Q Is he a witness for you and if not why not

A He is not a witness for me I dont know whether he would come, he lives so far off

Q Are you in his debt

A No Sir it ought to be the other way

Q Has any other person besides yourself any interest directly or indirectly in this claim

A No Sir not at all

Q How did you get your information in regard to the property that you claim was taken by the Federal Soldiers

A A Soldier named Johnston Called to me across the Street and Said an officer with a Squad of Soldiers have taken your Stock I was on duty and could not See any thing about the matter The next day I attempted to get to head quarters but had no pass, and could not get in I never got any vouchers or receipts for any of my Stock nor no pay. the only Satisfaction I ever got was about one week after my Stock was taken I Saw a Federal officer on my mare I Spoke to him about my mare, he Said you will be paid for your mare I am in a hurry and he rode way thats about all I have to Say or know about the matter

his
William X Hardin
mark

HDSr

Testimony of William Hardin, 23 Feb. 1878, claim of William Hardin, Adams Co. MS case files, Approved Claims, ser. 732, Southern Claims Commission, 3rd Auditor, RG 217 [I-187]. According to other documents in the same file, Hardin had submitted a claim for $570 as compensation for the livestock taken by Union soldiers. He was awarded $330.

185: Secretary of the Treasury to the Supervising Agent of the Treasury Department 1st Special Agency, Enclosing a Report from a War Department Special Inspector to the Adjutant General's Office

Treasury Department [*Washington*]. December 17th, *1863*.

Sir, I transmit a letter from General Wadsworth, together with a copy of his Report to the War Department on leased plantations. You have already had some conversation with him and with myself on the subject. The Secretary of War has as yet arrived at no definite conclusion in respect to the permanent policy to be adopted. In the meantime his order, committing the charge of abandoned plantations to the Supervising Special Agents, stands.[1] I am clearly of opinion that you should immediately proceed to lease these plantations substantially in accordance with the plan partially [executed] under the arrangements of General Thomas. You can designate Mr. Field as an Assistant Special Agent under you, and if you think proper others also, and provide them with the necessary clerical aid. I agree fully with the views expressed by General Wadsworth in his Report, and you will see the importance of prompt action. Mr. Field I think deserves great credit for his consideration of the colored people & for leasing, when he could, to them directly. They should all be got out of the camps and restored to their accustomed employments under the free labor system with as little delay as possible. As the season is advancing, please act promptly. Yours very truly,

HLS S: P: Chase

[*Enclosure*] Washington D.C. December 16th 1863

Sir I have the honor to report that, after addressing the Department from Cairo on the 19th of October last, I proceeded down the Mississippi River– On the 30th of October I reported to Adjutant General L. Thomas at Natchez Mississippi, returned with him up the River to Vicksburg & Goodrich's Landing & thence proceeded with him down the River to New Orleans, from New Orleans westwardly to Brashea City & Southerly along the banks of the River some fifty or Seventy five miles.

That I visited in the Mississippi Valley all Military Posts & other places where Colored Troops were stationed & had been, were being or might be raised, all camps or collections of colored Refugees & many Plantations on which they were employed. making the inspections required by my orders.[2]

. . . .

In compliance with that portion of my Orders requiring me to inspect all Camps, Plantations & other places where Colored Refugees are Collected or where there may be a Colored population, I have the honor to report furthur, that there are still remaining in the camps or Depots at the several military Posts on the River about twelve thousand Colored Refugees. It is among these people that nearly all the suffering & mortality incident to this great social change has existed & is still to be found.

While every effort has been made by the military Authorities & by Philanthropists to ameliorate the condition of the thousands of Freedmen who have flocked to our military Posts for protection, it is not to be denied that they are still subject in these Depots to great suffering, from the want of adequate shelter, medical attendance & the proper distribution of food & clothing, A large mortality has been the result. These evils will continue until the people thus gathered together can be removed on to Plantations where they will find comfortable houses, gardens & Employment. There are abandoned Plantations, with empty houses, adequate to the employment & shelter of these & even a much greater number. All that is wanting for their relief is Lessees to carry on the work.

Much of the mortality & suffering which has existed, resulted from the heartless course pursued by the large Slave holders in the region referred to. Taking their able-bodied & most valuable negroes, they fled to Georgia & Alabama on the one hand & to Texas on the other, leaving on the Plantations the women, children, aged & infirm without food, clothing or other supplies. Thus left exposed to the depredations of Guerrillas & other wandering outcasts, these unfortunate people had no alternative but to seek protection at the nearest Union Military Post. But what could be done for them here. Military Commandants had the utmost difficulty in getting supplies for their own troops, & especially for the sick & wounded. They had little time & small means to apply to the relief of these unfortunate Refugees. They gathered together in Camps without shelter & with little food & contracted there the diseases which have been the fruitful source of the mortality referred to. From these Camps, as far as possible, they have been removed to Plantations. The same evils, to some extent, followed them here, owing to the difficulty of procuring an adequate supply of food, clothing, medicines & medical attendance. These evils are only just now begining to be effectually removed & we have every reason to hope that the worst is over.

To charge, the evils which result from this great Social change, to the friends of the Union & of freedom, is not less preposterous & unjust, than it is to charge upon the brave men who have left their families & their homes, to uphold the national Flag, & the integrity of the Country, the blood & devastation of War.

In the midst of War, of marches, sieges & Battles, seldom surpassed in extent & in havoc, these unfortunate people were driven to us for protection & support. As our own Soldiers suffered from exposure, hunger & thirst, they suffered & as we hope to reap our reward by upholding our Government, they will receive theirs in the achievment of their freedom, without which life is of little worth, even to them.

Made helpless, ignorant & degraded by all the Arts of a base & cruel tyranny, they have still intelligence enough to see that those who would relieve their present sufferings by restoring them to a relentless bondage are not their friends but their enemies, as they are the enemies of all that is noble in the nature of man.

The System of leasing Abandoned Plantations & those of persons in open rebellion against the United States to loyal & trustworthy men is demonstrated by experience to be most condusive to the welfare of the Freedmen. It is of the highest importance that these Plantations should be occupied as fast as they are brought within our military Lines & freed from the inroads of the enemy.

The ability, sound discretion & integrity with which Adjutant General Thomas has discharged the important duties intrusted to him entitle him to the cordial gratitude of every patriot & friend of humanity, and it would, in my judgment, be a great calamity to interrupt the System of leasing Plantations inaugurated by him & carried out by the Commissioners Messrs. Field, Dent & Montague. Experience will doubtless suggest many alterations & improvements in this system. It will be recollected that it was commenced with little time for reflection, in the midst of active military operations, when no portion of the Country was entirely free from the danger of inroads by the enemy & when the large influx & destitute condition of the freed population made it indespensible that something should be done forthwith for their relief.

The means of the Lessees were limited & they have not been able to pay their laborers, their wages regularly. Men of large Capital were unwilling to embark in an enterprise so new & deemed so hazardous. Several of the leased Plantations were overrun by the enemy in the midst of the Season for cultivating the Crops. In spite of all these very serious draw backs, the System has been practically successful. The freed people are contented & willing & anxious to continue to labor for their support. They are recovering in health, from the effects of the great exposure & privations through which they have passed. The lessees have in almost every case been fairly remunerated & many have made large profits. They, with scarcely an exception, wish to renew their Leases & continue the enterprise. As they derive means from the sale of their Crops, they are paying the arrears of wages to their laborers, and laying in ample supplies of clothing, medicines & such comforts & humble luxuries as will stimulate the industry of the freed people.

As this System becomes more fully developed, the means of the Lessees enlarged, the Country more perfectly protected from the inroads of the enemy, the pressing need of relieving the Depots at Military Posts, of unemployed & destitute people flocking to them accomplished, many & important modifications should be introduced. The Lessees should be bound to provide medical attendance for the sick. Wages should be paid monthly, except a small reservation to protect the Lessee against the failure of the laborer to continue at work during the harvest season. Schools should be established by Lessees, prvision made for religious instruction & reading matter, for those able to read, should be placed within their reach. With more perfect protection from the enemy the Lessee should pay a larger rent, thus providing a fund to extend the System & support those not employed.

Several Plantations & parts of Plantations have been leased by Colored Lessees, who have been previously slaves, employed by their masters as Overseers or Drivers. Mr. Field, one of the Commissioners for leasing Plantations had favored this plan & generously aided the Lessees with means to commence their operations. I found that the lands thus leased had been as well worked & that the laborers were as well cared for & as contented as on any Plantation leased by white men. I trust that this policy will be continued.

It is by many deemed probable that a considerable portion of the African population of the South will eventually become Peasant Cultivators, that is, Cultivators of small holdings of from ten to fifty acres. The Cotton culture is admirably adapted to this system of labor. With ten or twenty acres, a family can raise all their own food & several bales of Cotton, selling it, in the seed, to Capitalists who with Gins & Presses prepare it for market. The feasibility of this plan has been, to a certain degree, demonstrated in Texas & East Tennessee. I respectfully recommend that this System be inaugurated to a moderate extent.

The Order issued by Adjutant General Thomas to place Arms & ammunition on every leased Plantation will have a most salutary effect in protecting them from the attacks of lawless Guerrillas, as well as in infusing into the freed people a manly self dependence for the maintenance of their rights.

To educate the children, & place arms in the hands of the Adults will be found the most efficient means of elevating a Race discouraged & debased by Centuries of cruel subjugation.

I can not deem it necessary to enter into an elaborate argument against the plan of conducting these abandoned Plantations by Government Agents & at Government Cost. It may have been sometimes expedient as a means of giving immediate employment & support to a destitute population, & under the extraordinarily high prices of Cotton & Sugar, may have been temporarily successful, but it is based on a vicious principle & cannot permanently succeed.

The policy of the Government as I understand it is to establish in the rebellious Districts & especially to line the banks of the Mississippi with a loyal population, one which recognizes the right as well as the efficacy of the Emancipation Proclamation, which receives it as a finality, which will inaugurate at once the regeneration of the African Race, restore the productiveness of the Country, make the people of the South homogeneous with those of the North, and give to the nation a Peace which will be lasting, because honorable & based upon Justice & wisdom.

The patience with which these unfortunate people bear their privations & their eagerness to find employment is highly commendable.

From Northern men or from thoroughly loyal Southern men I have heard no complaints that the Colored Refugees are not willing to work for wages.

Amidst many discouragements & disappointments as to the payment of their wages, much suffering & want from the inability to get medical supplies, clothing, & sometimes, even food, they have continued faithful at their toil until the Crop was made & the means of payment secured. But while they have thus cheerfully & confidingly labored for those they believed to be their friends, they have instinctively discovered that no small portion of their old Masters had not accepted the Proclamation as a finality & entertained a lingering hope that they would be able to restore the old system if not in form, in substance. To encourage such hopes would inflict the greatest possible injury upon both the white & black Races of the South.

The remotest prospect of freedom unfits the Black for Slavery. All the disorganization which can result from this great social change has already accrued. The improvement in the condition of the Black will begin when he is assured of his freedom, when he sees that his support & comfort depend upon his own industry & that he is respected & confided in as far as his conduct may seem to merit. The prosperity of his Employer must likewise depend upon the quiet & industry of the laborers. So long as he occupies the ambiguous position of paying wages to his laborers, but not fully recognizing the completeness of their freedom, he must suffer all the, to him, great annoyances & vexations of a change from the old system without reaping any of the benefits which history throughout the world has accorded to freedom.

Within a few months a Vast Army of Colored Soldiers will be organized & drilled under gallant & accomplished Officers. It can not be believed that these men will voluntarily lay down their arms & return to slavery, or allow their wives & children to be held in bondage.

This Government can not recede from the step which it has taken. To attempt to do so would be an act of infamy unparalleled in history. Barbaric nations have in all time captured & sold into Slavery their enemies but I know of no instance in which any people, however degraded, has purchased an ignominious Peace by selling into bondage its own Soldiers & friends.

It will naturally be asked, when can the production of Cotton be restored to the point it had reached under the old System. The answer must depend in a large degree upon the temper & disposition of the white population of the Cotton Region. If it adopts the new System in good faith & sets to work, with ordinary energy & industry to repair the devastations of war, I think it may be expected with great confidence that the production will overtake its former maximum in from three to five years. But if the whites cling to the idea that they can reestablish Slavery & throw impediments in the way of the new System, this result will be considerably retarded. It will nevertheless be attained.

The great profit of this culture, the general healthfulness of the country, the light & attractive character of the labor, suited eminently to women & children will soon draw a new population to the Cotton region. Lands will change hands, free labor will develope its matchless power & we shall only have to add a few years to the period I have named, to witness an extent of cultivation & production which never could have been attained under the old System. I am Sir Very Respectfully Your Obedient Servant

HLcS Ja[s] S. Wadsworth

S. P. Chase to Wm. P. Mellen, Esquire, 17 Dec. 1863, enclosing excerpts from Brig. Genl. Jas. S. Wadsworth to the Adjutant General U.S. Army, 16 Dec. 1863, Letters Received from the Secretary of the Treasury, Records of the General Agent, RG 366 [Q-142]. The letter from General Wadsworth, said to have been enclosed along with his report, is not in the file. The omitted portion of the report discussed the recruitment, military service, and pay of black troops in the Mississippi Valley. For a more candid assessment of the plantation-leasing system, in which Wadsworth confessed that his report to the Adjutant General's Office had been in part an apology for it, see above, doc. 107.

1 War Department General Order 331, issued October 9, 1863, had directed Union army officers to turn over to the supervising agents of the Treasury Department's special agencies all captured and abandoned "houses, tenements, lands, and plantations," except those required for military purposes. (*Official Records*, ser. 3, vol. 3, p. 872.)
2 On October 9, 1863, the War Department had ordered General James S. Wadsworth to inspect black troops in the Mississippi Valley, to examine conditions among "the women, children, infirm, and sick of the colored people," and to recommend measures for "the protection, maintenance, employment, and comfort of the colored population not organized into troops." (*Official Records*, ser. 3, vol. 3, pp. 872–73.)

186: Secretary of the Treasury to the Supervising Agent of the Treasury Department 1st Special Agency

Treasury Department [*Washington*]. December 27th, *1863*
Sir, Some days since I advised you, in executing the Order of the Secretary of War touching abandoned houses and plantations,[1] to follow, in the main, the System which had been adopted by Gen. Thomas.

Since then I have received important information concerning the practical operation of that System, and the condition of plantations and of the freedmen. Much of it from Mr. Yeatman of St. Louis.[2]

I am informed that two at least of the three Commissioners appointed by Gen. Thomas to lease plantations are themselves lessees. This is wrong. If you appoint Assistant Agents to take charge of this business of leasing, you will take care, I trust, that no one of them shall have the least pecuniary interest, direct or indirect, in plantations, or in supplies furnished for them, or in the results of the labor hired upon them. Clean hands and absolute disinterestedness are primary requisites for Agents connected with the disposition of these plantations. Let them be honest, conscientious, competent men, earnestly desirous for the amelioration and elevation of the freedmen, and ready to make sacrifice of comfort and pecuniary gain for the sake of doing good.

Mr. Yeatman has taken great interest in the welfare of our soldiers as a most active and efficient officer of the Western Sanitary Commission, and has of late given much special attention to the condition of the men made colored citizens, whose recent enfranchisement, in the midst of War, has exposed them to much suffering.

I have read with much interest a good deal of what he has written, and have conversed with him quite freely on the whole subject. No man has more impressed me by the sincerity of his humanity and the general soundness of his views. If I do not subscribe absolutely to all his suggestions, I am quite willing to commend all to your careful consideration; with the assurance that you will adopt such of them as you find expedient and practicable. –

There are some leading ideas which I especially approve.

All leases for the coming year, made under the authority of Gen. Thomas since he was notified of the Order of the Secretary of War,[3] and especially all leases, whenever made, by the Commissioners to one of their own number, should be regarded, I think, as void. Lessees from these Commissioners, however, not of their own number, who have taken leases in good faith, should be considered as entitled to preference in new leases, and as little occasion for complaint as possible should be given. –

In leasing plantations care should be especially taken of the interests of the laborers; and the lessees should be bound to prompt weekly or at least monthly payments of wages, and these wages should be sufficiently liberal to induce laborers to *desire* the employment. To every contract for labor the employee should be a party as well as the employer; and the practice which, as I learn, has obtained to some extent, of assigning the freedmen to labor on this or that plantation or with this or that person, with little or no regard to his consent, should be discontinued and broken up.

When it is found possible to lease plantations to associations or partnerships of the laborers themselves, the opportunity of doing so, should be promptly embraced.

So, too, when leases can be made of a part or parts of a plantation to a single freedman or other person or to two or three freedmen or other persons in partnership, there should not only be no hesitation but great readiness to make them.

Few things will more contribute to the improvement of the condition of the freedmen and to the productiveness of the country than their occupation of the soil as managers under leases made directly to them.

With the same view, proprietors of plantations should be encouraged to sell in small parcels of forty, eighty or a hundred and twenty acres to the freedmen, who can raise sufficient sums to make the necessary payments. I am not at present authorized to speak for the President, but I am very confident he would relieve the plantations of any proprietor remaining or coming to remain within our lines, and desirous to sell it in this manner, from the effects of the confiscation acts. You will, yourself, be warranted, under your present authority, in providing for the necessary surveys. To expedite matters, boundaries might be arranged and marked roughly at first, subject to correction or more regular measurement.

It will be well, I think, to commit the business of leasing and supervising plantations to Assistant Special Agents for Plantations, of whom there should be one for each State, and perhaps, in some cases, more than one. In case you should think it best to appoint more than one in any State, let the jurisdiction of each be limited to specified counties or parishes, and let all be required to report fully every month, and for each month within ten days of its close. These reports are important and should embrace all the suggestions of the practical experience of the Assistant Agents who make them. Until Congress shall place this whole business under definite legislative sanction, these Assistant Special Agents for Plantations may be considered as upon the same footing as to compensation and general responsibility as the Assistant Special Agents provided for in the General Regulations of September 11, 1863.[4]

I have thus given you the leading ideas which should, I think, be kept prominently in view. Details will readily occur to you, or will be suggested by Mr. Yeatman.

I wish Mr. Yeatman could be prevailed on to Act as General Assistant Agent and take the personal oversight of these matters in your Agency. But this is, I suppose, impossible. He desires to keep himself independent of official trammels, thinking he can thus accomplish most good; and perhaps in this he may be right. Possibly you may find Mr. Field a good and useful Assistant Special Agent. But all this belongs properly to you, and with you I am content to leave it. Very truly Yours,

HLS S: P: Chase

S. P. Chase to Wm. P. Mellen, Esquire, 27 Dec. 1863, Letters Received from the Secretary of the Treasury, Records of the General Agent, RG 366 [Q-143]. Chase's earlier letter to the supervising agent is printed immediately above, as doc. 185. The two commissioners of plantations who were themselves lessees were Robert V. Montague, a Louisiana unionist, and Lewis Dent, a Missourian; George B. Field was the third commissioner.

1 War Department General Order 331, issued October 9, 1863, had directed Union army officers to turn over to the supervising agents of the Treasury Department's special agencies all captured and abandoned "houses, tenements, lands, and plantations," except those required for military purposes. (*Official Records*, ser. 3, vol. 3, p. 872.)

2 James E. Yeatman, president of the Western Sanitary Commission, had toured the Union-occupied parts of the Mississippi Valley in the fall of 1863 and subsequently published both a scathing critique of the plantation-leasing

system and suggestions for its reform. See *A Report on the Condition of the Freedmen of the Mississippi, Presented to the Western Sanitary Commission, December 17th, 1863* (St. Louis, 1864), and *Suggestions of a Plan of Organization for Freed Labor, and the Leasing of Plantations along the Mississippi River . . .* (St. Louis, 1864). For a summary of Yeatman's report, see below, doc. 189n.

3 See note 1, above.

4 Issued by the Secretary of the Treasury, the regulations pertained to trade between the loyal and rebel states. To administer the regulations, five "special agencies" were established within the Union-occupied South, each staffed by a supervising special agent, one or more assistant special agents, and various subordinate agents. (U.S., House of Representatives, "Report of the Secretary of the Treasury, on the State of the Finances, for the Year Ending June 30, 1863," *House Executive Documents*, 38th Cong., 1st sess., No. 3, pp. 410–22.)

187: Testimony by the Acting Assistant Secretary of War before the American Freedmen's Inquiry Commission

New York, January 4, 1863 [1864].

Testimony of Charles A. Dana, Esq.

Q: From what you have seen of the refugee freedmen, what amount of guardianship do you think it wise and proper for the Gov't to exercise over them?

A Not much.

Q But some?

A They hire themselves into the service of the planters; and the only interference you want is the interference of laws to prevent their being abused and overworked. They are perfectly able to make their own bargains, and take care of themselves.

Q Do you think they need any guardianship that should be rather advisory than otherwise?

A That is the sort of guardianship that they naturally get through the clergymen among them, and their teachers. I don't think they need any official guardianship. Here is an industrious, saving peasantry; ready to work; all that they want is, to be sure that they are going to be paid; and the moment you give them the opportunity to work, with security, they will take care of themselves. They are a very timid people, and are more afraid to work where they would be exposed to guerrilla incursions than Irishmen, or any other class of laborers; but they are a frugal, prudent, and shrewd people – not an easy people to defraud or oppress.

Q The intelligence that comes to us from Louisiana is that the negroes are badly treated; that their wages are paid to them in the way of trade, and that they are defrauded in that way. Now, what I desire to ask is, whether you think it may not be necessary, as a temporary measure, to have those whose business it shall be, not to make contracts for them, except, perhaps, to put in writing such contracts as they may make, but, after the contracts are made, to see that they are carried out?

A That is undoubtedly desirable, in the present abnormal condition of the country. I think, that the moment peace is established, and things get upon a regular basis, as they will, these people will be able to take care of themselves, to a great extent. They are a shrewd people, in their small way. They are a great deal shrewder people, I tell you, the negroes of Tennessee, than the whites, and a great deal smarter people. They are more thrifty; they will accumulate property where the whites will remain poor. I refer to the small people – the men of the mountains – all Union men; they are not as shrewd in the management of their business as the negroes are in the management of theirs. The negro saves every cent, and accumulates money.

Q Where do these men of the mountains come from?

A They are mostly from North Carolina, originally. The stock is Scotch. I found a great many Scotch names among them.

Q As to the women and children, the families of soldiers who have enlisted, or of laborers who have been taken into the army or employed by the gov't or railroads, or families that have been abandoned – to what extent would you interfere in regard to them, and in what form?

A The question is more complicated in Tennessee than in Louisiana. In Louisiana, the women & children can find employment suitable to their strength on the cotton plantations, and pay their own way. A child ten years old can make its own living on the Mississippi. But in Tennessee, where the principal product is corn, & where they cannot have protection, they must do the best they can.

Q What would you think of this plan, in places where they could have protection: Put them on a farm, and give them cabins for each family; enclose, say a couple of acres for each family, and let the children, from 13 up to 18, & the old men from 45 to 55 or 60, & the elderly women, where they have not too many children, work from four to six hours a day on the farm, and the rest of the time, on their own acres, of which they should have the produce; follow the soldiers & laborers with an allotment system, and get what you could out of their wages for their families, and so organize a system for them somewhat corresponding to the care taken of the white soldiers at the North?

A The difficulty is, that these families are scattered over such a vast extent of country. Take the State of Tennessee: they are scattered all over that; and very thinly scattered. I don't see any objection to the plan. There are plenty of farms in the neighborhood of Nashville that might be taken. Take possession of one of them, and build the cabins. It would cost nothing.

Q Are there a great many abandoned plantations in the neighborhood of Nashville?

A I have not been about Nashville much, but it looks as though there were a great many.

Q What do they raise there?

A Corn and vegetables. They don't raise cotton in the neighborhood of Nashville – they can't. Until you get to the bottoms of the Tennessee, in the southern part of the middle district, and over on the Mississippi, you don't find cotton.

Q Is it safe to go to that portion of Tennessee where you can plant cotton?

A No. If you got a large farm there, it couldn't be planted safely. But go to Nashville, and take a large farm and raise vegetables, for the market, and you could make a fortune in a year, If you could get a smart fellow, who would take charge of 1500 or 2000 of these people, there is no doubt he could make them pay their way. It would be a great bother, and he would have to stand a great amount of vexation, from their shiftless and lazy ways of work; still, he could raise enough vegetables of all sorts to make it pay its way.

Q Now, there is a question which is very fundamental to this whole subject of the final disposition of these people, and that question has relation to the lands; because these people have got to live upon the lands, to begin with. Then you can never have in any country a democratic society, or a society substantially, practically free, where the land all belongs to a few people. What is your idea of the disposition of the abandoned or confiscated estates of rebels, as connected with the final settlement of these people? Have you ever thought about the matter?

A I have thought about it a good deal. What is your idea?

Col. McKaye These lands are subject to confiscation, & they should be confiscated. They will be sold under the order of Court, & they will be bought in by the highest bidder.

Mr Dana That depends upon the Government.

Col. McKaye These lands are confiscated to the Gov't, & the title goes to the Gov't; the Gov't can make what disposition they please of the lands.

Mr Dana I have not come to any clear conclusion as to what the gov't will do with these lands. There are two ways: one is, to do it, & the other is, not to do it. The tendency of modern society is, to let every man fight his own way; and that would lead the gov't to sell the lands to the highest bidder, & let the negroes find employment as laborers for wages, under laws which will protect them. The other way is, to give them each a little bit of land & a little cabin.

Mr Owen I don't agree with you, that there are only two ways. I think there is a middle course. If you put up the land in large portions, you virtually exclude the negroes. If you put them up in small holdings, of ten or fifteen acres, you are sure to get the negroes to buy.

Col. M[c]Kaye There is a question about that – whether it is good for a country to have its land cut up into small holdings.

Mr. Dana. There is another consideration – that the cultivation of cotton is better done on large plantations than small patches.

Mr Owen There is another consideration – that it is not at all an unprofitable thing to raise cotton on small patches, and sell it in the pod to those who will gin it.

Col M[c]Kaye It seems to me that a system of confiscation should be initiated at once, and that, in the mean time, the Gov't should hold these lands, and have a system of leasing them, in connection with the immediate care of these people.

A The difficulty is, that you cannot dispose of the lands early advantageously – cannot get anything like their fair value, until it is settled that the occupants are not to be harried by rebel invasion. When you have given the rebellion so nearly its finishing stroke that the conclusion is settled and apparent to every body, so that every body gives it up, then you can begin to confiscate and sell the lands; but you cannot until then. When you have got Atlanta and Mobile, or Atlanta and Savannah, and the whole of Lee's army prisoners, as Stanton expressed it the other day, without the trouble of taking care of them, then you can sell those lands; but in the mean time, the only thing you can do is to lease the lands and afford protection to the occupants.

Q When that is done, when, for instance, the question of the rebellion is settled, have you the idea that the valley of the Mississippi is to become at once a peaceful, orderly country?

A The valley of the Mississippi is a pretty bad place. It is a place where robbers and marauders can easily hide, & we are going to have a good deal of brigandage of that sort. Fellows who have been in one or other of the armies, and don't like to live by labor, and like that wild sort of life, will have a great chance there for some time to come. But that depends upon what inducements are held out to people that country. If you can get an industrial population there, they will put that down.

Q Have you not got to depend upon the colored population to settle the valley of the Mississippi and organize a system of defence?

A That, in my judgment, is the great object in enlisting colored troops, as we are now doing. I don't think the colored soldiers are going to render any service in putting down the rebellion; but they will be immensely serviceable in protecting the country. I think we shall settle it all up before they can be brought into the field.

Q There is one question I should like to ask you. I know it is a mere matter of opinion; still, I would like to have your opinion, because I think it lies at the bottom of this whole matter, though it is a good ways off. Have you any doubt that the two races, when the rebellion is closed and peace is restored, will be able to live in harmony, without any government interference?

A There is not the least doubt about it. Why should there be any quarrel between them? I was talking with Frank Blair a short time ago, in Tennessee, and he said that he foresaw a great deal of convulsion and violence when the rebellion was over, growing out of the antagonism between the two races. I did not discuss the matter with him, because I knew what his views were; but I did not share his apprehensions. I have some doubt about the capacity of the negro race to sustain itself in the long struggle for existence; some doubt whether they will increase or dwindle. I rather incline to the conclusion that it will gradually dwindle and go out, as the Indians, by the peaceful operation of natural causes, just as it does in New York and Canada. It is very possible the negro race may be perpetuated south of Mason & Dixon's line; but I don't care a copper whether it can or not. I don't think there is the least danger of violence or convulsion about it.

Q The question that concerns me [Col. McKaye][1] and I confess I am bothered about it, is as to the rights that should be given to these people to enjoy. Not that the negro may not, after a very short time, exercise political rights as well as other men, perhaps, and may be a great deal better than some other men; yet they are naturally a docile people, and very easily led; they are a people who will be for many years subject to white influence, in a very extraordinary degree.

A More than other laboring men – a great deal more.

Q Now if, when you have destroyed this great slave aristocracy of the South, you establish at once a great negro democracy, there is a new crop of demagogues to come up, who are the bane of all Republics & of all society; in short, they play the very devil everywhere. All these fellows will swear they have got negro blood in their veins, and so carry the negroes with them. What do you think of this question of political rights?

A It is a very important question. In the State of Mass^{ts} or New York, I should vote for allowing the negro his political rights, as a matter of abstract principle; but if I had to construct the State of Georgia, with a population of a million whites & five hundred thousand negroes, I would not give the negroes suffrage, except with certain qualifications.

Q You would have to construct it with the balance the other way – five hundred thousand whites, and a million of negroes.

A Take the State of Louisiana: there are a great many educated, wealthy negroes there, able to take care of themselves, and who ought really to enjoy political rights. The only means that ingenuity has discovered to arrange that is to have a property qualification

Q We have hit upon that, for that is the English method.

A It is universal in all countries where there is a desire to restrict the exercise of political rights. Up to 1830, free negroes in Tennessee voted without any qualification. But my idea is that that would not be advisable.

Q You were at Vicksburg, I believe, at the time of its surrender?

A Yes, Sir.

Q What became of the negroes who fled to our lines at that time?

A I only know that a great many of them were employed upon the plantations from Vicksburg up to Lake Providence – a distance of a hundred miles.

Q That is on the West side?

A Yes, Sir

Q Do you know any thing about what care was taken of them?

A No, Sir.

Q You do know, undoubtedly, how Gen. Grant feels on this matter of emancipation?

A Gen. Grant is an anti-slavery man.

Q What sort of an anti-slavery man?

A He is a man who says it would be a great crime to end the war without abolishing slavery.

. . . .

Q How is the rebellion to be finally settled, except by a proper disposition of the land, and a proper disposition of the slaves?

A Of course, you cannot settle it without a proper disposition of the land & the slaves, for the land and the slaves are the two great elements. I have not the least objection to reducing the white people to the most abject poverty. I want to have them punished, and they are punished.

Q The difficulty is, that there is no way in the world in which you can rehabilitate a proper loyal community, except by punishing the rebels?

A No. General Thomas, of Kentucky, who is one of the most

intelligent men I know, says there is no way to finish the rebellion except by driving out the white people of the South. I will tell you a very interesting fact. I have seen, first and last, fifty thousand prisoners of war, and as soon as they are captured, they are all (the number of exceptions is trifling,) the best of friends with our soldiers – living among them, good fellows and comrades, just as though they were serving in the same army. It is so everywhere. There is not a trace of animosity. There is no bitterness. They are perfectly ready to share their bread with our men, and our men are perfectly ready to share their bread with them. I have seen these men come in, a thousand or two thousand in a body, laughing and talking with the men they had been trying to kill a moment before – perfectly happy and contented – nothing to indicate animosity. I tell you that men who fight with each other in opposing armies are at heart always friends. They know each other's strength; they respect each other; they know that each risks his life, that each is brave, and it is a fraternity.

Q In your intercourse with these people, have you observed any indications of a disposition to come back into the Union?

A Well, if you talk with the officers, the burden of their song is – "We are never going to give up, and you can never subjugate us – you cannot subdue our spirit." But if you talk with the men, they will say, as one said the other day, "I don't see why we-uns should kill you-uns. We-uns are going to plant corn; would you-uns want to buy any?" Another man said – "I don't see what I am fighting for. I was never hurt. I never lost any thing. I don't know why I should fight the United States; the United States has never done any thing to me; but one must stand by his colors, you know."

Q In a general way, how does the Proclamation of the President[2] strike you?

A I think it is exceedingly judicious. I think it will have an important military effect in diminishing their armies. In Bragg's army, the amount of desertion is very great. The average that came into our lives was twenty a day for two months past; and the usual report of the men was, that eight ran away home for every one that came to us. But that you cannot depend on; for the idea of a deserter always is to tell the worst story he can of the army he deserts from; it justifies him. After the rebel defeat at Chattanooga, the desertion increased very rapidly. Riding down from Knoxville to Chattanooga the other day, with Gen. Sherman, we met in one day, I should say six different parties of deserters – three or five, and there was one party of fifteen or twenty. We stopped them in the road, and they would bring out the paper they had received from the first Provost Marshal they had come to, giving them permission to go home. They were Kentuckians and Tennesseeans, who wanted to get home, because they had got enough of it. They complained that their food was insufficient, but they didn't look it. I never saw any that showed it.

Q How were their clothes?

A They were about as well clothed as our men. Taking the average, they were not quite so ragged as the men of the army of the Cumberland. I will tell you another thing, in connection with the question of Mr. Owen. We have captured a great many Southern mails. We come down upon some little town, and go at once to the Post Office. We got a mail at Ringgold, another at Loudon, and all around we get them. A great many private letters are got, and they are all read. These letters were from the wives of men in the rebel army, from non-competent men to their brothers, and they were all to this effect: – "If we only had the old times back again! If we only our little house back again and the little farm, & every thing quiet and peaceful, and the children all at home!" And then, "What are we going to do? Our last steer was killed last week; there are not many hogs left, and we are likely not to have meat enough for the winter." And the people living in some city, like Atlanta, write that they have no means of getting any thing to eat. There was one letter taken at Ringgold from a woman in Atlanta to her husband in the army, in which she said, "There was nothing in the house for the children to eat, and a man came along and offered me five dollars to let him sleep with me. I took the money, to get our children bread. If you want to take the children away, you can do so; I shall not complain; here they are. I write this that you may know to what straits we are reduced."

Q Are there many negroes employed in the army at Chattanooga?

A There are a great many employed as officers' servants & as teamsters & grooms. I should think that in the army of Chattanooga, there are five thousand employed as laborers and servants – men whose places would have to be filled by white men, if they were withdrawn. I have a letter that I got from one of those mails in which the writer, who is a quartermaster, writing to a friend in Georgia, discusses the question of reconstruction. He does not give it any great encouragement, but yet he evidently would not be unwilling. There is no animosity; he is perfectly calm about it.

Q Does he say anything about slavery?

A No; they have no idea of abandoning slavery. They have not got to that yet. The number of people at the South who are willing to do what Gen. Gantt has done is very small.

HD

Excerpts from testimony of Charles A. Dana, Esq., before the American Freedmen's Inquiry Commission, 4 Jan. 1863 [1864], filed with O-328 1863, Letters Received, ser. 12, RG 94 [K-212]. Topical labels in the margins are omitted. The omitted portion concerned the personal habits and military tactics of General Ulysses S. Grant. Dana, an editor and correspondent for the *New-York Tribune*, had served as a War Department special investigator in the Mississippi Valley in 1863; his appointment as assistant secretary of war was confirmed by Congress on January 28, 1864. (*Official Records*, ser. 3, vol. 4, p. 1035.) Dana's interlocutors were James McKaye and Robert Dale Owen.

1 Brackets in manuscript.

2 The Proclamation of Amnesty and Reconstruction, issued December 8, 1863, which offered "full pardon" – including restoration of all property rights "except as to slaves, and in property cases where rights of third parties shall have intervened" – to most persons who had engaged in the rebellion, once they had taken an oath of allegiance to the United States that required their adherence to congressional acts and presidential proclamations respecting slavery. The proclamation also outlined a procedure whereby the loyal residents of a seceded state might establish a new state government and seek readmission to the Union. (*Statutes at Large*, vol. 13, pp. 737–39.)

188: Regulations Issued by the Supervising Agent of the Treasury Department 1st Special Agency

[*Memphis, Tenn.*] JANUARY 7, 1864.

Rules and Regulations for Leasing Abandoned Plantations and Employing Freedmen.

I. Said plantations, or such portions thereof as may be required, will be leased to good and loyal citizens, who have taken the oath subjoined to the foregoing contract:

II. Preference will be given to those wishing small tracts of land.

III. No lessee will be allowed to lease more than one abandoned plantation, and all shall be obliged to furnish satisfactory evidence of ability to stock and cultivate the quantity of land applied for.

IV. Owners of plantations who have taken the prescribed oath may occupy the same, and no charge will be made, except in cases where they employ the labor of freedmen, when payment of one cent per pound will be charged on all cotton grown by them, and a proportionate charge upon all other products of their labor, which will be applied to the support of aged, infirm, and helpless freed people, and for sanitary and educational purposes.

V. On all lands without improvements the lessee shall pay a rent of one cent per pound on all cotton, and a proportional charge upon other products grown by him, and for improved lands an additional rent will be required according to their value, having regard to location and improvements, which will be agreed on between the agent and the lessee, and in all cases where freed labor is employed, the lessee shall, in addition to the stipulated rent, contribute one cent per pound on all cotton grown by him, and a proportionate sum upon all other products of the labor, to the fund for the support of helpless and aged freed people, for educational and other purposes connected therewith.

VI. Freedman's Home Farms shall be established at convenient locations, which shall be under a superintendent appointed for the purpose, and shall be places–

First, Where all freed persons of the respective districts in which they are located, shall be registered and employed, until engaged or hired by other employers.

Second, As homes for the aged and infirm freedmen, and motherless children unable to perform labor.

VII. Planters, farmers, and other employers requiring laborers, shall make application to the Superintendent of the Freedman's Home Farms, who will furnish such as may be required. Persons employing fathers or mothers, must take with them such children or near relatives as may be dependent upon them, and desire to go.

VIII. All freed persons over the age of twelve years, who are capable of performing labor, will be required to work.

IX. All laborers shall be classified by the Superintendent as follows: 1. Sound persons from twenty to forty years of age, inclusive, shall be called No. 1 hands. 2. From fifteen to nineteen inclusive, and from forty-one to fifty, inclusive, shall be called No. 2 hands. 3. From twelve to fourteen, inclusive, and over fifty, No. 3 hands. Persons suffering from any physical defect or infirmity, shall be classified by the Superintendent, and wages for them designated.

X. Application for hands shall be made to Superintendents, with certificate or copy of contract showing number of acres leased and hands required. One No. 1 hand, or the equivalent in other grades of hands, shall be employed for every twelve acres of tillable land. The Superintendent to designate the proportionate numbers and grades of each sex to be selected, and the wages of No. 1 males shall be $25 per month; No. 2, $20; No. 3, $15. Nos. 1, 2, and 3 females, $18, $14, and $10.

In case any person employing freed persons to labor on plantations, shall wish to give any of those employed an interest in the profits resulting from working the same, in lieu of the regular wages above specified, and such persons shall desire to make a contract with the employer for a stipulated portion of such profits, in lieu of other wages, it may be done: Provided, however, that all such contracts shall be approved by the Superintendent of the Freedman's Home Farm, at which they are employed, or nearest which they may be located, and also by the Agent of the District, and that one cent per pound on all cotton raised, and a proportionate amount upon other products, shall be contributed for the support of the helpless, as provided in case of stipulated wages, and also that all necessary supplies for the employed shall be furnished to them by the employer, upon the same terms, and subject to the same conditions as in cases of payment of the regular wages above provided for.

XI. When lessees wanting laborers shall have made their selection, lists shall be prepared, and the employer and employee shall each sign a contract in duplicate in presence of a witness, one copy of which shall be retained and filed by the Superintendent.

XII. At the end of the year or period of time for which such contract shall be made, the lessee shall return the hands to the Farm from which they were taken, or account for them, and a full settlement shall then be made, he paying to his hands in cash such balance as may be due; and no cotton shall be sold or shipped without previous written permit of the Special Agent of the District, or the certificate of the Superintendent of the Farm from which they were hired, that wages have been fully paid.

XIII. Lessees shall provide, without charge, good and sufficient quarters for laborers employed, a separate tenement for each family, with proper regard for sanitary conditions, a sufficient supply of food, one acre of ground to each family of four or more persons, and also to others requiring it, in same proportion.

XIV. The lessee shall provide and keep on hand a sufficient supply of wholesome food, and suitable clothing for the employees and their families, which shall be sold to the laborers at the wholesale cost price, and ten per cent. thereon, keeping an account of the items with each laborer, which account shall be settled and approved by the Superintendent at the close of the year, at which time the balance due shall be paid. All accounts and invoices shall be open to inspection of the Superintendent and to the Special Agent of the District at all proper times.

XV. Laborers to be paid for full time unless they shall be sick, or voluntarily neglect to work. In cases of such sickness or neglect, the employer may report it to the Farm Superintendent within ten days after it occurs, who, upon being satisfied of such sickness or neglect, shall endorse the proper deduction therefor upon the contract. In case a person fails to labor as contemplated by the contract, the Superintendent upon being satisfied of the fact, shall receive him or her back at the Farm, and cancel the contract, upon payment by the employer of the amount properly due. Should a hand quit voluntarily, without consent of lessee, before the end of the term, the balance of wages to be forfeited, half to the employer, and half to the Government.

XVI. Where the lessee fails to furnish a proper supply of food or clothing, or does not furnish proper quarters, or overtasks his laborers, or otherwise abuses them, or violates his agreement, they shall have the right to appeal to the Superintendent, who may have the same corrected, by declaring the contract forfeited, and taking possession of the land, or by releasing the employees from their contract, in which latter case the lessee shall be required to pay all wages due, and shall be held responsible for half wages until other employment for the released employees can be obtained.

XVII. There shall be employment provided on the Freedman's Home Farms, for all who are able to work, for which no wages shall be paid; food and clothing being considered as an equivalent therefor, the labor performed being for the benefit of the occupants of the Farm, and the general good. The Superintendent may establish such rules for police and other purposes, as may be proper in conducting the Farm, and governing the persons connected therewith.

XVIII. Lessees shall only be required to pay half the monthly wages, either in money, provisions, or clothing, until the crops are sold. The first lien upon the crops shall be for the wages of the laborer, and provision will be made by the Superintendent, to secure the prompt payment of same.

XIX. The Supervising Agent, or such officer as shall be designated by him for that purpose, will from time to time examine invoices and accounts of lessees, and see that the rules are complied with.

XX. The use of the lash, paddle, and all other cruel modes of punishment shall not be permitted or inflicted by lessees or any one in their employment, upon the persons of any of the employees or their families.

XXI. Schools will be established in convenient localities, and all children between the ages of six and twelve years shall be required to attend them.

XXII. Persons desiring to employ mechanics, wood-choppers, or other laborers, must apply to the Superintendent of the Freedman's Home Farm, and all contracts for such labor shall be subject to his approval.

XXIII. All persons living together as husband and wife shall be legally married; they shall assume a family name, and Registers of marriages, births, and deaths shall be kept by the Superintendents, to whom the same shall be reported by the employers. And also of the names and location of all employers, together with the names of the persons employed by them, and of those living with them.

PDSr WM. P. MELLEN,

Rules and Regulations for Leasing Abandoned Plantations and Employing Freedmen, 7 Jan. 1864, Miscellaneous Papers, 1st Agency, RG 366 [Q-26]. Attached are the plantation lease agreement and oath referred to in the regulations. The oath required the lessee to swear allegiance to the United States, to take no further part in the rebellion, and to observe all congressional acts and presidential proclamations "touching slaves and the condition of slavery." The day after issuing the regulations, Mellen forwarded a copy to Secretary of the Treasury Salmon P. Chase, along with an assessment of "prospects for leasing plantations . . . this year." Noting that numerous would-be lessees were already making preparations to begin planting, Mellen indicated that he would endeavor to lease enough estates "to employ every freed person able to labor." He estimated that some 30,000 former slaves – the majority of whom were women, children, and "infirm" men – were available for plantation labor. "Most of the best class of labor" had either been "run off by their former masters, into Rebel lines" or enlisted into the Union army. Nevertheless, he predicted, "we can make the whole system self-sustaining." Mellen urged Chase to press for legislation that would consolidate the Treasury Department's control over matters involving former slaves – either the bill to create a bureau of emancipation that had recently been introduced in the House of Representatives, or an amendment to the Direct Tax Act of August 1861. "The care of the Freedmen and their labor are so intimately connected with the leasing of abandoned plantations," he argued, "that they should be united as one subject." Mellen also sought legal action to ensure the lessees' security of tenure, evidently fearing that the restoration of abandoned estates to returning owners, as proposed in President Lincoln's amnesty proclamation, would undercut the leasing system. Since "few, if any" plantations were likely to be sold for delinquent taxes under the Direct Tax Act, he advised Chase that "[w]e must look to the Confiscation Act or some other law to give title or long occupancy to others than the present owners." (Wm. P. Mellen to Hon. S. P. Chase, 8 Jan. 1863 [1864], #174 1864, Letters Received by the Division, ser. 315, Division of Captured Property, Claims, & Land, RG 56 [X-30].)

189: Commissioner of Plantations in the Department of the Tennessee to the Adjutant General of the Army

Vicksburg [*Miss.*] Jany 10th 1864

Dr General Your letter from Memphis of the 9th ult did not reach me until the first of this month.[1] In the meantime I waited in suspense as to what course should be pursued relative to leasing plantations the ensuing year, Your letter cleared up my doubts upon the subject and Mr Montague in conjunction with Col McDowall (Special Agent of the Treasury Dept) and myself under took the laborious and difficult task of examining into and passing upon nearly three hundred applications for Leasses, which we have just Concluded, and now to our surprise we learn through the latest public prints that Mess Jas E Yeatman and Mr Mellen are on their way hither to inaugurate a new and improved system, in other words the pet plan of Genl Hawkins of subdivision into one and two hundred acre lots, the absurdity of which (in the existing Condition of the Country) may be seen by the fact that since the amnesty of the Prest [2] Fourteen of the forty abandoned plantations leased by us last year have already been given up to their former owners. And I do not hesitate to express the belief that before the first of January next there will not be ten plantations between the mouths of the Arkansas and Red Rivers, that will not have been given up to their former owners, by some sort of compromise with the lessees of the present year, and the only real usefulness of the Commissioners or any other agents that may succeede them is by acting as an advisery Court bringing *applicants* for plantations and *owners* together and thus aid them in forming those amicable connections by which negro labor may be *at once* applied to the peaceful pursuit of agricultur under the direction of *loyal Northern men* upon harmonious terms with the *owners* of the soil, These partnerships are now forming in all directions some planters on the extreme border having obtained protection from Confederate Genls while his loyal partner as Lessee of the Govt obtains protection from our Commanders, and thus is beginning to be sown the seeds of an enduring and mutually advantageous reconstruction of the Union. I hope to see these union of interests fostered and extended as far as possible Altho I shall not be the future medium of inter-communication in this interesting and important business. yet I am happy to believe that the gentleman Col McDowall who has acted with and will probably succeede us is fully impressed with the importance of the matter, and entertains broad, intelligent and comprehensive views upon the whole subject, Mr Yeatman I judge from the pamphlet he has issued on the subject, has been manipulated by Genl Hawkins both of the plan adopted last spring and the fidelity of its execution.[3] It is probable you may obtain a copy of Mr Yeatman's report of Secy Chase or Hon H T Blow of Missouri. If so you will see at a glance and be able to refute its inaccuracies and misstatements and I write this mearly to call your attention to the subject while at Washington, I am engaged in closing up the affairs of the Commission during the past year which when done will be laid befor the Secry of War in a final report covering the whole ground. It affords me pleasure in being able to say to you in advance, that the wisdom of your plans and the success attending their execution against so many obsticles and under such unfavorable Circumstances, will leave you no cause to look back with regret at your agency in bringing about one of the most important movements of the times

I cannot close this communication without calling your attention to the Conduct of Gen[l] Hawkins and I do so the more reluctantly as you are aware his appointment was made at my earnest solicitation. with M[r] Stanton and youself. His course since his return in September has been one of not only systematic violation of the orders of his superior officers, but of persistant and I believe selfish opposition to the plans and policy adopted by the gvn[t], in leaving no means untried to misrepresent and bring into disrepute the action of not only the Gov[t] but its Lessees & Commissioners. If he had pursued and faught the enemy with half the energy he has the loyal citizens of his District, who are there by the invitation of the Gov[t], He would at least have escaped the imputation. he is now unde of being a Calumniator and a Coward. I trust his fitness for his present position will be thoroughly scrutenized before his confirmation as Brig General. I am glad to hear of your restoration to health and hope a long and happy life may reward your honorable Career I have the honor to be Your very Obt servt

ALS Geo B Field

Geo. B. Field to Genl. L. Thomas, 10 Jan. 1864, F-1 1864, Letters Received by Adjutant General L. Thomas, ser. 363, Colored Troops Division, RG 94 [V-77]. Ten days later, William P. Mellen, the supervising agent of the Treasury Department's 1st Special Agency, took charge of leasing plantations in the Mississippi Valley, under regulations that differed substantially from those established by Adjutant General Lorenzo Thomas in April 1863. (See above, docs. 162, 188, and below, doc. 197.) Field – who became the lessee of an estate near Natchez, Mississippi – continued to criticize Mellen's policy. The new treasury regulations, he warned Thomas, "are of a very radical, and I must say unwise character – especially the one giving laboring men twenty five dollars pr month which appears to me utterly subversive to the interests of goverment." "I cannot see how enlistments in the army can be made at ten dollars pr month – under the influence of such Compitition. The same difficulty will also occur in the Quarter Masters and Commissary Depts. how are they to obtain labor?" According to Field, "the Residents of the country" had begun to "look with favor" upon Thomas's system, but Mellen's regulations were creating "the greatest alarm" and had caused many prospective lessees to return to their homes in the North. Field shared their concern, and he predicted that "little will be done in the cultivation of plantations the present year – unless the present system is greatly modified." (Geo. B. Field to Genl. L. Thomas, 8 Feb. 1864, F-2 1864, Letters Received by Adjutant General L. Thomas, ser. 363, Colored Troops Division, RG 94 [V-78].) No "final report" by Field to the Secretary of War has been found in the records of the War Department.

1 Adjutant General Lorenzo Thomas's letter (dated December 8, 1863, in his volume of retained copies), had notified the commissioner of plantations that William P. Mellen, supervising agent of the Treasury Department's 1st Special Agency, was not yet prepared to take charge of plantation leasing for the 1864 season. Thomas had therefore authorized the commissioner to continue granting leases until further notice. (Adjutant General [Lorenzo Thomas] to George B. Field, Esq., 8 Dec. 1863, Letters & Telegrams Sent by L. Thomas, ser. 9, RG 94 [V-171].)

2 President Lincoln's Proclamation of Amnesty and Reconstruction, issued on December 8, 1863, which offered "full pardon" – including restoration of all property rights "except as to slaves, and in property cases where the rights of third parties shall have intervened" – to most persons who had engaged in the rebellion, once they had taken an oath of allegiance to the United States that required their adherence to congressional acts and presidential proclamations respecting slavery. (*Statutes at Large*, vol. 13, pp. 737–39.)

3 In early January 1864, James E. Yeatman, president of the Western Sanitary Commission, published a sharp criticism of the plantation-leasing system in the Mississippi Valley. Yeatman protested that the freedpeople had been forced to labor for Northern lessees who "treat them, so far as providing for them is concerned, far worse than their 'secesh' masters did," and that they received unreasonably low wages while the lessees reaped large profits. Charging that most lessees were "adventurers, camp followers, [and] 'army sharks,' " Yeatman condemned the practice of permitting them to operate "as many plantations as their cupidity may lead them to grasp." He urged that the estates instead be subdivided and rented in small tracts either to Northerners sympathetic to emancipation, or directly to those freedmen who possessed the means to operate a farm. Yeatman's recommendations owed much to General John P. Hawkins, commander of the District of Northeastern Louisiana, who had convinced him that "the true interest of our country, and justice to our loyal people, who have given their sons to the crushing out of this rebellion, require that they should have the opportunity to share in the fruits of their victories." (Yeatman, *A Report on the Condition of the Freedmen of the Mississippi, Presented to the Western Sanitary Commission, December 17th, 1863* [St. Louis, 1864].)

190: Two Applications by Mississippi Freedmen to the Commissioners of Plantations in the Department of the Tennessee

Vicksburg [*Miss.*] Jany 11th 1864

To the commissioners of Plantations. I the undersigned Josua Culverson, for Willis Culverson Lee Whaley, James Houston, Manuel Johns and Nathan Buckner, (Colored) represent that we have belonged to the plantation owned by Levi Culverson, that said

Culverson Abandoned his said place taking most of his negroes to Texas. over one year ago that we together with some twenty others have remained & wish to cultivate as much as we are able the Coming season Say About one hundred and fifty acres there are twelve double log cabins on the place, and about eight hundred acres of Cultivable land.

his
HDSr Josua X Culverson
mark

Vicksburg Miss, Jan[y] 19" 1864

To the U.S. Com[s] of Plantations, The undersigned a Colored Loyal Citizen of the United States hereby makes application to lease of the Government the present Year upon the prescribed termes. The Hunt Place on the Miss River near Tallula Conting About One hundred & fifty acres tillable land

his
HDSr Major X Whiteing
mark

[*Endorsement*] I Know the old man who makes the above application. he has resided on the above place for years, and has had full Control of the same. Col Eaton has given him permission to take some of his relations from the Contraband Camp to his home. I Know he has the means to support them. I will endorse the old Mans Honesty and Industry and think him fully Competant to manage the small place he applies for Theodore Fitler a Citizen of Issaquena Co Miss Vicksburg Jany 18. 1864

Josua Culverson to the Commissioners of Plantations, 11 Jan. 1864, and Major Whiteing to the U.S. Com's of Plantations, 19 Jan. 1864, Applications to Lease Plantations, Vicksburg District, 2nd Agency, RG 366 [Q-55]. George B. Field, a commissioner of plantations, witnessed Culverson's application; Fitler witnessed that of Whiteing. A notation on the wrapper of Culverson's application reads "Aworded conditionally"; there is no indication whether Whiteing's application was successful.

191: Northern Plantation Lessees to the Supervising Agent of the Treasury Department 1st Special Agency

Vicksburg Miss Jany. 13th 1864

Sir, We, the undersigned, loyal citizens of the United States and representing also a much larger number of the most loyal and patriotic citizens of the Northern States having been informed that it is proposed to adopt some regulations governing the operations upon abandoned plantations in the Valley of the Mississippi River which materially modify existing rules, would respectfully request that your Honor would allow us to present the following statement and that in your deliberations the same may receive as much regard as in the judgement of your Honor it may be entitled –

Toward the close of the last year the Rev. L. S. Livermore purporting to have been duly commissioned by the proper Authorities to arrange with loyal citizens of the Northern States for leasing plantations of the General Government, for the purpose of raising cotton, by his appeals through the press and public assemblies attracted our attention and through the representations contained in a circular signed by him, a copy of which is here with presented, prevailed upon us to organize companies, involving the withdrawal of ourselves from the comforts of our homes and our safe and pleasant occupations, and the direction of large amounts of capital from its ordinary channels, that we might engage in the business above indicated.

In order to estimate the amount of capital we should need to carry on one hundred acres, we had recourse to the estimates furnished by Mr. Livermore and which he assured us had by trial been prooved to be correct and reliable.

In these estimates we were assured that twelve (12) Hands would be furnished for every one hundred acres cultivated, at an average price of $5 per month, but that with these the lessee would be required to take six persons unfit for service and that in addition to the wages of $5 per month he should furnish the rations designated in the circular referred to for each one of the eighteen persons at an expense of 81¢ per week.

Also that the Government tax upon each pound of cotton would be one cent. Relying upon these statements we found that our expenses per 100 acres upon these items would be as follows – viz –

12 Hands at $5 per month for 12 mos	720.00
Rations for 18 Hands at 80¢ per wk for 52 wks	748.80
Gov. tax of 1¢ per lb on 40.000 lbs	400.00
Total –	$1868.80

After expending much time and money in making our selections of Plantations and arrangements to work the same, we have been informed that it is proposed to alter the above prices as follows– Hands shall receive $20 per month including rations and the tax to be increased to 2¢ per lb. Upon which our estimates will be as follows

12 Hands at $20 per mo for 12 mo[s]	2880.00
Gov. tax of 2¢ per lb on 40.000 lbs	800.00
Total–	$3680.00

Which would be an increase of expenditure upon each 100 acres of $1811.20 while if we are correctly informed the immense risk we incur both of life and capital is not lessened by means of adequate military protection–

We are also informed that 10 per cent upon the invoice cost of rations and clothing is the maximum amt allowed for cost of transportion, insurance, the labor of disbursement and the unavoidable loss attending the shipment and distribution of goods–

In the opinion of those who have had large experience in such matters in the present unsettled condition of the country, this loss or expenditure will amount to not less than fifty per cent upon invoice cost– If such were the case the difference of forty per cent upon all goods furnished to hands upon plantations would increase the outlay upon each 100 acres to at least $2200. more than we were informed by Mr. Livermore would be required.

In closing, while we lament the fact, if any such exists, that during the last year any of the race recently brought into the position of free men from cruel bondage, were deprived of any of their rights or treated with unkindness and while we desire that strict justice shall be meted out to the negro, we would respectfully request, that as we have embarked in the business under consideration, under direct invitation from the United States Government that no regulations be now introduced which will modify materially the plan or increase the outlay made known to us by Mr Livermore and in view of which we closed our business at the North and arranged to take part in this. All of which is most respectfully submitted by Your most Obedient Servants,

HLS [*19 signatures*]

Benj. Leos et al. to Hon. W. P. Mellen, 13 Jan. 1864, General Letters Received, Records of the General Agent, RG 366 [Q-150]. Alongside his name, each lessee indicated his home state. Twelve were from Illinois, four from Wisconsin, two from Ohio, and one from Indiana. Lark S. Livermore, the chaplain of a Wisconsin regiment, had served as a commissioner of plantations in the Department of the Tennessee in 1863. His circular, said to have been enclosed, is not in the file. No reply has been found in the letters-sent volumes of the supervising agent.

192: Contract between an Arkansas Farmer and Eight Arkansas Freedpeople

[*Jackson Co., Ark. January 26, 1864*]

This article of agreement entered into this 26th day of January A.D. 1864 between William R. Steen a white citizen aged 34 Years of the first part– and Caroline a colored woman aged 40 Years, Charity a colered woman aged 40 Years– Harriet a colered woman aged 20 Years, Milly a colored girl aged 14 Years, Jake a colored man aged 55 Years, Frank a colored man aged 40 Years, Juliet a colored woman aged 45 Years, Emeline a colored woman aged 25 Years of the Second part. all of Jackson County State of Arkansas: Witnesseth That said Wm R. Steen agrees to hire said above named colored women and men to work upon a farm cultivated by said Steen for the Year 1864, agreeing to give said women and men one third part of the crop raised upon the farm by their labor or the proceeds thereof to be divided between themselves as they may deem best in proportion to the labor performed by each, said Steen agreeing to subsist and clothe them and their children–and said colored women and men agreeing on their part to work and labor upon said farm for said Steen for the above stipulated price or part of the crop raised and further agreeing to work diligently and industriously to raise said crop and to behave themselves in an orderly manner, and obey all the laws that may be in force in the Land– Witness our hands the day and Year first above written

W R Steen
Caroline X Steen
Charity X Steen
Harriet X Steen
Milly X Steen
Jake X Steen
Frank X Steen

[*In the margin*] (Duplicate)

HDcSr

Contract between W. R. Steen and Caroline Steen et al., 26 Jan. 1864, Letters Sent, Reports, Affidavits, & Court Papers, ser. 348, Jacksonport AR Supt., RG 105 [A-2502]. Witnessed. All the "signatures" on this copy are in the same handwriting; neither Juliet nor Emeline, both of whom were listed in the contract, are among the signers.

193: Staff Assistant of the Superintendent of Freedmen for the State of Arkansas to the Superintendent

Helena Ark Feb 5th 1864

Sir By Special order VII Issued from your Office at Helena Ark dated 29th of Jany 1864 in which I was directed to proceed to Woodyard and Camps mouth of White River takeing five Boxes donated goods for distribution among the freed people at that point

I was also ordered to make a registration of all the Freed people congregated at that point classifying them according to the Suggestions of J. E. Yeatman of the W. S Com Decr 17th 1863[1]

And also to examine and report the condition quality and quantity of abandoned disloyal lands in the vicinity and agricultural implements if any

I have the Honor to make the following report

I embarked on the Steamer Bellfast on the 30th of Jany 1864 but owing to the severe gale on Sunday we did not reach the mouth of white river until monday morning 1st of Feb 1864

On my arrival I reported to Capt Pritchett on the Gunboat Tyler got the donated goods in a safe place at the cabin of Mr Jacob Hugus The Partner & foreman of Maj Love who are engaged keeping a goverment wood yard in which nearly all the labor is performed by colored people

I proceeded to make a careful registration of all the freed people in their employ and while doing so took care to note the condition of all their cabins their Bedding their clotheing furniture &c

And also to make enquiries as to compensation for labor performed and the charges made for provisions I found Their whole number including five persons in the employ of Samuel Griffin to be 183 souls and have classified them as follows

12	(twelve)	First	class	males
29	(twenty nine)	"	"	Females
11	(Eleven)	Second	class	males
14	(fourteen)	"	"	Females
14	(fourteen)	Third	Class	males
7	(seven)	"	"	Females

	Infirm and under age
39	males able for light labor
18	Females " " " "
1	male Totally unfit for labor
9	Boys under 12 years of age
29	Girls under 12 years of age
183	Total in camp

	Recapitulation
12	males of the first class
11	males of the second class
14	males of the Third class
37	Total males in good health
29	Females of the first class
14	Females of the second class
7	Females of the Third class
50	Total Females in good health
	Infirm and under age
49	males
47	Females
96	Total of the infirm & under age

Their cabins consist of an incongruous assemblage of miserable huts no attempt haveing been made towards introduceing any system whatever Their floors are on or quite near the ground they have no windows and are only lighted by holes in the roofs consequently in rainy weather most of their Scanty Bedding is wet their floors are damp and no wonder that from this little community they have already furnished one hundred and sixteen subjects for the Graveyard notwithstanding quite a number had been sent off sick

And in addition to other inconveniences a recruiting officer or as they termed them (De Pressers) came among them, and carried away twenty of the Best men leaveing some families without any men to assist them

Some of those women thus left alone with little children seemed discouraged whilst others were quite cheerful I will give a single instance one Martha Thompson eighteen years old had a small Babe when asked where her husband was replied he run away the first chance and joined the union army The next question asked was how she come there she replied her brother come with her but that the pressers took him I enquired how she made a liveing she replied that she left her baby with a neighbor and then went and piled cord wood she seemed cheerful and determined

I met with but few Cases of Sickness in camp

The people invariably said Messrs Love & Hugus had measured the wood that they cut and corded fairly and had paid them promtly every saturday night if they wished for their pay they also said that there had been at all times provisions on hand for sale but some of them complained of the prices that they had to pay Beef 12 cts pr lb pork 12 cts pr lb flour 7 cts pr lb meal 6 cts pr lb and some of the people complained of the prices of Clotheing Shoes $3.75c pr pair Blankets $5.00 a piece common coarse coats $12.00 pants $7.00 Shirts $3.00 As to the distribution of those donated goods I was careful when makeing the Registration to make a minute of the wants of the most destitute and sickly and if I could have had a room and some one to have assisted me I would have adopted the ticket System but haveing but little room and no assistance I made amongst the needy as near an equal distribut[ion] as I could make Then I gave out as rewards for industry the ballance on hand with the exception of a few articles for Small Boys that was not needed which I have returned

Most of the clothing was very thankfully received indeed but I heard of one woman expressing dissatisfaction with the Smallness of the donation

Those people had at one time begun a meeting house but after so many of the men were pressed they abandoned the undertakeing but they still have some religious meetings have hopes of happiness after death and all of them believe that President Lincoln is their friend

There is no Physician here to administer medicine to the sick neither is there any preparations being made for a school nor have those people had any Rations issued to them from the goverment they have relied solely upon their own industry for a support

The price paid for cutting and cording wood is one dollar pr cord other hands are paid for loading the waggons and 12: cts pr cord is paid for cording at the River after it is halled

The land on which this camp is situated once belonged to a man by the name of Cumby who died in 1857 his son and heir is said to be in the Rebel Army— his Widow Married a man whose name was Lane who was by some one of our Naval officers ordered to leave the Island as a disloyal man and he left

At the place Lane was then liveing at which is one and a half miles below the camp there is about 40 acres of cleared land but no fence the land is rather sandy— there is a pretty comfortable one story frame dwelling house a good cistern and several out houses then at the back of the cleared land there is several buildings

This place is at present occupied by a man by the name of Saml Griffin whose wife claims to have rented of Young Cumby but common report says that Lane and his wife are now liveing on Griffin's farm on the South Side of the Arkansas River while Saml Griffin and wife occupy his place on the Island

There is two broken plows and one old cultivator on the premises and a considerable amount of Bale rope and webbing for the cotton trade and indications of considerable buisness in that line haveing been done

And still further down and a little back from the River there is about fifteen acres of cleared land Mr Saml Griffin has engaged a man by the name of Graham to fence and cultivate the same this season

Then again above the camps towards White River there has been a field of some 60 or 80 acres that appears to have been abandoned some 4 or 5 years ago and is partly grown up with young timber

The Cumby estate consists of a large tract of land haveing a front on the Mississippi River about five miles on which there is a vast amount of hard wood now growing consisting of Pecan Gray ash and hackberry with some oak the higher part but seldom overflows more than two feet gradually growing lower back from the River until the overflow will average ten feet deep then there is a considerable pond that remains the whole year round

There is a Slough or cut off connecting the White and Arkansas Rivers of about 4 miles in length that is, at all times navigable when navigation is possible on the Arkansas now to include all the land from this cut off down to Napoleon where there has been recently a new cut off made by the Mississippi wearing its way in to the Arkansas would probably amount to not less than fourteen thousand Acres

There is a pressing demand for wood for govern[t] uses that will continue probably while the war lasts All of which is respectfully Submitted

ALS A W Harlan

A. W. Harlan to Maj. W. G. Sargent, 5 Feb. 1864, Retained Copies of Reports, Reports Received, & Miscellaneous Papers, ser. 379, Little Rock AR Supt. of Freedmen, RG 105 [A-2536].

1 In his widely circulated pamphlet, *Suggestions of a Plan of Organization for Freed Labor, and the Leasing of Plantations along the Mississippi River . . .* (St. Louis, 1864), James E. Yeatman, president of the Western Sanitary Commission, advocated a system of classification for agricultural laborers in which black men, women, and working-age children would be ranked according to sex and ability to labor, and be paid the following minimum wages per month: No. 1 men, $25; No. 2 men, $20; No. 3 men, $15; No. 1 women, $20; No. 2 women, $16; No. 3 women, $12; with children between the ages of twelve and fifteen rated as No. 3 hands.

194: Affidavit of a Mississippi or Louisiana Freedman

Natchez Miss March 3 1864

Sam[l] Goff, A freedman formally belonging to James Brabston owner of the Gilliard Plantation, Appeared in this Office, And made the following statement. The said Goff was employed by Dewitt C. Brown on or about the First day of December 1863 at the rate of Seven Dollars per Month with board and Clothing. Said Brown being Leasee of said Plan[t]: Said Goff has continued upon said plantation up to this time, And has lost no time through his own neglect And has received no money or Clothing from said Brown except one pair of Boots charged at seven Dollars, Worth about Three Dollars and fifty cents. The said Goff further states that there are Thirty four Other Grown Laborers employed on the Plantation, being Fourteen Men and Twenty Women, And Twenty three Children, About Eight of which have assisted in picking of Cotton. These hands have been moved to the Johnson and Carr Plantations by said Brown and have worked on each place under his orders. The said Brown agreed to pay to each hand 1/4¢ per pound in addition to their Monthly wages, All Goods and Groceries furnished to the hands by Brown were paid for in Cash by the hands at the time. said Goff bought One hundred and sixty pounds of Flour for Ten Dollars Cash, Four pounds of Coffee for Three Dollars Cash and Three pounds of sugar for Seventy five cents Cash.

The said Goff for himself and as agent for the Other hands requests that the said Brown be required to pay the wages due to them in to the hands of the Ast sp[c] Ag[t] for Plantations of this District. To be held by him for distrburstion

In Testimony where of the said Saml Goff has hereunto set his hand and Seal this 3[d] day of March 1864

his
HDcSr Samuel X Goff
mark

Affidavit of Samuel Goff, 3 Mar. 1864, Letters Received by Assistant Special Agents, Natchez District, 2nd Agency, RG 366 [Q-44]. The affidavit is headed "*Office of Ast Sp[c] Agt for Plantations Natchez District*," and was sworn before William Burnet, the assistant special agent. The previous day, Burnet had asked the provost marshal general of the Department of the Gulf to arrest Brown, who was reportedly in New Orleans selling cotton gathered by freedpeople whose wages he "has not paid and utterly refuses to pay." Brown was soon arrested and returned to the Natchez area, remaining in detention until March 10, when he "closed his a/c satisfactorily with the hands." (Wm. Burnet to Genl. Bowen, 2 Mar. 1864, Wm. Burnet to Capt. Grier, [early Mar. 1864], and Wm. Burnet to Capt. Walker, 10 Mar. [186]4, vol. 237

1/2, pp. 44–45, 47, 75, Press Copies of Letters Sent Relating to Abandoned and/or Confiscated Property, ser. 2295, Natchez MS Treasury Agent, RG 105 [A-9548].)

195A: Contract between an Arkansas Planter and an Arkansas Freedman

Little Rock Ark. March 1, /64

Copy of Lease to Wash Keats,

I have this day rented of Mrs. Maria Thibault of Pulaski county, State of Arkansas, that portion of her plantation upon which her dwelling house, and gin are situate and known as Walnut ridge. The said land is supposed to contain One Hundred acres of tillable land: for which I am to pay the sum of four dollars per acre and furnish vegetables and fruit for family use – the buildings, orchards &c to be kept in good condition while in my possession – The lease to expire on the last day of December 1864 –

The Gin house to be used by the different lessees of Mrs. Thibault[s] farm in ginning their respective crops,

The rent money to be paid after the crop is made, and before it is removed from said land –

his
Washington X Keats
mark

HDcSr

Contract between Mrs. Maria Thibault and Washington Keats, 1 Mar. 1864, Retained Copies of Reports, Reports Received, & Miscellaneous Papers, ser. 379, Little Rock AR Supt. of Freedmen, RG 105 [A-2533]. Witnessed. In the same file is a copy of a similar contract, also dated March 1, between Thibault and another freedman, Thomas Bass, who was to rent 150 acres of her plantation at $5 per acre and to have use of both the gin house and "half the buildings on the land leased by Washington Keats. The dwelling house included."

195B: Attorneys for an Arkansas Freedman to the Provost Marshal General of the Department of Arkansas

Little Rock Arkansas November 8th 1864

To Col. J. L. Chandler, Provost Marshal Gen[l] &c The undersigned, desire to ask your attention to the following statement of facts, and for such orders and relief, as may be consistent with justice and right in the premises.

In the spring of this year, one *Washington Keatts*, a negro, rented of Mrs Thibault, – now dead – one hundred acres of land, on which to plant cotton, corn &c. That said Washington, had horses, mules implements of agriculture [&] but owing to the fact, that he had formerly been a slave, he had little or no money to buy either food for himself or stock; and without which he would fail in making any crop at all.

Two white men, by the name of **Hoover*, and *Voss*,[1] agreed to *lend* Washington Keatts, money enough to secure the raising of the crop, and take in lieu thereof, a certain *portion of the crop*, when secured, That those two generous persons were soldiers, of the U.S. Army. Under this arrangement, advances were made to said Washington, and the crop raised in accordance with such understanding.

One, *Thomas Bass,* a negro, also rented land of Mrs Thibault, upon the same plantation, near to, or adjoining said Washingtons leasehold, That said *Bass*, having but few or any facilities, to cultivate the land, beyond his own personal labor, that said Washington took his teams and ploughed and cultivated the land to put in the crop, of Bass; while Bass would go and cut logs, clear the ground &c on Washingtons portion of the premises. This was an *exchange of labor*, agreed upon by the parties, and account kept of the number of days each assisted the other.

Early in the month of July, owing to the fact that Bass, did not work his own crop, he had no disposition to work in the crop of others. Washington informed him he would assit him no more, as his own crop would require all his attention, They settled up their respective exchange of work, and here matters ended as between them, Bass, by his want of industry lost his crop, Keatts, by great exertion, and the assistance referred to made a fair crop.

On the 10″ of July, Bass, in an advertisment, in the "National Democrat," says, "Thomas Bass, and W. Keatts have divided our crop" &c. see Exhibit "A". This being so, that certainly ended the matter, as between them, In the same adv^{t} he says, the "Partnership is disolved," – *A thing that never existed*; but, had it been so, there was also an end of that, Bass, went on to caution people, that "he was not responsible any longer" &c. gave up all idea of having anything more to do with Keatts, and his crop.

When cotton picking time comes on, Bass, *again* comes in as a claimant, on *Keatts* cotton – he Bass, having failed to raise but very little himself. The crop, so boastfully, "divided in July," was again *all unsettled in October.* Keatts comes out in an adv^{t} "declaring that he never formed any partnership" &c This appears to end the matter, at that time first referred to

Bass now complains that he has no crop, and asks for aid in some shape from the authorities, to do for him, what, from want of industry, he had failed to do for himself – to make him a crop –

Some person under Major Sargent, a private, or non Commissioned officer, undertook to investigate the matter. But little evidence appeas to have been taken; the main witnesses were not examined, or knew anything of what was going on. The rights of parties were set at naught, indeed, so flagrant was the injustice done, that the commission, or whatever it may be called, undertook to, and did convert itself into a *Landlord*, or rentor of land! They declared that Bass should take part of Keatts, lease, and Keatts, part of Bass, lease; cut it up into small fragments or parcels.!

Those persons that advanced money to Keatts, as herein stated, are cut out; the result of their money goes into the capacious pocket of Bass, and he appears to well understand it, and loudly boasts of it.

It can be proven, that Bass, now says, that the decision, has given him the *better* of Keatts *five thousand dollars,* and, "that it is of *no use* for Keatts to contend with him, for he has too many friends"

By the decision made, the rights of [third] parties are set aside, overlooked, trampled in the dust; and that of white men too, all tending to enrich Bass, at the expense of black and white persons alike. This surely was never intended by the persons having this matter in charge; and only needs to be presented to receive correction; from wrongs so glaring on their face.

It is therefore respectfully asked that an order be made, restraining Bass from converting this crop to his own use. That is, that Keatts receive *all the cotton raised upon the land rented by him*, and, in case any cotton has been sold or disposd of by Bass, that he immediately, account for any and all that was taken from the land of said Keatts. and for such other relief as shall seem best to further the ends of justice in this behalf, That the case be investigated upon its facts and merits, either by yourself or in such other manner, as shall be in accordance with the rules and regulations of your office, whether by special commission or otherwise.

T. D. W. Yonley,
HLSr John Wassell,

T. D. W. Yonley and John Wassell to Col. J. L. Chandler, 8 Nov. 1864, Letters & Orders Received, ser. 376, Little Rock AR Supt. of Freedmen, RG 105 [A-2533]. Yonley and Wassell, both of whose signatures are in the same handwriting, identified themselves as "attos. for Keatts." Enclosed and labeled "Exhibit 'A' " are handwritten copies of the newspaper advertisements by Bass (10 July 1864) and by Keatts (20 July 1864). In his advertisement, Keatts denied having entered into partnership with Bass: "Having plenty of room I have only permitted him to live on my premises to save him time, trouble and expense to build shanties to live in on the land he leased." Among several endorsements on the attorneys' letter is one by the provost marshal general of the Department of Arkansas, indicating that Major W. G. Sargent, superintendent of freedmen in the state of Arkansas, had promised to "give the matter careful attention" and that Wassell was willing to accept Sargent's arbitration. According to another letter in the same file, Sargent promptly set about investigating the dispute by requesting permission for Bass to bring witnesses through Union lines. (Maj. W. G. Sargent to Col. Garrett, 21 Nov. 1864.) No record of the original judgment or final disposition of the case has been found among Sargent's records (filed with those of the Arkansas Freedmen's Bureau) or among the records of the provost marshal of the Department of Arkansas.

1 Marginal notation at the bottom of the page, in the same handwriting as the text: "* not now in the service."

196: Treasury Department Special Agent for Skipwith's Landing District to the Supervising Agent of the Treasury Department 1st Special Agency, Enclosing a List of Plantations Leased Out by the Former

Skipwiths Landing Miss Mar. 11th 1864.

Sir. Your communication of the 8th inst, asking information in regard to number of Plantations leased, as to whether the price established by the Treasury Department to be paid the Freedmen are too high &c &c is before me.

In reply I respectfully beg leave to submit my report of buisiness transacted in this district from Jany. 12th to Feby 12th 1864 inclusive.

A synopsis of the tabular reports herewith enclosed shows the following result:

Number of Plantations Leased 41
" " " Occupied by owners or leased by owners under Government Rules, 37 Total 78.

Number of acres in Plantations as above		55,105
Requiring first class hands	4,409	
Infirm and helpless Negroes 3 to each no 1 hand	13,227	
Total number of colored persons		17,636

I would further remark that if such Military protection had been placed upon the Mississippi River as was promised in January, I could have leased every Plantation along the river in my district to good responsible Citizens of the Northern and Western States who came here in good faith, with the best endorsements and abundant means – to cultivate these Plantations in accordance with the rules prescribed by the Treasury Department – Some came singly, while others came representing organized companies of one hundred or more, who were ready to come in person as soon as advised so to do,

My intercourse with these men convinced me that they were not Speculators or unprincipled persons eager to enrich themselves at the expense of the Negro, but liberal minded philanthropic Gentlemen, who while they sought to make the cultivation of Cotton proffitable, at the same time regarded the rights of the Negro, and entertained toward him the principles of humanity and christianity,

I am asked if the lessees have not complained of the wages paid to the Freedmen under the Treasury rules as being too high? I reply emphatically no. In no single instance has a lessee made any such complaint. On the contrary, in every instance they have expressed a perfect willingness to pay the rates prescribed by the Government, and furthermore I feel justified in asserting that if I could have given applicants for lands any assurance of protection every Freedman woman and child capable of work in this district would have been employed on these Plantations, and been supporting themselves instead of being a burthen to the Government or demoralized marauders, living by theft and murder as many of them now are.

The absence of protection on the river has had a most disastrous influence upon many of these Negroes, and is rapidly working thier ruin. They collect in abandoned camps in large numbers and make a precarious living by chopping a little wood stealing Cotton, corn, mules &c on the abandoned Plantations. Many of them are armed with Government Guns, and they not unfrequently resort to murder and all manner of personal violence upon unprotected white persons. This in turn calls out the vengeance of those upon whom they transgress, and thus life and property are constantly jeopardized.

A demoralized camp of this kind exists upon the river opposite Skipwiths Landing.

Several hundred negroes were living there in filth and disease, with all manner of booty stolen from the surrounding country, Application was repeatedly made to them by lessees to work for them, but they declined. Last Sunday morning while I was on the Mississippi side of the river opposite thier camp thirty white men rode in upon them and fired indiscriminately among them. Four were killed instantly and twelve others wounded very badly. I have understood that these Negroes had murdered a white man sometime before in the vicinity for his money, and hence the attack upon them. This is but one instance of many.

On many of the abandoned Plantations that I have visited, I have found Negroes living in the quarters; and they generally expressed a desire to go to work. But if they leave thier homes and wander about, they collect in camps and soon become loathsome objects of Vice and disease. I am not aware of any cases, where persons have called upon Col. Eaton with my order for hands that he has not shown a readiness to respond, so far as in his power as regards furnishing transportation to the Contraband Camps.

But upon arriving at the camps, I have been told of several instances where persons were unable to procure the particular hands they desired. These were cases where persons went to the Contraband Camp at Dare's [*Davis*] Bend for hands they had formerly owned The Negroes expressed a desire to go, but were not allowed to do so for some technicality assigned by Lieut Bryant in charge, Mrs Dunbar, Mrs Bettie A Wilson and Mrs Henson, experienced this difficulty and came away without thier hands.

In several instances lessees experienced a difficulty, because the Negroes did not wish to go to work and no authority was used to make them go. M[r] Johns of Worthington's Landing could get no hands at Dare's [*Davis*] Bend for this reason.

My duties require me to visit every Plantation on the river in my district. It is necessary to appraise the property on these Plantations and inspect the books of the lessees, to see that the Freedmen are charged no more than the rates laid down by Government for Supplies. It is necessary to take charge of abandoned Cotton, Corn and Stock and for the lack of a boat to enable me to do so, the Government is daily loosing this property by having it Stolen,

While traversing the river on official buisiness the same boat could amply accomodate lessees in thier transportion, and if a uniform rate of freight and passage, were established, the amount thus earned by the boat would no doubt pay her expenses. And further in this connection I would remark that the interests of the Government imperatively demand a boat subject to my order. Lessees wishing to transport stock, supplies and hands to thier Plantations have to contend with many difficulties. Transient boats cannot be had when they are wanted in many instances and often they are unwilling to take on Stock and hands or unwilling to land where the lessees desire to, and when they reluctantly comply with the wishes of the lessee their charges are exhorbitant.

The passage money of a single person from Vicksburg to Skipwith Landing, is generally Ten Dollars. When a lessee has from ten to fifty mules and from twenty to a hundred hands with their baggage and Stores to transport at these rates, it will be seen that the sum required to pay freight and passage is enormous.

I have known lessees to be detained at Vicksburg for several days with thier hands and Stock on heavy expense, and then pay exhorbitant rates to get transportation, and soon after landing have stock and Stores captured by the guerrillas.

Owing to the difficulty in exploring the river under existing circumstances it has been impossible to obtain anything like a complete record of abandoned or occupied Plantations, such as I present has been compiled from personal observation or information from others who have been out.

There are hundreds of fine Plantations in my district of which I have yet obtained no record,

In conclusion allow me to say, that with the protection of the "Marine Brigade" and some fifteen hundred or two thousand troops judiciously Stationed along the river at once, there is time enough yet, this year to lease and successfully Cultivate a large portion of these abandoned Plantations.

Aside from the principle of economy which should induce prompt action on the part of the Government in this matter the dictates of humanity toward the Freedmen demand it.

They are the helpless, down-trodden Victims of this War – crushed between the two contending parties as corn is ground between the upper and nether millstone. Here is a field where they can at once be lifted from thier Misery and degradation, and, while they support themselves and contribute largely to the wealth of the Government, at the same time they may be greatly improved in thier condition and gradually elevated to the position they should occupy as intelligent human beings Respectfully

ALS A. M[c]Farland

[*Enclosure*] [*Skipwith's Landing, Miss. March 1864*]

Plantations leased by A. W. M[c]Farland, Asst. Special Agent for Plantations.

Date 1864		Plantation	Lessee.	Location of Plantation	No. Acres.	No. 1. Hands	Other persons to be Supported.	Remarks.
Jan'y	20	Barry Prince	Stephen C. Heurd	Issaquena Co. Miss.	900.	72.	216.	
"	"	Stono	J. B. Harris	Carroll Par. La.	600.	48.	144.	
"	"	Aldemer	Henry Smith	Washington Co. Miss.	1,100.	88.	264.	
"	23	George Ward	Smith, Lyday & Co.	"	500.	40.	120.	
"	"	Beard	John Fawn	Carroll Par. La.	500.	40.	120.	
"	"	Goza	J. A. Biddle	Washington Co. Miss.	800.	64	192.	
"	"	Helen Johnson	Wm. G. Munson	Issaquena Co Miss.	1,000.	80	240.	
"	"	Kiger	J. H. Hodges	"	400	32	96	
"	28	Ward or Parks	E. P. Bancroft	"	1,000.	80.	240.	
"	29	Sam. Chambley	J. H. Healy	Carroll Par. La.	300.	24.	72.	

Feb	1	Island 76.	Eddy & Wilbur	Bolivar Co. Miss.	3,000.	240.	720.	
"	"	Dr Mills	H. D. Callen	Issaquena Co. Miss.	175.	14	42	
"	2	Eustacia	A. H. Reed	"	800	64	192	
"	3	Knox	H. C. Freeman	Washington Co. Miss.	800	64	192	
"	5	Carson	J. C. Groshong	Carroll Par. La.	1,000	80	240	
"	8	Cottonwood	Mich. Morrissy	Washington Co. Miss.	300.	24	72	
"	"	Dr Langley	Belmont Perkins	Issaquena Co Miss.	700	56	168	
"	10	Balfour	Westly Brooks	"	150	12	36	Colored.
"	11	Gibson	T. B. Waddell	"	900	72	216	
"	18	Wilderness	A. Gates White	"	400	32	96	
"	"	Outpost	Henry Jackson	Carroll Par. La.	300	24	72	Colored.
"	19	Balfour	Sanch Lynce	Issaquena Co. Miss	250	20	60	"
"	"	Balfour	James Diggs	"	200	16	48	"
"	"	Howory	Wm. Thompson	"	200	16	48	"
"	24	Shipland	Theo. Fitler & al.	"	1,000	80	240	
"	27	Belzona	M. W. Bland	Washington Co. Miss	800.	64	192	
Feb	29	Chotard	Thos. D. Aylsworth & Co	Issaquena Co. Miss.	200.	16	48	
"	"	Savage	Wm. Gibson & Co.	Carroll Par. La.	500.	40	120	
"	"	Goodrich	O. H. Brewer & Co.	"	300.	24	72	
Mar	1	Hayes	D. Davis & Q Jenkins	Issaquena Co. Miss.	400	32	96	Colored.
"	2	Chotard	J. Smith & J. Batton	"	300	24	72	"
"	"	Nelson	Bristow Williams	"	400	32	96	"
"	3	Good Intent	Rich. Mullen	"	700	56	168	"
"	"	Sunnyside	Wm R. Smith	Chicot Co. Ark.	1,000	80	240	
"	"	Red Cap	W. A. Pattison	"	1,000	80	240	
"	"	Ford	Dr. A B Jones	"	1,000	80	240	
"	"	Omega	Isaac Wildy	Issaquena Co. Miss.	150	12	36.	Colored.
"	5	W. Sutton	T. W – Jepson	Carroll Par La.	600	48	144	
"	8	Reality	Sam[l] Turner	Issaquena Co Miss	100	8	24	"
"	"	Kelsau	H. Booker	"	100	8	24	"
"	9	Harris	John Lynch & Co	"	500	40	120	
				Totals	25,325	2,026.	6,078.	

HD

A. McFarland to Wm. P. Mellen, 11 Mar. 1864, enclosing list of Plantations leased by A. W. McFarland, Asst. Special Agent for Plantations, [Mar. 1864], Reports of A. McFarland, Skipwith's District, 2nd Agency, RG 366 [Q-39].

197: Supervising Agent of the Treasury Department 1st Special Agency to the Secretary of the Treasury

Cincinnati [*Ohio*], March 29 *1864.*

Sir I beg to refer you to my last report from Vicksburg dated March 10th in reference to the leasing of abandoned plantations and employment of Freedmen on the Mississippi[1]

In persuing the course therein indicated I have obtained from the Assistant Agents appointed to lease abandoned plantations on the Mississippi their respective reports, copies of which please find enclosed herewith.

The Rules and Regulations made by me Jany 7. 1864. concerning leasing abandoned plantations and employing Freedmen,[2] a copy of which I enclose herewith, were generally distributed and discussed along the Mississippi from Memphis to Natchez in January. On the

20" of that month we commenced leasing at Vicksburg under the rules and subject to the conditions thereof See copy blank lease on the sheet of rules enclosed.

The following abstract of the enclosed reports will show the number of acres leased by the respective agents, with the number of Freedmen they have applied for at contraband camps to labor under the rules and the number of young or otherwise helpless in the families of the hands applied for and to be disposed of with the hands thus applied for

Name and Location of Agent		No of Lessees	No of Acres Leased	No of Hands applied for	No in families of Hands	Date of Leases made
T. C. Callicot	Helena	28	3,910	321	963	Feby 10 to March 15
A. McFarland	Goodriches Landg	43	25,325	2,026	6078	Jany 20 to " 9
C. A. Montross	Vicksburg	209	100,294	8,270	24,811	" 20 to " 10
Wm Burnet	Natchez	35	37,200	4,650	13,950	" 22 to " 7
	Total	315	166,729	15,267	45,802	

I addition to the demand for labor of Freedmen by *lessees* of abandoned plantations along the Mississippi. large numbers of *owners* of plantations who have remained at home. or who have returned and taken the amnesty oath under the Presidents Proclamation,[3] have come in and agreed to employ their former slaves who have remained at home, and others if they could get them from the contraband camps at the wages and under the rules of January 7, including the contribution of one cent per pound on all cotton raised by them.

Many of the lessees had procured hands stock impliments and supplies and moved on to, and commenced working the plantations leased by them in January when the withdrawal by General Sherman of all military forces to which they had looked for protection produced the panic and general stampede of whites and blacks, of which you have already been advised. From that time the whole planting operations were almost entirely suspended until those engaged in them were re-assured as to military protection. During this time most of the lessees had waited hoping that protection would be given and ready to work as agreed when this should be done, if done in time. Some, tired of the delay and lateness of the season, left and returned North. But I feel certain that there will be a much larger demand for laborers than the numbers now within our lines will supply.

By the reports of the Agents of the Abandoned plantations respectively leased by them, you will see that the aggregate number of acres of such plantations so leased is 166.729 up to the 15th inst. At about that time such assurances of protection were given as will doubtless increase the number of such lessees.

The number of owners who have employed and will employ their former slaves and other freedmen under the rules will proberably be larger than the lessees. How much success will follow, will depend chiefly on the protection afforded. If that shall be regarded as at all adequate, I believe that even though the season is so far advanced 250,000 to 400,000 acres will be cultivated in cotton this year in the Mississippi Valley in the 1st Agency

I think it proper I should be placed right with the Secretary of War in the agency I have had in this matter under his order[4] since Dec 30., when I left here to execute my duties under it, and for that purpose submit the following statement in connection with my report

When in Vicksburg in January I submitted the rules and regulations dated January 7th under which I proposed acting, to Col. John Eaton of the "Invalid Corps" of colored troops and "General Superintendent of Freedmen" He most *heartily* approved of *every one* of them and so expressed himself several times *enthusiastically* in presence of Mr James E. Yeatman of St Louis, Asst Spl Agent McDowell of Vicksburg, Mr Geo B Field (former commissioner) of Natchez and others, He would have come up the River with me to order the troops of his corps, which was formed for the purpose of protecting the planting interest, down to such possitions as he thought best for the purpose, but was ill, and promiced to follow me as soon as he should be able.

I confidently expected his most hearty co-operation, but heard nothing from him until after my return from Washington. I met General Thomas at Louisville and from him learned that Col Eaton had been to the Front and had informed him that my rules and regulations were impracticable, that they were so unsatisfactory to persons who had gone down intending to lease and plant that they were all abandoning the business and going home and that unless he came forward and interposed, the whole freed people would be thrown upon the Government for support. General Thomas informed me that he was satisfied as to the correctness of this information and had telegraphed the President, and that he should at once go down the Mississippi and correct the mischief I had done. I assured him he had been misinformed and that I would follow him and demonstrate the falsehood of Col Eaton. I joined him at Memphis March 7, and we started thence down the River together. On board the boat after starting he showed me a telegram he had received at Louisville from the President as follows

Washington Feby 28 1864

Genl L. Thomas

I see your dispatch of yesterday to the Secretary of War I wish you would get to the Mississippi River at once and take hold of and be master of the contraband and leasing business. You understand it better than any other man does Mr Mellen's system is doubtless well intended but from what I hear I fear that if persisted in it would fall dead within its own entangled details. Go there and be the Judge. Mr Miles will probably follow you with something from me on this subject. But do not wait for him. Nor is this to induce you to violate or neglect any military order of the General in Chief or Secretary of War

(signed) A. Lincoln

My impulse on reading this was to regard it as superceding the order of the Secretary of War of Oct 9,[4] under which I had assumed to act, But believing that the false statements of Col Eaton had caused the trouble, and that the public interests demanded whatever aid I could render to make this years planting with free labor a success, and also feeling that it was due to my position as well as to you that I should vindicate myself, I proceeded with General Thomas.

The testimony of over 300 persons who had leased under my rules and many of whom had commenced operations under them before the withdrawal of protecting forces by General Sherman, and most of whom were still there and ready to go to work if the military protection could be given – the testimony of large numbers of owners of plantations who had agreed to work their own plantations with their former slaves and other freedmen upon the terms of compensation and contribution prescribed by my rules which leases and agreements were in writing and filed with the Agents making them, – the testimony of Judge Field, his former commissioner, in whom he has properly great confidence, that Col. Eaton had over and over again while the rules were being discussed (he, Judge Field, disapproving several of them) argued in favor of such as he opposed and expressed ardent approval of *all*, insisting that they were "the first steps in the right direction" – the assurance of the many lessees he saw ready to commence work under them if they could have military protection – satisfied General Thomas that he had been misinformed and that *protection* was the *only* question

He then proposed that for the sake of uniformity in my Agency and the 5th Agency, he would issue an order similar to that of General Banks in the Gulf Department,[5] adopting his rules in most respects but approving my rules and the contracts made with lessees and owners except as to compensation classification and police Regulations. To this I consented. His order was then issued,[6] a copy is enclosed.

This being done he obtained from General McPherson an assignment of two (2) Regiments of Infantry and two (2) battalions of Cavalry, and such of the "Invalid Corps" as could be availed for that purpose, to be detailed for protecting this planting interest

I hope now for prosperous gales and smoother sailing He

assured me of every assistance he can render and that if we do not move in perfect harmony it shall not be his fault. It is late, but the lessees and other planters at once made preperations to commence work as soon as the forces were in the positions assigned

I beg you to excuse the length of my report. I feel that a full explanation of matters should be made, and have given it as briefly as I could I am Very Respectfully Your Obt Servt

HLS Wm P. Mellen

Wm. P. Mellen to Hon. S. P. Chase, 29 Mar. 1864, M-78 1864, Letters Received by the Division, ser. 315, Division of Captured Property, Claims, & Land, RG 56 [X-53]. The documents said to have been enclosed are not in the file.

1 In his letter of March 10, William P. Mellen, the supervising agent, had reported a conference with Adjutant General Lorenzo Thomas, who in earlier correspondence with the Secretary of War had criticized the Treasury Department's administration of the plantation-leasing system. Charging that Thomas's complaints had been based upon incorrect information, Mellen declared that he would set forth the "*facts*" as to "why this great interest has failed." (Wm. P. Mellen to Hon. S. P. Chase, 10 Mar. 1864, M-61 1864, Letters Received by the Division, ser. 315, Division of Captured Property, Claims, & Land, RG 56 [X-50].)
2 See above, doc. 188.
3 The Proclamation of Amnesty and Reconstruction, issued December 8, 1863. For a summary of its provisions, see above, doc. 187n.
4 Presumably War Department General Order 331, issued on October 9, 1863, which instructed Union army officers to turn over to the supervising agents of the Treasury Department's special agencies all captured and abandoned "houses, tenements, lands, and plantations," except those required for military purposes. (*Official Records*, ser. 3, vol. 3, p. 872.)
5 General Order 23, issued by General Nathaniel P. Banks, commander of the Department of the Gulf, on February 3, 1864. (See above, doc. 109.) The Treasury Department's 5th Special Agency had jurisdiction over the southern Louisiana parishes that constituted the Department of the Gulf.
6 The adjutant general's order, issued March 11, 1864, is printed immediately below as doc. 198.

198: Order by the Adjutant General of the Army

Vicksburg, Miss., *March 11th, 1864.*

ORDERS, No. 9.

The following regulations, respecting the leasing of plantations within the limits of the military Division of the Mississippi, and the management of the Freedmen thereon, are published for the information and government of all concerned.

The rules adopted by Major General N. P. BANKS, in the Department of the Gulf,[1] have, for the sake of uniformity, been taken as a basis, with such modifications as the experience of the past year has dictated as most beneficial to the interest of this section of the country.

The occupation of the plantations and employment of the Freedmen, having been directed by the President of the United States, must be regarded as a settled policy of the Government, and it is the duty of all military commanders and troops to afford protection to the fullest extent to this most important interest whenever it can properly be done.

When steamboats are employed by proper authority, transporting Freedmen or supplies for plantations, such boats will not be taken possession of unless under an imperative necessity, and then only under the immediate order of the General in command of the Department, Corps, or District.

I. The enlistment of soldiers from plantations under cultivation in this Department, having been suspended by order of the Government, will not be resumed except upon direction of the same high authority.

II. Provost Marshals shall be distributed at convenient points in the neighborhood of leased plantations, whose duty it shall be to see that justice and equity is observed in all relations between employers of freedmen and those employed and to exercise such other police duties as shall be assigned to them by the District Commanders appointing them. The districts over which they shall exercise these duties shall be called Police Districts.

III. Provision will be made for the establishment of a sufficient number of schools, one at least for each of the police districts, for the instruction of colored children under twelve years of age, which, will be established by, and placed under the direction of the Superintendent of Public Education.

IV. Soldiers will not be allowed to visit plantations without the written consent of the Commanding Officer of the Regiment or Post to which they are attached, and never with arms, except when on duty, accompanied by an officer.

V. Plantation hands will not be allowed to pass from one place to another except under such regulations as may be established by the Provost Marshal of the Police District.

VI. Flogging and other cruel or unusual punishment are interdicted.

VII. Planters will be required, as early as practicable after the publication of these Regulations, to make a Roll of persons employed upon their estates, and to transmit the same to the Provost Marshal of the District. In the employment of hands, the unity of families will be secured as far as possible.

VIII. All questions between the employer and the employed, until other tribunals are established, will be decided by the Provost Marshal of the Police District, subject to appeal to the higher authorities.

IX. Sick and disabled persons will be provided for on the plantations to which they belong, except such as may be received in establishments provided for them by the government at the Freedmen's Home Farms, which establishments shall be under the exclusive control and direction of the respective Superintendents thereof, and all commanders of military forces, stationed thereon, will see that all proper military protection is afforded, and will aid in carrying out the police regulations thereof as desired by the Superintendents.

X. The unauthorized purchase of clothing, or other property, from laborers, will be punished by fine and imprisonment. The sale of whisky, or other intoxicating drinks, to them, or other persons, except under regulations established by the Commander of the District, will be followed by the severest punishment.

XI. The possession of arms, or concealed or dangerous weapons, without authority, will be punished by fine and imprisonment.

XII. Laborers shall render to their employer, between daylight and dark, ten hours in summer, and nine hours in winter, of respectful, honest, faithful labor, and receive therefor, in addition to just treatment, healthy rations, comfortable clothing, quarters, fuel, medical attendance, and instruction for children, wages per month as follows, payment of one half of which, at least, shall be reserved until the end of the year, and lessees will discourage all payment of monthly wages as far as it can be done without discontent, and reserve the same as above stated: The minimum wages for males over fourteen years of age, and competent to do a well man's work, ten dollars per month; for females over fourteen years of age, and competent to do a well woman's work, seven dollars per month; children from twelve to fourteen years of age, inclusive, and of those too feeble to earn full wages, half the above amounts will be paid, or a specified amount to be agreed upon by the employer and the employed, subject to the approval of the Superintendent of the Freedmen's Home Farm nearest thereto. Engineers and foremen, when faithful in the discharge of their duties, will be paid such additional sums as shall be agreed upon, and approved by the proper Home Farm Superintendent. This schedule of wages may be commuted by agreement between the employer and the employees, subject to approval as above. Wages will be deducted in case of sickness, and rations also, when sickness is feigned. Indolence, insolence, disobedience of orders, and crime, will be suppressed by forfeiture of pay – such forfeitures to go to the fund for the support of the helpless freed people – and such punishments as are provided for similar offences by Army Regulations. Sunday work will be avoided, when practicable, but when necessary, will be considered as extra labor, and paid at the rates specified herein.

XIII. When laborers are furnished with employment, they will be held to their engagement for one year, under the protection of the Government. In cases of attempted imposition, by feigning sickness, or stubborn refusal of duty, they will be turned over to the Provost Marshal of the Police Districts for labor upon the public works, without pay.

XIV. Laborers will be permitted to cultivate land on private account, as shall be agreed between them and the employers, subject to the approval of the Provost Marshal of the District. The encouragement of independent industry will strengthen all the advantages which capital derives from labor, and enable the laborer to take care of himself and prepare for the time when he can render so much labor for so much money, which is the great end to be attained.

XV. To protect the laborer from possible imposition, no commutation of his supplies will be allowed, except in clothing, which may be commuted at the rate of $3 per month. The crops will stand pledged, wherever found, for the wages of labor.

XVI. It is advised, as far as practicable, that employers provide for the current wants of their hands, by perquisites for extra labor, or by appropriation of land for share cultivation.

XVII. A FREE LABOR BANK will be established for the safe deposit of all accumulations of wages and other savings; and in order to avoid a possible wrong to depositors, by official defalcation, authority will be asked to connect the bank with a Treasury of the United States in the Military Division of the Mississippi.

XVIII. The rules and regulations of the Supervising Special Agent of the Treasury Department, dated January 7, 1864,[2] and the terms and conditions of all contracts made in pursuance thereof for leasing abandoned plantations and employing freedmen are hereby approved, except as to the classification and compensation of hands, and as to police matters, which shall be as herein provided.

XIX. The last year's experience shows that the planter and the negro comprehend the revolution. The overseer, having little interest in capital, and less sympathy with labor, dislikes the trouble of thinking, and discredits the notion that anything new has occurred. He is a relic of the past, and adheres to its customs. His stubborn refusal to comprehend the condition of things, occasioned most of the troubles of the past year. Where such incomprehension is chronic, reduced wages, diminished rations, and the mild punishments imposed by the Army and Navy, will do good.

XX. These regulations are based upon the assumption that labor is a public duty, and idleness and vagrancy a crime. No civil or military officer of the Government is exempt from the operation of this universal rule. Every enlightened community has enforced it upon all classes of people by the severest penalties. It is especially necessary in agricultural pursuits. That portion of the people identified with the cultivation of the soil, however changed in condition, by the revolution through which we are passing, is not relieved from the necessity of toil, which is the condition of existence with all the children of God. The revolution has altered its tenure, but not its law. This universal law of labor will be enforced upon just terms, by the Government, under whose protection the laborer rests secure in his rights. Indolence, disorder, and crime, will be suppressed. Having exercised the highest right in the choice and place of employment, he must be held to the fulfillment of his engagements until released therefrom by the Government. The several Provost Marshals are hereby invested with plenary powers upon all matters connected with labor, subject to the approval of the Commanding Officer of the District. The most faithful and discreet officers will be selected for this duty, and the largest force consistent with the public service detailed for their assistance.

XXI. Employers, and especially overseers, are notified, that undue influence used to move the Marshal from his just balance between the parties representing labor and capital, will result in immediate change of officers, and thus defeat that regular and stable system upon which the interests of all parties depend.

XXII. Successful industry is especially necessary at the present time, when large public debts and onerous taxes are imposed to maintain and protect the liberties of the people and the integrity of the Union. All officers, civil or military, and all classes of citizens who assist in extending the profits of labor, and increasing the products of the soil, upon which, in the end, all national prosperity and power depends, will render to the Government a service as great as that derived from the terrible sacrifices of battle. It is upon such consideration only that the Planter is entitled to favor. The Government has accorded to him, in a period of anarchy, a release from the disorders resulting mainly from insensate and mad resistance to sensible reforms, which can never be rejected without revolution, and the criminal surrender of his interests and power to crazy politicians, who thought by metaphysical abstractions to circumvent the laws of God. It has restored to him in improved, rather than impaired condition, his due privileges, at a moment when, by his own acts, the very soil was washed from beneath his feet.

XXIII. A more majestic and wise clemency history does not exhibit. The liberal and just conditions that attend it cannot be disregarded. It protects labor by enforcing the performance of its duty, and it will assist capital by compelling just contributions to the demands of the government. Those who profess allegiance to other governments will be required, as the condition of residence in the Military Division of the Mississippi, to acquiesce, without reservation, in the demands presented by Government as a basis of permanent peace. The non-cultivation of the soil, without just reason, will be followed by temporary forfeiture to those who will secure its improvement. Those who have exercised, or are entitled to the rights of citizens of the United States will be required to participate in the measures necessary for the re-establishment of civil government. War can never cease except as civil governments crush out contest, and secure the supremacy of moral over physical power. The yellow harvest must wave over the crimson field of blood and the representatives of the people displace the agents of purely military power.

XXIV. It is therefore a solemn duty resting upon all persons, to assist in the earliest possible restoration of civil government. Let them participate in the measures suggested for this purpose. Opinion is free and candidates are numerous. – Open hostility cannot be permitted. Indifference will be treated as crime, and faction as treason. Men who refuse to defend their country with the ballot box or cartridge box, have no just claim to the benefits of liberty regulated by law. All people not exempt by the law of nations, who seek the protection of the Government are called upon to take the oath of allegiance in such form as may be prescribed, sacrificing to the public good, and the restoration of public peace, whatever scruples may be suggested by incidental considerations. The oath of allegiance, administered and received in good faith, is the test of unconditional fealty to the government and all its measures, and cannot be materially strengthened or impaired by the language in which it is clothed.

XXV. The amnesty offered for the past, is conditioned upon an unreserved loyalty for the future, and this condition will be enforced with an iron hand. Whoever is indifferent or hostile, must choose between the liberty which foreign lands afford, the poverty of the rebel States, and the innumerable and inappreciable blessings which our Government confers upon its people.

May God preserve the Union of the States!
By order of the Secretary of War.

PDSr L. Thomas,

Adjutant General L. Thomas, Orders, No. 9, 11 Mar. 1864, A-246 1864, Letters Received, ser. 12, RG 94 [K-542]. On March 14, Adjutant General Thomas informed the Secretary of War that he had just issued new plantation regulations, "[a]fter full consultation" with William P. Mellen, supervising agent of the Treasury Department's 1st Special Agency, whose own regulations were thereby revised. Thomas was sure that his order was "satisfactory" to Mellen, "and will be so to the lessees." "With the military protection I shall be able to afford," he predicted, "I think the system will work well." (*Official Records*, ser. 3, vol. 4, pp. 176–77.) On March 23, Thomas changed that part of his order respecting provision of clothing to plantation laborers, releasing employers from the obligation to furnish it (or a monetary equivalent) and thereby requiring laborers to purchase clothing with their own means. (Adjutant General L. Thomas, Orders No. 14, 23 Mar. 1864, L. Thomas Letters & Orders, Generals' Papers & Books, ser. 159, RG 94 [V-62].)

1 General Banks's "rules" were embodied in his General Order 23, issued February 3, 1864. See above, doc. 109.
2 See above, doc. 188.

199: Treasury Department Special Agent for Natchez District to the Supervising Agent of the Treasury Department 1st Special Agency

[*Natchez, Miss.*] March 12th 1864

Copy

In addition to the above extract from my report of the 1st [1] I have the honor to say, that on Monday week last the Asst Supt of the Home Farm came in to inform me that the people who had been gradually increasing numbers engaging in the work assigned to them, had that morning refused to work and that the reason assigned by them was, that *Lieut. Howell* had been there the day before (Sunday) and had told them, they need not work unless they chose, and if they did work, they had a right to wages – That the Government intended to take care of them, and would not let any one force them to labor against their will,

I sent Dr. Weldon with the assists to Col Johnson to State the case, and ask an order that no Officer or Soldier be allowed to visit the Home Farm without a pass from himself or from me

Such an order was issued and since, matters have become more pleasant, and the people are gradually returning to work, We now have a large extent of Land cleared and ready for the plow, and have as many plows going as we have Mules and Harness for,

The evil counsils heretofore given have not yet lost thier effect entirely, and there are still cases of refusal to work, but each day reduces the number. The impressions, against going on to the Plantations seem to be more permantly fixed in thier minds and with some exceptions brought about by causes outside of my Knowledge, but *probably* a *Bonus*, to some one having influence over the people, the Lessees have not been able to secure Laborers from the Corrall or Farm,

It is proper to say here that those moved to the Farm have been the most helpless, with only such of the able bodied as were absolutely required for the purposes of the Farm and the care of the helpless,

It is true that most of the Lessees prefer the terms of Labor as fixed by Genl Banks and the Negroes themselves prefer, to be fed and clothed by the Employer,[2] but I have not found more than two or three of my Lessees that would not have been glad to take thier hands on *either* or indeed *any* terms, that would induce them to go,

The officers, heretofore having the control and protection of the contrabands have evidently been disappointed by the appointment of civilians to that duty, Whether this has had any share in creating the difficulties referred to, may be decided by others quite as well as by me, I merely state the facts as they come to me from observation, and from the reports of Lessees, and of my own employees,

I hand you herewith copies of orders given to Lessees on the Superintendent for details of Hands, More than Thirty such orders were issued but as they were all similar in import, it was not beleived essential to preserve Copies of every one issued.

I also hand you herewith a Copy of letter to Major Young Commdg Controband Camp,

In conclusion allow me to say that the almost countless difficulties confronting me at the outset have been gradually surmounted or are giving way before the System adopted in my District, and that if we can secure a *Military* order *requireing* all able bodied hands to find employment, which I doubt not Gen[l] Tuttle would readily issue, and with *protection* to Lesses from Guerillas, we shall not only make a large crop of Cotton and Corn in this District but the System will result in a triumphant success,

To sum up the entire result of my observation and experience, in a simple sentence, All we ask to insure success in this District is *protection* from the Military Authorities without interference: Give us that and I do not hesitate to say that "Providence permitting" we shall turn out 1/2 Million Bales of Cotton, and other Crops in proportion, while making material progress in elevating the character and ameliorrating the condition of the Freed People Respectfully your Obt Servt,

HLcSr W Burnet

W. Burnet to Hon. William P. Mellen, 12 Mar. 1864, Monthly Reports, Natchez District, 2nd Agency, RG 366 [Q-40]. Except for the extract of Burnet's March 1 report, no copies were retained of the documents said to have been enclosed. General James M. Tuttle, who Burnet believed would agree to issue an order requiring able-bodied freedpeople to "find" employment, was commander of U.S. forces at Natchez. Burnet's desire for such an order reflected the failure of his repeated attempts to induce residents of the home farm to accept employment as wage laborers on leased plantations. In the ensuing weeks, Burnet redoubled his efforts, but neither persuasion nor curtailment of rations accomplished his goal. In response to offers of plantation employment, the freedpeople all "claimed to be sick or ailing in some way—except Soldiers wives, who openly refused to work, on the ground that the Recruiting Officer promised them the government would take care of them." Yet, Burnet noted sardonically, "when a Lessee was known to be coming, (and by some means incomprehensible to me, they always find it out) those who were *too sick to work*, would pack up their movables, and walk off under a *fair Cart load*, to be seen no more for days, when one by one they would be found again in their quarters, to repeat the same operations." Only by stationing an armed guard to prevent such departures did Burnet manage to send "three Wagon Loads" of former slaves to a nearby plantation. (W. Burnet to Honb. W. P. Mellen, 27 Apr. [186]4, vol. 133, pp. 90–101, Reports of the Plantation Department, Natchez District, 2d Agency, RG 366 [Q-52].)

1 The earlier report had complained that freedpeople at the home farm near Natchez refused to "leave the Camp for Plantations" and were supported in their resistance by Arthur O. Howell, a lieutenant in the 64th USCI, "who notifies the people that they need not go unless they prefer, and that all who choose to stay will be taken care of as heretofore without labor." It also charged that some lessees had "procured hands by means of a *Bonus* or *head money* paid to parties having influence over the people." (Wm. Burnet, "Extract from my Report of March 1st 1864," Monthly Reports, Natchez District, 2nd Agency, RG 366 [Q-40].)

2 The military order that governed plantation labor in southern Louisiana, issued in February 1864 by General Nathaniel P. Banks, commander of the Department of the Gulf, required employers to provide food and clothing for their laborers, in addition to paying wages. (See above, doc. 109.) By contrast, the Treasury Department regulations that governed plantation labor in the Mississippi Valley required laborers to purchase their own food and clothing from their (higher) wages. (See above, doc. 188.) Unbeknownst to the special agent, however, this and other differences in policies for the two regions were being eliminated. On March 11, Adjutant General Lorenzo Thomas had re-

vised the treasury regulations, adapting and extending General Banks's policy to the territory embraced by the Military Division of the Mississippi (which included the Natchez area). (See above, docs. 197 and 198.)

200: Superintendent of Freedmen in the District of Vicksburg to the General Superintendent of Freedmen in the Department of the Tennessee and State of Arkansas

Vicksburg, Miss., March 14th *1864.*

Dear Sir: I enclose a Financial Statement of the Condition of the Freedmens Department under my charge, and also a consolidated morning report, showing the number of camps, their location, and the number of people now in them. You will see by the report that during the last week thirty seven hundred people have been removed from the camps to plantations. There has been since the 1st of January 1864 nearly nine thousand people sent out of the different camps to labor, yet the numbers now in camps is about as large as it was then. They are constantly coming in from the interior, and being sent to these camps for food and portection. So much so has this been the case, that I find in some of the camps that the hands employed at work near the camp, have changed four different times within thirty days. The object has been to make every well person work that came within the lines of the camp as long as they remaned, urgeing them to seek employment on plantations where they would be better paid for what they did, and find a more permanent home. I have found that some of my camps are composed of such old and profitless people to the planters, that they will not take them under any consideration.

At Paw Paw Island I have about one thousand people that are engaged in gardening and cutting wood, that I have heard planters say were entirely unfit for service on a plantations, as they would have to take such a large number in order to accomplish any work.

The camp at Omega Landing has been broken up, and the people distributed among the planters in the vicinity; this camp had been engaged in cutting wood, some of which still remains on the yard.

The camp at Goodrichs Landing is only temporary as the people will go on the plantations and find employment, as soon as it is safe for them to do so.

At Youngs Point the people have about one thousand cords of wood cut, but are now turning their attention to agriculture. Under the direction of M[r] Beard they have small pieces of ground allotted to them on which they have built houses and expect to raise vegetables for the Vicksburg market. But without the aid of the

Government to supply them with teams, implements, and rations, they must fail.

Opposite Vicksburg there is only about six hundred left in camp they being of that class that there is but few among them able to perform any kind of labor. They have seeds, mules, and implements, and are attempting to put in gardens.

Blakes Plantation has been leased, and large numbers from that camp have hired out on the plantations near by. I think it will be but a short time till that camp can be broken up entirely.

Davis Bend has about three thousand people of all classes there now. All that are able have been made work at something, although most of their time has been devoted to repairing their quarters and improving their camp. Nearly six thousand negroes have been shipped to this camp from time to time for a temporary home, but three thousand of them have found employment on plantations, and have left the camp.

The season being so far advanced when the plantations were leased, it was important for planters to have their hands immediately, and it being imposuble for them to get supplies from the North, it has been necusary for me to furnish supplies for the people in their transition from my camps to the Plantations, and also to leave them a small amount of provisions to prevent actual suffering. By the consent of the Chief Commissary of this Post I have furnished such supplies to a small extent, and charged the planters for the amunt, and turned over the proceeds to the Post Commissary. The whole amount of such sales will not exceed Eight hundred dollars.

You will see that the Financial Statement does not include the abandoned property gathered up by the Camps, or include the labor performed in building Homes imporving camps or putting in individual gardens, which amounts to a large amount of labor as it has been our constant aim to have them build comfortable houses and put in small gardens, in order to relieve the Government as much as possible of their support, and improve the sanitary condition of the camps

In the four items of Mules Horses Cattle and Wagons we have gathered up property to the amount of twenty thousand dollars, that otherwise would have been lost to the government by being destroyed and taken up by private parties.

I make the foregoing statement, not as a report of the operations of the Department or as an estimate of what has been done, but as an explination of its present condition as shewn by the enclosed Financial Statement and Morning report. I am Col Yours Respectfully

HLcSr — Sam[l] Thomas

Col. Saml. Thomas to Col. John Eaton Jr., 14 Mar. 1864, Miscellaneous Reports from Subordinate & Staff Officers, ser. 2029, General Supt. of Freedmen, MS Asst. Comr. Pre-Bureau Records, RG 105 [A-4012]. Endorsement. This copy is written on letterhead of the office of the general superintendent of freedmen. Evidently copies were not made of the enclosures; the financial statement and morning report are not in the file.

201: Circular by the General Superintendent of Freedmen in the Department of the Tennessee and State of Arkansas

VICKSBURG, MISS., March 26, 1864.

CIRCULAR.

WITH REFERENCE TO REQUIRING FREEDMEN TO LABOR ON PLANTATIONS.

I. The able bodied freed people must labor.

II. Those supported by the Government will be kindly advised to seek labor on plantations, under circumstances of safety. All persons, officers and others connected with the freedmen will use their best endeavors to induce them to accept of opportunities to labor.

III. The rations of all able bodied, not disposed to labor voluntarily, will at once be reduced one half.

IV. All able bodied, refusing to work, will be required to go to labor with properly authorized parties, under circumstances of safety. This requirement will be carried out without the use of harsh means.

V. The officers in charge will take command of a guard, and present with it; kindly assure the people that they must labor; if they refuse, the guard will be used as under similar circumstances in the control of white persons. The people have suffered all manner of trial; they are full of distrust and fear, but become attached to any persons, or to localities, where they have found safety and kindness. They will soon become as much attached to their new homes; the Government will be relieved of their support, and they will be in better health than when idle—besides contributing to the general good, and securing their own advancement in the arts and virtues of life.

PDSr JOHN EATON, JR.,

CIRCULAR, OFFICE GENERAL SUPERINTENDENT OF FREEDMEN, 26 Mar. 1864, enclosed in Major W. G. Sargent to A.A. General C. H. Dyer, 17 May 1864, Miscellaneous Letters & Reports Sent & Received, ser. 272,

Dist. of Little Rock, RG 393 Pt. 3 [C-254]. Colonel Eaton's circular was probably intended to clarify instructions he had issued one week earlier, which spelled out the duties of superintendents of freedmen in enforcing the labor regulations of Adjutant General Lorenzo Thomas. "For the purpose of protecting the Freedmen . . . on the one hand, and of giving trustworthiness to labor on the other," the superintendents were to ensure that each contract be "the free act of the parties," enforce the "inviolability" of the agreement, and adjudicate disputes between employers and employees. They were also instructed to "encourage" the enlistment of black men in the Union army, assist those freedpeople "disposed, and competent to carry on individual enterprise," and "require the industry of all others able to work." (INSTRUCTIONS TO SUPERINTENDENTS, OFFICE GENERAL SUPERINTENDENT OF FREEDMEN, DEPARTMENT TENNESSEE AND STATE OF ARKANSAS, 19 Mar. 1864, in the same file.)

202A: Superintendent of Freedmen in the District of Natchez to the Adjutant General of the Army, Enclosing an Order by the Health Officer at Natchez, a Letter from the Superintendent of Freedmen to the Commander of U.S. Forces at Natchez, and a Letter from the Superintendent of Freedmen to the Health Officer

Natchez, Miss., Mch 31st *1864.*

General Enclosed please find copies of two communications and the endorsements thereon to which I beg leave to call your attention. The enforcement of Surg. Kelleys Health order (which find enclosed) against a class I have petitioned for in the city is causing a vast Amount of Suffering and will still cause more. If individual enterprise among the colored people is going to be thus crushed their condition will be but little changed by their transition from bondage to freedmen – and that little change will be for the worse. Knowing you will give this matter that attention its importance demands I have the honor to be Very Respectfully Your obt Servant

ALS Geo. W. Young

[*Enclosure*] Health Office, NATCHEZ, MISS., March 19th, 1864.

TO PRESERVE THE GENERAL HEALTH of the troops stationed in the City of Natchez, and of the inhabitants, and to guard against the origination here, and the introduction of pestilential diseases the ensuing summer and autumn, it imperatively requires the *prompt, vigorous* and *steady* enforcement of the Sanitary Regulations heretofore prescribed in this City.

It is of the first and greatest importance and necessity that all causes tending to the engendering and dissemination of pestilential diseases here, so soon as their existence is known, shall be at once abated, or removed so far as practicable. It is to be apprehended that serious danger to the health of this City will result from the congregation within its limits of the large numbers of *idle* negroes which now throng the streets, lanes and alleys, and over-crowd every hovel. *Lazy* and *profligate,* unused to caring for themselves; thriftless for the present, and recklessly improvident of the future, the most of them loaf idly about the streets and alleys, prowling in secret places, and lounge lazily in crowded hovels, which soon become dens of noisome filth, the hot beds, fit to engender and rapidly disseminate the most *loathsome* and *malignant* diseases.

To prevent these evil effects it *is hereby ordered* that after the first day of April, 1864, no contraband shall be allowed to remain in the city of Natchez, who is not employed by some *responsible white person* in some legitimate business, and who does not reside at the domicil of his or her employer; and no contraband will be allowed to hire any premises in this city for any purpose whatever, and no other person will be allowed to hire such premises for the purpose of evading this order, nor allowed to hire or harbor any contraband who cannot satisfy the Health Officer that he or she needs the services of said contraband in some legitimate employment. All contrabands remaining in the city in contravention of this order after April 1st, will be removed to the contraband encampment.

The word contraband is hereby defined to mean all persons formerly slaves who are not now in the employ of their former owners.

Any evasion of this order will be punished more severely than the direct infraction of it, and all persons renting buildings to contrabands will be held responsible.

Persons drawing rations from U.S. Government are not supposed to need many *hired* servants. The number allowed to each family will be determined by the undersigned.

By order of A. W. KELLY,
Surgeon and Health Officer.

Approved: J. M. TUTTLE, Brig. Gen. Commanding District.
PDSr

[*Enclosure*] *Natchez, Miss.,* Mch 31st *1864.*

Gen'l. The Health Order as issued by Surgeon Kelley is I fear being put in force against many people of color for which it was not really intended – the draymen Hackmen and other tradesmen in the city. Some means ought to be devised to protect these as they are undoubtedly necessary to carry on the business of the Post and when they are Keeping themselves in a decent manner could not they in some way be permitted to remain? Hoping you will pardon me for calling your attention to this I have the honor to be Your obt Servant

ALcS Geo W. Young

[*Endorsement*] [*Natchez, Miss. March 31, 1864*] Refered to Sergeon Kelley Heath Officer (signed) J M Tuttle Brig Genl Comd.g.

[*Endorsement*] [*Natchez, Miss. March 31, 1864*] Draymen Hackmen Marketmen and those in legitamate employment of their masters and who reside on their *immediate premises* & those in employ of the military by proper authority will not in any way be interfered with. (signed) A. W. Kelley Surg. & H Off

[*Enclosure*] *Natchez, Miss.*, Mch 31st *1864*.

Major A. W. Kelley Health Officer The bearers of this are in "legitimate" business as the permission from the former Commanding Officers which I enclose and which please return to the men shows and according to Your endorsement on a note for information that I addressed to Genl Tuttle they ought not to be molested and yet their families have been turned out of doors so they inform me.

Please do what you can for them as I think some distinction ought to be made between the worthless and vagrant and those as capable of supporting and caring for themselves as thier *former* masters. I am, Major, Your Obt Sevant

ALcS Geo. W. Young

[*Endorsement*] [*Natchez, Miss. March 31, 1864*] If permission is given in one case it must be in another therefore this is disapproved. By order of Maj. Kelley (signed) Capt. M. Yeoman asst.

If any colored men or contrabands are permitted to remain in ther city they must reside on the premises of their employers By order of Maj. Kelley (signed) Capt. M Yeoman asst.

Sup't of Freedmen Geo. W. Young to Brig. Gen'l L. Thomas, 31 Mar. 1864, enclosing Order, Health Office, Natchez, Miss., 19 Mar. 1864, Major Geo. W. Young to Brig. Gen'l J. M. Tuttle, 31 Mar. 1864, and Major Geo. W. Young to Major A. W. Kelley, 31 Mar. 1864, Y-2 1864, Letters Received by Adjutant General L. Thomas, ser. 363, Colored Troops Division, RG 94 [V-86]. Major Kelly's order is in the form of a clipping from an unidentified newspaper. A notation on the wrapper indicates that Major Young's letter and its enclosures were simply filed by Adjutant General Lorenzo Thomas, to whom they were addressed. A search of the records of the Adjutant General's Office, including Thomas's records in the "Generals' Papers," revealed no evidence of further action by Thomas.

202B: Newspaper Account of a Protest by Northerners at Natchez, Mississippi, to the Commander of U.S. Forces at Natchez

[*?, Iowa*] May 5 [*1864*]

THE MILITARY ORDER ON THE FREEDMEN AT NATCHES.

Protest of the Missionaries.

General Tuttle issued an order that all free persons must hire themselves to white masters, or be banished the city. The Northern agents and missionaries at that place presented the following protest:

NATCHEZ, Miss., April 1, 1864.

General Tuttle:

SIR: The undersigned citizens of Natchez would respectfully ask you to modify the recent order of the Health Officer of this city, because of the manifold and manifest evils arising from its execution, as it is now carried out. It certainly cannot be the interest or policy of the Government of the United States at this time to alienate the colored people from it and make them its enemies. The colored soldier in the field hearing that his mother or his wife has been driven from her quiet and comfortable home, simply because she supported herself and was not dependent upon some white person, may feel less inclined to hazard his life in the cause of his country now struggling for *its life*, and many doubt whether the pledges made by the Government to him have been fulfilled. And it seems strange just now, when the Government is fighting for the principles of universal liberty, that a distinction should be made in this district in favor of those who have been slaveholders, and against well-doing and self-supporting freedmen.

In the execution of the order referred to, the most flagrant wrongs have been inflicted upon the better class of the freed people. An old woman who has lived fifty years in this city, and was not disturbed before, was driven at the point of the bayonet to the camp. Mothers who having young infants and attending to lawful business were arrested, and were not allowed to see their babes. Many persons in the employment of respectable white citizens, were driven from their houses, and no time allowed them to obtain certificates of being employed. Many others who had paid their taxes and rents in advance, and who had official and personal security of protection and safety, were suddenly turned out of their neat and comfortable houses, without any time allowed them to arrange their affairs, and driven away to the camp, without shelter or clothing for the night. Parents were driven away from their young children, and children coming out of school were driven away by soldiers without the knowledge of their parents. These wrongs have been inflicted upon a people already sufficiently oppressed and injured, and upon many of them because they are not in a state of servitude, whilst it is the evident policy and design of the Government to liberate and elevate them.

Signed by.

James Wallace, Missionary of the Reformed Presbyterian Church.

J. C. H. Feris, Missionary of the Reformed Presbyterian Church to Freedmen.

S. G. Wright, Missionary American Association, N.Y.

H. A. McKelvey, Northwestern Freedmen's Aid Commission, Chicago.

J. B. Weeks, Northwestern Freedmen's Aid Commission, Chicago.

J. G. Thorn, Agent Western Freedmen's Aid Commission, Cincinnati, Ohio, and Acting Agent National Freedmen's Relief Association, N.Y., and Western Sanitary Commission.

William G. Thompson, M.D., Assistant Surgeon, Freedmen.

After the general had read this paper, he said to them who presented it, "You appear to think that colored men have a great many more rights than white men." To which it was replied, "We did not; that we had never dreamed of them having more rights than white men, but we simply believed that a colored man or woman who decently and comfortably supported himself or herself in lawful employment, might be permitted to remain in the city." He then referred the paper to Dr. Kelly.

PD

Clipping from an unidentified [Iowa] newspaper, 5 May [1864], enclosed in Saml. Collins to his Excellency A. Lincoln, 6 May 1864, C-463 1864, Letters Received by General Grant, ser. 105, Hdqrs. in the Field, RG 108 [S-34]. Samuel Collins, a Presbyterian minister from Madison, Iowa, forwarded the clipping to President Lincoln with a covering letter asserting that military disaster had always followed the announcement of Union policies "bearing hard on the colored people." Collins regarded it as no coincidence that battle-field reverses in the Red River campaign had followed the order issued by Major A. W. Kelly, the "health officer" at Natchez, and approved by General James M. Tuttle, commander of U.S. Forces at Natchez (and unsuccessful Democratic candidate for governor of Iowa in 1863). "[L]et that diabolical order be reversed," Collins pleaded, "or the cup of our iniquity will soon run over and we will have neither a President to pray for, nor a Government to Support." Lincoln evidently referred the letter and its enclosure to the general-in-chief, without comment. Soon the uproar over Kelly's order was reverberating in the halls of Congress. On May 16, the House of Representatives passed a resolution, introduced by Josiah B. Grinnell of Iowa, instructing the Joint Committee on the Conduct of the War "to inquire as to the occasion of" the order. (Edward McPherson, *The Political History of the United States of America, during the Great Rebellion*, 2nd ed. [Washington, 1865], p. 253.) Beset with criticism, including well-founded allegations that he had abused his official position for personal gain, General Tuttle resigned his commission in June.

203: Affidavit of a Tennessee Freedman

Memphis Tenn. July 31st 1865

Statement of Clinton Hamilton,

I have been working for one George Howard a citizen living 5 miles South of Covington in Tipton County Tenn for the last nine years. and on the 4" day of this month I complained of being Sick and told the said Howard I could not work that day, The said Howard insisted that I Should go to work, and I told him the second time that I could not. the said Howard then ordered me to take off my clothes which I done, he Howard then gave me about two hundred blows on my back with a white oak Stick– I was to work for the said Howard in company with Eleven other colored persons, under the following Contract, Since March 1864, said Howard promised to divide equilly between the[se] above mentioned twelve persons five Bales of Cotton at Each Christmas which he Howard failed to do last Christmas, and he has not given me any thing for labor but one suit of Clothes worth Twenty dollars since March 1864–

HDSr

his
Clinton X Hamilton
mark

Affidavit of Clinton Hamilton, 31 July 1865, Affidavits & Statements, ser. 3545, Memphis TN Provost Marshal of Freedmen, RG 105 [A-6600]. Sworn before an assistant provost marshal of freedmen. In an endorsement dated August 13, 1865, the provost marshal of freedmen at Memphis directed that Howard be arrested and brought to trial, "together with the necessary witnesses to prove the facts in this case." Howard was evidently tried and found guilty; on August 16, 1865, he paid a fine of $100 for "whipping." ("Statement of fines recieved By Major A. T. Reeve Prov Marshal Freedmen . . .," 17 Aug. 1865, Miscellaneous Records, ser. 3546, Memphis TN Provost Marshal of Freedmen, RG 105 [A-6600].)

204: Circular by the Superintendent of Freedmen in West Tennessee

Memphis [*Tenn.*] April 4th 1864

Circular

A communication having been forwarded stating the fact that a large number of the families of Colored Soldiers were collected in the camps for Freedmen in the District of Memphis. and were being supported by the Goverment. The following endorsement was made by Brig. Genl L. Thomas Adjt Genl. U.S.A.

> Every company is entitled to a certain number of Laundresses. and the wives and children of Soldiers have no claim on the Goverment for rations
>
> "The families of Colored Soldiers are on the same footing as other Blacks. and I shall require them to work for their living. I am opposed to having large numbers of women and children around the stations of colored troops"
>
> (Signed) L Thomas
> Adjt Genl.
>
> Vicksburg
> March 26th /64

An opportunity now offers, for the employment of 1000 women and children at remunerative wages at a point on the River near Helena where they will be well protected and their interests looked after by the Local Superintendents appointed for the purpose of securing the interests of the Goverment, by improving the condition usefulness and character of the freed people, and they will endeavor to render available as far as possible, all efforts of volunteer laborers, and of charity looking to their good.

under existing orders the families of Colored Soldiers must be made self-supporting and I assure them in all kindness that it is for their interest to go voluntarily. all those that volunteer to labor will be sent to Helena where they can have daily communication by Boat with their husbands at Memphis.

Jno Phillips

HDcSr

Circular, Office Supt. Freedmen West Tenn., 4 Apr. 1864, Letters Received, ser. 2910, Organization of U.S. Colored Troops, Dist. of West TN, RG 393 Pt. 2 No. 183 [C-2204]. Colonel Phillips's efforts to remove former slaves – including the wives and children of black soldiers – from the Memphis contraband camps had been under way for several months. In early 1864, applications by plantation lessees for "a large number of Field hands" had led him to predict that he would be able to hire out at least 2,000 freedpeople from the camps by the first of March. (Lt. Col. Jno. Phillips, "Consolidated Report Department West Tennessee . . . ," [1 Feb. 1864], P-3 1864, Letters Received by Adjutant General L. Thomas, ser. 363, Colored Troops Division, RG 94 [V-89].) By that time, Phillips had also begun to remove the families of black soldiers from a settlement near Fort Pickering and relocate them "down river," presumably as plantation laborers. The commander of the black artillery regiment stationed at the fort warned that his men were "seriously allarmed" by the eviction of their families. (Col. I. G. Kappner to Lieut. Geo. A. Mason, 4 Mar. 1864, Letters Received, 3rd USCHA, Regimental Books & Papers USCT, RG 94 [G-9].) Officers of other black regiments voiced similar objections to requirements that soldiers' families work on plantations, whereas plantation lessees commended Phillips's readiness to supply them with laborers. (See, for example, below, doc. 206.)

205: Agent of the Cincinnati Contraband Relief Commission to the Headquarters of the Commission

Jeff Davis Mansion. [*Davis Bend, Miss.*] 4th Mo. 14th 1864.

Copy.

Esteemed Friends In the prosecution of my intended personal inspection of all and each one of the coloured family under my care on this beautiful and interesting portion of earth, I have to add to what I have already sent; that in another direction to what I have described is a settlement of negros on what is called the Lake plantation from a large sheet of water being there. the frame of a large good building is standing, ready for roof and siding which was intended for the Overseer to reside in, in the rear are a row of neat houses some twenty, for the coloured people.

They need clothes for changing and the women here begged loudly for colored handkerchiefs for their heads. I never have ordered any, but a few dozen I think would be well to have on hand, for every woman and many of the men constantly wear a bandage on their heads and some are disgustingly nasty. Their other most pressing needs are very similar to those of the other places I have mentioned. Around here I saw a many sheds filled with cotton unginned, there is a good gin, building & power, all on hand. I learnt the great trouble why it has not been cleaned and made marketable is that all so far who have had any thing to do with it, have invariably been attacked with the Cotton fever so effecting them that the proceeds generally get into the purses of the Overseers in lieu of being appropriated for the negro's benefit.

I intend to watch and try and stop such improper use of such property, the negros raised, worked, and gathered it in without any wages, it is theirs and I will help them to obtain it and plead their cause against all injustice.

They have no School here nor a suitable place for any.

Passing on for a mile and half brought me to another settlement and a most lovely spot called Wood's plantation of 1300 acres of nice land. Here were two classes of coloured people quite distinct and who pride themselves on dignity. Those occuping the neat and comfortable houses were generally well supplied unless it was with Shoes, which are universally needed. These are the slaves of the Estate, whilst around about are 100 of the wretched shanties or sheds which I described in mine of yesterday, these occupied by some who came in with Gen[l] Sherman, are miserable substitutes for residences and not fit to shelter cattle in during a storm, yet therein are our fellow creatures in all weathers subjected to disease, degradation and immorality. These need assistance in almost every thing. Please remember the far larger proportion of these settlements of negros are Women and children, old or crippled men only being left, the men mostly being obliged to enlist as soldiers in the U.S. army.

At this place I found and attended a large school of 200 children under excellent training of three young ladies Lee, Wallace and Finley. I heard a class spell, one read very nicely and one acquitted themselves creditably in Arithmetic. Their house needs enlarging and fitting up with benches, and they need a supply of books &c which I gave encouragement to them that I would in a short time supply.

I need for the Bend, 500 Childs Primer. 500 each McGuffie's Electic Speller & Reader. 500 Slates about 10 × 12 size, and 5 gross Pencils. There are two other large and interesting schools besides on the Bend, one at the Mills, and one at Lovells being equally divided in distance from the other places enables all the children to have an opportunity of attending, and it is gratifing to witness how eager they are to obtain it (learning). These schools have my best wishes, and they furnish good opportunities of giving religious & moral influences with their scholastic requirements, may we not hope these seasons will be blessed by the great Creator. The successful husbandman not only prepares the ground, sowing good seed, but he continues to work the land, keeping down injurious weeds &c. until the harvest is gathered in; so I believe the ultimate good of this people greatly depends upon their having christians for their caretakers, and when these have secured their confidence they should be very careful of leaving them, or from getting away from under the responsibility of being as it were the keeper of the minds and interest of many truly helpless.

I humbly trust through divine grace I clearly see and feel the weight of such responsibility, and if my Heavenly Father continues to bless with health of body and peace of mind, I see no way for myself but in a full reliance on Him for help and strength; faithfully continuing to labour for the benefit of the colored race, endeavouring to teach them the religion of the Bible; their duties as therein laid down, their obligations to their Maker, to their fellow man, to their families, and last though not least, their duties to themselves.

The extent of distance from one extreme point to the other is over seven miles, I very much wish to visit each place twice during the week if possible. To walk this distance and be exposed to the summers son, I could not bear; riding on horseback would not be less exposing to the heat, besides which I never learnt to ride on horseback, I shall frequently wish to carry a bundle of clothing &c to some object; that after mature consideration I have decided to very respectfully ask the Commission to furnish me a low priced second hand Covered Buggy for one horse, which I have no doubt will sell here for more than cost in Cin after one or two years using by me.

I know such can be frequently be obtained in cities I should also require a single sett of harness, the horse gov[t] will find or I can have one belonging to Gov[t] The harness should be well boxed up, else it would be stolen in coming here, and all directed care of Col J. Eaton Gen[l] Sup[t] of Freedmen Vicksburg. please send a piece of chain and pad lock & key to keep it from being used by any one but self.

There has been so many destroyed around here that they are very scarce and enormously high. It will come as goods for the Cont[d] being truly, wholly to benefit them, by increasing my facilities of spending more time amongst them, and saving my health and strength to labour for them.

I have no choice in the style &c all I want is use with shade from sun, and means of dispatch in getting from place to place. In respectfully submitting this to you I remain your friend

ALcS Henry Rowntree

Henry Rowntree to Esteemed Friends, 14 Apr. 1864, vol. 122, pp. 14–17, Letters Sent, ser. 2150, Davis Bend MS, RG 105 [A-9376]. In a letter to the commission written the previous day, Rowntree had described the condition of several thousand black refugees who had been shipped to Davis Bend after following General William T. Sherman's army from the interior of Mississippi to Vicksburg. Rowntree found the new arrivals suffering for want of food, shelter, and medical attention. In a cattle shed on one plantation lived thirty-five former slaves, including five women ("all Mothers") and twenty-nine children under twelve years of age. With only two quilts and a threadbare army blanket among them, they slept by huddling together "to keep one another warm and then throw the quilts over them." Elsewhere on Davis Bend, Rowntree counted nearly two thousand refugees crowded into 150 makeshift huts. In still other parts of the bend, he discovered one group of sixteen ex-slaves housed in a henhouse, and "many sleeping on small branches of trees." Some of the freedpeople had cleared land and begun to cultivate vegetables by the time of Rowntree's visit, but he predicted that famine and disease would take a fearsome toll. (Henry Rowntree to Esteemed Friends, 13 Apr. 1864, vol. 122, pp. 10–13, Letters Sent, ser. 2150, Davis Bend MS, RG 105 [A-9376].)

206: Northern Plantation Lessee to the Treasury Department Special Agent for Vicksburg District

Backulum, Madison Parish, La. May 7th 1864.

Dear Sir: In compliance with your request that I should state the results of my observation and experience as to the facilities afforded planters in obtaining hands for the cultivation of plantations, I would reply: –

That on my arrival in Vicksburg last January, I found that the difficulty of obtaining laborers was one of the most serious obstacles to the successful prosecution of the planting enterprize. Gentlemen in whose statements I have entire confidence, informed me that they had been from camp to camp with an order for hands, without being able to obtain a hand; although the camps were overflowing with unemployed laborers.

Having leased plantations near to Skipwiths Landing in company with Capt. A. H. Kelsey, I went to Memphis, preferring to bring hands three hundred miles rather than not obtain them. Col. Phillips who has charge of that Department, promised us that as soon as a prior order was filled, he would furnish ours. The next day I received news that our operations were broken up by guerrillas, which compelled me to withdraw the order. I have no doubt that Col. Phillips would have furnished us all the hands we wanted, although he was embarrassed by the interference of Officers of colored troops, who claimed that the wives of soldiers should be exempt from labor.

A few weeks since I became a lessee of this plantation, and being in want of hands I called at the Office of Col. Eaton, Superintendant of Freedmen, and obtained an order for fifty hands. The Officer in charge told me that there was a large number of unemployed persons in the camps in this vicinity. I presented my order to the superintendant of the camp opposite Vicksburg He told me that there was a large number of hands there who ought to work, and that he had tried hard to induce them to work, but without success. That he could not compel them to go with me, but that I was at liberty to take them if I could persuade them to go. Feeling that it would be useless for me to attempt where he had failed, after one or two trials, I returned to the Office of Col. Eaton. I stated to him my difficulty and requested an order requiring his Officer to furnish the hands. He replied that such order had already been given.[1] I then requested that he should see that it was executed. He wanted to know how *I* would execute such an order. I replied that it was not for me to advise or instruct him as to the manner in which his orders were to be executed, but that if I should receive an order from a superior officer, it would be executed. Upon this he accused me of bringing a ridiculous charge against his officer, and flung in my face the taunt that I had come here from the North for the purpose of making money (as though it was a crime). I told him that I came at the invitation of the Government, and all that I asked was that they should do what they had promised. He said that he had received a great many complaints like mine, and the question arises whether the difficulty is attributable to the unreasonable expectations of the complainants as to the non-performance of the duties of his Office. That this point may appear in a clearer light I will add that but a few days previous I read a notice signed by Col. Eaton, saying that there were 1,500. unemployed persons in camps near Vicksburg, and calling upon planters to send in their orders without delay.

The result of my interview was, that I got no hands, but got abuse. After a weeks delay and the sacrifice of time and *money*, I got a few hands, some of them sick, while the camps and home-farm are full of able-bodied persons, who do not average one day's work in three.

I have thus far given you facts rather than opinions. My opinion is that the military authorities in this vicinity desire that the planting enterprize (so long as the plantations are leased by the Treasury Department) shall prove a failure. I have facts to sustain this opinion which my present limits will not allow me to present. I intend to present them to the Member of Congress from my District; and ask that justice shall be rendered. Respectfully Yours

HLcSr H. Wilson

H. Wilson to C. A. Montross Esqr., 7 May 1864, Letters Received from Assistant Special Agents, Records of the General Agent, RG 366 [Q-167]. Wilson was not the only plantation lessee to complain about obstructions to labor procurement created by Colonel John Eaton, general superintendent of freedmen in the Department of the Tennessee and State of Arkansas, and his subordinate superintendents. One month earlier, C. A. Montross, the Treasury Department's special agent for Vicksburg District, had charged that the superintendents of freedmen were advising plantation laborers "to come in town to Col. Eatons Office" if they were dissatisfied with their employers or their working arrangements, and thereby causing the workers "to become disatisfied and quit their places." Eaton himself, complained Montross, "does not try in any way at all" to persuade the freedpeople on the "Home Farms" to hire out to lessees. (C. A. Montross to W. P. Mellen Esq., 7 Apr. 1864, Letters Received from Assistant Special Agents, Records of the General Agent, RG 366 [Q-167].) Montross's grievances against Eaton mounted as the season advanced. In late June 1864 – after guerrilla raids had driven laborers from the leased plantations, interrupted agricultural operations, and forced planters to search desperately for new hands – Montross pronounced it "all wrong, that the Lessees should be so put to it for help, when the Contraband Camps are full to overflowing." The lessees, who could not engage laborers even at $50 per month, were "almost becoming mutinous." Meanwhile, according to Montross, Eaton continued to insist that the residents of the camps "are all Freed-people" and that, consequently, the superintendents "cannot compel them to go out, and . . . must not let them starve." The former slaves, Montross declared, "will not, as a class, work, so long as they can get full rations from the Gov't." (C. A. Montross to W. P. Mellen, Esq., 24 June 1864, Letters Received from Assistant Special Agents, Records of the General Agent, RG 366 [Q-169].)

1 It is not known which particular order was cited by Colonel John Eaton, Jr. (the general superintendent of freedmen in the Department of the Tennessee and State of Arkansas), but his general policy had been announced in a March 1864 circular instructing his subordinates to "induce" freedpeople to accept offers of employment and "requir[ing]" the able-bodied to work for "properly authorized parties, under circumstances of safety." (See above, doc. 201.)

207: Northern Plantation Lessee to the Supervising Agent of the Treasury Department 1st Special Agency

Hubbard Plantation Helena Ark. May 12th 1864

I send you a few facts in regard to my plantation of 1040 acres, 4 miles South of Helena. My plantation has been called among plantation lessees the "Gem of the Miss, while the *gentle* inhabitants quietly despose of it as the "*D--n Tribune concern*"[1] I have practically demonstrated the policy of the Treasury rules – the fact that freedmen will work well if you pay them their wages and will be equinomical when thrown upon their own resources

– Map –

The enclosed map gives the geographical status of my plantation, besides the other plantations to the extent of 12000 acres under cotton cultivation

I rented my plantation of 1100 acres last March, Dr. J. B. Pinney – ex-President of Liberia and Secy American Colonization Society – joining [use] in one fourth or 230 acres out of the 1100.

Labor

My labor consists entirely of freed people – men women and children. I am working strictly according to the rules of the Supervising Special agent of the Treasury Department.[2] The rules and modifications of Adj. General Thomas (March 10th)[3] are not prctical among free people. They would do to govern slaves. I can not use them and get labor, cheerful and happy labor from the people. They will do for slave drivers, but they will not do in the employment of Freedmen

Why?

While the wages ($10. for men and #7.00 for women) look small and are small for the freedman, the actual cost is more through prodigality. If you still feed and cloth men like children or slaves, you can not teach them economy. They are not thrown upon their own resources. They are freedmen but not free. The first rules of the Supervising Special agent (#25 for men and #16 for women) are found by the prctical anti-slavery planter to be wise – politic and calculated to lift up and make free the colored people, while the rules of Adj. Gen. Thomas keep the negro still a slave in practice – a slave in responsibility – a slave in advancement.

Intelligent negroes will not work under them. They say "We used to work so in Secesh times." This is the strongest arguement against it. Under the Treasury rules I am truly astonished at the economy, saving care, happy hopeful content, and every day industry of the freedman

I would not stupidly maintain this fact if my labour stood idle in the fields

Looking Forward

Two thirds of the men on my plantation are looking forward to making their own crops next year, and are saving money to my actual knowledge, for I pay my people monthly, to do it. All around my plantation on the "home farms" are negroes working from ten (10) to one hundred and fifty acres of cotton, which will pay them from two thousand to $15.000.

Protection

There are two forts, one above my plantation called Ft. Freedman and one below called Ft. PINNEY. Each is manned [by] a company of invalide colored troops

These give all the protection to a reservation of 13000 acres and 4000 freedmen, which, if well protected will pay a revenue of $450000 to the government. To the rear of this reservation is Gen. Buford's strong fort – "Fort Retaliation" To this fort the loyal planters about Helena owe their real protection, their growing crops, stock and their very existence.

Whenever a raid is made upon the planters and their stock driven off, Gen. Buford raids on the rich secessionists beyond Big Creek, who harbor and feed the theiving bands. He generally returns just as much stock as the rebels carry away

My mules, 45 were all stolen by armed guerrillas once, and taken away to White River, and sold at auction among disloyal planters.

Whenever Gen Buford found one of my mules marked "C.L." he swept the plantation of all stock bringing in enough to supply all the planters who had suffered by guerrillas.

– My Fort –

I have a fort, *iron clad*, with 36 stand of arms and one cannon on my plantation. My men act doubly as a picket for Gen. Buford and as a guard over the plantation. Through my fort and guard several Rebel guerrillas have been killed.

FORT LANDON. 36 stand of arms. 1 cannon.

WE NEED MORE PROTECTION

General Buford has only 400 cavalry to defend the Helena Post and protect loyal plantations. He has done his best to protect us but his horses are jaded, and it is a hard thing to cope with the three hundred rebels continually harrassing the plantations and post.

Daily the guerrillas make inroads upon the plantations, capturing stock and harrassing the planters Almost every evening I have a fight with men trying to steal my mules.

Picking time

When the time comes for picking and ginning (1st of August) I fear a large Rebel scout will break us up. We can not defend our crops against twenty-five men though we can defend ourselves.

I should feel sure of success if we had one more company of invalides to station in a block house at the Ford and 25 cavalry to do independent scouting

– Treasury Rules –

The Treasury rules for supplying loyal planters from the North are admirably calculated. They protect the loyal planter, and hundreds of southern men seeing the advantage of the plan, are contracting with their labor under the rules.

13.000. Acres –

There are now 13.000 acres under cultivation in cotton between Long Lake and the Missippi This reservation will yield a revenue to the government of $450.000

This is the largest, best, and most systematic reservation planted on the Miss. this year by loyal planters and freed people.

We are naturally protected and every man is plucky and brave enough to defend himself.

This is national absorption. The thirty-six loyal planters about Helena are doing more to squelch out slavery and southern Aristocracy than four Regiments of troops.

If successful many of the lands will be purchased – and many loyal business houses will spring up – many news papers be established, schools established, and laborers, the heroes of the axe and the hoe will be kept tilling the soil as freemen – as citizens. Yours – [. . .]

M D Landon

ALS

M. D. Landon to Wm. P. Mellon, 12 May 1864, General Letters Received, Records of the General Agent, RG 366 [Q-153]. The map said to have been enclosed is not in the file.

1 The writer was a correspondent for the *New-York Tribune*.
2 See above, doc. 188.
3 Actually issued on March 11, 1864. See above, doc. 198.

208: Report by the Assistant Provost Marshal of Freedmen at Young's Point, Louisiana

[*Young's Point, La.*] June 13, 1864

Nolly Plantation one mile above Desoto Landing. Tilled in part by W. H. Shadburn who has 40. acres under actual cultivativation Viz All in cotton. And Said Shadburn Employs five hands in cultivating the Same. The condition of the crop is good and promising, and the Husbandry is unexceptionable

Miller Plantation Fifty acres under actual cultivation and tilled by the Firm Edward Jones, Jonas Brown and Emanuel Scott (col) All planted in corn and They employ 26 hands in cultivating the Same. The crop looks promising

Barnes plantation Adjoining Desoto Landing & Tilled in part by the firm Edward Jones, Jonas Brown & Emanuel Scott who have under actual cultivation one hundred and fifty acres viz 70 in corn 75 in Cotton and five in vegetables And they employ 26 hands in tilling the same. The condition of these crops is very promising and the tillage is good & husbandmanlike.

Also on Barnes Plantation Empero Satterfield (col) has 12 Acres planted in corn & vegetables Employs no hands. Corn looks well cultivation is good. Prospect encouraging

Beards Home Farm 2 miles west Desoto Landing. Planted and controlled as follows By the following colored persons

David Thomas has about 20 acres planted to corn and Garden vegetəbles, about 8 acres being in corn, and the balance in vegetables, condition of the corn not very good (for want of culture) that of the vegetables is quite good

Albert Bailey has about Ten acres planted as follows. Five in corn, and Five in Garden vegetables. condition of the vegetables is unexceptionable. that of the corn not so good (requiring culture)

Curtis Pollard has in charge about Forty acres planted thus about Twenty five acres in corn in good and promising condition, and Fifteen acres in garden vegetables also in fine order With about twelve assistants in cultivating the Land: the profits to be divided acording to the amt of stock and force each one produces in the said tillage of the tract (Character of these people appears to be very Good)

Jacob Truman Hunter has about one hundred and Seventy five acres under his charge. Planted as follows one hundred and twenty five to corn and fifty to garden vegetables The condition of the Garden vegetables is fine indeed that of the corn is generally very indifferent Most of it Just coming up Said Jacob Hunter (or Truman) Employs 37 Hands (at Govt rates or wages) viz 12 First class hands, and Fifteen Second class hands. All appearing to be opperating togather very harmoniously The chief point of objection being that few of them are paying sufficent attention to the cultivation of the corn crops Mostly being weedy and requiring plowing & hoing Said Hunter appears to be a fine Young Man

White Plantation 3 miles west of Desoto Landing and tilled by Capt Sweney & Whiteman and planted as follows. – Three hundred acres planted to cotton (and now in a very fair and promising condition) And twenty acres of elegant corn in a fine State of cultivation

Said Swaney & Wightman employ forty hands in the cultivation of the foregoing crops and all appear as far as visibly manifested to be satisfied with their employment and Employers This tract lies west and ajacent to the Birney Plantation and is partly situated on both sides of the Canal, also adjacent to the Beard Home Farm

Swaney & Wightman employ Eighteen First class hands & Twenty two second class & Pay to first class hands (men) $15 pr month & rations & Women 1st class $10 pr month & ration

Prices Rations Swaney & Wightman continued Pickle pork 18 cts pr pound and Bacon 20[cts] pr pound Flour $7.00 pr cwt., Sugar 30[cts] pr pound

Hogan Plantation Tilled in part by C. J. Swan (citizen) & Alex Stewart (Col) They also till (50) acres of the Birney Tract lying south & adjacent to the Hogan Place Planted as follows. On the Hogan Place Fifty acres planted to cotton & Twenty to corn (All in a fair State of cultivation) On the Birney Plantation Fifty acres in Cotton in a fair state of cultivation and giving fair promise of a crop.

Said Swan & Stewart employ in tilling this land 13 hands viz about 8 first class hands and Six of the Second class Paying first class male hands $10. pr month and rations Same class female $7 and rations Second class male $5 per month and rations This Plantation is Situated two miles due west from Desoto Landing

June 14, 1864

Home Farm on Birney Plantation
Tilled by the following persons to wit

Benjamin Freese

Tills Ten acres planted to corn now in tolerable order, employs no hands but his own family An industrious & honest man

John Turner

Tills Ten acres all planted to corn. crop Stands well on the ground, but is weedy and needs culture. A cunning Negro.

William Gibson

Tills Ten acres, all planted to corn and in medium condition, in both physical condition and culture

Solomon Holmes

Tills Ten acres all planted to corn, which he is in a very unpromising condition, very grassy and puny. said Holmes has a very poor chance, he being all the time sick and has no mule &c

Dennis Williams

Tills ten acres, all planted to corn. which in midling condition, in evry respect An honest man

J. Thornton Turner

Tills Fifteen acres all in corn, which is poor, (for want of culture) Said Turner is imbibing some lofty notions & neglecting his work & passes his time in riding around the country

Moses Ellis

Tills Seven acres in corn, which looks very poor, and Sadly in want of culture Said Moses Ellis is not a good man

Anthony Kelway

Has ten acres planted to corn, condition moderate. He has no mule and therefore not much chance. A fine old man

Arthur Walton

Has ten acres planted to corn. Condition midling Said Walton (of Co. E 9th La. A.D.) is a contentious fellow; midling honest

Peter Smith.

Has ten acres planted to corn, in good Condition. He has an old horse and puts on much Style A fine old man

Wilson Mingo (of Co E 9th La AD)

Tills ten acres in corn which is in fine order in all respects. A fine young man

Jack Findlay

Tills Six acres in corn, which is in middling condition being planted late Said Jack is one tricky man

Robt Hill

Has ten acres in corn, midling fair in condition. A fine industrious old man

John Henry

Has ten acres in corn, in excellent condition promising a fine crop

William Foster (Sexton)

Has 3 1/2 acres in corn and vegetables in promising condition Said Foster is likewise the Parson & Medicine man

Frank Sewell (Co. E 9 La. A.D.)

Has Six acres in corn, indifferent lacking culture greatly & Sewell is too trifling to give it the necessary labor. A Desperate character

Benjamin Gray

Has Seven Acres in corn and one in cotton, all indifferent in appearance (He has a lease of thirty acres) and appears to be a harmless indolent fellows

John Thomas

Has Six Acres in corn and Six acres in cotton. Corn rather [an?] indifferent in apperance a result of late planting &c

This finishes with the exception of some very fine gardens a Summary of the Agricultural condition of the Freedmans Home on Birneys' Plantation La Two miles below Desoto Landing.

The chief Obstaclle to the successful cultivation of this land has been an almost entire lack of teams & farming implements, and these people being too poor to buy and the consequence bad farming

Groves Plantation Partly tilled by Owen & Thurston. Situated on the river Four miles below Desoto Landing La This firm tills one hundred and Twenty five acres in cotton which Stands well on the ground but is Small and in a backward State. Also about twenty five acres in fine thrifty corn in Splendid State of cultivation They employ 14 regular hands in cultivating this crop (& 40 hands in cutting wood. In regular hand Employ Five 1st Class women & 3 1st Class men, one 3d Class girl rest all second Class. Paying 1st class men $13 pr month and rations. First class women $10 per month and rations & the other Classes in the same ratio &c Hands complain of not receiving very high measure & high prices Do not always pay Promptly

Biggs Plantation June 14, 1864

Tilled by Meany & Kennedy Situated five miles on the river below Desoto Landing Who have one hundred and fifty & 50 acres planted to corn (in fine condition in evry sense of the word) Said Kennedy & Meany have not employed their hands in any very regular way and do not enjoy very good repute as employers They have with the colored people the character of Defrauders They Have in cultivation about two hundred acres of fine corn in Splendid condition & culture And employ 14 hands viz 3 1st class Male hands & 5 1st Class Female hands the 2 2" class men & 3 2" clas women & 1 3d & Pay 1st Class males $25 pr month without rations &c 1st class women $ pr month without rations &c at Govt rates. Quarters first Quality

Plantation of Brown & Jonson

Joseph Sanders & Lucinda Washington (col) Have about 15 acres in corn in excellent condition & use no help outside their families

By Lease to Cook & Coleman (col) given Feb 15, 1864 for three hundred acres the said Cook & Coleman & co. consisting of Cook, Coleman, Madison Milyun, Bristol Washington, Daniel Bell, Zara

Berlin, Jeff. Jonson, Bartlett Corbin, James Randall, Emanuel Randall, Edmund Jackson, John Allen. Have in cultivation about Two hundred acres planted to corn. Some of which is good and part is very indifferent because of defective cultivation & drought Much of this corn gives promise of a fair crop. These appear to be fair and decent people. But lack mules and farming implements

Think perhaps 175 acres may cover the crop

Luke & Patrick Madden (citizens) have thirty acres of fine corn in an excellent state of cultivation Giving promise of a Splendid crop

AD

Report by [Sergeant Moses Proctor], 13 & 14 June 1864, Miscellaneous Records, ser. 2035, General Superintendent of Freedmen, MS Asst. Comr. Pre-Bureau Records, RG 105 [A-4018]. The outside wrapper labels the document "Report of Lessees & Plantations on Youngs Point" and identifies its author as Moses Proctor, "Serg't and Pro Marshal." The 9th Louisiana Infantry A.D. (designated 81st USCI in April 1864), of which several farmers on the Birney Plantation were said to be members, had been organized at Port Hudson, Louisiana, and performed garrison duty along the Mississippi River throughout its term of service.

209: Provost Marshal of Freedmen in the Department of the Tennessee to the Adjutant General of the Army

Vicksburg Miss June 15th 1864

Genl: In making out a report of the Provost Marshal business of the Department. I find it almost impossible to get at the figures necessary, as the Assistant Provost Marshals have been so engaged with the duties around them that they have not had time to furnish me with the facts. Their duties were new to them, and it required all the ability they could bring to bear upon the affairs of their districts to remedy the confusion existing at the time of their appointment. Their duties were not fully defined, and for some time they were not aware of what they really were. Planters gave them but little assistance, and often refused to comply with their request. The planting district under my supervision, extending from Lake Providence. La. to Natchez Miss was divided into eight sub-districts and a Lieutenant assigned to each district as Assistant Provost Marshal. They entered upon their duties April 15th and have been actively engaged ever since. By the removal of the troops two of the districts have been abandoned and the Provost Marshals relieved. Some of the sub-districts are necessarily so large that it is almost impossible for one man to attend to the business; but we have every man engaged that can be spared for the work

The planting region that is in cotton, is a line of plantations near the Mississippi, from Lake Providence to Natchez, seldom over three miles from the river. Most of them have been leased to Northern men by Agents of the Treasury Department, and are cultivated by freedmen that have come within our lines since our occupation of this country They are cultivated on the basis of General Orders No. 9. of the Secretary of War, by Adjutant General Thomas.[1] I make the following report from the Assistant Provost Marshals Reports, sent to me monthly:

Washington County Miss.

There were a large number of plantations leased in this county. during the spring; but lack of protection has forced all who were loyal, to leave. There are several thousand acres of cotton planted in this county, but by citizens who are on good terms with the leaders of the bands of rebels which infest the country, or in such small quantities that it does not attract their attention. The Provost Marshal does not visit the county, as it would be unsafe. During the spring, large numbers of people were sent to the plantations; but since that time they have nearly all returned, and found employment in safer localities The freedmen while there, run great risk of being carried off into slavery again; and after their return were unwilling to go to plantations at all for fear of the same result.

Goodrichs Landing, and Millikens Bend.

This district extends from Lake Providence to Vicksburg on the Louisiana side of the river, with a few plantations in Issaquena Co., Miss. There are fifty-one plantations embraced in this district 30970 acres of cotton planted. They furnish employment for 4456 hands and have in the aggregate of people 7720. It will be seen from this, that nearly three-fifths of the freedmen are working hands. There is a population of 200 white men in the capacity of superintendents clerks &c. A large portion of this district was cultivated last year, and furnished but few obstacles to the Northern Planter. There are but few Southern men in the district, and what are left are becoming reconciled to the new order of things, and are joining hands with the new men. Military protection for this district has been granted and but small loss has been sustained by the planters from the incursion of rebel bands. This section is one of the finest cotton-growing regions of the South; and from all appearances will prove as fruitful under the free labor exertions of Northern men as it ever did under the lash of the Southern slave driver

A great many cases of difficulties between the employer and employee are constantly referred to the Provost Marshal and keep two men busy hearing the complaints and adjusting their difficulties. This duty is laborious and requires great firmness on the part of the officer, to use the proper discrimination in the various cases that come before him. The records in the offices of the Assistant Provost Marshals in this district, show a report of 122 cases that have been brought before them and disposed of. The amount of fines imposed is large but as it has not all been collected, no report has been received. For the want of a proper place to confine criminals brought before them there has been some complaint of their leniency; but I am satisfied the interests of all parties have been weighed in their actions. The planters have complied with "Orders No. 9."[1] and "Regulations for Leasing Abandoned Plantations,"[2] and seem to manifest a willingness to comply with every rule or order that is for the good of the government or the freedmen employed by them. The plantations in this district are large – 1000 acres being the average size. Yet the lessees have not been able to get more than 600 acres planted. The cotton of this district will compare favorably with that of any along the river; and I believe the hands are as well fed and clothed as laborers elsewhere. There are a large number of negro lessees in this district who have leased from the Government and are doing well. The Government is supplying them with food, and doing what can be done under existing orders, to aid them They are, as a body, industrious, economical and determined in their efforts to sustain themselves

I should like before leaving this report, to mention the names of several planters who are making extra exertions to make a good field of cotton on liberal principles, dealing honestly with their freedmen laborers; but to any one visiting the field of labor such a planter is easily distinguished, by the fine condition of his cotton, the cleanliness of his plantation and gardens, the cheerfulness of his hands and their willingness to do anything they can for him.

Warren County Miss.

In this county from the Yazoo River to the Big Black there are thirty-three plantations; 11874 acres of cotton under cultivation; 1280 hands employed; and 2396 people in the aggregate. A large portion of this is by the owners of the land, in connection with Northern men who furnish the supplies. Vicksburg furnishing a good market for vegetables, a large amount of land is devoted to the culture of such vegetables as can be sold in the market. There are a large number of colored lessees in this county: but we have no returns from them, and can make no estimate of how much they are cultivating. This county being upland and very uneven it has not presented so many inducements for the culture of cotton, as the neighboring river bottoms. Those who have planted in this county have received good protection from the military authorities: as there has been until quite recently, a military post on the Big Black which made the county comparatively safe. The freedmen are healthy, contented and as a general thing, well treated by the lessees who employ them.

Davis Bend.

This Bend, containing about 8000 acres of land, is securely protected by three companies of soldiers stationed at the neck which connects it with the main land. There are only two lessees here, who are cultivating about 3000 acres of land. They employ about 250 hands and have in their quarters fully 1000 people.

A report made to me of one of the lessees that appeared in a former report, I am satisfied was false. The representations made to me were unjust, and I am glad of this opportunity to do Mr Phelps justice. His plantation is being as well conducted as any on the Bend, and I am in hopes his labors will be rewarded with success.

Two thousand acres are cultivated by negro lessees, supplied with material by the Government, and under the control of the Superintendent of Freedmen. The enterprise promises success. These lessees are as far advanced with their work, are as industrious, and have as good a prospect of succeeding as the white lessees around them

St Joseph

This is a colony located in the bend of Lake St Joseph, about 30 miles below Vicksburg. It was organized by Professor Winchell and J. A. Hawley, and commenced work about the 1st of March. They have met serious obstacles from the very beginning, and have had to contend with obstacles that would have disheartened less resolute men. Their plantations have been raided twice and two of their number murdered under the most brutal circumstances: yet they manifest a determination to face the storm, and carry out their project of raising cotton. They are more exposed than any other body of cotton planters and farther from help in case of trouble. They merit great praise for the determined manner in which they have battled for their possessions and deserve success

There are eight plantations under cultivation; 6047 acres planted in cotton, furnishing employment for 666 hands, and a home for 1400 people in the aggregate. They need more hands in order to succeed; but find trouble in getting them to go, owing to their exposed condition. They are men of experience and judgment, who have brought correct business principles to bear upon their work. There would not be a necessity for near as many Provost Marshals, if all the planters came here imbued with the same principles.

Waterproof

At this place there were troops stationed during the months of March and April which led lessees to lease plantations in the vicinity and commence the work of planting. About the last of April the troops were moved to Vidalia, La., and the planters were left at the mercy of the guerrillas. Six plantations were leased by Northern men, who bought stock and provisions and commenced work. Other places in the vicinity were carried on by their owners; but they only planted such an amount of land, as they thought the guerrillas would allow them to cultivate. After the troops left, the Northern lessees deserted their places and abandoned the enterprise; but not until they had been raided and robbed of everything they had invested. The Southern men who were at work are still there, and will be allowed to raise enough to support their families. There is but little cotton planted from this place up to Lake St Joseph, and but few freedmen; what few there are being old men and women who still stay around the old plantation quarters, too harmless to attract the attention of either party.

Natchez Miss.

This district extends from Marengo to Ashley, in Concordia Parish, La., on both sides of the river. On the Mississippi side there is but little done, as there is not protection sufficient outside the city limits, to insure planters in making investments. There are a number of freedmen on nearly every plantation in the district, whether it be abandoned or not; as they manage to raise a little garden, and live on what may be left by their former masters.

In Concordia Parish. La. along the Mississippi river from Marengo to Ashley, there is a tier of 34 plantations with 22590 acres of cotton under cultivation. They furnish employment for 2390 freedmen, with a population of 4312 people. The freedmen of this district are mostly made up of the original hands that have worked the plantations they are on, for years. This fact makes them work better and more contentedly, as they have the little community commonly known as "fellow servants" all together, as they have lived for years

Planters have not enough freedmen to cultivate what they have planted; and as the competition for hands increases, wages for their work go up, and actually settle the troublesome question of what wages shall be paid. A planter must pay well and punctually, or he will not get laborers to do his work

Early in the spring preparations were made for planting extensively; but the vigilance of the guerrillas has confined them to the narrow limits of what the military authorities can protect. The desolating influences of a large army, that have made a perfect waste of most of the cotton country above here, did not reach this district. The plantations are some of the finest in the South, being in fine order at the beginning of the year. Dwelling houses, negro quarters, fences, steam gins and saw-mills – all in good repair and ready for use.

Several raids have been made, and a large number of mules, horses and wagons carried off, besides valuable material that will cripple the planters losing it very much. During the week ending June 15th nine steam gins have been burned in the lower end of the district by the guerrillas, who seem to be determined to do what they can to thwart the project of raising cotton. Perhaps one-half of the plantations being worked in this district are not abandoned, but have been leased from the owners who have some share in the crop. The cotton was planted early, looks well, and as a general thing has been well cultivated. The combination of Yankee skill, and Southern experience will work a great improvement in raising cotton in this Valley.

Recapitulation

Number of plantations 162; number of acres of cotton in the whole district under my supervision 74.981; number of hands employed, 9.192; number of freed people living on the plantations. in the aggregate, 17319; number of white men engaged as superintendents, clerks, &c., 397.

Number of freedmen lessees, 180; acres in cultivation 5,870; hands employed exclusive of lessees. 380; people supported by lessees including hands employed, 1.280. This does not include many small pieces of ground being cultivated by one or two freedmen, who have no claim to their lands, except to occupy what they find abandoned, for their own use.

The above estimates of land under cultivation are made from the old calculation of the number of acres in the plantations that are being worked The constant changing of hands would make some variation from the above calculation; but the statement is as near correct as it is possible for me to get it.

Conclusion.

I find that the planters have not executed the form of contract between themselves and their hands. prescribed by this office, and by Orders No. 9, of the Secretary of War,[3] owing to the fact that they have had to change hands several times since they commenced work; and the labor of making these contracts has been so great, that my office has not had time to execute the part assigned to it, of furnishing the blanks and visiting the plantations to see the contracts executed. To remedy this as far as practicable, my Assistant Provost Marshals are required to visit every plantation in their districts once a week, and examine into the condition of the people and hear all complaints that may be made of neglect or failure of either party to fulfill his part of what is understood to be the regulation. The duty is arduous and perplexing. Nearly every form of complaint comes before them; and as far as I have received reports, the decisions of the Provost Marshals have been satisfactory to all parties. The wages of the freedmen for half the time worked have been paid up to June 1st, which gives satisfaction to all, except a few who are not contented in any position, and who, through stupidity, or a desire to be finding fault, complain of the wages not being paid, and tell hard stories of their treatment, which are not founded on facts. I find a desire among a considerable portion of the hands to change about; and to justify their desire, they invent stories, which if taken by themselves, would reflect upon the planters, and lead to the belief that serious abuses existed among them. I do not think this is the case. As a general thing, I find the planters as upright and just a body of men as can be found anywhere. I will venture the assertion that they will compare favorably with any body of business men of the same number. With a few exceptions they have treated their hands justly and humanely in all the transactions that have come to light and seem to do all they can to inculcate manliness and self-reliance on their laborers, rendering their labor dignified and respectable That the laborer is going to receive a large amount of money for his year's work is not claimed by any one. I cannot see how this would help him in gaining the place that some enthusiastic people would have him hurried into immediately. The best we can do is, to place his labor on an equal footing with white labor, and neither endow him with a fortune, nor open up his road to jump at once to ease or affluence, that he does not know how to use or enjoy. Guard him against imposition, give him his just dues at the end of each month, and if there is one able to carry on business for himself so construct rules as to assist him, and let him work his way up. Our country has enough to bear without undertaking the enormous task of starting out each freedman with a competency for the rest of his life. They are free but they must labor for the food they eat. and the clothes they wear. Capital does now, and will for some time to come carry on great enterprises; and a large portion of the human family, both white and black, must labor for this capital at regulated wages, without any direct interest in the result of the enterprise.

One of the terrors of the planting system has been the guerrillas, who lurked in swamps and canebrakes near the river, ready at any moment to pounce upon the planter, and destroy the fruits of his labor. The loss of life has not been great, as I find that there have been only eleven Northern, and seven Southern men killed while engaged in cultivating plantations since Jan'y 1st 1864.

The planting season this year has been very dry. The oldest

planters claim that it is an exception. Planters were late in getting arrangements made to start their plantations, owing to the different changes in the policy of the Government about leasing them. Great dissatisfaction existed in the beginning, and many went home disgusted with their efforts to obtain information as to the course that was to be pursued by the Government. Expectations were encouraged at one time, that there would be protection furnished; but military operations might demand the withdrawal of the troops, and the planters would be left at the mercy of the rebels. Most of the plantations were entirely destitute of everything except buildings and many were without these in adequate numbers to shelter their laborers. Forage, mules, provisions and tools must come from the North, and be brought through all the tortuous routine of trade regulations. Planters commenced planting cotton about the 1st of April and continued to the 1st of June. The largest amount of seed went into the ground the last week of April. and the 1st week of May. The ground was very dry during the months of April and May. making it almost impossible to prepare it for the seed. Seed planted during this dry weather did not come up very well; and what did come up remained at a stand still for some time after peering through the ground. Planters all replanted, and some even commenced anew, and put in a new crop about the last of May. The continued rains during the first part of June have brought this planting up, and it looks well. All have a good stand of cotton, although very uneven in height. It was difficult to get good seed, as all that could be procured was two years old, and had been subject to the wet weather which had rotted and made it unfit for use. At this time, (June 20th) most of the cotton has been worked over once. The lack of hands is being severely felt. There is not a plantation but what could take more hands, and actually needs more, to cultivate the crops properly. As a whole, the planters gained nothing by planting early crops this season. While they were losing for lack of rain to bring their cotton out of the ground they were gaining in being sure that the floods in the Mississippi would not sweep through the breaks in the levee and destroy their crops This must be a serious drawback the next season, if the levee is not repaired. I have the honor to be. Your obedient Servant

ALS Saml Thomas

Col. Saml. Thomas to Brig. Genl. L. Thomas, 15 June 1864, T-8 1864, Letters Received by Adjutant General L. Thomas, ser. 363, Colored Troops Division, RG 94 [V-70]. Colonel Thomas, commander of the 64th USCI, served simultaneously as provost marshal of freedmen in the Department of the Tennessee and as superintendent of freedmen in the District of Vicksburg; his letter is headed "Office Supt & Provost Marshal Freedmen."

1 See above, doc. 198.
2 See above, doc. 188.
3 See above, doc. 198.

210: Treasury Department Special Agent for Vicksburg District to the Supervising Agent of the Treasury Department 1st Special Agency

Vicksburg, Miss., July 9th *1864*

Sir, Something should be done with the men that are cutting wood from Abandoned Plantations, as many are cutting under authority from old Commanders, that was given at the time our Army was advancing down the River, and at enormous prices, for the sake of having wood for our Transports, but now wood is gotten out in larger quantities by Owners of Plantations on the River, and by authority of Cap't. D. N. Rusch, A.Q.M. Besides many of these wood-yards are run by men having charge of Contraband Camps; such is the case with Island N° 102.

A man by the name of Smith is furnished with help, and Sixty rations per day, from what is called the Contraband Camp on the Island, and for which he pays Col. Sam[l] Thomas 25¢ per Cord, on all wood cut, for the rations, and then divides with him the nett proceeds for all wood sold, this is not the only contraband camp that is used in this way, and hence the difficulty, "to some extent," in getting hands to leave these camps. The prospects are growing worse all the time, for want of help, thousands of acres will have to be abandoned, and many more will have to be abandoned, on account of Raids.

I leave here on the 14th for home, shall call on you, and hope to see you at Cincinnati I remain Your Ob't Servt.

HLS C. A. Montross

C. A. Montross to W. P. Mellen, Esq., 9 July 1864, Letters Received from Assistant Special Agents, Records of the General Agent, RG 366 [Q-172]. Marks resembling periods, but apparently not intended as punctuation, follow about half the words in the manuscript; they have been omitted. Military officials shared Montross's concern that the possibility of obtaining subsistence, physical security, and remunerative employment in the contraband camps and government wood yards was reducing the willingness of former slaves to work for plantation lessees. In June 1864, the assistant provost marshal of freedmen at Milliken's Bend, Louisiana, had attempted to counteract the attractions of the camps at Island 102 and Paw Paw Island (both in the Mississippi River, above Vicksburg) by discontinuing rations, "except to persons unable to labor on Plantations, persons employed on the Islands and such other persons as are needed in families to [take] care of old or sick people." His order achieved the intended result, inducing "[a] good many" former slaves to leave the islands for plantation employment. Nevertheless, he reported, "[h]ands are very scarce – All Lessees want more help." Moreover, the proprietor of the wood yard on Island 102, James Smith, had hired workers "in such a manner as to make it unfortunate for those wanting hands." "In employing women to cord wood and other work," Smith hired "Single women" instead of "the *wives* and daughters of Wood choppers – So that the females belonging to 66 Choppers are only a small portion of them employed." (Lt. D. McCall to Colonel Thomas, 27 June 1864, Letters Received, ser. 2037, Asst. Supt. of Freedmen, MS Asst. Comr. Pre-Bureau Records, RG 105 [A-4008].)

211: Statement of a Tennessee Freedman

Memphis, Tenn., Aug 4" *1865.*

Statement of MaKage MacKey }

In August 1864 – I met a man named Mr Neal as I after learned, in Memphis Tenn and he told me if I would go into the country with him he would pay and cloth me. I conscented to do so and got into his Wagon and he took me to his Home in Shelby County Tenn. near Union Church, and sold me to a man named Mr. James Smith, where I have been up to the present date, but made a crop for James Smith. I have asked Mr. Smith twice for money but each time he told me he had no money.

his
MacKage X MacKey
mark

HDSr

Statement of MacKage MacKey, 4 Aug. 1865, Affidavits & Statements, ser. 3545, Memphis TN Provost Marshal of Freedmen, RG 105 [A-6602]. On letterhead of the office of the provost marshal of freedmen at Memphis. A search of the records of the provost marshal of freedmen revealed no evidence of any action on MacKey's behalf.

212: Commander of a Mississippi Black Regiment to the Headquarters of the District of Vicksburg

Vicksburg, Miss., Sept 13th *1864.*

Colonel. I would respectfully Submit the following Statements for the consideration of the commanding General.

The innumerable huts of contrabands in the vicinity of the camps and fortifications are a nuisance besides being an expense to the Government. Their close proximity to the camps, give their occupants opportunity of obtaining Rations and clothing from the Soldiers. notwithstanding the Strict watchfulness of officers and the heavy penalty inflicted upon offenders.

How this class of people make their living is a problem. I would respectfully Suggest that from Six to Eight acres of ground between the fortifications and the picket lines be Selected for each family whereupon they may erect their Shanties. and raise a Sufficient quantity of vegetables to Support themselves. There are from four to five thousand acres of land susceptible of cultivation between the fortifications and picket lines.

This arrangement would also prove beneficial to the garrison. as in a Short period a sufficient quantity of vegetables would be produced to supply the market. I am Colonel Very Respectfully Your obt. Svt

HLS H Lieb

[*Endorsement*] Headqr[s] Dist of Vicksburg Sep 14″ 1864 Respectfully referred to Gen Hawkins and Col Eaton as to the propriety of moving all these people outside the main line By Command of Maj Gen Dana H C Rodgers AAG

[*Endorsement*] Head Qrs. 1st Division U.S.C.T. Vicksburg Miss. Sept 14 1864 I am in favor of moving some but not all of these people many earn a good living by chance work Those who are not doing well should be encouraged to move outside John P. Hawkins Brig. Gnl. Comd[g]

[*Endorsement*] Office General Supt Freedmen Vicksburg Miss., Sept 15, 1864. I agree with General Hawkins – "part in and part out." In that adjustment the difficulties lie. Thoroughly loyal, save in exceptional cases which can easily be detected, and indeed are detected among themselves and punished by a severe public sentiment of their own, in some instances amounting to persecution – the Freedmen are not only necessary to the industry of the cities whether garrisoned or not, but they constitute a social element cooperative with the Federal forces, giving information, adding strength, and greatly feared by the rebels among whom they live, as well as by the armed rebels who might make an attack. Many own considerable property. Notwithstanding the known difficulties of adjusting by order, the proportion of different classes in cities, experience previous to the occupation of Vicksburg taught us that these people should be allowed in town only so far as required by its virtuous industry. Various trials were made to secure this through the usual pass-offices, but all failed and the whole turned over to the Supts of Freedmen under whom with the instructions given, at several points very satisfactory results have been secured. First, the term of passes was limited, and some responsible party required to vouch fór the negro. As soon as one negro after another was found to be responsible and to conduct a legitimate business on his own responsibility the time was extended and no voucher required. All going outside the lines first secured the Superintendent's pass, subject to the approval of the Provost Marshal. Picket Officers were to let none in but what were reported at once to the Supt. None were to live or build houses in town without his permit, and after the cold season no rations were to be issued in town without his permission. A patrol guard reporting to him took all without passes.

He and his assistants were required to inspect the negro quarters; the towns were districted, and teachers and other volunteer laborers and the most intelligent colored people were organized into visiting parties so as to combine charitable with Governmental action. The people, unskilled in foreseeing the changes of trade, when profit appeared in any direction, would rush that way, not only as the sharpest speculators do, until they lost their means, but were reduced to suffering and those who constituted the foundation of that business were obliged to leave it. So, Superintendents were charged to study that the passes in no direction should overreach the demand, but to favor artizans in preference to others in order to reduce the expenses of articles of their manufacture – shoes &c. Indeed all the principles of social organization were studied, and every instrumentality tried, that could be of any service. Untold evils resulted from the presence of lewd women; to meet this, Marriage was started on the basis of the laws of the U.S., regular registration established,[1] regimental villages urged, for the wives of soldiers, out of town where each family could have a garden and all might cultivate Regimental Gardens.

Col Lieb co-operated decidedly. A rational idea of marriage was urged, so that all the family instincts, which so largely constitute the foundations of society, might come to our aid. Weeks of time have been spent by my officers upon the single matter of getting building lots for them out of town. Had there been no interference, I have no doubt the evils would have been reduced to their minimum before this, without violence and without harm. As it is, the improvement, to those who understand the facts, is great and marked, notwithstanding others have given permits to build in town and issued passes to lewd women and others who were refused by the Supt., that Regimental Commanders of troops have assumed to give passes to women to remain about the camps &c, and that some *opposed* efforts to secure the legal marriage of their soldiers; and blacks have often come through the picket lines and wandered where they chose without being reported.

The management in town connects itself with those out of town, their industry &c. But the statement of details would require a treatise instead of an endorsement. I am confident that the only thing required to remove the evils complained of and recall the evils wrought is the full support, on all hands, of the Supt of Freedmen, in the difficult task of faithfully discharging his duties. Without repeating the details of instructions to Superintendents, I would respectfully suggest that this matter be referred to Col. Samuel Thomas, who is familiar with all the details, with authority to locate houses and Regimental Villages, and that some title to the lots be devised and given which will not be revoked by any commanding Officer. Instead of 6 acres to each family I would suggest from 1/2 to 5 acres according to the industrial capacity of the family – the amount to be determined by the Superintendent.

I need not add that I should object to any indiscriminate expulsion of the people; or that I should take great care that no injustice or violence be done.

John Eaton Jr Colonel and General Superintendent of Freedmen for the Dept of the Tenn. and State of Ark.

Colonel H. Lieb to Lieut. Col. H. C. Rodgers, 13 Sept. 1864, Letters Received, ser. 2203, Dist. of Vicksburg, RG 393 Pt. 2 No. 127 [C-2216]. Colonel Lieb commanded the 5th USCHA, which had been recruited in the Vicksburg area and was garrisoning the city's fortifications. General John P. Hawkins, commander of the division of black troops that included the 5th USCHA, and General Napoleon J. T. Dana, commander of the District of Vicksburg, had already taken steps to encourage the settlement of freedpeople on the outskirts of the city. On September 7, 1864, in response to complaints that landowners were demanding "exorbitant rent" for vacant land outside Vicksburg, Hawkins (whose duties included supervision of "dwelling Shanties outside the line of Fortifications," most of which were inhabited by the families of black soldiers and sailors) had requested Dana's permission "to grant permits for locating shanties on any waste ground outside the fortifications," free of rent. The landlords' "exactions," he contended, threatened to keep the freedpeople "in a state of pauperage." "Nothing can be laid up by them and when sick Gov,ment must take care of them." General Dana had approved Hawkins's proposal, authorizing "indigent" freedpeople "to occupy vacant land so long as it is not required for actual use by owners," stipulating that the rent was not to exceed the amount of taxes on the land, and condemning "[t]he spirit shown by these land owners who wish to gouge the poor." (Brig. Genl. John P. Hawkins to Lt. Col. H. C. Rodgers, 7 Sept. 1864, and endorsement by Brig. Gl. N. J. T. Dana, [7? Sept. 1864], Brigade at Vicksburg, 1st Division, Letters & Orders Received by Forces under the Department of the Gulf, ser. 1753, Dept. of the Gulf, RG 393 Pt. 1 [C-608].)

1 For a sample page from a register of marriages of former slaves in the Vicksburg area, including three soldiers from the regiment commanded by Lieb, see *Freedom*, ser. 2: doc. 309.

213: Mississippi and Louisiana Planters and Northern Plantation Lessees to the General Agent of the Treasury Department Special Agencies

[*Vicksburg, Miss.? October? 1864*]

(copy)

Hon. W. P. Mellon Esq. General Agent Treas. Dept. We the undersigned, Planters and Government Lessees of Plantations, knowing the deep interest you take in the success of our Enterprize and confident that you will do all in your power to obviate in the coming season, some of the great and fatal obstacles, and protect us against the almost intolerable and unnecessary restrictions, we have to meet constantly. Beg leave to submit to your Kind consideration, with all due respect; the following Statement.

That we were induced to risk our fortunes, and our lives in the growing of Cotton by free labor, by the most solemn promise of Authorized Agents of the Government, that efficient protection, abundant labor, and every possible facility should be granted to make our efforts successfull. Nothing can be more dear to loyal patriotic men, than the honor and dignity of the Government.

And it is therefore with a feeling of shame that we must confess, that either the agents of the Government wilfully deceived us, or that we overestimated the power and the ability of the Authorities to carry out their declared policy

It is however universally know that we not only failed to obtain adequate protection or sufficient labor, but were surrounded with restriction in all our movements, and until now we cannot even go to our plantations without beseiging some officers Head quarters for hours or days to obtain a pass.

To avoid generalities and [*make?*] demonstrations of the justice of our complaints by facts, we beg leave to state, that the promise of Protection by strong military post at Skipwith, Goodrich Landing

Lake Providence, Millikens Bend, and other points, the additional patroling of the river by the Marine brigade and Gunboats, has never amounted to more than the placing of a feable garrison of colored soldiers in forts, at Goodrich Landing and Millikens Bend, so inefficient in numbers and equipments are these Troops, that men have been murdered, mules stolen and houses burned within two miles and in full sight of these Forts, by parties of guerillas numbering from six to two Hundred men.

Thus far from being any protection to us, they prove a source of constant annoyance and positive injury. Recruting officers invaded our plantations and robed us of the few able bodied hands we had obtained. Their families would either follow by stealth or be carried off, in some instances by forces or orders from Officers. Horses and mules were taken off on the most shallow pretences of military necessity by officers and soldiers, or stolen by straglers with no pretences whatever, and it seemed a matter of positive enjoyment and pride to most of them to hide and disguise our Stock, so that we have lost hundreds of valuable animals, without hope of recovery, & even in cases of absolute proof We had to submit to unnecessary difficulties and delays, and always obtain the ill will of officers with our property.

It is needless to say that our gardens were striped before harvest. We are perfectly willing to bear patiently the unavoidable and usual pilfering of soldiers, and ready to offer our property for the service of the Government and army in case of positive exigency; but we solemnly protest against being needlessly robbed and holding our property only by sufferance in case the comfort or whim of commanders. should not demand it.

We furthermore declare, that we were deceived by the promise of an abundant supply of labor, and facilities to obtain the same. In spite of almost painful exertions, and liberal expenditure of money, we could not obtian half the labor realy needed, and that too, after more than two thirds of the Lessees, discouraged by the obstinate and early opposition of the military commanders and the evident weakness of the Treasury Department had abandoned the enterprize. –

The reason for our failure in this respect, were the impressment of all able bodied men into military service the suffering of women & children in camps and in towns; the free and indiscriminate distribution of provisions to idle negroes; and the attempt of officers having charge of Government Carrals, to direct the labor into other channels.

There were no facilities to approach the negroes scattered at Davis Bend, and other so called Home Farms. The officers in charge were surly & unobliging; the negroes were camping over six or eight square miles of ground, and were only required to go with their full & free consent. Under these circumstances we could only obtain the most *worthless* class of labor. To secure even them we were obliged to support such a number of Disabled, sick aged & young, that our labor accounts, will show, that we could not get more than half the number we supported into the field.

The long delays occasioned by the attempts to harmonize the policy of the Treasury & war Departments, and agree upon regulations; the difficulty of obtaining labor, and getting supplies, brought the planting late into the season, and when an unfavorable rainy season demanded extra exertions, the inadequacy of labor obliged us to throw out, or abandon thousands of acres of good standing, cotton to the weeds.

Raiding parties encouraged by their success, and having little or no opposition, increased the frequency of their appearance; stole hundreds of mules, thousands of Dollars worth of goods, and carried off hundreds of negroes into slavery, and threatened, and demoralized the remainder; and although the extraordinary and unprecedented ravages of the army worm, occasioned by the lateness of the crop, reduced it to less than a fifteenths of an average yield. many of our number have hardly labor sufficient to secure the small remainder.

We also complain that the regulations & restrictions under which we labor are needlessly severe and formalities too complicated and expensive; it does not add in our opinion, to the solemnity or efficiency of the oath, to administer it on the most trivial occasion

We would respectfully direct your attention to the fact, that although we are fully engaged in carrying out the free labor system, we have to make oath that we will conform to the emancipation proclamation every time we wish to obtain only a few Dollars worth of supplies.

There seems a want of dignity in this system, and we would respectfully suggest that one oath; affirming that we would carry nothing but necessary supplies to our plantations, as binding as hundreds to the same effect.

But although the Treasury regulations are so stringent, and by the requirement of detailed restriction make it difficult to remedy omisions, and supply sudden or unforeseen demands, additional military restrictions have almost put it out of our power to supply our plantations, making the expense and labor of doing so, overdue and intolerable. There is unfortunately obvious a growing tendency among many of our army officers to consider, and treat every citizen in a Military district as a public enemy, or a creature to be regulated, snubbed, taxed, drafted, enrolled in Militia companies, and watched by detectives. And this tendency develops itself most fully at every change of Commanders, every new Commander has an administrative policy of his own, and carries it out, regardless of consequences. A flood of regulations, prohibitions, investigations, and Confiscation is the consequence.

We have borne these inconveniences without complaint as long as they did not interfere seriously with our business. We have now however reached the Climax of Military interference, and the Officers of the Treasury Department under whose auspices we commenced, and carried on our operations, seem to sit by, helplessly unable to protect us in our guaranteed rights, or preserve there own dignity.

We cannot take supplies to places without special pass, signed by the Commander in person, who can only be approached on Mondays, and Thursdays. We must ship all cotton to Vicksburg and pay five dollars per bale post tax, the additional freight, insurance, drayage storeage, and the personal attention required with shipment increases the cost of bringing our cotton to market fearfully, without counting the loss occasioned by delaying shipments, to a rapidly falling market. Nor is this all, large quantities of our cotton must be shipped in the seed to Vicksburg, to be ginned on account of the scarcity of Gin Houses on plantations. and we are now waiting transportation, exposed to the weather, and to rebel raids and the restrictions on navigation issued by our present Commander, are such, that we cannot obtain this transportation.

The consequence of this policy if persisted in, must certainly ruin us completely, and we shall be compelled to believe that it was intended to accomplish this result We would respectfully state that we are loyal citizens of the United States, and have supported the Government to the best of our ability. We have conscientiously complied with all orders of the Treasury, Army & Navy Departments, know to us; and have expended Millions of dollars, risked our lives, and lost many friends, and Employees, in the endeavor to carry out a declared policy of the United States Government.

We are engaged in our enterprize under fixed rules of the Treasury Department and we most solemnly protest against any change of those rules and regulations, or to any additionally taxes & restrictions whatsoever, arbitrary and unnecessary interferance of Military authorities in our business, and our property, and our liberty. Holding ourselves responsible that we shall do the duty as well as maintain the dignity of Americans citizens and most respectfully demand the fulfillment of obligations entered into by our government.

Lessees	Plantations	Acres –
[S]. A. Duke	"Out Post"	1.500
O. H. Brewer & Co	"Goodrich"	500
J. U. Green	"Mary land	600
A. Basginsdo	"Buzinsky"	500
P. P. Bailey	"Mohel Place"	800
Fred G. Burnham	"Warren Co"	1.000
Wm R. Greene	"Morr[n]ly"	1.000
Hamilton Borden	"Dick Wilson"	500
T. Borden	"Banner"	1.500
Q. A. Fisk	Forest Home	350
A. Mygatt	"Mr Dan M. Plent"	1 300
Edward Reed	White	400
Geo. P. Deweene	Mr H. Plantation	700
J. R. Barrett	Peck Plantation	800
W. Nichols	Mollett "	700
Wm Grant	Winn "	1 000
Gordon & Co	Duckford "	500
Madison Miller	McDowell "	600
Rockford Cottn Co	[. . .] Tensas Parsh	1.200
Geo W. Hall	Barefield and Bey	1.235
D. W. Jones & Co	Walls Plantation.	480
C. E. Hovey	Arlington	1.000
Wm Henry Wright	Willis	800
J. M. Wells	Dalkeith	900
J. H. Carter & Co	Joe Davis Plan	1.200
T. A. Marshall & Co	Milles Plan.	500

HLcSr

S. A. Duke et al. to Hon. W. P. Mellon Esq., [Oct.? 1864], enclosed in Wm. P. Mellen to Hon. W. P. Fessenden, 4 Nov. 1864, M-599 1864, Letters Received by the Division, ser. 315, Division of Captured Property, Claims, & Land, RG 56 [X-97]. The general agent, William P. Mellen, referred this copy of the petition to William P. Fessenden, Secretary of the Treasury, indicating in a covering letter that he knew "many of the signers" and considered them "generally men of character and means" whose views merited "the consideration of the Government." Acutely aware of the debate in Congress and the Lincoln administration concerning whether the War Department or the Treasury Department should be given authority over plantation leasing for the 1865 season, Mellen urged Fessenden to present the planters' grievances to the President. Mellen stressed "the importance of immediate action concerning the Cotton planting operations of another year. It is not fair either towards the freedmen or those supporting them to procrastinate longer."

214: Arkansas Farmer to the Treasury Department Special Agent for Helena District

Helena [*Ark.*] Oct 4th 1864

Dr Sir I am a loyal citizen of the U.S. Gov[rnmt] having taken the Oath of allegiance in January 1863 and to the best of my ability have observed it faithfully– I live in crittenden county Arks near the Miss river mid way between this place and Memphis. I have hired the servants on my farm for this present year– I am to pay out of the proceeds of the crop to Sam Hammonds and wife and four small children one hundred and thirty Dollars ($130.) and feed and clothe them gratutously– I pay Jane and Daughter with four helpless children one Hundred and Twenty five Dollars with supplies gratuitous–Sooky a cook Sixty Dollars and supplies and four others two men and two women who do not belong to me and are working for a part of the crop and food and clothing.

I would have entered into a contract as Government Lessee but the danger from bands of Confederate souldiers and Guerrillas was so great that I dared not incur it– The fact that they broke up all farms with a Governt contract is well know when they could reach them unprotected– This statement of my status and operations I hope Col will induce you readily to grant such supplies of food clothing, medicins and Bagging & Rope as will be necessary to the support of the place. And now the marauding bands who infested our county previous to this time having been expelled I am willing and ready to make any contract which the Governt may require for the year 1865.

Without the countenace and support of the Govemt officials in supplying the farm it is impossible to gather the crop or comply with the contra[ct] in paying the servants as the cold weather approaching cannot be endured without the necessary winter clothing & shoes I hope all the facts will be born in mind and the protection which I claim as a loyal citizen will be extended to me Very Respectfully your obt servt

HDS G Hammond

G. Hammond to Col. McDowel, 4 Oct. 1864, General Letters Received, Records of the General Agent, RG 366 [Q-156]. Sworn before Colonel John A. McDowell, the special agent. On the same day, a planter from Phillips County, Arkansas, made a similar appeal for supplies and offered a similar explanation of his failure to register the plantation as required by Treasury Department regulations. "[O]wing to the bands of Lawless Marauders and wandering souldiers claiming to be in the confederate service," he had "dared not let any willingness to hire the sevants be known for fear of personal violence and injury to the contrabands." Indeed, he claimed, "the servants understood the danger and did not desire a governt contract," so he had "bargained with them" and reached a private agreement to pay them "the tenth of the proceeds of the cotton crop and feed & clothe all on the place gratuitously." (E. T. Diamond to Col. McDowell, 4 Oct. 1864, General Letters Received, Records of the General Agent, RG 366 [Q-156].)

215: Mississippi Planter to the Secretary of the Treasury

Washington D.C. October 27" 1864

Sir Your petitioner, Irene Smith, a loyal citizen of the U. States, respectfully represents, that she and Alexander C. Bullitt are the owners of four cotton plantations in the state of Mississippi, three of which are in Washington Co. Miss: in what is commonly Known as Ky. Bend; & the fourth near Port Gibson in same state.

These plantations, were well stocked with every thing necessary for successful planting, & capable of producing 3000 Bales of cotton per annum. Your petitioner and A. C Bullitt were in peaceful occupancy of these plantations, & the owners of about six hundred slaves, when the Army of the United States in Feby. 1862 come upon the plantations in Washington Co. and forcibly took possession of almost every species of stock, & grain that were upon them, The union Army, or that portion of it which took possession of these plantations, was commanded by a Col, Clarkeright of Missouri, we claimed protection from an indiscriminate taking of our property, on the ground that we had been and were strictly loyal and peaceable citizens, had never given any aid or countenance to the Rebellion, His reply was, that the goverment needed the stock and grain, and that we could get paid by the goverment, He give us no receipt for anything he took, and some of his troops, robbed us of our silver plate, and committed great waste and destruction, Foraging parties afterward come and took part of what Col. Clarkeright left, till Capt Henry Coffman of the 101st Illinois Regiment, come, and seeing our destitute condition, offered us the protection to which American Citizens are justly entitled.

After the capture of Port Gibson by Genl Grant in the spring of 1863, the plantation near that place, was almost intirely stripped of every thing by the troops of his command, The amount of property taken and destroyed, on the four plantations, was worth at least *One Hundred Thousand Dollars*.

Beside this loss sustained by reason of our own Army, the Rebels burned some *three thousand Bales of Cotton* for us, leaveing only ten Bales out of part of two years crop,

On the 4" day of June 1863, we procured from Brig Genl. H. T.

Reed commanding Providence Post La, near to us, the following order Viz: "All officers and soldiers will respect the person & property of Mrs Irene Smith of Ky. Bend Mississippi She being a loyal woman and having already had much forage and other property taken from her plantation" Sgd, H. T Reed, Brig General Commanding.

Your petitioner would futher state, that she applied to Genl Grant, for protection which was promptly given to her, M[r] A. C. Bullitt & his wife Mrs Irene Bullitt which is as follows to wit:

> "Head Quarters Division of Miss.
> Nashville Tenn. Oct. 21st 1863.–
>
> All United States forces are commanded to respect the property & persons of the families of Mrs Irene Smith–& – Bullitt residing on the Mississippi River, in the State of Mississippi, at what is known as the Ky. bend.
>
> The stock, utensils & provisions will not be taken for military purposes from either of the three plantations of Mrs Smith, or from the plantations of Mr Bullitt, but all practicable protection will be given them by the Military
>
> Sgd, U. S. Grant
> Maj Genl. U.SA.
> Comdg.–"

Since the foregoing protection, we have not been molested by the troops of the U. States, and all facilities have been given to us for the protection of what little property was left.

Your petitioners now further state, that she, Mr Bullitt & Mrs Bullitt have remained on their plantations during the year 1861, 1862, 1863 & 1864. endeavoring to preserve in tact, their property, and demean themselves as good & loyal citizens.

After the proclamation of the President of the [*United States*] emancipating all the slaves in the states in Rebellion, almost every slave they owned was taken off by some of the agents of the goverment and conveyed on transports at the expense of the goverment to a camp of Contrabands below their plantations on the River, A few house servants, and a few old men and women remained to share with their former owners whatever fate awaited them.

At the time of this exode, the negroes laid hands on the farming utensils, carried away every thing their fancy suggested, and left almost nothing upon the plantations, In a few months they were in a very destitue condition, Many of them died in camp, others were sick, and in this state of sickness & destitution many of them returned to their former homes, made desolate when they left, Humanity & Christianity alike demanded of us, to share with them, the pittance left, accordingly they were kindly received and cared for, and they kept returning, until now, we have about 250 of them on the plantations,

Your petitioners notwithstanding the dangers on the River, has made several trips to Louisville Ky, for supplies of food & clothing, and also to New Orleans, for the same purpose;

under the late regulations[1] your petitioner & Mr Bullitt made arrangement with the goverment, to hire these negroes with some others as *freed men*, and during the current year, have cultivated three of the plantations, and have raised a crop of grain & cotton; Your petitioner further states, that many of these negroes were *entailed* by the late Benj Smith dec[d]; and it was the purpose of your petitioner & M[r] Bullitt to emancipate them so soon as they were sufficiently educated for selfprotection. To this end, a good Chapel was erected & preachers employed to hold divine service regularly on the Lords Day: Sunday Schools established & for many years they have enjoyed full & equal religious priviledges, with your petitioners: in the knowledge & worship of Almighty God, Many of these Colored persons were taught to read the word of God, and looked forward to a day not far distant, when they should share in all the blessings of that fredoom, for which they were being fitted: Your petioner would futher state, that forty or fifty of these *freedmen* are aged infirm, helpless women & children, whom they have been and are supporting without receiveing compensation;

In view therefore, of all the premises – your petitioner would humbly request that you grant to her and A. C Bullitt the priviledge of safe conduct to market, for all the cotton and produce which are on the plantations prepared & being prepared for shipment;

That you will also give her a permit to lay in a supply of Stores of food & clothing sufficient for the winter[s] supply. Your petitioner is now only allowed by the authorities, to purchase & receive a monthly allowance for these *freedmen*, to obtain which she or A. C. Bullitt has to be absent, almost all the time, no fears need be entertained of these supplies being taken by the Rebels, there are only a few Rebel Cavalry scouting down the River, that scarcely ever come on the plantations, there is no point near the plantations where any considerable rebel force have ever congregated, and your petitioner has no fears of the supplies ever being taken; Her interest & that of M[r] Bullitt in the supplie[s] thus purchased, is the best guarrantee for their safety we can offer,

Lastly, Your petitioner would state, that she has borrowed a large sum of money, with which former supplies have been purchased, & she is anxious to be permitted at the earliest day possible to ship her cotton & produce to market, and return with her winter supplies, and pay all her outstanding Obligations.

HLS Irene Smith

Irene Smith to Hon. W. P. Fessenden, 27 Oct. 1864, Letters Received by the Supervising Special Agent, 2nd Agency, RG 366 [Q-217]. According to other documents in the same file, William P. Fessenden, the Secretary of the Treasury, referred Smith's petition to a subordinate, who ruled that Smith and Bullitt could market their cotton if they received a permit from a treasury agent, but that they could not stockpile winter supplies for their plantations without violating regulations that prohibited shipment of more than one month's supplies at a time. Apparently that decision did not satisfy Fessenden; he forwarded the petition to William W. Orme, supervising agent of the Treasury Department's 2nd Special Agency (with headquarters at Memphis), instructing him to "act as you shall judge right, after considering the locality of the plantations, the virtual obligation of the Government to protect planters who employ freedmen under its rules, and the peculiar necessity for allowing supplies in greater quantity than are sufficient for a month, as regards this special case." Orme evidently sent a copy of Fessenden's letter to the surveyor of customs at Louisville, Kentucky (whose duties included the regulation of trade in Union-occupied portions of the Mississippi Valley), and in early December the surveyor–citing "the spirit" of that letter–authorized a shipment of winter supplies for Smith's plantations, consigning it to Orme for "final disposition." (H. A. Risley to Hon. Wm. P. Fessenden, 31 Oct. 1864; W. P. Fessenden to Wm. W. Orme, Esq., 5 Nov. 1864; W. D. Gallagher to Genl. Orme, 8 Dec. 1864.)

1 Presumably the plantation regulations of the Treasury Department's 1st Special Agency, issued January 7, 1864, and revised by order of the adjutant general of the army on March 11, 1864. (See above, docs. 188 and 198.)

216: Questionnaire Responses by Northern Plantation Lessees

[*Davis Bend, Miss. November? 1864*]

Answers to Questions for Planters
By J. H. Carter & Co
Lessees Joe Davis Plantation Davis Bend

1 Food

1 [*Specify the articles of food furnished to your employees.*] We has furnished generaly Bacon, Flour, Meal Fish & Molasses

2 [*Specify the proportion (or amount) of each.*] Say 10 a 12^{lb} Flour 4 a 8^{lb} Bacon 1 pt Molasses the amt. based upon the requirements of the receiver

3. [*How have the small children, infirm parents, or other dependents of*

those employed by you, been supplied with food?] The children, or infirm, dependent upon our hands, have been rationed in part by ourselves and in part by Govt. as our situation in this respect was peculiar, inasmuch as we took the hands that were in the quaters at the time we came to the plantation, & in many cases the non workers were largely predominant, 4. [*Have the rations of the sick been stopped?*] 5 [*What Sanitary stores have you supplied for the sick or feeble?*] Our sick hands we have continued in all cases to provide for, & when desired, have supplied them with whatever our private table stores contained,

2 Clothing We working under Orders No 9[1]

1 [*How has clothing been furnished to your hands?*] 2 [*What profit has been charged on the clothing sold them?*] 3 [*What has been its quality and sufficiency?*] 4 [*What plan would you recommend for clothing the Freedmen on plantations, in the future?*] Have charged our hands with whatever they required, at a profit or rather advance of 15 a 30 pr cent from invoice cost. We have always ordered good articles of their kind, and if the lessees would always do their duty this plan may be better than any other, but think it might be left discretionary with the lessee whether he should keep a supply of goods or Pay the money to the laborer to purchase where he would, for a store is a great source of annoyance and one we should wish to be rid of another season.[2]

No 3 Work

1. [*How many hours per day have your hands worked?*] 2 [*How many days per week?*] Our hands have labored on an average about 9 1/4 hours pr day, and we have had a fair degree of success in the time worked. but in the field the girls say from 14 a 20 years old have been much inclined to waste their time. Our experience shews middle aged hands much more reliable, 3 [*What success have you had in securing industry?*] 4 [*What methods have you of securing success.*] we have by exhorting & precept endeavored to inspire all with the desire to labor, & shew them their time was valuable, but as great a quickener to their zeal has been, to find the amt. to their credit insufficient to procure a coveted calico dress, or straw Hat. 5 [*Have your people labored in rainy or stormy weather?*] We have never worked the hands on stormy days. but have sometimes sent them out after showers. 6. [*What disposition to labor have they manifested as a class?*] 7. [*Does your success show any superiority of free over slave labor?*] But our experience shews that the same amt. of labor cannot be obtained under a free, as under a cumpulsory system of labor, this must be apparant to any person conversant with the working of the two systems, under the old regime, they were

aroused at dawn. in the field before sunrise & did not leave it until after dark, breakfast & dinner were eaten in the field, and the lash of the driver quickened the faculties of any hand disposed to shirk, or be lazy, Now they never go to the field until after sunrise, have two hours for dinner & leave the field at sunset, there is one third less time labored & full one third less daily labor performed now. than under the slave system, and it must continue to be so. and cotton, (if we succeed in destroying the cursed institution) can never be raised as cheaply again as it has been.

8 [*Is severity of manner, or profanity, necessary or useful in promoting industry?*] We think a planter more likely to succeed with his hands, by mild firm treatment, never allowing himself to be made angry by them, and avoiding all profane language, he must inspire their respect, and the man who is habitualy profane cannot command that of either white or black.

9 [*Do you see any improvement in their industrial habits?*] Our people have not felt that interest in laboring of late as would have been the case had the crop been secured, they have been discouraged at the prospect, as they well might be, and we have not tried to make them work.

No 4 [*Wages.*]

1 [*What rates have you paid?*] 2 [*How have they been paid?*] 3 [*What is the most judicious plan of compensation?*] 4 [*Would you leave the rate of wages, and the manner and time of payment entirely to the agreement of the parties?*] 5 [*Would you classify by their ages, without regard to capacity or diligence, and thus determine the pay of these classes?*] 6 [*Would you classify according to merit; fix a minimum price for each class, and allow the parties to contract at any price above that?*] We pay our hands as pr rates set forth in orders No 9[1] & we have given them money or goods as they desired or seemed expedient, and think the present plan perhaps as good as any, although it would be better after establishing a minimum rate for labor of the poorest sort, to allow the planter to make his own terms with his hands, and pay such wages as should be for his interest to secure the kind of labor he desired.

No 5 [*Sanitary Affairs.*]

1 [*How have your laborers been supplied with medicines and medical attendance?*] 2 [*Can you suggest any better plan?*] Our hands have been attended to with those under govt. care, by the Hospital physicians, & it is as good a plan as any to adopt at the Bend.[3]

No 7. [*Domestic Relations.*]

1 [*How have the people observed the social and family relations?*] 2 [*Have those living together as husband and wife, been*

instructed as to the duty of marriage, as required by the Order of the War Department?][4] 3 [*If so, with what effect?*] Perhaps one of the most revolting effects slavery has produced upon the negro, is their almost utter want of chastity or modesty, hence the marriage relation is as yet but a loose bond, and in many cases the parties refuse to be married, prefering the system of concubinage brought out from slavery. It will take stringent laws rigidly enforced to break up the licentious habits of this generation, and a patient teaching of the young will do much to eradicate such practices in the next generation.

4 [*What regard for truth and for the rights of property have your laborers shown?*] 5 [*What improvement can you report in these respects under your tuition?*] Stealing & Lying are other fruits of the accursed institution, it is natural for these people to commit both these offences, and we regret to say they are almost universal & no improvement has yet been shewn, The law & its penalties, must be brought to bear here with especial force & it is false philanthropy that would use other means with these peope, than with white offenders

6 [*Are the people generally disposed to remain on the plantations, or to roam abroad?*] Our people have troubled us but little by straying to other plantations, but a number have run away to Natchez.

No 8[5]

2 [*How do the mixed and unmixed races compare as laborers?*] We have no laborers of mixed blood on the place, hence can make no comparisons

3 [*In the present disturbed state of the country do you believe that the highest interests of the negro and his employer can be secured without military organization and instrumentalities?*] It appears to us the duty of the govt. to afford Military protection to the negroes & those who employ them, and also to take immediate steps to punish all offences committed by the freed people, that they may be brought to understand that *liberty is not license.* Every true friend of the negro must desire this, else the results can but be deplorable, and furnish the enemies of freedom much occasion to blaspheme[6]

ADS J. H. Carter & Co

J. H. Carter & Co., Answers to Questions for Planters, [Nov.? 1864], Miscellaneous Reports from Subordinate & Staff Officers, ser. 2029, General Supt. of Freedmen, MS Asst. Comr. Pre-Bureau Records, RG 105 [A-4015]. The italicized questions inserted in brackets are taken from a questionnaire that was circulated to 100 individual planters in the Vicksburg area, on both the Louisiana and Mississippi banks of the Mississippi River, and was also answered collectively by a group of planters near Helena, Arkansas. (For both the questions and a synopsis of the planters' responses, see John Eaton, *Report of the General Superintendent of Freedmen, Department of the Tennessee and State of Arkansas for 1864* [Memphis, 1865], pp. 28–33.) In the spring of 1864, J. H. Carter & Co. had listed 108 black laborers employed by them on the "Mill Quarters" of Joseph Davis's "Hurricane Plantation": 41 "Men" between the ages of ten and sixty and 67 "Women & Girls" from fourteen to sixty years old. Only two of the laborers (both women) bore the surname Davis. Beneath the list appeared the following notation: "The above embraces all the regular laborers employed on this date. many others have been with us for a brief period & left, either going away to other plantations with their kins folk, when the 'Bend' has been visited by planters in want of hands, or have hired themselves to the Negro farmers, on this and adjacent farms of the Govt. Some have found themselves unable to endure field Labor, & hence to day we have fewer *nominal* field hands employed, than at any time for six weeks past. We are now stringent in enforcing the rules & regulations relative to leaving the farm service, & hence expect fewer changes in the future." ("Roll of Laborers employed by J. H. Carter & Co. on the Hurricane Plantation. [North Half] belonging to Joseph Davis, Warren Co. Miss.," 28 May 1864, Miscellaneous Reports from Subordinate & Staff Officers, ser. 2029, General Supt. of Freedmen, MS Asst. Comr. Pre-Bureau Records, RG 105 [A-4015].) A census of freedpeople at Davis Bend, taken in August 1864, counted 101 at "Mill Quarters": 11 men, 43 women, and 47 children. It placed the total black population of Davis Bend at 2,325: 260 men, 928 women, and 1,137 children. ("Number of Freedmen in different Camps and Quarters on Davis Bend," 15 Aug. 1864, Miscellaneous Reports from Subordinate & Staff Officers, ser. 2029, General Supt. of Freedmen, MS Asst. Comr. Pre-Bureau Records, RG 105 [A-4015].)

1 Issued by Adjutant General Lorenzo Thomas on March 11, 1864. (See above, doc. 198.)
2 The questionnaire included a fifth question, to which Carter & Co. did not respond: "Have you sold them any gewgaws or trinkets?"
3 At this point, the questionnaire introduced a sixth topic, "Schools," which Carter & Co. omitted altogether. It comprised the following questions: "1. To what extent have your employees or their children attended school? 2. If none, or very little, why? 3. Have they otherwise received any instructions?"
4 Presumably Adjutant General Thomas's Order 9, which revised several provisions of the plantation regulations issued by the Treasury Department but approved others, including the twenty-third section, which required that "[a]ll persons living together as husband and wife shall be legally married." (See above, docs. 188 and 198.)
5 The questionnaire provided no topic for section 8. Its first question, to which Carter & Co. did not respond, was: "Is there any manifest improvement in their disposition to labor steadily, as the season advanced, and as they received compensation?"
6 The questionnaire included a fourth question, to which Carter & Co. did not respond: "Ought lessees of plantations who treat their laborers cruelly, to be suffered to renew their leases?"

217: Chaplain of the Post of Helena, Arkansas, to the Commander of the District of Eastern Arkansas

HELENA, ARK., NOV. 30TH, 1864.

GENERAL: Being deeply interested in the welfare of the colored people, and having had favorable opportunities for studying the workings of the policy pursued toward them, I have paid particular attention to the consideration of the question: "What is to be done with the colored people?"

And as the season is drawing near when the policy for the coming year is to be determined, I have much pleasure in complying with your request, that I should report tó you such suggestions as occur to me.

Last winter a definite plan was inaugurated. It has had as fair a trial, and been administered by as faithful and competent officers, as it is reasonable to expect will in general be obtained. What was that policy? How has it been pursued? What is the result? And what does this season's experience suggest for the ensuing year?

The policy was to cultivate the land upon the Mississippi river, furnishing regular and steady employment to the colored people; to insure to them fair compensation in wages, food and clothing; to train the adults to habits of industry and economy; to give to the children opportunity to obtain the rudiments of an education; to provide homes for the sick and infirm.

Government proposed to rent the abandoned plantations along the river. As it was impossible to protect so extended a line from the inroads of a savage and merciless foe, the land actually rented and cultivated was limited to a comparatively few localities, those easily defended.

The leases provide that schools shall be established on each plantation. They require the lessees to keep for, and sell to their laborers good and proper food and clothing. They regulate the amount of profit the lessees might charge, and establish rules to determine the proper cost of goods they were required to keep. They provide that such supervision should be maintained over the planters as would secure the observance of the above rules, and also protect both planters and laborers from injustice or oppression, and would secure peace and quietness. Now as to the workings of this humane and well designed plan.

But few localities were occupied. The tract below Helena was desirable: the land was good and easily defended. All of it was rented. The system was instituted under very favorable circumstances. The white lessees were generally fair, honorable men; professing kind feelings towards the negroes. Yet not a school has been established on a plantation, and I believe no effort made to establish one. No such supervision has been maintained as would prevent extortion, or ensure that the food and clothing furnished to the laborers should be good and substantial of its kind. No particular and persistent effort has been made to cultivate thriftiness and forethought, or, to protect the weak, ignorant and humble from injustice. No officer having care of the people has visited them at their homes, and from observation and inquiry made there, become familiar with the state of affairs there; no adequate and efficient means of redress has been afforded, and if injustice has been experienced, hedged in, on the plantation by a necessary system of passes it has had to be endured in silence.

The end of the season approaches. No kind and ever watchful care has sought to check the gratification of their childish appetites and desires; therefore, they have generally consumed the earnings of the year, and practically they are still slaves, though no one is obliged to provide for them when sick or disabled. They are in a measure without the benefit of slavery, while still subject to many of its disadvantages.

This picture is a sombre one, and were there no reverse side, the way would be dark; but land was rented in small lots to colored lessees, and their present condition solves the difficulty. While the laborers on the large plantations have not essentially improved their condition, the colored lessees have improved theirs. They have been industrious and self-denying; have become more considerate and calculating; have greater self-respect; are desirous of being themselves taught to read and write and qualified to manage their own affairs. They are anxious to have their children *well* educated. About thirty colored people leased land in this vicinity, and all of them have made money. Ten of them have realized thirty-one thousand ($31.000) from their crop. These ten did not have the most land: I mention them only because I know the result of their work.

All of the colored lessees have made more than a living, and will be ready to begin another year with capital that will enable them to work to better advantage than in the past. Besides these successful persons, the town contains many, who, by their industry, economy and good judgment, have made and saved money. They are traders, mechanics and laborers, and if let alone, will compete successfully with any people in the same walks in life. Encouraged by the success of the lessees, a large number of the negroes desire to rent land the coming season. The negroes are here and free. They cannot reasonably be expected, generally or willingly, immediately if ever, to remove to a foreign country. A large body of them are being trained to the use of fire-arms, and will not submit to laws that bear unjustly upon themselves or friends. Therefore, for the above reasons, if all reasons based upon humanity are set aside, we must try to elevate and fit them for the duties of citizenship – give them a fair chance of development, a fair opportunity to educate their children. To accomplish this most quickly, they must be concentrated into communities, in which they are encouraged to work on their own account and manage their own affairs.

Led by the above facts, I would respectfully suggest the following plan for your consideration.

Let such tracts of land be taken as are easily protected, and hold the land for a certain time, exclusively for leasing to colored people. The land lying between Helena and Oldtown on the South, and the tract adjacent to Helena, presents just this advantage. This I would take military possession of. I would pay the loyal owners a fair rent for their land, basing the rent on the value of the land and crop in fair seasons before the war, not upon the value it has had temporarily conferred upon it by military protection. To this rental I would add twenty-five per cent., and assess it upon the whole tract, averaging it *pro rata* per acre, and this would be the rate for the whole. I would hold the crops subject to the same taxes as this year, and for the same objects, viz: the support of Government, and for a fund for the infirm and needy freed people.

Rent the land to any law abiding colored persons, in such quantities as they show they have the means to cultivate. Provide that the oversight contemplated this year should be enforced in the future, so as to secure the establishment of schools; the just treatment of all parties – employers and employes; enforce the observance of law and the maintenance of good order; and secure that only a fair remuneration should be exacted for staple articles of food and clothing. I would in every possible way encourage individual effort and laudable ambition. This plan will encourage all, stimulate to industry, train to virtue, and produce a self supporting and self directing people, a comfort to themselves, and strength to the nation. Respectfully submitting this to your consideration, I am, General, very respectfully, Your Obedient Servant,

PLSr J. I. HERRICK,

Chaplain J. I. HERRICK to Brig. Gen'l. Buford, 30 Nov. 1864, enclosed in Brig. Gen'l N. B. Buford to Gen'l W. W. Orme, 27 Dec. 1864, #2274, Case Files of Claims for Cotton & Captured & Abandoned Property, ser. 370, Miscellaneous Division, RG 56 [X-513]. Herrick signed as chaplain of the 29th Wisconsin Infantry. Favorably impressed with Herrick's proposal, General Napoleon B. Buford, commander of the District of Eastern Arkansas, directed him to conduct an inspection of the plantations recommended for rental to former slaves. Herrick examined some thirty estates between Helena and Oldtown, Arkansas, that had either been abandoned by their Confederate proprietors or were owned by absentees. Emphasizing that the plantations, which contained more than 15,000 acres of tillable land, could be "easily protected by a very small force," Herrick suggested that they be seized "by military Authority, and devoted to the colored people." One of them, the "river plantation" of Confederate General Gideon J. Pillow, had already been put to such use. A portion was "occupied as a home for the colored paupers & is cultivated by hired colored laborers for the benefit of the Freedmens Department"; the remainder had been "let out in small lots to the colored people." (Post Chaplain J. I. Herrick to Brig. Genl. Buford, 26 Dec. 1864, in the same file.) On December 27, the day after Herrick made the report of his inspection, Buford forwarded a copy to William W. Orme, supervising agent of the Treasury Department's 2nd Special Agency (who administered the plantation-leasing system in the Helena area), along with this printed copy of Herrick's proposal.

218: Commander of the Military Division of West Mississippi to the Secretary of War

New Orleans [*La.*], Decr. 6. *1864.*

Sir: I have been prevented by disability from inviting your consideration at an earlier period to the plantation system in the valley of the Mississippi in its relations to the military occupation and military operations. When it was first commenced the force on the river was very large, and, under the assurances of protection which it was then thought proper to give, a large number of persons engaged in the cultivation of cotton and sugar.

Protections, leases and registers were extravagantly issued, and in many instances to cover plantations that were not, and have not, since the commencement of the rebellion, been within the limits of our permanent occupation.

Three classes of persons were engaged in these operations.

1" Loyal and respectable men from the north who embarked their capital and labor as a permanent investment, and a part of the original planters, who submitted themselves cheerfully to the change of circumstances.

2[d] Dishonest and unprincipled men who engaged in it for the opportunities it afforded for illegal trade with the enemy, or with the hope of securing large gains easily and rapidly.

3[d] A large part of the original planters who accepted the conditions imposed by the Government with the expectation that our occupation of the country would be temporary, and that they would be able, in the end, to secure not only their plantations but their slaves.

The withdrawal of a large part of the force in the valley consequent upon the operations of Generals Grant and Sherman has prevented the protection that was proper and appears to have been promised, and exposed the first class except those in the immediate vicinity of military posts, to raids of the enemy who found in these plantations a convenient source of supply for many of their wants. The restrictions upon trade and the general failure of the crops throughout the valley has disappointed the expectations of the second class and a majority of them have abandoned the plantations they had leased, leaving the negroes to run at large or throwing them back upon the Army or Treasury Department for care and support. The third class disappointed in their expectations of seeing the valley reoccupied by the rebels, have left, or are preparing leave, for points within the rebel lines taking the negroes with them for the purpose of reducing them again into a state of slavery.

The subject is one of grave difficulties. As at present managed it has not realized the results that were anticipated either for the Government or for the planters and has greatly embarrassed military operations. Complicated as it is with the future of the negroes I regard it as one of the most difficult problems we have yet to solve. It is idle to expect that, until the strength of the great rebel armies is effectually broken, troops can be spared for the purpose of giving protection to these interests to the extent that it is asked for by the planters and demanded by a proper regard for the welfare of the colored laborers on the plantations. As a question of the private interests of the planters it is of subordinate importance, but as a question involving the future welfare of an entire race it should be second only to the measures that are necessary for the suppression of the rebellion.

Regarding an increase of the force in this command as out of the question until the more important results are attained it is important to determine what other measures can be adopted that will best meet the desired ends. The policy to be adopted should be adopted by higher authority than that of the military Commander in order that it may be secured from the danger of change with every change of command.

The course that seems best calculated to work good results is that of subdividing the plantations and thus multiplying the interests connected with them for the purpose of attracting an active enterprizing and arms bearing population, and the establishment of a system of military colonies capable of protecting themselves against anything except an organized invasion. The colonists should be put into military organizations, armed and equipped at the expense of the United States and mustered into its service for the special duty of preserving order; protecting the plantations from raids and picketing the approaches from the districts under the control of the rebels. It is necessary that they should be mustered into the service in order to subject them to military control and to secure proper treatment for them if they should fall into the hands of the enemy. When employed in the protection of private interests they should receive no pay but if called upon to resist an invasion they should be placed on the same footing with other troops.

To guard against the plantations becoming the centers of unlawful trade with the enemy and to secure the negroes employed on them from the danger of falling into the hands of the enemy and being reduced to a state of slavery, no leases should be given for any plantation that is beyond the reach of military supervision and protection except in the cases where the lessees are able to maintain a force to protect themselves from raids and hold their [*positions?*] until they can be relieved. No plantations should be leased or registered without the Knowledge and approval of the commander of the District in which they are located.

I have authorized local organizations to be formed or directed the issue of arms and ammunition for the purposes above indicated and I propose to extend it whenever it can be done without danger that the means put into the hands of individuals will not be used against us, but the whole system should be so defined and fixed as not to expose the interests involved to embarrassment and loss by the changes and uncertainty to which they are now subjected I have the honor to be Very respectfully Your obdt servt

HLcSr Sgd Ed R. S. Canby

Maj. Genl. Ed. R. S. Canby to the Secretary of War, 6 Dec. 1864, enclosed in M.G.C. Ed. R. S. Canby to the Secretary of War, 7 Jan. 1865, W-109 1865, Letters Received, ser. 12, RG 94 [K-579]. On December 10, 1864, Secretary of War Edwin M. Stanton reminded General Canby of the importance of providing military protection for plantations along the Mississippi River that were operated by Northern lessees or loyal owners, "in order to afford proper and necessary supplies and security for planting of crops and securing them for the market." Stanton acknowledged that such use of Union forces should not "interfere with any military operation." Nevertheless, he emphasized, "the advantage of thus obtaining a supply of cotton for the market cannot very well be overestimated." He did not address Canby's proposal to subdivide the plantations into smaller units and arm their population for self-defense. (*Official Records*, ser. 1, vol. 41, pt. 4, p. 816.)

219: Tennessee Freedman to the Provost Marshal of Freedmen in the District of West Tennessee

[*Memphis, Tenn. December 2? 1865*]

Lieut. Gable Sullivan, a freedman, respectfully represents that, about last christmas he paid to one Aaron Jackson, of Shelby County, one hundred dollars, for hire of his (Gable's) wife for one year who had been the slave of said Jackson. The Said Gable respectfully asks that you issue your order to said Jackson to refund to him (Gable) the said sum of one hundred dollars, on the ground that Jackson had no right to the same, the woman being no longer under his Control according to the Military Laws – of the United States Very Respectfully

his
Gable X Sullivan
mark

HLSr

Gable Sullivan to Lieut. T. H. Ward, [2? Dec. 1865], Affidavits & Statements, ser. 3545, Memphis TN Provost Marshal of Freedmen, RG 105 [A-6623]. According to other documents in the same file, Sullivan had agreed to pay Jackson a total of $150 for "the hire" of Sullivan's wife Charlotte during the year 1865 – that is, for her release from Jackson's custody and from his claim to her labor. Sullivan had paid $100 on January 10, 1865, and promised to remit the balance twelve months later. However, on December 2, 1865, the provost marshal of freedmen directed Jackson to return the $100 payment, "less the amount of two months wages" (presumably for the period before February 22, 1865, when slavery was abolished in Tennessee), and to relinquish any claim to the remaining $50. Jackson disputed the judgment, contending that since the hire agreement predated the adoption of the constitutional amendment that abolished slavery in Tennessee, he was entitled to retain the $100 already paid by Sullivan. (Promissory note by [G?] Sullivan, 10 Jan. 1865; Lieut. T. H. Ward to Mr. Aaron Jackson, 2 Dec. 1865; J. T. Swayne to Gen. Dudley, 4 Dec. 1865.) No information about the final outcome has been found in the records of the provost marshal of freedmen.

220: Order by the Superintendent of Freedmen at Davis Bend, Mississippi

[*Davis Bend, Miss., early 1865?*]

The following *Rules and Regulations* will for the present be adopted for the *Government* of the *Freedmen* at *Davis Bend. Miss.*

I. The *Bend* with the exception of the *Jeff. Plantation* will be leased to those who seem willing and able to work lands upon their own accounts.

II Those wishing to work lands upon their own account will be required to form themselves into companies of from three to twenty five hands that are able to do their share of the labor. Before the land will be allotted, the companies will be registered, (in a book kept for that purpose.) together with the parents and children belonging to each member of the Company. At this time each company will be required to select one from their number who will be Known as the head of the company and who will transact the business for the entire company and no account will be Kept with any other partner.

III. After the companies are formed and registered no changes will be allowed except by the consent of two thirds of the members and the approval of the *Post Superintendent.*

IV No company will be allowed to hire hands to work for them, except by the consent of the Post Superintendent. Each hand that is registered with the company and remains with it through the season will pay their portion of the expense and receive their share of the profit.

V. Each company will be required to pay for all the rations they receive, and for the use of all horses, mules, and farming utensils they receive from Government.

Rations will be issued to companies only for the number registered.

VI In dividing land the quantity will be regulated according to the number of hands in the company— the number of acres to a hand will be regulated by the Post Superintendent.

VII The companies will be divided into colonies for which Superintendents will be provided and whose duty will be to see that every company in his colony work their ground in the proper manner. He will have a general Supervision over all the people in his colony. and all companies and people living within his colony will be subject to his orders.

VIII Any member of a company who shall refuse or neglect to perform his share of the labor, (except in cases of actual sickness) or shall absent himself from the company without their consent. can be reported to the Colony Superintendent, and if he think it proper will be turned over to work without pay until he is willing to work for himself.

IX The "Jeff Plantation" will be reserved and worked as a *Government Farm* where all hands that are not registered with companies can find employment with pay and rations.

X No rations will be issued on the Bend except to companies and those employed on the Government Farm. All those not able to work will be required to show a certificate to this effect from the surgeon in charge, or furnish their own rations.

XI All those having certificates of disability from the surgeon will be placed in a camp by themselves at some suitable place where they will be fed and properly cared for.

XII All crimes and disobedience of orders will be punished according to the nature of the offence. Thieves and robbers will when proved guilty be banished from the bend and sent to Big Black Island.

XIII. Heads of Companies who allow any of their members to steal from one another or from the Government will be dis[pen?]sed and sent from the Bend.

Great efforts must be made by all good men on the bend to change the present disgraceful and bad conduct of a large number of the negroes now living here who are Stealing, plundering, Killing stock, and living in idleness and vagrancy. Extreme measures for punishment will be adopted and vigorously carried out. All those interested in the welfare of the people, and who wish to see the Bend improve will assist the Superintendent in his efforts to bring about good order.

HDc

Rules and Regulations . . . for the Government of the Freedmen at Davis Bend. Miss., [early 1865?], vol. 122, pp. 23–24, Letter Sent, a General Order, & an Instruction, ser. 2150, Davis Bend MS, RG 105 [A-9535]. Probably issued by Captain Gaylord B. Norton, who had been appointed superintendent of freedmen at Davis Bend in September 1864 and served in that capacity through much of 1865. (Special Orders No. 7, Office Supt. and Pro. Mar. Freedmen, 18 Sept. 1864, vol. 75, p. 4, Special Orders Issued, ser. 2038, Asst. Supt. of Freedmen, MS Asst. Comr. Pre-Bureau Records, RG 105 [A-9535].)

221: Chaplain of a Black Regiment to the General Agent of the Treasury Department Special Agencies

Vicksburg [*Miss.*] Jan 14 1865

Sir I have charge of a Camp of Freedmen, of about 700 or 800 persons on the Valley Road just outside of the Picket lines–

They are now a heavy expense to the Gov[t] which might be relieved by a judicious disposition of their labor–

To secure this object, land is needed for them to work on, which can be had in their immediate neighborhood.

For this purpose, I respectfully request you to reserve the Cathel place, the Bearfield place, & the Edwards place, which last, I believe that Col. Thomas claims to control by a grant from the General

The people are exceedingly anxious for the success of this application.

I hope to accomplish by this means 1st the relief of government from a very Considerable expense. by the support of most of the people & 2nd their prosperity & improvement, by securing from this labor a some what better remuneration than ordinary wages, if we succeed, & in doing this to procure for them sufficient means, so as to relieve them from the embarrassments which hinder the success of those at Davis Bend, & 3′ to improve & stimulate & gratify the people, by a better style of management – In the hope of getting land the people have built houses under my direction, have a school house ready to put up, are getting gardens ready – & are hopeful for the future. Col. Thomas approves of my general plan, which I will display to you when I see you –

Col. Thomas will give us the wood yard there also –

I desire also to get a permanent grant of the Edwards place, with 50 acres of land for an Orphan Asylum –

Presuming that you will dispose of none of these lands till I can see you, I remain Your obedt Servt

ALS J. A. Hawley

Chapn. J. A. Hawley to Mr. Wm. P. Mellen, 14 Jan. 1865, General Letters Received, Records of the General Agent, RG 366 [Q-159]. Hawley, who was chaplain of the 63rd USCI (an "invalid" regiment composed of men recruited at various points in the Mississippi Valley), signed as "Asst in Charge of Freedn." William P. Mellen, the Treasury Department general agent, had already arranged to rent two of the estates in question to Northern lessees, and he denied Chaplain Hawley's application. However, at the urging of Colonel Samuel Thomas, superintendent of freedmen in the District of Vicksburg, the military commander of the Post of Vicksburg ordered Mellen to revoke the leases and reserve the property for occupancy by the freedpeople under Hawley's supervision. Thomas appointed the chaplain superintendent of the settlement, which became known as "Camp Hawley." The workers in the settlement organized themselves into thirteen squads "according to their preferences," each unit comprising from six to twenty-three "hands" and a "contractor or 'Chief of Squad.' " The squads grew cotton on tracts ranging from 20 to 150 acres, and almost every family also cultivated a garden, using seed furnished by Northern aid societies. Hawley arranged for a Memphis firm to furnish each squad with mules, tools, and provisions, in return for which the merchants would receive not only the cost of the supplies, but also one-half "the net profits of the crop." The remaining profits from each squad's crop were to be divided among its "hands." As it turned out, there was little to divide. At the end of the year, Hawley reported that springtime flooding, summertime drought, and the cotton-boll worm had dealt severe setbacks.

Moreover, unspecified "vicious influences" had led many of the laborers to neglect the crop "at the most critical time." Six of the thirteen squads ended the year in debt to the furnishing merchants, and the "cash dividends" earned by the others were in some cases "very small." Full hands in the most successful squad received the equivalent of 75¢ per working day. Still, despite the unfavorable weather and disadvantageous terms of credit, the freedpeople had managed to feed and clothe themselves, and, Hawley emphasized, they had "learned a valuable lesson of economy, & of the importance of good management – which may yet be worth more to them than a considerably larger percentage of profit." (Major D. Cornwell to Col. H. Lieb, 27 Apr. 1865, vol. 47/94 DMiss, pp. 77–82, Letters Sent by the Acting Assistant Inspector General, ser. 2225, Dist. of Vicksburg, RG 393 Pt. 2 No. 127 [C-2141]; Chaplain J. A. Hawley to Col. S. Thomas, 8 Dec. 1865, H-69 1865, Registered Letters Received, ser. 2052, MS Asst. Comr., RG 105 [A-9049].)

222A: General Superintendent of Freedmen in the Department of Mississippi and State of Arkansas to the Secretary of the Treasury

Washington D.C. Jan. 31st 1865

Sir; In accordance with the expectation & desire of your Dept. as communicated to me by Hon. Geo. Harrington Asst. Secy, in a note of Aug. 23d 1865 [*1864*], the crop raised by Freedmen under charge of the Gov't, has been gathered; the sales are nearly complete; full accounts will be rendered. A copy of the General Report has been forworded to you.[1] The facts gathered from all sources show that 1st the system adopted for the self-support of the infirm & dependent, would have been eminently successful had not the army worm destroyed the cotton. 2nd The Freedmen do best for themselves & the Gov't as independent cultivators of small farms, Those who warked for themselves, have raised on the average the most cotton per acre & have saved sums varying from one hundred dollars to ten thousand, while those who have worked for hire, have rarely laid up any[thing] & in many instances have returned to the Gov't for support. 3d Wages should not be regulated by classification by age or otherwise except as the Supt. for the purpose of guarding against fraud & abuse shall fix a minimum. the employer & employee being allowed to enter a free market. 4th Freedmen will go to labor willingly & work faithfully when free from the fear of barbarous guerrilla incursions; but that any pressed beyond security by lessees too intent on profit & too little careful of the negro, results not only in furnishing the enemy supplies & the massacre of negroes, & the abandonment of plantations but in evil to all by spreading a terror among them incompatable with steady & faithful service.

The note alluded to, expects me to continue these enterprises as inaugerated until your Dept. is prepared in all respects to assume control. I am informed by Hon. Mr. Harrington that you will not assume control at present. But a new season opens. I am anxious that it should start with all the advantages of the past year's experience. I am aware Congress is agitating the whole subject.

Will not the season take shape before any action? I would therefore respectfully ask your concurrence 1st in retaining present arrangements for the self-support of infirm & dependent. 2nd in securing occupancy of lands to Freedmen deemed by the Supt. competent to farm independently in preference to other lesses, 3d in assuring Freedmen that none will be expected to go beyond limits pronounced secure by the Depart Commander 4th in withdrawing regulations of price of labor from leases, leaving the supt. to fix a minimum to guard against abuse; and 5th The assurance from you that the Treas'y will pay for supply of medicines & medical attendance as agreed between Ajt Genl Thomas & the Agt of the Treas'y & provided in orders No. 1. Louisville Ky Jan. 1st 1865 Ajt Gnl Thomas –[2] Most respectfully your ob'dt serv't

ALS John Eaton Jr

Col. John Eaton Jr. to Hon. W. P. Fessenden, 31 Jan. 1865, E-88 1865, Letters Received by the Division, ser. 315, Division of Captured Property, Claims, & Land, RG 56 [X-108]. Both George Harrington's "note" of August 23, 1864, and the Secretary of the Treasury's reply to Eaton are quoted in doc. 222B, immediately below.

1 Presumably John Eaton, *Report of the General Superintendent of Freedmen, Department of the Tennessee and State of Arkansas for 1864* (Memphis, Tenn., 1865). (The Department of the Tennessee, over which Eaton's jurisdiction as general superintendent had extended, had been virtually abolished in November 1864 and most of its territory transferred to the Department of Mississippi.) Eaton's report, dated December 31, 1864, criticized the Treasury Department's administration of the plantation-leasing system for having encouraged "the spirit of speculation" among lessees while failing to guarantee the personal safety and legal protection of black laborers. It also pointed out that those ex-slaves who had worked independently as plantation lessees or urban artisans had ended the year in far better circumstances than those who had labored for wages on leased plantations. Eaton emphasized that the future of a reconstructed South depended in large measure on the policies adopted by the federal government toward the former slaves: "[W]hat is made of these

masses during the war, whether actually voters or not, must determine the status of these regions" after the conclusion of armed conflict.
2 The order, issued by Adjutant General Lorenzo Thomas, established procedures whereby the Treasury Department would reimburse the army for certain expenses connected with the medical care of freedpeople in the Department of Mississippi and the Department of Arkansas, particularly the cost of medical supplies and the wages of contract surgeons and nurses. (Orders No. 1, 1 Jan. 1865, L. Thomas Letters & Orders, Generals' Papers & Books, ser. 159, RG 94 [V-54].)

222B: General Superintendent of Freedmen in the Department of Mississippi and State of Arkansas to the Commander of the Department of Mississippi

Memphis, Tenn., Feb 24th *1865*

General; I beg leave to submit the following statement of the substance of the information in my possession derived from my official visits to Washington last Summer and the present Winter. Then the Freedmen Treasury Regulations had just been issued.[1]

In the absence of the Secretary, I inquired of his Assistant the Hon. Mr Harrington, how these regulations were to go into operation; and at his request stated the fact, that military authority alone could execute justice among or towards them. and had provided the supplies, medical, commissary, [&c,] for the assistance of the dependent; that I could not see how the Treasury with its own instrumentalities then in operation, was to accomplish the object of the Government any time, and especially then, as the season was progressing here at least, on a different plan. He agreed with me fully, and at once suspended the Regulations, writing the following note

"Treasury Department
August 11th 1864

W. P. Mellen Esq.
Gen. Agent. Treas'y Dep't. Cinn, O. –

Sir; Until further instructions all action under the regulations of July 29th (Ult.,) concerning Freedmen, will be suspended.

Very Respectfully
Geo. Harrington
Act'g Sec'y of Treasury."

After Mr Fessenden's return, and consultation with him I received the following note from Mr Harrington

"Treasury Department
August 23[d] 1864.

Col. John Eaton, Jr. –

Sir: The suspension of the Regulations whereby this Department contemplated taking immediate control of the Freedmen, has been approved by the Secretary.

In directing such suspension it was the expectation and desire of the Department that the system and arrangements heretofore inaugurated and now being prosecuted under you should be continued without interruption until the crops now in, are gathered and the present season closed and until this Department is prepared in all respects to assume such control under the law."

Very Respectfully,
Geo. Harrington
Asst Secretary of Treasury"

I might add that the general Regulations of the Treasury were signed by the President without his knowing that they contained anything in regard to Freedmen, and that I made at his request the statement of facts on which the Regulations were suspended

In January, calling upon the Treasury Department to know if they were ready to take up the Freedmen, Mr Harrington informed me that they were not.

Afterwards, at his suggestion, I addressed the Secretary a note, for the purpose of receiving an official reply. He answered as follows: –

Treasury Department
Feb 3[d] 1865.

Sir: – I have received your letter of the 31st Ult., offering certain suggestions concerning the management of the Freedmen.

No action in this direction can be taken by this Department, until the discussion of the matter, now pending in Congress, has resulted in some definite plan, and it is known under which Department of the Government the affairs of the Freedmen are to be placed.

I am, Very Respectfully
W. P. Fessenden
Secretary of the Treasury."

"Col. John Eaton.
Washington."

Showing his note to the President, he gave me the following order: –

Col Eaton: –

You will continue your supervision of Freedmen, over the same territory, and on the same principles, as in the past, making such improvements as experience may suggest, until legislation shall require some further change.

A. Lincoln."

Feb 10th 1865."

It will be seen by the above that the action proposed by the Gen'l Agent of the Treasury to Major General Canby[2] beyond the general wish of the President and Secretary, that the best should be done, was his individual proposition; The Regulations were suspended. The care with which General Canby's order takes up the subject, I think indicates the apprehensions before his mind.[3] I see the same in your order[4] and discover no essential difficulty in carrying the work forward as it now stands, excepting such impractical features as the classification of hands by age and not according to merit, and the absence in the Regulations themselves, of anything but civil authority, which is powerless in [the] very nature of military occupation I do not think the Government or the country would sustain an infringement upon the policy of your orders in regard to Davis' Bend and President's Island, and similar points of security set apart for Freedmen[5]

The conflict of speculative capital with the true interests of the Freedmen and military operations is readily and deeply felt.

Major General Canby's letter upon the subject of trade[6] received the highest and strongest commendation. I was called upon for statements, and had almost unlimited corroborative facts

This influence of speculation upon the policy of Emancipation was widely felt, and a strong feeling prevailed that the safeguard of the negro not only against it, but against the old slavocratic prejudices is in a just but temporary exercise of the war power.

This, however, was opposed by Mr Sumner and a few others. Working between the two ideas, a Bill establishing a separate Department for Freedmen and Abandoned Lands was reported by a conference committee, and passed the House by two majority

Another Bill, from the Military Committee, provided that the whole subject of Freedmen and refugees should be in charge of a Bureau established in the War Office, which should also control such abandoned lands as might be needed for their benefit leaving all details to be worked out by experience This Bill is also reported as having passed the House. This met most aptly the difficulties and conclusions suggested by my experience. The President and Secretaries did not see fit to influence legislation but I am confident their views look to the most simple and practical solution of the difficulties. I have the honor to be Genl., Very Respectfully Your Obd't Servant

HLS John Eaton Jr.

Col. John Eaton Jr. to Maj. Gen. N. J. T. Dana, 24 Feb. 1865, filed as C-115 1865, Letters Received, ser. 1920, Civil Affairs, Dept. of the Gulf, RG 393

Pt. 1 [C-742]. On letterhead of the "Office General Superintendent of Freedmen." Endorsements indicate that the commander of the Department of Mississippi, General Napoleon J. T. Dana, referred Eaton's letter to his superior officer, General Edward R. S. Canby, commander of the Military Division of West Mississippi, who in turn forwarded it to another subordinate, General Stephen A. Hurlbut, commander of the Department of the Gulf. On March 11, General Hurlbut issued plantation regulations that superseded and substantially revised those of the Treasury Department. (See above, doc. 138.) Within days, General Dana adopted Hurlbut's order for his own department, with minor "modifications adapted to local necessities" (chiefly those of administrative organization). "As the plantation interests of this Department and those of the Department of the Gulf are so intimately connected," Dana announced, "it is deemed advisable to establish in both commands uniform regulations for the employment of laborers, and to secure to the Planters and Freedmen, substantially, the same system by which to be governed." (General Orders, No. 34, Headquarters Department of Mississippi, 23 Mar. 1865, vol. 10 DMiss, General Orders & Circulars, ser. 2438, Dept. of MS, RG 393 Pt. 1 [C-2097].)

1 On July 29, 1864, four weeks after an act of Congress had charged the Treasury Department with providing "for the employment and general welfare of all [freedpeople] . . . within the lines of national military occupation," the Secretary of the Treasury had issued plantation regulations prepared by William P. Mellen, general agent of the department's special agencies. (*Statutes at Large*, vol. 13, pp. 375–78; and, for the regulations, see above, doc. 119.)

2 In early February 1865, Mellen had reissued the suspended regulations of July 29, 1864, after consulting with and securing the approval of General Edward R. S. Canby, commander of the Military Division of West Mississippi. (See above, doc. 137.)

3 General Order 13, issued by General Canby on February 1, 1865, had sanctioned Mellen's regulations, but required that the plantations worked in accordance with their provisions be confined to areas under actual Union control. Military commanders, Canby announced, would try to guard such plantations, but their protection would remain "subordinate" to calls upon troops for "offensive military operations." Plantation owners and lessees were "required to construct stockades or such other temporary defences as may be necessary to secure their laborers, stock and other property from . . . small raiding parties." Canby's order also directed commanders of the departments in his military division not to relinquish authority over the freedpeople until they had arranged with treasury officials "the term of transfer so as to avoid any embarrassment to either branch of the service." (See above, doc. 137.)

4 General Order 21, issued on February 16, 1865, by General Napoleon J. T. Dana, commander of the Department of Mississippi (which belonged to General Canby's military division), was designed "[t]o carry out the objects and intentions" of Canby's General Order 13. Dana's order required that planters secure his approval and that of the local district commander before operating any plantation under treasury regulations; warned that any planter who failed to construct the defenses mandated by Canby's order would "suffer the withdrawal of the approval from his lease and the forfeiture of his privileges"; and

directed that, until treasury officials made definite arrangements to assume supervision over the freedpeople, the general superintendent of freedmen (Colonel John Eaton, Jr.) and his subordinates were to continue in their duties "as at present." (*Official Records*, ser. 1, vol. 48, pt. 1, p. 870.)

5 In late 1864, General Dana had ordered that President's Island (in the Mississippi River immediately south of Memphis) and most of Davis Bend (on the east bank of the river, south of Vicksburg) be reserved for occupation exclusively by black people, requiring all white residents, except those with written military authorization, to leave the two areas. (Special Orders No. 9, Head Quarters Department of Mississippi, 16 Dec. 1864, vol. 11 DMiss, Special Orders, ser. 2441, Dept. of MS, RG 393 Pt. 1 [C-2168]; *Official Records*, ser. 1, vol. 41, pt. 4, pp. 437–38.)

6 In a letter of December 7, 1864, to the Secretary of War, General Canby had raised strong objections to opening Union lines to "promiscuous" commercial intercourse with areas still under Confederate control. Such trade, Canby had warned, would encourage unprincipled speculators to compromise the secrecy of Union military operations and would also allow the rebel army to obtain much-needed supplies more easily. (*Official Records*, ser. 1, vol. 41, pt. 4, pp. 785–87.)

223: Superintendent of Freedmen at Helena, Arkansas, to the Headquarters of the District of Eastern Arkansas

Helena, Arkansas, Feb: 9th, *1865*.

Captain. I respectfully make application for permission from the General Comd,g to Ship to W. W. Orme. at Memphis Tenn, the following Cotton owned by Freedpeople (colored)

3 (Three) Bales marked B&J. owned by Bill & Jones Wendle.
3 (Three) Bales marked ◇J owned by Martin & Mary Williams

7 (Seven) Bales marked L.D.C. owned by Porter Avant, Allen Avant, Billy Avant, and others– 4 (Four) Bales marked Jim C owned by Amanda Wendle, Scott, Rachel, Andrew, Anderson and Maryanne 10. (Ten) Bales marked D.X. owned by Aleck. Squire, Dempsey Stephen, William, Dick, Buck, Porter, Harry, Frank, Lotty & Sol, Dowd.

3 (Three) Bales marked B&X. owned by Moses, Anderson, Bob. George. Paul. & Spencer Bradley.

4 (Four) Bales marked "Bill C." owned by Sam, Sarah, George, Henry, Bill, Emmeline, Grandison, Mary White, Amelia, Sally, Nelson, Rachel, Edmund, John, Jem, Eliza & Marth Wendle. Very Respectfully Your Ob[t] Ser[t]

Henry Sweeney

HLcS

Capt. Henry Sweeney to Capt. T. C. Meatyard, 9 Feb. 1865, S-1 1865, Letters Received (Supplementary), ser. 4677, Dist. of Eastern AR, RG 393 Pt. 2 No. 299 [C-1820]. Sweeney signed as both a captain in the 66th USCI and superintendent of freedmen. William W. Orme was the supervising agent of the Treasury Department's 2nd Special Agency; his duties included regulating cotton shipments from Union-occupied parts of eastern Arkansas. A stamp on Captain Sweeney's letter signified that General Napoleon B. Buford, commander of the District of Eastern Arkansas, approved the shipment. In the same file are copies of several similar applications by Sweeney to ship small lots of cotton produced by freedpeople in the Helena area.

224: Contract between a Mississippi Landowner and Three Mississippi Freedmen

[*Warren County, Miss.?*] 17th day of March A.D. 1865.

Know all Men by these Presents, that I, Sarah C. Lane (Widow) of the first part, Have this day granted, bargained, and leased unto George W. Walton, Cato Darden & Ephraim Watkins (All colored) Eighty acres (more or less included within certain limits known to the parties) of my tract of land, from the date of these presents until the 1st day of January 1866.

The said tract of land is known & registered as the "Pleasant Hill" plantation, situated in the County of Warren in the State of Miss, between the Halls Ferry Road & Rail Road, and South East from Vicksburg. The portion of land so leased being the Eastern & Southern part of said tract.

The terms & conditions of this lease are, That the said Walton, Darden & Watkins are to have control & cultivate said land, for the time stated in above lease. They are to settle all government dues, and pay unto said Lane, as rent for said land, the sum of six Hundred ($600⁰⁰) dollars, Two Hundred ($200⁰⁰) dollars Cash, the receipt of which is hereby acknowledged, The balance, being Four Hundred ($400⁰⁰) dollars to be paid on or before the 1st day of September next.

Witness our hands & seals on this the 17th day of March A.D. 1865.

Sarah C, Lane
G. W. Walton
Cato Darden
HDcSr Ephaim Watkins

Contract between Sarah C, Lane and G. W. Walton et al., 17 Mar. 1865, Miscellaneous Records, ser. 2393, Vicksburg MS Special Agent of the Treasury Dept., RG 105 [A-9523]. Witnessed.

225: Mississippi and Louisiana Planters and Northern Plantation Lessees to the Superintendent and Assistant Provost Marshal of Freedmen in the District of Natchez

Natchez Miss, April 1, 1865.

To Major Geo. D. Reynolds Ass[t] Pro[v] Marshall of Freedmen The undersigned Registers, Lessees, & Managers of Plantations in your District, in view of the late order of Major Gen[l] Hurlbut relating to the support & paymnt of Freedmen employed on plant[n] [1] Respectfully beg to present the following ideas for your consideration – Heartily acquiessing in the managemnt of freedmen for their greatst good, we believe –

1st That by adhering to the existing contracts by us made with them, & approved by the Trea[s] & Military authorities – to them (the negroes) will be shown the best faith in carrying out properly enacted contracts, & hence give a good reason why they as freedmen should act honorably in fulfilling their part of the agreement, & thus as men – now free, learn the value of a contract. – Many of us have already made two contracts with our hands – first – according to the best light we had, made the same agreem[t], as for last year – & second, – after the promulgation of Mr. Melen's regulations,[2] – agreeably thereto. It was difficult to make the negroes understand, *why* it was necessary to make a new bargain when they understood that the first was to hold good for one year. & they considerd they were bounden by it. If a 3[d] agreemt must be made its effects will be very deleterious to them, & hinder much in prosecuting plan[tn] work at this hurried season – & many of them would not agree thereto.

2[d] Great dissatisfaction must arise from resorting to the clothing of Negroes, as they have for the past two years enjoyed the freedom they very much prize, of *buying* with their *own money*, whatever clothing they like, & while we *advise* them against buying light & useless articles, they are free to buy what they please. They will regard the change as nearer allied to the old slavery custom, (as it seems to us) & hence create dissatisfaction. Without cheerful satisfaction on their part, proper work can not be accomplished, nor due respect paid to laws & regulations – [hence] the desired effect to elevate & Christianize them, & the product of a crop upon which Gov[t] will realize a handsome rev[enue] will alike be defeated.

Thus showing that by our contracts, we are giving them an *equivalent* in *money* for their clothing, & that, this equivalent is really *better* than the clothing, we believe the *intent* of the order will be fully met by confirming contracts, already existing, where a fair compensation is agreed upon. –

We therefore desire your candid consideration of these facts, &

such action in the premises as will secure the continuance of the existing contracts.

HLS [*24 signatures*]

G. H. Lambdin et al. to Major Geo. D. Reynolds, 1 Apr. 1865, Unregistered Letters Received, ser. 2269, Natchez MS Asst. Comr. for the Southern Dist. of MS, RG 105 [A-9479]. The signatures, each in a different handwriting, included the names of four partnerships and one company; two signers identified themselves as lessees, two as agents, one as a manager, one as "Manager & Lessee," and one as "Reg[r]." The wrapper gives no indication of a reply, and the letters-sent volumes of the superintendent of freedmen at Natchez are no longer extant.

1 General Order 23, issued on March 11, 1865, by General Stephen A. Hurlbut, commander of the Department of the Gulf, required employers to furnish food and clothing to their laborers, in addition to wages. Hurlbut's policy superseded that established only one month earlier by the Treasury Department, which provided for higher wages, but required laborers to purchase their own food and clothing. (See above, docs. 119 and 138.)
2 Plantation regulations drafted by William P. Mellen, general agent of the Treasury Department's special agencies, in July 1864, but not put into effect until February 1865–only to be superseded shortly thereafter by General Hurlbut's order. (See above, doc. 119.)

226: Assistant Quartermaster of Freedmen at Vidalia, Louisiana, to the Superintendent and Assistant Provost Marshal of Freedmen in the District of Natchez

Vidalia La, April 15" *1865*.

Major, I have the honor to request that some definite arrangement be made for the Compensation of the Laborers employed by me as soon as this can conveniently be done. Receiving no pay and very poorly clothed, they are restless and dissatisfied which is much increased of late as they disliked the more to remove from Natchez as in so doing they lose the frequent opportunities of picking up odd change for jobs of labor enjoyed when they wer quartered at the business center of the Town.

As a result I have great difficulty in keeping my trains moving. at all, and delays occur in executing your Orders troublesome to others and extremely annoying to myself.

I think it equitable that my men should be paid the wages prescribed for hands on Plantations, and have accordingly noted the wages of Teamsters the same as 1st Class hands, and others at different rates on the accompanying list and my Mechanics at $10.00 additional to 1st Class. The Mechanics were promised this rate of pay by Lieut Thirds who first employed them.

I think the spring suit of Clothing should be worth $15.00 and it might probably be obtained from the Freedman's Store by giving vouchers.

Though indefinite promises to men who have so often been deceived are worse than useless, and there are many reasons why they should receive a part of their pay as soon as practicable, I believe I could secure efficient labor from all named on my list, by assuring them that they would certainly receive this Pay in any contingency unless stopped for carelessness or idleness.

This arrangement would make my Department a model of justice rather than of injustice and enable me promply and efficiently to execute all orders, without being beset by those constant perplexities and annoying circumstances which are almost aggravating enough to destroy the temper and worry out the life of any man who takes a pride in the prompt performance of duty. I am Major, With great respect, Your obedient servant,

ALS A. W. Williamson

2d Lt. A. W. Williamson to Maj. Geo. D. Reynolds, 15 Apr. 1865, Unregistered Letters Received, ser. 2269, Natchez MS Asst. Comr. for the Southern Dist. of MS, RG 105 [A-9478]. Williamson signed as a lieutenant in the 70th USCI, a black regiment composed largely of men recruited in the Natchez area. The "accompanying list" referred to in the letter is not in the file. No reply has been found; the letters-sent volumes of the superintendent of freedmen at Natchez are no longer extant.

227: Resolutions Adopted by a Meeting of Vicksburg, Mississippi, Freedpeople

[*Vicksburg, Miss. April 17, 1865*]

At a meeting in the presbyterian church April 17, 1865, of the self supporting Freedmen of the Post of vicksburg, the following preamble and resolutions were proposed and unanimously adopted,

Whereas the military authorities of this Department have kindly established for us a freedmen's store, with a view to better our condition, protect us from extortion, and place the means of subsistance within our reach, and whereas; a subsequent order has been issued, the effect of which is to deprive us, in a great measure, of these benefits, therefore be it

At a meeting in the presbyterian Church April 17. 1865, of the self supporting Freedmen of the Post of Vicksburg, the following preamble and resolutions were ~~unanimously~~ proposed and unanimously adopted,

Whereas the military authorities of this Department have kindly established for us a freedmen's store, with a view to better our condition, protect us from extortion and place the means of subsistance within our reach, and whereas; a subsequent Order has been issued. the effect of which is to deprive us. in a great measure of these benefits, therefore be it

Resolved

That the Freedmen's store kept by Ellet and Huggins, established under special Order No 27. Extract II. Head Quarters District of Vicksburg, is regarded by us as the most direct. the most feasible, and the most substantial effort that could be made for our relief, and that we have availed ourselves of its benefits with gratitude to God. and to those benevolent persons who have been instrumental in bringing it about

Resolved

Resolved
That through this instrumentality the price of all the necessaries of life have been greatly reduced and a better Chance given us to support ourselves by industry and economy.

Resolved
That we have therefore heard with sorrow and regret that subsequent Orders have been issued, requiring us to obtain a permit to purchase at that store before goods can be obtained, thereby imposing such a heavy tax upon our time as to deprive us, in a great measure, of the benefits which we believe were intended to be confered upon us

Resolved
That this shall be our petition to the military authorities, requesting them to rescind special order No 83. par IV. and allow us to purchase our goods as heretofore, without this great annoyance and inconvenience.

Resolved that our thanks are tendered to Gen Dana, Gen Smith, and Col. Samuel Thomas for their Kindness to us, and that a copy of these resolutions be sent to them

Henry Scott, sec

Document 227

Resolved

That the Freedmen's store kept by Ellet and Huggins, established under special order No 27, Extract II, Head Quarters District of Vicksburg,[1] is regarded by us as the most direct, the most feasible, and the most substantial effort that could be made for our relief, and that we have availed ourselves of its benefits with gratitude to God, and to those benevolent persons who have been instrumental in bringing it about

Resolved

That through this instrumentality the prices of all the necessaries of life have been greatly reduced and a better chance given us to support ourselves by industry and economy.

Resolved

That we have therefore heard with sorrow and regret that subsequent orders have been issued, requiring us to obtain a permit to purchase at that store before goods can be obtained, thereby imposing such a heavy tax upon our time as to deprive us, in a great measure, of the benefits which we believe were intended to be confered upon us

Resolved

That this shall be our petition to the military authorities, requesting them to rescind special order No 83, par IV,[2] and allow us to purchase our goods as heretofore, without this great annoyance and inconvenience.

Resolved that our thanks are tendered to Gen. Dana, Gen Smith, and Col Samuel Thomas for their kindness to us,[3] and that a copy of these resolutions be sent to them

HDS Henry Scott,

Resolutions adopted by "a meeting . . . of the self supporting Freedmen of the Post of vicksburg," [17 Apr. 1865], F-A-80 1865, Letters Received, ser. 2433, Dept. of MS, RG 393 Pt. 1 [C-2087]. Scott signed as secretary. The freedpeople's protest was evidently unavailing; a penciled notation, probably by a clerk at the headquarters of the Department of Mississippi, reads "File," and there is no evidence that Special Order 83 was rescinded or modified.

1 Issued on January 30, 1865, by General Cadwallader C. Washburn, commander of the District of Vicksburg, Special Order 27 had authorized P. C. Huggins and John A. Ellet to open a "Freedmen's Store" in Vicksburg. The two merchants were authorized to sell "exclusively to Contrabands" such merchandise "as may be necessary to supply the wants of this class," charging no more than 33 percent above wholesale prices in Vicksburg. The purpose of the store, Washburn had announced, was "to relieve the Contrabands from the system of extortion to which they are now subjected." (Special Orders, No. 27,

Head Quarters District of Vicksburg, 30 Jan. 1865, Orders & Circulars, ser. 44, RG 94 [DD-44].)

2 Issued on April 10, 1865, by General Morgan L. Smith, who had assumed command of the District of Vicksburg in February, Special Order 83 had noted disapprovingly that "certain white citizens have, in various ways, availed themselves of the benefits" of the freedmen's store. General Smith had therefore forbidden purchases at the store without a permit from the provost marshal of freedmen, probably to prevent black people from buying goods on behalf of white purchasers. (Special Orders No. 83, Head Quarters District of Vicksburg, 10 Apr. 1865, Orders & Circulars, ser. 44, RG 94 [DD-44].)

3 General Napoleon J. T. Dana, commander of the Department of Mississippi; General Morgan L. Smith, commander of the District of Vicksburg; Colonel Samuel Thomas, superintendent of freedmen in the District of Vicksburg.

228: Assistant Provost Marshal of Freedmen at De Soto Landing, Louisiana, to the Provost Marshal of Freedmen in the District of Vicksburg

De Soto La. April 21st 1865

Liut I have the honor to report that I began my duties at this place about the first of January 1865

On my arrival I found a considerable number of Freedmen here, who had been thrown out of employment by reason of the Union Forces evacuating the posts of Millikens Bend, and Goodriches Landing, There were some of them who had not been paid the wages due them for their last years labor, and they had left their homes in such haste that they were unable to bring with them the property which they had gathered around them during the year

They were thus made dependents for the time. or untill they could get employment, or the wages due them for labor

I believe that all the hands who were working last year on plantations have now been paid for their labor.

Rations

I issued rations to the old and infirm who had no person to support them to orphan children, to those who were crippled so as not to be able to do anything, and to some of those who were out of employment, and had not been paid for their last years work, so as to be able to support themselves

Those Freedmen who had been living for some time in the camp, resorted to all manner of trickery and deception to procure rations, and I found it extremely necessary to be very perticular in giving rations to prevent their imposing on me & drawing supplies under false pretences.

But although I used every precaution that I could devise, there were some who received rations who ought not to have had them. As soon as I found out that any person was imposing on me in that way, I immediately stopped their supply of subsistance and subjected them to various forms of punishment, such as I thought was best adapted to their case.

I have kept a record of all rations issued, which shows the name of the head of faimlies, the number of adults and children in each, and the number of rations issued to each family. To children under twelve years of age I issued half rations.

As soon as I found that any person who was drawing rations had got employment or had received their last years wages, I discontinued rations to them.

I found on commencing my duties that I had so much buisiness to attend to that I could not issue rations to the Freedmen oftener than twice per month as it took me two and a half to three days to make one issue.

I used my register to issue by which I found much more convenient than the system of issuing by tickets.

Settlement of cases of dispute,

As soon as the Freedmen acertained that there was some person here to whom they could look for an adjustment of their difficulties, they came in with their complaints very rapidly

Most of the cases brought before me were of debt, all of which I settled according to the best of my judgment It is unnecessary to state the nature of the rest of cases brought before me further than they were such as only persons who are very ignorant would have settled publicly.

Passes,

I have issued passes to Freedmen at an average of twenty per day, keeping a record of all passes issued White persons can not cross over the river from this side without passes– to such as are by some unforseen accident caught on this side without a pass, I have been giving passes to go over the river, and at the same time instructing them that they will be required to get a pass in Vicksburg if they wish to return

Untill Capt Wakeman was assigned to the Com$^{d.}$ of the Ldg, I did not issue passes to go through the lines but since he took Com'$^{d.}$ I have issued passes to go through his pickets subject to his approval

Division of lands to Freedmen,

About the first of march I commenced the division of the lands appropriated by Genl. Com'd'g. Disct for the establishing at this place of a Freedmens Home Colony I have given from this Office one hundred and ten memorandum Leases of which I have kept a

Register this register shows the number of each tract, to whom it has been assigned for cultivation, the number of acres it containes, of what plantation it is a part, and also the description of the tract as to its situation and bounderies

The one hundred and ten memorandum Leases above mentioned contain about one thousand three hundred acres of the
De Soto Hogan, White, and Burney plantations

I was prevented from finishing the division of the lands because of the high water, and the land undivided is now under water.

There is about two hundred and fifty acres of the Burney and White plantations which has not been divided, this land will probably be assigned to about fifteen persons.

Registry of Freedmen

I have almost completed the registry of the Freedmen who are supporting themselves by working in Home Colony, The registry of those who are otherwise employed, and the unemployed, I have began but am getting along rather slowly on account of the high water and disagreeable weather.

There has been since the first January about one hundred and fifty hands hired from these camp to work on plantations.

Hopeing this may set forth all the points on which you wish me to report, I remain Liut your Obd[t] Servt

ALS Ben F Cheney

Lt. Ben F. Cheney to Liut. Stuart Eldridge, 21 Apr. 1865, Miscellaneous Records, ser. 2035, General Supt. of Freedmen, MS Asst. Comr. Pre-Bureau Records, RG 105 [A-4017]. Three months earlier, in a census of four "Camps of Freedmen"in the De Soto Landing area – "Burney Camp," "Beards Levee," "Desoto Camp," and "Chapmans Woodyard" – Lieutenant Cheney had counted 2,238 people: 1,421 adults (903 "Self Supporting" and 518 "Destitutes") and 817 children (365 "Self Supporting" and 452 "Destitutes"). ("Census of the Camps of Freedmen at and around De Soto Landing, La," 20 Jan. 1865, Miscellaneous Records, ser. 2035, General Supt. of Freedmen, MS Asst. Comr. Pre-Bureau Records, RG 105 [A-4017].)

229: Report by a Plantation Lessee

[*Concordia Parish, La. May? 1865*]

Monthly Report Minorca Plantation, ~~County~~ Parish of Concordia, State of La, Months of Jan. Feby. Mch & April 1865.

No.	NAMES.	DATE OF ENTRY.	[illegible] LEAVING.	PAY PR. MONTH DOLLS.	PAY PR. MONTH CTS.	STOPPAGES. DOLLS.	STOPPAGES. CTS.	DEPENDANTS. Adults	DEPENDANTS. Chil'n.	REMARKS.
1	Albert Bradley	Jany	Apl 30	10	00	17	85	1		We did not commence to do much work untill about Midl Jany. & for some time the hands did not work well or [illegible] as & there has been more or less sickness among them
2	Christopher "	"	"	5	.	6	25	1		
3	Armistead "	Feby	"	5	.	4	.			
4	Wilson Johnson	Jany	"	10	.	12	85			
5	Elizabeth "	"	"	7	.	10	80		1	
6	Kitty "	"	"	3	50	6	80			
7	Henry Mason									Been Sick
8	Polly "									not worked any
9	Jim "	"	"	10	.	14	.			
10	Maloiny "	"	"	3	50	6	50			
11	William "									Not working
12	Adam Williams	"	"	10	.	15	.			
13	[illegible] Hamilton	"	"	10	.	18	35			Sick & absent
14	Alley "	"	"	5	.	7	15			
15	Frank Clement	"	"	10	.	17	35			
16	Minerva "	"	"	7	.	9	55			
17	Jim "	"	"	5	.	7	25			
18	Robt Robinson	"	"	10	.	10	.			
19	Ailey "									Not been working on the place most time
20	Isaac Porter	"	"	10	.	12	50			
21	Margaret "	"	"	7	.	8	85			
22	Henry Watkins	"	"	10	.	13	65	1		
23	Elijah Duncan	"	"	10	.	16	.	1	1	
24	Jackson Davis	"	"	10	.	11	35	1		
25	Jim Warren	"	"	10	.	16	65			
26	Sarah "	Mch	"	7	.	7	35			

I Certify, on Honor, That the above Report is correct.

.... Lessee.

Excerpt from V. A. Woolfolk, Monthly Report Minorca Plantation, [May? 1865], Records on Renting & Leasing of Abandoned Property, ser. 2030, General Supt. of Freedmen, MS Asst. Comr. Pre-Bureau Records, RG 105 [A-4013]. The first page of a five-page list, all on the same printed form, with handwritten insertions; the final page was signed by V. A. Woolfolk, the lessee. The list totals 133 persons employed on the plantation between January and April, 1865, of whom (judging by their given names) 64 were male and 69 female. Specialized positions were noted only for five men – three drivers, a blacksmith, and a hostler. Five workers received wages of more than $10 per month: one driver, $30; three men, including another driver and the blacksmith, $20 each; the third driver, $15. Of the remaining 122 laborers – men, women, and children – for whom wages were listed, thirty-one (all men) received $10 per month; eight (all men), $8; forty (all women), $7; twenty-one, $5; eight, $3.50; and fourteen, $2.50. In comments under the heading of "REMARKS," ten laborers were described as sick and seven as absent or otherwise not working, including one woman who "Cannot work any more"; one of the drivers had been "Dischg[d] Apl 24 – by his own request"; and one woman had died. On the final page appears the following comment: "Average working hours pr Day 7 – until latter part of April – got them up to 8 & occasionally 9 – " The report also enumerated a total of sixty-five "DEPENDANTS" (apparently only those not employed for wages), of whom thirty-four were adults and thirty-one children.

230: Mississippi Freedpeople to the Supervising Agent of the Treasury Department 2nd Special Agency

Tallahatchie river – State of Mississippi – [*June 15?, 1865*]

To General W. W. Orme Superintending Special Agent, Memphis –

Your petitioners would respectfully shew, that they are men of colour of African decent, who have been recognized by their late owners as free, under the proclamation of President Lincoln, and as freed-men are labouring for their own support and benefit, and that of their families; that about the close of the late military campaign in the state of Mississippi, the Rebel Soldiers were permitted to seize, or did, in their own strenght, seize upon, and convey away, what remained in this locality of the Cotton that had been purchased by the Rebel Government of Richmond; that said Cotton from having been exposed for one year without any shelter, had wasted & become rotten & worthless to the extent of 5/6th of its bulk and value, and that out of what was left by said Rebel Soldiers, or not burnt, your petitioners picked by hand, & with arduous labour, separated from the decayed & decaying Cotton, conveyed to the nearest Gin, repacked, rebaled & repressed, to the extent of Twenty six (26) Bales Cotton, which they herewith surrender upon your authority, to Erskine & Co, agents, & James Davis, Govermt aid, to be delivered to you at Memphis

Your petitioners respectfully alledge that they have by their labour saved what would have been entirely lost to the Government, by natural decay & exposure, or otherwise, as can be verified by an inspection of what remains, where this was saved; and they respectfully claim the most liberal compensation allowable under the circumstances, for their own benefit & to discharge obligations to others, (independent of their late owner,) incurred in thus saving, conveying to gin, repacking, covering & repressing said Cotton. And your petitioners will ever pray &c Signed by Jn° M. Dingall, in behalf of, & by request of,

HDSr [*36? signatures*]

William & Emily Sykes et al. to General W. W. Orme, 15 June 1865, Letters Received by the Supervising Special Agent, 2nd Agency, RG 366 [Q-216]. The signatures, all of which are in the same handwriting as the body of the letter, include the names of both men and women and appear to be listed according to family or household (most of them a husband and wife); because the petitioners are not consistently identified by both a given name and surname, the exact number of signers cannot be determined. A notation on the wrapper identified the petitioners as "The Freed-men on Robinson's Plantation." According to an endorsement dated June 15, 1865, written in the same handwriting as the letter and signed by James Davis, a "U.S. Government Aid" (presumably an official of the Treasury Department's 2nd Special Agency), John Dingall had sworn before Davis, on board the steamer *Free Stone*, that he had written the petition "at the request of the foregoing named Free persons of colour . . . from facts stated by them, and which, from what he personally knows and has learned from reliable sources, he verily, believes to be true–"

231A: Tennessee Freedman to the Freedmen's Bureau Superintendent for the Subdistrict of Memphis

Memphis, Tenn. Nov. 3d 1865

Gen. The undersigned, your petitioner, would respectfully represent and show that, in the year 1863, he had a verbal contract with his former master, John Herron, resident citizen of the county of Shelby, Tennessee, to the following effect, to wit; [*John*] Herron was to furnish land, teams, provisions and hands, for the purpose of raising a crop of cotton, in the ensueing year, 1864. He complied with the terms of his contract, with respect to the land, which is located about ten miles from the city – but furnished neither hands, teams, tools, nor provisions.

Your petitioner cultivated the land, providing everything requisite to that purpose, as enumerated in terms of contract, and expended \$700[oo], of his own money, by way of forwarding the enterprise; and produced for 1864, seven bales of cotton. After it was gathered and prepared for market, Herron represented to petitioner that, the country being subject to inroads by guerrillas, it would be dangerous for him, a colored man, to claim, or exercise the rights of ownership of such property; and proposed to your petitioner that if he would put the cotton in his hands, he would dispose of it to the best advantage, and divide the proceeds equally between himself and your petitioner.

Your petitioner's fears being operated upon by these representations, and by the general behaviour of Herron, he assented to the proposition. Herron, however, has never accounted for either cotton or proceeds, to any, the smallest degree.

Your petitioner would further represent that, in the present year, /65, he has continued working under same contract, and raised from ten to twelve bales of cotton, five of which are now here, baled up, and in market; that, two weeks ago, or thereabout, he instituted suit in the Freedmen's Bureau, to enforce his rights – that it was delayed from time to time, owing to some difficulty in procuring witnesses, who resided at a distance from the city. that the cause was finally set for hearing at 2 o'clock, Nov. 2[d] 1865, – when to the utter surprise of petitioner, the case was summarily disposed of prior to that hour, without the cognizance of either himself or attorney, – without giving him any remedy or redress, and in direct contravention of all known rules of right and justice.

Here, General, permit me most respectfully to submit that, it is an easy matter for any discerning man to perceive that this man Herron, shrewd, intelligent and unscrupulous, as he unquestionably is, has imposed upon and betrayed the weakness, the credulity and the ignorance of your petitioner; and that this becomes more palpable, when viewed in connection with the following circumstances, to wit: That, 1st, He (Herron) denies that any such contract as that hereinbeforementioned ever existed, and 2[d] That he is resorting to every artifice which an ingenious man can conjure up, in order to make such appear to be case. – and 3[d] That he claims that petitioner is now working his land for him at the rate of \$30[oo] pr month, independent of any such contract as that already explained.

Your petitioner therefore prays that the five bales of cotton before alluded to may be attached, and the case be properly tried, in pursuance of such directions as you may deem fit to give, before the Freedmen's Bureau, of this city. I have the honor, to remain, Gen. your most Obd't Svt.

Prince Herron,
By his ag't
HLSr Geo. Washington

Prince Herron to Gen. Dudley, 3 Nov. 1865, Affidavits & Statements, ser. 3545, Memphis TN Provost Marshal of Freedmen, RG 105 [A-6526]. Later the same month, Lieutenant T. H. Ward, the provost marshal of freedmen at Memphis, examined the case and, in attempting to determine the nature of the "contract" between Prince Herron and John Herron, recapitulated the events that led to the dispute: In early 1863, John Herron had gone to Memphis to persuade several of his former slaves, who had left him the previous year, to return to his plantation just outside the city, "promising them as an inducement that if they would remain with him, during the war . . . they should have half that was made, and be found in food, shelter & the means with which to make crops." Some of the former slaves had accepted these terms, and Herron had "set apart 20 acres of land to be cultivated in cotton for the negro laborers." Later in the spring of 1863, after the close of the season for planting cotton, Prince Herron had also returned to the plantation, having been promised by John Herron that he would "become a partner" in the cotton being cultivated by the former slaves. However, the other laborers objected to Prince Herron's receiving a share of the crop he had not planted, and he was instead permitted to raise corn on a separate tract. In the spring of 1864, some of the workers on the plantation made specific verbal agreements with John Herron respecting terms of employment for that year, while others – including Prince Herron – simply accepted their former owner's pledge that "he would 'do right by them,' . . . believing that right in that case was what had been promised them when they went to the place in 1863." On this assurance, Prince Herron made crops of cotton in both 1864 and 1865, furnishing his own team, provisions, and forage, and "hiring such help as he needed." The provost marshal of freedmen found in favor of Prince Herron, granting judgment in the amount of $910 for the 1864 crop, plus one-half the proceeds of nine bales produced in 1865. (Judgment in case of Prince Herron vs. John Herron, [13 Nov. 1865], Affidavits & Statements, ser. 3545, Memphis TN Provost Marshal of Freedmen, RG 105 [A-6526].) John Herron, however, appealed the case to the Freedmen's Bureau superintendent at Memphis; testimony from the appeal is printed immediately below as doc. 231B.

231B: Testimony before the Freedmen's Bureau Superintendent at Memphis, Tennessee, in a Case between a Tennessee Freedman and His Former Owner

[*Memphis, Tenn. December 1865*]

Prince Herron
vs. } Evidence
John Herron

Evidence for Plaintiff

Ira Herron, sworn, testified –

In the year 1863 – four hands made 13 bales of cotton – We worked under an agreement with John Heron – We were to get one half of all the crop we raised. There were [. . .] acres planted for the colored people, In November 1864 the price of cotton was from 90 cents to $1.[10] John Heron paid me by the month for 1865. I never heard John Heron say to Mose that he would not give the hands any part of the crop. He said he would give one half of the crop. He said to me he would give all alike. He said this after Prince went there – The hands worked a lot of about twelve acres in 1863 – Prince had no share in it – Prince made a corn crop in 1863 – Prince made 6 bales of cotton in 1864, and found every thing

Mr. Burdett sworn testified

I am a cotton merchant in the City of Memphis. Prince bought provisions for himself and hands for the last two years and paid for them himself – Prince brought one bale of cotton to me Nov. 5, 1864 At that date cotton was selling at St. Louis for $1.[12 1/2] to $1[28 1/2] – The shipment of this cotton was delayed on the instance of John Heron till February 1865 when he relinquished his claim to it, and it was then sold for 75[cts] a pound.

Mrs. White, sworn, testified

This year Prince furnished his own teams and supplies, all except 1/2 bushel of meal and some meat. I saw him pay hands he hired.

Granville Beverly sworn testified

Last year Prince made a crop on John Heron's land of between 8 and 9 Bales of cotton. Last summer he borrowed money on his own account to buy provisions. He made a crop of 6 or 7 bales that I know of. I saw him trading horses, and hiring hands, and supplying his own teams and provisions and I know from all this that he was not working by the month.

William Wilkinson – sworn testified

Prince made 9 bales of cotton this year upon John Heron's place. I heard John Heron tell Prince that if he would get Billy Brower to make out his account of his expenses he would pay it – Prince got Billy to make out the account and presented it to John Heron. John Heron said he would see him in hell before he would pay a dime of it. I was sitting in the wagon. Prince went into the house. There was some cotton of the crop made by Prince this year over what was put in the 9 bales – enough to make about half a bale. In November 1864 cotton was worth 1^{00} a pound.

N. J. White, sworn, testified –

Prince was his own boss. He furnished every thing himself, and went and came as he pleased and traded horses on his own account. I heard John Heron make a proposition to Prince to give him $30. and his wife $20. a month

Sam. Heron, sworn, testified

John Heron told me he had got Prince, Mose, and Ira to work on his plantation on halves and he to find them. He told me he would give me the same if I would go. I did not go. This was about March two years ago, when Prince first went there. I do not know whether Prince and Ira and Mose went together to John Herons place. Formerly belonged to Mr. Heron.

Sambo. Richmond, sworn testified.

I formerly belonged to John Heron. About 3 years ago, he promised me one half of all I could raise and make on his place, even to milk and butter if I would go back. He did not say for how long. He said this on Beall Street. Prince was not present.

Wilson Perkins, sworn, testified

I live in Memphis – I made crops on John Heron's place – This year he said he was to give me one half. I was to get supplies out to his place, as it was not registered.[1] He was to give me $50 a month for the work of my wife and 3 children, and the use of a mare. He told me he was to give the other hands one half and find them. It was at my house on Beal St. when this proposition was made. It was the last of April or first of May 1865. I did not conclude with his proposition – I just helped to plant for one month and three weeks.

Defence

A. R. Heron sworn testified

I am a brother of John Heron the defendant. I know all about my brother's calculations as to the colored people working on his plantation, because he talked to me and advised and consulted with me often on the subject. In 1862 immediately after the occupation of Memphis by the Federal troops his hands all left him and came into the City. A number of them had died– and my brother was anxious to get them back to work on his place. In 1863 my brother set apart 20 to 22 acres for the hands to work– Prince had not then come back– That year Prince found two horses[2] and cultivated a corn crop. He got all that crop but a few Roasting ears. My brother furnished supplies that year to all the hands except Prince. Prince killed hogs & was paid in hogs. The supplies furnished overrun the value of the crop. For 1864 my brother told me he would parcel out a piece of land to each of the hands or the families, and pay them wages in proportion to their work, Prince included. He settled with them at the end of the year, and paid 1st class hands $200. Prince had a team, and was paid more, as I understood from my brother– he was paid one bale of cotton more. He got more as I understood because he had a team, and worked well. Brother told Prince that he might raise cotton on a patch of about one acre, to pay off hirelings– think part of the cotton raised upon that patch went into the bale spoken of by Mr. Burdett. In 1865 the same plan was adopted, as I understood from my brother– He said he had authorized hands to hire laborers to work–he to pay expenses. There was no price fixed. The hands wanted to know what they would get. Prince was not among them that got supplies. Some of them picked cotton at $1.00 per hundred. Prince was not in the number. Brother gave Prince $65.00 to buy a horse. I know of no contract being made with Prince, except in 1863. as to corn crop. $10 per acre would be good rent for the land– In 1863 my brother's hands had left him, and he was anxious to get them back. I heard John Heron say that Prince controlled his own operations. I know from what my brother told me that all persons were to be reimbursed their expenses. I think about 17 acres were planted in cotton–30 acres in all– I heard my brother say that he never claimed that one bale of cotton which Mr. Burdett spoke about.

William Brower, sworn, testified:

I am Superintendent of John Heron's plantation, and have been such since May 1864. The hands, Prince included, worked to themselves. I do not know the terms under which Prince worked. In 1864 Prince had a small patch, and made one bale of cotton upon it. I ginned all the cotton that was made upon the plantation. Prince made five bales of cotton on the plantation in 1864– I talked with him frequently on the subject of the terms upon which he was working. He did not know what he was going to get. He said he would make sure of the 1 bale; that it was raised for hirelings. Prince told Heron that he wanted to come to an understanding – The hands picked 7900 pounds of cotton at $1 per pound. I saw Prince pay $70 to his hands that raised the crop. He also furnished the provisions and teams – Some of the provisions were bought before he commenced work. Heron furnished Prince for his hands 1 1/2 bushels meal and 312^{lbs} bacon this year. In 1865 Prince made 9 bales and part of a bale of cotton on Heron's plantation. Hands picked part of Prince's crop – 2456 pounds – it was put with other cotton raised on the plantation. This cotton was near gin & was being injured by mules & Prince had gone to work on Mrs White's crop. Prince hired the hands who raised his crop. Heron's books do not show any amounts paid by Prince to his hands – $10 per acre would be a good rent for that land – One half the crop is more than I would give. One half is more than is usual – Prince had one regular hand – sometimes he had 3 or 4. I made out the bill of his expenses for Prince – Heron refused to pay it – I do not know why – because it was larger than he expected it would be I suppose It was larger [than] the other hands the prices were higher

R. S. Jones sworn, testified:

Prince came with cotton to us in this city this fall, and afterwards came and claimed that John Heron owed him. He said that if Heron would pay him $280 and expenses he would quit even for friendships sake – That he wanted peace and wanted to ~~settle the matter so that when he met his old master John he could say to him "How do you do Master John as he had always done.~~ In July last John Heron wanted to go away up the river, and wanted to come to some understanding with the hands –

William Brewer recalled – testified:

John Heron's plantation is in Shelby County & the State of Tennessee. Heron furnished rope and bagging and hauled all the cotton to town – Prince traded horses and acted generally as his own boss – He kept about three horses all the time – Heron furnished some [feed], Prince had a few blacksmith tools – It was worth $20 to $24 to furnish bagging & Rope for a Bale of cotton & ginning to haul the cotton to town – Last year it was worth from $5 to $10 a load sometimes $2 1/2 to haul to the City.

Bill Heron sworn, testified:

I lived on Heron's place in 1863 – formerly belonged to him. I went out for $30 per month. I don't know the bargain made with Prince and others. I and Mose and Ira went out together Prince did not come out until the Cotton crop was in. Prince did not work in the same way as we did. We had patches– In 1864 Heron wanted the hands to come up and make a new bargain– Prince did not come up. Prince worked differently from a man working by the month. He hired his own hands and had a team of his own and furnished his own supplies. I don't know what bargain Prince and Heron made. Heron told Prince he could plant a small patch, about 1 acre, which would help pay his hands. Heron said if we made a big crop he would pay big pay. Finally the men were paid $200 and the women $100. Paid Prince one bale of cotton– Prince got this bale which was raised on the patch to pay his hands. Some time in June Mr. Heron came to us to make a bargain, but we did not make any then. In July, he said he was going up the river, and wanted to come to some understanding. I and Mose made a bargain. Heron was to settle expenses. Prince did not make a bargain– Heron has agreed to pay me $230. and Mose and wife $300. I heard Prince say if he could settle in peace he would rather. John Heron told him to make out his account for expenses, and he would settle with him as with the balance.

H. Dean–sworn, testified:

In December 1862 at the request of Mr. John Heron, I solicited his negroes to return– they had all left him. I talked with Bill and Mose– Heron told me to see Prince–that he would give him $30 pr month. Prince said he would go out and see Heron– Prince told me that he would give me $500 if I would swear for him– He did not tell me at the time what his contract was.

Ira–recalled.

I delivered 5 bales of the cotton raised by Prince in 1864 on Heron's plantation to Farrington & Howell in Memphis in November 1864. Cotton was then worth 95 ^{cents} to $1 ^{10} in Memphis.

Bill Herron Recalled (previous to Ira's last evidence.)

The Five Bales Raised by Prince in 1864 was carried to Jones & Co– I came in with the wagon. I brought five bales. Prince brought in one Bale. Ira told me I was mistaken that he carried Prince's cotton to Farrington & Howell.

Add to Ira's first evidence the following,

I wanted to work by the month because he (J. H.) had not fulfilled his bargain. He knows I was dissatisfied I told him so last year. If Prince gets judgement then I expect to have my rights too. I settled with Herron because I thought I could not help myself but I mean to have my rights yet. I meant you (A R. Herron) to think I did not know anything about the contract with Prince. I told you (A. R. Herron) that *there was not any contract by* which Prince was to have one half the crop, that was a week before the first trial. There was about Eight bales made in 1863 there were Ten or twelve hands ~~& Two Irishmen~~.

I certify that the preceding statement of Evidence & the above case is correct

HDS Jno A. Staley

Capt. Jno. A. Staley, Evidence in Prince Herron vs. John Herron, [Dec. 1865], enclosed in Bt. Maj. Genl. Clinton B. Fisk to Maj. General O. O. Howard, 28 Feb. 1866, Affidavits & Statements, ser. 3545, Memphis TN Provost Marshal of Freedmen, RG 105 [A-6526]. According to another document enclosed in the same covering letter, Captain Staley awarded Prince Herron a judgment of $1,076.15 for the cotton he raised in 1864, plus one-half of the 1865 crop. ("Prince Heron vs. John Heron, Judgment in case of appeal . . . ," [Dec. 1865].) John Herron then raised a new legal issue, arguing that Prince Herron had been a slave until February 1865, when slavery was abolished in Tennessee, and that the Freedmen's Bureau had no grounds upon which to enforce an agreement between a master and his slave. However, when Captain Staley sought advice on this question from General Clinton B. Fisk, assistant commissioner of the Freedmen's Bureau in Tennessee, Fisk ruled "that Mr John Herron may be held to his contract with Prince, for both law and equity are against him. The Courts of Tennessee, under the old Code even, would hold him to his agreement." (Capt. Jno. A. Staley to Bvt. Maj. Genl. Clinton B. Fisk, 19 Jan. 1866, and endorsement of Bt. Major Gen. Clinton B. Fisk, 23 Jan. 1866, Unregistered Letters Received, ser. 3522, Memphis TN Supt., RG 105 [A-6526].) John Herron's death in mid-January 1866 did not bring the case to an end. Shortly thereafter, the executor of his estate appealed Captain Staley's judgment to General Fisk, who, on February 3, reduced by $200 the amount due Prince Herron for 1864, but otherwise let the decision stand. John Herron's brother Abraham then appealed to General Oliver O. Howard, commissioner of the Freedmen's Bureau, who sustained Fisk's ruling. (Geo. E[v]. Montgomery to Brig. Genl. Clin. B. Fiske, [late Jan.? 1866], with endorsement of Bt. Lt. Col. J. E. Jacobs, 3 Feb. 1866, enclosed in Bt. Maj. Genl. Clinton B. Fisk to Maj. General O. O. Howard, 28 Feb. 1866, and endorsement of Asst. Adjt. Gen. Wm. Fowler, 27 Mar. 1866, all filed in Affidavits & Statements, ser. 3545, Memphis TN Provost Marshal of Freedmen, RG 105 [A-6526].) However, in April 1866, when General Benjamin P. Runkle, Freedmen's Bureau superintendent for the subdistrict of Memphis, attempted to execute the judgment against John Herron's estate, Abraham Herron sought an injunction from the U.S. district court. The federal judge refused to grant an injunction – but on the grounds that the act creating the Freedmen's Bureau authorized no judicial powers, and that, in any case, military tribunals had no legal standing after the end of the war, and hence no authority to render or enforce judgment. The judge warned that any bureau official who seized John Herron's property under the "pretext" of executing a judgment would be subject to arrest for trespass. General Fisk nevertheless ordered Runkle to collect the judgment. But when Abraham Herron appealed to still higher authority (President Andrew Johnson), the military commander of the Department of the Tennessee ordered Runkle to suspend further action pending the President's decision. (Bvt. Brig. Gen. Benj. P. Runkle to Lt. Col. J. E. Jacobs, 12 Apr. 1866, and endorsement of A.A. Genl. H. S. Brown, 19 Apr. 1866; A. R. Herron to His Excellency Andrew Johnson, [Apr. 1866], enclosing a clipping from an unidentified newspaper, [Apr. 1866]; and Maj. Genl. George Stoneman to Brvt. Brig. Genl. B. P. Runkle, 24 Apr. 1866, all in Affidavits & Statements, ser. 3545, Memphis TN Provost Marshal of Freedmen, RG 105 [A-6526].) No information about the final outcome has been found in the Tennessee records of the Freedmen's Bureau or in those of the bureau's national headquarters.

1 A plantation had to be registered with a treasury agent in order to obtain supplies.
2 That is, he supplied two horses of his own.

232: Tennessee Planter to the Freedmen's Bureau Subassistant Commissioner of the Subdistrict of Memphis

Shelby Co Tenn April 10th 1867

Maj Hendricks The Year before the war closed, it was almost a univeral thing for all farmers, to give those negroes who *still* remained with them, a cotton Patch for their fidelety, in remaining with them, – Cotton, that season commanded a fabulous price, a small cotton patch made considerable money – there were other planters that give some money, which amounted to the same thing

This year, several of the planters are recovering, before our magistrates; Judgements, for all monies, the negroes received that year – The magistrates, allege, that a decision of the supreme court of the state, Justifies them, in giving such a judgement – I have a very nice negro man and his wife living with me, this year his wife is sued, the trial to come off Saturday next, *I will have the trial put off until I hear from you*, to know whether it is lawful. or not, I presume you are posted in the matter please advise me what steps, to take in the matter, to avoid paying it, if it can be done, *Please answer at once direct as below.* you will recollect me, as a crippled man, that has troubled you so much, about some mislaid contracts Fraternally Yours

ALS Thomas, J, Ross

Thomas J. Ross to Maj. Hendricks, 10 Apr. 1867, R-8 1867, Registered Letters Received, ser. 3521, Memphis TN Subasst. Comr., RG 105 [A-6561]. Beneath his signature, Ross gave his address as Sulphur Wells Post Office. Later the same month, Ross informed the subassistant commissioner that the trial of the freedwoman had been twice postponed, and he reiterated his request for advice respecting judgments against former slaves for wartime wage payments. (Thomas J. Ross to Major Hendricks, [late Apr. 1867], R-9 1867, Registered Letters Received, ser. 3521, Memphis TN Subasst. Comr., RG 105 [A-6561].) No reply to either letter has been found in the volumes of letters sent by the subassistant commissioner.

Index